T0191650

Lecture Notes in Computer Science   12889

More information about this subseries at http://www.springer.com/series/7412

Yuxin Peng · Shi-Min Hu ·
Moncef Gabbouj · Kun Zhou ·
Michael Elad · Kun Xu (Eds.)

Image
and Graphics

11th International Conference, ICIG 2021
Haikou, China, August 6–8, 2021
Proceedings, Part II

 Springer

Editors

Yuxin Peng
Peking University
Beijing, China

Moncef Gabbouj
Tampere University
Tampere, Finland

Michael Elad
Technion – Israel Institute of Technology
Haifa, Israel

Shi-Min Hu
Tsinghua University
Beijing, China

Kun Zhou
Zhejiang University
Hangzhou, China

Kun Xu
Tsinghua University
Beijing, China

ISSN 0302-9743   ISSN 1611-3349 (electronic)
Lecture Notes in Computer Science
ISBN 978-3-030-87357-8   ISBN 978-3-030-87358-5 (eBook)
https://doi.org/10.1007/978-3-030-87358-5

LNCS Sublibrary: SL6 – Image Processing, Computer Vision, Pattern Recognition, and Graphics

This Springer imprint is published by the registered company Springer Nature Switzerland AG
The registered company address is: Gewerbestrasse 11, 6330 Cham, Switzerland

Preface

These are the proceedings of the 11th International Conference on Image and Graphics (ICIG 2021), which was supposed to be held in Haikou, China, during August 6–8, 2021, but was postponed due to COVID-19.

The China Society of Image and Graphics (CSIG) has hosted the series of ICIG conferences since 2000. ICIG is the biennial conference organized by the CSIG that focuses on innovative technologies of image, video, and graphics processing and fosters innovation, entrepreneurship, and networking. This time, the conference was organized by Hainan University. Details about the past conferences are as follows:

Conference	Place	Date	Submitted	Proceeding
First (ICIG 2000)	Tianjin, China	August 16–18	220	156
Second (ICIG 2002)	Hefei, China	August 15–18	280	166
Third (ICIG 2004)	Hong Kong, China	December 17–19	460	140
4th (ICIG 2007)	Chengdu, China	August 22–24	525	184
5th (ICIG 2009)	Xi'an, China	September 20–23	362	179
6th (ICIG 2011)	Hefei, China	August 12–15	329	183
7th (ICIG 2013)	Qingdao, China	July 26–28	346	181
8th (ICIG 2015)	Tianjin, China	August 13–16	345	170
9th (ICIG 2017)	Shanghai, China	September 13–15	370	172
10th (ICIG 2019)	Shanghai, China	August 23–25	384	183

For ICIG 2021, 421 submissions were received and 198 papers were accepted. To ease the search of a required paper in these proceedings, the accepted papers have been arranged into different sections according to their topic.

We sincerely thank all the contributors, who came from around the world to present their advanced work at this event. We would also like to thank all the reviewers, who carefully reviewed all submissions and made their valuable comments for improving the accepted papers. The proceedings could not have been produced without the invaluable efforts of the members of the Organizing Committee, and a number of active members of CSIG.

August 2021

Yuxin Peng
Shi-Min Hu
Moncef Gabbouj
Kun Zhou
Michael Elad
Kun Xu

Organization

Organizing Committee

General Chairs

Yaonan Wang	Hunan University, China
Laurence T. Yang	Hainan University, China
Ming Lin	University of Maryland at College Park, USA

Technical Program Chairs

Yuxin Peng	Peking University, China
Shi-Min Hu	Tsinghua University, China
Moncef Gabbouj	TUT, Finland
Kun Zhou	Zhejiang University, China

Organizing Committee Chairs

Mingming Cheng	Nankai University, China
Zhaohui Wang	Hainan University, China
Faouzi Alaya Cheikh	NTNU, Norway

Sponsorship Chairs

Rongrong Ji	Xiamen University, China
Yafeng Deng	Qihoo 360 Technology Co., Ltd., China

Finance Chair

Jing Dong	Institute of Automation, CAS, China

Special Session Chairs

Ioan Tabus	Tampere University, Finland
Jian Cheng	Institute of Automation, CAS, China

Award Chairs

Yirong Wu	Aerospace Information Research Institute, CAS, China
Ridha Hamila	Qatar University, Qatar
Jieqing Feng	Zhejiang University, China

Publicity Chairs

Sid Ahmed Fezza	INTTIC, Algeria
Zhi Jin	Sun Yat-sen University, China
Jimin Xiao	Xi'an Jiaotong-Liverpool University, China

Exhibits Chairs

Jinjian Wu	Xidian University, China
Drahansky Martin	Brno University of Technology, Czech Republic
Dong Wang	Dalian University of Technology, China

Publication Chairs

Michael Elad	Israel Institute of Technology, Israel
Kun Xu	Tsinghua University, China

Oversea Liaison Chairs

Yubing Tong	University of Pennsylvania, USA
Azeddine Beghdadi	University Sorbonne Paris Nord, France

Local Chair

Xiaozhang Liu	Hainan University, China

Tutorial Chairs

Hongkai Xiong	Shanghai Jiao Tong University, China
Yo-Sung Ho	GIST, South Korea
Zhanchuan Cai	MUST, Macau, China

Workshop Chairs

Yunchao Wei	UTS, Australia
Joaquín Olivares	University of Cordoba, Spain
Cheng Deng	Xidian University, China

Symposium Chairs

Chia-wen Lin	Tsing Hua University, Taiwan, China
Frederic Dufaux	CNRS, France

Website Chair

Zhenwei Shi	Beihang University, China

Area Chairs

Weihong Deng	Meina Kan	Huimin Lu	Hang Su
Jing Dong	Weiyao Lin	Wanli Ouyang	Hao Su
Hu Han	Risheng Liu	Jinshan Pan	Nannan Wang
Gao Huang	Jiaying Liu	Houwen Peng	Shuhui Wang
Di Huang	Si Liu	Xi Peng	Yunhai Wang
Xu Jia	Zhilei Liu	Boxin Shi	Xinchao Wang

Limin Wang
Dong Wang
Yunhai Wang
Yingcai Wu

Baoyuan Wu
Yong Xia
Guisong Xia
Junchi Yan

Shiqi Yu
Shanshan Zhang
Xi Sheryl Zhang
Xiaoyu Zhang

Liang Zheng
Xiaobin Zhu
Chao Zuo

Additional Reviewers

Haoran Bai
Xiaoyu Bai
Zhidong Bai
Bingkun Bao
Daniel Barath
Chunjuan Bo
Jintong Cai
Zewei Cai
Zhanchuan Cai
Anqi Cao
Jian Cao
Jianhui Chang
Di Chen
Han Chen
Hao Chen
Jinsong Chen
Shuaijun Chen
Wenting Chen
Xiaojun Chen
Xin Chen
Xiu Chen
Yang Chen
Yuanyuan Chen
Yuqing Chen
Zhibo Chen
Zhihua Chen
De Cheng
Yu Cheng
Zhanglin Cheng
Xiangtong Chu
Yang Cong
Hengfei Cui
Yutao Cui
Zhaopeng Cui
Enyan Dai
Ju Dai
Congyue Deng
Dazhen Deng

Jiajun Deng
Weijian Deng
Shangzhe Di
Jian Ding
Hao Du
Heming Du
Peiqi Duan
Yuping Duan
Jiahao Fan
Yao Fan
Yongxian Fan
Zejia Fan
Zhenfeng Fan
Sheng Fang
Xianyong Fang
Jieqing Feng
Qianjin Feng
Xiaomei Feng
Zunlei Feng
Chenping Fu
Jiahui Fu
Xueyang Fu
Jingru Gan
Difei Gao
Guangshuai Gao
Jiaxin Gao
Jun Gao
Ruochen Gao
Shang Gao
Ziteng Gao
Zhang Ge
Yuanbiao Gou
Heng Guo
Jie Guo
Senhui Guo
Xuyang Guo
Yingkai guo
Chunrui Han

Songfang Han
Xinzhe Han
Yahong Han
Yizeng Han
Zheng Han
Zhenjun Han
Shuai Hao
You Hao
Zhongkai Hao
Xiangyang He
Richang Hong
Yuchen Hong
Chenping Hou
JieBo Hou
Yunzhong Hou
Yuxuan Hou
Donghui Hu
Fuyuan Hu
Lanqing Hu
Peng Hu
Qingyong Hu
Ruimin Hu
Shishuai Hu
Yang Hu
Zhenzhen Hu
Yan Hu
Bao Hua
Haofeng Huang
Jun Huang
Shaofei Huang
Yan Huang
Zhenghua Huang
Zhenyu Huang
Xiaopeng Ji
Haozhe Jia
Mengxi Jia
Muwei Jian
Xinrui Jiang

Zeren Jiang
Zhiying Jiang
Lianwen Jin
Zhuochen Jin
Yongcheng Jing
Meina Kan
Yongzhen Ke
Jianhuang Lai
Nan Lai
Xing Lan
Hyeongmin Lee
Baohua Li
Boyun Li
Fenghai Li
Guozhang Li
Han Li
Hangyu Li
Hongjun Li
Jiaji Li
Ping Li
Ruihuang Li
Shuang Li
Wenbin Li
Wenhao Li
Yi Li
Yifan Li
Yixuan Li
Yunfan Li
Zekun Li
Zhuoshi Li
Zhuoxiao Li
Hao Liang
Min Liang
Zhifang Liang
Xin Liao
Zehui Liao
Yijie Lin
Chang Liu

Chenglin Liu
Hao Liu
Jie Liu
Jinyuan Liu
Liu Liu
Min Liu
Minghua Liu
Pengbo Liu
Qingshan Liu
Risheng Liu
Ruijun Liu
Shiguang Liu
Shuaiqi Liu
Si Liu
Wenyu Liu
Xuan Liu
Xuejing Liu
Yaohua Liu
Yaqi Liu
Yiguang Liu
Yipeng Liu
Yong Liu
Yu Liu
Yuchi Liu
Yunan Liu
Zhenguang Liu
Zimo Liu
Yang Long
Hongtao Lu
Hu Lu
Kaiyue Lu
Linpeng Lu
Tao Lu
Bin Luo
Weiqi Luo
Kai Lv
Youwei Lyu
Huimin Ma
Lizhuang Ma
Long Ma
Tengyu Ma
Xiaorui Ma
Xinzhu Ma
Yuhao Ma
Qirong Mao
Shitong Mao

Yongwei Miao
Weidong Min
Zhou Ning
Xuesong Niu
Weihua Ou
Xuran Pan
Guansong Pang
Bo Peng
Sida Peng
Xi Peng
Zhaobo Qi
Jiaming Qian
Rui Qian
Zhenxing Qian
Qingyang Wu
Jiayan Qiu
Xinkuan Qiu
Zelin Qiu
Zhong Qu
Wenqi Ren
Tushar Sandhan
Hanbo Sang
Nong Sang
Cai Shang
Shuai Shao
Zhiwen Shao
Chunhua Shen
Linlin Shen
Qian Shen
Yuefan Shen
Shurong Sheng
Haichao Shi
Jun Shi
Yongjie Shi
Zhenghao Shi
Zhenwei Shi
Shizhan Liu
Jaskirat Singh
Guoxian Song
Sijie Song
Bowen Sun
Haomiao Sun
Jiande Sun
Jianing Sun
Shitong Sun
Xiaoxiao Sun

Bin Tan
Haoteng Tang
Hong Tang
Shixiang Tang
Jun Tao
Zhou Tao
Yadong Teng
Zhan Tong
Jun Tu
Kurban Ubul
Thomas Verelst
Fang Wan
Renjie Wan
Beibei Wang
Bowen Wang
Ce Wang
Chengyu Wang
Di Wang
Dong Wang
Feipeng Wang
Fudong Wang
Guodong Wang
Hanli Wang
Hanzi Wang
Hongyu Wang
Hu Wang
Huiqun Wang
Jinwei Wang
Kaili Wang
Kangkan Wang
Kunfeng Wang
Lijun Wang
Longguang Wang
Mei Wang
Meng Wang
Min Wang
Qiang Wang
Runzhong Wang
Shengjin Wang
Shuhui Wang
Shujun Wang
Tao Wang
Dongsheng Wang
Wei Wang
Weizheng Wang
Wenbin Wang

Xiaoxing Wang
Xingce Wang
Xinhao Wang
Xueping Wang
Xun Wang
Yifan Wang
Yingqian Wang
Yongfang Wang
Yuehuan Wang
Zhengyi Wang
Zhihui Wang
Ziming Wang
Hongyuan Wang
Jinjia Wang
Jie Wei
Xiushen Wei
Ziyu Wei
Weifan Guan
Ying Wen
Di Weng
Shuchen Weng
Zhi Weng
Wenhua Qian
Kan Wu
Runmin Wu
Yawen Wu
Yicheng Wu
Zhongke Wu
Zizhao Wu
Zhuofan Xia
Fanbo Xiang
Tao Xiang
Wei Xiang
Wenzhao Xiang
Qinjie Xiao
Jingwei Xin
Xiaomeng Xin
Bowen Xu
Fang Xu
Jia Xu
Qian Xu
Shibiao Xu
Mingliang Xue
Xiangyang Xue
Xinwei Xue
Zhe Xue

Zhenfeng Xue

Ziyu Xue

Xuejuan Wu

Bin Yan

Xin Yan

Bangbang Yang

Hongyu Yang

Mouxing Yang

Qisen Yang

Shuo Yang

Xue Yang

Yiding Yang

Yifang Yang

Yuansheng Yao

Yue Yao

Jingwen Ye

Shuainan Ye

Yiwen Ye

Zhichao Ye

Wei Yin

Yongkai Yin

Zhaoxia Yin

Zhenfei Yin

Chengyang Ying

Di You

Baosheng Yu

Hongyuan Yu

Nenghai Yu

Zhenxun Yuan

Yuzhang Hu

Jiabei Zeng

Geng Zhan

Yinwei Zhan

Bohua Zhang

Boyuan Zhang

Cuicui Zhang

Jialin Zhang

Jianguo Zhang

Jiawan Zhang

Jie Zhang

Jing Zhang

Junxing Zhang

Kaihua Zhang

Pengyu Zhang

Pingping Zhang

Runnan Zhang

Shaoxiong Zhang

Shizhou Zhang

Songyang Zhang

Xiaoshuai Zhang

Xinfeng Zhang

Xinpeng Zhang

Xinyu Zhang

Yanan Zhang

Yanfu Zhang

Yanhao Zhang

Yaru Zhang

Yifan Zhang

Zhanqiu Zhang

Zhexi Zhang

Ziwei Zhang

Jie Zhao

Tianxiang Zhao

Wenda Zhao

Yan Zhao

Qian Zheng

Weishi Zheng

Chengju Zhou

Chu Zhou

Dawei Zhou

Guijing Zhu

Jianqing Zhu

Mingrui Zhu

Zijian Zhu

Yunzhi Zhuge

Junbao Zhuo

Contents – Part II

Face, Gesture, and Body Pose

Artificial Intelligence

A Calibration Strategy for Smart Welding

Min Chen[1,2], Zhiling Ma[1,2], Xu Chen[1], Muhammad Owais[1], and Yaohui Liu[2(✉)]

[1] Shenzhen Super-Accurate Vision Technology Co., Ltd., Shenzhen 518000, China
[2] Xiangnan University, Chenzhou 423000, Hunan, China
liu_yh@xnu.edu.cn

Abstract. Welding robots have been widely used in manufacturing process to substitute for human welders. In an effort to enhance their flexibility as well as accomplishing more efficient industrial welding, this paper proposes a novel calibrated strategy based on visual guidance for smart welding, which includes the camera calibration, the calibration of the laser plane, and the calibration of the hand-eye. The corresponding experimental results have demonstrated the effectiveness, dependability and efficiency of the calibration strategy.

Keywords: Welding robot · Image processing · Camera calibration · Hand-eye calibration

1 Introduction

Industrial Robots are currently using in multiple manufacturing areas. The most demanding areas for robotics are such as the handling, welding and assembly and manufacturing.

Welding technologies have been developed from the original hand worked craft to the modern systemic technical science, to realize automatic welding similar to welder. We need three essential technical steps. The first step is to sense and acquire information of the welding dynamic process (Chen and Lv 2014), this is as like human sensing organs for detecting interior and exterior condition as human being can; the second step is to identify the characteristics of the welding process, in simple words, the modeling of the welding dynamic process; the third one is to develop the human-brain like controller to reason controlling strategies. One of the main functions in modern welding manufacturing system, which can be case of easing welder's work, is to substitute or partially replace the physical force and brain calculation/function of a welder with concerns machines. In practical welding production, welding conditions are often changing like work-piece heat conduction and dispersion during welding process, which can bring on weld distortion and penetration odds.

Currently, there are two most frequent operating modes for welding robots, which are appropriate for use in a standardized, modular, strictly coordinated welding system (Zeng and Cao 2020). These two modes are the teaching mode, which is known as traditional ones, and the off-line programming mode. The teaching mode is based on teaching programming of human operators. It has encountered welding thermal deformation assembly errors or sometime has unfavorable factors which may significantly

© Springer Nature Switzerland AG 2021
Y. Peng et al. (Eds.): ICIG 2021, LNCS 12889, pp. 3–17, 2021.
https://doi.org/10.1007/978-3-030-87358-5_1

affect the quality of welding system. The off-line programming mode does not depend on sensor measurements for the duration of welding, the welding trajectories are set in advance by workers or concern peoples, and according to their setting values robot moves in accordance with the desired trajectory.

During teaching mode, it is also noticed that when welding various kinds of joints, it is essential to re-program robots which are not flexible. Therefore, automatic welding has become increasingly popular in modern manufacturing, and leads the revolution in welding industry, as it can intelligently run flexible production lines by online sensing, self-learning and auto-recognition (Li and Li 2017). It's also noticed that the welding environment might not be static in actual welding operations. Therefore, these two modes do not offer sufficient flexibility and robustness to handle such a complex and dynamic welding environment.

The author's Aviles-Viñas (2015) approach was based on the automatic generation of training data and the corresponding patterns. The main goal of their work was to learn the appropriate values for the welding parameters to generates specific bead geometries. Calibration vision system is used for generating patterns which are automatically register. System is trained to predict the width and height of the weld bead by using real data from exploring training and this is done by ANN.

Based on previous research, Dinham and Fang (2013) presented some further evolutions of the intelligentized technologies for robotics welding like multi-information acquirement of arc welding process, multi-information fusion algorithms for prediction of weld penetration; intelligentized modeling of welding process and robot system; intelligent control schemes for welding pool and penetration process; and the 3D seam tracking during robotic welding by combining arc sensing and visual sensing.

A vision system uses cameras and analyses images to obtain information and is used for monitoring the process at distance with all possibilities to interface during abnormal situations.

Vision sensing has provided better performance in terms of the richness of welding information, low cost and high reliability etc. (Zhang and Wen 2016). Thus, it has been utilized for multiple research subjects, such as seam penetration controlling, seam tracking and guiding of robotic welding and so on. Nevertheless, with the disturbance of arc light and surroundings, how to improve the real-time performance, stability and robustness of image system is still a huge challenge in terms of online image feature extraction.

The authors Gong et al. (2020) improved Kernelized Correlation Filter (KCF) Algorithm for tracking. The pre-trained deep convolutional neural network (CNN) is introduced in extracting the layer information respectively to describe the spatial and semantic features of the target. Experiments are performed on OTB-2015 benchmark datasets, and the results show that in comparison with the existing tracking algorithms, the proposed improved algorithm can deal with the challenges much better performance compared to original KCF and KCF-S method.

2 Background

The purpose to use the stereo vision is to take images of the weld joint from two different directions. The obtained images were input to an algorithm that calculates the 3D geometry of the joint, and the robot trajectory can be corrected.

The relationship between the robot base coordinate system and the measuring coordinate system of the laser vision sensor must be determined before using the sensor to collect weld position. This process is called hand–eye calibration (Zou and Chen 2018), which is significant for seam tracking because its accuracy will directly influence the finally welding quality. The problem of hand-eye calibration is also converted to a problem and works on;

The robot is controlled to observe the same reference point with different positions and orientations.

$$AX = XB \tag{1}$$

A and B represents the homogenous transformation matrix of the end effector and the homogenous transformation matrix of the Camera between robot's two relative positions, and X are the constants as well as unknown relationship between the robot flange and the sensor and finally find its solution by calculating the least square fit solution of an linear equation $CY = D$, but the author (Qiu 1995) show robustness is the most prominent feature of their method because it is very important because of usually impossible to obtain data which are not disturbed by noise in an actual application.

To improves the accuracy of the calibration results. The number of data should be increased as much possible. Thus, $AX = XB$ can be rewritten as;

The matrices A, B and X are composed of the orientation rotation matrix R and a translation vector T; (Fig. 1)

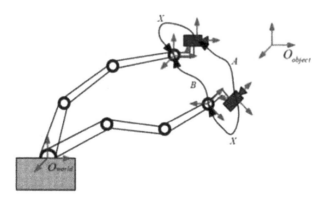

Fig. 1. Hand–eye calibration that can be formulated as an $AX = XB$ problem

$$\begin{pmatrix} R_{A_i} & T_{A_i} \\ 0^T & 1 \end{pmatrix} \begin{pmatrix} R_x & T_x \\ 0^T & 1 \end{pmatrix} = \begin{pmatrix} R_x & T_x \\ 0^T & 1 \end{pmatrix} \begin{pmatrix} R_{B_i} & T_{B_i} \\ 0^T & T \end{pmatrix} \tag{2}$$

The above equation can be divided into two separate sets of equations, which are a notation matrix equation:

$$R_{A_i} T_x + T_{A_i} = R_x R_{B_i} + T_x \tag{3}$$

The author (Li and Ma 2016) has developed a probabilistic approach to simultaneously obtain X and Y in the $AX = YB$ sensor calibration problem. Without a priori knowledge of the correspondence between $\{A_i\}$ and $\{B_j\}$, the proposed probabilistic method on Lie groups is used to constrain the possible solutions of X and Y to eight pairs of candidates. Given shifted data streams of $\{A_{i+s}\}$ and $\{B_j\}$, using the correlation theorem with Euclidean-group invariants, the correspondence is recovered to determine the correct solution among the eight candidates. In the numerical simulation, the method performs well with different sets of data samples. Lastly, we brought up a new approach to deal with completely disordered data sets and show its effectiveness in simulation. Future work will be to improve the prob method and investigate on its performance dealing with noisy scrambled data sets.

The author propose a marker-less hand-eye calibration method for high-fidelity 3D scanners by utilizing standardized design features on the robot flange, namely flange-based hand-eye calibration method. They proposed a novel use of the depth sensors for a direct hand-eye calibration with a reduced system error. Instead of using a calibration marker, the author adopted the existing, standardized features on the robot flange as the reference for the depth sensor. The calibration accuracy is found to be as high as the camera's, probing the hardware limit of the robot system (Wan and Song 2020).

The author (Dinham and Fang 2009) introduced a high-accuracy, high speed, simple, versatile, and fully autonomous technique for 3D robotics hand/eye calibration. High speed is recorded since; about $100 + 64N$ arithmetic operations to compute the hand/eye relationship after the robot finishes the movement, and incurs only additional 64 arithmetic operations for each additional station. This makes the current algorithm the fastest compared with the state of the art. The speed performance is especially attractive to those applications where the hand/eye configuration needs to be changed frequently.

KCF is tracking method, designed for perspective vision system, which based on an improved learning mechanism (Cai and Fan 2017). KCF method builds the training samples of the classifier through the cyclic offset and transforms the data matrix into a circular matrix, which avoids the matrix inversion and greatly reduces the computation complexity.

Generically the tracking task is to find similar features and regions of interest in subsequent images and make the predication about the position of the target in the next frame. This problem is challenging with a few training samples, fast moving objects and some other issues.

KCF was proposed by Joao f. Henriques, Ruicaseiro, Pedro Martins, and Jorge Batista in 2014 (Gong et al. 2020). The authors published a paper about this algorithm on a conference with relevant algorithm source code implementation. It takes kernel ridge regression classifier as the core, constructs a cyclic sample matrix to train the classifier, and makes the training data matrix have cyclic features after ingenious transformation of samples, so that it can be diagonalized by discrete Fourier transform, which can greatly reduce the amount of calculation, improve the operation speed, and make the algorithm meet the real-time performance requirements, so as to achieve the goal of fast and effective detection and tracking of the target (Wei et al. 2012). Because of the outstanding performance of the algorithm in both tracking effect and tracking speed, a large number of scholars are working on this algorithm. KCF tracker framework had been added to OpenCV library already, nowadays, a large number of visual tracking applications have adopted KCF algorithm.

KCF (Kernelized Correlation Filter Algorithm) is one of the faster tracking algorithms present in the literature (Giuffrida and Meoni 2019). Its power derives by the combination of the motion model with the appearance model. This combination permits identifying the object among different frames without losing the high performance given by the YOLOv2 neural network. The author (Giuffrinda, GlMeono, G) use the KCF algorithm. This technique permits to increase the frames rate and to improve the target tracking to avoid its loss during the movement. The Robot Movement Control System is responsible for controlling the movement of the robotic arm end-effectors to reach the desired object position. The information on the latter is inherited by the KCF, which tracks it frame by frame. YOLOv2 belongs to a broader class of algorithms note in literature as Artificial Intelligence algorithms.

In order to reduce the computational cost for image processing, only the area near to seams of images needs to be processed. Therefore, the ROI should be established. The author has described some methods for quickly establishing the ROI. Here the searching method, intensity accumulation method and predication and estimation for ROI are introduced as follows [Li Y, Wang Q]. where ROI is a portion of the image that can filter or perform some other operation on. It can be defined by creating a binary mask that has the same size as the original image to process with pixels that defines the ROI set to 1 and all other pixels set to 0. It has variety of methods to define more than one ROI in the image.

Hough transform techniques include morphological operations and Hough lines (Ketcham and Ganokratanaa 2015). Morphological operations affect the form, structure, and shape of an object in the image. Their operations are applied on the binary image and used in pre or post processing. Hough transform is a technique which can be used to isolate features of a particular shape within the image. It is mostly commonly used for the detection of regular curves such as lines, circles and ellipse.

Houghlines specifies the parameters/value pairs, including fillgap parameter that specific the distance between two line segments with the same Hough transform bin.

The author described the technique of image morphology in detecting and extracting the preliminary welding position for the period of the autonomous welding process. During the process, to start with visual sensing technology, which is used to capture the straight seam image, and secondly the image edges are detected by morphological corrosion edge detection algorithm, with which can retain the significant information while filter further interferences effectively at the same time. After that morphological processing algorithm is used to carry out the direction of filter by selecting the multidirectional linear structuring elements and to end with get the initial weld position point coordinates with the Hough transform (Wei et al. 2012). The algorithm is simple, rapid, self-adaptability with high accuracy for interferences except long lines so as to accomplish the entire process of detecting the initial welding position. It can meet the practical demands of automatic guidance for robotic welding.

The author (Wu et al. 2015) described the development of an image processing by the modified Hough algorithm which applied for seam tracking system in GMA (Gas metal arc) welding. To achieve this objective, image features in the procedure of welding processing were discussed and specially treated. Algorithms in the image processing were investigated to maximize the processing effect based on the modified Hough algorithm, which was quite cost efficient in line detection. Quantitative evaluations of the used algorithm were set up to acquire optimal image processing algorithm. Finally, a common image processing method was employed to verify efficiency of proposed image processing and extract the welding location in a shorten time for industrial application. It can be concluded the detected feature points and centerlines proved that this algorithm can be used for automatic GMA welding process as well as industrial applications.

The cheap binocular system attached on the end-effector is used for measurement without resorting to any additional costly measurement instrument (Wang and Lu 2015), a mirror is used to enlarge the view field of the binocular system to make the hand-eye calibration easy and practical. Their method could achieve an absolute positioning precision as high as 0.77 mm, with which the robot could find many different real applications in various fields such as measurements, welding, grabbing, etc. In addition, a 1.67-times-reaction between the absolute positioning precision of the robot and that of the binocular system implies that if a more precise camera system is used, the robot's absolute positioning precision could be further increased accordingly.

The author Zhang and Wen (2016) proposed an easy methodology to quickly extract several image features for the purpose of detecting the typical welding defects of Al alloy in pulsed GTAW. First, based on the idea of vision attention, the gray level statistics have been calculated for three image regions of interested (ROI) both from welding pool and back seam. Then, experience-driven based certain gray interval is chosen to extract its total number of pixel as the main monitoring parameters. Furthermore, the background noise is successfully removed by using the proposed pixel ratio algorithm as well as enhancing the ratio of signal to noise. The test results indicate that the proposed method has the ability of predicting and identifying welding defects of under penetration, surface oxidation, over penetration and burning through, which certainly improves the intelligent level of robotic welding.

3 Calibration Method and Models

3.1 Camera Calibration

Camera calibration is the process of calculating the intrinsic and extrinsic parameters of the cameras.

In Fig. 2, X, Y, Z are the coordinate axes to form the camera coordinate system, take C as the origin and X, Y as the coordinate axes to form the image coordinate system. It can be;

$$x = f\frac{X}{Z}, y = f\frac{Y}{Z} \tag{4}$$

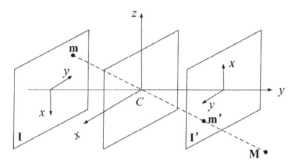

Fig. 2. Camera calibration model

Where x, y are the coordinates of the image point m on the image coordinate M.

$$Z\begin{bmatrix} x \\ y \\ 1 \end{bmatrix} = \begin{bmatrix} f & 0 & 0 & 0 \\ 0 & f & 0 & 0 \\ 0 & 0 & 1 & 0 \end{bmatrix} \begin{bmatrix} X \\ Y \\ Z \\ 1 \end{bmatrix} \tag{5}$$

The digital image coordinate (u, v) with pixel as the unit are used to replace the image coordinate (x, y) with the physical size as the unit.

$$\begin{cases} u = u_0 = s_x x \\ v = v_0 = s_y y \end{cases} \tag{6}$$

Where, (u_0, v_0) origin of the digital image coordinates.

Now (3), (4) can be write down in matrix form;

$$\begin{bmatrix} u \\ v \\ 1 \end{bmatrix} = \begin{bmatrix} k_u & 0 & u_0 \\ 0 & k_v & v_0 \\ 0 & 0 & 1 \end{bmatrix} \begin{bmatrix} X/Z \\ Y/Z \\ 1 \end{bmatrix} \tag{7}$$

Where $K_u = s_x f$ and $K_v = s_y f$ are the scaling factors in the X-axis and Y-axis directions of the imaging plane, and the matrix in the middle is the internal parameter of the camera.

When the image coordinate axes u and v are not vertical and the angle between them is θ, the internal parameter matrix K is:

$$K = \begin{bmatrix} k_u & k_u cot\theta & u_0 \\ 0 & k_v/sin\theta & v_0 \\ 0 & 0 & 1 \end{bmatrix} \tag{8}$$

When point M is expressed in world coordinates, the position conversion relationship between camera coordinate system and world coordinate system is shown in Eq. 7:

$$\begin{bmatrix} X \\ Y \\ Z \end{bmatrix} = R \begin{bmatrix} X_w \\ Y_w \\ Z_w \end{bmatrix} + t \tag{9}$$

Where (X_w, Y_w, Z_w) Is the coordinates of the object point m in the world coordinate system, R and t are the rotation matrix translation vectors of the two coordinate systems, which are called the external parameters of the camera.

According to formula (6) and Eq. (7), the transformation relationship from world coordinate to image coordinate is as follows:

$$Z \begin{bmatrix} u \\ v \\ 1 \end{bmatrix} = \begin{bmatrix} k_u & k_u cot\theta & u_0 \\ 0 & k_v/sin\theta & v_0 \\ 0 & 0 & 1 \end{bmatrix} [R|t] \begin{bmatrix} X_w \\ Y_w \\ Z_w \\ 1 \end{bmatrix} \tag{10}$$

3.2 Laer Calibration

The laser vision sensor is fastened on the front end of the torch and moves with it. The weld seam points, which are formed by laser stripes, can be captured by the camera of sensor and sent to computer to calculate their coordinates. Then the coordinate is sent to the robot for tracking. So, welding precision and efficiency can be improved through real-time weld position detection (Zou and Chen 2018).

The main purpose of vision sensing to recognizing welding surroundings, tracking seams, autonomously guiding as well as real-time intelligent control of Robotic welding process (Dinham and Fang 2013).

The laser calibration is mainly external parameter calibration that is to calculate the position parameters of the line structured light beam plane. (Liang and Jiahui 2018) The external parameters of the camera describe the position relationship between the camera coordinate system and the world coordinate system, while the laser external parameters describe the position relationship between the lines structured light plane and the camera coordinate. According to the content of camera calibration in the previous section, if the calibration plate plane is set as the plane of world coordinate system $Z_w = 0$, the position relationship between the current camera coordinate system and the world coordinate system can be obtained by using a calibration plate image, that is, the position of the calibration plate plane in the camera coordinate system. If the line structured light is projected on the plane of the calibration plate and the camera takes the image projected by the line structured light, the world coordinate of the projection point can be obtained from the image coordinates of the projection point of the line structured light according to the internal and external parameters of the camera, and then the camera coordinates of the projection point can be obtained according to the current external parameters. Keeping the relative position relationship between the laser and the camera unchanged and changing the relative position of the calibration plate and the camera, the camera coordinates of the projection points on the line structured light plane can be obtained, and the line structured light plane can be fitted by more than three projection points which are not collinear. The position of the line structured light plane in the camera coordinate system. Suppose that the projection point of the line structured light is $L_w = [X_w, Y_w, Z_w, 1]^T$ in the camera coordinate system. $L_c = [X_c, Y_c, Z_c, 1]^T$ in the space coordinate system, $1 = [u, v, 1]^T$.

According to $m = HM$ in the previous section, the transformation matrix H between the object point and the image point in the world coordinate system and the transformation matrix between the camera coordinate system and the world coordinate system $[R, t]$ can be obtained from a calibration plate image. Since the line structured light is projected on the plane of the calibration plate, the projection point of the line structured light has the same imaging rule that is According to the image coordinate 1 of line structured light projection, the camera coordinate can be obtained.

$$1 = HL_w \tag{11}$$

$$L_c = [R, t]L_w \tag{12}$$

According to image coordinate of the line structured light projection, the camera mark can be obtained.

$$L_c = [R, t]L_w = [R, t]H^{-1}1 \tag{13}$$

The position equation of linear structured light plan in camera coordinate system can be expressed as follow:

$$aX_c + bY_c + cZ_c + d = 0 \tag{14}$$

By changing the position of calibration plate, we can get the structured light on different planes. Assuming that the camera coordinate is $L_{ci} = [X_{ci}, Y_{ci}, Z_{ci}, 1]^T$, there are, $aX_{ci} + bY_{ci} + cZ_{ci} + d = 0$, can be written in matrix form;

$$\begin{bmatrix} X_{c1} & Y_{c1} & Z_{c1} & 1 \\ \vdots & \vdots & \vdots & \vdots \\ X_{ci} & Y_{ci} & Z_{ci} & 1 \\ \vdots & \vdots & \vdots & \vdots \\ X_{cn} & Y_{cn} & Z_{cn} & 1 \end{bmatrix} \begin{bmatrix} a \\ b \\ c \\ d \end{bmatrix} = 0 \tag{15}$$

Using the least square method to solve the following objective function, the position equation of the line structured light plane can be obtained;

$$c(a, b, c, d) = min \sum_{i=0}^{n} (\frac{a}{c}X_{ci} + \frac{b}{c}Y_{ci} + \frac{d}{c}Z_{ci})^2 \tag{16}$$

3.3 Hand-Eye Calibration

Due to flexibility and convenience, hand-eye serial robots are widely used in Industrial fields.

The "hand-eye" form is often used in the application of vision system to six axis serial robots, that is, the camera is fixed on the robot's tool. In some applications for measurement, the camera is the tool of the robot. The "eye" is given to the robot to measure the position of the target object on the robot benchmark, so as to facilitate the robot to operate the target object. The measurement of the target object is completed by phase, and the measurement result is based on the camera coordinate system. Assuming that the target object coordinate system is the world coordinate system, the position of the world coordinate system relative to the camera coordinate system is the external parameter of the camera, and the space coordinate of the target object can be converted into the camera coordinate system. In order to convert the position of the target object in the camera coordinate system into the robot base coordinate system, it is also necessary to know the relative position relationship between the camera coordinate system and the base coordinate system.

Since, the camera is fixed at the end of the robot, the position between the camera and the base of the robot is not fixed, but the position with the tool is relatively constant. The position of the tool in the base coordinate system can be obtained by the robot control system. Therefore, the position of the target object in the base coordinate system can be obtained by obtaining the position relationship between the camera and the tool. Robot hand-eye calibration is to get the relationship matrix between camera coordinate system and tool coordinate system.

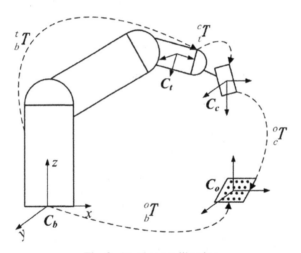

Fig. 3. Hand-eye calibration

The relationship between robot coordinate systems is shown in Fig. 3. C_0 is the target object coordinate system, that is, the world coordinate system, C_c is the camera coordinate system, C_t is the tool coordinate system, C_b is the base coordinate system, $_b^t T$ is the transformation matrix from the robot tool coordinate system to the base coordinate system, $_t^c T$ is the transformation matrix from the camera coordinate system to the tool coordinate system, and $_C^0 T$ is the transformation matrix from the world coordinate system to the camera coordinate system, $_b^0 T$ is the transformation matrix from the world coordinate system to the base coordinate system. Each transformation matrix has the following relations:

$$_b^o T = {}_b^t T {}_b^C T {}_b^O T \tag{17}$$

It can be obtained by the above formula;

$$_t^c T = {}_b^t T^{-1} {}_b^O T {}_c^0 T^{-1} \tag{18}$$

In general, $_b^t T$ is obtained by the robot control system, $_C^O T$. The external parameters of the camera can be measured by the camera, $_b^0 T$. It is the ultimate goal of hand eye calibration, which is difficult to obtain by measuring method. It is necessary to add a constraint condition F and solve at the same time $_t^c T$ and $_b^o T$, namely

$$\begin{cases} _b^0 T = {}_b^t T {}_t^c T {}_c^O T \\ f\left(_b^O T\right) = 0 \end{cases} \tag{19}$$

If the position of the target object relative to the base of the robot remains unchanged in multiple measurements, then the transformation matrix from the world coordinate system to the base coordinate system is a constant. If this is the constraint condition, then $f : {}_b^0 T_i = {}_b^0 T = {}_b^0 T_{i+1}$.

Equation (19) can be rewritten as follows:

$$_b^t T_i {}_t^c T {}_t^O T_i = {}_b^t T_{i+1} {}_t^c T {}_c^O T_{i+1} \tag{20}$$

$$_b^t T_{i+1}^{-1} {}_b^t T_i {}_t^c T = {}_t^c T_c^O T_{i+1} {}_c^o T_i^{-1} \tag{21}$$

Suppose, $A = {}_b^t T_{i+1}^{-1} {}_b^t T$, $B = {}_c^o T_{i+1} {}_c^o T_i^{-1}$, $X = {}_t^c T$, the Eq. (21) can be written as $AX = X$, its purpose of hand eye calibration is to solve the hand eye relationship matrix X.

4 Experiment and Results

ZEGE arc welding robot is used in our experimental setup. The system has included hardware and software parts. The processing of images is recorded by Camera.

In our experimental setup, we have done the following main tasks, the descriptions are under;

Image Processing
Transformation Image Coordinates to Camera Coordinate
Transformation Camera Coordinates to Robot Coordinate
To use these results in implement in real practical weld.

4.1 Image Processing

Image processing is done in the following five steps;

The coordinates of weld feature point on the image are extracted for the next step to convert the image coordinates to the manipulator coordinates. Traditional extraction method, based on the original drawing to find the characteristics of welding seam, full width processing speed is slow, and the interference caused by high misjudgment rate.

However, our method is based on the traditional method, adding an image tracker such as KCF to extract the main area of the welding seam, and only based on this area to do image preprocessing, filtering and feature extraction. The image processing speed and the robustness of weld location are greatly improved.

The main process is as follow:

Step 1. KCF
In this step, we got ROI region by use of KCF to ROI image tracking algorithm for finds the weld area of interest, as shown in below in Fig. 4(a).

In order to reduce the computational cost for image processing, only the area nearby seams of images is necessary to be processed. So the range of interest (ROI) should be detected.

The purpose to do this step is to extract the ROI area where the weld is located to reduce the time of Image processing and other environmental noise interference.

Step 2. Median Filtering
The main purpose of Median filtering is to remove isolated noise and retain image details.

Median filtering which shown in Fig. 4(b), adopts nonlinear method, which is very effective in smoothing pulse noise. Meanwhile, it can protect sharp edges of images and select appropriate points to replace the value of pollution points. Therefore, it has a good processing effect, good performance against salt and pepper noise and poor performance against Gaussian noise.

Step 3. Close Operations
The goal of this operation is to connect the laser image of the line and keep the original shape unchanged due to the influence of welding surface material absorption or sensor shooting angle. Close Operation is shown in Fig. 4(c). Mainly closed operation is equal to expansion operation then corrosion operation.

It can fill out the small cracks, discontinuities and holes in the foreground object, while the total position and shape remain unchanged.

Different sizes of Structural elements will lead to different filtering effects.

The selection of different structural elements leads to different segmentation that is, different features are extracted.

Step 4. Thinning
It's also called, Grayscale centroid method, shown in Fig. 4 (d).The aim of this step; the gray center of gravity of each line of line laser images is used to extract the frame of line laser image, which reduces the redundancy of data and facilities data processing.

Considering that the laser brightness distribution is the highest in the center and gradually decreases along the two sides, the grayscale centroid method is used to refine the image.

Step 5. Hough Transform
The final step of image processing is Hough Transform, since the weld feature identified is fillet weld, the intersection point of two straight lines are considered as the feature point. Hough transform is shown in Fig. 4(e).

Finally, results mark the location of feature point on the original drawing.

Since the weld feature identified is fillet weld, the intersection point of two straight lines is considered as the feature point.

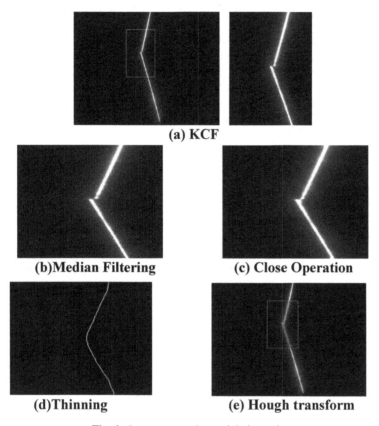

(a) KCF

(b)Median Filtering   (c) Close Operation

(d)Thinning   (e) Hough transform

Fig. 4. Image processing and their results

4.2 Transformation Image Coordinates to Camera Co-ordinate

Camera Calibration method is used to transformation of Image coordinates to Camera coordinate.

4.3 Transformation Camera Coordinates to Robot Coordinate

Hand-eye transformation is used to transform the Camera coordinate to Robot Coordinate.

5 Conclusion

Camera calibration and hand-eye calibration are key problems in the applications of vision robots. In this paper, we have defined our experimental process, through visual identification of welds and calculation of positions and attitudes of welds, automatic planning of welding path was carried out for welding of eight pipeline types. The three task includes; image processing which includes further total 5 steps; to get the image from camera source, ROI image through Deep Learning "KCF", to use Morphological processing for remove the noise, and then get thinning when noise removed well, using Hough line to get close point and finally the result, second task includes camera calibration method and final task for transformation camera coordinate to Robot coordinate, have used the eye-in hand calibration.

6 Future Work

Our future works include the following:

The Camera Calibration accuracy is related to the attitude, distance, pattern and size of the checkerboard. The calibration accuracy of linear laser sensor needs to be improved.

Camera attitude, shooting distance, robot arm attitude, different $AX = XB$ solution method, sample number and so on will all affect the result during calibration.

The positioning accuracy of welding seam need to be improved. Since the weld may actually be reflective materials, the interference in the image will increase and the positioning of various weld images will be expanded.

The position and attitude of the generated trajectory are interpolated and smoothed. At present, the sampling frequency of the trajectory is low, and dense point positions are required for the manipulator to move coherently. Moreover, for positions with large attitude changes, the welding attitude of the manipulator should be smoothen to ensure the stability of the welding.

The final process is the welding process. This project solved the positioning of the weld in the real space theory, but in fact, the actual welding process needs to be considered, such as the width of the weld needs to be calculated, and the trajectory trend of the weld in the real space, such as uphill or downhill, will directly affect the final welding effect.

Acknowledgment. This work was supported by China Construction Shenzhen and completed by Shenzhen Super-Accurate Vision Technology Co. LTD. The authors would like to thanks the staff of the company for their valuable suggestions and comments.

References

Cai, C., Fan, B., Weng, X., Zhu, Q., Su, L.: A target tracking and location robot system based on omnistereo vision. Ind. Robot. Int. J. https://doi.org/10.1108/IR-03-2017-0042

Chen, S., Lv, N.: Research evolution on intelligentized technologies for arc welding process. J. Manuf. Process. **16**, 109–122 (2014)

Dinham, M., Fang, G.: Autonomous weld seam identification and localisation using eye-in-hand stereo vision for robotic arc welding. Robot. Comput. Integr. Manuf. **29**(5), 288–301 (2013). https://doi.org/10.1016/j.rcim.2013.01.004

Giuffrida, G., Meoni, G., Fanucci, L.: A YOLOv2 convolutional neural network-based human-machine interface for the control of assistive robotic manipulators. Appl. Sci. **9**, 2243 (2019)

Wang, H., Lu, X., Hu, Z., Li, Y.: A vision-based fully-automatic calibration method for hand-eye serial robot. Ind. Robot. Int. J. **42**(1), 64–73. https://doi.org/10.1108/IR-06-2014-0352

Aviles-Viñas, J.F., Lopez-Juarez, I., Rios-Cabrera, R.: Acquisition of welding skills in industrial robots. Ind. Robot Int. J. **42**(2), 156–166. https://doi.org/10.1108/IR-09-2014-0395

Gong, J., Mei, Y., Zhou, Y.: Research on an improved KCF target tracking algorithm based on CNN feature extraction. In: 2020 IEEE International Conference on Artificial Intelligence and Computer Applications (ICAICA), Dalian, China, pp. 538–543 (2020). https://doi.org/10.1109/ICAICA50127.2020.9182522

Li, Y., Wang, Q., Xu, D., Yan, Z., Tan, M.: Recent developments on welding image processing and features extraction. Meas. Control **40**(5), 139–145 (2007). https://doi.org/10.1177/002029400704000502

Li, H., Ma, Q., Wang, T., Chirikjian, G.S.: Simultaneous hand-eye and robot-world calibration by solving the $AX=YB$ problem without correspondence. IEEE Robot. Autom. Lett. **1**(1), 145–152 (2016). https://doi.org/10.1109/lra.2015.2506663

Method and Application of Robot Trajectory tracking based on Line-structured Laser 3D Vision, Master thesis, Liang Jiahui, South China University Guangzhou China (2018)

Dinham, M., Fang, G.: A low cost hand-eye calibration method for arc welding robots. In: 2009 IEEE International Conference on Robotics and Biomimetics (ROBIO), Guilin, pp. 1889–1893 (2019).https://doi.org/10.1007/978-90-313-7627-8_10

Qiu, M.A.: A practical and robust method for hand-eye calibration. IFAC Proc. **28**(16), 275–280 (1995).https://doi.org/10.1016/S1474-6670(17)45191-3. ISSN 1474-6670

Ketcham, M., Ganokratanaa, T.: The analysis of lane detection algorithms using histogram shapes and Hough transform. Int. J. Intell. Comput. Cybern. **8**(3), 262–278 (2015). https://doi.org/10.1108/IJICC-05-2014-0024

Wan, F., Song, C.: Flange-based Hand-eye calibration using a 3D camera with high resolution, accuracy, and frame rate. Front. Robot. AI **7**, 65 (2020). https://doi.org/10.3389/frobt.2020.00065

Wei, S., Wang, J., Lin, T., et al.: Application of image morphology in detecting and extracting the initial welding position. J. Shanghai Jiaotong Univ. (Sci.) **17**, 323–326 (2012). https://doi.org/10.1007/s12204-012-1278-9

Wu, Q.-Q., et al.: A study on the modified Hough algorithm for image processing in weld seam tracking. J. Mech. Sci. Technol. **29**(11), 4859–4865 (2015). https://doi.org/10.1007/s12206-015-1033-x

Li, X., Li, X., Khyam, M.O., Ge, S.S.: Robust welding seam tracking and recognition. IEEE Sens. J. **17**(17), 5609–5617 (2017). https://doi.org/10.1109/JSEN.2017.2730280

Zou, Y., Chen, X.: Hand–eye calibration of arc welding robot and laser vision sensor through semidefinite programming. Ind. Robot **45**(5), 597–610 (2018). https://doi.org/10.1108/IR-02-2018-0034

Zhang, Z., Wen, G.: An easy method of image feature extraction for real-time welding defects detection. In: 2016 13th International Conference on Ubiquitous Robots and Ambient Intelligence (URAI), Xi'an, pp. 615–619 (2016). https://doi.org/10.1109/URAI.2016.7625790

Zeng, J., Cao, G.-Z., Peng, Y.-P., Huang, S.-D.: A weld joint type identification method for visual sensor based on image features and SVM. Sensors **20**(2), 471 (2020).https://doi.org/10.3390/s20020471

Brain Connectivity: Exploring from a High-Level Topological Perspective

Wei Sheng[1,2], Liang Li[1,2], Shaoqiang Han[1,2], Yunshuang Fan[1,2], Chong Wang[1,2], Qin Tang[1,2], Yuyan Chen[1,2], Qian Cui[2], and Huafu Chen[1,2(✉)]

[1] The Clinical Hospital of Chengdu Brain Science Institute, School of Life Science and Technology, University of Electronic Science and Technology of China, Chengdu, China
chenhf@uestc.edu.cn

[2] MOE Key Lab for Neuroinformation, High-Field Magnetic Resonance Brain Imaging Key Laboratory of Sichuan Province, University of Electronic Science and Technology of China, Chengdu, China

Abstract. How invariant structural architecture of brain coupling with variant functionality is still unclear in neuroscience. The previous exploration of relationships between large-scale structural and functional brain networks mainly focused on whole or partial statistical correlation, ignoring network context information, such as network topology structure. Here we applied a network representation learning approach to create high-order representations of structural or functional networks while preserving network context information for studying the function-structure coupling of the brain at topological subnetwork levels. We found that the structural and functional network obtained from the network representation learning method was more stable and more tightly coupled than those from the conventional correlation method, primarily distributed in high-order cognitive networks. Application on schizophrenia patients showed decoupling on the default-mode network, dorsal attention network, executive control network, and salience network, as well as the over-coupling on the sensorimotor network, compared with healthy controls. Overall, network representation learning can more effectively capture the higher-order coupling between brain structure and function and provides a good technical means for us to study mental illness.

Keywords: Brain connectivity · High-order representations · Schizophrenia

1 Introduction

In the past several decades, researches in neuroscience have shown that brain regions do not work in isolation [1]. The conjoint function of brain areas working together to support complex brain functions upon its relative fixed anatomical connectivity [2]. Recent evidence such as small-worldness and modularity in structural brain networks suggests that this stable architecture of the brain may reflect a balance between wiring costs and computational efficiency [3]. Furthermore, surveys conducted by Honey [4] have shown that the brain structure network is not identical to the function network, but

© Springer Nature Switzerland AG 2021
Y. Peng et al. (Eds.): ICIG 2021, LNCS 12889, pp. 18–29, 2021.
https://doi.org/10.1007/978-3-030-87358-5_2

is constrained by its factors. However, the ubiquitous degeneracy at the level of cognitive anatomy suggests that the relationship between human brain structure and function is more complex [5, 6].

Several attempts have been made to clarify the relationship between structure and function in the human brain summarized through a network perspective. Hermundstad [7] and Ekman [8] shows that flexible and facilitate functional network are due to the reconfiguration of those long-range connections which is constrained by structural connectivity. Some researchers have reported that the shortest paths [9] and other diffusion properties of the structure network [10, 11] can shape the functional networks. Nowadays, some literature has been published to demonstrate that all possible paths on structural connectivity determined the functional connectivity [12, 13]. Although these works further explored the weak and elusive rules that how anatomy constrains brain dynamics in the past decade, there remain some issues. On the other hand, graph neural networks (GNN) is an emerging technology that could be used in learning partial latent representation in network or reasoning about discrete entities and structure among lots of relationship-known objects [14, 15]. Recently, several works convert nodes and edges to a continuous space vector to tackle tasks such as node classification or link prediction on the network [16, 17]. Also, methods that represent parts of the network were proposed [18, 19]. Combined with that, many strategies have already been adopted and obtained success in the research of social networks [20], recommendation systems [21], and biomedical networks [22]. In this sense, introducing GNN into brain network research has attracted extreme attention as well, and hereby, it has resulted in some achievements [23].

In this paper, an approach named Sub2vec [19] was applied to capture the macroscopic relationship between brain subnetworks in a low-dimensional continuous vector space, to further explore their relationships such as coupling relation between structural and functional connectivity in subnetwork-level.

2   Materials and Methods

2.1   Participants and Data Acquisition

Datasets: The analyses were conducted on a dataset of 40 healthy participants (Dataset 1) and validated on an independent dataset of 37 healthy and 38 schizophrenia participants (Dataset 2).

Dataset 1. The study was approved by the research ethics committee of the University of Electronic Science and Technology of China and informed written consent from each participant was obtained before study inclusion. The MRI data of all participants were acquired using a 3T GE DISCOVERY MR750 scanner (General Electric, Fairfield Connecticut, USA) with an 8-channel prototype quadrature birdcage head coil. T1-weighted images, diffusion tensor imaging (DTI) and functional images parameters have been described in our previous study [24].

Dataset 2. Before the collection of MRI data, the study was registered in the Chinese Clinical Trial Registry (ChiCTR1800014844). All subjects were recruited from the Second Affiliated Hospital of Xinxiang Medical University. The MRI data of all participants were acquired using a 3T Siemens MRI scanner (Siemens Verio, Erlangen, Germany).

T1-weighted images, diffusion tensor imaging (DTI) and functional image parameters have been described in our previous study [25] (Table 1).

Table 1. Characteristics of demographic and clinical variables of dataset 2

	HC (N = 37)	SCZ (N = 38)	P value
Age (years)	25.12 ± 4.58	24.98 ± 4.76	0.56[a]
Gender (female/males)	21/16	26/12	0.30[b]
Education (years)	11.12 ± 2.8	10.4 ± 2.9	0.25[a]
Course (months)	8.29 ± 2.58		
PANSS positive symptoms	25.78 ± 3.60		
PANSS negative symptoms	18.32 ± 5.18		
PANSS general symptoms	48.29 ± 6.47		
PANSS total symptoms	92.39 ± 10.92		

HC, healthy controls; SCZ, schizophrenia; PANSS, positive and negative syndrome scale;
[a]Two-sample t-test.
[b]chi–square test.

2.2 Data Preprocessing

DTI data were processed using the Diffusion Toolkit and TrackVis software (http://tra ckvis.org/blog/tag/diffusion-toolkit/), and resting-state fMRI were preprocessed using Data Processing Assistant for Resting-State fMRI package (DPARSFA, http://www.res tfmri.net). The cerebral cortex was parcellated into a set of 246 regions of the human Brainnetcome Atlas [26]. More preprocessing details are same as our previous study [24, 25]. Dataset 1 and Dataset 2 are under the same data preprocessing.

2.3 Subnetwork Embedding

First, after structural and functional connectome construction based 246 nodes and divide them to 17 subnetworks, a subnetwork embedding algorithm is applied to transfer subnetworks of connectome into a low-dimension continuous vector representation, or subnetwork embedding (SE) (Fig. 1a–c). Next, we check the stability and effectivity of those SEs generated by sub2vec from structural and functional subnetworks on each participant for 500 iterations. Then, we demonstrate that SE is more stable and powerful to reflect the relationship between structural and functional subnetwork connectivity compared with the previous study. Lastly, we use SE to explore the difference between structure and function coupling among patients with schizophrenia and normal subjects.

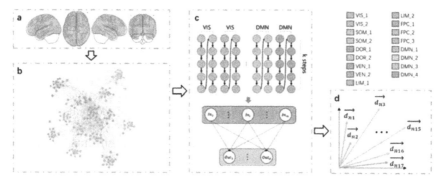

Fig. 1. Illustration of the pipeline about how to transform brain subnetwork into embedding space. **a)** The 17 sub-areas in the brain, each color represents a unique brain area. **b)** The inter-connections and intra-connections among 17 networks in the brain. **c)** The embedding procedure in subnetwork, each circle denotes a node in sub-network. The arrow between two nodes denotes the walks from one node to another in random walk sampling process. The bottom part denotes a shallow neural network that aims to learn latent representation from sampled node series. **d)** Each arrow that is a vector representation of a sub-network has a topological meaning.

2.4 SE-Based Identification

This identification was first performed across pairs of SE vectors consisting of structural SE vectors and functional SE vectors, with the requirement that the structural SE vectors and the functional SE vectors be taken from the same participant and in the same iteration: for example, structural SE vectors were used as the target and compared to a database of functional SE vectors. For each iteration of 500 iterations on each participant, one structural SE vector was selected from the target set and compared against each of the functional SE vectors in the database to find the maximally similar vector. The similarity was defined as the cosine similarity between the structural SE vector and the selected functional SE vector from the database. Once an identity had been predicted, the true identity of the target structural SE vector was encoded and that the sign was assigned a score of 1 if the predicted identity matched the true identity, or 0 if it did not. Within a target-database pair, each structural SE vector was tested against the database in an independent trial.

3 Results

3.1 The Stable Relationship Between SEs

To test whether SE can reflect the topological information stably, we mainly focused on examining the relationship among SEs. Following this, the stability of the relationship among SE vectors derived from structural or functional subnetworks in two different datasets is checked. The cosine similarity is computed between each pair of structural SE vectors in all iterations of each participant. This procedure resulted in a reconstruction of the structural subnetwork association matrix (structural embedding reconstruction).

Similarly, the functional embedding reconstruction is derived from the corresponding functional SE vectors through the cosine similarity metric.

To investigate the reliability of these two kinds of inter-connections separately, an index named Intra-class Correlation Coefficient (ICC) is computed on each kind of connection [27]. In previous studies, the ICC index was used to measure test-retest reliability [28, 29]. Therefore, we calculated ICCs of structural or functional embedding reconstruction in 500 iterations on each participant after the embedding reconstruction procedure.

For structural SE vectors of each participant, there are 500 structural embedding reconstructions generated from 17 structural SE vectors. In a word, the inter-connections build upon structural SE vectors are measured 500 times. Accordingly, for all structural embedding reconstructions of each participant, an ICC value can be computed. The same procedure was applied in all functional embedding reconstructions of this participant. These results are shown in Fig. 2a.

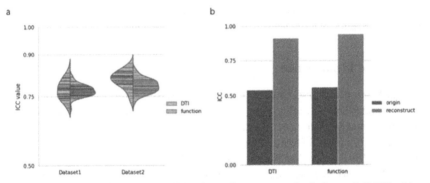

Fig. 2. Computed ICC values. **a)** The ICC values of reconstructed relations of all HC subjects, including the structural network and the functional network in two datasets. **b)** The ICC values of all subjects between traditional relations and reconstructed relations in two kinds of brain connectivity (DTI and function).

To further explore the interconnection issues in structural or functional SE vectors at the group level, we performed group-based ICC analysis on the two datasets. We assumed that if the SE vectors manage to capture high-order topological information of subnetworks, the constructed embedding reconstructions should be more stable in these participants compared with the traditional interconnections within subnetworks.

As implied by the above exploration, the relationship among structural or functional SE vectors encompass topological information of structural or functional subnetwork is pretty stable in 500 iterations for each participant. Accordingly, we averaged the 500 structural or functional embedding reconstructions as a representation of each participant. Since the interconnection between each pair of SE vectors is regarded as an entity and each participant in each dataset as a rater. Four ICC values were computed accordingly, and the reliability is compared between traditional interconnections in the subnetworks and embedding reconstructions to find whether there are significant differences in these two kinds of subnetwork interconnections. The steps are as follows:

First, an ICC value can be calculated in structural embedding reconstructions in all HC participants in Dataset 1 and Dataset 2. Next, another ICC value in functional embedding reconstructions is computed similarly. Then, equivalently to the results obtained from embedding reconstructions, two ICC values can be derived from traditional interconnections within the structural or functional subnetworks. Finally, a two-sample t-test was applied to support that the difference was statistically significant ($p < 0.01$). The result is shown in Fig. 2b.

3.2 Traditional Relationship Preserved in SE Vectors

As implied by the stability analysis, the relation between the learned SE vectors is pretty stable. To further explore the nature of SE vectors, a comparison between embedding reconstruction and traditional interconnections within the subnetworks is applied. We did not expect a perfect reconstruction of the traditional interconnections. Rather, we assumed that the high-level topological attributes captured by SE vector can be reflected in SE pair-wise relation. We checked the similarity between the averaged embedding reconstruction and traditional interconnections in the subnetworks. The results showed that dataset1: 0.584 ± 0.039 (DTI), 0.879 ± 0.084 (function); dataset2: 0.686 ± 0.028 (DTI), 0.886 ± 0.06 (function).

3.3 Comparison Between the Traditional and Reconstructed Coupling

We further investigate the relationship between structural SE vectors and corresponding functional SE vectors with a comparison of traditional subnetwork structure-function relation on a group level. Due to the structural and functional subnetworks of each participant are embedded into the identify Euclidean space, the cosine similarity can be used to measure the relation between structural SE vectors and functional SE vectors on each participant and in the same iteration. First, a relation between structural SE vectors and corresponding functional SE vectors on a group of participants was constructed as a reconstructed structure-function coupling. Then, the traditional structure-function coupling derived from traditional structural subnetworks and traditional functional subnetworks is constructed similarly. Finally, a comparison analysis between the reconstructed structure-function coupling and the traditional structure-function coupling is applied.

As stated prior, a SE-based identification to explore the reconstructed structure-function coupling on the group level is proposed. We tested identification across all possible pairs of SE vectors. In each case, the success rate was measured as the percentage of participants whose identity was correctly predicted out of the total number of subjects. After identification in SE vectors, we tested identification accuracy on traditional subnetworks similarly. The result is shown as follows:

To further analyze the differences between reconstructed structure-function coupling and origin reconstructed structure-function coupling, the differences in 17 subnetworks are examined individually. Moreover, a χ^2 test is applied to compare whether there exist differences between the traditional structure-function coupling and the reconstructed structure-function coupling. We just find significant difference in subnet 3, 6, 8, 16 in both datasets.

- Dataset1: subnet-3 ($\chi^2 = 15.39, p < 0.05$), subnet-6 ($\chi^2 = 30.13, p < 0.05$), subnet-8 ($\chi^2 = 9.43, p < 0.05$) and subnet-16 ($\chi^2 = 35.69, p < 0.05$).
- Dataset2: subnet-3 ($\chi^2 = 17.72, p < 0.05$), subnet-6 ($\chi^2 = 9.33, p < 0.05$), subnet-8 ($\chi^2 = 21.68, p < 0.05$) and subnet-16 ($\chi^2 = 20.74, p < 0.05$).

The result is shown in Fig. 3. According to the comparison, subnet-3, subnet-6, subnet-8 and subnet-16 are found distinctly different between traditional structural-functional coupling and reconstructed structural-functional coupling in both dataset1 and dataset2. While the reconstructed structural-functional coupling between dataset1 and dataset2 is consistent, subnet-3 ($\chi^2 = 0.79, p = 0.37$), subnet-6 ($\chi^2 = 0.95, p = 0.33$), subnet-8 ($\chi^2 = 0.31, p = 0.58$) and subnet-16 ($\chi^2 = 0.01, p = 0.94$).

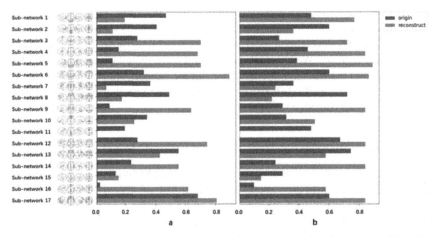

Fig. 3. The comparison of sub-network structural-functional coupling between traditional and reconstructed inter-connections. **a)** Structural-functional coupling between traditional and reconstructed inter-connections in dataset 1. **b)** Structural-functional coupling between traditional and reconstructed inter-connections in dataset 2.

3.4 Coupling in Schizophrenia

The high order topological contained in structure-function coupling provides a novel opportunity to bridge structure-function coupling and schizophrenia brain network abnormalities. One potential application is to explore whether exists differences in structure-function coupling between schizophrenia and healthy control. Especially, the SE-based identification can be applied in schizophrenias and compared with the healthy control group (Dataset 2). Then a two samples t-test can be used to find the significantly different subnetworks reflected by structural-functional coupling disorders.

We utilize sensorimotor network (subnet-3), attention network (subnet-6), salience network (subnet-8), and default mode network (subnet-16) in above as testbed to exemplifying the variation of the structure-function coupling according to corresponding SE vectors. It is commonly accepted that both functional and anatomical connectivity variants in large-scale networks of schizophrenia. Accordingly, we present a hypothesis that there exist differences in high order topological structure-function coupling between schizophrenia and healthy control. To test this hypothesis, we first compute the reconstructed structural-functional coupling in 17 subnetworks between schizophrenia and healthy control, then a two-sample t-test is applied to find the differences of coupling between schizophrenia and healthy control. After that, we observed that the attention network, salience network, and default mode network showed decreased structural-functional coupling, meanwhile the sensorimotor network showed increased structural-functional coupling in schizophrenia compared with healthy control. The result is shown in Fig. 4.

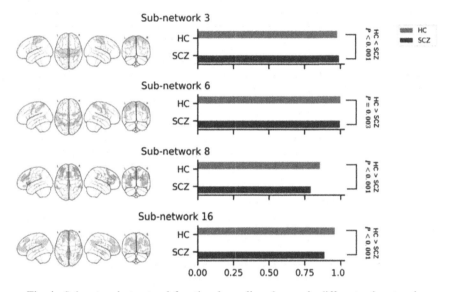

Fig. 4. Sub-network structural-functional coupling changes in different sub-networks.

4 Discussion

4.1 A Subsection Sample

As previously stated, apply the embedding approach that captures context structural topological information in brain networks holds great promise [30, 31]. In this work, we first use ICC measures to identify that the relationship between each pair of subnetwork embedding in an individual is pretty stable according to the previous standard [29]. Then, compared with the traditional connectivity of the subnetwork, we discovered that the connectivity derived from embedding is more stable among all two datasets no matter in the structural or functional brain. Although many researchers reported that brain structure shows a high degree of heterogeneity among individuals [32, 33], as well as brain function [34, 35]. This result indicates that our approach may find a high-order topological eigenmode of subnetwork both in brain structure and function overall participates. Besides, the moderate similarity between traditional and reconstructed subnetwork connectivity as well as a strong correlation in reconstructed structural-functional coupling could also provide another proof about our hypothesis.

However, previous studies focused on a direct statistical comparison between static brain structure and fluctuated functional activities [2]. Our study provides a local integration view to study the structural-functional coupling relation. We revealed several prominent subnetworks coupling that distinctively differs from the traditional coupling: the attention network, the default mode network, the sensorimotor network, and the silence network [36]. Those findings are highly consistent in two datasets and contribute to the major forte compared with traditional structural-functional coupling. The traditional structural-functional subnetwork coupling based on a statistical correlation only includes low-order topological patterns [37, 38], while the reconstructed coupling relationship contains high-order information in the network [15]. According to our observation, the strong coupling of the significant network in the traditional structure-function relationship indicates that there may be mainly low-order connection modes. Moreover, the coupling relation in the attention network, the default mode network, and the sensorimotor network may be mainly reflected in high-order connection patterns.

To capitalize on the high refined power of subnet embedding that contains multi-order in brain connectivity, we tested whether there exists a distinct variance between normal people and schizophrenia patients. We use the coupling between structural and functional subnetwork embeddings as a test-bed and compared schizophrenia patients with normal people. Compared with healthy controls, the decoupling of structure-function high-order relation discovered on the default mode network may be explained by a decrease in gray matter and deactivation within the subnetwork regions, which is consistent with previous studies [39, 40]. Similarly, the observed high-order decoupling on the salience network may be due to the reduced functional connectivity and fractional anisotropy among the salience network regions in schizophrenia patients reported in Wang's study [41]. Moreover, the attention network reported attentional deficits [42] also was the cause of decoupling in the high-order relationship. On the contrary, the widespread alterations in the connectivity with higher-order nodes discovered in Tobias's report [43] may be a reasonable interpretation of the over-coupling in high-order relation of the sensorimotor network. In line with previous work, our findings suggest that the aberrant changes in schizophrenia brain activity may result from a localized coupling disorder between anatomical structure and functional activity.

5   Conclusion

This study revealed network representation learning can more effectively capture the higher-order coupling between brain structure and function and provides a good technical means for us to study mental illness, and provide us with a new exploration perspective for understanding the constraints of structure on function.

Acknowledgments. This study was supported by the Key Project of Research and Development of Ministry of Science and Technology (2018AAA0100705), and the Natural Science Foundation of China (61533006, U1808204, 62036003, 81771919).

References

1. Freemon, F.R.: Histology of the nervous system of man and vertebrates. JAMA J. Am. Med. Assoc. **275**, 493 (1996)
2. Park, H.J., Friston, K.: Structural and functional brain networks: from connections to cognition. Science **342**, 1289 (2013)
3. Bullmore, E., Sporns, O.: The economy of brain network organization. Nat. Rev. Neurosci. **13**(5), 336–349 (2012)
4. Honey, C.J., et al.: Network structure of cerebral cortex shapes functional connectivity on multiple time scales. Proc. Natl Acad. Sci. USA **104** (2007). 6 pages
5. Edelman, G.M., Gally, J.A: Degeneracy and complexity in biological systems. Proc. Natl. Acad. Sci. USA **98**(24), 13763–13768 (2001)
6. Friston, K.J., Price, C.J.: Degeneracy and redundancy in cognitive anatomy. Trend Cogn. **7**, 151–152 (2003)
7. Hermundstad, A.M., et al.: Structural foundations of resting-state and task-based functional connectivity in the human brain. Proc. Natl. Acad. Sci. **110**(15), 6169–6174 (2013)
8. Ekman, M., et al.: Predicting errors from reconfiguration patterns in human brain networks. Proc. Natl. Acad. Sci. **109**(41), 16714–16719 (2012)
9. Goñi, J., et al.: Resting-brain functional connectivity predicted by analytic measures of network communication. Proc. Natl. Acad. Sci. **111**(2), 833–838 (2014)
10. Kuceyeski, A., et al.: The application of a mathematical model linking structural and functional connectomes in severe brain injury. Neuroimage Clin. **11**, 635–647 (2016)
11. Abdelnour, F., Voss, H.U., Raj, A.J.N.: Network diffusion accurately models the relationship between structural and functional brain connectivity networks. Neuroimage **90**, 335–347 (2014)
12. Gilson, M., et al.: Framework based on communicability and flow to analyze complex network dynamics. Phys. Rev. E **97**(5), 052301 (2018)
13. Robinson, P.A.J.P.R.E., Interrelating anatomical, effective, and functional brain connectivity using propagators and neural field theory. Phys. Rev. E **85**(1), 011912 (2012)
14. Scarselli, F., et al.: Computational capabilities of graph neural networks. IEEE Trans. Neural Netw. **20**(1), 81–102 (2008)
15. Perozzi, B., Al-Rfou, R., Skiena, S.: Deepwalk: Online learning of social representations. In: Proceedings of the 20th ACM SIGKDD International Conference on Knowledge Discovery and Data Mining (2014)
16. Zhang, D., et al.: Network representation learning: a survey. IEEE Trans. Big Data **6**(1), 3–28 (2018)
17. Chen, Y., Lu, H., Qiu, J., Wang, L.: A tutorial of graph representation. In: Sun, X., Pan, Z., Bertino, E. (eds.) ICAIS 2019. LNCS, vol. 11632, pp. 368–378. Springer, Cham (2019). https://doi.org/10.1007/978-3-030-24274-9_33
18. Dutta, A., et al.: Hierarchical stochastic graphlet embedding for graph-based pattern recognition, pp. 1–18 (2019)
19. Adhikari, B., Zhang, Y., Ramakrishnan, N., Prakash, B.A.: Sub2vec: feature learning for subgraphs. In: Phung, D., Tseng, V.S., Webb, G.I., Ho, B., Ganji, M., Rashidi, L. (eds.) PAKDD 2018. LNCS (LNAI), vol. 10938, pp. 170–182. Springer, Cham (2018). https://doi.org/10.1007/978-3-319-93037-4_14

20. Zang, C., Cui, P., Faloutsos, C.: Beyond sigmoids: The nettide model for social network growth, and its applications. In: Proceedings of the 22nd ACM SIGKDD International Conference on Knowledge Discovery and Data Mining (2016)
21. Ying, R., et al.: Graph convolutional neural networks for web-scale recommender systems. In: Proceedings of the 24th ACM SIGKDD International Conference on Knowledge Discovery & Data Mining (2018)
22. Gottlieb, A., et al.: PREDICT: a method for inferring novel drug indications with application to personalized medicine. Mol. Syst. Biol. **7**(1), 496 (2011)
23. Li, X., Dvornek, N.C., Zhou, Y., Zhuang, J., Ventola, P., Duncan, J.S.: Graph neural network for interpreting task-fmri biomarkers. In: Shen, D., Liu, T., Peters, T.M., Staib, L.H., Essert, C., Zhou, S., Yap, P.-T., Khan, A. (eds.) MICCAI 2019. LNCS, vol. 11768, pp. 485–493. Springer, Cham (2019). https://doi.org/10.1007/978-3-030-32254-0_54
24. Cui, Q., et al.: Dynamic changes of amplitude of low-frequency fluctuations in patients with generalized anxiety disorder. Hum. Brain Map. **4**(16), 1667–1676 (2019)
25. Han, S., Huang, W., Zhang, Y., Zhao, J., Chen, H.: Recognition of early-onset schizophrenia using deep-learning method. Appl. Inform. **4**(1), 1–6 (2017). https://doi.org/10.1186/s40535-017-0044-3
26. Fan, L., et al.: The human brainnetome atlas: a new brain atlas based on connectional architecture. Cereb. Cortex **26**, 3508–3526 (2016)
27. Shrout, P.E., Fleiss, J.L.: Intraclass correlations: uses in assessing rater reliability. Physcol. Bull. **86**(2), 420 (1979)
28. Shehzad, Z., et al.: The resting brain: unconstrained yet reliable. Cereb. Cortex **19**, 2209–2229 (2009)
29. Zuo, X.N., et al.: Reliable intrinsic connectivity networks: test-retest evaluation using ICA and dual regression approach. NeuroImage **49**, 2163–2177 (2010)
30. Richiardi, J., et al.: Machine learning with brain graphs: predictive modeling approaches for functional imaging in systems neuroscience. IEEE Signal Process. Mag. **30**(3), 58–70 (2013)
31. Rosenthal, G., et al.: Mapping higher-order relations between brain structure and function with embedded vector representations of connectomes. Nat. Commun. **9**(1), 1–12 (2018)
32. Amunts, K., et al.: Brodmann's areas 17 and 18 brought into stereotaxic space—where and how variable? Neuroimage **11**(1), 66–84 (2000)
33. Bürgel, U., et al.: White matter fiber tracts of the human brain: three-dimensional mapping at microscopic resolution, topography and intersubject variability. Neuroimage **29**(4), 1092–1105 (2006)
34. Rypma, B., D'Esposito, M.J.: The roles of prefrontal brain regions in components of working memory: effects of memory load and individual differences. Proc. Natl. Acad. Sci. **96**(11), 6558–6563 (1999)
35. Newman, S.D., et al.: Frontal and parietal participation in problem solving in the Tower of London: fMRI and computational modeling of planning and high-level perception. Proc. Natl. Acad. **41**(12), 1668–1682 (2003)
36. Buckner, R.L., et al.: The organization of the human cerebellum estimated by intrinsic functional connectivity. J. Neurophysiol. **106**(5), 2322–2345 (2011)
37. Honey, C.J., et al.: Predicting human resting-state functional connectivity from structural connectivity. Proc. Natl. Acad. Sci. **106**, 2035–2040 (2009)
38. Bullmore, E., Sporns, O.: Complex brain networks: graph theoretical analysis of structural and functional systems. Nat. Rev. Neurosci. **10**, 186–198 (2009)
39. Falkenberg, I., et al.: Failure to deactivate medial prefrontal cortex in people at high risk for psychosis. Eur. Physc. **30**, 633–640 (2015)
40. Salgado-Pineda, P., et al.: Correlated structural and functional brain abnormalities in the default mode network in schizophrenia patients. Schizophrenia Res. **125**(2–3), 101–109 (2011)

41. Wang, C., et al.: Disrupted salience network functional connectivity and white-matter microstructure in persons at risk for psychosis: findings from the LYRIKS study. Physchol. Med. **46**(13), 2771–2783 (2016)
42. Kai, W., et al.: Selective impairment of attentional networks of orienting and executive control in schizophrenia. Schizophrenia Res. **78**(2–3), 235–241 (2005)
43. Kaufmann, T., et al.: Disintegration of sensorimotor brain networks in schizophrenia. ScienceDirect. **33** (2016)

Hetero-STAN: Crowd Flow Prediction by Heterogeneous Spatio-Temporal Attention Network

Kai Fang, Enze Yang$^{(\boxtimes)}$, Yuxin Liu, and Shuoyan Liu

Institute of Computer Technologies Department,
China Academy of Railway Sciences, Beijing 100082, China

Abstract. Crowd flow prediction has involved in extensive applications like intelligent transportation and public safety, especially in metropolis where the crowd flow usually show high nonlinearities and complex patterns. Among the existing prediction methods, most of them suffer from (1) implicit long-term spatial dependency, (2) the external factors lack of crucial spatial attributes, (3) complex spatio-temporal dynamics with uncertain external conditions, which yield limited performance. This paper proposes a novel method using spatio-temporal attention network with heterogeneous feature enhancement. Specifically, heterogeneous feature enhancement introduces spatial mapping and Periodic Dilated Convolution (PDC), the former provides the dimension supplement of external factors while PDC could capture the correlations of both spatial and temporal domain. Moreover, a Spatio-Temporal Attention (STA) mechanism is proposed to further obtain the dynamic spatial-temporal correlations. Our framework is evaluated on several citywide crowd flow datasets, i.e. TaxiBJ, MobileBJ and TaxiNYC, the experimental results indicate the proposed method outperforms the state-of-the-art baselines by a satisfied margin.

Keywords: Crowd flow prediction · Periodic dilated convolution · Spatial mapping · Spatio-temporal attention

1 Introduction

With the rapid progress of urbanization, modernized metropolises engendered big challenges such as increased energy consumption, traffic congestion, frequent traffic accidents and air pollution. In recent years, sensing technologies and large-scale intelligent facilities have produced a variety of big data in citywide spaces, this could help to tackle the challenges of urbanization. Urban computing is a vision proposed in [16], which aims to reveal the huge of knowledge from big and heterogeneous data collected in urban spaces and solve the major citywide issues. As a significant topic in urban computing, the research of crowd flow and attribute has involved in intelligent transportation and smart city applications.

© Springer Nature Switzerland AG 2021
Y. Peng et al. (Eds.): ICIG 2021, LNCS 12889, pp. 30–41, 2021.
https://doi.org/10.1007/978-3-030-87358-5_3

Recently, with great achievement of intelligent sensing technique, citywide crowd and traffic flow information are generated in high-dimensional sequential data with high complexity, which naturally drive researchers to design advanced deep learning models to achieve superior performance to classical methodologies, it is possible to forecast crowd flow with heterogeneous big data.

According to Zhang et al. [15], crowd flow prediction is proved to make breakthrough progresses by convolutional neural network (CNN), which could effectively extract the spatial features of grid-based data, the inflow and outflow crowd map are measured by the number of people that move in or out of a citywide region. However, the distribution of crowd flow is affected by complicated spatio-temporal correlation, most existing methods show limited ability to simultaneously model the spatio-temporal features and dynamic correlations of external factors. To be specific, in real-life citywide transportation, people could move anywhere in a very short time, which brings implicit long-range spatial dependency. Besides, the external factors like weather and holidays have a significant impact on the distribution of the crowd, such data is merely indexed by date, yet the spatial attributes of external factors are also vital. Moreover, spatio-temporal dynamics with uncertain external condition brings much more difficulty in CNN-based feature fusion diagrams, the existing methods yield unsatisfied performance of prediction.

To address these limitations, a novel framework named Heterogeneous Spatio-Temporal Attention Network (Hetero-STAN) is proposed in this paper. Firstly, we introduce heterogeneous enhancement for multiple feature extraction, which includes spatial mapping of external factors and a periodic dilated convolution (PDC). Further, inspired by advanced attention mechanism, a spatio-temporal attention (STA) module is proposed to integrate the dynamic heterogeneous features. In all, the proposed framework makes a major contribution to research on crowd flow prediction by demonstrating:

- To study the crowd flow forecasting problem and model the spatio-temporal dependency of traffic, in this paper, we propose a novel framework named Hetero-STAN, which consists of heterogeneous enhancement and a spatio-temporal attention module.
- A periodic dilated convolution and spatial mapping are introduced in heterogeneous enhancement. Specifically, PDC could capture the correlations of various spatial scales and temporal spans, while spatial mapping provides the dimension supplement of external factors that have a certain impact on crowd distribution, such as weather and holidays.
- We develop a spatio-temporal attention mechanism to sequentially infers attention maps along spatial and temporal dimensions, which could learn the dynamic spatial-temporal correlations of heterogeneous crowd flow feature. Extensive experiments carried out on public crowd flow datasets verify that our model achieves the best prediction accuracy compared with the state-of-the-art baselines.

2   Related Works

Spatio-Temporal Prediction. Crowd flow prediction is a classic problem in transportation and operational research which are primarily based on queuing theory and simulations. Data-driven approaches for forecasting flow have received considerable attention, and more details can be found in a recent survey paper [8]. However, existing machine learning models either impose strong stationary assumptions on the data (e.g., auto-regressive model) or fail to account for highly non-linear temporal dependency [13]. In recent years, deep neural network models have been used for time series forecasting problem, models based on Auto Regressive Moving Average (ARMA) [1] focus on linear temporal modeling of time-series data next frame prediction problem in video analysis. With the great progress made by convolutional neural networks, the diagram of spatio-temporal prediction could be covered by forecasting region based mesh-grids of crowd flow. As a milestone, [15] Deep-ST is proposed to describe the dependency of spatio-temporal features. After that, [14] proposes ST-ResNet to model the spatial and temporal properties of crowd traffic inspired by ResNet [3]. Deep-ST and ST-ResNet utilize fully connected layers to extract the feature of external factors, which is lack of spatial association. According to DeepSTN [6], multi-scale feature maps contain hierarchical spatio-temporal semantics, the scheme of hand-craft multi-scale feature fusion could be optimized, yet the improvement of prediction accuracy is partly obtained by point of interests information. [5] formulates the density and in-out flow prediction problem comprehensively, then propose a family of deep learning models named VLUC-Nets, which utilizes Conv-LSTM as the basic component, and extend their network with feature pyramid for datasets with large spatial domain. Although the spatio-temporal features of the traffic data can be extracted, the correlation of heterogeneous feature is still limited in these models.

Attention Mechanism. Attention mechanisms introduced in [7], have been widely used in various domains such as natural language processing and image understanding due to their high efficiency and flexibility in modeling dependencies. The key idea of the attention mechanism is to select information that is relatively critical to the current task from all input. Over the last few years, several attempts [9] are explored to incorporate attention processing to improve the performance in computer vision tasks. Based on CNN, SENet [4] adaptively recalibrates channel-wise feature responses by explicitly modelling interdependencies between channels. However, the SE attention only considers encoding inter-channel information while neglects the importance of positional information, which is critical to capturing object structures in vision tasks [10]. CBAM [11] was proposed to sequentially infers attention maps along both channel and spatial dimensions, the attention maps are multiplied to the input feature map for adaptive feature refinement. Dual attention network (DANet) [2] aims to capture contextual dependence based on the self-attention module which adaptively integrate local features with their global dependencies. Motivated by spatio-temporal prediction diagram and attention mechanisms mentioned above, in this paper, we employ heterogeneous feature enhancement and the attention mechanisms to model the dynamic spatio-temporal patterns with external factors of the traffic data.

3   Methodology

In this section, the spatio-temporal prediction formulation is firstly introduced, then we focus on the proposed Heterogeneous Spatio-Temporal Attention Network.

3.1   Formulation of Spatio-Temporal Prediction

According to the definition of [15], the data of spatio-temporal prediction is consisted of Region and Inflow/Outflow.

Definition 1. *The citywide region data is partitioned into a number of fine-grained mesh-grids, citywide crowd and traffic information in a continuous time period can be represented with $H \times W$ grids based on the longitude and latitude, which indexed by timestamps, each grid indicates the same geographical size.*

Definition 2. *For each grid (x, y) lies at $x^t h$ row and $y^t h$ column, the inflow and outflow of the crowds at the tth time interval are defined respectively as:*

$$x^{in,i,j} = \sum_{Tr \in \mathbb{P}} |\{k > 1 | g_{k-1} \notin (i,j) \wedge g_k \in (i,j)\}| \tag{1}$$

$$x^{out,i,j} = \sum_{Tr \in \mathbb{P}} |\{k \geq 1 | g_k \in (i,j) \wedge g_{k+1} \notin (i,j)\}| \tag{2}$$

where $\mathbb{P}$ represents the collection of trajectories at the tth time interval. $Tr :$ $g_1 \rightarrow g_2 \rightarrow \cdots \rightarrow g_{|Tr|}$ and g_k indicates the geospatial coordinate, $g_k \in (i,j)$ means the g_k lies within grid (i,j), and vice versa. $|\cdot|$ denotes the cardinality of a set.

According to the definitions, crowd flow prediction could be formulated as: Given the historical observations $\{X_i | i = 1, 2, \cdots, n-1\}$, predict X_n.

As defined in [14], ST-ResNet contains four major components: closeness, period, trend and external factors. Each component leads to a predicted crowd flow map through a branch of residual units or a fully connected layer. Then, the model uses a fusion scheme which is a simple combination to aggregate all these predictions. The external factors of ST-ResNet contain weather, holiday event and metadata, which lead to one dimension feature vectors.

In this paper, a novel CNN-based framework is proposed to predict the inflow and outflow of the crowd. The overall pipeline is shown in Fig. 1, which consists of Heterogeneous feature enhancement and Spatio-Temporal Attention mechanism.

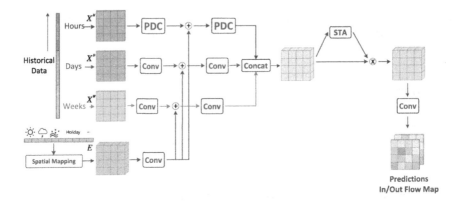

Fig. 1. The framework of proposed Hetero-STAN for crowd flow prediction. The external factors are firstly encoded by spatial mapping, a two-dimension external map is generated. A Periodic Dilated Convolution (PDC) is utilized to extract the feature of diverse spatial correlations within hours, and the Res-block in [14] are implied as "Conv". The heterogeneous feature map is fused by concatenatation, after that, the spatio-temporal correlation are further highlighted by proposed STA, the details will be discussed in following sections. The final prediction of in/outflow is obtained after a 1×1 convolution layer.

3.2   Heterogeneous Feature Enhancement

There are two processes in Heterogeneous Feature Enhancement, spatial mapping is provided for dimension supplement of external factors while a novel periodic dilated convolution is introduced to capture the correlations of both spatial and temporal domain.

Except for spatio-temporal features, the factors that represent the status and environment also have an impact on the distribution of crowd flow. These factors are counted as external vectors indexed by date in crowd flow datasets like TaxiBJ, MobileBJ, TaxiNYC, etc. Due to the limitation of the statistical means, the external factors are represented as one dimension feature vectors, which could not represent the specific location like:

- **Weather:** The regional impacts of rainfall or strong wind that affects the distribution of crowd flow.
- **Festival:** During the major holidays like the National Day and the Spring Festival, the crowd flow of places like shopping malls and railway stations could increase significantly.

In order to enrich the spatial attributes of external factors, we provide spatial mapping in Eq. (3):

$$E = f_{smap}(V_w^i, V_s^i), i = 1, 2, ..., n \tag{3}$$

where V_w^i, V_s^i is the external vectors indexed by certain date, and $f_{smap}(\cdot)$ indicates spatial mapping. To be specific, the dimension supplement achieved by spatial mapping is initialized with random spatial metrics, due to the distinction of impact area, the initialization are classified by radiation scale. For the external factors V_w with wide region impact, such as weather, regional spatial initialization is utilized to learn related external distribution maps. While the external factors of spot region V_s like railway stations and places of interest in holidays, the spatial maps are initialized by sparse metrics. The external maps E is learnable in end-to-end training process.

According to [14], ResUnit is leveraged to extract the features of spatio-temporal maps, which integrates the deep features of various time span. However, the long-range spatial dependence of crowd flow is significant, the dependence between features of layers is limited to the adjacent space by the fixed convolution scale.

In convolutional neural networks, receptive field is a concept that represents the scales of spatial features. The widely accepted strategies to expand the receptive field are of two aspects: i) A large kernel size could increase the mapping area of feature, yet it is not efficient because of the large parameters. ii) Dilated convolution proposed in [12], which is to extend the receptive field, yet the fixed dilation rate of kernel size is insufficient to collect adjacent relationship of crowd flow.

A Periodic Dilated Convolution (PDC) is introduced in this paper, the idea of periodically switching the dilated ratio of kernel size can effectively deal with the limitation of fixed-size dilated convolution. As shown in Fig. 2, assume that the feature map with a scale of $W \times H$, the dilated ratio of each $K \times K$ kernel is altered by the depth of convolution channel for mutil-scale and multi-range feature extraction.

The dependence of spatial features could be extracted by a periodical changed convolutional kernel with sharing weights, which enables the network to aggregate the rich nearby and remote spatial dependence. Semantics of multi-scale features can be fused by adjusting the pattern of convolution without introducing additional parameters and computational complexity, which is novel and efficient.

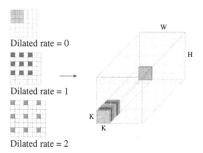

Fig. 2. An illustration of periodical dilated convolution. The dilated rate is periodically changed so that the receptive field is expanded accordingly.

In this paper, PDC is included in the process of heterogeneous feature enhancement. Note that the long-range spatial dependence is formed by the trajectory of efficient transportation like intercity railway and subways, these trajectory are usually relevant to temporal data in several hours. In other words, we only focus on capturing long-range spatial feature in closeness time spans.

To formulate the process of periodic dilated convolution, let the input feature map as a tensor $\chi \in \mathbb{R}^{C_{in} \times W \times H}$, where C_{in} is the number of input channels and W, H indicates the spatial scale of input feature map. Denote the convolution kernel as $\omega \in \mathbb{R}^{C_{out} \times C_{in} \times K \times K}$, the process of periodic dilated convolution could be formulated as:

$$(PDC)_{c,x,y} = \sum_{k=1}^{C_{in}} \sum_{i=-\frac{K-1}{2}}^{\frac{K-1}{2}} \sum_{j=-\frac{K-1}{2}}^{\frac{K-1}{2}} \omega_{c,k,i,j} \cdot \chi_{k,x+iD_{(c,k)}} \chi_{k,y+jD_{(c,k)}} \qquad (4)$$

where $D \in \mathbb{R}^{C_{out} \times C_{in}}$ is composed of channel-wise and filter-wise dilation rates in orthogonal dimensions. $D_{(c,k)}$ is associated with specific channel in one filter to support $\chi_{c,k,\cdot}$ as a unique kernel, the dilated rate could be represented periodically. By integrating spatial mapping and PDC in adjacent time spans, an enhanced heterogeneous feature map is fused as Eq. (5):

$$EH = f_{Hetero}(X^H, X^D, X^W, E) \qquad (5)$$

where EH indicates the Enhanced Heterogeneous feature map, X^H, X^D, X^W are the input feature maps sampled with the time spans of hours, days and weeks respectively. E denotes the external feature map obtained in Eq. (3).

As shown in Fig. 1, the process of heterogeneous enhancement is in the left part of the framework. To be specific, external feature map E is firstly obtained by spatial mapping, then the PDC is utilized for capturing both adjacent and distant spatial features within a few hours, while common convolution is utilized to extract the feature of X^D and X^W. Note that the external map E is added to three different temporal feature maps in the process of feature extraction, which the external attributes can be equally merged. Finally, we fuse the heterogeneous feature with a manipulation of concatenatation. Hence, the proposed heterogeneous enhancement could extend the spatial distribution of external factors and enrich the spatio-temporal feature correlation, which turns out to be an effective structure of feature extraction and fusion.

3.3   Spatio-Temporal Attention Mechanism

Recent studies on attention mechanism have demonstrated the remarkable effectiveness of channel and spatial domains, which have become a new trend of feature correlation and representation. According to the Squeeze-and-Excitation attention [4] and CBAM [11], both channel and spatial attributes could have a significant impact on the network performance. In the diagram of spatio-temporal prediction, channel attention could emphasize the temporal correlation while spatial attention further associates the dependence in various geographical scope. Benefit from attention mechanisms, this paper introduces a novel attention module for spatio-temporal feature fusion.

Global average pooling is the manipulation utilized in SE [4] that could assist the model in capturing global information, whereas, in the spatial domain, the spatial dependence among grids are squeezed. As mentioned in heterogeneous feature map, the correlation of temporal domain is constructed along with the direction of channel. In order to capture significant feature of long-range spatial dependence and dynamic time span, a Spatio-Temporal Attention (STA) module is introduced deal with this problem.

As shown in Fig. 3, firstly the global average pooling is factorized in horizontal and vertical direction. Obtained in Eq. (5), let the enhanced heterogeneous feature map $EH \in \mathbb{R}^{C \times W \times H}$ as input of spatio-temporal attention, two parallel average pooling are implied to encode each direction of spatial correlation and temporal feature in channels. For "H-Pooling" in Fig. 3 as an example, an $(H \times 1)$ kernel is implied to emphasize correlation vertically, and a direction-aware feature map of a scale of $C \times W \times 1$ is obtained. These two transformations could capture long-range dependence on different directions, compared to spatial attention used in CBAM, the separate pooling operation is provided with a larger receptive range and a more precise location.

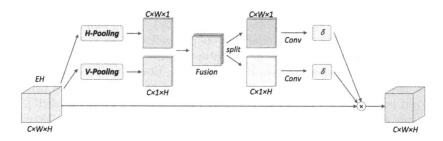

Fig. 3. The details of STA mechanism utilized to capture significant feature of long-range spatial dependence and dynamic time span.

Then, we use a concatenatation followed by a convolution layer to fuse the feature of two directions. After that, a secondary separation is implied to make full use of encoded positional information, where the crucial feature of crowd flow could be described in highlighted attention map. The relationship of temporal feature in channels could also be captured in this process.

Followed by a convolution layer and activation function, two attention map of horizontal $Att^H \in \mathbb{R}^{C \times W \times 1}$ and vertical $Att^W \in \mathbb{R}^{C \times 1 \times H}$ are obtained. Finally the output of the STA could be formulated as:

$$STA(EH) = EH \times Att^H \times Att^W \tag{6}$$

As shown in Fig. 1, the predicted crowd flow inflow/outflow map are generated by the final prediction layer, which could aggregate the feature along the direction of channel. The inflow/outflow grid map $\widehat{Y}$ of is predicted as:

$$\widehat{Y} = \sigma(f_{conv}(STA(EH))) \tag{7}$$

where $\sigma(\cdot)$ is the activation function of $Tanh$, $f_{conv}(\cdot)$ represents the 1×1 convolution layer. Proposed STA fuses the features of enhanced heterogeneous feature map in spatial and temporal domains, further, the long-range spatial dependence of two directions is highlighted, the attention along both the horizontal and vertical directions is applied. This process allows the STA to predict crowd flow more accurately.

4   Experiments and Analyses

In this section, the open source crowd flow prediction datasets are introduced, then the evaluation metrics and loss function are discussed, the experimental results are illustrated finally.

TaxiBJ is the dataset produced by Zheng Yu et al. in [15]. As a milestone of crowd flow prediction, trajectories are represented as grid maps and external vectors with time stamps. External factors are collected as a set of weather conditions and holidays. MobileBJ is another dataset collected from the most popular social network vendor in Beijing, China. TaxiNYC is a similar crowd in/out flow dataset created from the NYC-Taxi data in 2015. In the demand of crowd prediction task, the data is transformed as the definition of [15]. To make sure that the fairness of the experiments, external factors are collected as vectors as well.

Our model is trained and evaluated separately on the datasets. In the training process, our model is optimized via Adam with a weight decay of 0.0005 and momentum of 0.9. The learning rate is set to 0.001, where the batch-size is 64 on 4 Nvidia V100 graphics cards.

To evaluate the crowd flow prediction results, Root Mean Squared Error (RMSE) and Mean Absolute Error (MAE) are utilized to describe the differences between the predictions and ground-truth as in the Eq. (8) and (9):

$$RMSE = \sqrt{\frac{1}{n}\sum_{i}^{n}\left\|\widehat{Y}_i - Y_i\right\|^2} \tag{8}$$

$$MAE = \frac{1}{n}\sum_{i}^{n}\left|\widehat{Y}_i - Y_i\right|^2 \tag{9}$$

where the $\widehat{Y_i}$ indicates the predicted grid map of ith time interval and Y_i is the corresponding ground-truth. RMSE represents the differences between the prediction and the ground-truth, which is widely accepted to measure the loss of predicted vectors. Hence, RMSE is also utilized as the loss function in the process of training.

Table 1. Evaluation results on TaxiBJ and MobileBJ.

Model	TaxiBJ		MobileBJ	
	RMSE	MAE	RMSE	MAE
HA	45.01	24.48	122.36	50.31
VAR	22.88	13.79	61.25	43.78
ST-ResNet [14]	18.70	10.49	40.13	25.53
DeepSTN [6]	17.04	10.08	37.08	23.94
Hetero-STAN	**15.90**	**8.13**	**32.13**	**20.30**

Table 1 show the performance of crowd flow prediction baselines and proposed Hetero-STAN evaluated on TaxiBJ and MobileBJ. As mentioned above, RMSE and MAE are utilized in evaluation. Note that we use a compact strategy to generate the input gird maps, which the spatio-temporal data are sampled in the span of hours, days and weeks. Hence, the algorithm and models in our experiments are retrained with these settings and hyper parameters. HA means the methods of predicting crowd flow by historical average of inflow and outflow in the corresponding periods. Vector Auto-Regressive (VAR) captures the pairwise relationships among all flows. ST-Resnet is the landmark method of crowd flow prediction, which represents the CNN-based model baseline. DeepSTN is proposed to improve the performance of ST-ResNet, whereas, the proposed Hetero-STAN demonstrate the superiority to the state-of-the-art method, which outperforms DeepSTN $1 \sim 2$ in both RMSE and MAE. The results of MobileBJ indicate the similar distribution, the proposed model gains 32.13 RMSE and 20.30 MAE respectively, which gives a evidence of advantage performance of our model.

Table 2. Comparison of crowd flow prediction baselines and proposed structures evaluated on TaxiNYC. The Heterogeneous Feature Enhancement, Spatio-Temporal Attention mechanism are implied separately on base network, which could we obtain the proof of their effectiveness.

Model	TaxiNYC	
	RMSE	MAE
ST-ResNet [14]	12.34	5.63
DeepSTN [6]	11.73	4.94
Hetero + simple fusion	10.87	4.79
ResNet + STA	9.93	4.36
Hetero + STA	**8.89**	**4.03**

In order to investigate the effectiveness of proposed sub-modules, as illustrated in Table 2, our network is separated into Heterogeneous Enhancement (as "Hetero") and Spatio-Temporal Attention mechanism (as "STA"). Evaluated on TaxiNYC, the method of Heterogeneous Enhancement with a simple feature fusion scheme suggests a better performance than ST-ResNet, which shows the effectiveness of spatial mapping and PDC. For attention mechanism, we utilize the same feature extractor as ST-ResNet, then the STA is implied. Learned from the results, the proposed spatio-temporal attention achieves a significant precision compared with the baseline model. To aggregate the sub-modules, our Hetero-STAN ("Hetero + STA" in Table 2) gains a remarkable enhancement of 2.84 in RMSE and 0.91 in MAE than state-of-the-art DeepSTN. The effectiveness of proposed method are verified in the tables, which shows the superiority of our model.

5   Conclusion

In this paper, we present a novel crowd flow prediction framework based on convolution neural network, named Hetero-STAN. A heterogeneous enhancement for multiple feature extraction is introduced, which consists of spatial mapping for external factors and a periodic dilated convolution (PDC). In order to further capture the spatio-temporal correlations, we propose spatio-temporal attention (STA) module to integrate the dynamic features and highlight the key attributes of two directions. Corresponding experiments are conducted on public crowd flow datasets TaxiBJ and MobileBJ, the results demonstrate that the proposed model outperforms the state-of-the-art baseline by a large margin. Additionally, the effectiveness of the sub-modules are also verified on TaxiNYC.

Acknowledgment. This work was support by the fund of China Academy of Railway Sciences (DZYF20-14).

References

1. Box, G.E.P., Jenkins, G.M.: Time series analysis: forecasting and control. J. Time **31**(3) (2010)
2. Fu, J., et al.: Dual attention network for scene segmentation. In: IEEE Conference on Computer Vision and Pattern Recognition, CVPR 2019, Long Beach, CA, USA, 16–20 June 2019, pp. 3146–3154. Computer Vision Foundation. IEEE (2019)
3. He, K., Zhang, X., Ren, S., Sun, J.: Deep residual learning for image recognition. In: 2016 IEEE Conference on Computer Vision and Pattern Recognition, CVPR 2016, pp. 770–778 (2016)
4. Hu, J., Shen, L., Sun, G.: Squeeze-and-excitation networks. In: 2018 IEEE Conference on Computer Vision and Pattern Recognition, CVPR 2018, Salt Lake City, UT, USA, 18–22 June 2018, pp. 7132–7141. IEEE Computer Society (2018)
5. Jiang, R., et al.: VLUC: an empirical benchmark for video-like urban computing on citywide crowd and traffic prediction (2019)

6. Lin, Z., Feng, J., Lu, Z., Li, Y., Jin, D.: DeepSTN+: context-aware spatial-temporal neural network for crowd flow prediction in metropolis. In: Thirty-Thrid AAAI Conference on Artificial Intelligence, pp. 1020–1027 (2019)
7. Vaswani, A., et al.: Attention is all you need. In: Guyon, I., et al. (eds.) Advances in Neural Information Processing Systems 30: Annual Conference on Neural Information Processing Systems 2017, 4–9 December 2017, Long Beach, CA, USA, pp. 5998–6008 (2017)
8. Vlahogianni, E.I., Karlaftis, M.G., Golias, J.C.: Short-term traffic forecasting: where we are and where we're going. Transp. Res. Part C Emerg. Technol. **43**(1), 3–19 (2014)
9. Wang, F., et al.: Residual attention network for image classification. In: 2017 IEEE Conference on Computer Vision and Pattern Recognition, CVPR 2017, Honolulu, HI, USA, 21–26 July 2017, pp. 6450–6458. IEEE Computer Society (2017)
10. Wang, H., Zhu, Y., Green, B., Adam, H., Yuille, A., Chen, L.-C.: Axial-DeepLab: stand-alone axial-attention for panoptic segmentation. In: Vedaldi, A., Bischof, H., Brox, T., Frahm, J.-M. (eds.) ECCV 2020. LNCS, vol. 12349, pp. 108–126. Springer, Cham (2020). https://doi.org/10.1007/978-3-030-58548-8_7
11. Woo, S., Park, J., Lee, J.-Y., Kweon, I.S.: CBAM: convolutional block attention module. In: Ferrari, V., Hebert, M., Sminchisescu, C., Weiss, Y. (eds.) ECCV 2018. LNCS, vol. 11211, pp. 3–19. Springer, Cham (2018). https://doi.org/10.1007/978-3-030-01234-2_1
12. Yu, F., Koltun, V.: Multi-scale context aggregation by dilated convolutions. In: 4th International Conference on Learning Representations. ICLR (2016)
13. Yu, H.F., Rao, N., Dhillon, I.S.: Temporal regularized matrix factorization for high-dimensional time series prediction. In: Advances in Neural Information Processing Systems, pp. 847–855 (2016)
14. Zhang, J., Zheng, Y., Qi, D.: Deep spatio-temporal residual networks for citywide crowd flows prediction. In: Thirty-First AAAI Conference on Artificial Intelligence, pp. 1655–1661 (2017)
15. Zhang, J., Zheng, Y., Qi, D., Li, R., Yi, X.: DNN-based prediction model for spatio-temporal data. In: 24th ACM International Conference on Advances in Geographic Information Systems, pp. 92:1–92:4 (2016)
16. Zheng, Y., Capra, L., Wolfson, O., Yang, H.: Urban computing: concepts, methodologies, and applications. ACM Trans. Intell. Syst. Technol. **5**(3), 38:1–38:55 (2014)

UAV Track Planning Algorithm Based on Graph Attention Network and Deep Q Network

Xinyu Hu[1], Jingpeng Gao[1(✉)], and Zhiye Jiang[2]

[1] College of Information and Communication Engineering, Harbin Engineering University, Harbin, China
gaojingpeng@hrbeu.edu.cn
[2] National Key Laboratory of Science and Technology on Test Physics and Numerical Mathematics, Beijing Institute of Space Long March Vehicle, Beijing, China

Abstract. To solve the problem that the deviation of the Unmanned Aerial Vehicle (UAV) flight status data collected by the equipment during flight leads to the failure of the mission, this paper proposes a UAV track planning algorithm based on Graph Attention Network and Deep Q Network (DQN). Firstly, we use the camera to collect images and apply pre-trained ResNet to extract image features. Secondly, we adopt the Graph Attention Network to establish the connection between the sensor-measured flight state information and the actual flight state information. Thirdly, we build the optimization model of flight state. Moreover, based on the Deep Reinforcement Learning (DRL) theory, the DQN-based UAV track planning system is trained. Finally, the system combined the optimized flight state to complete the optimal flight action output to realize the track planning. Simulation results show that, compared with the original algorithm which is under the same flight conditions as the proposed algorithm, the velocity deviation rate of the proposed algorithm is improved by 46.79%, which can plan a high-quality track and has good engineering application value.

Keywords: UAV · Track planning · Graph Attention Network · Deep Q Network · Image processing

1 Introduction

Track planning is an important part of UAV's mission. To execute the mission successfully in a complex environment, the UAV needs to use a reasonable planning algorithm to obtain the track. In recent years, Reinforcement Learning (RL) algorithm has been successfully applied to the field of planning because of its excellent generalization [1]. The research in [2] used Sarsa(λ) algorithm to solve the logistics planning problem. The work in [3] applied the Q-learning algorithm to realize the optimal track planning of a mobile robot. However, Sarsa(λ) algorithm and Q-Learning algorithm are not capable of processing high-dimensional state space because the computational complexity will increase sharply once the state dimensions increase. Therefore DeepMind team proposed a DRL method based on Deep Q Network [4]. DQN algorithm uses a neural network to

© Springer Nature Switzerland AG 2021
Y. Peng et al. (Eds.): ICIG 2021, LNCS 12889, pp. 42–54, 2021.
https://doi.org/10.1007/978-3-030-87358-5_4

fit the Q value function and solves the problem that the increase of state data leads to difficulty in processing. But in the actual environment, the flight status information measured by sensors usually has deviation, which gives rise to the unstable track. Although the RL algorithm has generalization ability, it cannot solve this problem fundamentally.

With the development of Deep Learning, Graph Neural Network (GNN) appears in the academic field, which can deal with non-grid graph structure problems. GNN is often used to solve prediction problems because of its ability to express related information and to construct relationships by combining attributes and features of information. According to the multi-dimensional time-series relationship between the volume fraction of dissolved gas in transformer oil and time, reference [5] proposed a network event prediction method based on GNN. In addition, reference [6] showed a method that introduced a block design in GNN and was readily applied to the tasks of bioactivity prediction. Therefore, GNN has excellent capability in prediction. Thus GNN can be used to optimize the flight status of UAV, which can provide strong support for the field of track planning.

In this paper, the UAV track planning algorithm based on Graph Attention Network and Deep Q Network is proposed to optimize the flight state of UAV and plan the more accurate track. First of all, image features are extracted using pre-trained ResNet. Then, the graph structure relationship between sensor-measured state and image features is constructed. Moreover, the Graph Attention Network is trained to map the measured state to the optimized state. Furthermore, reasonable DRL elements are designed. And then, the DQN model of the UAV's track planning is trained. At last, combined with the flight state, which is optimized by the trained Graph Attention Network, the trained DQN model is applied to obtain more reliable flight movements and finally form the track.

The structure of this paper is organized as follows. Section 2 describes the track planning model based on Markov Decision Process. And we introduce the DQN-based UAV track planning algorithm in Sect. 3. Section 4 combines pre-training ResNet and Graph Attention Network to realize flight state optimization and build a UAV track planning system based on Graph Attention Network and DQN. After that, the training and simulation results are presented in Sect. 5. Finally, the conclusions are drawn in Sect. 6.

2 Track Planning Model Based on MDP

In Markov Decision Process (MDP) model, the state change at every time t is only related to the state and action at time $t-1$ which has nothing to do with the state and action before time $t-1$ [7]. MDP can be expressed as follows,

$$M = (S, A, P, R), \tag{1}$$

where S represents the set of all states of an agent in the environment, and A is the set of actions that an agent can perform in the corresponding state. P is the state transition probability of the agent, which is usually a matrix. Besides, R refers to the reward set for the agent. $r(s_t, a_t, s_{t+1}) \in R$ means the reward of the round, in which s_t and a_t represent the state and action of the agent at time t, respectively.

A track planning process, in which the UAV interacts with the environment to obtain flight movements and form flight tracks, can be regarded as a sequential decision-making process, which can be modeled by MDP. And then, the MDP problem can be solved by the RL algorithm.

3   UAV Track Planning System Based on DQN

To solve the problem of the MDP model of track planning, it is necessary to design reasonable RL basic elements according to the requirements of UAV's mission and apply an appropriate RL algorithm. Then the UAV can obtain the state from the actual environment and output the flight action to plan the track.

3.1   Basic Elements of Reinforcement Learning

By analyzing the formula (1), the basic elements of RL include the state of the agent, the action corresponding to the state, and the reward from the interaction between agent and environment after the action is performed. Therefore, in the context of UAV track planning, to design reasonable basic elements of RL needs to fully consider the mission requirements, maneuvering performance, and the interaction between UAV and the actual environment.

State Space. To evade obstacles in space, the UAV perceives the environmental information in real-time and can make flight actions based on the information. In consideration of the above requirements and the fact that UAV can obtain sensor-measured flight information during the actual flight, the current position and the direction of flight velocity of UAV are designed to be the state. Furthermore, the UAV can make decisions based on its current position and velocity by using the RL algorithm. After executing the flight actions, it can obtain the new position and new velocity to be reached at the next moment. Therefore, the state space of the UAV at any moment is expressed as follows,

$$S_t = ([x_{u,t}, y_{u,t}, z_{u,t}], [v_{x,t}, v_{y,t}, v_{z,t}]), \tag{2}$$

where $[x_t, y_t, z_t]$ is the coordinates position of the UAV in the space at time t, and $[v_{x,t}, v_{y,t}, v_{z,t}]$ is the partial velocity of the UAV in three directions at time t.

Action Space. From the perspective of flight dynamics, to evade the obstacle area during the flight, the UAV needs to change the direction of velocity during the flight. The UAV is set to fly at a uniform speed in this paper, so the direction of velocity can be changed by adjusting the flight direction. Thus we combine the action space of the UAV at any moment. The formula is expressed as,

$$A_t = (\varphi_t, \theta_t), \tag{3}$$

where φ_t and θ_t are the direction angle and the pitch angle of UAV, respectively.

Reward Function. The reward function in the RL algorithm is used to evaluate the effect of interaction between the agent and the environment. Accordingly, a reasonable set of reward functions can ensure the convergence of the network [8]. Under actual circumstances, the UAV needs to reach the destination successfully while evading the mountain obstacle during the flight course. Hence the reward function we designed mainly includes the following two aspects.

Positive Reward. The primary task of UAV track planning is to arrive at the mission destination successfully, so when the mission destination is within the detection range of UAV, the system feedback is rewarded positively to make the arrival trend more obvious. Thus we set a positive reward of reaching. The formula is as follows,

$$R_a = \begin{cases} 2 - \hat{N}(\|p_{t,t} - p_{u,t}\|) & \|p_a - p_{u,t}\| < d_{max} \\ -\hat{N}(\|p_a - p_{u,t}\|) & \|p_a - p_{u,t}\| \geq d_{max} \end{cases}, \qquad (4)$$

where $p_{u,t}$ and p_a represent the position coordinates and the destination of the UAV at time t, respectively. The operation $\| \cdot \|$ is to calculate its magnitude. $\hat{N}(\cdot)$ means to normalize. d_{max} represents the maximum detection range of the UAV.

Negative Reward. If the UAV collides with the mountain obstacle during the flight, the mission will be failed, so the negative reward of the obstacle is as follows,

$$R_o = \begin{cases} -(1 - \hat{N}(\|p_{u,t} - p_{o,t}\|)) & \|p_{u,t} - p_{r,t}\| \geq d_{max} \\ -1 & \|p_{u,t} - p_{r,t}\| < d_{max} \end{cases}, \qquad (5)$$

where $p_{o,t}$ is the coordinates of the mountain that is closest to the UAV at time t. Therefore, the reward function for UAV flight at any moment can be expressed as,

$$R_f = R_a + R_o \qquad (6)$$

3.2 Deep Q Network

DQN algorithm combines a neural network with the Q-Learning algorithm and uses a neural network to fit the Q value function, which solves the problem that Q-table is difficult to deal with complex state space. Therefore, DQN is applicable to the problem of high-dimensional state space, such as UAV track planning.

The agent interacts with the environment to get the experience (s, a, r, s'), which is stored in the experience replay pool for network learning. During the network learning, (s, a) is fed into the current Q network and s' is fed into the target Q network. Then the algorithm uses the method of the mean square error to calculate the DQN loss function according to Formula (7),

$$L(\omega) = E\left[\left(r + \gamma \max_{a'} Q(s', a', \omega) - Q(s, a, \omega)\right)^2\right], \qquad (7)$$

where γ is the discount factor. ω is the Q network weight parameter. $r + \gamma \max_{a'} Q(s', a', \omega)$ means the maximum Q value of the strategy obtained by the target Q network under the action a'. $Q(s, a, \omega)$ is the Q value of the current Q network. Then the gradient of the loss function can be calculated using Formula (8),

$$\nabla_\omega L(\omega) = E\left[\left(r + \gamma \max_{a'} Q(s', a', \omega) - Q(s, a, \omega)\right) \nabla_\omega Q(s, a, \omega)\right]. \qquad (8)$$

And then, the network parameters are updated by the gradient descent method to obtain the optimal Q value. Conventional method to minimize the loss function is using the neural network directly. However it will lead to the strategy learning of the agent unsteadily. So DQN introduces the target network. After some rounds of iteration, the network parameter ω of the current Q network is copied to the target Q network. Thus this mechanism improves the stability of the algorithm. Hence, DQN algorithm can obtain the optimal Q value $\max_a Q(s, a, \omega)$ every time the state s is received and obtain the optimal action a corresponding to the Q value.

3.3   System Model of Track Planning Based on DQN

Combined with the basic elements designed by Formulas (2)–(6), the DQN-based UAV track planning system is trained according to the above DQN algorithm principle. In application, the system can output the optimal action corresponding to the sensor-measured flight state in real-time so that the UAV can finally form the track. The system block diagram of the DQN-based UAV track planning is shown in Fig. 1.

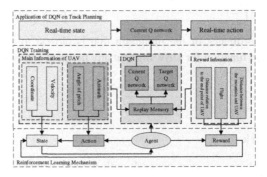

Fig. 1. This figure shows the block diagram of the DQN-based UAV track planning system.

4   Flight State Optimization Based on CNN and GAT

UAV's missions in complex environments require reliable flight trajectories. However, in actual flight, the flight status data measured by sensors typically have deviation, which makes the flight actions determined by the DQN algorithm poor and causes the UAV to fail the mission. To solve this problem, this section combines Convolutional Neural Network (CNN) and GNN to optimize the flight state of UAV. Hence DQN can make better flight actions and eventually form an accurate track.

4.1 Feature Extraction Based on Pre-trained ResNet

CNN has incomparable advantages over other technologies in image feature extraction. However, due to the limitation of experimental conditions, it is difficult to achieve CNN training with large sample conditions. With the development of Machine Learning, the emergence of Transfer Learning makes it possible to migrate multi-domain models. So the pre-trained CNN model can be used to solve the problems in related fields directly and avoid the situation that applying the CNN model requires a large number of samples. In contrast to regular CNN, ResNet detours the input information to the output, so the network only needs to learn the difference between input and output. Thus it has lower learning complexity and stronger feature extraction ability compared with other similarly deep networks.

Although the accurate change value of the flight state cannot be obtained from the image, the image information can be reflected by using pre-trained CNN to extract the image features. Therefore, the images collected by the camera in real-time can embody the real state changes during the flight and then indirectly reflect the impact of the actual environment on the flight of the UAV. Accordingly, this paper combines with the idea of Transfer Learning and utilizes the pre-training ResNet to extract the features of the images collected by the camera. Then the features are provided as input information for the state optimization model based on GAT. The diagram of the feature extraction model based on pre-trained ResNet is shown in Fig. 2.

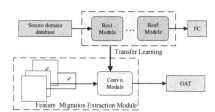

Fig. 2. This figure shows the block diagram of the feature extraction model based on pre-trained ResNet.

4.2 State Optimization Model Based on Graph Attention Network

As a generalization of Recurrent Neural Network, GNN can directly deal with more general graphs by modeling the dependency relationship between graph nodes [9], which makes a breakthrough in the research field related to graph analysis.

Among the evolution networks of GNN, the Graph Attention Network (GAT) introduces an attention mechanism, which avoids the shortcomings of previous approaches based on Graph Convolution Network. Each node of the GAT can pay attention to the characteristics of neighbor nodes and specify different weights for different nodes in its neighborhood implicitly, without the need for tedious matrix operation. Therefore, this paper builds the relationship between information and information by using GAT to establish the mapping relationship between the sensor-measured flight state and the real state of UAV in the actual flight process.

To show the importance of one node's information to another node's information, the correlation coefficient between each node and its direct neighborhood is calculated by Formula (9),

$$e_{ij} = a\left(W\,\overrightarrow{h_i}\,||\,W\,\overrightarrow{h_j}\right), j \in \mathcal{N}_i, \tag{9}$$

where e_{ij} represents the correlation degree of j to i. h_i refers to the i-th node. h_j is the neighborhood node of h_i. $\mathcal{N}_i$ is the neighborhood that h_j can take on. W represents the relationship between input features and output features which is refers to the required trained linear mapping matrix that shares parameters for each node. The operation $||$ means to splice. The function $a(\cdot)$ represents the process of mapping concatenated high-dimensional data to a real number which is achieved by the single-layer feedforward neural network.

After the correlation coefficient is obtained, the *LeakyReLU* activation function is used to map the input of the node to the output, and the correlation coefficient is normalized to avoid the *dyingReLU* problem, which is expressed in Formula (10) as,

$$\alpha_{ij} = \frac{\exp\left(LeakyReLU\left(e_{ij}\right)\right)}{\sum\limits_{k \in \mathcal{N}_i} \exp(LeakyReLU\left(e_{ik}\right))}, \tag{10}$$

where α_{ij} is the coefficient of attention of j to i.

In order to integrate the neighborhood information into each node, the adding weight of features is expressed by Formula (11),

$$\overrightarrow{h_i'} = \sigma\left(\sum_{j \in \mathcal{N}_i} \alpha_{ij} W \overrightarrow{h_j}\right), \tag{11}$$

where $\overrightarrow{h_i'}$ is the output eigenvector of the node h_i. $\sigma(\cdot)$ is the activation function.

To stabilize such a self-attention learning process, the extended mechanism of multi-head attention is introduced. The mechanism is expressed as follows,

$$\overrightarrow{h_i'}(K) = ||_{k=1}^{K} \sigma\left(\sum_{j \in \mathcal{N}_i} \alpha_{ij}^k W^k \overrightarrow{h_j}\right), \tag{12}$$

where α_{ij}^k is the attention coefficient calculated by the k-th attention mechanism. W^k represents the linear mapping matrix between the input and the output under the k-th attention mechanism. $\overrightarrow{h_i'}(K)$ is the output feature under the W^k mapping, which means that independent attention mechanisms are used to execute K times.

Thus the training of the GAT model is based on the complete graph information, which includes the graph structure to be trained, the initial features carried by each node, and the new features of each node through the operation of the attention mechanism. The mapping described by this operation is needed.

The data set of network training is constructed for training the GAT-based state optimization model. The data set contains the graph structure, node characteristics about input and output. The graph structure includes nodes, the edges between nodes, and the adjacency matrix representing the connection relationship between each node. The graph structure is expressed in Formula (13),

$$G = (H, E, U),\qquad(13)$$

where H is the set of nodes, the number of nodes is $2N + 3$, N is the frame number. E is the set of edges and W is the adjacency matrix of G. U can be obtained according to the topological relationship and connectivity of nodes in G.

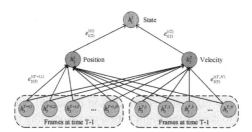

Fig. 3. This figure shows the graph structure.

The graph structure established under the mechanism of single independent attention is shown in Fig. 3. $h_3^{T-1,1}$ to $h_3^{T-1,N}$ represent N frame nodes at time $T - 1$. $h_3^{T,1}$ to $h_3^{T,N}$ represent N frame nodes at time T. h_2^1 and h_2^2 represent the node of position and velocity of the UAV, respectively. h_1^1 represents the node of UAV's state. $e_{1(2)}^{1(1)}$ refers to the attention correlation coefficients of the node h_2^1 to the node h_1^1. The meaning of other coefficients of edges is similar to $e_{1(2)}^{1(1)}$. Therefore, the graph structure can reflect the attribute relationship between sensor-measured flight state information and the image features of each frame collected by the camera.

Each node in the graph structure has its attributes and specific characteristics. Table 1 shows the attributes of nodes in the graph structure. And the feature vector set of all nodes can be comprehensively expressed as follows,

$$h = \{\overrightarrow{h_1}, \overrightarrow{h_2}, \cdots, \overrightarrow{h_{|H|}}\},\ \overrightarrow{h_i} \in \Re^D,\qquad(14)$$

where $\overrightarrow{h_i}$ is the eigenvector of the i-th node, and D is the eigenvector dimension.

Thus, the optimal mapping of the optimized flight state can be obtained by training according to the principle of the GAT attention mechanism.

Table 1. The attributes of the graph structure node.

Node	Attribute	Node	Attribute	Node	Attribute
h_1^1	State{position, velocity}	$h_3^{T-1,1}$	Frame 1 at time $T-1$	$h_3^{T,1}$	Frame 1 at time T
h_2^1	Position{p_{T-1}, p_T}	...	...	...	...
h_2^2	Velocity{v_{T-1}, v_T}	$h_3^{T-1,N}$	Frame N at time $T-1$	$h_3^{T,N}$	Frame N at time T

4.3 Track Planning System Based on Flight State Optimization

To meet the practical application of the optimized flight state, the state space of DQN is redesigned according to the state after feature extraction. Then the training is carried out again. Therefore, with the real-time flight position and velocity measured by sensors, using the trained GAT, the flight state optimization is carried out. Then the re-trained DQN algorithm is used to decide the flight action corresponding to the optimized flight state. At last, the system achieves better track planning. The block diagram of the UAV track planning system based on Graph Attention Network and Deep Q Network is shown in Fig. 4.

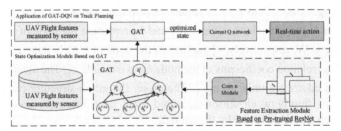

Fig. 4. This figure shows the block diagram of the UAV track planning system based on Graph Attention Network and Deep Q Network.

5 Simulation and Discussion

In this section, the UAV track planning algorithm based on Graph Attention Network and Deep Q Network we proposed is trained and simulated. The number of attention heads is 8, the dropout rate is 0.6, the learning rate for Adam is 5×10^{-3}, and the factor for regularization is 2.5×10^{-4}. Table 2 shows the main parameters of UAV flight. And Table 3 shows the main parameters of DQN training. Besides, this paper assumes that the UAV flies at a uniform speed and the camera frame number is 60. In addition, the operating system of the experimental equipment is Windows 10 (Microsoft, Redmond, WA, USA), the processor is intel® CoreTM i7-9700k (Intel, Santa Clara, CA, USA), and the simulation environment is Python 3.5.

Table 2. Relevant parameters of UAV flight.

Parameter	Value	Parameter	Value
Range of flight altitude (km)	[0.5, 8]	Flight area (km)	15 km * 15 km
Range of direction Angle (°)	[0, 180]	Flight velocity (m/s)	200
Range of pitch Angle (°)	[−90, 90]	Number of obstacles	4

Table 3. The main parameters of DQN training.

Parameter	Value	Parameter	Value
Episodes of training	10000	Discount factor γ	0.99
Size of replay memory	5000	Learning rate	2.5×10^{-4}

5.1 Evaluation Index

To verify the feasibility and reliability of the proposed algorithm, the relative velocity deviation rate is designed as the evaluation index to evaluate the accuracy of the track. We defined that the velocity deviation ϑ means the offset between the real-time flight velocity direction of the UAV and the radial direction of the destination. Then the velocity deviation rate can be obtained by the following formula,

$$v_o = \frac{\sum |\vartheta|}{t_{all}} = \frac{\sum \left| \frac{2}{\pi} \arccos \left(\frac{\overrightarrow{P_{destination} - P_t} \cdot \overrightarrow{v_t}}{\| \overrightarrow{P_{destination} - P_t} \| \cdot \| \overrightarrow{v_t} \|} \right) \right|}{t_{all}}, \tag{15}$$

where $p_{destination}$ is the coordinates of the destination, p_t is the position coordinates of the UAV at time t, v_t is the velocity direction of the UAV at time t, t_{all} is the time that UAV took for a single flight. Therefore, the smaller the v_o is, the more obvious the trend that UAV finish the mission.

Correspondingly, the relative velocity deviation rate is used to represent the degree of change of the two values. The formula is as follows,

$$RV(v_{o1}, v_{o2}) = \frac{|v_{o1} - v_{o2}|}{v_{o1}}, \tag{16}$$

where v_{o1} and v_{o2} are the values of velocity deviation rate obtained from two different flights. $RV(v_{o1}, v_{o2})$ represents the change degree v_{o2} relative to v_{o1}. The greater the $RV(v_{o1}, v_{o2})$ is, the greater the improvement v_{o2} relative to v_{o1}.

5.2 Training and Testing

The algorithm has a large random fluctuation during a large number of training processes, so it is not effective to display the reward convergence curve of all training rounds directly.

To demonstrate the training effect of the algorithm better, we averaged and normalized the sum of the rewards obtained from every 20 training rounds, and then the convergence curve of 10,000 iterations is replaced by 500 iterations.

We compare the training effect of the pre-optimized track planning system and the post-optimized track planning system for the flight state in this part. Under the condition of the main training parameters of DQN setting as shown in Table 3, Fig. 5 shows the training reward convergence curves of the two systems. As can be seen from Fig. 5, with the increase in the number of iterations, the normalized reward values in both cases tend to converge. For the GAT-DQN-based system, the normalized reward values tend to stabilize around 5,600 iterations, with the value incline to 0.8. But for the DQN-based system, the normalized reward values gradually converge around 6,800 iterations, with the value incline to 0.6. On the whole, it can be seen that the fluctuation of the DQN-GAT-based system training is smaller than the DQN-based system. It can be inferred that the flight state optimized by GAT composes the experience arrays better. Thus, under the condition of the same training parameters, its feedback can get a higher reward value, which improves the learning ability and convergence performance of the algorithm.

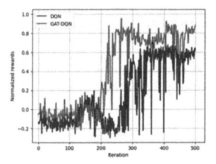

Fig. 5. This figure shows the training reward convergence curve.

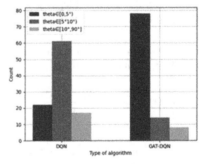

Fig. 6. This figure shows the distribution of the velocity deviation.

Then we compare the performance of the pre-optimized track planning system and the post-optimized track planning system for the flight state in this part. Under the condition of the main parameters of UAV flight setting as shown in Table 2, Fig. 6 shows

Table 4. The main parameters of DQN training.

Parameter	DQN-based UAV system	GAT-DQN-based UAV system
Average flight time (s)	92.51	66.76
Average velocity deviation rate	9.34%	4.97%
Relative velocity deviation rate	46.79%	

the distribution of the velocity deviation of the two systems. And Table 4 shows the performance index comparison of the two systems for testing 100 times. As can be seen from Fig. 6, the velocity deviation of the GAT-DQN-based system reached 78 times in the range of 0 to 5°. But the velocity deviation of the DQN-based system only reached 22 times. As shown in Table 4, the average flight time of the UAV is 66.76 s when the GAT-DQN algorithm is used for track planning, and the average flight time of the UAV is 92.51 s when the DQN algorithm is used. In terms of the average velocity deviation rate, the GAT-DQN-based system is 4.97%, which is 46.79% higher than that of the DQN-based system. It can be inferred that the DQN-based system with sensors measuring flight status makes a poor decision for flight movements. But the GAT-DQN-based system optimizes the sensor-measured information. Therefore, the GAT-DQN-based system can output excellent flight movements and form a track with higher quality. It also suggests that the GAT-DQN-based system can make the UAV reach the destination faster.

6 Conclusion

This paper proposes a UAV track planning algorithm based on Graph Attention Network and Deep Q Network, which reduce the flight state deviation measured by sensors when the UAV is flying in the actual environment. The algorithm that we proposed uses pre-trained ResNet to extract the features of the images captured by the camera to represent the actual flight state of the UAV. In addition, combined with the ability of GNN's information correlation, the algorithm realizes the optimization from sensor-measured flight state to actual flight state, which improves the adaptability of the UAV in the actual environment. Besides, according to the principle of Deep Reinforcement Learning, the state space, action space, and reward function based on the background of track planning are designed. In addition, the DQN algorithm is used to process the high-dimensional flight state and output the flight action corresponding to the optimized state, which makes the UAV plan an accurate track. The simulation and testing results show that the average velocity deviation rate of the proposed algorithm is improved by 46.79% than the original algorithm under the same flight conditions. Therefore, the algorithm we proposed enhances the adaptability of the UAV in the actual environment and provides a new idea for the application of image processing in the field of UAV track planning.

Acknowledgment. This work is funded by the International Exchange Program of Harbin Engineering University for Innovation-oriented Talents Cultivation and the State Key Laboratory of Complex Electromagnetic Environment Effects on Electronics and Information System (CEMEE) through researchers under Grant CEMEE2021K0103B.

References

1. Liu, C., Li, H., Tang, Y., et al.: Next generation integrated smart manufacturing based on big data analytics, reinforced learning, and optimal routes planning methods. Int. J. Comput. Integr. Manuf. **32**(9), 820–831 (2019)
2. Yu, T.: Sarsa(λ)-based logistics planning approximated by value function with policy iteration. J. Algorithms Comput. Technol. **9**(4), 449–466 (2015)
3. Ee, S., Pauline, O., Kah, C.: Solving the optimal track planning of a mobile robot using improved Q-learning. Robot. Auton. Syst. **115**(115), 143–161 (2019)
4. Fanyu, Z., Chen, W., Shuzhi, S.: A survey on visual navigation for artificial agents with deep reinforcement learning. IEEE Access **8**(11), 135426–135442 (2020)
5. Qiang, F., Yongchao, W.: Event prediction technology based on graph neural network. J. Phys. **1852**(4), 42037–42044 (2021)
6. Yuquan, L., Pengyong, L., Xing, Y., et al.: Introducing block design in graph neural networks for molecular properties prediction. Chem. Eng. J. **414**(3), 128817–129924 (2021)
7. Tuyen, P., Ngo, A., TaeChoong, C.: A deep hierarchical reinforcement learning algorithm in partially observable markov decision processes. IEEE Access **6**(3), 49089–49102 (2018)
8. Shixun, Y., Diao, M., Lipeng, G.: Deep reinforcement learning for target searching in cognitive electronic warfare. IEEE Access **7**(1), 37432–37447 (2019)
9. Zhihui, Z., Jingwen, L., Lingxiao, M., et al.: Architectural implications of graph neural networks. IEEE Comput. Archit. Lett. **19**(1), 59–62 (2020)

Object 6DoF Pose Estimation for Power Grid Manipulating Robots

Shan Du[1], Xiaoye Zhang[1,2,3], Zhongliang Li[1], Jingpeng Yue[2], and Qin Zou[1(✉)]

[1] School of Computer Science, Wuhan University, Wuhan, China
qzou@whu.edu.cn
[2] Electric Power Research Institute of Guangdong Power Grid Co., Ltd., Guangzhou, China
[3] China Southern Power Grid Technology Co., Ltd., GuangZhou, China

Abstract. This paper introduces a six degree-of-freedom (6DoF) pose estimation method for manipulating robots to construct a robust machine-vision system. Generally, 2DoF results obtained by traditional object detectors cannot meet the requirements of manipulating operations, where the posture of targets are additionally needed. Meanwhile, due to the sensitivity to light and the limitation to distance, the depth sensor of RGB-D cameras could not always be reliable. To overcome these problems, we study 6DoF pose estimation from a single RGB image. To reduce the complexity and computation, we divide the task into four stages, i.e., data collection and pre-processing, instance segmentation, keypoints prediction, and 2D-to-3D projection. We build the model with deep neural networks, and test it in practical manipulating tasks. The experimental results demonstrate the high accuracy and practicality of our method.

Keywords: 6DoF pose estimation · Instance segmentation · Deep learning · Manipulating robot

1 Introduction

In a power grid system, the maintenance of transmission lines is the most common and representative operation. It is a labor-intensive and dangerous work, which causes several fatal accidents every year. With the development and application of robot technologies, this problem is expected to be solved gradually. The robot technology could improve the efficiency of equipment operation and maintenance, enhance the safety of personnel, and increase the reliability of power grid operations.

This research was funded by China Postdoctoral Science Foundation under grant 2020M672529, and China Southern Power Grid Science and Technology Project under grant GDKJXM20192276, GDKJXM20184840 and NYJS2020KJ005-12.

© Springer Nature Switzerland AG 2021
Y. Peng et al. (Eds.): ICIG 2021, LNCS 12889, pp. 55–66, 2021.
https://doi.org/10.1007/978-3-030-87358-5_5

Nowadays, a number of researches have been conducted on electric power operation robots [3–5,12,17,19]. For example, the Canadian Hydropower Research Institute of Quebec has developed an overhead line inspection and repair robot capable of identifying and repairing single conductor defects; Japan's Hibot company has developed a non-contact inspection function for the internal and external damage of the conductor robot. A cable tunnel detection robot was developed by the University of Washington which can recognize fault location. Beside the above researches abroad, many studies have also been done in China, e.g., Wuhan University, Shenyang Institute of Automation, Chinese Academy of Sciences, Beihang University, Guangdong Power Grid, etc., have successively developed 110 kV, 500 kV overhead transmission line inspection robots and 110 kV, 220 kV robots for single conductor tension drainage clamp bolt fastening and vibration prevention hammer resetting, broken strands repairing, suspension insulators disassembling and installing, etc. Shenzhen Power Supply Bureau, Zhejiang Guozi Robot, Shenzhen Langchi and other units have developed a variety of cable tunnel inspection robots. Shandong Electric Power Research Institute and Shenyang Institute of Automation of Chinese Academy of Sciences have respectively developed robots for live work on distribution lines of 10 kV and below.

However, current robots for distribution lines have failed to achieve the goal of replacing humans with machines [10,21]. Since the low-level intelligence of machine has only poor environmental adaptability. One of the main technical reasons and difficulties is environmental perception and task positioning. Therefore, this paper focuses on this problem: a perception system for the 6DoF pose estimation of the electric manipulating robot.

Object pose estimation has always been a research hotspot. For example, some methods are based on the scale invariant feature matching transform algorithm, which is suitable for targets with rich local texture features [6,11,13,22]. However, when dealing with poor feature texture problems, these template-based matching or dense feature learning methods have shown some shortcomings: 1) sensitive to illuminance and occlusion; 2) cumbersome and time-consuming. Some recent methods [14,16,18] use CNNs to regress the 2D key-points, and then use Perspective-n-Point (PnP) algorithm to calculate 6D pose parameters. Although CNNs can predict these invisible keypoints by memorizing similar patterns, these methods also suffer from low robustness, especially when the actual scene changes, or the target itself has noise or changes in illumination. In such conditions, the prediction ability of these method will be significantly degraded [8,15].

This paper studies how to use machine vision to estimate the 6DoF pose of the target in an open environment, which expands the theory of deep learning-based pose estimation, studies the instance segmentation, keypoints prediction, and restore the target from a 2D view to a 3D pose. A framework for machine vision-based 6DoF pose estimation is designed, which builds the model on deep neural network and direction vector field, and realizes the image segmentation and pose estimation. It aims to provide practical solutions and technical supports for the manipulating robotics working in wild conditions.

2   6DoF Pose Estimation

This paper focuses on the electrical distribution lines manipulating robots, and tries to estimate the pose in all directions. The core difficulty lies in the outdoor operation environment. The commonly used 3DoF position coordinates cannot be well operated and 6DoF is needed . 6DoF includes x, y, z spatial coordinates and α, β, γ angle information. This information must be recognized to determine the angle and posture of the robotic arm to perform correct operations on the target.

By solving these problems independently, our method decomposes the 6D pose estimation task into four sub-tasks, in order to reduce the complexity. The overall workflow is shown in Fig. 1. Firstly, in the pre-processing stage, it performs a data augmentation process on the target, which is used to generate more data and improve the robustness and generalization ability of the network. Next, the instance segmentation network is utilized to obtain all known objects in the image Example. Then, for each object, the designed network with skip connections is used to estimate the 2D object coordinates. Finally, the PnP solution method is used to estimate the 6DoF pose of the target in 3-dimension environment.

2.1   Pre-processing Stage

The training process of deep neural networks requires a large amount of data, and the number of samples directly affects the recognition effect of the model. When the dataset is small, the trained model is prone to overfitting, which leads to a decrease in performance. Generally speaking, obtaining a massive data set is a prerequisite for training, and it is also the key to ensuring a good training effect. When a large number of samples could not be obtained easily, data augmentation is essential for training models, especially when we need to train intensive estimation tasks. In addition, data augmentation can help reduce data set bias and introduce novel examples for deep model training. One of the direct methods to perform data augmentation is to cut the target object from the existing limited data set and paste it on a random background. This paper also adopts such a technical solution.

This paper uses the original RGB image and mask data to extract object, and transform it to other scenes, and give the scaling, offset and other processing at the same time to achieve data augmentation. Considering that the target is rigid, and our task is to estimate the 6DoF pose, our data augmentation processing does not include stretch or flip. Because without considering the camera distortion, the predicted target will not be deformed such as stretching. Moreover, the flipping will introduce the wrong frame corner data information, so it is abandoned as well.

In most cases, the target may be at any angle and pose. Therefore, during training, it is necessary to effectively correlate the angle and pose data in order to achieve the effect of predicting all the obtained data. Among them, the main point is the association between keypoints, that is, each keypoint needs to be relatively fixed with the position of targets. These targets can also be associated with the corresponding keypoints even when the target is converted.

2.2   Instance Segmentation

The goal of instance segmentation is to classify and segment all known objects in the image. In this stage, we use the multi-task network cascade (MNC) [2] proposed by Dai et al. Based on CNN, it deals with instance-level semantic segmentation tasks [1]. In traditional multitasking methods, on the basis of sharing features, each task is performed at the same time. Each task does not interfere with each other and is completed independently. The output of the previous task in the MNC's multi-task cascading network will be used as the input of the next task, forming the cascading network shown in the figure below on the premise of sharing features.

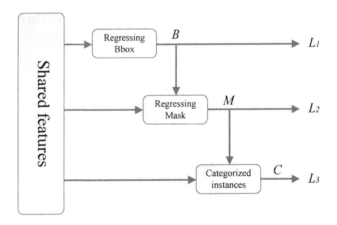

Fig. 1. Schematic diagram of instance segmentation

The shared feature map is learned from the first 13 layers of VGG-16. Each row in the figure above represents a task. Each task contains a loss, and the loss of the next task will also be affected by the previous tasks. MNC's back propagation algorithm can be used to complete the training of the whole model. However, the loss of each stage of the model is affected by the loss of the previous stage, and there is a spatial transformation in the ROI process. MNC has a network layer with differentiable spatial coordinates, which makes the gradient computable.

1) Regress the Bounding Box
In the first stage, the network proposes an instance frame without category. RPN predicts the position of bounding boxes and the object fraction by full

convolution. Use 3×3 convolution for dimension reduction and use two 1×1 convolutions to do classification and regression. The losses at this stage are as follows:

$$L_1 = L_1(B(\Theta)) \tag{1}$$

where Θ represents the parameters to be optimized in the network, B represents the output of the first stage. When $B = B_i$, $B_i = \{x_i, y_i, w_i, h_i, p_i\}$, x_i, y_i represents the center of the bounding box, and the width is w_i, height is h_i, score with p_i.

2) Segmentation at Pixel Level

Mask segmentation at pixel level is performed on the proposal of each bounding box. For the box generated in the first stage, ROI pooling is used to extract features. ROI pooling can generate fixed length features for any size of feature input. Two FC (fully connected) layers are added after each bounding box. The first FC reduces the dimension to 256, and the second one generates pixel level mask regression. The losses at this stage are as follows:

$$L_2 = L_2(M(\Theta)|B(\Theta)) \tag{2}$$

M is the output of this stage, representing a series of masks. $M = \{M_i\}$ and M_i is the output of logistic regression of $m \times m$ dimension. As mentioned earlier, this stage is affected by the first stage.

3) Instance Classification

Given the box in the first stage, the feature extraction is also carried out. Then the mask estimation of the second stage is used for binarization. The losses in the third stage are as follows:

$$L_3 = L_3(C(\Theta)|M(\Theta), B(\Theta)) \tag{3}$$

$C(*)$ is the predicted categorize of object.

Therefore, the total loss of instance segmentation is as follows:

$$L_m(\Theta) = L_1(B(\Theta)) + L_2(M(\Theta)|B(\Theta)) + L_3(C(\Theta)|M(\Theta), B(\Theta)) \tag{4}$$

2.3   Keypoints Prediction

The core of target 6DOF pose estimation is to predict the corners of the 3D circumscribed rectangle, that is, the keypoints. In this paper, each point on the target mask is used to predict the location of the keypoints, forming several direction vectors, and then the location of keypoints is obtained through the optimization algorithm.

More specifically, we perform two tasks: semantic segmentation and vector field prediction. For pixel p, our output is the semantic label associated with a specific object and the vector $v_k(p)$ representing the direction of 2D keypoint $x(k)$ from pixel p to target. Vector $v_k(p)$ is the offset between pixel point p and keypoint $x(k)$, namely $x(k)-p$. By using semantic tags and offsets, we obtain the target object pixels and add offsets to generate a set of keypoints assumptions.

Therefore, the position of keypoint is where the offset of $v_k(p)$ reaches the minimum.

$$L_k = min(\sum v_k(p)) \tag{5}$$

However, due to the interference of imprecise mask and other factors, there will be outliers in the prediction points. Therefore, in the post-processing stage, this paper introduces particle swarm optimization algorithm to remove outliers before predicting the position of corner points.

$$L_k = min(\sum PSO(v_k(p))) \tag{6}$$

L_k is the loss of the keypoints prediction network. Therefore, the final training loss function is:

$$L_{all} = L_m + \lambda \cdot L_k \tag{7}$$

Among them, λ is used to balance the weight of loss function of multitasking, and we set $\lambda = 0.5$ in this work.

2.4   2D-to-3D Projection

The PnP (Perspective-n-Point) problem [9,20] is as follow. Given the matching point pairs of n spatial 3D reference points to the camera image 2D projection points, and the coordinates of 3D points in the world coordinate system and 2D points in the image coordinate system are known, then the position and pose of the camera and the object need to be calculated.

PnP can calculate the coordinates of the corresponding points in the camera coordinate system according to the two-dimensional pixel coordinates and the corresponding three-dimensional space coordinates of the feature points in a single frame, as shown in Fig. 2. The coordinate transformation relationship of the target relative to the three-dimensional space coordinate system can be obtained. The position of any point of the target in the camera coordinate space can be obtained by this transformation relationship. Therefore, this paper uses the PnP method to estimate the 6DoF pose of the target in 3 dimension world coordinate. According to each frame of the collected image, the 3D space target pose is estimated. The final target pose is fitted by multiple sets of estimation results in order to improve the accuracy of pose estimation.

3   Experiments

The experiments are divided into three parts. The first part is the method of making power system clamp dataset. In the second part, we use the open-source dataset Linemod to verify the algorithm. In the third part, we do 6-DOF pose estimation experiment based on this dataset.

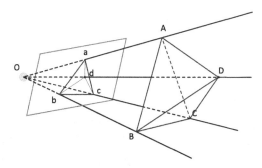

Fig. 2. 2D-to-3D projection sketch map

3.1   Design the Clamp's Dataset

Data is an important part of deep learning algorithm, so we need to build a 6-DOF data set for clamp in power system. We combine 2-D and 3-D information, construct 3-D data through 2-D data, then project the information of 3-D data into 2-D. At last, 2-D label is constructed. Specifically, first of all, the QR code is placed around the object that needs to build the data set, and the video recording is carried out to collect the image data. Then, using the location information of the QR code, the three-dimensional pose of the camera is calculated, and the transform-matrix of multiple images is calculated. Utilizing these matrices and image data, 3D model can be generated. The keypoints and mask information of the target object are determined in the 3D model. Finally, the 3D data is projected into the 2D data to realize the production process of the dataset.

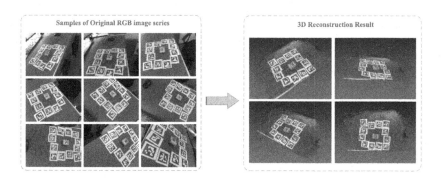

Fig. 3. 2D image collection and 3D construction

In this experiment, we placed Aruco QR code around the object and collected 1050 images. Some examples are shown in the Fig. 3. Next, the 3D data is generated by the QR code data information and image matching algorithm. Then, according to the clamp model scanned by the 3D scanner, as shown in Fig. 4, the frame corner data information of the clamp is mapped and calculated.

Afterwards, we take the image augmentation combined with the 3D scanning model of the clamp. As shown in Fig. 4, we changes different backgrounds to the clamp to improve the data complexity and enhance the robustness and generalization ability of the model.

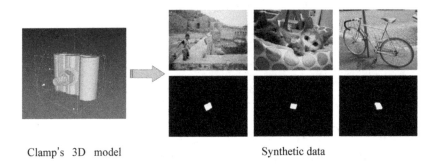

Clamp's 3D model   Synthetic data

Fig. 4. The 3D model and synthetic data

3.2   Results on Public Dataset Linemod

Linemod is the standard benchmark for 6D object pose estimation [6,7]. The Linemod dataset consists of image sequences of 13 objects, each of which contains the real ground pose of a single object of interest in a cluttered environment. CAD models of all objects are also provided. This dataset brings out many challenges in pose estimation: chaotic scenes, objects without texture and changes in lighting conditions.

In order to enhance the robustness of network model, we use the data augmentation in Sect. 2.1 to the original data, then train and verify the augmented data. Table 1 lists the quantitative results, and Fig. 5 shows some visual examples.

We can see that the prediction of mask is quite accurate, which is basically consistent with that of the ground truth, except for some differences in the contour. In the prediction of keypoints, the blue box is the ground truth, and the red box is prediction box. It can seen that there is only a slight difference between them. Next, we use two objective indexes to evaluate the algorithm.

Average Pixel Accuracy. This is an index for image segmentation. It represents the proportion of pixels in each class that are correctly classified, and then the average of all classes is calculated.

Pixel-Deviation in 2D Projection Images. This is an index for augmented reality, 6DoF pose estimation and other applications. If the average 2D distance between the projection of an object vertex and the estimated pose and the real pose on the ground is less than 5 pixels, the pose is considered correct.

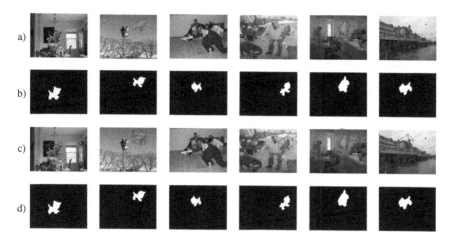

Fig. 5. Mask and 6DOF results on synthetic dataset Linemod. Note that, a) shows six synthesis samples, b) shows the ground-truth masks, c) shows the keypoints prediction (red lines) compared with ground truth (blue lines), and d) shows the predicted masks. (Color figure online)

Table 1. Prediction accuracy of the mask and 6DoF on composite dataset

Targets	Mask	6DoF
Ape	97.7	95.1
BenchVise	98.8	97.7
Camera	97.4	95.5
Can	97.1	96.3
Cat	99.6	99.3
Driller	99.2	97.2
Duck	98.1	94.1
EggBox	99.0	96.6
Glue	99.4	95.6
HolePuncher	99.3	99.6
Iron	97.1	96.1
Lamp	97.9	94.8
Phone	99.9	99.0
Avg	98.5	96.8

3.3   Results on Power Manipulating Robot

The clamp's results are shown in Fig. 6. Two scenes are demonstrate and the 6DoF pose estimation can be carried out no matter which angle the clamp is placed.

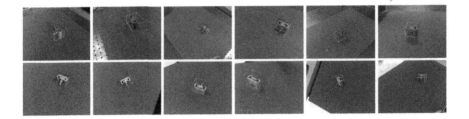

Fig. 6. Clamp's 6Dof results

Figure 7 shows a simulated on-site test environment. The operating robot is UR series, and the camera model is Intel Realsense D415. The camera is set up in the middle of the robot base, and another robot arm is used to control its angle and direction, so as to improve the adaptability of the robot to the environment. There is no need to perceive and operate at a specific angle and specific position, and it can be compatible with the ability to operate multiple cables in the same camera position.

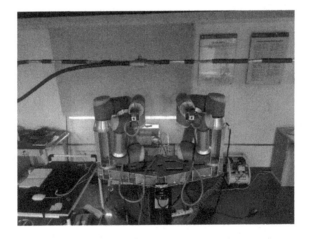

Fig. 7. Manipulating robot and power transmission line

The accuracy requirements of the robot's visual perception are that the displacement deviation is less than 1.5 cm and the angle deviation is less than 20°. It can be realized by using customized structural tools and high-frequency force control feedback provided by the control algorithm. The results of our measurement show that the displacement deviation is less than 1 cm and the angle deviation is less than 15°, which meets the requirements of the electric distribution lines manipulating robot for the accuracy of visual perception.

4   Conclusion

This paper introduced a method for 6DoF pose estimation for manipulating robots. The method included four steps, i.e., data collection and pre-processing, instance segmentation, keypoint prediction, and 2D-to-3D pose estimation. We predicted the positions of 8 keypoints by a deep neural network, and removed outliers by a particle swarm optimization algorithm. Finally, the PnP algorithm was used to realize the projection from 2D to 3D through the positions of 8 keypoints, and achieve the 6DoF pose estimation. Experimental results showed that, the proposed method held a high accuracy, and has very good application prospects in the perception system of manipulating robots for electric transmission line maintenance.

References

1. Cao, Y., Ju, L., Zou, Q., Qu, C., Wang, S.: A multichannel edge-weighted centroidal voronoi tessellation algorithm for 3D super-alloy image segmentation. In: IEEE Conference on Computer Vision and Pattern Recognition, pp. 17–24 (2011)
2. Dai, J., He, K., Sun, J.: Instance-aware semantic segmentation via multi-task network cascades. In: Proceedings of the IEEE Conference on Computer Vision and Pattern Recognition, pp. 3150–3158 (2016)
3. Dian, S., Liu, T., Liang, Y., Liang, M., Zhen, W.: A novel shrimp rover-based mobile robot for monitoring tunnel power cables. In: 2011 IEEE International Conference on Mechatronics and Automation. pp. 887–892. IEEE (2011)
4. Fan, F., Wu, G., Wang, M., Cao, Q., Yang, S.: Multi-robot cyber physical system for sensing environmental variables of transmission line. Sensors $18(9)$, 3146 (2018)
5. Griepentrog, H.W., Jaeger-Hansen, C.L., Dühring, K., et al.: Electric agricultural robot with multi-layer-control. In: Proceedings of International Conference of Agricultural Engineering (2012)
6. Hinterstoisser, S., et al.: Model based training, detection and pose estimation of texture-less 3D objects in heavily cluttered scenes. In: Lee, Kyoung Mu, Matsushita, Yasuyuki, Rehg, James M.., Hu, Zhanyi (eds.) ACCV 2012. LNCS, vol. 7724, pp. 548–562. Springer, Heidelberg (2013). https://doi.org/10.1007/978-3-642-37331-2_42
7. Kaskman, R., Zakharov, S., Shugurov, I., Ilic, S.: HomebrewedDB: RGB-D dataset for 6d pose estimation of 3d objects. In: Proceedings of the IEEE/CVF International Conference on Computer Vision Workshops (2019)
8. Kehl, W., Manhardt, F., Tombari, F., Ilic, S., Navab, N.: SSD-6D: making RGB-based 3D detection and 6D pose estimation great again. In: Proceedings of the IEEE International Conference on Computer Vision, pp. 1521–1529 (2017)
9. Lepetit, V., Moreno-Noguer, F., Fua, P.: EPNP: an accurate o(n) solution to the PNP problem. Int. J. Comput. Vis. $81(2)$, 155 (2009)
10. Li, Yi., Wang, Gu., Ji, Xiangyang, Xiang, Yu., Fox, Dieter: DeepIM: deep iterative matching for 6D pose estimation. Int. J. Comput. Vis. $128(3)$, 657–678 (2019). https://doi.org/10.1007/s11263-019-01250-9
11. Lowe, D.G.: Object recognition from local scale-invariant features. In: Proceedings of the Seventh IEEE International Conference on Computer Vision, vol. 2, pp. 1150–1157. IEEE (1999)

12. Lu, S., Zhang, Y., Su, J.: Mobile robot for power substation inspection: a survey. IEEE/CAA J. Automatica Sinica **4**(4), 830–847 (2017)
13. Ng, P.C., Henikoff, S.: SIFT: predicting amino acid changes that affect protein function. Nucleic acids Res. **31**(13), 3812–3814 (2003)
14. Pavlakos, G., Zhou, X., Chan, A., Derpanis, K.G., Daniilidis, K.: 6-DoF object pose from semantic keypoints. In: 2017 IEEE International Conference on Robotics and Automation (ICRA), pp. 2011–2018. IEEE (2017)
15. Peng, S., Liu, Y., Huang, Q., Zhou, X., Bao, H.: PVNet: pixel-wise voting network for 6DoF pose estimation. In: Proceedings of the IEEE/CVF Conference on Computer Vision and Pattern Recognition, pp. 4561–4570 (2019)
16. Rad, M., Lepetit, V.: BB8: a scalable, accurate, robust to partial occlusion method for predicting the 3D poses of challenging objects without using depth. In: Proceedings of the IEEE International Conference on Computer Vision, pp. 3828–3836 (2017)
17. Song, Y., Wang, H., Jiang, Y., Ling, L.: AApe-D: a novel power transmission line maintenance robot for broken strand repair. In: 2012 2nd International Conference on Applied Robotics for the Power Industry (CARPI), pp. 108–113. IEEE (2012)
18. Tekin, B., Sinha, S.N., Fua, P.: Real-time seamless single shot 6D object pose prediction. In: Proceedings of the IEEE Conference on Computer Vision and Pattern Recognition, pp. 292–301 (2018)
19. Wang, B., Chen, X., Wang, Q., Liu, L., Zhang, H., Li, B.: Power line inspection with a flying robot. In: 2010 1st International Conference on Applied Robotics for the Power Industry, pp. 1–6. IEEE (2010)
20. Wu, Y., Hu, Z.: PnP problem revisited. J. Math. Imag. Vis. **24**(1), 131–141 (2006)
21. Xiang, Y., Schmidt, T., Narayanan, V., Fox, D.: PoseCNN: a convolutional neural network for 6D object pose estimation in cluttered scenes. arXiv preprint arXiv:1711.00199 (2017)
22. Zhang, X., Ma, Y., Fan, F., Zhang, Y., Huang, J.: Infrared and visible image fusion via saliency analysis and local edge-preserving multi-scale decomposition. JOSA A **34**(8), 1400–1410 (2017)

Novel Augmented Reality System for Oral and Maxillofacial Surgery

Lele Ding[1], Long Shao[1], Zehua Zhao[1], Tao Zhang[2(✉)], Danni Ai[1(✉)], Jian Yang[1], and Yongtian Wang[1]

[1] Beijing Engineering Research Center of Mixed Reality and Advanced Display, School of Optics and Photonics, Beijing Institute of Technology, Beijing 100081, China
danni@bit.edu.cn
[2] Department of Oral and Maxillofacial Surgery, Peking Union Medical College Hospital, Beijing 100730, China

Abstract. Recently, in the field of surgical visualization, augmented reality technology has shown incomparable advantages in oral and maxillofacial surgery. However, the current augmented reality methods need to develop personalized occlusal splints and perform secondary Computed Tomography (CT) scanning. These unnecessary preparations lead to high cost and extend the time of preoperative preparation. In this paper, we propose an augmented reality surgery guidance system based on 3D scanning. The system innovatively designs a universal occlusal splint for all patients and reconstructs the virtual model of patients with occlusal splints through 3D scanning. During the surgery, the pose relationship between the virtual model and the markers is computed through the marker on the occlusal splint. The proposed method can replace the wearing of occlusal splints for the secondary CT scanning during surgery. Experimental results show that the average target registration error of the proposed method is 1.38 ± 0.43 mm, which is comparable to the accuracy of the secondary CT scanning method. This result suggests the great application potential and value of the proposed method in oral and maxillofacial surgery.

Keywords: Augmented reality · Surgical navigation · Occlusal splint · Three-dimensional reconstruction

1 Introduction

The traditional method of oral and maxillofacial surgery performs preoperative planning and operation simulation according to CT images, mainly relying on the prior knowledge and experience of the surgeon [1]. In recent years, researchers have studied several oral and maxillofacial surgical guidance systems based on augmented reality technology [2–6]. Wang et al. [7] used integral imaging technology to realize the 3D

L. Ding and L. Shao—These authors contributed equally to this work and should be considered co-first authors.

Y. Peng et al. (Eds.): ICIG 2021, LNCS 12889, pp. 67–79, 2021.
https://doi.org/10.1007/978-3-030-87358-5_6

display of the mandible virtual model, enhancing the depth perception during the surgical guidance process. Ma et al. [8] proposed an augmented reality display system based on integral videography. The system can provide a 3D image with full parallax and help surgeons directly observe the hidden anatomical structure with naked eyes. Through a half-silvered mirror, observers can directly perceive the real environment while receiving the reflected virtual content, avoiding the problem of hand–eye coordination during surgery. The marker-less image registration method used in AR scenes must usually extract the features of objects [9]. However, the process of extracting the boundary shape is complicated and time-consuming. Zhu et al. [10] designed personalized occlusal splints for each patient, achieving the superimposition of the virtual skull model on the patient by identifying fiducial marks and tracking patient displacement. This method has high precision and real-time performance that satisfy the intraoperative requirements. However, this method requires a significant amount of time to design an occlusal splint based on the CT data of each patient before the operation.

This study proposes an augmented reality system for oral and maxillofacial surgery. The proposed system uses a 3D scanner to perform 3D reconstruction. The virtual model is superimposed on the real object by tracking the reference image marker. The principal prototype of the system was tested on a skull phantom and cadaver mandibles. The results show that the accuracy of the proposed system meets the clinical needs. In addition, our method does not require patients to undergo secondary CT scans. Furthermore, we only need to design a universal occlusal splint for all patients to meet the surgery requirement. We summarize our contributions as follows. (1) A universal occlusal splint is designed for most patients, replacing the design of personalized occlusal splints for each patient, thereby greatly reducing the time and material costs. (2) Instead of secondary CT scanning, the virtual model is reconstructed by 3D scanning to achieve a "seamless" integration of the virtual and real situations. The influence of fusion precision and external factors om accuracy is analyzed from several aspects.

2   Experimental Setup

Figure 1 illustrates the setup of the proposed augmented reality display system. M represents the universal occlusal splint. A marker is pasted on the occlusal splint, which is rigidly fixed to the skull phantom. R represents the skull phantom. The size of the skull phantom is the same as that of a human skull. S represents the 3D scanner (Artec EVA, Canada), which is used to obtain the virtual model for the experiment. C represents the camera (sy8031, Shenzhen, China). The maximum frame number of video processing is 28 frames/s, and the resolution is 1080p. V represents a computer monitor, which is used to obtain the fusion view. Optical tracker N (NDI Polaris, Canada) and navigation tracking probe X are used to verify the fusion error.

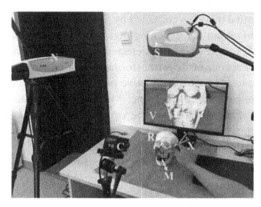

Fig. 1. Experimental setup for the developed augmented reality display system of oral and maxillofacial surgery. (N: Optical tracker, X: Probe, C: Camera, S: 3D scanner, V: Computer monitor, R: model, M: Occlusal splint)

3 Methods

3.1 System Framework

Figure 2 illustrates the framework of the proposed augmented reality display system for oral and maxillofacial surgery. The framework mainly includes the following parts: virtual model production, marker recognition, and fusion view generation.

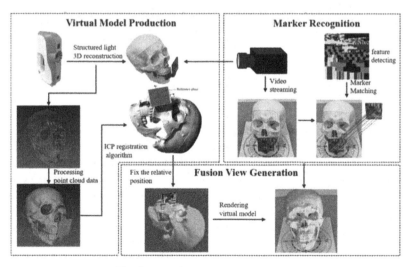

Fig. 2. Workflow of proposed system.

To obtain the virtual model, a universal occlusal splint with a marker is fixed with a skull phantom or a mandible. The virtual model is reconstructed using a 3D scanner, and the pose of the virtual model is corrected by the ICP registration algorithm. During marker recognition, to obtain the matching region between the marker and the input video stream, the ORB feature points are detected and saved, and the feature descriptor is calculated. The marker coordinate is transformed to the screen coordinate through the marker. To obtain the fusion view, the relative position between the virtual model and the marker is fixed similarly as the real scene. After recognizing the marker, the pose of the marker is calculated in real time, and the virtual object's pose is updated according to the marker. When measuring the fusion accuracy, quantitative results are obtained by the optical tracker and the navigation tracking probe.

3.2 Virtual Model Production

Universal Occlusal Splint Design
We collected the CT data of mandibles in 100 patients. Three-dimensional models of each mandible were reconstructed by threshold segmentation (Mimics) and surface reconstruction, as shown in Figs. 3(a), (b) and (c). The mandible dataset was constructed as follows:

$$\left\{ S_i = (x_{i1}, y_{i1}, z_{i1}, \ldots \ldots, \quad x_{im}, y_{im}, z_{im})^T | i = 1, 2, \ldots \ldots, 100 \right\} \qquad (1)$$

The 3D models of each mandible are composed of a set of points, where m denotes the total number of vertices on the mandibular model, and each vertex is represented by x, y, z; i indicates an index of 100 cases. The data volume of each mandible is down sampled. The statistical shape is established based on principal component analysis [11]. The average shape model is consequently obtained, as shown in Fig. 3(d), and f can be used to describe any 3D statistical shape in the mandibular training data set, as shown in Formula (2):

$$f = \overline{f} + \sum_{i=1}^{m-1} a_i b_i \qquad (2)$$

where f indicates the statistical shape parametric model of 100 mandible cases. $\overline{f}$ indicates the average 3D statistical shape matrix of the mandible. a_i indicates the eigenvector matrix describing the morphological changes of the first $m - 1$ principal components. b_i indicates the matrix describing the specific model parameters. The statistical shape model contains the structural features of 100 cases and can be used as a standard mandible template. As shown in Fig. 3(e), a 3D groove model, which is suitable for most people and can be fixed with the lower teeth of the template, is designed according to the template. To facilitate the identification of the marker during the virtual reality fusion process, a connecting rod is led out from the groove model. The end of the rod is designed as a square plane where the image marker can be placed. The recognition rate is higher when the marker size is set to 50 mm × 50 mm than other sizes. Therefore, the size of the square plane is designed to be 50 mm × 50 mm. Finally, the universal occlusal splint is 3D-printed, as shown in Fig. 3(f).

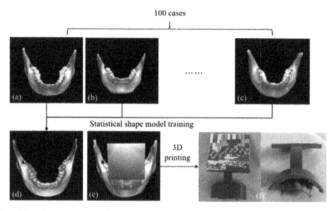

Fig. 3. Design of universal occlusal splint. (a) Segmentation and reconstruction of case1, (b) Segmentation and reconstruction of case2, (c) Segmentation and reconstruction of case100, (d) Statistical shape model of 100 cases, (e) Design universal occlusal splint based on statistical shape model, (f) 3D printed universal occlusal splint.

Virtual Model Pose Correction

The universal occlusal splint is fixed with the skull phantom to form a whole model, as shown in Fig. 4(a). The virtual skull model reconstructed by 3D scanning, which is consistent with the size of the real skull phantom, is shown in Fig. 4(b). The relative position between the virtual model and the marker is not unified in the virtual and real spaces. Therefore, their position relationship in the virtual and real spaces must be unified before obtaining the fusion view. We set up a reference plane plate with the same size as the square plane of the occlusal splint at the origin of the marker coordinate system. The reference plane plate and the occlusal splint are composed of point sets. We suppose that the point set on the reference plate is p_i, and the point set of the occlusal splint is represented by q_i. The ICP registration algorithm [12] is used to register the square plane of the occlusal splint with the reference plane. Consequently, the conversion matrix that minimizes E in Eq. (3) is obtained:

$$E = \sum_{i=1}^{N} |Tp_i - q_i|^2 \tag{3}$$

The virtual skull model is moved to the origin of the reference image marker coordinate system through transformation matrix T, as shown in Fig. 4(c). After identifying the image marker, the virtual model is correctly superimposed on the real environment according to the position and pose of the marker.

3.3 Marker Recognition

The ORB feature points [13, 14] of the image marker are extracted, and the BRIEF algorithm [15] is used to calculate the feature descriptors. All the feature points and the feature descriptors are stored as feature templates for determining whether the marker is included in the video stream frame.

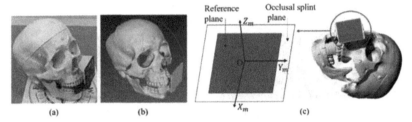

Fig. 4. Pose correction of virtual model. (a) Skull model with universal occlusal splint, (b) Virtual skull model obtained from 3D scanning, (c) Adjustment of position according to ICP registration algorithm.

Gray-scale processing is performed on the acquired input frame image to detect the feature points. The Hamming distance is used as the similarity measure to check the corresponding relationship between the marker and the input frame image. Feature matching is carried out afterward. $Y = y_0 y_1 \cdots y_n$ indicates the ORB descriptor marker. $X = x_0 x_1 \cdots x_n$ indicates the ORB feature descriptor of the input frame image. The Hamming distance is,

$$H = \|X - Y\| = \sum_{i=0}^{n} x_i \oplus y_i < \alpha \tag{4}$$

where α represents the threshold of the Hamming distance. When the Hamming distance between the two descriptors is greater than the threshold, the two images have a large error and the video stream has no marker. When the distance is less than the threshold, the part of the input frame image containing a large amount of feature information in the video stream can be determined, and the position of the marker can be identified.

3.4 Fusion View Generation

For the augmented reality system, the goal is to superimpose the virtual model in real space. Therefore, drawing the virtual model at the target coordinate position accurately is a particularly important step for the augmented reality system. $O\{X_m, Y_m, Z_m\}$, $C\{X_c, Y_c, Z_c\}$, $\{x_c, y_c\}$, and $\{x_d, y_d\}$ represent the marker, camera, ideal screen, and actual screen coordinates, respectively.

The marker coordinate system takes the center of the image marker as the origin. In Sect. 3.2, the coordinates of the virtual model and the marker are unified. In real space, the relative transformation matrix of the camera and the marker can be estimated by the pose of the marker. The augmented reality registration task is converted to calculate a spatial transformation relationship, mapping the relationship between the marker and screen coordinates. That is, the virtual and real space coordinates are connected. The fusion view is displayed on the actual screen coordinates. The transformation relation between the marker and camera coordinates follows the following formula:

$$\begin{bmatrix} X_c \\ Y_c \\ Z_c \\ 1 \end{bmatrix} = \begin{bmatrix} R_{11} & R_{12} & R_{13} & T_1 \\ R_{21} & R_{22} & R_{23} & T_2 \\ R_{31} & R_{32} & R_{33} & T_3 \\ 0 & 0 & 0 & 1 \end{bmatrix} \begin{bmatrix} X_m \\ Y_m \\ Z_m \\ 1 \end{bmatrix} = \begin{bmatrix} R & T \\ 0 & 1 \end{bmatrix} \begin{bmatrix} X_m \\ Y_m \\ Z_m \\ 1 \end{bmatrix} = T_{c2m} \begin{bmatrix} X_m \\ Y_m \\ Z_m \\ 1 \end{bmatrix} \quad (5)$$

where R denotes the rotation matrix, and T denotes the translation matrix. Ideally, the conversion relationship between the camera and ideal screen coordinates is as follows:

$$\begin{bmatrix} x_c \\ y_c \\ 1 \end{bmatrix} = \begin{bmatrix} f & 0 & 0 & 0 \\ 0 & f & 0 & 0 \\ 0 & 0 & 1 & 0 \end{bmatrix} \begin{bmatrix} X_c \\ Y_c \\ Z_c \\ 1 \end{bmatrix} \quad (6)$$

Given the linear distortion of camera lens, the result of pose estimation is the transformation relationship between the camera and actual screen coordinate systems:

$$\begin{bmatrix} x_d \\ y_d \\ 1 \end{bmatrix} = \begin{bmatrix} h_x f & h & u_0 & 0 \\ 0 & h_y f & v_0 & 0 \\ 0 & 0 & 1 & 0 \end{bmatrix} \begin{bmatrix} X_c \\ Y_c \\ Z_c \\ 1 \end{bmatrix} \quad (7)$$

where h_x, h_y indicates the scale factor. f indicates the camera's focal length. h indicates the distortion parameter. (u_0, v_0) indicates the camera's principal point coordinate. These parameters can be obtained by camera calibration. If T_{c2m} can be found by identifying the marker, then an accurate coordinate can be provided for the virtual model drawing [16].

4 Experiments and Results

4.1 Experiment on Skull Phantom

Verification Points Selection
The verification points on the obvious physical feature structure that originally exists must be selected. In addition, the selection of verification points on the skull phantom must consider whether these points have high coverage for direction and face shape when used as evaluation indexes. In the proposed system, the points covering most of the maxillofacial region are selected from the skull phantom. Two of the feature points are not selected as verification points because they are blocked by the square plane of the occlusal splint. The name and label of each verification point selected on the skull phantom are shown in Fig. 6(a). Among the points, points 1, 2, 4, 6, 7, and 9 are the verification points of the right half of the skull phantom, and points 2, 3, 5, 6, 8, and 10 are the verification points of the left half of the skull phantom.

Measurement Scheme

The processed virtual model is imported into the fusion view display module. When the marker is recognized, the virtual model is superimposed onto the real phantom. The initial scene of the skull phantom is shown in Fig. 5(a). For the virtual model that was smoothed in the process of structured light 3D reconstruction, the verification points selected on the real model were difficult to identify. Therefore, 11 verification points were added to the skeletal characteristic position of the skull phantom and highlighted. The superimposed effect is shown in Fig. 5(b). When collecting the virtual and real verification points for precision measurement, the skull virtual model data will affect the recognition of the verification points, which could lead to visual errors. Therefore, unnecessary virtual model data can be deleted, and only the verification points are retained. At this time, the effect after superimposition is shown in Fig. 5(c).

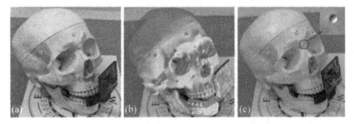

Fig. 5. The fusion view. (a) Original view, (b) Fusion view (reduce the transparency of virtual models), (c) Fusion view (keep only feature points).

The navigation probe was pointed to each of the verification points under the optical tracker, and the probe tip positions were saved. The virtual coordinate $P_{virtual} = (x_{iv}, y_{iv}, z_{iv})$ $(i = 1, 2, 3 \ldots \ldots n)$ and real coordinate $P_{real} = (x_{ir}, y_{ir}, z_{ir})(i = 1, 2, 3 \ldots \ldots n)$ of each verification point were then recorded. The absolute value of the distance between the virtual and real verification points is taken as the fusion error (target registration error (TRE)) [7, 17, 18] and used to evaluate the accuracy of the superimposed result.

$$TRE = \frac{1}{n} \cdot \sum_{i=1}^{n} \sqrt{(x_{iv} - x_{ir})^2 + (y_{iv} - y_{ir})^2 + (z_{iv} - z_{ir})^2} \qquad (8)$$

As shown in Fig. 6(b), the probe was first used to select the real space fiducial points, and the real coordinates P_{real} were recorded. Then, the corresponding virtual fiducial points were selected according to augmented reality fusion. The virtual coordinates $P_{virtual}$ were recorded. We took P_{real} and $P_{virtual}$ as a set of data, forming a complete set of data by recording each verification point separately in order [3]. In addition, we set the skull phantom rotation according to the angle disc to verify the fusion error under different angles. A complete set of data was obtained through measurements at intervals of $10°$ from $-60°$ to $+ 60°$ (Fig. 6(c)), and all data were recorded and then analyzed and sorted. We took TRE measurements under the same conditions in triplicates, and the mean values were calculated. All measurements were completed by the same operator.

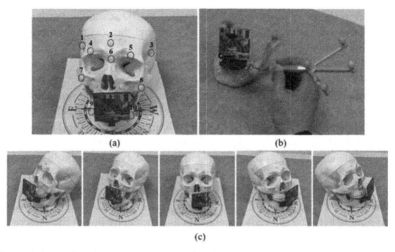

Fig. 6. Spatial coordinate data acquisition. (a) Nomenclature of skull models, (b) Measurement of the TRE on mandible, (c) Accuracy measurement under different angles (From left to right: −60°, −30°, 0°, 30°, 60°.

Comparison of the Accuracy in Three Methods

In reference [19], Chen et al. built a virtual skull model and designed a printed personalized occlusal splint based on the patient's CT images. They generated an integrated virtual model by nesting the virtual occlusal splint on the teeth shape. In reference [10], the skull phantom was fixed with the designed personalized occlusal splint, and the entire CT data was obtained by secondary scanning. The virtual model for the experiment was segmented from CT images, and the artificial marker was used for augmented reality display. Given that each verification point is visible at 0°, the TRE at 0° is the most suitable for verifying the overall average fusion accuracy. The TRE results of the proposed method and the methods in references [19] and [10] are shown in Table 1.

Table 1. TRE of three methods at 0°.

	Proposed method	Method of [19]	Method of [10]
TRE(mm)	1.38 ± 0.43	1.35 ± 0.77	0.77 ± 0.88

As shown in Table 1, the average fusion error of the proposed system is equivalent to that in reference [19], verifying the feasibility of the proposed system in guiding oral and maxillofacial surgery. The system in reference [10] has the highest fusion accuracy because its integrated model is derived from a second CT scan. However, a second CT scan increases the patient's radiation risk. The preoperative preparation in references [19] and [10] includes three processes: the CT scan, segmentation, and the reconstruction of the virtual model; personalized occlusal splint design; and printing. The proposed system saves in CT scan and modeling segmentation time. The establishment of the virtual model in the proposed system is completed by 3D scanning. Furthermore, the proposed system can reduce CT radiation exposure and the cost of medical treatment while ensuring accuracy.

Influence of Different Angles on Fusion Accuracy

The TRE of each fiducial point under different angles is measured to verify the influence of the angle om fusion accuracy. Figure 7 (a) shows the TRE of points 1, 2, 4, 6, 7, and 9 during skull phantom rotation from 0° to 60°. Figure 7(b) shows the TRE of points 2, 3, 5, 6, 8, and 10 during skull phantom rotation from −60° to 0°.

Figures 7(a) and 7(b) shows that the error of point 1 decreases as the angle increases, and the errors of points 2 and 6 increase with the angle. This phenomenon occurs because point 1 is located at the edge of the skull, and the angle between point 1 and the center line of the camera's field of view decreases as the model's rotation angle increases. The smaller the angle between the verification point and the center line of the camera's field of view is, the smaller the fusion error of the point will be [19]. Given that point 10 is nearest to the marker, the error range of point 10 is smaller than those of the other points, indicating that the nearer the point to the marker is, the more stable the fusion effect would be.

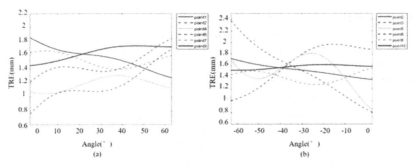

Fig. 7. Error distribution of TRE with angle at verification points. (a) Verification points of the left half of skull model, (b) Verification points of the right half of skull model.

4.2 Cadaveric Mandible Experiment

Four cadaveric mandible cases used in our experiment are collected from Peking Union Medical College Hospital. The measurement scheme was applied to the mandible of four cases to verify the stability and versatility of the proposed system. The feasibility of this method in practical medical applications was verified by measuring the fusion accuracy on the mandible cases.

Results and Analysis

The superimposition process between the virtual model and the real scene was performed at 0° because all verification points are visible the tracking effect the most stable at the 0° position. We selected several verification points that can be observed at the 0° position on the mandible in advance, as shown in Fig. 8(d). Four cadaveric mandible cases were selected for the experiment, and the measurement scheme employed was the same as that in the skull phantom experiment. The same universal occlusal splint was fixed on the mandible of the four cases. Then, the entire virtual models were reconstructed. After recognizing the image marker, the virtual model was superimposed onto the real environment, forming the "integrated image" on the monitor. The initial states of the mandible and the virtual model reconstructed by structured light are shown in Figs. 8(a) and 8(b), respectively, and the effect of overlay is shown in Fig. 8(c). The feature points are highlighted, the virtual model display is hidden, and only the verification points used to verify the accuracy of virtual real fusion are retained. The fusion effect is shown in Fig. 8(d). The results of TRE are shown in Fig. 9. The TREs of cases 1, 2 and 3 are less than 2 mm, satisfying the surgery requirement. The fluctuation of the TRE curve in Fig. 9 can be attributed to the following: the errors caused by manual measurement, image recognition, and the environmental lighting changes.

Fig. 8. Fusion of virtual and real body mandible. (a) Original view, (b) Virtual mandible model obtained from 3D scanning, (c) Fusion view (reduce the transparency of virtual models), (d) Fusion view (keep only feature points).

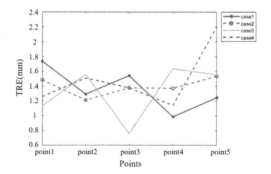

Fig. 9. TRE of all verification points in four cases.

5 Conclusion

This paper proposes a new augmented reality display system in oral and maxillofacial surgery. According to the statistical shape model of the mandible of 100 patients, a general occlusal splint was designed. The virtual model of the real phantom and cadaveric mandible cases were obtained by 3D scanning and positioned and tracked in real space based on the image marker. The fusion accuracy and feasibility of the proposed system were verified by comparison with the method in reference [19]. Surgeons can mark the planned surgical plan and the path of the surgery on the patient's 3D model before the operation using the proposed system. During the operation, the virtual model and the actual surgical area fusion view can be obtained easily when patients wear a universal occlusal splint. The trajectory marked by the doctor in advance will be displayed on the planned position in the real scene to assist the doctor in the operation. Experimental results show that the accuracy of the proposed system is within the allowable range of actual surgical error, with an average fusion error of 1.38 ± 0.43, proving the reliability of the proposed system. In addition, personalized splints and secondary CT scanning are no longer necessary in the proposed system. In summary, the proposed system has development potential for assisting surgeons in improving surgical accuracy and reducing operational difficulty.

Acknowledgement. This work was supported by the National Key R&D Program of China (2019YFC0119300), the National Science Foundation Program of China (62025104, 61901031), and Beijing Nova Program (Z201100006820004) from Beijing Municipal Science & Technology Commission.

Disclosures. The authors declare that there are no conflicts of interest related to this article.

References

1. Chana, J.S., Chang, Y.M., Wei, F.C.: Segmental mandibulectomy and immediate free fibula osteoseptocutaneous flap reconstruction with endosteal implants: an ideal treatment method for mandibular ameloblastoma. Plast. Reconstr. Surg. **113**(1), 80–87 (2004)
2. Ma, L., et al.: Augmented reality surgical navigation with accurate CBCT-patient registration for dental implant placement. Med. Biol. Eng. Comput. **57**(1), 47–57 (2018). https://doi.org/10.1007/s11517-018-1861-9
3. Gao, Y., Lin, L., Chai, G.: A feasibility study of a new method to enhance the augmented reality navigation effect in mandibular angle split osteotomy. J. Cranio-Maxillofac. Surg. (2019)
4. Badiali, G., Ferrari, V., Cutolo, F.: Augmented reality as an aid in maxillofacial surgery: Validation of a wearable system allowing maxillary repositioning. J. Craniomaxillofac. Surg. **42**(8), 1970–1976 (2014)
5. Mamone, V., Ferrari, V., Condino, S.: Projected augmented reality to drive osteotomy surgery: implementation and comparison with video see-through technology. IEEE Access **8**, 169024–169035 (2020)
6. Azimi, E., Song, T., Yang, C., et al.: Endodontic Guided treatment using augmented reality on a head-mounted display system. Healthc. Technol. Lett. **5**(5), 201–207 (2018)
7. Wang, J., Suenaga, H., Liao, H.: Real-time computer-generated integral imaging and 3D image calibration for augmented reality surgical navigation. Comput. Med. Imaging Graph. **40**, 147–159 (2015)
8. Ma, L., Fan, Z., Ning, G., Zhang, X., Liao, H.: 3D visualization and augmented reality for orthopedics. In: Zheng, G., Tian, W., Zhuang, X. (eds.) Intelligent Orthopaedics. Advances in Experimental Medicine and Biology, vol. 1093, pp. 193–205. Springer, Singapore (2018). https://doi.org/10.1007/978-981-13-1396-7_16

9. Wang, J., Suenaga, H.: Video see-through augmented reality for oral and maxillofacial surgery. Int. J. Med. Robot. Comput. Assist. Surg. (2017)
10. Zhu, M., Liu, F., Chai, G.: A novel augmented reality system for displaying inferior alveolar nerve bundles in maxillofacial surgery. Sci. Rep. **7**, 42365 (2017)
11. Lüthi, M.: Statismo-a framework for PCA based statistical models. Insight **1**,1–18 (2012)
12. Besl, P.J., Mckay, H.D.: A method for registration of 3-D shapes. IEEE Trans. Pattern Anal. Mach. Intell. **14**(2), 239–256 (1992)
13. Cui, X.: Augmented Reality Assistance System Framework Research Based on Boeing 737 Aircraft Pre-flight Maintenance, pp. 21–27. Civil Aviation University of China, Tianjin (2019)
14. Rublee, E., Rabaud, V., Konolige, K.: ORB: an efficient alternative to SIFT or SURF. In: International Conference on Computer Vision. IEEE (2012)
15. Calonder, M., Lepetit, V., Strecha, C., Fua, P.: BRIEF: binary robust independent elementary features. In: Daniilidis, K., Maragos, P., Paragios, N. (eds.) ECCV 2010. LNCS, vol. 6314, pp. 778–792. Springer, Heidelberg (2010). https://doi.org/10.1007/978-3-642-15561-1_56
16. Fischler, M.A., Bolles, R.C.: Random sample consensus: a paradigm for model fitting with applications to image analysis and automated cartography. Commun. ACM **24**(6), 381–395 (1981)
17. Jiang, T., Zhu, M., Chai, G., Li, Q.: Precision of a novel craniofacial surgical navigation system based on augmented reality using an occlusal splint as a registration strategy. Sci. Rep. **9**(1), 501 (2019)
18. Murugesan, Y.P., Alsadoon, A., Manoranjan, P.: A novel rotational matrix and translation vector algorithm: geometric accuracy for augmented reality in oral and maxillofacial surgeries. Int. J. Med. Robot. Comput. Assist. Surg. (2018)
19. Chen, L., Li, H., Shao, L.: An augmented reality surgical guidance method based on 3D model design. In: The 20th National Conference on Image and Graphics (NGIG), vol. 144, pp. 28–30 (2020)

A New Dataset and Recognition for Egocentric Microgesture Designed by Ergonomists

Guangchuan Li[1], Yue Liu[1,2($\boxtimes$)], Weitao Song[1], Cong Wang[1,3], and Yongtian Wang[1]

[1] Beijing Engineering Research Center of Mixed Reality and Advanced Display, School of Optics and Photonics, Beijing Institute of Technology, Beijing, China
`liuyue@bit.edu.cn`
[2] AICFVE of Beijing Film Academy, Beijing, China
[3] China Academy of Industrial Internet, Beijing, China

Abstract. Virtual and Augmented reality (VR/AR) are widely deployed in industrial, medical, educational, and entertaining fields. The design of interactive interfaces has an impact on usability, comfort, and efficiency. Hand controllers and gestures are popularly used in VR/AR devices. However, users may suffer from overloading on the upper extremities while raising the hand or controller. Therefore, we released a microgesture library with 19 microgestures designed by ergonomists. Users can perform microgestures for an extended duration by resting the forearm on the tables to reduce the load on the upper extremity. Additionally, we collected a microgesture dataset of 2900 samples and utilized the C3D model to recognize the microgesture dataset. Finally, we achieved a recognition accuracy of 93.4% on the microgestures dataset.

Keywords: Microgestures · VR/AR · Gesture recognition · Ergonomist · Dataset

1 Introduction

The acquisition of information for users was different while using VR/AR head-mounted displays (HMDs) compared to traditional devices such as cell phones, tablets, and projectors. The VR/AR techniques have the potential to change the way how we work or entertain in the future [1]. The design of interfaces for HCI is critical to user performance and usability. The interfaces based on hand controllers and mid-air gestures are built to bridge human and VR/AR systems. The use of a hand controller is similar to the operation of the gaming controller so learning difficulty is low for users. Besides, users can signal command with high accuracy, low latency, and tactile feedback while pressing the button on the

Granted by the Key-Area Research and Development Program of Guangdong Province (No. 2019B010149001), the National Natural Science Foundation of China (No. 61960206007) and the 111 Project (B18005).

Y. Peng et al. (Eds.): ICIG 2021, LNCS 12889, pp. 80–89, 2021.
https://doi.org/10.1007/978-3-030-87358-5_7

controller. Users may not be able to keep their attention on the hand controller while browsing information with VR/AR devices. Therefore, there are only a few buttons on the controller for users to press to avoid clicking the neighbor button. The interaction efficiency with a hand controller is limited by the number of buttons while users have to browse different menus and shift pages. Additionally, the controller weight is non-trivial and users can not afford to hold it for hours or longer. Moreover, the use of a hand controller contributes to motion sickness so hand gesture [2] as an alternative is attracting the attention of researchers.

Mid-air gestures are deployed in VR/AR devices like HoloLens and Magic Leap et al., and users can perform hand gestures without noticing the hands because of the proprioception. Meanwhile, users can perform dozens of hand gestures to commit commands efficiently without increasing the memory load. Hence, users can perform hand gestures to control the VR/AR devices efficiently. Nevertheless, the existing hand gestures were designed by users without ergonomic background and the repeated formation of hand gestures may be associated with health problems like disorders or even pain in the wrist. Further, users have to raise their hands in front of the camera because hands should appear in the limited field of view of the camera mounted on the devices. The raise of hands will increase the muscle load on the neck and shoulder so users may perceive fatigue on the upper extremities easily. Meanwhile, the lack of feedback has an impact on user input confidence while performing mid-air gestures compared to using a hand controller [3]. Researchers focus on designing microgestures with small hand or finger motions and users can rest the forearm or wrist on the table to reduce the muscle load on the neck and shoulder [4]. Users can interact with smart devices by microgestures for the long term in the future. However, performing microgestures are still potential to contribute to health risk while overextending or over flexing the wrist or finger joints. The microgestures designed by ergonomists can protect users from disorder or pain after performing gestures to interact with smart devices.

The primary purpose of the study was to propose a microgesture set designed by ergonomists for VR/AR systems that may improve usability and comfort. We utilized the deep learning model to recognize the microgesture dataset collected from 9 participants and demonstrated that the application of microgestures can be implemented based on visual methods. The microgestures dataset can be beneficial to researchers who try to design the interfaces based on the microgestures.

2   Realated Work

2.1   The Design of Gestures

The design and selection of gestures for HCIs are crucial to user comfort, and the popular method for designing gestures was to elicit the gestures from users proposed by Wobbrock et al. [5]. The proposed gesture set from users combing user behavior can decrease the cognitive load and improve usability. Rempel et al. [6] found that sign language interpreters have pain or disorders on the upper extremity because their profession is forming mid-air hand gestures repeatedly for many years. Therefore, the formation of gestures from users only may be associated with a health risk. Pereira et al. [7] proposed a 3D hand gesture set for common HCI tasks by evaluating the disorders caused by the hand or finger postures. So, the health risk for users is reduced while performing gestures without awkward postures. However, raising the hands to perform mid-air gestures for a prolonged time tires users on the neck and shoulder easily [8]. Chan et al. [9] proposed a single-hand microgesture set for ubiquitous cameras as accessories integrated on the smart devices everywhere and microgestures were elicited from the non-technical users. The microgestures consist of small finger motion which is hard to be observed by others and users can protect their input privacy while performing microgestures. Nevertheless, users have no experience in ergonomics and part of microgestures can not be performed by users without dexterity fingers. For example, drawing a circle on the palm with a thumb may be a difficult one for users.

2.2 Gesture Recognition

The accuracy and speed for recognizing the hand gestures are key to interaction efficiency and user comfort because high latency and misrecognition may frustrate users and incur wrong responses. The release of commercial depth sensors including Kinect, Leap Motion, and RealSense helps researchers to segment the region of interest like hand region from the clutter background, and the hand gesture recognition and hand pose reconstruction were implemented based on these devices [10, 11].

With the increase of dataset samples, deep learning models achieved state-of-the-art performance in visual problems including scene understanding, action recognition, and object segmentation. Therefore, dynamic gestures are utilized to recognize the dynamic gestures. RNN model [12] was used to recognize the dynamic gestures captured with depth, color, and stereo-IR camera from the third view. Wu et al. [13] designed the Dorsum Deformation Network to decode the hand gestures captured by an RGB camera mounted on the wrist to observe the movement of bones, muscle, and tendons of the backhand. Cao et al. [14] developed a recurrent 3D CNN model to recognize dynamic gestures from an egocentric view which demonstrates that the design of interfaces based on egocentric hand gestures captured with an RGB camera could be implemented. Beyond the algorithms, the sample size of the dataset is crucial to the model performance.

The dynamic gesture datasets were released to accelerate the application of hand gestures for HCI systems because the creation of the dataset is time costing and hard for researchers. The egocentric gesture dataset [15] and third view hand gesture dataset [16] was published openly. Moreover, the release of datasets poses a challenge for researchers, and they are inspired to develop algorithms specifically. However, there was a lack of a microgesture dataset. The release of a microgesture dataset can motivate researchers to focus on extracting the features of small hand or finger motion from microgesture sequences which can promote the application of the microgestures for HCI systems.

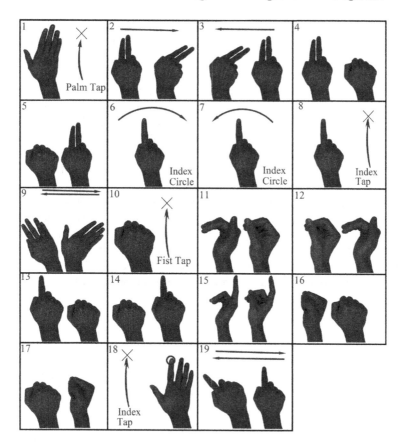

Fig. 1. Microgesture dataset and its literal description. Gesture 1: palm tapping on the table; gesture 2, 3: index and middle fingers swipe right, left; gesture 4, 5: index and middle fingers scratch toward, away; gesture 6,7: index finger moves in circle CW, CCW; gesture 8: index finger tapping on the table; gesture 9: palm scrolling on the table; gesture 10: fist tapping on the table; gesture 11, 12: thumb slides on the side of the index finger to the left/right; gesture 13, 14: index finger scratching toward, away; gesture 15: thumb tapping on the middle finger; gesture 16, 17: fist rotating from the neutral forearm to pronated forearm position or vice-versa; gesture 18: index finger tapping on the table with the palm on the table; gesture 19: index finger scratching on the table.

3   Methodology

3.1   Microgesture Set

The microgestures were designed by ergonomists who have experience in HCIs and health risk management which is different from prior elicitation studies [5,7,9]. The touch or non-touching gestures that appeared in publications or applied in commercial devices were collected in advance for the reason that the existing interaction paradigms impact user preference for gesture selection. Especially, touching devices are widely used in smart devices daily. Additionally, the static gestures were excluded while the systems may respond to them easily while users performing meaningless gestures. All the dynamic microgestures were designed with the forearm in the pronated (palm down) or neutral position (thumb-up) and the overextending or over flexing wrist or finger joints were avoided by following the suggestion from Rempel et al. [6]. Users can rest the forearm on the table while performing the microgestures which can reduce the muscle load on the upper extremities. Hence, users can interact with smart devices by microgestures for an extended duration without being fatigued. Considering the user interaction habits, the different types of microgestures were designed including click, swipe, and circle which are similar to the gestures used for smart devices. For example, users are accustomed to selecting the object by clicking the target on the screen. Therefore, we provided the gesture (*index finger clicks on the supporting surfaces with the forearm in the pronated position*) to complete the selection task. Finally, a microgesture set of 19 microgestuers was proposed and displayed graphically with literation in Fig. 1.

3.2   Microgesture Dataset

Deep learning methods are increasingly used in gesture recognition and the gesture dataset size is vital to the gesture recognition performance and efficiency of designed interfaces. In order to expand the use of proposed microgestures, we created an egocentric microgesture dataset captured by RealSense SR300 which was mounted on the front head to emulate the camera accessorized on the HMDs (Fig. 2). Nine participants were recruited from the university and asked to perform the 19 microgestures repeatedly. Finally, a dataset of 2900 microgestures with RGB and depth information was collected. Gesture 12 (*thumb slides on the index finger from left to right with the forearm in neutral position*) were dis-played in Fig. 3.

3.3   Microgesture Recognition

The proposed microgestures involving small hand or finger motions may be hard to be noticed so we implemented a microgesture recognition based on the deep learning method because of its state-of-the-art performance in action recognition. The 3D convolutional (Conv) layer performs very well in extracting spatiotemporal information from sequential frames which is popular across deep learning models. Tran et al. [17] built a C3D model with eight 3D Conv, five max-pooling, and 2 fully connected layers. The C3D model has more than 17.5 million parameters. All 3D Conv kernels are $3 \times 3 \times 3$ with stride 1 in both spatial and temporal dimensions. Microgetures consist of sequential hand or finger motions; thus we utilized the C3D model to recognize the microgesture dataset. The input shape for the C3D model is $16 \times 112 \times 112 \times 3$ where 16 denotes the frame length, 112 represents the image size, and 3 is the image channel. We set the batch size at 12 and the initial learning rate was set at 0.001. Cross-entropy was used to calculate the loss function while weight regularization was adopted to reduce the overfitting of the model to constrain the increase of the parameters. The image captured by RealSense SR300 with a size of 320×140 was reshaped to 128×128. To increase the robustness of the model, we cropped a region of 112×112 from the reshaped image randomly and the dropout rate was set to 0.5 during the model training. The C3D model was built on TensorFlow and trained with a GPU of 11 GB of memory (GeForce RTX 2080 Ti).

4   Results

80% of microgestures was used to train the C3D model while 20% of microgestures was used to test the C3D model. After training the C3D model to convergence, we achieved a training accuracy of 99.8% and a test accuracy of 88.6%. Therefore, the model was overfitted and the initialization of the model with millions of parameters may have an impact on model performance. The size of the microgesture dataset may limit the learning ability of the C3D model. Hong et al. [18] proposed the transfer learning methods to help researchers to train their model with a small size dataset based on model parameters pre-trained on a larger size dataset. We attempted to use the transfer learning method to improve the C3D model performance on the microgesture dataset. Tran et al. [17] released the C3D model parameters trained on a dataset named with sports 1M dataset of more than one million video clips [19]. We fine-tuned the model parameters with the microgesture dataset based on the parameters published by Tran et al. We achieved a test accuracy of 93.4% with an improvement of 4.8% on the test da-taset. The confusion matrix was displayed in Fig. 4. It was found that 16% of gesture 1 (palm taps on the table) was misrecognized as gesture 10 (fist taps on the table). From the egocentric view, gesture 1 and gesture 10 have the same motion trajectory which contributed to the misrecognition. The recognition accuracy of gestures 2, 3, 11, and 12 was relatively lower because the minor finger motion may be hard to be detected. So, the ability of the C3D model to extract the small difference in actions was not great as to capture large motions. We made an insight to visualize features

Fig. 2. Microgestures captured with Intel RealSense SR300

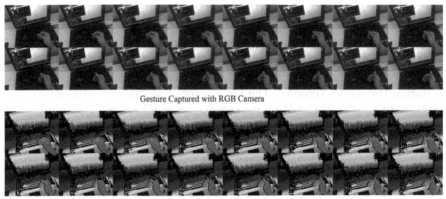

Gesture Captured with RGB Camera

Gesture Captured with Depth Camera

Fig. 3. The gesture 12 displayed in the form of RGB and colored depth

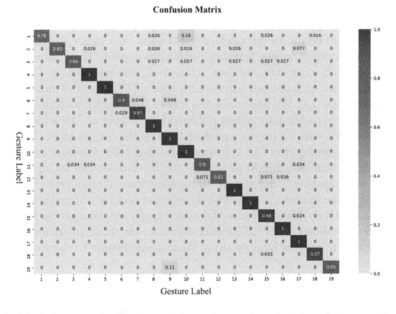

Fig. 4. Confusion matrix for recognizing microgesture training dataset with C3D model.

while the C3D model recognizing the gesture 12 (thumb slides on the index finger with the forearm in neutral position) and showed the features in Fig. 5. On layers 3, 4, and 5, the feature map showed that the direction of the thumb can be captured by the model and the spatial motion of the thumb was extracted as the high-level feature which was visualized in layer 7.

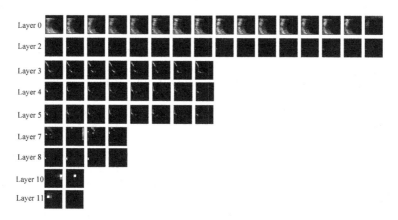

Fig. 5. The visualized feature of the 3D CNN layers from the C3D model while recognizing the gesture 12 (thumb sliding on the index finger from left to right).

5   Conclusion

AR/VR devices are potential to entertain, educate or train users while the interfaces has an impact on usability, comfort and interaction efficiency. To solve the problem that users may suffer from overload on the neck and shoulder while performing mid-air gestures or using a hand controller, A microgesture set designed by ergonomists was presented in this study to reduce the load and health risk to upper extremities while resting the arm on the supporting surface. Therefore, users can perform microgestures to control smart devices for an extended duration without being fatigued or induried. Besides, the minor finger or hand motion is not easy to be observed by others so interaction privacy is protected.

The microgesture dataset is vital to researchers and developers while designing the interfaces based on such microgestures. We created a microgesture dataset of more than 2900 samples captured with RGB and depth cameras. The C3D model was utilized to recognize the proposed microgestures and we achieved a recognition accuracy of 93.4% on the test part. Therefore, the application of microgestures for smart devices can be implemented based on the current deep learning methods visually. The release of the microgesture dataset and the trained C3D models will be beneficial to HCI researchers who may lack knowledge in complicated image processing algorithms and deep learning models. However, we observed that the ability of the C3D model to extract minor finger motions should be improved from the confusion matrix on the recognizing the microgesture dataset (Fig. 4). How to extract the small finger motion from the egocentric view visually is still a problem? So, the release of the microgesture dataset provides a new challenge for researchers to design the algorithms specifically to recognize the finger or hand motions accurately.

References

1. Guo, J., et al.: Mixed reality office system based on Maslow's hierarchy of needs: towards the long-term immersion in virtual environments. In: 18th IEEE International Symposium on Mixed and Augmented Reality, Beijing, pp. 224–235. IEEE (2019)
2. Saredakis, D., Szpak, A., Birckhead, B., Keage, H.A.D., Rizzo, A., Loetscher, T.: Factors associated with virtual reality sickness in head-mounted displays: a systematic review and meta-analysis. Front. Human Neurosci. **14**, 96 (2020)
3. Wang, Y., MacKenzie, C.L.: The role of contextual haptic and visual constraints on object manipulation in virtual environments. In: CHI 2000: Proceedings of the SIGCHI Conference on Human Factors in Computing Systems, pp. 532–539. ACM (2000)
4. Visser, B., Korte, E.D., Kraan, I.V.D., Kuijer, P.: The effect of arm and wrist supports on the load of the upper extremity during VDU work. Clin. Biomech. Supp. **1**(15), 34–38 (2000)
5. Wobbrock, J.O., Morris, M.R., Wilson, A.D.: User-defined gestures for surface computing. In: CHI 2009: Proceedings of the SIGCHI Conference on Human Factors in Computing Systems, pp. 1083–1092. ACM (2009)
6. Rempel, D., Camilleri, M.J., Lee, D.L.: The design of hand gestures for human-computer interaction: lessons from sign language interpreters. Int. J. Hum.-Comput. Stud. **10**(72), 728–735 (2014)
7. Pereira, A., Wachs, J.P., Park, K., Rempel, D.: A user-developed 3-D hand gesture set for human-computer interaction. Hum. Fact. **57**(4), 607–621 (2015)
8. Hincapié-Ramos J.D., Guo X., Moghadasian P., Irani P.: Consumed endurance: a metric to quantify arm fatigue of mid-air interactions. In: CHI 2014: Proceedings of the SIGCHI Conference on Human Factors in Computing Systems, pp. 1063–1072. ACM (2014)
9. Chan, C., Seyed, T., Stuerzlinger, W., Yang, X., Maurer, F.: User elicitation on single-hand microgestures. In: CHI 2016: Proceedings of the SIGCHI Conference on Human Factors in Computing Systems, pp. 3403–3414. ACM (2016)
10. Nai, W., Liu, Y., Rempel, D., Wang, Y.: Fast hand posture classification using depth features extracted from random line segments. Hum. Fact. **65**, 1–10 (2016)
11. Mueller, F., et al.: Real-time pose and shape reconstruction of two interacting hands with a single depth camera. ACM Trans. Graph. **38**(4), 1–13 (2019)
12. Molchanov P., Yang X., Gupta S., Kim K., Tyree S., Kautz J.: Online detection and classification of dynamic hand gestures with recurrent 3D convolutional neural networks. In: 2016 IEEE Conference on Computer Vision and Pattern Recognition (CVPR), pp. 4207–4215. IEEE (2019)
13. Wu W., Yuan Y., Yeo H., Quigley A., Koike H., Kitani K.M.: Back-hand-pose: 3D hand pose estimation for a wrist-worn camera via dorsum deformation network. In: Proceedings of the 33rd Annual ACM Symposium on User Interface Software and Technology, pp. 1147–1160. ACM (2020)
14. Cao, C., Zhang, Y., Wu, Y., Lu, H., Cheng, J.: Egocentric gesture recognition using recurrent 3d convolutional neural networks with spatiotemporal transformer modules. In: 2017 IEEE International Conference on Computer Vision (ICCV), pp. 3763–3771. IEEE (2017)
15. Zhang, Y., Cao, C., Cheng, J., Lu, H.: EgoGesture: a new dataset and benchmark for egocentric hand gesture recognition. IEEE Trans. Multimedia **5**(20), 1038–1050 (2018)

16. Materzynska J., Berger G., Bax I., Memisevic R.: The jester dataset: a large-scale video dataset of human gestures. In:2019 IEEE/CVF International Conference on Computer Vision Workshop (ICCVW), pp. 2874–2882. IEEE (2019)
17. Tran, D., Bourdev, L., Fergus, R., Torresani, L., Paluri, M.: Learning spatiotemporal features with 3D convolutional networks. In: 2015 IEEE International Conference on Computer Vision (ICCV), pp. 4489–4497. IEEE (2015)
18. Ng, H., Nguyen, V.D., Vonikakis, V., Winkler, S.: Deep learning for emotion recognition on small datasets using transfer learning. In:17th ACM International Conference on Multimodal Interaction, pp. 443—449. ACM (2015)
19. Andrej K., George T., Sanketh S., Thomas L., Rahul S., Li F.: Large-scale video classification with convolutional neural networks. In: 2014 IEEE Conference on Computer Vision and Pattern Recognition (CVPR), pp. 1725–1732. IEEE (2014)

Machine Learning Architectures and Formulations

Orthogonal Dual Graph Regularized Nonnegative Matrix Factorization

Jinrong He[1,2,3,4], Yanxin Shi[2], Zongwen Bai[4(✉)], and Zeyu Bao[5]

[1] Key Laboratory of Agricultural Internet of Things, Ministry of Agriculture and Rural Affairs, Northwest A&F University, Yangling 712100, Shaanxi, China
[2] College of Mathematics and Computer Science, Yan'an University, Yan'an 716000, China
[3] Shaanxi Key Laboratory of Agricultural Information Perception and Intelligent Service, Northwest A&F University, Yangling 712100, Shaanxi, China
[4] Shaanxi Key Laboratory of Intelligent Processing for Big Energy Data, Yanan University, Yan'an 716000, Shaanxi, China
ydbzw@yau.edu.cn
[5] University of Science and Technology of China, Hefei 230026, Anhui, China

Abstract. Nonnegative matrix factorization (NMF) is a classical low-rank approximation method of data matrix, which decomposes a high-dimensional data matrix into two nonnegative low-rank matrices, namely basis matrix and coefficient matrix. In order to capture the local geometric structure of original dataset, manifold learning methods are incorporated into NMF framework. Motivated by recent progress in dual graph regularization, by considering the geometric structures of both the data manifold and the feature manifold, Orthogonal Dual-graph NMF (ODNMF) algorithms were proposed, which imposed orthogonality constraints on basis matrix or coefficient matrix. Since the projection directions were mutually orthogonal, the representation power of data samples was enhanced, thus ODNMF methods are more robust for data clustering. The extensive experimental results on UCI, text and face image data sets have demonstrated the superiority of the proposed methods.

Keywords: Data representation · Nonnegative matrix factorization · Dual-graph regularization · Orthogonal projection

1 Introduction

Non-negative Matrix Factorization (NMF) is one of the most powerful tools in numerical computing, machine learning and data mining. By decomposing original high dimensional non-negative data matrix X into two low dimensional non-negative factors U and V, namely basis matrix and coefficient matrix, such that $X \approx UV^T$. Moreover, the additive reconstruction with nonnegative constraints can lead to a parts-based representation for images [1], texts [2], and microarray data [3] and so on.

To decompose the given data into a component part that encodes low-rank sparse principal features and a noise-fitting error part, Zhang et al. proposed a transductive low-rank and sparse principal feature coding (LSPFC) model to recover the low-rank and

© Springer Nature Switzerland AG 2021
Y. Peng et al. (Eds.): ICIG 2021, LNCS 12889, pp. 93–105, 2021.
https://doi.org/10.1007/978-3-030-87358-5_8

sparse subspaces jointly for robust data representation [4]. By imposing orthogonality constraints on NMF, Ding et al. proposed orthogonal non-negative matrix factorization (ONMF) method [5], which has been shown to work remarkably well for clustering tasks. Pompili et al. show that ONMF is mathematically equivalent to a weighted variant of spherical k-means [6]. Motivated by recent progress in manifold learning and orthogonal projection, in this paper we propose a novel algorithm, which called Orthogonal Graph Regularized Nonnegative Matrix Factorization (OGNMF), which combining orthogonal constraints and manifold regularization in a parts-based low-dimensional space.

From geometric perspective, the data samples are usually sampled from a low-dimensional manifold embedded in a high-dimensional ambient space. Based on such assumption, Cai et al. proposed graph regularized NMF (GNMF [7]) method, which incorporates the manifold learning into NMF for finding a compact low-dimensional representation to discover the latent semantics and intrinsic geometric structure in the dataset simultaneously. Since the sparse hypergraph inherits the merits of both the hypergraph model and sparse representation, S. Huang et al. proposed Sparse Hypergraph regularized NMF (SHNMF [8]) to exploit the high-order discriminant manifold information for data representation. In order to depict complex relations of samples, J. Wang et al. encoded different sample relations into multiple graphs and proposed Multiple Graph regularized NMF (MGNMF [9]). However, the process of multiple graphs construction is very time consuming. Motivated by recent study on sample diversity learning [10], C. Wang et al. proposed Graph regularized NMF with Sample Diversity (GNMFSD [11]), which incorporated label information into the graph to encode the intrinsic geometrical structures of the data space, then the discriminant power of the basis vectors is enhanced. By introducing an additional regression level, Mei et al. proposed a general method for including side information on the columns and rows in NMF, which can be used for time series recovery and prediction [12].

Recent works have shown that not only the original data samples are found to lie on a nonlinear low-dimensional manifold, which is called data manifold, but also the feature vectors lie on a manifold, which is called feature manifold [13]. Considering the duality between data samples and feature vectors, several dual-graph based data representation algorithms have been proposed and shown to be superior to traditional data manifold regularization based methods. Shang et al. [14] proposed graph Dual regularization Nonnegative Matrix Factorization (DNMF). In order to improve the overall performance of recommender systems, by encoding the side information from both users and items as two graph regularization terms, Yao et al. [15] proposed a dual-regularized model for one-class collaborate filtering. In order to estimate fraction of different land cover types from remote sensing imagery, Tong et al. [16] applied DNMF in hyperspectral unmixing and showed that DNMF has better performance than GNMF. Yang et al. [17] applied DNMF to discover real-world events from Flickr data. By imposing the L2,1-norm constraint on the self-representation coefficients matrix in data space, Shang et al. proposed self-representation based dual-graph regularized feature selection clustering (DFSC, [18]) and non-negative spectral learning and sparse regression-based dual-graph regularized feature selection (NSSRD, [19]). For incorporating the graph topology, Yankelevsky et al. [20] proposed a dual regularized dictionary learning method, which imposed a quadratic smoothness constraint on the dictionary bases and a manifold smoothness regularization on the sparse representations. Luo et al. proposed Dual-regularized Multi-view Non-negative Matrix Factorization (DMvNMF [21]) to deal with multi-view data, which can extract compatible and complementary information contained in multiple modality datasets, while preserve the geometric structures in both the data space and the feature space. In order to reduce the redundancy between bases and representations in GNMF model, He et al. proposed Orthogonal GNMF (OGNMF [22]), which incorporates three kinds of orthogonal constraints into GNMF model.

In summary, our main contributions in this paper are listed below.

(1) Orthogonal dual-graph regularized NMF models are proposed, in which three types of orthogonal constraints are added, including U orthogonal, V orthogonal and bi-orthogonal. In this way, the potential geometrical structural information can be preserved during the process of data representation, which can effectively enhance the discriminative ability of clustering.
(2) The multiplicative iterative updating rules derived from original NMF are used to optimize the proposed DNMF models.
(3) Comprehensive experiments on ten real world datasets are conducted to show the effectiveness of the proposed three algorithms, and demonstrate its advantage over other state-of-the-art methods.

The remainder of this paper is organized as follows. Section 2 briefly reviews the related works, such as NMF, ONMF and DNMF. In Sect. 3, we proposed three types of ODNMF models and their optimization algorithms. Extensive experiments are presented in Sect. 4. Finally, Sect. 5 concludes the paper.

2 Related Works

2.1 NMF

NMF aims to express each sample x_i as a linear combination of the basis vectors which are columns of U, namely, where v_j is the jth column $x_i = Uv_j$ of V. Such a factorization is generally obtained by minimizing the following cost function:

$$\min_{U,V} \|X - UV^T\|_F^2$$
$$s.t. \ u_{ij} \geq 0, v_{ij} \geq 0 \tag{1}$$

where $X = [x_1, x_2, \cdots, x_n] \in R^{d \times n}$ denotes the original data matrix, which contains n data samples with the dimensionality d, and $U \in R^{d \times r}$ denotes the basis matrix, $V \in R^{r \times n}$ denotes the coefficient matrix, where r is the reduced target dimensionality of projected low dimensional data. The NMF model (1) can be optimized by using following multiplicative updating rules [1]:

$$u_{ij} = u_{ij} \frac{(XV)_{ij}}{(UV^TV)_{ij}} \tag{2}$$

$$v_{ij} = v_{ij} \frac{\left(X^T U\right)_{ij}}{\left(VU^T U\right)_{ij}} \tag{3}$$

Since the objective function in (1) is not convex in both U and V, the above iterative updating rules can only find the local minimum of the objective function. The convergence of the optimization algorithm is proved in [1].

2.2 ONMF

ONMF is a variant of NMF, which approximate the data matrix with the product of two low-rank nonnegative matrices, one of which has orthonormal columns. For example, when the coefficient matrix V has orthonormal columns, the corresponding optimization model is

$$\min_{U,V} \left\| X - UV^T \right\|_F^2$$
$$s.t. \quad \begin{aligned} u_{ij} \geq 0, v_{ij} \geq 0 \\ V^T V = I \end{aligned} \tag{4}$$

Since the column vectors of coefficient matrix V is orthonormal, its power lies in the potential to generate sparser part-based decompositions of data with smaller basis vectors, that are easier to interpret.

The updating rules to optimize the above objective function (4) are given as follows

$$u_{ij} = u_{ij} \frac{(XV)_{ij}}{\left(UV^T V\right)_{ij}} \tag{5}$$

$$v_{ij} = v_{ij} \frac{\left(X^T U\right)_{ij}}{\left(VU^T XV\right)_{ij}} \tag{6}$$

2.3 GNMF

GNMF adds manifold learning into the classical NMF for finding a compact representation, in which the local geometric structure of data manifold is simulated by a neighborhood graph.

Let $G(X, W)$ denote a graph with vertex set $X = \{x_1, x_2, \cdots, x_n\}$ and weight matrix W whose entry W_{ij} denotes the similarity between sample x_i and x_j. There several ways to compute the similarity weight matrix W, and we use the Gauss kernel function as follows:

$$W_{ij} = \begin{cases} e^{-\frac{\|x_i - x_j\|_2^2}{t}} & x_i \in N_k(x_j) \vee x_j \in N_k(x_i) \\ 0 & otherwise \end{cases} \tag{7}$$

where $N_k(x_i)$ is the sample points set that contains the k nearest neighbors of x_i, and t is heat kernel parameter. Since G is an undirected graph, the weight matrix W is symmetric and the diagonal entries in W are all 0.

GNMF aims to learning a collection of nonnegative basis which can not only minimize the reconstruction error but also preserve the similarities between pairwise samples that encoded in neighborhood graph. Therefore, the optimal nonnegative basis U can be obtained via minimizing the following objective:

$$\min_{U,V} \left\| X - UV^T \right\|_F^2 + \lambda tr\left(V^T LV\right)$$
$$s.t. \ u_{ij} \geq 0, v_{ij} \geq 0 \tag{8}$$

where $L = D-W$ is the graph Laplacian matrix and D is a diagonal matrix whose entry is $D_{ii} = \sum_{j=1}^{n} W_{ij}$, W is the weight matrix to measure the similarity between the nearby data samples. The λ is a regularization parameter which balance the reconstruction error and graph embedding term. Since the graph embedding regularizer could smooth the variation between two samples with large similarity in the latent low-dimensional space, the performance of clustering based on GNMF can be effectively improved.

Similar to Eq. (2) and (3), the iterative updating rules to solve (8) are presented as follows:

$$u_{ij} = u_{ij} \frac{(XV)_{ij}}{\left(UV^T V\right)_{ij}} \tag{9}$$

$$v_{ij} = v_{ij} \frac{\left(X^T U + \lambda WV\right)_{ij}}{\left(VU^T U + \lambda DV\right)_{ij}} \tag{10}$$

2.4 DNMF

DNMF is an extension of GNMF, which imposed graph regularization on basis matrix and coefficient matrix to discover the geometrical structure of data. Similar to GNMF, DNMF constructed k nearest neighbor graph on data samples and feature vectors. Suppose the columns of data matrix X are $\{X_{:1}, X_{:2}, ..., X_{:N}\}$ and the weight between two neighborhood samples can be defined as:

$$[W^V]_{ij} = \begin{cases} 1 \text{ if } X_{:,j} \in N(X_{:,i}) \\ 0 \text{ otherwise} \end{cases} i, j = 1, ..., N \tag{11}$$

where $N(X_{:,i})$ is the k-th neighborhood sample of $X_{:,i}$. The graph Laplacian matrix is $L_V = D^V - W^V$, here D^V is diagonal matrix, whose diagonal elements are rows sum of W, i.e., $[D^V]_{ii} = \sum_j [W^V]_{ij}$.

Similarly, the rows of data matrix X are feature vectors, i.e., $\{X_{1,:}^T, X_{2,:}^T, ..., X_{N,:}^T\}$, and the weight between feature vectors can be defined as:

$$[W^U]_{ij} = \begin{cases} 1, \text{ if } X_{j,:}^T \in N(X_{i,:}^T) \\ 0 \ \text{otherwise} \end{cases} i, j = 1, ..., M \tag{12}$$

where $N(X_{i,:}^T)$ is the k-th feature vector of $X_{i,:}^T$., and the corresponding graph Laplacian matrix is $L_U = D^U - W^U$, here D^U is a diagonal matrix, and its element is row sum of W, i.e. $[D^V]_{ii} = \sum_j [W^V]_{ij}$.

Similar to GNMF, the DNMF model can be formulated as

$$J_{DNMF} = ||X - UV^T||^2 + \lambda Tr(V^T L_V V) + \mu Tr(U^T L_U U)$$
$$\text{s.t. } U \geq 0, V \geq 0 \tag{13}$$

where λ, μ are regularization parameters. When μ tends to 0, DNMF is equivalent to GNMF. When both the λ and μ tend to 0, DNMF is equivalent to NMF. The minimization process of objective function in Eq. (9) can be achieved through the following update rules:

$$U_{ij} = U_{ij} \frac{(XV)_{ij} + \mu (W^U U)_{ij}}{(UV^T V)_{ij} + \mu (D^U U)_{ij}} \tag{14}$$

$$V_{ij} = V_{ij} \frac{(X^T U)_{ij} + \lambda (WV)_{ij}}{(VU^T U)_{ij} + \lambda (DV)_{ij}} \tag{15}$$

3   Proposed Methods

Orthogonal projections have been proved to be more discriminative in most cases, since it can also release the correlation of the projection directions or low-dimensional representations. With orthogonal constraints on basis matrix and coefficient matrix, the performance of DNMF model on data clustering is improved. ODNMF inherits the advantages of ONMF and DNMF, it can capture the local similarity structures of data space and feature which are helpful for extracting the discriminative features, while preserving the global geometrical structure of data space which aims to contain the intrinsic information as much as possible.

3.1   ODNMF-U

Adding the orthogonal constraint on basis matrix U, we have the following orthogonal dual-graph regularized NMF with U orthogonality (ODNMF-U):

$$J_{ODNMF} = ||X - UV^T||^2 + \lambda Tr(V^T L_V V) + \mu Tr(U^T L_U U)$$
$$\text{s.t. } U \geq 0, V \geq 0, \ U^T U = I \tag{16}$$

The objective function in model (16) can be rewritten as:

$$\begin{aligned}
J_{ODNMF} &= tr((X - UV^T)(X - UV^T)^T) \\
&+ \lambda tr(V^T L_V V) + \mu tr(U^T L_U U) \\
&= tr(XX^T) - 2tr(XVU^T) + tr(UV^T VU^T)
\end{aligned}$$

$$+ \lambda tr(V^T L_V V) + \mu tr(U^T L_U U) \tag{17}$$

The partial derivatives of objective function (17) with respect to U and V are:

$$\begin{aligned} \nabla_U J &= [\nabla_U J]^+ - [\nabla_U J]^- \\ &= UV^T V - XV + \mu L_U U \\ &= \nabla_U \varepsilon + \mu L_U U \end{aligned} \tag{18}$$

$$\begin{aligned} \nabla_V J &= [\nabla_V J]^+ - [\nabla_V J]^- \\ &= VU^T U - X^T U + \lambda L_V V \\ &= \nabla_V \varepsilon + \lambda L_V V \end{aligned} \tag{19}$$

where $L_U = D^U - W^U$ and $L_V = D^V - W^V$, and their definitions are same as Eq. (11) and (12). Let $\nabla_U \varepsilon = UV^T V - XV$ and $\nabla_V \varepsilon = VU^T U - X^T U$, when imposing orthogonal constraint on U, then

$$\nabla_U \varepsilon = UV^T X^T U - XV \tag{20}$$

Substituting Eq. (20) into Eq. (18), we have the following updating rule on U,

$$U_{ij} = U_{ij} \frac{(XV)_{ij} + \mu \left(W^U U\right)_{ij}}{\left(UV^T X^T U\right)_{ij} + \mu \left(D^U U\right)_{ij}} \tag{21}$$

Similarly, the updating rule on V is,

$$V_{ij} = V_{ij} \frac{\left(X^T U\right)_{ij} + \lambda \left(W^V V\right)_{ij}}{\left(VU^T U\right)_{ij} + \lambda \left(D^V V\right)_{ij}} \tag{22}$$

3.2 ODNMF-V

By incorporating orthogonal constraint of the coefficient matrix V in DNMF model, we have the following ODNMF-V model,

$$\begin{aligned} J_{ODNMF} &= ||X - UV^T||^2 + \lambda tr(V^T L_V V) + \mu tr(U^T L_U U) \\ &\text{s.t. } U \geq 0, V \geq 0, \ V^T V = I \end{aligned} \tag{23}$$

The partial derivatives of objective function (23) with respect to U and V are same as in Eq. (18) and (19). Similarly, the orthogonal constraint on V can lead to the following formula,

$$\begin{aligned} \nabla_V \varepsilon &= [\nabla_V \varepsilon]^+ - [\nabla_V \varepsilon]^- \\ &= VU^T XV - X^T U \end{aligned} \tag{24}$$

Substituting Eq. (24) into Eq. (19), we have,

$$
\begin{aligned}
\nabla_v J &= [\nabla_v J]^+ - [\nabla_v J]^- \\
&= \nabla_v \varepsilon + \mu L_v V \\
&= V U^T X V - X^T U + \mu L_v V
\end{aligned}
\tag{25}
$$

Then the updating rules on V and U can be formulated as follows,

$$
V_{ij} = V_{ij} \frac{(X^T U)_{ij} + \lambda (W^V V)_{ij}}{(V U^T X V)_{ij} + \lambda (D^V V)_{ij}}
\tag{26}
$$

$$
U_{ij} = U_{ij} \frac{(X V)_{ij} + \mu (W^U U)_{ij}}{(U V^T V)_{ij} + \mu (D^U U)_{ij}}
\tag{27}
$$

3.3 ODNMF

ODNMF imposes the orthogonal constraints on both the basis matrix U and coefficient matrix V, which involves the following minimization problem,

$$
\begin{aligned}
J_{ODNMF} &= ||X - U V^T||^2 + \lambda tr(V^T L_v V) + \mu tr(U^T L_U U) \\
&\text{s.t. } U \geq 0, V \geq 0, \ V^T V = I, \ U^T U = I
\end{aligned}
\tag{28}
$$

The orthogonal constraints on the basis matrix U and coefficient matrix V provide a strong capability of simultaneously clustering rows and columns, which we call bi-orthogonal constraints. Combining update rules (21) in OGNMF-U and (26) in OGNMF-V, the update rules of OGNMF are given as follows

$$
V_{ij} = V_{ij} \frac{(X^T U)_{ij} + \lambda (W^V V)_{ij}}{(V U^T X V)_{ij} + \lambda (D^V V)_{ij}}
\tag{29}
$$

$$
U_{ij} = U_{ij} \frac{(X V)_{ij} + \mu (W^U U)_{ij}}{(U V^T X^T U)_{ij} + \mu (D^U U)_{ij}}
\tag{30}
$$

4 Experimental Results

In this section, we evaluate the effectiveness of our proposed ODNMF framework compared with the related matrix factorization methods including NMF, ONMF, GNMF.

4.1 Experimental Setting

To investigate the image clustering performances, two popular evaluation metric are used in the experiments, i.e., the clustering accuracy (AC) and the normalized mutual information (NMI) [10], that are defined as follows

$$AC = \frac{\sum_{i=1}^{n} \delta(l_i, \tau_i)}{n}$$

where δ is a cluster label indicator function, which equals 1 if the two entries are the same and equals 0 otherwise. l_i and τ_i denote the true label and predicted label.

$$NMI = \frac{MI(C, C')}{\max(H(C), H(C'))}$$

where C is the set of clusters from the ground truth, and C' is predicted clusters by clustering method. $H(\cdot)$ is the entropy of a set, and the mutual information $MI(C, C')$ between two sets of clusters C and C' is defined as

$$MI(C, C') = \sum_{c_i \in C, c_j' \in C'} p(c_i, c_j') \log \frac{p(c_i, c_j')}{p(c_i)p(c_j')}$$

where $p(c_i)$ and $p(c_j')$ are the probabilities of a sample belonging to the clusters c_i and c_j', respectively. $p(c_i, c_j')$ denotes the joint probability that the selected sample belongs to the clusters c_i as well as c_j' at the same time. The larger *AC* and higher *NMI* indicate a better clustering performance [6].

For the ODNMF methods, the neighborhood graph on data samples are set the same as those for GNMF, where the number of nearest neighbors of each sample is fixed as 5 and the regularization parameter in model (9), (12), (19) and (24) are empirically set as 100. After the low-dimensional data representations were produced by matrix factorization methods, the k-means clustering method was performed in the low-dimensional data space. All the experiments in this paper run in MATLAB R2015b on Win7 with 8G RAM and 3.4 GHz CPU.

4.2 Datasets Description

In our experiments, we use three types of datasets, including UCI datasets[1], text datasets, and face image datasets. For UCI datasets, MADELON is an artificial dataset, which was part of the NIPS 2003 feature selection challenge and containing data points grouped in 32 clusters placed on the vertices of a five dimensional hypercube and randomly labeled +1 or −1. CNAE9 is a highly sparse text dataset, which contains 1080 documents with 9 groups. Semeion is a handwritten digital dataset, which contains 1593 binary images

---

[1] http://archive.ics.uci.edu/ml/ .

created by 80 persons, and each image is with the size of 16 × 16. Hillvalley is a graphical dataset, and each sample contains 100 points of a 2D plane, and there are 606 samples in two groups, hill or valley. For text dataset, Tr31 dataset is a subset of TREC datasets[2] and Re1 is a subset of Reuters21578 dataset[3]. For face image dataset, UMIST dataset[4] consists of 575 images with 20 different persons, the number of which varies from 19 to 36. XM2VST dataset[5] contains 2950 samples with 295 persons, and YaleB dataset[6] used in our experiments is a subset of original YaleB dataset, containing 2414 images of 38 persons under 64 lighting conditions. ORL dataset[7] contains 400 images of 10 individuals, each of which contains 40 images that captured at different conditions, including shooting time, illuminations, expressions and some other facial details, such as with/without glasses. Some statistics of the four face image datasets are summarized in Table 1.

Table 1. The description of datasets used in the experiments

Datasets		#Samples	#Dimensionality	#Classes
UCI datasets	MADELON	4400	500	2
	CNAE9	1080	856	9
	Semeion	1593	256	10
	Hillvalley	606	100	2
Text dataset	Tr31	927	10128	7
	Re1	1657	3758	25
Face image dataset	UMIST	575	2576	20
	XM2VST	2950	2576	295
	YaleB	2414	1024	38
	ORL	400	1024	40

4.3 Results Discussion

The optimal clustering results on different datasets are reported in this section. The clustering accuracies are summarized in Table 2 and the NMI metrics are summarized in Table 3. The value in the parentheses is the optimal target dimensionality under which the method achieved the maximum evaluation metric. As can be shown, the proposed orthogonal DNMFs have better clustering performances than others in most cases. It

---

[2] https://trec.nist.gov/data.html.

[3] http://www.daviddlewis.com/resources/testcollections/reuters21578/.

[4] http://www.sheffield.ac.uk/eee/research/iel/research/face.

[5] http://www.ee.surrey.ac.uk/CVSSP/xm2vtsdb/.

[6] http://vision.ucsd.edu/~D.Leekc/ExtYaleDatabase/ExtYaleB.html.

[7] https://www.cl.cam.ac.uk/research/dtg/attarchive/facedatabase.html.

is worth noting that the original DNMF and orthogonal DNMF perform perfect on the Hillvalley dataset. This is because that the feature or attribute neighborhood information plays more role on identifying a Hill and a Valley on a 2D graph. However, on CNAE9, Tr31 and Re1 datasets, the traditional NMF method performs better than other methods, which indicates that dual-graph regularized NMFs are not suitable for text clustering tasks.

Table 2. The optimal clustering results (AC%)

Datasets	NMF	ONMF	DNMF	ODNMF-U	ODNMF-V	ODNMF
MADELON	54.20(78)	53.25(20)	52.40(3)	51.20(24)	58.45(2)	**59.00(2)**
CNAE9	**70.74(93)**	54.44(43)	63.89(9)	56.39(92)	64.26(37)	65.00(23)
Semeion	60.39(64)	52.48(14)	69.49(59)	69.93(16)	71.50(19)	**72.44(12)**
Hillvalley	68.65(2)	592.4(23)	**100.0(10)**	**100.00(10)**	**100.00(10)**	**100.0(10)**
Tr31	**58.36(64)**	50.05(6)	54.05(12)	54.48(12)	53.83(8)	52.64(8)
Re1	**43.39(94)**	42.31(74)	39.35(38)	38.32(76)	39.77(50)	40.43(16)
XM2VTS	17.29(31)	12.71(4)	15.80(44)	15.63(87)	**17.39(96)**	16.92(71)
UMIST	48.35(77)	33.91(8)	62.96(19)	63.30(23)	**63.65(69)**	63.13(34)
YaleB	16.20(91)	6.96(1)	32.97(18)	**33.35(16)**	13.09(21)	10.65(5)
ORL	56.50(76)	36.75(27)	55.50(65)	58.50(41)	**60.25(73)**	58.75(70)

Table 3. The optimal clustering results (NMI%)

Datasets	NMF	ONMF	DNMF	ODNMF-U	ODNMF-V	ODNMF
MADELON	0.51(78)	0.31(20)	0.17(36)	0.04(24)	2.10(2)	**2.36(2)**
CNAE9	**68.88(93)**	48.12(43)	63.26(64)	53.88(71)	64.84(6)	64.67(6)
Semeion	53.01(86)	47.32(14)	64.96(59)	63.83(16)	**66.70(20)**	65.73(12)
Hillvalley	10.29(2)	2.52(23)	**100.0(10)**	**100.0(10)**	**100.0(10)**	**100.0(10)**
Tr31	41.07(4)	36.79(6)	44.01(38)	42.93(38)	**44.58(8)**	43.98(14)
Re1	44.63(70)	**48.09(28)**	46.40(52)	45.68(52)	46.74(40)	47.21(16)
XM2VTS	61.17(10)	58.75(5)	60.20(66)	60.16(3)	**61.45(98)**	61.17(96)
umist	66.86(79)	48.13(8)	79.73(36)	79.69(52)	**80.18(35)**	79.66(83)
YaleB	27.63(86)	8.64(1)	**45.36(18)**	44.89(18)	20.88(5)	17.86(5)
ORL	74.18(59)	59.31(27)	73.03(65)	74.66(80)	**76.05(73)**	74.05(82)

5 Conclusions

Existing data representation methods are all carried out in data space. However, the information of feature space cannot be fully exploited. To compensate for this drawback, orthogonal dual-graph regularized NMF (ODNMF) is proposed by incorporating DNMF and ONMF. Orthogonal constraints on the basis matrix U and coefficient matrix V are incorporated as the additional condition, which can not only make full use of geometrical structural information underlying the data manifold, but also enhance the generalization performance and robustness of the proposed methods. Since ONMF are more robust to noise, and DNMF has good performance on data clustering, therefore, ODNMF can combine the advantages of ONMF and DNMF together, which has been confirmed on data clustering experiments. The theoretical analysis of the models will be investigated deeply in the future work.

Acknowledgement. This work is supported in part by National Natural Science Foundation of China under grant No. 61902339, by the Natural Science Basic Research Plan in Shaanxi Province of China under grants No. 2021JM-418, by Shaanxi Key Laboratory of Intelligent Processing for Big Energy Data in Yan'an University under grant No. IPBED14, by Doctoral Starting up Foundation of Yan'an University under grant No. YDBK2019-06, by Yan'an Special Foundation for Science and Technology (2019-01, 2019-13), by Collaborative education project supported by Google (202002107065) and Innovation and entrepreneurship training program for Shaanxi Provincial College Students (S202010719116, S202010719068).

References

1. Gao, H., Nie, F., Cai, W., Huang, H.: Robust capped norm nonnegative matrix factorization. In: Proceedings of the 24th ACM International Conference on Information and Knowledge Management, Melbourne, Australia, October 19–23 (2015)
2. Shi, T., Kang, K., Choo, J., et al.: Short-text topic modeling via non-negative matrix factorization enriched with local word-context correlations. In: Proceedings of the 2018 World Wide Web Conference on World Wide Web. International World Wide Web Conferences Steering Committee, pp. 1105–1114 (2018)
3. Kim, H., Park, H.: Sparse non-negative matrix factorizations via alternating non-negativity-constrained least squares for microarray data analysis. Bioinformatics **23**(12), 1495–1502 (2007)
4. Zhang, Z., Li, F., Zhao, M., et al.: Joint low-rank and sparse principal feature coding for enhanced robust representation and visual classification. IEEE Trans. Image Process. **25**(6), 2429–2443 (2016)
5. Ding, C., Li, T., Peng, W., Park, H.: Orthogonal nonnegative matrix t-factorizations for clustering. In: Proceedings of the 12th ACM SIGKDD International Conference on Knowledge Discovery and Data Mining, pp. 126–135. ACM (2006)
6. Li, B., Zhou, G., Cichocki, A.: Two efficient algorithms for approximately orthogonal nonnegative matrix factorization. IEEE Signal Process. Lett. **22**(7), 843–846 (2015)
7. Cai, D., He, X., Han, J., et al.: Graph regularized nonnegative matrix factorization for data representation. IEEE Trans. Pattern Anal. Mach. Intell. **33**(8), 1548–1560 (2011)
8. Huang, S., Wang, H., Ge, Y., et al.: Improved hypergraph regularized Nonnegative Matrix Factorization with sparse representation. Pattern Recogn. Lett. **102**(15), 8–14 (2018)

9. Wang, J.Y., Bensmail, H., Gao, X.: Multiple graph regularized nonnegative matrix factorization. Pattern Recogn. **46**(10), 2840–2847 (2013)
10. Xu, Y., Li, Z., Zhang, B., Yang, J., You, J.: Sample diversity, representation effectiveness and robust dictionary learning for face recognition. Inf. Sci. **375**(1), 171–182 (2017)
11. Wang, C., Song, X., Zhang, J.: Graph regularized nonnegative matrix factorization with sample diversity for image representation. Eng. Appl. Artif. Intell. **68**(2), 32–39 (2018)
12. Mei, J., De Castro, Y., Goude, Y., et al.: Nonnegative matrix factorization with side information for time series recovery and prediction. IEEE Trans. Knowl. Data Eng. **31**(3), 493–506 (2018)
13. He, J., Bi, Y., Liu, B., et al.: Graph-dual Laplacian principal component analysis. J. Ambient Intell. Humaniz. Comput. 1–14 (2018)
14. Shang, F., Jiao, L.C., Wang, F.: Graph dual regularization non-negative matrix factorization for co-clustering. Pattern Recogn. **45**(6), 2237–2250 (2012)
15. Ye, J., Jin, Z.: Dual-graph regularized concept factorization for clustering. Neurocomputing **138**, 120–130 (2014)
16. Yin, M., Gao, J., Lin, Z., et al.: Dual graph regularized latent low-rank representation for subspace clustering. IEEE Trans. Image Process. **24**(12), 4918–4933 (2015)
17. Yao, Y., Tong, H., Yan, G., et al.: Dual-regularized one-class collaborative filtering. In: Proceedings of the 23rd ACM International Conference on Conference on Information and Knowledge Management, pp. 759–768. ACM (2014)
18. Shang, R., Zhang, Z., Jiao, L., et al.: Self-representation based dual-graph regularized feature selection clustering. Neurocomputing **171**, 1242–1253 (2016)
19. Shang, R., Wang, W., Stolkin, R., et al.: Non-negative spectral learning and sparse regression-based dual-graph regularized feature selection. IEEE Trans. Cybern. **48**(2), 793–806 (2017)
20. Yankelevsky, Y., Elad, M.: Dual graph regularized dictionary learning. IEEE Trans. Signal Inf. Process. Over Netw. **2**(4), 611–624 (2016)
21. Luo, P., Peng, J., Guan, Z., Fan, J.: Dual regularized multi-view non-negative matrix factorization for clustering. Neurocomputing **294**(6), 1–11 (2018)
22. He, J., He, D., Liu, B., Wang, W.: Orthogonal graph regularized nonnegative matrix factorization for image clustering. In: Jin, H., Lin, X., Cheng, X., Shi, X., Xiao, N., Huang, Y. (eds.) BigData 2019. CCIS, vol. 1120, pp. 325–337. Springer, Singapore (2019). https://doi.org/10.1007/978-981-15-1899-7_23

Robust Recovery of Low Rank Matrix by Nonconvex Rank Regularization

Hengmin Zhang[1,2], Wei Luo[3], Wenli Du[2], Jianjun Qian[4], Jian Yang[4],
and Bob Zhang[1(✉)]

[1] Department of Computer and Information Science, University of Macau,
Macau 999078, People's Republic of China
`zhanghengmin@126.com, bobzhang@um.edu.mo`
[2] School of Information Science and Engineering, Key Laboratory of Advanced Smart
Manufacturing in Energy Chemical Process, Ministry of Education, East China
University of Science and Technology, Shanghai 200237, People's Republic of China
`wldu@ecust.edu.cn`
[3] College of Mathematics and Informatics, South China Agricultural University,
Guangzhou 510642, People's Republic of China
`cswluo@gmail.com`
[4] School of Computer Science and Engineering, Nanjing University of Science and
Technology, Nanjing 210094, China
`{csjqian,csjyang}@njust.edu.cn`

Abstract. As we know, nuclear norm based regularization methods
have the real-world applications in pattern recognition and computer
vision. However, there exists a biased estimator when nuclear norm
relaxes the rank function. To solve this issue, we focus on studying nonconvex rank regularization problems for both robust matrix completion
(RMC) and low rank representation (LRR), respectively. By extending
both to a general low rank matrix minimization problem, we develop a
nonconvex alternating direction method of multipliers (ADMM). Moreover, the convergence results, i.e., the variable sequence generated by
the nonconvex ADMM is bounded and its subsequence converges to
a stationary point. Meanwhile, its limiting point satisfies the Karush-
Kuhn-Tucher (KKT) conditions provided under some milder assumptions. Numerical experiments can verify the convergence properties of
the theoretical results and the performance shows its superiority on both
image inpainting and subspace clustering.

Keywords: Low rank matrix recovery · Nonconvex rank
regularization · Convergence analysis · Nonconve ADMM · KKT
conditions

1 Introduction

In recent years, recovering low rank matrix has the popular applications in
pattern recognition and computer vision. The commonly used methods include
robust principle component analysis (RPCA) [5], matrix completion (MC) [6],
robust matrix completion (RMC) [8], low rank representation (LRR) [19] and

© Springer Nature Switzerland AG 2021
Y. Peng et al. (Eds.): ICIG 2021, LNCS 12889, pp. 106–119, 2021.
https://doi.org/10.1007/978-3-030-87358-5_9

Table 1. Several ℓ_0-norm relaxations and their formulas of supergradient.

Names	$f_\lambda(\sigma_i), \sigma_i \geq 0$	$\partial f_\lambda(\sigma_i), \sigma_i \geq 0$
ℓ_p-norm [23]	$\lambda\sigma_i^p, p \geq 0$	$\begin{cases} +\infty, & \text{if } \sigma_i = 0 \\ \lambda p\sigma_i^{p-1} & \text{if } \sigma_i > 0 \end{cases}$
ETP [12]	$\frac{\lambda(1-\exp(-\theta\sigma_i))}{1-\exp(-\theta)}$	$\frac{\lambda\theta\exp(-\theta\sigma_i)}{1-\exp(-\theta)}$
Geman [13]	$\frac{\lambda\sigma_i}{\sigma_i+\theta}$	$\frac{\lambda\theta}{(\sigma_i+\theta)^2}$
Laplace [25]	$\lambda\left(1-\exp\left(-\frac{\sigma_i}{\theta}\right)\right)$	$\frac{\lambda}{\theta}\exp\left(-\frac{\sigma_i}{\theta}\right)$
Logarithm [11]	$\frac{\lambda\log(1+\theta\sigma_i)}{\log(1+\theta)}$	$\frac{\lambda\theta}{(1+\theta\sigma_i)\log(1+\theta)}$

their series of variants, e.g., [10,16,27,30]. Note that both RMC and LRR can be regarded as the extensions of both MC and RPCA, this work focuses on the studies of problem formulations, optimization algorithms and performance evaluations, respectively.

The original formulations of both RMC and LRR are firstly presented by

$$\min_{\mathbf{Z}} \lambda\text{rank}(\mathbf{Z}) + \|P_\Omega(\mathbf{D}) - P_\Omega(\mathbf{Z})\|_q^q, \tag{1}$$

$$\min_{\mathbf{Z}} \lambda\text{rank}(\mathbf{Z}) + \|\mathbf{D} - \mathbf{DZ}\|_\ell, \tag{2}$$

where $\lambda > 0$ is the regularization parameter, $\mathbf{D}$ is the data matrix, $P_\Omega(\mathbf{Z}_{i,j})$ equals to $\mathbf{Z}_{i,j}$ if $(i,j) \in \Omega$, otherwise, $P_\Omega(\mathbf{Z}_{i,j}) = 0$, rank$(\mathbf{Z})$ depends on the number of non-zero singular values of matrix $\mathbf{Z}$, both $\| \bullet \|_q^q$ (e.g., $q > 0$) and $\| \bullet \|_\ell$ (e.g., $\ell = \ell_1, \ell_2$ and ℓ_{21}-norm) can describe various residual styles (e.g., laplace, gaussian and column-elements). It follows from [5,6,8,19] that problems (1) and (2) are NP-hard and not solvable easily due to the nonconvex and nonsmooth properties of rank function, which can motivate us to produce the feasible solutions to obtain a low-rank solver.

In this work, we present a general nonconvex rank regularization problem, which can be written as the following form:

$$\min_{\mathbf{Z}} f_\lambda(\mathbf{Z}) + g(\mathbf{D} - \mathbb{A}(\mathbf{Z})), \tag{3}$$

where $\mathbb{A}(\cdot)$ is the linear mapping and $\mathbb{A}^*(\cdot)$ is its adjoint, $f_\lambda(\mathbf{Z})$ is the substitute of rank$(\mathbf{Z})$ and $g(\mathbf{D} - \mathbb{A}(\mathbf{Z}))$ measures the loss function. It is well-known that problem (3) is actually the extension of some existing low rank matrix recovery problems when substituting $f_\lambda(\mathbf{Z})$ by nuclear norm [6], Schatten-p ($p > 0$) norm [23], weighted Schatten-p ($p > 0$) norm [29,32] and weighted/truncated nuclear norm [14,15,24], respectively. Additionally, some convex and nonconvex ℓ_0-norm relaxations (e.g., Logarithm [11], Exponential Type Penalty (ETP) [12], Geman [13], ℓ_p-norm ($p > 0$) [23] and Laplace [25]), listed in Table 1, can be extended to relax the rank function by acting on the singular values of matrix $\mathbf{Z}$ [21,34]. The empirical results have shown that nonconvex methods usually perform better than convex ones for the matrix recovery from the incomplete data matrix and the corrupted matrix, respectively.

Table 2. The Model Names and Problem Formulations for RMC and LRR.

Names	Problem Formulations
RMC	$\min_{\mathbf{X},\mathbf{Z},\mathbf{E}} \sum\limits_{i=1}^{r} f_\lambda(\sigma_i(\mathbf{X})) + \sum\limits_{i=1}^{m}\sum\limits_{j=1}^{n} g(P_\Omega(\mathbf{E}_{i,j}))$ $s.t., \quad \mathbf{X} = \mathbf{Z}, \quad P_\Omega(\mathbf{Z}) + P_{\bar{\Omega}}(\mathbf{E}) = P_\Omega(\mathbf{D}).$
LRR	$\min_{\mathbf{X},\mathbf{Z},\mathbf{E}} \sum\limits_{i=1}^{r} f_\lambda(\sigma_i(\mathbf{X})) + \sum\limits_{j=1}^{n} g(\|\mathbf{E}_j\|_2)$ $s.t., \quad \mathbf{X} = \mathbf{Z}, \quad \mathbf{A}\mathbf{Z} + \mathbf{E} = \mathbf{D}.$

In the optimization process, one can choose accelerated proximal gradient algorithm (APG) [18,31], iteratively reweighed optimization algorithm (IROA) [20,21] and nonconvex ADMM [26,30,35]. Moreover, the local convergence properties can be guaranteed easily in most of existing literatures [4,14,20–22], while the global convergence ones can be achieved under some specific conditions, e.g., the Kurdyka-Łojasiewicz (KL) property and the coercive property [1–3,26,33] for the objective function.

Based on these statements, we list the main contributions as follows:

- **For the model formulation**, we unify a nonconvex low-rank matrix relaxation framework by extending both RMC and LRR, which can achieve nearly unbiased estimators over nuclear norm based regularization problems.
- **For the algorithm design**, developing nonconvex ADMM with two dual variables and without the linearized strategy, each subproblem can be guaranteed to achieve the closed-form solver, respectively.
- **For the theoretical analysis**, proving the variable sequence generated by nonconvex ADMM is bounded and its subsequence converges to a stationary point for the local convergence analysis, while at the same time its limiting point satisfies the Karush-Kuhn-Tucher (KKT) conditions under some milder assumptions.

Finally, numerical results can show better recovery performance of nonconvex methods than convex cases for real-world databases.

2   Problem Formulation and Its Optimization

To make the closed-form solver of each subproblem be computed easily, one can convert problem (3) into the following constrained problem

$$\min_{\mathbf{Z},\mathbf{E},\mathbf{X}} f_\lambda(\mathbf{X}) + g(\mathbf{E}), \quad s.t., \quad \mathbf{X} = \mathbf{Z}, \quad \mathbf{E} + \mathbb{A}(\mathbf{Z}) = \mathbf{D}, \tag{4}$$

where $\mathbf{X}$ and $\mathbf{E}$ are both auxiliary variables, and it can be regarded as the extended formulation of modified RMC and LRR, listed in Table 2. Using nonconvex ADMM to solve problem (4), we take the form of augmented Lagrange function as follows

$$\mathscr{L}_\mu(\mathbf{Z},\mathbf{E},\mathbf{X},\Lambda_1,\Lambda_2) = f_\lambda(\mathbf{X}) + g(\mathbf{E}) - \frac{1}{2\mu}\left(\|\Lambda_1\|_F^2 + \|\Lambda_2\|_F^2\right)$$

$$+ \frac{\mu}{2}\left[\left\|\mathbf{X} - \mathbf{Z} + \frac{\Lambda_1}{\mu}\right\|_F^2 + \left\|\mathbf{E} + \mathbb{A}(\mathbf{Z}) - \mathbf{D} + \frac{\Lambda_2}{\mu}\right\|_F^2\right], \tag{5}$$

where $\mu > 0$, both Λ_1 and Λ_2 are the dual variables. Given the k-th iteration variables $(\mathbf{Z}_k, \mathbf{E}_k, \mathbf{X}_k, \Lambda_{1,k}, \Lambda_{2,k}, \mu_k)$, then the $(k+1)$-th ones can be updated by

$$
\begin{cases}
\mathbf{Z}_{k+1} = \text{argmin}_{\mathbf{Z}} \frac{\mu_k}{2} \left[\left\| \mathbf{Z} - \widehat{\mathbf{X}}_{\Lambda_{1,k}}^k \right\|_F^2 + \left\| \mathbb{A}(\mathbf{Z}) - \widehat{\mathbf{E}}_{\Lambda_{2,k}}^k \right\|_F^2 \right] \\
\quad\quad = (\mathbf{I} + \mathbb{A}^*\mathbb{A})^{-1} \left(\widehat{\mathbf{X}}_{\Lambda_{1,k}}^k + \widehat{\mathbf{E}}_{\Lambda_{2,k}}^k \right) \quad\quad\quad\quad\quad\quad (6) \\
\mathbf{E}_{k+1} = \text{argmin}_{\mathbf{E}} \, g(\mathbf{E}) + \frac{\mu_k}{2} \left\| \mathbf{E} - \widehat{\mathbf{Z}}_{\Lambda_{2,k}}^{k+1} \right\|_F^2, \quad\quad\quad\quad\quad (7) \\
\mathbf{X}_{k+1} \in \text{argmin}_{\mathbf{X}} \, f_\lambda(\mathbf{X}) + \frac{\mu_k}{2} \left\| \mathbf{X} - \widehat{\mathbf{Z}}_{\Lambda_{1,k}}^{k+1} \right\|_F^2, \quad\quad\quad\quad (8) \\
\Lambda_{1,k+1} = \Lambda_{1,k} + \mu_k (\mathbf{X}_{k+1} - \mathbf{Z}_{k+1}), \quad\quad\quad\quad\quad\quad\quad (9) \\
\Lambda_{2,k+1} = \Lambda_{2,k} + \mu_k (\mathbf{E}_{k+1} + \mathbb{A}(\mathbf{Z}_{k+1}) - \mathbf{D}), \quad\quad\quad\quad (10) \\
\mu_{k+1} = \min (\rho\mu_k, \mu_{\max}), \ \rho > 1, \quad\quad\quad\quad\quad\quad\quad\quad (11)
\end{cases}
$$

where $\widehat{\mathbf{X}}_{\Lambda_{1,k}}^k = \mathbf{X}_k + \frac{\Lambda_{1,k}}{\mu_k}$, $\widehat{\mathbf{E}}_{\Lambda_{1,k}}^k = \mathbf{D} - \mathbf{E}_k - \frac{\Lambda_{2,k}}{\mu_k}$, $\widehat{\mathbf{Z}}_{\Lambda_{2,k}}^{k+1} = \mathbf{D} - \mathbb{A}(\mathbf{Z}_{k+1}) - \frac{\Lambda_{2,k}}{\mu_k}$, and $\widehat{\mathbf{Z}}_{\Lambda_{1,k}}^{k+1} = \mathbf{Z}_{k+1} - \frac{\Lambda_{1,k}}{\mu_k}$, the number of iterations heavily rely on the choice of ρ-values, in which the larger of ρ-values can lead to the less number of iterations. The subproblem (6) needs to solve the quadratic problem and the subproblem (8) needs to compute the proximal operators by fixed point iteration algorithm for various function formulations of $f_\lambda(\mathbf{X})$. Additionally, the optimal solver of subproblem (7) can be achieved from [28] for various choices of $g(\mathbf{E})$ (e.g., $\ell_1/\ell_2/\ell_{21}$ norm). Note that (5) is the augmented Lagrange function of problem (4) and $\| \bullet \|_F$ is the penalty term introduced from [7,14,19].

To optimize (8) for obtaining the closed-form solver, the generalized singular value thresholding (GSVT) operator [22] will be given as follows:

Proposition 1. *Suppose that* $\mathbf{Y} = \mathbf{U}Diag(\sigma(\mathbf{Y}))\mathbf{V}^T$ *is the singular value decomposition (SVD) of matrix* $\mathbf{Y} \in \mathbf{R}^{p \times q}$ *and* $Prox_\lambda^f(\cdot)$ *is a monotone proximal operator, we compute the GSVT operator by*

$$
\text{argmin}_{\mathbf{S} \in \mathbf{R}^{p \times q}} \sum_i f_\lambda(\sigma_i(\mathbf{S})) + \frac{1}{2}\|\mathbf{S} - \mathbf{Y}\|_F^2, \quad\quad\quad\quad (12)
$$

where the function $f_\lambda(\cdot) : \mathbf{R}^+ \to \mathbf{R}^+$*, and the optimal solver of minimization problem (12) is* $\mathbf{S}^* = \mathbf{U}Diag(\varrho^*(\mathbf{Y}))\mathbf{V}^T$ *with* $\varrho^*(\mathbf{Y}) = [\varrho_1^*(\mathbf{Y}), \varrho_2^*(\mathbf{Y}), ..., \varrho_r^*(\mathbf{Y})]$*, in which* $\varrho^*(\mathbf{Y})$ *satisfies* $\varrho_1^*(\mathbf{Y}) \geq \varrho_2^*(\mathbf{Y}) \geq ... \geq \varrho_r^*(\mathbf{Y})$ *for* $i = 1, 2, ..., r = min(p, q)$*, and* $\varrho_i^*(\mathbf{Y}) \in Prox_\lambda^f(\sigma_i(\mathbf{Y}))$ *as well as*

$$
Prox_\lambda^f(\sigma_i(\mathbf{Y})) = \text{argmin}_{\varrho_i} f_\lambda(\varrho_i) + \frac{1}{2}\|\varrho_i - \sigma_i(\mathbf{Y})\|_2^2. \quad\quad (13)
$$

By choosing various function parameters, e.g., p for ℓ_p-norm and θ for ETP, Geman, Laplace and Logarithm, respectively, we present the plotted curves in Fig. 1 through the function formulations and their supergradients given in Table 1. Furthermore, the plotted curves of proximal operators can be achieved by Proposition 1, which is computed by fixed point iteration strategy [16,22]

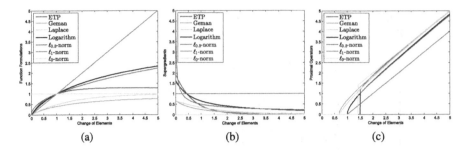

Fig. 1. The plotted curves of several convex and nonconvex ℓ_0-norm function formulations (a) and their supergradients (b) and proximal operators (c). Here, we set $\lambda = 1.0$, and $p \in \{0, 0.5, 1.0\}$ for ℓ_p-norm, and $\theta = 1.5$ for ETP, Geman, Laplace and Logarithm, respectively.

for several convex and nonconvex ℓ_0-norm relaxed functions of this work. These results can help us solving problem (3) directly or indirectly and then provide the convergence guarantees.

We can observe from subproblems (6)–(11) that multiple variables exist in nonconvex ADMM, the convergence guarantees [7] can not be easily given in general. To solve this issue, this work aims to provide the theoretical convergence guarantees for local analysis. The computational complexity mainly depends on matrix SVD and matrix multiplications. The involved parameters are given by choosing $\lambda \in \{0.001, 0.01, 0.1, 1.0, 5.0, 20.0\}$, $\rho \in \{1.1, 1.3, 1.5, 1.7, 1.9\}$, $\mu_0 \in \{0.001, 0.005, 0.01, 0.05, 0.1\}$ and $\mu_{\max} = 10^3$, respectively. The initial values variables are set as $(\mathbf{Z}_0, \mathbf{E}_0, \mathbf{X}_0, \varLambda_{1,0}, \varLambda_{2,0}, \mu_0)$. Finally, we set the stopping criteria by $\|\mathbf{X}_{k+1} - \mathbf{Z}_{k+1}\|_\infty \leq \epsilon$ and $\|\mathbf{E}_{k+1} + \mathbb{A}(\mathbf{Z}_{k+1}) - \mathbf{D}\|_\infty \leq \epsilon$ for $\epsilon = 1e-3$. Thus we can describe the detailed iteration procedure of nonconvex ADMM for solving problem (4) through the function formulation (5).

3   Convergence Analysis

The convergence analysis of nonconvex ADMM mainly depends on the updated rules, then the first-order optimality conditions are given as follows

$$
\begin{cases}
\mathbf{0} = \mathbb{A}^*(\varLambda_{2,k+1}) - \varLambda_{1,k+1} \\
\quad + \mu_k (\mathbf{X}_{k+1} - \mathbf{X}_k) + \mu_k \big[\mathbb{A}^*(\mathbf{E}_k) - \mathbb{A}^*(\mathbf{E}_{k+1})\big], & (14) \\
\mathbf{0} \in \partial g(\mathbf{E}_{k+1}) + \varLambda_{2,k+1}, & (15) \\
\mathbf{0} \in \partial f_\lambda(\mathbf{X}_{k+1}) + \varLambda_{1,k+1}, & (16)
\end{cases}
$$

where (14)–(16) are obtained from (9) and (10). We next prove the boundedness of sequence $\{(\mathbf{Z}_k, \mathbf{E}_k, \mathbf{X}_k, \varLambda_{1,k}, \varLambda_{2,k})\}$ and there exists at least one accumulation point, e.g., $(\mathbf{Z}_*, \mathbf{E}_*, \mathbf{X}_*, \varLambda_{1,*}, \varLambda_{2,*})$, which satisfies the KKT condition of $\mathscr{L}_\mu(\mathbf{Z}, \mathbf{E}, \mathbf{X}, \varLambda_1, \varLambda_2)$, i.e.,

$$
\mathbf{0} = \mathbb{A}^*(\varLambda_{2,*}) - \varLambda_{1,*}, \mathbf{0} \in \partial g(\mathbf{E}_*) + \varLambda_{2,*}, \mathbf{0} \in \partial f_\lambda(\mathbf{X}_*) + \varLambda_{1,*}. \tag{17}
$$

It should be special noted that the theoretical merits of this work are different from [26], in which for minimizing a nonconvex and possibly nonsmooth objective function, the latter considers one constraint while the former considers two constraints, and for proving the convergence guarantees, the latter provides the global analysis while the former presents the local analysis under some various assumptions.

Lemma 1. *Let* $\{\Theta_k = (\mathbf{Z}_k, \mathbf{E}_k, \mathbf{X}_k, \Lambda_{1,k}, \Lambda_{2,k})\}$ *be the sequence generated by nonconvex ADMM, and assume that* $\sum_{i=0}^{k} \frac{1}{\mu_i} < +\infty$ *holds. Then* $\{\Theta_k\}$ *is bounded.*

Proof. *Firstly*, we will prove that the dual variable sequence $\{(\Lambda_{1,k}, \Lambda_{2,k})\}$ is bounded. Then it follows from (15) and (16) that we have

$$-\partial g(\mathbf{E}_{k+1}) \ni \Lambda_{2,k+1}, \qquad -\partial f_\lambda(\mathbf{X}_{k+1}) \ni \Lambda_{1,k+1}, \qquad (18)$$

where $\partial f_\lambda(\mathbf{X}_{k+1}) = \mathbf{U}\Sigma\mathbf{Y}^T$ with $\Sigma_{ii} = \partial f_\lambda(\sigma_i)$ for $1 \le i \le \min\{m, n\}$. On the one hand, by the boundedness of $\partial f_\lambda(\sigma_i)^1$ [21], we can conclude from [4,17,36] that $\{\Lambda_{1,k+1}\}$ is bounded, and the supergradients of $f_\lambda(\sigma_i)$ is monotonically decreasing as in Fig. 1 (b).

On the other hand, to measure the residual styles, $g(\mathbf{E}_{k+1})$ may be $\ell_1/\ell_2/\ell_{21}$ norm in problem (4), e.g., when $g(\mathbf{E}_{k+1})$ is ℓ_1 norm, if it is nonsmooth only at 0 elements, we can define $\partial g(\mathbf{E}_{k+1}^{ij}) = 0$ if $\mathbf{E}_{k+1}^{ij} = 0$, and further get that $0 \le \partial g(\mathbf{E}_{k+1}^{ij}) \le mn$ is bounded. Similarly, when $g(\mathbf{E}_{k+1})$ is ℓ_2/ℓ_{21} norm, $\{\Lambda_{2,k+1}\}$ can also be proved boundedness.

Secondly, we prove that the sequence $\{(\mathbf{Z}_k, \mathbf{E}_k, \mathbf{X}_k)\}$ is bounded. Due that $\mathscr{L}_{\mu_k}(\mathbf{Z}, \mathbf{E}_k, \mathbf{X}_k, \Lambda_{1,k}, \Lambda_{2,k})$ is strongly convex with modulus at least $\mu_k(1 + \delta_\mathbb{A}^{\min})$ for $\mathbf{Z}$, and $\mathbf{Z}_{k+1}$ is the minimizer of subproblem (6), then we have

$$\mathscr{L}_{\mu_k}(\Theta_k) \ge \mathscr{L}_{\mu_k}(\mathbf{Z}_{k+1}, \mathbf{E}_k, \mathbf{X}_k, \Lambda_{1,k}, \Lambda_{2,k}) + \frac{\mu_k(1 + \delta_\mathbb{A}^{\min})}{2}\|\mathbf{Z}_{k+1} - \mathbf{Z}_k\|_F^2, \quad (19)$$

where $\delta_\mathbb{A}^{\min}$ is the smallest eigenvalue of $\mathbb{A}^*\mathbb{A}$. Since $\mathbf{E}_{k+1}$ and $\mathbf{X}_{k+1}$ are the minimizers of the subproblems (7) and (8) accordingly, then we can yield

$$\mathscr{L}_{\mu_k}(\mathbf{Z}_{k+1}, \mathbf{E}_k, \mathbf{X}_k, \Lambda_{1,k}, \Lambda_{2,k})$$
$$\ge \mathscr{L}_{\mu_k}(\mathbf{Z}_{k+1}, \mathbf{E}_{k+1}, \mathbf{X}_k, \Lambda_{1,k}, \Lambda_{2,k}) \qquad (20)$$
$$\ge \mathscr{L}_{\mu_k}(\mathbf{Z}_{k+1}, \mathbf{E}_{k+1}, \mathbf{X}_{k+1}, \Lambda_{1,k}, \Lambda_{2,k}) \qquad (21)$$
$$= \mathscr{L}_{\mu_{k+1}}(\Theta_{k+1}) - \frac{\mu_k + \mu_{k+1}}{2\mu_k^2}\left[\|\Lambda_{1,k+1} - \Lambda_{1,k}\|_F^2 + \|\Lambda_{2,k+1} - \Lambda_{2,k}\|_F^2\right], \quad (22)$$

---

[1] For ℓ_p-norm, if $\sigma_i = 0$, then $\partial f_\lambda(\sigma_i) = \{+\infty\}$, we can guarantee from the iteration rules for $\mathbf{X}_{k+1}$ in subproblem (8) that the rank of the generated sequence $\{\mathbf{X}_{k+1}\}$ is nonincreasing.

where " $=$ " holds from (9) and (10). By virtue of (19)–(22), we can get

$$
\mathscr{L}_{\mu_k}(\Theta_k) \geq \mathscr{L}_{\mu_{k+1}}(\Theta_{k+1}) + \frac{\mu_k(1 + \delta_{\mathbb{A}}^{\min})}{2}\|\mathbf{Z}_{k+1} - \mathbf{Z}_k\|_F^2
$$
$$
- \frac{\mu_k + \mu_{k+1}}{2\mu_k^2}\left[\|\Lambda_{1,k+1} - \Lambda_{1,k}\|_F^2 + \|\Lambda_{2,k+1} - \Lambda_{2,k}\|_F^2\right]. \tag{23}
$$

Thus, iterating the inequality (23) can conclude that

$$
\mathscr{L}_{\mu_0}(\Theta_0) \geq \mathscr{L}_{\mu_{k+1}}(\Theta_{k+1}) + \sum_{i=0}^{k} \frac{\mu_i(1 + \delta_{\mathbb{A}}^{\min})}{2}\|\mathbf{Z}_{i+1} - \mathbf{Z}_i\|_F^2
$$
$$
- \sum_{i=0}^{k}\left[\frac{\mu_i + \mu_{i+1}}{2\mu_i^2}\left(\|\Lambda_{1,i+1} - \Lambda_{1,i}\|_F^2 + \|\Lambda_{2,i+1} - \Lambda_{2,i}\|_F^2\right)^2\right]. \tag{24}
$$

Under the constraints on $\{\mu_k\}$ and (11), we can get that $\sum_{i=0}^{k}\frac{\mu_i+\mu_{i+1}}{2\mu_i^2} \leq \sum_{i=0}^{k}\frac{\rho+1}{2\mu_i} < +\infty$ and $\sum_{i=0}^{k}\frac{\mu_i}{2} \leq \frac{\rho\mu_{\max}-\mu_0}{\rho-1} < +\infty$ hold natually. Thus $\mathscr{L}_{\mu_{k+1}}(\Theta_{k+1})$ is bounded by the positive property of $\|\bullet\|_F$ and the boundedness of both $\mathscr{L}_{\mu_0}(\Theta_0)$ and $\{(\Lambda_{1,k}, \Lambda_{2,k})\}$. By the form of $\mathscr{L}_{\mu_{k+1}}(\Theta_{k+1})$, each term on the right-hand side of (5) is nonnegative and bounded, i.e., the sequences $\left\{\left\|\mathbf{X}_{k+1} - \mathbf{Z}_{k+1} + \frac{\Lambda_{1,k+1}}{\mu_{k+1}}\right\|_F^2\right\}$, $\left\{\left\|\mathbf{E}_{k+1} + \mathbb{A}(\mathbf{Z}_{k+1}) - \mathbf{D} + \frac{\Lambda_{2,k+1}}{\mu_{k+1}}\right\|_F^2\right\}$ and $\{f_\lambda(\mathbf{X}_{k+1}) + g(\mathbf{E}_{k+1})\}$ are all bounded. Thus, by the coercive property of objective function, we can achieve that $\{\mathbf{X}_{k+1}\}$ and $\{\mathbf{E}_{k+1}\}$ are both bounded.

Together with the boundedness of dual variables, we know that $\{\mathbf{Z}_{k+1}\}$ is bounded from (9), i.e., $\mathbf{Z}_{k+1} = \mathbf{X}_{k+1} - \frac{\Lambda_{1,k+1}-\Lambda_{1,k}}{\mu_k}$. Thus, the sequence $\{\Theta_k\}$ is bounded. □

Theorem 1. *Let* $\{\Theta_k = (\mathbf{Z}_k, \mathbf{E}_k, \mathbf{X}_k, \Lambda_{1,k}, \Lambda_{2,k})\}$ *be the sequence generated by nonconvex ADMM, and assume that* $\lim_{j\to+\infty} \mu_{k_j}(\mathbf{X}_{k_j+1} - \mathbf{X}_{k_j}) = \mathbf{0}$ *and* $\lim_{j\to+\infty} \mu_{k_j}(\mathbf{E}_{k_j} - \mathbf{E}_{k_j+1}) = \mathbf{0}$, *then any accumulation point* $\Theta_* = (\mathbf{Z}_*, \mathbf{E}_*, \mathbf{X}_*, \Lambda_{1,*}, \Lambda_{2,*})$, *it satisfies (17) as well as both* $\mathbf{X}_* = \mathbf{Z}_*$ *and* $\mathbf{D} = \mathbf{E}_* + \mathbb{A}(\mathbf{Z}_*)$.

Proof. It follows from the Bolzano-Weierstrass theorem [9] that, for the bounded sequence $\{\Theta_k\}$, there exists a subsequence $\{\Theta_{k_j}\} \subseteq \{\Theta_k\}$ and at least one accumulation point, denoted as Θ_*, such that $\lim_{j\to+\infty} \Theta_{k_j} = \Theta_*$, i.e.,

$$
\lim_{j\to+\infty} (\mathbf{Z}_{k_j}, \mathbf{E}_{k_j}, \mathbf{X}_{k_j}, \Lambda_{1,k_j}, \Lambda_{2,k_j}) = (\mathbf{Z}_*, \mathbf{E}_*, \mathbf{X}_*, \Lambda_{1,*}, \Lambda_{2,*}). \tag{25}
$$

By the updating rules of $(\Lambda_{1,k}, \Lambda_{2,k})$ and then setting $k = k_j$, we have

$$
\begin{cases}
\dfrac{\Lambda_{1,k_j+1} - \Lambda_{1,k_j}}{\mu_{k_j}} = \mathbf{X}_{k_j+1} - \mathbf{Z}_{k_j+1}, & (26) \\[3mm]
\dfrac{\Lambda_{2,k_j+1} - \Lambda_{2,k_j}}{\mu_{k_j}} = \mathbf{E}_{k_j+1} + \mathbb{A}(\mathbf{Z}_{k_j+1}) - \mathbf{D}. & (27)
\end{cases}
$$

Thus when μ_{k_j} sufficiently larger in both (26) and (27), we can get from the boundedness of $(\Lambda_{1,k}, \Lambda_{2,k})$ that $\mathbf{X}_* = \mathbf{Z}_*$ and $\mathbf{D} = \mathbf{E}_* + \mathbb{A}(\mathbf{Z}_*)$ hold naturally.

By the optimality condition for $\mathbf{Z}_{k_j+1}$ in subproblem (6), we yield from (14) that

$$
\mathbf{0} = \mathbb{A}^*(\Lambda_{2,k_j+1}) - \Lambda_{1,k_j+1} + \mu_{k_j}\left(\mathbf{X}_{k_j+1} - \mathbf{X}_{k_j}\right) + \mu_{k_j}\left[\mathbb{A}^*(\mathbf{E}_{k_j} - \mathbf{E}_{k_j+1})\right]. \tag{28}
$$

Combining (25), (28) with the given assumptions, it is easy to obtain

$$
\mathbf{0} = \mathbb{A}^*\left(\Lambda_{2,*}\right) - \Lambda_{1,*}. \tag{29}
$$

By virtue of both (15) and (16), we can conclude from [4] that (17) holds similarly.

Hence, the above results accord to the desired conclusions. In other words, the limiting point $(\mathbf{Z}_*, \mathbf{E}_*, \mathbf{X}_*, \Lambda_{1,*}, \Lambda_{2,*})$ satisfies the KKT conditions of function (5) and $(\mathbf{Z}_*, \mathbf{E}_*, \mathbf{X}_*)$ is a stationary point of problem (4), respectively. $\qquad\square$

4   Numerical Results

In this section, we will show the superiority of nonconvex rank regularization for both RMC and LRR problems (see Table 2) and present the theoretical results for the converged objective function. The model formulations are different from the existing works [21, 22], they are more general than the mostly related works [5, 6, 8, 17, 19, 23].

The evaluation criteria [19, 22, 32], e.g., peak signal-to-noise ratio (PSNR), relative error (RERR), subspace clustering accuracy (SCA) and normalized mutual information (NMI), will be taken into consideration for the real-world data, e.g., natural images and face images. The larger values of PSNR, SCA and NMI as well as the lower values of RERR, the better performance of the involved methods. The experimental settings and numerical comparisons are given as below.

- **Experimental descriptions for RMC**

– In the first experiment, it follows from [29] that the matrix $\mathbf{X} = \mathbf{U}_1\mathbf{U}_2$ with rank $\mathbf{r} = 20$ is given by the Matlab command normrnd for $\mathbf{U}_1 = $ normrnd$(0, 1, 200, \mathbf{r})$ and $\mathbf{U}_2 = $ normrnd$(0, 1, \mathbf{r}, 200)$, respectively. In this task, 10% of elements in matrix $\mathbf{X}$ are selected randomly to construct Ω as the missing set, we further represent the observed data matrix by $P_\Omega(\mathbf{X})$.

- *In the second experiment*, we apply RMC to the robust recovery of natural images, shown in Fig. 3, with two incomplete masks, i.e., text and blocks. These natural images have three channels, so we complete the missing pixel parts by the proposed methods on each channel (i.e., red, green, and blue) independently, and then combine them to achieve the optimal performance.

- **Experimental descriptions for LRR**

- *In the first experiment*, it follows from [20] that we need to generate 10 independent subspaces $\{\mathbf{S}_i\}_{i=1}^{k}$, whose bases $\{\mathbf{U}_i\}_{i=1}^{k}$ are constructed by the iteration rules $\mathbf{U}_{i+1} = \mathbf{T}\mathbf{U}_i$ for $1 \leq i \leq 10$. Also, we generate a random rotation matrix $\mathbf{T}$ by the Matlab command rand and a random column orthogonal matrix $\mathbf{U}_1$ having the dimension 200×20. Besides, each subspace has a rank number and an ambient dimension for 20 and 200 accordingly. In this task, we sample 20 data vectors from each subspace by $\mathbf{X}_i = \mathbf{U}_i\mathbf{C}_i$ with $\mathbf{C}_i$ being a 20×20 i.i.d. standard Gaussian matrix. And we randomly chose 20% samples corrupted by adding Gaussian noise with zero mean and standard deviation $0.5\|\mathbf{X}\|_F^2$.

- *In the second experiment*, the Extended Yale B database[2], which contains face images belonging to 38 subjects, will be used for the testing. By resizing each image into 32×32, one can use the first 5 and 10 subjects to form a raw matrix $\mathbf{D}$ with the size of 1024×320 and 1024×640, respectively, and then project them onto 100D, 200D, 100D and 200D subspace, respectively, by applying PCA technique. The SCA and NMI are both used to test the clustering performance. The optimal $\mathbf{X}_*$ will be used to construct an affinity matrix $\mathbf{W}$ by computing $(|\mathbf{X}_*| + |\mathbf{X}_*^\mathbf{T}|)/2$.

The visual and numerical results of both RMC and LRR methods on image inpainting and subspace clustering are presented in Figs. 2, 3 and 4 and Table 3, respectively. Based on them, we have the quantitative and qualitative observations as follows:

- Figures 2 and 4 show that the values of objective function induced from the first experiment of both RMC and LRR methods on the synthesis data through (5) have the nonincreasing property over the number of iterations for the ℓ_0-norm relaxations according to (a). Especially, for the ℓ_p-norm based both RMC and LRR methods, the objective values have the decreasing property with the increasing of ρ-values and μ_0-values through (b) and (c). Moreover, the number of iterations can be reduced when the ρ-values increase and the μ_0-values decrease, respectively.

---

[2] http://vision.ucsd.edu/leekc/ExtYaleDatabase/ExtYale.

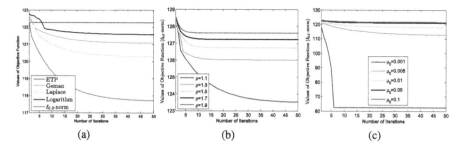

(a)   (b)   (c)

Fig. 2. The values of objective function (5) for RMC by nonconvex ℓ_0-norm relaxations (a), and $\ell_{0.5}$-norm with the parameters for various ρ-values (b) and μ_0-values (c), respectively.

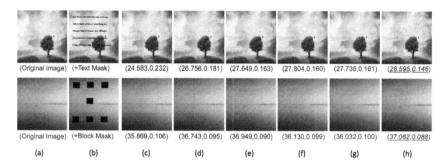

Fig. 3. The visual demonstrations and quantitative comparisons (PSNR and RERR) obtained by (c) ℓ_1, (d) $\ell_{0.5}$, (e) ETP, (f) Geman, (g) Laplace and (h) Logrithm (from left to right) based RMC for recovering the natural images (a) with text mask and multiple-block mask (b), respectively.

- Figure 3 shows the visual and numerical results for the qualitative and quantitative comparisons. For the recovered natural images, they seem to be very similar though there may exist some slight differences. For the evaluation criteria, we observe that the larger values of PSNR, the smaller values of RERR. These numerical values imply that the RMC methods involved nonconvex relaxations can achieve higher PSNR values than convex case related with ℓ_1-norm. The achieved results accord to the empirical sense. Among nonconvex ℓ_0-norm relaxations listed in Table 1, the Logrithm function based RMC method achieves the best recovery performance.
- Table 3 shows that the values of both SCA and NMI will decrease when the data classes and dimensions increase, respectively. Meanwhile, larger values of SCA correspond to larger values of NMI. The nonconvex relaxations will have higher clustering accuracy than convex case, e.g., ℓ_1-norm, for these LRR variants. In addition, we can observe that the induced LRR methods by ETP and Logarithm can obtain relatively better performance among these nonconvex relaxations.

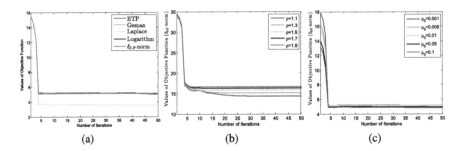

Fig. 4. The values of objective function (5) for LRR by nonconvex ℓ_0-norm relaxations (a), and $\ell_{0.5}$-norm with the parameters for various ρ-values (b) and μ_0-values (c), respectively.

Table 3. The quantitative results of SCA (%) and NMI (%) on the Extended Yale B database.

Relaxations	5 Classes		10 Classes	
	100 Dim	200 Dim	100 Dim	200 Dim
ℓ_1-	74.063	72.500	62.656	62.500
	62.807	*62.507*	*58.520*	*58.302*
$\ell_{0.5}$-	75.938	73.438	64.531	64.063
	63.489	*62.689*	*61.180*	*60.960*
ETP	80.938	78.125	65.156	64.561
	68.861	*65.812*	*61.701*	*61.377*
Geman	79.375	76.875	65.000	63.125
	67.470	*64.600*	*61.348*	*59.969*
Laplace	77.813	76.250	64.219	63.594
	64.246	*63.221*	*61.083*	*60.503*
Logarithm	<u>81.250</u>	<u>80.625</u>	<u>66.875</u>	<u>65.469</u>
	69.902	*68.152*	*61.967*	*61.781*

5   Conclusions

This paper mainly provides the convergence guarantees of nonconvex ADMM for solving a class of generalized nonconvex rank regularization problems, which can be regarded as the extension of both RMC and LRR problems. By relying on the updating rules and some milder assumptions, we first present the boundedness of two dual variables, and then analyse the local convergence result of the generated sequence. Performing numerical comparisons on both synthetic and real-world databases, the experimental results can maintain its consistency with the theoretic properties and show their efficiency over convex low-rank matrix regularization problems. In the future works, the generalized proximal operator formulations and the global convergence analysis are both the key issues for nonconvex optimization algorithms, which are the very challenging problems especially for the multi-variable cases [7].

Acknowledgements. The authors would like to thank the anonymous reviewers for their valuable comments. This work was supported in part by the National Natural Science Fund for Distinguished Young Scholars under Grant 61725301, in part by the National Science Fund of China under Grant 61973124, 61702197, 61876083, and 61906067, in part by the China Postdoctoral Science Foundation under Grant 2019M651415 and 2020T130191, and in part by the University of Macau under UM Macao Talent Programme (UMMTP-2020-01).

References

1. Attouch, H., Bolte, J., Svaiter, B.F.: Convergence of descent methods for semi-algebraic and tame problems: proximal algorithms, forward-backward splitting, and regularized Gauss-Seidel methods. Math. Program. **137**(1–2), 91–129 (2013)
2. Bolte, J., Daniilidis, A., Lewis, A.: The Lojasiewicz inequality for nonsmooth subanalytic functions with applications to subgradient dynamical systems. SIAM. J. Optim. **17**(4), 1205–1223 (2007)
3. Bolte, J., Sabach, S., Teboulle, M.: Proximal alternating linearized minimization for nonconvex and nonsmooth problems. Math. Program. **146**(1-2), 459–494 (2014)
4. Brbić, M., Kopriva, I.: ℓ_0-motivated low-rank sparse subspace clustering. IEEE Trans. Cybern. **50**(4), 1711–1725 (2020)
5. Candes, E., Li, X., Ma, Y., Wright, J.: Robust principal component analysis? J. ACM **58**(3), 1–37 (2011)
6. Candes, E., Tao, T.: The power of convex relaxation: near-optimal matrix completion. IEEE Trans. Infor. Theo. **56**(5), 2053–2080 (2010)
7. Chen, C., He, B., Ye, Y., Yuan, X.: The direct extension of ADMM for multi-block convex minimization problems is not necessarily convergent. Math. Program. **155**(1–2), 57–79 (2016)
8. Chen, Y., Jalali, A., Sanghavi, S., Caramanis, C.: Low-rank matrix recovery from errors and erasures. IEEE Trans. Infor. Theo. **59**(7), 4324–4337 (2013)
9. Clarke, F.: Optimization and nonsmooth analysis. Society for Industrial and Applied Mathematics (1990)
10. Dong, W., Wu, X.: Robust low rank subspace segmentation via joint ℓ_{21}-norm minimization. Neural Process. Lett. **48**(1), 299–312 (2018)
11. Friedman, J.H.: Fast sparse regression and classification. Int. J. Forecasting **28**(3), 722–738 (2012)
12. Gao, C., Wang, N., Yu, Q., Zhang, Z.: A feasible nonconvex relaxation approach to feature selection. In: Proceedings Association Advancement Artificial Intelligence (AAAI), pp. 356–361 (2011)
13. Geman, D., Yang, C.: Nonlinear image recovery with half-quadratic regularization. IEEE Trans. Image. Process. **4**(7), 932–946 (1994)
14. Gu, S., Xie, Q., Meng, D., Zuo, W., Feng, X., Zhang, L.: Weighted nuclear norm minimization and its applications to low level vision. Int. J. Comput. Vis. **121**(2), 183–208 (2017)
15. Hu, Y., Zhang, D., Ye, J., Li, X., He, X.: Fast and accurate matrix completion via truncated nuclear norm regularization. IEEE Trans. Pattern. Anal. Mach. Intell. **35**(9), 2117–2130 (2013)

16. Hu, Z., Nie, F., Tian, L., Li, X.: A comprehensive survey for low rank regularization. arXiv preprint arXiv:1808.04521 (2018)
17. Kang, Z., Peng, C., Cheng, Q.: Robust subspace clustering via tighter rank approximation. In: Proceedings ACM Conference Information and Knowledge Management (CIKM), pp. 655–661 (2012)
18. Lan, X., Zhang, S., Yuen, P.C., Chellappa, R.: Learning common and feature-specific patterns: a novel multiple-sparse-representation-based tracker. IEEE Trans. Image. Process. **27**(4), 2022–2037 (2018)
19. Liu, G., Lin, Z., Yan, S., Sun, J., Yu, Y., Ma, Y.: Robust recovery of subspace structures by low-rank representation. IEEE Trans. Pattern. Anal. Mach. Intell. **35**(1), 171–184 (2013)
20. Lu, C., Lin, Z., Yan, S.: Smoothed low rank and sparse matrix recovery by iteratively reweighted least squares minimization. IEEE Trans. Image. Process. **24**(2), 646–654 (2015)
21. Lu, C., Tang, J., Yan, S., Lin, Z.: Nonconvex nonsmooth low-rank minimization via iteratively reweighted nuclear norm. IEEE Trans. Image. Process. **25**(2), 829–839 (2016)
22. Lu, C., Zhu, C., Xu, C., Yan, S., Lin, Z.: Generalized singular value thresholding. In: Proceedings Association Advances Artificial Intelligence (AAAI), pp. 1805–1811 (2015)
23. Nie, F., Wang, H., Huang, H., Ding, C.: Joint Schatten-p norm and ℓ_p-norm robust matrix completion for missing value recovery. Knowl. Infor. Syst. **42**(3), 525–544 (2015)
24. Oh, T.H., Tai, Y., Bazin, J.C., Kim, H., Kweon, I.S.: Partial sum minimization of singular values in robust PCA: algorithm and applications. IEEE Trans. Pattern. Anal. Mach. Intell. **38**(4), 744–758 (2015)
25. Trzasko, J., Manduca, A.: Highly undersampled magnetic resonance image reconstruction via homotopic ℓ_p-minimization. IEEE Trans. Med. Image. **28**(1), 106–121 (2009)
26. Wang, Y., Yin, W., Zeng, J.: Global convergence of ADMM in nonconvex nonsmooth optimization. J. Sci. Comput. **78**(1), 29–63 (2019)
27. Wei, L., Wang, X., Wu, A., Zhou, R., Zhu, C.: Robust subspace segmentation by self-representation constrained low-rank representation. Neural. Process. Lett. **48**(3), 1671–1691 (2018)
28. Wen, F., Chu, L., Liu, P., Qiu, R.C.: A survey on nonconvex regularization-based sparse and low-rank recovery in signal processing, statistics, and machine learning. IEEE Access. **6**, 69883–69906 (2018)
29. Xie, Y., Gu, S., Liu, Y., Zuo, W., Zhang, W., Zhang, L.: Weighted Schatten-p norm minimization for image denoising and background subtraction. IEEE Trans. Image. Process. **25**(10), 4842–4857 (2016)
30. Yang, L., Pong, T., Chen, X.: Alternating direction method of multipliers for nonconvex background/foreground extraction. SIAM J. Imag. Sci. **10**(1), 74–110 (2017)
31. Yao, Q., Kwok, J.T., Gao, F., Chen, W., Liu, T.: Efficient inexact proximal gradient algorithm for nonconvex problems. In: Proceedings Association Advancement Artificial Intelligence (AAAI), pp. 3308–3314 (2017)
32. Zhang, H., Gong, C., Qian, J., Zhang, B., Xu, C., Yang, J.: Efficient recovery of low-rank matrix via double nonconvex nonsmooth rank minimization. IEEE Trans. Neural Netw. Learn. Syst. **30**(10), 2916–2925 (2019)

33. Zhang, H., Qian, F., Shang, F., Du, W., Qian, J., Yang, J.: Global convergence guarantees of (A)GIST for a family of nonconvex sparse learning problems. IEEE Trans. Cybern. https://doi.org/10.1109/TCYB.2020.3010960 (2020)
34. Zhang, H., Qian, J., Gao, J., Yang, J., Xu, C.: Scalable proximal Jacobian iteration method with global convergence analysis for nonconvex unconstrained composite optimizations. IEEE Trans. Neural Netw. Learn. Syst. **30**(9), 2825–2839 (2019)
35. Zhang, H., Yang, J., Qian, J., Luo, W.: Nonconvex relaxation based matrix regression for face recognition with structural noise and mixed noise. Neurocomput. **269**(20), 188–198 (2017)
36. Zhang, H., Yang, J., Shang, F., Gong, C., Zhang, Z.: LRR for subspace segmentation via tractable Schatten-p norm minimization and factorization. IEEE Trans. Cybern. **49**(5), 1722–1734 (2019)

Free Adversarial Training with Layerwise Heuristic Learning

Haitao Zhang[1], Yucheng Shi[1], Benyu Dong[1], Yahong Han[1(✉)],
Yuanzhang Li[2], and Xiaohui Kuang[3]

[1] College of Intelligence and Computing, and Tianjin Key Lab of Machine Learning,
Tianjin University, Tianjin, China
{haitaoz,yucheng,dby1997,yahong}@tju.edu.cn
[2] Beijing Institute of Technology, Beijing, China
popular@bit.edu.cn
[3] National Key Laboratory of Science and Technology on Information System
Security, Beijing, China

Abstract. Due to the existence of adversarial attacks, various applications that employ deep neural networks (DNNs) have been under threat. Adversarial training enhances robustness of DNN-based systems by augmenting training data with adversarial samples. Projected gradient descent adversarial training (PGD AT), one of the promising defense methods, can resist strong attacks. We propose "free" adversarial training with layerwise heuristic learning (**LHFAT**) to remedy these problems. To reduce heavy computation cost, we couple model parameter updating with projected gradient descent (PGD) adversarial example updating while retraining the same mini-batch of data, where we "free" and unburden extra updates. Learning rate reflects weight updating speed. Weight gradient indicates weight updating efficiency. If weights are frequently updated towards opposite directions in one training epoch, then there are redundant updates. For higher level of weight updating efficiency, we design a new learning scheme, layerwise heuristic learning, which accelerates training convergence by restraining redundant weight updating and boosting efficient weight updating of layers according to weight gradient information. We demonstrate that LHFAT yields better defense performance on CIFAR-10 with approximately 8% GPU training time of PGD AT and LHFAT is also validated on ImageNet. We have released the code for our proposed method LHFAT at https://github.com/anonymous530/LHFAT.

1 Introduction

Deep learning has been widely used in computer vision, natural language processing [12]. However, research has shown that DNNs are vulnerable to adversarial attacks [1,4,9,11,15], which could cause severe security issues. So the robustness of DNNs to adversarial attacks has drawn a lot of attention.

This work is supported by the NSFC (under Grant 61876130).

Y. Peng et al. (Eds.): ICIG 2021, LNCS 12889, pp. 120–131, 2021.
https://doi.org/10.1007/978-3-030-87358-5_10

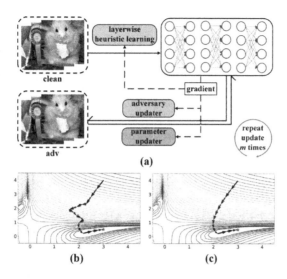

Fig. 1. Architecture of LHFAT (a) and comparison of gradient descent between other adversarial training methods (b) and our method LHFAT (c). LHFAT updates parameters and adversary simultaneously and utilizes layerwise heuristic learning which accelerates training convergence with higher weight updating efficiency.

Owing to the existence of adversarial attacks, various defense methods followed. One of the most effective and straightforward methods is adversarial training (AT) [4,10,11,16]. AT can be regarded as training with adversarial examples to minimize the probability of being fooled by adversarial samples [4,16]. Projected gradient descent adversarial training (**PGD AT**) is one of the most effective AT methods that can resist strong attacks [11], but problems remain for PGD AT. On account of extra iterative steps for adversarial sample generation, PGD AT costs much more for adversarial training compared with natural training. The training convergence of PGD AT is pretty slow. There is a recent work FreeAT [14] that can accelerate PGD AT. FreeAT eliminates the overhead cost of generating adversarial samples by updating projected gradient descent adversary (PGD) [11] with the gradient information computed when updating model parameters. However, FreeAT still has two limitations that influence convergence speed. Firstly, FreeAT neglects that different layers vary in learning ability for adversarial training. Secondly, the training convergence could be retarded due to the lack of adjustment of model weight updating. FreeAT requires updating model parameters m times for the same mini-batch of data in one training epoch. However, if the weight of specific layer is updated in opposite directions with high frequency in the same training epoch, then the redundant weight updating will fluctuate the adversarial training.

To solve the above problems, we propose **LHFAT** to improve FreeAT and further accelerate training convergence of PGD AT. As illustrated in Fig. 1, LHFAT accelerates PGD AT convergence by alleviating heavy computation burden of producing adversarial examples and training with layerwise heuristic learning for higher weight updating efficiency. Firstly, for diminishing the extra computation cost of generating adversarial samples, LHFAT couples model parameter updating with PGD adversary updating, where we "free" and unburden extra updates. Secondly, for differentiating layerwise learning ability and updating weight efficiently, layerwise heuristic learning in LHFAT restrains inefficient weight updating to reduce the adverse effect on training and boosting high efficient weight updating. We integrate layerwise heuristic learning with momentum-SGD [13] to form an efficient learning scheme.

Our proposed method LHFAT achieves better defense performance. LHFAT is about 13 times faster than PGD AT and 2 times faster than FreeAT on CIFAR-10. The effectiveness of LHFAT is also verified on ImageNet [3]. Experiments show that it requires larger magnitude of adversarial perturbation to fool the defense model trained with LHFAT, which indicates the defense ability of LHFAT is stronger.

2 Related Work

2.1 Adversarial Defense

There are many proposed methods for improving the robustness of DNNs.

Adversarial training [15] is a variant of empirical risk minimization problem, which aims to minimize the risk over adversarial examples [16]. The process of adversarial training is to inject generated adversarial samples into training data.

There are other kinds of defense using adversarial examples. MemGuard [8] utilizes adversarial examples to defend against black-box membership inference attack.

2.2 Adversarial Training

For adversarial defense, we only focus on AT in this paper. AT is one of the most straightforward and effective defense method. The procedure of AT can be seen as training with injected adversarial samples.

Vanilla AT [15] can be seen as augmenting training data by injecting adversarial samples.

There are various adversarial training methods subsequently. Projected gradient descent adversarial training (PGD AT) [11] improves vanilla AT by training with projected gradient descent adversary (PGD) [11]. Ensemble AT [16] explores the robustness of AT.

2.3 Training Acceleration

During training, mini-batch of data are forwarded through the network and loss is calculated. Then gradients are computed and backpropagated. Model parameters are updated and optimized with optimizer. Training can be accelerated according to the training process accordingly.

Increasing computation capacity and data parallel can speed up the training. Model compression [5], knowledge distillation [7], parameter pruning [6] and low-rank factorization [17] can accelerate the training. We design an efficient layerwise heuristic learning scheme, which is embedded in the training process. For fair comparison, we train the network with the same device in each part of our experiments.

2.4 Adversarial Training Acceleration

The training convergence of PGD AT [11] is slow because of heavy computation cost for iterative adversary updating steps and poor weight updating efficiency.

To accelerate PGD AT, a recent work FreeAT [14] retrains the network with the same mini-batch of data for m times in each training epoch and updates PGD adversary with the gradient calculated when updating network parameters. FreeAT can reduce the overhead cost of adversarial sample production. There is a concurrent work that is related with FreeAT. YOPO decouples the adversarial calculation and network parameter updating. Fast adversarial training (FastAT) [18] utilizes FGSM for adversarial training acceleration, but the defense performance and standard accuracy of FastAT is not that good.

3 Method

We will introduce threat model and our proposed method LHFAT in this section.

3.1 Adversarial Training

In this section, we introduce the detail of adversarial training. Adversarial training can be regarded as empirical risk minimization problem [16] as Eq. (1). The goal of adversarial training is to minimize the risk over adversarial examples. Adversarial training is training with clean data and corresponding adversarial examples generated by some adversarial attack. The algorithm process of vanilla adversarial training is shown in Algorithm 1. For evaluating robustness of adversarial training, we should use white-box adversarial attacks to evaluate the trained models [2]. We all evaluate our trained models in white-box evaluation settings in our paper.

$$f^* = \arg\min_{f \in F} \; \mathbb{E}_{(x, y_{true} \; \mathbb{D})} \left[\max_{\|x - x_{adv}\| \le \epsilon} L\left(f\left(x_{adv}\right), y_{true}\right) \right]. \tag{1}$$

Algorithm 1: Vanilla Adversarial training (Vanilla AT)

   Data: Training data x, label y, perturbation δ, training epochs N, learning rate
       η

   Result: Network parameter θ

1 **repeat**

2 | **for** *epoch* $\leftarrow$ *0 to N/m* **do**

3 | | **for** *mini-batch* $B \in X$ **do**

4 | | | $B^* \leftarrow generate\_adv(B, y, \theta)$;

5 | | | $\theta \leftarrow train(B, B^*, y, \theta, \eta)$;

6 | | **end**

7 | **end**

8 **until** *training converged*;

Layerwise Heuristic Learning. We now enlarge upon the learning scheme in LHFAT, layerwise heuristic learning. We design layerwise heuristic learning based on two reasons. The first one is that network layers vary in learning ability. And the second one is that there may exist redundant weight updating, if the weight is updated towards opposite directions frequently while retraining one mini-batch of data. Layerwise heuristic learning accelerates PGD AT by updating layerwise weight efficiently. Layerwise heuristic learning can be decomposed into two parts: layerwise heuristic regulation and learning with regulated layerwise learning rate. As illustrated in Fig. 2, the left part describes the training process of K-PGD AT. Mini-batch of data are forwarded through the network and then gradients are backpropagated. We obtain gradient w.r.t. weight (g_w) during each training iteration in one training epoch. Next, we calculate weight updating efficiency E_w^l of each trainable layer l with g_w. We restrain redundant weight updating by reducing learning rate ratio R_η^l of specific layer whose E_w^l is low. And we boost efficient weight updating by increasing R_η^l whose E_w^l is high. Learning rate for layer l_i is regulated according to $R_\eta^{l_i}$.

The following experiments will testify that different layers differ from learning ability.

Implementation Details of LHFAT. Subsequently, we describe the implementation details of LHFAT. We distinguish the network layers and give priority for learning to deep layers, so we initialize higher learning rate for deep layers, initial learning rate ratio (R_η^{init}) of each trainable layer l is calculated according to Eq. (2), where q is 0.9, n is the number of trainable layers, $i \in n$.

$$R_\eta^{init}(l_i) = (q + (1 - q) * i/n)^3 . \tag{2}$$

Total training epoch N is compressed to N/m because of retaining the same mini-batch of data m times. In this way, we keep total training iterations as constant N. Within each retraining iteration, the gradient g_θ of model parameters θ is calculated after backward. When training epoch is even, learning rate ratio R_η^l for each layer is set to $R_\eta^{init}(l)$. When epoch is odd, weight updating efficiency

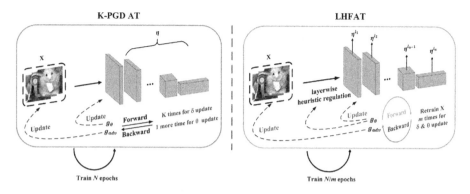

Fig. 2. Overview of our proposed method LHFAT and K-PGD AT. The process of K-PGD AT [11] is described in the left part of the figure. Mini-batch of images X are forwarded through the network. K-PGD AT requires K iterative steps to update PGD perturbation δ in each iteration during training. Then K-PGD AT trains with generated PGD adversarial examples and updates parameters θ with unified learning rate η. The right part of the figure depicts our method LHFAT. LHFAT retrains X for m times and couples PGD perturbation (δ) updating with parameter (θ) updating simultaneously so that LHFAT keeps the total training iterations as N. Layerwise heuristic regulation utilizes gradient g_θ information to regulate layerwise learning rate η^{l_i} to update parameters efficiently.

$E_w^{l_i}$ of specific layer l_i is calculated with Eq. (3), where $n_w^{l_i}$ is number of weights in layer l_i, m is the number of iterations in current epoch and $g_{jk}^{l_i}$ is the gradient of loss w.r.t. weight w_j for l_i in the k_{th} iteration. The gradient w.r.t. weight g_w is obtained when calculating g_θ.

$$E_w^{l_i} = \begin{cases} 0, & if \ g_w^{l_i} = 0 \\ \dfrac{\sum_{j=1}^{n_w^{l_i}} \left| \sum_{k=1}^{m} g_{jk}^{l_i} \right|}{\sum_{j=1}^{n_w^{l_i}} \sum_{k=1}^{m} \left| g_{jk}^{l_i} \right|}, & otherwise. \end{cases} \tag{3}$$

$E_w^{l_i}$ in Eq. (3) is normalized to $[0, 1]$:

$$E_w = \frac{E_w - min(E_w)}{max(E_w) - min(E_w)} \tag{4}$$

We sort E_w for all layers in ascending order. Then we divide layers into low E_w group (G^L) and high E_w group (G^H). To update weight efficiently, learning rate ratio R_η^l is regulated according to E_w with Eq. (5). If l_i is in the G^L group, we decrease $R_\eta^{l_i}$ to alleviate the impact of inefficient weight updating. And if

l_i is in the G^H group, we increase $R_\eta^{l_i}$ to boost efficient weight updating. This represents the process of layerwise heuristic regulation.

$$R_\eta^{l_i} = \begin{cases} (1 - C_m) * R_\eta^{l_i}, & if \ l_i \in G^L \\ (1 + C_a) * R_\eta^{l_i}, & if \ l_i \in G^H \end{cases} \tag{5}$$

where $i \in n$, C_m and C_a are corresponding to learning rate regulation coefficients.

Then different layer l_i learns with corresponding learning rate η^{l_i}, which is obtained with Eq. (6).

$$\eta^{l_i} = \eta_{base} * R_\eta^{l_i} * C_\eta, \tag{6}$$

where $i \in n$ and C_η is the coefficient of learning rate.

Within each training epoch, we utilize cosine annealing schedule for all layers as Eq. (7):

$$\eta_{it}^{l_i} = \eta_{min} + \frac{1}{2}(\eta_{max}^{l_i} - \eta_{min})\left(1 + \cos\left(\frac{T_{cur}}{T_i}\pi\right)\right), \tag{7}$$

where it is the it_{th} iteration in current training epoch, $i \in n$, $\eta_{max}^{l_i}$ is the value of η^{l_i} at the beginning of current epoch.

For updating parameters θ, we combine our layerwise heuristic learning with M-SGD. Different layer l_i learns with different learning rate η^{l_i}, therefore we apply layerwise M-SGD in LHFAT.

4   Experiments

In this section, we will compare our method with PGD AT [11] and FreeAT [14] using their publicly available code. We conduct experiments on CIFAR-10 and ImageNet [3] to verify that our proposed method LHFAT can accelerate PGD AT. LHFAT yields better performance than FreeAT and PGD AT with much less training time.

4.1   CIFAR-10 Experiments

In this section, we conduct experiments on CIFAR-10 and compare related adversarial training methods with our proposed method LHFAT. The CIFAR-10 dataset consists of $3 \times 32 \times 32$ images with 10 classes. There are 50000 training images and 10000 test images.

CIFAR-10 Experiment Settings. We conduct all CIFAR-10 experiments with one GeForce GTX 1080 Ti GPU. The batch size is 128. We train with WideResnet 34-10. Natural training denotes training the network without adversary. For PGD AT [11] and FreeAT [14], we train with their publicly released code. For FreeAT, $m = 8$ because it achieves comparable robustness levels of 7-PGD AT. For YOPO [19], we conduct related experiments using their publicly

Table 1. Comparison results on CIFAR-10. 7-PGD AT [11]: PGD adversarial training. FreeAT-8 [14]: free adversarial training. m is 8, which corresponds to 7-PGD AT. Ours: our adversarial training method LHFAT, $m = 8$.

Training	Evaluate			Training time (min)
	Clean	PGD-20	PGD-100	
Natural	**95.56**	0	0	428.50
7-PGD AT [11][a]	87.27	46.10	45.68	5514.48
FreeAT-10 [14][b]	83.27	46.14	44.60	790.02
FreeAT-8 [14]	86.27	46.65	46.05	779.02
YOPO [19][c]	85.95	46.42	44.84	476
Ours ($m = 10$)	84.04	**48.60**	**47.17**	448.65
Ours	86.19	47.82	46.17	**424.38**

[a] https://github.com/MadryLab/cifar10_challenge
[b] https://github.com/ashafahi/free_adv_train
[c] https://github.com/a1600012888/YOPO-You-Only-Propagate-Once

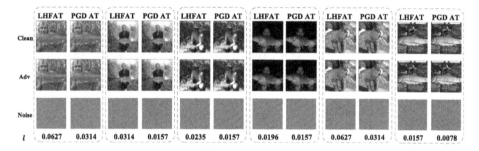

Fig. 3. PGD adversarial examples (fish class) built for defense models (ResNet50) trained with LHFAT and 2-PGD AT on ImageNet.

released code. For adversary settings, we adopt the same settings with FreeAT. For LHFAT, learning rate decays at epoch 12 and 18.

Comparison Results on CIFAR-10. For evaluation, we test the trained defense model with PGD-20 and PGD-100. We present comparison results in Table 1. As we can see, PGD AT [11] needs much longer training time. FreeAT [14] significantly reduces the training time of PGD AT and has comparable defense performance with 7-PGD AT. However, LHFAT has better defense performance than PGD AT and FreeAT. LHFAT accelerates PGD AT about 13 times and accelerates FreeAT about 2 times. When we increase m from 8 to 10, it means that there are more iterative steps for PGD adversarial examples generation, that is, defense performance of the trained model should be better. When $m = 10$, our proposed method LHFAT has reached better defense performance than FreeAT-10. For YOPO[19], we have tried to train WideResnet 34-10 three

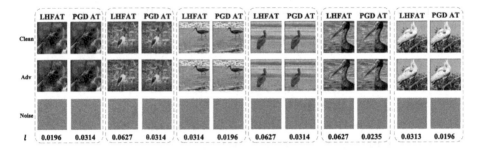

Fig. 4. PGD adversarial examples (bird class) built for defense models (ResNet50) trained with LHFAT and 2-PGD AT on ImageNet.

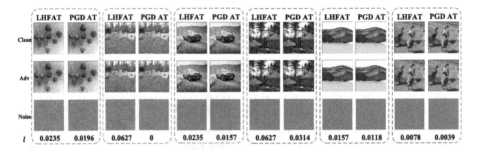

Fig. 5. BIM adversarial examples built for defense models (ResNet50) trained with LHFAT and 2-PGD AT on ImageNet.

times with their publicly released code and report the best result. Compared with YOPO, our method LHFAT is faster. And YOPO is more complicated for implementation than LHFAT. Our method LHFAT can be easily applied to complicated models and large scale of datasets.

4.2   ImageNet Experiments

For ImageNet experiments, we choose ILSVRC 2012 dataset. There 1000 classes of $3 \times 224 \times 224$ images in ILSVRC 2012 dataset. Due to high complexity of training on ImageNet, there are few AT research performing experiments on ImageNet.

ImageNet Experiment Settings. We conduct all ImageNet experiments on a single workstation with four GeForce RTX 2080 Ti GPUs. For all ImageNet experiments, we use the PyTorch pretrained ResNet models for adversarial training and the batch size is 256. For adversary settings, we use l_∞-PGD, step size $2/255$ and $\epsilon = 4/255$, which is identical with FreeAT [14]. For PGD AT [11] experiment, we adopt 2-steps PGD adversary because 2-PGD AT is comparable with FreeAT-4 on ImageNet. We set $m = 4$ in FreeAT and LHFAT experiments

Table 2. Comparison results on ImageNet. 2-PGD AT [11]. FreeAT-4 [14]. Ours: our adversarial training method LHFAT, $m = 4$.

Training	Evaluate					Training time (min)
	Clean	PGD-10	PGD-50	PGD-100	CW-100	
Natural	76.15	0	0	0	0	–
2-PGD AT	64.34	31.06	29.84	29.73	34.90	11640.99
FreeAT-4[a]	64.33	30.14	28.88	28.82	34.88	3320.72
YOPO [19]	–	–	–	–	–	–
Ours	**64.94**	**32.58**	**31.19**	**31.13**	**38.07**	**2954.30**

[a] Code at https://github.com/mahyarnajibi/FreeAdversarialTraining

for fair comparison. We train FreeAT for 23 epochs ($\lceil N/m \rceil = 23$). For LHFAT, initial learning rate is $5e - 3$ and decays 10 times at epoch 8 and 16.

Performance Comparison on Imagenet. We evaluate the trained defense models against PGD-10, PGD-50, PGD-100 and CW-100. In Table 2, our proposed approach LHFAT achieves better defense performance compared with 2-PGD AT and FreeAT. For ImageNet experiments, we use pretrained models for adversarial training, so the accelerate ratio is not as high as that on CIFAR-10. It shows that training with LHFAT is about 4 times and 11.03% faster than 2-PGD AT and FreeAT on ImageNet. For YOPO [19], the authors of YOPO did not conduct experiments on ImageNet, so we do not report the results of YOPO in ImageNet experiments. In Fig. 3, Fig. 4 and Fig. 5, Clean, Adv, Noise and l denote clean images, adversarial examples, adversarial noise and distance between clean image and adversarial image, respectively. As shown in Fig. 3 and Fig. 4, we choose two classes (fish and bird) of images in ImageNet validation set and use PGD to attack the trained defense model. It requires larger magnitude adversarial noises to fool the defense model trained with LHFAT than 2-PGD AT, which means that the model trained with LHFAT is more robust than PGD AT.   Considering that the defense performance of PGD AT is better than FreeAT on ImageNet, we make further comparison between PGD AT and our method LHFAT on ImageNet. It requires larger magnitude adversarial noises to fool the defense model trained with LHFAT than 2-PGD AT, which means that the model trained with LHFAT is more robust than PGD AT.

Training Convergence on ImageNet. Figure 6 shows the training process with ResNet50 on ImageNet. X-axis denotes the training time during adversarial training and Y-axis denotes the error rate. LHFAT converges about 4 times faster than 2-PGD AT, which shows that layerwise heuristic learning in LHFAT can accelerate adversarial training.

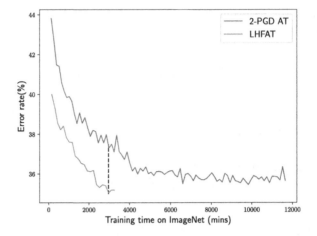

Fig. 6. Training results for 2-PGD AT and LHFAT on ImageNet. It shows that the training convergence of LHFAT is faster than PGD AT.

5 Conclusion

In this paper, we propose LHFAT for accelerating adversarial training. PGD AT is one of the most effective methods for defending against adversarial attacks. But PGD AT needs iterative steps to generate PGD adversarial examples for adversarial training. It increases much computation and time burden. However, LHFAT can mitigate the problems. LHFAT integrates adversary updating with model parameter updating and utilizes layerwise heuristic learning to improve adversarial training. Experiment results show that LHFAT significantly accelerates PGD AT and FreeAT and has better performance.

References

1. Cao, Y., et al.: Adversarial sensor attack on lidar-based perception in autonomous driving. In: CCS, pp. 2267–2281. ACM (2019)
2. Carlini, N., et al.: On evaluating adversarial robustness. CoRR abs/1902.06705 (2019)
3. Deng, J., Dong, W., Socher, R., Li, L., Li, K., Li, F.: ImageNet: a large-scale hierarchical image database. In: CVPR, pp. 248–255. IEEE Computer Society (2009)
4. Goodfellow, I.J., Shlens, J., Szegedy, C.: Explaining and harnessing adversarial examples. In: ICLR (Poster) (2015)
5. Han, S., Mao, H., Dally, W.J.: Deep compression: compressing deep neural networks with pruning, trained quantization and Huffman coding. arXiv preprint arXiv:1510.00149 (2015)
6. He, Y., Zhang, X., Sun, J.: Channel pruning for accelerating very deep neural networks. In: ICCV, pp. 1398–1406. IEEE Computer Society (2017)
7. Hinton, G.E., Vinyals, O., Dean, J.: Distilling the knowledge in a neural network. CoRR abs/1503.02531 (2015)

8. Jia, J., Salem, A., Backes, M., Zhang, Y., Gong, N.Z.: MemGuard: defending against black-box membership inference attacks via adversarial examples. In: CCS, pp. 259–274. ACM (2019)
9. Kurakin, A., Goodfellow, I.J., Bengio, S.: Adversarial examples in the physical world. In: ICLR (Workshop). OpenReview.net (2017)
10. Kurakin, A., Goodfellow, I.J., Bengio, S.: Adversarial machine learning at scale. In: ICLR (Poster). OpenReview.net (2017)
11. Madry, A., Makelov, A., Schmidt, L., Tsipras, D., Vladu, A.: Towards deep learning models resistant to adversarial attacks. In: ICLR (Poster). OpenReview.net (2018)
12. Redmon, J., Farhadi, A.: Yolov3: an incremental improvement. CoRR abs/1804.02767 (2018)
13. Ruder, S.: An overview of gradient descent optimization algorithms. CoRR abs/1609.04747 (2016)
14. Shafahi, A., et al.: Adversarial training for free! In: NeurIPS, pp. 3353–3364 (2019)
15. Szegedy, C., et al.: Intriguing properties of neural networks. In: ICLR (Poster) (2014)
16. Tramèr, F., Kurakin, A., Papernot, N., Goodfellow, I.J., Boneh, D., McDaniel, P.D.: Ensemble adversarial training: attacks and defenses. In: ICLR (Poster). OpenReview.net (2018)
17. Wang, W., Sun, Y., Eriksson, B., Wang, W., Aggarwal, V.: Wide compression: tensor ring nets. In: CVPR, pp. 9329–9338. IEEE Computer Society (2018)
18. Wong, E., Rice, L., Kolter, J.Z.: Fast is better than free: Revisiting adversarial training. In: ICLR. OpenReview.net (2020)
19. Zhang, D., Zhang, T., Lu, Y., Zhu, Z., Dong, B.: You only propagate once: accelerating adversarial training via maximal principle. In: NeurIPS, pp. 227–238 (2019)

Adversarial Attack with KD-Tree Searching on Training Set

Xinghua Guo[1], Fan Jia[2], Jianqiao An[2], and Yahong Han[2]($\boxtimes$)

[1] Nanjing Research Institute of Electronics Engineering (NRIEE), Nanjing, China
[2] College of Intelligence and Computing, and Tianjin Key Lab of Machine Learning,
Tianjin University, Tianjin, China
{kvjia,anjianqiao,yahong}@tju.edu.cn

Abstract. With the emergence of adversarial examples, target detection models based on deep learning have been found to be susceptible to well-designed input samples. Most adversarial examples are imperceptible to humans, but they will purposefully mislead the target detection system to produce various errors. This article provides a new idea of adversarial example generation: a method of adversarial attack based on training set data. In this paper, by establishing the training set KD-tree of the target model, it is used to retrieve the reference image that is closest to the original image and does not belong to the same category. By moving the image closer to the reference image, the purpose of constructing an adversarial example with a stronger attack ability is achieved. We show through experiments that moving the image closer to the training set image that is most similar to it can quickly achieve the attack effect with less disturbance.

Keywords: Adversarial attack · Adversarial example · Deep learning

1   Introduction

In recent studies, machine learning models including deep neural networks have shown high performance in image recognition tasks [1]. However, studies have shown that it is possible to guide any image recognition system to misclassify images by adding some imperceptible disturbances to the image, and this modification is basically indistinguishable by human observers [2].

As shown in Fig. 1, the typical purpose of countering attacks is to add natural disturbances (i.e. fast gradient symbols, fog and noise, etc.) to the image, so that the target model can misidentify the sample, but it is still correctly identified by the human eye.

The current black-box attack methods (such as modified boundary attacks [3]) are mainly to randomly set the starting point to move closer to the original image or add random noise from the original image, which makes it

This work is supported by the NSFC (under Grant 61876130).

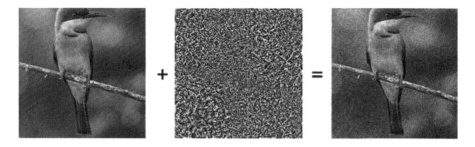

Fig. 1. Diagram of adversarial example generation process.

difficult to determine the direction of the attack. Therefore, the attack requires a large number of iterations and requires a lot of access to the target. Detector, so the required cost is higher [2]. Up to now, black-box attack methods are difficult to determine a specific attack direction at the beginning of the attack. Basically, they are randomly selected and continuously revised during the attack process. Therefore, it is necessary to find a way to determine the effective attack direction to reduce the query cost.

Based on the above reasons, this paper proposes a adversarial attack method based on the training set k-d tree. This method analyzes the training set data of the target detector and establishes the training set k-d tree. For each image to be attacked, the closest reference image in the training set that does not belong to the same category is found through retrieval, and noise is added to make the image to be attacked move closer to the reference image, and the position of the classification box of the detection model is combined to achieve The purpose of constructing a more powerful adversarial example. Since the target detector has a very high accuracy rate for the images in its training set, the attack direction determined by our method must cross at least one decision boundary, and the decision boundary is the closest to the image to be attacked.

The contribution of this method is mainly to provide a new idea to solve the problem that black-box confrontation attacks cannot determine an effective confrontation direction before the attack starts. By retrieving reference images from the training set, our method determines a reliable attack direction and saves the cost of continuously correcting the attack direction for black box attacks. And because the attack direction determined by the attack method in this article is unique for each image, the effect difference is small in repeated experiments. Our method can effectively complete the generation of adversarial examples in a small number of iterations. At the same time, for fast retrieval, we creatively use the data structure of k-d tree to store training set images to speed up retrieval.

2 Related Work

Researchers have done a lot of research on designing different adversarial attack methods to deceive the most advanced deep convolutional networks [4]. Attacks can be roughly classified into three categories:

(1) Gradient-based iterative attacks, such as a series of FGSM variants such as FGSM, I-FGSM, and VR-IGSM.
(2) Iterative attacks based on optimization, such as C&W (Carlini & Wagner)
(3) Attacks based on decision boundary, such as boundary attack.

2.1 Fast Gradient Sign Method (FGSM)

According to the linear characteristics of adversarial examples, as shown in Fig. 2, a practical method for generating adversarial examples using the linear behavior of adversarial examples appears [5].

Fig. 2. Diagram of FGSM's attack process.

The goal of FGSM is to deceive the classification of images by adding an inconspicuous small vector. By taking the sign of the gradient of the loss function related to the feature vector, the elements of the vector are obtained.

$$\eta = \varepsilon * sign(\nabla_x J(\theta, x, y)),\tag{1}$$

$J(\theta, x, y)$ is the cost function of training the neural network, η is the disturbance, θ is the network model parameter, x is the input, and y is the correct classification of the model target. This method can obtain a linear cost function and generate the optimal disturbance as shown in the above formula.

2.2 Optimization-Based Attack (C&W)

Carlini-Wagner introduced a method that can overcome defensive distillation. It proposes three powerful attacks against this latest promising defense algorithm [6]: l_0 attack, l_2 attack, and l_∞ attack. These three attacks showed a 100% success rate when finding adversarial examples on defensive distillation and non-distillation networks.

In order to improve the robustness of any neural network model to adversarial examples [6], defensive distillation technology is adopted. Carlini-Wagner proposed l_0 attack, l_2 attack, and l_∞ attack algorithms. The adversarial examples generated by these algorithms will lead to misclassification of the same label; therefore, they defeat the defensive distillation [7] with a 100% probability.

Carlini-Wagner applied these three attack methods to defensive distillation, proving that there is almost no difference in security between non-distilled networks and distilled networks.

2.3   Hot/Code Attack

Rozsa et al. are based on the idea of changing the input to increase the loss of the classifier, as described in FGSM [5] (see Sect. 4.2). [13] proposed an attack algorithm based on setting the value of the classification logarithm $Z'(x)$. We can then use the gradient relative to the input to push the input to produce the desired logarithm. The logarithm is modified so that the gradient of each category will point in the direction where the network output will increase the probability of the target ("hot") category and decrease the probability of the ground truth ("cold") category.

Intuitively, by maximizing these modified logits using the gradient rise on x, $Z(x)_{(t)}$ will increase (assuming it starts at a positive setpoint), and $Z(x)_y$ will decrease. Correspondingly, since the softmax function increases monotonically with respect to its logit input, the target model will predict the adversarial category with the likelihood $f(x)_{(t)}$, and decrease the likelihood $f(x)_{(y)}$ to predict the true category.

Once $Z'(x)$ is obtained and the gradient direction is extracted with respect to the input x, we use line search and bisecting search to search for the closest counter disturbance x' along these directions like the L-BFGS attack. Similarly, although the original author did not specify it explicitly, since the cold/hot attack is to find the closest opponent through the gradient line search, it will accordingly force the perceived similarity between x' and x according to the L_2 metric.

2.4   Boundary Attack

The boundary attack is an iterative algorithm based on rejection sampling [3], which is initialized at the image in the target class. In each step, the perturbation is sampled from the proposed distribution, thereby reducing the distance from the perturbed image to the original input. If the disturbance image is still in the target class, keep the disturbance. Otherwise, remove the disturbance. The performance of border attacks in image classification is comparable to the latest white box attacks of deep neural networks. However, due to the need for a large number of model queries, its cost is relatively high. In order to obtain a successful adversarial example that humans cannot distinguish, tens of thousands or even hundreds of thousands of model queries are needed [8].

3   Method

This article mainly proposes a method of adversarial example generation based on training set KD-tree.

This method builds a training set k-d tree by analyzing the training set data of the target detector. For each image to be attacked, the closest reference image in the training set that does not belong to the same category is found through retrieval. The image to be attacked is moved closer to the reference image by adding noise, and combined with the location of the classification box of the detection model to construct Adversarial examples with stronger attack capabilities.

The core method of this paper is to find the reference image that is closest to the image to be attacked in the training set. For a test picture, you need to find a picture that is relatively close to it as a reference for radial noise. For the closeness of the two pictures, use the following method to calculate. For an H * W 3-channel (RGB) image, we flatten it into a H * W * 3-dimensional high-dimensional vector, which is called the expansion vector of the original image. The similarity of two pictures is defined as the Euclidean distance of their expansion vectors, that is, the l_2 norm.

The radial noise reference of each picture must ensure that the higher the similarity, the better. We consider finding such a reference picture in the data set. Define the size of the data set as N, that is, the entire data set contains N pictures, and define the expansion vector dimension of a picture as K, that is, $K = H * W * 3$. We need to find a picture with the highest similarity to the original picture from the data set. If we use the method of violent enumeration, each reference image in the enumerated data set has $O(N)$ complexity. For each reference image, the complexity of calculating the Euclidean distance from the original image is $O(K)$. Therefore, the total time complexity is $O(NK)$. Since both N and K have a higher order of magnitude, the enumeration method needs to be further optimized.

We creatively propose to use the data structure of KD-tree to solve this problem. KD-tree (short for k-dimensional tree) [9] is a data structure that divides the K-dimensional data space. Mainly used in the search of key data in multi-dimensional space, such as range search and nearest neighbor search.

The problem to be solved in the method proposed in this paper is the nearest neighbor search, which can be accurately completed with KD-tree.

First, insert the expansion vector (K dimension) of each reference image in the data set into the initialized KD-tree in sequence. There are many ways to select the hyperplane. Therefore, there are many ways to initialize the KD-tree. We take The following method:

(1) With the depth of the tree, the axis is selected in turn as the dividing plane.
(2) The points are distinguished by the median of the axis coordinates of the vertical dividing plane and placed in the subtree.

The KD-tree generated by our method is a balanced binary tree, that is to say, the height of each leaf node is equivalent. Due to its balanced nature, the complexity of querying the nearest point is greatly reduced.

The KD-tree is constructed. For the image X_i to be attacked, the KD-tree is first used to query the training image X of the closest non-same category in $\tilde{X}$:

$$\tilde{X} = \underset{\tilde{X}}{argmin}(\|\tilde{X} - X_i\|_2), \tilde{X} \in Y. \tag{2}$$

We use the following algorithm to query the reference image with the closest Euclidean distance [10] from the original image expansion vector. Each reference image in the data set is regarded as a point in the KD-tree:

First, start from the root node and move down recursively. The method of determining whether to go left or right is the same as the method of inserting elements (if the input point is on the left side of the partition surface, it will enter the left child node, and if it is on the right, it will enter the right child node).

Then once you move to the leaf node, treat that node as the "current best point".

Next, unravel the recursion, and perform the following steps for each passing node:

(a) If the current point is closer to the input point than the current best point, it will be changed to the current best point [11].
(b) Check whether there is a closer point in the subtree on the other side, and if there is, look down from that node.

Finally, when the root node is searched, the nearest neighbor search is completed, and the reference image with the highest similarity is found.

According to the above algorithm, the reference image with the highest similarity to the original image in the data set can be found within $O(n^{2-1/K})$ complexity as a guide for radial noise. Next, we conduct an adversarial attack according to the determined direction: by adding radial and tangential noise, the original image is approached to the nearest base point, knowing that it crosses the decision boundary, and forms an adversarial example.

Construct initial radial noise z^* according to $\tilde{X}$:

$$z_i{}^* \leftarrow \tilde{x} - x_i. \tag{3}$$

Therefore, the initial radial noise is as follow:

$$z^* = \{z_1{}^*, z_2{}^*, \cdots z_n{}^*\}. \tag{4}$$

Then, the disturbance space can be constructed and obtained by randomly sampling the disturbance space, where is the amount of tangential disturbance in the process of adversarial example generation:

$$\eta \sim N(0, z_i{}^{*2}). \tag{5}$$

Algorithm 1. Adversarial attack based KD-tree

Input: Target DNN $F(x)$ and training set $Train$
      Original image X and its label Y
      The corresponding detection frame area U
      Max number of Original image R
      Nearest Neighbor Search Function $searchKNN()$
      Out-of-area noise removal function $detect()$
Output: Adversarial example x^* with compressed noise

1: Construct KD-tree T on the input training set $Train$;
2: **for** i in 1 to R **do**
3:     $x_i \in X, l_i \in Y, t_i = searchKNN(x_i, T)$;
4:     **while** $l_i^* = l_i$ **do**
5:         Get random perturbation $z \sim N(0, 1)$;
6:         Get random perturbation of original image size by linear interpolation $\tilde{z}$
7:         $z^* \longleftarrow \tilde{z} + \mu(x_i^* - x)$
8:         Only add noise to the region U to get a new adversarial example x_i^*
9:         $x_i^* \longleftarrow x_i^* + z^*$
10:       We only take the noise in the region U:
11:       $x_i^* = detect(l_i^*, U)$
12:     **end while**
13: **end for**
14: **return** x^*.

$$\eta = \{\eta_1, \eta_2, \cdots \eta_n\}. \tag{6}$$

Finally, adjust the amount of disturbance in the image detection frame, and generate a new adversarial example x' according to η:

$$x' = x' + T \cdot (\delta \cdot \frac{\eta}{\|\eta\|_2} - \varepsilon \cdot \frac{z^*}{\|z^*\|_2}). \tag{7}$$

δ is the tangential step length, and ε is the radial step length.

4 Experiments

4.1 Dataset Used in the Experiment

This method is tested on the VOC 2007 data set [12], which provides a data set containing 20 types of objects. Each picture is marked, and the marked objects include 20 objects including people, animals (such as cats, dogs, islands, etc.), vehicles (such as cars, boats, airplanes, etc.), and furniture (such as chairs, tables, sofas, etc.) category. VOC2007 contains 9,963 annotated pictures, composed of three parts train/val/test. We selected a total of 2358 images in the training set of a single target.

Fig. 3. Effect map of confrontation attack based on training set KD tree.

4.2   The Result of the Experiment

This method attacks the YOLOv3 target detection system on the VOC 2007 data set. We select 50 images of each category, a total of 1000 images to construct a KD tree, and based on this KD tree to fight the attack, the resulting effect is shown in Fig. 3. The first line in the figure is the original image, and the second line is the detection result of the original image. The third line is the adversarial example, and the fourth line is the test result of the adversarial example. The original image The adversarial example generated after the attack only adds disturbance and noise to the detection frame area, and the magnitude of the change is much smaller than the global change. At the same time, the detection frame of the adversarial example is obviously different from the original image.

At the same time, in order to better demonstrate the attack effect of this method, as shown in Fig. 4, we divide the attack process into four parts for display. The first picture is the starting point, which is the original picture. The last picture is the final adversarial example, and the middle two pictures are the effect pictures of the middle process of the attack. Since the number of attacks on each image is not equal, we have selected two images with the number of attacks being one-third and two-thirds of the total number of attacks for display. It can be seen from the figure that each iteration of the adversarial example has a certain impact on the detector during the generation process, until the decision boundary is crossed and the adversarial example is successfully generated.

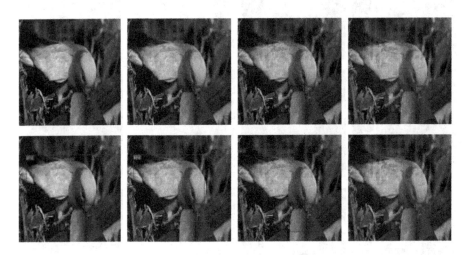

Fig. 4. Diagram of the adversarial attack process based on the KD tree of the training set.

4.3 Performance Evaluation

In order to evaluate the method in this paper quantitatively, we first define the successful adversarial example as the detection result. All the detection frames that contain the center point of the detection frame in the original image detection result are different from the original image.

Based on this standard, we conducted a comparative experiment on the number of images of each type in the training set, where the size of the disturbance was measured by the average L_2 distance between the adversarial example and the original image:

$$L_2 = \sqrt{\sum_{i=1}^{h*w*c} \frac{(x_i - x_i^*)^2}{h * w * c}}, \tag{8}$$

x is the original image, x^* is the adversarial example, and h, w, and c are the height, width and number of channels of the image.

The experiment uses a total of 500 images to attack, and the experimental results are shown in Table 1:

Table 1. Comparison test results of the number of images of each type in the KD tree of the training set.

Number of images	5	10	20	50
Number of iterations	325.622	295.630	272.952	243.556
L2 distance	8.637	8.355	7.836	7.264

With the increase in the number of images of each type in the training set, although the construction cost of the KD-tree increases, the number of attack iterations per image is significantly reduced, and the attack effect is also significantly improved. We used 50 images of each type in the training set to construct the KD-tree, and used boundary attacks for comparison. The experimental results are shown in Table 2. The number of iterations of our method Far smaller than border attacks. At the same time, because our method is a greedy algorithm, the degree of noise compression may be slightly inferior to the boundary attack after 20,000 iterations. But in terms of iteration cost, our method saves a lot of overhead.

Table 2. Experimental results of comparison between adversarial attacks and boundary attacks based on the KD tree of the training set.

Method	Ours	Boundary attack			
Iterations step	243.556	200	300	5000	20000
L2 distance	7.264	36.854	31.956	13.588	6.952

5 Conclusions

This paper proposes an innovative counterattack method based on the KD tree of the training set. Compared with other countermeasures against black box attacks, we only adjust the pixels in the current detection frame for each attack, and at the same time combine the training set with the closest reference image of the training set of the same category. Experiments show that by determining the radial attack direction and moving the image closer to the reference image of the training set that is most similar to it, the attack effect can be achieved in the fastest iterations, and the disturbance generated is also small.

References

1. Qiu, J., Wu, Q., Ding, G., et al.: A survey of machine learning for big data processing. EURASIP J. Adv. Signal Process. **1**, 67 (2016)
2. Ozdag, M.: Adversarial attacks and defenses against deep neural networks: a survey. Procedia Comput. Sci. **140**, 152–161 (2018)
3. Akhtar, N., Mian, A.: Threat of adversarial attacks on deep learning in computer vision: a survey. IEEE Access **6**, 14410–14430 (2018)
4. Kurakin, A., Goodfellow, I.J., et al.: Adversarial machine learning at scale. In: International Conference on Learning Representations (2017)
5. Goodfellow, I.J., Shlens, J., et al.: Explaining and harnessing adversarial examples. In: International Conference on Learning Representations (2015)
6. Papernot, N., McDaniel, P., Wu, X., et al.: Distillation as a defense to adversarial perturbations against deep neural networks. In: IEEE Symposium on Security and Privacy (SP), pp. 582–597. IEEE (2016)
7. Moosavi-Dezfooli, S.M., Fawzi, A., Frossard, P.: DeepFool: a simple and accurate method to fool deep neural networks. In: Proceedings of the IEEE Conference on Computer Vision and Pattern Recognition, pp. 2574–2582 (2016)
8. Hinton, G., Vinyals, O., Dean, J.: Distilling the knowledge in a neural network. Comput. Sci. **14**(7), 38–39 (2015)
9. Bentley, L.J.: Multidimensional binary search trees used for associative searching. Commun. ACM **18**(9), 509–517 (1975)
10. Xu, W., Evans, D., Qi, Y.: Feature squeezing: detecting adversarial examples in deep neural networks. In: Network and Distributed System Security Symposium (2018)
11. Meng, D., Chen, H.: MagNet: a two-pronged defense against adversarial examples. In: Proceedings of the 2017 ACM SIGSAC Conference on Computer and Communications Security, pp. 135–147 (2017)
12. Papernot, N., Mcdaniel, P., Goodfellow, I.: Transferability in machine learning: from phenomena to black-box attacks using adversarial samples (2016)
13. Rozsa, A., Rudd, E.M., Boult, T.E.: Adversarial diversity and hard positive generation. CoRR, vol. abs/1605.01775 (2016)

Mixup Without Hesitation

Hao Yu, Huanyu Wang, and Jianxin Wu$^{(\boxtimes)}$

State Key Laboratory for Novel Software Technology, Nanjing University,
Nanjing, China
wujx2001@nju.edu.cn

Abstract. Mixup linearly interpolates pairs of examples to form new
samples, which has been shown to be effective in image classification
tasks. However, there are two drawbacks in mixup: one is that more training epochs are needed to obtain a well-trained model; the other is that
mixup requires tuning a hyper-parameter to gain appropriate capacity.
In this paper, we find that mixup constantly explores the representation
space, and inspired by the exploration-exploitation dilemma, we propose mixup Without hesitation (mWh), a concise and effective training
algorithm. We show that mWh strikes a good balance between exploration and exploitation by gradually replacing mixup with basic data
augmentation. It can achieve a strong baseline with less training time
than original mixup and without searching for optimal hyper-parameter,
i.e., mWh acts as mixup without hesitation.

Keywords: Deep learning · Mixup · Exploration-exploitation dilemma

1 Introduction

Deep learning has made great breakthroughs in various computer vision problems such as image classification [4] and object detection [11]. However, requiring
lots of training data is the well-known drawback of deep learning, and data augmentation methods have partially alleviated this difficulty.

In particular, mixup, proposed by Zhang et al. [18], is based on virtual examples created by linearly interpolating two random samples and their corresponding labels, i.e.,

$$\begin{aligned}
\tilde{x} &= \lambda x_i + (1 - \lambda)x_j \\
\tilde{y} &= \lambda y_i + (1 - \lambda)y_j
\end{aligned} \tag{1}$$

where x_i and x_j are two data samples, and y_i and y_j are their labels. The mixing
coefficient λ is sampled from a beta distribution $\mathbf{Beta}(\alpha, \alpha)$. Mixup allows deep
learning models to train on a large number of virtual examples resulting from the
random combination, and the standard cross-entropy loss is calculated on the
soft-labels $\tilde{y}$ instead of hard labels. In general, mixup raises the generalization
of deep neural networks significantly, especially on small datasets [13].

However, it is also well-known that mixup suffers from slow convergence and
requires a sophisticated selection of the hyper-parameter α. In detail,

© Springer Nature Switzerland AG 2021
Y. Peng et al. (Eds.): ICIG 2021, LNCS 12889, pp. 143–154, 2021.
https://doi.org/10.1007/978-3-030-87358-5_12

- Mixup requires more epochs to converge. Since it explores more regions of the data space, longer training is required, e.g., it takes 200 epochs to train ResNet-50 on ImageNet with mixup, but a normal training routine of 90 epochs is sufficient [18]. Note that this observation not only exists in mixup, but can also be found in other data augmentation methods that strongly increase the complexity of training data [2,17].
- Mixup requires an α value to sample mixing coefficients. Different α values usually lead to big differences in model accuracy. Zhang et al. [18] mentioned that mixup improves performance better when $\alpha \in [0.1, 0.4]$, and larger α may cause underfitting. However, α greater than 1 tends to perform better in some cases [13]. In other words, the generalization ability of mixup is heavily affected by hyper-parameter selection, but choosing a suitable α is quite difficult.

In order to solve both difficulties, we propose mWh, which stands for **m**ixup **W**ithout **h**esitation (mWh). Instead of using mixup to augment data throughout the entire model training process, mWh accelerates mixup by periodically turning the mixing operation off, which also makes it robust to the hyper-parameter α. The contributions of mWh are:

- Through carefully designed experiments and observations, we show that mixup attains its accuracy improvement through boldly *exploring* the representation space. Basic data augmentation (e.g., flipping and cropping) focuses more on *exploiting* the space. Hence, mWh strikes a good exploration-exploitation trade-off, and achieves both high accuracy and training speed.
- We gain new benchmarks of image classification consistently. Regardless of whether epochs are doubled or not, mWh performs better than mixup.
- mWh is robust with respect to α. With a default α value, mWh performs consistently well in a variety of computer vision tasks.

2   Related Work

First, we briefly review data augmentation methods and the related works that inspired this paper.

One of the important problems in computer vision is training with a small amount of data, as deep learning models often overfit with small datasets. Data augmentation is a family of techniques to solve this difficulty, and basic data augmentation methods, such as horizontal reflection, rotation and rescaling, have been widely applied to many tasks and often boost the model accuracy. Mixup can be regarded as a kind of data augmentation method and it often enhances the generalization performance of CNNs. Mixup can also ease the over-confident prediction problem for deep neural networks [13]. Similar interpolation can be applied in semi-supervised learning [1] and model adversarial robustness [10] and domain adaptation [16]. Manifold mixup [14] shares similarities with mixup. It trains neural networks on linear combinations of hidden representations of training examples.

Apart from mixup, some novel data augmentation methods have recently been proposed, too. Some data augmentation approaches are based on searching, like AutoAugment [3] and Fast AutoAugment [9]. AutoAugment designs a search space to combine various data augmentation strategies to form a policy, but the whole search algorithm is very computationally demanding. Cutout [5] randomly masks out square regions of an input image during training. GridMask [2] improves the existing information dropping algorithms. Similar to mixup, CutMix [17] also involves two training samples: it cuts one image patch and pastes it to another training image. He et al. [6] analyze the distribution gap between clean and augmented data. They preserve the standard data augmentation and refine the model with 50 epochs after training DNNs with mixup.

Note that these elaborate methods change the original images significantly, and almost always elongate the training process, e.g., in Manifold mixup, Verma et al. [14] trained PreAct ResNet-18 for 2000 epochs in CIFAR-10 and CIFAR-100, but 100 epochs of training will be enough without Manifold mixup. CutMix and GridMask also need careful hyper-parameter selection. Although they often achieve higher accuracy than basic data augmentation, more training epochs lead to significantly inflated financial and environmental costs, which is the common and significant drawback of mixup and these methods. Hence, we propose mWh to solve this dilemma. Its goal is to achieve higher accuracy even without many epochs or hyper-parameter selection.

3   Mixup Without Hesitation (mWh)

We propose mWh in this section. First, we analyze the effect of mixup training and reveal its property. Then we propose mixup Without hesitation (mWh), a simple plug-and-play training strategy. Finally, we study the role of every stage as well as the influence of hyper-parameters in mWh.

3.1   Observations

We investigate the role mixup plays during training, and demonstrate that with *the combination of mixup and basic data augmentation*, mWh has the potential to retain the accuracy improvement brought by mixup, too.

Training neural networks involves finding minima of a high-dimensional non-convex loss function, which can be visualized as an energy landscape. Since mixup generates more uncertain data, it enlarges the sample representation space significantly, and *explores* more potential energy landscapes, so the optimization method can find a better locally optimal solution. However, the side effect of mixup is that it also brings instability during the training process. We trained PreAct ResNet-18 on CIFAR-10, and as Fig. 1 showed, we have two observations from the curves. The first one is: with mixup, the loss oscillates constantly on the original test dataset, but if the model is trained on the clean data, the curves are smoother. This phenomenon suggests that compared with basic data augmentation, mixup introduces higher uncertainty in the training process. The

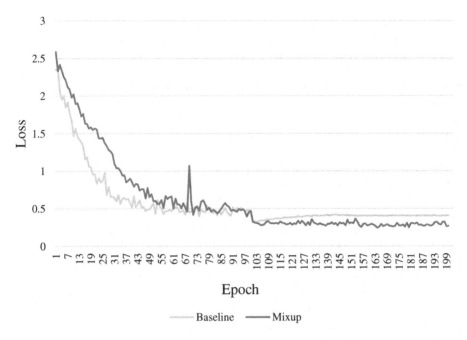

Fig. 1. Cross-entropy loss on the CIFAR-10 *test* set. We used PreAct ResNet-18 and $\alpha = 0.5$.

second one is: in the early training stage, mixup enlarges the test loss, which indicates it focuses on exploring the energy landscapes and will not fall into local optima prematurely.

However, in the later training stages, since the model gets closer to convergence, exploration must not be the main goal. Instead, we should switch to *exploiting* the current state using *basic data augmentation*. Results in Table 1 validate our motivations. We train PreAct ResNet-18 on CIFAR-100 with 100 epochs and set α as 1.0. The result demonstrates that using mixup only in the first 50 epochs is better. Hence, we conjecture that *mixup is effective because it actively explores the search space in the early epochs, while in the later epochs, mixup might be harmful.*

But, if we directly apply basic data augmentation after a model is trained with mixup [6], this refinement operation may end up with overfitting. We trained PreAct ResNet-18 with 200 epochs in CIFAR-10 and Tiny-ImageNet-200 with mixup, and refine the model with 25 epochs without mixup. Learning rate starts at 0.1 and is divided by 10 after 100 and 150 epochs, and we set the learning rate to be the same as that in the final epochs of the last stage during refinement. The results are shown in Table 2. We can observe that accuracy decreased after refinement, which indicates the number of refining epochs is difficult to control, and refining may lead to overfitting. Putting our observations and conjectures together, we propose to *gradually replace mixup with basic data*

Table 1. Accuracy (%) on CIFAR-100. Baseline means we train the model with basic data augmentation. Mixup means we apply mixup throughout the training process. First Half Mixup means the first half of epochs apply mixup but the last do not, and similarly, Second Half Mixup means we only apply mixup in the second half of epochs.

Methods	Top1	Top5
Baseline	74.20	92.53
Mixup	75.25	92.40
First Half Mixup	**75.87**	**93.10**
Second Half Mixup	72.50	91.04

Table 2. Accuracy (%) on PreAct ResNet-18, $\alpha = 0.5$.

Datasets	Mixup	+Refinement
CIFAR-10	**95.46**	95.30
Tiny-ImageNet-200	**60.73**	60.21

augmentation such that the learning algorithm gradually switches from exploration to exploitation, which is a good strategy to solve the *exploration-exploitation dilemma* [12] in our context.

3.2 Algorithm

The mWh algorithm is in Algorithm 1. We use a mini-batch instead of an epoch as the unit of execution. We denote the total number of mini-batches as m, and use two hyper-parameters p and q ($0 \leq p < q \leq 1$) to divide the whole training process into three stages, i.e.,

- First stage: from 1 to pm mini-batches, we train with mixup. Note that here we assume pm is an integer.
- Second stage: from $pm + 1$ to qm mini-batches, we alternate between mixup and basic data augmentation. If the last mini-batch does not apply mixup, the next one will, and vice versa.
- Third stage: from $qm + 1$ mini-batches to the end, we run mixup with probability ϵ, where ϵ decreases *linearly* from 1 to 0.

In the first stage, mWh lets the model explore a large portion of the sample representation space by consistently applying mixup.

The second stage is an exploration-exploitation trade-off. We periodically turn mixup on and off to avoid getting trapped in a local optimum prematurely. When we turn mixup off, the model will exploit the limited and promising region of the sample representation space with the hope of accelerating convergences. When we turn mixup on, the model will keep exploring more energy landscapes.

In the third stage, we gradually switch to exploitation, which is inspired by the ϵ-greedy algorithm [12]. We define an exploration rate ϵ that is initially set

---

Algorithm 1: The mWh Training Algorithm

Input: Training dataset $(\mathcal{X}, \mathcal{Y})$, number of training mini-batches m, two
       parameters p and q satisfying $(0 \leq p < q \leq 1)$, Beta distribution
       parameter α for mixup.

1   **for** $i = 1$ *to* m **do**
2   Draw a mini-batch (x_b, y_b).
3   **if** $i \leq pm$ **then**   *// First stage*
4          $(\tilde{x}_b, \tilde{y}_b) = \text{mixup}(x_b, y_b, \alpha)$
5   **else if** $i \leq qm$ **then**   *// Second stage*
6   **if** i is even **then**
7              $(\tilde{x}_b, \tilde{y}_b) = \text{mixup}(x_b, y_b, \alpha)$
8   **else**
9              $(\tilde{x}_b, \tilde{y}_b) = \text{basic\_augmentation}(x_b, y_b)$
10   **end if**
11   **else**   *// Third stage*
12         $\epsilon = \frac{m-i}{m(1-q)}$
13   Randomly generate threshold $\theta \in [0,1]$.
14   **if** $\theta < \epsilon$ **then**
15             $(\tilde{x}_b, \tilde{y}_b) = \text{mixup}(x_b, y_b, \alpha)$
16   **else**
17             $(\tilde{x}_b, \tilde{y}_b) = \text{basic\_augmentation}(x_b, y_b)$
18   **end if**
19   **end if**
20   Train model with mini-batch $(\tilde{x}_b, \tilde{y}_b)$.
21 **end for**

---

to 1. This rate is the probability that our model will use mixup. As ϵ decreases gradually, the model tends to choose exploitation rather than exploration.

Finding suitable values of p and q is essential. Note that we expect mWh to be robust and insensitive to hyper-parameters. Hence, we want to fix p and q in *all* experiments. Here we train ResNet-50 on ImageNet with 100 epochs and study the effect of different p and q. In these experiments, the default learning rate is 0.1 with a linear warmup for the first 5 epochs and divided by 10 after training 30, 60, 90 epochs. We set batch size to 256. In Table 3, we set q as 0.9 and explore the impact of different q. We also fix p as 0.6 and research the effect of q in Table 4. Especially, when q is equal to 1.0, we remove the third stage in mWh, and similarly, when q is 0.6, we apply the ϵ-greedy algorithm after the mini-batches of 60%. Based on our experimental results, although choosing different p and q does not have a significant effect on the outcome, 0.6 and 0.9 are a reasonable choice, so we always set $p = 0.6$ and $q = 0.9$.

Now we validate our framework by an ablation study on ImageNet. We train ResNet-50 on ImageNet with 100 epochs and set α as 0.5. All experiments apply mixup in the top 60% mini-batches. Table 5 contains several results and we try different strategies in Stage 2 and Stage 3. Different rows represent using different strategies to train the model. In particular, none indicates we apply basic data

Table 3. The influence of p on ImageNet.

p	0.5	0.6	0.7	0.8	0.9
$\alpha = 0.2$	**76.952**	76.948	76.814	76.856	76.894
$\alpha = 0.5$	76.782	76.854	**76.964**	76.754	76.736

Table 4. The influence of q on ImageNet.

q	0.6	0.7	0.8	0.9	1.0
$\alpha = 0.2$	76.854	76.814	76.792	**76.948**	76.742
$\alpha = 0.5$	76.792	**76.942**	76.894	76.854	76.716

Table 5. Accuracy (%) of ResNet-50 trained on ImageNet.

Stage 2	Stage 3	Top1	Top5
None	None	76.756	93.314
mixup	None	76.770	93.478
mixup	mixup	76.212	93.246
mixup	mWh	76.832	**93.504**
mWh	None	76.772	93.428
mWh	mixup	76.388	93.304
mWh	mWh	**76.854**	93.463

augmentation. When we apply mWh at Stage 2, it refers to the alternating of mixup and basic data augmentation between the mini-batches of 60 to 90%. Using mWh at Stage 3 means running mixup with a probability of ϵ in the final 10% of the mini-batches.

From Table 5, we can find no matter at what stage, applying mWh instead of mixup leads to higher accuracy. Especially, mixup reduces the performance of the model in Stage 3, which coincides well with results in Table 1 and our conjecture (mixup is harmful in later epochs). These results verify the effectiveness of our framework. Note that those results do not mean that our 3 stages setting is the best, maybe four stages or cosine decaying chance strategy performs better in some experimental results. After all, our contribution is a working algorithm that meets our goal (attain mixup accuracy with fewer epochs and insensitive to alpha).

4   Experiments

In this section, we evaluate the performance of mWh. We first conduct experiments to validate the effectiveness of mWh on four benchmark classification datasets. For a fair comparison, mWh used the same random seed as mixup. Then we show its transferability in CutMix [17]. The parameters p and q are always set to 0.6 and 0.9. All our experiments are conducted by PyTorch.

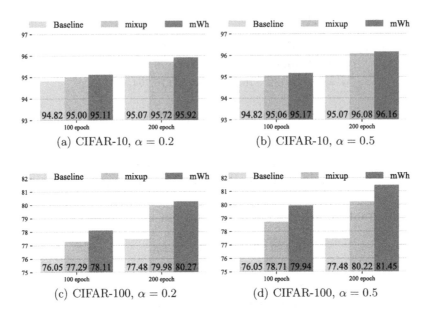

Fig. 2. Accuracy (%) on CIFAR-10, CIFAR-100 using mixup and mWh.

4.1   Experiments on Image Classification Tasks

First we will show the results on four small-scale datasets, i.e., CIFAR-10, CIFAR-100 [8] and CUB-200 [15]. Then the results on ImageNet will be presented.

We want to show that without doubled epochs and tuning hyper-parameters we can still get better performance in all datasets, so we follow the setting of Zhang et al. [18] but halve the training epochs. We also set α to 0.2 and 0.5 to illustrate mWh is robust to hyper-parameter selection. To further show the validity of mWh, we double the epochs and report the results, although it is not our primary focus.

Datasets: CIFAR-10 and CIFAR-100 [8] both consist of 50k training and 10k test images at 32×32 resolution. CIFAR-10 contains 5k training and 1k test images per class in a total of 10 classes, and CIFAR-100 has 100 classes containing 600 images each. For the CUB-200, it contains 200 categories of birds with 5,994 training and 5,794 testing images. The large-scale ImageNet ILSVRC-12 dataset consists of 1.28M training and 50K validation images of various resolutions.

Implementation Details: For CIFAR-10 and CIFAR-100, to provide a strong baseline we train DenseNet-121 [7] with the mini-batch size of 128 for 100 epochs. Learning rate starts at 0.1 and is divided by 10 after 50 and 75 epochs. Note that we also conduct experiments to double the epoch, i.e., we train the model with 200 epochs, and divide the learning rate by 10 after 100 and 150 epochs.

Table 6. Accuracy (%) on CUB-200. The first two groups of experiments are about training ResNet-18 from scratch and the rest are the fine-tuning experiments.

Method	$\alpha = 0.2$		$\alpha = 0.5$	
	Epochs	Accuracy	Epochs	Accuracy
Baseline	350	64.308	350	64.308
mixup	350	66.672	350	68.347
mWh	350	**67.535**	350	**70.297**
Baseline	175	62.858	175	62.858
mixup	175	**63.704**	175	64.118
mWh	175	**63.704**	175	**65.948**
Baseline	300	77.080	300	77.080
mixup	300	78.650	300	78.391
mWh	300	**79.272**	300	**79.185**
Baseline	150	76.345	150	76.345
mixup	150	78.236	150	78.219
mWh	150	**78.357**	150	**78.840**

For CUB-200, we use ResNet-18 and crop 224 * 224 patches as input images for training. For fair comparisons, we evaluate the strategy of training from scratch and fining tune. For training from scratch, we set the number of training epochs to be 175 and 300, and initialize the learning rate as 0.1, batch size as 32. A smoother cosine learning rate adjustment is applied. For fine-tuning, we train the model with 150 and 300 epochs. We set the learning rate as 0.001, batch size as 32. We also use a cosine schedule to scale the learning rate. The initialization ResNet-18 model is downloaded from the PyTorch official website.

To provide further evidence about the quality of representations learned with mWh, we evaluate it on ImageNet. We train ResNet-50 from scratch. For faster convergence we use NVIDIA's mixed-precision training code base with batch size 2048. The default learning rate is $0.1 * \frac{\text{batch size}}{256}$ with a linear warmup for the first 5 epochs and divided by 10 after training $30, 60, 90$ epochs when training 100 epochs, or after $60, 120$ and 180 epochs when training 200 epochs. We first randomly crop a patch from the original image and then resize the patch to the target size (224 * 224). Finally, the patch is horizontally flipped with a probability of 0.5.

Results: For CIFAR-10 and CIFAR-100, we summarize the results in Fig. 2. mWh consistently outperforms mixup and the baseline. And, mWh with 100 epochs consistently outperforms baseline with even 200 epochs. Note that on CIFAR-100, with a higher α, mWh boosts more accuracy. We think the reason is that the difference between the augmented data and the original data will be greater because of a higher α, so the empirical risk will decrease more after introducing basic data augmentation. This indicates mWh will bring more improvement with larger α, and this situation is particularly noticeable on more complex datasets.

Table 7. Accuracy (%) on ImageNet with ResNet-50.

Method	$\alpha = 0.2$		$\alpha = 0.5$	
	Epochs	Accuracy	Epochs	Accuracy
Baseline	200	76.392	200	76.392
mixup	200	**77.148**	200	77.838
mWh	200	77.098	200	**77.888**
Baseline	100	76.043	100	76.043
mixup	100	76.718	100	76.212
mWh	100	**76.948**	100	**76.854**

Table 6 shows the results on CUB-200, and similar to the previous experiments, we observe mWh is highly competitive when compared with mixup. When jointly applying mixup and basic data augmentation, mWh obtains the lowest Top-1 error in both training from scratch and fining tune.

Table 7 demonstrates the validation accuracy rates on the ImageNet dataset. mWh outperforms (or is on par with) mixup, mWh also exhibits its robustness to the hyper-parameter α. In the 100 epochs case, although mixup is effective when $\alpha = 0.2$, it is not effective when $\alpha = 0.5$ (only improves 0.169% over the baseline). However, mWh is consistently effective for different α values.

As the results have shown, mWh achieves the state-of-the-art performance when halving the epochs, and without deliberately selecting α we can still gain consistently better performance than mixup. Although mWh's goal is not to gain improvement with more epochs, our results show that mWh performs better than mixup when training time is doubled. These results indicate that without doubling epochs and selecting optimal α, mWh can still perform very well. The fact that with more epochs mWh performs better than mixup is a nice byproduct.

4.2   Transferability in CutMix

In order to provide insights into what makes mWh successful, we further study the transferability of mWh in CutMix. We examine the effect of mWh in CutMix for the image classification tasks.

Implementation Details: All of our following experiments share the same setting with previous ones. We train our strategy in CIFAR-10 and CIFAR-100. Note that different from mixup, we select α as 1 instead of 0.2. It is because according to the recommendation of Yun et al. [17], choosing α as 1.0 will achieve better performance. For providing strong baselines we set α to 1.0 and 0.5.

Results: The results of CutMix with mWh in CIFAR-10 and CIFAR-100 are shown in Fig. 3. mWh also brings considerable improvement, which proves the validity of our algorithm.

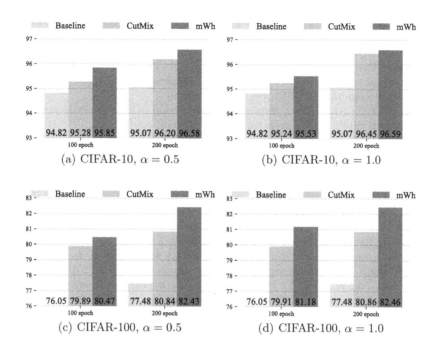

Fig. 3. Accuracy (%) on CIFAR-10, CIFAR-100 using CutMix and mWh in CutMix.

5   Discussion and Conclusion

In this paper, we proposed mixup Without hesitation (mWh), a simple but general training policy for effective training. We apply the strategy of reintroducing basic data augmentation to balance exploration and exploitation. Experimental results showed that mWh improves the convergence rate of various dataset instances and is robust to the hyper-parameter selection. It also gains remarkable improvement in different tasks and models compared with the baseline.

Many data augmentation algorithms used in computer vision have similar features as mixup. Therefore, One interesting future work is to extend the proposed algorithm to other augmentation algorithms.

Acknowledgements. This research was partially supported by the National Natural Science Foundation of China (61772256).

References

1. Berthelot, D., Carlini, N., Goodfellow, I., Papernot, N., Oliver, A., Raffel, C.A.: MixMatch: a holistic approach to semi-supervised learning. In: Advances in Neural Information Processing Systems, vol. 32, pp. 5049–5059 (2019)
2. Chen, P.: GridMask data augmentation. arXiv preprint arXiv:2001.04086 (2020)

3. Cubuk, E.D., Zoph, B., Mane, D., Vasudevan, V., Le, Q.V.: AutoAugment: learning augmentation strategies from data. In: The IEEE Conference on Computer Vision and Pattern Recognition (CVPR), pp. 113–123 (2019)

4. Deng, J., Dong, W., Socher, R., Li, L.J., Li, K., Fei-Fei, L.: ImageNet: a large-scale hierarchical image database. In: The IEEE Conference on Computer Vision and Pattern Recognition (CVPR), pp. 248–255 (2009)

5. DeVries, T., Taylor, G.W.: Improved regularization of convolutional neural networks with cutout. arXiv preprint arXiv:1708.04552 (2017)

6. He, Z., Xie, L., Chen, X., Zhang, Y., Wang, Y., Tian, Q.: Data augmentation revisited: rethinking the distribution gap between clean and augmented data. arXiv preprint arXiv:1909.09148 (2019)

7. Huang, G., Liu, Z., Van Der Maaten, L., Weinberger, K.Q.: Densely connected convolutional networks. In: The IEEE Conference on Computer Vision and Pattern Recognition (CVPR), pp. 4700–4708 (2017)

8. Krizhevsky, A., Hinton, G.: Learning multiple layers of features from tiny images. Technical Report, University of Toronto (2009)

9. Lim, S., Kim, I., Kim, T., Kim, C., Kim, S.: Fast AutoAugment. In: Advances in Neural Information Processing Systems, vol. 32, pp. 6662–6672 (2019)

10. Pang, T., Xu, K., Zhu, J.: Mixup inference: better exploiting mixup to defend adversarial attacks. In: International Conference on Learning Representations, ICLR (2019)

11. Ren, S., He, K., Girshick, R., Sun, J.: Faster R-CNN: towards real-time object detection with region proposal networks. In: Advances in Neural Information Processing Systems, vol. 28, pp. 91–99 (2015)

12. Sutton, R.S., Barto, A.G.: Reinforcement Learning: An Introduction, 2nd edn. MIT Press, Cambridge (2018)

13. Thulasidasan, S., Chennupati, G., Bilmes, J.A., Bhattacharya, T., Michalak, S.: On mixup training: improved calibration and predictive uncertainty for deep neural networks. In: Advances in Neural Information Processing Systems, vol. 32, pp. 13888–13899 (2019)

14. Verma, V., et al.: Manifold mixup: better representations by interpolating hidden states. In: International Conference on Machine Learning, pp. 6438–6447 (2019)

15. Welinder, P., et al.: Caltech-UCSD birds 200. Technical Report, California Institute of Technology (2010)

16. Xu, M., et al.: Adversarial domain adaptation with domain mixup. In: Proceedings of the AAAI Conference on Artificial Intelligence, pp. 6502–6509 (2020)

17. Yun, S., Han, D., Oh, S.J., Chun, S., Choe, J., Yoo, Y.: CutMix: regularization strategy to train strong classifiers with localizable features. In: Proceedings of the IEEE International Conference on Computer Vision, pp. 6023–6032 (2019)

18. Zhang, H., Cisse, M., Dauphin, Y.N., Lopez-Paz, D.: mixup: beyond empirical risk minimization. In: International Conference on Learning Representations, ICLR (2018)

An LDA and RBF-SVM Based Classification Method for Inertinite Macerals of Coal

Zihan Xue[1], Jing Cao[1], Peizhen Wang[1,3(✉)], Zihuan Yin[1], and Dailin Zhang[2]

[1] School of Electrical and Information Engineering, Anhui University of Technology,
Maanshan 243032, China
pzhwang@ahut.edu.cn
[2] Anhui Key Laboratory of Clean Conversion and Utilization,
Anhui University of Technology, Maanshan 243032, China
[3] Key Laboratory of Metallurgical Emission Reduction and Resources Recycling,
Ministry of Education, Anhui University of Technology, Maanshan 243032, China

Abstract. In view of the complicacy and the diversity of inertinite macerals of coal, a classification method based on linear discriminate analysis (LDA) and support vector machine (SVM) is proposed. Firstly, according to differences of texture and intensity among macerals, inertinite macerals are represented with texture related features as energy, entropy, moment, local smooth and intensity related features as contrast, mean, standard deviation, 3-order moment deviation. Then, by using LDA, the initial features are further extracted by means of maximizing the inter-class dispersion as well as minimizing intra-class scatter. Finally, a classifier based on SVM with radial basis function (RBF-SVM) is built for the automatic classification of inertinite macerals. Experimental results show that, textures employed in this paper can present inertinite macerals effectively; with LDA and RBF-SVM, the dimension of feature space is reduced and the accuracy of classification is increased obviously.

Keywords: Coal · Inertinite · Texture · Linear discriminant analysis · Support vector machine · Classification

1 Introduction

The performance of coal plays an important role in clean coal combustion, coking and gasification. Research shows that the microstructure of coal is related to its adsorption properties of CO, thermal crushing properties, cohesiveness, coal water slurry properties [1–3]. Therefore, it is of significance for the comprehensive utilization of coal by study the properties of coal from the microstructure level. In view of the time-consuming, heavy workload and the unavoidably subjective of the conventional manual and semi-manual method of macerals analysis, in recent years, methods of image processing are employed to analyze the macerals of coal. Mlynarczuk *et al.* [4] used the nearest neighbor method (NN), the k-nearest neighbor method (kNN) and the multilayer perceptron (MLP) to identify the

© Springer Nature Switzerland AG 2021
Y. Peng et al. (Eds.): ICIG 2021, LNCS 12889, pp. 155–166, 2021.
https://doi.org/10.1007/978-3-030-87358-5_13

maceral groups of coal, namely vitrinite, inertinite and liptinite, and also tried
to identify some non-organic minerals. Wang *et al.* [5] combined texture features
from local binary pattern (LBP) and gray level co-occurrence matrix to identify
the three major groups of coal maceral. However, they haven't implemented a
deeper identification of macerals within groups.

Inertinite is one of the important groups of coal macerals. For its complex
structure, Wang *et al.* [6,7] proposed an outline extraction method of the maceral area with structural elements and a visual clustering method to segment
regions of macerals. Grey level co-occurrence matrix, Tamura, contourlet transform, multifractal spectrum were also employed by the author's research group
in the previous work [8–11] to describe features of these macerals, but none of
these techniques can characterize them perfectly, especially for the features of
texture, owing to the complex structure of them and there are similar morphological features between some different macerals, and also there is a correlation
between them. If these features are combined simply for classification, it will
result in redundancy of feature information and high dimensionality of feature
space, which will increase the computation and reduce the accuracy of classification. Linear discriminate analysis (LDA) [12–14] is an effective method to select
features. It can not only reduce the dimension of feature space but also remain
the main information of training samples from the initial features extracted from
the microscopic image of coal. In the lower dimensional feature space, the inter-
class distance is maximized while the intra-class distance is minimized. So, LDA
is employed in this paper for the further extraction of initial features. Considering the limit of sample number of inertinite samples, and in order to obtain
higher classification accuracy in the low-dimensional space, a classifier is built
with support vector machine (SVM), which is suitable for small samples.

2   The Selection of Initial Features

The feature is the original property of an image. It can be a natural feature of
the direct perception of biological vision, or abstract features obtained by mathematical measurement transformation, including features of geometric, texture,
and so on.

2.1   Characteristic Analysis of Microscopic Image of Inertinite

Inertinite group of coal macerals mainly comes from woody fiber of plant or
remains fungus. They can be classified into eight typical categories of cribriform
fusinite, stellate fusinite, semifusinite, secretinite, funginite, macrinite, inertodetrinite and micrinite. In this paper, the microscopic images are obtained by
optical microscopy under oil immersion reflected light. Some typical microscopic
images of inertinite macerals are shown in Fig. 1.

From the typical microscopic images, it is not difficult to find that, macerals
of inertinite show different structures of striped, granular, reticular, circular or
other seemingly random but certain spatial distribution of the regular. The texture is one of the effective means to describe these complex surface structures

and boundary morphology of an image. Besides, there are distinct differences of brightness, namely gray level, between some of different macerals. In this paper, texture based features and gray level based features are selected as initial features to describe the characteristic of macerals within inertinite.

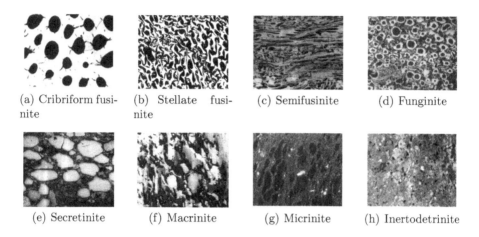

(a) Cribriform fusi-nite

(b) Stellate fusi-nite

(c) Semifusinite

(d) Funginite

(e) Secretinite

(f) Macrinite

(g) Micrinite

(h) Inertodetrinite

Fig. 1. Typical microscopic images of inertinite macerals

2.2 Texture Feature Extraction

We employ the gray level co-occurrence matrix based feature such as energy, entropy, moment of inertia and local stationary to describe the texture characteristic of macerals of inertinite.

The gray level co-occurrence matrix is based on the second-order conditional probability density of the image. For an image $f(x, y)$ with $A \times B$ pixels, each element (i, j) in the corresponding gray level co-occurrence matrix describes the frequencies of a pair of pixels with gray values i and j in the image of direction θ and distance l, marked as $P(i, j | l, \theta)$.

Based on the gray level co-occurrence matrix, the following five main feature parameters are defined.

(1) Energy

$$E = \sum_{i=0}^{L-1} \sum_{j=0}^{L-1} P^2(i, j | l, \theta) \tag{1}$$

where L denotes the gray level of the image. The energy mainly reflects the uniformity of the gray distribution and the degree of thickness of the texture.

(2) Entropy

$$H = - \sum_{i=0}^{L-1} \sum_{j=0}^{L-1} P(i, j | l, \theta) \lg P(i, j | l, \theta) \tag{2}$$

Entropy represents the amount of information contained in an image. It is used to describe the degree of non-uniform of the texture.

(3) Moment

$$I = \sum_{i=0}^{L-1}\sum_{j=0}^{L-1}(i-j)^2 P(i,j|l,\theta) \tag{3}$$

The moment is used to evaluate the gray-scale variation of the image. The finer the texture, the greater the moment.

(4) Local stationary

$$J = \sum_{i=0}^{L-1}\sum_{j=0}^{L-1}\frac{1}{1+(i-j)^2}P(i,j|l,\theta) \tag{4}$$

It measures the local variation of the texture, and the higher the value, the higher the local uniformity of the texture.

(5) Maximum probability

$$P_{\max} = \max\left[\frac{P(i,j|l,\theta)}{\sum_{i=0}^{L-1}\sum_{j=0}^{L-1}P(i,j|l,\theta)}\right] \tag{5}$$

It measures the percentage of cells with the highest number of occurrences of the texture.

2.3   Gray Level Distribution Based Feature Extraction

Brightness is one of the important basis for the manual distinguishment of macerals. To this end, some feature parameters are defined.

(1) Brightness ratio

$$g = \frac{\sum_{i\geq e}^{i\leq L-1}h(i)}{\sum_{i=0}^{L-1}h(i)} \tag{6}$$

where $h(i)$ represents the number of pixels whose gray value is i, and e is the gray level threshold. It is the ratio of the number of pixels within a set range to the total number of pixels of the image, which can reflect the relative brightness difference of different macerals and avoid the influence of the imaging light source.

(2) Mean

$$\mu = \sum_{i=0}^{L-1}ip(i) \tag{7}$$

where $p(i)$ is the probability of pixels with gray value i. It reflects the mean brightness of the image.

(3) Variance

$$\sigma = \sqrt{\sum_{i=0}^{L-1}(i-\mu)^2 p(i)} \tag{8}$$

It measures the deviation extent of gray values of pixels from the mean. In a way, it reflects the contrast of an image.

(4) 3-order moment deviation

$$\alpha = \frac{1}{\sigma^3}\sum_{i=0}^{L-1}(i-\mu)^3 p(i) \tag{9}$$

It reflects the degree of asymmetry or skewness of gray distribution, positive skew when $\alpha > 0$, and negative skew when $\alpha < 0$.

(5) Consistency

$$U(i) = \sum_{i=0}^{L-1} p^2(i) \tag{10}$$

A smoothing image is consistent with a large value of consistency.

(6) Kurtosis

$$\beta = \frac{1}{\sigma^4}\sum_{i=0}^{L-1}(i-\mu)^4 p(i) \tag{11}$$

The kurtosis indicates the degree of concentration of the gray-scale distribution or the degree of spike in the distribution curve. When $\beta > 0$, the distribution is more concentrated than the normal distribution, and with peak state; when $\beta = 0$, it is a normal distribution; when $\beta < 0$, the distribution is more dispersed than the normal distribution, and with low peak state.

3   Feature Extraction with LDA

Assuming that the original sample matrix is $X_{n \times m}$, n is the feature dimension, m is the number of samples. The sample is divided into c major classes. Where m_i is the number of samples belonging to class i, each samples are denoted as $x_1, x_2, \ldots, x_m$, n dimensional row vector for each one. x_k is the kth sample, $u = \frac{1}{m}\sum_{k=1}^{m} x_k$ is the mean of all samples, $u_i = \frac{1}{m_i}\sum_{x \in class\ i} x$ is the mean of sample class i. Then two matrixes are defined.

Inter-class dispersion matrix

$$S_b = \sum_{i=1}^{c} m_i(u_i - u)(u_i - u)^T \tag{12}$$

Intra-class dispersion matrix

$$S_w = \sum_{i=1}^{c}\sum_{x_k \in class i}(u_i - x_k)(u_i - x_k)^T \tag{13}$$

By introducing the Fisher discriminate criterion expression

$$J_{fisher}(\varphi) = \frac{\varphi^{\mathrm{T}} S_b \varphi}{\varphi^{\mathrm{T}} S_w \varphi} \tag{14}$$

and substituting s_b and s_w into the Eq. (14), we can be obtained

$$J_{fisher}(\varphi) = \frac{\sum\limits_{i=1}^{c} m_i \varphi^{\mathrm{T}} (u_i - u)(u_i - u)^{\mathrm{T}} \varphi}{\sum\limits_{i=1}^{c} \sum\limits_{x_k \in class i} \varphi^{\mathrm{T}} (u_i - x_k)(u_i - x_k)^{\mathrm{T}} \varphi} \tag{15}$$

The problem of finding the projection direction for the larger s_b and the smaller s_w is translated into the problem to find a lower dimensional space, where the ratio of the sum of the squares of the inter-class geometric distances and the sum of the squares of the intra-class geometric distances within the class is maximized when the sample is projected in the space.

Now, we should optimize the criteria function to find a set of vector to determine the projection matrix

$$W_{opt} = \arg \max_{\varphi} \frac{|\varphi^{\mathrm{T}} S_b \varphi|}{|\varphi^{\mathrm{T}} S_w \varphi|} \tag{16}$$

Let

$$\frac{\partial J_{fisher}(\varphi)}{\partial \varphi} = \frac{S_b \varphi (\varphi^{\mathrm{T}} S_w \varphi) - S_w \varphi (\varphi^{\mathrm{T}} S_b \varphi)}{(\varphi^{\mathrm{T}} S_w \varphi)^2} = 0 \tag{17}$$

then

$$S_b \varphi = J_{fisher}(\varphi) S_w \varphi \tag{18}$$

Let $J_{fisher}(\varphi) = \lambda$, then $S_b \varphi = \lambda S_w \varphi$. The problem above is transformed into the problem of solving the generalized eigenvector. If S_w is not equal to 0, it becomes solving $S_w^{-1} S_b \varphi = \lambda \varphi$. We obtain the column vector of W_{opt} as $S_b \varphi = \lambda S_w \varphi$. It has d largest eigenvalues correspond to the eigenvectors. Where φ is the transformation vector from the original sample space to the Fisher space, $\varphi = [\varphi_1, \varphi_2, \ldots, \varphi_d]$. The number of the optimal projection vectors is not large than that of classes minus one, $d \leq c - 1$.

4   Method of Classification

SVM is based on the VC dimension theory and structural risk minimization of statistical learning theory. VC dimension is a measure of function class, the higher the VC dimension, the higher the problem complexity, and structural risk is the sum of experience risk and confidence risk. Compared with the complexity of the problem, SVM algorithm requires a relatively small number of samples. It can find the best compromise between the complexity of the model and the learning ability based on the sample information. In this paper, SVM is employed to construct the classifier and classify the eight categories macerals of the inertinite group.

4.1 Construction of Classifier

Suppose that there is a sample set $\{(x_1, y_1), (x_2, y_2), ..., (x_Q, y_Q)\}$, where $x \in R^G$ is the input mode, G is the input space dimension, and $y \in \{\pm 1\}$ is the label of target output. Assuming that the optimal hyperplane is $w^T x_q + b = 0 (q = 1, ..., Q)$, the weight vector w and the offset b must satisfy the following constraints.

$$y_q(w^T x_q + b) \geq 1 - \xi_q \tag{19}$$

Where ξ_q is the relaxation variable, indicating the degree of deviation of the pattern from the ideal linearly separable problem. The goal of SVM is to find a hyperplane that minimizes the average error classification of training data. Define a cost function

$$\Phi(w, \xi) = \frac{1}{2}\|w\|^2 + C\sum_{q=1}^{N}\xi_q \tag{20}$$

Where C is the penalty coefficient which control the degree of punishment for the error classification samples, and N is the number of samples wrongly classified.

4.2 Selection of Kernel Function

For linearly indivisible problems, support vector machines map training sets from low-dimensional space to high-dimensional space. It realizes the transformation from nonlinear problem to linear problem. The choice of kernel function plays an important role in algorithm performance. Linear kernel, Polynomial kernel, Gauss kernel (RBF) and Sigmoid kernel are commonly used kernel functions. Compared with the polynomial kernel function, the RBF kernel needs fewer parameters, and it can avoid the case that the kernel matrix cannot convergence when the order of the polynomial is high. In addition, in a sense, RBF can cover the functions of linear or sigmoid kernel.

The RBF kernel is chosen here as the kernel function of SVM.

$$k\left(\|x - x_c\|\right) = e^{\left[-\|x - x_c\|^2 / (2\sigma)^2\right]} \tag{21}$$

Where, x_c is the center of kernel function, σ is the width of the function, it controls the radial range of the function.

5   Experiment and Result Discussion

The algorithm is implemented on the HPZ800 hardware platform by Visual C++ combined with OpenCV programming.

5.1 Implementation of Algorithm

The structure diagram of the classification model of inertinite macerals of coal is shown in Fig. 2. In this paper, eight categories of microscopic images are chosen as samples, which are from inertinite macerals of cribriform fusinite, stellate fusinite, semifusinite, secretinite, funginite, macrinite, inertodetrinite and micrinite. Each of 50 images for training, and 30 images for test. The image size is 180 × 170. In the calculation of the brightness ratio, the parameter e is empirically set to be 150. In the calculation of the gray level co-occurrence matrix, the gray level is reduced to eight levels to reduce the computational complexity, considering the premise of not affecting the texture description. In the construction of RBF-SVM classifier, the penalty coefficient C adjusts the learning machine of the confidence range and the empirical risk proportion in the determined feature space, and the value is between 0 and 1. The σ^2 mainly affects the complexity of the distribution of the sample data in the high-dimensional feature space. If it is chosen too big, the weight of high-order features decay very fast, which is equivalent to a low-dimensional subspace; if selected very small, it may lead to over-fitting problem. In this paper, we choose $C = 0.1$ and $\sigma = 0.09$ by experiments.

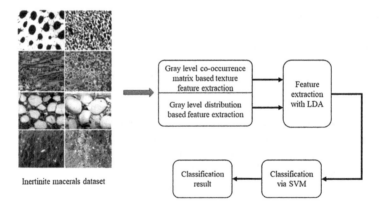

Fig. 2. The structure diagram of the LDA and RBF-SVM based classification method for Inertinite macerals of coal

5.2 Experimental Results and Discussion

Classification with the Initial Features. In order to investigate the effect of different kinds of features on the classification results, three experiments for classifying the eight maceral categories are performed with six gray statistical based features, five texture features and eleven total initial features, respectively.

Table 1 shows the results of classification with six gray-level statistical based features of mean, luminance ratio, standard deviation, 3-order moment deviation, consistency and kurtosis.

Table 1. Classification accuracy with 6 gray statistical based features /%.

Category	Training sample	Test sample
Semifusinite	100	91.67
Stellate fusinite	100	83.33
Cribriform fusinite	100	91.67
Inertodetrinite	100	91.67
Micrinite	100	97.00
Macrinite	100	50.00
Funginite	100	97.00
Secretinite	100	33.33

As can be seen from Table 1, with the gray-level statistical based features, the classification accuracy for micrinite, funginite can up to 97%, next for semifusinite, cribriform fusinite and inertodetrinite reach 91.67%. However, the classification accuracies of stellate fusinite, macrinite and secretinite are not so good, that may be owing to the large brightness jump of them.

Table 2 shows the results of classification with five texture features of energy, entropy, moment of inertia, local stationary, and maximum probability.

Table 2. Classification accuracy with 5 texture features /%.

Category	Training sample	Test sample
Semifusinite	100	83.33
Stellate fusinite	100	80.00
Cribriform fusinite	100	97.00
Inertodetrinite	100	76.67
Micrinite	100	80.00
Macrinite	100	91.67
Funginite	100	83.33
Secretinite	100	58.33

It can be found from Table 2 that with texture features, the classification accuracy of most categories are about 80%, the highest one is cribriform fusinite, up to 97%, except for secretinite. It means that texture features are effective for characterizing some macerals of inertinite, but not enough owing the existing of similar between some of them.

Table 3 gives the classification results with a total of 11 initial gray statistics based and the gray co-occurrence matrix based features as inputs of the SVM. As can be seen from Table 3, the classification with all initial features not only failed to improve the classification accuracy, but reduce it, particularly for the macerals of funginite and secretinite, because of the redundancy of information, which affect the accuracy of the classification.

Table 3. Classification accuracy with 11 initial features /%.

Category	Training sample	Test sample
Semifusinite	100	91.67
Stellate fusinite	100	83.33
Cribriform fusinite	100	91.67
Inertodetrinite	100	91.67
Micrinite	100	80.00
Macrinite	100	50.00
Funginite	100	28.33
Secretinite	100	33.33

Classification with Features Extracted by LDA. Table 4 shows the classification results of inertinite macerals with features after extracted with method of LDA.

Table 4. Classification accuracy with different dimension of LDA comprehensive features /%.

Category	Dimension					
	1	2	3	4	5	6
Semifusinite	93.33	93.33	93.33	93.33	100	100
Stellate fusinite	80.00	100	100	100	100	100
Cribriform fusinite	60.00	100	100	100	100	100
Inertodetrinite	46.67	66.67	66.67	73.33	86.67	86.67
Micrinite	100	100	100	100	100	100
Macrinite	66.67	100	100	100	100	100
Funginite	60.00	53.33	86.67	100	100	93.33
Secretinite	73.33	100	100	100	100	100

From Table 4, it can be found that when the dimension of extracted features is about 5, the over-all performance of classification for the total 8 categories is significantly higher than that of classification with the initial features. The accuracy of the classification is improved with the increase of the feature dimension. At the dimension of 5, the classification accuracy of most categories reaches 100%, besides maceral of inertodetrinite. But when the dimension is higher than 5, the accuracy of classification is no longer increased.

The Impact of Different Classification Models on the Results. In order to evaluate the accuracy of the classification method of inertinite macerals of coal based on LDA and RBF-SVM, this paper chooses the method based on PCA and RBF-SVM, the method based on multifractal spectrum [11] and the method based on extreme learning machine [15] for the comparison. The average accuracy of these four classification models for inertinite macerals of coal are shown in Table 5.

Table 5. The average accuracy of different classification models /%.

Method	Average accuracy
PCA and RBF-SVM	95.8
Multifractal spectrum [11]	95.3
Extreme learning machine [15]	96.7
Ours	98.3

Table 5 shows that the classification accuracy of the proposed method is higher than those of other classification methods. Therefore, the classification method based on LDA and RBF-SVM is more effective for the classification of inertinite macerals of coal.

6 Conclusion

According to the characteristics of the microscopic images of the inertinite of coal macerals, initial features of the inertinite group of coal macerals are extracted based on the gray-level co-occurrence matrix and the gray-level statistics. Owing to the redundancy of information and correlation between different macerals, initial features are further extracted and dimension of feature space is reduced with LDA. Each category is classified by using RBF-SVM, which is constructed with radial basis function as kernel function. Results show that: (1) In addition to the conventional brightness information, textures are one of the important features for describing the microstructure of inertinite of coal macerals; (2) It is difficult to obtain a desired effect by using initial feature parameters directly, and after combining the initial features, the classification accuracy is even remarkably reduced owing to the existence of information redundancy and correlation between different category of macerals; (3) LDA is an effective method for the feature extraction in this study. After extraction of the initial features with LDA, the dimension of feature space is reduced, and the classification accuracy is obviously improved. When the dimension of extracted features is about 5, the classification can achieve a perfect result. In addition, this method can provide a new reference for the study of the classification and identification of other groups of coal macerals.

Acknowledgement. This work was supported by the National Natural Science Foundation of China (number 51574004); Natural Science Foundation of the Higher Education Institutions of Anhui Province, China (number KJ2019A0085); Academic Foundation for Top Talents of the Higher Education Institutions of Anhui Province, China (number gxbjZD2016041).

References

1. Singh, A.K., Singh, M.P., Sharma, M., Srivastava, S.K.: Microstructures and microtextures of natural cokes: a case study of heat-affected coking coals from the Jharia coalfield, India. Int. J. Coal Geol. **71**(2–3), 153–175 (2007)
2. Guo, X., Tang, Y., Eble, C.F., Wang, Y., Li, P.: Study on petrographic characteristics of devolatilization char/coke related to coal rank and coal maceral. Int. J. Coal Geol. **227**, 103504 (2020)
3. Meng, F., Gupta, S., French, D., Koshy, P., Shen, Y.: Characterization of microstructure and strength of coke particles and their dependence on coal properties. Powder Technol. **320**, 249–256 (2017)
4. Mlynarczuk, M., Skiba, M.: The application of artificial intelligence for the identification of the maceral groups and mineral components of coal. Comput. Geosci. **103**(Jun), 133–141 (2017)
5. Wang, S., Zhu, X., Lyu, Q.: Coal rock macerals recognition based on RILBP-GLCM algorithm. Coal Technol. **36**(03), 142–144 (2017)
6. Wang, P., Ding, H., Liu, C., Zhang, K.: Coal microscope image contour extraction algorithm based on structuring elements. J. China Coal Soc. **39**, 285–288 (2014)
7. Wang, P., Chen, S., Zhang, D.: Coal micrograph segmentation based on visual clustering. In: 2011 9th World Congress on Intelligent Control and Automation, Taibei, pp. 683–687 (2011)
8. Wang, P., Ying, Z., Wang, G., Zhang, D.: A classification method of vitrinite for coal macerals based on the PCA and RBF-SVM. J. China Coal Soc. **42**(04), 977–984 (2017)
9. Wang, P., Reng, J., Du, C., Zhang, D.: Classification of macerals in exinite of coal based on Tamura features. J. Anhui Univ. Technol. (Nat. Sci.) **35**(02), 131–136 (2018)
10. Wang, P., Liu, J., Wang, W., Reng, J., Zhang, D.: Classification of macerals in exinite of coal based on contourlet transform. J. China Coal Soc. **43**(S2), 641–645 (2018)
11. Liu, M., Wang, P., Chen, S., Zhang, D.: The classification of inertinite macerals in coal based on the multifractal spectrum method. Appl. Sci. **9**(24), 5509 (2019)
12. Wang, X.: Review of linear discriminant analysis and principal component analysis and related research. J. Postgrad. Sun Yat-sen Univ. (Nat. Sci. Med. Ed.) **04**, 50–61 (2007)
13. Wang, S., Lu, J., Gu, X., Du, H., Yang, J.: Semi-supervised linear discriminant analysis for dimension reduction and classification. Pattern Recogn. **57**(C), 179–189 (2016)
14. Nie, F., Wang, Z., Wang, R., Wang, Z., Li, X.: Adaptive local linear discriminant analysis. ACM Trans. Knowl. Disc. Data **14**(1), 9.1-9.19 (2020)
15. Wang, P., Liu, M., Wang, G., Zhang, D.: Classification approach for inertinite of coking coal based on an improved extreme learning machine. J. China Coal Soc. **45**(09), 3262–3268 (2020)

A Weighted Non-convex Restoration Model for Hyperspectral Image

Yijun Yu and Min Li$^{(\boxtimes)}$

College of Mathematics and Statistics, Shenzhen Key Laboratory of Advanced
Machine Learning and Applications, Shenzhen University, Shenzhen 518060, China
1900201017@email.szu.edu.cn, limin800@szu.edu.cn

Abstract. Low-rank and sparsity are two popular regularization objects
in hyperspectral image restoration. To generalize this decomposition,
a weighted non-convex low-rank method is proposed by adopting nonconvex l_p-norm $(0 < p < 1)$ to recover the clean image more genuinely.
The noise term including Gaussian noise, impulse noise, stripes, and
deadlines, is assumed to be sparse, and the non-convex l_p-norm can better approach the l_0-norm when $0 < p < 1$. For the clean image underlying
a noised one, its low rank property is conducive to the capture of both
spatial and spectral information by applying l_p-norm to the bases of the
gradient of data. To remain faithful to the dissimilarity between the correlation along spatial and spectral directions, weights are assigned when
computing the difference in each direction. Although being non-convex,
the proposed model can be solved via ADMM algorithm. Extensive simulated experiments show that this model outperforms various existing
methods visually and quantitatively.

Keywords: HSI restoration · Low-rank · l_p-norm

1 Introduction

Hyperspectral imaging (HSI) is ubiquitous in remote sensing, which is applied
widely in civilian and military occasions [1]. However, HSI is inevitably corrupted
by noise during acquisition and transmission. Thereupon, HSI restoration has
been a fundamental research topic, which arouses the development of numerous
models and algorithms.

It is a common consensus for HSI restoration that every band corresponds
to a gray-scale image. Naturally, the existing methods for traditional gray-level
image processing are helpful to HSI denoising. Among these approaches, low-rank

This work was supported in part by the National Nature Science Foundation of
China (62072312, 61972264, 61872429, 61772343), in part by Shenzhen Basis Research
Project (JCYJ20180305125521534, JCYJ20170818091621856, JCYJ2017030214483
8601), in part by the Interdisciplinary Innovation Team of Shenzhen University (SZUG
S2021SEMINAR06, JG2020060), in part by National Nature Science Foundation of
Guangdong province (2019A1515010894).

© Springer Nature Switzerland AG 2021
Y. Peng et al. (Eds.): ICIG 2021, LNCS 12889, pp. 167–178, 2021.
https://doi.org/10.1007/978-3-030-87358-5_14

matrix approximation (abbreviated as LRMA) is very popular due to its superior theory and performance [14]. Zhang et al. explored the low-rank property of HSI by lexicographically ordering $3D$ structure into a $2D$ matrix [14,15]. Since more significant parts of data are mainly dependent on the larger singular values, Gu et al. integrated the weighted nuclear norm with band-to-band total variation (TV) for denoising (WNNM) [3]. Besides, to approximate rank function of HSI better, a weighted Schatten p-norm regularization is introduced into LRMA framework solved by generalized iterated shrinkage [13]. However, the above mentioned methods all ignore the spectral information, which is in fact the key component of HSI.

To alleviate the aforementioned issue, Wei et al. gave a unified spatial-spectral mixed-noise removal approach (LRTV) [5], in which TV regularization is used to characterize the spatial piecewise smoothness and nuclear norm to describe spectral low-rank property. Simultaneously, l_1-norm regularization is proposed for the sparse noise. Considering the multi-factor affiliation of HSI, some restoration models deem directly a noise HSI cube as a tensor. For example, Wang et al. presented a tensor-based HSI restoration method which combines tensor Tucker decomposition and l_1-norm regularization with an anisotropic spatial-spectral total variation (SSTV) in a unified framework (LRTDTV) [10].

Obviously, nuclear norm is usually the convex choice for describing low-rank and l_1-norm is the effective characterization for sparsity in the existing methods. In fact, processing image using non-convex regularizations has become a trend in recent years [16–19]. Motivated by this idea, we adopt non-convex l_p-norm $(0 < p < 1)$ as the low rank regularization imposed on the base of gradient, which can capture both spatial and spectral information. Moreover, different weights are assigned to treat gradient in different dimensions accordingly. In addition, the non-convex l_p-norm $(0 < p < 1)$ is given for the sparse term which is a more accurate approximation for l_0-norm than l_1-norm.

The remainder of this paper is organized as follows. In Sect. 2, we introduce some related works and preliminaries that are helpful in the proposed model. In Sect. 3, the new model is developed in detail and the corresponding optimization algorithm is illustrated. Extensive experimental results of HSI restoration are shown in Sect. 4. Finally, the paper ends with concluding remarks in Sect. 5.

2   Related Works and Preliminaries

In this section, we introduce some related works and necessary definitions which are used in the following sections.

An HSI image has three dimensions, which are respectively horizontal and lateral in terms of space, as well as spectral (or frontal for a three-order tensor) in spectrum. Not content with some models merely taking account correlation within spatial dimension, many researchers dedicate to the information both spectrally and spatially. Since low-rank and TV have respectively the properties of preserving edge information and enhancing piecewise smoothness, Rudin et al. devised TV-based regularization for gray-level images denoising [9]. In fact, this regularized term is used to characterize the sparsity of gradient.

In a few state-of-art HSI denoising methods, e.g. LRTDTV, HSI is expressed as a tensor. In this paper, tensors are denoted by the boldface Euler script letters, such as $\mathcal{A}$, and matrices by boldface capital letters, e.g. $\boldsymbol{A}$. A hyperspectral image is a three-order tensor $\mathcal{A} \in \mathbb{C}^{n_1 \times n_2 \times n_3}$ (in which n_1, n_2 are spatial size and n_3 is the number of spectral bands of HSI), and its (i, j, k)-th entry is denoted as $a_{i,j,k}$. Using Matlab notation, $\mathcal{A}(i, :, :), \mathcal{A}(:, i, :)$ and $\mathcal{A}(:, :, i)$ denote respectively the i-th horizontal, lateral and frontal slice [7]. The l_1-norm of $\mathcal{A}$ is given as $\|\mathcal{A}\|_1 = \sum_{i,j,k=1}^{n_1,n_2,n_3} |a_{i,j,k}|$ and the Frobenius norm as $\|\mathcal{A}\|_F = \sqrt{\sum_{i,j,k=1}^{n_1,n_2,n_3} |a_{i,j,k}|^2}$ [7]. The l_p-norm of $\mathcal{A}$ can be describe as $\|\mathcal{A}\|_p = (\sum_{i,j,k=1}^{n_1,n_2,n_3} |a_{i,j,k}|^p)^{\frac{1}{p}}$ [2]. In particular, when $p = 2$, the l_p-norm degenerates to the Frobenius norm which is the same as in matrix case.

Scores of HSI denoising methods treat the original data $\mathcal{Y} \in \mathbb{R}^{n_1 \times n_2 \times n_3}$ as a matrix by lexicographically ordering all the entries of each spectral slice $\mathcal{Y}(:, :, i)$ into columns and forming a Casorati matrix[1] $Y \in \mathbb{R}^{n_1 n_2 \times n_3}$ with the columns. Therefore, the HSI based on tensor representation can be processed using mature matrix calculations.

It is common sense that HSI is usually contaminated by Gaussian noise, impulse noise, dead lines, stripes and the other noise in real situations [4,5,14]. LRMR gave exact recovery of corrupted low-rank matrices, which can decompose an image as low-rank part and sparse component [11]. Whereupon, one has

$$Y = X + E, \tag{1}$$

where Y is the observed image, X is the underlying clean image, and E is the noise term. To extract X from Y, LRMR constructed the following optimization problem [11]:

$$\min_{X,E} \quad rank(X) + \lambda \|E\|_0 \quad s.t. \quad Y = X + E. \tag{2}$$

where $rank(\cdot)$ represents a low-rank metric, and $\|\cdot\|_0$ is l_0-norm which can be used to characterize sparsity, λ is positive trade-off parameter. However, solving (2) is NP-hard in many cases. Hence, this stimulates researchers to find the effective relaxed models.

It is the popular way that convex surrogates for low rank and sparsity are utilized in image processing, which corresponds to nuclear norm and l_1-norm respectively. To exploit the local piecewise smoothness in both spatial and spectral domains, LRTDTV proposed an SSTV metric [10]. The corresponding formulation can be expressed as:

$$\|\mathcal{X}\|_{SSTV} := \sum_{i,j,k=1}^{n_1,n_2,n_3} w_1|x_{i,j,k} - x_{i-1,j,k}| + w_2|x_{i,j,k} - x_{i,j-1,k}| + w_3|x_{i,j,k} - x_{i,j,k-1}|,$$

where w_1, w_2, w_3 are the weights along horizontal, vertical and spectral dimensions that control the regularization strength. This three-dimensional difference operator is denoted as $D_w(\mathcal{X})$.

---

[1] Casorati matrix is a matrix whose columns comprise vectorized bands of an HSI [5].

Motivated by this work, Peng et al. designed an enhanced 3DTV(abbreviated as E-3DTV) which encodes sparsity for bases of the gradient [8]. Specifically, this technique seeks to model sparse structure in the corresponding gradient maps when an HSI is transformed as a Casorati matrix. It is well known that an HSI has modes in spatial height, width and the spectrum. Thus, the difference calculated along the three modes of an HSI can be written as: $D_n(\mathcal{X}), n = 1, 2, 3$. Then $D_n(\mathcal{X})$ is unfolded into a Casorati matrix that is a gradient map: $G_n = unfold(D_n(\mathcal{X}))$. Since the original HSI is low-rank, and difference calculation and unfolding are linear operators, G_n is also low-rank which can be factorized into two smaller factor matrices:

$$G_n = U_n W_n^T, \quad n = 1, 2, 3, \tag{3}$$

where $U_n \in \mathbb{R}^{n_1 n_2 \times r}$, $W_n \in \mathbb{R}^{n_3 \times r}$ is orthogonal, and r is the rank of G_n. Obviously, the columns in U_n constitute a set of bases of G_n, and a sparsity measure for gradient map G_n is the sparse regularization for U_n [8]. Thus, the minimization problem can be formulated as:

$$\min_{X, U_n, W_n, E} \tau \sum_{n=1}^{3} \|U_n\|_1 + \lambda \|E\|_1, \tag{4}$$

$$s.t. \quad Y = X + E, \quad G_n = U_n W_n^T, \quad W_n W_n^T = I,$$

where $\|\cdot\|_1$ is l_1-norm, I is an identity matrix. Unfortunately, the existing works demonstrate that l_1-norm always over-penalize the large singular values and lead to deviation from the original solution [16–19].

To address this problem, more non-convex regularizations for low-rank term and sparse term are explored in image processing. Considering the low-rank and smoothness in both spatial and spectral dimensions, we propose to absorb non-convex l_p-norm $(0 < p < 1)$ into HSI restoration in this paper.

3   A Weighted Non-convex Low-Rank Model for HSI Restoration

The gradient map in (4) has low-rank structure, which is in essence equivalent to the sparsity of singular values of a matrix. Total variance is l_1-norm of gradient. A lot of research shows that sparsity can be better described by non-convex l_p-norm [20]. To better encode the sparsity of gradient, we propose to exploit non-convex l_p-norm with $0 < p < 1$ replacing l_1-norm. The l_p-norm of a matrix $M \in \mathbb{R}^{n_1 \times n_2}$ can be expressed as:

$$\|M\|_p = \left(\sum_{i,j=1}^{n_1, n_2} |m_{ij}|^p \right)^{\frac{1}{p}}. \tag{5}$$

Similarly, when describing the sparsity of noise, we choose l_p-norm ($0 < p < 1$) instead of convex l_1-norm. Using non-convex surrogate to replace both of the terms in (4) and imposing weights on gradient maps, a more general form for HSI restoration can be written as:

$$\min_{X, U_n, W_n, E} \quad \tau \sum_{n=1}^{3} \|U_n\|_p^p + \lambda \|E\|_p^p, \tag{6}$$

$$s.t. \quad Y = X + E, \quad G_{wn} = U_n W_n^T, \quad W_n W_n^T = I,$$

where τ and λ are trade-off parameters between the low-rank term and the sparse term, $G_{wn}(n = 1, 2, 3)$ are the unfolded gradient maps that can be described by the weighted difference operated on $\mathcal{X}$ along three different modes of the HSI, i.e. $G_{wn} = unfold(D_{wn}(\mathcal{X}))$. $D_{wn}(\mathcal{X}), n = 1, 2, 3$ denote weighted difference of $\mathcal{X}$ calculated along three dimensions. The (i, j, k)-th entry of $D_{wn}(\mathcal{X}), n = 1, 2, 3$ is

$$d_{w1,ijk} = w_1(x_{i,j,k} - x_{i-1,j,k}), d_{w2,ijk} = w_2(x_{i,j,k} - x_{i,j-1,k}), d_{w3,ijk} = w_3(x_{i,j,k} - x_{i,j,k-1}),$$

where w is the vector of weights. To solve the model (6) by ADMM algorithm, the corresponding augmented Lagrangian function is given by the following form:

$$\mathcal{L}(X, E, U_n, W_n, M_n, \Gamma) = \tau \sum_{n=1}^{3} \|U_n\|_p^p + \lambda \|E\|_p^p$$

$$+ \sum_{n=1}^{3} \langle M_n, G_{wn} - U_n W_n^T \rangle + \frac{\mu}{2} \|G_{wn} - U_n W_n^T\|_F^2 \tag{7}$$

$$+ \langle \Gamma, Y - X - E \rangle + \frac{\mu}{2} \|Y - X - E\|_F^2,$$

where $M_n, n = 1, 2, 3$ and Γ are Lagrange multipliers, μ is a positive coefficient. In ADMM algorithm, each variable is computed alternately while keeping the other variables fixed. In what follows, updating process of (7) is summarized concretely.

1) Updating X. Extracting all the terms containing X from (7), the sub-problem is obtained as follows:

$$X = \arg\min_{X} \sum_{n=1}^{3} \langle M_n, G_{wn} - U_n W_n^T \rangle + \frac{\mu}{2} \|G_{wn} - U_n W_n^T\|_F^2$$

$$+ \langle \Gamma, Y - X - E \rangle + \frac{\mu}{2} \|Y - X - E\|_F^2. \tag{8}$$

Optimization of (8) can be denoted by solving the linear system:

$$(\mu I + \mu \sum_{n=1}^{3} D_{wn}^* D_{wn})(X) = \mu(Y - E) + \Gamma + \sum_{n=1}^{3} D_{wn}^*(\mu U_n W_n^T - M_n), \tag{9}$$

where $D_{wn}^*(\cdot)$ denotes the transposition operator of $D_{wn}(\cdot)$. Set $N = \mu(Y - E) + \Gamma + \sum_{n=1}^{3} D_{wn}^*(\mu U_n W_n^T - M_n)$, using convolution theory [6], X can be calculated by (10). That is

$$X = \mathcal{F}^{-1}\left(\frac{\mathcal{F}(N)}{\mu \mathbf{1} + \mu T}\right), \tag{10}$$

where $T = \sum_{n=1}^{3} |\mathcal{F}(D_{wn})|^2$, $\mathcal{F}$ and $\mathcal{F}^{-1}$ symbolize fast Fourier transform and its inverse transform, $|\cdot|^2$ and the division are both calculated element-wisely.

2) Updating $U_n, n = 1, 2, 3$. To update U_n of (7), we have to solve the following subproblem:

$$
\begin{aligned}
U_n &= \arg\min_{U_n} \tau \|U_n\|_p^p + \langle M_n, G_{wn} - U_n W_n^T \rangle + \frac{\mu}{2} \|G_{wn} - U_n W_n^T\|_F^2 \\
&= \arg\min_{U_n} \tau \|U_n\|_p^p + \langle M_n W_n, G_{wn} W_n - U_n \rangle + \frac{\mu}{2} \|G_{wn} W_n - U_n\|_F^2 \tag{11} \\
&= \arg\min_{U_n} \tau \|U_n\|_p^p + \frac{\mu}{2} \|U_n - (G_{wn} + \frac{1}{\mu} M_n) W_n\|_F^2 .
\end{aligned}
$$

By applying the generalized soft-thresholding (GST) function $T_p^{GST}(\cdot; \cdot)$ [21], i.e.

$$T_p^{GST}(y; \lambda) = sign(y) max\{|y| - \lambda p |y|^{p-1}, 0\}, \tag{12}$$

we can find the closed-form solution of (11):

$$U_n = T_p^{GST}\left((G_{wn} + \frac{1}{\mu} M_n) W_n; \frac{\tau}{\mu}\right), \tag{13}$$

and the solution is calculated element-wisely.

3) Updating $W_n, n = 1,2,3$. Extracting the terms containing W_n from (7), fixing other variants as constants, we have

$$
\begin{aligned}
W_n &= \arg\min_{W_n} \langle M_n, G_{wn} - U_n W_n^T \rangle + \frac{\mu}{2} \|G_{wn} - U_n W_n^T\|_F^2 \\
&= \arg\min_{W_n} \frac{\mu}{2} \|U_n W_n^T - (G_{wn} + \frac{1}{\mu} M_n)\|_F^2 \tag{14} \\
&= \arg\min_{W_n} \langle (G_{wn} + \frac{1}{\mu} M_n)^T U_n, W_n \rangle .
\end{aligned}
$$

Set $Z = (G_{wn} + \frac{1}{\mu} M_n)^T U_n$ to simplify the equation. Since W_n is orthogonal, the global solution of (14) can be obtained in closed-form by the Theorem [12]:

Theorem 1 [12]: *For any given matrix $M \in \mathbb{R}^{n_1 \times n_2}$, V is an orthogonal matrix, the global solution of*

$$\min_{VV^T=I} \langle M, V \rangle \tag{15}$$

is $V = AC^T$, where $M = ABC^T$ is the SVD of M.

The solution of (14) can be written as:

$$\begin{cases} [A, B, C] = \mathtt{svd}(Z) \\ W_n = AC^T \end{cases} \tag{16}$$

4) Updating E. Extracting all terms containing E and regarding other variants as constants, we get

$$\begin{aligned} E &= \arg\min_E \lambda \|E\|_p^p + \langle \Gamma, Y - X - E \rangle + \frac{\mu}{2} \|Y - X - E\|_F^2 \\ &= \arg\min_E \lambda \|E\|_p^p + \frac{\mu}{2} \|E - (Y - X + \frac{1}{\mu}\Gamma)\|_F^2. \end{aligned} \tag{17}$$

The solution of (17) can be obtained using the generalized soft-thresholding(GST) function $T_p^{GST}(\cdot;\cdot)$ [21], i.e.

$$E = T_p^{GST}(H; \frac{\lambda}{\mu}) = sign(H)max\{|H| - \frac{\lambda}{\mu}p|H|^{p-1}, 0\}, \tag{18}$$

where $H = Y - X + \frac{1}{\mu}\Gamma$, and the solution is calculated element-wisely.

5) Updating Multipliers. Based on the ADMM algorithm, the multipliers $M_n(n = 1, 2, 3)$ and Γ can be given in the following form:

$$M_n = M_n + \mu(G_{wn} - U_n W_n^T) \tag{19}$$

$$\Gamma = \Gamma + \mu(Y - X - E). \tag{20}$$

4   Experiments and Discussion

To illustrate the effectiveness in HSI restoration of the proposed model, six simulated experiments are carried out in comparison with other methods, including WNNM [3], LRMR [14], LRTV [5], LRTDTV [10] and E-3DTV [8]. These five competing methods cover both matrix model and tensor model, convex regularization like nuclear norm in WNNM, and even total variation is included in LRTV, LRTDTV and E-3DTV. We adopt the six noise combination cases in [10] to simulate the noised image, and the origin data Indian Pines HSI, the size of which is $145 \times 145 \times 224$ can be downloaded online.[2]

The details of the six cases are showed in Table 1. For instance, in Case 4) zero-mean Gaussian noise with variance 0.75 is added in every band. In band 91–130, numbers of deadlines are randomly selected from 3 to 10, and width of deadline is randomly selected from 1 to 3. Impulse is added in each band with percentage 0.15.

---

[2] https://engineering.purdue.edu/~biehl/MultiSpec/hyperspectral.html.

Table 1. Cases of different noise mixture

Case	Gaussian	Deadlines (band 91–130)	Impulse	Stripes (band 161–190)
1)	N (0, 0.1)			
2)	N (0, 0.1)	Width 1–3, number 3–10		
3)	N (0, 0.075)		0.15	
4)	N (0, 0.075)	Width 1–3, number 3–10	0.15	
5)	0-mean, variance 0–0.2	Width 1–3, number 3–10	0–0.2	
6)	0-mean, variance 0–0.2	Width 1–3, number 3–10	0–0.2	Number 20–40

In all the experiments, the parameters in those competing methods are tuned in accordance with their defaults. In the proposed model, the restoration with $p = 2/3$ is better than that with $p = 1/2$ for l_p-norm so we only show the results with $p = 2/3$ for simplicity. Rank is set as $r = [13, 13, 13]$, and the coefficient of the regularization of low rank term as $\tau = 0.004\sqrt{n_1 n_2}$, where n_1, n_2 are spatial length and width of an HSI [8]. λ is defaulted as 1. For the weight w, the larger singular values are generally associated with major information, thus they should better be shrunk less [3]. As analysed in [10], in spatial modes, there are more and larger singular values than in spectral mode. Therefore, we did sensitivity analysis on spectral weight, while keeping both of the spatial weights at 1. Figure 1 shows the best selection of spectral weight for each case. It is obvious that when the spectral weight is set small (around 0.2), the proposed method manifests its best restoration performance in terms of the three indexes (which will be introduced in Sect. 4.2). All bands of the HSI are normalized into [0,1] for processing and will be adjusted back to the natural magnitude.

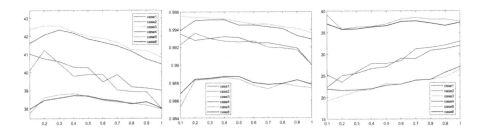

Fig. 1. The performance of spectral weights in terms of MPSNR, MSSIM and ERGAS.

4.1   Quantitative Comparison

To make quantitative comparison, three indexes are adopted to evaluate the performance objectively: the mean peak signal-to-noise ratio (MPSNR), mean structure similarity index (MSSIM), and Erreur Relative Globale Adimension-nelle de Synthese (ERGAS). ERGAS is a spectral-based evaluation measure.

The larger MPSNR and MSSIM are, and the smaller ERGAS is, the better the restoration methods perform. Table 2 lists the indexes of all competing methods under six noise cases, and all results are calculated by the average of 5 runs.

Table 2. Averaged Indexes of All Competing Methods under Six Noise Cases

Case	Index	Noise	WNNM	LRMR	LRTV	LRTDTV	E-3DTV	OURS
Case 1)	MPSNR	19.99	32.58	36.20	38.68	40.76	**42.33**	41.34
	MSSIM	0.3672	0.8420	0.9311	0.9853	0.9804	0.9910	**0.9935**
	ERGAS	233.99	57.65	36.85	28.47	23.02	24.32	**22.35**
Case 2)	MPSNR	19.34	32.46	35.67	38.04	40.54	**41.97**	41.22
	MSSIM	0.3592	0.8415	0.9291	0.9818	0.9895	0.9910	**0.9936**
	ERGAS	257.88	58.39	39.84	49.18	**23.44**	24.78	23.53
Case 3)	MPSNR	13.07	32.36	36.4	39.54	41.08	**43.13**	42.96
	MSSIM	0.1778	0.8786	0.9345	0.9866	0.9910	0.9928	**0.9959**
	ERGAS	520.53	59.71	36.04	35.22	21.98	22.55	**19.93**
Case 4)	MPSNR	12.92	32.29	35.76	38.75	40.72	42.68	**42.69**
	MSSIM	0.1784	0.8777	0.9316	0.9826	0.9906	0.9926	**0.9955**
	ERGAS	529.82	60.10	39.99	55.44	22.90	23.26	**20.39**
Case 5)	MPSNR	13.80	31.33	33.72	36.54	38.83	**40.80**	39.12
	MSSIM	0.2038	0.8445	0.8951	0.9742	0.9859	**0.9894**	**0.9894**
	ERGAS	500.68	66.39	50.16	72.52	28.66	**28.37**	35.12
Case 6)	MPSNR	13.73	29.97	33.42	36.35	38.63	**40.54**	39.08
	MSSIM	0.2022	0.8431	0.8918	0.9736	0.9852	0.9888	**0.9894**
	ERGAS	504.37	82.48	52.62	72.05	29.82	**28.87**	34.77

From the table, it is easy to find that the new model outperforms most of the state-of-the-art methods. To be concrete, MSSIM and MPSNR from the new method are either best or second to only the latest method. In a few cases, ERGAS of the proposed model ranked second or third of all methods, and is still comparable to the latest two methods. Thus, these results illustrate clearly the effectiveness of the proposed model.

4.2   Visual Quality Comparison

For generality, we show two sets of images under different mixed noise cases for visual comparison. Restoration results of band 36 under case 3) are shown in Fig. 2, and band 116 under case 5) in Fig. 3. We use pseudo color to make denoising outcome more clear visible.

It can be readily concluded from the sets of images that method WNNM and LRMR can remove part of the noise, but the outcomes are not satisfying.

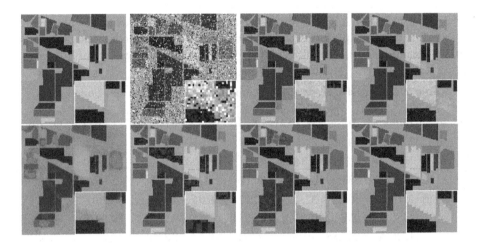

Fig. 2. Restoration results of the six compared methods, where the images from left to right represent: the original band 36, the noisy band of Case 3), WNNM, LRMR, LRTV, LRTDTV, E-3DTV and the proposed model.

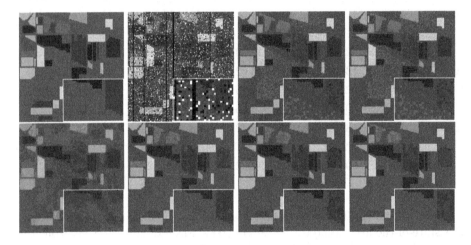

Fig. 3. Restoration results of the six compared methods, where the images from left to right represent: the original band 116, the noisy band of Case 5), WNNM, LRMR, LRTV, LRTDTV, E-3DTV and the proposed model.

Although LRTV can deal with subtotal noise, it over-smooths the image so that the edges are blurred. LRTDTV and E-3DTV eliminate plentiful noise and can retain some of the edges. The proposed method can not only remove most noise but also reserve most authentic edge information, which is illustrated graphically in Fig. 2 and Fig. 3 where a fixed subregion of each image is signed by a small rectangle and magnified in a larger one.

5 Conclusion

In this paper, a weighted non-convex low-rank model for HSI restoration is presented. Specifically, low rank structure in spatial and spectral dimensions is preserved via non-convex l_p-norm with $0 < p < 1$ imposed on the base of gradient and the noise term. Furthermore, restoration precision is improved when weights are assigned to encode the spatial and spectral correlation differently. Experiment results validate the superiority of the proposed model over the state-of-arts, especially for edge detail and MSSIM. In the future, we are interested in the refinement of this model and apply it to related problems like subspace clustering.

References

1. Goetz, A.F.: Three decades of hyperspectral remote sensing of the earth: a personal view. Remote Sens. Environ. **113**, S5–S16 (2009)
2. Goldfarb, D., Osher, S., Burger, M., Xu, J., Yin, W.: An iterative regularization method for total variation-based image restoration. Multiscale Model. Simul. **4**(2), 460–489 (2005)
3. Gu, S., Zhang, L., Zuo, W., Feng, X.: Weighted nuclear norm minimization with application to image denoising. In: 2014 IEEE Conference on Computer Vision and Pattern Recognition, pp. 2862–2869 (2014)
4. He, W., Zhang, H., Zhang, L., Shen, H.: Hyperspectral image denoising via noise-adjusted iterative low-rank matrix approximation. IEEE J. Sel. Top. Appl. Earth Obs. Remote Sens. **8**(6), 3050–3061 (2015)
5. He, W., Zhang, H., Zhang, L., Shen, H.: Total-variation-regularized low-rank matrix factorization for hyperspectral image restoration. IEEE Trans. Geosci. Remote Sens. **54**(1), 178–188 (2016)
6. Krishnan, D., Fergus, R.: Fast image deconvolution using hyper-laplacian priors. In: Bengio, Y., Schuurmans, D., Lafferty, J.D., Williams, C.K.I., Culotta, A. (eds.) Advances in Neural Information Processing Systems 22: 23rd Annual Conference on Neural Information Processing Systems 2009. Proceedings of a Meeting Held 7–10 December 2009, Vancouver, British Columbia, Canada, pp. 1033–1041. Curran Associates, Inc. (2009)
7. Lu, C., Feng, J., Chen, Y., Liu, W., Lin, Z., Yan, S.: Tensor robust principal component analysis with a new tensor nuclear norm. IEEE Trans. Pattern Anal. Mach. Intell. **42**(4), 925–938 (2020)
8. Peng, J., Xie, Q., Zhao, Q., Wang, Y., Yee, L., Meng, D.: Enhanced 3DTV regularization and its applications on HSI denoising and compressed sensing. IEEE Trans. Image Process. **29**, 7889–7903 (2020)
9. Rudin, L.I., Osher, S., Fatemi, E.: Nonlinear total variation based noise removal algorithms. Physica D **60**(1), 259–268 (1992)
10. Wang, Y., Peng, J., Zhao, Q., Leung, Y., Zhao, X., Meng, D.: Hyperspectral image restoration via total variation regularized low-rank tensor decomposition. IEEE J. Sel. Top. Appl. Earth Obs. Remote Sens. **11**(4), 1227–1243 (2018)

11. Wright, J., Ganesh, A., Rao, S.R., Peng, Y., Ma, Y.: Robust principal component analysis: exact recovery of corrupted low-rank matrices via convex optimization. In: Bengio, Y., Schuurmans, D., Lafferty, J.D., Williams, C.K.I., Culotta, A. (eds.) Advances in Neural Information Processing Systems 22: 23rd Annual Conference on Neural Information Processing Systems 2009. Proceedings of a Meeting Held 7–10 December 2009, Vancouver, British Columbia, Canada, pp. 2080–2088. Curran Associates, Inc. (2009)

12. Xie, Q., et al.: Multispectral images denoising by intrinsic tensor sparsity regularization. In: 2016 IEEE Conference on Computer Vision and Pattern Recognition (CVPR), pp. 1692–1700 (2016)

13. Xie, Y., Qu, Y., Tao, D., Wu, W., Yuan, Q., Zhang, W.: Hyperspectral image restoration via iteratively regularized weighted Schatten p-norm minimization. IEEE Trans. Geosci. Remote Sens. **54**(8), 4642–4659 (2016)

14. Zhang, H., He, W., Zhang, L., Shen, H., Yuan, Q.: Hyperspectral image restoration using low-rank matrix recovery. IEEE Trans. Geosci. Remote Sens. **52**(8), 4729–4743 (2014)

15. Zhou, T., Tao, D.: GoDec: randomized low-rank and sparse matrix decomposition in noisy case. In: Proceeding of the Twenty-Eighth International Conference on Machine Learning, pp. 33–40. International Machine Learning Society (IMLS) (2011)

16. Fan, J., Li, R.: Variable selection via nonconcave penalized likelihood and its Oracle properties. J. Am. Stat. Assoc. **96**, 1348–1361 (2001)

17. Nie, F., Wang, H., Cai, X., Huang, H., Ding, C.: Robust matrix completion via joint Schatten p-norm and l_p-norm minimization. IEEE International Conference on Data Mining, Brussels, Belgium, pp. 566–574 (2012)

18. Shang, F., Liu, Y., Cheng, J.: Scalable algorithms for tractable Schatten quasi-norm minimization. In: Computing Research Repository. arXiv:1606.01245 (2016)

19. Xu, C., Lin, Z., Zha, H.: A unified convex surrogate for the Schatten-p norm. In: The Thirty-First AAAI Conference on Artificial Intelligence, San Francisco, California, USA, pp. 926–932 (2017)

20. Shang, F., Cheng, J., Liu, Y., Luo, Z., Lin, Z.: Bilinear linear factor matrix norm minimization for robust PCA: algorithms and applications. IEEE Trans. Pattern Anal. Mach. Intell. **50**, 2066–2080 (2018)

21. Zuo, W., Meng, D., Zhang, L., Feng, X., Zhang, D.: A generalized iterated shrinkage algorithm for non-convex sparse coding. In: IEEE International Conference on Computer Vision, pp. 217–224 (2013)

Edge-Based Blur Kernel Estimation Using Sparse Representation and Self-similarity

Jing Yu[1], Lening Guo[1], Chuangbai Xiao[1(✉)], and Zhenchun Chang[2]

[1] Beijing University of Technology, Beijing 100124, China
{jing.yu,cbxiao}@bjut.edu.cn, lnguo@emails.bjut.edu.cn
[2] Tsinghua University, Beijing 100084, China

Abstract. Blind image deconvolution is the problem of recovering the latent image from the only observed blurry image when the blur kernel is unknown. In this paper, we propose an edge-based blur kernel estimation method for blind motion deconvolution. In our previous work, we incorporate both sparse representation and self-similarity of image patches as priors into our blind deconvolution model to regularize the recovery of the latent image. Since almost any natural image has properties of sparsity and multi-scale self-similarity, we construct a sparsity regularizer and a cross-scale non-local regularizer based on our patch priors. It has been observed that our regularizers often favor sharp images over blurry ones only for image patches of the salient edges and thus we define an edge mask to locate salient edges that we want to apply our regularizers. Experimental results on both simulated and real blurry images demonstrate that our method outperforms existing state-of-the-art blind deblurring methods even for handling of very large blurs, thanks to the use of the edge mask.

Keywords: Blind deconvolution · Deblurring · Sparse representation · Self-similarity · Cross-scale

1 Introduction

Motion blur caused by camera shake has been one of the most common artifacts in digital imaging. Blind image deconvolution is an inverse process that attempts to recover the latent (unblurred) image from the observed blurry image when the blur kernel is unknown. In general, for most of the work, the degradation is assumed that the observed image is the output of a linear shift invariant (LSI) system to which noise is added.

If the blur is shift-invariant, it can be modeled as the 2-D convolution of the latent image with the blur kernel:

$$y = h * x + v, \tag{1}$$

Scientific Research Common Program of Beijing Municipal Commission of Education (KM201910005029) and Beijing Natural Science Foundation (4212014).

where $*$ stands for the 2-D convolution operator, y is the observed blurry image, h is the blur kernel (or point spread function), x is the latent image and v is the additive noise. Then, removing the blur from the observed blurry image becomes a deconvolution operation. When the blur kernel is unknown, the blind deconvolution is a more severely ill-posed inverse problem. The key to the solution of the ill-posed inverse problem is proper incorporation of various image priors about the latent image into the blind deconvolution process. Non-blind image deconvolution seeks an estimate of the latent image assuming the blur is known. In contrast, blind image deconvolution tackles the more difficult, but realistic, problem where the degradation is unknown.

Despite over three decades of research in the field, blind deconvolution still remains a challenge for real-world photos with unknown kernels. Recently, blind deconvolution has received renewed attention since Fergus et al.'s work [1] and impressive progress has been made in removing motion blur only given a single blurry image. Some methods explicitly or implicitly exploit edges for kernel estimation [2–5]. This idea was introduced by Jia [2], who used an alpha matte to estimate the transparency of blurred object boundaries and performed the kernel estimation using transparency. Joshi et al. [3] predict sharp edges using edge profiles and estimate the blur kernel from the predicted edges. However, their goal is to remove small blurs, for it is not trivial to directly restore sharp edges from a severely blurred image. In [4,5], strong edges are predicted from the latent image estimate using a shock filter and gradient thresholding, and then used for kernel estimation. Unfortunately, the shock filter could over-sharpen image edges, and is sensitive to noise, leading to an unstable estimate.

Another family of methods exploit various sparse priors for either the latent image x or the motion blur kernel h, and formulate the blind deconvolution as a joint optimization problem with some regularizations on both x and h [1,6–10]:

$$(\hat{x}, \hat{h}) = \arg\min_{x,h} \left\{ \sum_* \omega_* \|\partial_* y - h * \partial_* x\|_2^2 + \lambda_x \rho(x) + \lambda_h \rho(h) \right\}, \qquad (2)$$

where $\partial_* \in \{\partial_0, \partial_x, \partial_y, \partial_{xx}, \partial_{xy}, \partial_{yy}, \cdots\}$ denotes the partial derivative operator in different directions and orders, ω_* is a weight for each partial derivative, $\rho(x)$ is a regularizer on the latent sharp image x, $\rho(h)$ is a regularizer on the blur kernel h, and λ_x and λ_h are regularization weights. The first term in the energy minimization formulation of blind deconvolution uses image derivatives for reducing ringing artifacts. Many techniques based on sparsity priors of image gradients have been proposed to deal with motion blur. Most previous methods assume that gradient magnitudes of natural images follow a heavy-tailed distribution. Fergus et al. [1] represent the heavy-tailed distribution over gradient magnitudes with a zero-mean mixture of Gaussian based on natural image statistics. Levin et al. [11] propose a hyper-Laplacian prior to fit the heavy-tailed distribution of natural image gradients. Shan et al. [8] construct a natural gradient prior for the latent image by concatenating two piece-wise continuous convex functions. However, sparse gradient priors always prefer the trivial solution, that is, the delta kernel and exactly the blurry image as the latent image estimate because the blur reduces the overall gradient magnitude. To tackle this problem, there are mainly two streams of research works for blind deconvolution. They use the maximum marginal probability estimation of h alone (marginalizing over x) to recover the true kernel [1,6,7] or optimize directly the joint posterior probability of both x and h by performing some empirical strategies or heuristics to avoid the trivial solution during the minimization [8–10]. Levin et al. [6,7] suggest that a MAP (maximum a posterior) estimation of h alone is well conditioned and recovers an accurate kernel, while a simultaneous MAP estimation for solving blind deconvolution by jointly optimizing x and h would fail because it favors the trivial solution. Perrone and Favaro [9,10] confirm the analysis of Levin et al. [6,7] and conversely also declare that total variation-based blind deconvolution methods can work well by performing specific implementation. In their work, the total variation regularization weight is initialized with a large value to help avoiding the trivial solution and iteratively reduced to allow for the recovery of more details. Blind deblurring is in general achieved through an alternating optimization scheme. In [9,10], the projected alternating minimization (PAM) algorithm of total variation blind deconvolution can successfully achieve the desired solution.

More present-day works often involve priors over larger neighborhoods or image patches, such as image super resolution [12], image denoising [13], non-blind image deblurring [14] and more. Gradient priors often consider two or three neighboring pixels, which are not sufficient for modeling larger image structures. Patch priors that consider larger neighborhoods (e.g., 5×5 or 7×7 image patches) model more complex structures and dependencies in larger neighborhoods. Image patches are usually overlapped with each other to suppress block effect. Sun et al. [15] use a patch prior learned from an external collection of sharp natural images to restore sharp edges. Michaeli and Irani [16] construct a cross-scale patch recurrence prior for the estimation of the blur kernel. Lai et al. [17] obtain two color centers for every image patch and build a normalized color-line prior for blur kernel estimation. More recently, Pan et al. [18] introduce the dark channel prior based on statistics of image patches to kernel estimation, while Yan et al. [19] propose a patch-based bright channel prior for kernel estimation.

Recent work suggests that image patches can always be well represented sparsely with respect to an appropriate dictionary and the sparsity of image patches over the dictionary can be used as an image prior to regularize the ill-posed inverse problem. Zhang et al. [20] use sparse representation of image patches as a prior for blur kernel estimation and learn an over-complete dictionary from a collection of natural images or the observed blurry image itself using the K-SVD algorithm. Li et al. [21] combine the dictionary pair and the sparse gradient prior with assumption that the blurry image and the sharp image have the same sparse coefficients under the blurry dictionary and the sharp dictionary respectively, to restore the sharp image via sparse reconstruction using the blurry image sparse coefficients on the sharp dictionary. The key issue of sparse representation is to identify a specific dictionary that best represents latent image patches in a sparse manner. Most methods use a database collecting enormous images as training samples to learn a universal dictionary. To make each patch of the latent image sparsely represented over such a universal dictionary, the database need involve massive training images, and thus this may lead to an inefficient learning and a potentially unstable dictionary. Meanwhile, the database needs to provide patches similar to the patches from the latent image, which cannot hold all the time. Alternatively, the dictionary is trained from the observed blurry image itself. However, the sparsity of the latent sharp image over the learned dictionary cannot be constantly guaranteed.

In this paper, we focus on an edge-based regularization approach for blind motion deblurring using patch priors. In our previous work, sparse representation and self-similarity are combined to work for image super resolution (SR) [12]. Super resolution approaches typically assume that the blur kernel is known (either the point spread function of the camera, or some default low-pass filter, e.g. a Gaussian), while blind deblurring refers to the task of estimating the unknown blur kernel. Michaeli and Irani [16] have showed image super resolution approaches cannot be applied directly to blind deblurring. In [22], we have proposed a blur kernel estimation method for blind motion deblurring using sparse representation and self-similarity of image patches as priors to guide the recovery of the latent image. In the previously proposed method, we construct a sparsity regularizer and a cross-scale non-local regularizer based on our priors. This method works quite well for a wide range of blurs but fails to deal with some extremely difficult cases. The edge-based method proposed in this paper is based on the observation that our regularizers often prefer sharp images to blurry ones only for image patches of salient edges. This fundamental observation enable us to build our regularizers on salient edge patches. Finally, we take an approximate iterative approach to solve the optimization problem by alternately updating the blur kernel and the latent image in a coarse-to-fine framework.

The remainder of this paper is organized as follows. Section 2 describes the background on sparse representation and multi-scale self-similarity. Section 3 makes detailed description on the proposed method, including our patch regularizers, our blind deconvolution model and the solution to our model. Section 4 presents experimental results on both simulated and real blurry images. Section 5 draws the conclusion.

2   Sparse Representation and Multi-scale Self-Similarity

2.1   Sparse Representation

Image patches can always be represented well as a sparse linear combination of atoms (i.e. columns) in an appropriate dictionary. Suppose that the image patch can be represented as $\mathbf{Q}_j \mathbf{X}$, here $\mathbf{Q}_j \in \mathbb{R}^{n \times N}$ is a matrix extracting the jth patch from $\mathbf{X} \in \mathbb{R}^N$ ordered lexicographically by stacking either the rows or the columns of x into a vector, and the image patch $\mathbf{Q}_j \mathbf{X} \in \mathbb{R}^n$ can be represented sparsely over $\mathbf{D} \in \mathbb{R}^{n \times t}$, that is:

$$\mathbf{Q}_j \mathbf{X} = \mathbf{D}\alpha_j, \|\alpha_j\|_0 \ll n, \tag{3}$$

where $\mathbf{D} = [\boldsymbol{d}_1, \cdots, \boldsymbol{d}_t] \in \mathbb{R}^{n \times t}$ refers to the dictionary, each column $\boldsymbol{d}_j \in \mathbb{R}^n$ for $j = 1, \cdots, t$ represents the atom of the dictionary $\mathbf{D}$, $\boldsymbol{\alpha}_j = [\alpha_1, \cdots, \alpha_t]^{\mathrm{T}} \in \mathbb{R}^t$ is the sparse representation coefficient of $\mathbf{Q}_j \mathbf{X}$ and $\|\boldsymbol{\alpha}_j\|_0$ counts the nonzero entries in $\boldsymbol{\alpha}_j$.

Given a set of training samples $\boldsymbol{s}_i \in \mathbb{R}^n, i = 1, \cdots, m$, here m is the number of training samples, dictionary learning attempts to find a dictionary $\mathbf{D}$ that forms sparse representations $\boldsymbol{\alpha}_i, i = 1, \cdots, m$ for the training samples by jointly optimizing $\mathbf{D}$ and $\boldsymbol{\alpha}_i, i = 1, \cdots, m$ as follows:

$$\min_{\mathbf{D}, \boldsymbol{\alpha}_1, \cdots, \boldsymbol{\alpha}_m} \sum_{i=1}^{m} \|\boldsymbol{s}_i - \mathbf{D}\boldsymbol{\alpha}_i\|_2^2 \quad \text{s.t. } \forall i \ \|\boldsymbol{\alpha}_i\|_0 \leqslant T, \tag{4}$$

where $T \ll n$ controls the sparsity of $\boldsymbol{\alpha}_i$ for $i = 1, \cdots, m$. The K-SVD method [23] is an effective dictionary learning method which solves Eq. (4) by alternately optimizing $\mathbf{D}$ and $\boldsymbol{\alpha}_i, i = 1, \cdots, m$.

We firstly use the K-SVD method [23] to obtain the dictionary $\mathbf{D}$. Then, we have to derive the sparse coefficient $\boldsymbol{\alpha}_j$ for the patch $\mathbf{Q}_j \mathbf{X}$. Equation (3) can be formulated as the following ℓ_0-norm minimization problem:

$$\min_{\boldsymbol{\alpha}_j} \|\mathbf{Q}_j \mathbf{X} - \mathbf{D}\boldsymbol{\alpha}_j\|_2^2 \quad \text{s.t. } \|\boldsymbol{\alpha}_j\|_0 \leqslant T, \tag{5}$$

where T is the sparsity constraint parameter. In our method, we obtain an approximation solution $\hat{\boldsymbol{\alpha}}_j$ for Eq. (5) by using the orthogonal matching pursuit (OMP) method [24].

As a matter of fact, the precision of the K-SVD method can be controlled either by constraining the representation error or by constraining the number of nonzero entries in $\boldsymbol{\alpha}_i$. We use the latter formulated in Eq. (4), because it is required in the OMP method [24]. In other words, the objective could be met by constraining the number of nonzero entries in the sparse representation coefficients $\boldsymbol{\alpha}_i$. Once the sparse coefficient $\hat{\boldsymbol{\alpha}}_j$ is derived by solving Eq. (5), the reconstructed image patch $\mathbf{Q}_j \hat{\mathbf{X}}$ can be represented sparsely over $\mathbf{D}$ through $\mathbf{Q}_j \hat{\mathbf{X}} = \mathbf{D}\hat{\boldsymbol{\alpha}}_j$.

2.2   Multi-scale Self-similarity and Non-local Regularization

Most natural images have properties of multi-scale self-similarity: structures from image fragments tend to repeat themselves at the same or different scales in natural images. In particular when small image patches are used, patch repetitions are found abundantly in multiple image scales of almost any natural image, even when we do not visually perceive any obvious repetitive structure. This is due to the fact that very small patches often contain only an edge, a corner, *etc.* [25]. Glasner et al. [25] have showed that almost any image patch in a natural image has multiple similar patches in down-scaled versions of itself.

Figure 1 schematically illustrates patch repetitions of self-similar structures both within the same scale and across different scales of a single image. For a patch of size 7×7 (marked with a red box) in Fig. 1(a), we search for its 5 similar patches (marked with blue boxes) in this image. Figure 1(b) shows close-ups of these similar patches within the same scale. In this example, the image is down-sampled by a factor of $a = 2$, as shown in Fig. 1(c). For the patch marked with a red box in Fig. 1(a) at the original scale, we also search for its 5 similar patches of the same size in Fig. 1(c), marked with blue boxes. Figure 1(d) shows close-ups of these similar patches searched from the down-sampled image, $i.e.$ cross-scale similar patches. The patches shown in Fig. 1 are displayed with clear repetitive structure in this image.

(a) Sharp image

(b) Similar image patches within the same scale

(c) Down-sampled image

(d) Similar image patches across different scales

Fig. 1. Patch repetitions occur abundantly both within the same scale and across different scales of a single image.

The non-local means was firstly introduced for image denoising based on this self-similarity property of natural images in the seminal work of Buades [26], and since then, the non-local means is extended successfully to other inverse problems such as image super resolution and non-blind image deblurring [27,28]. The non-local means is based on the observation that similar image patches within the same scale are likely to be appeared in a single image, and these same-scale similar patches can provide additional information. In our blind deconvolution model, we use similar image patches across different scales to construct a cross-scale non-local regularization prior by exploiting the correspondence between these cross-scale similar patches of the same image. Suppose that $X \in \mathbb{R}^N$ and $X^a \in \mathbb{R}^{N/a^2}$ represent the sharp image and its down-scaled version respectively, where N is the size of the sharp image, and a is the down-scaling factor. For each patch $\mathbf{Q}_j X$ in the sharp image X, we can search for its similar patches $\mathbf{R}_i X^a$ in X^a that the similarity is measured by the distance between $\mathbf{Q}_j X$ and $\mathbf{R}_i X^a$, here $\mathbf{Q}_j \in \mathbb{R}^{n \times N}$ and $\mathbf{R}_i \in \mathbb{R}^{n \times N/a^2}$ are matrices extracting the jth and the ith patch from X and X^a respectively, and n is the size of the image patch. The linear combination of the L most similar patches of $\mathbf{Q}_j X$ (put into the set $\mathcal{S}_j$) is used to predict $\mathbf{Q}_j X$, that is, the prediction can be represented as the following weighted sum:

$$\mathbf{Q}_j X \approx \sum_{i \in \mathcal{S}_j} w_i^j \mathbf{R}_i X^a, \tag{6}$$

where

$$w_i^j = \frac{\exp(-\|\mathbf{Q}_j X - \mathbf{R}_i X^a\|_2^2 / h)}{\sum_{l \in \mathcal{S}_j} \exp(-\|\mathbf{Q}_j X - \mathbf{R}_l X^a\|_2^2 / h)} \tag{7}$$

is the weight and h is the control parameter of the weight. It is noted from self-similarity that any patch can, in some way, be approximated by other similar patches of the same image. Obviously the difference between $\mathbf{Q}_j X$ and its prediction should be small and the prediction error can be used as the regularization in our blind deconvolution model (*i.e.* the cross-scale non-local regularizer).

3   Blind Deconvolution

3.1   Use of Cross-scale Self-similarity

We incorporate both sparse representation and self-similarity of image patches as priors into our blind deconvolution model to regularize the recovery of the latent image with these priors as regularizers. Since patches repeat across scales in natural images, our patch-based regularizers can depend on abundant patch repetitions across different scales of the same image. Typically we partition the latent image into small overlapping patches. For every patch of the latent image, we search for similar patches of the same size in a down-scaled version of itself. We construct a sparsity regularizer by sparsely representing the latent sharp image over the dictionary that these cross-scale similar patches are used as training samples to learn, denoted by $\mathrm{Reg}_c(x)$:

$$\mathrm{Reg}_c(x) = \sum_j \|\mathbf{Q}_j X - \mathbf{D}\alpha_j\|_2^2, \tag{8}$$

and a cross-scale non-local regularizer according to the correspondence between the latent image patch and its similar patches searched from the down-scaled latent image to enforce the recovery of sharp edges, denoted by $\mathrm{Reg}_s(x)$:

$$\mathrm{Reg}_s(x) = \sum_j \|\mathbf{Q}_j X - \sum_{i \in \mathcal{S}_j} w_i^j \mathbf{R}_i X^a\|_2^2, \tag{9}$$

where $\mathbf{D}$ is the learned dictionary for sparse representation, X is the vector-form notion of x, X^a is the down-scaled version of X by a factor a, $\mathbf{Q}_j X$ and $\mathbf{R}_i X^a$ represent the jth and the ith patch extracted from the latent image X and its down-scaled version X^a respectively, and $\mathcal{S}_j$ denotes the set of the p most similar patches of $\mathbf{Q}_j X$ searched from X^a. We only use similar image patches at down-sampled scales of the latent image to construct the non-local regularizer, without involving those within the same scale into our non-local regularizer.

The choice of training samples is very important for dictionary learning problem. Ideally the dictionary $\mathbf{D}$ should be trained from the patches sampled from the unknown latent sharp image. In our previous single-image super-resolution work [12], the dictionary is trained from the low-resolution image itself. Unfortunately, it is not a good choice for blind deblurring to learn a dictionary using the observed blurry image itself as training samples. This is because the dictionary trained from the blurry image cannot guarantee the sparsity of sharp image patches. In the previously proposed method [22], we used an adaptive over-complete dictionary trained from the down-scaled blurry image, more similar to the latent sharp image than the blurry image itself. In this paper, we present an improvement to collect training samples from the down-scaled latent image estimate, as will be detailed later.

We now provide illustration to account for the use of cross-scale self-similarity. Although patches repeat within and across scales of the sharp image, as illustrated in Fig. 1, the similarity diminishes significantly between the sharp image and its blurred counterpart. For the patch marked with a red box from the sharp image shown in Fig. 1(a), we still search for its 5 most similar patches from the blurry image (Fig. 2(a)) and its down-scaled version (Fig. 2(c)) by using block matching, respectively. Figure 2 shows that the patches from the down-scaled blurry image (Fig. 2(d)) that are more similar to the patch from the sharp image than the patches from the blurry image itself (Fig. 2(b)). This is because the blur effect tends to weaken at coarser scales of the image despite the strong blur at the original scale. It is easy to verify that down-scaling an image by a factor of a produces a-times sharper patches of the same size that are more similar to patches from the latent sharp image. Please refer to [16] for the proof.

Figure 3 illustrates the reason why similar patches across different scales are available for providing a prior for restoration. Suppose that $f(\boldsymbol{\xi})$ and $f(\boldsymbol{\xi}/a)$ are cross-scale similar patches and $f(\boldsymbol{\xi}/a)$ is an a-times larger patch in the sharp image, here $\boldsymbol{\xi}$ denotes the spatial coordinate. Accordingly, their blurry counterparts $q(\boldsymbol{\xi})$ and $r(\boldsymbol{\xi})$ are similar across image scales, and the size of $r(\boldsymbol{\xi})$ is a times as large as that of $q(\boldsymbol{\xi})$ in the blurry image. In Fig. 3, the blurry image is a times the size of its down-sampled version. Down-scaling the blurry patch $r(\boldsymbol{\xi})$ by a factor of a generates an a-times smaller patch $r^a(\boldsymbol{\xi})$. Obviously, $q(\boldsymbol{\xi})$ and $r^a(\boldsymbol{\xi})$ are of the same size and the patch $r^a(\boldsymbol{\xi})$ from the down-sampled image is exactly an a-times sharper version of the patch $q(\boldsymbol{\xi})$ in the blurry image. In such a case, $r^a(\boldsymbol{\xi})$ can offer much exact prior information for the recovery of $q(\boldsymbol{\xi})$. Figure 3 schematically demonstrates that the patches at coarser image scales can serve as a good prior, although it is an ideal case.

(a) Blurry image   (b) Similar patches in blurry image

(c) Down-sampled blurry image   (d) Similar patches in down-sampled blurry image

Fig. 2. Down-scaled blurry patches are more similar to the sharp patch than blurry patches at the original scale.

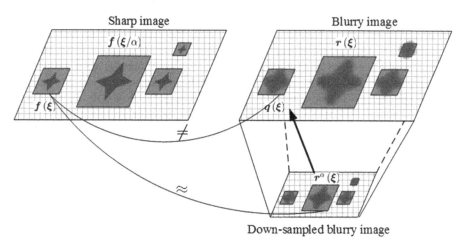

Fig. 3. Similar patches across different scales are available for providing a prior for restoration.

In summary, we incorporate effectively prior knowledge provided by cross-scale similar patches into our regularizers. As stated above, the down-scaled latent image estimate can provide sharper patches of the same size that are more similar to patches from the latent sharp image. In the sparsity regularizer, the dictionary is trained from sharper patches sampled from the down-scaled latent image estimate to make latent image patches well represented sparsely. In the cross-scale non-local regularizer, meanwhile, all latent image patches are optimized to be as close to their sharper similar patches searched from the down-scaled latent image estimate to enforce the sharp recovery of the latent image as possible.

3.2   Analysis on Regularizers

In regularization approaches, blind deconvolution is generally formulated as an energy minimization problem with appropriate regularizers, which tends to be minimal at the desired latent image. The regularizers are used to impose additional constraints on the optimization problem. They significantly benefit the solution of the blind deconvolution problem based on the condition that the regularization functions with respect to the sharp image x should be significantly smaller than those with respect to its blurry counterpart y. We will make the sparsity and the self-similarity comparison between the sharp image and the blurry image based on our patch regularizers respectively, and discuss whether the condition is satisfied or which patches satisfy this condition.

Sparsity Regularizer. First of all, we compare the sparsity regularization functions $\mathrm{Reg}_c(x)$ and $\mathrm{Reg}_c(y)$ with respect to the sharp image x and the blurry one y, respectively. For comparison, we generate the blurred image by the convolution of the sharp image shown in Fig. 1(a) with the averaging blur kernel. The dictionary is trained from patches sampled from the down-sampled blurry image. We calculate the values of the sparsity regularization functions with respect to the sharp image and several blurred images with blur kernels of varying sizes of 2×2, 3×3 and 5×5, respectively, which are averaged over all pixels, as shown in Table 1, where N is the size of the image, n is the size of image patch. The smaller the value, the smaller the sparse representation error. This means that the image is better represented over the learned dictionary. From Table 1, we can see that the sharp image has larger sparse representation error than any blurred image over the learned dictionary, and the larger blur corresponds to the sparser representation of the blurred image in terms of the entire image.

Then we compare the sparsity regularization functions with respect to the sharp image and the blurred counterpart on a patch-by-patch basis. Let $\mathcal{R}_c$ represent the set of pixels at which the sharp patch has smaller sparse representation error than the blurred one over the learned dictionary. That is,

$$\mathcal{R}_c = \{j |\ \|\mathbf{Q}_j X - \mathbf{D}\alpha_j\|_2^2 \leqslant \|\mathbf{Q}_j Y - \mathbf{D}\alpha_j\|_2^2\}, \tag{10}$$

where X and Y denote the vector notations of the sharp image x and the blurred image y respectively. Figure 4(a) shows the blurred image with the averaging blur

Table 1. Comparison of sparsity regularizer between sharp image and blurry images with blur kernels of different sizes.

	Sharp	2 × 2 blur	3 × 3 blur	5 × 5 blur
$\sqrt{\mathrm{Reg}_c(\cdot)/(N \cdot n)}$	5.40	3.70	2.70	1.72

Note: the intensity range is $[0, 1]$.

kernel of size 2×2. In Fig. 4(b), the set $\mathcal{R}_c$ are indicated with white pixels where the sharp patch achieves smaller sparse representation error than the blurred patch over the learned dictionary. From Fig. 4(b), we can see that the sparsity regularizer of the sharp image is smaller than that of the blurred image only for some certain patches. Intuitively, these regions comprised of white pixels coincide with edges and sharp changes in this image. It is believed that most image structures are often reflected around edges and areas of high variation. The optimal dictionary should produce sparsest representation of edge patches in the latent sharp image.

Non-local Regularizer. For the same reason, we compare the non-local regularization functions $\mathrm{Reg}_s(\boldsymbol{x})$ and $\mathrm{Reg}_s(\boldsymbol{y})$ with respect to the sharp image $\boldsymbol{x}$ and the blurry one $\boldsymbol{y}$, respectively. Similarly, we calculate the values of the non-local regularization functions with respect to the sharp image and the blurred images with blur kernels of varying sizes of 2×2, 3×3 and 5×5 respectively, averaged over all pixels, as shown in Table 2. The smaller the value, the smaller the prediction error. It means that there is stronger cross-scale self-similarity throughout the image. From Table 2, we can see that the sharp image reveals the weakest cross-scale self-similarity, and the blurred image with larger blur kernel displays stronger cross-scale self-similarity in terms of the entire image.

Table 2. Comparison of cross-scale non-local regularizer between sharp image and blurry images with blur kernels of different sizes.

	Sharp	2 × 2 blur	3 × 3 blur	5 × 5 blur
$\sqrt{\mathrm{Reg}_c(\cdot)/(N \cdot n)}$	0.0448	0.0385	0.0339	0.0271

Note: the intensity range is $[0, 1]$.

We still compare the non-local regularization functions with respect to the sharp image and the blurred counterpart on a patch-by-patch basis. Let $\mathcal{R}_s$ represent the set of pixels at which the sharp patch has smaller prediction error than the blurred one. That is,

$$\mathcal{R}_s = \{j| \ \|\mathbf{Q}_j\boldsymbol{X} - \sum_{i \in \mathcal{S}_j} w_i^j \mathbf{R}_i \boldsymbol{X}^a\|_2^2 \leqslant \|\mathbf{Q}_j\boldsymbol{Y} - \sum_{i \in \mathcal{S}_j} w_i^j \mathbf{R}_i \boldsymbol{Y}^a\|_2^2\}, \qquad (11)$$

where Y and Y^a denote the vector notation of the blurred image y and its down-sampled version by a factor of a. From Fig. 4(c), the set $\mathcal{R}_s$ indicated with white pixels is also roughly consistent with edges of the image. Our further observation shows that image edges do not always help kernel estimation when the scale of the edge is smaller than that of the blur kernel, while salient edges can effectively avoid the trivial solution and get an accurate blur kernel. We use Sun et al.'s strategy [15] (see the following edge mask M for more details) to detect and select salient edges of the blurred image, as is shown in Fig. 4(d).

It can be observed from the comparison of Figs. 4(c) and (d) that the cross-scale non-local regularizer of the sharp image is smaller than that of the blurred image roughly around salient edges. The blur alters to different extent edges of repetitive structures across different scales and thus deteriorates cross-scale self-similarity properties of edge structures in the blurry image.

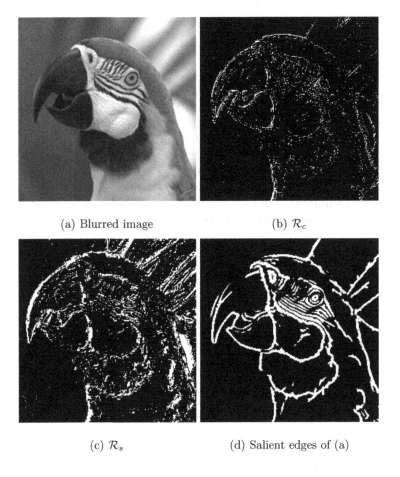

(a) Blurred image   (b) $\mathcal{R}_c$

(c) $\mathcal{R}_s$ (d) Salient edges of (a)

Fig. 4. Sharp image has stronger sparsity and cross-scale self-similarity than blurred image roughly around salient edges.

3.3 Modeling and Optimization

Although natural images generally have properties of sparsity and self-similarity, in the previous part, we have made detailed discussions on our two regularizers $\text{Reg}_c(\boldsymbol{x})$ and $\text{Reg}_s(\boldsymbol{x})$, and come to the conclusion that $\text{Reg}_c(\boldsymbol{x}) < \text{Reg}_c(\boldsymbol{y})$ and $\text{Reg}_s(\boldsymbol{x}) < \text{Reg}_s(\boldsymbol{y})$ are often satisfied only for image patches of salient edges. In other words, they only favor the sharp solution over the blurred one around salient image edges. In order to generate more exact solutions, our regularization constraints are only imposed on image patches of salient edges.

In this paper, we define the edge mask $\boldsymbol{M}$ according to the corresponding salient edge pixels, which is a binary mask indicating pixel locations that we want to apply our priors. We employ a heuristic process to detect and select salient edges of the latent image estimate during the optimization in a coarse-to-fine framework for kernel estimation and thus we do not present a joint energy minimization formulation of both the latent image $\boldsymbol{x}$ and the blur kernel $\boldsymbol{h}$. In each level of the image pyramid, we take an approximate approach to solve the optimization problem by directly alternating between optimizing the kernel $\boldsymbol{h}$ and the latent image $\boldsymbol{x}$.

1. Updating M

This step chooses pixel locations to apply our patch priors. Since our regularizers prefer the sharp image to the blurry one only around salient edges, in order to benefit the blur kernel estimation, we first detect and select useful salient edges. We adopt Sun et al.'s strategy [15] to filter the latent image estimate $\hat{\boldsymbol{x}}_k$ with a filter bank consisting of derivatives of Gaussians in eight directions and obtain the edge mask $\boldsymbol{M}$ by keeping the top 2% of pixel locations from the largest filter responses of the filter bank. In our model, regions outside the mask are weakly regularized by our patch priors, resulting in noise amplification in flat or smooth regions, and therefore the Gaussian low-pass filter are utilized before salient edge selection.

2. Updating h

In this step, we fix $\boldsymbol{x}_k$ and update $\boldsymbol{h}_{k+1}$. The minimization problem is defined with a Gaussian regularizer as:

$$h_{k+1} = \arg\min_{h} \left\{ \|\nabla \boldsymbol{y} - \boldsymbol{h} * (\nabla \boldsymbol{x}_k \odot \boldsymbol{M})\|_2^2 + \lambda_h \|\boldsymbol{h}\|_2^2 \right\}, \qquad (12)$$

where $\nabla = \{\partial_x, \partial_y\}$ denotes the spatial derivative operator in two directions, $\odot$ stands for the pixel-wise multiplication, and λ_h is the regularization weight to control the tradeoff between the fidelity to the observation model (as accounted for by the former term) and the smoothness of the estimated blur kernel (as reflected by the latter term). We multiply $\nabla \boldsymbol{x}_k$ by the mask $\boldsymbol{M}$ (*i.e.* $\nabla \boldsymbol{x}_k \odot \boldsymbol{M}$) to enforce that regions outside the mask do not participate in estimating $\boldsymbol{h}$. We only allow salient edges in the mask $\boldsymbol{M}$ to participate in the constraint of the observation model by setting the gradient $\nabla \boldsymbol{x}_k$ outside $\boldsymbol{M}$ to zero.

On the other hand, we take a common way to eliminate the influence of smooth or flat regions of the image on kernel estimation [4,5,15,17]. The pixels whose gradient magnitudes are less than a certain threshold in the intermediate latent image estimate are set to zero. Let τ denote a threshold of the gradient magnitude and N_h denote the size of the blur kernel. The threshold for truncating gradients is determined as follows. We construct the histograms of gradient magnitudes and directions for each $\partial_* \boldsymbol{x}_k$. Angles are quantized by $45°$, and gradients of opposite directions are counted together. Then, we find a threshold that keeps at least $r\sqrt{N_h}$ pixels from the largest magnitude for each quantized angle. We use 2 for r by default. To allow for inferring subtle structures during kernel refinement, we gradually decrease the value of the threshold τ in iterations by dividing by 1.1 at each iteration, to include more and more edges. Equation (12) excludes part of the gradients, depending jointly on the magnitude and the edge mask $\boldsymbol{M}$. In order to suppress the noise in flat or smooth regions, however, we do nothing on $\nabla \boldsymbol{y}$. This selection process reduces ambiguity in the following kernel estimation.

Equation (12) is a quadratic function of unknown $\boldsymbol{h}$, which has a closed-form solution for $\boldsymbol{h}_{k+1}$. We solve Eq. (12) in the Fourier domain by performing FFTs on all variables and setting the derivative with respect to $\boldsymbol{h}$ to zero:

$$\boldsymbol{h}_{k+1} = \mathcal{F}^{-1}\left(\frac{\overline{\mathcal{F}(\partial_x \boldsymbol{x}_k \odot \boldsymbol{M})}\mathcal{F}(\partial_x \boldsymbol{y}) + \overline{\mathcal{F}(\partial_y \boldsymbol{x}_k \odot \boldsymbol{M})}\mathcal{F}(\partial_y \boldsymbol{y})}{\mathcal{F}(\partial_x \boldsymbol{x}_k \odot \boldsymbol{M})^2 + \mathcal{F}(\partial_y \boldsymbol{x}_k \odot \boldsymbol{M})^2 + \lambda_h} \right), \qquad (13)$$

where $\mathcal{F}(\cdot)$ and $\mathcal{F}^{-1}(\cdot)$ denote the fast Fourier transform and inverse Fourier transform respectively, and $\overline{\mathcal{F}(\cdot)}$ is the complex conjugate operator.

3. Updating x

In this step, we fix $\boldsymbol{h}_{k+1}$, and given $\boldsymbol{x}_k$ update $\boldsymbol{x}_{k+1}$. With our patch priors as regularizers, we establish our regularizers on salient edge patches of the image, and get the following regularized minimization:

$$\boldsymbol{x}_{k+1} = \arg\min_{\boldsymbol{x}} \left\{ \|\nabla \boldsymbol{y} - \boldsymbol{h}_{k+1} * \nabla \boldsymbol{x}\|_2^2 + \lambda_c \frac{N}{|\boldsymbol{M}|} \sum_{j \in M} \|\boldsymbol{Q}_j \boldsymbol{X} - \boldsymbol{D}\boldsymbol{\alpha}_j\|_2^2 \right.$$

$$\left. + \lambda_s \frac{N}{|\boldsymbol{M}|} \sum_{j \in M} \|\boldsymbol{Q}_j \boldsymbol{X} - \sum_{i \in \mathcal{S}_j} w_i^j \boldsymbol{R}_i \boldsymbol{X}^a\|_2^2 + \lambda_g \|\nabla \boldsymbol{x}\|_2^2 \right\} \qquad , \qquad (14)$$

$$\text{s.t. } \forall j \ \|\boldsymbol{\alpha}_j\|_0 \leqslant T$$

where $|\boldsymbol{M}|$ is the number of non-zero elements in the mask $\boldsymbol{M}$, and N is the size of the latent image, $\boldsymbol{D}$ is the dictionary trained from the down-scaled latent image estimate, $\boldsymbol{X}$ is the vector notation of the latent image $\boldsymbol{x}$, $\boldsymbol{X}^a$ is the downsampled version of $\boldsymbol{X}$ by a factor of a, and λ_c, λ_s, and λ_g are regularization weights controlling the effect of the regularizers. In Eq. (14), the first term is the fidelity to the observation model, the second term is the sparsity regularizer, the third term is the cross-scale non-local regularizer, and the last term is the smoothness constraint of the estimated latent image.

Rearranging $\boldsymbol{y}$ in vector form, denoted by $\boldsymbol{Y} \in \mathbb{R}^N$, and rewriting the convolution of the blur kernel and the latent image in matrix-vector form, Eq. (14) can be rewritten as

$$X_{k+1} = \arg\min_{X} \left\{ \|G_x Y - H_{k+1} G_x X\|_2^2 + \|G_y Y - H_{k+1} G_y X\|_2^2 \right.$$

$$+ \lambda_c \frac{N}{|M|} \sum_{j \in M} \|Q_j X - D\alpha_j\|_2^2 + \lambda_s \frac{N}{|M|} \sum_{j \in M} \|Q_j X - \sum_{i \in S_j} w_i^j R_i X^a\|_2^2$$

$$\left. + \lambda_g(\|G_x X\|_2^2 + \|G_y X\|_2^2) \right\}$$

$$\text{s.t. } \forall j \ \|\alpha_j\|_0 \leqslant T$$
(15)

where G_x and $G_y \in \mathbb{R}^{N \times N}$ are the matrix forms of the partial derivative operators ∂_x and ∂_y in two directions respectively, and $H_{k+1} \in \mathbb{R}^{N \times N}$ is the blur matrix. Setting the derivative of Eq. (15) with respect to X to zero and letting $G = G_x^T G_x + G_y^T G_y$, we derive

$$\left[(H_{k+1}^T H_{k+1} + \lambda_g)G + (\lambda_c + \lambda_s)\frac{N}{|M|} \sum_{j \in M} Q_j^T Q_j\right] X_{k+1}$$

$$= H_{k+1}^T GY + \lambda_c \frac{N}{|M|} \sum_{j \in M} Q_j^T D\alpha_j + \lambda_s \frac{N}{|M|} \sum_{j \in M} Q_j^T \sum_{i \in S_j} w_i^j R_i X_{k+1}^a,$$
(16)

Since both sparse representation coefficients α_j and the down-sampled image X_{k+1}^a on the right-hand side of Eq. (16) depend on unknown X_{k+1}, Eq. (16) cannot be solved in closed form. Instead we approximately solve Eq. (16) with the following procedure:

(1) The K-SVD method [23] is used to attain the dictionary D by approximately solving Eq. (4). For each patch $Q_j X_k$ in X_k that the mask M selects, the OMP method [24] is used here to derive the sparse representation coefficient α_j over the dictionary D by approximately solving the following constrained minimization problem:

$$\hat{\alpha}_j = \arg\min_{\alpha_j} \|Q_j X_k - D\alpha_j\|_2^2 \quad \text{s.t. } \|\alpha_j\|_0 \leqslant T.$$
(17)

Since the sparse coefficient α_j on the right-hand side of Eq. (16) depends on unknown X_{k+1}, we approximate X_{k+1} using X_k to solve the sparse coefficient $\hat{\alpha}_j$ over the dictionary D.

(2) For the same reason, since X_{k+1} and its down-scaled X_{k+1}^a are both unknown, we approximate X_{k+1} and X_{k+1}^a using X_k and X_k^a respectively. For each patch $Q_j X_k$ in X_k that the mask M selects, we search for its similar patches $R_i X_k^a$, $i \in \hat{S}_j$ in the down-scaled image X_k^a of X_k, and use the linear combination of these similar patches $\sum_{i \in \hat{S}_j} \hat{w}_i^j R_i X_k^a$ to predict it. Here $\hat{S}_j$ and $\hat{w}_i^j$ are updated according to X_k and X_k^a.

(3) Equation (16) can be reformulated by substituting the sparse coefficient $\hat{\alpha}_j$, the set of similar patches $\hat{S}_j$ and the weights $\hat{w}_i^j$ derived from the above approximations into the right-hand side of Eq. (16), such that:

$$\left[(H_{k+1}^T H_{k+1} + \lambda_g)G + (\lambda_c + \lambda_s)\frac{N}{|M|} \sum_{j \in M} Q_j^T Q_j\right] X_{k+1}$$

$$= H_{k+1}^T GY + \lambda_c \frac{N}{|M|} \sum_{j \in M} Q_j^T D\hat{\alpha}_j + \lambda_s \frac{N}{|M|} \sum_{j \in M} Q_j^T \sum_{i \in \hat{S}_j} \hat{w}_i^j R_i X_k^a.$$
(18)

Since it is a linear equation with respect to X_{k+1}, Eq. (18) can be solved by direct matrix inversion or the conjugate gradient method. In our method, X_{k+1} are updated by solving it using the bi-conjugate gradient (BICG) method.

(4) **Repeat steps 1–3 until convergence or for a fixed number of iterations.**

3.4   Implementation

To speed up the convergence and handle of large blurs, following most existing methods, we estimate the blur kernel in a coarse-to-fine framework. We apply our alternating iterative minimization procedure described in Sect. 3.3 to each of the levels of the image pyramid constructed from the blurred image y. The blur kernel refinement starts from the coarsest level and works down to the finest level with the original image resolution. At the coarsest level, the latent image estimate is initialized with the observed blurry image. The intermediate latent image estimated at each coarser level is interpolated and then propagated to the next finer level as an initial estimate of the latent image to refine the blur kernel estimate in higher resolutions.

Different from [22], in which the dictionary is trained from patches randomly sampled from the down-scaled blurry image, in this paper, the dictionary is trained from edge patches sampled directly from the intermediate latent image estimated at the coarser scale, and iteratively updated once for each image scale during the solution. We do not pay attention to the sparsity of the entire image over the learned dictionary, but only the sparsity of edge patches in the image, for our sparsity regularizer prefers the sharp image to the blurred one only for edge patches.

Blind deconvolution in general involves two stages. The motion blur kernel h is firstly estimated by alternately updating the motion blur kernel h and the latent image x. The intermediate latent images estimated during the iterations have no direct influence on the final deblurring result, and only affect this result indirectly by contributing to the refinement of the blur kernel estimate $\hat{h}$. Then, the final deblurring result $\hat{x}$ is recovered from the given blurry image y with the estimated blur kernel $\hat{h}$ for the finest level by performing a variety of non-blind deconvolution methods, such as fast TV-ℓ_1 deconvolution [5], sparse deconvolution [6] and EPLL [29] *etc*.

We estimate the blur kernel h by the implementation of the pseudo-code outlined in Algorithm 1. We construct an image pyramid with L levels from the given blurry image y. The number of pyramid levels is chosen such that, at the coarsest level, the size of the blur is smaller than that of the patch used in the blur kernel estimation stage. Let us use the notation $\hat{x}_k^l$ for the intermediate latent image estimate, where the superscript l indicates the lth level in the image pyramid, while the subscript k indicates the kth iteration at each scale level. The iterative procedure starts from the coarsest level $l = 1$ of the image pyramid initialized with $\hat{x}_0^1 = y$. At each scale level $l \in \{1, \cdots, L\}$, we take the iterative procedure that alternately optimizes the motion blur kernel h and the latent image x as detailed in Sect. 3.3, which is implemented repeatedly until the convergence or for a fixed number of iterations. Then the outcome of updating the latent image at the lth level is upsampled by interpolation and then used as an initial estimate of the latent image for the next finer level $l+1$ to progressively refine the motion blur kernel estimate $\hat{h}$, which is repeated to achieve the final refinement of the blur kernel estimate $\hat{h}$ for the finest level.

Algorithm 1: Edge-Based Blur Kernel Estimation Using Sparse Representation and Self-Similarity

---

Input: Blurry image y
Output: Blur kernel estimate $\hat{h}$
Set down-scaling factor a, regularization weights λ_g, λ_c, λ_s, λ_h, size of patch n, size of dictionary t, sparsity constraint parameter T, number of similar patches p, convergence tolerance ϵ and maximum allowed number of iterations maxIters;
Build an image pyramid with L levels;
Initialize $\hat{x}_0^1 = y$;
Train dictionary $\mathbf{D}$ using $\hat{x}_0^1$;
Outer loop: for $l = 1$ to $l = L$ **do**   // for each level of image pyramid
    Initialize $k = 0$, gradient threshold τ;
    Inner loop: repeat   // for each iteration
        Predict the edge mask M;
        Compute blur kernel $\hat{h}_{k+1}^l$ using Eq. 13;
        Given $\hat{x}_k^l$, update latent image $\hat{x}_{k+1}^l$ by solving Eq. 18 using BICG;
        $\tau = \tau/1.1$; $k = k + 1$
    until $k >$ maxIters or $\|\hat{x}_k^l - \hat{x}_{k-1}^l\|_2^2 \leqslant \epsilon$;
    Update dictionary $\mathbf{D}$ using $\hat{x}_k^l$;
    Upscale image $\hat{x}_k^l$ to initialize $\hat{x}_0^{l+1}$ for the next finer level;
$\hat{h} = \hat{h}_k^L$; $\hat{x} = \hat{x}_k^L$.

In the blur kernel estimation process, we use the gray-scale versions of the blurry image y and the intermediate latent image estimate $\hat{x}$. Once the blur kernel estimate $\hat{h}$ has been obtained with the original image scale, we perform the final non-blind deconvolution with $\hat{h}$ on each color channel of y to obtain the deblurring result.

Finally, our method need perform deconvolution in the Fourier domain. To avoid ringing artifacts at the image boundaries, we process the image near the boundaries using the simple *edgetaper* command in Matlab.

4   Experiments

Several experiments are conducted to demonstrate the performance of our method. We first test our method on the widely used datasets introduced in [6] and [15], and make qualitative and quantitative comparisons with the state-of-the-art blind deblurring methods. Then we show visual comparisons on real blurry photographs with unknown blurs. The relevant parameters of our method are set as follows: the dictionary $\mathbf{D}$ is of size $t = 100$, and the sparsity constraint parameter $T = 4$, designed to handle image patches of size $n = 5 \times 5$, the number of iterations is fixed as 14 for the inner loop, and the regularization weights are empirically set to $\lambda_c = 0.04/n$, $\lambda_s = 0.04/n$, $\lambda_g = 0.003$ and $\lambda_h = 0.0003N$. As the down-scaling factor increases, image patches become sharper, but there exist less similar patches at the down-sampled scale. Following the setting of [16], the image pyramid is constructed with scale-gaps of $a = 4/3$ using down-scaling with a sinc function. Additional speed up is obtained by using the fast approximate nearest neighbor (NN) search of [30] in the blur kernel estimation stage, working with a single NN for every patch.

An additional important parameter is the size of the blur kernel. Small blurs are hard to solve if it is initialized with a very large kernel. Conversely, large blurs will be truncated if too small a kernel is used [1]. Following the setting of [15], we do not assume that the size of the kernel is known and initialize that the size of the kernel is 51×51 in most cases except for some extremely difficult cases. Experiment results on both simulated and real blurry images show the size of the blur kernel is generally not larger than 51×51 for most blurry images. Even though the input blurry image has a small blur kernel, our method is still able to obtain a good deblurring result, less sensitive to the initial setting of the kernel size.

4.1 Quantitative Evaluation with Reference to Ground Truth

We test our method on two publicly available datasets. One dataset, which is provided by Levin et al. [6], contains 32 images of size 255×255 blurred by real camera shake. The blurred images with spatially invariant blur and 8 different ground-truth kernels were captured simultaneously by locking the Z-axis rotation handle but loosening the X and Y handles of the tripod. The kernels range in size from 13×13 to 27×27. The other dataset provided by Sun et al. [15] comprises 640 natural images of diverse scenes, which were obtained by synthetically blurring 80 high-resolution images with the 8 blur kernels from [6] and adding 1% white Gaussian noise to the blurred images. We present qualitative and quantitative comparisons with the state-of-the-art blind deblurring methods [1,4,5,7,9,15,16,31–33].

We measure the quality of the blur kernel estimate $\hat{\mathbf{h}}$ using the error ratio measure ER [16]:

$$\mathrm{ER} = \frac{\|\mathbf{x} - \hat{\mathbf{x}}_{\hat{h}}\|_2^2}{\|\mathbf{x} - \hat{\mathbf{x}}_h\|_2^2},\tag{19}$$

where $\hat{\mathbf{x}}_{\hat{h}}$ corresponds to the deblurring result with the recovered kernel $\hat{\mathbf{h}}$, and $\hat{\mathbf{x}}_h$ corresponds to the deblurring result with the ground-truth kernel $\mathbf{h}$. The smaller ER corresponds to the better quality. In principle, if ER = 1, the recovered kernel yields a deblurring result as good as the ground-truth kernel.

On the dataset provided by Levin et al. [6], we compare our error ratios with those of Fergus et al. [1], Cho and Lee [4], Xu and Jia [5], Perrone and Favaro [9],

Levin et al. [7], Perrone et al. [33] and our previous method [22]. Figure 5 shows the cumulative distribution of the error ratio of our method compared with the other methods over the dataset of [6]. Levin et al. [7] use sparse deconvolution [6] to generate the final results, and observe that deconvolution results are usually visually plausible when their error ratios are below 3. Therefore, we standardize the final non-blind deconvolution by using sparse deconvolution [6] to obtain the results, for fair comparison. Table 3 lists the success rate and the average error ratio over 32 images for each method. The success rate is the percentage of images which achieve good deblurring results, that is, the percentage of images that have an error ratio below a certain threshold. On this dataset, the success rate is the percentage of the results under the error ratio of 3. Table 3 shows our method takes the lead with a success rate of 100%, a higher success rate than our previous method without considering salient edges [22]. Levin et al. [7], Perrone and Favaro [9] and Perrone et al. [33] initialize the size of the blur kernel with ground truth, while the size of the blur kernel is unknown for real scenes. Even so, our method still achieves a much higher success rate than the other methods over the dataset of [6].

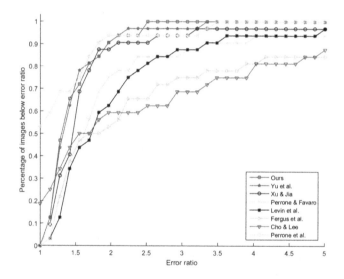

Fig. 5. Cumulative distributions of error ratios with different methods on the dataset of [6].

On this dataset provided by Sun et al. [15], we compare our error ratios with those of Cho and Lee [4], Xu and Jia [5], Levin et al. [7], Sun et al. [15], Michaeli and Irani [16], Cho et al. [31], Krishnan et al. [32] and our previous method [22]. Figure 6 shows the cumulative distribution of error ratios over the entire dataset for each method. We apply the blur kernel estimated by each method to perform deblurring with the non-blind deblurring method of [29] to recover latent images.

Table 3. Quantitative comparison of different methods over the dataset of [6].

	Success rate %	Mean error ratio
Ours	100	1.4433
Yu et al. [22]	96.88	1.4653
Perrone et al. [33]	93.75	1.2024
Xu and Jia [5]	93.75	2.1365
Perrone and Favaro [9]	87.50	2.0263
Levin et al. [7]	87.50	2.0583
Fergus et al. [1]	75.00	13.5268
Cho and Lee [4]	68.75	2.6688

It is empirically observed by Michaeli and Irani [16] that the deblurring results are still visually acceptable for error ratios ER $\leqslant 5$, when using the non-blind deconvolution of [29]. Table 4 lists the success rate (*i.e.*, an error ratio below 5) and the average error ratio over 640 images with different methods. Table 4 shows our method achieves the highest success rate and the lowest average error ratio followed by Michaeli and Irani [16] and Sun et al. [15]. Moreover, these two methods by Michaeli and Irani [16] and Sun et al. [15] take 9213 and 4899 s on average to process an image of size 1024×800 from this dataset respectively, and our method take 1823 1823 s, much faster than their methods.

Table 4. Quantitative comparison of different methods over the dataset of [15].

	Success rate %	Mean error ratio
Ours	96.56	2.1134
Yu et al. [22]	96.25	2.2047
Michaeli and Irani [16]	95.94	2.5662
Sun et al. [15]	93.44	2.3764
Xu and Jia [5]	85.63	3.6293
Levin et al. [7]	46.72	6.5577
Cho and Lee [4]	65.47	8.6901
Krishnan et al. [32]	24.49	11.5212
Cho et al. [31]	11.74	24.7020

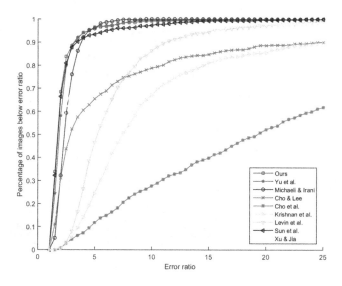

Fig. 6. Cumulative distributions of error ratios with different methods on the dataset of [15].

Figures 7 and 8 show qualitative comparisons of cropped results on two blurred images from the synthetic dataset of [15] by different methods. Compared with the other methods, our method usually obtains more accurate blur kernels, suffers from fewer ringing artifacts and restores more and sharper image details.

(a) Blurry image (b) Ground (c) Cho and Lee (d) Xu & Jia [5] (e) Krishnan et truth [4] al. [32]

(f) Cho et al. (g) Levin et al. (h) Sun et al. (i) Michaeli & (j) Our method [31] [7] [15] Irani [16]

Fig. 7. Qualitative comparison of different methods on a cropped image from the synthetic dataset of [15].

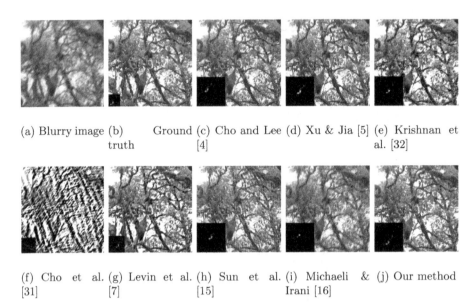

(a) Blurry image (b)   Ground (c) Cho and Lee (d) Xu & Jia [5] (e) Krishnan et
                truth   [4]   al. [32]

(f) Cho et al. (g) Levin et al. (h) Sun et al. (i) Michaeli & (j) Our method
[31]   [7]   [15]   Irani [16]

Fig. 8. Qualitative comparison of different methods on another cropped image from the synthetic dataset of [15].

4.2 Qualitative Comparison on Real Images

We also experiment with real blurry images which are blurred with unknown kernels. In this part, we process blurry images with very large blurs to demonstrate the robustness of our method. We recover the latent image from the observed blurry image by performing the non-blind deconvolution method of [29] in the deblurring stage once the blur kernel has been estimated. Several methods are terminated early during the iteration due to lack of memory caused by too large the blur kernel. Figure 9 shows a visual comparison example with the state-of-the-art blind deconvolution methods [5,9,15,18,19,32,33] on one blurred image from Kohler et al.'s dataset [34], at the bottom of which are close-ups of different parts of these images. The results illustrate a noticeable contrast improvement that our method recovers sharper edges and more fine details with negligible artifacts, and achieves better visual quality, as it estimates more accurate blur kernels. We observe from Fig. 9 that the deblurred images by Perrone et al. [9,33] suffer from ringing artifacts, and some fine details such as the fence and the lantern are not properly recovered by Pan et al. [18] and Yan et al. [19]. Figure 10 gives another visual comparison example with the state-of-the-art blind deconvolution methods [9,15,16,18,19,22,32,33,35,36]. The results show that our method can make better visual effect. Although Pan et al.'s method [18] restores fine details well, the result visually suffers from over-enhancement. In the above examples, the sizes of the blur kernels are empirically initialized to 151 × 151 and 91 × 91 respectively. Experimental results on real blurry photographs with

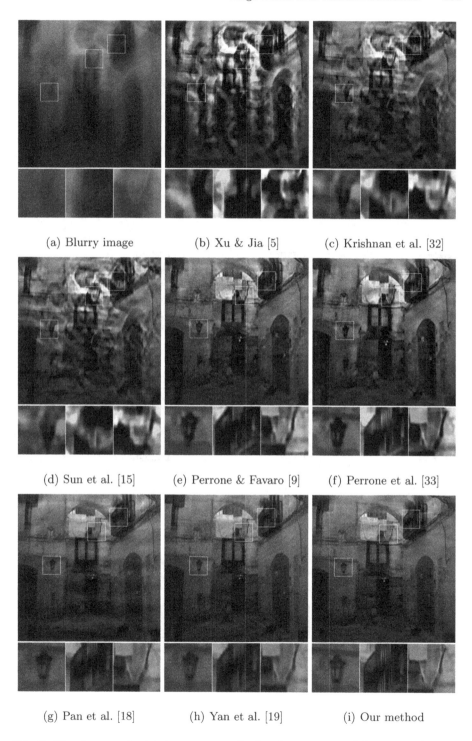

(a) Blurry image   (b) Xu & Jia [5]   (c) Krishnan et al. [32]

(d) Sun et al. [15]   (e) Perrone & Favaro [9] (f) Perrone et al. [33]

(g) Pan et al. [18]   (h) Yan et al. [19]   (i) Our method

Fig. 9. Visual comparison between our method and some state-of-the-art methods on real blurry image with unknown large blur.

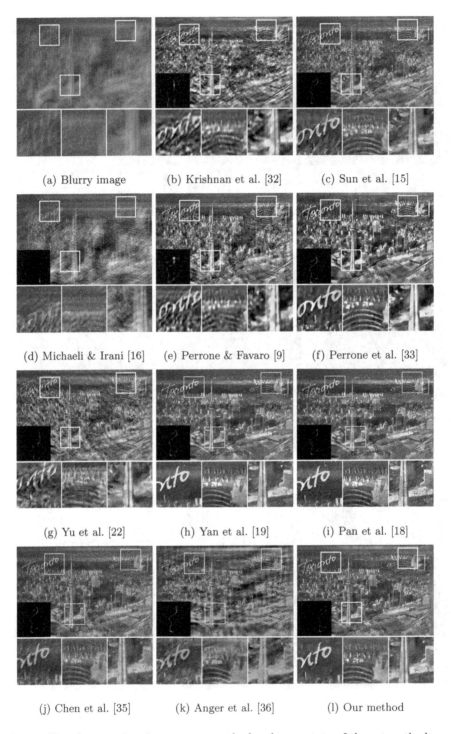

(a) Blurry image   (b) Krishnan et al. [32]   (c) Sun et al. [15]

(d) Michaeli & Irani [16]   (e) Perrone & Favaro [9]   (f) Perrone et al. [33]

(g) Yu et al. [22]   (h) Yan et al. [19]   (i) Pan et al. [18]

(j) Chen et al. [35]   (k) Anger et al. [36]   (l) Our method

Fig. 10. Visual comparison between our method and some state-of-the-art methods on another real blurry image with unknown large blur.

unknown large blurs validate that our method is quite robust to deal with large blurs.

When the blur is close to or even wider than the edge, the structure of the sharp edge will significantly change after blur. For such a highly blurred image, insignificant edges do not always provide useful information and instead mistake the kernel estimation. Nevertheless, large-scale structures are confused slightly by the blur due to their salient edges and provide informative edges for blur kernel estimation. Accordingly, it is more reasonable to obtain an accurate estimate of the blur kernel relying on salient edges. For small blurs, most of the edges are wider than the blur kernel and all helpful for kernel estimation besides salient edges. In this case, the edge-based method proposed in this paper only has a slight improvement over our previous method without considering salient edges [22]. But for large blurs, since insignificant edges could disturb kernel estimation and only salient edges around large-scale structures help kernel estimation, the edge-based method can achieve much better deblurring results and successfully handle severely blurred images.

5   Conclusion

In this paper, we have presented an edge-based blur kernel estimation method for blind motion deblurring unifying sparse representation and self-similarity of edge patches as image priors to guide the recovery of the latent image. We construct the sparsity regularizer and the cross-scale non-local regularizer based on our patch priors, exploiting thoroughly prior knowledge from similar patches across different scales of the latent image, and incorporate these two regularizers into our blind deconvolution model. We find that our regularizers prefer the sharp image to the blurred one only around salient edges, and accordingly impose our regularizers on salient edge patches of the image for blur kernel estimation. We have extensively validated the performance of our method, and it is able to deblur images with excessively large blur kernels.

References

1. Fergus, R., Singh, B., Hertzmann, A., Roweis, S.T., Freeman, W.T.: Removing camera shake from a single photograph. ACM Trans. Graph. (TOG) **25**(3), 787–794 (2006)
2. Jia, J.: Single image motion deblurring using transparency. In: IEEE Conference on Computer Vision and Pattern Recognition (CVPR), Minneapolis, Minnesota, USA, pp. 1–8. IEEE (2007)
3. Joshi, N., Szeliski, R., Kriegman, D.: PSF estimation using sharp edge prediction. In: IEEE Conference on Computer Vision and Pattern Recognition (CVPR), Anchorage, AK, pp. 1–8. IEEE (2008)
4. Cho, S., Lee, S.: Fast motion deblurring. ACM Trans. Graph. (TOG) **28**(5), 89–97 (2009)

5. Xu, L., Jia, J.: Two-phase kernel estimation for robust motion deblurring. In: Daniilidis, K., Maragos, P., Paragios, N. (eds.) ECCV 2010. LNCS, vol. 6311, pp. 157–170. Springer, Heidelberg (2010). https://doi.org/10.1007/978-3-642-15549-9_12

6. Levin, A., Weiss, Y., Durand, F., Freeman, W.T.: Understanding and evaluating blind deconvolution algorithms. In: IEEE Conference on Computer Vision and Pattern Recognition (CVPR), Miami, FL, pp. 1964–1971. IEEE (2009)

7. Levin, A., Weiss, Y., Durand, F., Freeman, W.T.: Efficient marginal likelihood optimization in blind deconvolution. In: IEEE Conference on Computer Vision and Pattern Recognition (CVPR), Colorado Springs, CO, USA, pp. 2657–2664. IEEE (2011)

8. Shan, Q., Jia, J., Agarwala, A.: High-quality motion deblurring from a single image. ACM Trans. Graph. (TOG) $27(3)$, 15–19 (2008)

9. Perrone, D., Favaro, P.: Total variation blind deconvolution: the devil is in the details. In: IEEE Conference on Computer Vision and Pattern Recognition (CVPR), Columbus, OH, pp. 2909–2916. IEEE (2014)

10. Perrone, D., Favaro, P.: A clearer picture of total variation blind deconvolution. IEEE Trans. Pattern Anal. Mach. Intell. $38(6)$, 1041–1055 (2016)

11. Levin, A., Fergus, R., Durand, F.E.D., Freeman, W.T.: Image and depth from a conventional camera with a coded aperture. ACM Trans. Graph. (TOG) $26(3)$, 70-es (2007)

12. Pan, Z., et al.: Super-resolution based on compressive sensing and structural self-similarity for remote sensing images. IEEE Trans. Geosci. Remote Sens. $51(9)$, 4864–4876 (2013)

13. Wang, M., Yu, J., Sun, W.: Group-based hyperspectral image denoising using low rank representation. In: 2015 IEEE International Conference on Image Processing (ICIP), pp. 1623–1627 (2015)

14. Jia, C., Evans, B.L.: Patch-based image deconvolution via joint modeling of sparse priors. In: IEEE International Conference on Image Processing (ICIP), Brussels, Belgium, pp. 681–684. IEEE (2011)

15. Sun, L., Cho, S., Wang, J., Hays, J.: Edge-based blur kernel estimation using patch priors. In: IEEE International Conference on Computational Photography (ICCP), Cambridge, MA, pp. 1–8. IEEE (2013)

16. Michaeli, T., Irani, M.: Blind deblurring using internal patch recurrence. In: Fleet, D., Pajdla, T., Schiele, B., Tuytelaars, T. (eds.) ECCV 2014. LNCS, vol. 8691, pp. 783–798. Springer, Cham (2014). https://doi.org/10.1007/978-3-319-10578-9_51

17. Lai, W.S., Ding, J.J., Lin, Y.Y., Chuang, Y.Y.: Blur kernel estimation using normalized color-line priors. In: IEEE Conference on Computer Vision and Pattern Recognition (CVPR), Boston, MA, United States, pp. 64–72. IEEE Computer Society (2015)

18. Pan, J., Sun, D., Pfister, H., Yang, M.H.: Blind image deblurring using dark channel prior. In: 2016 IEEE Conference on Computer Vision and Pattern Recognition (CVPR), Las Vegas, NV, USA, pp. 1628–1636. (2016)

19. Yan, Y., Ren, W., Guo, Y., Wang, R., Cao, X.: Image deblurring via extreme channels prior. In: 2017 IEEE Conference on Computer Vision and Pattern Recognition (CVPR), Honolulu, HI, USA, pp. 6978–6986. (2017)

20. Zhang, H., Yang, J., Zhang, Y., Huang, T.S.: Sparse representation based blind image deblurring. In: IEEE International Conference on Multimedia and Expo (ICME), Barcelona, Spain, pp. 1–6. IEEE (2011)

21. Li, H., Zhang, Y., Zhang, H., Zhu, Y., Sun, J.: Blind image deblurring based on sparse prior of dictionary pair. In: International Conference on Pattern Recognition (ICPR), Tsukuba, Japan, pp. 3054–3057. IEEE (2012)
22. Yu, J., Chang, Z., Xiao, C., Sun, W.: Blind image deblurring based on sparse representation and structural self-similarity. In: 2017 IEEE International Conference on Acoustics, Speech and Signal Processing (ICASSP), New Orleans, LA, USA, pp. 1328–1332. IEEE (2017)
23. Aharon, M., Elad, M., Bruckstein, A.: SVD: an algorithm for designing overcomplete dictionaries for sparse representation. IEEE Trans. Sig. Process. **54**(11), 4311–4322 (2006)
24. Tropp, J.A., Gilbert, A.C.: Signal recovery from random measurements via orthogonal matching pursuit. IEEE Trans. Inf. Theor. **53**(12), 4655–4666 (2007)
25. Glasner, D., Bagon, S., Irani, M.: Super-resolution from a single image. In: 2009 International Conference on Computer Vision (ICCV), Kyoto, Japan, pp. 349–356. IEEE (2009)
26. Buades, A., Coll, B., Morel, J.M.: A non-local algorithm for image denoising. In: 2005 IEEE Computer Society Conference on Computer Vision and Pattern Recognition (CVPR), San Diego, CA, United States, pp. 60–65. IEEE (2005)
27. Protter, M., Elad, M., Takeda, H., Milanfar, P.: Generalizing the nonlocal-means to super-resolution reconstruction. IEEE Trans. Image Process. **18**(1), 36–51 (2009)
28. Dong, W., Zhang, L., Shi, G., Wu, X.: Image deblurring and super-resolution by adaptive sparse domain selection and adaptive regularization. IEEE Trans. Image Process. **20**(7), 1838–1857 (2011)
29. Zoran, D., Weiss, Y.: From learning models of natural image patches to whole image restoration. In: IEEE International Conference on Computer Vision (ICCV), Barcelona, Spain, pp. 479–486. IEEE (2011)
30. Olonetsky, I., Avidan, S.: TreeCANN - k-d tree coherence approximate nearest neighbor algorithm. In: Fitzgibbon, A., Lazebnik, S., Perona, P., Sato, Y., Schmid, C. (eds.) ECCV 2012. LNCS, vol. 7575, pp. 602–615. Springer, Heidelberg (2012). https://doi.org/10.1007/978-3-642-33765-9_43
31. Cho, T.S., Paris, S., Horn, B.K.P., Freeman, W.T.: Blur kernel estimation using the radon transform. In: IEEE Conference on Computer Vision and Pattern Recognition (CVPR), Colorado Springs, CO, USA, pp. 241–248. IEEE (2011)
32. Krishnan, D., Tay, T., Fergus, R.: Blind deconvolution using a normalized sparsity measure. In: IEEE Conference on Computer Vision and Pattern Recognition (CVPR), Colorado Springs, CO, USA, pp. 233–240. IEEE (2011)
33. Perrone, D., Diethelm, R., Favaro, P.: Blind deconvolution via lower-bounded logarithmic image priors. In: Tai, X.-C., Bae, E., Chan, T.F., Lysaker, M. (eds.) EMMCVPR 2015. LNCS, vol. 8932, pp. 112–125. Springer, Cham (2015). https://doi.org/10.1007/978-3-319-14612-6_9
34. Köhler, R., Hirsch, M., Mohler, B., Schölkopf, B., Harmeling, S.: Recording and playback of camera shake: benchmarking blind deconvolution with a real-world database. In: Fitzgibbon, A., Lazebnik, S., Perona, P., Sato, Y., Schmid, C. (eds.) ECCV 2012. LNCS, vol. 7578, pp. 27–40. Springer, Heidelberg (2012). https://doi.org/10.1007/978-3-642-33786-4_3
35. Chen, L., Fang, F., Wang, T., Zhang, G.: Blind image deblurring with local maximum gradient prior. In: IEEE Conference on Computer Vision and Pattern Recognition (CVPR), Long Beach, CA, USA, pp. 1742–1750. IEEE (2019)
36. Anger, J., Facciolo, G., Delbracio, M.: Blind image deblurring using the l0 gradient prior. Image Process. On Line **9**, 124–142 (2019)

Normal Distribution Function on Descriptor Extraction

Jianhua Yin[1], Cong Liu[2], Jun Jiang[3], Jie Wen[1,4(✉)], Lihang Yang[5], and Shilong Zhu[5]

[1] School of Computer Science and Technology, Harbin Institute of Technology, Shenzhen 518055, China
[2] Shenzhen Institute of Artificial Intelligence and Robotics for Society, Shenzhen 518055, China
[3] Peng Cheng Laboratory, Shenzhen 518055, China
[4] Shenzhen Key Laboratory of Visual Object Detection and Recognition, Harbin Institute of Technology, Shenzhen 518055, China
[5] College of Big Data and Information Engineering, Guizhou University, Guiyang 550025, Guizhou, China

Abstract. The triplet-loss function is widely used in fields of descriptor extraction in recent years and owing to its good performance in various databases. However, some recent works make less effort on the relationship of adjacent descriptors from the same sample, which leads to the instability of descriptors and results in the mismatching problem in practical applications. To solve this problem, we introduce the topological relationship with the Normal Distribution Function (NDF) into the triplet loss function. The loss function establishes the relationship of descriptors from the same sample and considers the interrelation of descriptors from different types of samples. Furthermore, to increase the calculation speed, we normalize the algorithm NDF. Finally, we propose the triplet-loss function on three databases. These results demonstrate that our algorithm obtains better performance than state-of-the-art methods.

Keywords: Triplet-loss function · Topological relationship · Learned descriptors

1 Introduction

As a fundamental problem in computer vision, local descriptors have been widely used in three-dimensional reconstruction [1], biometrics [2], and SLAM [3, 4]. Local descriptors have good stability and uniqueness. For example, local descriptors are extracted and matched by the algorithm ORB [5], to improve the stability of three-dimensional reconstruction. SIFT [6], SURF [7], and ORB [5] are three famous and popular methods and have a wide application. However, these traditional methods generally cannot capture the high-level semantic information of the image. Due to the effectiveness of deep learning, many scholars [8, 9] are attracted to design the adaptive descriptor network. Generally,

Supported by National Natural Science Foundation of China (Grant No. 62006059), Guangdong Basic and Applied Basic Research Foundation (Grant No. 2019A1515110582), the National Key Research and Development Program of China (2020YFB2104304).

Y. Peng et al. (Eds.): ICIG 2021, LNCS 12889, pp. 206–215, 2021.
https://doi.org/10.1007/978-3-030-87358-5_16

the learned method contains two parts: descriptor extraction and loss function. The loss function, which can make the training model reach convergence, is the crucial part of the descriptor network. Siamese loss and triplet loss are the two main loss functions.

In recent years, the triplet loss function [10] has been widely used in learned descriptors and can mine the hard negative sample. However, recent works [10, 11] pay more attention to the relationship of descriptors from different types of samples and make less effort on the topological relation of descriptors from the same type of samples. The issue can cause the instability of descriptors, shown in Fig. 1 (a). The gray descriptors represent non-matching descriptors and the other types of color descriptors indicate matching pairs in the anchor and positive samples. Without topological constraint, the distance between non-matching descriptors is close to the distance between matching descriptors, which can cause instability of descriptors and results in mismatching. In order to improve the stability of the descriptor, we design a new triplet loss function, which considers the topological relationship of descriptors in the same sample by the Normal Distribution Function (NDF), shown in Fig. 1(b). In Fig. 1 (b), the distance between non-matching descriptors is exceeded to the distance of matching descriptors, and the algorithm can reduce the mismatching ratio of descriptors. Furthermore, to mine the hard-negative sample, we adopt the topological relationship with the algorithm NDF as the second-order constraint and select the relationship of descriptors from different types of samples as the first-order constraint. Moreover, the normalization processing is introduced to make the loss function value range from 0 to 1, which can save the memory space and reduce the calculation amount.

We can summarize the main contributions of the work as follows: (1) we design a two-order triplet loss function, which considers the topological relationship from the same sample and the interrelation of different types of samples. (2) we adopt a normalized algorithm to save memory space and reduce the amount of calculation. (3) Several experiments conducted on three types of datasets demonstrate that our algorithm performs better than the state-of-the-art methods.

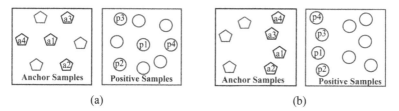

(a)   (b)

Fig. 1. Comparison between learned descriptors with (a) the previous method and (b) the algorithm NDF. In (a), the distance between matching descriptors pair (Blue and Red Descriptor) is not smaller than the distance between non-matching pairs (Grey Descriptor); In (b), the distance between matching descriptors pair is smaller than the distance between non-matching pairs. (Color figure online)

2 Related Work

As one of the main works in computer vision, local descriptors have gone through the development from the handcraft method to the learned method, and from the Siamese loss to the triplet loss. We mainly introduce some methods of local descriptors, and then analyze some current loss functions in this section.

As early as the 1990s, there were some works on local descriptor extraction. As the most famous handcraft method, SIFT [6] extracts feature descriptors by computing histograms with the gradient approach. Although the handcraft method can extract the descriptor, it lacks the semantic information of the image. In the past 20 years, many works [12, 13] have adopted the learned method to replace the handcraft method. Match-Net [12] is the first work to design a Siamese network to extract descriptors, including descriptor extraction and loss function. Some learned methods propose CNNs to generate local descriptors, such as TFeat [13], L2Net [14], HardNet [10], and DSM [11]. TFeat [13] demonstrates that mining negative samples can improve the performance of learned descriptors. L2Net [14] designs a seven-layer net-work structure and used the L2 distance to generate a unit norm descriptor. The architecture of L2Net is widely used in [10, 11, 15]. We also adopt L2Net as the descriptor extraction and redesign a new loss function.

The loss function plays a key role in the network structure, which can improve the convergence speed and reduce the prediction error in model training. HardNet [10] designs a triplet loss function in L2Net, which can minimize the distance between matching descriptors and enlarge the distance between non-matching descriptors. DOAP [9] introduces the optimized average precision into the learned binary and real-valued local feature descriptors and obtains more competitive results. Exp-TLoss [15] proposes the application of exponents to the triplet loss function in L2Net, and its excellent performance shows better generalization in many tasks. DSM [11] specifies a dynamic soft margin in L2Net to replace the hard-soft margin, which improves the performance of learned descriptors. Although these triplet-loss methods have achieved impressive performance, they ignore the topological relationship of neighboring descriptors in the same sample. This problem can lead to irregular spatial relationships of descriptors, thereby reducing the matching accuracy. To solve the above problem, we introduce the topological relationship with the algorithm NDF to the triplet loss, which can consider the influence of neighboring descriptors in the same sample.

3 Method

This section mainly describes the topological method with the algorithm NDF. The traditional triplet loss function methods only focus on the correlation of descriptors from different types of samples. These traditional methods failed to fully mine the hard-negative samples. To find the hard-negative sample, we adopt the topological relationship with the algorithm NDF to the triplet loss function. Furthermore, to reduce the amount of calculation, the new triplet loss function is normalized.

3.1 Triplet Loss Function

To better extract descriptors in image processing, it is generally assumed that the relationship of neighboring descriptors is linearly related and rigid. The Siamese-loss function only considers the relationship between positive samples and negative samples, while the triplet-loss function contains three different types of samples: anchor sample A, positive sample P, and negative sample N. p is a descriptor in the positive sample, and a is a descriptor of the anchor sample. $\{A, P\}$ is matching pairs, and $\{A, N\}$ is non-matching pairs. The triplet loss function can be expressed as follows:

$$L = \max(0, \mu + d_{\text{pos}} - d_{\text{neg}})$$ (1)

where, μ is the hyper-parameter, generally set as 1.0; d_{pos} is the correlation between matching descriptors in the positive samples; d_{neg} is the correlation between the non-matching descriptors in the negative samples. In the training model, the difference between d_{pos} and d_{neg} is used as the objective loss function. The purpose of the triplet loss function is to reduce the distance between matching descriptors and enlarge the distance between non-matching descriptors.

The negative loss function generally takes the distance between the non-matching descriptor pair as the evaluation parameter, and adopts the minimum value between the rows and columns of the Euclidean distance matrix D as the negative loss. In order to reduce the calculation memory, the matrix D is normalized. The negative loss function can be expressed as follows:

$$d_{\text{neg}} = \min\left(D, D^{'}\right)$$ (2)

where, D' is the transposed matrix of D.

This section mainly studies not only the correlation of descriptors from different types of samples, but also the topological relation of neighboring descriptors in the same sample. We adopt the correlation of descriptors from different types of samples as the first-order loss function, and the topological relationship of descriptors from the same sample as the second-order loss function. We adopt the diagonal elements in the two-order loss matrix as the positive loss function The positive loss function can be expressed as follows:

$$d_{\text{pos}} = \text{diag}(\lambda F_1 + (1 - \lambda)F_2)$$ (3)

where, F_1 is the first-order loss function $d(a, p)$ (Euclidean distance between two descriptors); F_2 is the second-order function. The parameter λ is a dynamic parameter. When $\lambda = 0$, the equation can only consider the second-order constraint; when $\lambda = 1$, the loss function degenerates to the first-order loss function. In this paper, we set $\lambda = 0.85$.

3.2 Topological Relationship with Normal Distribution

The traditional triplet loss function mainly focuses on the correlation of descriptors from different types of samples, and fails to pay enough attention to the topological relationship of descriptors in the same samples. The issue can lead to the instability of learned descriptors and affect their application, such as image recognition. This section focuses on the construction of the topological relationship of learned descriptors in the same samples and normalizing the function.

In Fig. 2, the gray descriptors represent non-matching descriptors and other color descriptors indicate matching descriptors (blue and red) in the anchor and positive samples. m descriptors are close to the descriptor a_1 in the anchor sample, and n descriptors are adjacent to the descriptor a_1 in the positive sample. Furthermore, k anchor descriptors match the corresponding positive descriptors. If the anchor descriptor a_i ($i = 1, 2, 3, 4$) matches the positive descriptor p_j ($j = 1, 2, 3, 4$), the difference value between $d(a_i, a_i)$ and $d(p_1, p_j)$ is equal to 0. The weight value between the grey descriptors and a_1 is 0. The weight parameter w means the relationship between a_1 and a_i ($i = 2, 3, 4$), which can match the corresponding positive descriptors.

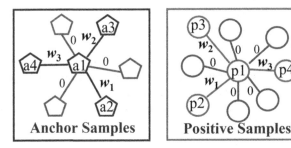

Fig. 2. Descriptors distribution of anchor samples and positive samples

The distance between matching descriptors is theoretically equal to 0, and the distance between non-matching descriptors is relatively large. However, the distance between matching descriptors is larger than 0 in practice, due to twisting, light, and other factors in the image. We propose the Normal Distribution Function (NDF) to construct the topological relationship of adjacent descriptors in the anchor sample, and anchor descriptors locate in the range of one standard deviation around the descriptor a_1, as shown in Fig. 3. We use this distribution function as the weight coefficient w_a, which can be expressed as follows:

$$w_a = \exp\left(-x^2/\sigma^2\right) \tag{4}$$

where x is the distance between the adjacent descriptor a_i ($i = 2, 3, 4$) and a_1; σ is the standard deviation of the distance x.

Similar to the distribution of anchor descriptors, we propose the Normal Distribution Function (NDF) as the weight coefficient w_p, which can be expressed as follows:

$$w_p = \exp\left(-y^2/\sigma^2\right) \tag{5}$$

where y is the distance the adjacent descriptor p_j ($j = 2, 3, 4$) and p_1; σ is the standard deviation of the distance y. In order to maintain the consistency of the weight parameter, the distance standard deviation σ is set to the same constant in formulas (4) and (5).

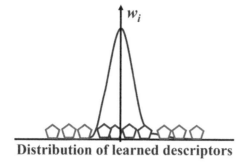

Distribution of learned descriptors

Fig. 3. The normal distribution of descriptors in the sample.

If there are k matching descriptors pairs in the anchor and positive samples, the distance matrix between matching descriptors can be expressed as follows:

$$D_{\text{w}} = \Sigma w_{\text{ak}} w_{\text{pk}} (x_{\text{k}} - y_{\text{k}})^2 \tag{6}$$

Due to the interference of non-matching descriptors, we will reduce the distance between matching descriptors and enlarge the distance between non-matching descriptors. Furthermore, in order to reduce the amount of calculation, we normalize the distance matrix. The new normalization distance matrix which means the second positive loss function can be expressed following as:

$$F_2 = 1 - \exp\left(-D_{\text{w}}^2\right) \tag{7}$$

4 Experiments

In this section, we propose three databases to verify the superiority of our algorithm NDF: UBC PhotoTourism [16], HPatches [17], and W1BS benchmark [18]. The benchmark UBC PhotoTourism can save training time and effectively improve the performance of learned descriptors and is used as a training dataset in many works. The dataset HPatches is a relatively complex dataset and we can adopt three types of subtasks to evaluate the performance of our descriptors. The benchmark W1BS adopts five different types of extreme conditions to evaluate the robustness of learned descriptors.

We introduce the algorithm NDF into the triplet loss function, which considers the topological relationship of adjacent descriptors. We adopt the triplet loss with our algorithm instead of the triplet loss in HardNet [10] and DSM [11] (denoted as HN + -NDF and DSM-NDF). The dataset UBC PhotoTourism has three subsets: Liberty, Yosemite, and Notredame. We use one subset as the training dataset, and the other two subsets as the test dataset. In the experiment, we use L2Net [14] as the network, which consists of convolutional layers, normalization layers, and Dropout. The batch size is set to 1024 and the learning rate decays is linearly selected from 0.1 to 0. The weight and momentum of Stochastic Gradient Descent (SGD) are 10^{-4} and 0.9, respectively. The image size required by L2Net is 32x32. Furthermore, each image is randomly flipped and rotated by 90, 180, and 270 degrees to increase the number of the dataset.

4.1 UBC Photo Tourism

UBC PhotoTourism dataset consists of Liberty, Notredame, and Yosemite. Generally, many works adopt the benchmark as the training dataset, which contains more than 100k matching and non-matching pairs and 400,000 standardized images. To evaluate the performance of different descriptors, we adopt FPR95 (the false positive rate of 0.95 accurate positive recall) as the evaluation parameter. The lower the FPR95, the better the performance. Finally, we compare HN + -NDF and DSM-NDF with some collection methods: DOAP [9], HardNet [10], DSM [11], L2Net [14], and DeepDesc [19], shown as in Table 1. In Table 1, the performance of learned descriptors trained by DSM -NDF is up to the best (FPR95 = 1.05). Furthermore, compared with original methods DSM and HardNet +, the mean FPR95 with our algorithm is reduced to 1.05 (DSM-NDF) and 1.22 (HN + -NDF), respectively. We can attribute the performance to the topological relationship with the algorithm NDF.

Table 1. Evaluating on the on the UBC PhotoTourism benchmark, and " + " denotes training with data augmentation.

Test	Liberty		Yosemite		Notredame		Mean
Train	Notredame	Yosemite	Liberty	Notredame	Liberty	Yosemite	
DeepDesc(2016)	1090		4.40		5.69		7.00
L2Net + (2017)	2.36	4.70	0.72	1.29	2.57	1.71	2.23
CSL2-Net + (2018)	1.71	3.87	0.56	1.09	2.07	1.30	1.76
DOAP + (2018)	1.54	2.62	0.43	0.87	2.00	1.21	1.45
HardNet(2018)	1.47	2.67	0.62	0.88	2.14	1.65	1.57
HardNet + (2018)	1.49	2.51	0.53	0.78	1.96	1.84	1.52
DSM + (2019)	1.21	2.01	0.39	**0.68**	1.51	1.29	1.18
HN + -NDF	1.23	2.19	0.38	0.73	1.52	1.26	1.22
DSM-NDF	**1.13**	**1.86**	**0.32**	**0.68**	**1.26**	**1.06**	**1.05**

4.2 HPatches

The HPatches dataset contains 59 sequences with geometric deformation and 57 scenes with illumination. Generally, we extract keypoints by Hessian, Harris, and DoG detectors from more than 1.5 million images, which divided into three levels of geometric noise: Easy, Hard, and Tough. Furthermore, we adopt three types of subsets (Image Matching, Patch Retrieval, and Patch Verification) to evaluate the performance. We use mAP as the evaluating parameter of the performance. The higher the mAP, the better the performance. We adopt the Liberty subset of the UBC PhotoTourism dataset as the training dataset.

We compare SIFT [6], DOAP [9], HardNet [10], and DSM [11] with HN + -NDF and DSM-NDF, shown in Fig. 4. As in Fig. 4, our methods are better than these original methods DSM and HardNet in many subsets. Furthermore, DSM-NDF achieved the best performance in the subtasks Patch Retrieval (mAP = 70.59) and Image Matching (mAP = 51.83), and achieved the second best in the subtask Patch Verification (mAP = 88.30). We attribute the good performance to the topological relationship with the algorithm NDF.

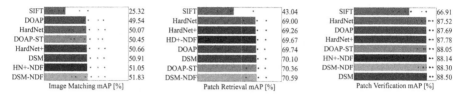

Fig. 4. Evaluating on the HPatches benchmark. ILLUM (×) and VIEWPT (◀) indicate the influence of illumination and viewpoint changes in matching task. DIFFSEQ (♦) and SAMESEQ (⋆) represent the source of negative examples in verification task. In all subtasks, three colors of points indicate three levels: easy (red), hard (green), tough (blue). (Color figure online)

4.3 Wide Baseline Stereo (W1BS)

We test our methods on the difficult conditions dataset W1BS, to evaluate the performance of learned descriptors. W1BS dataset consists of 5 parts: Appearance(A), Geometry(G), Illumination(L), Sensor(S) and Map to photo (map2photo). In this section, we adopt the subset Liberty as the training data, which are trained by two algorithms (HN + -NDF and DSM-NDF). We adopt mean Area Under Curve (mAUC) as the evaluation metric. The larger mAUC represents the better performance. We compare some state-of-the-art methods, including SIFT [6], HardNet [10], DSM [11] and Exp-Tloss [15], shown in Fig. 5. In Fig. 5, DSM-NDF (mAUC = 8.26) and HN + -NDF (mAUC = 8.31) are better than the original methods DSM (mAUC = 8.05) and HardNet + (mAUC = 8.30). Compared with these collection methods, the performance of HN + -NDF is up to the best in average image matching. Therefore, the experimental results on W1BS dataset also validate the effectiveness of the proposed method.

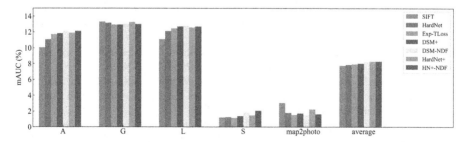

Fig. 5. Evaluating on the W1BS dataset.

5 Conclusion

In this work, we introduce the topological relationship with the algorithm NDF into the triplet loss function of HardNet + and DSM. The new triplet loss function with the algorithm NDF not only constructs the relationship of adjacent descriptors in the same samples, but also considers the interrelation of descriptors in different types of samples. We test our methods HN + -NDF and DSM-NDF on three different datasets and the performance of our descriptors in most tasks reaches state-of-the-art. These results demonstrate the generalization and application of our method.

Acknowledgement. This research is supported by National Natural Science Foundation of China (Grant No. 62006059), Guangdong Basic and Applied Basic Research Foundation (Grant No. 2019A1515110582), and the National Key Re-search and Development Program of China (2020YFB2104304).

References

1. Djordjevic, D., Cvetkovic, S., Nikoli´c, S.V.: An accurate method´for 3D object reconstruction from unordered sparse views. Signal Image Video Process. **11**(6) 1147–1154 (2017)
2. Zhang, B., Gao, Y., Zhao, S., Liu, J.: Local derivative pattern versus local binary pattern: Face recognition with high-order local pattern descriptor. IEEE Trans. Image Process. Publicat. IEEE Signal Process. Soc. **19**(2), 533–544 (2010)
3. Durrant-Whyte, H., Bailey, T.: Simultaneous localization and mapping (slam) part i. IEEE Robot. Autom. Mag. **13**(2) 99–110 (2006)
4. Durrant-Whyte, H.: Simultaneous localization and mapping (slam) part ii. IEEE Robot. Autom. Mag. **13**(3) 108–117 (2006)
5. Rublee, E., Rabaud, V., Konolige, K., Bradski, G.: ORB: an efficient alternative to sift or surf. In: International Conference on Computer Vision, pp. 2564–2571 (2011)
6. David, G.L.: Distinctive image features from scale-invariant keypoints. Int. J. Comput. Vis. **60**(2), 91–110 (2004)
7. Bay, H., Tuytelaars, T., Van, G.: Surf: speeded up robust features. In: European Conference on Computer Vision, pp. 404–417 (2006)
8. Simo-Serra, E., Trulls, E., Ferraz, L., Kokkinos, I., Fua, P., Moreno-Noguer, F.: Discriminative learning of deep convolutional feature point descriptors. In: International Conference on Computer Vision (ICCV), pp. 118–126 (2015)
9. He, K., Yan, L., Stan, S.: Local descriptors optimized for average precision. In: Proceedings of the IEEE Conference on Computer Vision and Pattern Recognition, pp. 596–605 (2018)
10. Mishchuk, A., Mishkin, D., Radenovic, F., Matas, J.: Working hard to know your neighbor's margins: local descriptor learning loss. In: Neural Information Processing Systems, pp. 4829–4840 (2017)
11. Zhang, L., Szymon, R.: Learning local descriptors with a CDF-based dynamic soft margin. In: International Conference on Computer Vision, pp. 2969–2978 (2019)
12. Han, X., Leung, T., Jia, Y., Rahul, S., Alexander, C.B.: Matchnet: unifying feature and metric learning for patch-based matching. In: Proceedings of the IEEE Conference on Computer Vision and Pattern Recognition, pp. 3279–3286 (2015)
13. Vassileios, B., Edgar, R., Daniel, P., et al.: Learning local feature descriptors with triplets and shallow convolutional neural networks. In: British Machine Vision Conference, pp. 119.1–119.11 (2016)

14. Tian, Y., Fan, B., Wu, F.: L2-net: deep learning of discriminative patch descriptor in euclide-an space. In: Proceedings of the IEEE Conference on Computer Vision and Pattern Recognition, pp. 6128–6136 (2017)
15. Wang, S., et al.: Better and faster: Exponential loss for image patch matching. In: International Conference on Computer Vision, pp. 4811–4820 (2019)
16. Brown, M., Winder, S.J.: Learning local image descriptors. In: Proceedings of the IEEE Conference on Computer Vision and Pattern Recognition, pp. 1–8 (2007)
17. Balntas, V., Lenc, K., Vedaldi, A., et al. Hpatches: a benchmark and evaluation of handcrafted and learned local descriptors. In: Proceedings of the IEEE Conference on Computer Vision and Pattern Recognition, pp. 3852–3861 (2017)
18. Mishkin, D., Matas, J., Perdoch, M., Lenc, K.: Wxbs: wide baseline stereo generalizations. In: Proceedings of the British Machine Vision Conference, pp. 12.1–12.12 (2015)
19. Edgar, S.-S., Eduard, T., Luis, F., et al.: Francesc, discriminative learning of deep convolutional feature point descriptors. In: International Conference on Computer Vision, pp. 118–126 (2015)

Supervised Non-negative Matrix Factorization Induced by Huber Loss

Ying Huang[1], Wen-Sheng Chen[1,2(✉)], Binbin Pan[1,2], and Bo Chen[1,2]

[1] College of Mathematics and Statistics, Shenzhen University, Shenzhen, China
{chenws,pbb,chenbo}@szu.edu.cn
[2] Guangdong Key Laboratory of Intelligent Information Processing,
Shenzhen University, Shenzhen, China

Abstract. Non-negative matrix factorization (NMF) has the ability for non-negative feature extraction and is successfully exploited for parts-based image representation. Most NMF-based algorithms utilize loss function with l_2-norm or Kullback-Leibler divergence to evaluate the quality of factorization. However, these measurements are sensitive to noise and outliers. Also, NMF is an unsupervised learning method and thus cannot acquire the desired performance in classification tasks. To address the problems of the NMF algorithm, this paper proposes a supervised non-negative matrix factorization (HSNMF) approach using Huber loss function, which is more robust to noise and outliers than l_2-norm. To enhance the discriminative power of NMF, we establish the objective function by incorporating two quantities including intra-class and inter-class information into the Huber loss function. The updating rules of HSNMF are derived using KKT conditions. The proposed HSNMF is shown to be convergent via the auxiliary function technique. Experimental results on face recognition demonstrate the robustness and superior performance of our algorithm when compared with the state-of-the-art algorithms.

Keywords: Non-negative matrix factorization · Huber loss · Supervised learning

1 Introduction

Non-negative matrix factorization (NMF) [1,2], proposed by Lee *et al.* in 1999, is an effective method for non-negative feature extraction. The basic idea of NMF is to represent image data using the linear combination of basis images under the non-negative constraint. It is equivalent to approximately decompose a non-negative data matrix into two low-rank non-negative factors, namely a basis matrix and a feature matrix, to achieve the purpose of parts-based image representation [1]. The traditional NMF model generally adopts the loss function with Frobenius norm or Kullback-Leibler (KL) divergence to estimate the quality of factorization. The principle of NMF has good interpretability and thus

© Springer Nature Switzerland AG 2021
Y. Peng et al. (Eds.): ICIG 2021, LNCS 12889, pp. 216–225, 2021.
https://doi.org/10.1007/978-3-030-87358-5_17

many variations of NMF [3–13] have been proposed to improve the performance of traditional NMF for different purposes, such as face recognition, clustering, and hyperspectral data analysis etc. Considering the adjacent graph structure of data, Cai *et al.* proposed a graph regularized NMF (GNMF) for image data representation [3]. He *et al.* presented a global and local structure based NMF algorithm by maximizing the nonlocal manifold structure while maintaining the local similarity of data [5]. Liu *et al.* proposed a dual locality preserving NMF method using Kullback-Leibler divergence [6]. Mani-NMF given by Chen *et al.* is based on the local manifold scatter and nonlocal manifold scatter [9]. But these approaches make use of the cost functions with Frobenius norm or KL-divergence, which are sensitive to noise and outliers. Therefore, some NMF-based approaches [10–13] have been presented to enhance the robustness of the traditional NMF algorithm. Huber loss is a function between l_1-norm and l_2-norm and is more robust to noise and outliers than l_2-norm. So, Du *et al.* proposed a Huber loss-based NMF, called HuberNMF [10], for data clustering. Wang *et al.* came up with another sparse graph Huber NMF [11] for cancer data analysis. Another loss with $l_{2,1}$-norm is also non-sensitive to noise because it does not amplify the value of noise and outliers. Kong *et al.* proposed a robust NMF(RNMF) algorithm using $l_{2,1}$-norm for image data clustering. Mao *et al.* employed correntropy induced metric to develop a robust graph NMF for image clustering [13]. However, most of the above-mentioned methods do not utilize the class label information and their performance will be degraded in classification tasks.

It can be seen that some of the aforementioned NMF algorithms encounter the non-robustness problem to noise and most of them have undesired performance in classification tasks because of failing to consider the class-label information. To address these problems of NMF, this paper proposes a novel supervised non-negative matrix factorization (HSNMF) approach using the Huber loss metric. We establish the objective function of the HSNMF model containing one reconstruction error term and two regularized terms, namely intra-class scatter and inter-class scatter. The reconstruction error is measured using Huber loss. The strategy of the class label-based scatters is to ensure the data from the same class have high similarity which is quantified via the intra-class scatter. While for the inter-class scatter, it makes the data from different classes be mutually separated as far as possible in the HSNMF feature space. The optimization problem is converted to two convex optimization sub-problems, which are solved to acquire the updating rules of HSNMF using KKT conditions. The proposed HSNMF algorithm is theoretically proved to be convergent. Our HSNMF algorithm achieves superior performance on face databases such as Yale and ORL databases under both noisy and non-noisy conditions.

The rest of this paper is organized as follows. Section 2 proposes our HSNMF algorithm. Experimental results are given in Sect. 3. Finally, Sect. 4 draws the conclusions.

2 Proposed HSNMF

This section will propose our HSNMF approach. The convergence of HSNMF algorithm is also discussed in this section.

2.1 HSNMF Model

Assume $X = [X_1, X_2, \cdots, X_s]$ is the training data matrix formed with s classes, where the kth class X_k contains n_k samples and $n = \sum\limits_{k=1}^{s} n_k$ is the total number of the training samples. The kernel matrix K can be calculated using RBF kernel function as

$$K = [k(x_i, x_j)]_{n \times n}, \tag{1}$$

where $k(x_i, x_j) = \exp(-\frac{\|x_i - x_j\|^2}{t})$ and $t > 0$ is the kernel parameter. Let $S = (S_{ij})_{n \times n}$ be the intra-class adjacency matrix, where

$$S_{ij} = \begin{cases} k(x_i, x_j), & \text{if } x_i, x_j \text{ from the same class} \\ 0, & \text{else} \end{cases} \tag{2}$$

and $\tilde{S} = (\tilde{S}_{ij})_{n \times n}$ be the inter-class adjacency matrix given by $\tilde{S} = K - S$. The non-negative feature vector of x_i is denoted by h_i. Two scatter quantities, namely Q and $\tilde{Q}$, are the intra-class scatter and the inter-class scatter, which are utilized to evaluate the degrees of dispersion of the intra-class data and inter-class data, respectively. HSNMF model will minimize the intra-class scatter and simultaneously maximize the inter-class scatter. We use the Huber loss $\delta(e)$ to resist the noise and establish the objective function $F(W, H)$ of HSNMF model as:

$$F(W, H) = \frac{1}{2} \sum_{i,j} \delta(X - WH)_{ij} + \frac{\alpha}{2} Q - \frac{\beta}{2} \tilde{Q}, \tag{3}$$

where $\delta(\cdot)$, Q and $\tilde{Q}$ are respectively given by

$$\delta(e) = \begin{cases} \frac{|e|^2}{2}, & |e| \leq c \\ c|e| - \frac{c^2}{2}, & \text{else,} \end{cases}$$

$$Q = \sum_{i,j=1}^{n} \|h_i - h_j\| S_{ij} = tr(HDH^T) - tr(HSH^T),$$

$$\tilde{Q} = \sum_{i,j=1}^{n} \|h_i - h_j\| \tilde{S}_{ij} = tr(H\tilde{D}H^T) - tr(H\tilde{S}H^T),$$

D and $\tilde{D}$ are two diagonal matrices with $D_{ii} = \sum\limits_{j=1}^{n} S_{ij}$ and $\tilde{D}_{ii} = \sum\limits_{j=1}^{n} \tilde{S}_{ij}$. The objective function (3) can be reformulated as:

$$F(W, H) = \frac{1}{2} \sum_{i,j} A_{ij} \cdot (X - WH)_{ij}^2 + \frac{\alpha}{2} [tr(HDH^T) - tr(HSH^T)]$$

$$- \frac{\beta}{2} [tr(H\tilde{D}H^T) - tr(H\tilde{S}H^T)], \tag{4}$$

where $A = (A_{ij})_{n \times n}$ is the auxiliary variable matrix, which only depends on the Huber loss function $\delta(\cdot)$ and

$$A_{ij} = \begin{cases} \frac{1}{2}, & \text{if } |X - WH|_{ij} \le c \\ \frac{c}{|X-WH|_{ij}} - \frac{c^2}{2|X-WH|_{ij}^2}, & \text{else} \end{cases} \tag{5}$$

The optimization problem of the proposed HSNMF is as follows:

$$\min_{W \ge 0, H \ge 0} F(W, H) \tag{6}$$

where $F(W, H)$ is defined by (4).

2.2 Update Rules of HSNMF

The optimization problem (6) can be converted to the following two convex optimization sub-problems:

$$\min_{H \ge 0} F_1(H) \quad \text{and} \quad \min_{W \ge 0} F_2(W),$$

where $F_1(H) = F(W, H)$ with W fixed and $F_2(W) = F(W, H)$ with H fixed. We focus on solving the problem $\min\limits_{H \ge 0} F_1(H)$ and first construct its Lagrange function shown below:

$$L_1(H) = \frac{1}{2} \sum_{j=1}^{n} (X_{\cdot j} - WH_{\cdot j})^T R_j (X_{\cdot j} - WH_{\cdot j}) + \frac{\alpha}{2} [tr(HDH^T) - tr(HSH^T)]$$

$$- \frac{\beta}{2} [tr(H\tilde{D}H^T) - tr(H\tilde{S}H^T)] + tr(\Phi^T H),$$

where R_j is a diagonal matrix with $R_j = diag(A_{\cdot j})$, Φ is the Lagrange multiplier matrix which has the same dimension as H. Set $\frac{\partial L_1(H)}{\partial H_{kj}} = 0$, namely,

$$\frac{\partial L_1(H)}{\partial H_{kj}} = (-W^T R_j X_{\cdot j} + W^T R_j WH_{\cdot j})_{kj} + \alpha(HD - HS)_{kj} - \beta(H\tilde{D} - H\tilde{S}) + \Phi_{kj} = 0.$$

Using KKT complementary slackness condition $H_{kj} \Phi_{kj} = 0$, we have

$$-H_{kj}(W^T R_j X_{\cdot j})_{kj} + H_{kj}(W^T R_j WH_{\cdot j})_{kj} + \alpha H_{kj}(HD - HS)_{kj} - \beta H_{kj}(H\tilde{D} - H\tilde{S})_{kj} = 0.$$

It yields from above equation that

$$H_{kj} = H_{kj} \frac{(W^T R_j X_{.j} + \alpha HS + \beta H\tilde{D})_{kj}}{(W^T R_j WH_{.j} + \alpha HD + \beta H\tilde{S})_{kj}} = H_{kj} \frac{[W^T(A \otimes X) + \alpha HS + \beta H\tilde{D}]_{kj}}{[W^T(A \otimes (WH)) + \alpha HD + \beta H\tilde{S}]_{kj}}$$

In a similar way, we acquire the update rule of W as:

$$W_{ik} = W_{ik} \frac{(X_{i.} P_i H^T)_{ik}}{(W_{i.} HP_i H^T)_{ik}} = W_{ik} \frac{[(A \otimes X)H^T]_{ik}}{[A \otimes (WH)H^T]_{ik}}.$$

The iterative formulas of our HSNMF method can be written in the following matrix form:

$$H \leftarrow H \otimes [W^T(A \otimes X) + \alpha HS + \beta H\tilde{D}] \oslash [W^T(A \otimes (WH)) + \alpha HD + \beta H\tilde{S}], \quad (7)$$
$$W \leftarrow W \otimes [(A \otimes X)H^T] \oslash [A \otimes (WH)H^T], \quad (8)$$
$$W \leftarrow W \oslash G.$$

where $G_{ij} = \sum_i W_{ij}$ and the entries of A are defined by (5).

2.3 Convergence of the Proposed HSNMF Algorithm

Using the auxiliary function technique [2], we can obtain the following convergence theorems.

Theorem 1. *For fixed W, $F_1(H_{.j})$ is nonincreasing under the following update rule:*

$$H_{.j} = H_{.j} \frac{(W^T R_j X_{.j} + \alpha HS_{.j} + \beta H\tilde{D}_{.j})}{(W^T R_j WH_{.j} + \alpha HD_{.j} + \beta H\tilde{S}_{.j})}.$$

Theorem 2. *For fixed H, $F_2(W_{i.})$ is nonincreasing under the following update rule:*

$$W_{i.} = W_{i.} \frac{(X_{i.} Q_i H^T)}{(W_{i.} HQ_i H^T)}.$$

The proofs of above theorems are omitted here for saving space.

2.4 HSNMF Algorithm

The proposed HSNMF algorithm for feature extraction and classification is designed in Algorithm 1.

3 Experimental Results

This section will report the experimental results on face recognition under nonnoisy and noisy conditions. The algorithms, including NMF [1], mani-NMF [9], and HuberNMF [10], are selected for comparisons. Two face databases, namely

Algorithm 1. HSNMF

Training Stage

Input: $X = [X_1, X_2, \cdots, X_s] \in R_+^{m \times n}$, parameters c, t, scatter parameters α, β, number of maximum iteration I_{max} and the number of feature r.

Output: $W \in R_+^{m \times r}, H \in R_+^{r \times n}$.

Step 1: Initialize W and H.

Step 2: Calculate $S, D, \tilde{S}, \tilde{D}$ defined in Sect. 2.1.

Step 3: Update A, W, H according to (5), (7), (8).

Step 4: If the iterative number attains I_{max}, the algorithm terminates and outputs W and H. Otherwise, return to Step 3.

Recognition Stage

Step 1: Compute the mean feature vector $\overline{H}_{\cdot k}$ from H and choose it as the representative of class k.

Step 2: For a testing sample y, its feature h_y is calculated via $h_y = W^+ y$, where W^+ is the pseudoinverse of W.

Step 3: If $l = \arg\min_k \|h_y - \overline{H}_{\cdot k}\|$, then y is assigned to class l.

Yale database and ORL database, are used for evaluations. Yale database contains 165 images for 15 people, each person has 11 images with different facial expressions such as normal, happy, sad, surprised, winking and etc. While for ORL database, it has 400 images from 40 individuals, each person has 10 images. Images for each person contain different facial expressions and different angles. The images of one person from Yale database or ORL database are shown in Fig. 1.

Fig. 1. Images of one person from Yale (left) and ORL (right) database.

3.1 Results on Non-noisy Images

On Yale database, we randomly choose $TN(TN = 2, 3, ..., 8)$ images of each person for training and the rest $(11 - TN)$ images from each person for testing. On ORL database, $TN(TN = 3, 4, ..., 9)$ images of each individual are randomly opted for training and the remaining $(10 - TN)$ images from each person for testing. Each experiment on two databases has been run for 10 times and the average results are recorded in Table 1 and Table 2, respectively. Table 1 gives the results on Yale database. It shows that the accuracy of our HSNMF increases from 79.56% with $TN = 2$ to 94.89% with $TN = 8$, while the accuracies of NMF, mani-NMF and HuberNMF increase from 72.67%, 74.37% and 75.63% with $TN = 2$ to 93.33%, 94.22% and 91.56% with $TN = 8$, respectively.

Table 1. Mean accuracy (%) versus Training Number (TN) on Yale database

TN	2	3	4	5	6	7	8
NMF	72.67	81.42	84.29	87.11	91.33	91.83	93.33
mani-NMF	74.37	82.42	84.86	89.00	91.33	91.83	94.22
HuberNMF	75.63	81.33	83.71	87.00	87.33	88.67	91.56
HSNMF	**79.56**	**87.00**	**89.24**	**91.33**	**93.47**	**92.33**	**94.89**

Table 2 tabulates the accuracies of different algorithms on ORL database. It reveals that the accuracy of the proposed HSNMF algorithm increases from 87.14% with $TN = 3$ to 96.50% with $TN = 9$. While for NMF, mani-NMF and HuberNMF algorithms, their accuracies increase from 85.07%, 86.00% and 86.18% with $TN = 3$ to 95.00%, 94.50% and 95.25% with $TN = 9$, respectively.

Table 2. Mean accuracy (%) versus Training Number (TN) on ORL database

TN	3	4	5	6	7	8	9
NMF	85.07	87.54	90.40	92.38	93.08	94.00	95.00
mani-NMF	86.00	88.25	92.35	92.00	93.50	95.13	94.50
HuberNMF	86.18	88.38	91.75	92.44	93.83	95.75	95.25
HSNMF	**87.14**	**89.83**	**93.60**	**94.06**	**95.17**	**96.00**	**96.50**

It can be seen that HuberNMF and mani-NMF algorithms outperform NMF algorithm in most cases, and our HSNMF method surpasses all the compared algorithms on both Yale database and ORL database. The results also imply that the proposed scatter quantities are beneficial for face classification.

3.2　Results on Noisy Images

This subsection will evaluate the performance of the proposed HSNMF approach under different Gaussian noises. Figure 2 shows facial images with Gaussian noise from Yale and ORL databases. We randomly select 5 non-noisy images from each person for training and the rest noisy images for testing. The testing images are contaminated using Gaussian noise with zero mean and σ variance ranging from 0 to 0.4. The experiment is repeatedly run 10 times and its average results are

Fig. 2. Images of one person from Yale (left) and ORL (right) databases with Gaussian noise.

calculated for comparisons. The recognition rates on Yale database and ORL database are respectively listed in Table 3 and Table 4, which demonstrate that when the variance σ of Gaussian noise increases from 0 to 0.4, the accuracies of all compared algorithms will decrease. On Yale database, the accuracy of our HSNMF method decreases from 90.67% to 60.89%, while NMF, mani-NMF and Huber-NMF algorithms decrease from 87.78%, 88.56% and 85.78% to 57.00%, 59.22% and 57.22%, respectively. We see that NMF has the worst performance and the proposed HSNMF method is more robust to Gaussian noises than all the other methods.

Table 3. Mean accuracy (%) versus Gaussian variance (σ) on Yale database

σ	0	0.05	0.1	0.15	0.2	0.25	0.3	0.35	0.4
NMF	87.78	84.90	82.67	77.33	74.11	70.56	61.67	54.44	57.00
mani-NMF	88.56	86.11	83.56	80.44	76.22	69.67	61.89	56.67	59.22
HuberNMF	85.78	85.44	81.56	76.22	78.00	73.11	63.22	60.00	57.22
HSNMF	**90.67**	**89.89**	**86.11**	**84.22**	**81.11**	**76.44**	**67.33**	**62.56**	**60.89**

Table 4 gives the results with different Gaussian noise on the ORL database. As the variance of noise increases from 0 to 0.4, the accuracy of our HSNMF method decreases from 93.65% to 70.00%, while the accuracies of NMF, mani-NMF, and Huber-NMF methods decrease from 90.45%, 91.40%, and 91.55% to 57.60%, 60.75%, and 69.10%, respectively. It shows that HuberNMF has better performance than other methods except for our HSNMF method. The proposed algorithm not only achieves the highest accuracies but also is robust to noise.

Table 4. Mean accuracy (%) versus Gaussian variance (σ) on ORL database

σ	0	0.05	0.1	0.15	0.2	0.25	0.3	0.35	0.4
NMF	90.45	88.15	83.90	80.60	76.85	73.70	68.70	61.20	57.60
mani-NMF	91.40	88.30	84.90	84.05	78.70	74.95	68.25	63.40	60.75
HuberNMF	91.55	90.70	87.80	87.05	82.85	80.35	76.45	69.15	69.10
HSNMF	**93.65**	**91.50**	**88.85**	**88.85**	**84.50**	**81.85**	**79.25**	**73.45**	**70.00**

4 Conclusions

This paper proposes a robust supervised non-negative matrix factorization (HSNMF) approach for face recognition. The HSNMF model is established using Huber loss and class label-based scatters. The Huber loss metric is utilized to resist noise and increase the robustness of our HSNMF algorithm. Two scatter quantities, namely, intra-class scatter and inter-class scatter, are constructed to enhance the discriminant power of the feature. We make use of KKT conditions to derive the iterative formulas of HSNMF and further prove the convergence of our algorithm. Two face databases are chosen to evaluate the performance of our HSNMF method. Experimental results have shown the robustness and effectiveness of the proposed HSNMF method.

Acknowledgments. This work was partially supported by the Stable Support Planning Project of Universities in Shenzhen (20200815000520001) and the Interdisciplinary Innovation Team of Shenzhen University. We would like to thank Olivetti Research Laboratory, Yale University for providing the facial image databases.

References

1. Lee, D.D., Seung, H.S.: Learning the parts of objects by non-negative matrix factorization. Nature **401**(6755), 788–791 (1999)
2. Lee, D.D., Seung, H.S.: Algorithms for non-negative matrix factorization. Neural Inf. Process. Syst. **13**(6), 556–562 (2001)
3. Cai, D., He, X., Han, J., Huang, T.S.: Graph regularized nonnegative matrix factorization for data representation. IEEE Trans. Pattern Anal. Mach. Intell. **33**(08), 1548–1560 (2011)
4. Guan, N., Tao, D., Luo, Z., Yuan, B.: Manifold regularized discriminative nonnegative matrix factorization with fast gradient descent. IEEE Trans. Image Process. **20**(7), 2030–2048 (2011)
5. He, M., Wei, F., Jia, X.: Globally maximizing, locally minimizing: regularized nonnegative matrix factorization for hyperspectral data feature extraction. In: 2012 4th Workshop on Hyperspectral Image and Signal Processing (WHISPERS), pp. 1–4 (2012)
6. Liu, F.: Dual locality preserving nonnegative matrix factorization for image analysis. In: 2012 IEEE International Conference on Granular Computing, pp. 300–303 (2012)
7. Meng, Y., Shang, R., Jiao, L., Zhang, W., Yang, S.: Dual-graph regularized nonnegative matrix factorization with sparse and orthogonal constraints. Eng. Appl. Artif. Intell. **69**, 24–35 (2018)
8. Wu, W., Kwong, S., Zhou, Y., Jia, Y., Gao, W.: Nonnegative matrix factorization with mixed hypergraph regularization for community detection. Inf. Sci. **435**, 263–281 (2018)
9. Chen, W.S., Wang, Q., Pan, B., Chen, B.: Nonnegative matrix factorization with manifold structure for face recognition. Int. J. Wavelets Multiresolution Inf. Process. **17**(02), 1940006 (2019)
10. Du, L., Li, X., Shen, Y.: Robust nonnegative matrix factorization via half-quadratic minimization. In: 2012 IEEE 12th International Conference on Data Mining, pp. 201–210 (2012)

11. Wang, C.Y., Liu, J.X., Yu, N., Zheng, C.H.: Sparse graph regularization non-negative matrix factorization based on Huber loss model for cancer data analysis. Front. Genet. **10**, 1054 (2019)
12. Kong, D., Ding, C., Huang, H.: Robust nonnegative matrix factorization using $l_{2,1}$-norm. In: Proceedings of the 20th ACM International Conference on Information and Knowledge Management, pp. 673–682 (2011)
13. Mao, B., Guan, N., Tao, D., Huang, X., Luo, Z.: Correntropy induced metric based graph regularized non-negative matrix factorization. Neurocomputing **204**, 172–182 (2016)

Small Sample Identification for Specific Emitter Based on Adversarial Embedded Networks

Wei Zhang[1,3], Li Jiang[2(✉)], Congzhang Ding[2], Huaizong Shao[3], Jingran Lin[3], and Chuan Chen[2]

[1] Key Laboratory of Electronic Information Control, Chengdu 610036, China
[2] College of Mechanical and Electrical Engineering,
Chengdu University of Technology, Chengdu 610059, China
[3] Univerisity of Electronic Science and Technology of China, Chengdu 611731, China

Abstract. The technology of specific emitter identification (SEI) has important military significance in electronic warfare. However, it is hard to obtain sufficient signal samples from the specific emitter in the electromagnetic environment of the battlefield. Therefore, it is a challenging issue to learn from a handful of samples to accurately identify complex and changeable emitter. A small sample identification method based on adversarial embedded networks is proposed to solve this problem. This method combines the improved generative adversarial networks (GAN) and the Convolutional neural networks (CNN) for classification. In the context of a handful of samples, high-quality simulation samples are generated by the generator in the generative adversarial networks to expand the available feature quantities of the model, thereby improving the recognition efficiency and accuracy. Through the training and testing of a small number of radar emitter data and communication station emitter data, the results show that the method just needs a small amount of data to achieve higher recognition accuracy.

Keywords: Specific emitter identification · Small sample · Adversarial embedded networks · Generative adversarial networks · Convolutional neural networks

1 Introduction

The technology of specific emitter identification (SEI) is one of the important means to obtain information control in modern information warfare [1–4]. The main task of SEI is to analyse the electromagnetic signals obtained from reconnaissance. According to the difference of the hardware of each equipment, the "fingerprint" characteristics of the transmitted electromagnetic signal are different from those of other equipment [5]. Therefore, the system, status, purpose,

Supported by National Natural Science Foundation of China under Grants U20B2070 and Sichuan Science and Technology Program under Grant 2020YFG0170.

© Springer Nature Switzerland AG 2021
Y. Peng et al. (Eds.): ICIG 2021, LNCS 12889, pp. 226–237, 2021.
https://doi.org/10.1007/978-3-030-87358-5_18

model, threat level, and other information of the specific emitters are determined. Thus, carrier tracking, surveillance, electronic jamming and military attack can be realized to the enemy-specific emitter.

The core steps of the SEI technology research mainly include signal feature extraction and classifier design [6–8]. The accuracy and efficiency of SEI are determined by the results of feature extraction and analysis of the received electromagnetic signals, which affect the effectiveness of electronic reconnaissance equipment. Therefore, how to extract the characteristic parameters which can completely characterize the "individual fingerprint characteristics" of the specific emitter from the electromagnetic signal is the research focus of the electronic reconnaissance system.

For fingerprint characteristics of individuals, the traditional manual extraction methods mainly extract the features of fractal dimension [9], wavelet transform, high-order spectrum [10], clutter and envelope [11]. However, the manual extraction methods for individual features have a high demand for professional knowledge, and are highly dependent on specific classification circumstances. With the development of artificial intelligence, there has been a breakthrough in using deep learning to identify specific emitter individuals. Deep neural networks can automatically and abstractly extract the characteristics of signals, and mine the data characteristics by the greedy layer-wise training method, which can effectively obtain the "fingerprint characteristics" of specific emitters for individual identification [7,12,13].

In [14], a full-automatic method for identifying seven Pulse Repetition Interval modulation types using CNN was proposed. The simulation results show that the identification method based on CNN not only improves the performance of the system but also is robust in the environment with loss and false pulse. An SEI algorithm based on deep learning architecture is proposed in [6]. A deep residual network is constructed to learn the Hilbert spectral image of the signal, and the residual architecture utilized effectively solves the degradation problem. To further extract the feature information hidden in the original signal, CNN, depth-limited Boltzmann machine and stacked auto-encoders (SAE) are applied to identify the specific emitter [15]. An individual radar emitter identification method based on deep learning and the SEI framework based on ensemble learning is mentioned in [16,17] respectively. In [18], a novel SEI algorithm based on joint depth time-frequency features is proposed. However, deep learning methods rely on a large number of data training, which can easily lead to dimensionality disaster. Therefore, feature extraction of data is required before data input into a deep learning network. To solve this problem, the CNN and SAE are combined to construct a denoising auto-encoder (DAE) for feature extraction, and the weight sharing characteristic of CNN and greedy layer-wise pre-training method are used to make the whole network have better generalization performance [19].

The electromagnetic environment of the battlefield is becoming increasingly complex in modern electronic warfare, and the modulation types and parameters of specific emitters are more complex and variable. New specific emitters and new working modes may appear at any moment. Therefore, it is hard to obtain sufficient specific emitter samples for the training of deep learning networks when reconnaissance conditions are limited. The problem of SEI under the condition of small samples is formed, which makes it tougher to identify complex and changeable specific emitters timely, quickly and accurately. In this paper, a small samples SEI method based on an adversarial embedded networks is proposed. This method combines the improved GAN and CNN classification network. In the case of a small number of time-frequency spectrogram samples, the accuracy of emitter recognition from small sample time-frequency spectrogram is improved by generating samples to assist the training classifier. In the end, the effectiveness of the method is verified by the measured data.

2   Formation of the Time-Frequency Spectrogram

The fine features of the emitter signal are generally concentrated in the frequency domain. Fourier transform is a commonly adopted analysis method in the frequency domain. However, the feature representation in the spectrum from the Fourier transform is global, which is unable to reflect the local signal characteristics along the time dimension. Therefore, this paper employs the short-time Fourier transform (STFT) to transform the original one-dimensional signal in the time domain to two-dimensional spectrogram in the time-frequency domain, where the characteristics of time and frequency domain can be obtained at the same time, so that the information hidden in the time series of a one-dimensional signal can be effectively and completely characterized. Let the signal be $x(t)$ and the sliding window function be $w(t)$, then the expression of STFT can be given by

$$X(t, f) = \int x(\tau)w(\tau - t)^{-j2\pi f\tau}d\tau \tag{1}$$

According to (1), the spectrogram is formed by performing a fast Fourier transform on a series of short-time frames which are separated from the original time-domain signal by using a window to slide over time. A sample original signal in the time domain and the corresponding spectrogram in the time-frequency domain are shown in Figs. 1 and 2.

3   Construction of Adversarial Embedded Network Model

The small sample recognition model of adversarial embedded networks combines the improved GAN and CNN classification network. The model structure is shown in Fig. 3, where X is a sample source data set, and Y is a small-scale sample data set. $label_x$ and $label_y$ are individual labels corresponding to signal samples. Meanwhile, D_x and D_y are discrimination models for image sources in the sample data sets X and Y. The Cy is a classifier for Y-type targets. In addition, G and F are generation models for realizing the mutual transformation of the sample data sets X and Y.

The detailed structure diagram of the adversarial embedded network based on GAN and CNN is shown in Fig. 4. Among them, $\hat{Y}$ represents the sample

$G(y, label_y)$ generated by the generator G conversion of the sample X, and $\widetilde{X}$ represents the reconstructed sample $F(\hat{Y}, label_x)$ generated by the generator F transformation of the generated sample $\hat{Y}$. Similarly, $\hat{X}$ represents the sample $G(Y, label_y)$ that the sample Y is converted by the generator F, and $\widetilde{Y}$ represents the reconstructed sample $G(\hat{X}, label_y)$ of the generated sample $\hat{X}$ transformed by the generator G. The discriminator D_y is used to discriminate whether the data comes from Y or $\hat{Y}$, and the discriminator D_x is utilized to discriminate whether the data comes from X or $\hat{X}$. C_y, which is trained by Y and $\hat{Y}$ together, is applied as a classifier to realize the classification task of Y. The network structure realizes the end-to-end training process by generating samples to assist the training of classifiers in the case of a handful of samples.

3.1   Generative Model

The generated models G and F have the uniform network structure as shown in Fig. 5, which mainly includes convolution layer module, residual network structure module and deconvolution layer module. An improvement to adding a category label constraint to the generated model is as follows.

$$G : input = [x, label_x]$$
$$F : input = [y, label_y] \tag{2}$$

Where x and y are the time-frequency diagrams of the data sets X and Y respectively. The label $label_x$ corresponding to x is duplicated and expanded to the size of the image x. $[x, label_x]$ indicates that the expanded $label_x$ is used as a new layer of a channel to be spliced with x as the input of the generated model G. Similarly, $[y, label_y]$ indicates that the expanded $label_y$ is utilized as a new layer of a channel to be spliced with y as the input of the generated model F.

The spliced data serving as the input of the generative network firstly passes through a plurality of convolution layer modules to extract high-order features, then passes through multiple residual error network structures. Ultimately, the

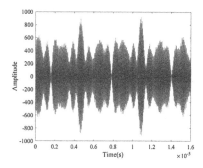

Fig. 1. A sample of original signal in time domain.

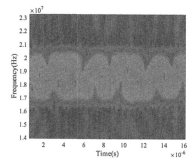

Fig. 2. A sample of spectrogram in time-frequency domain.

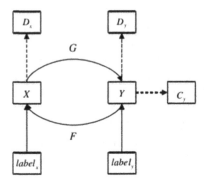

Fig. 3. The structure of the small sample recognition model for adversarial embedded network.

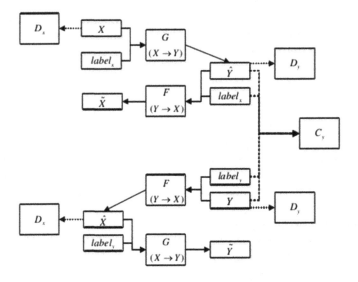

Fig. 4. The structure of the small sample recognition model for adversarial embedded network.

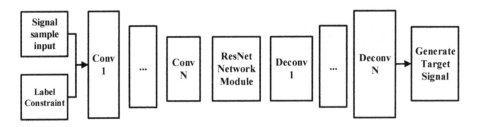

Fig. 5. The network structure of generation model for adversarial embedded network.

generated signal is output after passing through a plurality of deconvolution modules. Structural modules such as Conv1, ResNet module, and Deconv1 contain not only the necessary convolution operations but also other operations such as Batch Normalization and activation functions. The specific network structure can be correspondingly adjusted according to the practical application.

3.2   Discriminative Model

The network structures of the discriminative models D_x and D_y are the same, and the network structure diagram is shown Fig. 6. The network is a binary classification model, and the network structure mainly comprises a convolution layer module and a full connection layer module. When a signal is an input to the network, the high-order features are firstly extracted through the convolution layer module, then the final output is obtained through a plurality of full-connection layer modules. The network of the discriminative models is applied to determine whether that data is from a true sample or a false sample.

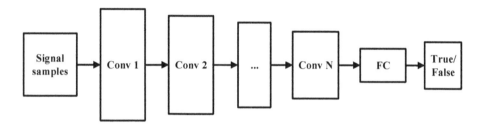

Fig. 6. The schematic diagram of network structure of discriminators D_x and D_y.

3.3   Classifier

The classifier C_y mainly realizes the classification function in the network. The selection range of classifier network structure is relatively extensive and flexible, such as CNN, ResNet and other existing classification network models can be selected. In addition, the relevant classification network can also be defined according to practical problems. For example, the CNN has utilized as the C_y classifier in this paper.

3.4   Objective Function and Loss Function

To make the samples of the generated enhanced signal similar to the real signal samples, two auxiliary loss functions are introduced to supervise the signal reconstruction. Different from the signal time-domain diagram which contains obvious boundaries and smooth regions, the signal frequency-domain diagram often contains a large number of details. Therefore, the discriminator is utilized to explicitly supervise the reconstruction of the signal frequency-domain diagram in the training process of the generator network and the discriminator network. In conclusion, the objective function of the proposed model can be expressed as Formula (2).

$$G^* = \min_{G} \min_{G} \max_{G} \max_{G} a \cdot L_{GAN}(G, D) + (L_{DATA}(G) + L_T(G)) \qquad (3)$$

where the first term $L_{GAN}(G, D)$ is the countermeasure loss, and the other two terms are the two auxiliary content losses. Furthermore, the hyper-parameter a is utilized to balance the countermeasure loss and the auxiliary loss.

The signal sample set is $Y : \{(y^1, label_y^1), (y^2, label_y^2), \cdots, (y^N, label_y^N)\}$, and the number of samples is N_1. The signal sample set is $X : \{(x^1, label_x^1), (x^2, label_x^2), \cdots, (x^N, label_x^N)\}$, and the number of samples is N_2. The cycle-consistency constraint parameters are λ_1 and λ_2, and the weights of the generated samples and the real samples to the objective function of the classification network are λ_3 and λ_4 respectively. In addition, the size of data batch is B. The optimization algorithm is Adam, and the learning rate is l_r. An adversarial embedded network based on GAN and CNN is employed to generate samples to train the classification network with a small amount of real data, thus improving the network performance. The whole network structure integrates the GAN improved network and the classification network into a whole. The end-to-end training can be performed. The specific algorithm flow is as follows.

1 The set and the label of real source sample $(x^j, label_x^j), j = 1, 2, \cdots, N_2$ and the set and the label of small sample $(y^i, label_y^i), j = 1, 2, \cdots, N_1$ are utilized as the input of the generation model G and F in the fusion network structure. Then the conversion learning of the real source sample and the small sample set can be performed.

2 The generation model (G,F) and the discrimination model (D_x,D_y) are trained alternately and iteratively to generate the countermeasure sample $\hat{y}$ from the model sample. $\hat{y}$ is consistent with the label of the corresponding real source sample x^j, which can be expressed as $(\hat{y}^j, label_x^j)$.

3 The combat samples, their labels and the real samples are utilized as the input of the classification network C_y in the combat embedding network structure. The network C_y is trained, and the C_y parameters are adjusted according to the classification error.

4 The process from step 1 to step 3 is repeated until the training results become stable, then the network training is completed.

5 The network C_y in the fusion network structure is extracted as the final classification model, which is utilized for small sample target recognition.

4 Radar Emitters Recognition

The training samples includes the original samples and the countermeasure samples generated by the built adversarial embedded network model. The ratio of the number of countermeasure samples to the original sample data is 1:4 as the total training samples of the adversarial embedded network. In other words, under the number of 100 pulse original samples and the number of 400 generated pulse enhanced adversarial samples, the simulator data of radar emitters is trained. The results of accuracy rate and loss rate are shown in Fig. 7. The loss rate caused by model training can decline smoothly. The reason is that the structure of the CNN utilized in the classification network of the adversarial embedded recognition model is relatively simple, so the training process of the model is relatively stable and the convergence is fast. After 30 rounds of training, the recognition accuracy is stable at about 82%.

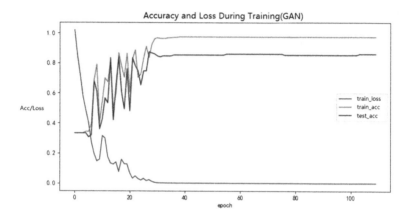

Fig. 7. The accuracy rate and loss rate of radar emitters recognition.

The confusion matrices of the adversarial embedded network model in the 5th, 20th, 50th and 100th rounds are shown in Fig. 8. There is a feature learning process at the beginning of the model training, and the individual feature differences of radar emitters have not been learned in the fifth round. As the training process continues, the adversarial embedded network model gradually completes the discrimination of individual features of Radar-1 and Radar-3 targets. The recognition effect is excellent, but the discrimination of Radar-2 targets is still in a completely chaotic state. After more than 50 rounds of training, the discrimination ability of Radar-2 has been significantly improved. The adversarial embedded network model has achieved excellent overall recognition results. After fine-tuning and optimization, the final training accuracy rate reaches 86.67%.

5 Communication Station Emitters Recognition

Similarly, under the number of 100 pulse original samples and 400 generated pulse enhanced countermeasure samples, the data of communication station emitters are trained. The accuracy rate and loss rate results are shown in Fig. 9.

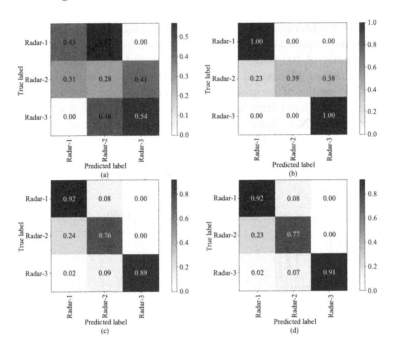

Fig. 8. The confusion matrices of GAN for radar emitters recognition. (a), (b), (c) and (d) denote the confusion matrix at the 5*th*, 20*th*, 50*th* and 100*th* rounds, respectively.

The training process of the communication station emitter is similar to the radar emitter, and the loss rate of model training can be smoothly reduced. The model training process is relatively stable.

The confusion matrices of the adversarial embedded network model in the 5*th*, 20*th*, 40*th* and 60*th* rounds are shown in Fig. 10. There is a feature learning process at the beginning of the model training, and the learning process of the communication station emitter is slightly faster than that of the radar emitter. In the fifth round, the target numbered Station-3 has been partially learned. The recognition accuracy rate has reached 82%, but the individual feature differences of the other two communication station emitters have not been learned yet. With the continuation of the training process, the adversarial embedded network model can distinguish the individual features of the three communication station emitters Station-1, Station-2 and Station-3, and the recognition accuracy is stable at about 86%. In the training process after more than 40 rounds, the recognition performance of the adversarial embedded network model has not been significantly improved. The reason is that the model has achieved nearly 100% accuracy on the training set since the 30*th* round. Moreover, new knowledge and individual fingerprint differences can no longer be learned from the training process, so the optimization model cannot be updated, leading to the obvious bottleneck of the embedded network in target recognition.

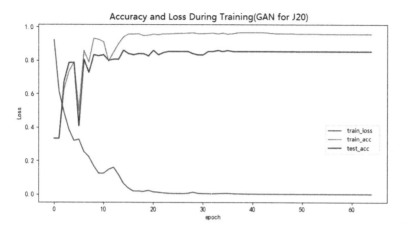

Fig. 9. The accuracy rate and loss rate of communication station emitters recognition.

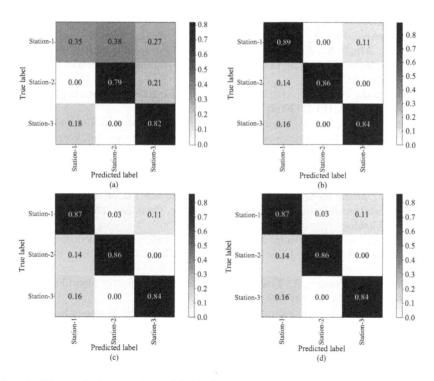

Fig. 10. The confusion matrices of GAN for communication station emitters recognition. (a), (b), (c) and (d) denote the confusion matrix at the 5th, 20th, 40th and 60th rounds, respectively.

6   Conclusion

Aiming at the issue that it is hard to identify a handful of multi-channel electromagnetic signals quickly in the battlefield electromagnetic environment, a small sample recognition algorithm based on adversarial embedded network is proposed. Above all, the small sample recognition model of the countermeasure embedding network is built, and the adversarial samples of a specific class are generated by utilizing the generative model with class label constraint in the generative adversarial network. Then, the small sample data of communication station emitters and radar emitters are trained and recognized, respectively. The accuracy and loss rate of target recognition verify the feasibility of the algorithm.

References

1. Sa, K., Lang, D., Wang, C., Bai, Y.: Specific emitter identification techniques for the internet of things. IEEE Access **8**, 1644–1652 (2019)
2. Talbot, K.I., Duley, P.R., Hyatt, M.H.: Specific emitter identification and verification. Technol. Rev. **1**, 113–133 (2003)
3. Gok, G., Alp, Y.K., Arikan, O.: A new method for specific emitter identification with results on real radar measurements. IEEE Trans. Inf. Forensics Secur. **15**, 3335–3346 (2020)
4. Matuszewski, J.: Specific emitter identification. In: 2008 International Radar Symposium, pp. 1–4. IEEE (2008)
5. Gong, J., Xu, X., Lei, Y.: Unsupervised specific emitter identification method using radio-frequency fingerprint embedded InfoGAN. IEEE Trans. Inf. Forensics Secur. **15**, 2898–2913 (2020)
6. Pan, Y., Yang, S., Peng, H., Li, T., Wang, W.: Specific emitter identification based on deep residual networks. IEEE Access **7**, 54425–54434 (2019)
7. Xiao, Y., Zhang Wei, X.: Specific emitter identification of radar based on one dimensional convolution neural network. J. Phys. Conf. Ser. **1550**, 032114 (2020). IOP Publishing
8. Huang, G., Yuan, Y., Wang, X., Huang, Z.: Specific emitter identification based on nonlinear dynamical characteristics. Can. J. Electr. Comput. Eng. **39**(1), 34–41 (2016)
9. Dudczyk, J., Kawalec, A.: Fractal features of specific emitter identification. Acta Phys. Pol. A **124**(3), 406–409 (2013)
10. Hadjileontiadis, L.J.: Continuous wavelet transform and higher-order spectrum: combinatory potentialities in breath sound analysis and electroencephalogram-based pain characterization. Philos. Trans. R. Soc. A Math. Phys. Eng. Sci. **376**(2126), 20170249 (2018)
11. Xu, S.: Individual radio transmitter identification based on spurious modulation characteristics of signal envelop. IEEE (2008)
12. Xu, J., Shen, W., Wang, W.: Individual recognition of communication emitter based on deep learning. In: 2018 12th International Symposium on Antennas, Propagation and EM Theory (ISAPE), pp. 1–4. IEEE (2018)
13. Liu, Z.M.: Multi-feature fusion for specific emitter identification via deep ensemble learning. Digital Signal Process. **110**, 102939 (2021)

14. Li, X., Huang, Z., Wang, F., Wang, X., Liu, T.: Toward convolutional neural networks on pulse repetition interval modulation recognition. IEEE Commun. Lett. **22**(11), 2286–2289 (2018)
15. Ding, L., Wang, S., Wang, F., Zhang, W.: Specific emitter identification via convolutional neural networks. IEEE Commun. Lett. **22**(12), 2591–2594 (2018)
16. Sun, W., Wang, L., Sun, S.: Radar emitter individual identification based on convolutional neural network learning. Math. Probl. Eng. **2021**, 5341940 (2021)
17. Shen, S., Sadoughi, M., Li, M., Wang, Z., Hu, C.: Deep convolutional neural networks with ensemble learning and transfer learning for capacity estimation of lithium-ion batteries. Appl. Energy **260**, 114296 (2020)
18. Li, H., Jing, W., Bai, Y.: Radar emitter recognition based on deep learning architecture. In: 2016 CIE International Conference on Radar (RADAR), pp. 1–5. IEEE (2016)
19. Ding, Y., Zhang, X., Tang, J.: A noisy sparse convolution neural network based on stacked auto-encoders. In: 2017 IEEE International Conference on Systems, Man, and Cybernetics (SMC), pp. 3457–3461. IEEE (2017)

Multi-mode Tensor Singular Value Decomposition for Low-Rank Image Recovery

Lanlan Feng, Ce Zhu$^{(\boxtimes)}$, and Yipeng Liu

School of Information and Communication Engineering, University of Electronic Science and Technology of China, Chengdu 611731, China
{eczhu,yipengliu}@uestc.edu.cn

Abstract. Tensor completion aims to recover the missing entries in multi-way data. Based on the low-rank assumption, many methods according to different tensor decomposition frameworks have been developed for image recovery. Recently emerging tensor singular value decomposition (t-SVD) can better characterize the low-rank structure for 3rd-order data, but it suffers from rotation sensitivity and demands for a higher-order version. As the high-order extension of matrix SVD, Tucker decomposition tries to extract low-rank information along each mode. Inspired by this, we extend t-SVD into an improved one called multi-mode tensor singular value decomposition, which can explore the low-rank information along different modes. Based on it, a convex multi-dimensional square model for tensor completion is proposed and solved by the classic alternating direction method of multipliers. Experimental results on color image and multispectral image completion demonstrate the superior recovery accuracy and competitive CPU time of our method compared with existing state-of-the-art ones.

Keywords: Tensor SVD · Tensor nuclear norm · Tucker decomposition · Tensor completion · Image recovery

1 Introduction

As the higher-order generalization of scalar, vector and matrix, tensor can better represent the multi-dimensional structure information in multi-way data, such as color image and multispectral image [8]. In most cases, the multi-way data have redundant information and low-rank tensor factorization is an efficient way to represent it using a few factors, which has a wide range of applications in many fields such as signal processing and machine learning. Tensor completion is one of them, which can recover the missing entries during data acquisition and transformation [13].

Supported in part by the National Natural Science Foundation of China (NSFC) under Grant 62020106011 and Grant U19A2052 and in part by the Sichuan Science and Technology Program under Grant 2019YFH008.

Current low-rank tensor completion methods can be divided into different categories according to different tensor decomposition frameworks, such as canonical polyadic (CP) decomposition [20], Tucker decomposition [5], tensor singular value decomposition (t-SVD) [14], tensor networks (tensor tree, tensor train, tensor ring, etc.) [1,6,12]. CP decomposition factorizes a tensor into the sum of a group of rank-one tensors and the CP rank is defined as the smallest number of rank-one tensors [8]. However, the CP rank is NP-hard to compute and cannot be accurately estimated [20]. Tucker decomposition, also called high-order singular value decomposition, can represent a multi-dimensional tensor as a core tensor multiplied by a factor matrix along each mode. Tucker rank is defined as a vector whose elements are the ranks of the factor matrices. As the rank minimization problem is NP-hard, it is usually relaxed into the convex nuclear norm minimization problem [3]. Based on the Tucker format, the sum of nuclear norm (SNN) for all mode-k unfolding matrices is proposed as a convex surrogate of the Tucker rank [10]. As the mode-k unfolding operator arranges the k-th mode of tensor as the row while the rest modes as the column of matrix, SNN method is usually extremely unbalanced and may result in poor performance.

Based on the t-product operation for three-way tensors (see the detail in Definition 3), tensor singular value decomposition (t-SVD) is proposed recently [4,8]. It can be easily computed by the fast Fourier transform (FFT) and the matrix SVDs. Based on t-SVD framework, the tensor nuclear norm (TNN) has been studied for the low-rank approximation problem. Compared with matrix SVD, t-SVD can better excavate low-rank structure in three-way tensor. However, in t-SVD, the low-rank information in the 3rd mode is not fully exploited and results in rotation sensitivity. Several improved versions have been studied in [11,21]. On the other hand, t-SVD can only process three-way data and effective higher-dimensional tensor decomposition framework is needed for improvement.

In this paper, motivated by the idea that Tucker decomposition is a high-order extension of matrix SVD, we expand t-SVD to a more compact multi-dimensional version called as multi-mode tensor singular value decomposition (MTSVD), which can more effectively exploit the correlations along all modes. The multi-dimensional tensor is decomposed as a core tensor, each mode of which is connected to a 3rd-order orthogonal factor tensor by t-product. Furthermore, benefiting from the square model for Tucker decomposition [17], which have been proven to have a lower bound for successful recovery than SNN, we propose a convex multi-dimensional tensor square model via TNN (MSTNN) for tensor completion and the classic alternating direction method of multipliers (ADMM) [2] is used for solution. Real experiments including color image completion and multispectral image completion have been conducted to evaluate the performance of the proposed method.

The rest of this paper is organized as follows. Section 2 gives some basic notations and preliminaries about t-SVD and Tucker decomposition. Then the proposed tensor decomposition MTSVD and the related model for tensor completion are presented in Sect. 3. In Sect. 4, two experiments are conducted to show the performance. Finally, we give the conclusions in Sect. 5.

2 Notations and Preliminaries

Firstly, some basic notations about this work are given briefly. A scalar, a vector, a matrix and a tensor are denoted by a, $\mathbf{a}$, $\mathbf{A}$, $\mathcal{A}$, respectively. $\mathbb{R}$ represents the fields of real numbers. Specially, for $\mathcal{A} \in \mathbb{R}^{I_1 \times I_2 \times I_3}$, $\mathcal{A}(:, :, i_3)$ and $\mathbf{A}^{(i_3)}$ represent the i_3-th frontal slices. Moreover, $\mathcal{A}(i_1, i_2, :)$ denotes the tube fiber of $\mathcal{A}$. We use $\hat{\mathcal{A}} = \mathrm{fft}(\mathcal{A}, [], 3)$ to represent the fast Fourier transform (FFT) along the 3-rd mode of $\mathcal{A}$. And $\mathcal{A} = \mathrm{ifft}(\hat{\mathcal{A}}, [], 3)$ stands for the inverse operation.

We define the matrix nuclear norm $\|\mathbf{A}\|_*$ as the sum of all singular values of $\mathbf{A} \in \mathbb{R}^{I_1 \times I_2}$, and $\|\mathcal{A}\|_F = \sqrt{\sum_{i_1, i_2, \cdots, i_n} a_{i_1, i_2, \cdots, i_n}{}^2}$ represents the Frobenius norm of the N-dimensional tensor $\mathcal{A} \in \mathbb{R}^{I_1 \times I_2 \times \cdots \times I_N}$.

Then we give the preliminaries related to Tucker decomposition in Definition 1 and 2 while Definition 3, 4, 5 and 6 are for tensor singular value decomposition.

Definition 1 (Mode-k unfolding and Mode-k product). *[8]   For $\mathcal{A} \in \mathbb{R}^{I_1 \times I_2 \times \cdots \times I_N}$, its mode-$k$ unfolding matrix is denoted as $\mathbf{A}_{(k)} \in \mathbb{R}^{I_k \times I_{k+1} \cdots I_N I_1 \cdots I_{k-1}}$. Combined with a matrix $\mathbf{B} \in \mathbb{R}^{J \times I_k}$, the mode-$k$ product is defined by $\mathcal{C} = \mathcal{A} \times_k \mathbf{B}$, $\mathcal{C} \in \mathbb{R}^{I_1 \times \cdots \times I_{k-1} \times J \times I_{k+1} \times \cdots \times I_N}$, whose elements are obtained by*

$$\mathcal{C}(i_1, \cdots, j, \cdots, i_N) = \sum_{i_k=1}^{I_k} \mathcal{A}(i_1, \cdots, i_k, \cdots, i_N) \mathbf{B}(j, i_k). \tag{1}$$

In matrix form, it can be represented as $\mathbf{C}_{(k)} = \mathbf{B} \mathbf{A}_{(k)}$.

Definition 2 (Tucker decomposition). *[8] Tucker decomposition, also called high-order singular value decomposition (HOSVD), can decompose an N-way tensor $\mathcal{A} \in \mathbb{R}^{I_1 \times I_2 \times \cdots \times I_N}$ into a core tensor multiplied by a factor matrix along each mode, which is formulated as:*

$$\mathcal{A} = \mathcal{G} \times_1 \mathbf{U}_1 \times_2 \mathbf{U}_2 \cdots \times_N \mathbf{U}_N, \tag{2}$$

where $\mathcal{G} \in \mathbb{R}^{R_1 \times R_2 \times \cdots R_N}$ is called as core tensor, $\mathbf{U}_n \in \mathbb{R}^{I_n \times R_n}, n = 1, \cdots, N$ are factor matrices which satisfy $\mathbf{U}_n^T \mathbf{U}_n = \mathbf{I}_{R_n}$, $R_n \leq I_n$. The Tucker rank is defined as a vector as $\mathrm{rank}_{tc}(\mathcal{X}) = (R_1, R_2, \cdots, R_N)$.

Definition 3 (T-product). *[4, 15] Given two tensors $\mathcal{A} \in \mathbb{R}^{I_1 \times I_2 \times I_3}$ and $\mathcal{B} \in \mathbb{R}^{I_2 \times J \times I_3}$, the t-product $\mathcal{C} = \mathcal{A} * \mathcal{B} \in \mathbb{R}^{I_1 \times J \times I_3}$ can be computed by*

$$\mathcal{C}(i, j, :) = \sum_{i_2=1}^{I_2} \mathcal{A}(i, k, :) \bullet \mathcal{B}(k, j, :), \tag{3}$$

where $\bullet$ denotes the circular convolution between two tubal fiber vectors.

It has been proven in detail that this t-product operator can be calculated by the matrix multiplication in the Fourier domain as $\hat{\mathbf{C}}^{(i_3)} = \hat{\mathbf{A}}^{(i_3)}\hat{\mathbf{B}}^{(i_3)}, i_3 = 1, \cdots, I_3$.

Definition 4 (Conjugate transpose, Orthogonal tensor, F-diagonal tensor). *[7, 14] For $\mathcal{A} \in \mathbb{R}^{I_1 \times I_2 \times I_3}$, the conjugate transpose is denoted as $\mathcal{A}^{\mathrm{T}} \in \mathbb{R}^{I_2 \times I_1 \times I_3}$, which is achieved by firstly conjugating transpose each of frontal slice and then reversing the order of frontal slices from 2 to I_3. $\mathcal{A}$ is called orthogonal when it satisfies $\mathcal{A}^{\mathrm{T}} * \mathcal{A} = \mathcal{A} * \mathcal{A}^{\mathrm{T}} = \mathcal{I}$, where $\mathcal{I}$ is identity tensor, whose first frontal slice is identity matrix and the rest are zero. $\mathcal{A}$ is called f-diagonal when each of frontal slice $\mathbf{A}^{(i_3)}, i_3 = 1, \cdots, I_3$ is a diagonal matrix.*

Definition 5 (T-SVD). *[8] For a three-way tensor $\mathcal{A} \in \mathbb{R}^{I_1 \times I_2 \times I_3}$, its tensor singular value decomposition (t-SVD) can be represents as*

$$\mathcal{A} = \mathcal{U} * \mathcal{S} * \mathcal{V}^{\mathrm{T}}, \tag{4}$$

where $\mathcal{U} \in \mathbb{R}^{I_1 \times I_1 \times I_3}$ and $\mathcal{V} \in \mathbb{R}^{I_2 \times I_2 \times I_3}$ are orthogonal tensors while $\mathcal{S} \in \mathbb{R}^{I_1 \times I_2 \times I_3}$ is a f-diagonal tensor. When eliminating non-zero elements, we have the skinny t-SVD as $\mathcal{A} = \mathcal{U}_s * \mathcal{S}_s * \mathcal{V}_s^{\mathrm{T}}$, which satisfy $\mathcal{U}_s \in \mathbb{R}^{I_1 \times R \times I_3}, \mathcal{S}_s \in \mathbb{R}^{R \times R \times I_3}, \mathcal{V}_s \in \mathbb{R}^{I_2 \times R \times I_3}, \mathcal{U}_s^{\mathrm{T}} * \mathcal{U}_s = \mathcal{V}_s^{\mathrm{T}} * \mathcal{V}_s = \mathcal{I}$. R is called as the tubal rank.

Based on t-product, this decomposition can be obtained by computing matrix SVDs in the Fourier domain. Then we can acquire

$$\hat{\mathbf{A}}^{(i_3)} = \hat{\mathbf{U}}^{(i_3)}\hat{\mathbf{S}}^{(i_3)}\hat{\mathbf{V}}^{(i_3)^{\mathrm{T}}}, i_3 = 1, \cdots, I_3. \tag{5}$$

Definition 6 (TNN). *[15, 19] Given a tensor $\mathcal{A} \in \mathbb{R}^{I_1 \times I_2 \times I_3}$ and the skinny t-SVD $\mathcal{A} = \mathcal{U}_s * \mathcal{S}_s * \mathcal{V}_s^{\mathrm{T}}$, the tensor nuclear norm (TNN) is defined as*

$$\|\mathcal{A}\|_* = \frac{1}{I_3}\|\hat{\mathcal{A}}\|_* = \frac{1}{I_3}\sum_{i_3=1}^{I_3}\|\hat{\mathbf{A}}^{(i_3)}\|_* = \frac{1}{I_3}\sum_{i_3=1}^{I_3}\sum_{r=1}^{R}\hat{\mathcal{S}}_s(r, r, i_3). \tag{6}$$

3   Method

Tucker decomposition tries to exploit the low-rank information along all modes, and the unbalance of Mode-k unfolding operator in Tucker decomposition will inevitably bring performance degradation in general. T-SVD can more effectively describe the low-rank structure of 3rd-order data compared with matrix SVD. However, it can only process third-order data, and deals with the 1st and 2ed modes by matrix SVD but leaves the third mode by FFT, so the results after decomposition will change with varying dimension orders. In this section, we first propose a new tensor decomposition framework called multi-mode tensor singular value decomposition (MTSVD). Then we introduce the related convex optimization models for tensor completion based on different nuclear norms minimization. Finally, a multi-dimensional square model via TNN (MSTNN) for tensor completion and the corresponding algorithm are presented in detail.

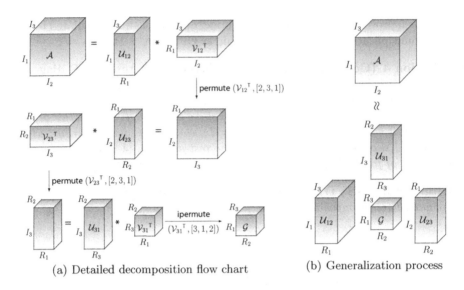

(a) Detailed decomposition flow chart   (b) Generalization process

Fig. 1. Multi-mode tensor singular value decomposition for a three-way tensor.

3.1 The Proposed Multi-mode Tensor Singular Value Decomposition

To more effectively exploit the correlations along all modes and obtain more compact low-rank tensor decomposition framework, we combine the advantage of Tucker decomposition and t-SVD, and propose a new tensor framework via t-product called MTSVD. For easy understanding, we give a detailed decomposition flow chart for an order-3 tensor in Fig. 1 (a). The first row shows the process to mainly extract the low-rank information in the first and second dimensions. Then we conduct the permutation operation and the second row shows the decomposition mainly for the second and third dimensions. Finally, the process in the last row is mainly for 1st and 2ed modes. Similar to the classic Tucker decomposition, we give the generalization decomposition in Fig. 1(b).

We first define the Mode-$(k, k+1)$ unfolding tensor and Mode-k t-product operation in Definition 7 and 8. Based on them, the proposed new MTSVD is elaborated in Definition 9.

Definition 7 (Mode-$(k, k+1)$ unfolding). *For a tensor $\mathcal{A} \in \mathbb{R}^{I_1 \times I_2 \times \cdots \times I_N}$, its mode-$(k, k+1)$ unfolding tensor is represented as $\mathcal{A}_{(k,k+1)} \in \mathbb{R}^{I_k \times I_{k+1} \times \prod_{s \neq k, k+1} I_s}$, whose frontal slices are the lexicographic ordering of the mode-$(k, k+1)$ slices of $\mathcal{A}$. Mathematically, the mapping relation of $(i_1, i_2, \cdots, i_N)$-th entry of $\mathcal{A}$ and (i_k, i_{k+1}, j)-th entry of $\mathcal{X}_{(k,k+1)}$ is*

$$j = 1 + \sum_{\substack{s=1 \\ s \neq k, s \neq k+1}}^{N} (i_s - 1) J_s \text{ with } J_s = \prod_{\substack{m=1 \\ m \neq k, m \neq k+1}}^{s-1} i_m.$$

Definition 8 (Mode-k t-product). *Given two tensors* $\mathcal{A} \in \mathbb{R}^{I_1 \times \cdots \times I_N}$ *and* $\mathcal{B} \in \mathbb{R}^{J \times I_k \times \prod_{s \neq k,k+1} I_s}$, *the mode-$k$ t-product* $\mathcal{C} \in \mathbb{R}^{I_1 \times \cdots \times I_{k-1} \times J \times I_{k+1} \times \cdots \times I_N}$ *is*

$$\mathcal{C} = \mathcal{A} *_k \mathcal{B}, \tag{7}$$

whose $(i_1, \cdots, j, \cdots, i_N)$*-th element in the Fourier domain is computed by*

$$\sum_{i_k=1}^{I_k} \hat{\mathcal{A}}_{(k,k+1)}(i_k, i_{k+1}, \prod_{\substack{s=1 \\ s \neq k, s \neq k+1}}^{N} i_s) \hat{\mathcal{B}}(j, i_k, \prod_{\substack{s=1 \\ s \neq k, s \neq k+1}}^{N} i_s). \tag{8}$$

Making use of the mode-$(k, k+1)$ unfolding operator in Definition 7, we can have the following property:

$$\mathcal{C}_{(k,k+1)} = \mathcal{B} * \mathcal{A}_{(k,k+1)}. \tag{9}$$

Definition 9 (Multi-mode tensor singular value decomposition). *Given a tensor* $\mathcal{X} \in \mathbb{R}^{I_1 \times I_2 \times \cdots \times I_N}$, *the multi-mode tensor singular value decomposition (MTSVD) can factorize it as*

$$\mathcal{A} = \mathcal{G} *_N \mathcal{U}_{N1} *_{N-1} \mathcal{U}_{(N-1)N} \cdots *_1 \mathcal{U}_{12}. \tag{10}$$

where $\mathcal{G} \in \mathbb{R}^{R_1 \times R_2 \times \cdots \times R_N}$ *is the core tensor,* $\mathcal{U}_{k(k+1)}(k = 1, 2, \cdots, N)$ *is the orthogonal three-way tensor, which mainly characterizes the low-rank information of mode k and $k+1$.*

3.2   The Related Convex Optimization Works

We first give the related convex optimization models for tensor completion. Based on Tucker decomposition, the sum of nuclear norm (SNN) minimization [5,10] model is proposed to recover an N-dimensional tensor $\mathcal{X} \in \mathbb{R}^{I_1 \times I_2 \times \cdots \times I_N}$:

$$\min_{\mathcal{X}} \sum_{n=1}^{N} \alpha_n \|\mathbf{X}_{(n)}\|_*, \quad \text{s.t. } \mathcal{X}_{\mathbf{\Omega}} = \mathcal{T}_{\mathbf{\Omega}}, \tag{11}$$

where $\mathbf{\Omega}$ is the index set of known entries. According to Definition 1, we can know that mode-n unfolding matrix $\mathbf{X}_{(n)} \in \mathbb{R}^{I_n \times I_{n+1} \cdots I_N I_1 \cdots I_{n-1}}, n = 1, \cdots, N$. The high unbalance of row and column of $\mathbf{X}_{(n)}$ will lead to poor performance.

In [17], a more square model has been proposed as

$$\min_{\mathcal{X}} \|\mathbf{X}_{[p]}\|_*, \quad \text{s.t. } \mathcal{X}_{\mathbf{\Omega}} = \mathcal{T}_{\mathbf{\Omega}}, \tag{12}$$

where $\mathbf{X}_{[p]} \in \mathbb{R}^{I \times J}$ is the square reshaping operator, which group any p modes as the first dimension I and the rest $(N - p)$ modes as the second one J. I and J should be as equal as possible in order to produce a more balanced matrix. Results both in theory and in numerical experiments, has shown that the square method can reduce the number of measurements for successful recovery required by SNN model.

Based on the t-SVD framework, the tensor completion model based on TNN [16] for a three-way data is represented as

$$\min_{\mathcal{X}} \|\mathcal{X}\|_{\text{TNN}}, \quad \text{s.t. } \mathcal{X}_{\Omega} = \mathcal{T}_{\Omega}. \tag{13}$$

For this tensor completion problem from uniform random sampling, it has been proved that, to recover a tensor with size $I_1 \times I_2 \times I_3$ with tubal rank R, the sample complexity is $O\left(R \max(I_1, I_2)I_3 \log^2(\max(I_1, I_2)I_3)\right)$ [16]. When the first and second modes differ large, the completion results will be affected.

3.3 The Proposed Multi-dimensional Square Model via TNN for Tensor Completion

Motivated by the square method about Tucker decomposition, we first generalize Mode-$(k, k+1)$ unfolding operator in Definition 7 into Mode-k square unfolding operator in Definition 10.

Definition 10 (Mode-k square unfolding). *For a multi-way tensor $\mathcal{A} \in \mathbb{R}^{I_1 \times I_2 \times \cdots \times I_N}$, its mode-$k$ square unfolding tensor $\mathcal{A}_{<k>} \in \mathbb{R}^{J_k \times J_{k+1} \times \prod_{s \neq k, k+1} I_s}$ can be obtained from its mode -$(k, k+1)$ unfolding tensor $\mathcal{A}_{(k,k+1)} \in \mathbb{R}^{I_k \times I_{k+1} \times \prod_{s \neq k, k+1} I_s}$ as follows*

$$\mathcal{A}_{<k>} = \text{reshape}(\mathcal{X}_{(k,k+1)}, J_k, J_{k+1}, [\,]), \tag{14}$$

which satisfies $I_k \times I_{k+1} = J_k \times J_{k+1}$, J_k and J_{k+1} are two integers that are as equal as possible.

Given the observed tensor $\mathcal{T} \in \mathbb{R}^{I_1 \times I_2 \times \cdots \times I_N}$ whose partial entries are missing, the task of tensor completion is to recover the original complete data $\mathcal{X} \in \mathbb{R}^{I_1 \times I_2 \times \cdots \times I_N}$, which is low-rank or approximately low-rank. In this paper, we propose a multi-dimensional square model via TNN (MSTNN) as follows

$$\min_{\mathcal{X}} \sum_{n=1}^{N} \alpha_n \|\mathcal{X}_{<n>}\|_{\text{TNN}} \quad \text{s.t. } \mathcal{X}_{\Omega} = \mathcal{T}_{\Omega}. \tag{15}$$

where $\|.\|_{\text{TNN}}$ is the classic TNN in Definition 6, the weighting vector $\alpha = [\alpha_1, \alpha_2, \cdots, \alpha_N]$ satisfies $\sum_{n=1}^{N} \alpha_n = 1, \alpha_n > 0, n = 1, 2, \ldots, N$.

The auxiliary variables $\{\mathcal{M}_n\}_{n=1}^{N}$ ($\{\mathcal{M}\}$ for convenience) are introduced to solve the problem (15), then we can obtain the following problem:

$$\min_{\mathcal{X}, \{\mathcal{M}\}} \sum_{n=1}^{N} \alpha_n \|\mathcal{M}_{n<n>}\|_{\text{TNN}}, \quad \text{s.t. } \mathcal{X}_{\Omega} = \mathcal{T}_{\Omega}, \mathcal{M}_n = \mathcal{X}, n = 1, 2, \ldots, N. \tag{16}$$

It can be solved by the classic alternating direction method of multipliers (ADMM) [2]. The augmented Lagrangian function can be formulated as

$$\mathfrak{L}(\mathcal{X}, \{\mathcal{M}\}, \Lambda_n) = \sum_{n=1}^{N} \alpha_n \|\mathcal{M}_{n<n>}\|_{\text{TNN}} + \sum_{n=1}^{N} \{\langle \Lambda_n, \mathcal{M}_n - \mathcal{X} \rangle + \frac{\gamma_n}{2} \|\mathcal{M}_n - \mathcal{X}\|_{\text{F}}^2\}$$

$$\text{s.t. } \mathcal{X}_{\Omega} = \mathcal{T}_{\Omega}.$$

$$\tag{17}$$

where $\{\Lambda_n\}_{n=1}^N$ ($\{\Lambda\}$ for convenience) are dual variables, $\gamma_n > 0, n = 1, \cdots, N$ is penalty operators. Each variable can be alternatively minimized while fixing the others. The key problems are the update of $\{\mathcal{M}\}$ and $\mathcal{X}$, whose details are presented as follows:

1) Subproblem with respect to $\{\mathcal{M}\}$: Extracting the items with respect to $\{\mathcal{M}\}$ from the Eq. (17), we need to solve:

$$\min_{\{\mathcal{M}\}} \sum_{n=1}^N \alpha_n \|\mathcal{M}_{n<n>}\|_{\text{TNN}} + \sum_{n=1}^N \{\langle \Lambda_n, \mathcal{M}_n - \mathcal{X} \rangle + \frac{\gamma_n}{2}\|\mathcal{M}_n - \mathcal{X}\|_{\text{F}}^2\} \quad (18)$$

which is equivalent to

$$\min_{\{\mathcal{M}\}} \sum_{n=1}^N \{\alpha_n \|\mathcal{M}_{n<n>}\|_{\text{TNN}} + \frac{\gamma_n}{2}\|\mathcal{M}_n - \mathcal{X} + \frac{\Lambda_n}{\gamma_n}\|_{\text{F}}^2\}. \quad (19)$$

Then we can get N independent subproblems:

$$\min_{\{\mathcal{M}\}} \alpha_n \|\mathcal{M}_{n<n>}\|_{\text{TNN}} + \frac{\gamma_n}{2}\|\mathcal{M}_{n<n>} - \mathcal{X}_{<n>} + \frac{\Lambda_{n<n>}}{\gamma_n}\|_{\text{F}}^2, \ n = 1, \cdots, N. \quad (20)$$

Utilizing the tensor singular value threshold (t-SVT) operator [15], when the iteration is k, each subproblem has the closed-form solution:

$$\mathcal{M}_{n<n>}^{k+1} := \text{tsvt}_{\frac{\alpha_n}{\gamma_n}}\left(\mathcal{X}_{<n>}^k - \frac{\Lambda_{n<n>}^k}{\gamma_n}\right). \quad (21)$$

Let the t-SVD of $\mathcal{A}$ is $\mathcal{A} = \mathcal{U} * \mathcal{S} * \mathcal{V}^{\text{T}}$, then the t-SVT operator with respect to τ is defined as $\text{tsvt}_\tau(\mathcal{A}) = \mathcal{U} * \mathcal{S}_\tau * \mathcal{V}^{\text{T}}$, where $\mathcal{S}_\tau = \text{ifft}\left((\hat{\mathcal{S}} - \tau)_+, [], 3\right)$, $t_+ = \max(t, 0)$.

Then the transformation between $\mathcal{M}_n$ and $\mathcal{M}_{n<n>}$ can be represented as $\mathcal{M}_n = \text{t-fold}(\mathcal{M}_{n<n>}), n = 1, 2, \cdots, N$.

2) Subproblem with respect to $\mathcal{X}$: When the related items about $\mathcal{X}$ are extracted from the Eq. (17), we can get the following optimization problem:

$$\min_{\mathcal{X}} \sum_{n=1}^N \{\langle \Lambda_n, \mathcal{M}_n - \mathcal{X} \rangle + \frac{\gamma_n}{2}\|\mathcal{M}_n - \mathcal{X}\|_{\text{F}}^2\}, \quad \text{s.t. } \mathcal{X}_{\boldsymbol{\Omega}} = \mathcal{T}_{\boldsymbol{\Omega}}. \quad (22)$$

The difficulty of the problem (22) is the solution of elements outside the index set $\boldsymbol{\Omega}$, we can take the derivation and set it to zero. Then we can obtain

$$\mathcal{X}^{k+1} := \begin{cases} \sum_{n=1}^N \{\Lambda_n^k + \gamma_n^k \mathcal{M}_n^{k+1}\}/\sum_{n=1}^N \gamma_n^k, & (i_1, \cdots, i_n) \notin \boldsymbol{\Omega} \\ 0, & (i_1, \cdots, i_n) \in \boldsymbol{\Omega}. \end{cases} \quad (23)$$

Finally, we summarize the algorithm for the MSTNN for tensor completion in Algorithm 1.

Algorithm 1: ADMM for MSTNN

Input: $\mathcal{T} \in \mathbb{R}^{I_1 \times I_2 \times \cdots \times I_N}$.

Initialize: $\mathcal{X}, \mathcal{M}_n, \Lambda_n, \gamma_n, n = 1, \cdots, N$.

while not converged **do**

    1. Update $\mathcal{M}_{n<n>}^{k+1}$ according to equation (21), $n = 1, \cdots, N$;

    2. $\mathcal{M}_n^{k+1} = \text{t-fold}(\mathcal{M}_{n<n>}^{k+1}), n = 1, \cdots, N$;

    3. Update $\mathcal{X}^{k+1}$ according to equation (23);

    4. Update $\Lambda_n^{k+1} := \Lambda_n^k + \gamma_n(\mathcal{M}_n^{k+1} - \mathcal{X}^{k+1}), n = 1, \cdots, N$.

    5. Check the convergence condition: $\|\mathcal{X}^{k+1} - \mathcal{X}^k\|_{\mathrm{F}}^2 / \|\mathcal{X}^k\|_{\mathrm{F}}^2 \leq \epsilon$.

end while

Output: $\mathcal{X}$.

---

4   Applications

In order to demonstrate the efficiency of the proposed MSTNN method, we compare it with five start-of-the-art methods including FBCP [20] (based on CP decomposition), Square [17] and HaLRTC [10] (based on Tucker decomposition), TNN [16] and WSTNN [21] (based on the t-SVD). We choose the parameters $\alpha = [0.01, 1, 1]/2.01, \gamma = 0.06 \times \alpha, \epsilon = 10^{-3}$ and conduct two experiments including color image completion and multispectral image (MSI) completion. The common evaluation index peak signal-to-noise ratio (PSNR) is computed to measure the recovery accuracy and the CPU time is also presented. All experiments are realized using MATLAB R2020a software on a computer with Intel i7-8700K CPU and 16 GB RAM.

airplane   sails   barbara   house   lena   peppers   sailboat   tulips

Fig. 2. Original images.

4.1   Color Image Completion

We choose 8 color images with the same size $256 \times 256 \times 3$ for comparison [9,18]. The details of these images have been shown in Fig. 2. Given a tensor $\mathcal{T} \in \mathbb{R}^{I_1 \times I_2 \times \cdots \times I_N}$, we randomly choose P entries from $\mathcal{T}$, then the sample ratio (SR) is defined as $\text{SR} = P / \prod_{n=1}^{N} I_n$. Figure 3 shows the comparison results in terms of PSNR and CPU time with different sample ratios from 5% to 50% with step 5% on 8 color images. No matter what the sample ratio is, MSTNN can obtain the highest PSNR values. Meanwhile, the CPU time consumed by the proposed method decreases as the sampling rate increases and the convergence

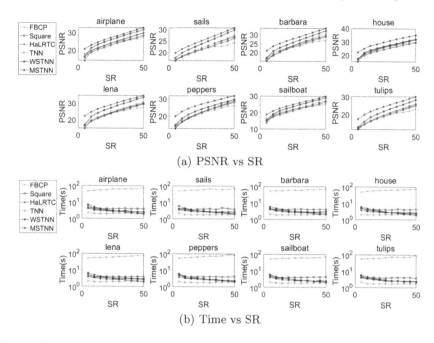

(a) PSNR vs SR

(b) Time vs SR

Fig. 3. Comparison of different methods (FBCP, Square, HaLRTC, TNN, WSTNN and MSTNN) with different sample ratios from 5% to 50% on 8 color images.

speed is relatively fast especially compared with FBCP method based on CP decomposition. Figure 4 also gives the completion results of several examples with different sample ratios 5%, 10% and 20%. It shows that MSTNN can recover more details compared with other start-of-the-art methods.

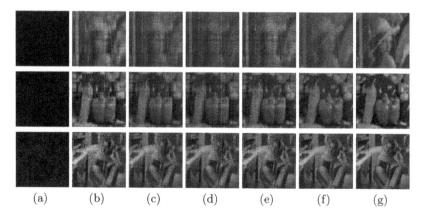

(a)   (b)   (c)   (d)   (e)   (f)   (g)

Fig. 4. Recovery results by different methods with varying sample ratios 5%, 10% and 20% form top to bottom. (a) Observed images; (b) FBCP [20]; (c) Square [17]; (d) HaLRTC [10]; (e) TNN [16]; (f) WSTNN [21]; (g) **MSTNN**.

4.2 Multispectral Image Completion

In this subsection, 20 multispectral images (MSI) with the same size $512 \times 512 \times 31$ in CAVE dataset[1] are chosen for experiment. Due to the high computational complexity of the FBCP method on this group of experiment, we will not compare it here. When we set the SR as 3%, the results of PSNR value and CPU Time recovered by five methods on 20 testing MSIs have been shown in Fig. 5. For each sample, the PNSR value obtained by the proposed method is best while the CPU time is not large. To sum up, the proposed MSTNN method can achieve the best recovery accuracy and the convergence speed is also competitive.

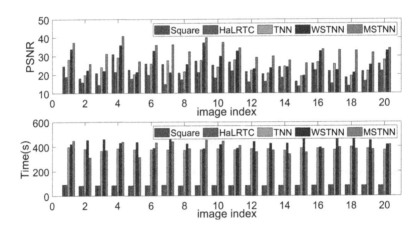

Fig. 5. Comparison of the PSNR and CPU time of different methods on 20 MSIs.

5 Conclusions

In this paper, based on the newly defined mode-$(k, k + 1)$ unfolding tensor and mode-k t-product operation, we propose a new multi-mode tensor singular value decomposition (MTSVD). Then we further develop mode-k square unfolding tensor and propose a convex multi-dimensional square model via TNN for tensor completion. ADMM is used for solving this optimization model. Numerical experiments show that our method can achieve a better accuracy performance and a competitive convergence speed compared with the state of-the-art tensor completion methods.

References

1. Bengua, J.A., Phien, H.N., Tuan, H.D., Do, M.N.: Efficient tensor completion for color image and video recovery: low-rank tensor train. IEEE Trans. Image Process. **26**(5), 2466–2479 (2017)

---

[1] https://www.cs.columbia.edu/CAVE/databases/multispectral/.

2. Boyd, S., Parikh, N., Chu, E.: Distributed Optimization and Statistical Learning via the Alternating Direction Method of Multipliers. Now Publishers Inc, Norwell (2011)
3. Cai, J.F., Candès, E.J., Shen, Z.: A singular value thresholding algorithm for matrix completion. SIAM J. Optim. **20**(4), 1956–1982 (2010)
4. Feng, L., Liu, Y., Chen, L., Zhang, X., Zhu, C.: Robust block tensor principal component analysis. Signal Process. **166**, 107271 (2020)
5. Gandy, S., Recht, B., Yamada, I.: Tensor completion and low-n-rank tensor recovery via convex optimization. Inverse Probl. **27**(2), 025010 (2011)
6. Huang, H., Liu, Y., Long, Z., Zhu, C.: Robust low-rank tensor ring completion. IEEE Trans. Comput. Imaging **6**, 1117–1126 (2020)
7. Kilmer, M.E., Martin, C.D.: Factorization strategies for third-order tensors. Linear Algebra Appl. **435**(3), 641–658 (2011)
8. Kolda, T.G., Bader, B.W.: Tensor decompositions and applications. SIAM Rev. **51**(3), 455–500 (2009)
9. Li, X.T., Zhao, X.L., Jiang, T.X., Zheng, Y.B., Ji, T.Y., Huang, T.Z.: Low-rank tensor completion via combined non-local self-similarity and low-rank regularization. Neurocomputing **367**, 1–12 (2019)
10. Liu, J., Musialski, P., Wonka, P., Ye, J.: Tensor completion for estimating missing values in visual data. IEEE Trans. Pattern Anal. Mach. Intell. **35**(1), 208–220 (2012)
11. Liu, Y., Chen, L., Zhu, C.: Improved robust tensor principal component analysis via low-rank core matrix. IEEE J. Sel. Top. Signal Process. **12**(6), 1378–1389 (2018)
12. Liu, Y., Long, Z., Zhu, C.: Image completion using low tensor tree rank and total variation minimization. IEEE Trans. Multimedia **21**(2), 338–350 (2018)
13. Long, Z., Liu, Y., Chen, L., Zhu, C.: Low rank tensor completion for multiway visual data. Signal Process. **155**, 301–316 (2019)
14. Lu, C., Feng, J., Chen, Y., Liu, W., Lin, Z., Yan, S.: Tensor robust principal component analysis: exact recovery of corrupted low-rank tensors via convex optimization. In: Proceedings of the IEEE Conference on Computer Vision and Pattern Recognition, pp. 5249–5257 (2016)
15. Lu, C., Feng, J., Chen, Y., Liu, W., Lin, Z., Yan, S.: Tensor robust principal component analysis with a new tensor nuclear norm. IEEE Trans. Pattern Anal. Mach. Intell. **42**(4), 925–938 (2019)
16. Lu, C., Feng, J., Lin, Z., Yan, S.: Exact low tubal rank tensor recovery from gaussian measurements. In: Proceedings of the 27th International Joint Conference on Artificial Intelligence, pp. 2504–2510 (2018)
17. Mu, C., Huang, B., Wright, J., Goldfarb, D.: Square deal: lower bounds and improved relaxations for tensor recovery. In: International Conference on Machine Learning, pp. 73–81 (2014)
18. Yokota, T., Zhao, Q., Cichocki, A.: Smooth parafac decomposition for tensor completion. IEEE Trans. Signal Process. **64**(20), 5423–5436 (2016)
19. Zhang, Z., Aeron, S.: Exact tensor completion using t-SVD. IEEE Trans. Signal Process. **65**(6), 1511–1526 (2016)
20. Zhao, Q., Zhang, L., Cichocki, A.: Bayesian CP factorization of incomplete tensors with automatic rank determination. IEEE Trans. Pattern Anal. Mach. Intell. **37**(9), 1751–1763 (2015)
21. Zheng, Y.B., Huang, T.Z., Zhao, X.L., Jiang, T.X., Ji, T.Y., Ma, T.H.: Tensor n-tubal rank and its convex relaxation for low-rank tensor recovery. Inf. Sci. **532**, 170–189 (2020)

Hyperspectral Anomaly Detection Based on Tensor Truncated Nuclear Norm and Linear Total Variation Regularization

Xiangbo Wang[1], Zebin Wu[1], Yang Xu[1(✉)], Zhihui Wei[1], and Lei Xia[2]

[1] School of Computer Science and Engineering, Nanjing University of Science and Technology, Nanjing 210094, China
xuyangth90@njust.edu.cn
[2] China Railway Shanghai Group Co., Ltd., Shanghai 200071, China

Abstract. Hyperspectral image (HSI) anomaly detection aims to separate abnormal targets and background, traditional HSI processing approaches are based on the matrixes and vectors. However, the spatial-spectral structure is destroyed in this way. In contrast with matrix-based methods, HSI, owing to its own structural characteristics, can use third-order tensor to describe its spatial-spectrum features more accurately. In this paper, we proposed a novel method based on tensor truncated nuclear norm and linear total variation regularization, and achieved outstanding result. Specifically, the background part is expressed linearly with the elements in the dictionary matrix, and the representation coefficients are stored in a tensor, which has low-dimensional structure and constrained by tensor truncated nuclear norm. As truncated nuclear norm removed the influence of smaller singular values of background tensor, the robustness of the model has been enhanced. What's more, linear total variation regularization (LTV) is adopted to exploit the smooth prior knowledge of the background tensor and a specific norm regularization is used to constrain the sparse property of the anomaly tensor in our model. Finally, extensive experiments demonstrate that proposed method and optimal algorithm are both effective.

Keywords: Anomaly detection · Low-rank representation (LRR) · Tensor truncated nuclear norm · Total variation regularization

1 Introduction

Hyperspectral image is a narrow-band continuous spectrum image obtained by imaging spectrometer. It provides richer information for earth observation missions and expands the depth of human cognition of the world. Hyperspectral image processing has attracted increasing interest in various fields such as ecological monitoring, mineral survey, urban remote sensing research and so on [1]. Among them, hyperspectral anomaly detection, which focuses on distinguishing specific targets from various backgrounds, has been successfully used in many fields of HSI research.

© Springer Nature Switzerland AG 2021
Y. Peng et al. (Eds.): ICIG 2021, LNCS 12889, pp. 250–261, 2021.
https://doi.org/10.1007/978-3-030-87358-5_20

According to the different background modeling methods and technical means, there are three categories of existing hyperspectral anomaly detection approaches: statistical-based detection model, geometric-based detection modeling and deep-learning-based detection model. The Reed-Xiaoli (RX) algorithm [2] is a benchmark method of target detection in the HSI field. This algorithm believes that background information in the HSI conforms to multivariate Gaussian distribution, it solves the Mahalanobis distance between the pixel to be measured and the spectral mean value of the surrounding background pixels to get the detection result. Many scholars had improved the basic RX from various aspects, for example, according to the different size of selected background region, there are global-RX (GRX) modeling from the entire image and local-RX (LRX) based on the dual-window. However, this statistical-based model has two defects. For one thing, multivariate Gaussian distribution is difficult to meet in the real situations. For another, RX algorithm ignores the dense sampling of the spectrum and the non-linearity of the spectrum curve, and does not fully utilize the rich information of the spectrum dimension. Sparse and low-rank matrix decomposition opened up a new perspective for hyperspectral image processing and various low-rank methods have been employed in HSI anomaly detection. The most popular matrix decomposition method is robust principal component analysis (RPCA) [3]. The original RPCA was designed to describe the low-dimensional property, and now is often used for anomaly detection, denoising, etc. RPCA-RX [4] models the background part based on the low-rank structure and then applies RX algorithm to detect the anomaly targets with sparse attributes. The low-rank representation (LRR) [6] is another HSI representation method, compared to RPCA, LRR is more consistent with linear mixed model of HSI. The first time it was used to HSI target detection is Low-rank and sparse representation (LRASR) [5] algorithm, where a dictionary is constructed and the dictionary should contain only background spectra as much as possible, and the representation coefficient was constrained by nuclear norm. However, existing anomaly detection methods often only consider the spectral characteristics, the spatial information and structural characteristics of HSI are neglected.

Recently, as an efficacious tool for overall analysis of high-dimensional data, tensor analysis can effectively extract the integrated information of HSI, and tensor description has achieved successful results in various image processing procedures, such as feature extraction [11], noise reduction [12], image restoration [13], data Compression [14], etc. Many algorithms using tensors have also appeared in the field of target detection. Tensor matched subspace detector (TMSD) [19] is a new framework to distinguish multi-pixel target with tensorial representation. This method makes use of tensor subspace projection, which is obtained by three predetermined mapping matrices with orthogonal direction. Coskewness detector (COSD) [20] is another tensor-based algorithm of small target detection which can obtain the single target distribution result without iteration. COSD utilized coskewness tensor and it can be seen as an extension of RX. However, many tensor-based anomaly detection methods only use tensors for data preprocessing, such as tensor-based multiway filtering proposed in [21], it is applied on the original tensor to eliminate the influence of noise thereby improving the detection result.

Most previous detection algorithms utilizing low-rank approximate representation can only characterize the spectral correlation prior, while the spatial correlation between neighboring pixels of background was not taken into account. Prior structure encoded by total variance (TV) operator is widely used in HSI processing, LRTDTV [22] is a restoration method, it characterizes the prior information by spatial-spectral TV operator and recovers clear images from noise interference.

In this paper, a new method focusing on anomaly detection of HSI utilizing tensor truncated nuclear norm and linear total variation regularization (TNNLTV) is proposed. As HSI can be represented as a cube data, we use improved LRR model to separate the whole HSI data into two three-order tensors, representing background and anomaly respectively, then adopted tensor truncated nuclear norm and linear total variation norm (LTV) to constrain the low-rank structure and smooth prior of the background, which improved the accuracy of background modeling. The anomaly part is the residuals between the original data and the recovered background part, it can be constrained by $l_{1,1,2}$ norm regularization. Finally, we conducted lots of experiments to demonstrate that our method can obtain the most accurate result among all the comparison methods.

2 Tensor Notations

In this section, we focus on introducing several tensor concepts proposed in [7–10]. We use tensor $\mathcal{X} \in \mathbb{R}^{h \times w \times d}$ to represent an HSI, where h, w, d denote rows, columns, and number of spectral bands respectively. Slicing operation refers to extracting a matrix from a tensor. We use $\mathcal{X}^{(k)}$ as representation of frontal slice in the kth and $\mathcal{X}(:, :, k)$ is the MATLAB notation of it. A tensor can be flattened into a matrix along one mode and this process is usually written as: $unfold_i(\mathcal{X}) = X_{(i)}. fold_i(X_i) = \mathcal{X}$ is the inversion operator. Similar to matrix, the corresponding tensor Frobenius norm is $\|\mathcal{X}\|_F \overset{def}{=} \left(\sum_{ijk} |x_{ijk}|^2 \right)^{1/2}$.

- Definition 1 (n-mode product): $\mathcal{X} \times_k A$ represents the n-mode product. The two terms in the formular represent tensor $\mathcal{X} \in \mathbb{R}^{n1 \times n2 \times \cdots \times nd}$ and matrix $A \in \mathbb{R}^{m \times nk}$. Elementwise, we have:

$$(\mathcal{X} \times_k A)_{i_1 i_2 \cdots i_{k-1} j i_{k+1} \cdots i_d} = \sum_{i_k=1}^{n_k} x_{i_1 i_2 \cdots i_d} a_{ijk}, 1 \le i_1 \le n_1, \cdots, 1 \le i_d \le n_d, 1 \le j \le m.$$

$$(1)$$

- Theorem 1: For $\mathcal{X} \in \mathbb{R}^{p \times q \times r}$, the tensor singular value decomposition is written as $\mathcal{X} = \mathcal{B} * \Sigma * \mathcal{C}^*. \Sigma \in \mathbb{R}^{p \times q \times r}$ is a f-diagonal tensor and front slices of Σ are diagonal matrixes. $\mathcal{B} \in \mathbb{R}^{p \times p \times r}$ and $\mathcal{C} \in \mathbb{R}^{q \times q \times r}$ are orthogonal tensors.
- Definition 2 (tensor nuclear norm): For $\mathcal{X} \in \mathbb{R}^{p \times q \times r}$, its Fourier transform form is $\overline{\mathcal{X}}$. To obtain tensor nuclear norm $\|\mathcal{X}\|_*$, we first calculate singular values of $\overline{\mathcal{X}}$ and then add all singular values of each frontal slice.
- Definition 3 (tensor truncated nuclear norm, TNN): The TNN definition of tensor $\mathcal{X} \in \mathbb{R}^{p \times q \times r}$ is: $\|\mathcal{X}\|_r = \|\mathcal{X}\|_* - \max_{\substack{\mathcal{G}^* \mathcal{G}^T = I \\ \mathcal{H}^* \mathcal{H}^T = I}} tr(\mathcal{G}^* \mathcal{X}^* \mathcal{H})$. In this expression, $\mathcal{G} = \mathcal{B}(:, 1:t, :)^T$ and $\mathcal{H} = \mathcal{C}(:, 1:t, :)^T$. $\mathcal{B}, \mathcal{C}$ are orthogonal obtained by t-SVD of $\mathcal{X}$.

Along the second mode of them, we can truncate the first t columns to obtain $\mathcal{G}$ and $\mathcal{H}$.

3   Proposed Methods

In this section, the proposed method TNNLTV and the optimization procedures of it are introduced in detail.

3.1   TNNLTV for Anomaly Detection

Improved Tensor-LRR Model.   Given an HSI tensor $\mathcal{X} \in \mathbb{R}^{h \times w \times d}$, there are obviously different spectral features between anomaly pixels and the surrounding background area. This means an HSI can be seen as composed of two parts, representing background and anomaly respectively in the following form:

$$\min_{\mathcal{S},\mathcal{A}} \beta rank(\mathcal{S}) + \lambda ||\mathcal{A}||_{1,1,2}$$
$$\text{s.t. } \mathcal{X} = \mathcal{L} + \mathcal{A}, \mathcal{L} = \mathcal{S} \times_3 U \tag{2}$$

where $\mathcal{L} \in \mathbb{R}^{h \times w \times d}$ is the background tensor and $\mathcal{A} \in \mathbb{R}^{h \times w \times d}$ denotes the anomaly tensor. Inspired by LRR, there is a strong correlation among background pixels composed of several ground materials, the background information can be expressed linearly by elements from background dictionary but the detection target cannot. We represent the background tensor $\mathcal{L}$ by the mode-3 product of dictionary matrix $U \in \mathbb{R}^{d \times n}$ and coefficient tensor $\mathcal{S} \in \mathbb{R}^{h \times w \times n}$. In our method, dictionary U should contains all object types on the ground and the coefficient tensor $\mathcal{S}$ should be the lowest-rank expression, then the spectral space of original background is able to be regarded as the combination of several low-rank subspaces corresponding to the various object types. From this we can get a well-structured and clean background tensor.

The anomaly pixels stored in the sparse tensor $\mathcal{A}$, which is considered to be tube-wise sparse. Tensor tube-wise sparse can be seen as the amount of non-zero tubes along a certain dimension of given tensor [8]. We adopt $l_{1,1,2}$ norm regularization as sparse constraint for $\mathcal{A}$. For a 3-d tensor, we treat a tube along the third dimension $\vec{a} \in \mathbb{R}^{1 \times 1 \times d}$ as a vector and then $l_{1,1,2}$ norm regularization is defined as $||\mathcal{A}||_{1,1,2} = \sum_{i,j} ||\mathcal{A}(i,j,:)||_F$.

Detection Model Based on Tensor TNN.   As usual, detection algorithms adopt nuclear norm to replace rank function because solving rank function is NP-hard. The general approximate method is to flatten the tensor into a matrix and use nuclear norm in matrix form to represent tensor nuclear norm. In this way, the spatial structure is intermingled.

According to t-SVD [8], for a low-rank image like the background tensor, the larger singular values of it can contain most of the raw background information, while the smaller singular values are approximately equal to 0. The large probability of the small singular values is due to the effect of observed noise and errors caused by the observation process, so they are not helpful for background modeling. So as to describe the low-rank composition of background tensor more accurately and enhance the robustness of the model, we use the tensor truncated nuclear norm as constraint of background coefficient tensor S, so that perform a better low-rank estimation on it. With definition of tensor TNN and singular value thresholding operator in [10], we first obtained orthogonal tensor $\mathcal{B}$ and $\mathcal{C}$ by t-SVD of S, then selected t larger columns along the second dimension of $\mathcal{B}$ and $\mathcal{C}$ to get $\mathcal{G}$ and $\mathcal{H}$, we denote the operations as: $\mathcal{G} = \mathcal{B}(:, 1 : t, :)^T, \mathcal{H} = \mathcal{C}(:, 1 : t, :)^T$. During the iterative optimization procedure, we can update (2) with the follow model based on the above discussion:

$$
\min_{S, \mathcal{A}} \beta\left(||S||_* - Tr(\mathcal{G} * S * \mathcal{H}^T)\right) + \lambda ||\mathcal{A}||_{1,1,2}
$$
$$
\text{s.t. } \mathcal{X} = \mathcal{L} + \mathcal{A}, \mathcal{L} = S \times_3 U
$$
(3)

Linear Total Variation for Background Tensor. Since the background pixels do not change drastically, the background tensor has smooth prior along its spatial mode [18]. Thus, we add a liner total variation (LTV) regularization of the background tensor to fully utilize its spatial priors. We unfolded the background tensor $\mathcal{L}$ along mode-1 and mode-2 to obtain $L_{(1)}$ and $L_{(2)}$, then the LTV can be formulated as:

$$
||\mathcal{L}||_{\text{LTV}} = ||D_H L_{(1)}||_F^2 + ||D_W L_{(2)}||_F^2
$$
(4)

where $D_H \in \mathbb{R}^{(h-1) \times h}, D_W \in \mathbb{R}^{(w-1) \times w}$ are defined as the following equations:

$$
D_H = \begin{bmatrix} 1 & -1 & & \\ & 1 & -1 & \\ & & \ddots & \ddots \\ & & & 1 & -1 \end{bmatrix}, D_W = \begin{bmatrix} 1 & -1 & & \\ & 1 & -1 & \\ & & \ddots & \ddots \\ & & & 1 & -1 \end{bmatrix}.
$$
(5)

Then, we can rewrite the model as:

$$
\min_{S, \mathcal{J}, \mathcal{A}} \beta\left(||S||_* - Tr(\mathcal{G} * S * \mathcal{H}^T)\right) + \lambda ||\mathcal{A}||_{1,1,2} + \frac{1}{2}||\mathcal{L}||_{\text{LTV}}.
$$
$$
\text{s.t. } \mathcal{X} = \mathcal{L} + \mathcal{A}, \mathcal{L} = S \times_3 U
$$
(6)

In this model, dictionary U was constructed by the strategy in [5]. $\lambda > 0$ and $\beta > 0$ are tradeoff parameters between low-rank and sparse terms.

3.2 ADMM Optimization Algorithm

To make the objective function separable and unconstraint, we introduce auxiliary variables $\mathcal{Q} = S$, $M_1 = L_1 = unfold_1(\mathcal{L})$, $M_2 = L_2 = unfold_2(\mathcal{L})$, and Lagrange multipliers $\mathcal{Y}_{i,i=1,2}$, $P_{i,i=1,2}$ and then we can construct the augmented Lagrange function of problem (6):

$$
Lag(S, \mathcal{Q}, \mathcal{A}, M_1, M_2, \mathcal{G}, \mathcal{H}, \mathcal{Y}_{i,i=1,2}, P_{i,i=1,2}, \mu)
$$
$$
= \beta(||S||_* - Tr(\mathcal{G} * \mathcal{Q} * \mathcal{H}^T)) + \lambda ||\mathcal{A}||_{1,1,2} + \frac{1}{2}(||D_H M_1||_F^2 + ||D_W M_2||_F^2)
$$
$$
+ \frac{\mu}{2}(||\mathcal{X} - S \times_3 U - \mathcal{A} + \frac{\mathcal{Y}_1}{\mu}||_F^2 + ||S - \mathcal{Q} + \frac{\mathcal{Y}_2}{\mu}||_F^2 + \sum_{i=1}^{2}||M_i - L_i + \frac{P_i}{\mu}||_F^2
$$
(7)

where μ is a positive penalty scalar.

We have the following recursion to solve the above problems.

1. Update $\mathcal{S}$: We set

$$f(\mathcal{S}) = \frac{\mu}{2}(||\mathcal{X} - \mathcal{S} \times_3 U - \mathcal{A} + \frac{\mathcal{Y}_1}{\mu}||_F^2 + ||\mathcal{S} - \mathcal{Q} + \frac{\mathcal{Y}_2}{\mu}||_F^2 + \sum_{i=1}^{2}||M_i - L_i + \frac{P_i}{\mu}||_F^2. \tag{8}$$

Then we can easily transform this subproblem into the following form:

$$\mathcal{S}_{k+1} = \arg\min_{\mathcal{S}} \beta||\mathcal{S}||_* + < \nabla_{\mathcal{S}} f(\mathcal{S}_k), \mathcal{S} - \mathcal{S}_k > + \frac{\eta_1 \mu_k}{2}||\mathcal{S} - \mathcal{S}_k||_F^2$$

$$= \arg\min_{\mathcal{S}} \beta||\mathcal{S}||_* + \frac{\eta_1 \mu_k}{2} \times ||\mathcal{S} - \mathcal{S}_k + [-(\mathcal{X} - \mathcal{S}_k \times_3 U - \mathcal{A}_k + \frac{\mathcal{Y}_{1,k}}{\mu_k}) \times_3 U$$

$$+ (\mathcal{S}_k - \mathcal{Q}_k + \frac{\mathcal{Y}_{2,k}}{\mu_k})/\eta_1]||_F^2 \tag{9}$$

Where $\eta_1 = ||U||_F^2$, and we use the partial differential of f, denoted by $\nabla_{\mathcal{S}} f$, as a first-order approximation at previous iterations to replace the quadratic term, and finally add a proximal term.

2. Update $\mathcal{Q}$: Extracting all terms of $\mathcal{Q}$:

$$\mathcal{Q}_{k+1} = \arg\min_{\mathcal{J}} -\beta Tr(\mathcal{G}_k * \mathcal{Q}_k * \mathcal{H}_k^T) + \frac{\mu_k}{2}||\mathcal{S}_{k+1} - \mathcal{Q}_k + \frac{\mathcal{Y}_{2,k}}{\mu_k}||_F^2, \tag{10}$$

the closed-form solution of problem (10) is:

$$\mathcal{Q}_{k+1} = \mathcal{S}_{k+1} + \frac{\mathcal{Y}_{2,k}}{\mu_k} + \frac{\beta(\mathcal{G}_k \mathcal{H}_k^T)}{\mu_k}. \tag{11}$$

3. Update M_i: Extracting all terms of M_1:

$$M_{1,k+1} = \arg\min_{M_1} \frac{1}{2}||D_H M_{1,k}||_F^2 + \frac{\mu_k}{2}||M_{1,k} - L_{1,k} + \frac{P_{1,k}}{\mu_k}||_F^2, \tag{12}$$

the closed-form solution of M_1:

$$M_{1,k+1} = \mu_k \left(D_H D_H^T + \mu_k I_H\right)^{-1} L_{1,k} + \frac{P_{1,k}}{\mu_k}. \tag{13}$$

Similarly, the closed-form solution of M_2 is:

$$M_{2,k+1} = \mu_k \left(D_W^T D_W + \mu_k I_W\right)^{-1} L_{2,k} + \frac{P_{2,k}}{\mu_k}. \tag{14}$$

4. Update $\mathcal{A}$: Consider all terms of $\mathcal{A}$, we easily derive:

$$\mathcal{A}_{k+1} = \arg\min_{\mathcal{A}} \lambda||\mathcal{A}||_{1,1,2} + \frac{\mu_k}{2}||\mathcal{X} - \mathcal{S}_{k+1} \times_3 U - \mathcal{A}_k + \frac{\mathcal{Y}_{1,k}}{\mu_k}||_F^2. \quad (15)$$

Then $\mathcal{A}$ can be gained by formula (16) where $\mathcal{R}_k = \mathcal{X} - \mathcal{S}_{k+1} \times_3 U + \mathcal{Y}_{1,k}/\mu_k$:

$$\mathcal{A}_{k+1}(p,q,:) = (1 - \frac{\lambda}{\rho||\mathcal{R}_k(p,q,:)||})_+ \mathcal{R}_k(p,q,:), \, p = 1, 2, ..., d. \quad (16)$$

5. Update $\mathcal{G}, \mathcal{H}$: $\mathcal{G}$ and $\mathcal{H}$ can be obtained by singular value thresholding operator:

$$[\mathcal{G}_{k+1}, \Sigma, \mathcal{H}_{k+1}] = SVDs(\mathcal{Q}_{k+1}, t). \quad (17)$$

6. Update L:$\mathcal{L}_{k+1} = \mathcal{S}_{k+1} \times_3 U$, then

$$L_{1,k+1} = unfold_1(\mathcal{L}_{k+1}), \, L_{2,k+1} = unfold_2(\mathcal{L}_{k+1}) \quad (18)$$

7. The Multiplier $\mathcal{Y}_i$ and P_i can be updated by:

$$\begin{cases} \mathcal{Y}_{1,k+1} = \mathcal{Y}_{1,k} + \mu_k(eq1) \\ \mathcal{Y}_{2,k+1} = \mathcal{Y}_{2,k} + \mu_k(eq2) \end{cases}, \begin{cases} eq1 = \mathcal{X} - \mathcal{S}_{k+1} \times_3 U - \mathcal{A}_{k+1} \\ eq2 = \mathcal{S}_{k+1} - \mathcal{Q}_{k+1} \end{cases}, \quad (19)$$

$$P_{i,k+1} = P_{i,k} + M_{i,k+1} - L_{i,k+1}, i = 1, 2. \quad (20)$$

Finally, the iteration will continue until convergence has been achieved. The complete algorithm of TNNLTV is organized in Algorithm 1.

Algorithm 1 optimization for TNNLTV
Input: HSI tensor $\mathcal{X}$, background dictionary matrix U, parameters $\lambda > 0, \beta > 0$
Initialize: $\mathcal{Q} = \mathcal{S} = \mathcal{A} = 0, \mathcal{Y}_1 = \mathcal{Y}_2 = 0, P_1 = P_2 = 0, \mu_0 = 0.01, \mu_{max} = 10^{10}$,

$\rho = 1.1, \varepsilon = 10^{-6}, \eta = ||U||_2^2$, max $Iter = 100$

1: **While** $||\mathcal{X} - \mathcal{S}_{k+1} \times_3 U - \mathcal{A}_{k+1}||_F / ||\mathcal{X}||_F \geq \varepsilon$ do:

2:    Update variable $\mathcal{S}_{k+1}$ using Eq.8 and Eq.9;

3:    Update variable $\mathcal{Q}_{k+1}$ using Eq.11;

4:    Update variable $M_{i,k+1}$ using Eq.13 and Eq.14;

5:    Set $\mathcal{R}_k = \mathcal{X} - \mathcal{S}_{k+1} \times_3 U + \mathcal{Y}_{i,k}/\mu_k$ then update variable $\mathcal{A}_{k+1}$ using Eq.16;

6:    Update variable $\mathcal{G}_{k+1}$ and $\mathcal{H}_{k+1}$ using Eq.17;

7:    Get current $\mathcal{L}_{k+1} = \mathcal{S}_{k+1} \times_3 U$, update variable $L_{1,k+1}$ and $L_{2,k+1}$ using Eq.18;

8:    Update Lagrange Multiplier $\mathcal{Y}_i$ and P_i using Eq.19 and Eq.20;

9:    Update μ using $\mu_{k+1} = \min(\mu_{max}, \rho\mu_{k+1})$;

10: **end while**
Output: the required tensor $\mathcal{S}_k, \mathcal{A}_k$.

4 Experiment

4.1 Data Sets Description

Two data sets including simulated and real data sets were employed in different experiments to demonstrate the effectiveness of TNNLTV method introduced above. All the experiments were implemented with MATLAB2019a. The two data sets were generated in accordance with data set over San Diego, CA, USA which was collected by the Airborne Visible/Infrared Imaging Spectrometer (AVIRIS) sensor [5]. For the purpose of eliminating the influence of artificial factors, we removed the bad bands from original 224 spectral channels and retained 186 available bands for experiments. For simulated data set, we selected a region of size 100×100, among the given pixels of the background with spectrum p, we implanted specific abnormal pixels fractionally with the spectrum of q as follows:

$$\varsigma = \tau \cdot q + (1 - \tau) \cdot p. \tag{21}$$

In formula (21), τ is a specified abundance fraction. In the anomaly array, τ is fixed in the same row and is setting to increasing values in the range of $\{0.05, 0.1, 0.2, 0.4\}$ for different rows. In this simulated data set, there are 16 anomalous targets shown in Fig. 1(b) and the false color image of this data set is presented in Fig. 1(a).

The second data set is taken from the up-left region of San Diego image with a size of $100 \times 100 \times 186$. The three planes are marked as abnormal targets to be detected as shown in Fig. 1(d), they contain a total of 57 pixels. It should be noted that the boundary of the aircraft is composed of mixed pixels while the center pixels are pure. A color representation is shown in Fig. 1(c).

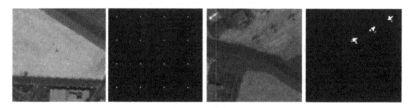

Fig. 1. (a) image scene for Simulated dataset (b) ground truth for Simulated dataset (c) image scene for San Diego (d) ground truth for San Diego

4.2 Performance

In this part, we conducted some contrast experiments using other anomaly detection methods, including RPCA-RX [4], LRASR [5], LSMAD [15], GTVLRR [16] and TRPCA [17] to compared with proposed TNNLTV. We set parameters K = 15 and P = 20 for these algorithms to learn background dictionary, including LRASR, GTVLRR and TNNLTV. The performances of the anomaly detection methods are evaluated by commonly used evaluation indicators: receiver operating characteristic (ROC) curve and the area under the curve (AUC).

β and λ are two regularization parameters which have an important impact on the result of TNNLTV. We chose β in the range of {0.001,0.01,0.1,0.5,1,1.5,2.5}, chose λ in the range of {0.5,1,3.5,6.5,8.5,10.5,12} for simulated data set and {0.005,0.05,0.1,0.2,0.5,1,2.5} for real data set. Figure 2 shows the obtained performance while jointly taking two parameters into consideration. In our experiments, we set λ = 6.5 for simulated data set experiment and λ = 0.04 for real San Diego data set experiment, and β = 1.0 for both of them.

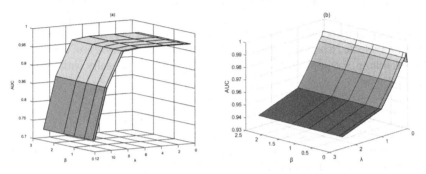

Fig. 2. Joint consideration of β and λ (a)simulated data set (b) San Diego data set

In Fig. 3, experiment results for the simulated data set are shown. Visually, all detection methods can distinguish background and anomalies in high abundance fraction pixels, while the proposed TNNLTV can detect the targets in the low abundance fraction pixels more clearly. Specially, when the specified abundance fraction is set to 0.05, only TNNLTV give the clear map of anomaly pixels. As shown in Fig. 5(a), the ROC curve of TNNLTV is closest to the upper left corner and our model achieved the highest detection probability among all the compared methods. Moreover, the AUC value of TNNLTV is highest as shown in the first row of Table 1. The value of TNNLTV is 0.04 higher than the second highest sore achieved by LSMAD.

We illustrate the color detection maps of the real San Diego data set in Fig. 4. The target planes are displayed more prominently using proposed TNNLTV method. It can be seen from the ROC curve in the Fig. 5(b), the detection rate of LSMAD is a little higher than TNNLTV when false alarm rate is between 0.1 and 0.25, but in general, the TNNLTV method converges faster and the detection effect is best. Although there is not much difference from the ROC graph, RPCA-RX and LSMAD cannot show the large anomaly targets such as airplanes distinctly judging from Fig. 4. Further, as is shown in the second line of Table 1, TNNLTV achieves the highest AUC value for quantitative results.

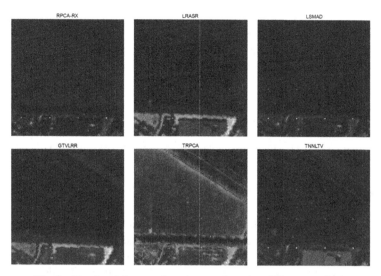

Fig. 3. Simulated data set detection results using different methods

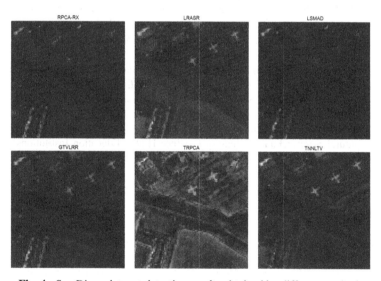

Fig. 4. San Diego data set detection results obtained by different methods

Table 1. AUC value comparison of two data sets

Dataset	RPCA-RX	LRASR	LSMAD	GTVLRR	TRPCA	TNNLTV
Simulated	0.8708	0.9239	0.9320	0.9093	0.8272	**0.9738**
San Diego	0.9395	0.9787	0.9742	0.9746	0.9832	**0.9906**

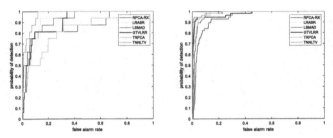

Fig. 5. ROC obtained by different algorithms (a)Simulated dataset (b)San Diego dataset

5 Conclusion

In this paper, the TNNLTV method for hyperspectral anomaly detection is proposed. In TNNLTV algorithm, tensor truncated nuclear norm is used to constraint the coefficient of background dictionary, it can more accurately approximate the rank function of background tensor and enhance the robustness of the model effectively. Besides, we use LTV regularization to represent the piecewise-smooth prior of the background tensor and use $l_{1,1,2}$ norm regularization to constraint tube-wise sparse of anomaly tensor. Finally, extensive experiments on different data sets were conducted, the detection consequents demonstrated that our detection algorithm yields superior performance.

Acknowledgments. This work was supported in part by the National Natural Science Foundation of China (61772274, 62071233, 61671243, 61976117), the Jiangsu Provincial Natural Science Foundation of China (BK20180018, BK20191409), the Fundamental Research Funds for the Central Universities (30917015104, 30919011103, 30919011402, 30921011209), and in part by the China Postdoctoral Science Foundation under Grant 2017M611814, 2018T110502, the Key Projects of Natural Science Fund of Jiangsu Province Higher Education Institutions of China [grant number 19KJA360001].

References

1. Goetz, F.-H.: Three decades of hyperspectral remote sensing of the earth: a personal view. Remote Sens. Environ. **113**, S5–S16 (2009)
2. Reed, I.S., Yu, X.: Adaptive multiple-band CFAR detection of an optical pattern with unknown spectral distribution. IEEE Trans. Acoust. Speech, Signal Process. **38**(10), 1760–1770 (1990)
3. Wright, J., et al.: Robust Principal Component Analysis: Exact Recovery of Corrupted Low-Rank Matrices (2009)
4. Sun, W., Liu, C., Li, J., Lai, Y.M., Li, W.: Low-rank and sparse matrix decomposition-based anomaly detection for hyperspectral imagery. J. Appl. Remote Sens. **8**(1), 083641 (2014)
5. Yang, X., Zebin, W., Li, J., Plaza, A., Wei, Z.: Anomaly detection in hyperspectral images based on low-rank and sparse representation. IEEE Trans. Geosci. Remote Sens. **54**(4), 1990–2000 (2016)
6. Liu, G., Lin, Z., Yu, Y.: Robust subspace segmentation by low-rank representation. In: International Conference on Machine Learning. DBLP (2010)

7. Xu, Y., Wu, Z., Chanussot, J., et al.: Joint reconstruction and anomaly detection from compressive hyperspectral images using mahalanobis distance-regularized tensor RPCA. IEEE Trans. Geosci. Remote Sens. **56**(5), 2919–2930 (2018)
8. Zhang, Z., et al.: Novel methods for multilinear data completion and de-noising based on tensor-SVD. In: 2014 IEEE Conference on Computer Vision and Pattern Recognition. IEEE (2014)
9. Kolda, T.G., Bader, B.W.: Tensor decompositions and applications. SIAM Rev. **51**(3), 455–500 (2009)
10. Xue, S., Qiu, W., Liu, F., Jin, X.: Low-rank tensor completion by truncated nuclear norm regularization. In: 2018 24th International Conference on Pattern Recognition (ICPR), Beijing, pp. 2600–2605 (2018). https://doi.org/10.1109/ICPR.2018.8546008
11. Zhong, Z., et al.: Discriminant tensor spectral–spatial feature extraction for hyperspectral image classification. IEEE Geosci. Remote Sens. Lett. **12.5**, 1028–1032 (2017)
12. Lin, T., Bourennane, S.: Survey of hyperspectral image denoising methods based on tensor decompositions. EURASIP J. Adv. Signal Process. **2013**(1), 1–11 (2013). https://doi.org/10.1186/1687-6180-2013-186
13. Lu, C., Feng, J., Chen, Y., et al.: Tensor robust principal component analysis: exact recovery of corrupted low-rank tensors via convex optimization (2017)
14. Li, R., Pan, Z., Wang, Y.: Correlation-based initialization algorithm for tensor-based HSI compression methods. arXiv (2019)
15. Zhang, Y., et al.: A low-rank and sparse matrix decomposition-based mahalanobis distance method for hyperspectral anomaly detection. IEEE Trans. Geosci. Remote Sens. **54**, 1376–1389 (2016)
16. Cheng, T., Wang, B.: Graph and total variation regularized low-rank representation for hyperspectral anomaly detection. IEEE Trans. Geosci. Remote Sens. **58**(1), 391–406 (2020)
17. Chen, Z., Yang, B., Wang, B.: A preprocessing method for hyperspectral target detection based on tensor principal component analysis. Remote Sens. **10**(7), 1033 (2018)
18. Li, L., Li, W., Qu, Y., Zhao, C., Tao, R., Du, Q.: Prior-based tensor approximation for anomaly detection in hyperspectral imagery. IEEE Trans. Neural Netw. Learn. Syst. https://doi.org/10.1109/TNNLS.2020.3038659
19. Liu, Y., Gao, G., Yanfeng, G.: Tensor matched subspace detector for hyperspectral target detection. IEEE Trans. Geosci. Remote Sens. (2016). https://doi.org/10.1109/TGRS.2016
20. Geng, X., Sun, K., Ji, L., et al.: A high-order statistical tensor based algorithm for anomaly detection in hyperspectral imagery. Sci. Rep. **4**, 6869 (2014). https://doi.org/10.1038/srep06869
21. Bourennane, S., Fossati, C., Cailly, A.: Improvement of target detection based on tensorial modelling. In: 2010 18th European Signal Processing Conference, pp. 304–308 (2010)
22. Wang, Y., Peng, J., Zhao, Q., Leung, Y., Zhao, X., Meng, D.: Hyperspectral image restoration via total variation regularized low-rank tensor decomposition. IEEE J. Sel. Topics Appl. Earth Observ. Remote Sens. **11**(4), 1227–1243 (2018). https://doi.org/10.1109/JSTARS.2017.2779539

Face, Gesture, and Body Pose

Deep Human Pose Estimation
via Self-guided Learning

Zhuowei Xu and Miaohui Wang[✉]

College of Electronics and Information Engineering,
Shenzhen University, Shenzhen, China

Abstract. The existing human pose estimation (HPE) models show good performance, but also reflect a pair of contradictions between the computational complexity and prediction performance. To address this dilemma, this paper proposes a novel HPE training approach via self-guided learning (SGL). Specifically, a dual model training is designed to get the model-temporal ensemble learning to fuse the knowledge from a new guidance model. Moreover, a self-guided joint loss is considered with the key-point attention enhancement and self-guided compensation. Experimental results show that the proposed SGL method not only has a lower computation cost, but also achieves a higher prediction precision.

1 Introduction

Human pose estimation (HPE) is not only a hot research topic, but also a challenging task in the field of computer vision. With the development of various deep convolutional neural network (CNN) methods, the existing HPE schemes have achieved promising performance [14]. However, various large-scale models reflect the contradiction between the prediction performance and computational complexity. High-performance models are often very complex, while simple models have low accuracy. The reason is that most of the existing HPEs focus on improving the prediction accuracy but ignoring the computational complexity. As a result, the practical deployment of large-scale models shows poor scalability and cost-effectiveness [23]. This is an urgent task to investigate the reduction of the computational complexity while maintaining the prediction accuracy as much as possible.

The existing solutions roughly fall into three categories. In the first category, some novel network architectures with efficient computing or memory operation are designed into HPE tasks, such as ResNet [5] to SimpleBaseline [20], Dense-Net [7] to DensePose [1], EfficientNet [16] to EfficientPose [4]. The second is to quantize the weights from 32-bit floating-point to low-depth representation [8]. This kind of method is usually independent of computer vision (CV) tasks, and

This work was supported in part by Natural Science Foundation of Guangdong Province (No. 2019A1515010961 and No. 2021A1515011877), and in part by Natural Science Foundation of Shenzhen City (No. 2021A1515011877 and No. JCYJ20180305124209486).

© Springer Nature Switzerland AG 2021
Y. Peng et al. (Eds.): ICIG 2021, LNCS 12889, pp. 265–274, 2021.
https://doi.org/10.1007/978-3-030-87358-5_21

pays more attention to model compression. As for the third category, training strategies are presented to improve the performance of a deep model [21, 23]. It is very attractive to improve the model efficiency via the training strategy, because such a scheme is often applicable to many HPE models. Thus, the training strategy is the focus of our investigation (Fig. 1).

| (a) Original | (a) +SGL | (b) Original | (b) +SGL |
| (c) Original | (c) +SGL | (d) Original | (d) +SGL |

Fig. 1. Visual prediction comparisons of primary and SGL models. The left side is the output of the primary model, and the right side is the output of the model trained by SGL. It is observed that the model trained by SGL learns the key-point representations better for the usual occasion, unique pose content, multi-pose estimation and crowd pose estimation.

Recently, a simple and effective method, namely knowledge distillation (KD) [6], has been introduced into HPE. A complex model (teacher) is employed to provide the training guidance in the joint training, with intent to bring the prediction accuracy improvement of the on-going trained model (student). However, some recent studies [3, 22] point out that the existing KD methods are not satisfactory. One main challenge is the selection of the teacher model [3]. A complex teacher model with the excellent performance can bring the improvement in the student model. However, it also can be a disastrous knowledge transfer. Another hard nut to crack is the divergence between the teacher and student models, which is largely reflected in the topological structure to affect the knowledge transfer [22]. Moreover, the frozen teacher model is usually well trained, which makes the divergence between the teacher model and the student model further widened.

In this paper, inspired by the ensemble learning [17], we design a self-guided training learning (SGL) approach for HPE. As an illustration in Fig. 2, dual models use the same network structure and scale to ensure the topology consistency. It is noted that these dual models only keep the difference in the training weights, and use the different weight update strategies in different phases. Moreover, SGL adopts a model-temporal ensemble guidance to learn a better feature representation by leverage different models and different temporal phases. Furthermore, a self-guided joint loss is designed based on the key-point attention mechanism and guidance compensation. Finally, We integrate the proposed SGL into the training of CPN [2], SimpleBaseline [20] and HRNet [15] as an example. Experiments on the challenging COCO human pose estimation dataset, show that SGL achieves promising performance in balancing the prediction accuracy and the computational complexity.

The reminder of this paper is organized as follows. Section 2 provides the relate work. Section 3 presents the details of the proposed SGL method. Section 4 describes the experiments, and Sect. 5 concludes this work.

2   Related Work

In recent years, some improved deep learning methods [3,6,9,10,13,17,21,23] have been investigated to improve the prediction performance and reduce the computational complexity, which can be roughly categorized into self-ensemble learning and knowledge distilling.

2.1   Self-Ensemble

Self-ensemble learning is proposed to learn the general visual features from a large-scale unlabeled data without manual labeling through the implicit ensemble learning [9]. The key of the self-ensemble is to learn a better feature representation from training experience.

Laine et al. [10] first proposed the temporal ensembling model to improve the prediction accuracy and robustness by minimizing the mean-square-error between the network predictions under different input augmentations. Relying heavily on the dropout regularization and versatile augmentations, these methods are realized as an implicit self-ensemble in training, with the purpose of improving the model efficiency and robustness. Inspired by this, Tarvainen et al. [17] proposed a mean teacher that averages model weights instead of label predictions, to form a target-generating teacher model, where the temporal ensemble is transferred to the teacher model, and thus the consistency loss is added in training.

Previous HPE methods hardly considered the self-ensemble method. As far as we know, this paper is the first work to improve the computing efficiency of HPE model by self-ensemble method under the supervised learning. Inspired by the existing self-ensemble work, we propose a new self-ensemble method for human pose estimation based on the human key-points.

2.2   Knowledge Distilling

Knowledge Distilling [6] is proposed to transfer the knowledge into a new model that is easier to deploy, on the purpose of improving the efficiency without additional operating costs. It sheds new light on improving the performance from the perspective of the training strategy, so that lower computation cost and higher performance can be achieved simultaneously.

Radosavovic *et al.* [13] proposed a data distillation for HPE. The ensembled predictions from a single model were applied to multiple transformations of an unlabeled image, which were used as automatically annotated data to train a student model.

Recently, Zhang *et al.* [23] proposed a fast pose distilling (FPD) method by compressing the hourglass [12] model and the traditional model distillation. Based on the FPD method, integral knowledge distillation (IKD) [21] greatly expanded the perspectives of the distillation mechanism via the logit distillation, feature distillation, and structural distillation.

Although the aforementioned studies of knowledge distilling have improved the efficiency of the HPE models, it still can be further improved. For instance, the student and teacher models in knowledge distillation have different network structures, which leads to the topology inconsistency. This inconsistency greatly makes the teacher model prevent the student from learning [3]. In order to solve this problem, we propose a novel training approach by guidance learning. Different from the previous knowledge distillation, the architecture of the two models maintains the same network structure.

3   Proposed Self-guided Learning

In this section, we describe the proposed SGL method, which contains an original training model as the source model, and a self-guided learning model as the guidance model. The source and guidance models are completely consistent in the network design (e.g., structure, scale, etc.), but different in the learned weights. The source and guidance models are trained via model-temporal ensemble guidance learning and self-guided joint loss.

3.1   Problem Formulation

As mentioned above, our goal is to fuse more information during training so that a better feature representation can be learned on human key-points without additional deployment costs. Given an input image I with the human pose information, the output prediction of model $\mathcal{M}$ should close to the ground-truth position, and it is expressed as:

$$\mathcal{M}(I;\ \mathrm{SGL})^* = \arg\min_{\mathrm{SGL}} \sum_{k=1}^{K} \left\| \mathcal{M}(I;\ \mathrm{SGL})_k - \left(x_{gt|k},\ y_{gt|k}\right) \right\|_2, \qquad (1)$$

where $\mathcal{M}(I;\ \mathrm{SGL})_k$ represents the coordinate prediction for the k-th key-point from $\mathcal{M}$, $\left(x_{gt|k},\ y_{gt|k}\right)$ denotes the ground-truth coordinate, and $\mathcal{M}(I;\ \mathrm{SGL})^*$ represents the optimal key-point coordinate prediction.

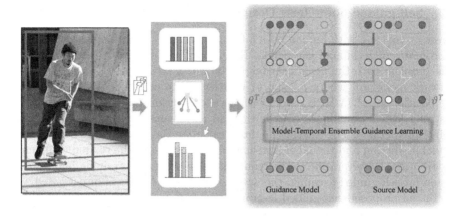

Fig. 2. Overall Framework. A complete model-temporal ensemble guidance learning is constructed by the key-point attention enhancement and self-guided compensation.

3.2 Model-Temporal Ensemble Guidance Learning

In the dual-model training, inappropriate learning guidance is present in most existing knowledge distillations where the topology inconsistency will seriously affect the training efficiency. We address this problem by introducing a learnable guidance model. On the one hand, the guidance model fundamentally solves the problem of inconsistency. On the other hand, the guidance model enlarges the learning space, and more information is collected and fused.

In this section, a model-temporal ensemble learning guidance is designed to learn the multi-model and multi-temporal-phase training information. In each training iteration, the guidance model will merge the training information from different models and different temporal phases, which can be transferred to the source model via the self-guided loss. A new information fusion will be conducted on each training iteration, which makes the source model get a more efficient guidance.

It is witnessed that the learned weights contain the information with respect to the model ensemble [17]. In view of this, we propose to adopt a time average of model weights as the learning strategy to guide the training:

$$\theta^T = \frac{T-1}{T} \sum_{t=1}^{T-1} (1+\sigma^t)\vartheta^t + \frac{(1+\sigma^T)\vartheta^T}{T}, \quad |\sigma^t - \frac{1}{\zeta \times (t+1)}| < 0, \quad (2)$$

where θ^T is the weight of guidance model in the iteration T, ϑ^T is the weight of source model, σ^t is the independent de-smoothing hyper-parameter $(t = 1, \cdots, T)$ controlled by ζ for a proper threshold.

The updated model at the end of each training iteration provides a new guidance for the next iteration. In fact, the updated guidance is helpful to integrate the global training experience, especially for the fusion accumulation of the topological structure characteristics, and the temporal training experience.

3.3   Self-guided Joint Loss Design

Given an image I with human pose information, HPE aims to detect the spatial coordinates of K human key-points. Recent methods [2,12,15,19,20] transform this problem to estimate a heat-map group $\{h_m\}_K$ via a convolution neural network model m, where $h_{m|k}(x, y)$ represents the confidence of key-point at the position (x, y). A HPE model with excellent performance usually represents a strong logical confidence distribution, so as to generate more accurate key-points predictions. The existing methods calculate the training loss between the model prediction and the label heat-map directly to learn the related confidence distribution. However, due to the requirement of additional training information fusion for self-guided learning, the design of new overall loss is investigated.

In the proposed self-guided learning, the dual models are consistent in the network structure, which indicates the same key-point representation learning. As a result, the self-guided learning is limited to the estimation of some key-points that are not easy to detect and identify. Therefore, we introduce a key-point attention mechanism to enhance the sensitivity of key-points. Moreover, the additional information from the guidance model allows a richer feature representation learning. We introduce a learning compensation through the divergence between the dual models. Specifically, we design a self-guided joint loss $\mathcal{L}$ with the key-point attention enhancement and self-guidance compensation as

$$\mathcal{L} = \frac{1}{K} \sum_{k=1}^{K} \left[(1 + \psi_k) \left\| h_{gt|k} - h_{s|k} \right\|_2^2 + \left\| h_{g|k} - h_{s|k} \right\|_2^2 \right], \tag{3}$$

where $h_{gt|k}$, $h_{s|k}$ and $h_{g|k}$ are the ground-truth heat-map, output heat-map from source model and guidance model, respectively; ψ_k is an enhancement factor, and α is the self-guided factor, which is set as 0.4 according to our experimental result.

3.4   Overall Framework

The SGL framework integrates the model-temporal ensemble to maximize key-point prediction performance. Among them, we train the source model as a target, and introduce the guidance model for model-temporal ensemble. The guidance model is designed to leverage multi-model training information shared across different training progress - a benefit not offered by the existing HPEs as far as we known.

As illustrated in Fig. 2, the SGL mechanism is summarized as followed. As the first step of each training epoch, an input video frame with human pose information is fed into the source and guidance models. Two groups of heat-maps will be obtained, which are the predictions from the source and guidance models, respectively. Then, the divergence between the predicted heat-maps and the ground-truth is computed via the self-guided joint loss, which is responsible for a continuous key-point attention enhancement and self-guidance compensation.

After that, both models learn from the self-guided joint loss through a gradient back propagation. The guidance model will provide the merged knowledge through self-guidance compensation in the next iteration.

4   Experimental Results

4.1   Implementation Details

We conduct the experiments based on CPN [2], SimpleBaseline [20], and HRNet [15] in this section.

For CPN and SimpleBaseline, we adopt a ResNet-50 as the backbone. For HRNet, we adopt HRNet-W18s and HRNet-W18 [18] as the backbones. HRNet-W18s and HRNet-W18 are two light-weight HRNets, in which the widths of the related parallel sub-networks are 18, 36, 72 and 144, respectively. Moreover, HRNet-W18s has a less number of basic blocks than HRNet-W18.

The MSCOCO 2017 dataset [11] is used in our experiments. In the training and testing, we keep the same setting suggested in [2,15,20].

4.2   Evaluation Metric

The object key-point similarity (OKS) [11] is employed to evaluate the model performance, which is defined as:

$$OKS = \frac{\sum_i exp(-d_i^2/2\,s^2 k_i^2)\delta(v_i > 0)}{\sum_i \delta(v_i > 0)}, \tag{4}$$

where d_i is the Euclidean distance between each detected key-point and its corresponding ground-truth, v_i is the visibility flag of the ground-truth, s is the object scale, and k_i is a per-key-point constant that controls falloff. Based on the OKS score, we further provide the standard average precision and recall scores: AP (the mean of AP scores at OKS = 0.50; 0.55; . . . ; 0.90; 0.95), AP^{50} (AP at OKS = 0.50), AP^{75} (AP at OKS = 0.75), AP^M (AP for medium objects), AP^L (AP for large objects), and AR (the mean of recalls at OKS = 0.50; 0.55; . . . ; 0.90; 0.95). The AP is the primary challenge metric in the MSCOCO key-point detection.

4.3   Overall Performance

The comparison results of the proposed SGL with some state-of-the-art HPE methods are provided in Table 1. Our CPN+SGL (denoted as "**+SGL**") obtains an AP score of 71.6, and gains a promotion of 0.4 AP score from CPN (71.2). Moreover, SimpleBaseline with SGL achieves an 0.8 AP improvement (73.2). Our HRNet-W18s+SGL, trained from scratch, obtains a 70.3 AP score, achieving a promotion of 4.5 improvement from HRNet-W18s (65.8). HRNet-W18+SGL obtains an AP score of 74.3 with only 2.91 GFLOPs and 9.32M parameters. Experimental results show that SGL is suitable for many HPE methods.

Table 1. Comparisons of between the proposed SGL and the corresponding state-of-the-art methods on MSCOCO 2017. #Params and FLOPS are calculated only for the pose estimation network.

Methods	#Params	GFLOPs	AP	AP^{50}	AP^{75}	AP^M	AP^L	AR
CPN	27.0M	6.20	71.2	91.4	78.3	68.5	75.6	74.4
+SGL	27.0M	6.20	**71.6(+0.4)**	91.4	**79.2**	**68.7**	**76.1**	**74.6**
SimpleBaseline	34.0M	8.99	72.4	91.5	80.4	69.7	76.5	75.6
+SGL	34.0M	8.99	**73.2(+0.8)**	**92.5**	**81.5**	**70.3**	**77.5**	**76.1**
HRNet-W18s	3.75M	1.83	65.8	90.5	75.9	63.7	69.7	69.7
+SGL	3.75M	1.83	**70.3(+4.5)**	90.5	**78.0**	**67.6**	**74.0**	**73.2**
HRNet-W18	9.32M	2.91	73.5	92.5	81.4	71.1	77.5	76.5
+SGL	9.32M	2.91	**74.3(+0.8)**	**92.6**	**81.5**	**71.3**	**78.3**	**77.0**

Table 2. Comparison results of HRNet-W18s with dvarious dual-model training methods on MSCOCO 2017. #Params and FLOPS are calculated only for the pose estimation network.

Methods	#Params	GFLOPs	AP	AP^{50}	AP^{75}	AP^M	AP^L	AR
HRNet-W18s	3.75M	1.83	65.8	90.5	75.9	63.7	69.7	69.7
HRNet-W48	**63.6M**	14.6	77.1	93.6	84.7	74.1	81.9	79.9
+FPD(48)	3.75M	1.83	69.5(+3.7)	90.5	77.0	67.2	73.2	72.6
+IKD(48)	3.75M	1.84	70.0(+4.2)	90.5	77.3	67.4	**74.7**	**73.3**
+SGL	3.75M	1.83	**70.3(+4.5)**	90.5	**78.0**	**67.6**	74.0	73.2

Moreover, various dual-model training methods based on HRNet-W18s are conducted on the MSCOCO dataset. For comparison purpose, two dual-model training methods FPD [23] and IKD [21] are evaluated in the experiments. As shown in Table 2, the first and third rows show the original prediction results of HRNet-W18s and HRNet-W48. The fourth row shows the result of the FPD method (denoted as "+FPD(48)"), where HRNet-W18s trained with the teacher model HRNet-W48 achieves a promotion of 3.7 (65.8 to 69.5). The fifth row shows that the IKD method achieves an AP score of 4.2. At the same time, our SGL method achieves the best performance (70.3) with the same amount of weights.

4.4   Ablation Study

Effect of Self-guided Factor α. The self-guided factor α balances the proportion of various losses in the self-guided training. We study the balance key between the losses with key-point attention and guidance compensation by controlling the self-guided factor α in Eq. (3).

As shown in Fig. 3, HRNet-W18 achieves the best performance using $\alpha = 0.4$. When $\alpha > 0.7$, the performance of SGL shows a decline. The reason is that when α increases, the compensation from self-guidance will lead to an excessive deviation of the training loss. This suggests that an accurate α value greatly affects the performance of SGL.

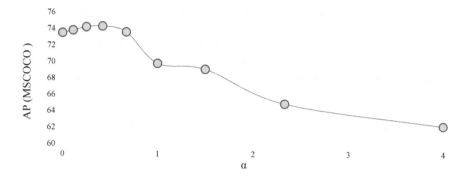

Fig. 3. Comparison results of SGL with various α.

5 Conclusion

This paper introduces a novel self-guided learning (SGL) for human pose estimation, where a guidance model adopts the same network structure to provide the guidance in the learning of the source model. Experiments show that it provides a significant performance improvement on several state-of-the-art HPE methods.

References

1. Alp Güler, R., Neverova, N., Kokkinos, I.: Densepose: dense human pose estimation in the wild. In: IEEE Conference on Computer Vision and Pattern Recognition (CVPR), pp. 7297–7306 (2018)
2. Chen, Y., Wang, Z., Peng, Y., Zhang, Z., Yu, G., Sun, J.: Cascaded pyramid network for multi-person pose estimation. In: IEEE Conference on Computer Vision and Pattern Recognition (CVPR), pp. 7103–7112 (2018)
3. Gou, J., Yu, B., Maybank, S.J., Tao, D.: Knowledge distillation: a survey. arXiv preprint arXiv:2006.05525 (2020)
4. Groos, D., Ramampiaro, H., Ihlen, E.: Efficientpose: scalable single-person pose estimation. arXiv preprint arXiv:2004.12186 (2020)
5. He, K., Zhang, X., Ren, S., Sun, J.: Deep residual learning for image recognition. In: IEEE Conference on Computer Vision and Pattern Recognition (CVPR) (2016)
6. Hinton, G., Vinyals, O., Dean, J.: Distilling the knowledge in a neural network. In: NIPS Deep Learning and Representation Learning Workshop (2015)
7. Iandola, F., Moskewicz, M., Karayev, S., Girshick, R., Darrell, T., Keutzer, K.: Densenet: implementing efficient convnet descriptor pyramids. arXiv preprint arXiv:1404.1869 (2014)
8. Jacob, B., et al.: Quantization and training of neural networks for efficient integer-arithmetic-only inference. In: IEEE Conference on Computer Vision and Pattern Recognition (CVPR), pp. 2704–2713 (2018)
9. Jing, L., Tian, Y.: Self-supervised visual feature learning with deep neural networks: a survey. IEEE Trans. Pattern Anal. Mach. Intell. (2020)
10. Laine, S., Aila, T.: Temporal ensembling for semi-supervised learning. arXiv preprint arXiv:1610.02242 (2016)

11. Lin, T.-Y., et al.: Microsoft COCO: common objects in context. In: Fleet, D., Pajdla, T., Schiele, B., Tuytelaars, T. (eds.) ECCV 2014. LNCS, vol. 8693, pp. 740–755. Springer, Cham (2014). https://doi.org/10.1007/978-3-319-10602-1_48

12. Newell, A., Yang, K., Deng, J.: Stacked hourglass networks for human pose estimation. In: Leibe, B., Matas, J., Sebe, N., Welling, M. (eds.) ECCV 2016. LNCS, vol. 9912, pp. 483–499. Springer, Cham (2016). https://doi.org/10.1007/978-3-319-46484-8_29

13. Radosavovic, I., Dollár, P., Girshick, R., Gkioxari, G., He, K.: Data distillation: Towards omni-supervised learning. In: IEEE Conference on Computer Vision and Pattern Recognition (CVPR), pp. 4119–4128 (2018)

14. Simonyan, K., Zisserman, A.: Very deep convolutional networks for large-scale image recognition. arXiv preprint arXiv:1409.1556 (2014)

15. Sun, K., Xiao, B., Liu, D., Wang, J.: Deep high-resolution representation learning for human pose estimation. In: IEEE Conference on Computer Vision and Pattern Recognition (CVPR) (2019)

16. Tan, M., Le, Q.V.: Efficientnet: rethinking model scaling for convolutional neural networks. arXiv preprint arXiv:1905.11946 (2019)

17. Tarvainen, A., Valpola, H.: Mean teachers are better role models: weight-averaged consistency targets improve semi-supervised deep learning results. In: Neural Information Processing Systems (NIPS) (2017)

18. Wang, J., et al.: Deep high-resolution representation learning for visual recognition. IEEE Trans. Pattern Anal. Mach. Intell. (2020)

19. Wei, S.E., Ramakrishna, V., Kanade, T., Sheikh, Y.: Convolutional pose machines. In: IEEE Conference on Computer Vision and Pattern Recognition (CVPR), pp. 4724–4732 (2016)

20. Xiao, B., Wu, H., Wei, Y.: Simple baselines for human pose estimation and tracking. In: European Conference on Computer Vision (ECCV), September 2018

21. Xu, X., Zou, Q., Lin, X., Huang, Y., Tian, Y.: Integral knowledge distillation for multi-person pose estimation. IEEE Signal Process. Lett. **27**, 436–440 (2020)

22. Yang, Y., Qiu, J., Song, M., Tao, D., Wang, X.: Distilling knowledge from graph convolutional networks. In: IEEE Conference on Computer Vision and Pattern Recognition (CVPR), pp. 7074–7083 (2020)

23. Zhang, F., Zhu, X., Ye, M.: Fast human pose estimation. In: IEEE Conference on Computer Vision and Pattern Recognition (CVPR) (2019)

Binary Convolutional Neural Networks for Facial Action Unit Detection

Mengyi Liu[1,2], Fei Wan[1,2], and Ruicong Zhi[1,2(✉)]

[1] School of Computer and Communication Engineering, University of Science and Technology Beijing, Beijing, China
zhirc@ustb.edu.cn
[2] Beijing Key Laboratory of Knowledge Engineering for Materials Science, Beijing, China

Abstract. Facial Action Unit (AU) detection is essential for automatic emotion analysis. However, most AU detection researches pay attention to real-valued deep neural networks, which include heavy multiplication operations and require high computation and memory. In this paper, we propose binary convolutional neural networks for AU detection. The main contributions of our work include the following two aspects: (1) we propose a multi-layer decision fusion strategy (MDFS), which combines multiple prediction channels to produce the final result. (2) MDFS is encoded with binary parameters and activations (BMDFS) instead of real values to reduce memory cost and accelerate convolutional operations. Our proposed method is evaluated on BP4D database. MDFS and BMDFS obtain the overall F1 score of 65.5% and 54.8%, respectively. Moreover, BMDFS achieves 32× memory saving and 4.6 × speed up compared to real-valued models. Experimental results show that our approach achieves promising good performance.

Keywords: Action unit detection · Multi-layer decision fusion · Binary weights · Binary activations

1 Introduction

Facial expression recognition (FER) has attracted increasing attention in the last decades and has been widely applied in many fields such as security, clinic, and robotics. Six basic emotions exist universally regardless of cultures and race. FER of these six basic emotions base on message judgment of facial behavior. However, relationships between message-judgment methods and human facial expressions are not universal, so it is insufficient for the comprehensive study of facial recognition. Facial Action Coding System (FACS) [1] is the most comprehensive and extensive method in popular facial behavior measurements. FACS encode facial movements by the combination of action units (AUs) and make emotion categories much wider.

Facial action unit detection plays an essential part in facial expression analysis. For example, happiness is usually the combination of AU12 and AU6, while the combination of AU1, AU2, AU5 and AU26 generally represents surprise. Recently, many AU detection approaches have been proposed and can be categorized into two classes: conventional methods and deep learning algorithms. Zhi et al. [2] gave a comprehensive

© Springer Nature Switzerland AG 2021
Y. Peng et al. (Eds.): ICIG 2021, LNCS 12889, pp. 275–287, 2021.
https://doi.org/10.1007/978-3-030-87358-5_22

survey of the issues including face detection and registration, facial action representation, facial AUs feature extraction and AUs classification. Simultaneously, Martinez et al. [3] systematically surveyed components of AU detection: pre-processing, feature selection and machine analysis of facial actions.

Currently, Convolutional Neural Networks (CNNs) are widely applied in AU detection task, which are trained on power-hungry and expensive Graphic Processing Units (GPUs) and is unsuitable for the applications on mobile devices. Therefore, there are growing demands to reduce the computational complexity and speed-up tasks. In this paper, a binary-weight network is utilized for AU detection. The main contributions of our proposed method include: (1) we design a multi-layer decision fusion strategy (MDFS) based on ResNet-18 to improve the representational capability of facial features. Moreover, different weights are applied to combine multiple prediction channels to produce the final result. (2) MDFS is encoded with binary parameters (BMDFS) and adopted in AUs detection for the first time. BMDFS quantizes both parameters and activations by the sign function, and we focus on piecewise polynomial function as an accurate approximation during the inference process. We demonstrate that our method is comparable to many full precision networks, while our method can save more memory and accelerate convolutional operations.

2　Related Work

We roughly group conventional AU detection methods into four categories according to facial features:

Appearance Features: Appearance features focus on facial color and texture information. Popular approaches include Gabor wavelets and Local Binary Patterns (LBP). Gabor wavelets can detect multi-directional and multi-scale texture information, and are robust to illumination changes and small registration errors, but has high complexity and identity bias. Applying Gabor filters to the difference between neutral face and expression image can reduce identity difference [4]. Tian et al. [5] proposed a Gabor-wavelet-based method for automatic AU recognition and compared it with geometric-based features. LBP is a non-parametric gray level descriptor, which is insensitive to gray change with less computation. LBP has been improved to promote AU analysis, such as Sobel-LBP [6], LGBP [7], STLBP [8]. Huang et al. [9] conducted a comprehensive review of LBP-based face image analysis.

Geometry Features: Geometry features describe changes in facial organs. Different AU has different effects on the same organ. For example, AU12 is to pull the lip corner, while AU15 depresses it. Therefore, facial landmark localization is significant in geometry feature extraction. Automatic Face Analysis (AFA) system based on permanent and transient facial features, and multi-state models tracked facial features, including lips, eyes, brows, cheeks [10]. Pantic et al. [11] explored a multidetector-based method for facial landmark localization, extracting profile-contour fiducial points for AU detection. Geometry features are independent of light conditions, easy to extract, and computed simply. However, they cannot detect subtle facial features like texture changes, depend on high accuracy of facial feature point location.

Hybrid Features: To improve AU recognition, some researches combined different feature extraction methods. Combining geometry and appearance features can enhance system performance, which conveys complementary information well [12, 13]. Ming et al. [14] utilized the fusion features based on a multi-kernel Support Vector Machine for the automatic AU intensities estimation, which demonstrates hybrid features outperform the mono-type feature. Local features mainly express subtle facial changes, while the global features strongly adjust whole face changes. To take the advantage of both, Chang et al. [15] applied manifold learning to characterize global and local information discriminatively.

Deeply Learnt Features: In the last decade, deep learning boosts the performance of many computer vision tasks, and deeper information can be learned and revealed from training images.

Local Features: Different AUs occur in various regions of the face, so regional features have a great effect on AU detection. Zhao et al. [16] constructed DRML to address region learning and multi-label learning, and a region layer was designed to capture facial local appearance changes. EAC-Net [17] was proposed to predict AUs reliably by adding enhancing layers (E-Net) and cropping layers (C-Net) to VGG network [18]. E-Net was a combination of attention layer and skipping layer. C-Net is similar to the region layer in DRML, aiming to learn AU-related features by independent convolutional layers. A region pooling layer was designed after a fully convolutional layer by [19], capturing regional features separately. Shao et al. [20] introduced JAA-Net and designed a hierarchical and multi-scale region learning module to learn features of each local region with different scales to adapt multi-scale AUs.

Dynamic Features: Features with temporal information can better describe facial textures. Hu et al. [21] introduced CCT involving two stages: CCB (cross-concat block) to adapt to distributions of AUs and LSTM (Long Short-Term Memory) to capture temporal dependencies. Mei et al. [19] designed a novel deep neural network where regional features are fed into several stacks of LSTMs to integrate temporal dependency. In FEAR 2015, the best approach [22] combined CNN and BLSTM (Bi-directional LSTM) to jointly learn different features in a deep learning manner. Li et al. [23] fused static CNN features with an LSTM-based temporal fusion recurrent net, which made AU detection task better improved than static images.

3 Proposed Method

The structure of our proposed method is shown in Fig. 1, consisting of three components: (1) Fine-tuned ResNet-18[24] network (FRES): fine-tuned pre-trained models are applied universally. We adopt ResNet-18 to have good image representations. (2) Multi-layer decision fusion strategy (MDFS): multi-layer features are extracted for each image and different weights are applied to combine multiple prediction channels for the final result; (3) Encoded MDFS with binary parameters (BMDFS): BMDFS replaces real-valued convolutional operations in MDFS with binary parameters, and piecewise polynomial function is adopted as an approximation of sign function to avoid being non-differentiable.

3.1 Fine-Tuned ResNet-18

Fine-tuning pre-training models have been proved to be effective in many fields, such as object detection [25] and emotion recognition [26]. We use ResNet-18 as a pre-trained model, which is designed for ImageNet and fine-tuned on extra AU images.

The modified ResNet-18 model is our baseline, which contains 17 convolutional layers and 1 fully connected layer. The first convolutional layer employs a kernel size of 7×7, and the rest is divided into four units. Each unit consists of two basic blocks, with 2 convolutional layers, and 3×3 kernels [27]. We keep convolutional layers' parameters of the pre-trained model. The fully connected layer is modified to 1 to match single AU detection. Sigmoid operation is applied to decide the presence of AUs.

3.2 MDFS: Multi-layer Decision Fusion Strategy

Low-level features in CNNs represent shallow features, while high-level features have richer semantic information and stronger resolution ability. AU detection task has high demands for facial details and requires multi-level information to express features. The output of different CNN layers represents diversity characteristics, which can implement complementary information and enhance recognition accuracy. Therefore, we propose MDFS to train three classifiers, and finally, obtain a weighted fusion result under combined action. Each image is fed into the network illustrated in Fig. 1, and features are extracted from three different units. Each unit is followed by an output layer, consisting of a fully connected layer and a sigmoid layer, and the final result is the fusion of output with weights which can be calculated as:

$$P = \sum_{i=1}^{3} p_i w_i \tag{1}$$

where p_i refers to the probability of each output layer, and w_i denotes the weight assigned to each prediction.

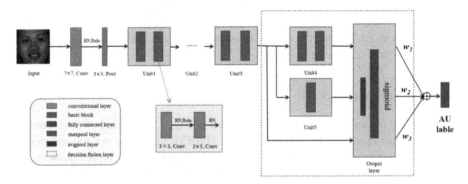

Fig. 1. Architecture of the proposed method.

Three different fusion strategies, as shown in Fig. 2, are designed to investigate the effectiveness of MDFS. Fusion_A, Fusion_B, and Fusion_C combine prediction channels of unit3 and unit4, the first basic block of unit4 and unit4, unit3, unit4, and the first basic block of unit4, respectively.

We know that the features leaned by a higher-level convolutional layer can better represent facial details. Thus, the weight of the higher-level is given a larger value, and the weights of different stages are 0.5, 0.3, 0.2 from the high-level to low-level layer. Finally, we set a threshold as 0.5 tasked with splitting AU into two classes.

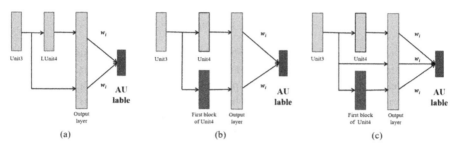

Fig. 2. The architecture of the proposed method. Three different combinations of results. (a) Fusion_A: the combination of prediction channels of unit3 and unit4. (b) Fusion_B: the combination of prediction channels of unit4 and the first basic block of unit4. (c) Fusion_C: the combination of prediction channels of unit3, unit4, and the first basic block of unit4.

3.3 BMDFS: MDFS with Binary Weights

Deep learning sometimes is limited to its computational complexity of parameter redundancy. The bottleneck could be broken by neural network pruning [28–30], weight quantization [31–34], and other methods. To overcome the mentioned problems in AU detection, we propose BMDFS with binary parameters in each basic block which can save memory training time compared with real-valued methods.

In regular CNNs, the convolutional operation is defined as:

$$y = W^T a \tag{2}$$

where W and a are vectors in $R^{\in n}$, W is the weight filter and a is the input vector computed by the previous layer.

We aim to binary real-valued weights and activations in CNNs, the quantization operation is computed as:

$$x_b = \alpha sign(x_r) = \begin{cases} +\alpha, \text{ if } x_r \geq 0 \\ -\alpha, \text{ otherwise} \end{cases} \tag{3}$$

where x_r indicates 32-bit real-valued parameters including weight W_r and activation a_r, and x_b are corresponding binary-valued parameters. α is a scaling factor.

Then the convolutional operations can be reformulated as:

$$y = \alpha_w \alpha_a (W_b \oplus a_b) \tag{4}$$

where $\oplus$ denotes XNOR operations, subscripts w and a of α indicate weight and activations.

The sign function is not continuously differentiable, which makes it incompatible with backward propagation. Therefore, we utilize a simple computed approximation function whose derivative is a piecewise linear function to replace it, as Eq. (5).

$$a_b = \begin{cases} a_r^2 + 2a_r & if \ a_r \in [-1, 0) \\ a_r^2 - 2a_r & if \ a_r \in [0, 1) \\ sign(a_r) & otherwise \end{cases} \tag{5}$$

Firstly, we take the advice of XNOR-Net [31] into consideration and real weights are utilized in the first convolutional layer and output layer. As parameters in both layers only account for a small part of the total parameters, the performance will be reduced due to information loss. Then, we adopt binary weights and activations in each basic block and save the trained model whose parameters are not binary. Finally, we convert the weights into 1 or -1 and save the binary model.

We only perform binarization operations with weights and activations in the basic block. Some parameters are kept real-valued in these parts, such as the first convolution layer, the last fully-connected layer, and 1×1 convolution in short-cut. They can enhance network representational capacity with small numbers of parameters. Similar to the basic block settings in [32], as shown in Fig. 3, we divide the original basic block (left) into two to enhance network representational capacity, and the new basic block (right) only includes one convolutional layer.

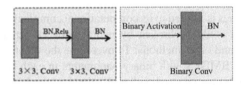

Fig. 3. Designed basic block. Left: basic block in real-value networks; Right: basic block in binary-value networks.

Compared to regular CNNs with 32-bit real-valued parameters, 1-bit CNNs replace convolution operations with XNOR and bit counting operations. Therefore, binary networks can save much computation cost by removing float-point multiplication. Moreover, 1-bit CNNs can also save $32\times$ memory cost relative to 32-bit CNNs.

4   Experiments

Firstly, we describe the facial dataset and experimental implementation, then the performances of binary neural networks were compared with approaches well-applied in AU detection.

4.1 Datasets and Settings

We evaluate our proposed method on BP4D dataset for AU detection task. Our experiments are based on the subject-independent strategy, which is more practical and challenging than the subject-dependent. BP4D dataset [35] is a high-resolution spontaneous facial expression database, which contains 2D videos and 3D videos of 41 participants, including 18 males and 23 females. Each subject is associated with eight tasks, and each task represents an emotion. There are 328 videos and around 14000 usable frames with labeled AUs. Similar to the experiment settings in [16, 17, 20], we split the dataset into three folds according to various subjects and try to balance the ratio of males and females. We adopt the three-fold cross-validation method for the experiment, and each fold refers to the train set, validation set and test set respectively. For each AU, the ratio of positive and negative samples is set around 1:2 based on positive. If the number of negative samples is less than twice the positive samples, the negative samples are expended by data augmentation. If not, the negative samples are randomly selected to balance the radio.

Settings: Images are normalized to $224 \times 224 \times 3$ to meet the input of ResNet18. Our proposed method is implemented using Pytorch and trained with Adam with a learning rate of 0.0001 and batch size of 32. The output of sigmoid is a probability between 0 and 1, we regard 0.5 as a threshold and judge the occurrence of AUs. The average F1 score and accuracy are utilized as evaluation.

4.2 Experimental Results

We regard the ResNet-18 network as the baseline and compare our proposed method against commonly used AU detection approaches, including traditional approaches and deep learning approaches.

MDFS Method: MDFS method fuses the results from different units of the basic network. In our experiments, four models are trained: Fine-tuned ResNet-18, Fusion_A, Fusion_B, and Fusion_C, and the corresponding average F1 score with three-fold cross-validation of 12 AUs in BP4D database is shown in Fig. 4. As is seen in Fig. 4, MDFS results outperform fine-tuned ResNet-18, which demonstrates ResNet-18 can learn deep

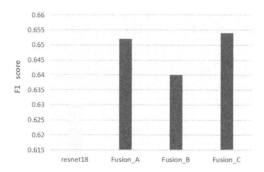

Fig. 4. F1 score of three fusions.

features and deeper features to better represent facial information. Fusion_C strategy achieves the highest F1 score.

Table 1 reports the comparison of SOTA on BP4D database, and the best result is in bold. It is shown that our proposed method performs best under the subject-independent protocol. In Table 1, DRML, EAC-Net, and JAA-Net are convention-based methods, and the rest are hand-craft methods. We also observe that deep learning methods are superior to traditional approaches. We pick these methods to verify the following questions: (1) are deep learning approaches more descriptive than hand-craft ones? (2) compared to SOTA, could the proposed MDFNet provide a more effective way to improve the performance of AU detection?

DRML was proposed by Zhao et al. [16] with a region layer to capture local appearance changes for different facial regions. As Table 1 shown, DRML performed better than traditional machine learning methods including LSVM, JPML, and CPM. Moreover, MDFS method gains on F1 score for all AUs compared to DRML, and the highest increment is 43.4% (AU24), the lowest is 3.4% (AU17). Concurrently, MDFS method is compared to some outperformed deep learning algorithms, such as EAC-Net and JAA-Net. MDFS performs better for most of AUs, and the average F1 score achieves 65.5%, which is 9.5% and 5.4% higher than EAC-Net and JAA-Net, respectively. These experimental results confirm the effectiveness of MDFNet.

Table 1. F1 score on BP4D dataset.

AU	LSVM[16]	JPML[36]	CPM[37]	DRML[16]	EAC-Net[17]	JAA-Net[20]	MDFS
1	0.232	0.326	0.434	0.364	0.390	0.472	**0.587**
2	0.228	0.256	0.407	0.418	0.352	0.440	**0.535**
4	0.231	0.374	0.434	0.430	0.486	0.549	**0.572**
6	0.272	0.423	0.592	0.550	0.761	**0.775**	0.691
7	0.471	0.505	0.613	0.670	0.729	**0.746**	0.724
10	0.772	0.722	0.621	0.663	0.819	**0.840**	0.794
12	0.637	0.741	0.685	0.658	0.862	**0.869**	0.827
14	0.643	0.657	0.525	0.541	0.588	**0.619**	0.589
15	0.184	0.381	0.340	0.332	0.375	0.436	**0.579**
17	0.330	0.400	0.543	0.480	0.591	**0.603**	0.514
23	0.194	0.304	0.395	0.317	0.359	0.427	**0.713**
24	0.207	0.423	0.378	0.300	0.358	0.419	**0.734**
Avg	0.353	0.459	0.500	0.483	0.559	0.600	**0.655**

Binary Operations: Convolutions are multiply-accumulators, calculating weighted sums of input data which make deep learning algorithms suffer from out-of-memory due to their computational complexity of parameter redundancy. In our experiments, we adopt 1-bit XNOR-count operations to replace 32-bit floating-point multiply accumulations. The numbers of parameters about convolution and BN are computed as in Eq. (6) and Eq. (7), respectively.

$$P_c = K_h \times K_w \times C_{in} \times C_{out} \tag{6}$$

$$P_b = 2 \times C_{out} \tag{7}$$

where $K_h \times K_w$ is the size of the convolution kernel, C_{in} is the number of the input channel, C_{out} is the number of output channels.

We keep real-valued weights and activations in these parts: the first convolution layer, the last fully-connected layer, and 1×1 convolution in short-cut. They can enhance network representational capacity with small numbers of parameters. Table 2 shows the details of parameter calculation on ResNet-18, where Equ denotes how to calculate the number of parameters. The required memory of full-precision ResNet18 and BMDFS is shown in Fig. 5. BMDFS saves memory usage by 31 times in comparison with full-precision ResNet18 theoretically. As the operation of XNOR is much faster than float point multiplication, BMDFS can save time cost.

Table 2. Numbers of parameter calculation on ResNet-18.

Renet18	Operation	C_{in}/C_{out}	Kernel size	Equ	Parameters	Memory (B) BMDFS/MDFS
unit1	conv1	3/64	(7,7)	$7 \times 7 \times 3 \times 64$	9408	37632/1176
	bn1	64/64	None	2one	128	512/16
	conv1	64/64	(3,3)	$3 \times 3 \times 64 \times 64$	36864	147456/4608
	bn1	64/64	None	2one	128	512/16
			......			
unit2	conv1	64/128	(3,3)	$3 \times 3 \times 64 \times 128$	73728	294912/9216
	bn1	128/128	None	2one1	256	1024/32
			......			
unit3	conv1	128/256	(3,3)	$3 \times 3 \times 128 \times 256$	294912	1179648/36864
	bn1	256/256	None	2one2	512	2048/64
			......			
unit4	conv1	256/512	(3,3)	$3 \times 3 \times 256 \times 512$	1179648	4718592/147456
	bn1	512/512	None	2one5	1024	4096/128
			......			

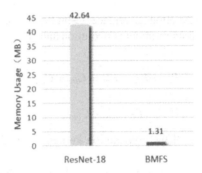

Fig. 5. Memory usage of full-precision ResNet18 and BMDFS.

Our BMDFS is also applied for AU detection on BP4D as is illustrated in Table 3. MDFS outperformed BMDFS with 19.5% in F1 score. However, BMDFS achieves up to 31.5 × memory saving compared with MDFS as Fig. 5 demonstrated.

As shown in Table 3, BMDFS outperforms all traditional approaches in the average F1 score, which demonstrates deep learning methods provide deep features to better detect AUs. As for deep learning methods, BMDF achieves 6.5% higher average F1 score than DRML with much memory saving. BMDFS does not achieve the best performance. However, it reduces computation cost and memory usage than full-precision networks, which is highly worthwhile for mobile devices.

Table 3. F1 score of BMDFS on BP4D dataset.

	AU1	AU2	AU4	AU6	AU7	AU10	AU12	AU14	AU15	AU17	AU23	AU24	Avg
MDFS	0.587	0.535	0.572	0.691	0.724	0.794	0.827	0.589	0.579	0.514	0.713	0.734	0.655
BMDFS	0.504	0.506	0.502	0.454	0.582	0.710	0.707	0.496	0.492	0.406	0.565	0.651	0.548

5   Conclusion

In this paper, we propose MDFS, a weighted multi-layer decision fusion strategy, which combines multiple prediction channels to produce the final result for single AU detection. We compare three combinations of different units to select the better-performance as the final fusion strategy. We evaluate our method on BP4D dataset and compare F1 score against other approaches. Experiment results illustrate that our method achieves better performance compared with others. We further encode MDFS with binary parameters and activations (BMDFS), which can not compete with the state-of-the-art performance of deep real-valued networks. However, BMDFS reduces computation and memory cost, and it can help the deployment of deep networks in mobile devices. Our future work will focus on improving performance based on binary networks for AUs detection.

Acknowledgement. This work was supported by the National Research and Development Major Project [grant numbers: 2017YFD0400100], the National Natural Science Foundation of China [grant numbers: 61673052], the Fundamental Research Fund for the Central Universities of China [grant numbers: numbers: FRF-TP-20-10B, FRF-GF-19-010A, FRF-IDRY-19–011]. The computing work is supported by USTB MatCom of Beijing Advanced Innovation Center for Materials Genome Engineering.

References

1. Ekman, P., Rosenberg, E.L.: What the Face Reveals: Basic and Applied Studies of Spontaneous Expression using the Facial Action Coding System (FACS). Oxford University Press, USA (1997)
2. Zhi, R., Liu, M., Zhang, D.: A comprehensive survey on automatic facial action unit analysis. Vis. Comput. **36**(5), 1067–1093 (2019). https://doi.org/10.1007/s00371-019-01707-5
3. Martinez, B., Valstar, M.F., Jiang, B., Pantic, M.: Automatic analysis of facial actions: a survey. IEEE Trans. Affect. Comput. **13**(9), 1–22 (2017)
4. Bazzo, J.J, Lamar, M.V.: Recognizing facial actions using Gabor wavelets with neutral face average difference. In: Sixth IEEE International Conference on Automatic Face and Gesture Recognition, Seoul, Korea: IEEE, pp. 505–510 (2004)
5. Tian, Y., Kanade, T., Cohn, J.F.: Evaluation of Gabor-wavelet-based facial action unit recognition in image sequences of increasing complexity. In: Proceedings of Fifth IEEE International Conference on Automatic Face Gesture Recognition. Washington, DC, USA: IEEE, pp. 229–234 (2002)
6. Zhao, S., Gao, Y., Zhang, B.: Sobel-lbp. In: 2008 15th IEEE International Conference on Image Processing. San Diego, USA: IEEE, pp. 2144–2147 (2008)
7. Senechal, T., Rapp, V., Salam, H., Seguier, R., Bailly, K., Prevost, L.: Facial action recognition combining heterogeneous features via multikernel learning. IEEE Trans. Syst. Man Cybern. Part B (Cybernetics) **42**(4), 993–1005 (2012)
8. Zhang, S., Yao, H., Liu, S.: Dynamic background modeling and subtraction using spatio-temporal local binary patterns. In: 2008 15th IEEE International Conference on Image Processing. San Diego, USA: IEEE, pp. 1556–1559 (2008)
9. Huang, D., Shan, C., Ardabilian, M., Wang, Y., Chen, L.: Local binary patterns and its application to facial image analysis: a survey. IEEE Trans. Syst. Man. Cybern. Part C **41**(6), 765–781 (2011)
10. Tian, Y.I., Kanade, T., Cohn, J.F.: Recognizing action units for facial expression analysis. IEEE Trans. Pattern Anal. Mach. Intell. **23**(2), 97–115 (2001)
11. Pantic, M., Rothkrantz, L.J.M.: Facial action recognition for facial expression analysis from static face images. IEEE Tran. Syst. Man Cybern. Part B: Cybern. **34**(3), 1449–1461 (2004)
12. Nicolle, J., Bailly, K., Chetouani, M.: Facial action unit intensity prediction via hard multi-task metric learning for kernel regression. In: 2015 11th IEEE International Conference and Workshops on Automatic Face and Gesture Recognition (FG). Ljubljana, SloveniaI: IEEE, pp. 1–6 (2015)
13. Nicolle, J., Bailly, K., Chetouani, M.: Real-time facial action unit intensity prediction with regularized metric learning. Image Vis. Comput. **52**, 1–14 (2016)
14. Ming, Z., Bugeau, A., Rouas, J.L., Shochi, T.: Facial action units intensity estimation by the fusion of features with multi-kernel support vector machine. In: 2015 11th IEEE International Conference and Workshops on Automatic Face and Gesture Recognition (FG). Ljubljana, SloveniaI: IEEE, pp. 1–6 (2015)

15. Chang, W.Y., Chen, C.S., Hung, Y.P.: Analyzing facial expression by fusing manifolds. Asian Conference on Computer Vision, pp. 621–630. Springer, Heidelberg (2007). https://doi.org/10.1007/978-3-540-76390-1_61

16. Zhao, K., Chu, W., Zhang, H.: Deep region and multi-label learning for facial action unit detection. In: 2016 IEEE Conference on Computer Vision and Pattern Recognition, pp. 3391–3399 (2016)

17. Li, W., Abtahi, F., Zhu, Z., Yin, L.: EAC-Net: deep nets with enhancing and cropping for facial action unit detection. IEEE Trans. Pattern Anal. Mach. Intell. 40(11), 2583–2596 (2018)

18. Simonyan K., Zisserman, A.: Very deep convolutional networks for large-scale image recognition. arXiv preprint arXiv:1409.1556 (2014)

19. Mei C., Jiang F., Shen R., Hu, Q.: Region and temporal dependency fusion for multi-label action unit detection. In: 2018 24th International Conference on Pattern Recognition (ICPR), pp. 848–853 (2018)

20. Shao, Z., Liu, Z., Cai, J., Ma, L.: Deep adaptive attention for joint facial action unit detection and face alignment. In: Ferrari, V., Hebert, M., Sminchisescu, C., Weiss, Y. (eds.) ECCV 2018. LNCS, vol. 11217, pp. 725–740. Springer, Cham (2018). https://doi.org/10.1007/978-3-030-01261-8_43

21. Hu, Q., Jiang, F., Mei, C., Shen, R.: CCT: a cross-concat and temporal neural network for multi-label action unit detection. In: 2018 IEEE International Conference on Multimedia and Expo (ICME). IEEE (2018)

22. Jaiswal, S., Valstar, M.: Deep learning the dynamic appearance and shape of facial action units. In: IEEE Winter Conference on Applications of Computer Vision(WACV), pp. 1–8 (2016)

23. Li, W., Abtahi, F., Zhu, Z.: Action unit detection with region adaptation, multi-labeling learning, and optimal temporal fusing. In: 2017 IEEE Conference on Computer Vision and Pattern Recognition (CVPR), pp. 6766–6775 (2017)

24. He, K., Zhang, X., Ren, S., Sun, J.: Deep residual learning for image recognition. In: IEEE Conference on Computer Vision and Pattern Recognition, pp. 770–778 (2016)

25. Girshick, R.: Fast R-CNN. In: IEEE International Conference on Computer Vision, 1440–1448 (2015)

26. Li, W., Abtahi, F., Zhu, Z.: A deep feature based multi-kernel learning approach for video emotion recognition. In: ACM International Conference on Multimodal Interaction, pp. 483–490 (2015)

27. Shen, F., Xu, Y., Liu, L., Yang, Y., Huang, Z., Shen, H.: unsupervised deep hashing with similarity-adaptive and discrete optimization. IEEE Trans. Pattern Anal. Mach. Intell. (99),1 (2018).

28. Molchanov, P., Tyree, S., Karras, T., Aila, T., Kautz, J.: Pruning convolutional neural networks for resource efficient inference. In: International Conference on Learning Representations (2016).

29. Liu, Z., Li, J., Shen Z., Huang, G., Yan, S., Zhang, C.: Learning efficient convolutional networks through network slimming. In: International Conference on Computer Vision(ICCV) (2017).=

30. Zhuang, Z., et al.: Discrimination-aware channel pruning for deep neural networks. In: 32nd Conference on Neural Information Processing Systems (NeurIPS) (2018)

31. Rastegari, M., Ordonez, V., Redmon, J., Farhadi, A.: XNOR-Net: imagenet classification using binary convolutional neural networks. In: Leibe, B., Matas, J., Sebe, N., Welling, M. (eds.) ECCV 2016. LNCS, vol. 9908, pp. 525–542. Springer, Cham (2016). https://doi.org/10.1007/978-3-319-46493-0_32

32. Liu, Z., Wu, B., Luo, W., Yang, X., Liu, W., Cheng, K.-T.: Bi-Real Net: enhancing the performance of 1-bit cnns with improved representational capability and advanced training algorithm. In: Ferrari, V., Hebert, M., Sminchisescu, C., Weiss, Y. (eds.) ECCV 2018. LNCS, vol. 11219, pp. 747–763. Springer, Cham (2018). https://doi.org/10.1007/978-3-030-01267-0_44

33. Courbariaux, M., Hubara, I., Soudry, D., El-Yaniv, R., Bengio, Y.: BinaryNet: training deep neural networks with weights and activations constrained to $+1$ or -1. arXiv: 1602.02830v3 (2016)

34. Li, Z., Ni, B., Zhang, W., Yang, X., Wen, G.: Performance guaranteed network acceleration via high-order residual quantization. In: 2017 IEEE International Conference on Computer Vision (ICCV). IEEE Computer Society (2017)

35. Zhang, X., et al.: BP4D-Spontaneous: a high-resolution spontaneous 3D dynamic facial expression database. Image Vis. Comput. **32**(10), 692–706 (2014)

36. Zhao, K., Chu, W.-S., Torre, F., Cohn, J.F., Zhang, H.: Joint patch and multi-label learning for facial action unit detection. In: IEEE Conference on Computer Vision and Pattern Recognition, pp. 2207–2216 (2015)

37. Zeng, J., Chu, W.-S., Torre, F., Cohn, J.F., Xiong, Z.: Confidence preserving machine for facial action unit detection. In: IEEE International Conference on Computer Vision, pp. 3622–3630 (2015)

Efficient Example Mining for Anchor-Free Face Detection

Chengpeng Wang[1], Chunyu Chen[2], Siyi Hou[2], Ying Cai[3], and Menglong Yang[2(✉)]

[1] Wisesoft Inc., Chengdu, China
[2] School of Aeronautics and Astronautics, Sichuan University, Chengdu, China
mlyang@scu.edu.cn
[3] College of Electronic and Information, Southwest Minzu University, Chengdu, China

Abstract. How to select the most suitable samples for face detection model training is considered to be a core procedure to improve the performance of the model.
including the provision of Gtboxes, the matching of Gtboxes and feature points,
and the label assignment of feature points. In this paper, we propose a novel anchor-
free face detector based on efficient example mining (EEM). Firstly, Introduction a
density variable to measure the number of feature positions that can be matched for
each Gtboxes of different scales. Secondly, we propose an adaptive multi-scale
ERF Prior for probabilistic label assignment which is totally anchor-free. The
proposed methods are implemented on Caffe. Extensive experiments on popular
benchmarks WIDER FACE demonstrate that the performance of EEM training
based on Mobilenet-v1 is close to the state-of-the-art face detectors.

Keywords: Face detection · Anchor-free · Example mining · Label assignment

1 Introduction

Face detection is a fundamental step of face recognition system. The Viola-Jones face
detector [1] which is regarded as a landmark real-time detector appeared as early as
a decade ago, it uses cascade classifiers, adaBoost algorithm and Harr-like handcraft
feature. After that, a lot of work focused on how to design a more effective handcraft
feature. For example, ACF [2] and CCF [3]. The deformable part models (DPM) [4]
focus on the relationship between local and global features, but it is still a handcraft.

Until the appearance of deep learning, face detection has breakthrough by using the
rich features of abstract levels which automatic extracted by the convolutional neural
network (CNN). However, many algorithms (joint cascade [5], cascade CNN [6], faceness
[7]) are still based on the traditional cascade detection framework.

The R-CNN detection algorithm based on end-to-end optimization has better performance, which is a two-stage detector. People have been trying to optimize to make it
faster, so Fast R-CNN [8] and Faster R-CNN [9] appeared one after another. There are
also face detectors based on faster RCNN [10, 39]. Benefit from the one-stage detector,
such as SSD [11] and yolo [12], Face detectors (SSH [13], pyramid box [14], faceboxes
[15]) can run in real applications with high accuracy and fps.

Y. Peng et al. (Eds.): ICIG 2021, LNCS 12889, pp. 288–300, 2021.
https://doi.org/10.1007/978-3-030-87358-5_23

With the development of detectors, the detection framework has gradually formed and developed the following parts besides the backbone. Neck Network: The feature fusion module fuses the high- and low-level features with different abstractions, such as FPN [16], PAN [17], HRNet [18]. The feature enhancement module enhances the span range of the effective receptive field in one feature pyramid layer, such as RFB [19], FEM [20]. AutoFEM [21] integrates feature fusion and feature enhancement. Head Network: Classification and regression bounding box. Anchor-based method regression box from a series of pre-set anchors and anchor-free method regression box from some feature point like corner or center.

Anchor was first proposed in faster R-CNN for region proposal and it was widely used in one stage detector after that. As more and more dense anchors distribution design become the bottleneck of performance improvement, anchor-free method which regression bounding box is directly from position attracts people's attention for object detection once again. However, compared with anchor-based method, anchor-free is not widely used in face detection. Although we can benefit from the development of object detection, there are still some differences between face detection and object detection.

Different from general object detection, face detection has symbiotic relationship with body outside the Gtbox which make effective receptive field (ERF) [22, 41] wider. Based on the inertial thinking of object detection by sliding window, it is considered that object detection is to classify images in the sliding window with different positions and scales. However, the research of small face detection [14] found that the bounding box is only used for location, the areas inside and outside the bounding box can be used for classification. The range of effective receptive field is not the same as Gtbox, but varies with the face scale, Anchor-based method can adjust the range of effective receptive field for matching Gtbox by setting IoU threshold which is a handcraft experience value. Generally, the IoU threshold for small face matching is set relatively low [23]. Many anchor-free methods use Gtbox to represent this ERF range roughly. Inspired by the adaptive training sample selection method [24, 25], we forward propagation to calculate the score of each feature positions and build probability distribution for those scores in a range containing body, then the prior of different scale faces is segmented adaptively by Gaussian Mixture Model.

The contributions of this paper are summarized as below:

1) Introduction a density variable to measure the number of feature positions that can be matched, the Gtboxes of different scales can match to almost the same number of feature positions according to this variable.
2) Propose adaptive multi-scale ERF prior setting for probabilistic label assignment. It can automatically find the appropriate prior for Gtboxes of various scales.
3) Achieving excellent performance on WIDER FACE compared with the state-of-the-art methods with common training equipment.

2 Related Work

2.1 Anchor Free Detection

Early one-stage detector yolo-v1 didn't use anchor for Gtbox matching, it divides the input image into an S × S grid. The grid cell which contains the center of a Gtbox is responsible for detecting that object. Densebox [34] label a filled circle located in the center of a face bounding box as positive region, predicts distance from positive location to left-top and right-bottom corners of the bounding box. CenterNet [35] assign the center pixel of a bounding box as positive and regress size from the point. FCOS [26] limit the range of bounding box as positives and directly regress four distances from all positive locations. center-ness is used to down-weight the low-quality bounding boxes predicted by a location far from the center of an object. Foveabox [31] use Scale Assignment and Object Fovea to limit the range of positives on feature pyramidal levels. and learn a transformation that maps the networks localization at cell (x, y) in the feature maps to the Gtbox. CSP [33] assign the location where an object's center point falls as positive which similar to yolo-v1, other location surrounding the positive are defined as negatives with a Gaussian mask to reduce the ambiguity.

2.2 Label Assignment

The early anchor-based detection algorithm uses IoU threshold to assign positive and negative samples, They and the anchor-free detection algorithm in the previous section all belong to hand-crafted label assignment.it is difficult to optimization parameters and design strategy.

In recent years, aiming at how to dynamic assign label rather than a fixed way for anchor-based method, a lot of face detection algorithms have made some exploration. SRN [28] calculate the Focal loss [38] for more samples under a wider IoU threshold for the first step of STC, only those samples that remain after the first step filtering will be used for the second step. DSFD [20] integrate novel anchor assign strategy into data augmentation. Hambox [37] mine sufficient and effective anchors at the end of forward propagation during training.

Some methods consider the label assignment as a maximum likelihood estimation procedure for probability distribution. FreeAnchor [29] select top-ranked anchors in terms of their IoU and use a mean-max function to select the best anchor. ATSS [24] automatically assign label according to IoU mean and the standard deviation from a set of close anchors, PAA [25] calculate anchor scores and choose Gaussian Mixture Model (GMM) to model the anchor score distribution.

Although these methods do not use IoU as threshold to assign label, they still use the IoU to select anchor candidates which constitute prior positive. Autoassign [30] is a differentiable label assignment strategy which abandon anchor completely, but it use Center Prior which is hand-crafted, it is difficult to adapt to face detection framework with large scale variation.

3 Efficient Example Mining

3.1 Pipeline

Figure 1 shows the pipeline of the algorithm which is a classic one stage detection framework, and the common feature fusion module and feature enhancement module are integrated. Mobilenet-v1 is used as the backbone. The feature pyramid is constructed

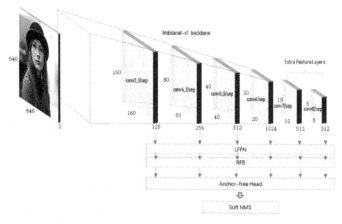

Fig. 1. EEM framework

by six levels $(P_1P_2P_3P_4P_5P_6)$. The feature fusion module adopts LFPN similar to that in paper [14]. Using other more advanced modules may improve the detection performance, including FPN [16] PAN [17] or high-resolution network [18]. The feature enhancement module adopts the classic RFB structure to enhance the span of receptive field of a feature layer.

The original SSD adopts the anchor-based matching strategy. The label assignment with IoU sorting has been proved to be unreasonable [24]. The initial position of anchor has little effect on the regression of detection box, but it is the corresponding feature point that play a decisive role in essence. Inspired by the PAA [25], we propose a novel adaptive label assignment. Using offline Gaussian Mixture Model to find the prior of various scale faces. during training, Gaussian Model (GM) is established for each Gtbox within the prior. We directly regress the distance between the edge of the bounding box and location (x, y) which is similar to FCOS [26], and normalize the distance with $S_{l-basic}$, as shown in Eq. [1]. In Eq. [2] we calculate a localization score (S_{loc}) and a classification score (S_{conf}). The localization loss(loc_loss) is Smooth L1 loss, the confidence loss is the softmax loss(conf_loss) over 2 classes for face detection. The difference between PAA and EEM is that PAA retains anchor. PAA used IoU sorting for hand-crafted prior setting and uses the IoU loss to regress the detection box.

$$left = \frac{x-x_0^i}{S_{l-basic}} \quad top = \frac{y-y_0^i}{S_{l-basic}}$$
$$right = \frac{x_1^i-x}{S_{l-basic}} \quad bottom = \frac{y_1^i-y}{S_{l-basic}} \quad (1)$$

$$S_{loc} = \exp(loc_{loss})$$
$$S_{conf} = \exp(conf_{loss}) \quad (2)$$
$$S_{pos} = S_{loc} \cdot S_{conf}^\lambda$$

The original SSD select negative samples according to according to sorting classification score when mining hard examples. We extend this process by selecting positive samples according conf and loc score. Firstly, Gaussian Mixture Model (GMM) is used to divide prior positive according to different Gtbox scales. The process is offline due to GMM needs a lot of statistical data to obtain accurate parameters. Gaussian Model (GM) is established in the range of the prior positive for each Gtbox. The value greater than the mean value is regarded as positive, and the rest as negative. The detail is discussed in Sect. 3.3.

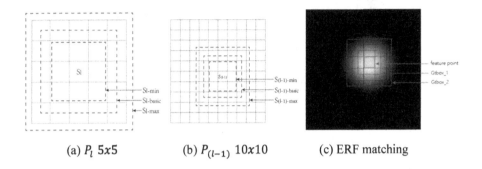

(a) P_l 5x5   (b) $P_{(l-1)}$ 10x10   (c) ERF matching

Fig. 2. (a) (b) Scale assignment limits which feature level can be matched by Gtbox of various sizes

3.2 Density Balance Scale Assignment

Utilizing the IoU threshold in anchor-based method, the matched feature points will be concentrated in several adjacent feature levels, as shown in Fig. 3(b)(c). The anchor-free method matches the feature points and the Gtbox according to their position relationship. If the feature points of all feature levels are included, the large Gtbox will contain more feature points than the small Gtbox, as shown in Fig. 3(d).

Inspired by the scale assignment in Foveabox [31], We set the corresponding basic scale (S_{basic}) for each feature level, enlarge or narrow the scope of S_{basic} ranging from S_{min} to S_{max}. According to the Eq. [3], when $\eta = \sqrt{2}$, the scale is divided as shown in Fig. 2, $S_{(l-1)-max} = S_{l-min}$, The scale space is divided into L continuous disjoint subspaces.

On feature level P_l, the resolution is n^2 and $S_l = 1/n^2$. We use the feature matching density D_l approximately indicates that Gtbox can match how many feature points in the feature level P_l. If different S_{gtbox} has similar D_{all}, the assignment is fair to any size of Gtbox. As shown in Table 1, $\eta = \left(\sqrt{2}\right)^n$. When n = 1, each feature level has the same feature density distribution, but the number of feature points can be matched is less. When n = 3, the number of feature points that can be matched by large-size Gtbox increases, while the number of feature points that can be matched by small-size Gtbox decreases, resulting in the unbalanced matching.

The experimental results in paper [31] Table 2 show that $\eta = 2$ has the best performance. The experimental results in Fig. 4 of paper [30] show that the feature response of a certain scale target will concentrate on the adjacent feature level. We abandoned the scales far away from $S_{l-basic}$ and set $\eta = 2$, which takes into account the balance and quantity of sample matching.

However, PPA [25] and ATSS use larger scales. It can be seen from Table 1 that when n is large, the number of feature points that cabe matched by small Gtbox and large Gtbox will be greatly different. Although they could set the super parameter Top-k to limit the number of feature points selected in each level. This is one of the reasons why small targets are difficult to detect.

$$\begin{aligned}
S_{l-basic} &= 16 \cdot S_l \\
S_{l-min} &= S_{l-basic}/\eta^2 \\
S_{l-max} &= S_{l-basic} \cdot \eta^2 \\
S_{gtbox} &\in \left[S_{l-basic}/\eta^2, S_{l-basic} \cdot \eta^2 \right] \\
D_l &= S_{gtbox}/S_l
\end{aligned} \tag{3}$$

Table 1. Matching density in each feature levels when η is different.

η	S_{gtbox}	D_{l-2}	D_{l-1}	D_l	D_{l+1}	D_{l+2}	D_{all}
$\sqrt{2}$	$[S_{min},S_{mid}]$	/	/	[8, 16]	/	/	[8, 16]
	$[S_{mid},S_{max}]$	/	/	[16, 32]	/	/	[16, 32]
$\left(\sqrt{2}\right)^2$	$[S_{min},S_{mid}]$	/	$[8 \times 4, 16 \times 4]$	[8, 16]	/	/	[40, 80]
	$[S_{mid},S_{max}]$	/	/	[16, 32]	[16/4,32/4]	/	[20, 40]
$\left(\sqrt{2}\right)^3$	$[S_{min},S_{mid}]$	$[8 \times 4 \times 4, 16 \times 4 \times 4]$	$[8 \times 4, 16 \times 4]$	[8, 16]	[8/4,16/4]	/	[170, 340]
	$[S_{mid},S_{max}]$	/	$[16 \times 4, 32 \times 4]$	[16, 32]	[16/4,32/4]	[(16/4)/4, (32/4)/4]	[85, 170]

3.3 Multi-scale ERF Prior

Figure 3 shows the various priors. The prior and label assignment of various algorithms are shown in Table 2. ATSS select top_k feature points the closest to the center of Gtbox for each level. PAA select top_k feature points corresponding to the anchors which have the largest IoUs. Because each feature level takes anchors, the super parameter top_k has little effect on the coverage of feature points. FCOS, FoveaBox [31] and CSP directly take feature points in the Gtbox box as the prior, and manually specify positive and negative through different strategies. Hambox [37] divides the prior by IoU threshold and mining positive with loc loss.

Inspired by the paper [30] Fig. 4 and FSAF [32], we let each Gtbox adaptively select the appropriate feature points on the appropriate feature level. The steps are as follows:

1) As shown in Fig. 4, the rough prior in level P can be simply set as the inscribed ellipse of Gtbox. The Euclidean distance between the center of Gtbox and the feature point

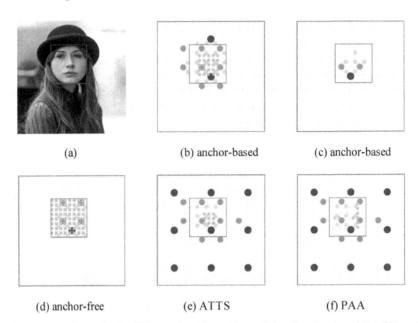

(a) (b) anchor-based (c) anchor-based

(d) anchor-free (e) ATTS (f) PAA

Fig. 3. Feature points prior for different algorithms. The traditional anchor-based ((a) (b)) method uses an IoU threshold for division, which not only limits the range of feature levels, but also realizes the selection of feature point in a feature level. (b) iou_thre $= 0.4$, (c) iou_thre $= 0.2$. (e) is ATTS, top_k $= 9$. (e) is PAA, top_k $= 9$.

Table 2. Prior and label assignment

	SSD	Foveabox	CSP	Hambox	ATTS	PAA	EEM
Prior	IoU threshold	Gtbox	Gtbox	IoU threshold	Each level top_k distance	Each level top_k IoU	Offline GMM
Label	All	Center part	Center point	loc loss	GM	GMM	GM

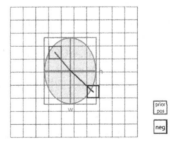

Fig. 4. The distance between Gtbox and the feature points in different levels

is calculated by Eq. [4]. The width and height of Gtbox are w and h. When ellipse $<$ $=$ 1 and k $=$ 0, the feature points are in the prior. Equation [5] is used for normalization. When overlap $\in$ (0,1], the feature point is in the range of ellipse. This overlap looks similar to the value of SSD when calculating the IoU of Gtbox and anchor.

$$ellipse = \frac{(x_1 - x_2)^2}{\left(k \cdot w + \frac{w}{2}\right)^2} + \frac{(y_1 - y_2)^2}{\left(k \cdot h + \frac{h}{2}\right)^2} \tag{4}$$

$$overlap = 1 - ellipse \tag{5}$$

2) PAA [25] dynamically establishes GMM for each Gtbox. However, it is difficult to obtain accurate modeling parameters due to the number of feature points corresponding to one Gtbox is limited. So, we use offline method to Establish GMM for Gtboxes in training set by various sizes, as shown in Fig. 5(a). Setting k of Eq. [4] be 0.5, we statistics the feature point probability distribution within ellipse containing face and body.

3) After obtaining the prior positive, the Gaussian Model (GM) for each Gtbox is established during training. The feature points above the mean value are set as positive samples, and those lower than are set as negative samples. as shown in Fig. 3(b)(c).

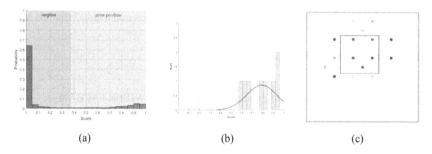

(a)   (b)   (c)

Fig. 5. Separate feature points using their probabilities

4 Experiments

4.1 Dataset

WIDER FACE [36] dataset is a face detection benchmark dataset. it consists of 32,203 images which labeled 393,703 faces with a high degree of variability in scale, pose, expression, illumination and occlusion. WIDER FACE dataset is organized based on 61 event classes. For each event class, it randomly selects 40%/10%/50% data as training, validation and testing sets. We use the training set to train our face detector and perform evaluations on the validation and test sets.

4.2 Implementation Details

Baseline

We build our face detector baseline based on SSD [11].

The existing face detectors that achieve state of the art results on WIDER FACE mostly use complex backbone such as ResNet-50, They usually rely on GPUs with large memory, such as multiple parallel Tesla V100. We use Mobilenet-v1 as the backbone to ensure that it can be trained and applied on ordinary equipment. The backbone is initialized by pre-trained model on the ImageNet classification task.

EEM-320: Add 3 extra feature layers after backbone and use 320^2 as network input to construct a 5-level feature pyramid with size of $80^2 40^2 20^2 10^2 5^2$. EEM-640: Add another extra feature layer to EEM-320 and change the network input to 640^2, a 6-level feature pyramid with size of $160^2 80^2 40^2 20^2 10^2 5^2$ can be constructed. Increasing the resolution of the lowest feature level is helpful to detect face with smaller size.

We use a data augmentation similar to Mosaic described in YOLOv4 [27]. We use hard example mining described in SSD, The proportion of positive and negative is 1:3. $\lambda = 1$ in Eq. [2]. During inference, the prediction boxes with score above 0.005 go through soft NMS to generate final results.

Optimization

Our models are trained on 4 NVIDIA GTX 1080ti GPUs. batch_size is 1, iter_size is 16, mini_batch (=batch_size* iter_size) is 16. We use SGD with 0.9 momentum. base_lr is set to 0.001 and decreased 10X at iteration 70k, the training ended at 120k iterations. our experiments are implemented on caffe-ssd. all the codes and trained models will be available in the future.

Analysis Multi-scale ERF Prior.

Table 3. The results of different prior assignment on WIDER FACE Val set

	Prior	Scale	Easy	Medium	Hard
EEM-320	Gtbox	3.2	0.897	0.831	0.419
	GMM	3.2	0.9	0.841	0.431
	GMM-GM	3.2	0.905	0.851	0.458

The evaluation results of EEM-320 on WIDER FACE Val set are shown in Table 3. Face detection is a kind of target detection with symbiotic relationship, where the face appears is often connected with the body. The feature point outside Gtbox can also help for classification, especially for small face. For multi-scale face detection, the size of the effective receptive field (ERF) is variable, as shown in Fig. 3(c), and the prior cannot be set according to the same standard. Meanwhile, directly establish GMM for each Gtbox may lead to inaccurate modeling parameters due to the insufficient number of feature points, thus affecting the selection of positive samples.

Comparisons to the State-of-the-Arts

Figure 6 shows the evaluation results between EEM-640 and CSP which are anchor-free based for single-scale testing. CSP adopts ResNet-50 as backbone, training on 8 GPUs with 2 images per GPU. EEM-640 adopts Mobilenet-v1 as backbone, training on 4 GPUs with 1 image per GPU. However, the results show that EEM-640 is close to the performance of CSP.

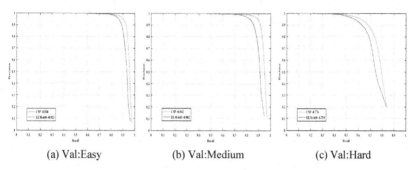

| (a) Val:Easy | (b) Val:Medium | (c) Val:Hard |

Fig. 6. Precision-recall curves on WIDER FACE validation sets

Considering the uncontrollable factors of multi-scale testing, it is difficult to form an effective comparison because of the great influence on the evaluation results. We simply use the single model for single-scale testing. As shown in Table 4, The backbone has a significant impact on performance but it relies on GPUs, the lightweight network we trained on the common equipment also achieved more ideal performance.

Most of the faces in hard validation set are very small, the detection rate is affected by the resolution of the bottom level of the feature pyramid. However, increasing the resolution will sharply increase the consumption of GPUs memory during training. As shown in Table 4, the precision on hard set is not high for single-scale testing. People always use multi-scale testing to increase the resolution at the bottom of the feature level. The detection performance is shown in Fig. 7.

Table 4. Performance comparisons on the WIDER FACE validation set

Method	Backbone	Easy	Medium	Hard
Retinaface [40]	ResNet-50	0.951	0.943	0.844
SRN	ResNet-50	0.93	0.873	0.713
CSP	ResNet-50	0.948	0.942	0.774
DSFD	ResNet-152	0.951	0.942	0.851
SSH	VGG-16	0.921	0.907	0.702
EXTD	Mobilenet-v1	0.851	0.823	0.672
LFFD [22]	other	0.91	0.881	0.78
EEM-640	Mobilenet-v1	0.923	0.902	0.739

Fig. 7. The results of our EEM-640 with detector confidence above 0.1 is shown in this figure. Zoom in for more details.

5 Conclusion

In this work, an efficient example mining method is presented for anchor-free face detector training. We analyze the essence of anchor-based and anchor-free methods in feature point matching. The label assignment algorithm based on probability is relatively rough in setting a prior, which does not conform to the large-scale variation of face detection, so we propose an adaptive multi-scale ERF prior. Meanwhile, Gaussian Mixture Model is changed to offline statistics based to improve the accuracy of modeling parameters. Experiments showed that the proposed methods achieved excellent detection performance without consuming a large number of GPUs for training.

Acknowledgment. This work was supported in part by the National Natural Science Foundation of China under Grant U1933134, in part by the Sichuan Science and Technology Program under Grant 2018JY0602 and Grant 2018GZDZX0024, and in part by the Fund of Sichuan University under Grant 2018SCUH0042.

The Fundamental Research Funds for the Central Universities, Southwest Minzu University (2020PTJS27004).

References

1. Viola, P., Jones, M.: Rapid object detection using a boosted cascade of simple features. In: CVPR (2001)

2. Yang, B., Yan, J., Lei, Z., Li, S.Z.: Aggregate channel features for multi-view face detection. In: International Joint Conference on Biometrics (2014)
3. Yang, B., Yan, J., Lei, Z., Li, S.Z.: Convolutional Channel Features. In: ICCV (2015)
4. Felzenszwalb, P., McAllester, D., Ramanan, D.: A discriminatively trained, multiscale, deformable part model. In: CVPR (2008)
5. Chen, D., Ren, S., Wei, Y., Cao, X., Sun, J.: Joint cascade face detection and alignment. In: Fleet, D., Pajdla, T., Schiele, B., Tuytelaars, T. (eds.) ECCV 2014. LNCS, vol. 8694, pp. 109–122. Springer, Cham (2014). https://doi.org/10.1007/978-3-319-10599-4_8
6. Li, H., Lin, Z., Shen, X., Brandt, J., Hua, G.: A convolutional neural network cascade for face detection. In: CVPR (2015)
7. Yang, S., Luo, P., Loy, C.C., Tang, X.: From facial parts responses to face detection: a deep learning approach. In: ICCV (2015)
8. Girshick, R.: Fast R-CNN. In: ICCV (2015)
9. Ren, S., He, K., Girshick, R., Sun, J.: Faster R-CNN: towards real-time object detection with region proposal networks. In: Advances in Neural Information Processing Systems, pp. 91–99 (2015)
10. Sun, X., Wu, P., Hoi, S.C.: Face detection using deep learning: an improved faster RCNN approach. Neurocomputing **299**, 42–50 (2018)
11. Liu, W., et al.: SSD: single shot MultiBox detector. In: Leibe, B., Matas, J., Sebe, N., Welling, M. (eds.) ECCV 2016. LNCS, vol. 9905, pp. 21–37. Springer, Cham (2016). https://doi.org/10.1007/978-3-319-46448-0_2
12. Redmon, J., Divvala, S., Girshick, R., Farhadi, A.: You only look once: unified, real-time object detection. In: CVPR (2016)
13. Najibi, M., Samangouei, P., Chellappa, R., Davis, L.S.: SSH: single stage headless face detector. In: ECCV (2017)
14. Tang, X., Du, D.K., He, Z., Liu, J.: PyramidBox: A context-assisted single shot face detector. In: Ferrari, V., Hebert, M., Sminchisescu, C., Weiss, Y. (eds.) ECCV 2018. LNCS, vol. 11213, pp. 812–828. Springer, Cham (2018). https://doi.org/10.1007/978-3-030-01240-3_49
15. Zhang, S., Zhu, X., Lei, Z., Shi, H., Wang, X., Li, S.Z.: FaceBoxes: a CPU real-time face detector with high accuracy. In: International Joint Conference on Biometrics (2017)
16. Lin, T.Y., Dollár, P., Girshick, R., He, K., Hariharan, B., Belongie, S.: Feature pyramid networks for object detection. In: CVPR (2017)
17. Guo, C., Fan, B., Zhang, Q., Xiang, S., Pan, C.:AugFPN: improving multi-scale feature learning for object detection. arXiv preprint arXiv:1912.05384 (2019)
18. Sun, K., Xiao, B., Liu, D., Wang, J.: Deep high-resolution representation learning for human pose estimation. In: CVPR (2019)
19. Liu, S., Huang, D., Wang, Y.: Receptive field block net for accurate and fast object detection. In: Ferrari, V., Hebert, M., Sminchisescu, C., Weiss, Y. (eds.) ECCV 2018. LNCS, vol. 11215, pp. 404–419. Springer, Cham (2018). https://doi.org/10.1007/978-3-030-01252-6_24
20. Li, J.: DSFD: dual shot face detector. In: CVPR (2019)
21. Zhang, B.: ASFD: Automatic and scalable face detector. arXiv preprint arXiv:2003.11228 (2020)
22. He, Y., Xu, D., Wu, L., Jian, M., Xiang, S., Pan, C.: Pan:LFFD: a light and fast face detector for edge devices. arXiv preprint arXiv:1904.10633
23. Zhang, S., Zhu, X., Lei, Z., Shi, H., Wang, X., Li, S.Z.: S3FD: single shot scale-invariant face detector. In: ICCV (2017)
24. Zhang, S., Chi, C., Yao, Y., Lei, Z., Li, S.Z.: Bridging the gap between anchor-based and anchor-free detection via adaptive training sample selection. In: CVPR (2020)
25. Kim, K., Lee, H.S.: Probabilistic anchor assignment with IoU prediction for object detection. In: Vedaldi, A., Bischof, H., Brox, T., Frahm, J.-M. (eds.) ECCV 2020. LNCS, vol. 12370, pp. 355–371. Springer, Cham (2020). https://doi.org/10.1007/978-3-030-58595-2_22

26. Tian, Z., Shen, C., Chen, H., He, T.: FCOS: fully convolutional one-stage object detection. In: ICCV (2019)
27. Bochkovskiy, A., Wang, C.Y., Liao, H.Y.M.: YOLOv4: optimal speed and accuracy of object detection. arXiv preprint arXiv:2004.10934 (2020)
28. Chi, C., Zhang, S., Xing, J., Lei, Z., Li, S.Z.: Selective refinement network for high performance face detection. In: AAAI (2019)
29. Zhang, X., Wan, F., Liu, C., Ji, R., Ye, Q.: FreeAnchor: learning to match anchors for visual object detection. In: NeurIPS (2019)
30. Zhu, B., et al.: AutoAssign: differentiable label assignment for dense object detection. arXiv preprint arXiv:2007.03496 (2020)
31. Kong, T., Sun, F., Liu, H., Jiang, Y., Li, L., Shi, J.: FoveaBox: beyond anchor-based object detector. IEEE Trans. Image Process. **29**, 7389–7398 (2020).
32. Zhu, C., He, Y., Savvides, M.: Feature selective anchor-free module for single-shot object detection. In: CVPR (2019)
33. Liu, W., Hasan, I., Liao, S.: Center and scale prediction: a box-free approach for pedestrian and face detection. In: CVPR (2019)
34. Huang, L., Yang, Y., Deng, Y., Yu, Y.: DenseBox: unifying landmark localization with end to end object detection. arXiv preprint arXiv:1509.04874 (2015)
35. Zhou, X., Wang, D., Krähenbühl, P.: Objects as points. arXiv preprint arXiv:1904.07850v2
36. Yang, S., Luo, P., Loy, C.C., Tang, X.: WIDER FACE: a face detection benchmark. In: CVPR (2016)
37. Liu, Y., Tang, X., Wu, X., Han, J., Liu, J., Ding, E.: HAMBox: delving into online high-quality anchors mining for detecting outer faces. In: CVPR (2020)
38. Lin, T.Y., Goyal, P., Girshick, R., He, K., Dollár, P.: Focal loss for dense object detection. In: IEEE Transactions on Pattern Analysis and Machine Intelligence, pp. 318–327 (2020)
39. Jiang, H., Learned-Miller, E.: Face detection with the faster R-CNN. In: IEEE International Conference on Automatic Face & Gesture Recognition (2017)
40. Deng, J., Guo, J., Zhou, Y., Yu, J., Kotsia, I., Zafeiriou, S.: Retinaface: Single-stage dense face localisation in the wild. arXiv preprint arXiv:1905.00641 (2019)
41. Luo, W., Li, Y., Urtasun, R., Zemel, R.: Understanding the effective receptive field in deep convolutional neural networks. In: NeurIPS (2016)

6D Object Pose Estimation with Mutual Attention Fusion

Lu Zou, Zhangjin Huang[(✉)], and Naijie Gu

University of Science and Technology of China, Anhui 230026, China
`zhuang@ustc.edu.cn`

Abstract. 6D object pose estimation from RGB-D images has achieved excellent performance in recent years. Since RGB-D images contain both RGB data and depth data, how to learn a comprehensive representation from these two modalities is an obstacle to achieving accurate pose estimation. Many existing works integrate RGB and depth information through either simple concatenation, or element-wise multiplication at the pixel level or feature level, ignoring the interaction between these two modalities. In order to address this problem, in this paper, we adopt the self-attention mechanism to model the relationship between different modalities, and propose a mutual attention fusion (MAF) block to interact the features in the two modalities, thereby producing a concise and robust RGB-D representation. Comprehensive experiments on the LineMOD and YCB-Video datasets demonstrate that the proposed approach achieves superior performance over previous works, yet remains efficient and easy to use.

Keywords: 6D object pose estimation · Cross-modality data · Self-attention mechanism · Iterative refinement

1 Introduction

6D object pose estimation refers to predicting the 3D rotation and translation from object space to camera space, which is a fundamental problem in real-world applications, such as robotic grasping and manipulation [15]. The problem is challenging due to background clutters and occlusion between objects, etc.

Over the years, much effort has been invested in 6D object pose estimation. Traditional methods such as [4] employed hand-crafted features to establish the correspondences between the object's known 3D model and the 2D pixel locations. However, such empirical features are sensitive to changing illumination conditions and scenes with occlusions. With the explosive growth of deep learning, many studies applied Deep Neural Networks (DNNs) to this task. Some of these methods treat pose estimation as a classification problem, and train DNNs to classify the image features into discretized pose space [18], while other methods detect 2D keypoints as intermediate representations of 6D pose, and compute 6D pose by using the Perspective-n-Point algorithm via 2D-3D correspondences [10,14]. Most of these approaches were built upon the 2D projections,

© Springer Nature Switzerland AG 2021
Y. Peng et al. (Eds.): ICIG 2021, LNCS 12889, pp. 301–313, 2021.
https://doi.org/10.1007/978-3-030-87358-5_24

however, errors that are small in 2D projections can be large in real 3D space, which reduces the reliability of these methods in complicated scenes [10].

As more and more RGB-D datasets are available, some researchers [6,7,17] proposed to simultaneously use RGB and depth images to enhance the accuracy of pose estimation. Considering that the distributions of RGB and depth data are different, how to effectively integrate RGB and depth modalities is an urgent problem to be solved. Nevertheless, existing approaches roughly perform cross-modality fusion at the input, feature or decision levels. For example, directly concatenate RGB and depth values, and feed the 4-channel data into a multi-stage model to produce pose estimations [6,7]. Recently, Wang *et al.* [17] designed a two-branch framework to exploit the features from both RGB and depth images separately, and merge the features of different modalities via a fully connected layer. Despite achieving considerable improvement, this work does not take full advantage of the interactive information existing in different modalities. In this paper, we aim to estimate the 6D object pose through robust and comprehensive feature representations. Specifically, we propose a novel cross-modality feature aggregation method, which models the feature interaction within RGB and depth modalities to enhance the performance of 6D pose estimation.

Our contributions can be summarized as follows:

- We present a novel cross-modality aggregation approach named mutual attention fusion (MAF) with the utilization of self-attention mechanism [16].
- With the assistance of MAF, our 6D object pose estimation algorithm can learn concise and robust feature representations in complicated scenes.
- Experiments demonstrate that the proposed approach achieves better performance than previous works on both the LineMOD [3] and YCB-Video datasets [18] as well as high-efficiency.

2   Related Works

2.1   Pose from RGB Images

6D pose estimation from RGB images has been intensively studied in recent years. Classical methods such as [4] have shown that pose estimation can be achieved by detecting and matching keypoints with known object models. However, these methods rely heavily on hand-crafted features which are not robust to low-textured objects and cluttered environments [12]. Recently, many works apply deep learning techniques to this task due to its robustness to environment variations. Tekin *et al.* [14] proposed to first detect the keypoints of the object, and then solve a Perspective-n-Point problem for pose estimation. The key to this approach is to predict the global characteristics of the object. As a result, it cannot effectively deal with objects with occlusions.

To address the above problems, Zakharov *et al.* [20] estimated a dense 2D-3D correspondence map between the input image and object models. Peng *et al.* [10] presented to predict a unit vector at each pixel pointing towards keypoints. More recently, Song *et al.* [13] improved [10] by utilizing keypoints, edge vectors, and symmetry correspondences to express different geometric information in the input image. The aforementioned methods help to address the issue of occlusion, however, due to the lack of depth information, they are still inferior to RGB-D based methods in terms of detection accuracy.

2.2 Pose from RGB-D Image

With the emergence of cheap 3D sensors, the amount of available 3D data (e.g., RGB-D images) has tremendously increased. The depth image provides geometric information of the 3D objects. Therefore, it can further improve the performance of 6D pose estimation with the assistance of depth information. Conventional RGB-D based methods mainly utilized depth information in three ways. First of all, RGB and depth modalities are acquired at separate stages [18], that is, a coarse 6D pose is first predicted from a RGB image, followed by the Iterative Closest Point (ICP) algorithm [1] using a depth image for refinement. Secondly, RGB and depth modalities are merged together at the early stage in the network [9], where the depth map is treated as another channel and concatenated with RGB channels. Recently, Wang *et al.* [17] proposed DenseFusion, which converts the depth image into 3D point clouds, and directly processes the 3D point clouds through PointNet architecture [11]. DenseFusion has achieved state-of-the-art performance while reaching almost real-time inference speed. However, it incorporates the characteristics of the two modalities in a straightforward manner, which is not sufficient to capture their inherent correlations.

In this work, we propose to exploit the complementary characteristics of RGB and depth modalities through self-attention mechanism [16]. In the experiment, we will show that the proposed method enables efficient exploitation of cross-modality feature fusion, and achieves great performance as well as high-efficiency.

3 Method

3.1 Overview

Given a set of known objects, 6D object pose estimation aims at predicting the rigid transformation from the object coordinate system to the camera coordinate system. Without loss of generality, we denote it as a rigid transformation matrix p, where $p \in SE(3)$. Specifically, p is composed of a 3D rotation matrix $R \in SO(3)$ and a 3D translation vector $t \in \mathbb{R}^3$, and $p = [R|t]$.

As shown in Fig. 1, our pose estimation network consists of four stages. First, the network takes the aligned RGB and depth images as input, which are encoded into color embeddings F^{rgb}, and geometric embeddings F^{geo}, respectively. Then, the feature embeddings in the two modalities interact through the proposed MAF block and are merged together to generate a cross-modality RGB-D representation F^{maf}. Next, the pose predictor processes the conjoint feature embeddings to obtain the per-point prediction $p_i = [R_i|t_i]$ with a confidence score c_i. Finally, the pose hypothesis with the maximum confidence score is further refined through the pose refiner to get the final pose prediction $\hat{p} = [\hat{R}|\hat{t}]$. The details about each stage are discussed as follows.

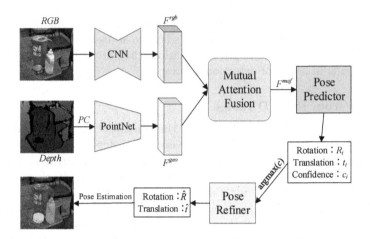

Fig. 1. The overall framework of our pose estimation network.

3.2 Pixel(Point)-Wise Feature Extraction

Given an aligned RGB and depth image pair, we first perform semantic segmentation on the RGB image to extract the mask of each object presented in the scene. Then, the RGB and depth images are cropped by the bounding box calculated by the segmentation mask of the RGB image. Next, the cropped depth image is converted into point clouds (PC) $w.r.t.$ the camera intrinsic parameters. After that, two feature extraction branches process the cropped RGB image and point clouds respectively to obtain modality-independent feature embeddings.

For semantic segmentation, we utilize the segmentation network introduced in PoseCNN [18] to obtain pixel-wise semantic labels. For the RGB branch, the segmented regions are passed through a CNN-based encoder-decoder architecture to generate pixel-wise color embeddings. For the point cloud branch, the 3D points are passed to a PointNet-like [11] feature encoder to obtain point-wise geometric embeddings (without STN [5], avg-pooling instead of max-pooling).

3.3 Mutual Attention Fusion

Since RGB and depth images exist in different spaces, it is essential to learn a joint representation of different modalities. We propose a cross-modality aggregation block (MAF) based on the self-attention mechanism [16] to interact the features from both modalities. As shown in Fig. 2, MAF contains several linear projection layers, a mutual attention mechanism, and an addition operation.

Specifically, given modality-independent feature embeddings F^{rgb}, and F^{geo}, these two modalities feature embeddings are first passed through two separate linear projection layers to get a series vectors query $Q_r(Q_g)$, key $K_r(K_g)$, and value $V_r(V_g)$ according to the standard self-attention mechanism [16], where $V_r, K_r, Q_r = \mathbf{MLP}(F^{rgb})$, $V_g, K_g, Q_g = \mathbf{MLP}(F^{geo})$. Then, the mutual attention mechanism is applied to retrieve the information from context vectors (key

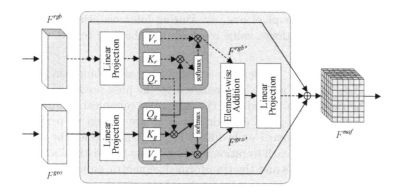

Fig. 2. The architecture of the proposed mutual attention fusion block.

K_g and value V_g) of the depth stream related to the query vector Q_r of the RGB stream and vice versa. Specifically, it calculates attention weights of the RGB feature in the depth modality and the attention weights of the depth feature in the RGB modality, and respectively generates the corresponding cross-modality features $F^{rgb'}$ and $F^{geo'}$. After the mutual attention mechanism, features of each modality are merged together via a feature addition operation and a linear projection layer, and finally they are concatenated with cross-modality features F^{rgb} and F^{geo} to get the final cross-modality representation F^{maf}.

$$F^{rgb'} = \mathbf{MutualAtt}(\mathbf{Softmax}(\frac{Q_g K_r^T}{\sqrt{d_r}})V_r), \tag{1}$$

$$F^{geo'} = \mathbf{MutualAtt}(\mathbf{Softmax}(\frac{Q_r K_g^T}{\sqrt{d_g}})V_g), \tag{2}$$

$$F^{maf} = \mathbf{Concat}(\mathbf{MLP}(F^{rgb'} + F^{geo'}), F^{geo}, F^{rgb}), \tag{3}$$

where d is the dimension of each query, $1/\sqrt{d}$ implements the scaled-dot product term achieve the numerical stability of the attention operations. The mutual attention mechanism establishes the interaction between different modalities, and the features obtained through this process can benefit from the modality discrepancy more than fusing the features extracted from the modalities directly.

We argue that there is one insight of applying the mutual attention mechanism in our model, that is, the RGB and depth images are aligned, therefore, the color pixels and point clouds are one-to-one correspondence, which makes their interaction with each other through the mutual attention mechanism effective and straightforward.

3.4   Pose Estimation and Refinement

Pose Estimation. We feed the fused cross-modality feature representation into an MLP-like pose predictor to produce the object's 6D pose with a corresponding confidence value in a per-pixel manner. During inference, the pose hypothesis with the maximum confidence value is selected as the final result.

Iterative Refinement. We develop a pose refiner as explained in [17] for pose refinement. The initial pose $[R_0|t_0]$ predicted by the pose predictor is utilized to transform the input point cloud into the estimated canonical coordinate frame, and the original RGB feature embeddings F^{rgb} are reused to perform point-wise fusion with the geometric embeddings F_{trans}^{geo} computed for the transformed point cloud PC_{trans}. At each iteration, we first apply the MAF block to fuse the original RGB embeddings and the transformed geometric embeddings. Then, an MLP-like pose residual estimator is employed to output a residual pose $w.r.t.$ the previous pose prediction. Next, the residual pose is applied to the current point cloud to get a new transformed point cloud, which will be fed into the next iteration. After K iterations, the final pose is derived as:

$$\hat{p} = \prod_{k=0}^{K} [R_k|t_k]. \tag{4}$$

The pseudocode of the pose refiner is shown in Algorithm 1.

Algorithm 1: The Algorithm of Pose Refiner

    Input: K, PC_{trans}, F^{rgb}, F_{trans}^{geo}, $[R_0|t_0]$
    Output: $\hat{p}$
1 $k \leftarrow 0$;
2   **while** $k <= K$ **do**
3   **if** $k == 0$ **then**
4 $F_k^{geo} \leftarrow F_{trans}^{geo}$;
5 $PC_k \leftarrow PC_{trans}$;
6 $\hat{p} \leftarrow [R_0|t_0]$;

7   **else**
8 $F_k^{maf} \leftarrow$ **MutualAttentionFusion**(F^{rgb}, F_{k-1}^{geo});
9 $[R_k|t_k] \leftarrow$ **PoseResEstimator**(F_k^{maf});
10 $PC_k \leftarrow PC_{k-1} \cdot [R_k|t_k]$;
11 $F_k^{geo} \leftarrow$ **PointNet**(PC_k);
12 $\hat{p} \leftarrow \hat{p} \cdot [R_k|t_k]$;

13 $k \leftarrow k + 1$;

14 **return** $\hat{p}$

3.5 Training Objective

We use the ADD (Eq. (5)) and ADD-S (Eq. (6)) loss functions to train the whole network. For asymmetric objects, the ADD loss is defined as the distance between the points sampled from the object model in the ground-truth pose and the corresponding points on the same model transformed by the predicted pose. For symmetric objects, the ADD-S loss is an ambiguity-invariant pose error metric, which aims at minimizing the distance between each point on the estimated model orientation and the nearest point on the ground-truth model.

$$\mathcal{L}_i^p = \frac{1}{M} \sum_j \| (Rx_j + t) - (\hat{R}_i x_j + \hat{t}_i) \|, \tag{5}$$

$$\mathcal{L}_i^p = \frac{1}{M} \sum_j \min_{0<m<M} \| (Rx_j + t) - (\hat{R}_i x_m + \hat{t}_i) \|, \tag{6}$$

where x_j represents the j-th point of the M randomly sampled 3D points from the object's 3D CAD model, $p = [R|t]$ is the ground-truth pose, and $\hat{p} = [\hat{R}|\hat{t}]$ is the predicted pose through the network. We follow [17] to add a confidence variable c_i to each pixel to help select the hypothesis that is most likely to be the correct pose. As a result, the total loss function is derived as

$$\mathcal{L} = \frac{1}{N} \sum_i (\mathcal{L}_i^p c_i - w \ln(c_i)), \tag{7}$$

where N is the number of dense-pixel features sampled from the segmented object regions, and w is a weighting hyperparameter that balances $\mathcal{L}_i^p$ and c_i.

4   Experiments

4.1   Datasets and Evaluation Metrics

We conduct experiments on two widely used 6D pose benchmarks: the LineMOD [3] and YCB-Video [18] datasets to evaluate our approach. The LineMOD dataset contains 15 low-textured objects in over 18,000 real images with well-annotated ground truth 6D poses, we only use 13 objects with the same training and testing splits as previous works. The YCB-Video dataset consists of 21 objects with different shapes and textures. It has 92 RGB-D videos annotated with segmentation masks and 6D poses, where 80 videos are used for training and 12 for testing. The 80,000 synthetic images are also included during training.

For evaluation metrics, we evaluate the presented method using two standard metrics: the average distance of model points (ADD) for non-symmetric objects and the average closest point distance (ADD-S) for symmetric objects. The calculation of ADD and ADD-S metrics can refer to Sect. 3.5.

4.2   Implementation Details

We implement the proposed approach in PyTorch framework and train it using a desktop NVIDIA GeForce RTX 2080Ti GPU.

The RGB image encoding network consists of ResNet-18 [2] as the encoder and 4 up-sampling layers as the decoder to restore the feature resolution. In order

Table 1. Quantitative evaluation of 6D Pose on ADD-S metric on the LineMOD dataset. Objects with bold name are symmetric.

	PoseCNN [18]	PVNet [10]	CDPM [8]	Point Fusion [19]	Dense Fusion [17]	Hybrid Pose [13]	Ours (MAF)
ape	77.0	43.6	64.4	70.4	92.3	77.6	**93.2**
ben.	97.5	99.9	97.8	80.7	93.2	**99.6**	94.3
cam.	93.5	86.9	91.7	60.8	94.4	95.9	**96.5**
can	**96.5**	95.5	95.9	61.1	93.1	93.6	95.2
cat	82.1	79.3	83.8	79.1	**96.5**	93.5	**96.5**
driller	95.0	96.4	96.2	47.3	87.0	**97.2**	87.4
duck	77.7	52.6	66.8	63.0	92.3	87.0	**95.0**
egg.	97.1	99.2	99.7	**99.9**	99.8	99.6	**99.9**
glue	99.4	95.7	99.6	99.3	**100.0**	98.7	99.7
hole	52.8	82.0	85.8	71.8	92.1	92.5	**94.0**
iron	98.3	**98.9**	97.9	83.2	97.0	98.1	98.3
lamp	97.5	**99.3**	97.9	62.3	95.3	96.9	96.0
phone	87.7	92.4	90.8	78.8	92.8	**98.3**	96.5
MEAN	88.6	86.3	89.9	73.7	94.3	94.5	**95.6**

Fig. 3. Visualization results of estimating the poses for the LineMOD dataset of Dense-Fusion [17] and our network.

to capture the geometric features, a variant of PointNet [11] is implemented as 1D-convolutions with ReLUs, with kernel size of 1 and stride of 1. The pose residual estimator consists of 4 fully connected layers that directly output the pose residual from the global dense feature obtained by our MAF block. We follow DenseFusion [17] to use $K=2$ iterations at the refinement process, and set the threshold for starting the refinement process to 0.013. We train the network with Adam with an initial learning rate of 0.0001 and a batch size of 8. After the loss of the pose predictor network drops below 0.016, then a decay of 0.3 is applied to further train the pose refiner.

4.3 Evaluation on LineMOD Dataset

The quantitative results of our method on the LineMOD dataset are reported in Table 1. Compared with [8,10,13,17–19], Ours (MAF) achieves an average accuracy of 95.6%, which is 1.3% improvement over the baseline approach: DenseFusion [17], 1.1% improvement over the latest work [13], and significantly outperforms the other approaches. Especially for those low-texture objects, the performance has been greatly improved compared to the baseline, such as *phone*(3.7%), *duck*(2.7%), *camera*(2.1%), and *can*(2.1%). Figure 3 visualizes some sample estimations (*ape, can,* and *driller*) predicted by DenseFusion [17] and our approach (MAF). As shown in the figure, our pose estimation results are better than DenseFusion [17].

4.4 Evaluation on YCB-Video Dataset

Table 2 shows our quantitative results in terms of ADD(-S) AUC for all the 21 objects on the YCB-Video dataset. To ensure a fair comparison, we utilize the same segmentation masks as PoseCNN [18]. As shown in the table, our network is superior to the state-of-the-art methods [17–19] on most of the objects. In addition, it outperforms PointFusion [19] by 9.5%, PoseCNN+ICP [18] by 0.4% and DenseFusion [17] by 0.3% in terms of mean accuracy. Note that our model suffers from performance degradation on objects *051_large_clamp* and *052_extra_large_clamp* because they are highly similar in appearance and usually appear in the same scene and overlap with each other. Therefore, the segmentation network is confused by these two objects, which leads to segmentation errors and ultimately affects the overall pose estimation performance.

We also report the qualitative results of our approach and give a comparision with PoseCNN+ICP [18] and DenseFusion [17]. The results are shown in Fig. 4. As the figure shows, PoseCNN+ICP [18] and DenseFusion [17] fail to estimate the correct poses of the objects such as *large_clamp, banana,* and *power_drill* due to occlusion, while our network can predict the correct poses.

4.5 Ablation Study

In order to verify the effectiveness of the proposed MAF block, we conduct ablation studies on the YCB-Video dataset. Table 3 summarizes the results.

As the table shows, our pose estimation network without iterative refinement achieves an improvement of 1.0% compared to that in DenseFusion [17]. In addition, with the integration of the presented pose refiner, our network gains an additional 1.2% performance improvement, which is 0.3% better than DenseFusion [17]. In summary, the proposed cross-modality aggregation block helps to improve the performance of pose estimation.

4.6   Efficiency Analysis

On the YCB-Video dataset, our method runs at about 38 FPS with a single Nvidia GTX 2080Ti GPU, compared to DenseFusion [17] which runs at about 43 FPS. In summary, our approach is almost the same as DenseFusion in time efficiency and it is approximately 100 times faster than PoseCNN+ICP [18].

Table 2. Quantitative evaluation of 6D Pose on ADD-S metric on the YCB-Video dataset. Objects with bold name are symmetric.

	PointFusion [19]	PoseCNN [18]	DenseFusion [17]	Ours (MAF)
002_master_chef_can	90.9	95.8	**96.4**	95.8
003_cracker_box	80.5	92.7	95.5	**96.1**
004_sugar_box	90.4	**98.2**	97.5	97.9
005_tomato_soup can	91.9	94.5	**94.6**	94.5
006_mustard_bottle	88.5	**98.6**	97.2	97.7
007_tuna_fish_can	93.8	97.1	96.6	97.0
008_pudding_box	87.5	**97.9**	96.5	97.1
009_gelatin_box	95.0	**98.8**	98.1	98.6
010_potted_meat_can	86.4	**92.7**	91.3	91.4
011_banana	84.7	**97.1**	96.6	96.4
019_pitcher_base	85.5	97.8	97.1	97.5
021_bleach_cleanser	81.0	**96.9**	95.8	96.4
024_bowl	75.7	81.0	88.2	89.2
025_mug	94.2	95.0	97.1	96.6
035_power_drill	71.5	**98.2**	96.0	95.8
036_wood_block	68.1	87.6	89.7	92.7
037_scissors	76.7	91.7	**95.2**	93.0
040_large_marker	87.9	97.2	**97.5**	97.8
051_large_clamp	65.9	**75.2**	72.9	73.5
052_extra_large_clamp	60.4	64.4	69.8	69.9
061_foam_brick	91.8	**97.2**	92.5	96.2
ALL	83.9	93.0	93.1	**93.4**

Table 3. Ablation analysis of different model components on the YCB-Video dataset.

	DenseFusion [17]	Ours	DenseFusion [17]	Ours (MAF)
Iterative refinement	✗	✗	✓	✓
ALL	91.2	**92.2**	93.1	**93.4**

Fig. 4. Visualization results of estimating the poses for the YCB-Video dataset of PoseCNN + ICP [18], DenseFusion [17] and our network.

5   Conclusion and Future Work

In this paper, we propose a novel cross-modality aggregation method for 6D object pose estimation from RGB-D images. A mutual attention fusion (MAF) block is introduced to model the interaction of RGB and depth modalities. Therefore, features from different modalities can exchange information via the mutual attention mechanism, and be fused into a conjoint cross-modality representation. The proposed method is simple yet effective, and demonstrates superior performance over previous works on both the LineMOD and YCB-Video datasets. In future work, we will focus on one-stage object pose estimation and improving the semantic segmentation accuracy when detecting objects.

Acknowledgement. This work was supported in part by the National Key R&D Program of China (No. 2018YFC1504104), the National Natural Science Foundation of China (Nos. 71991464/71991460, and 61877056), and the Fundamental Research Funds for the Central Universities of China (No. WK5290000001).

References

1. Besl, P.J., McKay, N.D.: Method for registration of 3-D shapes. In: Sensor Fusion IV: Control Paradigms and Data Structures, vol. 1611, pp. 586–606. International Society for Optics and Photonics (1992)
2. He, K., Zhang, X., Ren, S., Sun, J.: Deep residual learning for image recognition. In: Proceedings of the IEEE Conference on Computer Vision and Pattern Recognition, pp. 770–778 (2016)

3. Hinterstoisser, S., et al.: Multimodal templates for real-time detection of texture-less objects in heavily cluttered scenes. In: 2011 International Conference on Computer Vision, pp. 858–865. IEEE (2011)

4. Hinterstoisser, S., et al.: Model based training, detection and pose estimation of texture-less 3D objects in heavily cluttered scenes. In: Lee, K.M., Matsushita, Y., Rehg, J.M., Hu, Z. (eds.) ACCV 2012. LNCS, vol. 7724, pp. 548–562. Springer, Heidelberg (2013). https://doi.org/10.1007/978-3-642-37331-2_42

5. Jaderberg, M., Simonyan, K., Zisserman, A., Kavukcuoglu, K.: Spatial transformer networks. arXiv preprint arXiv:1506.02025 (2015)

6. Kehl, W., Milletari, F., Tombari, F., Ilic, S., Navab, N.: Deep learning of local RGB-D patches for 3D object detection and 6D pose estimation. In: Leibe, B., Matas, J., Sebe, N., Welling, M. (eds.) ECCV 2016. LNCS, vol. 9907, pp. 205–220. Springer, Cham (2016). https://doi.org/10.1007/978-3-319-46487-9_13

7. Li, C., Bai, J., Hager, G.D.: A unified framework for multi-view multi-class object pose estimation. In: Proceedings of the European Conference on Computer Vision (ECCV), pp. 254–269 (2018)

8. Li, Z., Wang, G., Ji, X.: CDPN: coordinates-based disentangled pose network for real-time RGB-based 6-DoF object pose estimation. In: Proceedings of the IEEE International Conference on Computer Vision, pp. 7678–7687 (2019)

9. Michel, F., et al.: Global hypothesis generation for 6D object pose estimation. In: Proceedings of the IEEE Conference on Computer Vision and Pattern Recognition, pp. 462–471 (2017)

10. Peng, S., Liu, Y., Huang, Q., Zhou, X., Bao, H.: PVNet: pixel-wise voting network for 6DoF pose estimation. In: Proceedings of the IEEE Conference on Computer Vision and Pattern Recognition, pp. 4561–4570 (2019)

11. Qi, C.R., Su, H., Mo, K., Guibas, L.J.: Pointnet: deep learning on point sets for 3D classification and segmentation. In: Proceedings of the IEEE Conference on Computer Vision and Pattern Recognition, pp. 652–660 (2017)

12. Shin, Y., Balasingham, I.: Comparison of hand-craft feature based SVM and CNN based deep learning framework for automatic polyp classification. In: 2017 39th Annual International Conference of the IEEE Engineering in Medicine and Biology Society (EMBC), pp. 3277–3280. IEEE (2017)

13. Song, C., Song, J., Huang, Q.: Hybridpose: 6D object pose estimation under hybrid representations. In: Proceedings of the IEEE/CVF Conference on Computer Vision and Pattern Recognition, pp. 431–440 (2020)

14. Tekin, B., Sinha, S.N., Fua, P.: Real-time seamless single shot 6D object pose prediction. In: Proceedings of the IEEE Conference on Computer Vision and Pattern Recognition, pp. 292–301 (2018)

15. Tremblay, J., To, T., Sundaralingam, B., Xiang, Y., Fox, D., Birchfield, S.: Deep object pose estimation for semantic robotic grasping of household objects. arXiv preprint arXiv:1809.10790 (2018)

16. Vaswani, A., et al.: Attention is all you need. In: Advances in Neural Information Processing Systems, pp. 5998–6008 (2017)

17. Wang, C., et al.: Densefusion: 6D object pose estimation by iterative dense fusion. In: Proceedings of the IEEE Conference on Computer Vision and Pattern Recognition, pp. 3343–3352 (2019)

18. Xiang, Y., Schmidt, T., Narayanan, V., Fox, D.: PoseCNN: a convolutional neural network for 6d object pose estimation in cluttered scenes. arXiv preprint arXiv:1711.00199 (2017)

19. Xu, D., Anguelov, D., Jain, A.: Pointfusion: deep sensor fusion for 3D bounding box estimation. In: Proceedings of the IEEE Conference on Computer Vision and Pattern Recognition, pp. 244–253 (2018)
20. Zakharov, S., Shugurov, I., Ilic, S.: DPOD: dense 6D pose object detector in RGB images. arXiv preprint arXiv:1902.11020 (2019)

Attention-Guided Siamese Network for Clothes-Changing Person Re-identification

Zhanxiang Feng[1], Sien Huang[1], and Jianhuang Lai[1,2,3,4(✉)]

[1] School of Computer Science and Engineering, Sun Yat-sen University,
Guangzhou, China
{fengzhx7,stsljh}@mail.sysu.edu.cn, huangsen3@mail2.sysu.edu.cn
[2] Guangzhou Xinhua University, Guangzhou, China
[3] Guangdong Province Key Laboratory of Information Security Technology,
Guangzhou, China
[4] Key Laboratory of Machine Intelligence and Advanced Computing,
Ministry of Education, Guangzhou, China

Abstract. Person re-identification (re-id) has achieved significant progresses in recent years. However, the existing methods generally assume that the clothes of pedestrians remain unchanged throughout the surveillance periods, which is contradict to realistic environment where pedestrians may change their clothes. Current re-id techniques may encounter a dramatic performance degradation when the pedestrians change the clothes. In this paper, we propose a novel attention-guided siamese network (AGS-Net) to solve the cross-clothes re-id challenge. The AGS-Net integrates the visual and contour information together by developing a dual-branch structure, among which one extracts powerful features from raw inputs while the other learns robust features from the sketch image. Moreover, we exploit the attention modules to emphasize reliable identity-related features considering changing clothes and avoid generating features sensitive to clothes. Specifically, we propose a clothes-change invariant constraint to learn clothes-invariant features. Experimental results verify the effectiveness of our approach.

Keywords: Person re-identification · Cross-clothes person re-id · Attention mechanism

1 Introduction

Person re-identification (re-id) aims to associate pedestrians across changing camera views. With the necessity in intelligent video surveillance, re-id has been a hot research topic and achieved great progresses in recent years. Researchers have proposed many approaches to improve the performance of re-id techniques, including metric learning [7,15], hand-crafted features [20,32], and deep learning structures [5,10,25]. With the development of deep networks and the emergence of large-scale datasets [18,33,35], re-id techniques have achieved impressive

This project was supported by Natural Science Foundation of China (61902444, 62076258).

Y. Peng et al. (Eds.): ICIG 2021, LNCS 12889, pp. 314–325, 2021.
https://doi.org/10.1007/978-3-030-87358-5_25

breakthroughs. However, the existing studies are based on the assumption that the pedestrians wear same clothes across different cameras. Nevertheless, this assumption may not work in realistic applications. A person may change the wearing while moving across disjoint surveillance devices for certain reasons. E.g., a person may get dressed/undressed because of the sudden change of the weather. Particularly, a person will be more likely to change the clothing with time elapsing. Besides, some people such as the criminals may change the clothes intentionally to fool the recognition systems and to escape from the arrestment. The above challenge is called the cross-clothes re-id problem.

Because of the cross-clothes visual discrepancy, the cross-clothes re-id issue is challenging for conventional re-id models which focus on the appearance features, and leads to a serious degradation in recognition performance. Recently, some researchers have made pioneering efforts to tackle with the cross-clothes re-id task [19,27,29,30]. Although these studies have improved the robustness of deep features against changing clothes, the recognition performance for cross-clothes re-id is still far from satisfactory.

In this paper, we propose a novel Attention-Guided Siamese Network (AGS-Net) to tackle with the cross-clothes problem by mitigating while keeping identity-related characteristics. The AGS-Net contains a dual-stream architecture, namely the visual stream and the sketch stream, to exploit both the visual features and the contour features simultaneously. The raw input images contain rich information for extracting discriminative features for different identities, whereas the sketch images contain contour information that is invariant to the changing clothes. Therefore, combining the visual features and the sketch features is valuable for learning features that are both distinguishing and robust in terms of cross-clothes re-id. Furthermore, we incorporate an attention module into the AGS-Net to pay more attention to areas that contain identity-related features invariant to clothes changes, and ignore features that are affected by the clothing. Specifically, we adopt the Position Attention Module (PAM) and Channel Attention Module (CAM) to learn extensive attention information. Finally, we design a novel cloth-invariant constraint to shrink the discrepancy between pedestrians wearing different clothes. Experimental results prove that the proposed approach is effective in improving the performance of cross-clothes re-id models, and outperforms the state-of-the-art methods. We also conduct feature visualization to verify that the AGS-Net focuses on discriminant features that are invariant to clothes changes.

2 Related Work

2.1 Person Re-identification

Re-id has attracted large amount of research interests in the last decade, and researchers have made enduring efforts to tackle with the challenges of re-id task. Generally, the current literature can be divided into two categories. One is the early studies which mainly focus on extracting appearance features using hand-crafted features [9,21] or drawing discriminative representations through metric

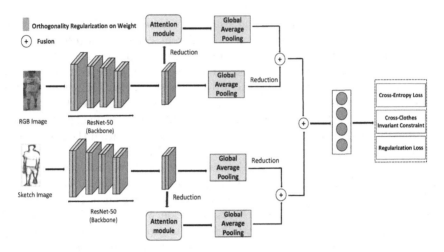

Fig. 1. Overview of our framework. The AGS-Net adopts a dual-stream structure to extract visual features and the sketch features respectively. The visual features and sketch features are fed into an attention module and fused together to obtain the final representation.

learning tricks. Because of the dramatic visual variations across pedestrians from changing viewpoints, the performance of the hand-crafted features is far from satisfactory. Another is deep learning based methods [3,6,16]. In recent years, deep learning based re-id methods have achieved significant breakthroughs and dramatically improved the performance of re-id models. Particularly, deep networks have achieved impressive progresses when dealing with appearance variations such as illuminations [1] changing and occlusions [34] changing. Nevertheless, the current researches focus on utilizing visual cues, especially the color information. Therefore, when the pedestrians change their clothes, deep networks may extract misleading features, resulting in serious performance degradation. In our work, we focus on designing a novel framework to break the above limitations and improve the discrimination ability of deep networks against the cross-clothes re-id task.

2.2   Cross-Clothes Person Re-identification

Cross-clothes person re-id aims to recognize a specific human being with different outfits across disjoint cameras. Recently, some preliminary attempts are made to solve the challenges brought by changing clothes. Wan et al. [27] address the cross-clothes challenges by emphasizing human face and combining the global information with partial features. However, only using facial characteristics is too weak because human face may be blurred in many situations, such as low resolution or high exposure. Yu et al. [30] propose to combine biometric features and clothes features. Li et al. [19] introduce the generative adversarial network (GAN) to extract person body shape feature. Qian et al. [22] remove the dependency on clothing information and use shape-embedding module to get human structural features. Yang et al. [29] introduce a learning-based spatial polar transformation (SPT) layer to learn body feature from human contour sketch in a polar coordinate space. However, most of the above methods only consider the appearance variations caused by changing clothes. E.g., Yang et al. [29] only use the sketch images to extract features. Although the contour features are invariant to cross-clothes changes, the color information is abandoned by the above works, which may lead to poor performance for traditional re-id. Furthermore, the raw images contain rich discriminant information which is crucial for cross-clothes re-id. Based on the above discussions, we propose to extract both discriminant identity-related features and cross-clothes invariant features to solve the cross-clothes challenges. Moreover, we intend to exploit attention mechanism to avoid learning disturbing features from the raw inputs.

3 Methodology

3.1 Network Structure

The overall architecture of the AGS-Net is shown in Figure 1. We propose a siamese network to tackle with the cross-clothes challenge. The siamese network is formed by a dual-stream structure, namely the visual stream and the contour stream. Notably, for both the visual stream and the contour stream, we adopt ResNet-50 [12] as the baseline network to extract backbone features. The major challenge of the cross-cloth re-id problem lies in the appearance variations of the pedestrians caused by changing clothes. When changing clothes, the visual characteristics of a pedestrian becomes quite different. Such a problem makes cross-clothes re-id more difficult for current re-id models which pay too much attention to visual cues, such as color and texture. Inspired by Yang et al. [29], we intend to take the sketch image as one of the input image, to extract robust body shape feature embedding. Because contour features show its invariance confronted by color changing situations. Although the contour features are robust to the variations of clothes or color, many identity-related cues are lacked in the sketch image. E.g., the color of the body parts. Such information is greatly important for extracting discriminative features. Furthermore, the color information is crucial for general re-id task, regardless of clothes changing. Only using sketch images as inputs is adverse to learning distinguishing features for traditional re-id, and is undesirable because a generalized model should work for both general re-id and cross-clothes re-id. Taking the above analysis into consideration, we propose to adopt the RGB images as the inputs of another stream, namely the visual stream, to learn identity-related features, including the features of body parts, faces, hairs and so on. As the contour features and the visual features are complementary to each other, we can obtain a more robust feature representation by integrating these two kinds of features into a united dual-stream network architecture.

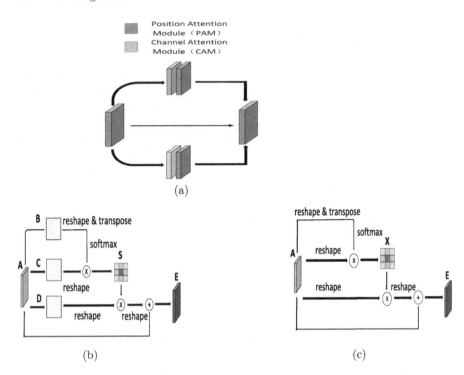

Fig. 2. (a) The detail of the Attention Module. Features extracted from the baseline network are fed into CAM module and PAM module respectively. The input features and the features derived from the CAM and PAM modules are concatenated to obtain the output features. (b) The structure of Position Attention Module (PAM). (c) The structure of Channel Attention Module (CAM).

3.2   Attention Module

As mentioned above, we extract discriminative identity-related features using RGB inputs. However, the RGB images contain disturbing information when dealing with the cross-clothes re-id problem. E.g., the color of the clothes is harmful for learning robust cross-clothes features. Meanwhile, the RGB images also contain important identity-related information that is robust to clothes changes, e.g., the color of the body parts, the hairs, and the texture of pedestrians. To extract robust and discriminant features in cross-clothes person re-id and avoid the negative influences of the clothes-related features, we take advantage of the attention mechanism to force the model to concentrate on person correlative areas and to ignore disturbing features, such as the color of the clothes or the background. As shown in Fig. 2, the proposed attention mechanism contains three branches. Features extracted from the backbone model are fed into CAM module and PAM module [11] respectively. The input features and the features derived from the CAM and PAM modules are concatenated at last, to obtain the output features.

Position Attention Module (PAM). As a consensus, features extracted by deep CNN contain semantic information. In cross-clothes re-id, a person is largely covered by his or her clothes, which means that the most features of the pedestrians are related to the clothes in terms of the spatial domain. The pixels concerning clothes share similar semantic contexts, such as color, texture, shape and etc. To eliminate the influence of clothes, we adopt the Position Attention Module (PAM) to grab and converge pixels with similar semantic information so that deep networks can focus on extracting features from areas irrelevant to clothes.

First, we send feature maps into convolution layers with batch normalization and ReLU activation to get feature maps B, C, D. Then we get the spatial position map by combing the feature map B and C. Finally, we fuse the input features with the attention-weighted features to obtain the attention outputs. Denote the output features maps of the backbone network $A \in R^{C \times H \times W}$. The spatial position map $S \in R^{(H \times W) \times (H \times W)}$ is computed as follows:

$$s_{ij} = \frac{\exp(B_i \cdot C_j)}{\sum_{i=1}^{H \times W} \exp(B_i \cdot C_j)} \tag{1}$$

where s_{ij} refers to the correlation or impact between position i and j, H and W is the height and width of the input image. The attention map S can be regarded as the pixel affinity matrix. The calculation of output E is as follows:

$$E_i = \beta \sum_{i=1}^{H \times W} (s_{ij} D_j) + A_i \tag{2}$$

where A_i is the ith position of the original input features A, and β is a weighted hyperparameter learning to adjust the impact of PAM.

Channel Attention Module (CAM). Similar to PAM, CAM is used to gather those semantically related features in different channels. The structure of the CAM is similar to the PAM. The CAM module measures the impact of features between channels. Denote the input as $A \in R^{C \times H \times W}$, where C is the sum of channels and $H \times W$ is the size of channel feature map X. The formula of the CAM is also similar to that of Eq. 1 and Eq. 2, which can be written as follows:

$$x_{ij} = \frac{\exp(A_i \cdot A_j)}{\sum_{i=1}^{C \times C} \exp(A_i \cdot A_j)} \tag{3}$$

$$E_j = \alpha \sum_{i=1}^{H \times W} (x_{ji} A_i) + A_j \tag{4}$$

3.3   Loss Function

The visual variations between different clothes is the major challenge for the cross-clothes person re-id. To address such a problem, we design a novel constraint called Cross-Clothes Invariant Constraint (CCIC) to narrow the gap

Table 1. Comparing with state-of-art methods on PRCC.

Methods	Camera A and C (Cross Clothes)			Camera A and B (Same Clothes)		
	Rank 1	Rank 10	Rank 20	Rank 1	Rank 10	Rank 20
LBP [21] + KISSME [15]	18.71	58.09	71.40	39.03	76.18	86.91
HOG [9] + KISSME [15]	17.52	49.52	63.55	36.02	68.83	80.49
LOMO [20] + KISSME [15]	18.55	49.81	67.27	47.40	81.42	90.38
LBP [21] + XQDA [20]	18.25	52.75	61.98	40.66	77.74	87.44
HOG [9] + XQDA [20]	22.11	57.33	69.93	42.32	75.63	85.38
LOMO [20] + XQDA [20]	14.53	43.63	60.34	29.41	67.24	80.52
Shape Context [2]	11.48	38.66	53.21	23.87	68.41	76.32
LNSCT [28]	15.33	53.87	67.12	35.54	69.56	82.37
Alexnet (RGB) [14]	16.33	48.01	65.87	63.28	91.70	94.73
VGG16 (RGB) [23]	18.21	46.13	60.76	71.39	95.89	98.68
HA-CNN (RGB) [17]	21.81	59.47	67.45	82.45	98.12	99.04
PCB (RGB) [25]	22.86	61.24	78.27	86.88	98.79	99.62
Alexnet (Sketch) [14]	14.94	57.68	75.40	38.00	82.15	91.91
VGG16 (Sketch) [23]	18.79	66.01	81.27	54.00	91.33	96.73
HA-CNN (Sketch) [17]	20.45	63.87	79.58	58.63	90.45	95.78
PCB (Sketch) [25]	22.48	61.07	77.05	57.36	92.12	96.72
SketchNet (RGB + Sketch) [31]	17.89	43.70	58.62	64.56	92.09	97.84
Deformable Conv. [8]	25.98	71.67	85.31	61.87	92.13	97.65
STN [13]	27.47	69.53	83.22	59.21	91.43	96.11
PRCC [29]	34.38	77.30	88.05	64.20	92.62	96.65
AGS-Net	**39.60**	72.90	81.50	**93.40**	99.26	99.73

between features extracted from the same pedestrian with clothes changing. The CCIC is proposed to make the features extracted from the same pedestrian with different clothes as close as possible in the feature space. Particularly, we adopt the cosine constraint to shrink the cross-clothes discrepancy to learn cross-clothes invariant representations. Denote x_i^A, x_i^B as the ith pedestrian wearing different clothes A and B, where $f(x_i^A)$ refers to features of the pedestrian, the CCIC loss can be formulated as follows:

$$L_{CCIC} = \frac{\sum_{i=1}^{N} f(x_i^A) f(x_i^B)}{\sqrt{\sum_{i=1}^{N} f(x_i^A)} \sqrt{\sum_{i=1}^{N} f(x_i^B)}} \tag{5}$$

Notably, we calculate a judgment matrix M_{id} using value 0 and 1 to distinguish whether the features are from the same pedestrian or from different pedestrians. 0 denotes that features are from different identities while 1 means that features are from the same id.

$$M_{id} = \begin{cases} 1, & x_i^A(id) = x_j^B(id), i = 1, ..., N, j = 1, ...N \\ 0, & \text{otherwise} \end{cases} \tag{6}$$

Table 2. Ablation Study of AGS-Net on PRCC.

Methods	Cross clothes		Same clothes	
	Rank 1	Rank 10	Rank 1	Rank 10
baseline + sketch	18.39	58.32	37.25	82.73
baseline + RGB	19.43	52.38	74.80	97.28
baseline + sketch + RGB	21.20	53.82	66.41	88.01
baseline + RGB + sketch + CAM	34.94	62.49	91.04	98.63
baseline + RGB + sketch + PAM	36.75	59.78	92.16	98.73
AGS-Net (xent)	37.47	69.77	92.74	99.13
AGS-Net	**39.60**	72.90	**93.40**	99.26

Eventually, we measure the average distance between pedestrians with clothes changing using the following formula:

$$L_{CCIC} = avg(L_{CCIC} \cdot M_{id}) \tag{7}$$

Notably, we employ the cross-entropy loss with label smoothing [26] to learn discriminative features. The formula can be written as follows:

$$L_{xent} = (1 - \epsilon)y + \frac{\epsilon}{N} \tag{8}$$

where ϵ is a small positive number, and y denotes the softmax output of the input image. N is the number of classes.

Besides, inspired by studies [6,24], we apply a regularization term on weights of the framework to reduce the feature correlations across different layers to strengthen the representative capacity of deep networks. Consequently, the overall objective function of the AGS-Net is composed by a cross entropy loss, a cross-clothes constraint Loss and a weights-regularized loss [6]. The formula of the overall loss function is listed as follows:

$$L = \gamma_{xent}L_{xent} + \gamma_{ow}L_{O.W} + \gamma_{ccic}L_{CCIC} \tag{9}$$

where L_{xent} refer to the cross entropy loss, $L_{O.W}$ denotes the regularization term on weights, γ_{xent}, γ_{ow} and γ_{ccic} are hyper-parameters to adjust the impact of each loss.

4 Experiments

4.1 Dataset

PRCC [29] is a large-scale dataset for cross-clothes re-id. It contains 33698 images of 221 identities with variations on clothes, illumination, occlusion pose and viewpoint, captured by three camera. Besides, PRCC provides the corresponding contour sketch images to the RGB images. The dataset is divided into training set and test set with 150 and 71 people respectively. Specially, the test set contains three parts, A set, B set and C set, where A set is the query set, and B, C sets are the gallery sets. B set contains images without changing clothes, while C set consists of cross-clothes images.

4.2 Training

Taking the ImageNet-pretrained ResNet-50 as our backbone, we finetune the model with two-step transfer learning algorithm [4]. We first use freeze-training fro 10 epochs only with cross entropy loss. Then we open all layers for the rest, and the batch-size is set to 64. We apply rank-k matching accuracy to evaluate our method.

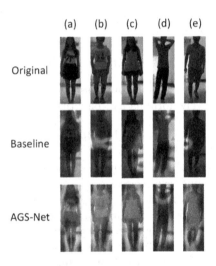

Fig. 3. Visualization of feature maps from Baseline and AGS-Net.

4.3 Comparison with State-of-the-Art Methods

Table 1 demonstrates the comparison results between AGS-Net and the state-of-the-art methods. The compared methods can be divided into two categories: models based on hand-crafted features or deep-learning models. AGS-Net achieves the best rank-1 accuracy for both the cross-clothes (39.6%) and same-clothes settings (93.4%), proving its superiority against other state-of-the-art methods. Obviously, the hand-crafted features perform poorly on PRCC because of the lack of discrimination ability. Besides, deep learning methods, such as VGG16 [23] and PCB [25], perform well for the same-clothes setting. But their performance degrade significantly, because deep-learning based models pay too much attention on color information. As listed, SketchNet [31] adopts both RGB and sketch images as inputs. However, AGS-Net outperforms Sketch-Net by a large margin. Because the AGS-Net takes the advantage of the attention module and the cross-clothes invariant constraint. The work of PRCC [29] achieves the competitive performance against AGS-Net, considering the cross-clothes protocol (34.4% V.S. 39.6%). However, the recognition performance of PRCC is much lower than AGS-Net, when considering the same-clothes settings (64.2% V.S. 93.4% in rank-1 accuracy). The experiment proves that merely using sketch images as inputs is harmful for general re-id tasks, and the proposed approach is adaptive for any application scenarios.

4.4   Ablation Study of AGS-Net

In this section, we conduct ablation experiments to verify the effects of each component in AGS-Net on PRCC. Seven variants are then constructed on top of the baseline: **1)** baseline + sketch, which only takes the sketch images as inputs; **2)** baseline + RGB, which only takes the RGB images as inputs; **3)** baseline + RGB + sketch, which use both RGB and sketch images as inputs to form a siamese network without any attention module; **4)** baseline + PAM, which implements the PAM module with the siamese network; **5)** baseline + CAM, which integrates the CAM module into the siamese network; **6)** AGS-Net (xent), our proposal without CCIC; **7)** AGS-Net, the proposed approach.

From Table 2, we can draw three conclusions: **1)** Combining visual features and contour sketch features leads to better recognition performance. **2)** Either PAM or CAM remarkably improves the recognition performance. Integrating two attention mechanisms can further strengthen the discriminative power of deep networks and achieve further improvement. **3)** The CCIC is proven effective for learning reliable cross-clothes invariant representations and dramatically improves the performance of deep networks against the cross-clothes challenges.

4.5   Visualization of Attention Module

Finally, we conduct visualization to show the effects of the AGS-Net. Figure 3 illustrates the visualization results. In the training set of PRCC dataset, pedestrians may change their clothes. We take five people as examples. As shown in Fig. 3, the baseline network pay more attention to the background, which is not affected by the variations of clothes. However, the background contains no identity-related information, which leads to poor classification performance using the baseline model. Notably, the AGS-Net focuses on areas containing rich person-related information, which is robust under the clothes-changing condition. Moreover, the AGS-Net pays less attention to the clothes and alleviates the impact of the background areas. E.g., the attention regions generated by AGS-Net emphasize the legs, the arms, the heads, the hairs, and the body shapes. Consequently, the proposed approach reach a balance, concentrating on features that are both identity-related and cross-clothes invariant while ignoring features concerning clothes and the background.

5 Conclusion

This paper proposes an attention-guided siamese network (AGS-Net) to solve the cross-clothes re-id problem. The AGS-Net develops a dual-branch network structure to integrate both visual features and contour features into a united framework. Furthermore, the AGS-Net exploits the attention module and design a cross-clothes invariant constraint to learn discriminant and cross-clothes invariant features. Experiments demonstrate that AGS-Net achieves superior performance for both cross-clothes and same-clothes settings.

References

1. Bak, S., Carr, P., Lalonde, J.F.: Domain adaptation through synthesis for unsupervised person re-identification. In: ECCV (2018)
2. Belongie, S., Malik, J., Puzicha, J.: Shape matching and object recognition using shape contexts. IEEE TPAMI **24**(4), 509–522 (2002)
3. Chen, D., Yuan, Z., Chen, B., Zheng, N.: Similarity learning with spatial constraints for person re-identification. In: CVPR (2016)
4. Chen, H., et al.: Deep transfer learning for person re-identification. In: BigMM (2018)
5. Chen, S., Guo, C., Lai, J.: Deep ranking for person re-identification via joint representation learning. IEEE TIP **25**(5), 2353–2367 (2016)
6. Chen, T., et al.: Abd-net: attentive but diverse person re-identification. In: ICCV (2019)
7. Chen, Y., Zhu, X., Zheng, W., Lai, J.: Person re-identification by camera correlation aware feature augmentation. IEEE TPAMI **40**(2), 392–408 (2018)
8. Dai, J., et al.: Deformable convolutional networks. In: ICCV (2017)
9. Dalal, N., Triggs, B.: Histograms of oriented gradients for human detection. In: CVPR (2005)
10. Feng, Z., Lai, J., Xie, X.: Learning view-specific deep networks for person re-identification. IEEE TIP **27**(7), 3472–3483 (2018)
11. Fu, J., et al.: Dual attention network for scene segmentation. In: CVPR (2019)
12. He, K., Zhang, X., Ren, S., Sun, J.: Deep residual learning for image recognition. In: CVPR (2016)
13. Jaderberg, M., Simonyan, K., Zisserman, A., Kavukcuoglu, K.: Spatial transformer networks. In: NIPS (2015)
14. Krizhevsky, A., Sutskever, I., Hinton, G.E.: Imagenet classification with deep convolutional neural networks. ACMMM (2017)
15. Köstinger, M., Hirzer, M., Wohlhart, P., Roth, P.M., Bischof, H.: Large scale metric learning from equivalence constraints. In: CVPR (2012)
16. Li, D., Chen, X., Zhang, Z., Huang, K.: Learning deep context-aware features over body and latent parts for person re-identification. In: CVPR (2017)
17. Li, W., Zhu, X., Gong, S.: Harmonious attention network for person re-identification. In: CVPR (2018)
18. Li, W., Zhao, R., Xiao, T., Wang, X.: Deepreid: deep filter pairing neural network for person re-identification. In: CVPR (2014)
19. Li, Y.J., Luo, Z., Weng, X., Kitani, K.M.: Learning shape representations for clothing variations in person re-identification. arXiv preprint arXiv:2003.07340 (2020)

20. Liao, S., Hu, Y., Xiangyu Zhu, Li, S.Z.: Person re-identification by local maximal occurrence representation and metric learning. In: CVPR (2015)
21. Ojala, T., Pietikäinen, M., Harwood, D.: A comparative study of texture measures with classification based on featured distributions. Pattern Recognit. **29**(1), 51–59 (1996)
22. Qian, X., et al.: Long-term cloth-changing person re-identification. arXiv preprint arXiv:2005.12633 (2020)
23. Simonyan, K., Zisserman, A.: Very deep convolutional networks for large-scale image recognition. arXiv preprint arXiv:1409.1556 (2015)
24. Sun, Y., Zheng, L., Deng, W., Wang, S.: SVDNet for pedestrian retrieval. In: ICCV (2017)
25. Sun, Y., Zheng, L., Yang, Y., Tian, Q., Wang, S.: Beyond part models: person retrieval with refined part pooling (and a strong convolutional baseline). In: ECCV (2018)
26. Szegedy, C., Vanhoucke, V., Ioffe, S., Shlens, J., Wojna, Z.: Rethinking the inception architecture for computer vision. In: CVPR (2016)
27. Wan, F., Wu, Y., Qian, X., Chen, Y., Fu, Y.: When person re-identification meets changing clothes. In: CVPRW (2020)
28. Xie, X., Lai, J., Zheng, W.S.: Extraction of illumination invariant facial features from a single image using nonsubsampled contourlet transform. Pattern Recognit. **43**(12), 4177–4189 (2010)
29. Yang, Q., Wu, A., Zheng, W.S.: Person re-identification by contour sketch under moderate clothing change. IEEE TPAMI (2019)
30. Yu, S., Li, S., Chen, D., Zhao, R., Yan, J., Qiao, Y.: Cocas: a large-scale clothes changing person dataset for re-identification. In: CVPR (2020)
31. Zhang, H., Liu, S., Zhang, C., Ren, W., Wang, R., Cao, X.: Sketchnet: sketch classification with web images. In: CVPR (2016)
32. Zhao, R., Ouyang, W., Wang, X.: Unsupervised salience learning for person re-identification. In: CVPR (2013)
33. Zheng, L., Shen, L., Tian, L., Wang, S., Wang, J., Tian, Q.: Scalable person re-identification: a benchmark. In: ICCV (2015)
34. Zheng, W.S., Li, X., Xiang, T., Liao, S., Lai, J., Gong, S.: Partial person re-identification. In: ICCV (2015)
35. Zheng, Z., Zheng, L., Yang, Y.: Unlabeled samples generated by GAN improve the person re-identification baseline in vitro. In: ICCV (2017)

Cross-domain Person Re-identification Based on the Sample Relation Guidance

Yue Zhang[1,2], Fanghui Zhang[1,2], Shichao Kan[1,2], Linna Zhang[3], Jiaping Zong[1,2], and Yigang Cen[1,2(✉)]

[1] Beijing Jiaotong University, Beijing, China
{17112065,18112013,16112062,18120333,ygcen}@bjtu.edu.cn
[2] Beijing Key Laboratory of Advanced Information Science and Network Technology, Beijing, China
[3] School of Mechanical engineering, Guizhou University, Guiyang, China

Abstract. The existing mainstream cross-domain person re-identification (Re-ID) methods mainly focus on reducing the deviation of the generated pseudo labels, and they did not introduce veracious label information for algorithm training on the unlabeled target domain. In this paper, we propose a new sample relation guidance (SRG) method. Specifically, the sample relation is a real label, which represents a definite positive sample pairs' relation or negative sample pairs' relation. Here, we construct a triple-branch network to form sample relation labels to improve the expressive power of features. In addition, the potential relationship of target domain label loss and source domain label loss is explored, and an adaptive adjustment label loss (ADLL) method is proposed, which effectively improves the generalization performance of the model. Extensive experiments over three benchmarks proved that our method outperforms the state-of-the-art methods.

Keywords: Person Re-ID · UDA · Cross-domain · Contrastive learning

1 Introduction

Person re-identification (Re-ID), as one of the most representative image retrieval applications, aims to retrieve the same pedestrian under different non-overlapping cameras. With the development of deep learning, the technologies of person Re-ID have obtained high performance on some public datasets. However, they strongly rely on the assumption that all the data belong to a same domain. When a model is trained on a labeled data set and tested on a new unlabeled data set, the performance will deteriorate dramatically. Recently, some works

Supported in part by the National Natural Science Foundation of China under Grant 61872034, 62062021, 61972030, and 62011530042, in part by the Beijing Municipal Natural Science Foundation under Grant 4202055, in part by the Natural Science Foundation of Guizhou Province under Grant [2019]1064.

Y. Peng et al. (Eds.): ICIG 2021, LNCS 12889, pp. 326–337, 2021.
https://doi.org/10.1007/978-3-030-87358-5_26

have shown that designing deep architectures with contrastive learning to solve unsupervised domain adaption (UDA) problem can achieve better performance. But these methods are developed for the situation that the same class images are distributed in different domains, i.e., the source domain and target domain have similar labels. In reality, the persons in different domains are different.

The UDA methods developed in literature for person Re-ID mainly include domain migration methods [1–3] and pseudo-label-based methods [4–7]. The former aims to reduce the distribution difference between the datasets of the source domain and target domain, so that the model trained in the source domain can be applied to the target domain. The latter is based on the generated pseudo-label to conduct supervision training and focuses on designing clustering algorithms. Recently, most researchers focus on reducing the deviation of the generated pseudo labels, but they did not introduce veracious label information for the algorithm training on the unlabeled target domain.

Motivated by the above observations, in this paper, we propose a new unsupervised domain adaptive person re-identification method based on a contrastive learning network, named the sample relation guidance (SRG) method. The proposed SRG is a real label, which represents a definite positive or negative relationship between the sample pairs. Specifically, different from the existing two-branch domain adaptive method, the proposed SRG framework is a triple-branch network, which contains three inputs: the source domain, the target domain, and the target domain with data augmentation. For the training of the target domain, the source domain images are taken as negative samples, and the enhanced images of the target domain are taken as positive samples. After obtaining triplet samples, we can effectively decrease the intra-class distance and push away the inter-class distance. In addition, we explore the relationship between the label loss of the source domain and target domain so as to improve the generalization performance of the model. Our contributions are summarized as follows:

- We propose a new cross-domain adaptation method for person re-identification based on the contrastive learning network, named sample relation guidance (SRG) method, which can provide accurate relation labels to improve the expression of features.
- We propose an adaptive adjustment label loss (ADLL) method, which effectively improves the generalization performance of the model.
- We evaluate our model on the Market-1501, DukeMTMC-reID, and MSMT17 datasets. Extensive experiments demonstrated the effectiveness of the proposed framework.

2   Related Work

2.1   Unsupervised Domain Adaptation for Person Re-ID

Unsupervised domain adaptation (UDA), which focuses on the knowledge transfer from a labeled dataset to another unlabeled one. With the development of deep learning, many methods have been proposed for the cross-domain person UDA problem. From the perspective of models, the existing UDA methods for person Re-ID mainly include two categories. One is the model invariant method. For example, style transfer method, it maps target domain data to source domain (e.g. PTGAN [2], SPGAN [3], ATN [8], and CR-GAN [22]) to reduce inter-domain differences. This type of method employs GAN network to learn domain-specific features for style transfer, but there is a gap in the performance of style transfer compared with the state-of-the-art methods.

Another type of category is the model migration method. [9,12,17,20] developed a camera-aware domain adaptation method to reduce distribution discrepancy between source and target domains. [18,21,25] aimed to design a generalizable person ReID framework that model is trained on source domain yet is able to perform well on the target domain. [6,15] developed the progressive unsupervised learning method to transfer pre-trained deep representations to unseen domains. In addition, the pseudo-label-based method has achieved the state-of-the-art performance for UDA to date, which employs a clustering method to cluster the features of samples, and then the pseudo-label of each sample is designated as supervision information to update the network. The main challenge of clustering-based methods is how to learn more discriminative features and improve the precision of pseudo-labels. [4] proposed MMT to generate more robust soft labels via mutual mean-teaching. [9,10] exploits the local features of unlabeled samples to assign pseudo labels. [7] adopt self-paced contrastive learning with hybrid memory gradually creates more reliable clusters. These methods focus on reducing the influence of false label noise, without introducing veracious labels for training.

2.2   Contrastive Learning

Contrastive learning is widely used in unsupervised deep learning, which measures the similarity between the images through comparative learning to train the network. For the person Re-ID task, [13] proposed a joint learning framework that disentangles id-related/unrelated features and enforces adaptation to work on the id-related feature space exclusively. [14] proposed a dissimilarity-based maximum mean discrepancy loss for aligning pair-wise distances. [3] proposed to preserve the self-similarity of an image before and after translation, and the domain-dissimilarity of a translated source image and a target image. [1] explored global distance-distributions separation constraint over the two distributions of positive and negative samples after clustered. [26] presented an AD-Cluster technique that estimates and augments person clusters in target domains and enforces the discrimination ability of re-ID models with the augmented clusters. Different from the existing methods, we construct a triple-branch network. The different forms of the same image in the target domain are taken as positive sample pairs, and the images in the source domain are taken as negative samples. By measuring the distance between positive and negative samples, different pedestrians can be distinguished and the same pedestrians can be recognized.

3   Methodology

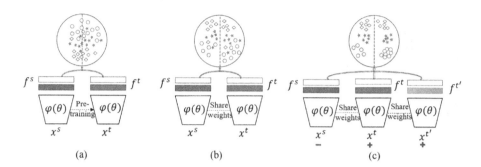

Fig. 1. Different unsupervised domain migration network frameworks, model migration from the labeled source domain (x^s) to the unlabeled target domain (x^t). (a) The model is pre-trained on the source domain, and fine-tuned by the target domain. (b) Source domain and target domain are co-trained together. (c) Source domain and target domain are co-trained together by the explicit positive and negative sample relation labels. + represents positive sample label, − represents negative sample label.

Common domain migration network mainly includes two types. The first one is performing pre-training in the source domain and then fine-tuning the model by the unlabeled target domain (Fig. 1(a)). Another one is co-training the source domain with labels and the target domain without labels (Fig. 1(b)) together. The accuracy of the latter reaches the most advanced performance. As shown in Fig. 1, (a) adopts a two-step training manner. The model is first trained by the source domain alone, and then the obtained model is used as the pre-training model to train the target domain. There are two problems with this kind of method. One is that it cannot distinguish whether the image comes from the source domain or the target domain, in other words, the domain-specific features learned from the source domain will change with the training of the target domain. Second, it can not accurately distinguish the different classes in the target domain due to the inaccurate guidance of pseudo-labels as supervision information. (b) adopts asynchronous synchronous training, which effectively alleviates the model deviation caused by inaccurate guidance of pseudo labels in the target domain. The trained model can distinguish whether one image is from the source domain or the target domain. It has a good ability to recognize the person in the source domain. But it can not generate a clear dividing line for different classes of the target domain. That's because it lacks real labels to guide the training of the network.

Based on this, we propose a new sample relation guidance (SRG) method (as shown in Fig. 1 (c) and Fig. 2), by introducing the data augmentation branch of the target domain, combining with the source domain branch and the target domain branch to form an authentic positive or negative sample relation label.

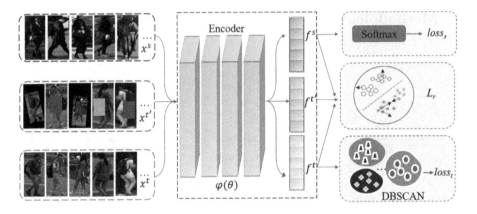

Fig. 2. The detailed network structure diagram of the proposed sample relation guidance (SRG) method.

As same as Fig. 1 (b), the target domain has no additional annotation information. The original image of the target domain and its augmentation image belong to a same class, while the source domain image and the target domain image constitute the negative sample pairs. Therefore, the obtained sample relation labels can guide the network to learn the intra-class distribution and inter-class distribution of the target domain in the right way.

3.1   The Network Framework

Given a set of n labelled source images $\mathcal{X}^s = \{x_1^s, x_2^s, ..., x_n^s\}$, $\mathcal{Y}^s = \{y_1^s, y_2^s, ..., y_n^s\}$ represents the corresponding labels. Let S and T represent source domain and target domain, respectively. The set of m unlabelled target images is defined as $\mathcal{X}^t = \{x_1^t, x_2^t, ..., x_m^t\}$. The set of m unlabelled target images with its augmentation is defined as $\mathcal{X}^{t'} = \left\{x_1^{t'}, x_2^{t'}, ..., x_m^{t'}\right\}$. We incorporate the person attention module into the encoder Φ_θ. The purpose of adding attention module is to make the features pay more attention to pedestrians. Therefore, we can get the pedestrian feature f^s of the source domain, and correspondingly the pedestrian feature f^t ($f^{t'}$) of the target domain T (the target domain T' after augmentation). The potential relationship between domains is helpful to further inference and identify pedestrians. We regard the samples x^t and $x^{t'}$ as a positive sample pair relation, and x^t and x^s as a negative sample pair relation. The sample relation loss $\mathcal{L}_r$ is as follows:

$$\mathcal{L}_r = \sum_{i,j}^{n,m} \left[\left\| f_j^t - f_j^{t'} \right\|_2^2 - \left\| f_i^s - f_j^t \right\|_2^2 \right] \tag{1}$$

Here, our task is to enlarge the distances among the pedestrians of different identities, and reduce the distance among pedestrians of the same identity. For the source domain, the final output of the pedestrian attention network will be classified by two FC layers, the cross-entropy loss will be applied to compute the loss between predicted label $\hat{\mathcal{Y}}^s$ and the real label $\mathcal{Y}^s$, as follows:

$$loss_s = \frac{1}{n} \sum_{i=1}^{n} -[\, y_i^s log\hat{y}_i^s + ((1 - y_i^s) log(1 - \hat{y}_i^s))\,] \tag{2}$$

The application of classification loss allows the model to learn the distinguish ability among different classes.

For the target domain, both the labels predicted by the encoder network and the labels generated by the clustering method contain a lot of noise. Therefore, the mean square error (MSE) of the output features f^t and their corresponding class centers' features c^t is used as label loss to update the parameters, the loss can be computed as:

$$loss_t = \frac{1}{m} \sum_{i=1,j=1}^{m,k} \left| f_i^t - c_j^t \right|^2 \tag{3}$$

Here, k is the cluster number. $\mathcal{C} = \{c_j\}_{j=1}^{k}$ represents the corresponding person feature of the class center j, which improves the model's ability to identify pedestrians of a same identity by calculating feature difference.

3.2   Adaptive Weight Adjustment for the Label Loss

The label loss of the whole network includes the source domain label loss ($loss_s$) and the target domain label loss($loss_t$). Through experiments, we explore four relationships between $loss_s$ and $loss_t$: (1) When $loss_s$ is small, $loss_t$ is large. It may lead to the model over-fitting and its generalization performance is poor. (2) When $loss_s$ is large, and $loss_t$ is large. It may lead to the model under-fitting because of the model doesn't converge. (3) When $loss_s$ is large, $loss_t$ is small. The trained model has good generalization performance but its accuracy needs to be improved. (4) When $loss_s$ is small, $loss_t$ is small. The trained model has good generalization performance with excellent accuracy. The label loss can be computed as:

$$\mathcal{L}_l = \gamma loss_s + (1 - \gamma) loss_t \tag{4}$$

Based on the above observations, we carefully investigate the relationship between $loss_s$ and $loss_t$, and find when $loss_s$ is large and $loss_t$ is small, the network will focus on optimizing $loss_s$. Then the $loss_s$ will fall rapidly, which will lead to model over-fitting. Therefore, we need to increase the weight of $loss_t$ to weaken the optimization of $loss_s$, and strengthen the optimization of $loss_t$ by network. Thus, we propose an adaptive weight adjustment for the label loss so that model can be trained well. In this work, we find that when $loss_s > 2 \times loss_t$,

Table 1. Evaluation on Market-1501 and DukeMTMC-reID (DukeMTMC) data sets.

Methods		DukeMTMC→Market-1501				Market-1501→ DukeMTMC			
		mAP	top-1	top-5	top-10	mAP	top-1	top-5	top-10
PUL [15]	TOMM (2018)	20.5	45.5	60.7	66.7	16.4	30.0	43.4	48.5
TJ-AIDL [16]	CVPR (2018)	26.5	58.2	74.8	81.1	23.0	44.3	59.6	65.0
SPGAN [3]	CVPR (2018)	22.8	51.5	70.1	76.8	22.3	41.1	56.6	63.0
HHL [17]	ECCV (2018)	31.4	62.2	78.8	84.0	27.2	46.9	61.0	66.7
ARN [18]	CVPRW (2018)	39.4	70.3	80.4	86.3	33.4	60.2	73.9	79.5
ECN [19]	CVPR (2019)	43.0	75.1	87.6	91.6	40.4	63.3	75.8	80.4
UCDA [20]	ICCV (2019)	30.9	60.4	–	–	31.0	47.7	–	–
PDA-Net [21]	ICCV (2019)	47.6	75.2	86.3	90.2	45.1	63.2	77.0	82.5
CR-GAN [22]	ICCV (2019)	54.0	77.7	89.7	92.7	48.6	68.9	80.2	84.7
PCB-PAST [6]	ICCV (2019)	54.6	78.4	–	–	54.3	72.4	–	–
SSG [9]	ICCV (2019)	58.3	80.0	90.0	92.4	53.4	73.0	80.6	83.2
ECN++ [23]	TPAMI (2020)	63.8	84.1	92.8	95.4	54.4	74.0	83.7	87.4
MMCL [24]	CVPR (2020)	60.4	84.4	92.8	95.0	51.4	72.4	82.9	85.0
SNR [25]	CVPR (2020)	61.7	82.8	–	–	58.1	76.3	–	–
AD-Cluster [26]	CVPR (2020)	68.3	86.7	94.4	96.5	54.1	72.6	80.5	85.5
MMT [4]($k-means$)	ICLR (2020)	71.2	87.7	94.9	96.9	65.1	78.0	88.8	92.5
MMT [4]($DBSCAN$)	ICLR (2020)	73.8	89.5	96.0	**97.6**	62.3	76.3	87.7	91.2
Proposed SRG		**76.3**	**90.8**	**96.7**	97.5	**68.7**	**82.4**	90.4	**92.8**
Proposed SRG+re-ranking		90.1	93.4	96.3	97.3	78.6	84.4	**90.5**	92.4

we need to adjust the weight γ. In other cases, the weight of $loss_s$ and $loss_t$ can be the same. The weight γ update method is as follows:

$$\gamma = (1-p) \times 0.5 + p \times \left(1 - \left\lceil \frac{q_s}{q_t} \right\rceil \times \xi\right) \qquad (5)$$

Here, if $loss_s > 2 \times loss_t$, then $p = 1$, otherwise $p = 0$. q_s represents the number of the query images in the source domain test set. q_t represents the number of the query images in the target domain test set. $\xi = 0.05$ is the weight regulation coefficient. The first term on the right-hand side of the equation means that $loss_s$ and $loss_t$ have the same weight when $loss_s \leq 2 \times loss_t$. The latter represents the weight automatically calculated according to the number of query images in the target domain and source domain.

4   Experiment

4.1   Datasets and Evaluation Protocol

In this paper, we adopt MSMT17 [27], Market-1501 [29] and DukeMTMC-reID [28] datasets to evaluation our model. MSMT17 contains 32,621 bounding boxes of 1,041 identities in the training set, and the testing set contains 11,659 query

Table 2. Performance comparison with state-of-the-art methods on the MSMT17 dataset with training on the Market-1501 dataset.

Methods		MSMT17→Market-1501				Market-1501→ MSMT17			
		mAP	top-1	top-5	top-10	mAP	top-1	top-5	top-10
PTGAN [2]	CVPR (2018)	–	–	–	–	2.9	10.2	–	24.4
MAR [11]	CVPR (2019)	40.0	67.7	81.9	87.3	–	–	–	–
PAUL [10]	CVPR (2019)	40.1	68.5	82.4	87.4	–	–	–	–
ECN [19]	CVPR (2019)	–	–	–	–	8.5	25.3	36.3	42.1
SSG [9]	ICCV (2019)	–	–	–	–	13.2	31.6	–	49.6
SSG++ [9]	ICCV (2019)	–	–	–	–	16.6	37.6	–	57.2
ECN++ [23]	TPAMI (2020)	–	–	–	–	15.2	40.4	53.1	58.7
MMCL [24]	CVPR (2020)	–	–	–	–	15.1	40.8	51.8	56.7
CASCL [12]	ICCV (2020)	35.5	65.4	80.6	86.2	–	–	–	–
DG-Net++ [13]	ECCV (2020)	64.6	83.1	91.5	94.3	22.1	48.4	60.9	66.1
D-MMD [14]	ECCV(2020)	50.8	72.8	88.1	92.3	13.5	29.1	46.3	54.1
MMT [4]	ICLR (2020)	75.6	89.3	95.8	97.5	24.0	50.1	63.5	69.3
Proposed SRG (wihtout re-ranking)		**77.4**	**91.5**	**96.6**	**97.8**	**24.5**	**53.2**	**67.8**	**73.1**

bounding boxes of 3,060 identities. Market-1501 consists of 751 persons in the training set. The test set consists of 750 persons, including 3,368 query images. DukeMTMC-reID consists of 702 people in the training set. And it contains 2,228 queries and 17,661 gallery images. Source dataset with labels, and target dataset without labels are used for training. We follow the standard evaluation protocol, a domain is chosen as a source, and the rest is chosen as the target. Mean average precision(mAP) and cumulative matching characteristic (CMC) [29] are applied to evaluate our proposed models' performances on the target-domain dataset.

4.2   Experimental Settings

We set a mini-batch size as 64 with 4 GPUs for training our models. We adopt an ImageNet-pre-trained ResNet-50 as the backbone for the encoder. Following the clustering-based UDA methods, we use DBSCAN for clustering before each epoch. We use the same number of SGD optimizer with a step learning rate decay scheduler. The image size is 128×256, the learning rate is 3.5×10^{-4}, the weight decay parameter is 5×10^{-4}. The methods of data enhancement mainly include random clipping, horizontal flipping, and random erasing.

4.3   Comparison with the State-of-the-Art Methods

In this section, for all methods, we tune the corresponding hyper-parameters of the proposed framework and report the best results. Our method is compared with the state-of-the-art domain adaptation methods on different domain adaption tasks, including DukeMTMC-reID→ Market-1501, Market-1501→ DukeMTMC-reID, MSMT17→ Market-1501, and Market-1501→ MSMT17.

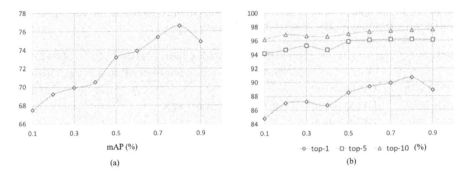

Fig. 3. The influence of adaptive weight γ of target domain for MSMT17→Market-1501 dataset.

The Table 1 shows the results of DukeMTMC-reID→ Market-1501 and Market-1501→ DukeMTMC-reID. When Market-1501 dataset is used as the target domain, and DukeMTMC-reID dataset is used as the source domain, compared with the MMT (DBSCAN) algorithm, the mAP, top-1, top-5, and top-10 of our method are improved by 2.5%, 1.3%, 0.7%, −0.1%, respectively. After re-ranking method is applied to our method, mAP and top-1 will reach 90.1%, 93.4% respectively. When DukeMTMC-reID is used as the target domain and Market-1501 is used as the source domain, our method achieves a large margin improvement. Compared with MMT (DBSCAN), mAP, top-1, top-5, and top-10 of our method are improved by 6.4%, 6.1%, 2.7%, 1.6%, respectively. After re-ranking is applied, mAP and top-1 can reach 78.6%, 84.4% respectively, which is comparable to the results of supervised learning.

MSMT17 is a very challenging dataset. We also conduct experiments on the MSMT17 dataset. The results are shown in Table 2. For the case that MSMT17 dataset is used as the source domain, the domain adaptation results on the Market-1501 dataset obtained by our proposed method are also superior to other algorithms. Among them, compared with MMT (DBSCAN), mAP, top-1, top-5, and top-10 are improved by 1.8%, 2.2%, 0.8%, 0.3%, respectively. For the case that MSMT17 dataset is used as the target domain, compared with MMT, mAP, top-1, top-5, and top-10 are improved by 0.5%, 3.1%, 4.3%, 3.8%, respectively. The experimental results further demonstrate that our method can learn more discriminative features.

4.4   Influence of Parameters

Adaptive Label Loss Weight. The impacts of the feature weight γ on MSMT17→ Market-1501 dataset are shown in Fig. 3, the horizontal axis represents the value range of γ ($\gamma \in [0.1, 0.9]$), and the vertical axis represents the corresponding accuracy of mAP, top-1, top-5, and top-10. The MSMT17 dataset including 11, 659 query images, the Market-1501 dataset includes 3, 368 query images, so $\left\lceil \frac{q_s}{q_t} \right\rceil = 4$. With the increase of γ value, mAP, top-1, top-5 and

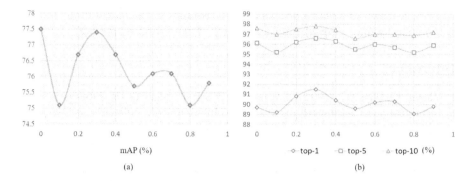

Fig. 4. Comparison of results obtained from sample relation loss $\mathcal{L}_r$ with different weights w_t for MSMT17→Market-1501 dataset.

top-10 also increased continuously. The result reaches the highest value around $1 - \left\lceil \frac{q_s}{q_t} \right\rceil \times \xi = 0.8$, and then begins to decline. This also shows that our adaptive label weight can effectively balance the losses in the source domain and target domain, so that the learned model can achieve good generalization performance.

Sample Relation Loss Weight. We investigate the effect of sample relation loss $\mathcal{L}_r$ with different weights w_t ($w_t \in [0, 0.9]$), $w_t = 0$ indicates that no sample relation loss is included. As shown in Fig. 4, mAP, top-1, top-5, and top-10 change with the change of weight. The fluctuation of accuracy is related to the initialization of the model, but after many experiments, the corresponding best results are obtained for each weight for comparison. As it can be seen from Fig. 4(a), the obtained mAP by the model at $w_t = 0.3$ is lower than the model without $\mathcal{L}_r$ of 0.1%. But the top-1 is much higher than the model without $\mathcal{L}_r$ of 1.8%. Generally speaking, top-1, top-5, and top-10 are more intuitive to evaluate the performance of the algorithm for image search. Here, top-1, top-5, and top-10 achieved the peak at $w_t = 0.3$, which further proves the effectiveness of adding sample relation loss.

5   Conclusion

Recently, for the target domain without labels, there is a lack of real and accurate labels to guide model training, so we introduced sample relation labels to guide the network to learn the feature distribution of inter-class and intra-class. In particular, we constructed a triple-branch network: the source domain and target domain features were used to construct negative sample relation, and the target domain and its augmentation constructed positive sample relation. Based on this, the recognition model obtained better generalization performance. In addition, we studied the relationship between the target domain label loss and the source domain label loss, and proposed an adaptive adjustment weight method of the loss weight, which provided a new idea for the training of the model in the future. Experimental results proved the effectiveness of the proposed method.

References

1. Zheng, L., Shen, L., Tian, L., Wang, S., Wang, J., Tian, Q.: Scalable person re-identification: a benchmark. In: 2015 IEEE International Conference on Computer Vision (ICCV), Santiago, Chile, pp. 1116–1124 (2015). https://doi.org/10.1109/ICCV.2015.133
2. Wei, L., Zhang, S., Gao, W., Tian, Q.: Person transfer GAN to bridge domain gap for person re-identification. In: 2018 IEEE/CVF Conference on Computer Vision and Pattern Recognition, Salt Lake City, UT, USA, pp. 79–88 (2018). https://doi.org/10.1109/CVPR.2018.00016
3. Deng, W., Zheng, L., Ye, Q., et al.: Image-image domain adaptation with preserved self-similarity and domain-dissimilarity for person re-identification. In: Proceedings of the IEEE Conference on Computer Vision and Pattern Recognition, pp. 994–1003 (2018)
4. Ge, Y., Chen, D., Li, H.: Mutual mean-teaching: pseudo label refinery for unsupervised domain adaptation on person re-identification. arXiv preprint arXiv:2001.01526 (2020)
5. Song, L., Wang, C., Zhang, L., et al.: Unsupervised domain adaptive re-identification: theory and practice. Pattern Recognit. **102**, 107173 (2020)
6. Zhang, X., Cao, J., Shen, C., et al.: Self-training with progressive augmentation for unsupervised cross-domain person re-identification. In: Proceedings of the IEEE/CVF International Conference on Computer Vision, pp. 8222–8231 (2019)
7. Ge, Y., Chen, D., Zhu, F., et al.: Self-paced contrastive learning with hybrid memory for domain adaptive object re-id. In: Advances in Neural Information Processing Systems (2020)
8. Liu, J., Zha, Z.J., Chen, D., et al.: Adaptive transfer network for cross-domain person re-identification. In: Proceedings of the IEEE/CVF Conference on Computer Vision and Pattern Recognition, pp. 7202–7211 (2019)
9. Fu, Y., Wei, Y., Wang, G., et al.: Self-similarity grouping: a simple unsupervised cross domain adaptation approach for person re-identification. In: Proceedings of the IEEE/CVF International Conference on Computer Vision, pp. 6112–6121 (2019)
10. Yang, Q., Yu, H.X., Wu, A., et al.: Patch-based discriminative feature learning for unsupervised person re-identification. In: Proceedings of the IEEE/CVF Conference on Computer Vision and Pattern Recognition, pp. 3633–3642 (2019)
11. Yu, H.X., Zheng, W.S., Wu, A., et al.: Unsupervised person re-identification by soft multilabel learning. In: Proceedings of the IEEE/CVF Conference on Computer Vision and Pattern Recognition, pp. 2148–2157 (2019)
12. Wu, A., Zheng, W.S., Lai, J.H.: Unsupervised person re-identification by camera-aware similarity consistency learning. In: Proceedings of the IEEE/CVF International Conference on Computer Vision, pp. 6922–6931 (2019)
13. Zou, Y., Yang, X., Yu, Z., et al.: Joint disentangling and adaptation for cross-domain person re-identification. arXiv preprint arXiv:2007.10315 (2020)
14. Mekhazni, D., Bhuiyan, A., Ekladious, G., Granger, E.: Unsupervised domain adaptation in the dissimilarity space for person re-identification. In: Vedaldi, A., Bischof, H., Brox, T., Frahm, J.-M. (eds.) ECCV 2020. LNCS, vol. 12372, pp. 159–174. Springer, Cham (2020). https://doi.org/10.1007/978-3-030-58583-9_10

15. Fan, H., Zheng, L., Yan, C., et al.: Unsupervised person re-identification: clustering and fine-tuning. ACM Trans. Multimedia Comput. Commun. Appl. (TOMM) **14**(4), 1–18 (2018)
16. Wang, X., Girshick, R., Gupta, A., et al.: Non-local neural networks. In: Proceedings of the IEEE Conference on Computer Vision and Pattern Recognition, pp. 7794–7803 (2018)
17. Zhong, Z., Zheng, L., Li, S., et al.: Generalizing a person retrieval model hetero-and homogeneously. In: Proceedings of the European Conference on Computer Vision (ECCV), pp. 172–188 (2018)
18. Li, Y.J., Yang, F.E., Liu, Y.C., et al.: Adaptation and re-identification network: an unsupervised deep transfer learning approach to person re-identification. In: Proceedings of the IEEE Conference on Computer Vision and Pattern Recognition Workshops, pp. 172–178 (2018)
19. Zhong, Z., Zheng, L., Luo, Z., et al.: Invariance matters: exemplar memory for domain adaptive person re-identification. In: Proceedings of the IEEE/CVF Conference on Computer Vision and Pattern Recognition, pp. 598–607 (2019)
20. Qi, L., Wang, L., Huo, J., et al.: A novel unsupervised camera-aware domain adaptation framework for person re-identification. In: Proceedings of the IEEE/CVF International Conference on Computer Vision, pp. 8080–8089 (2019)
21. Li, Y.J., Lin, C.S., Lin, Y.B., et al.: Cross-dataset person re-identification via unsupervised pose disentanglement and adaptation. In: Proceedings of the IEEE/CVF International Conference on Computer Vision, pp. 7919–7929 (2019)
22. Chen, Y., Zhu, X., Gong, S.: Instance-guided context rendering for cross-domain person re-identification. In: Proceedings of the IEEE/CVF International Conference on Computer Vision, pp. 232–242 (2019)
23. Zhong, Z., Zheng, L., Luo, Z., et al.: Learning to adapt invariance in memory for person re-identification. IEEE Trans. Pattern Anal. Mach. Intell. (2020)
24. Wang, D., Zhang, S.: Unsupervised person re-identification via multi-label classification. In: Proceedings of the IEEE/CVF Conference on Computer Vision and Pattern Recognition, pp. 10981–10990 (2020)
25. Jin, X., Lan, C., Zeng, W., et al.: Style normalization and restitution for generalizable person re-identification. In: Proceedings of the IEEE/CVF Conference on Computer Vision and Pattern Recognition, pp. 3143–3152 (2020)
26. Zhai, Y., Lu, S., Ye, Q., et al.: Ad-cluster: augmented discriminative clustering for domain adaptive person re-identification. In: Proceedings of the IEEE/CVF Conference on Computer Vision and Pattern Recognition, pp. 9021–9030 (2020)
27. Wei, L., Zhang, S., Gao, W., et al.: Person transfer GAN to bridge domain gap for person re-identification. In: Proceedings of the IEEE Conference on Computer Vision and Pattern Recognition, pp. 79–88 (2018)
28. Ristani, E., Solera, F., Zou, R., Cucchiara, R., Tomasi, C.: Performance measures and a data set for multi-target, multi-camera tracking. In: Hua, G., Jégou, H. (eds.) ECCV 2016. LNCS, vol. 9914, pp. 17–35. Springer, Cham (2016). https://doi.org/10.1007/978-3-319-48881-3_2
29. Zheng, L., Shen, L., Tian, L., et al.: Scalable person re-identification: a benchmark. In: Proceedings of the IEEE International Conference on Computer Vision, pp. 1116–1124 (2015)

Large-Scale Target Detection and Classification Based on Improved Candidate Regions

Runping Xi[1,2,3], Qianqian Han[1,2,3(✉)], Gaoyun Jia[1,2,3], and Xuefeng Kou[4]

[1] School of Computer Science and Techology, Northwest Polytechnical University, Xi'an 710072, China
[2] National Engineering Laboratory of Integrated Aero-Space-Ground-Ocean Big Data Application Technology, Xi'an 710129, China
[3] Shaanxi Provincial Key Laboratory of Speech and Image Information Processing, Xi'an 710129, China
[4] Shaanxi Baocheng Aviation instrument Co., Ltd., Baoji, China

Abstract. Target detection of aerial images has become a frontier subject of concern in the image processing field. Using existing method to detect and classify large-scale building objects in aerial images, the accuracy is still a little low. This is mainly because the current method does not make full use of the prior information of the target to be detected, so there are too much redundant information in the candidate box. In this paper, our own dataset were built and then utilize the Hough transform to filter out the images that may exist in the sequence image. For images with dense lines or circles, it is possible that there is an artificial building target which will be detected, otherwise it is excluded directly. Besides, this paper exploits significance analysis from the filtered image and then extract the area of interest where the potential target is located. The results of the above-mentioned processing lay a good foundation for the subsequent detection and classification which can help improve the accuracy.

Keywords: Target detection · Significance analysis · Hough transform

1 Introduction

In recent years, one of the important topics in the field of aerial image recognition is how to obtain useful information from images efficiently and accurately. With the rapid development of science and technology, computer vision technology and drone technology have developed rapidly. Convolutional neural network (CNN)

Supported by: [1] the National Natural Science Foundation's project "Research on Multi-source Image Cooperative Detection Method Based on Biological Vision for UAV Groups" (No. 61572405). [2] Major Science and Technology Project of Shaanxi Province "Development and application demonstration of Apple's quality and safety supervision and traceability system based on the Internet of Things".

Y. Peng et al. (Eds.): ICIG 2021, LNCS 12889, pp. 338–350, 2021.
https://doi.org/10.1007/978-3-030-87358-5_27

is a model of extended neurocognitive machines. The idea based on the Region-CNN (RCNN) detection method is to select the area where the target may exist from the image in advance. Then put the candidate area into the CNN to extract the features. In the end, classify and identify the object. Faster RCNN improves the candidate region generation method that can make the candidate region completed on the GPU. The result shows it can greatly reduce the detection time without affecting the detection accuracy. Its structure removes the image segmentation method extraction based on CNN. The steps of the target possible region are realized by adding a new network-RPN (Region Proposal Network) in the CNN. The overall detection process is shown in Fig. 1.

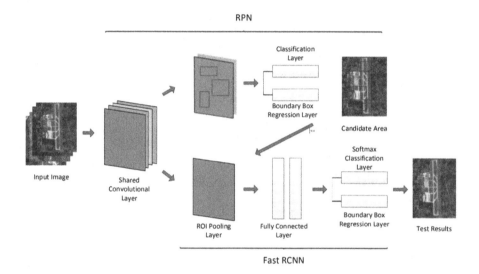

Fig. 1. Faster RCNN detection process.

Based on the Faster RCNN algorithm, we can detect, recognize and classify the target objects from the massive photos taken by UAV. But the RPN network needs to search for the candidate areas of all the pixels one by one [1–4]. This computation is relatively time-consuming. More-over, the generated suggestion box is based on the entire image and does not make full use of the apriori information of the target to be detected. Therefore, there are still too many redundant information in the candidate frame.

For the detection of large man-made structures such as airports, oil depots, bridges and so on, it is considered that these targets are of great significance in view of the great difference among the targets, the surrounding environment and the unique geometry of each target. Thus saliency detection mechanism can be introduced into the detection of these large-scale targets, which can achieve the purpose of extracting the target candidate areas. Meanwhile, it can overcome the shortcomings of the conventional methods which use the sliding window to detect the pixels one by one, resulting in too slow speed. Otherwise, it solve the problem that inaccurate positioning of building targets in amplitude images [5–9]. After obtaining the area of interest of the potential target, the features will be extracted and classified by the Faster RCNN network, finally identify the target.

This paper use the Hough transform to detect whether there is a target as a preliminary screening, which can reduce the processing and analysis of the image without the target, and accelerate the detection speed. It is considered that there is a target to be detected when there is a dense linear and circular image, otherwise excluded directly. Then saliency analysis on these remaining images to extract the candidate areas where the potential targets are located. The flow is shown in Fig. 2.

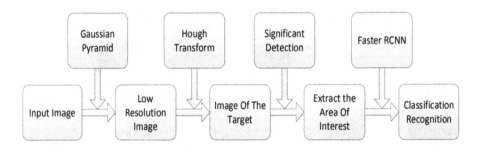

Fig. 2. Flow chart of large-scale target detection in aerial image.

2   Improved Hough Transform

The Hough transform is used to detect whether there is a target for a preliminary screening, which can reduce the processing and analysis of the image without a target, and speed up the detection speed. For the image with dense straight lines and circles, it is considered that there may be a target to be detected, otherwise it is ruled out directly.

2.1   Classical Hough Transform

Hough transform is a geometric feature extraction technology in image processing, and it is not affected by the image rotation. It transforms the image coordinate space into the parameter space, and calculates the local maximum of the cumulative result through a voting algorithm that will achieve a straight line and curve fitting, its main role is to detect from the image which has a certain characteristic of the geometric shapes, such as lines, circles and so on [10]. In Cartesian coordinates, a straight line can be expressed as an equation:

$$y = kx + b \tag{1}$$

This means that a straight line in the parameter space k–b, i.e. a point that can determine a linear cluster with parameters k, b. Based on the above theory, the binarized image can be edge-detected firstly, and each non-zero pixel point in the image is mapped to a parameter plane as a straight line. Therefore, when Hough transformation is performed on all points on the image, the detected straight line must be the point where the straight line intersects the most in the parametric plane, and all lines can be detected by traversing the entire image. However, in practical applications, since k = ∞ (infinite slope) cannot be represented, the Cartesian coordinate system is usually converted into a polar coordinate system. The straight line can use the parametric equation shown in Eq. 2.

$$\rho = xcos + ysin \tag{2}$$

In polar coordinate system, the method of transforming polar coordinate points into Hough space lines is shown in Fig. 3.

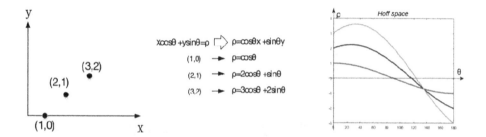

Fig. 3. Schematic diagram of converting polar coordinates to Hough space.

The Hough transform is also suitable for detecting curve whose function representation has been known. Because if the equation of the curve is known in the plane coordinate system, the corresponding parameter representation can be found and one point in the image coordinates can be mapped to the corresponding curve or surface in the parameter space. When using the Hough transform to detect a circle, the circle's space coordinate representation should be converted into a parameter space representation firstly. The general equation for the known circle is shown in Eq. 3.

$$(x - a)^2 + (y - a)^2 = r^2 \tag{3}$$

Where (a, b) is the center of the circle and r is the radius of the circle.

Convert the circle in the plane rectangular coordinate space to the parameter space, then a point (x,y) on the circle in the plane corresponds to a three dimensional cone surface with a change in height r in the parameter space, as shown in the left figure of Fig. 4. In the Cartesian coordinate system, a circle passing any point corresponds to a three-dimensional cone in the parameter space. When Cartesian coordinates are converted to the parameter space, and a point on the same circle corresponds to a three-dimensional cone surface, it must intersect at a point (a_0, b_0, r_0) where the height is r_0. By detecting this point, three parameters of the circle can be obtained and the corresponding circle can be found.

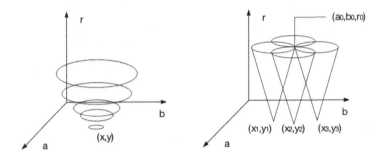

Fig. 4. The spatial representation of the parameter.

The effect of treating the oil field with the Hough transform is shown in Fig. 5. The first subfigure is the original image, and the next subfigure is the image after edge detection. The third is the image after Hough transform.

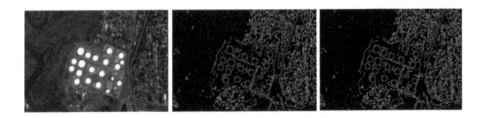

Fig. 5. Hough transform.

2.2 Improved Hough Transform

Because the parameter space of the Standard Hough transform needs three variables, obviously, the amount of calculation will be large, and the running memory and speed will be affected. The gradient direction can be used to find the center of the circle quickly and reduce unnecessary blind search in the improved method, but for most gray-scale images, the target after edge extraction still has a certain width. There are still many pixel points used to search for the center of the circle coordinates, so the problem of calculation amount has not been solved well. In this paper, we combine the Standard Hough transform and the unique properties of the circle to improve the efficiency of the operation by reducing the

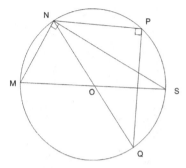

Fig. 6. Finding the center of a circle according to its characteristics.

dimension. The improved algorithm is divided into two steps: first find out the center of the circle, and then determine the radius.

As shown in Fig. 6, starting from a certain point m in the edge of a circle, according to a certain fixed direction, for example, a point N is taken out of n points clockwise, and a passing point N is taken as the vertical line of line MN. The vertical line must intersect the circle at a point S, connecting point M and point S, which is a diameter of the circle. According to the nature of the circle, the line must pass through the center of the circle. Starting from point N, a point P is taken out of n points clockwise again. Make a straight line perpendicular to the segment NP, and the straight line must intersect a point Q on the circle, connecting point N and point Q. Similarly, NQ also passes through the center of the circle. In this way, the intersection of segment MS and segment NQ must be the location of the center of the circle. According to the above principle, combined with the voting mechanism in Hough transform, the accumulator of the center point will be increased every time the center point is determined. When the search is finished, the coordinate value that reaches the preset threshold in the accumulator is the center coordinate. Then, from the non-zero pixels around the center of all the candidate circles, the radius is determined according to the degree of support for the center. Because the two-dimensional coordinate values are stored in the accumulator, compared with the Standard Hough transform, the one-dimensional is reduced, which greatly saves the storage space and calculation time. As shown in Fig. 7, this is the result pictures which might contain targets detected by improved Hough transform.

3 Significance Test

In the research of visual saliency target detection, visual attention mechanism is the focus of researchers' attention, and target saliency extraction works according to visual attention mechanism [11].

Fig. 7. Detection result by improved Hough transform.

Human visual attention mechanism can focus limited cognitive resources on the important information in the scene and suppress those relatively unimportant information. The current visual attention mechanism includes two kinds of visual models: one is the pre-attention mechanism with bottom-up control strategy; the bottom-up information processing is mainly the visual stimulation contained in the image, which has nothing to do with the high-level knowledge related to human brain tasks; the top-down information processing involves not only the prior knowledge of the target, the preparatory knowledge of the scene, but also the high-level knowledge of emotion, intention, expectation, motivation, etc.

In this paper, we use the bottom-up attention mechanism, the method of calculating visual saliency based on random sampling [12], which first samples the image into some random regions of interest, then calculates the saliency of each part on these regions, and finally fuses all regions. The flow chart is shown in Fig. 8. For an RGB image, the Gaussian filter is used to filter it first and transform it from RGB space to lab space. Compared with other color spaces, lab space is closer to human's neural visual space and is considered as the standard color space for calculating saliency image. Several windows are randomly generated in each of the three channel images because of the saliency area or objects The volume may appear in the image in any position and size, so the randomly generated strategy helps the generated window contain all areas as much as possible, then calculate the ratio of the area of each window to the sum of gray scale, and then calculate the saliency mapping of each window and each pixel; finally, the method of Euclidean distance is used to fuse the saliency value

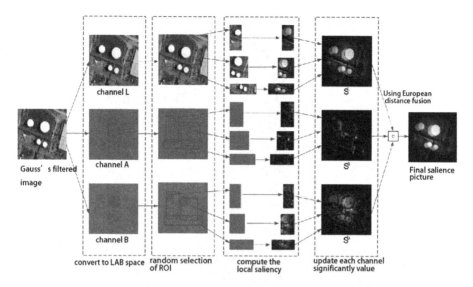

Fig. 8. Flow chart of visual significance detection based on random sampling.

of lab channel into the saliency map, and The final saliency map is generated after the value is normalized to [0,255].

The salience picture calculated by above method is shown in Fig. 9. After image segmentation, the result of candidate area generated by the method in this paper can be seen in the rightest part of Fig. 9. It is obvious that the segmentation effect is good, which can be used as the basis for subsequent classification and recognition.

4   Analysis of Experimental Results

4.1   Experimental Setting

In network structure shown in Fig. 1, this paper uses small-scale ZFNet [13] and another medium-scale VGGNet [14] as the shared convolution layer, respectively. They were run in two different experimental environments: the PC and the server built by the lab. The hardware and software environment used is shown in Table 1.

In this paper, the initial data set of airport oil depot target is constructed by using the image of Internet and the satellite image captured by Google Earth. The collected image data set includes 780 airport targets, 897 oil depot targets, 408 bridge targets, including 2085 images, covering a variety of samples in each type of typical targets. After change processing and equalization, the experimental data set contains 4680 airport targets, 5382 oil depot targets, 4496 bridge targets, including 14558 images.

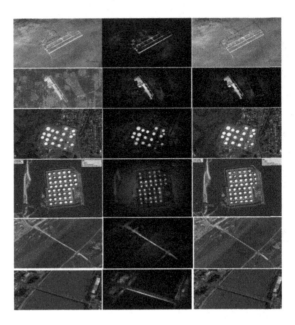

Fig. 9. Extracting candidate regions from large scale images.

Table 1. Software and hardware environment used in the experiment.

Project	ZF + Faster RCNN	VGG + Faster RCNN
Processor Inter	Inter i7-2600k 3.40 GHz	Xeon E5-2640v4 3.40 GHz
RAM	8GBz	64GB
Memory	GTX 970 (4G)	Tesla K40 (12G)
Operating System	Windows 7	centos 7
Deep learning framework	Caffe	TensorFlow
Data processing software	MATLAB R2016b	Python 3.0

4.2 Training Setting

The goal of the detection and classification contains three categories including airport, oil depot and bridge. Therefore the output of the input layer, the candidate area layer and the classifier is set to 4. The output of the bounding box regression layer is the four coordinate parameters of the bounding box, so its output is set to 16. Other parameters including the initial learning rate and the stepsize are set as shown in Table 2.

Table 2. Parameter settings of network training.

Parameter name	Value
base_lr	0.001
Gamma	0.1
Stepsize	50000
Display	20
Momentum	0.9
iter_size	2

4.3 Classification Network Experiment Results

As shown in Fig. 10, the time spent in each image test in the test set is changed. For the convenience of viewing data, the running time under the two shared convolutions is displayed in the coordinate system of different scales. Under the shared convolution of ZF network, the total time consumed is 25.372 s. On average, one image is tested every 75 ms, and the processing time of each image is relatively uniform. As a whole, under the training of small-scale network ZF, classification detection can meet the real-time requirements to a certain extent. But under the shared convolution of VGG network, the total time consumed is 198.503 s, and it needs to complete an image test every 0.589 s on average. From this analysis, it can be seen that VGG network is difficult to meet the real-time requirements of classification and detection. Considering the hardware and software environments of ZF network and VGG network, it can be concluded that the time cost of ZF network is much less under the same conditions.

Consider that the SSD network [15] is also a good network for detection. Therefore, the two networks mentioned above are compared with the SSD network. For the airport, oil depot and Bridge targets in the self-built database, the accuracy of SSD network and two different shared convolution networks is

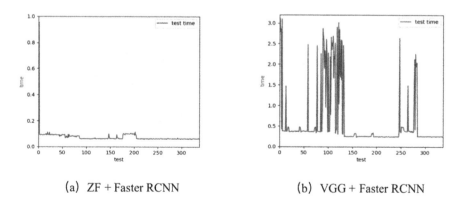

(a) ZF + Faster RCNN   (b) VGG + Faster RCNN

Fig. 10. Extracting candidate regions from large scale images.

shown in Table 3. It can be seen that compared with SSD method, the accuracy of the improved Faster RCNN algorithm is significantly improved. On the basis of VGG network with medium complexity, VGG + Faster RCNN is 10% points higher than SSD, and the effect is very obvious. And in the case of 80000 iterations, the classification detection rate of the two Faster RCNN networks is high, and the difference is only 4.56%, which can meet the requirements of classification detection.

Table 3. Accuracy of various targets in different shared convolution layers.

Scheme	Airport	Oil depot	Bridge	mAP
SSD	0.8575	0.7809	0.8335	0.8115
ZF + Fast RCNN	0.8733	0.8045	0.8537	0.8689
VGG + Fast RCNNN	0.9229	0.8861	0.9106	0.9145

As shown in Figs. 11 and 12, the detection results of different classified targets in different shared convolutions are shown. It can be seen from the figure that most of the targets can be distinguished and detected by the classification algorithms under the two network structures, but for some targets whose profile information is not too obvious, ZF algorithm still has the situation of missing detection, while VGG algorithm can distinguish this well because of more network structure layers, such as ZF model in Fig. 12(d).

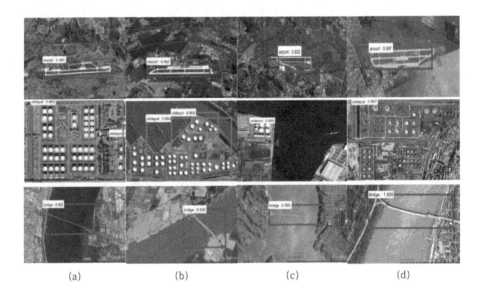

(a)   (b)   (c)   (d)

Fig. 11. Test results under ZF model.

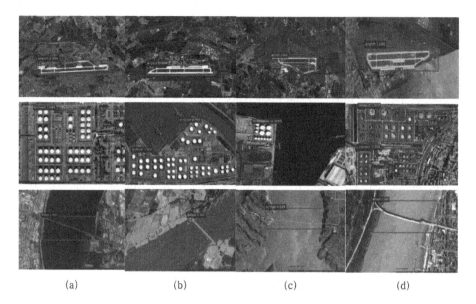

(a)   (b)   (c)   (d)

Fig. 12. Test results under VGG model.

5 Summary

In order to improve the efficiency and accuracy of detection and classification of large-scale targets such as airport el al. in aerial photos from UAV, this paper proposes a region of interest extraction strategy based on the combination of image prior structure features and visual significance detection, which can quickly find potential targets from large-scale UAV images area. Considering that the structural information of the target to be detected is the main feature for the category classification, the original image is reduced to a low-resolution image through the Gaussian pyramid firstly. Then the region of interest of the target is extracted by the combination of the prior structural feature of the image and the visual significance detection. Finally, the candidate region is generated by RPN network. The processing of Faster RCNN identifies the category of the target. The experimental results show that the ROI extraction strategy proposed can detect the potential target area in UAV aerial image quickly, eliminate a large number of redundant information in the image, and accelerate the speed of detection and classification.

References

1. Sun, W., Cheng, H., Qiu, R.: Remote sensing image target localization algorithm. Infrared Technol. **10**, 831–835 (2015)
2. Wang, H., Dong, Y., Yuan, B.: An effective line extraction algorithm in aerial image. J. Wuhan Univ. (Inf. Sci. Edn.) **37**(2), 160–164 (2012)

3. Wang, H.: Research on target recognition and tracking technology of UAV based on visual perception. Beijing Institute of Technology (2015)

4. Tong, X.: Research on moving target detection and tracking method of aerial video. Northwestern Polytechnical University (2015)

5. Sarkar, S., Duncan, K.: Relational entropy-based saliency detection in images and videos. In: IEEE International Conference on Image Processing. IEEE (2013)

6. Dapeng, L., Longsheng, W.: Saliency remote sensing image object detection model based on visual attention mechanism. Comput. Eng. Appl. **50**(19), 11–15 (2014)

7. Meng, L.: Saliency detection for color image based on visual attention mechanism. Appl. Res. Comput. **30**(10), 3159–3161 (2013)

8. Numano, S., Enami, N., Ariki, Y.: Task-driven saliency detection on music video. In: Jawahar, C.V., Shan, S. (eds.) ACCV 2014. LNCS, vol. 9009, pp. 658–671. Springer, Cham (2015). https://doi.org/10.1007/978-3-319-16631-5_48

9. Wu, F.J., Wei, C.C., Guan, S.Q.: Tool wear detection based on visual saliency mechanism. Appl. Mech. Mater. **602–605**, 1891–1894 (2014)

10. Leavers, V.F.: Which Hough transform? CVGIP Image Underst. **58**(2), 250–264 (1993)

11. Itti, L., Koch, C.: A saliency-based search mechanism for overt and covert shifts of visual attention. Vis. Res. **40**(12), 1489–1506 (2000)

12. Lei, Y., Ji, M.: A study of the classification of imbalanced data streams based on random balance sampling. J. Yunnan Univ. Nationalities (Nat. Sci. Edn.) **027**(001), 63–68 (2018)

13. Trecvid, Q.A., Related, S.: Visualizing and Understanding Convolutional Networks [104]

14. Simonyan, K., Zisserman, A.: Very deep convolutional networks for large-scale image recognition. Computer Science (2014)

15. Liu, W., Anguelov, D., Erhan, D., et al.: SSD: Single Shot MultiBox Detector. Springer, Cham (2016)

Joint Face Detection and Landmark Localization Based on an Extremely Lightweight Network

Yuxiang Liu⬤, Chen Chen⬤, Maojun Zhang$^{(\boxtimes)}$⬤, Jingbei Li⬤, and Wei Xu

College of Systems Engineering, National University of Defense Technology, Changsha, China
mjzhang@nudt.edu.cn

Abstract. Face detection and landmark localization are necessary steps in most face applications. At present, the method based on deep learning has shown obvious advantages in effect. However, most neural networks are computationally expensive and require special hardware for acceleration. To widely applied in real-world tasks, it is necessary to design a tiny model with fewer parameters, less computation cost, and fine performance. Therefore, we propose an extremely lightweight backbone for building a YOLOv3-style joint face detection and landmark localization model while compressing the parameters to the 0.15M level. We compare the proposed face detector with representative methods on the public benchmark. The results show that our proposed method can achieve performance much close to the representative face detector while a two-thirds reduction in the numbers of parameters and the computing costs. Moreover, our model has a lower failure rate (10%) of landmark localization and more robust.

Keywords: Face detection · Facial landmark localization · Lightweight model.

1 Introduction

There is an increasing number of scenarios where face information needs to be used to improve efficiency or increase security, such as intelligent security and face payment systems. These applications are all dependent on fast and accurate face recognition technology. For various face information analysis applications, the face detection and landmark localization are the most crucial steps. Although several excellent face detection and alignment methods have been proposed, the numbers of model parameters are relatively large, resulting in massive storage space and computation required for inference. The devices used in many application scenarios, such as FPGAs and IoT terminal chips, are greatly limited in their computational resources. Therefore, it is not possible to deploy huge

This research was partially supported by National Basic Enhancement Research Program of China under key basic research project, National Natural Science Foundation (NSFC) of China under project No. 61906206, 62071478.

deep neural network models in these devices. In this paper, we investigate how to reduce the model parameters and computation costs while keeping detection accuracy within an affordable range.

This paper addresses the problem of oversized and computationally intensive models by designing a lightweight, multi-task network that jointly learns face detection and landmark localization. We will introduce our work in the following three parts.

- We design an extremely lightweight backbone with only 50 k parameters, which can provide abundant visual features for face detection under limited resources.
- We build an Extremely Lightweight Face detector (ELFace) which can jointly detect face and predict landmark based on our extremely lightweight backbone. The FLOPs of our model are less than 137 M under the input image of 320×240.
- To obtain the optimal weights of each loss and data augmentation configuration, we use Tree-structured Parzen Estimator (TPE) [2] to search for the best value. Furthermore, through the Proximal policy optimization (PPO) algorithm [20], we get a more suitable feature fusion layer structure for a better trade-off between performance and model size.

2   Related Work

Face Detection is a fundamental problem in face recognition and a significant research area in computer vision. Many excellent methods have emerged in general object detection in recent years [7,18], and face detection has made great progress [14,16] on top of general object detection. Face detection is characterized by a small variation in the detected face region's aspect ratio, usually between 0.5 and 1.5. However, the entire face region scale varies considerably, from just a dozen pixels for small faces to several thousand pixels for large faces. Current state-of-the-art methods [14,22] mostly use a one-stage framework, which uses scaling on a feature pyramid after intensive sampling. Compared to two-stage methods [3,25], the models are generally more lightweight and have a faster inference speed while maintaining good detection accuracy. Therefore, to compress the numbers of parameters as much as possible and increase inference speed, we used a one-stage framework for the network structure design.

Face Landmark Localization algorithm is designed to automatically identify the location of key points in a facial image or video that describe the unique facial components (e.g., the center of the eyes). The Dlib [10] open library is the most popular manual-feature-based extractor for facial landmark localization, mainly using the ensemble method of regression trees proposed by Kazemi and Sullivan [9]. Another kind of method adopts deep neural networks. Sun [21] first proposed a cascaded network structure to extract facial landmarks. This method coarsely extracted facial landmarks in a deeper network at first and then optimized the results using an external network. Since then, many researchers have investigated how to use CNNs to extract facial landmarks. MTCNN [26] took this idea and proposed a deep cascaded multi-task framework that exploits the inherent correlation between face detection and alignment. This model consists of three networks, to detect face boxes with five facial landmarks from coarse to fine. Besides, other researchers proposed several targeted loss function for the coordinate regression problem in the facial landmark. Feng proposed Wingloss [5] aiming to improve deep neural networks training with a small to medium range of error. To reduce the impact of manual annotation noise on the training procedure, Rwing loss [6] omits minimal errors by rectifying the loss function around zero. The method that currently achieves the best performance is HRNet [23], which uses deeply high-resolution representation learning for visual recognition.

Lightweight Model has recently gained considerable development. Researchers have designed several various two-stage or one-stage lightweight detectors to apply deep-learning-based methods on numerous scenarios with limited computational resources. ThunderNet [15] designed a lighter backbone and utilized efficient RPN context enhancement modules and spatial attention modules. Light-Head R-CNN [12] used thin feature maps and inexpensive R-CNN subnets to make the head as light as possible. MobilenetV3 [8] inherited the deep convolution and extends it with linear bottlenecks and reverse residuals while adding NAS(Neural Architecture Search) techniques to obtain a more suitable network structure. The above methods achieve a trade-off between accuracy and model size, but we aim to develop a face detector with extremely few parameters and computational costs.

3 ELFace

The current mainstream neural network mainly consists of a backbone to extract features and the output modules to respond to a specific task. Besides, the neck network is added between the backbone and the output layer to fuse the output feature maps from the backbone in some tasks. We also used this backbone, neck layer, output layer framework to build the lightweight model, and the whole pipeline is shown in Fig. 1.

3.1 Network Architecture

Backbone is the foundation of the whole network and plays a vital role in feature extraction of later face detection and landmark localization. Inspired by the generic detector YOLOv3 [17], we design our backbone based on the Darknet-53 framework. Also, drawing on the idea of residual networks, we design a series of blocks containing multiple convolutional layers. We use shortcut and route layers to connect the front and back feature layers, as shown in Fig. 2. The input feature maps of the convolution unit are divided into two parts. One part is processed directly by the max-pooling layer, and the other part is processed by an iterative body consisting of multiple blocks to obtain more feature information. Finally, the outputs of the two branches are fused. In the upper branch, each

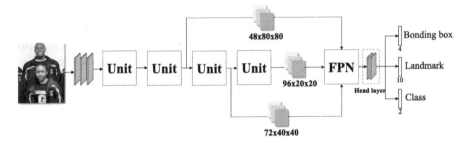

Fig. 1. The framework of our ELFace: The entire network consists of backbone, FPN, and Head layer. Assuming the input image is 640×640, the first three convolutional layers of the backbone first downsample the input image. Then four sequentially connected feature extraction units are used to extract multi-scale features, and the 8-,16-and 32-fold downsampled feature maps are fed into the FPN for feature fusion. The feature maps are then converted into 16-dimensional by the head layer. Eventually, the output is the class, bounding box, and landmark.

block processes the feature map similarly. First, the feature map is downsampled by a convolutional layer of stride 2. And then, four blocks are connected in a series to extract deeper visual information. Additionally, to smoothly obtain a downsampled feature map of the input image, we added a stream convolutional layer between the input and the Unit.

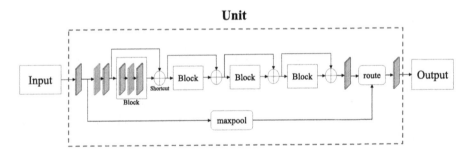

Fig. 2. A convolutional unit in the backbone, which consists of two branches. The yellow quad represents a 3×3 convolutional layer and the blue represents a 1×1 convolutional layer. Each block has the same structure. After the operation of a block is completed, sum its output and input. Then input the result into the next block, and so on.

Neck Layer is used to fuse the features extracted from the backbone. We choose the popular FPN [13] structure to fuse the low-level features with the high-level features. This design allows the information from the multi-scale layers to be fully utilized, thus improving performance.

Head Layer consists of a set of convolutional layers and an output layer. First, convolutional layers convert the three scales fused feature maps to the feature map with the same channels. The converted feature map is then transmitted to the final output layer, which is processed by the regressor (or decoder) into a set of sixteen-dimensional tensors that include the face boxes (x, y, w, h), the class (if it is a face region, we consider it as positive and set it to 1; otherwise, we set it to 0), the confidence (range in [0,1]) and five facial landmarks (p1x, p1y,..., p5x, p5y).

3.2   Loss Function

Training a model that simultaneously detects faces and predicts face landmarks can be seen as a multi-tasking process. Therefore we use the typical joint optimization approach of multiple loss functions. Four targeted loss functions are used for each part of the output, and the individual loss is eventually weighted and summed to form the total loss for optimization.

Bounding Box Loss: For YOLOv3 style object detection networks, the number of anchor groups is limited, so it is usual to encounter a situation where the predicted box does not overlap with the ground truth at all. *Giou* [19] is aimed to solve this problem. It tends to find a minimum closed region C to enclose the prediction box and truth box. The overall calculation is shown in the following Eq. 1 and 2, where *IoU* denotes the intersection ratio of the predicted box to the actual box. And A_c denotes the total area of the region C.

$$GIoU = IoU - \frac{A_c - U}{A_c} \tag{1}$$

$$L_{Box} = 1 - GIoU \tag{2}$$

Point Loss: To predict the five facial landmarks, the distance between the predicted point coordinates and the true value is usually calculated directly by *L1* or *L2* Loss. Feng et al. [5] compared various loss functions and found that loss functions such as *L1* and *L2* Loss performed well for large errors but failed to optimize for small or medium range errors. As a result, we replace *L1* and *L2* with *Wingloss* [5], which can behave as a logarithmic function with an offset for small errors while as *L1* Loss for large errors. We can define such a composite loss function as:

$$L_{point} = Wing(x) = \begin{cases} w\ln(1 + |x|/\epsilon), & \text{if } |x| < w \\ |x| - C & \text{otherwise} \end{cases} \tag{3}$$

where the range of the non-linear parts is set to $(-W, W)$ using a non-negative number W, ϵ limiting the curvature of the non-liner region, $C = w - w\ln(1 + W/\epsilon)$ is a constant for the linear and non-linear components [5].

Class and Objective Loss: As only the face needs to be detected in this task, the face and background can be considered a binary classification problem. Therefore, we use *BCE With Logits Loss* to calculate the classification loss and confidence loss.

$$loss(z, y) = mean\{l_0...l_{N-1}\} \tag{4}$$

$$l_n = -(y_n * \log(\delta(z_n)) + (1 - y_n) * \log(1 - \delta(z_n))) \tag{5}$$

With Eq. 2 3 and 5, the total loss funcion is defned as:

$$L_{total} = \alpha * L_{box} + \beta * L_{point} + \lambda * L_{cls} + \gamma * L_{obj} \tag{6}$$

where α, β, λ, γ represents the weights of each loss function.

3.3   Parameters and Architecture Optimizing

The joint face detection and landmark localization model may have large differences in the magnitude of the loss values between tasks during training. Simultaneously, some hyper-parameters such as learning rate and data enhancement may also affect the final performance to some extent. Therefore, we use the TPE optimization algorithm [2] based on the probabilistic model to simultaneously find more suitable weights for each loss and other configurations.

Table 1. Comparison of the number of parameters and FLOPs

Model	Feature fusion	Parameters	FLOPs(M)
MTCNN	–	481,336	571
RetinaFace	–	426,608	383
MobileNetV3-YOLOv3	–	393,816	274
ELFaceV1	conv3+conv1	133,386	107
ELFaceV2	conv1+conv3	133,386	97
ELFaceV3	conv1+conv1	100,618	87
ELFace	conv3+conv3	166,154	137

After completing the entire model, we find that the number of parameters in the neck layer, which is the feature fusion layer, accounted for half of all parameters. To further optimize the network structure, we choose PPO [20] to search the network structure, mainly for the FPN module. We hope to minimize the number of parameters while maintaining the model performance. We design several kinds of structures for merge1, merge2, the two feature fusion modules. The number of parameters and FLOPs for each model is shown in the following Table 1. The conv1 represents a 1×1 convolutional kernel for feature fusion, and conv3 is a 3×3 convolutional kernel. We calculated the FLOPS by using a 3-channel 320×240 image as the input image. As shown in the following table, we can see that our proposed model has a significant reduction in the number of model parameters and computational complexity. The performance of each model is shown in detail in Sect. 4.3.

4   Experiment

In this section, we first introduce the implementation details and experiment configurations of the proposed method. Secondly, we compare our approach with the several representative methods on the benchmark dataset.

4.1   Dataset

The most popular benchmark dataset in face detection is WIDER FACE [24], which consists of 32,203 images and 393,703 face bounding boxes with a high degree of variability in scale, pose, expression, occlusion, and illumination. To train a detector capable of localizing face and landmarks simultaneously, RetinaFace [4] filled in the data gaps by manually annotating five face landmarks on the training set of the WIDER FACE [24] dataset. Therefore, we also used this dataset as training data. Moreover, the WIDER FACE [24] test set faces can be categorized into three difficulty levels (i.e., Easy, Medium, and Hard) based on the detection rates of EdgeBox [28].

Annotated Facial Landmarks in the Wild (AFLW) [11]contains the facial landmarks annotations for 24,386 faces, and we use the same test subset as AFLW-Full protocol [27]. Our experiments extracted five landmarks - the left eye and right eye center, the tip of nose, and the left and right corner of mouth - as our test data.We adopt the widely used Normalised Mean Error (NME) metric to evaluate the facial landmark localization performance. For the AFLW dataset, we follow Zhu et al. [27] to use the face box size to normalized the NME. Additionally, the failure rate is defined as the proportion of the test images with NME higher than 1×10^{-2}. Finally, we evaluate the computational efficiency of our face detector.

4.2   Implementation Details

Data Augmentation: To perform data augmentation, we randomly flipped each training image with the probability of 50% and randomly rotated each training image between $[-30, 30]$ degrees. For bounding box perturbation, we randomly panned the top left and bottom right corners of the original face bounding box given by the training sample. Besides, We perform random scaling for training images, with a minimum of 67% of the original size and a maximum of 150% of the original size. In addition to random cropping, we also enhance the training dataset by applying photometric color distortion.

Training and Testing Details: The experiments were conducted on a server with Intel Core i7 6700 k CPU @4.00 GHz, 64 GB RAM, and one NVIDIA GeForce RTX 2080Ti. We adopt Adam as the optimizer and weight decay is set at 0.0005, and batch size of 32. The learning rate starts from 1×10^{-3}, and the training process is terminated at 300 epochs.

We use the TPE [2] Tuner in the Microsoft NNI [1] toolkit to search for the optimal learning rates and weights for each loss. At the same time, we search for the most suitable data augmentation configurations within a pre-defined range. Then we use the PPO [20] Tuner to find a more suitable structure for the FPN layer.

4.3   Evaluation Results

Face Detection: For the face detection task, we compared our model with the state-of-the-art method on the validation set of WIDER FACE[24], and the results are shown in the following Table 2. The RetinaFace [4] equip the MobileNet-0.25 backbone. And the YOLOv3 model using MobileNetV3 as the backbone. As can be seen, ELFaceV1 and ELFaceV2 have similar performance for the same number of parameters, while ELFaceV3 has the least number of parameters. However, the performance of ELFaceV3 reduces to an excessively low level. Eventually, our ELFace get a great trade-off between model size and performance.

Table 2. Evaluation results on WIDER FACE val [24]

Model	Easy	Medium	Hard
RetinaFace [4]	**0.879**	**0.807**	0.641
MobileNetv3-YOLOv3	0.832	0.796	0.553
ELFaceV1	0.698	0.670	0.562
ELFaceV2	0.687	0.679	0.556
ELFaceV3	0.534	0.493	0.231
ELFace	0.787	0.727	**0.652**

Five Facial Landmark Localization: We compare our methods with the classical MTCNN and the two methods mentioned earlier on the landmark task. Given the experimental results in face detection, we have only compared the results of the ELFace tests. The NME for each landmark, the overall NME, and the Failure Rate (the NME threshold at 10%) for the tests conducted on the test set of AFLW are shown in the Table 3, where Left Eye Center(LEC) and Right Eye Center(REC) mean center points of the left and right eyes respectively, Left Mouth Corner(LMC) and Right Mouth Corner(RMC) are the corners of the left and right mouths, and Nose means the tip of the Nose. The overall NME of MTCNN [26] and RetinaFace [4] is lower, but the Failure Rate of our methods shows an obvious advantage. That means that our model has a much lower probability of predicting large deviations. Although the overall NME is higher, our model performance more robust to faces in various poses. It is worth noting that this is achieved with a two-thirds reduction in the number of parameters.

Table 3. Comparison of the NME and Failure rate

Model	LEC	REC	Nose	LMC	RMC	NME(%)	Failure rate(10%)
MTCNN [26]	2.53	2.64	3.12	2.74	2.79	2.75	13.31
RetinaFace [4]	2.16	2.03	2.29	2.27	2.31	**2.21**	9.37
MobileNetv3-YOLOv3	5.61	5.49	5.59	5.32	5.27	5.51	7.12
ELFace	4.92	5.01	5.18	5.21	5.24	5.20	**4.92**

5 Conclusion

In this paper, we propose an extremely lightweight backbone network, and a joint face detection and landmark detection model is designed by combining the FPN structure with ideas from YOLOv3 [17]. The TPE algorithm based on the probabilistic model is used to optimize the Hyper-parameter, while the PPO algorithm is to search for the structure of the feature fusion layer in training. In the end, we reduce the number of parameters and the computing cost by more than two-thirds, maintaining an acceptable level of performance. Moreover, our methods can reach higher robustness on relatively specific images. Further research may focus on how existing models can be ported and optimized for some common mobile platforms.

References

1. Microsoft NNI(neural network intelligence) (2021). https://github.com/Microsoft/nni
2. Bergstra, J., Bardenet, R., Bengio, Y., Kégl, B.: Algorithms for hyper-parameter optimization. In: 25th annual conference on Neural Information Processing Systems (NIPS 2011), vol. 24. Neural Information Processing Systems Foundation (2011)
3. Chi, C., Zhang, S., Xing, J., Lei, Z., Li, S.Z., Zou, X.: Selective refinement network for high performance face detection. In: Proceedings of the AAAI Conference on Artificial Intelligence, vol. 33, pp. 8231–8238 (2019)
4. Deng, J., Guo, J., Ververas, E., Kotsia, I., Zafeiriou, S.: Retinaface: Single-shot multi-level face localisation in the wild. In: Proceedings of the IEEE/CVF Conference on Computer Vision and Pattern Recognition, pp. 5203–5212 (2020)
5. Feng, Z.H., Kittler, J., Awais, M., Huber, P., Wu, X.J.: Wing loss for robust facial landmark localisation with convolutional neural networks. In: Proceedings of the IEEE Conference on Computer Vision and Pattern Recognition, pp. 2235–2245 (2018)
6. Feng, Z.H., Kittler, J., Awais, M., Wu, X.J.: Rectified wing loss for efficient and robust facial landmark localisation with convolutional neural networks. Int. J. Comput. Vis. **128**, 1–20 (2019)

7. Girshick, R.: Fast R-CNN. In: Proceedings of the IEEE International Conference on Computer Vision, pp. 1440–1448 (2015)
8. Howard, A., et al.: Searching for mobilenetv3. In: Proceedings of the IEEE/CVF International Conference on Computer Vision, pp. 1314–1324 (2019)
9. Kazemi, V., Sullivan, J.: One millisecond face alignment with an ensemble of regression trees. In: Proceedings of the IEEE Conference on Computer Vision and Pattern Recognition, pp. 1867–1874 (2014)
10. King, D.E.: Dlib-ml: a machine learning toolkit. J. Mach. Learn. Res. **10**, 1755–1758 (2009)
11. Koestinger, M., Wohlhart, P., Roth, P.M., Bischof, H.: Annotated facial landmarks in the wild: a large-scale, real-world database for facial landmark localization. In: 2011 IEEE International Conference on Computer Vision Workshops (ICCV workshops), pp. 2144–2151. IEEE (2011)
12. Li, Z., Peng, C., Yu, G., Zhang, X., Deng, Y., Sun, J.: Light-head r-cnn: In defense of two-stage object detector. arXiv preprint arXiv:1711.07264 (2017)
13. Lin, T.Y., Dollár, P., Girshick, R., He, K., Hariharan, B., Belongie, S.: Feature pyramid networks for object detection. In: Proceedings of the IEEE Conference on Computer Vision and Pattern Recognition, pp. 2117–2125 (2017)
14. Najibi, M., Samangouei, P., Chellappa, R., Davis, L.S.: SSH: single stage headless face detector. In: Proceedings of the IEEE International Conference on Computer Vision, pp. 4875–4884 (2017)
15. Qin, Z., et al.: ThunderNet: towards real-time generic object detection on mobile devices. In: Proceedings of the IEEE/CVF International Conference on Computer Vision, pp. 6718–6727 (2019)
16. Ranjan, R., Patel, V.M., Chellappa, R.: Hyperface: a deep multi-task learning framework for face detection, landmark localization, pose estimation, and gender recognition. IEEE Trans. Pattern Anal. Mach. Intell. **41**(1), 121–135 (2017)
17. Redmon, J., Farhadi, A.: Yolov3: an incremental improvement. arXiv preprint arXiv:1804.02767 (2018)
18. Ren, S., He, K., Girshick, R., Sun, J.: Faster R-CNN: towards real-time object detection with region proposal networks. IEEE Trans. Pattern Anal. Mach. Intell. **39**(6), 1137–1149 (2016)
19. Rezatofighi, H., Tsoi, N., Gwak, J., Sadeghian, A., Reid, I., Savarese, S.: Generalized intersection over union: a metric and a loss for bounding box regression. In: Proceedings of the IEEE/CVF Conference on Computer Vision and Pattern Recognition, pp. 658–666 (2019)
20. Schulman, J., Wolski, F., Dhariwal, P., Radford, A., Klimov, O.: Proximal policy optimization algorithms. arXiv preprint arXiv:1707.06347 (2017)
21. Sun, Y., Wang, X., Tang, X.: Deep convolutional network cascade for facial point detection. In: Proceedings of the IEEE Conference on Computer Vision and Pattern Recognition, pp. 3476–3483 (2013)
22. Tang, X., Du, D.K., He, Z., Liu, J.: Pyramidbox: a context-assisted single shot face detector. In: Proceedings of the European Conference on Computer Vision (ECCV), pp. 797–813 (2018)
23. Wang, J., et al.: Deep high-resolution representation learning for visual recognition. IEEE Trans. Pattern Anal. Mach. Intell. (2020)
24. Yang, S., Luo, P., Loy, C.C., Tang, X.: Wider face: a face detection benchmark. In: Proceedings of the IEEE Conference on Computer Vision and Pattern Recognition, pp. 5525–5533 (2016)
25. Zhang, C., Xu, X., Tu, D.: Face detection using improved faster rcnn. arXiv preprint arXiv:1802.02142 (2018)

26. Zhang, K., Zhang, Z., Li, Z., Qiao, Y.: Joint face detection and alignment using multitask cascaded convolutional networks. IEEE Sig. Process. Lett. **23**(10), 1499–1503 (2016)
27. Zhu, S., Li, C., Loy, C.C., Tang, X.: Unconstrained face alignment via cascaded compositional learning. In: Proceedings of the IEEE Conference on Computer Vision and Pattern Recognition, pp. 3409–3417 (2016)
28. Zitnick, C.L., Dollár, P.: Edge boxes: locating object proposals from edges. In: Fleet, D., Pajdla, T., Schiele, B., Tuytelaars, T. (eds.) ECCV 2014. LNCS, vol. 8693, pp. 391–405. Springer, Cham (2014). https://doi.org/10.1007/978-3-319-10602-1_26

Extremely Tiny Face Detector
for Platforms with Limited Resources

Chen Chen⬤, Maojun Zhang⬤, Yang Peng, Hanlin Tan⬤,
and Huaxin Xiao$^{(\boxtimes)}$⬤

College of Systems Engineering, National University of Defense Technology,
Zunyi, China
xiaohuaxin@nudt.edu.cn

Abstract. Face detection is a fundamental step for face analysis tasks. In recent years, deep learning-based algorithms in face detection have grown rapidly. Most neural networks are computationally expensive and rely on graphics processing units, falling to be applied in practical applications. This paper explores the principles of designing tiny models and proposes an extremely tiny face detector based on the tiny-YOLOv3 framework, introducing new network structures such as Cross-Stage-Partial-connections (CSP), depthwise convolution, and Spatial Pyramid Pooling (SPP). The number of parameters is less than 10k, and the storage is less than 50Kb by using half-precision float point (FP16) for each parameter. Furthermore, each layer's peak memory usage is under 0.07MB, leading the model to be accessible to various platforms. The experiments on a subset of the WIDER FACE dataset and Open Images Dataset V4 (OID) show that the proposed face detector can achieve comparable performance to the more massive face detectors heavier in model size and floating-point operations.

Keywords: Face detectoin · Real-time · Loss function · Computational efficiency

1 Introduction

Face-based authentication and recognition can be employed in many scenarios, such as smart surveillance, biometrics authentication, and the Internet of Things (IoT). The first stage in face recognition is generally to detect and locate the faces in images or videos. Therefore, face detection is one of the key steps in the application of face recognition systems. Due to mobile devices and terminals' popularity, face-based authentication and recognition are becoming more and more convenient. However, the computing resources of such devices are heavily limited, especially for FPGA and intelligent chips. Furthermore, many real-world applications only need fast but relatively accurate face predictions under appointed conditions such as specified distance or input image size. In the past few years, deep CNNs have demonstrated great improvement in various computer vision tasks, such as image classification [20], segmentation [1] and

© Springer Nature Switzerland AG 2021
Y. Peng et al. (Eds.): ICIG 2021, LNCS 12889, pp. 362–373, 2021.
https://doi.org/10.1007/978-3-030-87358-5_29

object detection [10,11,16,17,22]. As an important branch of object detection, face detection can inherit many successful techniques from generic object detection. The state-of-the-art face detectors can handle various faces with difficult challenges such as rotation and occlusion.

While these methods achieved impressive detection performance, they commonly suffer from two main problems in real-world applications. One is the large number of parameters and floating-point operations (FLOPs). Most real-world tasks capture images in a fixed direction, eliminating multi-scale issues but requiring a high inference speed. Conventional face detectors often pay much attention to precision and adopt prevalent classification networks such as VGG-16 [20], ResNet-50 [5] as their backbone to enhance the diversity of feature representations, which requires huge storage spaces. The second problem, from the memory usage perspective, is the limited computation resources. For most detectors, a larger resolution of input and multi-scale detecting can dramatically boost the performance. However, these operations occupy a high memory usage peak for certain layers. Few detectors are targeted to improve the performance with specified input size.

This paper proposes an extremely tiny face detector (ETFD) for various platforms with limited resources, resolving the two mentioned problems. Our goal is to design an extreme fast face detector with few computation resources for industry application where the scale of face regions are approximately fixed. We follow the one-stage detector tiny-YOLOv3 [16] framework to build our detector. Several convolutional layers and modified CSPNet [23] are combined to build our backbone. The CSPNet can achieve a richer gradient combination while reducing the amount of computation. By replacing the generic convolution operation with depthwise separable convolution [6], we can further decrease the number of parameters and control it around 0.009 million. We also select a series of more suitable anchor boxes and use a novel loss function. On a customized subset of WIDER FACE dataset [26] and OID [8], we achieved better detection accuracy than tiny-YOLOv3 and ten times faster. The main contributions of our work can be summarized as three folds:

- We propose an extremely tiny and efficient face detection model, which can significantly reduce the parameter size and provide abundant feature information. The model is easily trained on GPU equipment and transplanted onto other platforms.
- We design a lightweight backbone network with around 9K of parameters, and the inference speed of one image is within 2 MS on CPU. We also control each layer's memory usage under 0.07 Mb, which meets the demands of various platforms.
- We gain more suitable anchor boxes by k-means clustering and propose a new regression loss function for face detection.

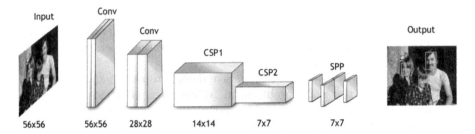

Fig. 1. The overall framework of the proposed method. The input image first gets downsampled by four streaming convolutional layers and then sent to the main iterative body, CSP1, and CSP2, to get rich information. An SPP-like module further processes the output to get information on different resolutions. Finally, a YOLO detection head is adopted to get final predictions.

2   Related Wroks

Face Detection has been an important research topic since the initial stage of computer vision researches. Some representative face detectors based on hand-craft features such as Haar features [22] and deformable part model (DPM) [13] are typical algorithms and achieved decent performance. While deep learning has become dominant, many face detection methods are built with different CNN structures. MTCNN [29] uses three cascade CNNs to detect faces and predicts five landmarks to gain more robust face positions. Faceness-Net [27] adopts a two-stage framework where the first stage generates multi facial parts via attribute-aware networks and the second stage refines the coarse predictions by a multi-task CNN. Recent face detectors have applied the techniques from generic object detectors including Faster-RCNN [17], SSD [11], FPN [10], YOLOv3 [16]. FDNet [28] is based on Faster-RCNN with a lighter head and other tricks, including multi-scale training and deformable convolution. SSH [14] is improved on SSD but draws different layers in VGG-16 for face detection. YOLO-face [3] expands YOLOv3 with a larger backbone and modifies the anchors to fit face detection. The mentioned methods are mostly GPU-based and commonly use a large classification network as their feature extractor. These classification networks learn abundant feature representations with a large number of parameters exceeding 20 million. Face detection should be as much smaller as possible because users generally want their applications not to exceed a few tens of Mb.

Lightweight Generic Object Detectors are aimed at the conditional situation with limited resources. Various two-stage and one-stage lightweight detectors are proposed. Thundernet [15] designs a much lighter backbone and exploits an efficient RPN context enhancement module and spatial attention module. Light-Head R-CNN [9] uses a thin feature map and cheap R-CNN subnet to make the head as light as possible. Mobilenetv2-SSD [19] inherits depthwise convolution [6] and extends it with linear bottleneck and inverted residuals. Pelee [25] is designed to meet strict constraints on memory which follows the connectivity pattern and some of the key design principles of DenseNet [7]. The mentioned methods achieve a relevant trade-off between accuracy and model size. However, we aim to develop a detector with a much smaller number of parameters and computational resources.

3   Extreme Tiny Face Detector

YOLOv3 is a typical one-stage generic object with a powerful backbone, darknet-53. Aimed to compress the model size without losing too much performance, we use its simplified version, tiny-YOLOv3, as our framework. We improved the backbone with depthwise convolution, CSP, and SPP as shown in Fig. 1. We also refined anchor boxes and loss functions to make them more suitable for fast and accurate face detection on limited resources.

3.1   Backbone

Backbone plays a critical role in feature extraction and face localization. For generic object detector YOLOv3, the framework includes a backbone network, namely Darknet-53, for feature extraction; three detection heads for multi-scale predictions, and an embedded FPN is used as the neck to connect them. Darknet-53 consists of multi-scales of residual blocks as ResNet. Shortcut and route layers are used for layer connections. Compared with the ResNet series, darknet-53 is more powerful and more efficient, achieving similar performance to ResNet-152 but two times faster. Low-level features are merged with high-level features via FPN structure. This design can fully utilize the information from multi-scale layers, thus boosting the performance.

Tiny-YOLOv3 aimed to perform object detection with a lighter backbone. Tiny-Darknet-53 has fewer 3 × 3 and 1 × 1 convolution layers and ResBlocks. We believe that residual blocks provide much more semantic information compared to the streaming structure in tiny-YOLOv3. We replace CSPNet with conventional ResNet taking both the performance and the size of the detector into consideration. The accuracy is greatly degraded after lightweightening, while CSPNet can maintain sufficient accuracy after such operation. CSPNet achieves a richer gradient combination while reducing the amount of computation by partitioning the base layer's feature map into two parts and then merging them through a proposed cross-stage hierarchy [24]. We use two CSPNet blocks of different scales. As illustrated in Fig. 2, the input feature maps for CSP1 are divided into two parts. A max-pooling layer directly processes one part, and the other part is processed by an iterative body to get more feature information. The output of the two operations is finally concatenated. The iterative body processes the feature map similarly. We add a few streaming convolution layers before the residual bodies to smoothly get downsamples of input images. After the feature extracting, we follow SPPNet [4] to build the neck. The SPP-like structure applies different sizes of receptive fields to get richer information of different resolutions. One unique property of this module is that this method achieves comparable performance to FPN but much less cost in our task. Given consideration of the application scenarios, we only retain one detection head. With the mentioned modifications, we further decrease the size to 50Kb and. Experiments in Sect. 4 illustrate that the improved backbone has remarkably promoted the performance for face detection.

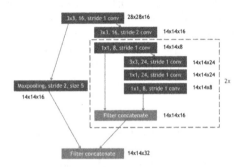

Fig. 2. Structure of CSP1. The rectangles are operation layer and the sizes of output for each layer are denoted behind.

3.2   Anchor Boxes Refinement for Face Detection

The scales and ratios of anchor boxes are very important hyper-parameters in object detection. The shape of anchor boxes should be highly related to the detected targets. For general object detection, the shape of anchor boxes should contain various kinds of shapes. Empirically, for most faces, the height of most faces is always larger than the width. Therefore, the shape of anchor boxes for face detection should be refined for face detection.

Aimed to select anchor boxes appropriate for face detection, we run k-means clustering on the WIDER FACE training dataset to get the dimensions of bounding boxes. The iterative steps are as follows: 1) We randomly set k clustered anchor boxes as initial clustering centers, subsequently calculating the IoU of the k anchor boxes and all other anchor boxes. The distances of anchor boxes are measured with IoU, and all the face labels are divided into k clusters. 2) We then take the mean values of the k class anchor box sizes are the new initial clustering center for the next round. 3) Steps 1) and 2) are iterated until convergence or preset iteration times. In our experiments, we set the number of initial clustering centers k to 3. The final 3 anchor shapes are: (8,7); (15,15); (34,35).

3.3 Loss Refinement

To train the model, YOLOv3 optimizes a multi-part loss function that is composed of three parts. The loss function is defined as follows:

$$L = \lambda_c \sum_i L_c(c_i, c_{gt}) + \lambda_b \sum_i L_b(b_i, b_{gt}) + \lambda_e L_e \tag{1}$$

where the i is referred to each anchor. And the first term of Eq. 1 is the classification loss L_c, which is a binary cross-entropy loss between target and background. The second term is the sum of the squared error loss of coordinates for bounding box regression. The last term is the prediction score by logistic regression. YOLOv3 sets the distribution of the three terms with equal importance to 1:1:1. However, when referring to face detection, the issue deteriorated to binary classification. To make the loss function more suitable for face detection, we revise the hyperparameters $\lambda_c = 2$, $\lambda_b = 1$ and to $\lambda_e = 1$. Generally, the Intersection of Union (IoU) of predictions and targets is commonly used as the optimizer metric, while Mean Square Error (MSE) is used for regression loss. However, it is hard to optimize MSE and maximize the IoU value in one trail as revealed in [18]. To compensate for this, a generalization of IoU (GIoU) is proposed [18] as a new metric for optimizing MSE and maximizing the metric itself, which is defined as follows:

$$\text{GIoU} = \text{IoU} - \frac{A_c - U}{A_c} \tag{2}$$

where A_c is the smallest enclosing convex set of the predicted location and the ground truth. We improve the classification loss by introducing a weighted GIoU loss, defined as:

$$L_c = \sum_{x,y,w,h} \sum (|c_{pred} - c_{target}| + \alpha\text{GIoU})^2 \tag{3}$$

where the x, y, w and h are the locations and sizes of bounding boxes and we set the α to 0.2 empirically.

4 Experiments and Discussion

4.1 Experimental Setting

Datasets: We build a customized dataset from WIDER FACE [26] and OID [8]. WIDER FACE dataset is a recently released dataset and is similar to the in-the-wild face detection situation. The data are collected from the Internet with manually cleaning, consisting of 393,703 face-bound box annotations in 32,203 images. Specifically, the dataset contains various challenges such as small scales, severe occlusions, and extreme poses. The whole dataset is divided into three subsets according to the difficulties of detection. The whole database is split into three subsets, namely training (40%), validation (20%), and testing (40%). OID contains 9.2M images collected from Flicker with unified annotations. The dataset offers more than 600 classes of objects with various scales. We collected

6150 images from WIDER FACE and 4230 images from OID for training, 1580 and 620 images for testing, respectively. We cropped images from the original dataset and set the scale of images in the customized dataset to 640 × 480. All of the face regions in the images are over 50 × 50 and fully contained.

Training and Variations: We trained our proposed model on an NVIDIA GeForce RTX 2080Ti GPU. The input image size was set to 56 × 56, and the batch size is set to 64. We use SGD as the optimizer with momentum set to 0.95 and weight decay set to 0.005. The learning rate is set to 10^{-3} for the first $20k$ iterations, 10^{-4} for next $25k$ iterations, and the last $5k$ iterations are trained with 10^{-5}. To make the model more versatile and generalizable, we used three data augmentation methods, including random color jittering, flips, and random crops. The LeakyReLU is adopted as our activation function. We also designed two variations which apply different recurrent scheme, namely ResNet and DenseNet. Both of the variations have two recurrent bodies and are trained as identical parameters with the proposed method.

4.2   Evaluation Results

The results in Table 1 show some variations of the proposed method that achieved comparable performance to the baseline model. For a fair comparison, we trained the listed models from scratch at the fixed input size at 56 × 56 with hyperparameters in the referred articles. The tiny-YOLOv3 detector is less capable of predicting the exact location of faces with small-scale inputs. Simultaneously, ETFD shows quite better performance, which means that the learned anchor ratios are more reasonable. When compared to STOA face detectors, PyramidBox, our proposed model *ETFD-CSP* achieved lower results. The margin between PyramidBox and the proposed model on our customized dataset is 4.1%. We notice that PyramidBox is designed for running on GPU while the proposed method is for running on limited resources, thus offering a more decent trade-off with 5000 times fewer parameters. We also compared MemoryPeak(MP) in the last column of Table 1. We can easily observe that most tiny models do not consider the memory peak usage, a critical tache applying to a limited source environment. The proposed model cost 0.07 memory usage at the peak, meeting the most development environment's demands.

4.3   Effects of Various Design Choices on the Performance

In this section, we conduct extensive experiments on our dataset to validate each component of the proposed face detector to improve performance. In the following experiments, the detector's input size in the test phase is still fixed to 56 × 56 pixels. Without special notice, we apply LeakyReLU as the activation function and SGD as the optimizer.

Table 1. Quantitative comparison on customized dataset.

Model	Params(M)	FLOPs(M)	mAP	CPU	MP(MB)
Tiny-YOLOv3 [16]	4.7	92	65.41	348ms	18.52
Pelee [25]	0.9	267	63.76	261ms	32.75
MobileNet-SSD [6]	4.1	473	68.18	475ms	14.88
MobileNetV2-SSD [19]	3.0	291	69.05	428ms	13.71
S3FD + MobileFaceNet [2]	1.2	612	70.90	311ms	85.04
PyramidBox [21]	48.2	11370	75.87	693ms	293.43
ETFD-CSP	0.009	2.4	71.72	5ms	0.07
ETFD-ResNet	0.014	5.5	69.28	17ms	0.56
ETFD-DenseNet	0.011	3.9	70.03	12ms	1.20

Effect of Main Components in Backbone. First, we study each main component's effect in the backbone, namely Depthwise Convolution (DC), CSP module, and SPP module. For comparison, we follow ResNet to build a detector with the same number of iterative bodies. From Table 2, we note that although the performance mAP is slightly decreased by applying Depthwise convolution, the number of parameters is excessively reduced, which is adequate for real-world applications. We observe that CSPNet demonstrates a greater ability to increase the detector accuracy and shrink the model's size due to various improvements. Furthermore, SPP contributes 0.82 point improvement on mAP in the cost of 0.4k of parameters as an acceptable trade-off.

Table 2. Effects of main components in backbone

DC	CSPNet	SPP	ResNet	FPN	mAP	Parameters(k)
	✓	✓			71.93	71.5
✓		✓	✓		69.48	13.6
✓	✓				70.90	9.1
✓	✓			✓	71.13	9.4
✓	✓	✓			71.72	9.5

Effect of Maxpooling Layer. For most CNN-based detectors, max-pooling layer (M) and convolution layer with stride = 2 (C) are often substituted for each other. Detectors with extremely low parameters should clearly distinguish the difference in performance. Generally speaking, max-pooling enjoys lower parameters and a bigger receptive field while convolution layers possess high inference speed. Two places in the entire model involve the choice between the max-pooling layer and the convolution layer. One is in the CSP module, and the other is in the SPP module. The basic choice is to use a max-pooling layer for both structures as the original method did. As listed in Table 3, we note that the replacement in SPP contributes to the result while the interchange in the CSP module dramatically harms the performance. We assume that in the CSP module, the max-pooling layer maintains more information, thus better for feature extraction. Original SPP uses a max-pooling layer to collect information on different scales of receptive fields. However, in our model, the feature map's size is too small to apply the max-pooling operation. Otherwise, convolution operation with different kernel sizes is fitter to integrate information on different scales.

Table 3. Effects of maxpooling layer

CSP	SPP	mAP	Parameters(k)
M	M	71.17	0
C	C	70.40	+0.7
C	M	68.99	+0.4
M	C	71.72	+0.3

Effect of Different Features on Training. We further study the effect of different data augmentation strategies on training. We test conventional data augmentation techniques and some novel strategies, including MixUp, Mosaic. Different activation functions are also considered, such as ReLU, LeakyReLU, Swish, and Mish.

Table 4. Effects of data augmentation strategies

Crop	Flip	Jittering	MixUp	Mosaic	LeakyReLU	mAP
✓				✓		70.01
	✓			✓		70.59
		✓			✓	70.14
			✓		✓	69.57
				✓	✓	69.22
✓	✓	✓			✓	71.72
✓	✓	✓	✓	✓	✓	70.88

As shown in Table 4, for the included data augmentation strategies with LeakyRelu, the conventional methods such as crop, flip, and color jitter all have contributed to the detector's performance. MixUp has little impact on the result, while when we are introducing Mosaic, the training process becomes unsteady and hard to convergence. We assume that Mosaic and MixUp are aimed at generic object detection where varied categories of targets need to be detected within one image, which is not applicable in our task. The Mish activation function is slightly better than the other three methods, as illustrated. However, we did not use Mish because this activation is not efficiently supported on microcontrollers.

4.4   Implementation on Prototyping Platforms

To further illustrate the practicality of ETFD, we transfer several models onto the prototyping platform. We adopt Raspberry Pi (RP) [12] as the development environment. RP is a small, cheap, and hackable computer board power by an Advanced RISC Machine (ARM) structure. The RP can be programmed both with Linux OS and Android. Its central and graphics processing units, audio and communications hardware, and memory chip, are built onto a single component. We use its third version plus as our experiment platform. The GPU is Broadcom Video core-IV, and the CPU of this type is Broadcom BCM2837B0@1.4Ghz with 1GB RAM. The models implemented on the board include one conventional method, Viola-Jones detector, and two CNN-based methods, MobileNetV2-SSD and ETFD. Figure 3 shows the average power usage and FPS on the RP board.

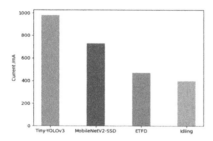

Fig. 3. Raspberry Pi power usage of idling and running different models.

5   Conclusions

This paper proposed a novel face detector for IoT devices that significantly reduces the model sizes while achieving comparable detection accuracy. Following the detection framework of tiny-YOLOv3, we modified its backbone with several techniques to reduce the vast amount of the network parameters and boost the performance for real-world tasks. We also renew the anchor sizes and loss function to make the model more suitable for face detection. Experiment results showed that our model outperforms the baseline model with hundreds time smaller parameters and FLOPS without a pre-trained model. We further test our model on a prototyping platform to valid the adaptivity and flexibility for running in a challenging environment. Further research can be either conducted to polish more complex limiting conditions and propose more robust and accurate methods.

Acknowledgement. FITC: This research was partially supported by National Basic Enhancement Research Program of China under key basic research project, National Natural Science Foundation (NSFC) of China under project No. 61906206, 62071478.

References

1. Chen, L.-C., Zhu, Y., Papandreou, G., Schroff, F., Adam, H.: Encoder-decoder with Atrous separable convolution for semantic image segmentation. In: Ferrari, V., Hebert, M., Sminchisescu, C., Weiss, Y. (eds.) ECCV 2018. LNCS, vol. 11211, pp. 833–851. Springer, Cham (2018). https://doi.org/10.1007/978-3-030-01234-2_49
2. Chen, S., Liu, Y., Gao, X., Han, Z.: Mobilefacenets: efficient CNNs for accurate real-time face verification on mobile devices. In: Chinese Conference on Biometric Recognition, pp. 428–438 (2018)
3. Chen, W., Huang, H., Peng, S., Zhou, C., Zhang, C.: YOLO-face: a real-time face detector. Vis. Comput. **37**, 805–813 (2020)
4. He, K., Zhang, X., Ren, S., Sun, J.: Spatial pyramid pooling in deep convolutional networks for visual recognition. IEEE Trans. Pattern Anal. Mach. Intell. **37**(9), 1904–1916 (2015)
5. He, K., Zhang, X., Ren, S., Sun, J.: Deep residual learning for image recognition. In: Computer Vision and Pattern Recognition, pp. 770–778 (2016)
6. Howard, A., et al.: MobileNets: efficient convolutional neural networks for mobile vision applications. In: Computer Vision and Pattern Recognition, arXiv (2017)
7. Huang, G., Liu, Z., Maaten, L.V.D., Weinberger, K.Q.: Densely connected convolutional networks. In: Computer Era (2017)
8. Kuznetsova, A., Rom, H., Alldrin, N., Uijlings, J., Ferrari, V.: The open images dataset V4: unified image classification, object detection, and visual relationship detection at scale. Int. J. Comput. Vis. **128**(4), 1956–1981 (2020)
9. Li, Z., Peng, C., Yu, G., Zhang, X., Deng, Y., Sun, J.: Light-head R-CNN: in defense of two-stage object detector (2017)
10. Lin, T., Dollar, P., Girshick, R., He, K., Hariharan, B., Belongie, S.: Feature pyramid networks for object detection. In: Computer Vision and Pattern Recognition, pp. 936–944 (2017)
11. Liu, W., et al.: SSD: single shot multibox detector. In: European Conference on Computer Vision, pp. 21–37 (2016)
12. Maksimovic, M., Vujovic, V., Davidovic, N., Milosevic, V., Perisic, B.: Raspberry PI as internet of things hardware: performances and constraints. In: IcETRAN (2014)
13. Mathias, M., Benenson, R., Pedersoli, M., Van Gool, L.: Face detection without bells and whistles. In: Fleet, D., Pajdla, T., Schiele, B., Tuytelaars, T. (eds.) ECCV 2014. LNCS, vol. 8692, pp. 720–735. Springer, Cham (2014). https://doi.org/10.1007/978-3-319-10593-2_47
14. Najibi, M., Samangouei, P., Chellappa, R., Davis, L.S.: SSH: single stage headless face detector. In: International Conference on Computer Vision, pp. 4885–4894 (2017)
15. Qin, Z., et al.: ThunderNet: towards real-time generic object detection on mobile devices. In: International Conference on Computer Vision, pp. 6718–6727 (2019)
16. Redmon, J., Farhadi, A.: YOLOv3: an incremental improvement. In: Computer Vision and Pattern Recognition, arXiv (2018)

17. Ren, S., He, K., Girshick, R., Sun, J.: Faster R-CNN: towards real-time object detection with region proposal networks. In: Neural Information Processing Systems 2015, pp. 91–99 (2015)
18. Rezatofighi, H., Tsoi, N., Gwak, J.Y., Sadeghian, A., Reid, I., Savarese, S.: Generalized intersection over union: a metric and a loss for bounding box regression. In: 2019 IEEE/CVF Conference on Computer Vision and Pattern Recognition (CVPR) (2020)
19. Sandler, M., Howard, A., Zhu, M., Zhmoginov, A., Chen, L.: MobileNetv 2: inverted residuals and linear bottlenecks. In: Computer Vision and Pattern Recognition, pp. 4510–4520 (2018)
20. Simonyan, K., Zisserman, A.: Very deep convolutional networks for large-scale image recognition. In: The Visual Computer (2014)
21. Tang, X., Du, D.K., He, Z., Liu, J.: PyramidBox: a context-assisted single shot face detector. In: Ferrari, V., Hebert, M., Sminchisescu, C., Weiss, Y. (eds.) ECCV 2018. LNCS, vol. 11213, pp. 812–828. Springer, Cham (2018). https://doi.org/10.1007/978-3-030-01240-3_49
22. Viola, P.A., Jones, M.: Rapid object detection using a boosted cascade of simple features. Comput. Vis. Pattern Recogn. 1, 511–518 (2001)
23. Wang, C.Y., Mark Liao, H.Y., Wu, Y.H., Chen, P.Y., Hsieh, J.W., Yeh, I.H.: CSP-Net: a new backbone that can enhance learning capability of CNN. In: Proceedings of the IEEE/CVF Conference on Computer Vision and Pattern Recognition Workshops, pp. 390–391 (2020)
24. Wang, C., Liao, H.M., Yeh, I., Wu, Y., Chen, P., Hsieh, J.: CSPNet: a new backbone that can enhance learning capability of CNN. In: Computer Vision and Pattern Recognition, arXiv (2019)
25. Wang, R.J., Li, X., Ling, C.X.: Pelee: a real-time object detection system on mobile devices. In: Advances in Neural Information Processing Systems, pp. 1963–1972 (2018)
26. Yang, S., Luo, P., Loy, C.C., Tang, X.: Wider face: a face detection benchmark. In: Computer Vision and Pattern Recognition, pp. 5525–5533 (2016)
27. Yang, S., Luo, P., Loy, C.C., Tang, X.: Faceness-Net: face detection through deep facial part responses. IEEE Trans. Pattern Anal. Mach. Intell. 40(8), 1845–1859 (2018)
28. Zhang, C., Xu, X., Tu, D.: Face detection using improved faster RCNN. In: Computer Vision and Pattern Recognition, arXiv (2018)
29. Zhang, K., Zhang, Z., Li, Z., Qiao, Y.: Joint face detection and alignment using multitask cascaded convolutional networks. IEEE Signal Process. Lett. 23(10), 1499–1503 (2016)

Multi-pose Facial Expression Recognition Based on Unpaired Images

Bairu Chen, Yibo Gan, and Bing-Kun Bao[✉]

College of Telecommunications and Information Engineering, Nanjing University
of Posts and Telecommunications, Nanjing, China
bingkunbao@njupt.edu.cn

Abstract. Giving machines the ability to perceive human emotions and enable them to recognize our emotional states is one of the important goals to realize human-computer interaction. In the past decades, facial expression recognition (FER) has always been a research hotspot in the field of computer vision. However, the existing facial expression datasets generally have the problems of insufficient data and unbalanced categories, leading to the phenomenon of over-fitting. To solve this problem, most methods employ the generative adversarial network (GAN) for data augmentation, and achieve good results in facial image generation. But these works focus only on facial identity or head poses, which are not robust for the transformation of facial expression recognition from the laboratory environment to unconstrained scenes. Therefore, we employ the disentangled representation learning to obtain facial feature representation, so as to reduce the impact of pose changes and identity biases on FER. Specifically, the generator uses the encoder-decoder structure to map each face image to two latent spaces: the pose space and the identity space. In each latent space, we disentangle the target attribute from other attributes, and then concatenate corresponding feature vectors to generate a new image with one person's identity and another person's pose. Experimental results on Multi-PIE and RAFD datasets show that the proposed method can obtain high quality generated images and effectively improve the recognition rate of facial expressions.

Keywords: Facial expression recognition · Generative adversarial network · Disentangled representation learning

1 Introduction

Facial expression is used to convey emotional states and intentions for human beings, universally, naturally and powerfully [5]. Due to the practical importance of FER in pain assessment, driver fatigue monitoring, lie detection and many other human-computer interaction systems [15], a great deal of research has been done on facial expression recognition, aiming to classify facial emotions into seven basic expressions, such as happy, angry, sad, disgust, fear, surprise and neutral.

© Springer Nature Switzerland AG 2021
Y. Peng et al. (Eds.): ICIG 2021, LNCS 12889, pp. 374–385, 2021.
https://doi.org/10.1007/978-3-030-87358-5_30

Although deep learning methods have made great progress in facial expression recognition [19,20,22], there are still huge challenges in FER application. On one hand, deep neural network needs sufficient training data to avoid overfitting. However, most of the existing face datasets are taken in the laboratory environment and annotated by hand, which is time-consuming and laborious. Besides, the category and number of facial expressions are limited, leading to the modest recognition rate of facial expressions. On the other hand, facial expression features vary with individual identity, lighting, head pose and other factors, which is also quite difficult for computer recognition.

At present, most of the methods are based on generative adversarial network for data augmentation, and have achieved good results in facial image generation. However, they usually focus only on facial identity or head poses, which are not robust. For example, in Fig. 1, (a) uses a face image as input to synthesize the subject's facial images with different expressions in any pose [27], and the identity of the output image is single. For (b), although using two face images with different identities as input to realize the exchange of facial expressions among different subjects, the influence of poses on facial expressions is ignored. In view of this, we need to take both pose changes and identity biases into account to further enrich the generated face images, so as to expand the face datasets and improve the expression recognition rate. Therefore, this paper focuses on the multi-pose facial expression recognition based on unpaired images.

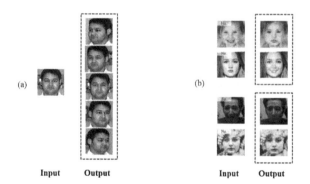

Fig. 1. Examples of face synthesis via CG-FER and GA-FER model respectively.

For multi-pose FER, traditional methods generally fall into three paradigms [27]: (1) Extract features unrelated to pose as facial expression representation. (2) Perform pose normalization for facial images. (3) Establish distinct classifiers for each specific pose. The success of these methods is largely attributed to the high quality of feature extraction. However, existing facial expression recognition methods are mostly based on manual visual features, which are susceptible to the influence of illumination and individual differences, and cannot well cope with the nonlinear facial changes caused by poses [1,6].

For identity bias, existing methods are divided into two categories: one is to learn identity invariant features [17,25,28]; the other is to minimize identity bias by learning distinct model for each specific person [4,26]. The former relys on identity-related image pairs which are difficult to obtain in the real world; the latter is also infeasible due to the lack of annotated facial images.

To address the above issues, we take both pose changes and identity biases into account, proposing the multi-pose FER based on unpaired images. In this paper, the disentangled representation learning is adopted to map each face image to two latent spaces: pose space and identity space. When inputting two images with different identities, a new facial image is generated by concatenating one person's identity vector and another person's pose vector into the decoder. In addition, a classifier is embedded in our model to facilitate image synthesis and facial expression recognition.

To sum up, this paper makes the following contributions:

(1) An end-to-end generative adversarial network is proposed to realize the pose exchange between different identity face images and facial expression recognition.
(2) The disentangled representation learning is applied to obtain facial feature representation, so as to reduce the impact of pose changes and identity biases on FER.

2 Related Work

2.1 Facial Expression Recognition

Facial expression is an important way to convey emotions in nonverbal communication. The process of FER is divided into three steps: image preprocessing, feature extraction and facial expression classification. How to extract the features of facial images effectively is the key step of facial expression recognition. The early FER is to manually extract facial expression features by designing feature extraction algorithm. It includes appearance model algorithm based on landmarks location for face modeling, as well as extraction algorithm based on local features, such as Local Binary Pattern (LBP) [31], Weber Local Descriptor (WLD) [29], multi-feature fusion, Garbor wavelet transform [23] and so on. These artificially designed extraction methods may lose part of the information of images, and are not robust enough for illumination and image scale.

With the success of deep neural network in the field of image classification and recognition, the research on FER based on deep learning has been carried out one after another. However, the training of deep convolutional neural network requires abundant data, and the lack of data will make the model unable to obtain sufficient information, resulting in the phenomenon of over-fitting. Therefore, it is extremely urgent to study the expansion of facial expression datasets. Yan et al. [24] proposed to use GAN for virtual expression images synthesis. Nirkin et al. [18] proposed the FSGAN based on RNN [2] to exchange faces. Zhang et al. [27] proposed a joint pose and expression model to generate images with different expressions in any pose. Nowadays, improving the expression recognition rate via generating a large number of facial images has become one of the research hotspots, but these jobs either focus on pose or identity, which are not suitable for unconstrained scenes. Therefore, this paper overcomes both pose changes and identity biases to generate facial expression images with one person's identity and another person's pose.

2.2 Generative Adversarial Network (GAN)

In 2014, Ian Goodfellow [8] applied the idea of generative adversarial learning to unsupervised learning and proposed a new generative model, GAN. The network uses an unsupervised method to learn the distribution of samples, and generates highly realistic composite data, which is widely used in the field of image. GAN is a kind of neural network which is trained by game theory. In other words, GAN is trained by adversarial learning of generator and discriminator. Using this characteristic of GAN to train the existing datasets, it can generate the artificial samples which are very similar to training samples, just meeting the requirement of expanding the facial expression datasets. Therefore, it is worth studying how to use adversarial network to effectively expand facial expression datasets to alleviate the impact caused by insufficient data and unbalanced categories.

Kaneko et al. [12] added an additional filter structure to CGAN to control the generation of different facial attributes. Similarly, Choi et al. [3] proposed that StarGAN could also be used to generate different facial attributes, such as different hair colors, different ages, different expressions, etc. Although there are many work related to face synthesis, most of them are unable to decouple multiple facial attributes at the feature level, and are confined to paired images of the same person for training. Therefore, this paper proposes a multi-pose facial expression recognition based on unpaired images to decouple facial pose and identity information at the feature level.

3 Proposed Method

3.1 Facial Expression Synthesis and Recognition

We propose an end-to-end facial expression recognition model to realize pose interchange among different facial images with different identities based on generative adversarial network (GAN). The framework of the model is shown in Fig. 2. Before passing a facial image into the model, we first use the "lib face detection" algorithm with 68 points to detect the face. After preprocessing, we input the face image into the encoder to learn the identity and pose representation, and then the corresponding feature vectors are concatenated together and input into the decoder. By adversarial learning between generator and discriminator, a new image with one person's identity and another person's pose can be generated when two face images with different identities are input to the model. Then the original images and the generated images are fed into the classifier for multi-pose facial expression recognition.

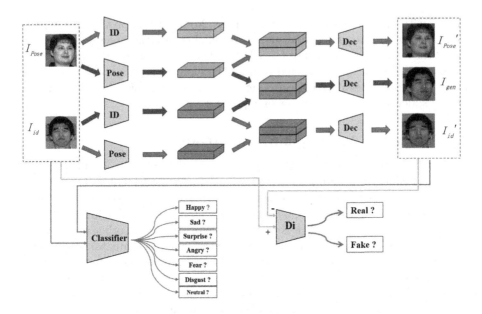

Fig. 2. The overall architecture of our facial expression synthesis and recognition model.

3.2 Network Architecture

Generator. To decouple pose and identity, we employ a two-branch generator network, processing two input streams separately. As shown in Fig. 2, the identity encoder specifically captures identity information, while the pose encoder exclusively captures pose information. Then concatenate the identity and pose features together and feed them into the decoder. In summary, the generator can be expressed as:

$$I_{gen} = G\left(E_i\left(I_{id}\right), E_p\left(I_{pose}\right)\right) \tag{1}$$

Where I_{pose} and I_{id} represent the pose reference image and identity reference image respectively. E_p is the pose encoder, which is composed of continuous Conv - Norm - ReLU blocks, while E_i is the identity encoder, consisting of consecutive Conv - ReLU blocks.

Discriminator. In order to make the model work, we also need a discriminator for adversarial training. With the size of input images larger, the receptive field of a single discriminator is limited. To solve this problem, we use multi-scale discriminators: D_1 denotes the discriminator working at a larger scale, guiding the generator to synthesize facial tiny details, while D_2 is responsible for processing the overall image content to avoid distortion of the generated images.

Classifier. For the classifier, we adopt a deep model, which ensures that the features are not affected by interference factors at each layer, and always maintains the discriminative information related to the recognition task. In this paper, VGGNet-19 network [21] is adopted as the classifier.

3.3 Loss Functions

Decoupling Loss. We use decoupled learning mechanism to control image generation based on identity and pose latent spaces. As shown in Fig. 2, given two images I_{id} and I_{pose} with different identities, the identity information of I_{id} and the pose information of I_{pose} need to be retained respectively to generate image $I_{gen} = G\left(E_i\left(I_{id}\right), E_p\left(I_{pose}\right)\right)$. In order to supervise that the image generated by the model is consistent with the input image in terms of basic facial features, we minimize the L1 distance between I_{gen} and I_{id} :

$$L_{dis} = \left\| I_{id} - G\left(E_i\left(I_{id}\right), E_p\left(I_{pose}\right)\right) \right\|_1 \tag{2}$$

Reconstruction Loss. Because there are many potential solutions to minimize decoupling loss, it alone may not achieve the desired goal. Therefore, in order to guarantee that the pose/identity encoder only encodes the pose/identity information, we require model reconstruction I_{pose} and I_{id} :

$$L_{recon} = \left\| I_{id} - G\left(E_i\left(I_{id}\right), E_p\left(I_{id}\right)\right) \right\|_1 + \left\| I_{pose} - G\left(E_i\left(I_{pose}\right), E_p\left(I_{pose}\right)\right) \right\|_1 \tag{3}$$

Classifier Loss. After synthesizing the facial images, original images and generated images are fed into the classifier for facial expression recognition. Here, we adopt a softmax cross-entropy loss for constraint:

$$L_c = -E\left[-y^e \log C\left(G\left(I\right), y^e\right) - y^e \log C\left(I, y^e\right)\right] \tag{4}$$

Adversarial Loss. In generative adversarial network, the generator is responsible for making the generated sample distribution fit the real sample as much as possible, while the discriminator is to judge whether the input sample comes from the real or the generated. In order to promote the antagonistic game between generator and discriminator, we use multi-scale discriminators. D_1 and D_2 work for different image scales, so as to improve the quality of the generated image and make them more realistic visually. Specifically, we train the generator and discriminator to optimize the following objective function:

$$L_{adv} = \sum_{i=1}^{2} \min_{G} \max_{D_i} E\left[\log D_i\left(I, y\right) + \log\left(1 - D_i\left(G\left(I, y\right), y\right)\right)\right] \tag{5}$$

Total Loss. Combined with all the above loss functions, our model forms the following min-max optimization problem:

$$\min_{G,C} \max_{D_i} \alpha L_{dis} + \beta L_{recon} + L_c + L_{adv} \tag{6}$$

Where, α and β represent the weight of each loss. The whole learning and training process is an iterative optimization of generator and discriminator.

4   Experimental Results

4.1   Datasets

The proposed multi-pose facial expression recognition model based on unpaired images is evaluated on the following two public facial expression datasets:

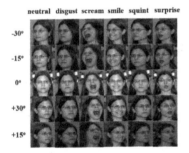

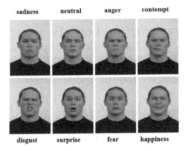

Fig. 3. An example of Multi-PIE images   **Fig. 4.** An example of RAFD images

Multi-PIE. [9] The Multi-PIE is used to evaluate face recognition in a controlled environment with changes in pose, illumination, and expression. It contains images of 337 subjects from 15 different perspectives, with six different emotions: disgust, neutral, scream, smile, squint or surprise. In our experiment, we use 270 subjects in five different poses $(-30, -15, 0, +15, +30)$. Similar to [7], we selected 6,124 face images as training data and 1,531 images as test data. Figure 3 is an example of facial expression images in Multi-PIE.

RAFD. [14] The dataset includes images of 67 subjects of different ages, genders and skin colors in eight different expressions (anger, disgust, fear, happiness, sadness, surprise, contempt and neutral). Each facial expression image corresponds to three different eye directions, and a total of 8,040 facial images are used. Figure 4 shows an example of eight basic expression images. Following the setting in [16], we selected 4,824 facial images of 8 kinds of expressions under three poses $(-45, 0, +45)$, including 3,888 training images and 936 testing images.

4.2   Implementation Details

We construct the network according to the flowchart shown in Fig. 2. First, we employ the "lib face detection" algorithm to cut out the faces, and then resize the images as 224×224. The face pixel value is normalized to $[-1,1]$. To make the model training stable, we design the structure of generator and discriminator with reference to [30]. Specifically, the pose encoder is composed of continuous Conv - Norm - ReLU blocks, while the identity encoder consists of consecutive Conv - ReLU blocks, which are respectively responsible for decoupling the identity and pose characteristics. The decoder, on the other hand, consists of seven deconvolution layers that convert the concatenated vectors into the generated image $I_{gen} = G\left(E_i\left(I_{id}\right), E_p\left(I_{pose}\right)\right)$. For the discriminator D_i, we apply batch normalization following each convolution layer. We use Adam optimizer [13] to train our model, and the learning rate is 0.0002.

4.3   Quantitative Results

4.3.1 Experiments on the Multi-PIE Dataset

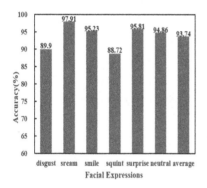

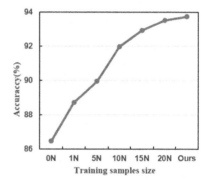

Fig. 5. Facial expression recognition results of Multi-PIE dataset

Fig. 6. Influence of the number of training samples on recognition rate

The facial expression recognition results of our proposed model on Multi-PIE is shown in Fig. 5, with an average FER accuracy of 93.74% in the last column. As can be seen from the graph, compared to other emotions, scream, smile, surprise and neutral are easier to be recognized with accuracy over 93%, which texture changes are more obvious. Among all expressions, the most difficult to be recognized is squint, with the recognition rate of only 88.72%.

Table 1 shows the comparison between our method and the current state-of-the-art methods on the Multi-PIE dataset. The average FER accuracy of each method under all poses are listed in the last column. These methods can be divided into two categories: (1) face expression recognition based on manual features (KNN, LDA, LPP, D-GPLVM, GPLRF, GMLDA, GMLPP, MVDA, DS-GPLVM); (2) face expression recognition based on deep learning (ResNet50 [10], DesNet121 [11], CG-FER, GA-FER).

Table 1. Comparison with existing methods on Multi-PIE dataset.

Methods	Poses					Average
	−30	−15	0	+15	+30	
kNN	80.88	81.74	68.36	75.03	74.78	76.15
LDA	92.52	94.37	77.21	87.07	87.47	87.72
LPP	92.42	94.56	77.33	87.06	87.68	87.81
D-GPLVM	91.65	93.51	78.70	85.96	86.04	87.17
GPLRF	91.65	93.77	77.59	85.66	86.01	86.93
GMLDA	90.47	94.18	76.60	86.64	85.72	86.72
GMLPP	91.86	94.13	78.16	87.22	87.36	87.74
MvDA	92.49	94.22	77.51	87.10	87.89	87.84
DS-GPLVM	**93.55**	**96.96**	82.42	89.97	90.11	90.60
ResNet50	87.54	87.71	84.21	85.90	87.54	86.58
DesNet121	87.71	87.88	84.54	86.23	86.89	86.65
CG-FER	90.76	94.72	89.11	93.09	91.30	91.80
GA-FER	93.07	93.77	**92.83**	92.21	**95.13**	93.40
Ours	93.42	94.78	92.81	**93.15**	94.53	**93.74**

For the first category, the FER results of KNN, LDA, LPP, D-GPLVM, GPLRF, GMLDA, GMLPP, MVDA and DS-GPLVM are provided by [10]. The FER accuracy of our method on the Multi-PIE dataset is 93.74%, which is 17.59% ∼ 3.14% higher than that of the methods in [10]. For the second category, compared with the four deep learning-based methods, our model still has an improvement of 7.16% ∼ 0.34%. Here, GA-FER is trained for increasing the FER rate, through the synthesis of a large number of facial images under different expressions. Different from this method, ours mainly focus on the variable head poses, generating an image with one person's identity and another person's pose. Moreover, except adversarial loss and classifier loss, the proposed model also adopts L1 loss to constrain the discrepancy between generated images and original images. In general, these factors lead to an improvement in expression recognition rate with our method.

Besides, we train the classifier with different number of face images on the Multi-PIE dataset to evaluate the influence of data size on recognition rate. The overall performance of our model is shown in Fig. 6, where m × N (denoted as mN) means that m times generated images are selected, and then they train our model with the original images. 0 × N means that only the original images are used to train the classifier. As can be seen from the graph, with the number of training samples increasing, the FER accuracy is improved, which further indicates the necessity of data augmentation, and also verifies the effectiveness of our facial expression synthesis model.

4.3.2 Experiments on the RAFD Dataset

The results of different poses and expressions on the RAFD dataset are shown in Table 2, which the last column and the bottom row respectively represent the average recognition accuracy of each pose and each expression. The bottom right 81.56% represents the average FER results of our model on RAFD. Of the eight emotions, happiness, anger, surprise and disgust are more likely to be recognized, while the most difficult to be recognized are fear and neutral. To explain this phenomenon, we look closely at face images and find that fear and neutral facial movements are relatively few compared to other expressions, making them difficult to be recognized.

Table 2. Facial expression recognition results on RAFD dataset.

	Happiness	Sadness	Anger	Surprise	Disgust	Fear	Contempt	Neutral	Average
−45	90.5	77	92	85	85	67	75.5	63	79.38
0	95	80	94.5	92	92	72.5	80.5	67	84.19
+45	92	74.5	90.5	87.5	92.5	70.5	77	64.5	81.13
Average	92.5	77.17	92.33	88.17	89.83	70	77.67	64.83	81.56

Table 3. Comparison with existing methods on RAFD dataset.

Methods	Poses		Average
	Angle	Number	
sLDA	(−45, 0, +45)	3	63.3
TDP	(−45, 0, +45)	3	63.7
Multi-SVM	(−45, 0, +45)	3	66.13
TDP-Zhang	(−45, 0, +45)	3	75
VGG16	(−45, 0, +45)	3	72.82
VGG19	(−45, 0, +45)	3	73.5
ResNet50	(−45, 0, +45)	3	74.75
DenseNet121	(−45, 0, +45)	3	74.2
Ours	(−45, 0, +45)	3	**81.56**

In the experiment, we compare our model with existing methods on RAFD dataset, including SLDA, TDP, Multi-SVM, TDP-Zhang (related results are provided in [16]) and VGG16 [21], VGG19 [21], ResNet50 [10] and DenseNet121

[11]. As can be seen from Table 3, our model has a great improvement compared with the methods based on manual features (such as sLDA and TDP), which proves that the features extracted by deep learning methods can achieve better results when dealing with nonlinear facial changes. At the same time, for classic deep learning models such as VGG16 and VGG19, our method still has an improvement of 8.74% ~ 6.81%, fully indicating the synthesis of effective facial expression images via generative adversarial network plays an important role in promoting the FER task.

5   Conclusion

Based on generative adversarial network, we present an end-to-end model for face image synthesis and expression recognition simultaneously. Through the disentangled representation learning, we extract the facial identity information and pose, so as to overcome the challenges brought by pose changes and identity biases. Experiments on Multi-PIE and RAFD demonstrate the effectiveness of the proposed model. In the future, we will further consider the impact of illumination and occlusion on expression recognition, and consider how to expand the seven basic expressions to more complex and varied expressions, so that the study of expression recognition will be closer to real-world scenes.

Acknowledgment. This work was supported by the National Key Research & Development Plan of China 2020AAA0106200, the National Natural Science Foundation of China under Grant 61936005, 61872424, the Natural Science Foundation of Jiangsu Province (Grants No BK20200037).

References

1. Bengio, Y., Courville, A.C., Vincent, P.: Unsupervised feature learning and deep learning: a review and new perspectives. CoRR, p. 2012 (2012)
2. Berglund, M., Raiko, T., Honkala, M., Kärkkäinen, L., Vetek, A., Karhunen, J.T.: Bidirectional recurrent neural networks as generative models. In: NIPS, pp. 856–864 (2015)
3. Choi, Y., Choi, M., Kim, M., Ha, J.W., Kim, S., Choo, J.: StarGAN: unified generative adversarial networks for multi-domain image-to-image translation. In: CVPR, pp. 8789–8797 (2018)
4. Chu, W.S., De la Torre, F., Cohn, J.F.: Selective transfer machine for personalized facial expression analysis. TPAMI **39**(3), 529–545 (2016)
5. Darwin, C., Prodger, P.: The Expression of the Emotions in Man and Animals. Oxford University Press, Oxford (1998)
6. Ding, C., Tao, D.: A comprehensive survey on pose-invariant face recognition. TIST **7**(3), 1–42 (2016)
7. Eleftheriadis, S., Rudovic, O., Pantic, M.: Discriminative shared Gaussian processes for multiview and view-invariant facial expression recognition. TIP **24**(1), 189–204 (2014)
8. Goodfellow, I.J., et al.: Generative adversarial networks. arXiv preprint: 1406.2661 (2014)

9. Gross, R., Matthews, I., Cohn, J., Kanade, T., Baker, S.: Multi-pie. Image Vis. Comput. **28**(5), 807–813 (2010)
10. He, K., Zhang, X., Ren, S., Sun, J.: Deep residual learning for image recognition. In: CVPR, pp. 770–778 (2016)
11. Huang, G., Liu, Z., Van Der Maaten, L., Weinberger, K.Q.: Densely connected convolutional networks. In: CVPR, pp. 4700–4708 (2017)
12. Kaneko, T., Hiramatsu, K., Kashino, K.: Generative attribute controller with conditional filtered generative adversarial networks. In: CVPR, pp. 6089–6098 (2017)
13. Kingma, D.P., Ba, J.: Adam: A method for stochastic optimization. arXiv preprint: 1412.6980 (2014)
14. Langner, O., Dotsch, R., Bijlstra, G., Wigboldus, D.H., Hawk, S.T., Van Knippenberg, A.: Presentation and validation of the Radboud faces database. Cogn. Emotion **24**(8), 1377–1388 (2010)
15. Li, S., Deng, W.: Deep facial expression recognition: a survey. In: IEEE Transactions on Affective Computing. https://doi.org/10.1109/TAFFC.2020.2981446
16. Mao, Q., Zhang, F., Wang, L., Luo, S., Dong, M.: Cascaded multi-level transformed Dirichlet process for multi-pose facial expression recognition. Comput. J. **61**(11), 1605–1619 (2018)
17. Meng, Z., Liu, P., Cai, J., Han, S., Tong, Y.: Identity-aware convolutional neural network for facial expression recognition. In: FG, pp. 558–565. IEEE (2017)
18. Nirkin, Y., Keller, Y., Hassner, T.: FSGAN: subject agnostic face swapping and reenactment. In: Proceedings of the IEEE/CVF International Conference on Computer Vision, pp. 7184–7193 (2019)
19. Parkhi, O.M., Vedaldi, A., Zisserman, A.: Deep face recognition (2015)
20. Schroff, F., Kalenichenko, D., Philbin, J.: FaceNet: a unified embedding for face recognition and clustering. In: CVPR, pp. 815–823 (2015)
21. Simonyan, K., Zisserman, A.: Very deep convolutional networks for large-scale image recognition. arXiv preprint: 1409.1556 (2014)
22. Taigman, Y., Yang, M., Ranzato, M., Wolf, L.: Deepface: closing the gap to human-level performance in face verification. In: CVPR, pp. 1701–1708 (2014)
23. Tian, Y.l., Kanade, T., Cohn, J.F.: Evaluation of Gabor-wavelet-based facial action unit recognition in image sequences of increasing complexity. In: FG, pp. 229–234. IEEE (2002)
24. Yan, Y., Huang, Y., Chen, S., Shen, C., Wang, H.: Joint deep learning of facial expression synthesis and recognition. TMM **22**(11), 2792–2807 (2019)
25. Yang, H., Ciftci, U., Yin, L.: Facial expression recognition by de-expression residue learning. In: CVPR, pp. 2168–2177 (2018)
26. Yang, H., Zhang, Z., Yin, L.: Identity-adaptive facial expression recognition through expression regeneration using conditional generative adversarial networks. In: FG, pp. 294–301. IEEE (2018)
27. Zhang, F., Zhang, T., Mao, Q., Xu, C.: Joint pose and expression modeling for facial expression recognition. In: CVPR, pp. 3359–3368 (2018)
28. Zhang, K., Huang, Y., Du, Y., Wang, L.: Facial expression recognition based on deep evolutional spatial-temporal networks. TIP **26**(9), 4193–4203 (2017)
29. Zhang, Z., Wang, L., Zhu, Q., Chen, S.K., Chen, Y.: Pose-invariant face recognition using facial landmarks and weber local descriptor. Knowl. Based Syst. **84**, 78–88 (2015)
30. Zhang, Z., Song, Y., Qi, H.: Age progression/regression by conditional adversarial autoencoder. In: CVPR, pp. 5810–5818 (2017)
31. Zhong, L., Liu, Q., Yang, P., Liu, B., Huang, J., Metaxas, D.N.: Learning active facial patches for expression analysis. In: CVPR, pp. 2562–2569 (2012)

Keypoint Context Aggregation
for Human Pose Estimation

Wenzhu Wu[1,2], Weining Wang[1,2], Longteng Guo[1,2], and Jing Liu[1,2(✉)]

[1] National Laboratory of Pattern Recognition, Institute of Automation,
Chinese Academy of Sciences, Beijing, China
[2] School of Artificial Intelligence, University of Chinese Academy of Sciences,
Beijing, China
wuwenzhu2019@ia.ac.cn, {weining.wang,longteng.guo,jing.liu}@nlpr.ia.ac.cn

Abstract. Human pose estimation has drawn much attention recently, but it remains challenging due to the deformation of human joints, the occlusion between limbs, etc. And more discriminative feature representations will bring more accurate prediction results. In this paper, we explore the importance of aggregating keypoint contextual information to strengthen the feature map representations in human pose estimation. Motivated by the fact that each keypoint is characterized by its relative contextual keypoints, we devise a simple yet effective approach, namely Keypoint Context Aggregation Module, that aggregates informative keypoint contexts for better keypoint localization. Specifically, first we obtain a rough localization result, which can be considered as soft keypoint areas. Based on these soft areas, keypoint contexts are purposefully aggregated for feature representation strengthening. Experiments show that the proposed Keypoint Context Aggregation Module can be used in various backbones to boost the performance and our best model achieves a state-of-the-art of 75.8% AP on MSCOCO test-dev split.

Keywords: Human pose estimation · Keypoint context · Feature augmentation

1 Introduction

Multi-person human pose estimation aims at recognizing and localizing the anatomical keypoints of all persons in a given image. As one of the most fundamental tasks in computer vision, it serves as a key component for many other vision applications, including human action recognition, human-computer interaction, virtual or augmented reality, etc. Despite the noticeable improvements achieved in this area by advanced deep learning techniques [7, 8, 17, 18, 20, 22, 25, 30], pose estimation still remains extremely challenging. It is still difficult to locate the keypoint coordinates precisely, due to the variation of clothing, the occlusion between the limbs and the deformation of human joints under different poses.

To address the above problems, full utilization of contextual information has been widely concerned. A line of previous works focus on exploring multi-scale

© Springer Nature Switzerland AG 2021
Y. Peng et al. (Eds.): ICIG 2021, LNCS 12889, pp. 386–396, 2021.
https://doi.org/10.1007/978-3-030-87358-5_31

contextual information to enhance the performance of keypoint localization. [15, 20] aggregated multi-scale contexts that generated from well-designed interactions among feature maps of different levels and resolutions. Another line of works are from the perspective of promoting the information communication within a local scope. [6] designed a hierarchical visual attention scheme to zoom in a smaller body part, which generated a specific attention map for each body joint. [1] proposed a novel network - RSN, which aims to learn delicate local representations by efficient intra-level feature fusion.

Although the existing works exploit contextual information from different perspectives, none of them explore keypoint areas as context. However, keypoint context is crucial for precise keypoint localization. Each position on the feature map contains different keypoint information, for example, a specific pixel may contain more characteristics of the left shoulder than the left ankle. Therefore, more characterized keypoint context information aggregation helps to make more accurate localization for prediction. Motivated by this, in this paper, we propose a Keypoint Context Aggregation Module (KCAM) to leverage the relationships between pixels and its contextual keypoints.

For each pixel on the image, KCAM can effectively learn the relationships between it and all human keypoints, thus we can aggregate the keypoint representations purposefully for the current pixel according to their relationships. The augmented feature can lead to more accurate localization. The whole scheme for KCAM can be summarized as follows. Firstly, we obtain a rough keypoint localization result, which can be considered as soft keypoints. Secondly, based on the coarse keypoint localization, we acquire the informative keypoint representations. Thirdly, we compute the relationship between each pixel and all keypoint representations. For the last step, for each pixel, we aggregate keypoint representations purposefully according to the calculated relationships, thus obtaining the augmented feature representation. The augmented feature is then used for final precise keypoint localization. We evaluate the proposed method on the benchmark dataset MSCOCO [16], and experimental results demonstrate the effectiveness of KCAM.

In summary, our main contributions are three-fold as follows:

- We propose a Keypoint Context Aggregation Module for human pose estimation, which can effectively aggregate representative and informative keypoint contextual information for reasonable feature augmentation and conduce more accurate keypoint localization results.
- Keypoint Context Aggregation Module can serve as a model-agnostic refinement method, which can be easily applied to the existing pose estimation methods.
- Our method outperforms state-of-the-art methods on the challenging benchmark MSCOCO dataset for human pose estimation.

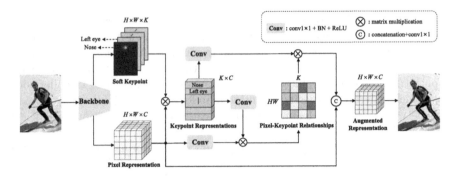

Fig. 1. Illustration of the pipeline of our proposed Keypoint Context Aggregation Module. (a) Acquire rough localization results for soft keypoint areas with intermediate supervision. (b) Obtain the informative keypoint representations. (c) Compute keypoint contextual representations and acquire the aggregated representation. (d) Concatenate original feature representation and the aggregated representation, followed by a conv 1 × 1 layer to get the final augmented feature representation.

2   Related Work

Multi-person Pose Estimation. For multi-person pose estimation, it can be classified into top-down and bottom-up methods. Top-down methods [4,9,11,24–26,29] construct human body poses by detecting the people first and then apply single-person pose estimators to predict the keypoints for each person. Different from top-down methods, bottom-up methods [2,5,10,13,14,19,21,23] detect all the body joints in one image first and then group them into individual poses. In the top-down pipeline, the number of people in the input image will directly affect the computing time. The computing speed for bottom-up methods is usually faster than top-down methods since they do not need to detect the pose for each person separately.

Relational Context. Previous works always explore the relationships among different keypoints. Zhang et al. [31] build a pose graph directly on keypoint heatmaps and use Graph Neural Network for modeling, which only considers the relationship between heatmap weights at the same location, while et al. [27] build pose graph considering the visual features at the position of corresponding keypoints. The above methods are dedicated to strengthening the relationships between keypoints. However, our approach is quite different, that we explore the relationships between feature maps and keypoints.

Coarse-to-Fine Pose Estimation. Various coarse-to-fine pose estimation schemes have been developed to gradually refine the result heatmaps from coarse to fine. Carreira et al. [3] refine pose estimation by predicting error feedback at each iteration, [1,2,20] design a cascaded architecture for mining multi-stage prediction. Our approach in some sense can also be regarded as a coarse-to-fine scheme. The difference lies in that we use the coarse segmentation map for generating a contextual representation instead of directly used as an extra representation.

3   Proposed Method

The overall pipeline of our method is illustrated in Fig. 1. First of all, the input image is sent to the backbone network. Then, taking the backbone output as input, the proposed Keypoint Context Aggregation Module can be summarized as: Firstly, heatmap regression network is applied to acquire rough localization results, which are considered as soft keypoint areas. Secondly, based on the keypoint areas, we obtain the informative keypoint representations. Thirdly, we compute the relationships between each pixel on the feature map and all keypoint representations. Then, we aggregate the feature representations with keypoint context through the computed relationships. Finally, with feature fusion, we acquire the augmented features for precise localization.

3.1   Keypoint Representations

Considering that we will leverage keypoint areas information to augment feature representations, it is essential to roughly locate the keypoint first. We predict K keypoint areas $\{G_1, ..., G_K, G_k \in \mathbb{R}^{H \times W}\}$ from the output feature map $F \in \mathbb{R}^{C \times H \times W}$ of the input image I. Each keypoint area can be described as a 2D heatmap whose per-pixel value g_{ik} indicates the probability of the k-th ($k = 1, 2, ...K$) keypoint's presence at this location i. In order to get more accurate location, we use intermediate supervision here and take the keypoints Guassian maps as ground-truth.

After obtaining the soft keypoint areas, we acquire the keypoint representations $R \in \mathbb{R}^{K \times C}$ through the following formulation:

$$R_k = \sum_{i=1}^{HW} g_{ik} f_i \tag{1}$$

where g_{ik} is the normalized degree for i-th pixel belonging to the k-th keypoint and $f_i \in \mathbb{R}^{1 \times C}$ indicates the representation of this pixel. And $R_k \in \mathbb{R}^{1 \times C}$ is the representation for k-th keypoint.

3.2   Pixel-Keypoint Relationships

In order to model rich contextual relationships, we encode contextual keypoint information into pixel features, thus enhancing feature representations capability. First, we compute the relationships between the feature of each pixel and keypoint representations. Given the original visual feature $F \in \mathbb{R}^{C \times H \times W}$, keypoint representations $R \in \mathbb{R}^{K \times C}$, we firstly feed it into a convolution layer to generate two new features as $F' \in \mathbb{R}^{C \times H \times W}, R' \in \mathbb{R}^{K \times C}$, respectively. After reshaping F to $\mathbb{R}^{C \times N}$, where $N = W \times H$ we apply a matrix multiplication between the transpose of F' and R', and apply a softmax layer to calculate the relationships $S \in \mathbb{R}^{N \times K}$ between pixels and keypoint representations:

$$S_{ij} = \frac{exp(F'_i \times R'_j)}{\sum_{j=1}^{K} exp(F'_i \times R'_j)} \tag{2}$$

where S_{ij} indicates j-th keypoint's impact on i-th pixel. The greater the attention weight is, the more the pixel is related with the corresponding keypoint representation.

3.3   Augmented Representation

Meanwhile, keypoint representations $R \in \mathbb{R}^{K \times C}$ is fed into a convolution layer to generate a new feature $R'' \in \mathbb{R}^{K \times C}$. Based on the above attention map, we compute the aggregated representation $E \in \mathbb{R}^{C \times H \times W}$ as the weighted sum of projected keypoint representations:

$$E_i = \sum_{j=1}^{K} S_{ij} R''_j \tag{3}$$

Then, We combine F and E through concatenation operation, and feed it to a conv 1×1 layer to get the final feature representation $A \in \mathbb{R}^{C \times H \times W}$. The resulting features are used for final keypoints localization.

3.4   Overall Loss Function

The overall loss is composed of two keypoints heatmap losses: one for intermediate supervision result, the other for the final output. The loss function can be described as:

$$L = \alpha L_{inter} + L_{output} \tag{4}$$

where the hyperparameter α is set to 0.2. Both L_{inter} and L_{output} are computed as:

$$L = \frac{1}{N} \sum_{n=1}^{N} \sum_{x,y} ||P_n(x,y) - G_n(x,y)||_2 \tag{5}$$

where $P_n(x,y)$ and $G_n(x,y)$ represent the predicted and the ground-truth confidence maps at the pixel location (x,y) for the n-th keypoint, respectively.

4   Experiments

4.1   Dataset

Our experiments are conducted on human keypoint detection task of the large-scale benchmark MSCOCO dataset [16]. The dataset contains over 200K images and 250K person instances labeled with 17 keypoints. Following the common practice [1], we train our model on MSCOCO trainval dataset (includes 57K images and 150K person instances) and validate on MSCOCO minival dataset (includes 5000 images). We report our main results on the test-challenge set (20K images). Unless specified, we only make use of the human keypoint annotations without bounding-boxes. The performance is computed with Average Precision (AP) based on Object Keypoint Similarity (OKS).

4.2 Implementaion Details

We use two different input sizes (256×192, 384×288) in our experiments. We initialize the backbones using the model pre-trained on ImageNet. Meanwhile, we initialize the Keypoint Context Aggregation Module randomly. The data augmentation includes random rotation ($[-40°, 40°]$), random scale ($[0.5, 1.5]$), and flipping. Following [28], half-body data augmentation is also involved. All models are trained using 4-GPU machines, with a batch size of 128 images. Batch normalization is used in our network. We use the Adam optimizer [12]. The base learning rate is set as 5e-4, and is dropped to 5e-5 and 5e-6 at the 170th and 200th epochs, respectively. The training process is terminated within 210 epochs.

We use the same person detectors provided by SimpleBaseline [29] for both validation and test-dev set. Following the same techniques used in [4], we also predict the pose of the corresponding flipped image and average the heatmaps to get the final prediction; a quarter offset in the direction from the highest response to the second highest response is used to obtain the final location of the keypoints.

4.3 Ablation Studies

We conduct the empirical analysis on MSCOCO validation set. Unless specified, all the ablation experiments are based on the backbone of Resnet-50 with the input size of 256×192.

Table 1. Influence of the soft keypoint supervision scheme. We can find that the soft keypoint supervision scheme is important for the performance.

Method	AP	AP_{50}	AP_{75}	AP_M	AP_L
w/o supervision	70.19	89.59	78.10	66.27	76.99
w/ supervision	**71.87**	**89.77**	**79.89**	**68.26**	**78.45**

Keypoint Region Supervision. We study the influence of the supervision for keypoint areas. We modify our approach by removing the supervision on the soft keypoint areas. We keep all the other settings unchanged and report the results in the Table 1. From the result, we can see that the performance decreased by a large margin without the intermediate supervision. Thus, it can be inferred that the intermediate supervision for the keypoints is crucial for KCAM. The reason is that more accurate localization of the keypoint areas will lead to more informative and representative keypoint representations.

Table 2. Influence of the different feature fusion operations. We can find that concatenation operation is the most effective.

Method	AP	AP_{50}	AP_{75}	AP_M	AP_L
Concatenation	**71.87**	89.77	**79.89**	**68.26**	78.45
Element-wise addition	71.77	89.82	79.41	68.11	**78.50**
w/o fusion	70.94	**89.92**	79.37	67.22	77.61

Feature Fusion. We explore the fusion operation for aggregating the original visual features and the augmented features. Here we discuss the influence of several different ways to fuse these two features. We finally choose the fusion operation which achieves the better performance on AP metric, for AP metric is an overall metric for measuring human pose estimation model performance and is much more important than other metrics. As shown in Table 2, feature concatenation achieves an AP of 71.87, which slightly surpasses element-wise addition operation by an AP of 0.1. Additionally, we study the result of only using the augmented features for final prediction, whose performance decreased by an AP of 0.93. The above results show that the feature fusion is necessary and concatenation operation leads to better performance.

Visualization Analysis. As shown in Fig. 2, we visualize the relationships between the chosen pixel (indicated by stars) and contextual keypoint areas (indicated by circles). Red, blue and other colors denote 1, 0, and the values between them, respectively. The closer to red, the more related to the current keypoint. So the left one shows us, the center point of the person is more relevant to the shoulder and hip, which is spatially closer to it. From the right one we can conclude that, the point on the left calf is more related to the keypoints on limbs. The above results further show that our proposed method effectively aggregates the keypoints context. Incorporating with the keypoint context helps to distinguish the keypoint type for the current pixel. Figure 3 illustrates some results generated using our method. In multi-person scenes, keypoints occluded by clothes or other limbs can also be accurately located.

4.4   Comparison with State-of-the-Art

We compare our method with top-performers including G-RMI [22], CPN [4], HigherHRNet [5], SimpleBaseline [29], and HRNet [25]. Table 3 shows the accuracy results of these state-of-the-art methods and KCAM on the MSCOCO test-dev set. In this test, we use the person detection results from [29]. We have

Fig. 2. Visualization of the relationships between the chosen pixel and contextual keypoint areas. The circles indicate the keypoint areas, while the star indicates the chosen pixel. Red, blue and other colors denote 1, 0, and the values between them, respectively. (Color figure online)

Fig. 3. Visualization of the results predicted by our models.

observed that KCAM with HRNet-W48 at the input size of 384 × 288 achieves the best accuracy. Specifically, compared with the best competitor (HRNet-W48 with the same input size), KCAM further improves AP by 0.3. The result again illustrates the effectiveness of our method.

Table 3. Comparisons on MSCOCO test-dev dataset. (+) indicates models ensembled.

Method	Backbone	Input size	AP	AP_{50}	AP_{75}	AP_M	AP_L
CMU-Pose [2]	–	–	61.8	84.9	67.5	57.1	68.2
Mask-RCNN [7]	ResNet-50-FPN	-	63.1	87.3	68.7	57.8	71.4
G-RMI [22]	ResNet-101	353×257	64.9	85.5	71.3	62.3	70.0
AE [19]	–	–	65.5	86.8	72.3	60.6	72.6
PersonLab [21]	–	–	68.7	89.0	75.4	64.1	75.5
HigherHRNet [5]	HRNet-W48	640×640	70.5	89.3	77.2	66.6	75.8
CPN [4]	ResNet-Inception	384×288	72.1	91.4	80.0	68.7	77.2
CPN+ [4]	ResNet-Inception	384×288	73.0	91.7	80.9	69.5	78.1
SimpleBaseline [29]	ResNet-152	384×288	73.7	91.9	81.1	70.3	80.0
HRNet-W48 [25]	HRNet-W48	384×288	75.5	92.5	83.3	71.9	81.5
Ours	HRNet-W48	384×288	**75.8**	**92.7**	**83.6**	**72.3**	**81.8**

5 Conclusion

In this work, we have proposed a Keypoint Context Aggregation Module for human pose estimation, which can effectively aggregate representative and informative keypoint contextual information for reasonable feature augmentation and conduce more accurate keypoint localization results. We empirically show that our approach brings consistent improvements on MSCOCO benchmark.

References

1. Cai, Y., et al.: Learning delicate local representations for multi-person pose estimation. In: Vedaldi, A., Bischof, H., Brox, T., Frahm, J.-M. (eds.) ECCV 2020. LNCS, vol. 12348, pp. 455–472. Springer, Cham (2020). https://doi.org/10.1007/978-3-030-58580-8_27
2. Cao, Z., Simon, T., Wei, S.E., Sheikh, Y.: Realtime multi-person 2D pose estimation using part affinity fields. In: CVPR, pp. 7291–7299 (2017)
3. Carreira, J., Agrawal, P., Fragkiadaki, K., Malik, J.: Human pose estimation with iterative error feedback. In: CVPR, pp. 4733–4742 (2016)
4. Chen, Y., Wang, Z., Peng, Y., Zhang, Z., Yu, G., Sun, J.: Cascaded pyramid network for multi-person pose estimation. In: CVPR, pp. 7103–7112 (2018)
5. Cheng, B., Xiao, B., Wang, J., Shi, H., Huang, T.S., Zhang, L.: Higherhrnet: scale-aware representation learning for bottom-up human pose estimation. In: CVPR, pp. 5386–5395 (2020)
6. Chu, X., Yang, W., Ouyang, W., Ma, C., Yuille, A.L., Wang, X.: Multi-context attention for human pose estimation. In: CVPR, pp. 1831–1840 (2017)
7. He, K., Gkioxari, G., Dollár, P., Girshick, R.: Mask R-CNN. In: ICCV, pp. 2961–2969 (2017)
8. Huang, J., Zhu, Z., Guo, F., Huang, G.: The devil is in the details: delving into unbiased data processing for human pose estimation. In: Proceedings of the IEEE/CVF Conference on Computer Vision and Pattern Recognition, pp. 5700–5709 (2020)

9. Iqbal, U., Gall, J.: Multi-person pose estimation with local joint-to-person associations. In: Hua, G., Jégou, H. (eds.) ECCV 2016. LNCS, vol. 9914, pp. 627–642. Springer, Cham (2016). https://doi.org/10.1007/978-3-319-48881-3_44

10. Jin, S., et al.: Differentiable hierarchical graph grouping for multi-person pose estimation. In: Vedaldi, A., Bischof, H., Brox, T., Frahm, J.-M. (eds.) ECCV 2020. LNCS, vol. 12352, pp. 718–734. Springer, Cham (2020). https://doi.org/10.1007/978-3-030-58571-6_42

11. Jin, S., et al.: Whole-body human pose estimation in the wild. In: Vedaldi, A., Bischof, H., Brox, T., Frahm, J.-M. (eds.) ECCV 2020. LNCS, vol. 12354, pp. 196–214. Springer, Cham (2020). https://doi.org/10.1007/978-3-030-58545-7_12

12. Kingma, D.P., Ba, J.L.: Adam: a method for stochastic gradient descent. In: ICLR, pp. 1–15 (2015)

13. Kocabas, M., Karagoz, S., Akbas, E.: Multiposenet: fast multi-person pose estimation using pose residual network. In: ECCV, pp. 417–433 (2018)

14. Kreiss, S., Bertoni, L., Alahi, A.: Pifpaf: composite fields for human pose estimation. In: CVPR, pp. 11977–11986 (2019)

15. Li, W., et al.: Rethinking on multi-stage networks for human pose estimation. arXiv preprint arXiv:1901.00148 (2019)

16. Lin, T.-Y., et al.: Microsoft COCO: common objects in context. In: Fleet, D., Pajdla, T., Schiele, B., Tuytelaars, T. (eds.) ECCV 2014. LNCS, vol. 8693, pp. 740–755. Springer, Cham (2014). https://doi.org/10.1007/978-3-319-10602-1_48

17. Luvizon, D.C., Tabia, H., Picard, D.: Human pose regression by combining indirect part detection and contextual information. Comput. Graph. **85**, 15–22 (2019)

18. Moon, G., Chang, J.Y., Lee, K.M.: Posefix: model-agnostic general human pose refinement network. In: CVPR, pp. 7773–7781 (2019)

19. Newell, A., Huang, Z., Deng, J.: Associative embedding: end-to-end learning for joint detection and grouping. In: NeurIPS, pp. 2277–2287 (2017)

20. Newell, A., Yang, K., Deng, J.: Stacked hourglass networks for human pose estimation. In: Leibe, B., Matas, J., Sebe, N., Welling, M. (eds.) ECCV 2016. LNCS, vol. 9912, pp. 483–499. Springer, Cham (2016). https://doi.org/10.1007/978-3-319-46484-8_29

21. Papandreou, G., Zhu, T., Chen, L.C., Gidaris, S., Tompson, J., Murphy, K.: Personlab: person pose estimation and instance segmentation with a bottom-up, part-based, geometric embedding model. In: ECCV, pp. 269–286 (2018)

22. Papandreou, G., et al.: Towards accurate multi-person pose estimation in the wild. In: CVPR, pp. 4903–4911 (2017)

23. Pishchulin, L., et al.: Deepcut: joint subset partition and labeling for multi person pose estimation. In: CVPR, pp. 4929–4937 (2016)

24. Qiu, L., et al.: Peeking into occluded joints: a novel framework for crowd pose estimation. In: Vedaldi, A., Bischof, H., Brox, T., Frahm, J.-M. (eds.) ECCV 2020. LNCS, vol. 12364, pp. 488–504. Springer, Cham (2020). https://doi.org/10.1007/978-3-030-58529-7_29

25. Sun, K., Xiao, B., Liu, D., Wang, J.: Deep high-resolution representation learning for human pose estimation. In: CVPR, pp. 5693–5703 (2019)

26. Umer, R., Doering, A., Leibe, B., Gall, J.: Self-supervised keypoint correspondences for multi-person pose estimation and tracking in videos. arXiv preprint arXiv:2004.12652 (2020)

27. Wang, J., Long, X., Gao, Y., Ding, E., Wen, S.: Graph-PCNN: two stage human pose estimation with graph pose refinement. In: Vedaldi, A., Bischof, H., Brox, T., Frahm, J.-M. (eds.) ECCV 2020. LNCS, vol. 12356, pp. 492–508. Springer, Cham (2020). https://doi.org/10.1007/978-3-030-58621-8_29

28. Wang, Z., et al.: Mscoco keypoints challenge 2018. In: Joint Recognition Challenge Workshop at ECCV (2018)
29. Xiao, B., Wu, H., Wei, Y.: Simple baselines for human pose estimation and tracking. In: ECCV, pp. 466–481 (2018)
30. Zhang, F., Zhu, X., Ye, M.: Fast human pose estimation. In: CVPR, pp. 3517–3526 (2019)
31. Zhang, H., et al.: Human pose estimation with spatial contextual information. arXiv preprint arXiv:1901.01760 (2019)

Clothes-Independent Identity Feature Learning for Long-Term Person Re-identification

Kunfeng Chen, Lei Shi, Zhisong Pan$^{(\boxtimes)}$, Jiabao Wang, and Xi Zhan

Army Engineering University of PLA, Nanjing 210007, China

Abstract. Long-term person re-identification (Re-ID) aims to retrieve the same pedestrian captured by different cameras over a long-duration, which is faced with the challenge of changing clothes. Existing traditional person ReID methods always assume that pedestrians hardly change clothes and focus clothes-dependent identity feature, thus they cannot achieve ideal recognition performance if this assumption is untenable. To alleviate the influence of clothes-changing, this paper proposes a dual-attribute fusion network (DAFN) learning clothes-independent identity feature. In DAFN, the original RGB image, gray-scale image and contour image of a pedestrian are utilized as the input. With the help of our proposed clothes-independent self-attention modules (CSM), the discriminative clothes-independent identity feature can be extracted. At the same time, lightweight feature-enhanced self-attention modules (FSM) are designed in DAFN to improve the robustness of feature representation. Empirical studies show that the DAFN proposed in this paper achieves state-of-the-art performance on long-term person ReID benchmark.

Keywords: Person re-identification · Long-term · Clothes-changing · Self-attention · Dual-attribute fusion

1 Introduction

The goal of person re-identification (Re-ID) is to retrieve images of a particular person cross different cameras at different times and locations. As a key task in computer vision research, person Re-ID is widely applied in intelligent surveillance and video analysis. In recent years, based on the progress of neural network [4] and feature metric learning [11,13], we can get more discriminative pedestrian information through deep learning [23]. Hence, person Re-ID has more and more innovation and breakthrough, and achieves high accuracy on the relevant datasets [12,15,22]. These existing person Re-ID methods seem to perform well, but most of them often assume that pedestrians hardly change clothes, which is obviously not in line with the complex real world. RGB images are often utilized as the input of existing traditional person Re-ID methods, thus the color information of clothing naturally becomes the key information when

© Springer Nature Switzerland AG 2021
Y. Peng et al. (Eds.): ICIG 2021, LNCS 12889, pp. 397–409, 2021.
https://doi.org/10.1007/978-3-030-87358-5_32

extracting features. However, if these traditional methods meet someone have changed clothes, the person will be easy to be matched with another person wearing similar clothes.

Considering the technical requirement that pedestrians may change clothes, existing works have proposed some enlightening methods, while there are also shortcomings in them. Xue et al. [18] solve it by diluting clothing and emphasizing face information. Face information has a high distinction, so adding the constraints of face recognition can well find the target pedestrian. However, the long-distance shooting cannot get clear faces, and the side face is often obtained from walking human body, leading to face recognition with low accuracy. Zheng et al. [23] separately encode each pedestrian image into appearance code and structure code, designing a discriminator sharing the appearance encoder with the generator, and use the generated data to improve the learned person Re-ID feature. However, the complex and difficult training of the Generative Adversarial Network (GAN) model is a drawback that cannot be ignored. Furthermore, some literatures also mention video-based person Re-ID [5] or gait recognition [2], which utilize the video sequence of someone to capture the action characteristics. These methods make good use of the discrepancy of different pedestrians during dynamic process, which is helpful to extract discriminative identity feature. However, some pedestrians appear in the camera view for a shot time occasionally, so it is difficult to reflect the complete gait cycle. Hence, it is still necessary to solve person Re-ID based on single-frame image. Recently, Yang et al. [19] found that the contour images exclude the influence of clothes and can bring better recognition results when exploring long-term person Re-ID. Inspired by this, we consider that the gray-scale images also have similar effect with the contour images, which can also make the model pay more attention to the pedestrian information unrelated to the color of the clothes. Moreover, the gray-scale images have greater information mining potential.

In order to achieve an end-to-end long-term person Re-ID system based on clothes-independent identity feature, we firstly propose to jointly utilize the original RGB images, gray-scale images and contour images as the input. Accordingly, we introduce two clothes-independent self-attention modules (CSM) to mine invariant information in the gray-scale/contour images and the original RGB images, so that two kinds of generated information-strengthen images are obtained. Because different generated images have different attributes, a dual-attribute feature fusion strategy is applied in our feature extractor. Therefore, the deep neural network proposed in this paper is named as dual-attribute fusion network (DAFN). In addition, AGW [20] proves that when the attention modules are inserted between the residual layers of ResNet50 feature extractor, more robust feature can be extracted, which gives us some profitable ideas. Nevertheless, the huge amount of computation introduced by the non-local attention module [16] in AGW is a problem that cannot be ignored. Afterwards, inspired by the "pyramid idea" in SIFT [8] and YOLO [3], we design a lightweight feature-enhanced self-attention module (FSM) utilizing the dilated convolution pyramid. As shown in relevant experimental results, FSM obtains a higher effect in person Re-ID than non-local attention module with less computation. Therefore, our method in this paper has the following contributions:

(1) We propose a novel method to take three heterogeneous images as input, and utilize clothes-independent self-attention modules (CSM) to get two kinds of generated images with different attributes, which can strengthen the representation of pedestrian feature unrelated to clothes.
(2) As for our feature extractor, we propose a dual-attribute feature fusion method to fully mine the different attribute identity information contained in the two kinds of generated images. Besides, we design a lightweight feature-enhanced self-attention module (FSM) in feature extractor, which can improve the robustness of feature representation with less computation.
(3) An end-to-end trained dual-attribute fusion network (DAFN) is proposed, which is effectively applied to the task of long-term person Re-ID. And it achieves state-of-the-art performance on long-term person ReID benchmark.

2 Proposed Method

2.1 Overview

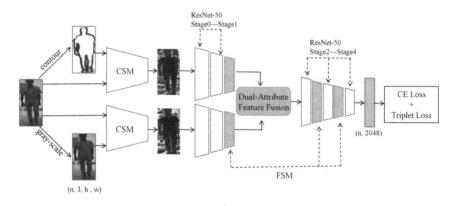

Fig. 1. The overall architecture of our proposed DAFN. Give a RGB image, we firstly convert it to gray-scale and contour image, and utilize two CSMs to get two generated images. Then, these generated images are sent to ResNet50-based feature extractor and realize dual-attribute feature fusion. In addition, we design FSM inserted into ResNet50 to make pedestrian feature more robust.

We propose a dual-attribute fusion network (DAFN) with clothes-independent self-attention modules (CSM) and lightweight feature-enhanced self-attention modules (FSM) to solve the clothes-changing problem of long-term person Re-ID. In this work, we utilize RGB images, contour images, and gray-scale images as input. The RGB images are directly derived from the pedestrian detection result of the surveillance videos. The contour images are obtained by processing the RGB images utilizing the edge detection method [17], and the gray-scale images are obtained by the gray-scale operation on the RGB image. Accordingly, the I/O approach of our work can be end-to-end. The overall architecture of our method is illustrated in Fig. 1.

At first, the RGB images are input into the network and converted into gray-scale images and contour images respectively. Then the two pairs of heterogeneous images, i.e., RGB images and contour images, RGB images and gray-scale images, are respectively sent to two CSMs. The purpose of this operation is to transfer the clothes-independent feature contained in the contour or gray-scale images into the RGB images. Therefore, two generated three-channel images are obtained. Subsequently, we send the two generated three-channel images to ResNet50-based feature extractor. In the first several convolutions of ResNet50, the low-level features of the two generated images are extracted respectively. To realize dual-attribution feature fusion, the low-level feature maps of the two branches are concatenated together firstly. We then apply a convolution layer with 1×1 kernel size to reduce the channel number of fused feature map to its 1/2. Subsequently, it is sent to the remaining convolution layers of the feature extractor. According to the practice, ResNet50 is regarded as five stages, namely Stage0 (shallow convolution layers) and Stage1–Stage4 (residual convolution layers). Based on experimental results, the best performance is achieved when the features are fused at Stage1. In addition, we add FSM after Stage1, Stage2 and Stage3 to extract more robust pedestrian features and improve the performance of our person Re-ID algorithm.

2.2   Clothes-Independent Self-Attention Module (CSM)

Exciting researches show that the effect of using RGB image as input is the best without considering changing clothes. Yang et al. [19] confirmed that the contour images are conducive to the implementation of long-term person Re-ID influenced by clothes changing. The reason is contour images abandon the clothing information of pedestrians, and the contour of pedestrians is unique discriminative information under not large range of clothing change. Consequently, we believe that the biggest difference between people who change their clothes is color change. So, if the gray-scale image is used too, we can get better color-independent feature, namely, clothes-independent feature. Thus, in order to implement a long-term person Re-ID algorithm with better recognition performance under the condition of changing clothes and not changing clothes, we consider using RGB images, gray-scale images and contour images as joint input. How can we make full use of these three heterogeneous images?

Attention mechanism plays an important role in computer vision, which can guide convolutional neural networks to learn the most informative feature. Among them, some studies use channel attention to learn the relationship between channels. e.g., Hu et al. [6] proposed an SE (Squeeze-and-Excitation) attention module that assigns weights to each channel. Inspired by this, we designed a Clothes-Independent Self-Attention Module (CSM), as Fig. 2 below shows.

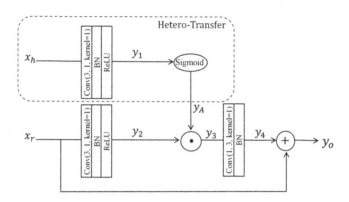

Fig. 2. The architecture of CSM. In this module, x_r donates the input of RGB images, and x_h is for heterogeneous image (gray-scale and contour) input. Hetero-Transfer in the top half of this architecture diagram represents the transfer of information from a heterogeneous image to an RGB image. Firstly, we reduce the dimension of the three-channel images (x_h and x_r) to the single-channel images (y_1 and y_2). Secondly, a Sigmoid operation is apply for the single-channel image (y_1) to compute attention mask (y_A). Then, reconstructing the weighted image from single channel (y_3) to three channel (y_4). Finally, After adding x_r and y_4, we can get y_o, as the output of CSM.

The CSM has two inputs and one output. x_h is used to input contour image or gray-scale image, and x_r is used to input RGB image. The output of CSM is a generated three-channel image y_o. The channel number of x_h and x_r is firstly reduced by the convolution layer with 1×1 convolution kernel size. Then Batch Normalization layer transformation and ReLU activation are performed to obtain a single-channel image y_1 and y_2. After a Sigmoid operation on y_1, the attention mask y_A is obtained. We compute element-wise dot product with attention mask y_A and y_2 to achieve information transfer of heterogeneous images (Hetero-transfer). Then the result is upgraded to three channels, so y_4 is obtained. Finally, adding the original RGB image x_r with y_4 and we can get the output result y_o. The overall procedure of CSM is presented in Algorithm 1.

Algorithm 1. The overall procedure of CSM

Require: The input contour or grayscale image x_h and the input RGB image x_r.

Ensure: y_o, which is the generated three-channel image from CSM.

1: $y_o \leftarrow x_r + y_4$

2: $y_4 \leftarrow Conv3(BN(y_3))$. Here, Conv3 is a convolution layer with 1×1 convolution kernel, and its input is one channel and output is three channels.

3: $y_3 \leftarrow y_2 \cdot y_A$

4: $y_A \leftarrow Sigmoid(y_1)$

5: $y_1 \leftarrow Conv1(BN(ReLU(x_h)))$, $y_2 \leftarrow Conv2(BN(ReLU(x_r)))$. Here, Conv1 and Conv2 are convolution layers with 1×1 convolution kernel, and theirs input is three channels and output is one channel.

2.3 Lightweight Feature-Enhanced Self-attention Module(FSM)

AGW [20] proves that inserting non-local attention modules in ResNet50 can effectively improve the performance of feature extractor. But the amount of computation introduced by non-local attention module is a disadvantage cannot be ignored. Can we find a simple and effective alternative to non-local attention?

In convolutional neural networks, the size of the receptive field determines the region size of the information obtained in the convolutional process. The larger receptive field is, the more global information is obtained. Although increasing the size of convolution kernel can expand the receptive field and obtain more global information, it will lead to an increase in the number of parameters. In order to expand the receptive field without increasing the number of parameters, Yu et al. [21] proposed the dilated convolution. Moreover, inspired by the "pyramid idea" in SIFT [8] and YOLO [3], we propose a Lightweight Feature-enhanced Self-Attention Module (FSM) via the dilated convolution pyramid, to enhance the scale invariant features of appearance in ResNet50. FSM's architecture is illustrated in Fig. 3.

The input of FSM is the feature map of each stage output in ResNet50-based feature extractor. We first construct a pyramid structure using four dilated convolution layers and the dilated rates are 1, 2, 3 and 4, respectively. Specifically, the first dilated convolution layer is conventional convolution, and its convolution kernel size is set to 1×1, and the convolution kernel size of the other three dilated convolution layers is set to 3×3. In each dilated convolution layer, the dimension of the output channel is reduced to $1/2$ of its input channel. Secondly, the output feature maps from the four convolution layers are concatenated in channels direction. In order to keep the dimension of input and output feature map consistent, the dimension of output channels is reduced as the original feature map. The attention mask is obtained by Sigmoid operation on the dimension-reduced feature map. Then, element-wise dot product is computed between the original feature map and attention mask. Finally, the results of the element-wise dot product and the original feature map are added to obtain the final output of FSM.

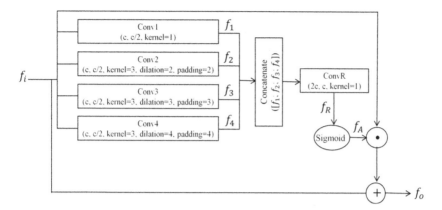

Fig. 3. The architecture of FSM. f_i donates the input of FSM, which is the feature map of each stage output in ResNet50-based feature extractor. $Conv1$, $Conv2$, $Conv3$ and $Conv4$ are four dilated convolution layers with different dilated rates, and the feature maps of their outputs are f_1, f_2, f_3, f_4. After concatenating these feature maps in the direction of channels and reducing the dimension of channels ($Conv_R$), we apply Sigmoid operation on dimension-reduced feature map (f_R) to compute attention mask (f_A). Then, by weighted fusion of feature maps(f_i and f_A), the output of FSM (f_o) is obtained.

2.4 Loss Function

In order to extract discriminative feature for identification during learning, we utilize Cross Entropy (CE) loss function to optimize the classification result, and Triplet loss function is applied for distance metric learning. Luo et al. [9] analyzed that CE loss and Triplet loss face convergence problem when the two losses acted on the same feature. In DAFN, the feature vectors for calculating Triplet loss functions are extracted directly from ResNet50-based feature extractor. Then using Batch Normalization layer to transform the feature and calculate CE loss function.

The formula of the CE loss function is:

$$L_{CE} = -\sum_{i=1}^{N} p\left(x_i\right) \log q\left(x_i\right) \tag{1}$$

Where x_i refers to the i_{th} input image, $p(x_i)$ refers to its real label, and $q(x_i)$ is the predicted label obtained after the feature vector through the Softmax layer.

The formula of the Triplet loss function is:

$$L_{Tri} = \frac{1}{n} \sum_{a \in batch} \left[\alpha + \max_{p \in A} d_{a,p} - \min_{n \in B} d_{a,n}\right]_+ \tag{2}$$

It means that for all samples (a) of an input batch, in the training process, the distance of feature vectors between a and its similar samples ($p \in A$) is narrowed, and the distance of feature vectors between a and its different samples ($n \in B$) is widened. In Eq. (2), α means the boundary threshold of triple loss, $d(a,p)$ and $d(a,n)$ denotes the metric function of feature distance(similarity). $[]_+$ means that if the calculation result in square brackets is less than 0, it is denoted as 0.

Therefore, the overall loss function calculation formula in the training process can be expressed as follows:

$$L = L_{CE} + L_{Tri} \tag{3}$$

3   Experiments and Analysis

3.1   Dataset and Evaluation Metrics

We use the PRCC (Person Re-id under moderate Clothing Change) dataset [19] to evaluate the effectiveness of our method for long-term person re-identification. The dataset contains 33698 images belonging to 221 pedestrians. These images were captured from three camera views (A, B and C). In PRCC, the pedestrian with the same identity wears the same clothes in view A and view B, and different clothes in view A and view C. Like other related methods, we use the images of 150 pedestrians in PRCC as training samples, and the images of remaining 71 pedestrians for test. We utilize images in view B or C as query images and images in view A as gallery images during testing. A single-shot retrieval method is adopted, that is, randomly selecting only one image of each identity pedestrian in gallery. We take Rank-k as a performance evaluation method to record the test results under the conditions of $B \rightarrow A$ (without clothes-change) and $C \rightarrow A$ (with clothes-change).

3.2   Implementation Details

The experiments are conducted on two NVIDIA GeForce 1080Ti GPU, and the methods are implemented using the PyTorch 1.7 toolbox. The pedestrian images are resized to 384×128. The batchsize is set to 64 during the training process, that is to say, four pedestrians are randomly selected, and then 16 images for each pedestrian are chosen. The margin of Triplet loss is set to 0.3. The SGD algorithm is used as the optimizer with a momentum of 0.9. The network is trained for 80 epochs with a warm-up strategy for the first ten epochs. The learning rate lr(t) at epoch t is computed according to Eq. (4).

$$lr(t) = \begin{cases} 0.035 \times \frac{t}{10} & if\ t \leq 10 \\ 0.035 & if\ 10 < t \leq 20 \\ 0.0035 & if\ 20 < t \leq 50 \\ 0.00035 & if\ 50 < t \leq 80 \end{cases} \tag{4}$$

3.3   Performance Analysis of Various Image Input Methods

In order to explore the role of RGB images, gray-scale images and contour images in person Re-ID system, we have compared the method of inputting only a kind of images into ResNet50, and the method of inputting two or three kind of images into ResNet50 through CSM and fusing feature maps at Stage0 of ResNet50. The experimental result is shown in Table 1.

Table 1. The performance of each image input method

Image input methods			Performance (Rank-1)	
RGB	Gray-scale	Contour	$B \to A$	$C \to A$
+			74.80%	19.43%
	+		70.42%	18.57%
		+	37.25%	18.39%
+	+		76.34%	31.26%
+		+	75.28%	34.39%
+	+	+	**83.23%**	**36.21%**

This result indicate that if there is no change of clothes, the deep neural network will more depend on the clothes information to identify pedestrians. Once some changes of clothes happen, the clothes information will become out of action. Therefore, we consider that the comprehensive use of RGB images, gray-scale images, and contour images can make good use of the clothes-independent identity of heterogeneous images and avoid the above shortcomings. The experimental result of "RGB + Gray-scale + Contour" in the table can also validate our viewpoint.

3.4   Performance Analysis of Various Feature Fusion Methods

After determining that the image input method is "RGB + Gray-scale + Contour" and adding CSM, in order to seek the feature fusion position for the two-branch networks, we have made some attempts at the five positions after Stage0 to Stage4 of ResNet50. The relevant experimental result is illustrated in Fig. 4.

Therefore, we select the position after Stage1 for feature fusion. As illustrated in Fig. 2, after the three images pass through CSM, the two generated images are sent to our ResNet50-based feature extractor. After extracting low-level features of each branch before Stage1, these feature maps is fused to extract high-level features.

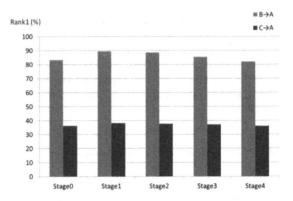

Fig. 4. The performance of each fusion method for DAFN

3.5   Performance Analysis of Various FSM Inserting Methods

After determining the image input mode and the location of the dual-attribute feature fusion, we designe the following experiment to explore where to insert FSM. For ResNet-50's five stages, FSM is first inserted after each stage. And then selecting the top two locations with high scores under clother-changing condition to insert FSM at the same time. Similarly, the top three and the top four locations with high scores are selected for experiment. In addition, we compared FSM and non-local attention module in the same location. Experimental results are shown in Table 2.

Table 2. The performance of each method of inserting FSM.

Inserting methods	$C \rightarrow A$ (Rank-1)		$B \rightarrow A$ (Rank-1)	
	FSM	Non-local	FSM	Non-local
Stage0	38.17%	38.45%	90.02%	87.23%
Stage1	38.25%	37.94%	90.81%	86.31%
Stage2	38.54%	38.31%	90.67%	88.23%
Stage3	38.90%	37.35%	90.73%	89.27%
Stage4	38.03%	38.42%	90.21%	90.04%
Stage2+Stage3	39.02%	–	90.97%	–
Stage1+Stage2+Stage3	**39.52%**	–	**91.73%**	–
Stage1+Stage2+Stage3+Stage4	38.93%	–	91.20%	–

According to Table 2, we can see that, if the attention module is inserted in only one location, FSM (38.90%) is better than non-local (38.45%). When we select more locations to insert FSM, "Stage1+Stage2+Stage3" can be the optima inserting method. Consequently, we design DAFN as Fig. 1.

3.6   Comparison with State-of-the-Arts

To verify the effectiveness and advancement of our proposed method, we conducted comparative experiment with some existing methods on the PRCC dataset. These methods include manual feature method: LBP [10], HOG [1], KISSME [7], classical depth method: ResNet50 [4] (RGB), PCB[14](RGB), and the best method SPT + ASE in existing related work [19]. We recorded the result in Table 3.

Table 3. The comparative experimental result on the PRCC dataset.

Methods	$C \to A$		$B \to A$	
	Rank-1	Rank-10	Rank-1	Rank-10
LBP [10]+KISSME [7]	18.71%	58.09%	39.03%	76.18%
HOG [1]+KISSME [7]	17.52%	49.52%	36.02%	68.83%
ResNet50 [4] (RGB)	19.43%	52.38%	74.80%	97.28%
PCB [14] (RGB)	22.86%	61.24%	86.88%	98.79%
SPT+ASE [19]	34.38%	77.30%	64.20%	92.62%
Our Method	**39.52%**	**80.02%**	**91.73%**	**98.67%**

It can be seen that the Rank-1 of our method is more than about 20% higher than that of our baseline method ResNet50 (RGB) under the conditions of changing clothes and not changing clothes. Compared with the current best method SPT+ASE, the performance of our method is also significantly advanced. Therefore, it can be proved that our method is effectively applied to the long-term person re-identification task by a simple and effective means.

4   Conclusion

In this paper, we propose a dual-attribute fusion network to realize long-term person re-identification. Firstly, the original RGB images, gray-scale images and contour images are utilized as input. With the help of two clothes-independent self-attention modules, discriminant clothes-independent feature are effectively mined without losing the original image information. In addition, we design lightweight feature-enhanced self-attention modules inserted into feature extractor, which make feature representation more robust. The experimental results of our proposed method on the dataset of long-term person Re-ID are significantly better than other existing methods. Hence, this method can provide a simple and effective idea for further research in this field.

References

1. Dalal, N., Triggs, B.: Histograms of oriented gradients for human detection. In: 2005 IEEE Computer Society Conference on Computer Vision and Pattern Recognition (CVPR 2005), vol. 1, pp. 886–893. IEEE (2005)
2. Fan, C., et al.: Gaitpart: temporal part-based model for gait recognition. In: Proceedings of the IEEE/CVF Conference on Computer Vision and Pattern Recognition, pp. 14225–14233 (2020)
3. Farhadi, A., Redmon, J.: Yolov3: an incremental improvement. Computer Vision and Pattern Recognition (2018)
4. He, K., Zhang, X., Ren, S., Sun, J.: Deep residual learning for image recognition. In: Proceedings of the IEEE Conference on Computer Vision and Pattern Recognition, pp. 770–778 (2016)
5. Hou, R., Chang, H., Ma, B., Shan, S., Chen, X.: Temporal complementary learning for video person re-identification. In: Vedaldi, A., Bischof, H., Brox, T., Frahm, J.-M. (eds.) ECCV 2020. LNCS, vol. 12370, pp. 388–405. Springer, Cham (2020). https://doi.org/10.1007/978-3-030-58595-2_24
6. Hu, J., Shen, L., Sun, G.: Squeeze-and-excitation networks. In: Proceedings of the IEEE Conference on Computer Vision and Pattern Recognition, pp. 7132–7141 (2018)
7. Koestinger, M., Hirzer, M., Wohlhart, P., Roth, P.M., Bischof, H.: Large scale metric learning from equivalence constraints. In: 2012 IEEE Conference on Computer Vision and Pattern Recognition, pp. 2288–2295. IEEE (2012)
8. Lowe, D.G.: Distinctive image features from scale-invariant keypoints. Int. J. Comput. Vision 60(2), 91–110 (2004)
9. Luo, H., et al.: A strong baseline and batch normalization neck for deep person re-identification. IEEE Trans. Multimedia (2019)
10. Ojala, T., Pietikäinen, M., Harwood, D.: A comparative study of texture measures with classification based on featured distributions. Pattern Recogn. 29(1), 51–59 (1996)
11. Paisitkriangkrai, S., Shen, C., Van Den Hengel, A.: Learning to rank in person re-identification with metric ensembles. In: Proceedings of the IEEE Conference on Computer Vision and Pattern Recognition, pp. 1846–1855 (2015)
12. Ristani, E., Solera, F., Zou, R., Cucchiara, R., Tomasi, C.: Performance measures and a data set for multi-target, multi-camera tracking. In: Hua, G., Jégou, H. (eds.) ECCV 2016. LNCS, vol. 9914, pp. 17–35. Springer, Cham (2016). https://doi.org/10.1007/978-3-319-48881-3_2
13. Shen, Y., Xiao, T., Li, H., Yi, S., Wang, X.: End-to-end deep kronecker-product matching for person re-identification. In: Proceedings of the IEEE Conference on Computer Vision and Pattern Recognition, pp. 6886–6895 (2018)
14. Sun, Y., Zheng, L., Yang, Y., Tian, Q., Wang, S.: Beyond part models: person retrieval with refined part pooling (and a strong convolutional baseline). In: Proceedings of the European Conference on Computer Vision (ECCV), pp. 480–496 (2018)
15. Wei, L., Zhang, S., Gao, W., Tian, Q.: Person transfer GAN to bridge domain gap for person re-identification. In: Proceedings of the IEEE Conference on Computer Vision and Pattern Recognition, pp. 79–88 (2018)
16. Xia, B.N., Gong, Y., Zhang, Y., Poellabauer, C.: Second-order non-local attention networks for person re-identification. In: Proceedings of the IEEE/CVF International Conference on Computer Vision, pp. 3760–3769 (2019)

17. Xie, S., Tu, Z.: Holistically-nested edge detection. In: Proceedings of the IEEE International Conference on Computer Vision, pp. 1395–1403 (2015)

18. Xue, J., Meng, Z., Katipally, K., Wang, H., van Zon, K.: Clothing change aware person identification. In: Proceedings of the IEEE Conference on Computer Vision and Pattern Recognition Workshops, pp. 2112–2120 (2018)

19. Yang, Q., Wu, A., Zheng, W.S.: Person re-identification by contour sketch under moderate clothing change. IEEE Trans. Pattern Anal. Mach. Intell. (2019)

20. Ye, M., Shen, J., Lin, G., Xiang, T., Shao, L., Hoi, S.C.: Deep learning for person re-identification: a survey and outlook. IEEE Trans. Pattern Anal. Mach. Intell. (2021)

21. Yu, F., Koltun, V.: Multi-scale context aggregation by dilated convolutions. arXiv preprint arXiv:1511.07122 (2015)

22. Zheng, L., Shen, L., Tian, L., Wang, S., Wang, J., Tian, Q.: Scalable person re-identification: a benchmark. In: Proceedings of the IEEE International Conference on Computer Vision, pp. 1116–1124 (2015)

23. Zheng, Z., Yang, X., Yu, Z., Zheng, L., Yang, Y., Kautz, J.: Joint discriminative and generative learning for person re-identification. In: Proceedings of the IEEE/CVF Conference on Computer Vision and Pattern Recognition, pp. 2138–2147 (2019)

Lightweight Non-local High-Resolution Networks for Human Pose Estimation

Congcong Zhang[1], Ning He[2(✉)], Qixiang Sun[1], Xiaojie Yin[2], Kang Yan[2], Yuzhe He[1], and Wenjing Han[2]

[1] Beijing Key Laboratory of Information Service Engineering, Beijing Union University, Beijing, China
[2] Smart City College, Beijing Union University, Beijing, China
xxthening@buu.edu.cn

Abstract. Human pose estimation is one of the fundamental tasks in computer vision, applied in areas such as motion recognition, games, and animation production. Most of the current deep network models entail deepening the number of network layers to obtain better performance. This requires computational resources that exceed the computational capacity of embedded and mobile devices, thereby limiting the practical application of these approaches. In this paper, we propose a lightweight network model that incorporates the idea of Ghost modules. We design Ghost modules to replace the base modules in the original high-resolution network, thus reducing the network model parameters. In addition, we design a non-local high-resolution network that is fused in the 1/32 resolution stage of the network. This enables the network to acquire global features, thus improving the accuracy of human pose estimation and reducing the network parameters while ensuring the accuracy of the model. We verify the algorithm on the MPII and COCO datasets and the proposed model achieves a 1.8% improvement in accuracy while using 40% fewer parameters compared with the conventional high-resolution network.

Keywords: Human pose estimation · Non-local module · Lightweight network · Ghost module · High-resolution network

1 Introduction

The human pose estimation task entails detecting key parts of the human body or limb joint parts in a given image or video and outputting the parameters (relative position relationships of individual joint points) related to all or some limbs of the human body. Human pose estimation is a fundamental technique required for several practical applications such as human action recognition [1], human-computer interaction, and pose tracking. At present, the mainstream research focus regarding the human pose estimation network is to increase the network width and depth, or increase the input image size to improve the accuracy of human pose estimation. These augmentations are not feasible for practical applications because they require vast computational resources far

© Springer Nature Switzerland AG 2021
Y. Peng et al. (Eds.): ICIG 2021, LNCS 12889, pp. 410–422, 2021.
https://doi.org/10.1007/978-3-030-87358-5_33

beyond the computational capacity of embedded and mobile devices. Therefore, improving the accuracy of the output, while reducing the parameters of the network model, is an essential challenge.

The human pose estimation task can be divided into two main implementation strategies: top-down and bottom-up. The top-down approach relies on a detector to detect human stances and generate a bounding box for a single human body, and then transform the problem into a series of single-human pose estimations. Xiao et al. [2] proposed simple baseline networks for multi-person pose estimation and tracking. Newell et al. [3] proposed the stacked hourglass network to efficiently fuse features of different scales. Specifically, the hourglass module is structured as a convolutional de-convolution module with residual connections. The effectiveness of the hourglass network structure has inspired subsequent researchers to deploy modules similar to the hourglass network structure. For example, Yang et al. [4] proposed a pyramid residual module based on the hourglass approach to improve the robustness to scale changes in body parts. Chen et al. [5] proposed the cascaded pyramid network (CPN) method, which fuses RefineNet and the feature pyramid network (FPN) to further improve the accuracy of predicting key-points. The top-down approach unifies detection frames of different sizes into one scale for learning, and is therefore relatively insensitive to human scale and applicable to small scales. However, this method requires highly accurate target detection, the number of people in the image has a greater impact on the amount of computation, and detector errors can significantly affect the accuracy of pose estimation.

Unlike the top-down approach, the bottom-up approach starts by finding all of the key-points of the human body in the image, i.e., all the heads, knees, left hands, and other parts relevant to the task. These key-points are then joined together to form a whole body. Pishchulin et al. [6] proposed DeepCut to model the allocation problem as an integer linear program (ILP) problem in a fully connected graph. Insafutdinov et al. [7] proposed DeeperCut to estimate human key-points using a deeper ResNet [8] network, while using incremental optimization strategies to improve the efficiency of human pose estimation. Levinkov et al. [9] proposed two local search algorithms that can monotonically converge to a local optimum, providing a feasible solution to the ILP problem. Varadarajan et al. [10] proposed a greedy allocation algorithm to reduce the complexity of the ILP problem. Cao et al. [11] proposed OpenPose, which uses the relationship between key-points modeled as part affinity fields (PAFs) for better and faster allocation of key-points. The semantic part segmentation proposed by Xia et al. [12] focuses on the clustering of key-point components. The hallucinating visual instances in total absentia (HVITA) method proposed by Qiu et al. [13] an end-to-end deep approach that explicitly looks into the global semantics within the image. Yang et al. [14] proposed a prediction of dynamics through a graph neural network that explicitly accounts for both spatial-temporal and visual information. The bottom-up approach is not affected by the error of target detection and the computational effort is independent of the number of people in the image, rendering it more efficient. However, the method is more sensitive to the scale of the target in the image, and it usually struggles with small scale human bodies in the image.

Network lightweight methods are usually divided into three approaches: lightweight network parameters, network trimming, or direct design of lightweight networks.

Lightweight network parameters entail reducing the number of network parameters characterized in the network. Binary Connect [15] can compress the size of the network model by a factor of 32, but these methods usually result in a lower-accuracy network. Network clipping is often applied to compress network models, reducing the complexity of the network while preventing overfitting of the network model. Zhao et al. [16] achieved network structure optimization through two stages of pruning and merging, and combined this approach with the grey-scale correlation analysis method, improving the numerical effectiveness of the network. It is also possible to design a more lightweight network model structure directly. Iandola et al. [17] used the bottleneck structure to design a lightweight network structure with a resulting accuracy comparable to AlexNet, while the size of the network parameters was only 1/50th of AlexNet.

This study uses a direct approach to design lightweight networks to reduce network parameters. The model proposed in this paper is based on the high-resolution network structure [18]. We use the Ghost network structure [19] to design the Ghost module instead of the original base module in the high-resolution network, thereby significantly reducing the network parameters. Then, we obtain the non-local network module by improving on the non-local neural network proposed by Wang et al. [20]. The non-local network module is fused in the 1/32 resolution stage of the base network to enable the network to acquire global features, thus improving the accuracy of human pose estimation. The effectiveness of the proposed method is verified on the MPII dataset [21] and the COCO human pose estimation dataset [22].

2 Related Work

2.1 Human Pose Estimation Methods

Traditional convolutional neural networks for key-point heatmap estimation consist of a backbone network, similar to a classification network, where the main body fuses multi-scale information in a high-to-low and low-to-high resolution manner. For example, hourglass [3] recovers high resolution information through a symmetric low-to-high resolution process; cascaded pyramid networks (CPN) [5] construct a cascaded pyramid model to obtain multi-scale features, which are then upsampled to high resolution for pose estimation; simple baseline [2] uses transposed convolutional layers to generate high-resolution feature representations; Deepercut [7] uses inflated convolution to make the process of recovering high resolution lightweight. The traditional human pose estimation network structure is shown in Fig. 1. Traditional human pose estimation network structure.

The model proposed reduces the number of network parameters while improving the accuracy of the pose estimation. The selected backbone network structure of the model is the high-resolution network (HRNet), which was proposed by Sun et al. of the University of Science and Technology of China and Microsoft Research Asia [18] in 2019. HRNet is a parallel structure that enhances high-resolution feature information by concatenating high-resolution to low-resolution convolutions in parallel and performing multi-scale fusion by repeated cross-parallel convolutions. HRNet consists of four parallel sub-networks, where the resolution of the same sub-network features does not vary with depth, and the resolution of the parallel sub-network feature maps is successively

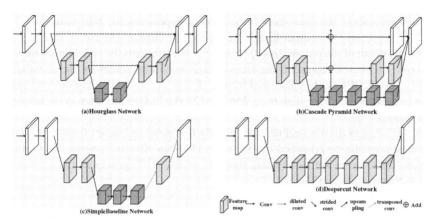

Fig. 1. Traditional human pose estimation network structure

reduced by half, while the number of channels doubles. The depth of HRNet can be divided into four phases. In between each phase, a fusion module fuses feature information of different resolutions to increase the feature representation performance of the network. Figure 2 shows the structure of the HRNet network. The convolution of different resolutions enables the extraction of different regional fine-grained features, and there is complementarity between these extracted features. Fusing features of different resolutions facilitates the extraction of representative human features.

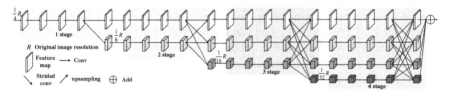

Fig. 2. HRNet network structure with four stages

2.2 Ghost Network Module

Deploying neural networks on embedded devices is difficult because of the inherent memory and computing power limitations. We improve the Ghost convolution proposed by Han et al. [19] to obtain the Ghost module, which can obtain a small set of intrinsic feature maps by ordinary convolution, and then obtain the final output feature maps by constant mapping and simple linear transformation. This greatly reduces the computational effort required for the model. For example, take the input data $X \in \mathbb{R}^{c \times h \times w}$, where c represents the number of channels of the input data, and h and w are the height and width of the input data, respectively. The operation used to generate an arbitrary convolutional layer of n feature mapping is shown in Eq. (1).

$$Y = X * f + b \tag{1}$$

where $*$ represents the convolution operation, b represents the bias term, and $Y \in \mathbb{R}^{h' \times w' \times n}$ represents the output feature map with one channel (h' and w' represent the height and width of the output data). $f \in \mathbb{R}^{c \times k \times k \times n}$ represents the convolution filter for this layer, and $k \times k$ represents the size of the convolution kernel for the convolution filter f. The FLOPs can be calculated from $n \cdot h' \cdot w' \cdot c \cdot k \cdot k$. Because the number of filters and channels is very high (e.g., 256 or 512), the FLOPs are often in the hundreds of thousands.

A well-trained deep neural network usually has many redundant feature maps, and the Ghost convolution proposed by Han et al. [19] can effectively solve this problem. Suppose there are m intrinsic feature maps $Y' \in \mathbb{R}^{h' \times w' \times m}$ generated from the initial convolution as shown in Eq. (2).

$$Y' = X * f' \tag{2}$$

where the convolution filter is $f' \in \mathbb{R}^{c \times k \times k \times m}$, where $m \leq n$. The other hyperparameters such as the convolution kernel, step size, and space size remain the same as in the original convolution. To obtain the required n feature maps, a series of linear operations are used to generate s Ghost features on the intrinsic feature map Y', as shown in Eq. (3).

$$y_{ij} = \Phi_{i,j}\left(y'_i\right), \forall i = 1, \ldots, m, j = 1, \ldots, s \tag{3}$$

where y'_i represents the i-th intrinsic convolutional map in the convolutional map Y', and $\Phi_{i,j}$ represents the j-th Ghost feature map y_{ij} generated using the j-th linear operation. This means that y'_i can have one or more Ghost feature maps, and the last linear operation $\Phi_{i,s}$ is a constant mapping that maintains the intrinsic features. $n = m \cdot s$ feature maps $Y = \left[y_{11}, y_{12}, \ldots, y_{ms}\right]$ can be obtained as the output data of the Ghost model using Eq. (3). As shown in Fig. 3, Ghost convolution includes an identity map and $m \cdot (s - 1) = \frac{n}{s} \cdot (s - 1)$ linear operations. Ideally, the parameters of ordinary convolution and Ghost convolution are shown in Eq. (4), that is, Ghost convolution can replace ordinary convolution operations. This reduces the number of parameters by a factor of s.

$$r_c = \frac{n \cdot c \cdot k \cdot k}{\frac{n}{s} \cdot c \cdot k \cdot k + (s - 1) \cdot \frac{n}{s} \cdot d \cdot d} \approx \frac{s \cdot c}{s + c - 1} \approx s \tag{4}$$

For the network model proposed in this paper, we design the Ghost module as shown in Fig. 3, which is similar to the original base module in HRNet. The Ghost module consists of two Ghost convolutions. The first Ghost convolution acts as an extension layer to increase the number of channels and is followed by batch normalization (BN) and the activation function (rectified linear unit) to accelerate the training process. The second Ghost convolution reduces the number of channels to the original number of channels. The two Ghost convolutions are connected by a deep convolution with a step size of two, again increasing the BN at each layer, and finally using a shortcut to connect the input and output according to the principles of residual networks.

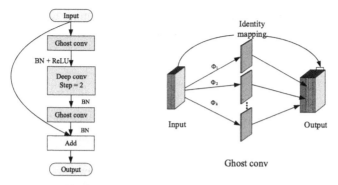

Fig. 3. Ghost module and Ghost convolution

2.3 Non-local Network Module

HRNet is the optimal network architecture for human pose estimation, combining accuracy and a suitable number of network parameters. However, HRNet uses convolutional neural networks (CNN) for feature extraction, just like traditional networks. Due to the structural characteristics of the human body's nodes, the full range of human features cannot be effectively obtained locally using traditional convolutional extraction. However, by adding global features, the full range of human pose features can be better extracted, thus improving the accuracy of human pose estimation. To obtain the global features of the human pose, Wang et al. [20] combined the characteristics of the non-local mean and proposed a generalized, simple, non-local network module that can be directly embedded into the current network. Equation (5) describes the non-local network module.

$$y_i = \frac{1}{C(x)} \sum_{\forall j} f(x_i, x_j) g(x_j) \tag{5}$$

where x is the input signal and y is the output signal of the same size as x. i is the index of the output location (in space, time, or space-time) to be computed. j is the index of an enumeration of all possible locations. The binary function f calculates the number of correlation coefficients (representing relationships, e.g., proximity) between x_i and all x_j. The unitary function g computes a representation of the input signal at position j. The response is normalized by the factor $C(x)$. Unlike the convolution operation, the non-local operation considers all position factors $(\forall j)$. The function g uses a linear embedding function $g(x_j) = W_g x_j$, where W_g is a learnable weight matrix, implemented in the experiments with a 1×1 convolutional layer.

This approach incorporates the non-local network module and HRNet. The non-local network module is encapsulated and defined as shown in Eq. (6):

$$z_i = W_z y_i^+ x_i \tag{6}$$

Combining the above equations and specific experimental parameters, the non-local network module designed in this paper is shown in Fig. 4. Equation (6) indicates that the non-local network can directly fuse the global information in the image and output richer semantic information. The module can add global features while maintaining the same parameters at the input and output of the network, with no change in the number of parameters or in the speed of computation.

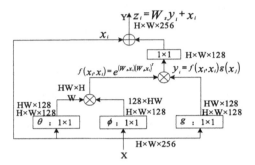

Fig. 4. Non-local network module

3 Lightweight HRNet Model

Combining the analysis of the above Ghost network module structure and the non-local network module, we propose a lightweight fusion of the non-local network module of HRNet (Non-Local block with Ghost Network, NGHRNet). The resulting model structure is shown in Fig. 5. The network consists of four phases and the main network structure is similar to that of HRNet. In this paper the base module of the original HRNet is replaced by the Ghost module. A smaller resolution indicates stronger semantic information. To better access the underlying features and to compensate for the decrease in accuracy resulting from the reduction in network parameters, this paper incorporates the non-local network module on the fourth branch of the network. That is, we add the non-local network module at the 1/32 resolution stage.

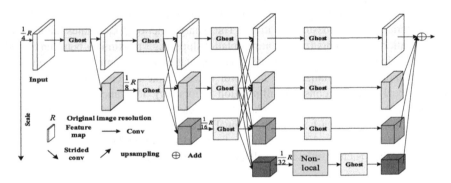

Fig. 5. HRNet architecture incorporating the Ghost module

The inputs to the non-local modules of the specific HRNet network are $265 \times 8 \times 8$, after the weight transformation to obtain $(HW \times 128)$ and $(128 \times HW)$. This can reduce the number of channels, reduce the amount of computation, allow transposing of operations, and facilitate matrix multiplication. The process calculates the similarity between the two transformation operations according to the function in Eq. (5). The same operation is performed for the function f. Finally, the features commonality can be further highlighted by a *softmax* operation, and then restored to the original number of channels by 1×1 convolution.

4 Experimental Results and Analysis

4.1 Experimental Environment and Dataset

The experimental environment consists of an Ubuntu 18.04 64-bit operating system, 12G of RAM, and an RTX2080Ti graphics card. The software platform uses Cuda 10.0.130, Cudnn 7.5, Pytorch 1.4, and Python 3.6. The network pre-training model uses parameters pre-trained on the ImageNet dataset.

The COCO dataset consists of more than 200,000 sample images, including 250,000 human targets and 17 labeled pose key-points. The evaluation standard is the average precision (AP) based on the object key-point similarity (OKS). The MPII human body pose dataset is extracted from YouTube videos. Among them, we use 30,000 human body instances for training and 10,000 human body instances for testing. Each human body has 16 labeled key-points, which are based on PCKh@0.5 (percentage of correct key-points of head, 0.5 is the normalization factor) as the evaluation standard.

4.2 Evaluation Indicators and Training Strategies

PCKh Evaluation Criteria [21]: The detection accuracy is obtained by clearly defining the boundaries corresponding to each person in the test image.

$$PCKh(k) = \frac{1}{N} \sum_{i=1}^{N} \begin{cases} 1, \left(T_k^i - \hat{T}_k^i\right) \leq rs_h \\ 0, \left(T_k^i - \hat{T}_k^i\right) > rs_h \end{cases} \tag{7}$$

where $PCKh(k)$ is the PCKh value of the k-th key-point. The label value of the k-th human key-point in the i-th image is T_k^i, the prediction result of the corresponding key-point is $\hat{T}_k^i$, and the total number of samples is N.

OKS Evaluation Criteria [22]: On the basis of the COCO evaluation index OKS, the AP measure is normalized for different key-point types and body size dimensions, and represents the average similarity between key-points. OKS is defined in Eq. (8).

$$OKS = \frac{\sum_i exp\left(-d_i^2/2s^2k_i^2\right)\delta(v_i > 0)}{\sum_i \delta(v_i > 0)} \tag{8}$$

where d is the Euclidean distance between the true coordinate $\theta^{(p)}$ and the predicted coordinate $\hat{\theta}^{(p)}$, $d = \hat{\theta}^{(p)} - \theta_2^{(p)2}$, s is the area occupied by the human body in the image, k_i is the normalization factor, and $\delta(v_i > 0)$ is equal to one when the visibility of the key-point is greater than zero. For human pose estimation, AP represents the average accuracy, and is defined in Eq. (9).

$$AP^t = \frac{\sum_p \delta\left(OKS_p > t\right)}{\sum_p 1}$$
(9)

where t is the threshold treatment for a given OKS, set as (0.50, 0.55,..., 0.90, 0.95), and the prediction accuracy is calculated from the OKS metrics of the characters in all of the images in the test set.

In this paper, we use the Adam optimizer and set the learning rate according to published settings [2], with the base learning rate set to 10^{-3} and reduced to 10^{-4} and 10^{-5} at the 170th epoch and 200th epoch, respectively. The final training process ends at 210 epochs. For the MPII data, the enhancement and training strategy was consistent with that of the COCO dataset. To facilitate comparison with other mainstream methods, the MPII dataset images were cropped and adjusted to a fixed input size of 256×256 in this paper.

5   Experimental Results and Analysis

The experimental results on the MPII validation set are shown in Table 1. Our approach achieves an accuracy improvement of 0.2 percentage points compared with the baseline experimental results of HRNet. According to the literature [18], the reason for this small improvement is the saturation of the accuracy of the MPII dataset.

Table 1. Experimental results on the MPII validation set (PCKh@0.5).

Method	Head	Shoulder	Elbow	Wrist	Hip	Knee	Ankle	Total
Hourglass [3]	96.5	96.0	90.3	85.4	88.8	85.0	81.9	89.2
CPN [5]	96.5	96.0	90.4	86.0	89.5	85.2	82.3	89.6
Deepercut [7]	95.6	95.9	90.7	86.5	89.9	86.6	82.5	89.8
HRNet [18]	97.1	95.9	90.3	86.4	89.1	87.1	83.3	90.3
Ours	**97.3**	**96.0**	**90.9**	**86.8**	**89.2**	**87.5**	**83.0**	**90.5**

The experimental results on the COCO dataset are shown in Table 2. Our method achieves the highest accuracy of 76.9% for an image input size of 256×192. Furthermore, even with a 32-channel network, the accuracy of our method still exceeds that of HRNet's 48-channel network. Our method using a 48-channel network achieves the highest accuracy of 78.0% for an image input size of 384×228. Our proposed network uses far fewer network parameters than the HRNet baseline network.

This paper focuses on human key-point estimation and the visual experimental results are shown in Fig. 6. We use visualization tools for the COCO dataset to link the estimated human key-points. We include human pose estimation results for different viewpoints, single people, multiple people, and different target sizes. The MPII dataset shows the localized human key-points.

Table 2. Experimental results on COCO val2017

Method	Backbone	Input size	#Params	FLOPs	AP	AP50	AP75	AP^M	AP^L	AR
Hourglass [3]	Hourglass	256 × 192	25.1M	14.3G	66.9	–	–	–	–	–
CPN [5]	ResNet-50	256 × 192	27.0M	6.2G	68.6	–	–	–	–	–
CPN + OHKM [5]	ResNet-50	256 × 192	27.0M	6.2G	69.4	–	–	–	–	–
SimpleBaseline [2]	ResNet-50	256 × 192	34.0M	8.9G	70.4	88.6	78.3	67.1	77.2	76.3
SimpleBaseline [2]	ResNet-101	256 × 192	53.0M	12.4G	71.4	89.3	79.3	68.1	78.1	77.1
SimpleBaseline [2]	ResNet-152	256 × 192	68.6M	15.7G	72.0	89.3	79.8	68.7	78.9	77.8
HRNet W32 [18]	HRNet-W32	256 × 192	28.5M	7.1G	74.4	90.5	81.9	70.8	81.0	79.8
HRNet W48 [18]	HRNet-W48	256 × 192	63.6M	14.6G	75.1	90.6	82.2	71.5	81.8	80.4
Ours-W32	**NGHRNet**	**256 × 192**	**14.6M**	**4.3G**	**76.2**	**92.6**	**83.6**	**72.0**	**81.7**	**81.1**
Ours-W48	**NGHRNet**	**256 × 192**	**33.5M**	**7.87G**	**76.9**	**93.2**	**83.9**	**72.6**	**82.0**	**81.9**
SimpleBaseline [2]	ResNet-152	384 × 228	68.6M	35.6G	74.3	89.6	81.1	70.5	79.7	79.7
HRNet W32 [18]	HRNet-W32	384 × 228	28.5M	16.0G	75.8	90.6	82.7	71.9	82.8	81.0
HRNet W48 [18]	HRNet-W48	384 × 228	63.6M	32.9G	76.3	90.8	82.9	72.3	83.4	81.2
Ours-W32	**NGHRNet**	**384 × 228**	**14.6M**	**8.4G**	**77.6**	**92.9**	**83.2**	**73.1**	**83.5**	**81.9**
Ours-W48	**NGHRNet**	**384 × 228**	**33.5M**	**17.1G**	**78.0**	**93.2**	**84.4**	**74.1**	**84.4**	**82.0**

Fig. 6. Detection examples for COCO and MPII datasets

5.1 Ablation Experiments

In this paper, we used a 32-channel width network as the skeleton network with an input image size of 256 × 192 pixels, and we conducted our experiments on COCOval2017. First, we conducted the ablation experiments for the lightweight network, and the corresponding results are shown in Table 3. The initial base modules of HRNet were replaced with Ghost modules according to the principle of stage-by-stage replacement, with zero representing the initial network architecture with no replacement of the HRNet modules by Ghost modules. The non-local network modules were fused with stage four of the network and the original number of network parameters, 28.5 M, was eventually reduced to 14.0 M.

Table 3. Lightweight network ablation experiment

Ghost module replacement stage	#Params	FLOPs	AP
0	29.1M	7.1 G	76.7
1	22.9 M	6.0 G	76.5
1 2	18.8 M	5.1 G	76.4
1 2 3	16.0 M	4.6 G	76.3
1 2 3 4	14.6 M	4.3 G	76.2

A non-local module was inserted from the highest resolution to the lowest resolution stage, and the corresponding experimental results are shown in Table 4. In this experiment, the main network architecture is a lightweight network and zero represents the case where there are no fused non-local network modules. The average precision increases as follows as the non-local module is added at lower resolution stages: 74.2%, 74.4%, 75.2%, 75.5%, and 76.2%. Thus, adding the non-local module at the lowest resolution of the network results in the optimal accuracy.

Table 4. Non-local network module ablation experiment

Stage	#Params	FLOPs	AP
0	14.3 M	4.3 G	74.2
1	14.3 M	4.3 G	74.4
2	14.4 M	4.3 G	75.2
3	14.5 M	4.3 G	75.5
4	14.6 M	4.3 G	76.2

6 Conclusion

In this paper, we propose a lightweight non-local high-resolution network for human pose estimation. The non-local module in this model achieves robust and accurate human pose estimation by acquiring global features. The Ghost module replaces the base module in the high-resolution network, effectively reducing the number of network parameters. Experiments on the MPII and COCO datasets demonstrate that the proposed method can improve the pose estimation accuracy while reducing the number of model parameters. In comparison with other methods, the proposed method achieves higher accuracy results with lower computational requirements. Our future research will address further reducing the number of parameters in the network while improving the accuracy.

References

1. Yan, S., Xiong, Y., Lin, D.: Spatial temporal graph convolutional networks for skeleton-based action recognition. In: Proceedings of the AAAI Conference on Artificial Intelligence, pp. 7444–7452 (2018)
2. Xiao, B., Wu, H., Wei, Y.: Simple baselines for human pose estimation and tracking. In: Proceedings of the European Conference on Computer Vision, pp. 466–481 (2018)
3. Newell, A., Yang, K., Deng, J.: Stacked hourglass networks for human pose estimation. In: European Conference on Computer Vision, pp. 483–499. Springer, Cham (2016). https://doi.org/10.1007/978-3-319-46484-8_29
4. Yang, W., Li, S., Ouyang, W., et al.: Learning feature pyramids for human pose estimation. In: Proceedings of the IEEE International Conference on Computer Vision, pp. 1281–1290 (2017)
5. Chen, Y., Wang, Z., Peng, Y., et al.: Cascaded pyramid network for multi-person pose estimation. In: Proceedings of the IEEE Conference On Computer Vision And Pattern Recognition, pp. 7103–7112 (2018)
6. Pishchulin, L., Insafutdinov, E., Tang, S., et al.: Deepcut: joint subset partition and labeling for multi person pose estimation. In: Proceedings of the IEEE Conference on Computer Vision and Pattern Recognition, pp. 4929–4937 (2016)
7. Insafutdinov, E., Pishchulin, L., Andres, B., et al.: Deepercut: a deeper, stronger, and faster multi-person pose estimation model. In: European Conference on Computer Vision. Springer, Cham pp. 34–50 (2016)
8. He, K.M., Zhang, X.Y., Ren, S.Q., et al.: Deep residual learning for image recognition. In: Proceedings of the IEEE Conference on Computer Vision and Pattern Recognition, pp. 770–778 (2016). https://doi.org/10.1007/978-3-319-46466-4_3
9. Levinkov, E., Uhrig, J., Tang, S., et al.: Joint graph decomposition & node labeling: problem, algorithms, applications. In: Proceedings of the IEEE Conference on Computer Vision and Pattern Recognition, pp. 6012–6020 (2017)
10. Varadarajan, S., Datta, P., Tickoo, O.: A greedy part assignment algorithm for real-time multi-person 2D pose estimation. In: 2018 IEEE Winter Conference on Applications of Computer Vision (WACV). IEEE, pp. 418–426 (2018)
11. Cao, Z., Simon, T., Wei, S.E., et al.: Realtime multi-person 2D pose estimation using part affinity fields. In: Proceedings of the IEEE Conference on Computer Vision and Pattern Recognition, pp. 7291–7299 (2017)
12. Xia, F., Wang, P., Chen, X., et al.: Joint multi-person pose estimation and semantic part segmentation. In: Proceedings of the IEEE Conference on Computer Vision and Pattern Recognition, pp. 6769–6778 (2017)

13. Qiu, J., Yang, Y., Wang, X., Tao, D.: Hallucinating visual instances in total absentia. In: Vedaldi, A., Bischof, H., Brox, T., Frahm, J.-M. (eds.) ECCV 2020. LNCS, vol. 12350, pp. 264–282. Springer, Cham (2020). https://doi.org/10.1007/978-3-030-58558-7_16

14. Yang, Y., Ren, Z., Li, H., Zhou, C., Wang, X., Hua, G.: Learning dynamics via graph neural networks for human pose estimation and tracking. In: Proceedings of the Computer Vision and Pattern Recognition (CVPR) (2021)

15. Rastegari, M., Ordonez, V., Redmon, J., et al.: Xnor-net: imagenet classification using binary convolutional neural networks. In: European Conference on Computer Vision, pp. 525–542. Springer, Cham (2016). https://doi.org/10.1007/978-3-319-46493-0_32

16. Zhao, R., Tang, C.Q., Liu, W.L., et al.: A new BP neural network pruning algorithm based on grey relational analysis. Technol. Innov. Appl. **13**, 17–18 (2016)

17. Iandola, F.N., Han, S., Moskewicz, M.W., et al.: SqueezeNet: AlexNet-level accuracy with 50x fewer parameters and< 0.5 MB model size [EB/OL] (2016). https://arxiv.org/pdf/1602.07360.pdf

18. Sun, K., Xiao, B., Liu, D., et al.: Deep high-resolution representation learning for human pose estimation. In: Proceedings of the IEEE/CVF Conference on Computer Vision and Pattern Recognition, pp. 5693–5703 (2019)

19. Han, K., Wang, Y., Tian, Q., et al.: GhostNet: more features from cheap operations. In: Proceedings of the IEEE/CVF Conference on Computer Vision and Pattern Recognition, pp. 1580–1589 (2020)

20. Wang, X., Girshick, R., Gupta, A., et al.: Non-local neural networks. In: Proceedings of the IEEE Conference on Computer Vision and Pattern Recognition, pp. 7794–7803 (2018)

21. Andriluka, M., Pishchulin, L., Gehler, P., et al.: 2D human pose estimation: new benchmark and state of the art analysis. In: Proceedings of the IEEE Conference on Computer Vision and Pattern Recognition, pp. 3686–3693 (2014)

22. Lin, T.-Y., et al.: Microsoft coco: common objects in context. In: Fleet, D., Pajdla, T., Schiele, B., Tuytelaars, T. (eds.) ECCV 2014. LNCS, vol. 8693, pp. 740–755. Springer, Cham (2014). https://doi.org/10.1007/978-3-319-10602-1_48

Occluded Animal Shape and Pose Estimation from a Single Color Image

Yiming Xie[1], Yunqi Zhao[1], Shijian Jiang[1], Jiangyong Hu[1],
and Yangang Wang[1,2(✉)]

[1] School of Automation, Southeast University, Nanjing, China
`yangangwang@seu.edu.cn`
[2] Shenzhen Research Institute of Southeast University, Shenzhen, China

Abstract. This work addresses the problem of the animal shape and pose estimation from an occluded image. Most of exisiting 3D animal reconstruction methods focus on an automatic and accurate framework in normal conditions, but ignore some exceptional occasions, such as occlusion, which limits the practical applications of estimating the animal shape and pose to a large extent. In this paper, we introduce a random elimination strategy from fully annotated joints and propose a deep neural network for SMAL parameters regression from the partial joints. Our proposed method can effectively deal with the reconstruction of animals under the scenario of an occluded image. We have conducted extensive experiments and results demonstrate that our 3D animal shape and pose estimation method can yield good performance on occluded images.

Keywords: Occluded situation · Animal shape and pose estimation · Deep learning

1 Introduction

Animal welfare is a concern of importance for business and society, with an estimation of 70 billion animals living under human care [12]. Besides, the real-time monitoring and protecting of some endangered species is also of high significance, which provides biologists and conservationists with information about animal health and behavior. Monitoring and assessment of animal health and behavior can be assisted by obtaining accurate measurements of an individual's shape and pose. These measurements should not disturb the normal activities of animals and should be still effective in spite of complicated environmental conditions. There have been several methods for animal reconstruction with a view to the improvements of either data acquisition methods or model refinement methods in normal conditions. However, those existing methods cannot effectively deal with occasions where the animal is

This work was supported in part by Shenzhen Fundamental Research Program under Grant JCYJ20180306174459972, Natural Science Foundation of Jiangsu Province under Grant BK20180355 and the Fundamental Research Funds for the Central Universities.

Y. Peng et al. (Eds.): ICIG 2021, LNCS 12889, pp. 423–433, 2021.
https://doi.org/10.1007/978-3-030-87358-5_34

occluded, which makes the estimation of animal shape and pose quite limited in practical applications.

In this paper, we address the occluded problem using a regression network from partial key points to parameters of the SMAL model [21] (A Skinned Multi-Animal Linear Model), combining machine learning and 3D model fitting. Firstly, we employ the latest DeepLabCut [11] software package to train a joints detector to obtain the 2D joints positions of the input color image. Then, we simultaneously use the Mask R-CNN [4] to train a network for silhouettes extraction. Based on the work of Biggs [2], we can regress the parameters of the SMAL model from full joints annotations and silhouette, which, however, cannot handle the occluded occasions. In order to solve the occluded problem, we introduce a method of training a regression network from partial joints to parameters of the SMAL model. We adopt a random elimination measure to the full joints annotations to obtain a partial-joints annotated image, which is still in the mapping relationship with parameters of the SMAL model acquired from the last step. Subsequently, we use the partial joints and the corresponding parameters of the SMAL model to train the regression network, which can obtain the parameters of the SMAL model only from part of the joints. The experimental results of the estimation of shape and pose on occluded images in Sect. 4 demonstrate the effectiveness of our proposed method to deal with the occluded occasions. In summary, the main contributions of our method can be concluded as follows:

- We propose a novel 3D animal shape and pose estimation framework based on a single color image to predict the 3D animal model parameters, which achieves the state-of-the-art performance on occluded animal images.
- We propose an idea of using partial key points for regression network training to deal with the occluded problem in the reconstruction of animals, which effectively improves the accuracy of the animal shape and pose estimation.

2   Related Work

2.1   Human 3D Pose and Shape Estimation

There has been a lot of work in the field of 3D human pose prediction, and the work closely related to our project is the model SMPL [9], which is also an important model in the 3D reconstruction of the human body. The standard model of animals, SMAL [21], is transformed from SMPL with some deformations. SMPL is a low-dimensional parametric model, and the structure of this model gives ideas for the design of SMAL, i.e., constructing a model with multiple parameters. Also, since this is a low-dimensional model, it can be obtained using parameters generated by a neural network trained on a smaller number of images. There have been many works carried out using this model, Tan [16] trained a network capable of learning parameters from contours to SMPL model pose and shape, Pavlakos [13] used a two-stage architecture based on 2D key points and contours to predict the pose and shape of the SMPL model, and so on.

An obvious advantage of human 3D reconstruction over animal 3D reconstruction is that the former has numerous indoor datasets with true values, while the animal datasets are collected in the wild. In terms of acquisition of human outdoor dataset, von Marcard [10] used IMU sensors and video to obtain an outdoor dataset of human 3D pose and shape, and Varol [17] created a fully synthetic 3D pose and shape dataset. In the case of animals, the idea of wearing a device to detect posture and shape is not desirable because of the large range of motion and the complexity of the environment, which makes the device easy to drop.

2.2 Animal Pose and Shape Estimation

There has been an extensive body of prior work related to joint position prediction for human subjects. Earlier work used graphical approaches such as pictorial structure models [1,5,14], which have since been replaced with deep learning-based methods [11,15]. Few works predict animal joint positions directly owing to the lack of annotated data, although Mathis et al. [11] demonstrate the effectiveness of human pose estimation architectures for animal domains.

One of the earliest works in the field of animal 3D reconstruction was done by Cashman and Fitzgibbon [3], but their work was limited to small classes of objects (e.g., dolphins, pigeons) and did not include skeletons. Their work also demonstrated the use of 2D contours, which is key to our approach. Kanazawa [7] learned a deformable model for cats and horses. Kanazawa [8] predicted the 3D shape and texture of birds from pictures, but they did not reconstruct the pose of the birds.

Zuffi et al. [21] extended the SMPL model to animals and proposed a standard model SMAL for animals, which is closely related to our work. Based on this, they further proposed the SMALR model [20], which improved the optimization step of model vertex positions, but this model is still based on manual extraction of contours and annotation of key points. Biggs [2] automatically fit the SMAL model to the picture by training a joint detector on the synthetically generated contours. Favreau et al. apply PCA to silhouette images to extract animal gaits from video sequences. The task of predicting silhouette images from 2D input has been effectively used as a proxy for regressing 3D model parameters for humans [6,16] and other 3D objects [18]. However, this method requires very accurate segmentation and is not robust to occlusions. Recently, Zuffi et al. [19] built the SMALST model using images synthesized from real horses and virtual backgrounds as a dataset, but the actual results were not good.

3   Method

An overview of the proposed method is shown in Fig. 1. We use partial joints from the full joints annotated image to represent the occluded animal body, and animal shape and pose estimation is finally formulated by obtaining parameters of the SMAL model.

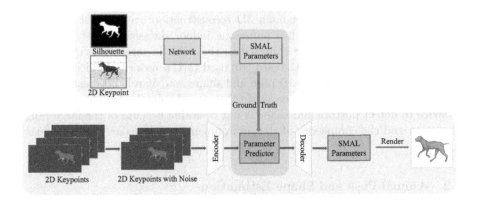

Fig. 1. Overview of the proposed method. (a) In the beginning, we obtain the SMAL model parameters based on the 2D keypoints and silhouette referring to the SMALify [2] method, which are assumed the ground truth. (b) After that we discard the 2D keypoints randomly to simulate the occlusion situation, and the remaining keypoints are fed into the parameter prediction network for training. (c) The SMAL parameters obtained from partial keypoints in the training process are compared with the ground truth for network optimization. (d) The SMAL model are rendered to obtain the reconstructed 3D model.

First of all, we use DeepLabCut software package, which is a deep convolutional network combining pretrained ResNet and deconvolutional layers to learn the 2D joints positions from a single color image. Simultaneously, we learn the animal silhouettes from Mask R-CNN network. Based on the work of Biggs [2], we can regress the parameters of the SMAL model from full joints annotations and silhouette, which, however, cannot handle the occluded occasions. Then we introduce a random elimination measure to obtain partial joints annotations, and we also introduce a regression network to regress the parameters of the SMAL model only from partial joints of the body, which can effectively deal with the estimation of animal shape and pose of an occluded image. Our method does not require manual key points annotations when testing and the accuracy can be dramatically improved targeting on occluded animal reconstruction problem.

3.1 3D Animal Model

We follow the previous 3D animal reconstruction methods, using the Skinned Multi-Animal Linear (SMAL) model of Zuffi et al. [21] to represent the animal body, which is learned from a small set of 3D scans of toy figurines in arbitrary poses. The SMAL model is a statistical shape model, which is a function $M(\beta, \theta, \gamma)$ of shape β, pose θ, and translation γ. β is a vector of the coefficients of the learned PCA shape space, $\theta \in R^{3N} = \{r_i\}_{i=1}^{N}$ is the relative rotation, expressed with Rodrigues vectors, of the joints in the kinematic tree, and γ is the global translation applied to the root joint. The SMAL function returns a 3D mesh, where the model template is shaped by β, articulated by θ and shifted by γ.

3.2 Estimation from Silhouettes and Full 2D Joints

2D Joints and Silhouettes Estimation. We train a Mask R-CNN [4] to extract the silhouettes of the input images. And we use the DeepLabCut [11] toolbox to predict the 2D joints positions of the input color image. DeepLabCut is a deep convolutional network combining two key ingredients from algorithms for object recognition and semantic segmentation: pretrained ResNets and deconvolutional layers. Instead of the classification layer at the output of the ResNet, deconvolutional layers are used to up-sample the visual information and produce spatial probability densities.

Optimization of SMAL Model. For the optimization process of parameters of the SMAL model, we use a deep neural network to obtain the mapping relationship from joints to parameters of the SMAL model. We divide the loss function in the network training into two parts, the joints reprojection loss and the contour loss (Fig. 2).

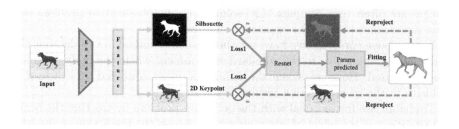

Fig. 2. Optimization of the SMAL model. (a) Extract the features by encoding the input RGB image and obtain the joint positions and silhouette from the corresponding detector. (b) The obtained contour and joint positions are fed into the network for training to get the SMAL model parameters.

Joints reprojected loss L_{joints} refers to the L2 loss calculated by comparing the 2D projection of the key points of the predicted 3D model with the real labels, which can be expressed as:

$$L_{joint}(\beta, \theta, \gamma; \hat{J}) = \left\| \hat{J} - J(\beta, \theta, \gamma) \right\|_2$$

Where β, θ, γ stands for the shape, pose and translation parameters of the SMAL model respectively, $\hat{J}$ refers to the joint labels and $J(\beta, \theta, \gamma)$ is the reprojection of the joints of the predicted 3D model.

Contour loss $L_{silhouette}$ refers to the L2 loss calculated by comparing the 2D projection of the silhouette of the predicted 3D model with the real one, which can be expressed as:

$$L_{silhouette}(\beta, \theta, \gamma; \hat{S}) = \left\| \hat{S} - S(\beta, \theta, \gamma) \right\|_2$$

Where β, θ, γ stands for the shape, pose and translation parameters of the SMAL model respectively, $\hat{S}$ refers to the silhouette ground truth and $S(\beta, \theta, \gamma)$ is the reprojection of the silhouette of the predicted 3D model. In summary, the loss function of the entire network is:

$$L = \varphi L_{joints} + \gamma L_{silhouette}$$

Among them, φ, γ are the hyperparameters of the corresponding loss functions, which are used to balance the value of each loss function.

3.3   Joints Estimation of an Occluded Image

As we know, the living environment of animals is often in the wild, and its changes are often very complex. The solution to the obscuration problem is of great significance in the 3D reconstruction of animals.

In the above two steps we have got the predicted animal 3D model, but this model is only applicable to the standard environment where the body of animal is not obscured. However, when the animal is object-obscured, it will lead to problems in the reconstruction results as shown in Fig. 4.

Therefore, we further deal with the occlusion problem by treating the occlusion situation as the effect of environmental noise on the prediction of the joint points, resulting in the failure to predict the full joint points under partial occlusion. We add noise randomly to the predicted nodes in standard pose and remove some key points to simulate the occlusion situation, which in turn increases the robustness of the network to adapt to the animal 3D reconstruction problem in the occlusion situation.

Specifically, we use heatmap to represent each joint point, and for the prediction results of joint points, we randomly set the heatmap of some joint points to zero to simulate the occlusion cases. The noise adding process is shown in Fig. 3.

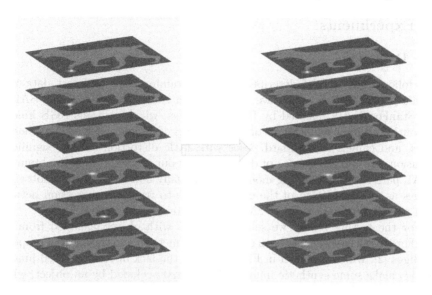

Fig. 3. Add noise to the full joint annotations for partial joint annotations.
The 2D keypoints are randomly discarded to simulate the occlusion occasions.

3.4   Regression of the Parameters of SMAL

At the same time, we find that the contour features in the occlusion case are detrimental to the parameter prediction, and the discontinuous contour information leads to outliers in the parameter prediction of the model, which plays a great negative role in our parameter prediction. Therefore, we choose to discard the contour features and establish the direct mapping relationship from the joint positions to the SMAL parameters through the model parameter regression module according to the idea of human 3D reconstruction.

For the regression module of SMAL model parameters, we use a deep learning network to establish the regression relationship between the articulated points with occlusion and the SMAL model parameters. We feed the joint heatmaps with occlusion effect into the network encoder for encoding, and use the predicted SMAL model parameters obtained in Sect. 3.2 as the ground truth. We use an error feedback iterative network for iterative optimization of parameters to make them approximate the ground truth, to build a regression network from only partial key points to the complete SMAL model parameters.

Furthermore, we define the loss of SMAL model parameter estimation as the MSE between the estimated value and the ground truth:

$$Loss = \left\| \hat{M} - M(\beta, \theta, \gamma) \right\|_2$$

Where $\hat{M}$ is the ground truth of SMAL model parameters and $M(\beta, \theta, \gamma)$ is the prediction of SMAL parameters obtained from Sect. 3.2.

4 Experiments

4.1 Datasets

The following is a brief description of the training data and test data used in this paper. In this paper, we use the open source animal dataset BADJA and StanFordExtra released by Benjamin Biggs, which contains RGB images, contours, and joint annotations of several kinds of animals such as dogs, horses, bears, and camels in standard poses with little distortion and no significant occlusion. We use a sequence of dog images as our training input to obtain our SMAL parameters predicting model. We manually add noise to the unobscured images as our simulation of the obscured case to train our regression network from partial joints positions to SMAL parameters in the obscured case.

For the testing phase, we selected images with object occluded from the StanFordExtra to test using both our proposed method and the method proposed by Biggs [2], which is shown in Fig. 4. Due to the lack of real occluded images, we also make some synthetic images with animal occluded by an object, which are shown in Fig. 5.

4.2 Implementation Details and Error Metrics

Implementation Details. In the process of solving the SMAL model parameters in the standard case, we first use the joint annotations in the dataset to train the joint detector in DeepLabCut, and use the mask annotations in the dataset to train the contour detector in Mask-RCNN. We use a 256×256 sized RGB image as the input, and combine the joint annotation and contour annotation to obtain the SMAL model parameters with the Smalify method for optimization as the ground truth. In the training process of obscured cases, we use the joint annotations with noise as input, the predicted SMAL model parameters as output, and the ground truth is the standard SMAL model parameters obtained in the previous step. We use ResNet to establish the regression relationship between the input and output, and use Adam as the optimizer, setting the learning rate to 10e-4 and the number of iterations to 150 on a 2080ti GPU.

Error Metrics. We evaluate the performance of the network quantitatively and use the mean vertex error to quantify the error of the reconstructed animal model.

$$\varepsilon = \frac{1}{N} \sum_{i=1}^{N} \sqrt{\|v_i - \hat{v}_i\|^2}$$

N is the number of all vertices of the 3D model, v is the predicted vertices of the 3D model, and $\hat{v}$ is the ground truth of the 3D model vertices.

Input   Silhouette and Keypoints   3D Reconstruction from Two Views

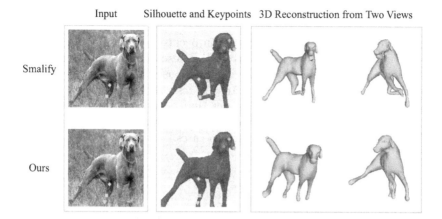

Fig. 4. Comparison Results. We compare our proposed method with SMALify [2]. (a) The results in the first line come from SMALify, which has a poor performance in the case of occlusion. (b) The results in the second line come from our method, which is more robust to occlusion and has more reasonable results.

Fig. 5. Results from Synthetic Images. Referring to the idea from SMALST [19], we synthesize images with occlusion from datasets released by Biggs and feed them into the network for reconstruction. Some of our reconstructed results are shown in Fig. 5, and we can see that our proposed method performs quite well on occluded images.

4.3   Experiment Results

We compare our model with Smalify [2] in occlusion cases and the results are shown in Fig. 4 and Fig. 5. The reconstruction results of our model in occlusion cases are more reasonable and do not show serious distortion.

In addition, we have conducted extensive tests on our model. Animal reconstruction was performed in occlusion cases, and some results are shown in Fig. 5. We can see that our method can yield good performance on occluded images and have good robustness to the occlusion cases.

5   Conclusion

In this paper, we propose an effective solution to the estimation of animal shape and pose from an occluded image, which achieves good performance on test images. In order to simulate the obscured situation, we adopt a random elimination measure to the joint annotations. Specifically speaking, we add noise randomly to the predicted nodes in standard pose and remove some key points to simulate the occlusion situation. Besides, we also introduce a parameter regression network only from partial joints to parameters of the SMAL model. In order to obtain the ground truth of the 3D model, we first employ the full joints and silhouette supervision to train a deep neural network. And when we train the regression network from partial joints, we discard the supervision of silhouette for better results. The experimental results on datasets show the effectiveness of our method.

References

1. Andriluka, M., Roth, S., Schiele, B.: Monocular 3D pose estimation and tracking by detection. In: IEEE Conference on Computer Vision and Pattern Recognition (CVPR), pp. 623–630 (2010)
2. Biggs, B., Roddick, T., Fitzgibbon, A., Cipolla, R.: Creatures great and smal: recovering the shape and motion of animals from video. In: Asian Conference on Computer Vision (ACCV) (2018)
3. Cashman, T.J., Fitzgibbon, A.W.: What shape are dolphins? Building 3D morphable models from 2D images. IEEE Trans. Pattern Anal. Mach. Intell. **35**(1), 232–244 (2012)
4. He, K., Gkioxari, G., Dollár, P., Girshick, R.: Mask R-CNN. In: IEEE International Conference on Computer Vision (ICCV), pp. 2961–2969 (2017)
5. Johnson, S., Everingham, M.: Clustered pose and nonlinear appearance models for human pose estimation. In: British Machine Vision Conference (BMVC), pp. 12.1–12.11 (2010)
6. Kanazawa, A., Black, M.J., Jacobs, D.W., Malik, J.: End-to-end recovery of human shape and pose. In: IEEE Conference on Computer Vision and Pattern Recognition (CVPR), pp. 7122–7131 (2018)
7. Kanazawa, A., Kovalsky, S., Basri, R., Jacobs, D.: Learning 3D deformation of animals from 2D images. Comput. Graph. Forum **35**(2), 365–374 (2016)

8. Kanazawa, A., Tulsiani, S., Efros, A.A., Malik, J.: Learning category-specific mesh reconstruction from image collections. In: European Conference on Computer Vision (ECCV), pp. 371–386 (2018)

9. Loper, M., Mahmood, N., Romero, J., Pons-Moll, G., Black, M.J.: SMPL: a skinned multi-person linear model. ACM Trans. Graph. (TOG) **34**(6), 1–16 (2015)

10. von Marcard, T., Henschel, R., Black, M.J., Rosenhahn, B., Pons-Moll, G.: Recovering accurate 3D human pose in the wild using IMUs and a moving camera. In: European Conference on Computer Vision (ECCV), pp. 601–617 (2018)

11. Mathis, A., et al.: Deeplabcut: markerless pose estimation of user-defined body parts with deep learning. Nat. Neurosci. **21**(9), 1281–1289 (2018)

12. Mekouar, M.A.: 15. food and agriculture organization (FAO). Yearb. Int. Environ. Law **24**(1), 587–602 (2013)

13. Pavlakos, G., Zhu, L., Zhou, X., Daniilidis, K.: Learning to estimate 3D human pose and shape from a single color image. In: IEEE Conference on Computer Vision and Pattern Recognition (CVPR), pp. 459–468 (2018)

14. Pishchulin, L., Andriluka, M., Gehler, P., Schiele, B.: Poselet conditioned pictorial structures. In: IEEE Conference on Computer Vision and Pattern Recognition (CVPR), pp. 588–595 (2013)

15. Reinert, B., Ritschel, T., Seidel, H.P.: Animated 3D creatures from single-view video by skeletal sketching. In: Graphics Interface (GI), pp. 133–141 (2016)

16. Tan, J.K.V., Budvytis, I., Cipolla, R.: Indirect deep structured learning for 3D human body shape and pose prediction. In: British Machine Vision Conference (BMVC), pp. 15.1–15.11 (2017)

17. Varol, G., et al.: Learning from synthetic humans. In: IEEE Conference on Computer Vision and Pattern Recognition (CVPR), pp. 109–117 (2017)

18. Wiles, O., Zisserman, A.: Silnet: single-and multi-view reconstruction by learning from silhouettes. arXiv preprint arXiv:1711.07888 (2017)

19. Zuffi, S., Kanazawa, A., Berger-Wolf, T., Black, M.J.: Three-d safari: learning to estimate zebra pose, shape, and texture from images in the wild. In: IEEE/CVF International Conference on Computer Vision (ICCV), pp. 5359–5368 (2019)

20. Zuffi, S., Kanazawa, A., Black, M.J.: Lions and tigers and bears: Capturing non-rigid, 3D, articulated shape from images. In: IEEE Conference on Computer Vision and Pattern Recognition (CVPR), pp. 3955–3963 (2018)

21. Zuffi, S., Kanazawa, A., Jacobs, D.W., Black, M.J.: 3D menagerie: modeling the 3D shape and pose of animals. In: IEEE Conference on Computer Vision and Pattern Recognition (CVPR), pp. 5524–5532 (2017)

Adaptively Fusing Complete Multi-resolution Features for Human Pose Estimation

Yuezhen Huang[1], Dong Wei[2], Yinan Liu[2(✉)], Xiaofeng Jin[2], Yuheng Huang[2], and Tianshi Xu[2]

[1] Guangzhou Radio Group, Guangzhou, Guangdong, China
[2] GRG Banking Equipment Co., Ltd., Guangzhou, Guangdong, China
liuyinan@grgbanking.com

Abstract. Multi-resolution features are important for image-based human pose estimation. In this paper, we present a method to exploit complete information from feature maps of neural network in different resolutions to improve the accuracy of human pose estimation. The proposal, namely Adaptively Complete Multi-Resolution Feature Fusion (AdaCMRFF), is based on a high-resolution network (HRNet). AdaCM-RFF fuses all feature maps based on the adaptive parameters which can preserve useful information of different resolution feature maps when fusing into a specific resolution feature map. Firstly, different resolution feature maps are resized to the same shape by sampling and convolution strategies. The fused weight parameters are then generated through 1×1 convolutions and softmax function which operate on above feature maps. Finally, the feature maps and fused parameters are added to make a new feature map. AdaCMRFF is equipped on all the stages of HRNet to retain handy information of all the feature maps. A series of experiments are conducted on two mainstream human pose estimation datasets, includes COCO2017 and CrowdPose dataset present the effect of the proposed method.

Keywords: Human pose estimation · HRNet · Feature fusion

1 Introduction

Human pose estimation is a very important and challenging topic in computer vision, which aims to detect 2D human key points (e.g. eyes, elbows, knees, *etc.*) from images and locate them in the correct positions of the images. Human pose estimation plays a considerable role in many applications, such as human behavior understanding, animation and augmented reality, etc. Also, it is a very useful tool for higher-level task such as motion tracking [21], human action recognition [5] and person re-id [7].

Recently, convolution neural networks (CNNs) have caught great attention due to the excellent capability in image classification [9,19] and object detection

© Springer Nature Switzerland AG 2021
Y. Peng et al. (Eds.): ICIG 2021, LNCS 12889, pp. 434–445, 2021.
https://doi.org/10.1007/978-3-030-87358-5_35

[14,17,18]. With these excellent network models and the openness of the conventional datasets [1,12,13], human pose estimation is developed rapidly recent years. Currently, more and more algorithms have been proposed to promote the detection accuracy of human keypoints and the accuracy is constantly improved. However, some hard human key points are still hard to be detected and located because of objection occlusion, various backgrounds and illumination.

There is a vast literature on human pose estimation methods in deep learning that can be categorized into two parts: top-down methods [15,20,21], bottom-up methods [4,10,22]. Top-down methods take an image with an accurate human bounding box as input and then detect the key points of a single human. Since top-down methods can crop and resize the detected person bounding boxes, they have great performances on datasets such as MPII [1], COCO [13] and CrowdPose [12]. By contrast, bottom-up methods detect and locate the persons key points from a complete image, and then group all the key points into person instances.

Most of the existing network architectures are based on high-resolution to low-resolution, and then localize human key points by recovering high-resolution representation from low-resolution representation. HRNet [20] is proposed to maintain high-resolution features during the entire human pose estimation process. However, the fuse approach of HRNet is simple and it just resize the heatmaps of different resolutions and use element-wise sum method to generate high and low resolution heatmaps. This approach may affect the combination of useful information at each resolution feature and useless information is kept, reducing the accuracy of human key point detection especially when the information of heatmaps is not enough.

In this paper, we propose a method, named Adaptively Complete Multi-Resolution Feature Fusion (AdaCMRFF), to keep the useful information in each resolution and fuse them into different resolution feature maps. The key idea of our proposed method is to allow the network to learn the features of different resolution and adaptively keep more useful information as much as possible. For the heatmap features at a certain resolution, features of other resolution are resized into the same resolution, and then the weight of each spatial position in these features are trained to learn. Finally, these features are integrated with learned weight. AdaCMRFF is equipped on all the stages of HRNet to retain handy information of all the feature maps, so that complete features in different resolutions can be exploited. Furthermore, the implementation of AdaCMRFF blocks is brief and the cost of network computation increases less.

To demonstrate the performances of our proposed method (AdaCMRFF), we comprehensively evaluate it with two mainstream human pose detection datasets including CrowdPose and COCO. The experimental results show that the performance of the proposed method is better than that of HigherHRNet in bottom-up approaches. Additionally, we use the proposed AdaCMRFF blocks in HRNet of top-down methods and the accuracy of human key point detection is improved.

2 Related Work

2.1 Top-Down Methods for Human Pose Estimation

The methods based on graph model and tree model achieve a good result for traditional human pose estimation. These methods are simple but they need to design specifically handcrafted features for the images. However, when in the complex and diversity scenes, these methods cannot detect human key points accurately.

Inspired by the distinguished algorithms of objection detection, some researchers employ them to human pose estimation. Cascaded pyramid network (CPN) [3] structure is proposed to use GlobalNet and RefineNet to detect key points efficiently. Xiao et al. [21] built a simple yet effective structure named Simple Baseline which utilizes a few deconvolutional layers in the ResNet to produce heatmaps for human key points high-resolution representations.

Most of the above methods take the images as input and obtain high-resolution output by performing down-sampling and up-sampling, while the HRNet [20] structure enhances high-resolution representation. HRNet maintain high-resolution representation by multi-scale fusion, which improves the accuracy of human pose estimation.

2.2 Bottom-Up Methods for Human Pose Estimation

As distinguished from top-down approaches, bottom-up methods have two main steps. They first need to extract local features from images and predict human body joint candidates, then assemble the joint candidates to build final pose representations with part association strategies for individual bodies. Cao et al. [2] proposed a network named OpenPose for human pose estimation, which uses CPMs to predict the heatmaps of human key points and builds Part Affinity Fields (PAFs) to associate the key points to every person. OpenPose outperforms the previous methods but it has poor performance on low resolution images and occluded scenes. Since high-resolution features contain enough information of images, Cheng et al. [4] adopted HRNet as the backbone and introduced Higher Resolution Network (HigherHRNet) to maintain high-resolution representation, which generates deconvolved high-resolution heatmaps to improve the key points detection accuracy of low-resolution images.

3 Proposed Method

Human pose estimation aims to detect the locations of K keypoints from an Image. Many methods estimate K heatmaps of size $W^{'} \times H^{'}$ from an Image of size $W \times H$ and predict the location of keypoint by the K heatmaps. HRNet is one of the state-of-the-art networks in human pose estimation, which retains high resolution heatmaps during the process. The design of HRNet can get abundant high resolution feature representation and detect the key points of human bodies more accurately. For the above advantages of HRNet, we apply Adaptively

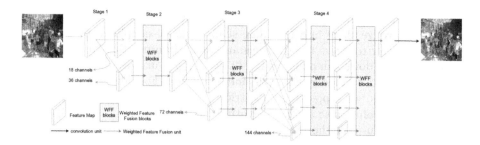

Fig. 1. The architecture of our proposed network. We replaced the fusion blocks of HRNet with our proposed Adaptively Complete Multi-Resolution Feature Fusion blocks.

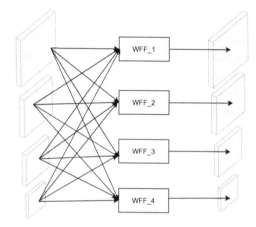

Fig. 2. The adaptively complete multi-resolution feature fusion blocks of stage 4 in the proposed architecture.

Complete Multi-Resolution Feature Fusion to it and demonstrate the functions of Adaptively Complete Multi-Resolution Feature Fusion. The architecture of our proposed method are shown in Fig. 1.

As shown in Fig. 1, we utilize Adaptively Complete Multi-Resolution Feature Fusion (AdaCMRFF) blocks to replace the fusion blocks of HRNet. We take the AdaCMRFF blocks of stage 4 as example to illustrate how the AdaCMRFF blocks work. As shown in Fig. 2, the inputs of AdaCMRFF blocks are the different resolution feature maps and the sizes of highest and lowest resolution feature maps are $H \times W \times C$ and $H/8 \times W/8 \times 8C$ respectively. All the feature maps enter different AdaCMRFF blocks and then generate different resolution feature maps according to some rules of AdaCMRFF blocks.

To further explain AdaCMRFF blocks, we take the third AdaCMRFF block in stage 4 for example, as shown in Fig. 3. We denote the feature maps of the resolution in stage 4 as $x^n, n = 1, 2, 3, 4$. For each level feature map x^n, we resize it to the same shape as that of x^3. Since the feature maps have different resolutions and channels, we use up-sampling, down-sampling and convolution strategies to resize them into the same shape. For up-sampling, we use 1×1 convolution layer to resize the channels and apply interpolation to upscale the resolutions. For down-sampling with $1/2$, we simply utilize convolution layer with a stride of 2 to modify channels and resolution. For down-sampling with $1/2$ or $1/4$ ratios, we supplement a 2-stride or 4-stride max pooling layer and use 2-stride convolution to resize the feature maps.

In order to fuse all the feature maps adaptively, we generate the weights which learned from the feature maps. The fuse method can be formulized as follows:

$$y_{ij}^l = \sum_{n=1}^{N} \alpha_{ij}^{ln} x_{ij}^{ln}, \tag{1}$$

where y_{ij}^l represents the vector of output feature maps y^l at (i,j) position among channels. N stands for the number of feature maps, and α_{ij}^{ln} denotes the learned weight for the feature maps at level l. x_{ij}^{ln} is the (i,j) position feature vector of the resized feature map which is resized from x^n to x^l. α_{ij}^{ln} is a scalar parameter and shared across all the channels of feature map x^n to x^l. In order to normalize the weight α_{ij}^{ln}, we make the condition as follows:

$$\sum_{n} \alpha_{ij}^{ln} = 1, \tag{2}$$

where $\alpha_{ij}^{ln} \geq 0$. Here we use softmax function to normalize the weights:

$$\alpha_{ij}^{ln} = \frac{e^{\lambda_{ij}^{ln}}}{\sum_{n} e^{\lambda_{ij}^{ln}}}, \tag{3}$$

where λ_{ij}^{ln} can be obtained by 1×1 convolution layers from the resized feature map x_{ij}^{ln} and can be learned through back-propagation.

With the Adaptively Complete Multi-Resolution Feature Fusion blocks, different resolution feature maps are adaptively integrated at each resolution level and the important features can be much preserved after fusing.

4   Experiments Results

To verify the effectiveness of the proposed method, we conduct experiments on two widely used keypoint detection datasets: COCO dataset [13] and CrowdPose dataset [12]. We describe our experimental settings and report the results of evaluation metric for human pose estimation.

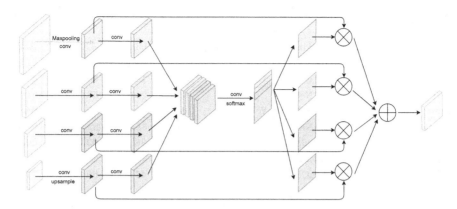

Fig. 3. The details of the third Adaptively Complete Multi-Resolution Feature Fusion block of stage 4.

4.1 The Experimental Settings

All experiments in this paper are conducted in the same environment, with Pytorch 1.6 and four NVIDIA 1080Ti GPUs. In the training process, Adam optimizer is used to update the weights and the learning rate is set as 1e-3 and dropped to 1e-4 and 1e-5 at the 200th and 260th epoch respectively both on the COCO dataset and CrowdPose dataset. The training stops at the 300th epoch. Our proposed method adopts the loss function of HigherHRNet and use the heatmap loss and the grouping loss as the loss function. We crop the human detection boxes from the datasets images and resize them to a fixed size 512×512. Meanwhile, we apply some data augmentation strategies include horizontal flipping, random rotation in and random scaling in (0.65, 1.35). For AdaCMRFF-W18 and AdaCMRFF-W32, we use the pretrained models which trained on ImageNet. As for AdaCMRFF-W24 and AdaCMRFF-W28, we use random initialization to initial parameters. In the testing process, we directly evaluate the models on the dataset without flipping and multi-scale strategies. Besides, the evaluation metric for compared methods is Object Keypoint Similarity (OKS):

$$OKS = \frac{\sum_i \exp(-d_i^2/2s^2k_i^2)\delta(v_i > 0)}{\sum_i \delta(v_i > 0)}, \tag{4}$$

where d_i^2 stands for the distance of ground-truth keypoint location and predicted location, s and k_i denote the scale and control parameters respectively, and v_i implies the visibility flag of person keypoint. For COCO dataset and CrowdPose dataset, we adopt the average precision as the criteria to assess human pose estimation quality, including AP (the mean AP at OKS = $0.50, 0.55, \ldots, 0.90, 0.95$), AP^{50} (AP at OKS = 0.50) and AP^{75} (AP at OKS = 0.75).

Table 1. Experimental results among different networks on CrowdPose test dataset

Model	Backbone	Pretrain	Params	GFLOPs	AP	AP^{50}	AP^{75}
HrHRNet-W18 [4]	HRNet-W18	Y	9.35M	19.42	58.1	83.9	64.1
Ours (AdaCMRFF-W18)	AdaCMRFF-W18	Y	**9.37M**	**19.53**	**58.2**	**84.1**	**64.2**
HrHRNet-W24 [4]	HRNet-W24	N	16.31M	29.66	57.9	83.3	64.1
Ours (AdaCMRFF-W24)	AdaCMRFF-W24	N	**16.33M**	**29.75**	**58.1**	**83.6**	64.0
HrHRNet-W28 [4]	HRNet-W28	N	22.01M	38.03	62.3	83.8	66.6
Ours (AdaCMRFF-W28)	AdaCMRFF-W28	N	**22.04M**	**38.09**	62.3	**83.9**	66.5
HrHRNet-W32 [4]	HRNet-W32	Y	28.64M	47.65	65.9	86.4	70.6
Ours (AdaCMRFF-W32)	AdaCMRFF-W32	Y	**28.67M**	**47.69**	**66.0**	86.4	**70.7**

4.2   Experiments on CrowdPose Dataset

The CrowdPose [12] dataset is composed of 20,000 images, containing about 80,000 person instances with 14 keypoints. The dataset is split into three parts: train, validation and test subset and the proportion of them is 5:1:4. Crowd-Pose has more crowded scenes than the COCO keypoint, posing more challenges to pose estimation methods. We train on train and validation subset (12,000 images, 43,400 persons) and evaluate on test subset (8,000 images, 29,000 persons). Besides AP, AP^{50} and AP^{75}, we also utilize AP^E, AP^M and AP^H (AP for easy, medium and hard objects) to evaluate the results on CrowdPose dataset.

Table 1 compares the results of our proposed AdaCMRFF method with HigherHR-Net [4] using different channels. (i) With more channel information, the performance of keypoint detection becomes better. For example, AdaCMRFF-28 model improves the AdaCMRFF-24 results by 4.2 AP and 2.5 AP^{75}. However, the parameters and GFLOPs of AdaCMRFF-28 increase appropriately 5.71M and 8.24 respectively. (ii) Compared with HigherHRNet on a certain channel, the AP roughly increases 0.1 point but the parameters and GFLOPs only raise 0.1% and 0.2%. (iii) Compared with AdaCMRFF-18 and AdaCMRFF-24, a pretrained model helps to obtain a better accuracy. From the results we can observe that HigherHRNet network can improve the performance after implementing our proposed AdaCMRFF blocks. The reason is that AdaCMRFF blocks preserve more useful information in both high-resolution feature maps and low-resolution feature maps.

Compared with other bottom-up methods for human pose estimation, the results are shown in Table 2. In contrast to openpose [2] network, our proposed method with AdaCMRFF-W18 backbone performs better on test dataset. The AP^E, AP^M and AP^H results of AdaCMRFF-18 is 3.3, 9.7 and 18.2 points higher than that of openpose respectively. Compared with Mask-RCNN and AlphaPose, our AdaCMRFF-32 model has the best performance on different evaluation metrics. The results show that AdaCMRFF model performs much better with small scales thanks to its higher resolution heatmaps. Besides, our proposed method has a better result on AP than that of HigherHRNet. The reason is that our AdaCMRFF method can preserve more useful information in both high-resolution feature maps and low-resolution feature maps.

Table 2. Experimental results among networks on CrowdPose test dataset

Model	Backbone	Input size	AP	AP^{50}	AP^{75}	AP^E	AP^M	AP^H
openpose [2]	–	–	–	–	–	62.7	48.7	32.3
Mask-RCNN [8]	Hourglass	512	60.4	83.0	66.2	–	–	
AlphaPose [6]	–	–	61.0	81.3	66.0	71.2	61.4	51.1
HrHRNet-W18 [4]	HRNet-W18	512	58.1	83.9	64.1	66.3	58.2	50.5
Ours(AdaCMRFF-18)	AdaCMRFF-W18	512	**58.2**	**84.1**	**64.2**	**66.0**	**58.4**	**50.9**
HrHRNet-W32 [20]	HRNet-W32	512	65.9	86.4	70.6	73.3	66.5	57.9
Ours(AdaCMRFF-32)	AdaCMRFF-W32	512	**66.0**	**86.4**	**70.7**	**73.0**	**66.7**	**56.0**

Table 3. Experimental results among bottom-up networks on COCO validation dataset

Model	Backbone	Input size	AP	AP^{50}	AP^{75}	AP^M	AP^L
openpose [2]	–	–	65.3	85.2	71.3	–	–
HGG [11]	Hourglass	512	60.4	83.0	66.2	–	–
PersonLab [16]	ResNet-152	601	54.1	76.4	57.7	40.6	73.3
PersonLab [16]	ResNet-152	1401	66.5	86.2	71.9	62.3	73.2
HrHRNet-W32 [20]	HRNet-W32	512	67.1	86.1	73.0	61.5	76.0
Ours (AdaCMRFF-32)	AdaCMRFF-W32	512	**67.2**	**86.1**	**73.1**	**61.4**	**76.2**

4.3 Experiments on COCO Dataset

The COCO [13] dataset contains over 200,000 images and 250,000 person instances labeled with 17 keypoints. We train our model on COCO train2017 dataset, including 57K images and 150K person instances. We evaluate our approach on the val2017 set which contains 5000 images and 6352 person instances. Besides AP, AP^{50} and AP^{75}, we also utilize AP^M (AP for medium objects) and AP^L (AP for large objects) as the evaluate metric for COCO dataset. In the following experiments, we compare our human pose estimation model with other networks.

Table 3 lists the keypoints detection results on COCO validation dataset. From the results, we can observe that our AdaCMRFF-32 model improves 1.9 AP as compared with openpose [2] network. Meanwhile, our proposed model with smaller input size outperforms PersonLab [16] of size 601 × 601 and 1401 × 1401 by +2.9 and + 0.7 AP respectively. Equipped with AdaCMRFF blocks, our proposed network gets 0.1 AP higher than HigherHRNet-W32.

Table 4. Experimental results among top-down networks on COCO validation dataset

Model	Backbone	Input size	Params	GFLOPs	AP	AP^{50}	AP^{75}
8-stage Hourglass [15]	8-stage Hourglass	256 × 192	25.1M	14.3	66.9	–	–
CPN [3]	ResNet-50	256 × 192	27.0M	6.2	68.6	–	–
CPN + OHKM [3]	ResNet-50	256 × 192	27.0M	6.2	69.4	–	–
SimpleBaseline [21]	ResNet-50	256 × 192	34.0M	8.9	70.4	88.6	78.3
SimpleBaseline[21]	ResNet-101	256 × 192	53.0M	12.4	71.4	89.3	79.3
SimpleBaseline [21]	ResNet-152	256 × 192	68.6M	15.7	72.0	89.3	79.8
HRNet-W18 [20]	HRNet-W18	256 × 192	9.31M	2.97	72.4	89.3	80.0
Ours (AdaCMRFF)	AdaCMRFF-W18	256 × 192	**9.33M**	**2.99**	**72.7**	**89.6**	**80.2**
HRNet-W32 [20]	HRNet-W32	256 × 192	28.48M	7.11	74.4	90.5	81.9
Ours (AdaCMRFF)	AdaCMRFF-W32	256 × 192	**28.53M**	**7.13**	**74.5**	**90.6**	**81.9**
SimpleBaseline [21]	ResNet-152	384 × 288	68.6M	35.3	74.3	89.6	81.1
HRNet-W18 [20]	HRNet-W18	384 × 288	9.31M	6.68	74.3	89.7	81.4
Ours (AdaCMRFF-18)	AdaCMRFF-W18	384 × 288	**9.33M**	**6.72**	**74.5**	**90.0**	**81.7**
HRNet-W32 [20]	HRNet-W32	384 × 288	28.48M	15.98	75.8	90.6	82.5
Ours (AdaCMRFF-32)	AdaCMRFF-W32	384 × 288	**28.53M**	**16.02**	**75.9**	**90.6**	**82.6**

4.4   Experiments on HRNet Top-Down Method

To further verify the performance of AdaCMRFF, we add the AdaCMRFF blocks into HRNet which is one of the state-of-the-art top-down method for human pose estimation. We conduct experiments on COCO dataset and report the results in Table 4. Compared with other models of the input size 256×192, our proposed model AdaCMRFF-32 reaches 74.5 AP on COCO validation dataset, which outperforms other models. Compared with Hourglass [15] model, the AP of our smaller model is 5.5 point higher, and both the parameters and GFLOPs are much smaller. Besides, compared to CPN model w/o and w/ OHKM, our proposed AdaCMRFF-18 model, with less parameters and lower computational cost, has 4.1 and 3.3 points improvement at AP accuracy, respectively. Considering SimpleBaseline [21] model with different backbones, our larger network, AdaCMRFF-32, obtains significant increasements: 4.1 points at AP accuracy gain for ResNet-50 backbone with comparable parameters and GFLOPs, and 1.8 points improvements for ResNet-152 backbone whose parameters and GFLOPs are larger than our proposed AdaCMRFF-32 model. As for the input size 384 × 288, AdaCMRFF-18 and AdaCMRFF-32 achieves 74.5 and 75.9 AP, which gain 1.8 and 1.5 improvements respectively compared to the results of the input size 256 × 192.

Comparing with HRNet network, our AdaCMRFF model, trained with the input size 256 × 192 and 18 channels, is 0.3 AP and 0.3 AP^{50} higher but only increases 0.2% computational cost. Equipped with AdaCMRFF blocks, our method can preserve more useful information in both high-resolution feature maps and low-resolution feature maps, especially when the channel information of feature maps is less. Meanwhile, the parameters and the computational cost of our AdaCMRFF method increase marginally. Fig. 4 demonstrate the keypoints detection results on some images of COCO dataset.

Fig. 4. The visualization results of some images for human pose estimation.

5   Conclusion

In this work, we introduce a feature fusion method called Adaptively Complete Multi-Resolution Feature Fusion (AdaCMRFF) based on HRNet for human pose estimation. AdaCMRFF considers the different importance among different resolution feature maps and aims to improve the accuracy of human keypoints detection. On one hand, the weights of AdaCMRFF for different resolution feature maps can learned adaptively so the useful information of features are preserved when merging them to a specific resolution feature map. On the other hand, the implementation of AdaCMRFF blocks is brief and the increased computational cost is marginal so AdaCMRFF is concise to equip on other networks. The experimental results on COCO and CrowdPose dataset show that the employment of AdaCMRFF blocks improves the accuracy of human keypoints location.

References

1. Andriluka, M., Pishchulin, L., Gehler, P., Schiele, B.: 2D human pose estimation: new benchmark and state of the art analysis. In: Proceedings of the IEEE Conference on computer Vision and Pattern Recognition, pp. 3686–3693 (2014)
2. Cao, Z., Hidalgo, G., Simon, T., Wei, S.E., Sheikh, Y.: Openpose: realtime multi-person 2D pose estimation using part affinity fields. IEEE Trans. Pattern Anal. Mach. Intell. **43**(1), 172–186 (2019)
3. Chen, Y., Wang, Z., Peng, Y., Zhang, Z., Yu, G., Sun, J.: Cascaded pyramid network for multi-person pose estimation. In: Proceedings of the IEEE Conference on Computer Vision and Pattern Recognition, pp. 7103–7112 (2018)
4. Cheng, B., Xiao, B., Wang, J., Shi, H., Huang, T.S., Zhang, L.: Higherhrnet: scale-aware representation learning for bottom-up human pose estimation. In: Proceedings of the IEEE/CVF Conference on Computer Vision and Pattern Recognition, pp. 5386–5395 (2020)
5. Das, S., Sharma, S., Dai, R., Bremond, F., Thonnat, M.: VPN: learning video-pose embedding for activities of daily living. In: Proceedings of the European Conference on Computer Vision, pp. 72–90 (2020)
6. Fang, H.S., Xie, S., Tai, Y.W., Lu, C.: RMPE: regional multi-person pose estimation. In: Proceedings of the IEEE International Conference on Computer Vision, pp. 2334–2343 (2017)
7. Gao, S., Wang, J., Lu, H., Liu, Z.: Pose-guided visible part matching for occluded person ReID. In: Proceedings of the IEEE/CVF Conference on Computer Vision and Pattern Recognition, pp. 11744–11752 (2020)
8. He, K., Gkioxari, G., Dollar, P., Girshick, R.: Mask R-CNN. IEEE Trans. Pattern Anal. Mach. Intell. **42**(2), 386–397 (2020)
9. He, K., Zhang, X., Ren, S., Sun, J.: Deep residual learning for image recognition. In: Proceedings of the IEEE Conference on Computer Vision and Pattern Recognition, pp. 770–778 (2016)
10. Huang, J., Zhu, Z., Guo, F., Huang, G.: The devil is in the details: delving into unbiased data processing for human pose estimation. In: Proceedings of the IEEE/CVF Conference on Computer Vision and Pattern Recognition, pp. 5700–5709 (2020)
11. Jin, S., et al.: Differentiable hierarchical graph grouping for multi-person pose estimation. In: Proceedings of the European Conference on Computer Vision, pp. 718–734 (2020)
12. Li, J., Wang, C., Zhu, H., Mao, Y., Fang, H.S., Lu, C.: Crowdpose: efficient crowded scenes pose estimation and a new benchmark. In: Proceedings of the IEEE/CVF Conference on Computer Vision and Pattern Recognition, pp. 10863–10872 (2019)
13. Lin, T.Y., et al.: Microsoft coco: common objects in context. In: Proceedings of the European Conference on Computer Vision, pp. 740–755 (2014)
14. Liu, W., et al.: SSD: single shot multibox detector. In: Proceedings of the European Conference on Computer Vision, pp. 21–37 (2016)
15. Newell, A., Yang, K., Deng, J.: Stacked hourglass networks for human pose estimation. In: Proceedings of the European Conference on Computer Vision, pp. 483–499 (2016)
16. Papandreou, G., Zhu, T., Chen, L.C., Gidaris, S., Tompson, J., Murphy, K.: Personlab: person pose estimation and instance segmentation with a bottom-up, part-based, geometric embedding model. In: Proceedings of the European Conference on Computer Vision, pp. 282–299 (2018)

17. Redmon, J., Divvala, S., Girshick, R., Farhadi, A.: You only look once: unified, real-time object detection. In: Proceedings of the IEEE Conference on Computer Vision and Pattern Recognition, pp. 779–788 (2016)
18. Ren, S., He, K., Girshick, R., Sun, J.: Faster R-CNN: towards real-time object detection with region proposal networks. In: Advances in Neural Information Processing Systems, pp. 91–99 (2015)
19. Sandler, M., Howard, A., Zhu, M., Zhmoginov, A., Chen, L.C.: Mobilenetv 2: inverted residuals and linear bottlenecks. In: Proceedings of the IEEE Conference on Computer Vision and Pattern Recognition, pp. 4510–4520 (2018)
20. Sun, K., Xiao, B., Liu, D., Wang, J.: Deep high-resolution representation learning for human pose estimation. In: Proceedings of the IEEE/CVF Conference on Computer Vision and Pattern Recognition, pp. 5693–5703 (2019)
21. Xiao, B., Wu, H., Wei, Y.: Simple baselines for human pose estimation and tracking. In: Proceedings of the European Conference on Computer Vision, pp. 466–481 (2018)
22. Zhang, F., Zhu, X., Dai, H., Ye, M., Zhu, C.: Distribution-aware coordinate representation for human pose estimation. In: Proceedings of the IEEE/CVF Conference on Computer Vision and Pattern Recognition, pp. 7093–7102 (2020)

Multi-view Gait Recognition by Inception-Encoder and CL-GEI

Chongdong Huang[1], Yonghong Song[2][(✉)], and Chen Wu[1]

[1] School of Software Engineering, Xi'an Jiaotong University, Xi'an, China
{huang22112211,wuchen12345}@stu.xjtu.edu.cn
[2] Institute of Artificial Intelligence and Robotics,
Xi'an Jiaotong University, Xi'an, China
songyh@mail.xjtu.edu.cn

Abstract. To solve multi-view problem in gait recognition, some methods based on Generative Adversarial Networks (GANs) are proposed. These methods mainly transformed multi-view gait features with walking variations into a common view without these variations. However, the direct pixel-to-pixel transformation would result to inefficient and inaccurate. Moreover, the transformed features often did not preserve enough identification information which would lead to accuracy decline. Besides, Gait Energy Image (GEI) often loses temporal information of sequences. To address these problems, Inception-encoder is proposed to extract effective gait features into feature vectors which are invariant to views and other walking variations by adopting generative constraints from GANs. To preserve more identification information, identification constraints is adopted from labels. Furthermore, inception model is embedded into the encoder for improving representation ability. Moreover, CL-GEI is proposed to preserve more temporal information. Experiments on CASIA-B and OU-ISIR prove the competitive performance of the combination of Inception-encoder with CL-GEI compared with the state-of-the-art.

Keywords: Generative adversarial networks · Gait recognition · View transformation

1 Introduction

Gait is the unique biometric feature that can identify humans from a far distance [9] with advantages like non-cooperation with subjects, hard to fake and obtainable at a distance [21], compared with other biometric features such as fingerprint, iris and face. However, gait recognition suffers from various difficult challenges including changes of view, occlusion such as bags and clothing, walking speed and so on [5,21]. Among these variations, view is one of the great factors that influences accuracy of gait recognition, which is the multi-view problem.

To alleviate influences of multi-view with other walking variations, some researchers adopted generative adversarial networks (GANs) to transform gait

© Springer Nature Switzerland AG 2021
Y. Peng et al. (Eds.): ICIG 2021, LNCS 12889, pp. 446–460, 2021.
https://doi.org/10.1007/978-3-030-87358-5_36

features under different view angles with other variations into a common view without these variations [5, 20] and Gait Energy Image (GEI) [7] is the usually used gait features. However, firstly, direct pixel-to-pixel transformation would result to inefficiency and inaccuracy because the instability of generation of GANs which would generate inaccurate distortion of human body. Secondly, the lacked identification information would lead to accuracy decline. Because of the vanishing gradient problem, it is not enough to identify only by discriminators. In the end, GEI often lacks temporal information because of the simple averaging process.

Faced with disadvantages above, the first design target in the paper is to extract gait features into feature vectors which should be invariant with variations such viewing angles, bags and clothes etc. Generating of feature vectors instead of images avoids distortion and inaccurate image parts. To achieve this target, the generative constraints is adopted from GANs [10] to generate target features. Another design target is that these feature vectors should preserve enough identification information for high recognition accuracy. Therefore, identification constraints is adopted from labels by encoding identification information into the encoder. To further improve performance and the ability of nonlinear expression, this paper proposed some improvements listed as follows:

1) Proposing inception-encoder to extract invariant gait features. There are two constraints for the encoder: generative constraints from GANs [10] and identification constraints from labels. Inception model [14] is embedded into the encoder to improve representation ability. To further improve performance, CBAM [18], an attention model is embedded in inception model as well.
2) Proposing an encoding rule for building up only one discriminator which combining training targets of two discriminators from [20] to learn joint distribution of real/fake and identification effectively.
3) Proposing CL-GEI to obtain temporal and spatial information by building up an auto-encoder by ConvLSTM [11].

The network architecture is illustrated in Fig. 1. The input gait feature is encoded into feature vector by encoder firstly. Then the feature vector is input into the decoder to generate the target image. The target image comes from training set (real) or the generated image (fake). Combined with source image sampled from training set, the concatenation feature is input into discriminator for judgement. The output of discriminator is the joint probability of real/fake and identification. Besides, the label is encoded into encoder for identification information. After training, only the encoder is left as the feature extraction model to generate feature vectors for matching.

Proposed method is evaluated on two large gait databases which proves the competitive performance compared with the state-of-the-art. The rest of this paper is organized as follows. Related work is reviewed in Sect. 2. Section 3 presents the proposed inception-encoder and CL-GEI. Experimental results are analyzed in Sect. 4. Conclusions are concluded in Sect. 5.

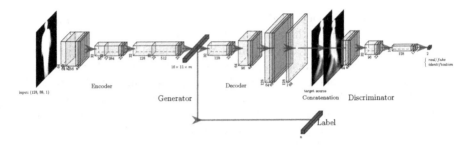

Fig. 1. The proposed network architecture is composed of four sub-networks: encoder, decoder, discriminator and label layer. The encoder encodes input gait features into feature vector. The decoder maps feature vector into target image. The discriminator receives concatenated image for judgement. The label layer encodes label information into the encoder.

2   Related Work

2.1   Multi-view Gait Recognition

Traditional methods in multi-view gait recognition could be classified into three categories: 3D reconstruction of human body, view-invariant gait features and projection of view transformation.

Deep learning methods could be divided into two categories: discriminative networks and generative networks [15]. Discriminative networks aim at optimizing discrimination capability of various variations by learning discriminant subspace or metrics [15]. [19] made a comprehensive study on cross-view gait recognition with deep convolutional neural networks (CNNs) and proposed three types of CNN networks which achieved state-of-the-art outcomes. [12] proposed GEINet with an eight-layer CNN network. [17] proposed a 3D CNN network with eight layers to solve multi-view problem. [15] proposed a siamese network with a pair of inputs and contrastive loss for verification and a triplet network with a triplet of inputs and triplet ranking loss for identification. However, discriminative networks usually hard to convergence because it must learn discriminant subspace for adapting various variations directly.

Generative networks transform gait features under different views with other variations to a common view without these variations for better matching. [20] proposed GaitGAN based on generative adversarial networks (GANs) to generate invariant gait images under side view with normal clothing and without carrying bags. [21] proposed stack progressive auto-encoder (SPAE) to extract invariant gait feature using only one model which is robust to view, clothing and carrying condition variation. [5] proposed multi-task generative adversarial networks (MGANs) for learning view-specific feature representations based on assumption of view angle manifold and a multi-channel gait template called period energy image (PEI). Generative networks alleviate various variations into a common variation which results to faster convergence. But there still exists shortcomings of generative networks. On one hand, pixel-to-pixel or frame-to-frame transformation leads to inefficient and inaccurate. On the other hand, unsupervised learning loses identification information which results to lower recognition accuracy.

2.2 Generative Adversarial Networks

Generative adversarial networks (GANs) [3] is composed of two models: generative model G and discriminative model D. G captures the data distribution P_z and D estimates the probability that the data comes from training set (real) or the generation from G (fake). Real data is x and corresponding distribution is P_{data}. Both generator and discriminator are iteratively optimized against each other in a minimax game as follows:

$$\min_G \max_D E_{x \sim P_{data}}[\log D(x)] + E_{z \sim P_z}[\log 1 - D(G(z))] \tag{1}$$

However, original GANs has disadvantages such as instability, generating images from random noise, lacking identification information etc. [1] proposed WGAN with a cost function of wasserstein distance to improve stability and alleviate mode collapse. [10] proposed DCGAN for training deep convolutional generator and discriminator networks with implement of up-sampling and down-sampling by strided convolutions. [8] proposed a conditional GANs by feeding labels into both the discriminator and generator as an additional input layer.

Different from methods above, the feature extraction model is regarded as an encoder which samples data from training set so that it generates z constrained in source domain. Besides, generator in original GANs is seemed as the decoder which directs the transformation direction by gradients so that encoder is preserved for generating features with target domain information encoded in the end. It is worth noticing that GaitGAN [20] direct transformed inputs into target images. But the generation is often inefficient because of the pixel-to-pixel process and direct template matching of target images. Proposed method encodes gait information into feature vectors which would avoid the image distortion and direct template matching. It also builds up an encoding rule to combine the training targets together and train in only one discriminator. In addition, different from input labels directly, identification information is encoded into encoder by gradients in proposed method.

3   Method

3.1   Constraints on Feature Extraction Model

As shown in Fig. 2, the feature extraction model is combined with the generative network in original GANs as the generator, i.e. the encoder-decoder model. On one hand, decoder directs the training direction of encoder, that is to transform features under various views with other variations into view $90°$ with normal walking which is the best view for recognition because of more dynamic information [21]. On the other hand, encoder constrains the sampling space of variable z which is sampled from training set. Sampling from a random space of z is one of the reasons of instability of GANs. By constraining sampling space of z, generator could have better performance than original GANs. Different from GaitGAN [20], the final target of proposed generator is to generate intrinsic vectors which is the best representation of gait features instead of target images directly. Because of instability of GANs discussed in Sect. 2.2, these unstable influence factors in image generation would result in accuracy decline for matching. In the contrary, encoding information into vectors avoids such inaccurate distortion in two-dimensional image space.

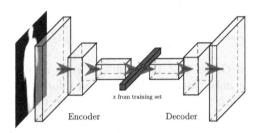

Fig. 2. Sketch map of generator.

As for the discriminator, GaitGAN [20] adopted two discriminative networks: real/fake discriminator for determining whether input image is real and identification discriminator for judging whether input source image and generated image are the same person. This paper adopts the thoughts above, but the significant difference is that the proposed method learns the joint distribution of real/fake and identification in only one discriminator. The major reason is that there exists inner relationship between these two discrimination targets, i.e. what ever source image or real or fake image is definitely corresponded to a specific person. Therefore, both two discrimination targets could be trained jointly which would further save parameters and space.

As depicted in Fig. 3, output of the discriminator is a two-dimensional vector. The first elements represents real/fake and the second one represents identification. The input of the discriminator is the concatenated images where the source image is sampled from training data randomly under view 90° with normal walking (ground truth) and the target image is under various views with different variations (real) or generated by generator (fake). Moreover, because discriminator outputs two elements, an encoding rule is proposed. For the real image, if the variations are satisfied with the source image, the first element is 1, otherwise is 0. If the image and the source image are the same person, the second element is 1, otherwise is 0. As for the fake image, all the elements should be 0.

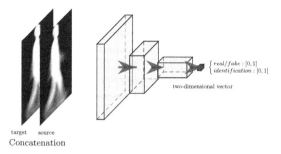

target   source
Concatenation

Fig. 3. Sketch map of discriminator.

The detailed rule is listed as follows, where "nm" represents normal walking:

$$
\begin{cases}
real \to nm\ and\ 90° \begin{cases} yes \to same\ person \begin{cases} yes:11 \\ no:10 \end{cases} \\ no \to same\ person \begin{cases} yes:01 \\ no:00 \end{cases} \end{cases} \\
fake:00
\end{cases}
$$

[8] proposed a conditional GANs by putting labels into both discriminator and generator as an additional input layer. Different from that, proposed method direct encodes identification information into the network by reverse gradients. For input m samples $[X_1, X_2, ..., X_m]$ and labels $[Y_1, Y_2, ..., Y_m]$ which are represented by one-hot encoding, the cross entropy loss function of output L and gradients solved with softmax activation function of output weights W are listed in Eq. 2. Function f represents transformation operation of input sample X. Because the reverse gradient contain label Y in equation, the identification information is encoded in the encoder by reverse gradients with chain rules.

$$
L(f(X), Y) = \frac{1}{m} \sum_{i=1}^{m} Y_i^T \log f(X_i)
$$
$$
\frac{\partial L}{\partial W} = \frac{1}{m} \sum_{i=1}^{m} (f(X_i) - Y_i)
$$

(2)

An additional full connected layer with the same dimension of labels is appended to the top of the feature extraction model for encoding identification information into the output vector.

3.2 Inception-Encoder: Improve Representation Ability by Inception Model

To achieve higher performance, the feature extraction model should have strong representation ability of input features with these training targets. Therefore, the inception model [14] is adopted. The inception model is embedded after each convolution layer. In each block, the convolution layer is regarded as sampling and linear mapping of input features. For input feature maps, inception model integrates features by channels by 1×1 convolution filters into multiple branches with different size of filters for different scale features. For output feature maps, the multi-scale features from branches are concatenated by channels.

To further improve performance of the feature extraction model, CBAM [18], an attention model is adopted to embed into the inception model as well. On one hand, embedding CBAM into the inception model constructs another structure of network in network which further improves the capability of nonlinear expression. On the other hand, CBAM makes inception model have attention ability to extract more effective features. The 1×1 convolution layer is replaced by CBAM to produce attention outputs.

3.3   CL-GEI: Learning Temporal Information of Gait Sequences by ConvLSTM

Gait energy image (GEI) is a widely used feature representation of gait by simply computing the averaging image of frames in one complete gait period [7]. Therefore, one of essential disadvantages of GEI is the lack of temporal information because of the simple averaging operation. The method in [2] built an auto-encoder by long short-term memory (LSTM) to recover sequence representation but had weakness to obtain spatial information because of one dimensional inputs. Therefore, ConvLSTM [11] is adopted to extract temporal as well as spatial information from gait sequences.

The construction of ConvLSTM auto-encoder is similar with [11], that is to adopt two ConvLSTMs as encoder and decoder with kernel size 1×1 in encoder. Once the ConvLSTM auto-encoder trained, the hidden state of last layer in each time is obtained as the representation of each frame. A gait feature of a sequence, which is called CL-GEI, is calculated by averaging the hidden states of all frames as follows:

$$CL - GEI = \frac{1}{N} \sum_{i=1}^{N} H_i \tag{3}$$

3.4   Network Architecture

As shown in Fig. 1, the network architecture is divided to three parts: generator, discriminator and label. The generator is composed of two models: encoder and decoder.

In encoder, the input is one gait feature image and the output is the one-dimensional feature vector extracted from input feature. For each convolution block, the order of components is: a convolution layer, a inception model, an activation layer and a batch normalization layer. Firstly, the kernel size is set to 3×3 for all the convolution layers. Secondly, the strides of the first two convolution layers are set to 2 for down sampling while strides of the last convolution layer is set to 1 for making the full connected layer connect to the full receptive fields. As for the inception model, the number of filters for all convolution layers in inception model are set to the same value with the convolution layer in each convolution block, i.e. 64, 96, 128. The reason is to obtain strong representation ability while control the scale of parameters. Besides, the dimension of output layer must be multiple of 16×11 so that it could be up-sampled to the size 128×88 as same as the original image by 3 deconvolution layers with strides of 2 in decoder, where the multiple m turns to be the channel dimension. In the end, PReLU [4] is adopted to learn parameters of rectifiers adaptively.

The decoder and discriminator have a common similar network structure: a convolution (or deconvolution) layer, a PReLU layer and a batch normalization layer. For decoder, it has a reshape layer in the front to reshape input vector into feature maps and a deconvolution layer with kernel size 1×1 in the end to generate the target image. For discriminator, it has a concatenation layer in the front to concatenate the source and target image by channels. For the fully connected layer of label, n represents the dimension of label.

3.5 Training

The training method is similar with GANs [3] but has two extra steps. Firstly, to encode identification information into the encoder, the encoder is trained before the generator. Secondly, since the source images with variations could be obtained, i.e. the same people of the input with normal walking under view $90°$, the generator could have an extra training procedure with the output of these variations to stabilize the generation of GANs for better accuracy and faster convergence. The training details are listed in Algorithm 1 and the definitions are listed here: L is the label layer, E is the encoder, G is the generator, D is the discriminator, S_n and L_n represent n images and labels sampled from training set with various variations, S_n' and L_n' represent images and labels which are sampled from training set with normal walking under view $90°$ in disorder, S_n'' is images which have the same condition with S_n' but are the same people with S_n and in order, T_n is images generated by G, L_r is the encoding rule results applied on L and L' and L_f for fake labels, $V_{n_1}^g$ is n_1 vectors generated by E under view g of data $S_{n_1}^g$ and $V_{n_2}^k$ is n_2 vectors under view k of data $S_{n_2}^k$.

For matching, the nearest neighbor classifier with L2 norm is applied. For ith feature vector v_i^g in $V_{n_1}^g$ and jth vector v_j^k in $V_{n_2}^k$, the similarity is calculated as follows:

$$d(v_i^g, v_j^k) = \left\| v_i^g - v_j^k \right\|_2 \tag{4}$$

4   Experiments

4.1   Datasets

Two famous large public gait databases are adopted for evaluation in the paper: CASIA-B [13] and OU-ISIR [6]. CASIA-B contains 124 subjects with 11 views where the range of views is from $0°$ to $180°$ with $18°$ disparity between each

Algorithm 1. The training procedure of proposed method.

Input: S_n, L_n, S_n', L_n', S_n'', $S_{n_1}^g$ and $S_{n_2}^k$.
Output: $V_{n_1}^g$ and $V_{n_2}^k$.
1: **for** number of training iterations **do**
2:     ▷ train discriminator
3:         $L_r = encoding\ rule(L_n, L_n')$
4:         $L_f = filling\ zeros$
5:         $\min \left\| L_r - D(S_n, S_n') \right\|_2$
6:         $T_n = G(S_n)$
7:         $\min \left\| L_f - D(T_n, S_n') \right\|_2$
8:     ▷ train encoder
9:         $\min \| L_n - L(E(S_n)) \|_2$
10:    ▷ train generator
11:        fix D
12:        $\min \left\| S_n'' - G(S_n) \right\|_2$
13:        $\min \left\| L_r - D(G(S_n), S_n') \right\|_2$
14: **end for**
15: $V_{n_1}^g = E(S_{n_1}^g),\ V_{n_2}^k = E(S_{n_2}^k)$
16: matching $V_{n_1}^g$ and $V_{n_2}^k$

two adjacent views. Under each view, each subject has 10 video sequences which consist of 6 normal walking sequences, 2 walking sequences with bags and 2 with coats. OU-ISIR dataset contains 4007 subjects with range of views from 55° to 85° and 10° disparity between two adjacent views. Each subject has two sequences with no walking variations, one for gallery and the other for probe.

As for dataset settings, for CASIA-B, similar with [20], the first 62 subjects are put into the training set and the remaining 62 subjects into the testing set. In the testing set, the first 4 normal walking sequences of each subjects are regarded as the gallery set and the others as the probe. For OU-ISIR, similar with [19], five-fold cross-validation is applied. All subjects are divided into five parts randomly. In each time, one set is for testing and the others are for training. In the end, the average classification rates are recorded.

4.2 Model Settings

The structure of model and hyper-parameters are depicted in Sect. 3.4. For the hyper-parameter of multiple m, $m = 4$ is set in the paper for enough feature representation while saving parameters and space. As for activation and loss functions, softmax and binary cross entropy function is adopted for discriminator, softmax and categorical cross entropy function for label, tanh and mean squared error function for generator and ConvLSTM auto-encoder. In the end, the rmsprop [16] optimizer is adopted for adapting learning rates automatically. For view transformation, in CASIA-B, all the views are transformed to view 90° with normal walking, and in OU-ISIR, all the views are transformed to 85°

which is close to 90°. Based on experiments, batch size is set to 8 and training iterations are set to 6,000 for CASIA-B and 10,000 for OU-ISIR.

4.3   Comparison on Influence Factors

The proposed method starts at a simple feature extraction model discussed in Sect. 1, and then improves by adopting modifications step by step. As shown in Table 1 and Table 2, there are two essential evaluating indicators here, where the first one is the average results of each view by averaging all the values of all gallery views corresponding to a probe view, described in Table 1. The indicator of averaging points out the total performance of proposed model, which means averaging values rise when most of multi-view results rise. The second one is the worst results of each view, at the point of maximized view disparity between gallery with probe, described in Table 2. The indicator of worst represents how the model improves in the worst condition. The first five rows of each table discuss the base structure of proposed model and extra training steps which all based on GEI, and the remaining discuss further performance improvement and comparison of different input features, i.e. GEI and CL-GEI.

Table 1. Averaging performance on CASIA-B. The second to fifth rows represent successive modifications on previous row.

	Probe view										
	0	18	36	54	72	90	108	126	144	162	180
Base model	17.23	14.00	11.80	10.78	13.56	10.70	13.86	12.17	11.80	15.76	15.91
1+one discriminator	23.02	22.73	27.35	28.23	30.13	30.79	32.92	30.50	28.81	23.90	21.92
2+label+training encoder	50.44	58.72	64.74	64.30	61.95	54.69	61.29	63.42	60.78	56.16	46.48
2+extra training generator	47.21	55.87	65.32	65.84	62.24	55.79	62.17	66.13	62.61	55.57	46.99
2+label+training generator	55.50	68.70	79.69	77.49	70.75	67.23	70.01	76.03	74.56	70.31	58.87
5+inception+GEI	59.75	72.95	80.94	79.11	73.39	67.23	72.73	78.30	77.64	71.63	60.63
5+inception+CL-GEI	64.52	74.41	80.50	78.08	73.02	68.11	72.65	77.49	79.47	73.83	61.66
5+inception+cbam+GEI	**64.88**	**76.32**	**85.19**	80.35	74.34	67.60	73.68	**81.67**	79.11	71.48	60.56
5+inception+cbam+CL-GEI	64.52	74.19	83.50	**80.72**	**76.17**	**69.35**	**74.93**	80.57	**80.28**	**78.81**	**64.44**

Table 2. Worst performance on CASIA-B. The second to fifth rows represent successive modifications on previous row.

Gallery/Probe	Views with maximized disparity										
	0/90	18/90	36/180	54/180	72/180	90/180	108/180	126/0	144/0	162/90	180/90
Base model	1.61	0.00	1.61	1.61	3.23	3.23	3.23	4.84	3.23	1.61	0.81
1+one discriminator	2.42	4.84	2.42	1.61	2.42	0.00	4.84	2.42	3.23	4.84	1.61
2+label+training encoder	8.06	29.84	38.71	25.00	21.77	9.68	13.71	25.81	35.48	16.94	11.29
2+extra training generator	12.90	28.23	41.13	25.00	20.97	21.77	20.16	24.19	32.26	25.81	12.90
2+label+training generator	20.16	41.13	60.48	39.52	33.87	26.61	32.26	36.29	39.52	42.74	19.35
5+inception+GEI	20.97	42.74	56.45	42.74	34.68	24.19	33.87	39.52	52.42	**45.16**	18.55
5+inception+CL-GEI	**24.19**	45.16	58.06	47.58	31.45	29.84	34.68	**46.77**	61.29	33.87	23.39
5+inception+cbam+GEI	20.97	**47.58**	58.87	35.48	33.87	24.19	33.06	45.16	57.26	36.29	20.16
5+inception+cbam+CL-GEI	**24.19**	43.55	**66.13**	**54.84**	**36.29**	**30.65**	**37.90**	44.35	**62.90**	43.55	**27.42**

Compared the first row with the second row, the second results outperforms the first one about 15% in first table, which verifies the advantage of one discriminator learning joint distribution of real/fake. Though the single discriminator improves averaging performance, it has nearly no contribution to maximized view disparity in second table for two reasons: the inadequate use of labels of discriminator discussed in Sect. 3.1 and unstable generation of GAN depicted in Sect. 2.2 and Sect. 3.5. Compared the third and fourth row with the second one, these two modifications improve averaging performance about 30% independently. Firstly, these comparisons verify the significant performance of adopting labels and extra training step of generator with source image. Secondly, these two modifications have similar performance on averaging level combining the comparison on the third with the fourth row in Table 1. The reason is that the source image implies partial identification information since it is the same person to transform to. Besides, compared the third and the fourth row in Table 2, extra training step of generator is much stable than the combination of labels with original GANs because it points out the explicit transformation direction obviously, i.e. the normal walking condition under view 90°. Therefore, it could stable the generation of GANs for improvement. In the end, compared the fifth with the second, third and fourth row, results outperforms about 40% to second row and about 10% to second and third row, which means the explicit direction of transformation with identification information achieves the further significant improvement of performance.

For the last four rows, in Table 1, compared the sixth and eighth row with the fifth, the result indicates that the inception model improves performance because of its strong feature representation by ability of nonlinear expression and multi-scale features. Moreover, CBAM further achieves improvement because it further strengths nonlinear expression by structure of network in network and attention mechanism for extracting features more effectively described in Sect. 3.2. In Table 2, these outcomes are at the similar level, which means inception model and CBAM have nearly no contribution to maximized view disparity. But compared the seventh and ninth row with the fifth, sixth and eighth row in Table 1, CL-GEI further improves averaging performance about 2%. In the last row in Table 2, combining CBAM and CL-CEI, the worst performance is improved definitely about 5%. Analyzing these results, on one hand, ConvLSTM extracts more temporal and spatial information than GEI discussed in Sect. 3.3. On the other hand, the attention mechanism of CBAM therefore could pay more attention to the features applied by attention. Though results are not sufficient to address improvement of inception model with attention and CL-GEI in Table 1 and Table 2, the more detailed comparisons are discussed in Sect. 4.4 and Sect. 4.5.

4.4   Comparison on CASIA-B

To evaluate the performance of proposed method comprehensively, SPAE [21], GaitGAN [20] and MGANs [5] are adopted for comparison because they are the most recent state-of-the-art methods.

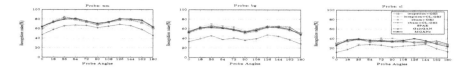

Fig. 4. The average performance of multi-view with compared methods under three conditions on CASIA-B.

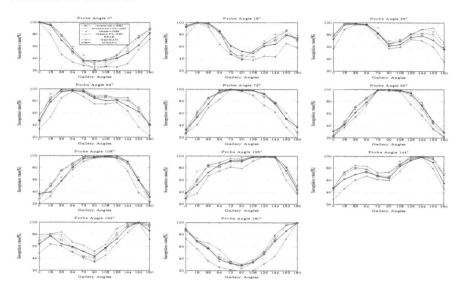

Fig. 5. Fully comparison with compared methods of each view under normal walking condition on CASIA-B.

The average performances of multi-view are listed in Fig. 4. Compared with others, the trends of curves illustrate proposed method outperforms SPAE and GaitGAN about 10%, which further prove the better performance of proposed method in solving multi-view problem. As for MGANs, proposed one is in the same level with MGANs in averaging, but in Fig. 5, the fully comparison of each view, proposed method is not lower than MGANs in some views. Moreover, it outperforms MGANs about 3% of most of views, especially from view 126° to 180°. In addition, proposed method outperforms SPAE and GaitGAN of all the outcomes among all views. Therefore, the results definitely proves the better performance than compared methods.

In summary, there are two reasons which lead to high performance of proposed method. The first is the adopted training constraints and inception model discussed in Sect. 4.3. The second reason is the adoption of CBAM model. By combining CL-GEI and CBAM, the weakness of CL-GEI is improved apparently. Based on attention mechanism of CBAM, the model could focus on truly useful information so that the final performance is improved.

The first advantage of proposed method is to use only one uniform model to handle all variations in multi-view gait recognition. Compared with SPAE and MGANs, the proposed network could be trained integrally with more simple structure. Only the encoder is used finally and all views are transformed to 90° directly. The second is that GaitGAN directly matched the generated images while proposed method matches extracted feature vectors so that proposed network avoids the inaccuracy of generation and the inefficiency of matching.

4.5 Comparison on OU-ISIR

CNNs [19], MGANs [5] and 3in+2diff [15] are adopted for evaluating performance of proposed method on OU-ISIR. As listed in Table 3, compared with CNNs and MGANs, proposed method outperforms them among all results, specially about 15% at pair 55° to 85° and 5% at pair 85° to 55°, and about 5% in averaging, which proves the better performance of proposed method of multi-view under large subjects condition. As for the fusion network 3in+2diff, results are listed in Table 4. On one hand, though proposed method drops about 0.3% in averaging compared to 3in+2diff, it outperforms about 1% of differences from 0° to 20°, which illustrates that proposed one still have advantages in dealing with multi-view. On the other hand, compared with the single networks (3in and 2diff), proposed method outperforms them about 1.5% of 3in and 0.2% of 2iff, which still proves the better performance. Therefore, by evaluating on OU-ISIR, proposed method has higher performance of multi-view under large subjects condition with only one uniform model.

Table 3. Full comparison of each view on OU-ISIR.

Probe	Gallery	CNNs	MGANs	Proposed
55°	55°	98.8 ± 0.1	–	**100.0 ± 0.0**
55°	65°	98.3 ± 0.1	99.4 ± 0.1	**99.9 ± 0.1**
55°	75°	96.0 ± 0.1	96.1 ± 0.3	**99.1 ± 0.2**
55°	85°	80.5 ± 0.4	77.9 ± 0.4	**95.5 ± 0.4**
65°	55°	96.3 ± 0.2	97.7 ± 0.1	**99.8 ± 0.1**
65°	65°	98.9 ± 0.2	–	**100.0 ± 0.0**
65°	75°	97.3 ± 0.0	98.5 ± 0.1	**99.9 ± 0.1**
65°	85°	83.3 ± 0.3	84.4 ± 0.5	**99.6 ± 0.2**
75°	55°	94.2 ± 0.2	94.8 ± 0.1	**98.3 ± 0.1**
75°	65°	97.8 ± 0.2	98.9 ± 0.1	**99.9 ± 0.1**
75°	75°	98.9 ± 0.0	–	**100.0 ± 0.0**
75°	85°	85.1 ± 0.1	86.4 ± 0.3	**99.9 ± 0.1**
85°	55°	90.0 ± 0.5	86.9 ± 0.6	**94.2 ± 0.5**
85°	65°	96.0 ± 0.3	97.4 ± 0.3	**99.4 ± 0.0**
85°	75°	98.4 ± 0.1	99.5 ± 0.1	**99.9 ± 0.1**
85°	85°	98.9 ± 0.1	–	**100.0 ± 0.0**
Mean		92.4	93.2	**99.1**

Table 4. Comparison with 3in+2diff on OU-ISIR.

	View difference				Mean
	0	10	20	30	
3in	98.5	98.2	96.4	92.3	97.1
2diff	99.1	99.0	98.0	95.1	98.3
3in+2diff	99.2	99.2	98.6	**97.0**	**98.8**
Proposed	**100.0**	**99.9**	**99.1**	94.9	98.5

5 Conclusion

This paper has proposed a feature extraction model called inception-encoder to generate invariant features of view and other variations with adequate identification information encoded and strong representation ability of intrinsic gait features. The encoder directly generates feature vectors instead of target images for avoiding inefficiency and inaccuracy of generation of images. The invariant characteristic is provided by generative constraints by adopting GANs. The adequate identification information is provided by labels by reverse gradients. The inception model is adopted to improve representation ability. To further improve performance, firstly, an encoding rule is proposed for only one discriminator to learn the joint distribution of real/fake and identification. Secondly, CBAM, an attention model is embedded into the inception model for further improving nonlinear expression and obtaining attention ability. Thirdly, an extra training step is applied on generator to stable the generation of GANs. Moreover, this paper further has proposed an effective gait feature called CL-GEI extracted from ConvLSTM auto-encoder to preserve more temporal and spatial information. Experimental results prove that proposed method achieves the competitive performance compared with the state-of-the-art on CASIA-B and OU-ISIR dataset.

References

1. Arjovsky, M., Chintala, S., Bottou, L.: Wasserstein GAN (2017)
2. Feng, Y., Li, Y., Luo, J.: Learning effective gait features using LSTM. In: 2016 23rd International Conference on Pattern Recognition (ICPR), pp. 325–330. IEEE (2016)
3. Goodfellow, I.J., et al.: Generative adversarial nets. In: International Conference on Neural Information Processing Systems (2014)
4. He, K., Zhang, X., Ren, S., Jian, S.: Delving deep into rectifiers: Surpassing human-level performance on imagenet classification (2015)
5. He, Y., Zhang, J., Shan, H., Liang, W.: Multi-task GANs for view-specific feature learning in gait recognition. IEEE Trans. Inf. Forensics Secur. **14**(1), 102–113 (2018)
6. Iwama, H., Okumura, M., Makihara, Y., Yagi, Y.: The OU-ISIR gait database comprising the large population dataset and performance evaluation of gait recognition. IEEE Trans. Inf. Forensics Secur. **7**(5), 1511–1521 (2012)

7. Ju Han, B.B.: Individual recognition using gait energy image. IEEE Trans. Pattern Anal. Mach. Intell. **28**(2), 316–322 (2006)

8. Mirza, M., Osindero, S.: Conditional generative adversarial nets. Computer Science, pp. 2672–2680 (2014)

9. Nixon, M.S., Tan, T., Chellappa, R.: Human Identification Based on Gait. Springer, New York (2006). https://doi.org/10.1007/978-0-387-29488-9

10. Radford, A., Metz, L., Chintala, S.: Unsupervised representation learning with deep convolutional generative adversarial networks. Computer Science (2015)

11. Shi, X., Chen, Z., Hao, W., Yeung, D.Y., Woo, W.C.: Convolutional LSTM network: a machine learning approach for precipitation nowcasting. In: International Conference on Neural Information Processing Systems (2015)

12. Shiraga, K., Makihara, Y., Muramatsu, D., Echigo, T., Yagi, Y.: Geinet: view-invariant gait recognition using a convolutional neural network. In: International Conference on Biometrics, pp. 1–8 (2016)

13. Shuai, Z., Zhang, J., Huang, K., Ran, H., Tan, T.: Robust view transformation model for gait recognition. In: IEEE International Conference on Image Processing (2011)

14. Szegedy, C., Vanhoucke, V., Ioffe, S., Shlens, J., Wojna, Z.: Rethinking the inception architecture for computer vision. In: Computer Vision and Pattern Recognition (2016)

15. Takemura, N., Makihara, Y., Muramatsu, D., Echigo, T., Yagi, Y.: On input/output architectures for convolutional neural network-based cross-view gait recognition. IEEE Trans. Circuits Syst. Video Technol. **29**(9), 2708–2719 (2017)

16. Tieleman, T., Hinton, G.: Lecture 6.5-rmsprop: divide the gradient by a running average of its recent magnitude. COURSERA: Neural Netw. Mach. Learn. **4**(2), 26–31 (2012)

17. Wolf, T., Babaee, M., Rigoll, G.: Multi-view gait recognition using 3D convolutional neural networks. In: IEEE International Conference on Image Processing, pp. 4165–4169 (2016)

18. Woo, S., Park, J., Lee, J.Y., So Kweon, I.: CBAM: convolutional block attention module. In: Proceedings of the European Conference on Computer Vision (ECCV), pp. 3–19 (2018)

19. Wu, Z., Huang, Y., Wang, L., Wang, X., Tan, T.: A comprehensive study on cross-view gait based human identification with deep CNNs. IEEE Trans. Pattern Anal. Mach. Intell. **39**(2), 209–226 (2016)

20. Yu, S., Chen, H., Reyes, E.B.G., Poh, N.: GaitGAN: invariant gait feature extraction using generative adversarial networks. In: Computer Vision and Pattern Recognition Workshops (2017)

21. Yu, S., Chen, H., Wang, Q., Shen, L., Huang, Y.: Invariant feature extraction for gait recognition using only one uniform model. Neurocomputing **239**, 81–93 (2017)

Facial Action Unit Detection Based on Transformer and Attention Mechanism

Wenyu Song[1,2], Shuze Shi[1,2], and Gaoyun An[1,2(✉)]

[1] Institute of Information Science, Beijing Jiaotong University, Beijing 100044, China
{20120313,19120306,gyan}@bjtu.edu.cn
[2] Beijing Key Laboratory of Advanced Information Science and Network Technology,
Beijing 100044, China

Abstract. Facial Action Unit (AU) detection is a key step in facial expression recognition and analysis. The recent AU detection methods usually use well-designed complex networks based on CNN or RNN. Here, we propose a novel facial action unit detection network based on Transformer and Attention Mechanism named TAM-Net, which combines the attention mechanism with the Transformer structure. Firstly, since the facial AU is an atomic muscle of the face, which usually occurs in a relatively fixed region, we introduce a fixed-position attention mechanism to explicitly guide the feature learning of the region of interest. Secondly, we also propose an attention adjustment mechanism to adaptively refine the attention map based on label information. Finally, the Transformer based on self-attention has been applied to many Computer Vision tasks and has achieved good performance, so we introduce the popular Transformer structure to automatically learning the relationship between different facial AUs. Experiments on the challenging BP4D dataset show that the proposed method achieves competitive results.

Keywords: Facial AU detection · Transformer · Attention mechanism

1 Introduction

Facial expressions are one of the important external manifestations of human emotions. Accurate recognition of facial expressions and inferring the emotions of others based on this is extremely important for the establishment of complete and effective social communication. Facial expressions are expressed through different combinations of basic facial muscles (i.e., facial AUs) [5]. Therefore, a robust facial AU detection system is of great significance for accurately analyzing facial expressions.

The essence of AU detection task is multi-label image classification. In recent years, many advanced methods for AU detection have been proposed, mainly

Supported by the Fundamental Research Funds for the Central Universities 2021YJS044, and the National Natural Science Foundation of China (62072028 and 61772067).

© Springer Nature Switzerland AG 2021
Y. Peng et al. (Eds.): ICIG 2021, LNCS 12889, pp. 461–472, 2021.
https://doi.org/10.1007/978-3-030-87358-5_37

based on a well-designed deep learning network, which realizes the detection target of AU by learning different levels of features. Since AU usually occurs in a relatively fixed position of the face, we introduce a fixed-position attention mechanism to explicitly guide the feature learning of the region of interest of AUs. However, the attention of the predefined position may not be able to fully adapt to the actual facial AU feature learning. So we propose an adaptive adjustment module to fine-tune the predefined attention to obtain higher-precision detection results. In recent years, the Transformer structure, which has been widely used in the field of machine translation, has also begun to be used in the field of Computer Vision, so we consider using the Self-Attention mechanism of the Transformer to automatically mine the relationship between facial AUs to guide AU detection.

In this paper, our main contributions are as follows:

- A novel AU detection network is proposed which combines the attention mechanism with the Transformer structure, and automatically learns the relationship between AU with the Self-Attention mechanism of the Transformer;
- The proposed attention adjustment module can fine-tune the pre-defined fixed position attention according to the label information, thereby adaptively refining the attention map;
- Experiments conducted on the BP4D [24] dataset show that our proposed method achieves competitive results.

2   Related Work

At present, many AU detection methods have been proposed. Traditional AU detection methods [4,14,25] mainly rely on the appearance features and geometric features extracted manually. Shan et al. [14] empirically evaluated facial representations using statistical local features, Local Binary Patterns and constructed an enhanced LBP to extract the most recognizable LBP features. The experimental results show that the best detection performance is obtained with the help of a support vector machine classifier with enhanced LBP features. Dalal et al. [4] showed that grids of histograms of oriented gradient (HOG) descriptors were significantly better than the existing feature sets for human detection. Most traditional methods fail to make full use of the correlation between AU and facial features, so Zhao et al. [25] introduced Joint-Path and Multi-label Learning (JPML) to address these issues.

With the development of deep learning, a large number of experiments have shown what deep learning networks can unsupervised learn higher-level representations from data, thereby obtaining higher performance improvements. Especially as deep Convolution Neural Networks (CNN) are widely used in various image processing tasks, many facial AU studies have also made full use of the feature learning capabilities of CNN, and various CNN-based facial AU detection models have been designed. Li et al. [9] proposed a face AU detection method based on deep learning, which is implemented by adding two new networks, an enhancement layer, and a cropping layer, to a pre-trained CNN model. So that it can effectively learn feature enhancement and region clipping functions, and then get a significant performance improvement.

However, due to the complexity of human expressions and the particularity of facial AU, learning image features by designing a complex CNN framework may not be enough to capture local specific AU information, and the symbiotic relationship between AUs is usually ignored. Therefore, most of the recently proposed face AU detection frameworks introduce an attention mechanism. Shao et al. [15] designed an end-to-end deep learning framework, combined AU detection and face alignment, and proposed an adaptive attention learning network that adaptively refined the attention map for each AU.

The Transformer was proposed by Google [21]. The Transformer is a network structure different from RNN and CNN because it completely uses the Self-Attention mechanism. It is widely used in the processing of sequence data, especially in the field of natural language processing such as language modeling and machine translation. Recent, many works that apply the Transformer to the field of computer vision have been proposed, and they have achieved good performance. Carion et al. [2] applied the Transformer structure to the field of target detection, and the experimental results on the popular COCO datasets [10] proved the performance improvement brought by this method. Wang et al. [22] demonstrated a simpler and faster video instance segmentation framework built upon Transformers, achieving competitive accuracy. By consulting relevant information, we found that there is no application of the Transformer in the field of facial AU detection, so we consider applying the Transformer structure to the task of facial AU detection, so we consider applying the Transformer structure to the task of AU detection, and use the Self-Attention mechanism to automatically learn the potential relationship between facial AU.

3 Method

In this section, our new framework for facial AU detection is introduced. First, we will make a general introduction to the entire framework. Then, we will describe the details of each module separately. Finally, we will introduce the loss functions used in the method.

3.1 Network Structure

In this paper, we propose a new facial AU detection framework based on attention mechanism and Transformer structure. Figure 1 shows the overall framework of the proposed method, which is mainly divided into three modules: the Fixed-Attention Module (FA-Net), the adaptive Attention Adjustment Module (AA-Net) and the Transformer Structure. In the proposed method, we use the aligned face image and the AU label of the image as the input of the network. Note that the AU label of 1 indicates that this AU occurs, and the AU label of 0 indicates that the AU does not occur.

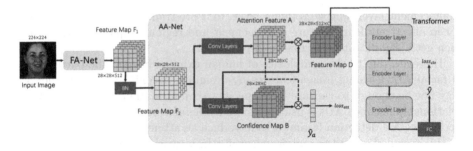

Fig. 1. The overall framework of TAM-NET proposed by us includes the Fixed-Attention Net (FA-Net), the Attention Adjustment Net (AA-Net) and the Transformer structure. The input of the whole framework is a 224×224 face image.

First, in order to effectively extract the depth features of the image, we use the pre-trained model VGG-19 [19] in the image classification task as our backbone network to learn multi-level features. Here, we first fine-tune the VGG-19 network to adapt to the AU detection. Then, we use the facial landmark position information to assign attention weights to the occurrence positions of each AU in the image to explicitly guided the learning of AU local region features. Next, we use an adaptive attention adjustment module, AA-Net, to adjust the predefined attention, which uses the ground-truth of the AU labels to supervise the adjustment of the attention map. Finally, we use the Transformer structure to automatically learn the relationship between AUs to guide facial AU detection. AU detection results are output through a set of fully connected layers designed. In Sect. 3.2–3.4, we will introduce the details of each module.

3.2   FANet: Fixed-Attention Net

In this module (FA-Net), we use the pre-trained VGG-19 [19] model to learn deep features, and fine-tune the original network structure to adapt to the task of facial AU detection. The general structure based on CNN is usually globally equal when learning deep features. In the facial AU detection task, it is necessary to distinguish the region of interest from other facial regions, so we need to pay more attention to the possible occurrence of AU area. Here we refer to the ideas in EAC-Net [9] and use a predefined attention map to guide the learning of deep features. Specifically, we first find the center position coordinates of each AU according to the relationship between the facial landmarks in and the center of AUs. With this coordinate as the center, a rectangular area with a size of 11×11 is selected as the region of interest of each AU. The weight of the corresponding pixel in the area is shown in Eq. 1:

$$w = 1 - 0.095 \times d_m \tag{1}$$

where d_m is the Manhattan distance to the AU center. Therefore, we get the predefined attention maps.

Next, in order of fully integrate the global depth feature and the predefined attention map, we refer to the skipping layer structure in [9], as shown in Fig. 2. The features obtained by the first two convolution layer groups pass through two parallel paths. One way is to multiply the attention map and the feature map, the other way is to directly obtain a new feature map through a group of convolution layers. Finally, the two results are summed to obtain the features that are fused with the attention map. This structure is applied to the third and fourth convolution layer groups, and the output of the FA-Net module is obtained in the end.

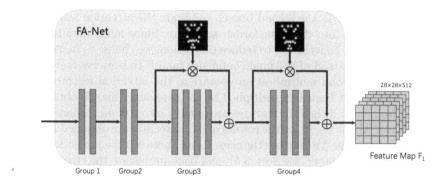

Fig. 2. The structure of Fixed-Attention Net (FA-Net). We use some layers of VGG-19 [19] as the backbone network for feature extraction.

3.3   AA-Net: Attention Adjustment Net

Since the pre-defined attention map we get according to the fixed position and weight may not be completely suitable for the actual AU detection task. Especially for the non-rigid structure of the human face, the feature map fused with attention may need adaptive learning and adjustment to obtain more accurate detection results. Because the essence of facial AU detection is the problem of multi-label image classification, here we refer to the relevant research on the application of attention mechanism in multi-label image classification tasks [23,27], and propose an adaptive Attention Adjustment module (AA-Net) (see Fig. 3) based on label semantic information. We hope to refine the attention of AU through image-level supervision.

Specifically, we designed two branches in this module. For the first branch, our goal is to automatically learn feature maps containing attention information, so we designed three convolution layers with kernel sizes of 1×1, 3×3 and 1×1. The two convolution layers are followed by the ReLU activation function. Then we use the softmax function as shown in Eq. 2 to obtain the attention feature map A

$$a_{i,j}^l = \frac{exp\left(o_{i,j}^l\right)}{\sum_{i,j} exp\left(o_{i,j}^l\right)}, A \in R^{28 \times 28 \times C} \tag{2}$$

where $o_{i,j}^l$ is the attention value of the l-th AU before normalization at the position of (i,j), and $a_{i,j}^l$ is the attention value after normalization. For the other branch, our goal is to obtain a confidence map to supervise the refinement of the attention map. Therefore, we use two 1×1 convolution layers to reduce the dimension of the feature map from FA-Net. Here we use two multiplication operations. For the first multiplication operation, the attention feature map A generated by the first branch is multiplied by the output confidence map T of the first convolution layer in the second branch to obtain the attention feature map D that will be input into the Transformer structure. Since many details will be lost when using 1×1 convolution to reduce dimension, we choose to multiply the confidence map T instead of the final confidence map B to preserve more global features. For the second multiplication operation, the attention feature map A generated by the first branch is multiplied by the confidence map B obtained by the second branch, and then the features are merged into a C-dimensional vector (the number of AUs is C), using the results of AU detection are obtained by using the attention features. We only use the error $loss_{att}$ between the prediction result and the ground-truth label (see Sect. 3.5), and back-propagate the error to guide the learning of model parameters. The final AU detection is not directly related to the prediction result.

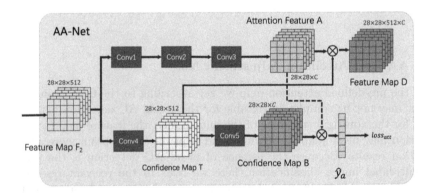

Fig. 3. The Attention Adjustment Net (AA-Net) proposed by us. It is used to supervise the refinement of attention maps.

3.4   Transformer Structure

In order to fully learn the correlation between facial AUs, we use the Transformer to automatically learn the potential relationship of facial AUs with the help of its Self-Attention mechanism. Since the original design of the Transformer structure was to be used in the field of machine translation, we adjusted its structure in order to adapt the Transformer structure to tasks in the image field. Figure 4 shows the Transformer structure we used in TAM-Net which is different from the original structure of the Transformer in [21]. Facial AU detection is essentially an image-level task, so we only use the Encoder module instead of the Decoder module. Considering the particularity of the facial AU detection task, the attention maps obtained by the previous module is used as the input of Transformer module. As input, each attention map is independent of each other and its position relation is not needed to be considered here, so we do not use the Positional Encoding module to learn the position embedding information.

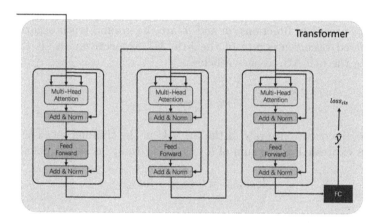

Fig. 4. The Transformer structure used in our method. It is mainly composed of three identical Encoder-Layers, each of which includes two sub-layers, the multi-head self-attention mechanism and the simple feed-forward network.

Specifically, the Encoder we use consists of N = 3 identical blocks. Each block has two sub-layers. The first is a multi-head self-attention mechanism, and the second is a simple feed-forward network with fully connected positions. Residual connections are used around the two sub-layers [7], and both follow a layer normalization [1]. In order to unify the dimension of the residual connection, the dimension of the output of the two sub-layers is 512. For details of these two modules, see [21]. In order to get the detection result of AU, we use C fully connected layers (the number of AU is C). Finally, the prediction results of each AU are output $\hat{y}$.

3.5   Loss Functions

In our experiment, since AU detection is a binary classification problem, we use the commonly used binary cross-entropy loss. Since the occurrence rate of each AU in the dataset is extremely unbalanced, here we use a weighted multi-label cross-entropy loss function. The first loss function is used in the adaptive Attention Adjustment module (AA-Net) to supervise the refinement of the attention map. The specific formula is as follows:

$$loss_{att} = -\sum_{l=1}^{C} w_i [y^l \log\left(\hat{y}_a^l\right) + (1 - y^l)\log(1 - \hat{y}_a^l)] \quad (3)$$

The second loss function is applied to the final AU detection, similar to Eq. 3, written as:

$$loss_{cls} = -\sum_{l=1}^{C} w_l \left[y^l \log\left(\hat{y}^l\right) + \left(1 - y^l\right)\log\left(1 - \hat{y}^l\right)\right] \quad (4)$$

In the above two loss functions, y^l and $\hat{y}^l$ are the ground-truth occurrence rate and predicted occurrence rate of the l-th AU, respectively. w_l is the weight assigned to the l-th AU, as shown below:

$$w_l = \frac{\frac{1}{r_l}}{\sum_{i=1}^{C} \frac{1}{r_i}} \quad (5)$$

where r_i is the occurrence rate of the i-th AU in the training set. The final loss function is expressed as the sum of $loss_{att}$ and $loss_{cls}$, as shown below:

$$loss_{sum} = loss_{att} + loss_{cls} \quad (6)$$

4   Experiment

In this section, we will introduce the dataset, evaluation metrics, and details of the experiment used in our experiment. In the end, we analyze the advantages of our proposed method by comparing the results of our experiment with other facial AU detection methods.

4.1   Datasets and Evaluation Metrics

Datasets. In our experiments, we used the dataset BP4D-Spontaneous [24], which has been widely used in facial AU detection. BP4D-Spontaneous, referred to as BP4D, is a spontaneous facial expression database jointly established by Binghamton University and the University of Pittsburgh. There are 41 subjects, including 18 male subjects and 23 female subjects. Each subject needs to participate in 8 meetings, and each meeting captures their spontaneous facial movements induced by emotions through 2D and 3D video. These videos were shot under constrained conditions, with good near-frontal lighting and a simple background. A total of 328 videos were obtained, and 12 AUs were encoded. The facial AU label of each frame is obtained through FACS [5], and the number of effective AU frames in each video ranges from several hundred to several thousand. There are approximately 140,000 frames with AU occurrence labels in the entire BP4D dataset.

Evaluation Metrics. In our experiment, F1-score [20] and accuracy are selected as the algorithm performance evaluation metrics for AU detection. F1-score is a commonly used performance evaluation metric in image classification problems. It is defined as the harmonic average of precision and recall. F1-score is between 0 and 1. The higher the F1-score, the better the performance of the model. To compare the performance with other algorithms, we calculated the F1-score and accuracy of 12 AUs in the BP4D dataset, as well as their average value on all AUs.

4.2   Implementation Details

We choose VGG-19 as the backbone network for deep feature learning. We use the facial landmarks provided in the BP4D dataset to align the input face images and adjust the aligned face images to a size of 224 × 224. The Adam optimizer with an initial learning rate of 1e-4 and a weight decay of 5e-4 is used to jointly optimize FA-Net, AA-Net, and the Transformer structure. For the scheduling of the learning rate, we set the learning rate to be reduced by half every two epochs. We set the batch size to 36, use 3-fold crossValidation, and train 6 epochs for each fold. Our code is based on the Pytorch deep learning framework, and all experiments are performed on a NVIDIA GTX 1080Ti GPU.

4.3   Comparison of AU Detection Methods

In order to verify the effectiveness of our proposed method, we compare it with other AU detection methods. Including traditional feature-based AU detection methods LSVM [6] and JPML [25], deep learning-based methods DRML [26], EAC [9], DSIN [3], CMS [13], GA [8], LP [12], ARL [17], MTLRT [18], JÂA [16], and graph-based methods AU-GCN [11]. The data we compare here directly quote the results recorded in these papers.

Table 1. F1 Score Comparison of AU Detection on BP4D Dataset

Method	Source	AU1	AU2	AU4	AU6	AU7	AU10	AU12	AU14	AU15	AU17	AU23	AU24	Avg
LSVM [6]	JLMR2008	23.2	22.8	23.1	27.2	47.1	77.2	63.7	64.3	18.4	33.0	19.4	20.7	35.3
JPML [25]	CVPR2015	32.6	25.6	37.4	42.3	50.5	72.2	74.1	65.7	38.1	40.0	30.4	42.3	45.9
DRML [26]	CVPR2016	36.4	41.8	43.0	55.0	67.0	66.3	65.8	54.1	36.7	48.0	31.7	30.0	48.3
EAC [9]	TPAMI2018	39.0	35.2	48.6	76.1	72.9	81.9	86.2	58.8	37.5	59.1	35.9	35.8	55.9
DSIN [3]	ECCV2018	51.7	40.4	56.0	76.1	73.5	79.9	85.4	62.7	37.3	62.9	38.8	41.6	58.9
CMS [13]	FG2019	49.1	44.1	50.3	79.2	74.7	80.9	88.3	63.9	44.4	60.3	41.4	51.2	60.6
GA [8]	FG2020	42.8	41.6	48.9	**81.5**	73.2	79.5	**89.1**	**67.3**	43.7	55.5	44.7	52.0	60.0
LP [12]	CVPR2019	43.4	38.0	54.2	77.1	76.7	83.8	87.2	63.3	45.3	60.5	48.1	54.2	61.0
ARL [17]	TAC2019	45.8	39.8	55.1	75.7	77.2	82.3	86.6	58.8	47.6	62.1	47.4	**55.4**	61.1
MTLRT [18]	ICSP2020	51.3	**48.6**	55.8	74.6	72.5	83.3	88.2	62.7	46.2	**64.5**	44.8	52.2	62.0
JÂA [16]	IJCV2021	**53.8**	47.8	58.2	78.5	75.8	82.7	88.2	63.7	43.3	61.8	45.6	49.9	62.4
AU-GCN [11]	MMM2020	46.8	38.5	**60.1**	80.1	**79.5**	**84.8**	88.0	**67.3**	52.0	63.2	40.9	52.8	62.8
TAM-Net	-	49.3	47.0	58.7	77.6	78.2	82.9	87.4	63.4	**52.8**	62.1	**48.3**	47.6	**62.9**

In Table 1 and Table 2, we list the F1-score and accuracy of all 12 AUs of various methods on the challenging BP4D dataset respectively. We can see that our proposed TAM-Net is better than the other methods mentioned above. Methods such as JÂA [16] also use an adaptive adjustment mechanism, but TAM-Net has achieved better performance, indicating that using the Transformer to automatically learn AU relationships is helpful for facial AU detection performance. Finally, we also compare TAM-Net with the graph-based method AU-GCN. Although we did not use the prior AU co-occurrence relationship in the graph method, we still achieved good performance. This shows that the Transformer has effectively learned the potential correlation of AUs and also proves the advantages of the method we proposed.

Table 2. Accuracy Comparison of AU Detection on BP4D Dataset

Method	Source	AU1	AU2	AU4	AU6	AU7	AU10	AU12	AU14	AU15	AU17	AU23	AU24	Avg
LSVM [6]	JLMR2008	20.7	17.7	22.9	20.3	44.8	73.4	55.3	46.8	18.3	36.4	19.2	11.7	32.2
JPML [25]	CVPR2015	40.7	42.1	46.2	40.0	50.0	75.2	60.5	53.6	50.1	42.5	51.9	53.2	50.5
DRML [26]	CVPR2016	55.7	54.5	58.8	56.6	61.0	53.6	60.8	57.0	56.2	50.0	53.9	53.9	56.0
EAC [9]	TPAMI2018	68.9	73.9	78.1	78.5	69.0	77.6	84.6	60.6	78.1	70.6	81.0	82.4	75.2
CMS [13]	FG2019	55.9	67.7	71.5	**81.3**	71.9	77.3	**87.4**	57.4	71.6	73.7	74.6	84.1	72.9
ARL [17]	TAC2019	73.9	76.7	80.9	78.2	74.4	79.1	85.5	62.8	84.7	**74.1**	82.9	85.7	78.2
MTLRT [18]	ICSP2020	76.7	81.8	80.8	77.4	70.4	**79.3**	86.9	64.6	82.1	73.6	80.4	86.0	78.3
JÂA [16]	IJCV2021	75.2	80.2	82.9	79.8	72.3	78.2	86.6	**65.1**	81.0	72.8	82.9	**86.3**	78.6
TAM-Net	-	**77.5**	**82.8**	**83.0**	78.6	**75.7**	77.7	86.3	65.0	**85.5**	73.6	**83.5**	85.2	**79.5**

Figure 5 shows the refined attention maps obtained for our method. As can be seen from Fig. 5, the adaptive attention adjustment mechanism proposed by us captures the region of interest of AU more accurately. And by comparing with EAC-Net [9], we can find that applying an adaptive adjustment module on the fixed attention mechanism is effective.

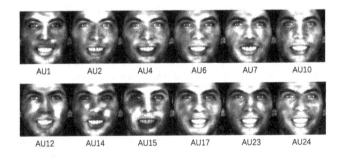

Fig. 5. The refined attention maps generated by the TAM-Net. Areas of higher brightness had higher levels of attention, and areas of lower brightness had lower levels of attention.

5   Conclusion

In this paper, we propose a novel facial action unit detection framework that combines the attention mechanism with the Transformer structure, called TAM-Net. On the one hand, while using a fixed-position attention mechanism to explicitly guide the feature learning of the region of interest, we also proposed an attention adjustment module to adaptively refine the attention map according to the label information. On the other hand, we introduced the Transformer structure to automatically learn the correlation between different facial AUs. Experiments show that our method has achieved competitive results on the challenging BP4D dataset.

References

1. Ba, J.L., Kiros, J.R., Hinton, G.E.: Layer normalization. arXiv preprint arXiv:1607. 06450 (2016)
2. Carion, N., Massa, F., Synnaeve, G., Usunier, N., Kirillov, A., Zagoruyko, S.: End-to-End object detection with transformers. In: Vedaldi, A., Bischof, H., Brox, T., Frahm, J.-M. (eds.) ECCV 2020. LNCS, vol. 12346, pp. 213–229. Springer, Cham (2020). https://doi.org/10.1007/978-3-030-58452-8_13
3. Corneanu, C., Madadi, M., Escalera, S.: Deep structure inference network for facial action unit recognition. In: Proceedings of the European Conference on Computer Vision (ECCV), pp. 298–313 (2018)
4. Dalal, N., Triggs, B.: Histograms of oriented gradients for human detection. In: 2005 IEEE Computer Society Conference on Computer Vision and Pattern Recognition (CVPR'05), vol. 1, pp. 886–893. IEEE (2005)
5. Ekman, R.: What the Face Reveals: Basic and Applied Studies of Spontaneous Expression using the Facial Action Coding System (FACS). Oxford University Press, USA (1997)
6. Fan, R.E., Chang, K.W., Hsieh, C.J., Wang, X.R., Lin, C.J.: Liblinear: a library for large linear classification. J. Mach. Learn. Res. 9, 1871–1874 (2008)
7. He, K., Zhang, X., Ren, S., Sun, J.: Deep residual learning for image recognition. In: Proceedings of the IEEE Conference on Computer Vision and Pattern Recognition, pp. 770–778 (2016)
8. Lakshminarayana, N., Setlur, S., Govindaraju, V.: Learning guided attention masks for facial action unit recognition. In: 2020 15th IEEE International Conference on Automatic Face and Gesture Recognition (FG 2020), pp. 465–472. IEEE (2020)
9. Li, W., Abtahi, F., Zhu, Z., Yin, L.: Eac-net: deep nets with enhancing and cropping for facial action unit detection. IEEE Trans. Pattern Anal. Mach. Intell. 40(11), 2583–2596 (2018)
10. Lin, T.Y., et al.: Microsoft COCO: common objects in context. In: Fleet, D., Pajdla, T., Schiele, B., Tuytelaars, T. (eds.) ECCV 2014. LNCS, vol. 8693, pp. 740–755. Springer, Cham (2014). https://doi.org/10.1007/978-3-319-10602-1_48
11. Liu, Z., Dong, J., Zhang, C., Wang, L., Dang, J.: Relation modeling with graph convolutional networks for facial action unit detection. In: Ro, Y.M., et al. (eds.) MMM 2020. LNCS, vol. 11962, pp. 489–501. Springer, Cham (2020). https://doi.org/10.1007/978-3-030-37734-2_40

12. Niu, X., Han, H., Yang, S., Huang, Y., Shan, S.: Local relationship learning with person-specific shape regularization for facial action unit detection. In: Proceedings of the IEEE/CVF Conference on Computer Vision and Pattern Recognition, pp. 11917–11926 (2019)

13. Sankaran, N., Mohan, D.D., Setlur, S., Govindaraju, V., Fedorishin, D.: Representation learning through cross-modality supervision. In: 2019 14th IEEE International Conference on Automatic Face & Gesture Recognition (FG 2019), pp. 1–8. IEEE (2019)

14. Shan, C., Gong, S., McOwan, P.W.: Facial expression recognition based on local binary patterns: a comprehensive study. Image Vis. Comput. **27**(6), 803–816 (2009)

15. Shao, Z., Liu, Z., Cai, J., Ma, L.: Deep adaptive attention for joint facial action unit detection and face alignment. In: Proceedings of the European Conference on Computer Vision (ECCV), pp. 705–720 (2018)

16. Shao, Z., Liu, Z., Cai, J., Ma, L.: Jaa-net: joint facial action unit detection and face alignment via adaptive attention. Int. J. Comput. Vis. **129**(2), 321–340 (2021)

17. Shao, Z., Liu, Z., Cai, J., Wu, Y., Ma, L.: Facial action unit detection using attention and relation learning. IEEE Transactions on Affective Computing (2019)

18. Shi, S., An, G., Ruan, Q.: Multi-scale region with local relationship learning for facial action unit detection. In: 2020 15th IEEE International Conference on Signal Processing (ICSP), vol. 1, pp. 252–256. IEEE (2020)

19. Simonyan, K., Zisserman, A.: Very deep convolutional networks for large-scale image recognition. arXiv preprint arXiv:1409.1556 (2014)

20. Valstar, M.F., et al.: Fera 2015-second facial expression recognition and analysis challenge. In: 2015 11th IEEE International Conference and Workshops on Automatic Face and Gesture Recognition (FG), vol. 6, pp. 1–8. IEEE (2015)

21. Vaswani, A., et al.: Attention is all you need. arXiv preprint arXiv:1706.03762 (2017)

22. Wang, Y., et al.: End-to-end video instance segmentation with transformers. arXiv preprint arXiv:2011.14503 (2020)

23. Wu, F., et al.: Weakly semi-supervised deep learning for multi-label image annotation. IEEE Trans. Big Data **1**(3), 109–122 (2015)

24. Zhang, X., et al.: Bp4d-spontaneous: a high-resolution spontaneous 3D dynamic facial expression database. Image Vis. Comput. **32**(10), 692–706 (2014)

25. Zhao, K., Chu, W.S., De la Torre, F., Cohn, J.F., Zhang, H.: Joint patch and multi-label learning for facial action unit detection. In: Proceedings of the IEEE Conference on Computer Vision and Pattern Recognition, pp. 2207–2216 (2015)

26. Zhao, K., Chu, W.S., Zhang, H.: Deep region and multi-label learning for facial action unit detection. In: Proceedings of the IEEE Conference on Computer Vision and Pattern Recognition, pp. 3391–3399 (2016)

27. Zhu, F., Li, H., Ouyang, W., Yu, N., Wang, X.: Learning spatial regularization with image-level supervisions for multi-label image classification. In: Proceedings of the IEEE Conference on Computer Vision and Pattern Recognition, pp. 5513–5522 (2017)

Unsupervised Detailed Human Shape Estimation from Multi-view Color Images

Huayu Zheng[1], Kangkan Wang[1,2,3(✉)], Wei Li[1], and Jian Yang[1,2]

[1] Key Lab of Intelligent Perception and Systems for High-Dimensional Information of Ministry of Education, Nanjing University of Science and Technology, Nanjing, China
{wangkangkan,119106010661,csjyang}@njust.edu.cn
[2] Jiangsu Key Lab of Image and Video Understanding for Social Security, School of Computer Science and Engineering, Nanjing University of Science and Technology, Nanjing, China
[3] State Key Lab for Novel Software Technology, Nanjing University, Nanjing, China

Abstract. This paper presents a novel framework to estimate detailed human body shape from color images in an unsupervised manner. It is a challenging task due to factors such as variations in human shapes, occlusion, and cloth details. The existing methods are mainly supervised and require a large number of ground truth real training data which is usually hard to obtain. To solve this problem, we propose an unsupervised detailed human shape estimation method from multi-view color images. Specifically, we first predict the depth map for the source view through robust photometric consistency with different views. Then, we predict the initial SMPL model from the color image and refine it by an iterative error feedback regressor based on point clouds of the predicted depth map. Finally, the refined SMPL model is deformed to fit the details (i.e., clothes and faces) on the point clouds to recover the detailed human shapes which are represented by adding a set of offsets to the SMPL model. The experimental results on different dataset demonstrate that our method outperforms the state-of-the-art methods and achieves higher reconstruction accuracy.

Keywords: Detailed human shape estimation · Unsupervised deep learning · Photometric consistency

1 Introduction

Detailed human shape estimation has a variety of applications in robotics, augmented reality (AR), and virtual reality (VR). Along with development of computer vision, recovering 3D human shape from color images has drawn much attention in recent years. However, estimating detailed human models directly from color images is still a challenging problem due to factors such as variations in human shapes and poses, and serious occlusion.

The Skinned Multi-Person Linear (SMPL) model proposed in [14] is a statistical body shape model, which is parameterized by a set of parameters. Lots of methods [2,3,10,12,13] predict the SMPL parameters to reconstruct human

© Springer Nature Switzerland AG 2021
Y. Peng et al. (Eds.): ICIG 2021, LNCS 12889, pp. 473–484, 2021.
https://doi.org/10.1007/978-3-030-87358-5_38

models from a single color image through convolutional network. But the parametric shape is of low-fidelity, and unable to reconstruct cloth details. Another collection of methods [7,19,20] learn the implicit functions which query a 3D point's occupancy by leveraging features from the input image. These methods then reconstruct human models from dense, continuous occupancy fields via Marching Cubes [15]. But they are limited to the resolution of 3D point space and have huge consumption in GPU memories. Besides, all methods above are supervised and need a large number of labeled datasets to train the network.

In this paper, we propose a novel unsupervised detailed human shape estimation framework from multi-view color images. In the proposed framework three modules are combined to reconstruct detailed human bodies. The first module uses CNN to extract features of multi-view images and wrap them to the source view to generate the 3D volume features, then predict the depth map through the photometric consistency. The second module takes the color image to predict the initial SMPL model, but the result is inaccurate due to lack of depth information. Then the SMPL model is refined through point clouds of the predicted depth map. The third module applies the non-rigid deformation to obtain the detailed human shape by adding a set of offsets representing the cloth details to the SMPL model. The experimental results on various datasets of dressed humans, such as CAPE [16] and CMU Panoptic Dataset [9], demonstrate the effectiveness of our method. In summary, the main contributions of the proposed method are as follows:

1. We propose a novel unsupervised detailed human shape estimation framework from multi-view color images, which can predict the detailed human models and achieve the state-of-the-art performance on human shape estimation.

2. We train the network and estimate the depth map by a fully unsupervised manner, which takes the photometric consistency of multi-view images as supervisory signal.

3. We estimate the detailed human model based on point clouds of the predicted depth map, which improves the reconstruction accuracy.

2   Related Work

2.1   Undressed Parametric Model Estimation

With the simplicity and flexibility of the SMPL model [14], there has been substantial work on estimating the parametric models. Bogo et al. [3] proposed SMPLify to estimate the position of the corresponding 2D human joints and recover SMPL parameters by minimizing the error between 2D projection of model joints and the detected 2D joints. Besides taking joints location as a constraint, many methods also used segmentation information to improve the quality of results. Kanazawa et al. [10] proposed an end-to-end framework for recovering a 3D human model from a color image, which directly extracted features from the images and recovered the SMPL pose parameters through regression. Kolotouros et al. [12] used model fitting to reduce reconstruction error based on

Unsupervised Depth Estimation

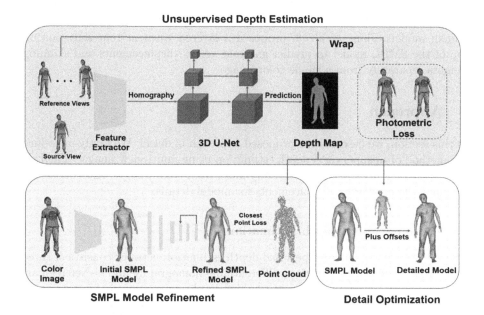

Fig. 1. Overview of the proposed framework. Our framework can reconstruct the detailed 3D human models from multi-view images in an unsupervised way. The unsupervised depth estimation module extracts image features and predicts the depth map using the photometric consistency in multi-view images. Based on the predicted depth map, the SMPL model refinement module regresses accurate parameters of the SMPL model by an iterative linear regressor. The detail optimization module obtains a set of offsets representing the cloth details to reconstruct detailed meshes through the point cloud of the predited depth map.

Kanazawa's work [10]. In addition to directly regressing SMPL model parameters, some recent works also used other methods to predict 3D human models. Kolotouros et al. [13] proposed a Graph CNN architecture to predict human meshes, which first attached the latent space feature by encoding images to 3D vertex coordinates of a template mesh and then predicted the mesh vertex coordinates using a convolutional mesh regression.

2.2   Detailed Parametric Model Estimation

In recent years, 3D human shapes with details are reconstructed from color images based on the SMPL model. Zhu et al. [28] specified the SMPL model to high resolution and deformed the details using joints, silhouette and lighting information together. Alldieck et al. [1] used an extra offset layer to extend the SMPL model and reconstructed detailed human models through semantic segmentation images. Except for using offset to represent details, some works also reconstructed garments and combined them with undressed models to recover detailed models. Ma et al. [16] modeled the clothing as a displacement layer and parameterized structure of clothing on the SMPL mesh to generate clothed human models. Jiang et al. [8] proposed a layered garment representation on top of the SMPL model to predict garment vertex displacements and skinning weights separately from a single color image.

3   Approach

In this section, we describe the proposed approach in detail. We firstly introduce the method of unsupervised depth estimation using multi-view images. Then we reconstruct the undressed human body mesh from color images. Afterwards, we optimize the per-vertex displacements for model details.

3.1   Unsupervised Depth Estimation

The architecture of our unsupervised depth estimation network consists of three parts, namely feature extraction, differentiable homography and U-Net regularization. The feature extraction extracts high-level representation of images using share-weighted CNN networks. Then a cost volume is constructed by the differentiable homography [26]. After that, the 3D U-Net regularization is used to regularize the volume. Finally, the depth map is obtained from the cost volume through the *soft argmin* operation.

We train the depth estimation network with the photometric consistency loss [11]. Given a main view image I_s and some other view images $\{I_v^1, ..., I_v^m\}$, the network can output a depth map D_s in the main view. For I_s and another view image I_v^m with their intrinsic parameter K and extrinsic parameter T, I_s can be warped to another view m:

$$\hat{I}_s^m = KT(D_s \cdot K^{-1} \cdot I_s) \tag{1}$$

And a binary mask V_s^m is generated, indicating vaild pixel in $\hat{I}_s^m$. Then we can calculate a photo-consistency specifying that the warpped image should match the source image. Therefore, our photometric loss in mth view is defined as:

$$L_{photo}^m = \left(\left\| (I_s - \hat{I}_s^m) \right\| + \left\| (\nabla I_s - \nabla \hat{I}_s^m) \right\| \right) \odot V_s^m, \tag{2}$$

where $\odot$ denotes element-wise multiplication operation and ∇ denotes the gradient of the image.

Besides the photometric loss, we also introduce the measure proposed in [25] called structured similarity $(SSIM)$ to calculate loss L_{SSIM} and regularization loss L_{reg} refered to [17]. Our photometric loss can supervise the network in a pixel-level and SSIM works in a patch-level. The regularization term ensures that the depths in neighbor pixel change smoothly.

$$L_{SSIM} = \sum_m^M [1 - SSIM(I_s, I_s^m)] \cdot V_s^m, \tag{3}$$

$$L_{reg} = e^{-|\nabla I_s|} \cdot |\nabla D_s|, \tag{4}$$

So the final loss for unsupervised depth estimation network is formulated as:

$$L = \alpha \sum_{m}^{M} L_{photo}^{m} + \beta L_{SSIM} + \delta L_{reg}, \tag{5}$$

where α, β and δ are hyperparameters to control the significance of corresponding losses.

The predicted depth maps can be converted to point clouds which are used as the pseudo groundtruth to supervise training in the following steps.

3.2 SMPL Model Refinement

SMPL model [14] uses an 85-D vector Θ consisting of pose parameter θ, shape parameter β and translation t to generate a mesh with 6890 vertices. It is a statistical parametric differentiable model that can represent various human shapes under natural conditions.

HMR [10] has successfully predicted the SMPL parameter. However, HMR use images as input, which has a poor performance when occlusion happens. Hence we first estimate a SMPL model using the HMR from the input image to capture a rough human pose and shape. Then to align the SMPL model to the pseudo groundtruth, we design a regression network to learn an increment $\Delta\Theta$ based on the initial SMPL model parameter Θ. The SMPL model refinement network takes the SMPL mesh as input, then uses PointNet++ [18] to generate 1024-D high-dimensional features. After, three full connected layers as an iterative error feedback regressor [4] is used to predict the increment $\Delta\Theta$.

Chamfer distance [6] usually is used to computer the average distance between two meshes, but it is inappropriate to train our refinement network since point cloud as groundtruth is partial in our experiments and some points in the mesh do not have any corresponding points in the point cloud. To solve this problem, we use the function $F(v_m, v_p)$ proposed in [24] to measure the error between the predicted mesh M and the point cloud P generated from depth map. Besides, we also use L_{prior} to supervise our training. L_{prior} is an adversarial prior [5] which can tell whether the predicted SMPL parameters correspond to a real body and effectively prevent implausible 3D meshes. So the loss of The SMPL model refinement is represented as:

$$L = \lambda_1 \sum_{\substack{v_m \in M \\ v_p \in P}} F(v_m, v_p) + \lambda_2 L_{prior}, \tag{6}$$

where λ_1 and λ_2 are weights of corresponding losses.

3.3 Detail Optimization

The limitation of SMPL model is lack of details. Inspired by previous works [1,2,27], our human body model uses a set of offsets $d \in \mathcal{R}^{6890 \times 3}$ to represent the clothing details of human bodies on top of the SMPL model.

To obtain the correct offsets, we first use the predicted SMPL parameters as the initial solution and then optimize the offsets to align the mesh M to the point cloud P. We define a function $E(\theta, \beta, t, d)$ to present the error of predicted mesh.

$$E(\theta, \beta, t, d) = \omega_{data} \sum_{v_p \in P} D(v_p, M) + \omega_{lap} E_{lap} + \omega_{off} E_{off}, \qquad (7)$$

where ω_{data}, ω_{lap} and ω_{off} are weights respectively.

The Eq. (7) will be minimized by solving correct offsets d. The $D(v_p, M)$ represent the distance from the vertex of point cloud P to the mesh M. Considering the point cloud P is incomplete, we only computer the distance from P to M. E_{lap} is a laplacian regularization term, which is a constraint of deformation, and is defined as:

$$E_{lap} = \sum \|v_{l,o} - v_{l,p}\|_1, \qquad (8)$$

where $v_{l,o}$ and $v_{l,p}$ are the Laplacian coordinates [21] of the original and predicted vertices. And the E_{off} is a regularization term meaning the offsets are usually small when the SMPL model has aligned to the point cloud. The term is defined as:

$$E_{off} = \sum_{i \in V} |d_i|. \qquad (9)$$

4   Experiments

4.1   Datasets

The CAPE [16] is a dataset of dressed human body meshes, which has 10 male subjects and 5 female subjects with large variations in pose and a wide range of common garments, and has various cloth details. Then we use texture images from SURREAL [23] to render the dressed meshes. We map the textures to the meshes through texture coordinates and render the mesh from $\{0, -15, +15, +30\}$ degrees along the Y-axis. Totally we render approximately 100,000 color images as our training dataset. To test our method on real data, we also use the CMU Panoptic Dataset [9]. CMU Panoptic Dataset has 31 synchronized HD videos with their camera parameters captured in the real scene. We generate about 14,000 images from the dataset to finetune our model.

4.2   Implementation Details and Error Metrics

Implementation Details. For depth estimation, we use the 768*768 color images from 4 different views as inputs. An eight-layer 2D CNN is applied to the feature extractor, where the strides of layer 3 and 6 are set to two to divide the feature towers into three scales. For the SMPL model refinement, a three-layer network in PointNet++ [18] is used to downsample input points to $\{1024, 512, 128\}$ and finally generates an 1024-D vector. The hyperparameters used in our network are $\alpha = 12$, $\beta = 6$, $\delta = 1.8$, $\lambda_1 = 60$, $\lambda_2 = 1$, $\omega_{data} = 100$, $\omega_{lap} = 10$ and $\omega_{off} = 0.1$. The learning rates in three steps are $1 * 10^{-3}$, $1 * 10^{-5}$ and $5 * 10^{-3}$, respectively. We train and test all three steps on a single NVIDIA GTX 2080Ti GPU. The total number of iterations of unsupervised depth estimation is set to 20 and the SMPL model refinement is set to 100.

Error Metrics. We conduct a quantitative and qualitative evaluation of the network. We use the Mean Average Vertex Error (MAVE) over all vertices to qunatify the reconstruction error:

$$\varepsilon = \frac{1}{N} \sum_{i=1}^{N} \sqrt{\|v_i - \hat{v}_i\|_2^2}, \tag{10}$$

where N is the number of vertices in the reconstruction model, $\hat{v}$ is the vertex on the predicted 3d human models, and v is the corresponding groundtruth. Moreover, following [22], we also compute the accuracy in different error thresholds to evaluate the quality of reconstructed details.

4.3   Comparison with State-of-the-Art Methods

In order to verify the performance of the method proposed in this paper, we compare it with three state-of-the-art methods including HMR [10], HMD [28] and PIFu [19] on the same test set. HMR predicts the parametric SMPL model. But the parameters are inaccurate since color images have ambiguities when occlusion happens. While our method can overcome this problem by the predicted depth map. HMD reconstructs detailed human meshes from a single image. The network first use HMR to predict the SMPL model and then generate more detail, so it has the same problem when HMR fails to work. Instead our method can align the SMPL model to the point clouds of predicted depths through refinement network, which provides better results for the following detail optimization, and thus our method achieves best performance in all experiments. PIFu uses pixel-aligned implicit functions to represent human bodies but it is easy to cause body part missing due to the lack of global shape robustness. 3D meshes reconstructed by HMD and PIFu have different topological structure compared to the groundtruth. For a fair comparison, we uniformly search the closest points from reconstructed meshes to calculate the MAVE. The quantitative results are shown in Table 1.

Table 1. Reconstruction errors and accuracy with different methods on the same test set of CAPE.

Methods	Accuracy (%)			MAVE (cm)
	1.0 cm	2.0 cm	4.0 cm	
HMR [10]	10.69	31.36	53.16	5.82
HMD [28]	11.41	32.64	59.17	5.21
PIFu [19]	15.74	38.79	62.10	4.37
Ours	**30.93**	**68.74**	**89.18**	**2.16**

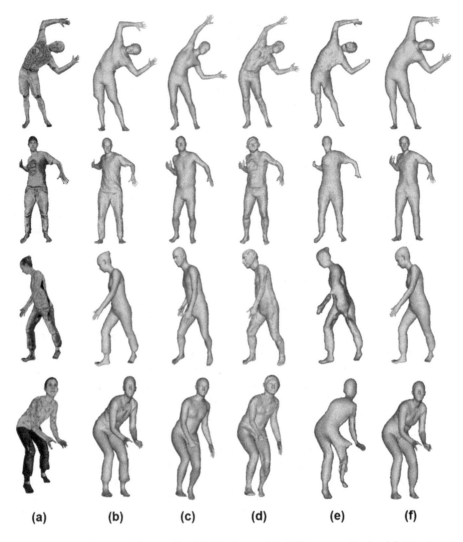

(a)   (b)   (c)   (d)   (e)   (f)

Fig. 2. Experiment results on the CAPE data with different methods. (a) The input image. (b) The groundtruth. (c) HMR [10]. (d) HMD [28]. (e) PIFu [19]. (f) Ours.

4.4   Ablation Study

We also analyse the effectiveness of our SMPL model refinement and detail optimization. In Table 2, we provide three experimental results for proving the significance of our SMPL model refinement and detail optimization. "w/o Ref" means that we do not use SMPL refinement to align models and "w/o Opt" means we do not optimize any details. The first line in Table 2 is the result without aligning to the predicted point clouds and directly optimize for details, and it has a large error when solving the offsets without aligning the SMPL model to the point clouds, as shown in the Fig. 3(c). The second line in Table 2 is the result without detail optimization. Althought the reconstructed mesh is well aligned, apparently the results also has a larger error due to lack of details compared to baseline, as shown in the Fig. 3(d). The baseline is with both the second step and the third step. Evidently it obtains the best performance in our experiments, as shown in the Fig. 3(e).

Table 2. Reconstruction errors and accuracy with different settings of our approach.

Methods	Accuracy(%)			MAVE(cm)
	1.0 cm	2.0 cm	4.0 cm	
Ours(w/o Ref)	20.17	51.02	79.89	2.95
Ours(w/o Opt)	24.71	58.24	81.85	2.73
Ours(Baseline)	**30.93**	**68.74**	**89.18**	**2.16**

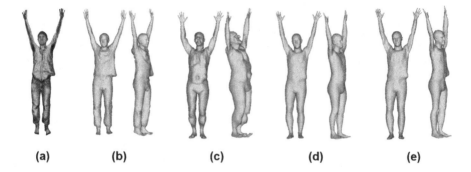

Fig. 3. An example of our ablation experiment result on the CAPE data in the front view and left view respectively. (a) The input image. (b) The groundtruth. (c) The result of Ours (w/o Ref). (d) The result of Ours (w/o Opt). (e) The result of Ours (Baseline)

4.5 Test on Real Dataset

Generally there is a large domain gap between the real data and training data. We generate about 14,000 images from CMU Panoptic Dataset [9] in 10 different views and split them to the training set and the test set. Then we train our network unsupervisedly on the training set and test our method after the training. Figure 4 shows our results on the test set.

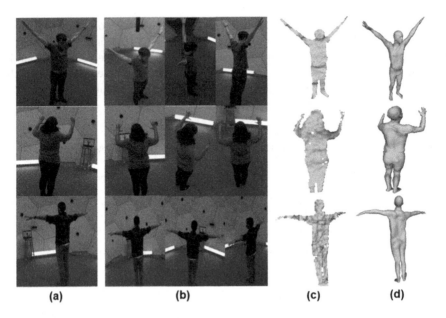

Fig. 4. Some examples of our results on the CMU Panoptic Dataset. (a) The source view image. (b) 3 different reference view images. (c) The mesh from predicted depth map. (d) The result of our method.

5   Conclusion

In this paper, we propose a novel unsupervised detailed human mesh reconstruction framework from multi-view color images, which achieves the state-of-the-art performance on human shape estimation. We first use CNN to extract features of multi-view images and wrap them to the source view, and then predict the depth map through the photometric consistency. After that, we use HMR to predict the initial SMPL model and refine it to align the point cloud generated by depth map. Afterwards we apply non-rigid deformation to fit the model to the point clouds to recover the detailed human models. The experimental results on different datasets (such as CAPE and CMU Panoptic Dataset) show the effectiveness of our method.

Acknowledgements. This work was supported in part by the Fundamental Research Funds for the Central Universities (NJ2020023), in part by the Open Project Program of State Key Laboratory of Virtual Reality Technology and Systems of Beihang University (No.VRLAB2021C03), and in part by the Open Project Program of the State Key Lab of CAD&CG of Zhejiang University (Grant No.A2106).

References

1. Alldieck, T., Magnor, M., Bhatnagar, B.L., Theobalt, C., Pons-Moll, G.: Learning to reconstruct people in clothing from a single RGB camera. In: Proceedings of the IEEE/CVF Conference on Computer Vision and Pattern Recognition, pp. 1175–1186 (2019)
2. Alldieck, T., Magnor, M., Xu, W., Theobalt, C., Pons-Moll, G.: Video based reconstruction of 3D people models. In: Proceedings of the IEEE Conference on Computer Vision and Pattern Recognition, pp. 8387–8397 (2018)
3. Bogo, F., Kanazawa, A., Lassner, C., Gehler, P., Romero, J., Black, M.J.: Keep It SMPL: automatic estimation of 3D human pose and shape from a single image. In: Leibe, B., Matas, J., Sebe, N., Welling, M. (eds.) ECCV 2016. LNCS, vol. 9909, pp. 561–578. Springer, Cham (2016). https://doi.org/10.1007/978-3-319-46454-1_34
4. Carreira, J., Agrawal, P., Fragkiadaki, K., Malik, J.: Human pose estimation with iterative error feedback. In: Proceedings of the IEEE Conference on Computer Vision and Pattern Recognition, pp. 4733–4742 (2016)
5. Fish Tung, H.Y., Harley, A.W., Seto, W., Fragkiadaki, K.: Adversarial inverse graphics networks: learning 2D-to-3D lifting and image-to-image translation from unpaired supervision. In: Proceedings of the IEEE International Conference on Computer Vision, pp. 4354–4362 (2017)
6. Groueix, T., Fisher, M., Kim, V.G., Russell, B.C., Aubry, M.: 3D-coded: 3D correspondences by deep deformation. In: Proceedings of the European Conference on Computer Vision (ECCV), pp. 230–246 (2018)
7. He, T., Collomosse, J.P., Jin, H., Soatto, S.: Geo-pifu: geometry and pixel aligned implicit functions for single-view human reconstruction. In: Larochelle, H., Ranzato, M., Hadsell, R., Balcan, M., Lin, H. (eds.) Advances in Neural Information Processing Systems 33: Annual Conference on Neural Information Processing Systems 2020, NeurIPS 2020, December 6–12, 2020, virtual (2020)
8. Jiang, B., Zhang, J., Hong, Y., Luo, J., Liu, L., Bao, H.: BCNet: learning body and cloth shape from a single image. In: Vedaldi, A., Bischof, H., Brox, T., Frahm, J.-M. (eds.) ECCV 2020. LNCS, vol. 12365, pp. 18–35. Springer, Cham (2020). https://doi.org/10.1007/978-3-030-58565-5_2
9. Joo, H., et al.: Panoptic studio: a massively multiview system for social interaction capture. IEEE Transactions on Pattern Analysis and Machine Intelligence (2017)
10. Kanazawa, A., Black, M.J., Jacobs, D.W., Malik, J.: End-to-end recovery of human shape and pose. In: Proceedings of the IEEE Conference on Computer Vision and Pattern Recognition, pp. 7122–7131 (2018)
11. Khot, T., Agrawal, S., Tulsiani, S., Mertz, C., Lucey, S., Hebert, M.: Learning unsupervised multi-view stereopsis via robust photometric consistency. arXiv preprint arXiv:1905.02706 (2019)
12. Kolotouros, N., Pavlakos, G., Black, M.J., Daniilidis, K.: Learning to reconstruct 3D human pose and shape via model-fitting in the loop. In: 2019 IEEE/CVF International Conference on Computer Vision, ICCV 2019, Seoul, Korea (South), October 27 - November 2, 2019, pp. 2252–2261 (2019)
13. Kolotouros, N., Pavlakos, G., Daniilidis, K.: Convolutional mesh regression for single-image human shape reconstruction. In: Proceedings of the IEEE/CVF Conference on Computer Vision and Pattern Recognition, pp. 4501–4510 (2019)
14. Loper, M., Mahmood, N., Romero, J., Pons-Moll, G., Black, M.J.: Smpl: a skinned multi-person linear model. ACM Trans. Graph. (TOG) 34(6), 1–16 (2015)

15. Lorensen, W.E., Cline, H.E.: Marching cubes: a high resolution 3d surface construction algorithm. In: Stone, M.C. (ed.) Proceedings of the 14th Annual Conference on Computer Graphics and Interactive Techniques, SIGGRAPH 1987, Anaheim, California, USA, July 27–31, 1987, pp. 163–169. ACM (1987). https://doi.org/10.1145/37401.37422

16. Ma, Q., et al.: Learning to dress 3D people in generative clothing. In: Computer Vision and Pattern Recognition (CVPR) (2020)

17. Mahjourian, R., Wicke, M., Angelova, A.: Unsupervised learning of depth and ego-motion from monocular video using 3D geometric constraints. In: Proceedings of the IEEE Conference on Computer Vision and Pattern Recognition, pp. 5667–5675 (2018)

18. Qi, C.R., Yi, L., Su, H., Guibas, L.J.: Pointnet++: Deep hierarchical feature learning on point sets in a metric space. arXiv preprint arXiv:1706.02413 (2017)

19. Saito, S., Huang, Z., Natsume, R., Morishima, S., Kanazawa, A., Li, H.: Pifu: pixel-aligned implicit function for high-resolution clothed human digitization. In: The IEEE International Conference on Computer Vision (ICCV), October 2019

20. Saito, S., Simon, T., Saragih, J.M., Joo, H.: Pifuhd: multi-level pixel-aligned implicit function for high-resolution 3D human digitization. In: 2020 IEEE/CVF Conference on Computer Vision and Pattern Recognition, CVPR 2020, Seattle, WA, USA, June 13–19, 2020, pp. 81–90. IEEE (2020)

21. Sorkine, O.: Differential representations for mesh processing. Comput. Graph. Forum $25(4)$, 789–807 (2006). https://doi.org/10.1111/j.1467-8659.2006.00999.x

22. Tang, S., Tan, F., Cheng, K., Li, Z., Zhu, S., Tan, P.: A neural network for detailed human depth estimation from a single image. In: Proceedings of the IEEE/CVF International Conference on Computer Vision (ICCV), October 2019

23. Varol, G., et al.: Learning from synthetic humans. In: Proceedings of the IEEE Conference on Computer Vision and Pattern Recognition, pp. 109–117 (2017)

24. Wang, K., Zhang, G., Yang, J., Bao, H.: Dynamic human body reconstruction and motion tracking with low-cost depth cameras. Vis. Comput. $37(3)$, 603–618 (2021)

25. Wang, Z., Bovik, A., Sheikh, H., Simoncelli, E.: Image quality assessment: from error visibility to structural similarity. IEEE Trans. Image Process. $13(4)$, 600–612 (2004). https://doi.org/10.1109/TIP.2003.819861

26. Yao, Y., Luo, Z., Li, S., Fang, T., Quan, L.: Mvsnet: depth inference for unstructured multi-view stereo. In: Proceedings of the European Conference on Computer Vision (ECCV), pp. 767–783 (2018)

27. Zhang, C., Pujades, S., Black, M.J., Pons-Moll, G.: Detailed, accurate, human shape estimation from clothed 3D scan sequences. In: Proceedings of the IEEE Conference on Computer Vision and Pattern Recognition, pp. 4191–4200 (2017)

28. Zhu, H., Zuo, X., Wang, S., Cao, X., Yang, R.: Detailed human shape estimation from a single image by hierarchical mesh deformation. In: Proceedings of the IEEE Conference on Computer Vision and Pattern Recognition (CVPR) (2019)

Device-Adaptive 2D Gaze Estimation: A Multi-Point Differential Framework

Runtong Li[1], Huimin Ma[2]($^{(\boxtimes)}$), Rongquan Wang[2], and Jiawei Ding[2]

[1] Tsinghua University, Beijing 100084, China
lirt19@mails.tsinghua.edu.cn
[2] University of Science and Technology Beijing, Beijing 100083, China
{mhmpub,rongquanwang}@ustb.edu.cn, g20209474@xs.ustb.edu.cn

Abstract. Eye tracking system on mobile devices is important for many interactive applications. However, since models are usually customized with limited types of devices and new devices have totally different physical parameters, it is hard to generalize over unseen devices. In this paper, we present a device-adaptive 2D gaze estimation algorithm based on differential prediction. We reformulate the gaze estimation as a relative position prediction problem between the input image and calibration images, which skips the estimation for camera parameters and makes models easily generalize over devices. To tackle the new challenge, this work proposes a framework which jointly trains a differential prediction module and an aggregation module for ensembling the predictions from multiple calibration points. Experiments show that the framework outperforms baseline models constantly on open datasets with only 3–5 calibration points.

Keywords: Adaptive gaze estimation · Neural networks · Differential prediction

1 Introduction

Gaze indicates the attention of human eyes, which is widely applied in mental states analysis. Besides, it is an important technique which can be applied to many areas such as human-computer interaction [11], virtual reality, and medical care [9].

Great improvements are made [1,7,8,22] in the gaze estimation field, due to the emergence of large-scale datasets such as GazeCapture [13], TabletGaze [10], etc. These works are mostly appearance-based, which use low-resolution images taken from the front camera of the device to estimate the movement of the eyes. The main advantage of such methods is the low requirement for device configuration, and as a consequence they are convenient for common usage. The success of deep learning in computer vision influences the task a lot, and

Supported by National Natural Science Foundation of China(No.U20B2062); Beijing Municipal Science and Technology Project(No.Z191100007419001).

Y. Peng et al. (Eds.): ICIG 2021, LNCS 12889, pp. 485–497, 2021.
https://doi.org/10.1007/978-3-030-87358-5_39

convolutional neural networks are widely used to extract eye features and shown to perform well.

However, popular 2D datasets are collected with limited types of mobile ends, on which the device-specific physical parameters are fixed or easy to obtain. Models based on them naturally use the camera space coordinates as the output [7,8,13], and a further step is needed to transform them into the screen space. We note that these parameters such as relative position between the front camera and screen are important for the deployment of gaze estimation models, because generally there may be some information displayed on the screen and we want to know the user attention at the pixel level. Collecting these parameters or gathering datasets on unseen devices is hard and impractical. Unfortunately, previous works usually neglect this problem and lose the generality to some content.

Instead of obtaining more data sources, another potential solution to device generalization is to do calibration, which is widely utilized in the field to justify the person-specific bias. Though calibration is seldom used to do device calibration in previous works, related methods such as SVR, linear adaption, and finetuning the neural networks [13,15] can do such device transformation. However, even training a naive linear adaptor on top of the model relies on new data of high quality, and they usually need too many calibration points (more than 9) to get satisfactory results. Besides, finetuning a neural network on mobile devices requires large memory and the time consumption is hard to tolerate. Above all, how to develop an efficient framework, which leverages the advantage of appearance-based methods and can be generalized to different devices, is a challenging and important task.

In this paper, we propose a multi-point differential framework to solve the above problem. The contributions of this work lie in three key aspects. (1) To predict the on-screen coordinates, the 2D gaze estimation problem is reformulated in a differential approach. Instead of getting more data, the approach relies on convenient user interaction. (2) Based on the new formulation, a deep learning framework, DAGE (**D**evice-**A**daptive **G**aze track**E**r), is designed which can dynamically aggregate predictions from multiple calibration points to further boost the performance. (3) Experiments show that our method not only solves the generalization problem but obtains competitive results with baseline models. We also investigate the effectiveness of each proposed module.

2   Related Works

Gaze estimation problem is usually divided into two categories: 2D gaze estimation and 3D gaze estimation. The former aims to predict the 2D location on a plane [7,8,10,13], while the latter focuses on predicting a 3D vector which represents the gaze orientation of the subject [5,20,21]. For the 3D vector, one more step is needed to transform it into the 2D location on the device screen, and we try to predict 2D coordinates directly in this work.

Appearance-Based Gaze Estimation. Approaches to solve gaze estimation problems generally include model-based methods and appearance-based methods. The model-based methods try to model the structure of eyeballs from the perspective of geometry [2,3,6,16]. Early methods use infrared systems to localize the center of the pupil and contour of the iris, which is accurate enough but relies on high-resolution images to analyze the features of the eye region, and is inconvenient for mobile usage. Besides, methods based on such systems usually predict 3D gaze vector and is projected onto the screen as the result. The performance of these methods highly depends on many factors such as the quality of input data, geometric modeling of eyeballs, and sometimes even the estimation of head pose [19]. In contrast, the appearance-based methods take mid or low-resolution images of eyes as the input and are more suitable for common usage. With the development of deep learning techniques and the emergence of gaze datasets, convolutional neural networks are widely used to solve the problem [4,13,18,24]. For instance, TabletGaze [10] is collected on Samsung Galaxy tablets, which is relatively small and contains only 51 subjects in unconstrained environments. And GazeStare [7] is collected with Samsung Galaxy S8+, in which the illumination conditions, body postures, and head pose varied a lot. They are all collected on specific devices, which makes models trained on them unsuitable for others. [13] reported the first large-scale dataset, GazeCapture, for eye tracking, which contains around 1500 subjects together with more than 2.5M frames. They also developed a model called iTracker as a benchmark in the field. Firstly, face bounding boxes and two eyes bounding boxes were detected in the input image. Then iTracker took face image, two eyes image, and face grid as the inputs, and predicted the 2D gaze location relative to the front camera. The error of iTracker was around 2 cm and 3 cm tested on phones and tablets separately without calibration. SAGE [8] was develop based on the iTracker model. It tried to prevent the model from overfitting and introduced some device-specific parameters, which eventually achieved around 25% better accuracy than iTracker. Besides, knowledge distillation and pruning skills are used to further improve the robustness of the model [7].

Personalized Calibration. Early methods are mostly person-independent, which means models with the same parameters are used for different subjects. However, different subjects have different facial features and eye structures, so novel faces without user-specific calibration may lead to bad performance. Calibration is used to alleviate the personal variance in estimation, and lots of experiments show its effectiveness [8,13–15]. In these works, new subjects are asked to gaze on several predefined locations, and their facial images along with the location labels are recorded to personalize the trained models. For example, SVR can be trained on top of the iTracker model for new subjects [13]. And in some works, calibration images are combined with few-shot learning skills. The calibration images and coordinates can be embedded in neural networks to obtain lower error [8] (around 1.37 cm on smartphones and 2.10 cm on tablets with 9 calibration points). And [15] proposed to estimate the angle difference based on the calibration for 3D gaze estimation to eliminate personal bias. However, though great improvements on accuracy are obtained in these works, a further step is needed to transform the coordinates from the original model output space (usually the coordinates originated from the camera) to new device screen space, which is a necessary but rarely studied process for the model deployment. [23] argued the device adaption as well and proposed device-specific CNN architecture to solve the 3D vector estimation. To the best of our knowledge, this work is the first to tackle device calibration in 2D gaze estimation and aims to develop a framework which can fit with common devices.

3   Proposed Method

3.1   Problem Formulation

Given the query image I_q taken by the front camera as the input, some previous methods try to predict the coordinates (x_q^c, y_q^c) originated from the camera. Since the images are taken by the camera, it is reasonable to take camera's position as the reference point on different devices, as we discussed before. In this way, a further step is needed to transform the predicted coordinates into the screen space (x_q^s, y_q^s). Some other methods directly predict coordinates in screen space under the assumption that the device is fixed [10]. Our goal is to use the screen space as the output directly without prior knowledge about camera location parameters. In the rest of the paper, the coordinates are all in screen space if no specification.

Calibration is the process to collect user-specific data and the model learns personal patterns using such data to make better predictions. We argue that this process can be used to do device generalization for 2D gaze estimation in a differential way. Given a set of calibration images $\{I_{calib\_k} | 1 \leq k \leq n\}$, together with the labeled gaze location set $\{(x_k, y_k)\}$, we try to predict the relative location $(\Delta x_k, \Delta y_k)$ between the query image I_q and each calibration image I_{calib_k}. And the query location could be represented as $(x_k + \Delta x_k, y_k + \Delta y_k)$. Then, motivated by the model ensemble methods, an aggregation module is designed to combine these coordinates as the query result (x_q, y_q).

3.2   Model Architecture

Figure 1 presents an overview of our framework. The subject firstly gazes at the calibration points on the screen, and the camera takes images containing the face region at the same time. At the inference stage, the framework predicts the relative gaze position between the query image and calibration images using **differential prediction module**. Then an **aggregation module** is used to combine the results: a weight predictor is responsible for judging the importance for each prediction and the weighted sum of them is calculated as the final result. Details are explained as the following.

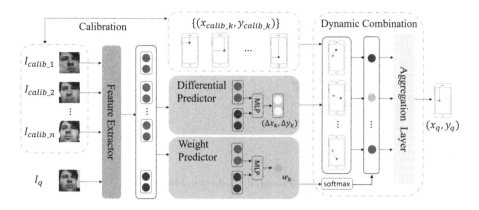

Fig. 1. Overview of our framework (best viewed in color) (Color figure online)

Differential Prediction Module. Many CNNs are developed as the feature extractors for facial features representation in previous works. We use SAGE [8] as our feature extractor because of its nice performance. We note that the original SAGE takes the camera space as the output, and our framework aims to make it device-adaptive. SAGE takes two eye images together with their bounding box coordinates as the input. We remove the device-specific affine transformation matrix in it, because it is not available on new devices. We calculate the normalized eye bounding box area as a new handcrafted feature. We change some parameters of convolution layers for better performance. We also remove the final FC layer in SAGE to get the embeddings of the facial images. We denote the modified SAGE as *mSAGE*. Note that the extractor could be replaced by any other CNN architecture.

$$\mathbf{emb}_q = f_{mSAGE}(I_q)$$
$$\mathbf{emb}_{calib\_k} = f_{mSAGE}(I_{calib\_k}) \tag{1}$$

After constructing the feature extractor, we need to predict the relative position between the query image and each calibration image in pair-wise manner. We simply concatenate the embeddings of two images and add a Multi-Layer Perceptron (MLP) on top of them, which predicts the relative position $(\Delta x_k, \Delta y_k)$.

$$(\Delta x_k, \Delta y_k) = MLP_{diff}(\mathbf{emb}_q, \mathbf{emb}_{calib\_k}) \tag{2}$$

Aggregation Module. Next, an aggregation module is needed to combine the results given by each calibration point. First, a weight predictor is used to determine the importance of each calibration point. Then, we aggregate the coordinates according to the weights. In this paper, we try three pooling methods for weight calculation as following.

(1) Mean Pooling. The final result is calculated by taking the average of all the calibration results. This method supposes that each calibration point has

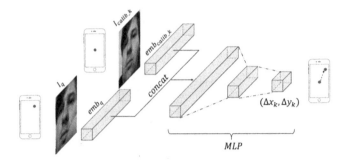

Fig. 2. Differential Prediction Module

equal contributions.

$$w_k = \frac{1}{n}$$
$$(x_q, y_q) = \sum_k w_k(x_k + \Delta x_k, y_k + \Delta y_k) \tag{3}$$

(2) MLP Pooling. We add an MLP to the concatenated image embeddings to decide the calibration point weight, and a softmax layer is used to make the weights follow a pseudo distribution.

$$w_k = \frac{exp(MLP_{wgt}(\mathbf{emb}_{calib\_k}, \mathbf{emb}_q))}{\sum_j exp(MLP_{wgt}(\mathbf{emb}_{calib\_j}))}$$
$$(x_q, y_q) = \sum_k w_k(x_k + \Delta x_k, y_k + \Delta y_k) \tag{4}$$

(3) Attention Pooling. We do inner-product for query embeddings with each calibration embeddings, which calculates the similarity between them. A softmax layer is added as well.

$$w_k = \frac{exp(\mathbf{emb}_{calib\_k} \cdot \mathbf{emb}_q)}{\sum_j exp(\mathbf{emb}_{calib\_j} \cdot \mathbf{emb}_q)}$$
$$(x_q, y_q) = \sum_k w_k(x_k + \Delta x_k, y_k + \Delta y_k) \tag{5}$$

Training Procedure. Our framework optimizes the differential prediction module and aggregation module jointly. For each training step, we put the query image together with n calibration images into the network, and the network predicts the coordinates. We use Mean Squared Error (MSE) as the loss function and do back propagation to update the parameters. We emphasize that the change of reference coordinate system won't influence the value of the error term because the relative distances between points are constant. The inference procedure process is similar to the training phase. The whole process is summarized in Algorithm 1.

Algorithm 1: Training and Inference Procedure

Input: dataset; hyper-parameters.

Output: model weights; predictions for test set.

1 // training procedure

2 **for** $i = 1$: *number of steps* **do**

3   Sample a batch of query images from dataset $\{I_q\}$;

4   For each query image I_q, sample n calibration images $\{I_{calib\_k}\}$;

5   Do forward and backward propagation;

6   Update parameters;

7 **end**

8 // inference procedure

9 **for** *each test sample* **do**

10   **if** *unseen subject or device* **then**

11   do calibration to get $\{I_{calib\_k}\}$;

12   **end**

13   Take image I_q by the front camera;

14   Forward the neural network.

15 **end**

---

4 Experiments

4.1 Setup

Dataset Description . We use GazeCapture [13], a large-scale dataset for eye tracking, to evaluate our model. The dataset was collected on iPhones and iPads from 1474 subjects. The subjects were asked to gaze at several fixed points on the screen, and the front camera recorded their face images at the same time. Following the dataset split settings in [8,13], 150 subjects are held out for the evaluation step.

Evaluation Metric. We use Euclidean Distance in centimeters between the ground-truth point and prediction point as the metric. Moreover, we report the error term for phones and tablets separately.

Implementation Detail. The framework is implemented using Pytorch [17]. We use Adam optimizer [12] in all experiments. We set the initial learning rate to $1e - 5$, β_1 to 0.9 and β_2 to 0.999. We train all the models for 25 epochs with a batch size of 128. Different from [8,13], we use no data augmentation in our work because they didn't report related details such as hyper-parameter settings. To mimic the procedure of calibration for each subject, we randomly sample data from his/her own image sets with the same device orientation.

4.2 Performance Comparison

Since most previous models are sensible to device changes and can't fit into our settings, we implement the following methods as our baselines for comparison.

(1) **Support vector regression (SVR)**. An SVR model was trained on top of iTracker to make the personal calibration [13]. SVR with a linear kernel is insensible to the coordinates drift, so it can be used on top of the feature extractor to do the device calibration as well.

(2) **Least Absolute Shrinkage and Selection Operator (LASSO)**. Because it is ill-posed to estimate weights from limited calibration points, we use LASSO to regularize the weights.

(3) **Gaussian kernel averaging (Gauss)**. Gaussian kernel averaging can be used to combine the results given by different calibration images as [15] did, which is similar to the nearest neighbor thoughts. We set the Gauss distribution to $\mathcal{N}(0, 0.5)$ for its best performance after trying different choices.

(4) **mSAGE**. We also report the performance of mSAGE without calibration for comparison, which predicts the coordinates originated from the camera.

Table 1. Performance Comparison (cm)

# of Pts	DAGE		SVR		LASSO		Gauss		mSAGE	
	Phone	Tablet	Phone	Tablet	Phone	Tablet	Phone	Tablet	Phone	Tablet
2	**2.06**	**3.32**	3.12	6.38	3.20	6.53	3.14	6.56	2.16	3.15
3	**1.87**	**2.98**	2.88	5.43	2.81	5.23	2.78	5.65		
5	**1.73**	**2.68**	2.40	4.07	2.42	4.04	2.41	4.57		
9	**1.59**	**2.43**	1.99	2.97	2.08	3.31	2.12	3.62		

Results are presented in Table 1, and we make the following observations and discussions.

(1) Our model outperforms all the baseline models consistently. Compared with SVR, our model reduces the error from 1.99 cm to 1.59 cm on phone and from 2.97 cm to 2.43 cm on tablets with 9 calibration points.

(2) For all the tested models, more calibration points lead to significant improvements. However, We find that our model performs well even with only 3 points while the baseline models need 9 points to get comparable results. Besides, for LASSO and Gauss, we need to try different parameter settings to obtain good performance.

(3) The SVR, LASSO, and Gauss play a role both in device and person calibration. The training process of them is independent of the training of the feature extractor and the performance is tightly related to the number of calibration points. However, our model trains the two parts jointly, so it can leverage the total dataset to optimize the aggregation module, which takes the advantage of deep neural networks.

(4) Our model obtains comparable results with mSAGE. However, we note that our method takes the screen space coordinates as the output and is easier for deployment on different devices.

4.3   Components Analysis

To further understand the components in our model, we conduct related studies for the aggregation module and device orientation choice.

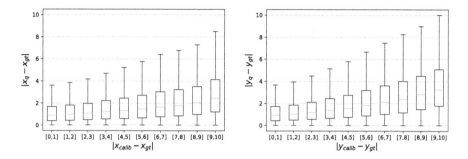

Fig. 3. Error Box Plot

Differential Prediction Module Analysis. We separate the differential prediction module from the whole model and test the module in the pair-wise manner (each query image with only one calibration image). We calculate the box plot between the ground-truth differential and the prediction error at x-axis and y-axis separately. Results are shown in Fig. 3. We can see from the figure that, as the calibration point goes far from the gaze point, the error grows as well. The reason might be that the features of the query image are too different from that of the calibration image, and it is hard for the model to make a precise prediction. And this phenomenon gives us the basic principle to choose calibration points, that we should set calibration points uniformly on the screen so that the query can find near enough calibration points all the time. Moreover, we can roughly observe from the figure that, the error at the y-axis is higher than the x-axis. We argue it is because that the horizontal eyeball movement is more significant than the vertical movement, which corresponds with human cognition.

Table 2. Performance Comparison (cm)

# of Pts	Mean		Attn		MLP	
	Phone	Tablet	Phone	Tablet	Phone	Tablet
3	1.95	3.06	1.93	3.10	1.87	2.98
5	1.86	2.92	1.84	2.86	1.73	2.68
9	1.77	2.78	1.67	2.58	1.59	2.43

Aggregation Module Influence. As we mentioned above, we try three methods to do the aggregation, which are Mean Pooling (Mean), MLP Pooling (MLP), and Attention Pooling (Attn). Results are shown in Table 2. We observe that MLP performs best under all circumstances (e.g. device type and the number of calibration points) and Mean performs worst most of the time. This indicates that the model can automatically learn the relation between the query image and the calibration images, and decide the weights for the combination. We also find that MLP is better than Attn constantly. We discuss that Attn can pay attention to similar embeddings, while MLP can analyze the relation based on statistics in the whole dataset not just limited to similar points.

Table 3. Device orientation influence (cm)

# of Pts	Orientation		Free	
	Phone	Tablet	Phone	Tablet
3	1.87	2.98	2.22	3.55
5	1.73	2.68	2.07	3.31
9	1.59	2.43	1.98	3.09

4.4 Discussions and Visualization

Device Orientation Influence. We re-train the models without the device orientation constrain (the screen orientation should be the same when taking query and calibration images), and the results are shown in Table 3. We can observe that, the performance of the model degrades drastically without the constrain. To explain the phenomenon, we draw the distribution of differential in Fig. 4, in which index o denotes orientation constrain, f denotes free from constrain. As shown, long tail is more obvious in the unconstrained curves, which is a challenge for neural networks without enough data.

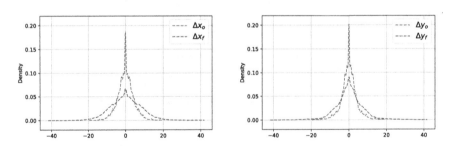

Fig. 4. Distribution of Differential.

Training Manner Analysis. The model was trained in the pair-wise manner and the results from different calibration points were combined at the inference stage in [15]. This pipeline breaks the integrity of the model and limits its power. In our framework, the aggregation module serves as a part of the model and can be trained with any number of calibration points. We show how this property influences performance. We test different combinations of calibration points, the results are shown in Table 4, where Tr denotes the number of calibration points used in the training phase, and Ts denotes that in the test phase. We observe that, even with the same Ts, lower error is obtained when using higher Tr. And this indicates the necessity to go beyond pair-wise training manner.

Table 4. Training manner influence.

	Tr = 3		Tr = 5		Tr = 9	
	Phone	Tablet	Phone	Tablet	Phone	Tablet
Ts = 3	1.87	2.98	1.84	2.88	1.80	2.92
Ts = 5	1.77	2.80	1.73	2.68	1.68	2.63
Ts = 9	1.70	2.67	1.65	2.53	1.59	2.43

Algorithm Complexity Analysis. The features of calibration points can be computed and cached after collecting the images. As a consequence, the time consumption of one inference consists of three parts: running feature extractor for the query image, predicting the relative position based on query embedding and calibration embeddings, and aggregating the results from multiple calibration points. Since the MLP in our framework is relatively shallow, the main bottleneck of speed lies on the feature extractor.

5   Conclusion

In this paper, we propose a framework for 2D gaze estimation, which skips the camera parameters estimation and can easily generalize over different devices. Experiments show that our method outperforms the baseline models constantly. We also investigate the effectiveness of the components in our framework. We think this work moves a further step towards general mobile gaze estimations.

References

1. Brousseau, B., Rose, J., Eizenman, M.: Accurate model-based point of gaze estimation on mobile devices. Vision **2**(3), 35 (2018)
2. Chen, J., Ji, Q.: 3D gaze estimation with a single camera without ir illumination. In: 2008 19th International Conference on Pattern Recognition, pp. 1–4 (2008)

3. Chen, J., Ji, Q.: Probabilistic gaze estimation without active personal calibration. In: 2011 IEEE Conference on Computer Vision and Pattern Recognition (CVPR), pp. 609–616 (2011)

4. Cheng, Y., Lu, F., Zhang, X.: Appearance-based gaze estimation via evaluation-guided asymmetric regression. In: Proceedings of the European Conference on Computer Vision (ECCV), pp. 100–115 (2018)

5. Deng, H., Zhu, W.: Monocular free-head 3D gaze tracking with deep learning and geometry constraints. In: 2017 IEEE International Conference on Computer Vision (ICCV), pp. 3162–3171 (2017)

6. Guestrin, E., Eizenman, M.: General theory of remote gaze estimation using the pupil center and corneal reflections. Biomed. Eng. IEEE Trans. **53**, 1124–1133 (2006)

7. Guo, T., et al.: A generalized and robust method towards practical gaze estimation on smart phone. International Conference on Computer Vision Workshop, ICCVW 2019 (2019)

8. He, J., et al.: On-device few-shot personalization for real-time gaze estimation. In: International Conference on Computer Vision Workshop, ICCVW 2019, pp. 1149–1158 (2019)

9. Holzman, P.: Eye-tracking dysfunctions in schizophrenic patients and their relatives. Arch. General Psychiatry **31**, 143 (1974)

10. Huang, Q., Veeraraghavan, A., Sabharwal, A.: Tabletgaze: dataset and analysis for unconstrained appearance-based gaze estimation in mobile tablets. Mach. Vis. Appl. **28**(5–6), 445–461 (2017)

11. Jacob, R.J., Karn, K.S.: Eye tracking in human-computer interaction and usability research: ready to deliver the promises. In: The Mind's Eye, pp. 573–605. Elsevier (2003)

12. Kingma, D., Ba, J.: Adam: a method for stochastic optimization. Computer Science (2014)

13. Krafka, K., et al.: Eye tracking for everyone. In: 2016 IEEE Conference on Computer Vision and Pattern Recognition (CVPR), pp. 2176–2184 (2016)

14. Lindén, E., Sjöstrand, J., Proutière, A.: Appearance-based 3d gaze estimation with personal calibration. CoRR abs/1807.00664 (2018)

15. Liu, G., Yu, Y., Mora, K.A.F., Odobez, J.M.: A differential approach for gaze estimation. IEEE Trans. Pattern Anal. Mach. Intell. **43**(3), 1092–1099 (2021)

16. Ogawa, T., Nakazawa, A., Nishida, T.: Point of gaze estimation using corneal surface reflection and omnidirectional camera image. IEICE Trans. Inform. Syst. **101**, 1278–1287 (2018)

17. Paszke, A., et al.: Pytorch: an imperative style, high-performance deep learning library. In: Wallach, H., Larochelle, H., Beygelzimer, A., d'Alché-Buc, F., Fox, E., Garnett, R. (eds.) Advances in Neural Information Processing Systems, vol. 32, pp. 8024–8035. Curran Associates, Inc. (2019)

18. Sugano, Y., Matsushita, Y., Sato, Y.: Learning-by-synthesis for appearance-based 3D gaze estimation. In: 2014 IEEE Conference on Computer Vision and Pattern Recognition, pp. 1821–1828 (2014). https://doi.org/10.1109/CVPR.2014.235

19. Valenti, R., Sebe, N., Gevers, T.: Combining head pose and eye location information for gaze estimation. IEEE Trans. Image Process. **21**(2), 802–815 (2012)

20. Yu, Y., Liu, G., Odobez, J.: Improving few-shot user-specific gaze adaptation via gaze redirection synthesis. In: 2019 IEEE/CVF Conference on Computer Vision and Pattern Recognition (CVPR), pp. 11929–11938 (2019)

21. Zhang, X., Sugano, Y., Fritz, M., Bulling, A.: Appearance-based gaze estimation in the wild. In: 2015 IEEE Conference on Computer Vision and Pattern Recognition (CVPR), pp. 4511–4520 (2015)
22. Zhang, X., Sugano, Y., Fritz, M., Bulling, A.: It's written all over your face: full-face appearance-based gaze estimation. In: 2017 IEEE Conference on Computer Vision and Pattern Recognition Workshops (CVPRW), pp. 2299–2308 (2017)
23. Zhang, X., Huang, M.X., Sugano, Y., Bulling, A.: Training person-specific gaze estimators from user interactions with multiple devices. In: Proceedings of the 2018 CHI Conference on Human Factors in Computing Systems, pp. 1–12. Association for Computing Machinery (2018)
24. Zhang, X., Sugano, Y., Fritz, M., Bulling, A.: Mpiigaze: real-world dataset and deep appearance-based gaze estimation. IEEE Trans. Pattern Anal. Mach. Intell. **41**(1), 162–175 (2017)

Dual Gated Learning for Visible-Infrared Person Re-identification

YuHeng Huang, JinCai Xian$^{(\boxtimes)}$, Dong Wei, XiaoFeng Jin, and TianShi Xu

GRG Banking Equipment Co., Ltd., Guangzhou, GuangDong, China
xianjincai@grgbanking.com

Abstract. Visible-infrared person re-identification (VI-ReID) is a crucial part of open world ReID task, targeting at cross-modality pedestrian retrieval between visible and infrared images. Its large intra-class variation and cross-modality discrepancy lead to difficulty in discriminated representation learning. In this paper, we investigate adaptive neurons deactivation technique to improve VI-ReID model performance and propose two auxiliary training schemes. First, we present a one-stream module (gated module, GM) and its corresponding training scheme (gated learning, GL), to assist model training by adaptive neuron deactivation. Based on GM and GL, we design two-stream module (dual gated module, DGM) and its corresponding training scheme (dual gated learning, DGL) for further utilizing deactivated neurons in GL. During inference, GL and DGL are abandoned, resulting in no extra computation cost. Extensive experiments are performed on SYSU-MM01 and RegDB dataset to demonstrate the superiority of GL and DGL approach. Experimental results show that our proposed methods achieve significant improvement.

Keywords: VI-ReID · Gated learning · Dual gated learning

1 Introduction

Person re-identification (Re-ID) is an important task in surveillance, aiming at solving person retrieval problem across disjoint cameras [1]. Take a given query image of specific person, the goal of Re-ID is to track the same person in different cameras, various time and distinct positions [5]. With the most recent deep learning technology, existing methods [8,9,20] show great performance in visible image Re-ID. However, the dependency on brightness limits its application in real world scenario.

As a complement, infrared camera works well under low lightness condition, yielding research interest on visible-infrared ReID (VI-ReID). VI-ReID aims to bridge the gap between visible and infrared ReID by matching images of person captured by visible and infrared cameras [3,27]. Due to the large visual difference in modality and cameras setting, Vi-ReID suffers from large variations in both intra-modality and cross-modality. Recently, [16] tempts to study cross-modality matching for Visible-near infrared face recognition, but worse performance is shown in VI-ReID due to the huge difference among persons.

© Springer Nature Switzerland AG 2021
Y. Peng et al. (Eds.): ICIG 2021, LNCS 12889, pp. 498–508, 2021.
https://doi.org/10.1007/978-3-030-87358-5_40

Existing VI-ReID methods can be categorized into three types. [2,4,21,22, 24] extract shared features between visible and infrared images to re-identify person via one-stream [2,21,22] or two-steam network [4,24]. Besides, some works integrate different modalities to learn discriminant representation by transferring to the same modal [12] or conducting images generated by GAN [19,21] to deal with modality discrepancy. In addition, [10,14] introduce re-ranking technique to modify initial ranking list to achieve better searching results. Nevertheless, the learning is easily affected by noisy samples and large discrepancy across two modalities, leading to less discriminated feature representation learning.

To alleviate the discrepancy between two modalities, we propose a novel training module to assistant training procedure. Existing methods like dropout [18] or ReLU encourages neuron deactivation in a random or simple manner, which might suffer from underfitting caused by unduly deactivated neurons. Base on this observation, we propose two auxiliary training schemes, named gated learning and dual gated learning. Our main idea is to allow model to deactivate neurons automatically in the final feature representation during training procedure. Gated learning introduces gated module to deactivate part of neurons, resulting in better and robust features learning. Dual gated module develops a two-stream module to further utilize the deactivated neurons in gated module to learn extra information.

Our main contributions are as follows:

- We propose gated module and gated learning to assist model training via dynamic neuron deactivation.
- We propose dual gated module and dual gated learning to further utilize deactivated neurons for feature representation learning.
- We evaluate our proposed methods on two VI-ReID dataset, SYSU-MM01 and RegDB, and achieve competitive results to existing methods.

2   Related Work

Single modality person re-identification targets at matching the same person from different visible cameras [11]. With the advanced deep learning technology, existing methods reach the human-level performance [1,8,9,11,20]. These methods either extract global feature from whole person image without extra cue, aggregate partial-level to represent human local information, or apply auxiliary features, like attributes. Nevertheless, most existing methods are developed to handle single modality scenario, which show low performance on cross modality task due to its large discrepancy across modality.

Visible-infrared person Re-ID is a open world task which aims to match person images from visible cameras and infrared images. Existing methods can be categorized into three main types: shared feature extraction, image transformation and re-ranking.

Shared feature extraction is developed to extract shared features between visible and infrared images. [22] proposed a one-stream network with zero-padding strategy to extract shared features between visible images and infrared images for

Re-ID. In addition, [26] proposed a two-stream network with non-local attention mechanism and general mean pooling. Recently, [25] proposed dynamic dual-attentive aggregation learning method to enhance intra-modality and inter-modality representations learning. [13] focused on attention mechanism and proposed a joint loss function for eliminating cross modality discrepancy.

Image transformation address cross modality discrepancy by converting images in different modality to the same. [2] proposed a cmGAN to reduce cross-modality distance between visible and infrared images. [21] reduced modality and appearance discrepancies separately instead of simultaneously. Besides, [19] proposed AlignGAN to exploit pixel alignment and feature alignment. Instead of developing a GAN model with heavy weights, [12] introduces a self-supervised lightweight network to transform visible and infrared image to X-modality.

Re-ranking is a wildly studied field to improve person Re-ID performance by modifying initial rank list in an automatic manner. [10] proposes to make use of successive similarity graph reasoning and mutual nearest-neighbor reasoning to mine cross modality samples. [14] mines cross-modality samples by utilizing modality-specific feature of cross modality sample with the closest distance.

3   Proposed Method

3.1   Base Model

We perform our proposed methods on a two-stream network [26], as shown in Fig. 1. The network is separated into two streams, one for visible image, another one for infrared image. The first two convolution blocks are parameter specific for both two streams, which captures modality-specific low-level features. Then, these low-level feature are feed into successive convolution blocks with shared parameters to capture shared features for both visible and infrared image. Finally, a parameter-shared batch normalization layer is added as in [15]. Note that it the feature extracted from batch normalization that is adopted for similarity computation at test time.

The combination of metric, classification and auxiliary loss is adopted to optimize model parameters during training, denoted as

$$L = L_m + L_c + \alpha L_{aux}, \qquad (1)$$

where L_m, L_c, L_{aux} are metric loss, classification loss and auxiliary loss, respectively. α is a factor to weight L_{aux} which is the loss in auxiliary training scheme. When α equals 0, training scheme becomes baseline. As shown in Fig. 1, the feature before batch normalization is feed into metric loss and the feature after batch normalization is feed into classification loss. Classification loss encourages an identity-invariant feature representation. Metric loss improves the relationships among different person images across the two modalities. Auxiliary loss utilizes gated mechanism to improve model performance. In the paper, cross entropy loss and triplet loss are adopted as classification and metric loss.

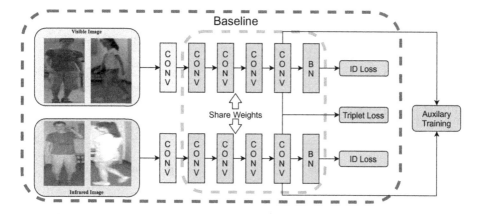

Fig. 1. Model training scheme

3.2 Gated Learning

In order to improve model performance, we propose a novel feature selection learning mechanism for VI-ReID, namely Gated Learning (GL), as shown in Fig. 3. GL adopts feature selected by Gated Module (GM) for subsequent model optimization.Different from random neuron dropping in Dropout [18], GM mines inner relation among features by deactivating part of neurons.

As shown in Fig. 2, GM employs a structure with two FC layers to generate binary mask for neuron deactivation. The input of GM is extracted from the final convolution block, denoted as $x \in R^c$. x is feed into a fully connected (FC) layer with ReLU activation, then another FC layer and binary function are used to generate binary mask to drop neurons in x, denoted as

$$s = x \cdot g(W_2, f(W_1, x)), \qquad (2)$$

where $W_1 \in R^{c \times \frac{c}{r}}$ and $W_2 \in R^{\frac{c}{r} \times c}$ denote the weights of the first and second FC layer, $f(.)$ refers to ReLU. $g(.)$ is a binary function to generate binary mask to drop neurons, denoted as

$$g(x) = \begin{cases} 1, & \text{if } x > 0; \\ 0, & \text{if } x <= 0. \end{cases} \qquad (3)$$

During training, feature from both two modalities are feed into GM for further training with triplet loss, namely Gated Learning (GL, as shown in Fig. 3). In inference, GM is abandoned, resulting no computation increasement.

3.3 Dual Gated Learning

Dual gated learning (DGL) is a further developed version of GL. During the training process of GL, part of neurons is dropped adaptively, which might

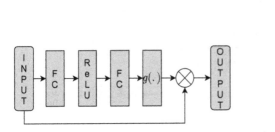

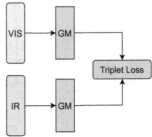

Fig. 2. Gated module   **Fig. 3.** Gated learning

affects training results caused by undue neuron deactivation. DGL utilizes the deactivated neurons in GL for further training.

As shown in Fig. 4, DGM is a two-stream structure module. One stream is the original GM, namely cross-stream, whose output is feed into triplet loss with both infrared and visible images. Another stream produces a binary mask as in cross-stream, and then multiplies the negation of the binary mask in cross-stream to generate orthogonal mask, named intra-stream.

As shown in Fig. 5, features from two modalities are feed into different losses. Features from cross-stream are jointly feed into a triplet loss as the same as GL. However, features from intra-stream are not feed into one triplet loss. Once these two streams are optimized in the same way, they are prone to suffer from performance reduction. Therefore, features from intra-stream are separately feed into two different triplet losses to learn a easier target, i.e. preson ReID in single modality.

Thus, L_{aux} in DGL is defined as follow

$$L_{aux} = L_{cross} + \beta(L_{inf} + L_{vis}), \tag{4}$$

where L_{cross} is the loss for cross-stream, L_{inf} and L_{vis} are the loss in intra-stream standing for infrared and visible intra-modality loss. β is the weight of L_{inf} and L_{vis}. When $\beta = 0$, DGL degrades to GL.

4   Experiment Results

4.1   Experiment Settings

The proposed method is evaluated on two VIS-IR ReID dataset, SYSU-MM01 and RegDB. Mean average precision (mAP), standard cumulative matching characteristic (CMC) is adopted as evaluation metrics.

SYSU-MM01 [22] is a large-scale RGB-infrared cross modality dataset for person re-identification. It contains 491 persons with 287628 RGB images and 12792 infrared images, which are captured by 2 infrared cameras and 4 RGB cameras. Half of the cameras are set for indoor scenes while the others are set for outdoor scenes. There are two modes for testing, all-search and indoor-search. In indoor-search mode, the gallery set contains the images captured by 2 RGB

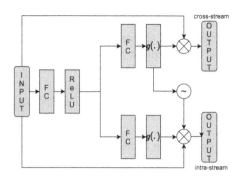
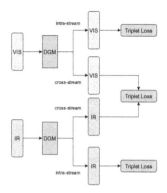

Fig. 4. Dual gated module   **Fig. 5.** Dual gated learning

cameras in indoor scenes. All-search task is a more difficult task because the gallery set contains the images captured by 4 RGB cameras in both indoor and outdoor scenes. Details on experimental settings can be found in [22].

RegDB [17] is a person re-identification dataset with both visible and infrared images for the same person. It contains 412 persons, and there are 10 RGB images and 10 thermal images respectively for each person. Dataset is randomly split into training set and testing set. During testing, images from one modality are considered as query while images from another modality are treated as gallery. Evaluation metrics are computed on both visual-thermal and thermal-visual pattern. This procedure is repeated for 10 trials to attain stable results as in [23].

Our proposed method is implemented in PyTorch. For comparison convenience, ResNet50 [7] is adopted as our backbone for VI-ReID. All parameters are initialized with the pre-trained ImageNet model, following [26]. Input images are resized to 288 × 144. Random cropping and horizontal flipping are adopted in training procedure. SGD optimizer with momentum parameter set to 0.9, is adopted for optimization. The learning rate is set to 0.1 and decays by 0.1 at 30th epoch and at 50th epoch, with a total 80 epochs and warm-up strategy [15] is adopted. During training procedure, every batch contains 8 random identities with 4 visible and 4 infrared images, i.e. 64 images per batch.

4.2 Comparison with Existing Methods

To evaluate the efficiency of our proposed methods, we compare the performance of our proposed methods with existing VI-ReID methods on two public datasets, SYSU-MM01 and RegDB.

As shown in Table 1, B+DGL achieves the best performance in rank-1 and mAP in both all-search and indoor-search mode. Compared to base model, the mAP of B+GL increases 2.05% in all-search mode and 3.20% in indoor-search mode, while the mAP of B+DGL increases 5.32% in all-search mode and 6.36% in indoor-search mode, demonstrating the effectiveness of GL and DGL.

As shown in Table 2, base model gains improvement from both GL and DGL. And simliar to other methods, our proposed methods get worse performance in infrared-to-visible task than visible-to-infrared task. However, different from SYSU-MM01 dataset, DGL gains slightly less improvement than GL in RegDB dataset. Actually, DGL provides an extra stream for single modality learning. Due to the tiny single modality variation of the same person in RegDB , this extra stream cannot provide effective assistance for model training and causes slight performance dropping.

Table 1. Comparison results (%) with existing methods on SYSU-MM01 datasets on two different settings. B denotes base model.

Mode	All Search				Indoor Search			
Method	r = 1	r = 10	r = 20	mAP	r = 1	r = 10	r = 20	mAP
Zero-Pad [22]	14.80	54.12	71.33	15.95	20.58	68.38	85.79	26.92
HCML [23]	14.32	53.16	69.17	16.16	24.52	73.25	86.73	30.08
cmGAN [2]	26.97	67.51	80.56	31.49	31.63	77.23	89.18	42.19
eBDTR [24]	27.82	67.34	81.34	28.42	32.46	77.42	89.62	42.46
D^2RL [21]	28.9	70.6	82.4	29.2	–	–	–	–
MSR [4]	37.35	83.40	93.34	38.11	39.64	89.29	**97.66**	50.88
AlignGAN [19]	42.4	85.0	93.7	40.7	45.9	87.6	94.4	54.3
AGW [26]	47.50	84.39	92.14	47.65	54.17	91.14	95.98	62.97
Xmodal [12]	49.92	**89.79**	**95.96**	50.73	–	–	–	–
B	47.27	83.89	91.94	46.26	49.53	88.38	95.38	57.96
B+GL	49.43	85.50	92.91	48.33	52.79	90.63	96.16	61.16
B+DGL	**53.06**	87.48	94.23	**51.58**	**56.75**	**91.30**	96.80	**64.32**

4.3   Ablation Study

Neuron Deactivation. As a neuron deactivation technique, our proposed methods are similar to dropout. However, our methods drop neurons adaptively instead of randomly. As shown in Table 3, both GL and DGL outperformance base method and dropout which points out the superiority of our proposed methods. Compared with ReLU, GL gains less improvement than ReLU, but DGL gets the best performance.

Squeeze Ratio. The squeeze ratio r introduced in GM and DGM is a hyper parameter which allows us to verify the compactness of feature representation. To investigate the effectiveness of r, we conduct experiments with different r in DGL. The comparison in Table 4 shows the model performance with various squeeze ratio on SYSU-MM01 dataset in all-search mode. With the help of DGL under different r settings, models gain better performance than original model. The setting of $r = 64$ achieves the best performance, indicating that a compact feature representation might results in better performance.

Table 2. Comparison results (%) with existing methods on RegDB datasets on two different settings.

Mode	Visible to Infrared				Infrared to Visible			
Method	r = 1	r = 10	r = 20	mAP	r = 1	r = 10	r = 20	mAP
Zero-Pad [22]	17.75	34.21	44.35	18.90	16.63	34.68	44.25	17.82
HCML [23]	24.44	47.53	56.78	20.08	21.70	45.02	55.58	22.24
eBDTR [24]	34.62	58.96	68.72	33.46	34.21	58.74	68.64	32.49
HSME [6]	50.85	73.36	81.66	47.00	50.15	72.40	81.07	46.16
D^2RL [21]	43.4	66.1	76.3	44.1	–	–	–	–
MSR [4]	48.43	70.32	79.95	48.67	–	–	–	–
AlignGAN [19]	57.9	–	–	53.6	56.3	–	–	53.4
Xmodal [12]	62.21	83.13	91.72	60.18	–	–	–	–
DDAG [25]	69.34	86.19	91.49	63.46	68.06	85.15	90.31	61.8
AGW [26]	70.05	86.21	91.55	66.37	70.49	**87.12**	**91.84**	**65.90**
B	68.75	85.29	90.92	63.46	67.38	84.35	89.79	61.78
B+GL	**72.58**	**87.79**	**92.59**	**66.68**	**70.90**	86.20	91.19	65.07
B+DGL	72.39	87.59	92.28	66.32	69.99	86.23	90.92	63.90

Table 3. Comparison results (%) with different deactivation methods

Method	r = 1	r = 10	r = 20	mAP
Base	47.27	83.89	91.94	46.26
Dropout	48.61	84.96	92.64	47.26
ReLU	50.31	87.20	93.90	49.53
GL	49.43	85.50	92.91	48.33
DGL	53.06	87.48	94.23	51.58

Table 4. Comparison results (%) with different squeeze ratio

Ratio r	r = 1	r = 10	r = 20	mAP
2	52.52	86.77	93.80	50.68
4	50.56	86.39	93.44	49.05
8	51.60	86.39	94.12	50.81
16	52.55	87.17	94.10	51.06
32	52.77	88.18	94.45	51.62
64	53.39	88.39	94.48	52.44
128	52.76	87.91	94.23	51.61
Original	47.27	83.89	91.94	46.26

Auxiliary Loss Ratio. In order to test the impact of auxiliary α loss ratio in DGL, we set experiments with different α in SYSU-MM01 dataset on all-search mode. As shown in Fig. 6, rank-1 and mAP increase monotonically when $\alpha < 1$, and reach the peak at $\alpha = 1.0$. When $\alpha > 1$, model performance drops. Therefore, we suggest adopting $\alpha = 1$ as the primary option for DGL.

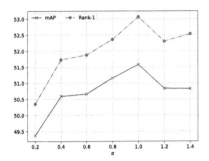

Fig. 6. Comparison results (%) with differnt auxiliary loss ratio

5   Conclusion

In the paper, we focus on visible-infrared person re-identification task. Two auxiliary training schemes are presented, which improve model performance without any extra computation cost. First, we propose gated learning mechanism to learn feature representation through adaptive neurons dropping. Base on gated learning, we design dual gated learning to utilize deactivated neurons in GL for further feature representation learning. We demonstrates the superiority of proposed methods with the experiment results on two public datasets, SYSU-MM01 and RegDB.

References

1. Chen, Y.C., Zhu, X., Zheng, W.S., Lai, J.H.: Person re-identification by camera correlation aware feature augmentation. IEEE Trans. Pattern Anal. Mach. Intell. **40**(2), 392–408 (2017)
2. Dai, P., Ji, R., Wang, H., Wu, Q., Huang, Y.: Cross-modality person re-identification with generative adversarial training. In: IJCAI. vol. 1, p. 2 (2018)
3. Dollár, P., Wojek, C., Schiele, B., Perona, P.: Pedestrian detection: a benchmark. In: 2009 IEEE Conference on Computer Vision and Pattern Recognition, pp. 304–311. IEEE (2009)
4. Feng, Z., Lai, J., Xie, X.: Learning modality-specific representations for visible-infrared person re-identification. IEEE Trans. Image Process. **29**, 579–590 (2019)
5. Gheissari, N., Sebastian, T.B., Hartley, R.: Person reidentification using spatiotemporal appearance. In: 2006 IEEE Computer Society Conference on Computer Vision and Pattern Recognition (CVPR'06), vol. 2, pp. 1528–1535. IEEE (2006)
6. Hao, Y., Wang, N., Li, J., Gao, X.: Hsme: hypersphere manifold embedding for visible thermal person re-identification. Proc. AAAI Conf. Artif. Intell. **33**, 8385–8392 (2019)
7. He, K., Zhang, X., Ren, S., Sun, J.: Deep residual learning for image recognition. In: Proceedings of the IEEE Conference on Computer Vision and Pattern Recognition, pp. 770–778 (2016)
8. Hou, R., Ma, B., Chang, H., Gu, X., Shan, S., Chen, X.: Interaction-and-aggregation network for person re-identification. In: Proceedings of the IEEE/CVF Conference on Computer Vision and Pattern Recognition, pp. 9317–9326 (2019)

9. Hou, R., Ma, B., Chang, H., Gu, X., Shan, S., Chen, X.: Vrstc: occlusion-free video person re-identification. In: Proceedings of the IEEE/CVF Conference on Computer Vision and Pattern Recognition, pp. 7183–7192 (2019)

10. Jia, M., Zhai, Y., Lu, S., Ma, S., Zhang, J.: A similarity inference metric for rgb-infrared cross-modality person re-identification. arXiv preprint arXiv:2007.01504 (2020)

11. Leng, Q., Ye, M., Tian, Q.: A survey of open-world person re-identification. IEEE Trans. Circ. Syst. Video Technol. **30**(4), 1092–1108 (2019)

12. Li, D., Wei, X., Hong, X., Gong, Y.: Infrared-visible cross-modal person re-identification with an x modality. Proc. AAAI Conf. Artif. Intell. **34**, 4610–4617 (2020)

13. Li, Y., Xu, H.: Deep attention network for rgb-infrared cross-modality person re-identification. In: Journal of Physics: Conference Series, vol. 1642, p. 012015. IOP Publishing (2020)

14. Lu, Y., et al.: Cross-modality person re-identification with shared-specific feature transfer. In: Proceedings of the IEEE/CVF Conference on Computer Vision and Pattern Recognition, pp. 13379–13389 (2020)

15. Luo, H., et al.: A strong baseline and batch normalization neck for deep person re-identification. IEEE Trans. Multimedia **22**(10), 2597–2609 (2019)

16. Mudunuri, S.P., Venkataramanan, S., Biswas, S.: Dictionary alignment with re-ranking for low-resolution nir-vis face recognition. IEEE Trans. Inform. Forensics Secur. **14**(4), 886–896 (2018)

17. Nguyen, D.T., Hong, H.G., Kim, K.W., Park, K.R.: Person recognition system based on a combination of body images from visible light and thermal cameras. Sensors **17**(3), 605 (2017)

18. Srivastava, N., Hinton, G., Krizhevsky, A., Sutskever, I., Salakhutdinov, R.: Dropout: a simple way to prevent neural networks from overfitting. J. Mach. Learn. Res. **15**(1), 1929–1958 (2014)

19. Wang, G., Zhang, T., Cheng, J., Liu, S., Yang, Y., Hou, Z.: Rgb-infrared cross-modality person re-identification via joint pixel and feature alignment. In: Proceedings of the IEEE/CVF International Conference on Computer Vision, pp. 3623–3632 (2019)

20. Wang, J., Zhu, X., Gong, S., Li, W.: Transferable joint attribute-identity deep learning for unsupervised person re-identification. In: Proceedings of the IEEE Conference on Computer Vision and Pattern Recognition, pp. 2275–2284 (2018)

21. Wang, Z., Wang, Z., Zheng, Y., Chuang, Y.Y., Satoh, S.: Learning to reduce dual-level discrepancy for infrared-visible person re-identification. In: Proceedings of the IEEE/CVF Conference on Computer Vision and Pattern Recognition, pp. 618–626 (2019)

22. Wu, A., Zheng, W.S., Yu, H.X., Gong, S., Lai, J.: Rgb-infrared cross-modality person re-identification. In: Proceedings of the IEEE International Conference on Computer Vision, pp. 5380–5389 (2017)

23. Ye, M., Lan, X., Li, J., Yuen, P.: Hierarchical discriminative learning for visible thermal person re-identification. In: Proceedings of the AAAI Conference on Artificial Intelligence, vol. 32 (2018)

24. Ye, M., Lan, X., Wang, Z., Yuen, P.C.: Bi-directional center-constrained top-ranking for visible thermal person re-identification. IEEE Trans. Inform. Forensics Secur. **15**, 407–419 (2019)

25. Ye, M., Shen, J., Crandall, D.J., Shao, L., Luo, J.: Dynamic dual-attentive aggregation learning for visible-infrared person re-identification. In: European Conference on Computer Vision (ECCV) (2020)

26. Ye, M., Shen, J., Lin, G., Xiang, T., Shao, L., Hoi, S.C.: Deep learning for person re-identification: a survey and outlook. IEEE Transactions on Pattern Analysis and Machine Intelligence (2021)
27. Zhong, Z., Zheng, L., Cao, D., Li, S.: Re-ranking person re-identification with k-reciprocal encoding. In: Proceedings of the IEEE Conference on Computer Vision and Pattern Recognition, pp. 1318–1327 (2017)

Biological and Medical Image Processing

Dual Attention Guided R2 U-Net Architecture for Right Ventricle Segmentation in MRI Images

Lei Jiang[1,2], Hengfei Cui[1,2(✉)], Chang Yuwen[1,2], and Yanning Zhang[1]

[1] National Engineering Laboratory for Integrated Aero-Space-Ground -Ocean Big Data Application Technology, School of Computer Science, Northwestern Polytechnical University, Xi'an 710072, China
hfcui@nwpu.edu.cn

[2] Centre for Multidisciplinary Convergence Computing (CMCC), School of Computer Science, Northwestern Polytechnical University, Xi'an 710072, China

Abstract. Right ventricle segmentation plays an important role in the computer-aided diagnosis of heart diseases. However, due to the small area of right ventricle and limited dataset, the performances of the existing deep learning segmentation methods are not good enough. For some small areas of right ventricle that are difficult to segment, we apply a novel dual attention module on the decoding path of Dilated R2 U-net to extract better feature representations in this work. The dual attention module in this work is divided into position attention module and channel attention module. The positional attention module suppresses the irrelevant feature representations in the feature map and enhances the useful feature representations to improve the sensitivity and prediction accuracy of the model. The channel attention module enhances the interdependence of the feature representation of channels by gathering the information of the associated channels in the feature map. We use dilated convolutions to expand the receptive field of the model. By adding dual attention modules, our model shows higher precision than Dilated U-net on the Right Ventricle Segmentation Challenge (RVSC) test dataset.

Keywords: Medical imaging · Right ventricle segmentation · Dual attention · U-Net · Computer-aided diagnosis

1 Introduction

Cardiovascular diseases have become one of the most serious diseases threatening human health. Cardiovascular diseases include coronary heart disease (heart attack), cerebrovascular disease (stroke), hypertension (increased blood pressure), peripheral vascular disease , rheumatic heart disease, congenital heart disease, and heart Failure. An important indicator for measuring the standard of heart health is ejection fraction (EF), and one important step of measuring ejection fraction is Ventricle image segmentation, that is, detecting the endocardium and epicardium in the end-diastolic (ED) and end-systolic (ES). The

© Springer Nature Switzerland AG 2021
Y. Peng et al. (Eds.): ICIG 2021, LNCS 12889, pp. 511–522, 2021.
https://doi.org/10.1007/978-3-030-87358-5_41

manual segmentation of cardiac CT or MRI images by doctors is time-consuming and labor-intensive, and is heavily dependent on the doctor's personal judgment and clinical experience, and cannot be repeated. Therefore, it is an urgent task to develop a set of automated ventricular segmentation technology for MRI data.

Fully Convolutional Neural Network (FCN) [1] is the first end-to-end model applied to semantic segmentation: set an image of any size as input, and output the corresponding segmentation map of the same size. Because the encoder reduces the resolution of the input image by 32 times, it is difficult for the decoder to produce accurate segmentation results. U-net [2] modified and expanded the architecture of FCN, added decoders encoders which are paired, and used skip connections between encoders and decoders of the same size to obtain more semantic information. DeepLab [3] provided many useful techniques for the existing network structure to improve precision of the output results, mainly including parallel atrous convolutions with different dilate rates, atrous spatial pyramidal pooling [4] and using CRF to improve the final output. Zhao [5] proposed the Pyramid Pooling Module, which divides the feature map into sub-regions of different sizes to perform average pooling and then concatenate the results. In recent years, some research works [6,7] tried to replace or improve the basic unit of U-net in encoding path and decoding path to obtain more accurate segmentation results; other research works [8] focus on improving the skip connection structure of the U-net to obtain richer semantic information.

The Attention method [9] was first proposed to deal with the challenge of translating long sentences in machine translation, but in recent years this method has been widely used in the field of computer vision. Inspired by the Non-local module, DANet [10] uses a dual attention module which includes the position attention module and the channel attention module to obtain rich contextual information. The position attention module selectively strengthens the relationship between similar features at different locations on the feature map, and the channel attention module selectively strengthens the connection between interdependent channel maps. While DANet is able to obtain global semantic information, each point of the feature map will generate one attention map with (H×W) weights for the position attention module, which greatly increases the usage of GPU memory. In response to the shortcomings of DANet, CCNet [11] has been improved, which captures global attention information through the recursive Criss-Cross attention map. Compared to DANet, the attention map corresponding to each point of the feature map only brings (H+W−1) weights. Compared with DANet, CCNet is more friendly to GPU memory and more computationally efficient, but it ignores the channel attention. Interlaced Sparse Self-Attention [12] avoids the large matrix operation of the positional attention module of DANet to reduce the usage of GPU memory, but it lowers the accuracy of image segmentation. SENet [13] and Enc-Net [14] introduce channel attention by weighting the channel map. Inspired by SENet, some recent works in the field of medical image segmentation try to add SE block to U-net to obtain better results.

Tran [15] first applied FCN for ventricular segmentation in short-axis MRI images. ACNN [16] incorporated prior knowledge of anatomical shapes into CNN by using convolutional auto encoder and T-L network to learn non-linear compact representation of the underlying anatomy. Panchaud [17] uses constrained variational autoencoder (cVAE) to shift the anatomically invalid shape to the closest valid shape. The existing U-net-based medical image segmentation methods have some shortcomings. Attention U-net [18] merges attention gate into the decoding path of U-net, but the receptive field of the model is small, and it lacks the strong feature representation like R2 U-net, while the global information of the image cannot be obtained by the latter. The existing methods which apply attention mechanism to the U-net model mostly only focus on position attention [18] or channel attention, for the large matrix calculation of the dual attention module in DANet [10] takes up a lot of GPU memory, which is difficult to apply to the U-net. At the same time, the right ventricle segmentation data set is small, which makes weak generalization ability of existing models.

Based on the shortcomings of the above methods, we use R2 U-net [6] (Recurrent Residual Convolutional Neural Network based on U-net models) as backbone network, and add dilated convolution [19] to its bottom layer to increase the receptive field of the model. Meanwhile, one newly designed dual attention module is added to the decoder of the R2 U-net, which combines the position attention module of the Attention U-net [18] and the channel attention module of the DANet [10]. It avoids the large matrix operation of the position attention module in DANet, therefore occupies less GPU memory and guarantees to obtain the global information of the feature map.

2   Methodologies

2.1   Baseline Model R2 U-Net

R2 U-net [6] is a variant of the U-net, replacing the original double layer 3×3 convolution unit with a recursive residual convolutional unit in encoding and decoding path. The overall network structure (Fig. 1) is composed of the encoding path on the left, skip connection, and the decoding path on the right. The encoder in the encoding path is composed of one recursive residual unit, activation function (ReLu) and one pooling layer; the decoder in the decoding path is composed of the transposed convolution, one recursive residual unit and activation function (ReLu). After each down-sampling, the size of the image becomes $1/4$, and the length of the channel becomes twice the original. The skip connection enables the fine positional information of the bottom layer and the abstract information of the high layer in the encoding path to be connected with the corresponding features in the decoding path, which is helpful for the circulation and synchronization of information at each layer. The depth the R2 U-net model is reduced from 4 to 3, because our right ventricle image is only half the size of the image in the original paper. Compared with the left ventricle, the image of the right ventricle is often more difficult to segment: the shape of the right ventricle of different patients is more complex and variable, and the thin walls sometimes fuse with surrounding tissues. Therefore, we use a recursive residual convolution structure to extract better feature representations to obtain better segmentation results. The recursive residual convolution structure is shown in Fig. 2. The input feature map passes through two recursive convolution layers, and the activation function is ReLu; we use zero padding to maintain the feature size.

2.2   Dilated Convolution

Because the network model we use is relatively shallow, the receptive field cannot cover all the image even in the deepest convolutional layer, which may cause the final segmentation result to misclassify some noise on the image as part of the ventricle. For this reason, we add 5 layers of dilated convolutions [19] to the bottom layer of the R2 U-net to increase the receptive field exponentially without deepening the network or adding additional convolutional layers which may increase network parameters inefficiently. This is conducive to extracting better global features and providing richer semantic information for subsequent attention modules. Compared with ordinary convolution whose points are closely connected, the dilated convolution adds a parameter, that is, the dilate rate, which

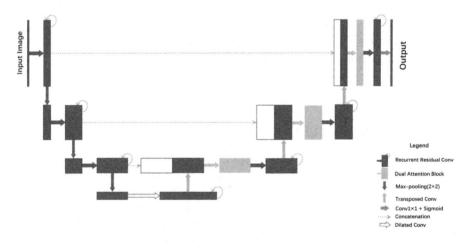

Fig. 1. Dilated R2 U-net with dual attention block. The whole network is based on U-net architecture with recurrent residual convolutional units on the encoding and decoding path. On the bottom of the network, we add 5 layers of dilated convolution to expand the receptive field. On the decoding path we add the dual attention module after the concatenation operation and before the recurrent residual convolutional units.

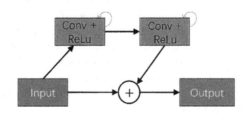

Fig. 2. Recurrent Residual convolutional unit.

means the distance between the points of the convolution kernel. By increasing the dilated rate exponentially, the dilated convolution effectively expands the receptive field of the model.

The calculation formula for the receptive field is as follows:

$$RF_{l+1} = RF_l + (kernel\_size_{l+1} - 1) \times feature\_stride_l * dilate_{l+1} \quad (1)$$

l is the serial number of the dilated convolution layers. RF_l is the receptive field of the layer l; dilate rate is initially 1, and then increases by 2^{l-1} times.

2.3   Dual Attention Module

In order to capture rich semantic information, U-net takes a standard CNN architecture to gradually down-sample the feature map, and combines fine detail of positional information with abstract feature information through skip connections. However, for small areas with irregular shapes, it tends to maintain relatively higher recall rate and lower precision rate. In order to reduce false positive predictions, we use the position attention module and the channel attention module to obtain spatial and channel attention information respectively. As shown in Fig. 2, we add the dual attention module after the concatenation operation and before the recurrent residual convolutional unit of each layer in the decoding path, to obtain the low-level position information of the original encoder aggregated at each layer and the high-level abstract feature information delivered by the lower decoder. The dual attention module is shown in Fig. 3.

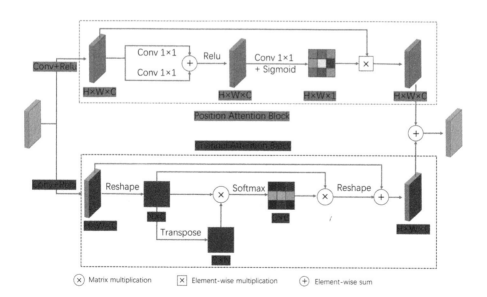

Fig. 3. Dual attention module.

The position attention module we use borrows the idea of attention gate [18], which suppresses irrelevant features by weighting the feature map in the H and W dimension. Through the sigmoid operation and the 1×1 bottleneck layer, the attention coefficients of the same size as the input performs element-wise multiplication with the input features, which avoids large-scale matrix operations. The channel attention block refers to the cam [10] module. It uses a mechanism similar to self-attention to capture the channel dependency between any two channel mappings. Each channel of feature map is related, and the cam module strengthens the related channels to enhance specific semantic features. By replacing the more computationally intensive position attention module in the original DANet with the less computationally intensive attention gate, the dual attention module we use can be easily attached to any layer of the U-net network without causing too much burden on GPU, while ensuring the stability of model training.

2.4   Implementation Details and Loss Function

We implement our model based on Keras, the model is trained on a single Nvidia RTX2080Ti GPU with adam optimizer, learning rate is set to 0.0001, and the training time is 600 epochs for the best performance. The batch size is set to 8 due to graphical memory limitations. We did not use batch normalization or dropout regularization, for the experiment found that it cannot improve the precision. The loss function used for training is the unweighted pixel-wise cross entropy:

$$L = -\sum_{c=1}^{M} y_c \log(p_c) \tag{2}$$

M is the number of classes, for the right ventricular segmentation data set, M is 2; y_c is the one-hot matrix of the original label, 0 represents the background, 1 represents the ground truth, and p_c is the probability of the predicted sample belonging to the category. We have also tried the weights cross entropy loss and dice loss but only to find out the unweighted pixel-wise cross entropy performs better.

3   Results

3.1   Dataset and Data Preprocessing

The dataset we use is RVSC (2012 Right Ventricle Challenge). The training set is MRI images of the right ventricle of 16 patients. It contains 243 pre-segmented pictures with size of 216×256 pixels. In the training process, we take 1/5 of the training data as the validation set. The test set additionally contains images of 32 patients.

Each image is normalized first. In order to prevent the model from overfitting during the training process due to the small training data, we used random transformation on the training data, that is, random rotation; shearing, flipping, scaling and other data enhancement operations. In addition, we performed elastic deformation [20] and shuffle operation on the training data.

3.2 Evaluation Metrics

The Dice coefficient is a function used to measure the similarity of two sets, the value range is $[0, 1]$:

$$dice(X, Y) = \frac{2|X \cap Y|}{|X| + |Y|} \tag{3}$$

In semantic segmentation tasks, X represents original image and Y presents the predicted image. The higher the dice coefficient, the more accurate the result of segmentation.

Hausdorff distance is a measure to describe the similarity between two sets of points, and it is a function of the distance between two sets of points. Suppose there are two sets of $A = \{a_1, a_2, ..., a_p\}$ and $B = \{b_1, b_2, ..., b_q\}$, the definition of Hausdorff distance between set A and set B is:

$$H(A, B) = max(h(A, B), h(B, A)) \tag{4}$$

where $h(A, B)$ means the Hausdorff distance from set A to set B:

$$h(A, B) = \max_{a \in A}\{\min_{b \in B}\{d(a, b)\}\} \tag{5}$$

The function $d(a, b)$ is the Euclidian distance between point a and b in set A and set B respectively. $h(B, A)$ is similar to $h(A, B)$. Smaller Hausdorff distance means higher precision of the segmentation results.

3.3 Results on RVSC Dataset

Table 1 presents the comparison of segmentation results on RVSC test set. Compared with FCN, our method significantly reduces the Hausdorff distance, and the dice coefficient is higher than other state-of-the-art methods. Compared with Dilated U-net, the average dice coefficient of our model increases by about 3% in segmenting endocardium, and 2% in segmenting epicardium.

Table 1. Segmentation results on RVSC test set.

Method	Dice Index (endo)	Dice Index (epi)	Hausdorff Dist (mm) (endo)	Hausdorff Dist (mm) (epi)
FCN	0.84 (0.21)	0.86 (0.20)	8.86 (11.27)	9.33 (10.79)
U-Net	0.79 (0.28)	0.77 (0.30)	–	–
Dilated DenseNet	0.83 (0.22)	0.85 (0.20)	–	–
Dilated U-Net	0.84 (0.21)	0.88 (0.18)	–	–
Our method	**0.874 (0.132)**	**0.902 (0.110)**	**6.081 (13.287)**	**5.684 (5.855)**

Figure 4 shows the learning curve of several models in endocardial segmentation. Compared with U-net and Dilated U-net, our method obtains the fastest learning speed. The Loss of the U-net model in the training set and the validation set is significantly higher than the other two models. The original U-net model is difficult to extract sufficient feature representations for the RVSC data set, and the receptive field is small, so the segmentation precision is low; the dice coefficient of U-net model in the training set is higher, but significantly lower than that of other models in the validation set, indicating that due to the small data in the training set, U-net exhibits over-fitting characteristics during the training process. Compared with U-net, Dilated U-net has increased the receptive field of the model, and has significantly improved training accuracy and model generalization ability. Due to the inherent instability of the attention model, the learning curve of the attention model occasionally fluctuates greatly during the training process, but our model can extract better feature representations and faster learning speed than Dilated U-net. From Table 1 we can see that the generalization ability of our model is better than that of Dilated U-net.

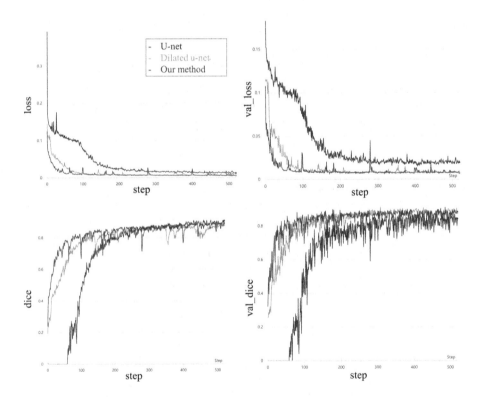

Fig. 4. Learning curves of U-net, Dilated U-net and our model.

3.4   Ablation Study

As shown in Table 2, in order to verify the performance of the attention model, we implemented several different experiments. Dilated U-net is trained with the adam optimizer, the learning rate is set to the default value of 0.001, and the batch size is set to 22, because we found that this parameter setting can get the best results. Channel means replacing the dual attention module in Fig. 3 with the channel attention module, and position means replacing it with the position attention module. The basic model we use, Dilated R2 U-net, has been improved compared to Dilated U-net in segmentation results. For example, the dice coefficient of endocardial segmentation is 0.856, which is 1% higher than that of Dilated U-net. The dice coefficients of endocardial segmentation using the channel attention module or position attention module alone are 0.868 and 0.865 respectively, which are about 1% higher than the Dilated R2 U-net. The finally results of dice coefficient using dual attention model in endocardial segmentation is 0.874. Compared with the single-channel attention model, the dice coefficient is increased by about 1%.

Table 2. Ablation study on RVCS test set, Channel represents channel attention module, Position represents position attention module.

	Dice Index (endo)	Dice Index (epi)	Hausdorff Dist (mm) (endo)	Hausdorff Dist (mm) (epi)
Dilated U-Net	0.847 (0.185)	0.874 (0.159)	8.431 (17.153)	9.425 (18.992)
Dilated R2 U-Net	0.856 (0.150)	0.883 (0.145)	8.178 (17.785)	8.221 (18.941)
Channel	0.868 (0.167)	0.896 (0.142)	6.806 (15.790)	6.774 (13.811)
Position	0.865 (0.180)	0.898 (0.145)	8.447 (24.403)	7.542 (19.103)
Dual attention	**0.874 (0.132)**	**0.902 (0.110)**	**6.081 (13.287)**	**5.684 (5.855)**

3.5   Visualization Results

For some large areas, even U-net can show good segmentation results, but when faced with complex scenes and some small areas, our model performs greater advantages. Figure 5 shows some visual examples of segmenting the endocardium by U-net and other models. We can see that U-net performs very poorly for the small region segmentation results of complex scenes, and always predicts irrelevant regions as ground truth. This is because the original U-net model has a small receptive field, and at the same time the lack of sufficient feature representation makes it very error-prone even to segment some large areas with complex shapes. Dilated R2 U-net increases the receptive field on the basis of U-net, and enhances the feature representation, making its segmentation result significantly better than U-net. The segmentation results of the Dilated R2 U-net in the first and third rows avoid the situation where irrelevant regions are predicted as ground truth, because the dilated convolution structure increases the receptive field of the model.

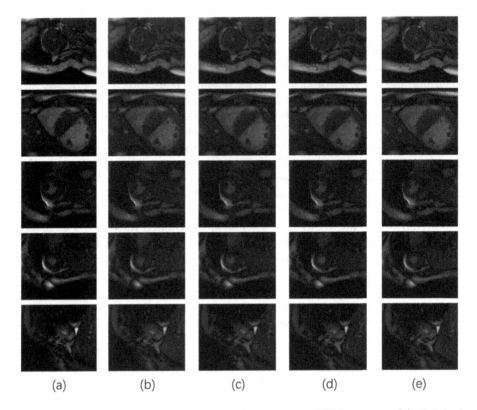

(a)   (b)   (c)   (d)   (e)

Fig. 5. Visualization results of some complex areas on RVSC test set. (a): Original image; (b): U-net; (c): Dilated R2 U-net; (d): Our method; (e): Ground truth.

Although Dilated R2 U-net has obtained good results for some difficult regions, it can be seen from the first, third, and fifth rows of Fig. 5 that it is not good enough for segmenting some small regions; in the fourth row, the model still predicts irrelevant small areas as ground truth, which shows that simply increasing the receptive field cannot completely eliminate segmentation errors, and the model lacks certain anatomical prior knowledge. Based on the rich semantic information provided by the dilated convolutions, our method applies a novel dual attention module on the decoding path of Dilated R2 U-net to extract better feature representations, which can obtain higher precision. The positional attention model suppresses the irrelevant feature representations in the feature map and enhances the useful feature representations to improve the sensitivity and prediction accuracy of the model; the channel attention module enhances the interdependence of the feature representation of channels by gathering the information of the associated channels in the feature map. By adding dual attention modules, our model shows higher precision than Dilated R2 U-net in small area segmentation, and completely avoids the situation where unrelated area predictions are included in the prediction results in the fourth row.

4   Conclusion

In this work we propose to apply a novel dual attention module to the U-Net structure for right ventricle segmentation. To solve the problem that some small areas of the right ventricle are difficult to segment, we use the R2 U-net model that can extract better feature representation than U-Net. We add the dual attention module to the decoding path of the backbone network, which is able to receive rich semantic information provided by bottom layers and skip connections. For the situation where there are few data for right ventricular segmentation, we use dilated convolutions to expand the receptive field of the model, and at the same time perform data enhancement operations for the training set to prevent the model from overfitting. The proposed method is tested on the public RVSC dataset, experimental results show that our proposed method outperforms state-of-the-art methods.

Our model still lacks enough ability to segment some complex-shaped structures and small regions. We will try other data enhancement methods, and improve the segmentation results by adding anatomical constraints or using 3D models. Further test in other open-source datasets like Automated Cardiac Diagnosis Challenge (ACDC) will be performed in the future.

Acknowledgment. The study was supported in part by the National Natural Science Foundation of China under Grants 61801393, 61801391 and 61801395, and in part by the Fundamental Research Funds for the Central Universities under Grant 3102020QD1001.

References

1. Jonathan, L., Evan, S., Trevor, D.: Fully convolutional networks for semantic segmentation. In: Proceedings of the IEEE Conference on Computer Vision and Pattern Recognition, pp. 3431–3440 (2015)
2. Ronneberger, O., Fischer, P., Brox, T.: U-Net: convolutional networks for biomedical image segmentation. In: Navab, N., Hornegger, J., Wells, W.M., Frangi, A.F. (eds.) MICCAI 2015. LNCS, vol. 9351, pp. 234–241. Springer, Cham (2015). https://doi.org/10.1007/978-3-319-24574-4_28
3. Chen, L.-C., Zhu, Y., Papandreou, G., Schroff, F., Adam, H.: Encoder-decoder with atrous separable convolution for semantic image segmentation. In: ECCV (2018)
4. He, K., Zhang, X., Ren, S., Sun, J.: Spatial pyramid pooling in deep convolutional networks for visual recognition. In: ECCV (2014)
5. Zhao, H., et al.: Pyramid scene parsing network. In: Proceedings of the IEEE Conference on Computer Vision and Pattern Recognition (2017)
6. Alom, M.Z., et al.: Recurrent residual convolutional neural network based on U-net (R2 U-net) for medical image segmentation. arXiv preprint arXiv:1802.06955 (2018)
7. Jin, Q., et al.: DUNet: a deformable network for retinal vessel segmentation. Knowl.-Based Syst. **178**, 149–162 (2019)

8. Zhou, Z., Rahman Siddiquee, M.M., Tajbakhsh, N., Liang, J.: UNet++: a nested U-Net architecture for medical image segmentation. In: Stoyanov, D., et al. (eds.) DLMIA/ML-CDS -2018. LNCS, vol. 11045, pp. 3–11. Springer, Cham (2018). https://doi.org/10.1007/978-3-030-00889-5_1

9. Bahdanau, D., Kyunghyun, C., Yoshua, B.: Neural machine translation by jointly learning to align and translate. arXiv preprint arXiv:1409.0473 (2014)

10. Fu, J., et al.: Dual attention network for scene segmentation. In: Proceedings of the IEEE Conference on Computer Vision and Pattern Recognition (2019)

11. Huang, Z., et al.: Ccnet: Criss-cross attention for semantic segmentation. In: Proceedings of the IEEE International Conference on Computer Vision (2019)

12. Huang, L., et al.: Interlaced sparse self-attention for semantic segmentation. arXiv preprint arXiv:1907.12273 (2019)

13. Hu, J., Li, S., Gang, S.: Squeeze-and-excitation networks. In: Proceedings of the IEEE Conference on Computer Vision and Pattern Recognition (2018)

14. Zhang, H., et al.: Context encoding for semantic segmentation. In: Proceedings of the IEEE Conference on Computer Vision and Pattern Recognition (2018)

15. Tran, P.V.: A fully convolutional neural network for cardiac segmentation in short-axis MRI. arXiv preprint arXiv:1604.00494 (2016)

16. Oktay, O., et al.: Anatomically constrained neural networks (ACNNs): application to cardiac image enhancement and segmentation. IEEE Trans. Med. Imaging **37.2**, 384–395 (2017)

17. Painchaud, N., et al.: Cardiac segmentation with strong anatomical guarantees. In: IEEE Trans. Med. Imaging **39.11**, 3703–3713 (2020)

18. Oktay, O., et al.: Attention U-net: Learning where to look for the pancreas. arXiv preprint arXiv:1804.03999 (2018)

19. Yu, F., Vladlen, K.: Multi-scale context aggregation by Dilated convolutions. arXiv preprint arXiv:1511.07122 (2015)

20. Simard, P.Y., Steinkraus, D., Platt, J.C.: Best practices for convolutional neural networks applied to visual document analysis. Icdar, vol. 3, no. 2003 (2003)

Global Characteristic Guided Landmark Detection for Genu Valgus and Varus Diagnosis

Lingfeng Ma[1], Chuanbin Liu[1], Sicheng Zhang[2], Yizhi Liu[3],
and Hongtao Xie[1(✉)]

[1] School of Information Science and Technology,
University of Science and Technology of China, Hefei 230026, China
htxie@ustc.edu.cn
[2] Anhui Provincial Childrens Hospital, Hefei 230026, China
[3] Hunan University of Science and Technology, Xiangtan 411100, China

Abstract. Genu valgus and varus (GVV) are common orthopedic deformities for children. The fundamental step for GVV diagnosis is to locate and identify anatomical landmarks in X-rays. However, it is quite challenging for both humans and computers to accurately detect the landmarks, due to the lack of distinctive position clues. In this paper, we develop a deep learning method named GVV-Net to tackling this issue by fully exploiting the *global* information inherent in the bones, such as the *stable structure features* and the *slender shape features*. Firstly, we propose the Spatial Dependency Mining (SDM) module for capturing the long-range latent dependency and providing global structural information as a supplementary position clue. Secondly, we develop the Vertical Information Aggregation (VIA) module providing a holistic view to help the network perceive more informative regions, which coincides with the slender shape of bones. Besides, we construct the first public dataset with 1555 X-ray images for deep learning research. We achieve an accurate performance in landmark detection with 1.764 mm in point error. The experimental results verify that our method can be reliable assistance for clinical application of GVV.

Keywords: Genu valgus and varus · Landmark detection · Medical imaging

1 Introduction

Nowadays, accurate and reliable anatomical landmark detection is a fundamental task in medical imaging [1], which also plays a critical role in the diagnosis of *Genu Valgus and Varus* (GVV) deformities.

GVV are the most common orthopedic deformities [2–4] in children. The diseases may cause serious consequences such as arthritis and even disability if not caught and treated early. Specifically as illustrated in Fig. 1(a), genu varus means the distal end of a tibia bends inward relative to the knee joint, while genu

© Springer Nature Switzerland AG 2021
Y. Peng et al. (Eds.): ICIG 2021, LNCS 12889, pp. 523–534, 2021.
https://doi.org/10.1007/978-3-030-87358-5_42

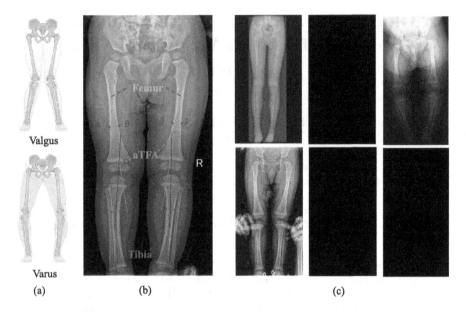

Fig. 1. The diagnosis of GVV deformities. (a) is a schematic diagram of GVV deformities, referenced from [6]. (b) shows the method to measure the aTFA of the lower extremities. The red crosses denote the location of landmarks. (c) represents some difficult examples. [Better viewed in color.] (Color figure online)

valgus is the opposite. And a critical approach for diagnosing GVV deformities is to identify the relative position between a femur and a tibia from X-ray images of the lower extremities. Figure 1(b) presents a clinical diagnosis approach of GVV which measures the *Anatomical Tibiofemoral Angle* (aTFA) [5] of the lower extremities according to the landmarks. The aTFA means the angle between the femoral and tibial axis lines, as illustrated with the green and blue lines in Fig. 1(b). Each axis line is obtained by four corresponding landmarks, including two corner points ("C" and "D" for example in the left femur) and two edge points ("A" and "B"). The connecting line between their midpoints constitutes the axis of the bone. Therefore, detecting these anatomical landmarks in X-ray images is a critical step for GVV diagnosis.

However, it is a challenging task to accurately detect the landmarks since there are several difficult barriers. Firstly, local neighborhood areas around the landmarks lack distinctive features and position information, bringing difficulty in determining their location. For example, edge points (like "A" and "B" in Fig. 1(b)) are labeled at the smooth boundary areas without distinctive position clues, thus they are harder to be accurately detected. Secondly, there is inevitable noise interference surrounding the bones in X-rays, as shown in Fig. 1(c), which appears because of various reasons, such as intensity caused by soft tissue reflection, low contrast from improper imaging, interference by other objects, etc. The noise exacerbates difficulty to sense the accurate location of landmarks. Thirdly, there exists a serious mismatch problem between the shape of region of interest and the receptive field of convolutional networks. It is obvious that the bones, i.e. femurs and tibias, are long and narrow in the vertical direction, while operations in networks including convolution and pooling often have square kernels, thus generating square receptive field. This mismatch conflict causes networks to perceive the irrelevant regions and then incorporates more background noise. In a word, all of these problems show that *only relying on local features hinders accurately detecting the landmarks.*

While the local neighborhoods around landmarks cannot yield effective local position features, the human lower limb skeleton presents a stable global structure, which is an effective constraint for landmark detection. In this paper, we explore the acquisition of *global* information to supplement the deficiencies of local features. Generally, we develop a novel convolutional neural network named GVV-Net. It contains a Spatial Dependency Mining (SDM) module and a Vertical Information Aggregation (VIA) module, investigating the *stable structure features* and the *shape features* of bones for landmark detection. Firstly, the bones show a stable morphological structure from a global perspective, such as the stable bone orientation and the stable upper-and-lower structure between femur and tibia. Therefore, we develop the SDM module to excavate global structural information. Secondly, the slender shape of bones, which is crucial for accurate landmark detection, is always easily ignored in general approaches. Thus, we propose the VIA module forcing the receptive field to adapt to the shape of region of interest. Moreover, in order to encourage the further research in the GVV automatic diagnosis, we construct a large-scale dataset including 1555 X-ray images of the lower extremities with fine annotations. To the best of our knowledge, this is the first X-ray dataset for GVV diagnosis and it will be public soon.

In summary, the main contributions of the paper are as follows:

- We propose an end-to-end framework named GVV-Net, targeting for accurately detecting anatomical landmarks in X-ray images of lower extremities. The GVV-Net addresses the difficulty of the lack of position cues in local features by capturing the global information.
- We propose the SDM and VIA modules in the GVV-Net, which investigating the *stable structure features* and the *shape features* of bones for landmark detection respectively.
- We construct the first large-scale dataset for GVV diagnosis containing 1555 X-ray images of lower extremities, which will be public for open research.

2   Related Work

In this section, we introduce some related works including landmark detection methods and GVV diagnosis in X-rays.

2.1   Landmark Detection Methods

Deep learning methods have achieved remarkable performance in the general landmark detection task by regressing heatmap, which treats a spatial neighborhood around landmarks as positive samples. For example, Newell et al. [7] have proposed a stacked hourglass network to fuse features from different stages. Xiao et al. [8] have provided a simple but useful network named SimpleBaseline, which applies the ResNet as its backbone to extract features. Sun et al. [9] have proposed a high-resolution network named HR-Net for landmark detection. The HR-Net maintains high resolution feature maps in the whole pipeline and aggregates multi-resolution information in every stage to get accurate results. All these methods have made achievements on general detection tasks due to their ability to explore local features. However, they have limited performance when directly applied in GVV diagnosis because local features do not yield sufficient position information. In this paper, we also apply a heatmap-based method while fully mines the inherent global characteristics of bones to overcome the problems in this task.

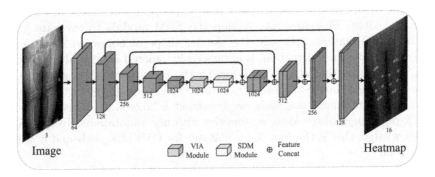

Fig. 2. The illustration of the entire structure of the GVV-Net, which applies U-Net [10] as the backbone.

2.2   GVV Diagnosis in X-Rays

X-ray is the common and useful metric to diagnose GVV. Thus, many studies have been conducted to analyze GVV based on X-rays. Yoo et al. [5] have investigated the development of the aTFA in Korean children. Silva et al. [11] have presented several approaches to diagnose GVV in X-ray images such as measuring the mechanical axis deviation and using the joint orientation angle. Bakshi et al. [12] have applied deep learning to *"correctly draw a boundary between a physiologically normal knee and a genu valgus"*. However, they only use the neural network as a decision-making system for classification ("Normal" or "Abnormal"). Besides, they have failed to use the spatial information in the X-ray images. In this paper, we train an end-to-end network to detect landmarks for GVV diagnosis, fully exploiting the global spatial information between bones.

3   Method

Figure 2 illustrates the overall architecture of the proposed GVV-Net for landmark detection in X-ray images. Firstly, we convert the detection of a landmark to regression of a heatmap activated at the landmark's neighborhood. Then we use a simple backbone, U-Net [10], to learn local spatial features. Secondly, the VIA module forces the network to perceive more information in the vertical direction to match the shape of bones. Moreover, we apply the SDM module to mine global structural information for landmarks. Finally, we realize an end-to-end network to accurately detect anatomical landmarks in X-rays images of lower extremities for GVV diagnosis.

3.1   Heatmap Based Landmark Detection

The purpose of the landmark detection is to detect the location of K keypoints from an image. In order to make full use of spatial information around the landmarks, we convert the target from landmark coordinates to K heatmaps $\{H_1, H_2, ..., H_K\}$ as previous works [7,8]. Each heatmap H_k is generated by applying 2D Gaussian centered at the location of corresponding k-th landmark. That is,

$$H_k(i, j) = \exp\{-\frac{(i - i_k^*)^2 + (j - j_k^*)^2}{2\sigma^2}\}. \tag{1}$$

Here, (i_k^*, j_k^*) denotes the coordinate of the k-th landmark. σ is the standard deviation of 2D Gaussian, as well as the range of local neighborhood around the landmark. With the heatmap target, the network can obtain guidance from the local neighborhoods rather than the individual landmarks, thus exploiting the spatial information.

3.2   Vertical Information Aggregation (VIA)

There is a mismatch problem between slender shape of region of interest and the square receptive fields in convolutional networks. This problem incorporates useless information from noisy background and limits the ability to capture long-range dependency especially in the vertical direction.

Therefore, in order to match the shape characteristic of bones, we explore to enlarge the receptive field so that the network can perceive more informative regions in the vertical direction. Motivated by this idea, we propose the simple yet effective VIA module. The structure is presented in Fig. 3(a). A unilateral pooling operation is first applied on the feature maps to aggregate information in the vertical direction. Denoting the features as $X \in \mathbb{R}^{H \times W \times C}$, we can compute the output $Y \in \mathbb{R}^{W \times C}$ as,

$$y_j = \frac{1}{H} \sum_{i=1}^{H} x_{i,j}. \tag{2}$$

Here, $x_{i,j}$ is the vector at i-th row j-th column in X and y_j is the j-th vector in Y. Then information interaction is performed between different columns via a

1D convolution layer. After that, we obtain a column weight $\omega \in \mathbb{R}^{W \times C}$, which indicates the importance of each column in each channel. The weight improves the original feature X by element-wise multiplication.

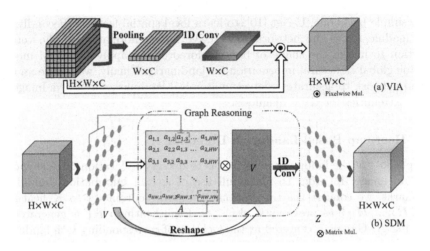

Fig. 3. The detailed structure of the proposed VIA and SDM modules. (a) is VIA module for enlarging the receptive field to perceive more informative regions in the vertical direction. (b) is the SDM module for learning the latent global dependency via graph reasoning. The orange lines give examples for calculating the affinity between graph nodes.

With this module, the GVV-Net gains larger receptive field in the vertical direction and perceive more informative regions, according with the slender shape of bones.

3.3 Spatial Dependency Mining (SDM)

It is difficult to accurately detect the landmarks only relying on the local features because the smooth boundary areas around the landmarks lack distinctive information. And the inevitable background noise further damages the local information that the network can obtain.

To address this issue, we investigate the global structural information to provide supplementary information for deficiencies of local features. Inspired by this idea, we develop a simplified graph reasoning method and propose the SDM module for the high-level features. The structure of the module is shown in Fig. 3(b). We first build a fully-connected graph directly on the feature space (i.e. regarding each pixel in the spatial grid as a node in the graph). For the input features $X \in \mathbb{R}^{H \times W \times C}$, a graph $\mathcal{G} = (V, E)$ with HW nodes is constructed with V as the set of nodes and E as the set of edges. Here, H, W and C denote the height, width and channels respectively. In this way, information can be exchanged between every pixel not just between adjacent pixels. As the previous work [13], a single-layer graph convolution is formulated as,

$$Z = \sigma(A_g V \Theta). \tag{3}$$

Here, $A_g \in \mathbb{R}^{HW \times HW}$ denotes the adjacency matrix passing information between nodes and $\Theta \in \mathbb{R}^{C \times C}$ is the trainable weight matrix of status updating function. $V \in \mathbb{R}^{HW \times C}$ is the input node features and $Z \in \mathbb{R}^{HW \times C}$ is the updated node features. $\sigma(\cdot)$ is a non-linear activation function. For simplicity, we exploit the affinity matrix $A \in \mathbb{R}^{HW \times HW}$ between nodes to approximate the adjacency matrix in Eq. (3). We compute the affinity between any two nodes as

$$a_{i,j} = (W_\theta \boldsymbol{x}_i)^T (W_\phi \boldsymbol{x}_j). \tag{4}$$

Here, $a_{i,j}$ is the value at i-th row j-th column of the matrix A. i and j are two positions in the graph ($1 \leq i, j \leq HW$), while $\boldsymbol{x}_i$ and $\boldsymbol{x}_j \in \mathbb{R}^C$ denote the feature vectors at corresponding position respectively. W_θ and W_ϕ are the weights of two 1×1 convolutional layers (omitted in the figure). During training, the matrix A learns latent dependency between each node. Then this latent information is distributed to each node and update their status through a transformation Θ via Eq. (3). The latter can be realized by a 1-D convolution. Finally, all nodes in the graph will be arranged regularly and restored to a feature map in the grid space.

With the SDM, every pixel in the feature maps is able to receive necessary information from all other pixels and we can deeply mine the global latent dependency between pixels.

3.4 Loss Function

The final prediction heatmaps are generated with K channels (where K is equal to the number of landmarks). Each landmark can be determined as the location of the maximum value point in the corresponding channel and the aTFA of the lower extremities can be computed.

We apply the Mean Square Error (MSE) loss function to supervise the network. The MSE is computed between prediction maps and ground-truth heatmaps at every channel, i.e.,

$$L_{MSE} = \frac{1}{K} \sum_{k=1}^{K} \frac{1}{HW} \parallel \sum_{i,j} \boldsymbol{M}_k(i,j) - \boldsymbol{H}_k(i,j) \parallel_2^2 . \tag{5}$$

Here, K means the number of landmarks and H, W denote the height and width of the maps respectively. $\boldsymbol{M}_k$ and $\boldsymbol{H}_k$ denote the prediction map and groundtruth heatmap of k-th landmark.

4   Experiments

4.1   Dataset

It is worth noting that a public dataset with sufficient X-ray images is important for GVV diagnosis with deep learning techniques. But there is currently no publicly available high-quality dataset for the task. Accordingly, we construct a large-scale dataset containing X-ray images of lower extremities with fine annotation for research. We collect 1555 X-ray images from a hospital for the dataset. Then we convert the original DICOM files to visible JPEG images with the pixel spacing of each image as 0.288 mm. After labeled by orthopedists, we randomly divide the dataset into a training set with 1244 images and a testing set with 311. To the best of our knowledge, the dataset is the first large-scale dataset for GVV and it will be public soon.

4.2 Experiments Setup

Experiments are carried out based on an open source deep learning framework, PyTorch. We use 2 GPUs to train the model for 100 epochs in total. During training process, we apply the Adam [14] optimizer with $betas = (0.9, 0.999), eps = 1e - 8$. The learning rate is initially set at 0.001, and it is multiplied by 0.1 every 50 epochs. Before feeding the images into the network, we apply some data augmentation approaches, including resizing images to 704×384, randomly rotating and randomly horizontal flipping. For hyperparameters, the number of landmarks K is equal to 16. The σ of groundtruth heatmap is set to 6 pixels.

4.3 Evaluation Metrics

We apply the average Point Error (PE) to evaluate the mean error of every landmark and every image as

$$PE = \frac{1}{NK} \sum_{n=1}^{N} \sum_{k=1}^{K} \parallel L_{n,k} - L_{n,k}^* \parallel_2. \tag{6}$$

Here, N and K represent the number of test images and landmarks respectively, L denotes the prediction results and L^* is the location of manually labeled landmarks. Besides the average evaluation, we also need to access the distribution of prediction results. Then the Successful Detection Rate (SDR) is used to calculate the proportion of points with errors within a certain range z to the total landmarks,

$$SDR = \frac{|\{Pd : \parallel L_{n,k} - L_{n,k}^* \parallel_2 \le z\}|}{NK} \times 100\%. \tag{7}$$

As shown in Fig. 1(a), the aTFA can be computed according to the coordinates of landmarks. Then, Angle Error (AE) is used to access the accuracy of angles similar as Eq. (6).

$$AE = \frac{1}{2N} \sum_{n=1}^{N} \sum_{k=1}^{2} \parallel A_{n,k} - A_{n,k}^* \parallel_2. \tag{8}$$

Here, $k = 0, 1$ denotes the aTFA of right and left legs. N is the total number of images in test set. A and A^* represent the angles obtained by prediction results and groundtruth, respectively.

Table 1. Performance comparison with state-of-the-art landmark detection algorithms.

Method	Left femur				Left tibia				Right femur				Right tibia				PE (mm)	AE
	A	B	C	D	E	F	G	H	I	J	K	L	M	N	O	P		
HRNet [9]	2.79	2.85	1.31	1.12	1.37	1.14	2.73	2.69	2.72	2.83	1.31	1.20	1.19	1.47	2.86	2.98	2.04	1.34°
SimpleBaseline [8] - Res50	2.70	2.87	1.43	1.26	1.58	1.29	2.83	2.95	2.95	2.98	1.33	1.46	1.30	1.72	3.17	3.14	2.18	1.53°
SimpleBaseline [8] - Res101	2.90	2.97	1.20	1.21	1.42	1.21	2.66	2.70	2.97	2.99	1.38	1.37	1.32	1.46	2.86	2.90	2.10	1.43°
SimpleBaseline [8] - Res152	2.84	2.87	1.57	1.24	1.74	1.21	2.81	2.71	2.91	2.93	1.30	1.37	1.18	1.36	2.91	2.90	2.12	1.50°
Hourglass [7] - stack 2	2.89	3.02	1.29	1.09	1.35	1.13	3.18	3.01	3.05	3.14	1.15	1.33	1.08	1.37	3.00	3.15	2.13	1.48°
Hourglass [7] - stack 8	2.80	2.95	1.25	1.18	1.45	1.20	2.75	2.74	2.76	2.80	1.24	1.20	1.09	1.24	2.84	2.86	2.02	1.29°
U-Net [10]	2.91	2.95	0.86	1.03	1.22	1.01	3.04	2.98	3.00	3.08	1.00	0.90	0.83	1.15	3.07	3.12	2.01	1.23°
U-Net++ [15]	2.88	2.96	0.89	0.89	1.11	0.85	3.05	2.94	2.96	3.01	0.92	0.89	0.78	1.18	3.15	3.22	1.98	1.20°
GVV-Net	**2.57**	**2.71**	**0.77**	**0.85**	**1.10**	**0.77**	**2.60**	**2.57**	**2.70**	**2.78**	**0.84**	**0.78**	**0.73**	**1.00**	**2.70**	**2.76**	**1.76**	**0.93°**

4.4   Performance Evaluation

We have conducted a series of experiments on the proposed dataset. Here, we evaluate the performance of our GVV-Net from two aspects, landmark detection and angle measurement.

Landmark Detection: In Table 1, we compare the performance with some state-of-the-art algorithms designed for the general landmark detection task, including the HRNet [9], SimpleBaseline [8], Hourglass [7] and U-Net [10,15] family. From the perspective of average error of all landmarks, the GVV-Net achieves the best performance of 1.76 mm in PE, outperforming the other networks. Moreover, we analyze the performance of each landmark, where "A"-"P" indicate the points shown in Fig. 1. As in Table 1, the edge points (for example "A" and "B") show worse performance than the corner points (such as "C" and "D" in left femur) in all approaches. There indeed exist challenges to sense the smooth local boundary areas around the edge points. Meanwhile, compared to the more complex variants such as U-Net++ [15], U-Net [10] achieves almost the same performance in landmark detection. This indicates that U-Net is powerful enough to learn local features. The GVV-Net can boost further performance in landmark detection than these U-Net family networks, demonstrating the vital role of global information in this task.

It is noted that simply increasing the complexity of the network, such as SimpleBaseline [8] and Hourglass [7] series, cannot get satisfactory improvements. The performance of SimpleBaseline with ResNet-152 is even slightly worse than the ResNet-101. The more complex networks often only reduce the error of some landmarks, while increasing the error of other landmarks. On the contrary, our GVV-Net shows large improvements in both corner and edge landmarks than other networks. These results demonstrate that the proposed network has a better performance to sense the smooth boundary areas.

In addition, we present the distribution of landmark detection results by SDR in Fig. 4. First of all, most of landmarks (about 95%) can be located within the error at 4 mm for these approaches. In addition, the GVV-Net shows its advantage when the error is smaller than 2 mm. This result means the GVV-Net not only obtains better performance in average error but also locates more landmarks with smaller error.

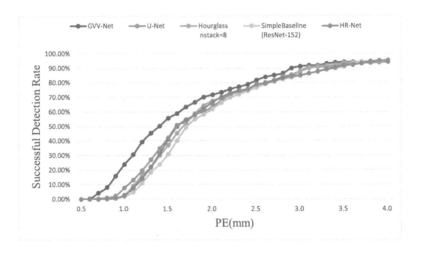

Fig. 4. The SDR performance comparison with other networks.

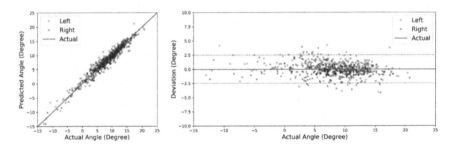

Fig. 5. The aTFA prediction results of GVV-Net. [Best viewed in color] (Color figure online)

Angle Measurement: Here, we further analyze the results of aTFA prediction. The last column in Table 1 presents the mean absolute angle errors obtained by different networks. From the table, our GVV-Net gets both accurate landmark coordinates and angle measurement ($0.93°$ in AE) than other methods. This means that our method can have better performance in automatic diagnosis of GVV. Beyond the absolute error, we also present the relative distance between the predicted results and ground truth. As shown in Fig. 5 (a), the distribution of predicted angles is close to a line with slope of 1, i.e., the actual angle. From Fig. 5 (b), most of angles can be measured within an error of $2.5°$. These angle prediction results demonstrate the superiority and robustness of the GVV-Net.

4.5   Ablation Study

Ablation study is conducted in order to demonstrate the effectiveness of the proposed modules. As illustrated in Table 2, it is clear that both the SDM and VIA modules have contributions to the improvements. The SDM module decreases the

Table 2. Ablation study on the effect of the proposed modules.

Method	SDM	VIA	HIA	Params (M)	Flops (G)	PE (mm)	AE (degree)
U-Net++ [15]				36.6	529.7	1.981	1.196°
U-Net [10]				34.5	251.2	2.010	1.228°
	✓			36.6	253.3	1.920	1.024°
		✓		38.7	252.4	1.896	1.009°
			✓	38.7	252.4	1.938	1.075°
	✓	✓		40.8	254.5	**1.764**	**0.933°**

PE from 2.010 mm to 1.920 mm and it also reduces the AE from 1.228° to 1.024°. Similarly, the VIA module reduces the PE and the AE results by 0.114 mm and 0.219° respectively. More importantly, the effect of these two modules can promote each other that the complete GVV-Net (the last row) further boosts the performance. From the perspective of computational complexity, our modules also show their advantages. For example, the SDM-only (3rd row) and VIA-only networks (4rd row) have a number of parameters close to the U-Net++ [15] (1st row), while only having half number of the Flops and better detection performance than the latter. This means that the performance improvement comes from our successful capture of the latent global information, not only due to more calculations.

To further investigating the performance of VIA, we conduct an experiment by using a module with the same structure as VIA except for the different pooling direction, named horizontal information aggregation (HIA, the 5th row). Despite having the similar computational complexity, the VIA module achieves better performance in PE (1.896 mm vs 1.938 mm) and AE (1.009° vs 1.075°) than HIA, which demonstrating the effectiveness of the vertical information in our network.

5   Conclusion

In this paper, we propose the novel GVV-Net for detecting anatomical landmarks in X-ray images of lower extremities. Due to the lack of distinctive position clues, it is difficult for deep learning methods to accurately detect the landmarks only relying on the local features. The GVV-Net fully exploits the stable structure features and the slender shape features by the SDM and VIA to learn the global information as a supplement to the deficiency of useful local features. Besides, it is worth noted that we construct the first large-scale dataset with 1555 X-ray images for GVV diagnosis and it will be public soon for further research. Our work can be an inspiration for anatomical landmark detection tasks on medical images.

Acknowledgements. This work is supported by the National Nature Science Foundation of China (62022076,61976008), the Key Project of Hunan Provincial Education Department (19A172) and the Fundamental Research Funds for the Central Universities under Grant WK3480000011.

References

1. Liu, C., Xie, H., Zhang, S., Xu, J., Sun, J., Zhang, Y.: Misshapen pelvis landmark detection by spatial local correlation mining for diagnosing developmental dysplasia of the hip. In: Shen, D., et al. (eds.) MICCAI 2019. LNCS, vol. 11769, pp. 441–449. Springer, Cham (2019). https://doi.org/10.1007/978-3-030-32226-7_49

2. Silva, M.S., Fernandes, A.R.C., Cardoso, F.N., Longo, C.H., Aihara, A.: Radiography, CT, and MRI of hip and lower limb disorders in children and adolescents. Radiographics **39**(3), 779–794 (2019)

3. GugenheimJr, J.J., Brinker, M.R.: Bone realignment with use of temporary external fixation for distal femoral valgus and varus deformities. JBJS **85**(7), 1229–1237 (2003)

4. White, G.R., Mencio, G.A.: Genu valgum in children: diagnostic and therapeutic alternatives. JAAOS-J. Am. Acad. Orthop. Surg. **3**(5), 275–283 (1995)

5. Yoo, J.H., Choi, I.H., Cho, T.J., Chung, C.Y., Yoo, W.J.: Development of tibiofemoral angle in Korean children. J. Korean Med. Sci. **23**(4), 714–717 (2008)

6. Knee alignment difference. https://allhealthpost.com/valgus-vs-varus/

7. Newell, A., Yang, K., Deng, J.: Stacked hourglass networks for human pose estimation. In: Leibe, B., Matas, J., Sebe, N., Welling, M. (eds.) ECCV 2016. LNCS, vol. 9912, pp. 483–499. Springer, Cham (2016). https://doi.org/10.1007/978-3-319-46484-8_29

8. Xiao, B., Wu, H., Wei, Y.: Simple baselines for human pose estimation and tracking. In: Ferrari, V., Hebert, M., Sminchisescu, C., Weiss, Y. (eds.) ECCV 2018. LNCS, vol. 11210, pp. 472–487. Springer, Cham (2018). https://doi.org/10.1007/978-3-030-01231-1_29

9. Sun, K., Xiao, B., Liu, D., Wang, J.: Deep high-resolution representation learning for human pose estimation. In: Proceedings of the IEEE Conference on Computer Vision and Pattern Recognition, pp. 5693–5703 (2019)

10. Ronneberger, O., Fischer, P., Brox, T.: U-net: convolutional networks for biomedical image segmentation. In: Navab, N., Hornegger, J., Wells, W.M., Frangi, A.F. (eds.) MICCAI 2015. LNCS, vol. 9351, pp. 234–241. Springer, Cham (2015). https://doi.org/10.1007/978-3-319-24574-4_28

11. Silva, M.S., Fernandes, A.R., Cardoso, F.N., Longo, C.H., Aihara, A.Y.: Radiography, CT, and MRI of hip and lower limb disorders in children and adolescents. Radiographics **39**(3), 779–794 (2019)

12. Bakshi, S., et al.: An investigative analysis on mapping x-ray to live using convolution neural networks for detection of genu valgum. Open Access Libr. J. **5**(11), 1 (2018)

13. Chen, Y., Rohrbach, M., Yan, Z., Yan, S., Feng, J., Kalantidis, Y.: Graph-based global reasoning networks. In: 2019 IEEE/CVF Conference on Computer Vision and Pattern Recognition (CVPR), pp. 433–442 (2019)

14. Kingma, D.P., Ba, J.: Adam: a method for stochastic optimization. arXiv preprint arXiv:1412.6980 (2014)

15. Zhou, Z., Rahman Siddiquee, M.M., Tajbakhsh, N., Liang, J.: UNet++: a nested u-net architecture for medical image segmentation. In: Stoyanov, D., et al. (eds.) DLMIA/ML-CDS -2018. LNCS, vol. 11045, pp. 3–11. Springer, Cham (2018). https://doi.org/10.1007/978-3-030-00889-5_1

Data-Dependence Dual Path Network for Choroidal Neovascularization Segmentation in SD-OCT Images

Jiasen Ke[1], Zexuan Ji[1(✉)], Qiang Chen[1], Wen Fan[2], and Songtao Yuan[2]

[1] School of Computer Science and Engineering,
Nanjing University of Science and Technology, Nanjing 210094, China
jizexuan@njust.edu.cn
[2] Department of Ophthalmology, The First Affiliated Hospital with Nanjing Medical University, Nanjing 210029, China

Abstract. Choroidal neovascularization (CNV) is a typical clinical manifestation of age-related macular degeneration (AMD) and an important factor leading to blindness in AMD patients. Automated CNV lesion segmentation based on SD-OCT images has important research significance for clinical diagnosis. We propose a data-dependence dual path network (D3PNet) for CNV segmentation by designing an expansive path, a guidance path and a novel feature fusion strategy. In the expansive path, the data-dependent upsampling method and the proposed upsampling strategy would preserve more detail information and make the obtained features more diversified. In the guidance path, a deformable module is proposed to generate the saliency maps and lead the model focusing on the contours. Finally, we design a novel feature fusion method by regarding the saliency maps as the attention mechanism of hierarchical features to amplify the beneficial features and suppress the useless ones. Experimental results demonstrate the superior performances and reliabilities of the proposed network comparing with state-of-the-art methods.

Keywords: SD-OCT · CNV · Deep learning · Medical image segmentation

1 Introduction

Age-related macular degeneration (AMD) is an important cause of blindness worldwide, and its incidence increases with the aging of society. AMD is a progressive chronic disease that occurs in the central retina, and is usually divided into non-exudative (dry) and exudative (wet) [1]. Choroidal neovascularization

This work was supported by National Natural Science Foundation of China under Grant No. 62072241, and in part by Natural Science Foundation of Jiangsu Province under Grants No. BK20180069, and in part by Six talent peaks project in Jiangsu Province under Grant No. SWYY-056.

Y. Peng et al. (Eds.): ICIG 2021, LNCS 12889, pp. 535–546, 2021.
https://doi.org/10.1007/978-3-030-87358-5_43

(CNV) is a common symptom of exudative AMD. The development and related manifestations of CNV, such as subretinal hemorrhage, fluid exudation, retinal pigment epithelium detachment, or other harmful symptoms [2], are the most common causes for vision loss or vision distortion.

For CNV treatment, quantitatively and objectively accurate analysis of retinal structure and pathology can assist ophthalmologists to better plan treatment intervals and reduce the risk of patients [3]. The early diagnosis tools for CNV lesions are fluorescein angiography (FA) and indocyanine green angiography (ICGA). However, FA and ICGA are invasive, which greatly limits the corresponding practical applications [4].

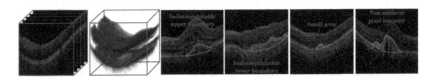

Fig. 1. An example of ST-OCT cube containing CNV lesions. The images from left to right show the original ST-OCT images, 3D visualization by marking CNV lesions as blue, and four different B-scans with different defects that CNV lesion suffers. (Color figure online)

Benefiting from high axial differentiation, spectral-domain optical coherence tomography (SD-OCT) reveals the high resolution internal spatial appearance of the retina in three-dimensional manner and has become accessible for researchers and clinicians in evaluating the retinal lesions [5]. As shown in the first image in Fig. 1, OCT imaging scales the macular area into a longitudinal 3D cube composed of hundreds of axial slices (B-scans). CNV represents the growth of new blood vessels from the choroid, which extends through the break of Bruch's membrane to the avascular outer retina. Compared with other retinal diseases, CNV lesions have more complicated pathological features and diverse structures as shown from the third to the sixth images in Fig. 1. Due to the diversity of CNV, most CNV segmentation or detection algorithms focus on dealing with the projection image of SD-OCT images [6].

In the field of automatic CNV segmentation, Lee et al. proposed a Markov random field model for interactive segmentation by integrating a semi-parametric conditional mixture model in a framework of transductive learning and inference [7]. Fahmy et al. used a navel gamma variable model to model the image intensity of different time frames to capture the temporal changes of the fluorescein dye in the early, mid, and late phases [8]. Tsai et al. utilized Adaboost to learn intensity values and intensity changes in multiple time intervals from the FA sequence to describe the typical leakage characteristics of CNV lesions [9].

Recently, deep learning further promotes the development of medical image analysis. The classical semantic segmentation networks, such as FCN [10], U-net [11], Deeplab v3 [12] and RefineNet [13], have been widely used in medical image area. In order to solve the problem of the variable scale of the lesion area, Zhang et al. introduced a multi-scale parallel branch convolutional neural network (CNN) [14]. Wang et al. designed two different networks CNV-M and CNV-V to identify and segment CNV, in which the CNV-M segments the CNV membrane and outputs a mask corresponding to its location to assist the CNV-V segmentation [15]. Xi et al. used a structural prior learning method based on sparse representation-based model to improve the distinctiveness between lesions and background, then constructed a multi-scale CNN for CNV segmentation [16].

The above segmentation models can accurately locate CNV lesions. However, due to the diverse shapes and complex structures of CNV lesions, the non-CNV tissues or lesions in the retina would easily confuse the CNNs and further limit the corresponding accuracy especially for the boundaries of CNV lesions. Although the multi-scale method is an effective solution to improve the segmentation accuracy, it is still not satisfactory for the boundary description of CNV lesions. Therefore, in this paper, we design a semantic segmentation network by guiding the model focusing on the contour of the lesion to further improve the CNV segmentation accuracy in SD-OCT images. The motivations and contributions can be summarized as follows:

Detailed Texture Preserving: To obtain accurate segmentation result, it is necessary to coordinate the use of abstract and detailed features. The down-sampling operations involved in CNNs would reduce the resolution of features and smooth many detailed features. In order to preserve the detailed features, the networks like Deeplab try to directly reduce the down-sampling operations, which would introduce a large number of intermediate variables and result in a high computational complexity. In this paper, we attempt to preserve the detailed information from the perspective of upsampling. By adopting the data-related upsampling method, the proposed upsampling stage would restore the detailed information lost and avoid the increasing of calculations.

Contour Information Emphasizing: The weak boundary problem of CNV lesions is a very challenging issue. Therefore, the network needs to be guided to focus on the contour fitting. In this paper, saliency maps are generated to emphasize the location of the possible lesion area. Deform blocks are stacked to form the guidance path to lead saliency maps to highlight contours.

Multi-scale Feature Fusion: Previous feature fusion strategies such as direct concatenation or accumulate of features, would lead to a compromise between useful and useless features. So, we design a novel feature fusion method by regarding the saliency maps as the attention mechanism of hierarchical information to amplify the beneficial features and suppress the useless ones.

2   Method

2.1   Overview

Figure 2 shows the architecture of the proposed model. The proposed model introduces three parts, i.e. the expansive path in the blue box, the guidance path in the green box and the feature fusion in the red box. In the expansive path, The proposed upsampling strategy would recover the detailed information from the perspective of upsampling. In the guidance path, deformable blocks stacked with Dupsampling method are proposed to generate the saliency maps and lead the model focusing on the contour information. In the feature fusion part, we regard the saliency maps as the attention mechanism of hierarchical information.

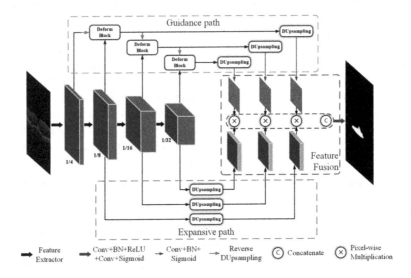

Fig. 2. The architecture of our model. (Color figure online)

2.2   Expansive Path

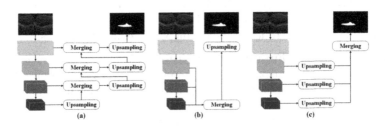

Fig. 3. The illustrations of feature merging strategy in (a) U-Net, (b) DU-Net [17], (c) D3PNet.

As shown in Fig. 3(a), most related works, such as FCN, U-Net, RefineNet, adopt the strategy of synchronous upsampling and feature merging in which the data-independent upsampling is widely utilized. In order to combine features with different resolutions, the network continuously performs feature merging stage by stage. However, data-independent upsampling methods can hardly recover the detailed information lost in the downsampling while enlarging the feature resolution. Suppose the features need to be upsampled by eight times using bilinear interpolation, in a 8×8 receptive area after upsampling, only the center feature is learned by the network, and the values of other locations are calculated from the features of the surrounding locations. The surrounding eigenvalues have a linear relationship, which is inconsistent with the actual situation.

Data-dependent upsampling (DUpsampling) method [17] is designed by using redundant channels to reconstruct features and perform upsampling. Based on the assumption that the feature itself contains structural information, DUpsampling method takes advantages of the redundancy in the channel space to expand feature size. As shown in Fig. 3(b), in DU-Net, the features from different stages are firstly downsampled to the same size of the features in the last stage and concatenated, then the fused features are up-sampled to obtain the final results (Fig. 4).

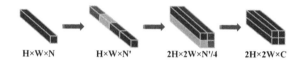

H×W×N   H×W×N'   2H×2W×N'/4   2H×2W×C

Fig. 4. The illustrations of data-dependent upsampling.

In this paper, we propose a new upsampling strategy as shown in the Fig. 3(c), in which the DUpsampling method is directly utilized to expand the features from different stages to its original size. Then the hierarchical features are fused. In this way, features from different layers can be trained more independently, which facilitates the model to obtain better feature combinations. In addition, because the feature maps of each layer is directly upsampled to avoid additional downsampling operation, our method can preserve more detailed information.

2.3   Guidance Path

The goal of the guidance path is to generate saliency maps to emphasize the location of the retinal lesions, which would further lead the model to focus on the contours. As shown in Fig. 5, comparing with the conventional convolution, the Deformable convolution [18] can guide its own deformation by learning affiliated convolutional layers as the offset of the convolution. Therefore, the deformable convolutions would automatically learn the geometric deformation and guide the sampling position to the irregular targets, which would enhanced the geometric transformations and lead the model adapting to the complex shapes.

Considering the characteristic of deformable convolution, the proposed network integrates deformable convolution into the saliency map generation module

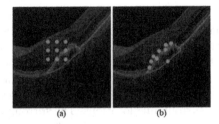

Fig. 5. The comparison between (a) standard convolution and (b) deformable convolution. The blue box in the figure indicates the size of the receptive field in the case of standard convolution, and the red point indicates the sampling location. (Color figure online)

Fig. 6. The structure of deform block.

to improve the shape fitting ability of the saliency map. As shown in Fig. 6, based on the residual structure of ResNet, the deformable convolutions are utilized to replace the convolutions in each block. Two continues modified residual modules are stacked to form a deform block, whose outputs are utilized in two ways:

In each stage, the output of deform block is firstly scale-reduced by utilizing the inverse process of DUpsampling, and concatenated with the features of the next stage. Then the combined features are fed into the next deform block.

Moreover, the outputs of deform blocks in each stage are fed into the DUpsampling module to generate the saliency maps for the feature fusion.

2.4 Feature Fusion

Conventional feature fusion methods include concatenation and addition of features. However, the corresponding combinations of features are generally not optimal, and all the features are indiscriminately processed. Therefore, the result would be a compromise between useful and useless features. To further filter features, in this paper, we design a new feature fusion strategy by multiplying the feature maps obtained by expansive path with the saliency maps obtained by guidance path, respectively. The guidance path can be regarded as an attention mechanism for hierarchical features. Then the concatenated features are used to produce the final segmentation results.

3 Experiments

The experiments were conducted on a linux server with NVIDIA GeForce RTX 2080 Ti GPU, and 32.0 GB RAM. The running environment was built under conda 4.3.30, with python3.6.4 and pytorch. To ensure the reliability of the experimental results, we conducted 10-fold cross-validation on the dataset and took the average value of the cross-validation as the final result. The experiment was designed in a patient-independent manner, which meant that in each fold, the data of one patient was used as the test set and the data of others was used as the training set. Besides, to better illustrate the characteristics of our model, we conducted the ablation experiments on the proposed model by adding one component at a time, which could reveal the influence of each part of our model.

The whole dataset contains 10 patients with 140 cubes. All patients were aged between 50 and 81. They were all treated with 3+ prn treatment. The whole dataset were acquired with a Cirrus OCT device (Carl Zeiss Meditec, Inc., Dublin, CA) from Jiangsu Province Hospital by recording a $6 \times 6 \times 2\,\mathrm{mm}^3$ macular area in the horizontal, vertical, and axial directions. The size of each cube is $1024 \times 512 \times 128$. Specifically, the B-scans are slices along the vertical direction, where a cube-scan can be divided into 128 B-scans. The CNV ground truth was annotated mainly by one expert and were given joint conformation for many times by multiple experts to guarantee its precision.

To evaluate the proposed method, we compared it with state-of-the-art methods, including FCN, U-Net, AU-net [19], DANet [20], Deeplab v3, RefineNet, CE-Net [21]. In order to measure the quality of the segmentation results, four evaluation criteria were utilized, including Dice coefficient (DC), underestimated ration (UR), overestimated ratio (OR) and absolute area difference (AAD). The Dice coefficient is used to calculate the degree of overlap between two regions. UR and OR are used to indicate whether the inaccurate segmentation is due to over-segmentation or under-segmentation. AAD is used to measure the difference in the absolute value of size of two areas. Their definitions are as follows:

$$DC = \frac{2|S_1 \cap S_2|}{|S_1| + |S_2|} \qquad UC = \frac{|S_1| - |S_1 \cap S_2|}{|S_1| + |S_2| - |S_1 \cap S_2|}$$

$$OC = \frac{|S_2| - |S_1 \cap S_2|}{|S_1| + |S_2| - |S_1 \cap S_2|} \qquad AAD = |Area(S_1) \cap Area(S_2)|$$

where S_1 and S_2 indicate the regions inside the segmented CNV contour produced by segmentation method and grader, respectively. The operators $\cap$ and $\cup$ indicate union and intersection. For the DC metric, higher value indicates better performance. For the others, lower value indicates better result.

Table 1. Quantitative results for all the comparison methods.

Index	DC	UR	OR	AAD
FCN	65.62 ± 6.60	17.47 ± 12.23	33.15 ± 10.73	0.062v0.053
U-Net	66.63 ± 9.40	17.57 ± 12.44	31.51 ± 14.11	0.068 ± 0.042
AU-net	69.82 ± 7.70	20.00 ± 11.06	25.69 ± 10.56	0.060 ± 0.043
DANet	72.56 ± 5.59	19.28 ± 10.61	23.35 ± 9.02	0.052 ± 0.043
Deeplab v3	74.07 ± 5.21	15.23 ± 10.38	25.53 ± 7.74	0.055 ± 0.052
RefineNet	75.86 ± 2.34	$\mathbf{9.43 \pm 5.62}$	29.13 ± 6.32	0.054 ± 0.028
CE-Net	76.78 ± 3.74	12.52 ± 8.69	24.80 ± 7.28	0.051 ± 0.037
D3PNet	$\mathbf{80.06 \pm 2.29}$	13.19 ± 6.03	$\mathbf{19.90 \pm 7.40}$	$\mathbf{0.043 \pm 0.032}$

Table 1 lists the quantitative results of all methods. As shown above, our method achieves 80.06%, 13.19%, 19.90% and 0.043 in terms of DC, UR, OR and AAD, and performs best on DC, OR and AAD. As conventional semantic segmentation methods, both FCN and U-Net cannot adapt to the shape variability of CNV segmentation and the corresponding results are not satisfactory enough. By introducing attention module, AU-net can suppress the characteristic response of irrelevant background regions and produces improved results. DANet proposes a dual attention network to capture the global feature dependence. Deeplab v3 can adapt to multi-scale changes through the ASPP module. RefineNet attempts to refine the coarse high-level semantic features by exploiting low-level features. CE-Net proposes a context extractor that contains a dense atrous convolution block and a residual multi-kernel pooling block to generate more high-level semantic feature maps. All of the above networks can obviously improve the segmentation accuracies. Comparatively, the proposed model can produce the best segmentation results except UR. Although CE-Net and RefineNet can obtain lower UR, the OR and UR of our method are more balanced.

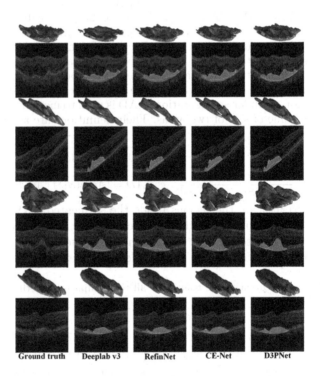

Fig. 7. Visual comparisons of different methods. In each case, the first row shows the 3D segmentation surfaces, and the second row shows the B-scan segmentation results. The red lines circle out ground truth. The red and yellow areas indicate the over- and under-segmentation. The blue areas indicates the areas where are segmented correctly. (Color figure online)

Figure 7 shows the qualitative comparison between our method and other well-performance methods including Deeplab v3, RefineNet and CE-Net among four cases selected from different patients. For the first case, the proposed model performs best at the lower boundary and corners. For the second case, all the other network fail to distinguish the small area on the left of the lesion and their 3D surfaces have obvious deformation. For the third patient, all the three comparison methods divide the lesions into two discontinuous areas for the B-scan, and cannot produce smooth and continuous 3D surfaces. For the last case, both Deeplab v3 and RefineNet fail to locate the left part of the lesions in the B-scan example. The over- and under-segmentation areas obtained by CE-Net are much larger than those of the proposed model. By comparison, the proposed network can produce the most similar results with the ground truth.

Table 2. Quantitative results for the ablation study.

Index	DC	UR	OR	AAD
D3PNet-1	74.60 ± 7.18	14.97 ± 10.34	24.92 ± 11.16	0.054 ± 0.046
D3PNet-2	76.57 ± 3.54	17.89 ± 8.65	19.83 ± 9.28	0.049 ± 0.039
D3PNet	80.06 ± 2.29	13.19 ± 6.03	19.89 ± 7.40	0.043 ± 0.032

In next section, we designed an ablation study by implementing two additional networks to demonstrate the effectiveness of the proposed modules, i.e. the proposed model without the expansive path (D3PNet-1) and the proposed model without guidance path (D3PNet-2). Table 2 reports the evaluation scores of this experiment. Comparing with networks such as DANet, both D3PNet-1 and D3PNet-2 can further improve the segmentation accuracy, which indicates that both paths proposed in our model are efficient in improving CNV segmentation accuracies. D3PNet-1 can alleviate over-segmentation, but introduces more under-segmentation, and D3PNet-2 can greatly solve the under-segmentation. There is an obvious improvement of complete D3PNet compared with D3PNet-1 and 2, which further indicates the effectiveness of the feature fusion strategy.

Figure 8 shows the visualization results of the ablation experiment on the four examples. The first column in Fig. 8 is the histogram of the cubes' segmentation accuracy, and the other three columns shows the 2D segmentation results from corresponding cubes. Comparing the results of D3PNet-1 and D3PNet-2, based on the DUNet, the upsampling strategy in D3PNet-2 can retain more detailed information for the network. However, the DUpsampling obtains the feature of $n \times n \times C'$ by reconstructing a $1 \times 1 \times C$ feature, and there is no correlation among the $n \times n$-sized regions in the upsampled result, which would lead to the problem of rasterization. This leads to the fact that although the evaluation index has been improved, the final results would produce boundary jitter problem. With utilization of the guidance path, the above problems can be alleviated. The generated saliency maps emphasize the location of the lesion, which reduces the over- and under-segmentations. Moreover, the proposed fusion strategy can improve the smoothness of the segmentation boundaries. Therefore, the final segmentation results obtained by the D3PNet can better fit the actual lesion.

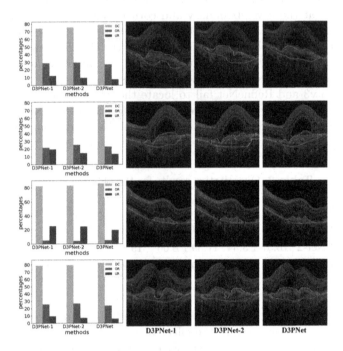

Fig. 8. Visual comparisons for ablation study. The first column is the histogram of the cube segmentation accuracies, and the other three columns show the corresponding 2D segmentation results. The red and yellow lines indicate the contours of ground truth and segmentation results. (Color figure online)

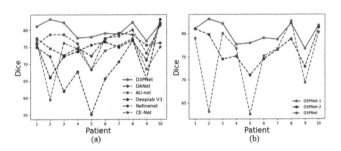

Fig. 9. The cross-validation results for (a) comparison and (b) ablation experiments.

Finally, we present the 10-fold cross-validation results for both experiments. As shown in Fig. 9, the proposed model achieves the best segmentation accuracies for most folds in both experiments, indicating its reliability and generalization.

4 Conclusion

This paper proposes a deep network for CNV lesion segmentation. Considering the unique pathological representations of CNV lesions, we design the network from three aspects, including preserving detailed information, emphasizing contour information and optimizing feature fusion. To this end, we proposes the D3PNet by designing an expansive path, a guidance path and a novel feature fusion strategy. With the utilization of DUpsampling method, the proposed expansive path can preserve more detailed information. The deform blocks are constructed in the guidance path to learn the geometric deformation information of the lesion, and lead the model focusing on the contours of the lesions to generate saliency maps. The proposed feature fusion method can amplify the beneficial features and suppress the useless ones. Experiments demonstrate the superior performances and reliabilities of the proposed network. How to further overcome the problem of rasterization will subject to our future research.

References

1. Lim, L.S., Mitchell, P., Seddon, J.M., Holz, F.G., Wong, T.Y.: Age-related macular degeneration. Lancet **379**(9827), 1728–1738 (2012)
2. Grossniklaus, H.E., Green, W.R.: Choroidal neovascularization. Am. J. Ophthalmol. **137**(3), 496–503 (2004)
3. Framme, C., Panagakis, G., Birngruber, R.: Effects on choroidal neovascularization after anti-VEGF upload using intravitreal ranibizumab, as determined by spectral domain-optical coherence tomography. Invest. Ophthalmol. Vis. Sci. **51**(3), 1671–1676 (2010)
4. Cavallerano, A.A.: Ophthalmic fluorescein angiography. Optom. Clin. Official Publ. Prentice Soc. **5**(1), 1–23 (1996)
5. Bruyère, E., et al.: Spectral-domain optical coherence tomography of subretinal hyperreflective exudation in myopic choroidal neovascularization. Am. J. Ophthalmol. **160**(4), 749–758 (2015)
6. Li, Y., Niu, S., Ji, Z., Fan, W., Yuan, S., Chen, Q.: Automated choroidal neovascularization detection for time series SD-OCT images. In: Frangi, A.F., Schnabel, J.A., Davatzikos, C., Alberola-López, C., Fichtinger, G. (eds.) MICCAI 2018. LNCS, vol. 11071, pp. 381–388. Springer, Cham (2018). https://doi.org/10.1007/978-3-030-00934-2_43
7. Lee, N., Laine, A.F., Theodore Smith, R.: Bayesian transductive Markov random fields for interactive segmentation in retinal disorders. In: Dössel, O., Schlegel, W.C. (eds.) World Congress on Medical Physics and Biomedical Engineering, 7–12 September 2009, Munich, Germany, pp. 227–230. Springer, Heidelberg (2009). https://doi.org/10.1007/978-3-642-03891-4_61
8. Fahmy, A.S., Abdelmoula, W.M., Mahfouz, A.E., Shah, S.M.: Segmentation of choroidal neovascularization lesions in fluorescein angiograms using parametric modeling of the intensity variation. In: 2011 IEEE International Symposium on Biomedical Imaging: From Nano to Macro, pp. 665–668. IEEE (2011)
9. Tsai, C.-L., Yang, Y.-L., Chen, S.-J., Chan, C.-H., Lin, W.-Y.: Automatic characterization and segmentation of classic choroidal neovascularization using adaboost for supervised learning. In: IEEE Nuclear Science Symposuim & Medical Imaging Conference, pp. 3610–3612. IEEE (2010)

10. Long, J., Shelhamer, E., Darrell, T.: Fully convolutional networks for semantic segmentation. In: Proceedings of the IEEE Conference on Computer Vision and Pattern Recognition, pp. 3431–3440 (2015)

11. Ronneberger, O., Fischer, P., Brox, T.: U-net: convolutional networks for biomedical image segmentation. In: Navab, N., Hornegger, J., Wells, W.M., Frangi, A.F. (eds.) MICCAI 2015. LNCS, vol. 9351, pp. 234–241. Springer, Cham (2015). https://doi.org/10.1007/978-3-319-24574-4_28

12. Chen, L.-C., Papandreou, G., Schroff, F., Adam, H.: Rethinking atrous convolution for semantic image segmentation. arXiv preprint arXiv:1706.05587 (2017)

13. Lin, G., Milan, A., Shen, C., Reid, I.: RefineNet: multi-path refinement networks for high-resolution semantic segmentation. In: Proceedings of the IEEE Conference on Computer Vision and Pattern Recognition, pp. 1925–1934 (2017)

14. Zhang, Y., et al.: MPB-CNN: a multi-scale parallel branch CNN for choroidal neovascularization segmentation in SD-OCT images. OSA Continuum **2**(3), 1011–1027 (2019)

15. Wang, J., et al.: Automated diagnosis and segmentation of choroidal neovascularization in OCT angiography using deep learning. Biomed. Opt. Express **11**(2), 927–944 (2020)

16. Xi, X., et al.: Automated segmentation of choroidal neovascularization in optical coherence tomography images using multi-scale convolutional neural networks with structure prior. Multimedia Syst. **25**(2), 95–102 (2019)

17. Tian, Z., He, T., Shen, C., Yan, Y.: Decoders matter for semantic segmentation: Data-dependent decoding enables flexible feature aggregation. In: Proceedings of the IEEE/CVF Conference on Computer Vision and Pattern Recognition, pp. 3126–3135 (2019)

18. Dai, J., et al.: Deformable convolutional networks. In: Proceedings of the IEEE International Conference on Computer Vision, pp. 764–773 (2017)

19. Oktay, O., et al.: Attention U-Net: learning where to look for the pancreas. arXiv preprint arXiv:1804.03999 (2018)

20. Fu, J.: Dual attention network for scene segmentation. In: Proceedings of the IEEE/CVF Conference on Computer Vision and Pattern Recognition, pp. 3146–3154 (2019)

21. Zaiwang, G., et al.: CE-Net: context encoder network for 2D medical image segmentation. IEEE Trans. Med. Imaging **38**(10), 2281–2292 (2019)

A Novel Feature Fusion Network
for Myocardial Infarction Screening Based
on ECG Images

Pengyi Hao, Xin Yin, Fuli Wu[✉], and Fan Zhang

School of Computer Science and Technology, Zhejiang University of Technology,
Hangzhou, China
{haopy,fuliwu}@zjut.edu.cn

Abstract. Myocardial infarction (MI) is a type of cardiovascular diseases (CVDs) with high mortality. Early diagnosis and treatment are crucial to improve survival rate. At present, electrocardiogram (ECG) is a common method for clinical diagnosis of MI, but it requires rich experiences. Hence it is meaningful to design an approach that can screen the MI automatically. In this paper, a feature fusion network is proposed for MI screening based on ECG images, which is composed of heartbeat detection module, local and global feature extraction module, feature fusion and classification module. Firstly, heartbeats are detected from ECG images. Then, heartbeats features are extracted as local features, at the same time, the features extracted from the corresponding ECG image are thought as global features. Finally, classification is designed for judging the input ECG is MI or normal based on fused features. Experiments on two ECG image datasets show the robust performance of the proposed method for MI screening at 99.34% of accuracy, 99.78% of specificity, and 99.64% of sensitivity.

Keywords: MI screening · Convolutional neural network · Feature fusion

1 Introduction

Cardiovascular disease is the number one cause of death in the world, there are about 422.7 million people diagnosed and 17.92 million died in 2015 alone [17]. Myocardial infarction (MI) is a type of CVDs with high mortality. If it is not diagnosed and treated in time, it will further damage the function and structure of the heart, and even make the people die quickly. The early diagnosis of MI can be conducted with an electrocardiogram (ECG). However, the difference between normal ECG and abnormal ECG is very small. It is time-consuming and subjective for a doctor to analyze an electrocardiogram, moreover, some important features in the ECG may be overlooked. Hence, an effective computer-aided diagnosis system can be employed to reduce subjective variabilities in the diagnosis and the time taken in the analysis of ECG signals.

© Springer Nature Switzerland AG 2021
Y. Peng et al. (Eds.): ICIG 2021, LNCS 12889, pp. 547–558, 2021.
https://doi.org/10.1007/978-3-030-87358-5_44

Most of works have been done by incorporating machine learning approaches. These methods can be generally divided into two main parts: (i) feature extraction and selection, (ii) classification. Wavelet transform is one of the widely used approaches to extract features from raw ECG signals [6,9]. Low dimensional feature vectors are obtained by using some statistical methods such as Principal Component Analysis (PCA) and Linear Discriminant Analysis (LDA) [15]. KNN, SVM and Logistic regression are some commonly used classifiers [2,10,18,19]. For example, Acharya et al. [2] studied MI detection and localization with KNN classifier. Sharma et al. [19] used lead II, III and aVF signals to differentiate inferior MI from healthy controls. Kumar et al. [10] explored SVM algorithm for the classification of normal ECG and MI ECG.

Deep learning has made great progress in recent years, a growing number of researchers begin to use deep learning to do the ECG classification task. Some researchers regard ECG signal as a kind of sequential data, so they choose recurrent neural networks for ECG signal classification [20,21]. For example, Yildirim et al. [21] used LSTM for 5 types of heartbeats classification based on ECG signals. Convolutional neural network (CNN) is one of the most commonly used structure to classify ECG signal [1,3,12,13,16]. For instance, Rajpurkar et al. [7] implemented a 34-layer CNN to detect arrhythmic heartbeats. Acharya et al. [3] proposed a 9-layer CNN to distinguish 5 categories of heartbeats. Lodhi et al. [12] designed a 20-layer CNN model using voting strategy to detect MI based on 12-leads signal. Lui et al. [14] developed an MI classifier that combined both CNN and LSTM based on single lead recording.

Most studies are based on one-dimensional ECG signals. However, it is not easy to get the original ECG signals out of the hospital and even in hospital. From the viewpoint of patients, they can only get the printed ECG images. So, doing analysis directly on ECG images is necessary and meaningful. In this study, we focus on MI screening from ECG images, especially from the printed ECGs. A novel MI screening architecture is proposed, which can not only convert ECG signals to be ECG images and then analysis ECG images, but also directly analysis the printed ECGs with 12 leads. In the proposed approach, heartbeats are detected from ECG images, then features of heartbeats are extracted as local features, at the same time, the features extracted from the corresponding ECG image are thought as global features. Finally, feature fusion is explored to further improve the performance of judging the input ECG is MI or normal. The proposed ECG screening approach has excellent automatic feature extraction ability and does not need hand-designed features. It does not need to do preprocessing in this work, which means that the procedure of analysis can be greatly simplified and the information of the data can be retained as much as possible. Experiments on a public dataset and a private dataset have proved the effectiveness of the proposed approach.

2   Method

The overview of procedure is shown in Fig. 1. The model takes the grayscale ECG images as input. For each input image, it can be described as $I_{ecg} \in R^{c \times w \times h}$,

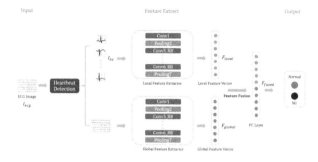

Fig. 1. Overview of the proposed approach

c, w and h represents the channel, width and height of it. Firstly, heartbeats are detected on I_{ecg}, we let $\{I_b^i\}_{i=1}^k$ denote the k heartbeat images, where $I_b^i \in R^{c_b \times m \times n}$ represents the i-th heartbeat image, c_b, m and n is the channel, width and height of it. And then the k heartbeat images are stacked according to the channel dimension to get stacked heartbeats $I_{bs} \in R^{c_b' \times m \times n}$, c_b' is the channel of I_{bs}. Secondly, two feature extractors are designed to extract features, one is used to extract local features from I_{bs}. We call local feature vector as $F_{local} \in R^\alpha$, α represents the size of F_{local}. The other one is explored to extract global features from I_{ecg}. We call global feature vector as $F_{global} \in R^\beta$, β is the size of F_{global}. Finally, the ECG image is classified into normal and MI based on the fused feature $F_{fused} \in R^\gamma$, γ is the size of F_{fused}.

2.1 Heartbeat Detection

In order to obtain a great detection accuracy and acceptable detection speed, we choose Faster R-CNN [4] as our heartbeat detection module. It is mainly composed of the convolution layers, region proposal networks (RPN), ROI pooling and classification layer. Among them, the convolution layers are expected to obtain the feature map of ECG images. Then, heartbeat bounding boxes are generated by RPN. After that, feature maps of bounding boxes extracted by ROI pooling are sent to the subsequent classification layer. Finally, the classification layer outputs the category of bounding box and gets precise coordinates with bounding box regression. In order to obtain the higher accuracy heartbeats, we keep the first 10 bounding boxes for each ECG image by sorting based on their probabilities. Figure 2 gives an example of heartbeat detection.

2.2 Feature Extraction

Considering that ECG images are not very complicated, using complex and deep structure may cause overfitting problem and waste computing resource, so we choose the modified ResNet18 [8] as our feature extractor. Table 1 shows the details of it. For global feature extractor, it receives I_{ecg} with the shape of $1 \times 224 \times 224$. After a series of convolution operations, we get a feature map

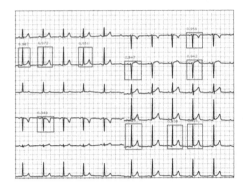

Fig. 2. ECG image with heartbeats bounding boxes (these numbers represent the probability of the corresponding bounding box is considered as heartbeat)

Table 1. The details of feature extractor. Residual blocks are shown in brackets. (kernel number is abbreviated as k, stride is abbreviated as s)

Layer name	Output size	Local feature extractor	Global feature extractor
Conv1	112 × 112	10 × 7 × 7, k = 64, s = 2	1 × 7 × 7, k = 64, s = 2
Pooling2	56 × 56	3 × 3, max-pooling, s = 2	
Conv3_RB	56 × 56	$\begin{pmatrix} 3 \times 3, k = 64 \\ 3 \times 3, k = 64 \end{pmatrix} \times 2$	
Conv4_RB	28 × 28	$\begin{pmatrix} 3 \times 3, k = 128 \\ 3 \times 3, k = 128 \end{pmatrix} \times 2$	
Conv5_RB	14 × 14	$\begin{pmatrix} 3 \times 3, k = 256 \\ 3 \times 3, k = 256 \end{pmatrix} \times 2$	
Conv6_RB	7 × 7	$\begin{pmatrix} 3 \times 3, k = 512 \\ 3 \times 3, k = 512 \end{pmatrix} \times 2$	
Pooling7	1 × 1	7 × 7, max-pooling	Avg-pooling

with the shape of $512 \times 7 \times 7$. It is more suitable for choosing avg-pooling because we want to get more comprehensive features from ECG image. Hence this extractor finally outputs the F_{global} with the size of 512. For local feature extractor, it receives I_{bs} with the shape of $10 \times 224 \times 224$. We replaced avg-pooling in global feature extractor with max-pooling, since we want to emphasize the most valuable information in the heartbeat images. The final output is F_{local} with the size of 512.

2.3 Feature Fusion

Features are the most vital and important information for any excellent classification. The accuracy of the classifier depends largely on the quality of final features. Therefore, in order to obtain the best representation of ECG images, we combine local feature vector and global feature vector. There are two commonly used strategies of feature combination: concatenate and summation. The concatenate indicate that F_{local} and F_{global} joint together. It can be described as Eq. 1. The summation means that F_{local} and F_{global} apply element-wise addition. It can be described as Eq. 2.

$$F_{fused} = F_{local} \oplus F_{global}, \gamma = \alpha + \beta \tag{1}$$

$$F_{fused} = F_{local} + F_{global}, \gamma = \alpha = \beta \tag{2}$$

2.4   Model Training

Considering that we don't have sufficient ECG images, hence we decide to apply transfer learning technology to all modules' training in this paper. We divide the training process into two parts: single module training and integration training.

Single module training means that we train each module separately, so that they can achieve their best performance. For the training of detection module, we first load its pre-trained parameters on COCO dataset [11], then continue to train it on our private dataset. Finally, we get the well trained detection module that can detect heartbeats on ECG image. For the training of two feature extractors. Firstly, we implement two ResNet18 and load its pre-trained parameters on ImageNet dataset. Secondly, we train them on heartbeat images and ECG images separately with Cross-entropy loss function and Adam optimizer. Finally, we remove their last fully connected layer and consider the remaining structure as feature extractor.

Integration training is aiming to integrate above sub-modules into proposed method and make good use of the local and global features. Therefore, by freezing all the parameters of heartbeat detection module, we fine-tune two feature extractors with a smaller learning rate, and update the weights of the last fully connected layer with a larger learning rate. More specifically, we initialize the learning rate of two feature extractors and the last fully connected layer to be $1e-5$ and $1e-2$ respectively. Then we update it twice in the subsequent training. After training for 40 epochs, we get the final well-trained model that has excellent classification ability.

3   Experiments

3.1   Dataset

Public Dataset: PTB Diagnostic ECG Database is a publicly available dataset [5]. It consists of ECG recordings from 200 subjects, including 148 MI and 52 healthy subjects, each subject contains one to five records, and each record has 12 leads of signals. Each signal is sampled 1000 Hz. We use sliding window to cut the original signal into a series of signal slices with a length of 5 s. In order to balance the number of normal and MI samples, the stride for normal and MI samples is 1 s and 3 s separately. Finally, we arrange 12 leads signal according to the standard format of ECG, and generate 22338 ECG images, including 9114 normal and 13224 MI,

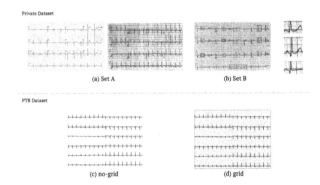

Fig. 3. Examples of ECG images in the two datasets, (a) and (b) are come from private dataset, (c) and (d) are come from PTB dataset

which is named as "no-grid" subset. Based on this subset, we add a standard grid on each image to generate "grid" subset. In the experiments, we will compare the classification performances on these two different ECG images to explore which kind of ECG image is best for MI screening. Figure 3 gives some examples.

Private Dataset: Zhejiang Second People's Hospital of China provided us 2031 printed 12-lead ECG images from distinct patients, among which there are 981 MI images and 1050 normal images. Each image does not contain personal information about the patient. The images have been annotated by several cardiologists and rechecked by an expert. We denote this dataset to be "Set A". They also provided us another 565 ECG images. Each of them has several heartbeat bounding boxes which indicate each heartbeat belongs to normal or abnormal. We crop the heartbeats according to bounding box annotations, resulting in a set of heartbeat images, denoted as "Set B", where there are 5459 heartbeat images, including 2381 normal and 3078 abnormal. Figure 3 gives some examples.

3.2 Evaluation Criteria

All the experiments in this work were implemented with PyTorch 1.2 under Ubuntu 18.04 operating system. All the experiments applied 5-fold cross-validation strategy to ensure that results are relatively accurate. We use four common criteria including accuracy (acc), sentisitivity (sen), specificity (spe), and positive predictive value (ppv) to evaluate the proposed approach. TP is the number of MI correctly classified, TN is the number of normal correctly classified, FP indicates normal classified as MI, and FN indicates MI classified as normal.

$$Accuracy(acc) = \frac{TN + TP}{TN + TP + FN + FP}, Sensitivity(sen) = \frac{TP}{TP + FN}$$

$$Specificity(spe) = \frac{TN}{TN + FP}, Positive\ Predictive\ Value(ppv) = \frac{TP}{TP + FP}$$

Table 2. Heartbeat image classification on set B of private dataset (Acc_{train} means training accuracy and the remaining four scores without subscript represent the testing scores).

Model	Acc_{train}	Acc	Sen	Spe	Ppv
ResNet18	88.06	**84.26**	**84.24**	**85.38**	**88**
ResNet34	88.63	83.79	83.33	83.79	87.09
ResNet50	89.12	82.78	82.55	82.06	85.75

3.3 The Structure of Local Feature Extractor

By classifying normal or abnormal heartbeat images, the structures of local feature extractor will be evaluated and the most suitable structure will be selected. We trained different structures of CNNs like ResNet18, ResNet34 and ResNet50 on the set B of private dataset. Results are shown in Table 2. From this table, we can see that the testing accuracy, sensitivity, specificity and ppv score of ResNet18 are the best, achieved 84.26%, 84.24%, 85.38% and 88% separately. In addition, the gaps of training accuracy and testing accuracy on ResNet18 is 3.8%, in comparison, the gap of training accuracy and testing accuracy on ResNet34 and ResNet50 are 4.84% and 6.34% respectively. It is obvious to find that ResNet18 with fewer layers not only has better performance than ResNet34 and ResNet50, but also has the smallest gap between training accuracy and testing accuracy. It indicates that ResNet18 is enough to extract features from heartbeat images and has the better generalization performance.

3.4 The Structure of Global Feature Extractor

In order to find the most suitable structure for extracting global features, we trained several structures of ResNet on the public dataset and the private dataset (set A). Results are shown in Table 3. First, all the evaluations are significantly higher than the classification using heartbeat images. It implies that the whole ECG images can provide much richer features than heartbeat images. Secondly, we can obviously find that the accuracy, sensitivity, specificity, ppv scores of classification on public dataset are higher than those on private dataset. There may be two reasons. The first reason is that the ECG images in public dataset are directly generated from ECG signals which have better qualities than the ECG images in private dataset where the images are obtained by scanning the printed ECG images. The second reason is that the number of ECG images coming from private dataset is much less than those in public dataset.

Finally, by comparing the accuracy, sensitivity, specificity, ppv scores of no-grid and grid ECG images in public dataset, we can find that the performances of ResNet18, ResNet34, and ResNet50 on these two kinds of ECG images are close. The accuracy on the grid images is slightly higher than that on no-grid images. We believe that is because the effective features of the ECG images are relatively few, and the image without grid is too clean, which is not conductive to improve the generalization ability. In ResNet18, the training accuracy on no-grid and

Table 3. Normal and MI ECG image classification on two datasets (Acc_{train} means training accuracy and the remaining four scores without subscript represent the testing scores).

Model	Dataset		Acc_{train}	Acc	Sen	Spe	Ppv
ResNet18	Public	No-Grid	99.98	98.12	97.86	**99.49**	99.64
		Grid	99.86	**98.5**	**98.57**	98.4	98.92
	Private	Set A	96.67	94.14	93.17	**95.05**	**94.73**
ResNet34	Public	No-Grid	99.97	97.56	97.21	99.52	**99.66**
		Grid	99.89	98.18	97.88	99.47	99.63
	Private	Set A	97.03	**94.29**	**95.62**	93.05	92.81
ResNet50	Public	No-Grid	99.98	97.21	97.07	98.86	99.22
		Grid	99.88	98.35	98.06	98.77	99.15
	Private	Set A	97.16	91.73	92.16	91.33	91.51

grid dataset achieved 99.98% and 99.86% respectively, the testing accuracy on no-grid and grid dataset have declined 1.86% and 1.36% respectively compared to the training accuracy. It is indicated that the model trained with grid dataset have better generalization ability and can achieved higher scores on testing. Moreover, the testing accuracy of ResNet18 has the least decrease compared with the training accuracy. Hence, based on comprehensive consideration, ResNet18 is chose as our global feature extractor.

3.5 Learning Rate

Choosing a suitable learning rate is a vital step in model training. We applied a multistep learning rate strategy in single module training and integration training. It means that we can set different learning rates in different stages of model training. We divide single model training and integrated training into three stages and apply a larger learning rate on stage1, then reduce the learning rate at stage2 and stage3. The specific learning rate configuration is shown in Table 4, and the loss curves in training and testing phase are shown in Fig. 4.

Every loss curve can be divided into two parts, using only global features, and using both global and local features. When using only global features, we can clearly see that when learning rate is changed from $1e-3$ to $1e-4$, both losses are significantly declined especially test loss. And when learning rate is changed from $1e-4$ to $1e-5$, both losses are still declined, but it is no longer obvious. For integration training and testing, we also change the learning rate twice, but the curve tells us that the change of learning rates cannot further reduce loss. It indicates that multistep learning rate strategy can improve the result to a certain extent. Moreover, from Fig. 4 we can find that there is significant decline between single module training/testing and integration training/testing. It indicates that the local features of the heartbeat image do help to expand the global features of the ECG images, and generate new features that are more conducive to the classifier.

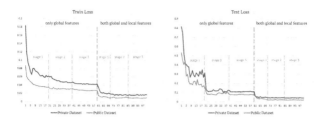

Fig. 4. Loss curves of training and testing.

Table 4. Configuration of learning rates.

	Single module training	Integration training	
	Feature extractors	Feature extractors	Classification layer
Stage1	1e−3	1e−5	1e−2
Stage2	1e−4	1e−6	1e−3
Stage3	1e−5	1e−7	1e−4

3.6 The Types of Feature Fusion

In order to figure out which type of feature fusion is more suitable, we trained our proposed model based on two types of feature fusion. Table 5 shows the results that trained on public dataset ("Grid") and private dataset (set A). "Concat" and "Sum" in the table represent the type of concatenating and the type of summation respectively. For both two datasets, we can see that the performance of model based on two different fusion types are relatively close. The evaluation scores based on "Concat" is little higher than those based on "Sum". The reason may be that "Concat" can not only combine local and global feature, but also not damage the relative integrity of these two features.

3.7 The Performance of the Proposed Approach

Based on the above experiments, we find the optimal structure of our proposed model, where both two feature extractors are modified ResNet18 and feature fusion type is concatenate. In this experiment, we trained our proposed model on public dataset ("Grid") and private dataset (set A) with multistep learning rate strategy. As is shown in Table 5, the final scores of the proposed model have achieved 99.34% of accuracy, 99.64% of sensitivity, 99.78% of specificity and 99.85% of positive predictive value on public dataset, 98.86% of accuracy, 98.88% of sensitivity, 98.57% of specificity and 98.49% of positive predictive value on private dataset.

At present, there are many related researches on the classification of MI based on ECG signals. Table 6 presents the various studies about the classification of MI based on the public database (PTB). All these methods are focus on heartbeats came from single or several leads, it can be noted from Table 6 that

Table 5. Classification results based on different feature fusions.

Dataset	Fusion Type	*Acc*	*Sen*	*Spe*	*Ppv*
Grid	Concat	**99.34**	**99.64**	**99.78**	**99.85**
	Sum	99.13	99.45	98.76	99.15
Set A	Concat	**98.86**	**98.88**	**98.57**	**98.49**
	Sum	98.67	98.62	98.08	98.38

Table 6. Comparison with MI classification approaches from ECG signals based on PTB dataset. The scores of proposed have been bolded.

Study/Year	Lead/Class	Acc	Sen	Spe
Acharya et al. [2] 2016	12 Lead Normal and MI of 10 types	98.74	99.55	99.16
Kumar et al. [10] 2018	Lead-II Normal and MI	99.31	99.62	98.12
Sharma et al. [19] 2018	Lead-II, III and aVF Normal and IMI	98.84	99.35	98.29
Lodhi et al. [12] 2018	12 Lead Normal and MI	93.53	93.71	–
Sadhukhan et al. [18] 2018	Lead-II, III and V2 Normal and MI	95.6	96.5	92.7
Lui et al. [14] 2018	Lead-I Normal, MI other CVD and noisy data	–	92.4	97.7
Proposed	12 Lead Normal and MI	**99.34**	**99.64**	**99.78**

the proposed method performed better than other studies. So, we can believe that our method can understand the underlying of ECG images, thus we might be able to accurately classify the ECG images.

4   Conclusions

In this paper, we proposed an excellent MI screening approach based on ECG images by fusing local features and global features. According to extensive experiments, our modified ResNet18 was used to extract local features and global features. Two kinds of features are fused as concatenate type, and then were fed into classifier for judging MI or normal ECG. By extensive comparisons, our proposed model achieved excellent performance of ECG image classification. For the future, we plan to enhance the adaptability of proposed model for ECG image with different qualities and formats, so that it can play an important role in future healthcare.

Acknowledgements. This work is supported by National Natural Science Foundation of China under grants No.61801428.

References

1. Acharya, U.R., Fujita, H., Oh, S.L., Hagiwara, Y., Tan, J.H., Adam, M.: Application of deep convolutional neural network for automated detection of myocardial infarction using ECG signals. Inf. Sci. **415**, 190–198 (2017)
2. Acharya, U.R., et al.: Automated detection and localization of myocardial infarction using electrocardiogram: a comparative study of different leads. Knowl.-Based Syst. **99**, 146–156 (2016)
3. Acharya, U.R., et al.: A deep convolutional neural network model to classify heartbeats. Comput. Biol. Med. **89**, 389–396 (2017)
4. Girshick, R.: Fast R-CNN. In: Proceedings of the IEEE International Conference on Computer Vision, pp. 1440–1448 (2015)
5. Goldberger, A., et al.: Components of a new research resource for complex physiologic signals. PhysioToolkit Physionet PhysioBank (2000)
6. Güler, İ, Übeylı, E.D.: ECG beat classifier designed by combined neural network model. Pattern Recogn. **38**(2), 199–208 (2005)
7. Hannun, A.Y., et al.: Cardiologist-level arrhythmia detection with convolutional neural networks. Nat. Med. **25**(1), 65–69 (2019)
8. He, K., Zhang, X., Ren, S., Sun, J.: Deep residual learning for image recognition. In: 2016 IEEE Conference on Computer Vision and Pattern Recognition (CVPR), vol. 1, pp. 770–778. IEEE Computer Society (2016)
9. Ince, T., Kiranyaz, S., Gabbouj, M.: A generic and robust system for automated patient-specific classification of ECG signals. IEEE Trans. Biomed. Eng. **56**(5), 1415–1426 (2009)
10. Kumar, M., Pachori, R.B., Rajendra Acharya, U.: Automated diagnosis of atrial fibrillation ECG signals using entropy features extracted from flexible analytic wavelet transform. Biocybernetics Biomed. Eng. **38**(3), 564–573 (2018)
11. Lin, T.-Y., et al.: Microsoft COCO: common objects in context. In: Fleet, D., Pajdla, T., Schiele, B., Tuytelaars, T. (eds.) ECCV 2014. LNCS, vol. 8693, pp. 740–755. Springer, Cham (2014). https://doi.org/10.1007/978-3-319-10602-1_48
12. Lodhi, A.M., Qureshi, A.N., Sharif, U., Ashiq, Z.: A novel approach using voting from ECG leads to detect myocardial infarction. In: Arai, K., Kapoor, S., Bhatia, R. (eds.) IntelliSys 2018. AISC, vol. 869, pp. 337–352. Springer, Cham (2019). https://doi.org/10.1007/978-3-030-01057-7_27
13. Lu, W., Hou, H., Chu, J.: Feature fusion for imbalanced ECG data analysis. Biomed. Signal Process. Control **41**, 152–160 (2018)
14. Lui, H.W., Chow, K.L.: Multiclass classification of myocardial infarction with convolutional and recurrent neural networks for portable ECG devices. Inf. Med. Unlocked **13**, 26–33 (2018)
15. Martis, R.J., Acharya, U.R., Min, L.C.: ECG beat classification using PCA, LDA, ICA and discrete wavelet transform. Biomed. Signal Process. Control **8**(5), 437–448 (2013)
16. Ponomaryov, V., Li, J., Si, Y., Xu, T., Jiang, S.: Deep convolutional neural network based ECG classification system using information fusion and one-hot encoding techniques. Math. Probl. Eng. **2018**, 7354081–7354091 (2018)
17. Roth, G.A., et al.: Global, regional, and national burden of cardiovascular diseases for 10 causes, 1990 to 2015. J. Am. Coll. Cardiol. **70**(1), 1–25 (2017)
18. Sadhukhan, D., Pal, S., Mitra, M.: Automated identification of myocardial infarction using harmonic phase distribution pattern of ECG data. IEEE Trans. Instrum. Meas. **67**(10), 2303–2313 (2018)

19. Sharma, L.D., Sunkaria, R.K.: Inferior myocardial infarction detection using stationary wavelet transform and machine learning approach. SIViP **12**(2), 199–206 (2017). https://doi.org/10.1007/s11760-017-1146-z
20. Tan, J.H., et al.: Application of stacked convolutional and long short-term memory network for accurate identification of cad ECG signals. Comput. Biol. Med. **94**, 19–26 (2018)
21. Yildirim, Ö.: A novel wavelet sequence based on deep bidirectional LSTM network model for ECG signal classification. Comput. Biol. Med. **96**, 189–202 (2018)

Semi-supervised Attention-Guided VNet for Breast Cancer Detection via Multi-task Learning

Yiyao Liu[1], Yi Yang[2], Wei Jiang[3], Tianfu Wang[1], and Baiying Lei[1(✉)]

[1] National-Region Key Technology Engineering Laboratory for Medical Ultrasound, Guangdong Key Laboratory for Biomedical Measurements and Ultrasound Imaging, School of Biomedical Engineering, Health Science Center, Shenzhen University, Shenzhen 518060, China
leiby@szu.edu.cn
[2] Guangdong Medical University, Zhanjiang 524023, China
[3] Department of Ultrasonics, Huazhong University of Science and Technology Union Shenzhen Hospital, Shenzhen 518052, China

Abstract. Due to the rapid increase incidence of breast cancer, automated breast volume scanner (ABVS) is developed to detect breast cancer rapidly and accurately, which can automatically scan the whole breast with less manual operation. However, it is challenging for clinicians to segment the tumor region and further identify the benign and malignant tumors from the ABVS images since it has the large image size and low data quality. For this reason, we propose an effective 3D deep convolutional neural network for multi-task learning from ABVS data. Specifically, a new VNet structure is designed using deep attentive module for performance boosting. In addition, a semi-supervised mechanism is introduced to address the issue of insufficient labeled training data. Due to the difference of the tumor size, we create a two-stage process and fit the small size tumor via volume refinement block for further performance improvement. The experimental results on our self-collected data demonstrate that our model has achieved Dice coefficient of 0.764 for 3D segmentation and F1-score of 81.0% for classification. Our network outperforms the related algorithm as well.

Keywords: 3D breast cancer detection · Automated breast volume scanner · Multi-task learning · Semi-supervised mechanism · Deep attentive module

1 Introduction

According to estimation from the World Health Organization (WHO) in 2015, the incidence rate of breast cancer has reached the second place among all cancers [1]. Among females, breast cancer is the most commonly diagnosed cancer and the leading cause of cancer death. It is clinically meaningful to diagnose the breast cancer more accurate and earlier because of its high incidence and life-threating effect. As a novel method to deliver a 3D visual image of the whole breast, automated breast volume scanner (ABVS)

© Springer Nature Switzerland AG 2021
Y. Peng et al. (Eds.): ICIG 2021, LNCS 12889, pp. 559–570, 2021.
https://doi.org/10.1007/978-3-030-87358-5_45

[2] is developed as a new technology to identify the suspicious breast tumor. However, the clinicians take huge amounts of time for breast tumor contouring, which also requires the experience and operation skills. Also, the breast tumor tends to have various sizes and shapes, and the low data quality causes the segmentation error and classification difficulty.

To address these issues and alleviate the intensity of doctors' work for tumor contouring, various automatic methods have been proposed for segmentation based on neural network methods. For example, Chen et al. applied a 3D fully convolutional network (FCN) for intervertebral disc segmentation [3] and Jesson et al. segmented the brain tumor using a 3D FCN as well [4]. Moreover, Geng et al. applied a feature pyramid network (FPN) [5] for prostate segmentation. Later, Wang et al. proposed a deep attentive feature network (DAF) [6] by improving FPN with attentive mechanism, which can obtain better prostate segmentation results. Apart from FPN based framework, UNet [7] is another appropriate structure for medical image segmentation, which can maintain the semantic information from high layer and the detail feature from low layer by a skip-connection between encoder and decoder. Due to the merits of UNet, Ronneberger et al. first made use of UNet in biomedical area, and then Li et al. applied an improved UNet for liver segmentation on magnetic resonance imaging [8]. Furthermore, many other researchers also used networks based on UNet for medical image segmentation [9–11]. In addition, researchers designed VNet [12] for 3D volume segmentation. To further improve the segmentation performance, some researchers integrate the attention module [13] into segmentation network. Attention mechanism can redistribute the weights of features by training so that the network can focus more on the region of interest when attention module becomes deeper. Therefore, Jiang et al. applied a mixed attention mechanism for liver segmentation in computed tomography volumes [14]. For research on ABVS data, Wang et al. designed a deep supervision network with a novel loss function for breast cancer detection on ABVS data [15]. Multi-task learning [16] has important clinical significance in medical image processing. For example, researchers can obtain the tumor region to discriminate benign and malignant tumors simultaneously. Zhou et al. designed a multi-task framework via VNet for breast tumor segmentation and classification in ABVS dataset [17]. Due to the scarcity of medical imaging data, researchers apply the semi-supervised mechanism for medical image segmentation [18], they generate the pseudo segmentation by forward propagating the augmented images and using the pseudo label for back propagation of loss.

In this study, to address the challenge for ABVS segmentation and tumor classification due to its large image size and low data quality, we propose a deep attentive VNet with multi-task learning. Also, due to the lack of labeled data, a semi-supervised mechanism is incorporated into training process. Experimental results on our self-collected ABVS data shows that our 3D multi-task network achieves quite promising results, which achieves a Dice coefficient of 0.764 and F1-score of 81.0%. In summary, this work has three main contributions: 1) We devise a segment-expert network to fit multi-task learning with a novel deep attentive module (AM) to synthesize the detail information and semantic information for performance improvement. 2) We adopt a semi-supervised training strategy (SS) due to the limited labeled data. 3) We design a volume refine block (VRB) for improving the performance on small tumor.

2   Method

Figure 1 shows the flowchart of the proposed 3D multi-task deep attentive network. The network consists of encoder, decoder, deep attentive block and volume refine block. The multi-task learning contains two main tasks of classification and segmentation, and an auxiliary task of feature reconstruction.

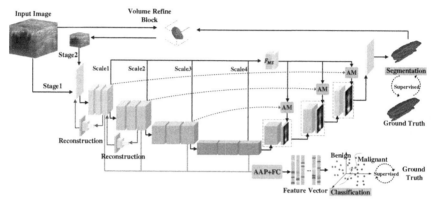

Fig. 1. Architecture of the proposed 3D multi-task deep attentive network, which includes the volume refine block, deep attentive module and three tasks. AAP denotes the adaptive average pooling, FC denotes the fully connected network, AM denotes the deep attentive module and F_{MS} denotes the multi-scale feature.

2.1   Proposed Network Architecture

The backbone of our model is VNet, which fits 3D volumetric image. In each encoder block, we apply up to two feature extractor, which contains 3D convolutional layers, batch normalization layers and rectified linear unit [19] layers. Furthermore, each decoder block possesses an adaptive upsample layer to meet different input sizes in stage 2 and an additional concatenation layer. To classify the benign and malignant tumors, we adopt four 3D adaptive average pooling layers ($1 \times 1 \times 1$) for channel-wise feature extraction, and then apply two fully connected layers for mapping features and classifications. Apart from the two main tasks, an auxiliary task is designed for feature extraction.

2.2   Deep Attentive Module

The feature maps from shallow layers contain the detail texture and margin information of tumor, and the feature maps from deep layers catch the high-level semantic information [20]. Figure 2 illustrates the proposed deep attentive module which is combined with the multi-scale attention map and local feature.

To integrate the detail information and semantic information, a branch of the attentive module concatenates each feature from different stages of encoder, which generates the multi-scale feature via resample layer, $1 \times 1 \times 1$ convolutional layer, group normalization and ReLU layer. Simultaneously, another branch acquires element-wise summation of the corresponding encoder and decoder feature via $1 \times 1 \times 1$ convolutional layer and to explore the local attention map via a sigmoid activation layer. Next, the module combines the multi-feature and local attention map to synthesize the multi-local attention map. Ultimately, by element-wise multiplying the attention map and the local feature from encoder, we can obtain the attention-guided feature. The process of forming the attention-guided feature:

$$\mathcal{F} = \left[\sigma\left(\mathcal{F}_i^s \oplus \mathcal{F}_i^l\right) \otimes \left(\sum_i^N \otimes \mathcal{F}_i^s\right)\right] \times \mathcal{F}_i^s, \tag{1}$$

where $\mathcal{F}$ represents the attention-guided can be described as the formula feature, $\mathcal{F}_i^s$ denotes the feature comes from each scale and $\mathcal{F}_i^l$ denotes the feature comes from the decoder. $\oplus$ is the element-wise summation, $\otimes$ is the concatenate operation, $\times$ means the element-wise multiplying and σ is sigmoid function. In the backbone network, we utilize the attention-guided feature as the residual connection to concatenate with the decoder feature.

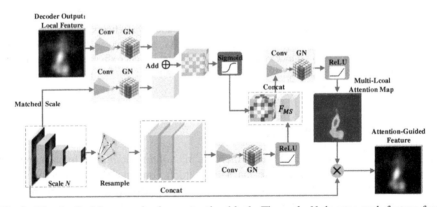

Fig. 2. The detailed framework of our attention block. The scale N denotes each feature from different stages of encoder and F_{MS} denotes the multi-scale feature. GN means the group normalization layer and Concat denotes the concatenate operation.

2.3 Semi-supervised Mechanism

Generally, medical data lacks the label information and reading medical clinical images is time-consuming due to the lack of experienced clinicians. Particularly, it is difficult to analyze images because of the small tumor size and low quality of ABVS image. Apart from utilizing the unlabeled data, semi-supervised learning can also improve the generalization ability of the model [21]. For this reason, we integrate a novel semi-supervised mechanism into the training process, which is shown in Fig. 3.

We denote the labeled data as $S_l\{x_i, seg_i, cls_i\}$ and denote the unlabeled data as $S_u\{x_i, \_, cls_i\}$, $S_u\{x_i, seg_i, \_\}$ and $S_u\{x_i, \_, \_\}$, which represent the data with classification label only, the data with segmentation label only and the data without neither classification nor segmentation label, respectively.

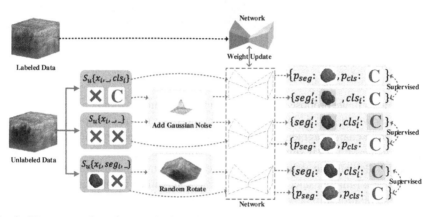

Fig. 3. The proposed semi-supervised mechanism. The unlabeled data was divided into three parts: $S_u\{x_i, \_, cls_i\}$, $S_u\{x_i, \_, \_\}$ and $S_u\{x_i, seg_i, \_\}$. We use two different augmentation methods: adding Gaussian noise and rotation.

Three different kinds of unlabeled data are augmented by different methods. The $S_u\{x_i, \_, cls_i\}$ and $S_u\{x_i, \_, \_\}$ are added Gaussian noise while $S_u\{x_i, seg_i, \_\}$ is rotated. In the training, we put the augmented unlabeled data in the forward propagation to obtain the pseudo segmentation label as seg_i' and pseudo classification label as cls_i'. To calculate the loss function, the original unlabeled data are put into the network to produce the predicted segmentation as p_{seg} and predicted classification as p_{cls}. After that, the loss is calculated by prediction and the hybrid label which is combined with real and pseudo label:

$$\mathcal{L} = \mathcal{L}_{cls}\{p_{cls}, (cls_i or cls_i')\} + \mathcal{L}_{seg}\{p_{seg}, (seg_i \ or \ seg_i')\} + \mathcal{L}_{recon}. \tag{2}$$

2.4 Volume Refine Block

The large range of tumor volume difference is a great challenge in our study. According to our statistics, the volume of tumor is from 1.51×10^2 to 1.18×10^6 mm^3, and leading to poor results for small tumors by such a huge difference. From Fig. 4, we can intuitively understand the huge difference in tumor volume. In the preprocess, we crop the original image data into the same size ($64 \times 256 \times 256$) due to the limitation of Graphics Processing Unit (GPU) memory. However, putting the same size image into network training will reduce the accuracy of segmentation and classification. Because the image can only contain limited texture and margin information of a small tumor but abundant useless background.

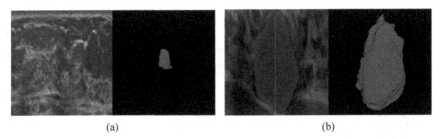

Fig. 4. The small tumor (a) and huge tumor (b) display in 2D and 3D vision.

To address it, we propose a novel two-stage model and a volume refine block (VRB) which is shown in Fig. 5. In the stage 1, the network utilizes the pre-cropped image and emerges a coarse segmentation. Then putting the coarse segmentation and the pre-cropped image into VRB simultaneously for volume refinement. In the VRB, first, the block will calculate the volume ratio of the coarse tumor segmentation to the entire image for small tumors selection. We generate a maximum connected domain by considering the relationship between the center element and its 26 nearest neighbors. And composing a cube boundary based on the maximum connected domain. Finally, the module will re-crop the image according to the cube boundary and put it into the stage 2 for a delicately segmentation and classification. The result of this operation reduces the irrelevant background information and improve the performance of the model.

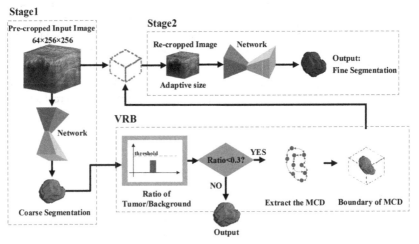

Fig. 5. The workflow of volume refine block. The MCD denotes the maximum connected domain and VRB denotes volume refine block.

2.5 Multi-task Learning with Hybrid Loss

In our study, we propose a novel multi-task learning loss, which can produce a better result efficiently. The segmentation network will focus on the margin and inner feature of tumor, and these features promote the classification performance. In addition, another auxiliary reconstruction task is effective for the feature extraction process.

The segmentation task works on the pixel level scale and classification task works on the tumor level or pixels aggregation level. We think when the classification task makes a macroscopic classification of the tumor, it is meaningful for the segmentation task to classify at the pixel level. And the segmentation task will help to refine the volume to reduce the abundant useless background information and makes more accurate on classification. The auxiliary reconstruction task works for restricting the feature extraction process.

To achieve it, we design a hybrid loss function by associating segmentation, classification tasks and the auxiliary feature reconstruction task. In segmentation task, two types of loss functions, binary cross entropy loss (BCELoss) and Dice loss are involved, which are defined as:

$$\mathcal{L}_{bce} = \sum_{i=0}^{k=1} \left(-y_i * \log y_i - (1 - y_i) \log(1 - y_i) \right) \tag{3}$$

$$\mathcal{L}_{dc} = 1 - \frac{2 * \left| \hat{Y}_i \cap Y_i \right|}{\left| \hat{Y}_i \right| + |Y_i|}, \tag{4}$$

where $\mathcal{L}_{bce}$ is a binary cross entropy loss, y_i denotes the classification ground truth. The Dice loss is represented by $\mathcal{L}_{dc}$, $\hat{Y}_i$ means the predicted segmentation region and Y_i is the real tumor region labeled by clinicians.

In classification task, to solve the imbalance of category, the focal loss [22] was introduced into our network as classification task loss, which is defined as:

$$\mathcal{L}_{cls} = -\frac{1}{n} \sum_{i=1}^{n} \left[\alpha y_i (1 - p_i)^\gamma \log(p_i) + (1 - \alpha)(1 - y_i) p_i^\gamma \log(1 - p_i) \right], \tag{5}$$

where y_i denotes the classification label, p_i denotes the possibility of prediction, n represents the total number of samples, α reduces the impact of loss on the larger party and γ always be set to 2.

To reduce the loss of information, we apply the L2 loss between the reconstruction feature and original feature as:

$$\mathcal{L}_{recon} = \| F_{recon} - F_{ori} \|_2, \tag{6}$$

where $\mathcal{L}_{recon}$ denotes the loss of reconstruction task, F_{recon} represents the reconstruction feature and F_{ori} is original feature.

The final hybrid loss is formulated as:

$$loss = \lambda_1 \mathcal{L}_{bce} + \lambda_2 \mathcal{L}_{dc} + \lambda_3 \mathcal{L}_{cls} + \lambda_4 \mathcal{L}_{recon}, \tag{7}$$

where λ_1, λ_2, λ_3 and λ_4 are the weights of are set to 0.3, 1.0, 4.0 and 0.2 empirically.

3 Experiment

Dataset. In this study, we have 92 valid volumes with labels, and we perform histogram equalization for preprocessing. Since data has the huge amount of volume, each volume is cropped into ($64 \times 256 \times 256$) by the center of tumor to utilize GPU.

Implementation Details. The experiment is carried out by 5-fold cross validation. We use the PyTorch framework to train the models on a single TITAN RTX GPU with 24GB memory. During the training process, the initial learning rate is set to 10^{-4} and utilizes a learning rate decay mechanism with 0.85 decay coefficient. We set 200 epochs for experiments and in each epoch the batch size is set to 1 for fitting the different input size in stage2 and the limitation of GPU memory.

Results and Comparison with Other Methods. To further verify the effectiveness of our network, we compare it with several current models such as UNet, 3D FCN, 3D PSP, VNet and DAF network. The comparison results on segmentation task via the combination of 5-fold cross validation are shown in Table 1. From Table 1, it shows that our model has achieved the best score among all networks on segmentation task. We can see that our model has the highest mean Dice coefficient as formula (8) of 0.764. Furthermore, in other metrics, our model also performs quite well and is almost close to the best score in terms of Jaccard similarity coefficient and 95% Hausdorff distance (HD_95) as formula (9) and (10). Additionally, DAF also has a relatively good segmentation score, but the scores of original UNet and VNet are not satisfactory.

$$Dice = \frac{2 * \left| \hat{Y}_i \cap Y_i \right|}{\left| \hat{Y}_i \right| + |Y_i|}, \tag{8}$$

$$Jaccard = \frac{\left| \hat{Y}_i \cap Y_i \right|}{\left| \hat{Y}_i \cup Y_i \right|}, \tag{9}$$

$$HD\_95 = max \left\{ \underset{\hat{y}_i \in \hat{Y}_i}{max} \underset{y_i \in Y_i}{min} d\left(\hat{y}_i, y_i\right), \underset{y_i \in Y_i}{max} \underset{\hat{y}_i \in \hat{Y}_i}{min} d\left(\hat{y}_i, y_i\right) \right\}, \tag{10}$$

Where $\hat{Y}_i$ means the predicted segmentation region, Y_i is the real tumor region labeled by clinicians, $\hat{y}_i$ and y_i is the boundary element in $\hat{Y}_i$ and Y_i respectively. And $d(\hat{y}_i, y_i)$ means the distance between the $\hat{y}_i$ and y_i.

To have a more intuitive interpretation, we visualize the results of the segmentation in two ways. Figure 6 is the 3D segmentation results with different methods. Each column of Fig. 6 shows different volumes image, and images in the first row are the results of UNet, the second column are the results of VNet, the third column are results of 3D PSP, the fourth column are the results of DAF and the last column are the results of our model. The color in Fig. 6 represents the distance between the prediction and ground truth, where red and blue denotes the further distance and green denotes closer distance.

Table 1. Segmentation comparison with different methods. The Seg-PRE, Seg-SEN and Seg-SPE are the pixel level precision, sensitivity and specificity.

Method	Dice	Jaccard	Seg-PRE	Seg-SEN	Seg-SPE	HD_95(vox)
3D FCN	0.632 ± 0.106	0.470 ± 0.112	0.623 ± 0.191	0.726 ± 0.163	0.970 ± 0.192	25.3 ± 12.0
UNet	0.612 ± 0.146	0.456 ± 0.144	0.510 ± 0.176	$\mathbf{0.886 \pm 0.159}$	0.971 ± 0.206	19.9 ± 12.1
VNet	0.608 ± 0.141	0.451 ± 0.145	0.553 ± 0.246	0.839 ± 0.158	0.949 ± 0.393	21.7 ± 10.9
3D PSP	0.628 ± 0.120	0.468 ± 0.122	0.616 ± 0.200	0.720 ± 0.156	$\mathbf{0.980 \pm 0.148}$	21.8 ± 11.2
DAF	0.734 ± 0.115	0.592 ± 0.131	$\mathbf{0.726 \pm 0.164}$	0.813 ± 0.141	0.973 ± 0.446	15.8 ± 14.3
Ours	$\mathbf{0.764 \pm 0.104}$	$\mathbf{0.624 \pm 0.096}$	0.711 ± 0.177	0.791 ± 0.144	0.977 ± 0.224	$\mathbf{10.7 \pm 5.2}$

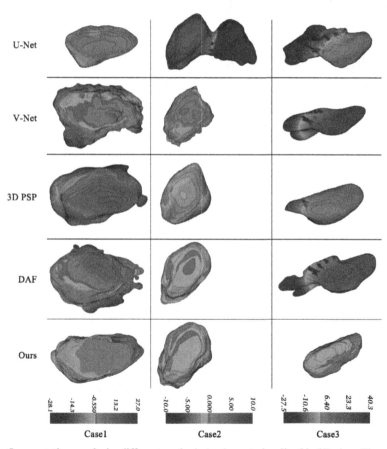

Fig. 6. Segmentation results by different methods (each row) visualized in 3D view. The red area indicates the predicted boundary is out of the real boundary, the blue area indicates the predicted boundary is inside the real boundary, and green area indicates close to the real segmentation. (Color figure online)

Figure 7(a) is the 2D segmentation visualization results with different methods, where each column denotes different volumes image. The upper images are from the original data. In Fig. 7(a), the pictures above are cropped original images with the ground truth in red area. In the pictures below, the red line is ground truth, the blue line is labeled by VNet, the yellow line is labeled by UNet, the purple line is labeled by 3D PSP, the pink line is labeled by DAF network and the green line is labeled by our model. We can see that the green line is always the closest to the ground truth.

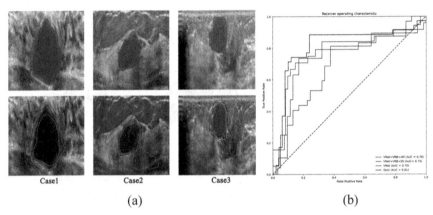

Fig. 7. (a) Segmentation results by different methods visualized in 2D view. The pictures above are cropped original images with the ground truth in red area. The red line is ground truth, the blue line is labeled by VNet, the yellow line is labeled by UNet, the purple line is labeled by 3D PSP, the pink line is labeled by DAF network and the green line is labeled by our model. (b) ROC curves and AUC metrics of different modules. Our method is the green curve which reaches the AUC of 0.81. (Color figure online)

Ablation Studies. In order to illustrate the effectiveness of each module clearly, we have performed numerous ablation experiments. Table 2 shows the effectiveness of different modules. As for the classification task, we get the accuracy of 82.4%, the precision of 74.4%, recall of 88.9%, AUC of 0.81 and F1-score of 81.0%. We can observe that designed modules improve the performance greatly. From Table 2, it is obvious that VRB significantly improves the performance on both classification and segmentation tasks, because the small volume tumor can have great impact on the results. Furthermore, the attentive module raises the results of the segmentation tasks and semi-supervised mechanism is meaningful in the network. Figure 7(b) shows the receiver operating characteristic (ROC) and the area under ROC curve (AUC) which manifests the designed modules contribute to classification task.

Table 2. Ablation studies in segmentation and classification tasks. AM denotes the deep attentive module, SS denotes the semi-supervised mechanism and VRB denotes the volume refine block. The baseline method is VNet.

AM	SS	Task VRB	SEG Dice(%)	Jaccard(%)	HD_95(vox)	CLS Acc	Rec	Pre	F1-Score
x	x	x	0.608 ± 0.141	0.451 ± 0.145	21.7 ± 10.9	0.647	0.688	0.524	0.595
√	x	√	0.745 ± 0.111	0.598 ± 0.132	11.6 ± 7.8	0.670	0.680	0.629	0.653
x	√	√	0.722 ± 0.119	0.587 ± 0.129	14.3 ± 13.2	0.635	0.692	0.600	0.642
√	√	√	0.764 ± 0.104	0.624 ± 0.096	10.7 ± 5.2	0.824	0.889	0.744	0.810

4 Conclusion

In this paper, we propose a novel network based on VNet with innovative modules which aims at breast tumor segmentation and classification. To achieve this, we integrate deep attentive module, volume refine block and multi-task learning method into VNet. We design a semi-supervised learning in training process due to a lack of labeled data. To this end, we address the 3D segmentation and classification challenge of various sizes of tumor and low data quality in ABVS data. The experimental results illustrate that our model can deliver the most satisfactory tumor segmentation and classification performance compared with other models.

Acknowledgements. This work was supported partly by National Natural Science Foundation of China (Nos. 62001302 and 61871274), Key Laboratory of Medical Image Processing of Guangdong Province (No. 2017B030314133), Guangdong Basic and Applied Basic Research Foundation (Nos. 2021A1515011348, 2019A1515111205), and Shenzhen Key Basic Research Project (Nos. JCYJ20170818 094109846, JCYJ20190808145011259, RCBS20200714114920379).

References

1. Bray, F., Ferlay, J., Soerjomataram, I., et al.: Global cancer statistics 2018: GLOBOCAN estimates of incidence and mortality worldwide for 36 cancers in 185 countries. CA Cancer J. Clin. **68**(6), 394–424 (2018)
2. Schmachtenberg, C., Fischer, T., Hamm, B., et al.: Diagnostic performance of automated breast volume scanning (ABVS) compared to handheld ultrasonography with breast MRI as the gold standard. Acad. Radiol. **24**(8), 954–961 (2017)
3. Chen, H., Dou, Q., Wang, X., Qin, J., Cheng, J.C.Y., Heng, P.-A.: 3D fully convolutional networks for intervertebral disc localization and segmentation. In: Zheng, G., Liao, H., Jannin, P., Cattin, P., Lee, S.-L. (eds.) MIAR 2016. LNCS, vol. 9805, pp. 375–382. Springer, Cham (2016). https://doi.org/10.1007/978-3-319-43775-0_34
4. Jesson, A., Arbel, T.: Brain tumor segmentation using a 3D FCN with multi-scale loss . In: Crimi, A., Bakas, S., Kuijf, H., Menze, B., Reyes, M. (eds.) BrainLes 2017. LNCS, vol. 10670, pp. 392–402. Springer, Cham (2018). https://doi.org/10.1007/978-3-319-75238-9_34
5. Geng, L., Li, S.M., Xiao, Z.T., et al.: Multi-channel feature pyramid networks for prostate segmentation, based on transrectal ultrasound imaging. Appl. Sci.-Basel **10**(11), 12 (2020)

6. Wang, Y., Dou, H., Hu, X., et al.: Deep attentive features for prostate segmentation in 3D transrectal ultrasound. IEEE Trans. Med. Imaging **38**(12), 2768–2778 (2019)

7. Ronneberger, O., Fischer, P., Brox, T.: U-Net: Convolutional Networks for Biomedical Image Segmentation. In: Navab, N., Hornegger, J., Wells, W., Frangi, A. (eds.) Medical Image Computing and Computer-Assisted Intervention – MICCAI 2015. MICCAI 2015. Lecture Notes in Computer Science, vol. 9351. Springer, Cham (2015). https://doi.org/10.1007/978-3-319-24574-4_28

8. Agarwal, R., Diaz, O., Llado, X., et al.: Lesion segmentation in automated 3d breast ultrasound: volumetric analysis. Ultrason Imaging **40**(2), 97–112 (2018)

9. Çiçek, Ö., Abdulkadir, A., Lienkamp, S.S., Brox, T., Ronneberger, O.: 3D U-Net: learning dense volumetric segmentation from sparse annotation. In: Ourselin, S., Joskowicz, L., Sabuncu, M.R., Unal, G., Wells, W. (eds.) MICCAI 2016. LNCS, vol. 9901, pp. 424–432. Springer, Cham (2016). https://doi.org/10.1007/978-3-319-46723-8_49

10. Dong, X., Lei, Y., Wang, T., et al.: Automatic multiorgan segmentation in thorax CT images using U-net-GAN. Med. Phys. **46**(5), 2157–2168 (2019)

11. Oktay, O., Schlemper, J., Folgoc, L.L., et al.: Attention u-net: Learning where to look for the pancreas. arXiv:1804.03999 (2018)

12. Milletari, F., Navab, N., Ahmadi, S.-A.: V-net: fully convolutional neural networks for volumetric medical image segmentation. In: 2016 fourth international conference on 3D vision (3DV), pp. 565–571. IEEE (2016)

13. Du, J.C., Gui, L., He, Y.L., et al.: Convolution-based neural attention with applications to sentiment classification. IEEE Access **7**, 27983–27992 (2019)

14. Jiang, H., Shi, T., Bai, Z., et al.: Ahcnet: An application of attention mechanism and hybrid connection for liver tumor segmentation in CT volumes. IEEE Access **7**, 24898–24909 (2019)

15. Wang, Y., Wang, N., Xu, M., et al.: Deeply-supervised networks with threshold loss for cancer detection in automated breast ultrasound. IEEE Trans Med Imaging **39**(4), 866–876 (2020)

16. Vandenhende, S., Georgoulis, S., Proesmans, M., et al.: Revisiting multi-task learning in the deep learning era. arXiv:2004.13379 (2020)

17. Zhou, Y., Chen, H., Li, Y., et al.: Multi-task learning for segmentation and classification of tumors in 3D automated breast ultrasound images. Med. Image Anal. **70**, 101918 (2021)

18. Li, X., Lequan, Y., Chen, H., Chi-Wing, F., Xing, L., Heng, P.-A.: Transformation-consistent self-ensembling model for semisupervised medical image segmentation. IEEE Trans. Neural Netw. Learn. Syst. **32**(2), 523–534 (2021). https://doi.org/10.1109/TNNLS.2020.2995319

19. Glorot, X., Bordes, A., and Bengio, Y.: Deep sparse rectifier neural networks. In: Proceedings of the Fourteenth International Conference on Artificial Intelligence and Statistics, pp. 315–323. JMLR Workshop and Conference Proceedings (2011)

20. Woo, S., Park, J., Lee, J.-Y., Kweon, I.S.: CBAM: convolutional block attention module. In: Ferrari, V., Hebert, M., Sminchisescu, C., Weiss, Y. (eds.) ECCV 2018. LNCS, vol. 11211, pp. 3–19. Springer, Cham (2018). https://doi.org/10.1007/978-3-030-01234-2_1

21. Ragesh, R., Sellamanickam, S., Lingam, V., et al.: A Graph Convolutional Network Composition Framework for Semi-supervised Classification. arXiv:2004.03994 (2020)

22. Lin, T.-Y., Goyal, P., Girshick, R., et al.: Focal loss for dense object detection. In: Proceedings of the IEEE International Conference on Computer Vision, pp. 2980–2988 (2017)

Cross-Domain Transfer Learning for Vessel Segmentation in Computed Tomographic Coronary Angiographic Images

Ruirui An[1], Tao Han[1], Yining Wang[2(✉)], Danni Ai[1(✉)], Yongtian Wang[1], and Jian Yang[1]

[1] Beijing Engineering Research Center of Mixed Reality and Advanced Display, School of Optics and Photonics, Beijing Institute of Technology, Beijing 100081, China
danni@bit.edu.cn

[2] Department of Radiology, Peking Union Medical College Hospital, Chinese Academy of Medical Sciences and Peking Union Medical College, Beijing 100730, China

Abstract. Segmenting coronary arteries in computed tomographic angiography images is an essential procedure for coronary artery disease diagnosis. However, it still remains challenging due to the insufficient annotation data for supervised deep learning methods. To solve this problem, we propose a novel cross-domain transfer learning network to adaptively transfer knowledge learned from public liver vessel dataset for coronary artery segmentation. The signed distance map learning task is joined to enforce the network to transfer tubular structure knowledge from the liver vessel. Moreover, an adaptive feature-selection module is used to determine the optimal fine-tune strategy for every target sample. We conduct ablation experiments to demonstrate the effectiveness of the auxiliary task and module. We also compare the proposed method with other state-of-the-art transfer learning and segmentation methods. Results showed that our method achieve the best performance on accurate coronary artery segmentation. Our method achieves the best *Dice* score of 81.60%, an improvement of at least 1% with respect to other methods.

Keywords: Transfer learning · Cross domain · Coronary artery segmentation

1 Introduction

Coronary artery disease (CAD), which is mainly caused by atherosclerosis, has become one of the most serious threats to human health. Computed tomography angiography (CTA) can provide high-resolution 3D visualization of the coronary arteries and is a non-invasive imaging modality, which has been a popular way to diagnose CAD [1, 2]. Accurate vessel segmentation is an essential procedure for disease diagnosis. Deep learning methods, especially CNNs have shown tremendous potential for performing medical image segmentation task. However, vessel extraction in CTA still remains challenging due to (a) insufficient training data, as annotation of CTA image is time-consuming and

© Springer Nature Switzerland AG 2021
Y. Peng et al. (Eds.): ICIG 2021, LNCS 12889, pp. 571–583, 2021.
https://doi.org/10.1007/978-3-030-87358-5_46

difficult without professional training, and (b) low contrast, noise, and other pseudo vessel structures in CTA images.

In recent years, researchers have studied various excellent approaches to solve these problems, which can be classified into two categories: learning-free methods and learning-based methods. Learning-free methods, such as enhancement-based methods [3, 4], region-growing approaches [5, 6], and level set methods [7, 8], do not need ground truth annotation, so insufficient data is not a problem for them. However, these methods extract blood vessels on the basis of hand-designed feature filters, causing intolerable over-segmentation or under-segmentation in vessel prediction masks.

Learning-based methods, especially Unet and its variants [9–11], have shown excellent ability for medical image segmentation. These supervised deep learning methods need abundant annotation data to avoid over-fitting and obtain ideal results. However, as we mentioned before, publicly accessible annotated datasets for coronary artery segmentation task are scarce. Data augmentation [10, 12–16] and transfer training [17–19] have served as two effective approaches to tackle this problem. Traditional data augmentation operations [10, 13], such as rotation, scaling, random elastic deformations, gamma correction, and Gaussian noise, have become generally-used tricks for reducing overfitting and improving test performance. However, the improvement is limited due to the large similarity between original data and augmented examples. Synthetic data augmentation methods [14–16] are emerging with the rapid development of GANs. For instance, SC-GAN [14] exploits publicly available annotated retinal vessel images to synthesize images consisting of coronary background, retinal vessels, and coronary arteries. These generated images are used to train coronary artery segmentation network. However, it is difficult to synthesize coronary CTA images that contain complex structures. For transfer learning methods, natural images are widely used as the source domain for medical image classification [17, 18], but are not regularly seen in medical image segmentation. Moreover, pre-trained 2D models are not suitable for 3D medical images due to the absence of spatial information. Med3D [19] builds a large 3D medical dataset from different domains and trains a general segmentation network, but it does not perform well on vessel extraction.

In order to obtain more accurate vessel trees with limited training data, we propose a novel transfer learning framework to adaptively transfer knowledge from publicly available liver vessel dataset [20]. We consider transfer strategy and feature similarity to improve the performance of the network on target task. An adaptive feature-selection module (AFSM) is applied to decide which layers of the pre-trained model should be fine-tuned or frozen for each input sample, different from common fine-tune strategies [18, 21, 22]. Moreover, due to the similar tubular structure between liver vessels and coronary arteries, the segmentation network combines the signed distance map (SDM) learning task [23] for coronary artery extraction.

The contributions of this study are as follows: 1) we propose a novel cross-domain transfer learning method, which is a new attempt to transfer from distant medical domain for vessel segmentation; 2) AFSM, a novel transfer strategy, is applied to adaptively decide which layers of the pre-trained model should be fine-tuned or frozen for each input sample; and 3) we additionally join SDM learning task to encourage the network to transfer structure knowledge from pre-trained model and improve the performance of vessel boundary prediction.

2 Methods

2.1 Network Architecture

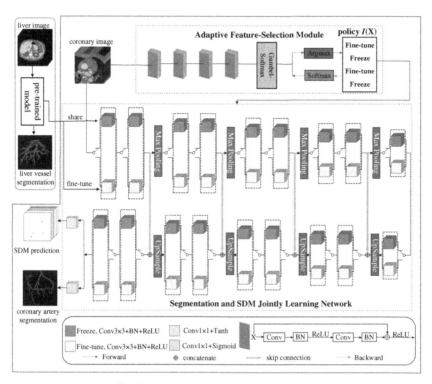

Fig. 1. The proposed network architecture.

We design a novel cross-domain transfer learning framework based on feature adaptation as shown in Fig. 1. In the source domain, we focus on training a Unet pre-trained model on liver vessel data (source data). Due to the large z-axis spacing of the liver image, 3D Unet is not suitable for the spatial knowledge transfer. Therefore, a 2D segmentation structure is chosen. In order to take advantage of the spatial and contextual information, the inputs are composed of eight channels of continuous slices from CTA images. In the target domain, the pre-processed images are first put into AFSM that contains four residual blocks [24] to make decisions to freeze or fine-tune parameters for each layer of the segmentation and SDM jointly learning (SSJL) network during training. Finally, the pre-processed images dynamically swap the SSJL network on the basis of the above decisions. We create a parameter-frozen network branch and a trainable branch. Both are initialized with the parameters of the pre-trained model. Compared with the pre-trained model, the coronary artery segmentation network combines an additional SDM output besides segmentation mask to transfer knowledge about tubular structure features.

2.2 AFSM

Fine-tuning has become the most widely used approach for transfer learning. However, the number of layers to freeze during fine-tuning is still determined artificially or by conducting several experiments, which is time-consuming and a waste of resources. Moreover, every target input instance may suit different fine-tuning strategies to achieve optimal performance. Therefore, an input-dependent approach that can automatically determine whether the layer should be fine-tuned is extremely meaningful. Inspired by SpotTune [26], we apply the policy network of SpotTune as AFSM to generate freeze or fine-tune decisions. Different from SpotTune, we focus on a Unet-like model instead of ResNet for the task network, as the former consists of an encoder, decoder, and skip connection that can combine low-level and high-level features, which is beneficial for medical image segmentation.

In order to avoid vanishing gradients, ResNet blocks are applied in AFSM. The output of the ResNet blocks contains two channels that describe the probability distribution of two categories (freeze or fine-tune). Gumbel Softmax trick[25] is used to draw samples from the categorical distribution α_1 and α_2 in the following way. A random variable G that has a standard Gumbel distribution, is defined as $G = -\log(-\log(U))$, where U is with uniform distribution. G_1 and G_2 are first sampled from $Gumbel(0,1)$. Then, the discrete output decision is generated as follows:

$$I = \operatorname*{argmax}_{i}\big[log\alpha_i + G_i\big](i = 1, 2) \tag{1}$$

It would be difficult to optimize the overall network with back-propagation as the output decisions are discrete. Argmax operation is replaced with softmax to make the network calculate gradients. The output vector O for softmax operation is calculated as follows:

$$O_i = \frac{\exp((log\alpha_i + G_i)/\tau)}{\sum_{i=1}^{2} \exp((log\alpha_i + G_i)/\tau)}(i = 1, 2) \tag{2}$$

where τ is a parameter that controls the discreteness of O.

2.3 SSJL Network

Given a point in image space, the absolute value of SDM is calculated by the distance between the point and the nearest vascular boundary point. The vessel belongs to tubular structure, which can be described by centerline and radius. The inside vessel points with the maximum absolute SDM value which represents radius of the cross-section form the centerline. Therefore, the SDM learning task is beneficial for the network to transfer structure knowledge from the pre-trained model owing to the high-level analogous tubular feature between source and target data.

As the accurate SDM prediction for the pixels close to the vessel is more important than those far away from the vessel, the original definition of SDM is adjusted to place more attention on the vessels and their surroundings. The SDM is newly defined as:

$$\phi(x) = \begin{cases} 0, x \in S \\ -\inf_{y \in S} ||x - y||, x \in \Omega_{in} \\ +\inf_{y \in S} ||x - y||, x \in \Omega_{out} \text{and} \inf_{y \in S} ||x - y|| \leq 10 \\ 10, x \in \Omega_{out} \text{and} \inf_{y \in S} ||x - y|| > 10 \end{cases} \tag{3}$$

where x, and y denote an arbitrary point in images and the corresponding nearest boundary point, respectively. S represents the surface of the vessel. Ω_{in} and Ω_{out} denote the region inside and outside the vessel, respectively. For the outside points greater than 10 from the nearest boundary point, the SDM value is set to 10. The sign indicates either inside or outside the vessel.

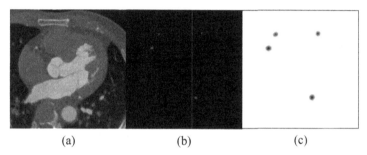

(a)   (b)   (c)

Fig. 2. Ground Truth masks for network training. (a) is a slice of original CTA image. (b) is the vessel segmentation ground truth of (a). (c) is the corresponding SDM generated from (b).

Given an input sample X and the corresponding segmentation ground truth mask Y_{seg}, the ground truth SDM Y_{SDM} is generated by Danielsson's algorithm[27] on the basis of Y_{seg} and then normalized to $[-1, 1]$, as shown in Fig. 2.

During training, the output of the k-th convolution layer in the SSJL network is calculated as follows:

$$x_k = I_k(X)F_k(x_{k-1}) + (1 - I_k(X))\hat{F}_k(x_{k-1}) \tag{4}$$

where F_k and $\hat{F}_k$ indicate the frozen layer and the replicated layer that can be optimized during training, respectively. $I_k(X)$ is a binary value generated by AFSM and decides whether x_{k-1} should go into the frozen layer F_k or fine-tuned layer $\hat{F}_k$.

We train SDM learning task using the L_1 loss between prediction $\hat{Y}_{SDM}$ and ground truth. The loss is expressed as follows:

$$\mathcal{L}_{SDM} = \frac{1}{N} \sum_{i=1}^{N} \left| \hat{Y}_{SDM}(x_i) - Y_{SDM}(x_i) \right| \tag{5}$$

where N indicates the total number of pixels in X and x_i represents a pixel in the sample X.

For the segmentation task, due to the class imbalance between the coronary artery and the background, dice loss [11] that is suitable for tasks with uneven samples is used as object function. The calculation formula is defined as follows:

$$\mathcal{L}_{seg} = 1 - \frac{2 \sum_{i=1}^{N} \left(Y_{seg}(x_i) * \hat{Y}_{seg}(x_i) \right)}{\sum_{i=1}^{N} \left(Y_{seg}^2(x_i) + \hat{Y}_{seg}^2(x_i) \right)} \tag{6}$$

where $\hat{Y}_{seg}$ denotes the coronary artery segmentation prediction of the network.

In the end, the total loss for the SSJL network is given by

$$\mathcal{L}_{total} = \mathcal{L}_{seg} + \lambda * \mathcal{L}_{SDM} \tag{7}$$

where λ controls the relative importance of the SDM learning task. During training, we set $\lambda = 0.001$.

3 Experiments and Results

3.1 Datasets and Metrics

The public liver vessel dataset is used as source data to provide knowledge for the target domain. The liver vessel dataset consists of 303 training data with annotated vessels and 140 test images. The size of the CTA data is $512 \times 512 \times D$, where D represents the number of slices (ranging from 24 to 181). There are many irrelevant slices without blood vessels at the beginning and the end of images. Therefore, only valid slices are extracted to participate in network training. Forty coronary CTA images used in our experiment are collected from Peking Union Medical College Hospital. Among them, 30 are used as the training set, and the remaining are used as the test set. The slice number of these images ranges from 207 to 410, and the size of each slice is 512×512. The masks of ground truth are annotated manually.

In this paper, *Dice*, *Sensitivity*, and *Precision* are used to evaluate the performance of the coronary artery segmentation results. The equations of the three metrics are as follows:

$$Dice = \frac{2 \times TP}{2 \times TP + FP + FN} \tag{8}$$

$$Sensitivity = \frac{TP}{TP + FN} \tag{9}$$

$$Precision = \frac{TN}{FP + TN} \tag{10}$$

where TP, FP, and FN refer to true positive, false positive and false negative, respectively. *Sensitivity* and *Precision* respectively measure the degree of under-segmentation and over-segmentation for prediction. *Dice* is a trade-off between *Sensitivity* and *Precision*, and is used to gauge the similarity between ground truth and segmentation mask.

3.2 Implementation Details

The original images and segmentation ground truth masks used in our experiment are normalized to [0,1]. The SDM ground truth is generated by the methods introduced in Sect. 2.2, as shown in Fig. 2. The channel of AFSM blocks is set to 64, 128, 256, and 512. We use the PyTorch 1.4.0 library to implement the whole pipeline. Adam solver is used to optimize the network model with an initial learning rate of 0.001, which is reduced by a factor of 10 in every 20 epochs. The model is trained for 80 epochs on a single NVIDIA GPU (NVIDIA GTX 3090), and the batch size is set to 8.

3.3 Ablation Research

In this section, we study the effectiveness of the auxiliary SDM learning task and AFSM in the proposed method on coronary artery segmentation. Detailed ablation experiments are conducted to demonstrate contributions qualitatively and quantitatively and consist of the following parts:

a) w/o SDM (w/o S): the proposed network without SDM prediction task
b) w/o AFSM (w/o A): the proposed network without AFSM
c) w/o SDM and AFSM (w/o S&A): only segmentation network, which is the proposed network without SDM prediction and ASFM

The qualitative results of ablation experiments are shown in Fig. 3. As can be seen, the proposed method is able to obtain more accurate segmentation masks. The SDM learning task is beneficial to predict the boundary of vessels and avoid over-segmentation around coronary arteries, as shown in Fig. 4. It is extremely necessary because it can prevent the interference of venous vessels to a certain extent. However, it is not suitable for small vessels because the SDM value of points inside small vessels is infinitely close to 0, which is the value of the boundary. The transfer strategy with AFSM improves the performance of small vessels segmentation, benefitting from the features learned from the small liver vessels. However, the prediction masks exhibit terrible over-segmentation due to the blurred boundary of liver vessels. The proposed method combines the advantages of the SDM learning task and AFSM to improve the performance of coronary artery segmentation.

As shown in Table 1, *Dice* of the proposed method improves by 3.5% with respect to the baseline segmentation network, which is the proposed network without SDM prediction and AFSM (w/o S&A). The SDM learning task and AFSM achieve an improvement of 2.5% and 2%, respectively, in terms of *Dice* compared with the baseline network. Although the proposed network without SDM prediction achieves the best *Sensitivity* score, it faces serious over-segmentation. The proposed method considers the advantages of SDM and AFSM to obtain optimal segmentation results. Therefore, the SDM prediction task and AFSM are both effective for vessel extraction.

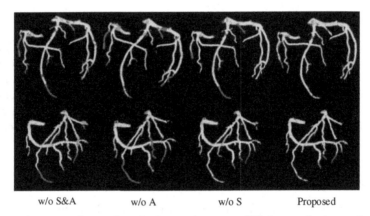

w/o S&A   w/o A   w/o S   Proposed

Fig. 3. Ablation comparison and qualitative results on two CTA images. In the results, red and green represent ground truth and coronary artery segmentation mask, respectively. The overlap between ground truth and segmentation results is shown in yellow color. (Color figure onlline)

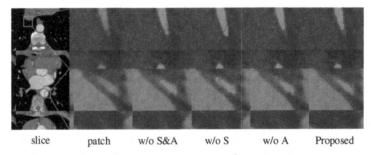

slice   patch   w/o S&A   w/o S   w/o A   Proposed

Fig. 4. Ablation comparison on the coronary artery boundary. The vessel segmentation is shown in green color, the vessel boundary ground truth is shown in red color. (Color figure onlline)

Table 1. Ablation study of the proposed method on coronary CTA images.

Methods	Dice (%)	Sensitivity (%)	Precision (%)
w/o S	79.02	**89.35**	71.23
w/o A	79.51	83.45	76.52
w/o S&A	78.07	85.19	72.55
Proposed	**81.60**	86.42	**77.71**

3.4   Comparison with Other Transfer Learning Methods

As the proposed network mainly focuses on transfer learning and aims to achieve positive transfer from liver vessels, we compare our method with other transfer learning methods. Standard Fine-tune [21] is a classic method to optimize all parameters on the target domain when the target data are sufficient. When the target data are limited, fine-tuning part layers are commonly used. According to Fine-tune Unet [28], fine-tuning all Unet blocks except block 5 results in the optimal performance for ultrasound image segmentation. The recently proposed Med3D [19] trains a general backbone for 3D medical image segmentation and classification. The pre-trained backbone trained on numbers of 3D medical images is used as the encoder and the decoder is designed by ourselves for comparison.

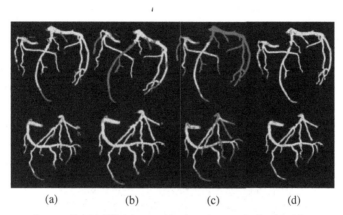

| (a) | (b) | (c) | (d) |

Fig. 5. Segmentation results of different transfer learning methods. (a)–(d) represent Standard Fine-tune, Fine-tune Unet, Med3D and our method, respectively.

The qualitative segmentation results of these methods are shown in Fig. 5. Standard Fine-tune performs poorly as the target domain has insufficient training data. Fine-tune Unet exhibits under-segmentation. Med3D performs poorly on coronary artery segmentation because the vessel-like training data of Med3D are limited and the decoder still needs to be trained from scratch on the target domain. Our method outperforms the other transfer learning methods on coronary artery segmentation in CTA images.

Table 2. Comparison of segmentation accuracy with various transfer learning methods.

Methods	Dice (%)	Sensitivity (%)	Precision (%)
Standard Fine-tune	77.67	**86.57**	70.94
Fine-tune Unet	80.73	84.52	**77.82**
Med3D	53.38	47.66	64.96
Proposed	**81.60**	86.42	77.71

Our method obtains the best score in terms of *Dice* metric, as shown in Table 2. Besides, the proposed method obtains the similar *Sensitivity* score with Standard Fine-tune. This finding indicates that the proposed method obtains the most accurate and complete coronary artery segmentation masks. Standard Fine-tune faces serious over-segmentation. Fine-tune Unet obtains great performance overall, but it faces under-segmentation. Therefore, the proposed method is better than the other transfer learning methods.

3.5   Comparison with Other Segmentation Methods

In order to demonstrate the advantages of the proposed method for coronary artery segmentation, we conduct another set of comparative experiments, including 3D Unet [9] and RE-Net [20]. 3D Unet is designed for 3D medical image segmentation, which extends Unet [10] architecture by replacing all 2D operations with corresponding 3D counterparts. RE-Net is proposed to segment the cerebrovascular images from magnetic resonance angiography images. A reverse edge attention module is used to discover the missing edge features effectively, which is important for segmentation.

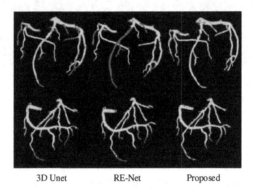

3D Unet   RE-Net   Proposed

Fig. 6. Qualitative comparison of the proposed method with 3D Unet and RE-Net.

Figure 6 illustrates the qualitative results of these methods. As can be seen, our method has the best performance with respect to 3D Unet and RE-Net. Besides, Table 3 shows our method achieves improvements of all measures. The training data are insufficient to achieve great performance for supervised deep learning network. Therefore, our method performs better compared with other segmentation methods.

Table 3. Quantitative comparison with other segmentation methods.

Methods	Dice (%)	Sensitivity (%)	Precision (%)
3D Unet	79.24	86.01	74.00
RE-Net	78.16	84.71	73.08
Proposed	**81.60**	**86.42**	**77.71**

4   Conclusion

In this study, we propose a novel cross-domain transfer learning method to achieve significant positive transfer on target domain task. The proposed method combines SDM learning task to encourage the network to transfer structure knowledge from the source domain. Moreover, AFSM is used to adaptively determine freeze or fine-tune parameters for every layer of the SSJL model on the basis of the input samples. We conduct three sets of experiments to demonstrate the excellent performance of the proposed method qualitatively and quantitatively. The proposed method achieves an improvement of at least 1% in *Dice* with respect to other methods.

Acknowledgements. This work was supported by the National Science Foundation Program of China [62071048, 61901031, 61971040].

References

1. Huang, W., Lu, H., Lin, Z., Su, H., Liang, Z.: Coronary artery segmentation by deep learning neural networks on computed tomographic coronary angiographic images. In: 2018 40th Annual International Conference of the IEEE Engineering in Medicine and Biology Society (EMBC) (2018)
2. Meinel, F.G., Ii, R.B., Zwerner, P.L., Cecco, C.D., Schoepf, U.J.: Coronary computed tomographic angiography in clinical practice: state of the art. Radiol. Clin. North Am. **53**, 287–296 (2015)
3. Zhao, J., et al.: Automatic Segmentation and Reconstruction of Coronary Arteries Based on Sphere Model and Hessian Matrix using CCTA Images. J. Phys.: Conf. Ser. **1213**, 042049 (2019). https://doi.org/10.1088/1742-6596/1213/4/042049
4. Zhou, C., et al.: Automated coronary artery tree extraction in coronary CT angiography using a multiscale enhancement and dynamic balloon tracking (MSCAR-DBT) method. Comput. Med. Imaging Graph. **36**, 1 (2012). https://doi.org/10.1016/j.compmedimag.2011.04.001
5. Tian, Y., Pan, Y., Duan, F., Zhao, S., Wang, Q., Wang, W.: Automated segmentation of coronary arteries based on statistical region growing and heuristic decision method. Biomed. Res. Int. **2016**, 1–7 (2016). https://doi.org/10.1155/2016/3530251
6. Chen, Y., Cao, Q., Zhuang, Z., Yang, Z., Luo, L., Toumoulin, C.: 3-D coronary vessel extraction using a novel minimum path based region growing. In: Kamel, M., Campilho, A. (eds.) ICIAR 2013. LNCS, vol. 7950, pp. 502–509. Springer, Heidelberg (2013). https://doi.org/10.1007/978-3-642-39094-4_57
7. Taghizadeh Dehkordi, M., Doost Hoseini, A.M., Sadri, S., Soltanianzadeh, H.: Local feature fitting active contour for segmenting vessels in angiograms. IET Comput. Vision **8**, 161–170 (2014). https://doi.org/10.1049/iet-cvi.2013.0083
8. Sun, K., Chen, Z., Jiang, S.: Local morphology fitting active contour for automatic vascular segmentation. IEEE Trans. Biomed. Eng. **59**, 464–473 (2012). https://doi.org/10.1109/TBME.2011.2174362
9. Çiçek, Ö., Abdulkadir, A., Lienkamp, S.S., Brox, T., Ronneberger, O.: 3D U-net: learning dense volumetric segmentation from sparse annotation. In: Ourselin, S., Joskowicz, L., Sabuncu, M.R., Unal, G., Wells, W. (eds.) MICCAI 2016. LNCS, vol. 9901, pp. 424–432. Springer, Cham (2016). https://doi.org/10.1007/978-3-319-46723-8_49

10. Ronneberger, O., Fischer, P., Brox, T.: U-net: convolutional networks for biomedical image segmentation. In: Navab, N., Hornegger, J., Wells, W.M., Frangi, A.F. (eds.) MICCAI 2015. LNCS, vol. 9351, pp. 234–241. Springer, Cham (2015). https://doi.org/10.1007/978-3-319-24574-4_28

11. Milletari, _F_, Navab, N., Ahmadi, S.A.: V-Net: fully convolutional neural networks for volumetric medical image segmentation. In: 2016 Fourth International Conference on 3D Vision (3DV) (2016)

12. Tajbakhsh, N., Jeyaseelan, L., Li, Q., Chiang, J.N., Wu, Z., Ding, X.: Embracing imperfect datasets: a review of deep learning solutions for medical image segmentation. Med. Image Anal. **63**, 101693 (2020). https://doi.org/10.1016/j.media.2020.101693

13. Sirinukunwattana, K., et al.: Gland segmentation in colon histology images: the glas challenge contest. Med. Image Anal. **35**, 489–502 (2017). https://doi.org/10.1016/j.media.2016.08.008

14. Yu, F., et al.: Annotation-free cardiac vessel segmentation via knowledge transfer from retinal images. In: Shen, D., et al. (eds.) MICCAI 2019. LNCS, vol. 11765, pp. 714–722. Springer, Cham (2019). https://doi.org/10.1007/978-3-030-32245-8_79

15. Tang, Y., et al.: CT image enhancement using stacked generative adversarial networks and transfer learning for lesion segmentation improvement. In: Shi, Y., Suk, H.-I., Liu, M. (eds.) MLMI 2018. LNCS, vol. 11046, pp. 46–54. Springer, Cham (2018). https://doi.org/10.1007/978-3-030-00919-9_6

16. Fu, C., et al.: Three dimensional fluorescence microscopy image synthesis and segmentation. In: 2018 IEEE/CVF Conference on Computer Vision and Pattern Recognition Workshops (CVPRW). pp. 2302–23028. IEEE, Salt Lake City, UT (2018). https://doi.org/10.1109/CVPRW.2018.00298

17. Shin, H.-C., et al.: Deep convolutional neural networks for computer-aided detection: cnn architectures, dataset characteristics and transfer learning. IEEE Trans. Med. Imaging. **35**, 1285–1298 (2016). https://doi.org/10.1109/TMI.2016.2528162

18. Tajbakhsh, N., et al.: Convolutional neural networks for medical image analysis: full training or fine tuning? IEEE Trans. Med. Imaging. **35**, 1299–1312 (2016). https://doi.org/10.1109/TMI.2016.2535302

19. Chen, S., Ma, K., Zheng, Y.: Med3D: Transfer Learning for 3D Medical Image Analysis (2019)

20. Simpson, A.L., et al.: A large annotated medical image dataset for the development and evaluation of segmentation algorithms. arXiv:1902.09063 [cs, eess] (2019)

21. Girshick, R., Donahue, J., Darrell, T., Malik, J.: Rich feature hierarchies for accurate object detection and semantic segmentation. In: 2014 IEEE Conference on Computer Vision and Pattern Recognition. pp. 580–587. IEEE, Columbus, OH, USA (2014). https://doi.org/10.1109/CVPR.2014.81

22. Yosinski, J., Clune, J., Bengio, Y., Lipson, H.: How transferable are features in deep neural networks? Eprint Arxiv. **27**, 3320–3328 (2014)

23. Xue, Y., et al.: Shape-Aware Organ Segmentation by Predicting Signed Distance Maps. arXiv:1912.03849 [cs] (2019)

24. He, K., Zhang, X., Ren, S., Sun, J.: Deep residual learning for image recognition. In: 2016 IEEE Conference on Computer Vision and Pattern Recognition (CVPR). pp. 770–778. IEEE, Las Vegas, NV, USA (2016). https://doi.org/10.1109/CVPR.2016.90

25. Maddison, C.J., Mnih, A., Teh, Y.W.: The Concrete Distribution: A Continuous Relaxation of Discrete Random Variables. ICLR (2017)

26. Guo, Y., Shi, H., Kumar, A., Grauman, K., Feris, R.: SpotTune: transfer learning through adaptive fine-tuning. In: 2019 IEEE/CVF Conference on Computer Vision and Pattern Recognition (CVPR) (2019)

27. Danielsson, P.-E.: Euclidean distance mapping. Comput. Graph. Image Process. **14**, 227–248 (1980). https://doi.org/10.1016/0146-664X(80)90054-4

28. Amiri, M., Brooks, R., Rivaz, H.: Fine-tuning U-Net for ultrasound image segmentation: different layers, different outcomes. IEEE Trans. Ultrason., Ferroelect., Freq. Contr. 67, 2510–2518 (2020). https://doi.org/10.1109/TUFFC.2020.3015081

Frequency-Based Convolutional Neural Network for Efficient Segmentation of Histopathology Whole Slide Images

Wei Luo[1,2], Yushan Zheng[2(✉)], Dingyi Hu[1,2], Jun Li[1,2], Chenghai Xue[3,4], and Zhiguo Jiang[1,2]

[1] Image Processing Center, School of Astronautics,
Beihang University, Beijing 100191, China
luowei0701@buaa.edu.cn

[2] Beijing Advanced Innovation Center for Biomedical Engineering,
Beihang University, Beijing 100191, China
yszheng@buaa.edu.cn

[3] Tianjin Institute of Industrial Biotechnology,
Chinese Academy of Sciences, Tianjin 300308, China

[4] Wankangyuan Tianjin Gene Technology, Inc., Tianjin 300220, China

Abstract. CNN-based methods for WSI segmentation are time-consuming under the limits of communication bandwidth and memory usage, due to the high pixel resolution of WSIs. In this paper, we propose a novel framework for accelerating the segmentation of digital histopathology WSIs in the frequency domain. Based on the characteristics of the JPEG format in data storage and transmission on the existing digital histopathological diagnosis cloud platform, we extract DCT coefficients from the JEPG decoding and compress them into the DCT feature cubes by a frequency selection block. Based on the DCT feature cubes, we propose an extremely light-weighted model named Efficient DCT-Network (EDCT-Net). The size of the input data, as well as the bandwidth requirement for CPU-GPU transmitting, for EDCT-net reduces by 96% compared to the common CNN-based methods. And, the number of model parameters and the floating-point operations (FLOPs) for EDCT-Net decreases by 98% and 94% compared to the baseline method. The experimental results have demonstrated that our method achieves a Dice score of 0.811 with only 8 frequency channels in the task of endometrial histopathology WSI segmentation, which is comparable with state-of-the-art methods.

Keywords: Histopathology WSI · Segmentation · DCT · Image compression

1 Introduction

Digital histopathology whole slide images (WSIs) become popular in the modern cancer diagnosis. The diagnosis based on digital WSIs is time-consuming and

© Springer Nature Switzerland AG 2021
Y. Peng et al. (Eds.): ICIG 2021, LNCS 12889, pp. 584–596, 2021.
https://doi.org/10.1007/978-3-030-87358-5_47

laborious for pathologists due to the high pixel resolution of WSIs. In this case, an increasing number of computer-aided histopathology diagnosis technologies are developed to assist the pathologists in clinical diagnosis.

Recently, automatic methods based on deep learning have widely used for WSI analysis [2,3,6,18,21–23]. And cancerous region segmentation is always a popular and challenging topic. In the case of high pixel resolution, it is hard to directly segment the entire WSIs by common deep learning models for the limitations of recent CPU and GPU capacities. Therefore, the WSIs are generally divided into image patches and then fed into the deep learning model for inference. There are two typical strategies to achieve the segmentation of WSIs. The one is using end-to-end fully convolutional networks (FCNs) [10,14] such as U-Net [12], CRFs [20], DeepLab [4] and SegNet [1], which produce correspondingly-sized segmentation results for these patches and then mosaicked to obtain the WSI segmentation result. The other is based on convolutional neural networks (CNNs) [9,13,17], e.g. GoogleNet [15], ResNet [5] and DenseNet [8]. The classes of the patches are predicted by CNNs, then aggregated together into the segmentation result. Whereas, for both of the above strategies, the computation amounts are heavy when facing the large-scale whole slide images. Simultaneously, because the RGB-format patches are generally pre-processed on the CPUs and then transmitted to the GPUs/AI accelerator in the convolutional inference, the communication bandwidth between the CPU and the GPU/AI limits the analysis speed. To reduce the bandwidth and computational amount, the general and simplest way is to down-sample the input image. But it will result in a significantly decrease in the segmentation accuracy [14].

In the practical applications, the tiles of WSIs are commonly stored and transmitted on cloud platforms as compression data following the JPEG standard. The compressed data stream needs to be decoded into the RGB-format data in the sequence of unzigzag, Huffman decoding, IDCT, etc. following the JPEG standard before used for image analysis and processing. It is notable that the discrete cosine transformation (DCT) coefficients generated in the process of JPEG decoding are informative and potential to develop efficient deep learning models for histopathology patterns recognition. Especially for digital WSIs, all the image content nearly locates on one imaging plane and thereby the same structures, such as nuclei, occupies a consistent number of pixels in the WSI. In this case, one specific DCT frequency indicates a fixed image pattern. Based on the prior knowledge, we could greatly reduce the computational complexity of histopathology whole slide image analysis and meanwhile achieve a comparable accuracy by building a framework in the frequency domain.

In this paper, we propose a novel framework for fast segmentation of digital histopathology WSIs in the frequency domain. The proposed framework is illustrated in Fig. 1. Compared to the existing methods [3], we truncate the decoding process and directly extract the DCT coefficients from the JPEG-compressed data as the input of the deep learning model. Meanwhile, a frequency selection block is designed to compress the DCT coefficients into DCT feature cube, which is tens of times smaller than the corresponding RGB-format data.

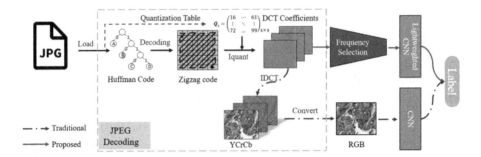

Fig. 1. The illustration of the proposed method, where the purple dotted arrow is the data flow of the deep learning methods based on RGB-format data, the red solid arrow is the data flow of the proposed Efficient DCT-Network (EDCT-Net), and the green dotted box is the process of JEPG decoding. (Color figure online)

Furthermore, since the DCT feature cube is with smaller width and height, we build an extremely light-weighted convolutional neural network named Efficient DCT-Network (EDCT-Net) for fast classification of histopathology image patches and also for the segmentation of digital WSIs. Our methods were evaluated on a large-scale endometrial WSI dataset. The experimental results have demonstrated that the proposed framework greatly reduces the computational complexity of whole slide image analysis and meanwhile achieve a comparable performance with the existing methods. The contribution of this paper can be summarized as:

1) We proposed a novel framework for efficient segmentation of digital histopathology WSIs in the frequency domain based on the JPEG compression standard. The JPEG-compressed image data is first decoded to obtain the DCT coefficients, then DCT feature cube is generated based on frequency selection of the DCT coefficients, and finally a light-weighted CNN, EDCT-Net, is trained to classify the DCT feature cubes. Compared to the existing methods based on RGB-format CNNs, the size of the input data, as well as the bandwidth requirement for CPU-GPU transmitting, is reduced by tens of times, the number of model parameters and the floating-point operations (FLOPs) decreases by 98% and 94% compared to the baseline method.

2) We studied the frequency selection for compression in the frequency domain. The comprehensive experiments have shown that a small part of low frequency data stored most of the discriminative information for histopathology patterns recognition. The proposed EDCT-Net achieved a Dice score of 0.811 with only 8 frequency channels in the task of endometrial histopathology WSI segmentation, which is comparable with the state-of-the-art RGB-based CNNs.

The remainder of this paper is organized as follows. Section 2 introduces the methodology of the proposed method. The experiment are presented in Sect. 3. Section 4 summarizes the contribution.

2   Method

The proposed framework involves 1) DCT coefficients extraction, 2) the frequency selection, 3) the Efficient DCT-Network, and 4) WSI segmentation based on EDCT-Net, which are detailed in this section.

2.1   DCT Coefficients Extraction

The JPEG standard is widely used for photographs and internet graphics compression. The standard encoding process defined by JPEG is as follows: 1) Convert RGB to YCbCr for each pixel, 2) Convert the Y, Cb and Cr channels into chunks of blocks in 8×8 pixels, then apply Discrete Cosine Transformation (DCT) to each block and use quantization to compress the resulting block, 3) Use Zig-zag encoding to flatten the 8×8 matrix into one-dimensional data, then apply run-length and Delta encoding, and 4) Use Huffman encoding to generate the binary stream. As shown in Fig. 1, the decoding process is the reverse of the encoding process.

In this paper, we truncate the decoding process of histopathology images to obtain the DCT coefficients. Letting $\mathbf{I} \in \mathbb{R}^{H \times W \times 3}$ denote an image patch in size of $H \times W$ in the WSI, the DCT coefficients of Y, Cb and Cr channels for $\mathbf{I}$ are represented as $\mathbf{D}^Y$, $\mathbf{D}^{Cb}$ and $\mathbf{D}^{Cr}$. Specifically,

$$\mathbf{D}^c = \begin{pmatrix} \mathbf{B}_{11}^c & \cdots & \mathbf{B}_{1N_c}^c \\ \vdots & \ddots & \vdots \\ \mathbf{B}_{M_c 1}^c & \cdots & \mathbf{B}_{M_c N_c}^c \end{pmatrix}, c = Y, Cb, Cr, \tag{1}$$

where $\mathbf{B}_{ij}^c \in \mathbb{R}^{8 \times 8}$ represents the 64 frequency channels transformed from the 8×8 block in the i-th row and j-th column, and M_c and N_c denote the rows and columns in the c-th channel. Notice that the size of DCT coefficients matrix for the Y channel is larger than that for the Cr and Cb channels because of different sampling mode. Specifically in our study, the height and width of $\mathbf{D}^Y$ are the same as $\mathbf{I}$, while the height and width of $\mathbf{D}^{Cb}$ and $\mathbf{D}^{Cr}$ are half of $\mathbf{D}^Y$.

2.2   Frequency Selection Block

In the frequency selection block, the 8×8 blocks in $\mathbf{D}^Y$, $\mathbf{D}^{Cb}$ and $\mathbf{D}^{Cr}$ are first flattened into one-dimensional vectors while keep their spatial relations (as shown in Fig. 2). Then, the DCT coefficients matrics are rescaled into 192 channels (as shown in Fig. 2c), where each channel represents one frequency. Afterwards, the DCT frequency cubes can be defined as $\widetilde{\mathbf{D}}^Y \in \mathbb{R}^{H/8 \times W/8 \times 64}$, $\widetilde{\mathbf{D}}^{Cb} \in \mathbb{R}^{H/16 \times W/16 \times 64}$ and $\widetilde{\mathbf{D}}^{Cr} \in \mathbb{R}^{H/16 \times W/16 \times 64}$. Finally, these cubes are concatenated after upsampling the $\widetilde{\mathbf{D}}^{Cb}$ and $\widetilde{\mathbf{D}}^{Cr}$ to the same size as $\widetilde{\mathbf{D}}^Y$. The concatenated DCT frequency cube is formulated as:

$$\widetilde{\mathbf{D}} = [d_0^Y, d_1^Y, \ldots, d_{63}^Y, d_0^{Cb}, d_1^{Cb}, \ldots, d_{63}^{Cb}, d_0^{Cr}, d_1^{Cr}, \ldots, d_{63}^{Cr}] \in \mathbb{R}^{H/8 \times W/8 \times 192}$$
$$\tag{2}$$

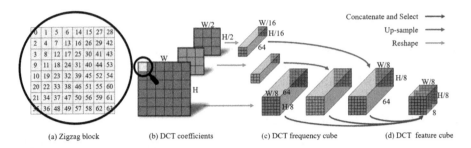

Fig. 2. The data processing pipeline of frequency selection block, where (a) is the Zigzag block of the each pixel in the original (b) DCT coefficient, the orange, green and blue cubes are from Y, Cb and Cr respectively, (c) is the DCT frequency cube generated after reshaping and up-sampling, (d) is the DCT frequency cube (Color figure online)

where $d_k^c \in \mathbb{R}^{H/8 \times W/8}$ is the k-th frequency channel from $\widetilde{\mathbf{D}}^c$. Notice that $\widetilde{\mathbf{D}}$ maintains the same size with the image $\mathbf{I}$. The main different is that majority frequency channels of $\widetilde{\mathbf{D}}$, especially the high-frequency channels, are occupied by zero. We suppose that these zero-occupied channels are less informative and therefore less effective for histopathology image recognition. To reduce the size of the data, we propose keeping the informative channels and meanwhile discard the less-informative channels in the frequency selection stage. Generally, the final frequency feature cubes are formulated as $\mathbf{F} \in \mathbb{R}^{H/8 \times W/8 \times M}$, where $M = M_Y + M_{Cb} + M_{Cr}$ is the total number of selected frequency channels with $M_c, c = Y, Cb, Cr$ denotes the number of selected channel for the c-th color channel.

In our experiments, an original $224 \times 224 \times 3$ RGB-format image is finally converted into a DCT feature cube of size $28 \times 28 \times M$. The compression ratio is $M/192$. This conversion can be efficiently processed by a CPU during the data preparation for deep learning frameworks.

2.3   Efficient DCT-Network (EDCT-Net)

EfficientNets are a family of models which can be scaled up to any target resource constraints in a more principled way while maintaining model efficiency [16]. EfficientNet-b0 is the base network structure, which is a popular light-weighted model to develop efficient applications. In this paper, the EfficientNet-b0 is used as the baseline model for histopathology image patch classification. Moreover, considering the shape of the proposed DCT feature cube ($28 \times 28 \times M$), we defined a more light-weighted version of EfficientNet-b0 by discarding the first 4 MBConv blocks and named it as Efficient DCT-Network (EDCT-Net). EDCT-Net has much fewer layers and narrower width than EfficientNet-b0, but can achieve higher accuracy and faster speed than EfficientNet-b0 for the DCT feature cubes introduced in the previous section.

2.4 CNN-Based Segmentation for Histopathology Images

After training the EDCT-Net, the segmentation of cancerous regions from a WSI can be achieved by feeding the patches generated by the sliding window paradigm into the EDCT-Net. Specifically, the size of the window is 224 × 224 with the step of 224. Then, the probability map for the WSI is generated by aggregating the prediction scores of all the patches. Next, the segmentation result is obtained by the threshold operation after up-sampling the probability map to the same size of the WSI. Finally, to refine the segmentation result, an open operation followed by a hole filling operation was used as the post-processing.

3 Experiments

3.1 Dataset and Settings

To study the effectiveness and feasibility of the proposed framework for efficient WSI segmentation, we collected a large-scale endometrial dataset containing 1288 WSIs. These WSIs were categorized to 5 types of endometrial pathology, including Normal, Well-differentiated Endometrioid adenocarcinoma (WDEA), Moderately differentiated Endometrioid adenocarcinoma (MDEA), Low differentiated Endometrioid adenocarcinoma (LDEA), and Serous. All the WSIs were scanned under a lens of 20x, and were well annotated by pathologists, as shown in Fig. 3. We randomly selected 772 samples for training, 193 for validation and 323 samples for testing.

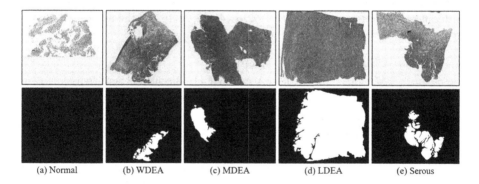

(a) Normal   (b) WDEA   (c) MDEA   (d) LDEA   (e) Serous

Fig. 3. Instances in the endometrial WSI dataset, where (a) is Normal, (b) is Well-differentiated Endometrioid adenocarcinoma, (c) is Moderately differentiated Endometrioid adenocarcinoma, (d) is Low differentiated Endometrioid adenocarcinoma, (e) is Serous, and the ground-truth for the cancerous regions are provided on the second row.

Image patches in size of 224 × 224 pixels were sampled from the WSIs and labeled according to the pathologists' annotations. Specifically, 728,659 patches are obtained from the training WSIs, 184,905 patches from the validation WSIs, and 393,870 patches from testing WSIs. In the experiments, the Normal samples were regarded as the negative and WDEA, MDEA, LDEA, and Serous were regarded as the positive. The sensitivity, specificity, and accuracy for the binary classification were used as the metrics. The segmentation of the WSI was achieved according to Sect. 3.3. The Dice Score (DSC) was used as the segmentation metric, which is formulated as

$$DSC = \frac{2TP}{FP + 2TP + FN},$$
(3)

where TP, FP, and FN denotes the number of true positive pixels, false positive pixels and false negative pixels, respectively.

All the algorithms were implemented in python with Pytorch. The experiments conducted on a computer with 2 CPUs of Intel Xeon and 2 GPUs of Nvidia Geforce 2080Ti.

3.2 Patch Classification Based on DCT Coefficients

We first conducted experiment to verify the hypothesis that the frequency data within the DCT coefficients represents consistent information of histopathology WSIs. As mentioned in the Sect. 2, each $224 \times 224 \times 3$ RGB-format patch is transformed by the feature selection block into DCT feature cube in size of $28 \times 28 \times M$ and used as the input to CNNs.

Table 1. The classification results on patches using DCT feature cubes as inputs with different M settings, where $M = 192, 64, 40, 32, 24, 16, 8$ is the number of selected frequency channels.

No.	Channel settings				Metrics		
	M	M_Y	M_{Cb}	M_{Cr}	Accuracy (%)	Specificity	Sensitivity
1	192	64	64	64	90.67	**0.90**	0.92
2	64	64	0	0	89.39	0.86	**0.93**
3		0	64	0	88.73	0.89	0.88
4		0	0	64	84.94	0.87	0.83
5	40	40	0	0	89.33	0.88	0.91
6	32	32	0	0	89.25	0.86	**0.93**
7	24	24	0	0	89.68	0.89	0.90
8		8	8	8	**91.06**	0.89	**0.93**
9	16	16	0	0	89.45	**0.90**	0.89
10	8	8	0	0	89.02	0.87	0.91
11		4	2	2	90.67	0.89	0.92

The Effect of the Frequency Channels. In this experiment, we explored the importance of each frequency extracted from Y, Cr, Cb channel. We selected different number of frequency channels for patch classification by setting M to 192, 64, 40, 32, 24, 16, 8, respectively. The detailed channels used for each color channel and the corresponding classification performance for the test set are shown in Table 1. The accuracy of $M_Y, M_{Cb}, M_{Cr} = [64, 64, 64]$ achieves at 90.67% when using all the frequency channels for the classification, which can be regarded as the baseline of the DCT-based models. The results for $M = 64$ indicate that the frequency channels from Y play a more important role in the classification than those from Cb and Cr. Interestingly, $M_Y, M_{Cb}, M_{Cr} = [8, 8, 8]$ achieves an accuracy of 91.06%, which is the best among all the experimental settings. Moreover, when we further reduced the channels to 8, it still maintains an accuracy of 90.67%, which is equivalent to the baseline. It demonstrates that in these 192 frequency channels, the features contained in the lower-frequency channels are more informative for classification. In contrast, higher-frequency channels contain less important information and may perform as the noise in the classification task.

Table 2. The classification results on patches when the number of selected frequency channels is $M = 8$, and K_Y, K_{Cb}, K_{Cr} defines the index of the selected frequency channels from Y, Cr, Cb respectively.

No.	Channel settings			Metrics		
	K_Y	K_{Cb}	K_{Cr}	Accuracy (%)	Specificity	Sensitivity
1	0,1,2,3,4,5	0	0	90.56	0.88	**0.93**
2	0,1,2,3	0,1	0,1	90.67	**0.89**	0.92
3	0,1,2,3	0,2	1,3	90.34	**0.89**	0.91
4	0,2,4,6	0,1	0,1	90.48	0.88	**0.93**
5	0,1,3,5	0,1	0,1	**90.75**	**0.89**	0.92
6	0,1	0,1,2	0,1,2	90.42	0.90	0.91

Channel Selection for the Efficient DCT-Net. For the reason of building efficient segmentation framework, we determined retaining 8 frequency channels as the input setting of the EDCT-Net. However in the above experiments, we simply selected the top-lower-frequency channels. To pursue a higher accuracy, we conducted experiments to decide the eight specific channels. The results are presented in Table 2. It is obvious that the best accuracy is 90.75% when $K^Y = \{0, 1, 3, 5\}$, $K^{Cb} = \{0, 1\}$, $K^{Cr} = \{0, 1\}$, where K^Y, K^{Cb} and K^{Cr} denote the indexes of the selected channels for Y, Cb, and Cr, respectively. Finally, we used this solution that achieves the best accuracy in the following experiments.

As shown in Fig. 4, we reconstruct the RGB-format images from different remaining frequency channels of the DCT feature cubes. It illustrates that more higher frequency channels are reserved, more edge details will be in the reconstructed image. The images in Fig. 4 (e-h) are reconstructed by only 8 frequency channels. It shows only the rough structure of the histopathology images can be reconstructed. Nevertheless, such rough information delivers comparable recognition performance with the baseline strategy. The results indicate the rough but crucial structures and spatial position relations of the nuclei could be more important than the high-frequency information in the considered task.

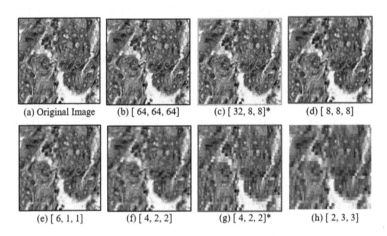

Fig. 4. The RGB-format images reconstructed by the remaining frequency channels. (a) is the original image, (b), (d), (e), (f) and (h) are constructed by the top M_Y, M_{Cb}, M_{Cr} lower frequency channels from Y, Cb and Cr respectively. The yellow bounding box (c)is the selection scheme of DCTNet, while blue bounding box (d) is the selection scheme which achieves highest accuracy, and the red bounding box (g) is the selection scheme of the Efficient DCT-Network (EDCT-Net). The * denotes that the selection scheme of it is based on a certain subset of frequency index. (Color figure online)

Table 3. The comparison of classification performance between the proposed EDCT-Net and baselines.

Model	#Params($\times 10^6$)	#FLOPs($\times 10^8$)	Accuracy	Specificity	Sensitivity
Efficientnet-b0 [16]	4.0	3.9	**92.60**	**0.91**	0.94
Mobilenet-v3 [7]	2.7	0.6	92.21	0.90	**0.95**
Shufflenet-v2 [11]	1.3	1.5	92.22	**0.91**	0.94
DCTNet [19]	23.50	12	90.34	0.87	0.93
EDCT-Net (ours)	0.08	0.23	91.43	0.90	0.93

Comparison with the Existing Classification Methods. Then, we compared the proposed EDCT-Net with the state-of-the-art methods, including the light-weighted networks (EfficientNet-b0 [16], Mobilenet-v3 [7], Shufflenet-v2

[11]) and another model based on DCT input (DCTNet [19]). Except DCTNet, all methods take RGB-format image as inputs. The input size of the RGB-based CNNs is $224 \times 224 \times 3$. The input of DCTNet is DCT feature cubes of $28 \times 28 \times 48$ size. The construction of DCT feature cubes refer to the [19]. As shown in the Table 3, the proposed EDCT-Net achieves an accuracy of 91.43%, which is 1.17% inferior to the EfficientNet-b0. However, the EDCT-Net contains only 0.08×10^6 parameters, which is 2.0% of Efficientnet-b0, 3.0% of Mobilenet-v3 and 6.2% of Shufflenet-v2. Meanwhile, the FLOPs of EDCT-Net is 0.23×10^8, which is about 5.8% of the EfficientNet-b0 and 2% of DCTNet [19]. All the above results have demonstrated that the proposed method is effective in histopathology image classification and is rather computational efficient than the existing light-weighted methods.

3.3 WSI Segmentation Based on Efficient DCT-Net

Finally, we evaluated the segmentation performance of the model for the 323 testing WSIs. The input format, normalized input size, dice score (DSC), accuracy for different models, average inference time for each WSI are presented in Table 4. It shows that our method achieves a DSC of 0.811 and a pixel accuracy of 0.810, which are comparable with the other RGB-based methods and superior to the DCT-based DCTNet. It is notable that the normalized input size of the proposed is 0.04 while the EfficientNet-b0 [16], Mobilenet-v3 [7], and Shufflenet-v2 [11] are 1.00 and DCTNet [19] is 0.25. Namely, the proposed EDCT-Net reduces the data scale required to be uploaded to the GPU by 96%, when compared to the RGB-based methods. This substantial reduction breaks through the bandwidth bottleneck between the CPU and the GPU, and thereby accelerating the speed of segmentation for histopathology WSIs. With the same batchsize setting, our method is more than 50% faster than the baselines and still has the potential to increase batchsize for a faster analysis. It is very significant to develop high data-efficient applications for WSI analysis.

Table 4. The segmentation performance of the proposed EDCT-Net, where normalized input size is the ratio of input sizes of the methods to that of EfficientNet-b0.

Model	Input format	DSC	Accuracy	Normalized input size	Time
Efficientnet-b0 [16]	$224 \times 224 \times 3$ RGB	**0.832**	**0.811**	1.00	23.3 s
Mobilenet-v3 [7]	$224 \times 224 \times 3$ RGB	0.827	0.809	1.00	19.6 s
Shufflenet-v2 [11]	$224 \times 224 \times 3$ RGB	0.821	**0.811**	1.00	19.3 s
DCTNet [19]	$28 \times 28 \times 48$ DCT	0.804	0.806	0.25	17.7 s
EDCT-Net	$28 \times 28 \times 8$ DCT	0.811	0.810	**0.04**	11.3 s

Figure 5 visualizes several segmentation instances of WSIs for the EfficientNet-b0 [16], Mobilenet-v3 [7], Shufflenet-v2 [11], DCTNet [19] and the proposed EDCT-Net. As shown in the last row, our model can be found better on segmenting isolated small tissue areas.

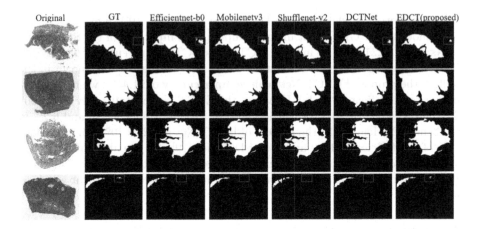

Fig. 5. Examples of segmentation results on the endometrial dataset. The first column is the original WSIs, the second column is the ground-truth, and the remaining columns are the segmentation results of the five methods respectively.

4   Conclusion

In this paper, we propose an efficient framework for recognition and segmentation of digital histopathology WSIs in the frequency domain. Our method utilizes the DCT coefficients from the JPEG standard to achieve the classification and segmentation for WSIs. The experimental results have demonstrated that the lower frequency channels contain the sufficient information for recognition while the higher frequency has less information and may introduce noise. The proposed EDCT-Net achieves a Dice score of 0.811 with only 8 frequency channels in the task of endometrial histopathology WSI segmentation. More comprehensive experimental results show that the bandwidth requirement for CPU-GPU transmitting, is reduced by 96% and the number of model parameters and the floating-point operations (FLOPs) decreases by 98% and 94% when compared to the baseline method. Our future work will focus on applying the DCT coefficients to the compression and classification of WSIs.

Acknowledgment. This work was partly supported by the National Natural Science Foundation of China (Grant No. 61771031, 61901018, and 61906058), partly by China Postdoctoral Science Foundation (No. 2019M650446) and partly by Tianjin Science and Technology Major Project (Grant No. 18ZXZNSY00260).

References

1. Badrinarayanan, V., Kendall, A., Cipolla, R.: SegNet: a deep convolutional encoder-decoder architecture for image segmentation. IEEE Trans. Pattern Anal. Mach. Intell., 1 (2017)

2. Bandi, P., et al.: From detection of individual metastases to classification of Lymph Node Status at the patient level: the CAMELYON17 challenge. IEEE Trans. Med. Imaging **38**(2), 550–560 (2019)

3. Bejnordi, B.E., et al.: Diagnostic assessment of deep learning algorithms for detection of lymph node metastases in women with breast cancer. JAMA **318**(22), 2199–2210 (2017)

4. Chen, L.C., Papandreou, G., Kokkinos, I., Murphy, K., Yuille, A.L.: DeepLab: semantic image segmentation with deep convolutional nets, Atrous convolution, and fully connected CRFs. IEEE Trans. Pattern Anal. Mach. Intell. **40**(4), 834–848 (2018)

5. He, K., Zhang, X., Ren, S., Sun, J.: Deep residual learning for image recognition. In: 2016 IEEE Conference on Computer Vision and Pattern Recognition (CVPR) (2016)

6. Hollon, T.C., et al.: Near real-time intraoperative brain tumor diagnosis using stimulated Raman histology and deep neural networks. Nat. Med. **26**(1), 52–58 (2020)

7. Howard, A., et al.: Searching for mobilenetv3. In: 2019 IEEE/CVF International Conference on Computer Vision (ICCV) (2020)

8. Huang, G., Liu, Z., Laurens, V., Weinberger, K.Q.: Densely connected convolutional networks. IEEE Computer Society (2016)

9. Lerousseau, M., et al.: Weakly supervised multiple instance learning histopathological tumor segmentation. In: Martel, A.L., et al. (eds.) MICCAI 2020. LNCS, vol. 12265, pp. 470–479. Springer, Cham (2020). https://doi.org/10.1007/978-3-030-59722-1_45

10. Long, J., Shelhamer, E., Darrell, T.: Fully convolutional networks for semantic segmentation. IEEE Trans. Pattern Anal. Mach. Intell. **39**(4), 640–651 (2015)

11. Ma, N., Zhang, X., Zheng, H.-T., Sun, J.: ShuffleNet V2: practical guidelines for efficient CNN architecture design. In: Ferrari, V., Hebert, M., Sminchisescu, C., Weiss, Y. (eds.) Computer Vision – ECCV 2018. LNCS, vol. 11218, pp. 122–138. Springer, Cham (2018). https://doi.org/10.1007/978-3-030-01264-9_8

12. Ronneberger, O., Fischer, P., Brox, T.: U-net: convolutional networks for biomedical image segmentation. In: Navab, N., Hornegger, J., Wells, W.M., Frangi, A.F. (eds.) MICCAI 2015. LNCS, vol. 9351, pp. 234–241. Springer, Cham (2015). https://doi.org/10.1007/978-3-319-24574-4_28

13. Sun, S., Jiang, B., Zheng, Y., Xie, F.: A comparative study of CNN and FCN for histopathology whole slide image analysis. In: Zhao, Y., et al. (eds.) ICIG 2019. LNCS, vol. 11902, pp. 558–567. Springer, Cham (2019). https://doi.org/10.1007/978-3-030-34110-7_47

14. Sun, S., Yuan, H., Zheng, Y., Zhang, H., Hu, D., Jiang, Z.: Cancer sensitive cascaded networks (CSC-NET) for efficient histopathology whole slide image segmentation. In: IEEE 17th International Symposium on Biomedical Imaging (ISBI) (2020)

15. Szegedy, C., Wei, L., Jia, Y., Sermanet, P., Rabinovich, A.: Going deeper with convolutions. IEEE Computer Society (2014)

16. Tan, M., Le, Q.: EfficientNet: rethinking model scaling for convolutional neural networks. In: International Conference on Machine Learning, pp. 6105–6114 (2019)

17. Tokunaga, H., Teramoto, Y., Yoshizawa, A., Bise, R.: Adaptive weighting multi-field-of-view CNN for semantic segmentation in pathology, pp. 12589–12598 (2019). https://doi.org/10.1109/CVPR.2019.01288

18. Veta, M., et al.: Predicting breast tumor proliferation from whole-slide images: the TUPAC16 challenge. Med. Image Anal. **54**, 111–121 (2019)

19. Xu, K., Qin, M., Sun, F., Wang, Y., Chen, Y.K., Ren, F.: Learning in the frequency domain (2020)
20. Zheng, S., et al.: Conditional random fields as recurrent neural networks. In: 2015 IEEE International Conference on Computer Vision (ICCV) (2015)
21. Zheng, Y., Jiang, B., Shi, J., Zhang, H., Xie, F.: Encoding histopathological WSIs using GNN for scalable diagnostically relevant regions retrieval. In: Shen, D., et al. (eds.) MICCAI 2019. LNCS, vol. 11764, pp. 550–558. Springer, Cham (2019). https://doi.org/10.1007/978-3-030-32239-7_61
22. Zheng, Y., et al.: Diagnostic regions attention network (DRA-Net) for histopathology WSI recommendation and retrieval. IEEE Trans. Med. Imaging **40**(3), 1090–1103 (2021)
23. Zheng, Y., et al.: Feature extraction from histopathological images based on nucleus-guided convolutional neural network for Breast Lesion classification. Pattern Recogn. **71**, 14–25 (2017)

MR Image Denoising by FGMM Clustering of Image Patches

Zhaoyin Shi and Long Chen$^{(\boxtimes)}$

Faculty of Science and Technology, University of Macau, Macau SAR, China
yc07456@umac.mo, longchen@um.edu.mo

Abstract. The general procedure of image denoising is solving an inverse problem with some statistic prior information as the regularization. We propose a novel noise removal method for Magnetic Resonance (MR) images based on the Fuzzy Gaussian Mixture Model (FGMM) Clustering of image patches. In this method, the FGMM, which is an extension of the Gaussian Mixture Model (GMM), has been trained using overlapping clean patches randomly selected from the image database firstly. Then the objective function, which is the sum of the image corruption model and the prior model, is constructed. We optimize the objective using the "Half Quadratic Splitting" method and obtain an expression of iteration to restore the whole image. Finally, we use the proposed method to denoise Magnetic Resonance (MR) images. The experimental results show that the proposed method achieves good performance in MR image denoising.

Keywords: Magnetic resonance images · Clustering · Image denoising · Fuzzy Gaussian Mixture Model · Image patches

1 Introduction

Magnetic Resonance Imaging (MRI) [1,4,17] has become one of the mainstream medical image acquisition methods. Clinicians can quickly diagnose diseases and find lesions using Magnetic Resonance (MR) images. The presence of the noise obeying Rician distribution [23], will have a significant impact on the accurate analysis of MRI images, and affect the results of subsequent diagnosis and medical treatment. So, denoising MR images and improving its peak signal-to-noise ratio (PSNR) is extremely important for clinical diagnosis.

Most representative methods of MR image denoising can be roughly divided into two categories, including Spatial domain methods and transform domain methods. Among Spatial methods, median filtering [16], mean filtering [10,23], and Wiener filtering [15] have significant performance in removing specific types of noise such as salt and pepper noise, impulse noise, and Gaussian white noise,

Supported by Macau Science and Technology development fund (FDCT): FDCT/196/2017/A3.

etc. Simultaneously, the non-local means (NLM) [2,3,9,13,17] method, which makes full use of the non-local redundant in formation of images and has satisfactory performance on image de-noising. However, due to the slow calculation speed it is difficult for NLM methods to meet the requirements of contemporary clinical diagnosis timeliness. Transform domain methods are aimed at transforming the image from the pixel domain to the frequency domain through Fourier transform [20], wavelet transform [21] or other transform methods [8,25], to denoise in the frequency domain, and then inversely transform it to the pixel domain to complete image denoising.

Besides these classic methods, other methods based on prior information of natural images, such as local smoothness [24], non-local self-similarity [18], sparsity [7], and statistical characteristics [26], etc. also have received wide attention. Zoran and Weiss [26] have proved that the image patch-based model is a powerful tool named Expected Patches log likelihood (EPLL) with the Gaussian Mixture Model (GMM) prior for whole image restoration. They proved that if we can train better image patch prior, it will provide better support for image denoising tasks.

Fuzzy clustering has been widely used in image segmentation [11] and edge detection [22]. However, fuzzy clustering models generally do not have probabilistic properties, so it is rarely used as a priori model in image denoising. In this manuscript, we try to introduce the fuzzy Gaussian mixture model (FGMM) into the task of MR images denoising as image patch prior. The trained FGMM Clustering [14] model over patches is used to construct a cost function as a regularization. And we optimize it through "Half Quadratic Splitting" [5,12] optimization method to restore the whole image. Experimental results show that the proposed method performs well in MR images denoising and has the improvement of PSNR than EPLL.

2   FGMM Clustering and Image Patches Clustering Prior

FGMM is a powerful clustering tool with widespread application in various domains, where the objective function is the C-means type with entropy regularization [14,19]:

$$J = \sum_{i=1}^{N}\sum_{k=1}^{K}\mu_{ki}d_{ki} + \gamma\sum_{i=1}^{N}\sum_{k=1}^{K}\mu_{ki}\,ln\,\frac{\mu_{ki}}{\pi_k}$$

$$s.t. \begin{cases} \sum_{k=1}^{K}\mu_{ki} = 1 \quad \forall i = 1,2,...,N \\ \sum_{k=1}^{K}\pi_k = 1 \end{cases} \tag{1}$$

Here, z_i is the $i\,th$ sample, μ_{ki} is the membership of $z_i \in k\,th$ cluster, π_k is the weight of the $k\,th$ cluster, γ is the parameter, which controls the fuzziness of the model and d_{ki} is the dissimilarity function yields following expression:

$$d_{ki} = -ln\,\mathcal{N}(z_i|v_k, \Sigma_k) \tag{2}$$

$\mathcal{N}(z_i|v_k, \Sigma_k)$ is the Gaussian distribution density function, v_k and Σ_k are the mean and covariance of the k-th cluster.

Introducing the Lagrange Multiplier Algorithm, we can obtain the parameters' estimations as following:

$$\mu_{ki} = \frac{\pi_k\,exp\left(-\frac{1}{\gamma}d_{ki}\right)}{\sum_{h=1}^{K}\pi_h\,exp\left(-\frac{1}{\gamma}d_{hi}\right)} \tag{3}$$

$$\pi_k = \frac{1}{N}\sum_{j=1}^{N}\mu_{kj} \tag{4}$$

$$v_k = \frac{\sum_{j=1}^{N}\mu_{kj}z_j}{\sum_{j=1}^{N}\mu_{kj}} \tag{5}$$

$$\Sigma_k = \frac{\sum_{j=1}^{N}\mu_{kj}(z_j - v_k)(z_j - v_k)^T}{\sum_{j=1}^{N}\mu_{kj}} \tag{6}$$

We notice that when $\gamma = 1$, the FGMM is the same as GMM. However, when $\gamma \neq 1$, the FGMM can be regarded only as a clustering model, instead of a probability mixture density model [14]. So, in the paper, we try to use the FGMM to denoise images, which is an extension of the EPLL and at the same time, we will discuss the impact of the fuzziness of the model on image denoising performance, to obtain the better prior model. The details of the optimization of FGMM can be found in [14].

To train a FGMM, we select over 1×10^6 patches with 8×8 size randomly from the MR image data from the BrainWeb [6] as the training set with their DC removed. In the training process, we set the number of clusters to 100, fuzziness parameter $\gamma = [0.3, 0.4, 0.5, 0.8, 1.0, 1.2]$. The obtained model after training contains rich prior information since it was trained over a large number of clear MR image patches. For any untrained MR image patch, it should satisfy the constraint of the FGMM clustering structure as much as possible. In other words, for image denoising tasks, we try to find a reconstructed image in which every patch is close to the corrupted image patch, subject to the constraints of minimizing the FGMM prior:

$$\begin{aligned} J_F(z) =& \gamma\sum_{k=1}^{K}\mu_{ki}ln\frac{\mu_{ki}}{\pi_k} \\ &+ \sum_{k=1}^{K}\mu_{ki}\left[\frac{\omega}{2}ln\,2\pi + \frac{1}{2}ln\,|\Sigma_k|\right. \\ &\left. + \frac{1}{2}(z_i - v_k)^T\Sigma_k^{-1}(z_i - v_k)\right] \end{aligned} \tag{7}$$

Here, $\omega = 8 \times 8$ is the number of pixels in each image patch.

3   Image Denoising Based on the FGMM Clustering of Image Patches

3.1   Optimization

The basic idea of our method is to try to minimize the FGMM prior while still close to the corrupted image. Assume that the image corrupted model is defined by following:

$$y = \mathbf{A}x + \epsilon \tag{8}$$

where x is an original image and y is the corrupted image (observation image), $\mathbf{A}$ is the corrupted matrix and ϵ is random noise with standard deviation σ. According to the detail in Sect. 2, we construct the cost function as:

$$f(x|y) = \frac{\lambda}{2}\|\mathbf{A}x - y\|_2^2 + J_F(x) \tag{9}$$

Equation (9) is optimization objective function of whole images. The dimensionality of whole images is too huge to optimize. In order to optimize Eq. (9), we use the "Half Quadratic Splitting", introducing image patches, as an alternative optimization method to reduce the optimization difficulty.

Firstly, a set of auxiliary variables $\{z^i\}_1^N$ is introduced to approximate the overlapping patches $\mathbf{R}_i x$, yielding the following cost function:

$$
\begin{aligned}
C(x, z|y) =& \frac{\lambda}{2}\|\mathbf{A}x - y\|_2^2 + \sum_{i=1}^{N} \left\{ \frac{\beta}{2}\|\mathbf{R}_i x - z^i\|_2^2 \right. \\
&+ \left. \sum_{j=1}^{K} \frac{\mu_{ki}}{2}(z_i - v_k)^T \Sigma_k^{-1}(z_i - v_k) \right\} \\
&+ Const
\end{aligned}
\tag{10}
$$

λ and β are both parameters It should be noted that as $\beta \to \infty$, $\mathbf{R}_i x$ is restricted to be equal to z^i and the solution of Eq. (10) will converge to the solution of Eq. (9). So, we set $\beta = \frac{1}{\sigma^2}[1, 4, 8, 16, 32, 64]$ as an increasing sequence, and transform the Eq. (10) into a two-step optimization.

For each fixed value of β, optimize Eq. (10) can be carried out in the following two steps:

– Solving x while keeping z^i

For this step, the third term on the right side of Eq. (10) is a constant, so the whole optimization problem becomes the extreme point problem of solving the quadratic function of x. Take the derivative of x Eq. (10), set it to 0 and solve the result yielding the following equation:

$$
\begin{aligned}
\hat{x} =& (\lambda \mathbf{A}^T \mathbf{A} + \beta \sum_{i=1}^{N} \mathbf{R}_i^T \mathbf{R}_i)^{-1} \\
& (\lambda \mathbf{A}^T y + \beta \sum_{i=1}^{N} \mathbf{R}_i^T z^i)
\end{aligned}
\tag{11}
$$

– Solving z^i given x

For this step, the first term of Eq. (10) is a constant. Similarly, we can obtain the following equation:

$$\hat{z}_i = \left(\beta \mathbf{I} + \sum_{k=1}^{K} \mu_{ki} \mathbf{\Sigma}_k^{-1} \right)^{-1}$$
$$\left(\beta \mathbf{R}_i x + \sum_{k=1}^{K} \mu_{ki} \mathbf{\Sigma}_k^{-1} v_k \right) \tag{12}$$

Due to the numbers of patches and clusters are both large, it is difficult to take out each μ_{ki} from the membership matrix $U = [\mu_{ki}]^{K \times N}$ to calculate the weighted average of $\mathbf{\Sigma}_k^{-1}$ and $\mathbf{\Sigma}_k^{-1} v_k$. Therefore, we choose the component k^* corresponding to the maximum membership μ_{ki} for each patch z_i to substitute the weighted average:

$$\hat{z}_i = \left(\sigma^2 \mathbf{I} + \mathbf{\Sigma}_{k^*} \right)^{-1}$$
$$\left(\mathbf{\Sigma}_{k^*} \mathbf{R}_i x + \sigma^2 \mathbf{I} v_{k^*} \right) \tag{13}$$

About the maximum membership, we use the following equation to estimate:

$$k^* = arg \max_k \mu_{ki}, \forall i = 1, 2, ..., N$$
$$\mu_{ki} = \frac{\pi_k [\mathcal{N}(z_i | v_k, \mathbf{\Sigma}_k)]^{\frac{1}{\gamma}}}{\sum_{h=1}^{K} \pi_h [\mathcal{N}(z_i | v_h, \mathbf{\Sigma}_h)]^{\frac{1}{\gamma}}} \tag{14}$$

3.2 Details

Now, we have obtained a complete algorithm for restoring images from noisy images based on the FGMM clustering prior of image patches. Some details should be noted.

When we set $\gamma = 1$, and use the clustering with the largest membership for approximation, the proposed is the same with EPLL totally. So, our method can be regarded as an extension of EPLL. Meanwhile, because the proposed method using the clustering model——FGMM, which has no probabilistic meaning in most cases, it is more universal than EPLL.

About the choice of β, we estimate the value of $\beta = \frac{1}{\sigma^2} \cdot [1, 4, 8, 16.31, 64]$ according to the initial observation image y, in which noise level σ is a constant. According to [26], in each iteration step for the fixed β, the current noise level $\sigma \approx \sqrt{\frac{1}{\beta}}$. In other words, in Eq. (13), σ is the current noise level estimated by the current β, rather than the initial noise level. As for λ, we set $\lambda = \frac{\omega}{\sigma^2}$ is a constant according to the initial noise level and the size of each image patch.

The detailed algorithm is shown in the following Algorithm 1.

Algorithm 1. Image denoising using the FGMM clustering

1: Select images and divide them into overlapping patches as the training set to construct the FGMM clustering.
2: **Input**: corrupted image $x^{(l)} = y$, set parameters β, and λ, the number of iterations equal to 0.
3: Fix β at $\beta^{(l+1)}$.
4: **Z step**: divide $x^{(l)}$ into overlapping patches $\{z^i\}_1^N$, then denoise the image patches according to Eq. (13), and obtain $z^{(l+1)}$.
5: **X step**: Denoise the whole image according to Eq. (11), and obtain $x^{(l+1)}$.
6: The number of iterations $l = l + 1$.
7: Repeat 3-6 until the traversal of β is complete.
8: **Output**: final denoised image $\hat{x}$.

---

4   Experiments

We conduct some comparative experiments to test the performance of the proposed image denoising method based on the FGMM clustering of image patches. All experiments are carried out on MR images from the BrainWeb [6] Database. Patches we used in the work contain 8×8 pixels. For the FGMM clustering prior, we randomly select 98 images from the Database and divided them into 1×10^6 overlapping image patches, with their DC removed, all black or all white image patches removed and the same patches removed. After all of these steps, we obtain 6 FGMM prior with $\gamma = [0.3, 0.4, 0.5, 0.8, 1.0, 1.2]$ respectively.

At the beginning of the experiment, we choose 8 additional images as test images, which are different from above 98 images, shown in the following Fig. 1:

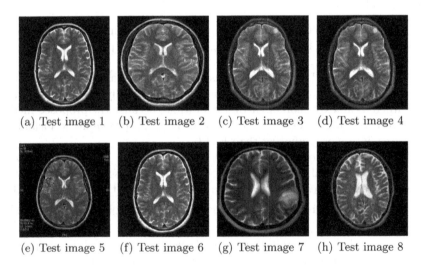

(a) Test image 1   (b) Test image 2   (c) Test image 3   (d) Test image 4

(e) Test image 5   (f) Test image 6   (g) Test image 7   (h) Test image 8

Fig. 1. The test set of MR images

Firstly, we add Gaussian noise to the test images, with the noise level setting $\sigma = 25$, using the 6 established prior models to implement the proposed denoising method. The result is shown in the Table 1. The proposed method has better denoising performance in the test images with Gaussian noise than EPLL ($\gamma = 1$). The FGMM with $\gamma = 0.5$ has the best performance in the most cases.

Table 1. The PSNR results with Gaussian noise

No	γ					
	1.2	1 (GMM)	0.8	0.5	0.4	0.3
1	31.0489	31.2053	31.2600	**31.3893**	31.2805	30.1186
2	25.8619	26.1727	26.2336	**26.3857**	26.0896	25.0122
3	30.6136	30.6564	30.8870	**30.9384**	30.8547	30.6132
4	30.5058	30.7494	30.8597	**31.0281**	30.8025	30.6890
5	28.2489	28.5550	**28.7637**	28.7553	27.9526	27.5773
6	31.0209	31.1906	31.2704	**31.3741**	31.2877	30.1369
7	29.8978	30.1421	30.1414	**30.3646**	30.1785	29.9660
8	28.0790	28.2204	28.2775	**28.4139**	28.3720	27.7946

Then, Fig. 2 shows the details of denoising performance in the test image 1 with added $\sigma = 50$ Gaussian noise, and at the same time, we compare the result with three popular filter methods, including Median filter, and Average filter and Winner filter. As the noise level σ increases, the advantages of the proposed method become more obvious.

Finally, We also add Rician noise to the test image 7 and conduct the comparison experiments on the its denoising. Our method also achieves good performance, as shown in Fig. 3.

5 Dsiscussion

In this work, we propose an image denoising method based on the FGMM clustering of image patches, and we conduct experiments using the proposed method to denoise MR images and achieve good performance.

The proposed method can be regarded as an extension of EPLL. The FGMM cannot be used as a density function, only used as a clustering model, and therefore, the proposed method has more general applicability. We also have following conclusions through experiments:

- When $\gamma = 0.5$, the proposed method can achieve the best performance in most cases.
- The proposed method is better than EPLL in both Gaussian noise and Rician noise reduction.
- The proposed method can also complete the denoising tasks for images with Rician noise.

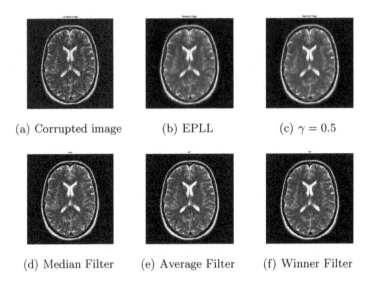

(a) Corrupted image   (b) EPLL   (c) $\gamma = 0.5$

(d) Median Filter   (e) Average Filter   (f) Winner Filter

Fig. 2. Examples of denoising the test image 1; (a) is the initial image added Gaussian noise with $\sigma = 50$, and its PSNR equals to 14.16; (b) is the denoising image using EPLL, and its PSNR equals to 27.15; (c) is the denoising image using the proposed method, and its PSNR equals to 27.38; (d) is the denoising image using Median filter, and its PSNR equals to 21.73; (e) is the denoising image using Average filter, and its PSNR equals to 23.41; (f) is the denoising image using Wiener filter, and its PSNR equals to 24.71;

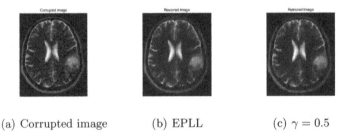

(a) Corrupted image   (b) EPLL   (c) $\gamma = 0.5$

Fig. 3. Examples of denoising the test image 7; (a) is the initial image added Rician noise with $\sigma = 25$, and its PSNR equals to 20.65; (b) is the denoising image using EPLL, and its PSNR equals to 24.48; (c) is the denoising image using the proposed method, and its PSNR equals to 24.62;

After all, we should notice that the image patches is converted to the vectors in the optimization of FGMM. This ignores the spatial relationship between pixels and may cause a large amount of information loss. Therefore, in future work, we will try to establish a model that considers the spatial relationship of pixels and apply it to image denoising.

References

1. Ahishakiye, E., Gijzen, M.B.V., Tumwiine, J., Obungoloch, J.: A dictionary learning approach for noise-robust image reconstruction in low-field magnetic resonance imaging. In: 2020 IST-Africa Conference (IST-Africa), pp. 1–12, May 2020. iSSN: 2576-8581
2. Alekya, K., Vijayalakshmi, K., Radha, N., Nandan, D.: Colour image de-noising analysis based on improved non-local mean filter. In: Kumar, A., Mozar, S. (eds.) ICCCE 2020. LNEE, vol. 698, pp. 1169–1178. Springer, Singapore (2021). https://doi.org/10.1007/978-981-15-7961-5_108
3. Buades, A., Coll, B., Morel, J.M.: Non-local means denoising. Image Process. Line **1**, 208–212 (2011)
4. Chen, Z., Zhou, Z., Adnan, S.: Joint low-rank prior and difference of Gaussian filter for magnetic resonance image denoising. Med. Biolog. Eng. Comput. **59**(3), 607–620 (2021)
5. Cheng, K., Du, J., Zhou, H., Zhao, D., Qin, H.: Image super-resolution based on half quadratic splitting. Infrared Phys. Technol. **105**, 103193 (2020)
6. Collins, D.L., et al.: Design and construction of a realistic digital brain phantom. IEEE Trans. Med. Imaging **17**(3), 463–468 (1998). https://doi.org/10.1109/42.712135. Conference Name: IEEE Transactions on Medical Imaging
7. Dong, W., Li, X., Zhang, L., Shi, G.: Sparsity-based image denoising via dictionary learning and structural clustering. In: CVPR 2011, pp. 457–464, June 2011. https://doi.org/10.1109/CVPR.2011.5995478. iSSN: 1063-6919
8. Goyal, B., Agrawal, S., Sohi, B., Dogra, A.: Noise Reduction in MR brain image via various transform domain schemes. Res. J. Pharm. Technol. **9**(7), 919 (2016). https://doi.org/10.5958/0974-360X.2016.00176.1
9. Guo, L., Chen, L., Chen, C.L.P.: Shadowed non-local image guided filter. In: Ninth International Conference on Graphic and Image Processing (ICGIP 2017), vol. 10615, p. 1061552. International Society for Optics and Photonics, April 2018. https://doi.org/10.1117/12.2302633. https://www.spiedigitallibrary.org/conference-proceedings-of-spie/10615/1061552/Shadowed-non-local-image-guided-filter/10.1117/12.2302633.short
10. Guo, L., Chen, L., Li, T., Chen, C.L.P.: Fuzzy non-local image guided filter and averaging. In: 2017 International Conference on Fuzzy Theory and Its Applications (iFUZZY), pp. 1–6, November 2017. https://doi.org/10.1109/iFUZZY.2017.8311801. iSSN: 2377-5831
11. Guo, L., Chen, L., Wu, Y., Chen, C.L.P.: Image guided Fuzzy C-means for image segmentation. In: 2016 International Conference on Fuzzy Theory and Its Applications (iFuzzy), pp. 1–6, November 2016. https://doi.org/10.1109/iFUZZY.2016.8004969. iSSN: 2377-5831
12. He, R., Zheng, W., Tan, T., Sun, Z.: Half-quadratic-based iterative minimization for robust sparse representation. IEEE Trans. Pattern Anal. Mach. Intell. **36**(2), 261–275 (2014). https://doi.org/10.1109/TPAMI.2013.102. Conference Name: IEEE Transactions on Pattern Analysis and Machine Intelligence
13. Heo, Y.C., Kim, K., Lee, Y.: Image denoising using non-local means (NLM) approach in magnetic resonance (MR) imaging: a systematic review. Appl. Sci. **10**(20), 7028, January 2020
14. Ichihashi, H., Miyagishi, K., Honda, K.: Fuzzy c-means clustering with regularization by K-L information. In: 10th IEEE International Conference on Fuzzy Systems. (Cat. No.01CH37297), vol. 2, pp. 924–927, December 2001. https://doi.org/10.1109/FUZZ.2001.1009107

15. Kalavathi, P., Priya, T.: Removal of impulse noise using Histogram-based localized wiener filter for MR brain image restoration. In: 2016 IEEE International Conference on Advances in Computer Applications (ICACA), pp. 4–8, October 2016. https://doi.org/10.1109/ICACA.2016.7887913

16. Lin, L., Meng, X., Liang, X.: Reduction of impulse noise in MRI images using block-based adaptive median filter. In: 2013 IEEE International Conference on Medical Imaging Physics and Engineering, pp. 132–134, October 2013. https://doi.org/10.1109/ICMIPE.2013.6864519

17. Manjón, J.V., Coupé, P., Buades, A.: MRI noise estimation and denoising using non-local PCA. Med. Image Anal. **22**(1), 35–47 (2015)

18. Manjón, J.V., Coupé, P., Buades, A., Louis Collins, D., Robles, M.: New methods for MRI denoising based on sparseness and self-similarity. Med. Image Anal. **16**(1), 18–27 (2012)

19. Miyamoto, S., Umayahara, K.: Fuzzy clustering by quadratic regularization. In: 1998 IEEE International Conference on Fuzzy Systems Proceedings. IEEE World Congress on Computational Intelligence (Cat. No.98CH36228), vol. 2, pp. 1394–1399, May 1998. https://doi.org/10.1109/FUZZY.1998.686323. iSSN: 1098-7584

20. Mustafi, A., Ghorai, S.K.: A novel blind source separation technique using fractional Fourier transform for denoising medical images. Optik **124**(3), 265–271 (2013)

21. Nayak, D.R., Dash, R., Majhi, B.: Brain MR image classification using two-dimensional discrete wavelet transform and AdaBoost with random forests. Neurocomputing **177**, 188–197 (2016)

22. Orujov, F., Maskeliūnas, R., Damaševičius, R., Wei, W.: Fuzzy based image edge detection algorithm for blood vessel detection in retinal images. Appl. Soft Comput. **94**, 106452 (2020)

23. Singh, D., Kaur, A.: Fuzzy based fast non local mean filter to denoise Rician noise. Mater. Today Proc. (2021)

24. Wang, H., Cen, Y., He, Z., He, Z., Zhao, R., Zhang, F.: Reweighted low-rank matrix analysis with structural smoothness for image denoising. IEEE Trans. Image Process. **27**(4), 1777–1792 (2018). https://doi.org/10.1109/TIP.2017.2781425. Conference Name: IEEE Transactions on Image Processing

25. Wei, H., Chen, L., Xu, L.: Tensor decomposition for poisson image denoising. In: 2019 International Conference on Fuzzy Theory and Its Applications (iFUZZY), pp. 158–162, November 2019. https://doi.org/10.1109/iFUZZY46984.2019.9066222. iSSN: 2377-5831

26. Zoran, D., Weiss, Y.: From learning models of natural image patches to whole image restoration. In: 2011 International Conference on Computer Vision, pp. 479–486. IEEE, Barcelona, November 2011. https://doi.org/10.1109/ICCV.2011.6126278. http://ieeexplore.ieee.org/document/6126278/

3D-Resnet Fused Attention for Autism Spectrum Disorder Classification

Xiangjun Chen[1(✉)], Zhaohui Wang[1], Faouzi Alaya Cheikh[2], and Mohib Ullah[2]

[1] School of Computer Science and Cyberspace Security, Hainan University, Haikou, China
[2] The Norwegian Colour and Visual Computing Laboratory, Norwgian University of Science and Technology, Trondheim, Norway

Abstract. Autism spectrum disorder (ASD) is a neuro development condition, early diagnosis of ASD traits is indispensable for applying effective treatment. Analysis of ASD based on deep learning (DL) has become an active research topic in the field of medical image analysis. However, the classification performance of the DL models is severely affected by the class imbalance of medical images. Recently, the combination of attention mechanism and Convolutional Neural Network (CNN) has significantly improved the performance of numerous classification and recognition tasks. Therefore, the attention mechanism has a promising prospect in improving the performance of CNN-based ASD diagnosis. This paper proposes a 3D-ResNet model with an attention subnet for ASD diagnosis. The model is constructed by the residual attention module, which is designed to mask redundant regions that are irrelevant to ASD diagnostic classification during the feature extraction process. The fMRI from Autism Imaging Data Exchange (ABIDE) was applied as the datasets and the experimental results show that the performance of the proposed approach is significantly better than that of conventional DL models.

Keywords: ASD diagnosis · Class imbalance · Attention mechanism · 3D · ResNet · Classification · ABIDE

1 Introduction

Autistic spectrum disorder (ASD) is a common mental development disorder characterized by cognitive delays, repetitive behaviors, and social deficits. ASD generally occurs in children of 2 and 3 years old and the cause of ASD is uncertain. In the world, there is a prevalence of ASD that ranges between 6 and 16 per 1000 children [1]. Due to the lack of typical medical tests and the intricacies of pathogenic factors, diagnosis is often intractable. Early identification of ASD is essential for patients. Efficient diagnosis of ASD can save time for education and treatment. Early intervention can also reduce a lot the energy and material consumption, and obtain good therapeutic results.

Unfortunately, the pathological description of ASD lacks precise definition. The conventional ASD diagnosis method is based on statistical behavior observation, e.g., the Autism Diagnosis Observation Schedule (ADOS) has been extensively applied in

© Springer Nature Switzerland AG 2021
Y. Peng et al. (Eds.): ICIG 2021, LNCS 12889, pp. 607–617, 2021.
https://doi.org/10.1007/978-3-030-87358-5_49

ASD screening [2, 3]. However, this diagnostic method is not only time-consuming and labor-intensive but also affected by the subjective bias of the diagnostician.

More recently, a large amount of radiographic imaging data have been accumulated with the rapid development of imaging technologies, e.g. MRI, CT, X-Ray, PET, etc. Therefore, disease diagnosis research based on radiographic imaging data has become feasible, and various disease diagnosis methods have emerged, e.g. analysis of neurological diseases in functional magnetic resonance imaging (fMRI), X-ray based fracture examination, and computer tomography (CT) diagnosis of lung diseases, etc.

Due to the successful diagnosis of Alzheimer's disease and schizophrenia based on magnetic resonance imaging (MRI), more researchers have realized that brain abnormalities of psychiatric patients are significantly reflected in functional magnetic resonance imaging (fMRI) [4, 5]. The biomarkers hidden in the high-dimensional Spatio-temporal signals in fMRI could separate healthy subjects from psychiatric patients. The effective extraction of this high-dimensional information is very intractable, and the analysis of fMRI data of brain diseases has always been challenging. As shown in Fig. 1, Due to the brain MRI of ASD patients lacks obvious pathological features, even a professional psychiatrist can hardly identify ASD patients with naked eyes. Consequently, there is an urgent need for more advanced computer technology to automatically exploit the deep features of radiographic images.

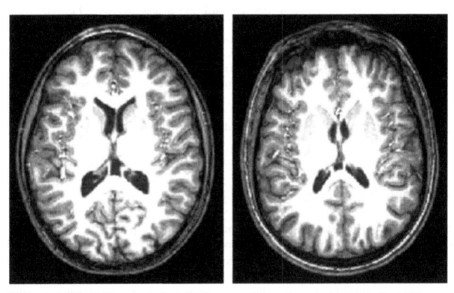

Fig. 1. Axial head MRI sample: the left is the normal control group, the right is the ASD group.

The rise of AI allows radiographic images to be transformed into extractable image features, with the purpose of quantitatively describing the image features that cannot be identified by the naked eye, leading to the concept of Radiomics. Radiomics - the high-throughput mining of large amounts of image information from radiographic images [6]. Most of the early research based on Radiomics was realized by machine learning technology, e.g. the most widely applied SVM (support vector machines) [7] in machine learning (ML) classifiers. A variety of medical image classification tasks can be solved by SVM based on different image features, e.g. SVM is introduced to ASD classification based on individual variation in functional connectivity [8, 9]. The efficiency of disease diagnosis can be improved to a certain extent with the aid of ML. However, so far, medical image analysis of brain disorders based on ML has been challenging due to the radiographic data characteristics such as structural complexity, nonlinear separability, and high dimensionality [10]. Therefore, more advanced technologies are needed to improve the robustness of computer-aided complex disease diagnosis tasks.

In the past decade, Deep learning (DL) technology has demonstrated tremendous potential in image processing and analysis. As a representative of deep learning approaches, CNN is widely used in medical image classification [11–13]. Given its excellent performance in feature extraction and the end-to-end learning strategy, CNN has been widely introduced in fMRI-based ASD diagnosis in recent years. Several CNN-based studies have achieved promising results in identifying individuals with ASD and normal controls. For example, Jain [14] deployed graph CNN on fMRI, and its accuracy rate was 70.23%. An element layer based on BrainNetCNN was proposed by Brown et al. [15]. In particular, they used an anatomically informed, data-dependent layer to improve model accuracy. To incorporate single volume images into research to take advantage of the richness of data, an image generator was designed by Ahmed [16] to generate single volume brain images from the whole-brain image. Then, an amended CNN was introduced for classification. The results of a 5-fold cross-validation showed that the model has achieved state-of-the-art performance on ABIDE. Xu et al. [17] combined Long-short term memory (LSTM) with CNN to fuse the patterns of temporal variation related to ASD, and they confirmed that the behavioral characterization of brain activity can better discover the cause of ASD. To distinguish ASD from normal controls based on input data from fMRI between regions of interest, an fully connected neural network (FCNN) was proposed by Hu et al. [18]. Recently, a CNN-based architecture to help in the diagnosis of ASD using fMRI data that are collected from a response to a speech experiment was developed by Haweel et al. [19], and excellent accuracy of 80% was achieved on 100 samples (50 ASD, 50 TD).

Although the above methods have made tremendous progress, there is still room for improvement. Severe class imbalance usually exists in medical images, typically the lesion area only occupies a few pixels of the image. To suppress irrelevant regions in the feature extraction process, an attention mechanisms is introduced to improve the classification accuracy and save computing resources. Lately, several network architectures based on attention mechanism were proposed for medical image classification. Li et al. [20] fused attention into CNN for glaucoma detection, which selectively exploits lesion features via attention prediction subnets. Ypsilantis et al. [21] proposed a stochastic attention-based model to determine which regions should be visually explored and conclude whether a specific radiological abnormality exists or not. Moreover, In the field of CNN-based ASD diagnosis, most studies [14–19] are limited to 2D kernels. Due to the great spatial complexity of MRI of ASD patients, 2D-CNNs cannot fully exploit sufficient image features [22]. Research reveals that compared to 2D-CNN, CNN with 3D convolution kernels can learn enough spatial features from the original data [23].

This paper proposes a 3D-CNNs with attention mechanism for ASD diagnosis, which aims to replace the method of screening ASD based on behavioral characteristics with a deep learning model. With the layers go deeper, the attention activation from different modules will change adaptively [24], so as to achieve the improvement of model performance and the saving of computing resources. Meanwhile, very deep networks can be constructed by combining the residual module of the attention subnet. Moreover, the introduction of 3D convolutional kernels can make full use of the spatial information of medical images. The attention subnet can generate an attention map based on original features to mask the regions in the feature map output by the residual block. Experimental results show that compared to methods in the literature, the proposal achieved excellent classification performance.

The leftover of the paper is organized as follows: Section 2 discusses the proposed method in detail; In Sect. 3, the experiment and discussion of the proposal including the dataset are presented. Finally, the conclusions are drawn in Sect. 4.

2   Proposal Network

In this section, an overview of the proposed network for ASD classification is first introduced. Then the residual attention module which combines the attention subnet with the residual block is introduced in detail. Finally, the Attention subnet of the model is described in detail.

2.1   Overview of the Framework

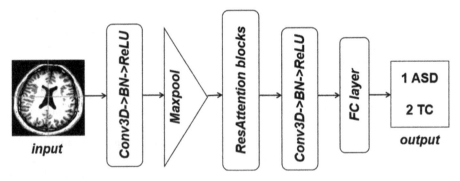

Fig. 2. The framework of the proposal

The framework of the proposal is shown in Fig. 2. The residual module integrated with the attention subnet will be applied as the main block in the framework, which is to be discussed in Sect. 2.2. The number of residual attention modules is determined by comparative experiments, which will be demonstrated in Sect. 3.2. The attention subnet is integrated with the residual module in 3D-ResNet [25] for reducing the redundancy of images, which is to be discussed in Sect. 2.3.

As shown in Fig. 2, three-dimensional brain fMRI as the input of the model, while the output is two predicted labels (1) ASD patient and (2) normal control group. Note that all convolutional layers in the model are followed by batch normalization and ReLU function for increasing the nonlinearity of the model, such that the convergence rate can be sped up. The training process of the model is a supervised end-to-end format.

2.2 Residual Attention Module

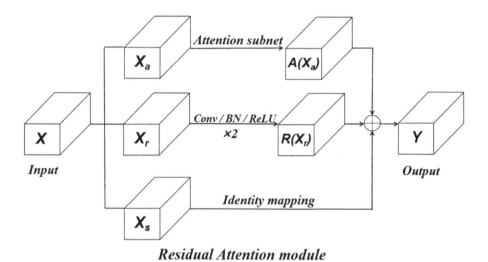

Residual Attention module

Fig. 3. The architecture of residual attention module

Residual attention modules are applied as the main module to construct the Network, the full module is illustrated in Fig. 3. As shown in Fig. 3, in each module, the yielded attention map is used to weight the feature map extracted by convolution to mask the redundant area. Specifically, the input of the residual attention module is tensor X with dimension: $104 \times 128 \times 88$, it will be fed to three parts (the input X of different parts is represented as X_a, X_r, X_s). First, X_a is sent to the attention subnet, and the output is attention map $A(X_a)$ (the specific process will be discussed in the next section). Meanwhile, X_r is sent to the residual module in parallel with the attention subnet for feature extraction and output $R(X_r)$. Afterward, we add the output of the two branches to make the redundant region in features be refined by attention map. Lastly, we add the weighted result of $R(X_r)$ and $A(X_a)$ to X_s through the identity mapping to get the output Y of the residual attention module, the dimension of Y is $104 \times 128 \times 88$. Note that the identity mapping in the last step uses the residual principle.

After the original features pass through the residual attention module, the redundant features irrelevant to ASD classification are be inhibited.e

$$Y = A(X_a) \oplus R(X_r) + X_s. \tag{1}$$

2.3 Attention Subnet

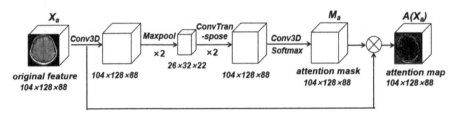

Fig. 4. The architecture of attention subnet.

The attention subnet is integrated with the residual module to generate the attention maps of the brain images to improve model accuracy. The structure of the attention subnet is shown in Fig. 4. Specifically, the original feature map X_a of the brain fMRI obtained by a convolution and max-pooling operation as the input of the model, which is represented by the tensor of size $104 \times 128 \times 88$. First, the input tensor is fed to one convolutional layer with a kernel size of $3 \times 3 \times 3$ for exploiting the hierarchical features, the result of the convolution is a feature map with constant dimensions. Meanwhile, the feature map extracted by convolution will pass through two max-pooling layers, the purpose is to compress the features. The depth of down-sampling is determined by a comparative experiment, which will be explained in Sect. 3.2. After down-sampling, features of a size of $26 \times 32 \times 22$ are obtained. Then, up-sampling with the same depth of deconvolution operation is performed to revert to the original feature map dimensions. Afterward, the convolution operation is used to further extract the features and feed the feature map into the softmax function to output the attention mask M_a. The role of softmax is to scale each element of the attention mask to $(0,1)$. Lastly, the attention map $A(X_a)$ is obtained by weighting the original feature X_a and the attention mask M_a.

In the next stage, $A(X_a)$ will be added to the output of the residual block to refine the redundant features in its output. Noteworthy, the attention map $A(Xa)$ can be used not only to serve as a feature selector during the forward inference process but also as a gradient update filter during the backward propagation process. Hence, the attention subnet can prevent wrong gradients to update the parameters. The predicted attention map can be fused with the feature map output by the residual block, thereby effectively focusing the activation of the network on the salient region.

3 Experiments and Results

3.1 Datasets

The fMRI from Autism Imaging Data Exchange (ABIDE) [26] was introduced as the experimental datasets. The ABIDE datasets aggregates and openly share 1112 existing fMRI datasets from 539 individuals with ASDs (autism, Asperger, and pervasive developmental disorder) and 573 age-matched normal controls (5–64 years). Most of the included subjects were adolescents (median age was 13 years), and one-third of them were diagnosed with ASD. In this study, only the MRI scans collected from 500 individuals are used to evaluate the proposed method, where the ASD patient's label is 1, and the normal controls label is 0.

The dimension of each brain MR scan sample in ABIDE set is $208 \times 256 \times 176$, the image format is.nii which is a standard neuroimaging format. Figure 5 shows the scanning of a sample in different directions.

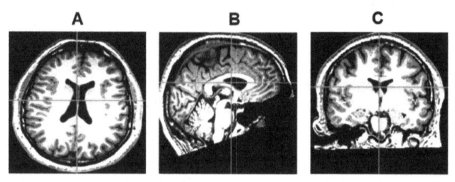

Fig. 5. Sample of ABIDE. Each sample includes three planes: (A) Axial, (B) Sagittal, (C) Coronal.

3.2 Classification Results and Discusion

To evaluate the proposed method, two comparative experiments were implemented. One is to explore the rationality of the proposed model via setting various numbers of residual attention modules and the adoption of different structures in the Attention subnet. In another experiment, the classification performance of the proposed algorithm was verified by comparison with methods from the literature.

The model weights were optimized by the cross-entropy loss and Adam optimizer with learning rate of 0.001, and momentum of 0.9. Models were trained for 50 epochs, and the epoch with the best accuracy on the validation was selected. The confusion matrix is obtained by comparing the classified labels and gold-standard labels, from which true negative (TN), false negative (FN), true positive (TP), and false positive (FP) are calculated to quantify the performance of the proposed method. Then, the accuracy, sensitivity, and specificity of the model are calculated as follows

$$
\begin{aligned}
\text{accracy} &= \frac{TP + TN}{TP + TN + FP + FN} \\
\text{sensitivity} &= \frac{TP}{TP + FN} \\
\text{specificity} &= \frac{TN}{TN + FP}
\end{aligned}
\tag{2}
$$

Exploration of Structural Rationality: The first experiment is implemented to explore its impact on model performance via designing several architectures with different numbers of residual attention modules stacked orderly in the network. Figure 5 shows the model classification accuracy when stacking different numbers of structures on the ABIDE dataset. From the chart, it can be observed that when the number of residual attention modules in the network is less than 3, the performance is poor. The network achieved its best performance when the number of residual attention modules is set to 3. However, the classification accuracy began to decline with the continuous increase of the number of residual attention modules involved. Consequently, in the next experiment, the number of modules in the network is set to 3.

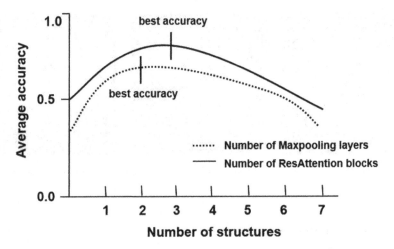

Fig. 6. The relationship between model accuracy and the number of structures.

In addition, different depth auto-encoding structures were tried to explore the rationality of the proposed attention subnet design. Specifically, the best feature is obtained by downsampling the features extracted by the convolutional layer through max-pooling, and then the predicted attention map is output through the ConvTranspose operation of the same depth.

Max-pooling layers of different depths (up-sampling has the same number of layers as down-sampling) are tried, and the accuracy of the models under different numbers of max-pooling layers is reflected in Fig. 6. From the chart, it can be observed that when the depth of the down (up) sampling layers are less than 2, the performance is poor. The reason for this result is that some redundant features are not fully removed. Similarly, when the number of down (up) sampling layers are more than 2, the network performance drops again. This is probably due to excessive downsampling, resulting in the loss of some important features. Therefore, the down (up) sampling layer in the attention subnet are set to 2 in the next experiment.

Model Performance Comparison: The second experiment is implemented to demonstrate the performance of the proposal. Table 1 compares the model metrics of the proposed method with different ASD classification models. To demonstrate the advantages of automatic feature extraction of deep learning, the differences between SVM and the proposed methods are compared, and the results reveal that the deep learning model can automatically exploit more high-dimensional related features. Meanwhile, to demonstrate the advantages of 3D kernels compared to 2D kernels, the performance between BrainNetCNN with 2D kernels and the proposed methods are compared, and the results prove that the proposal can make better use of the spatial features of the data. The 3D-ResNet with the same depth as the proposed network was used on the same datasets to demonstrate the influence of the attention subnet on the performance of the model. Compared with the 3D-ResNet the proposed model has superior performance, which confirms the positive effect of the attention subnet in masking the redundant features. The performance of 3D-AlexNet integrated with the attention subnet on ABIDE is also used for comparison. The results reveal that under the same model depth, the performance of 3D-AlexNet is much lower than the proposed model. The reason for this phenomenon probably is the vanishing/exploding gradient occurring when training the deep 3D-AlexNet, which demonstrates the advantage of introducing the residual structures in the proposal.

Table 1. Performance of different models on ABIDE.

Metrics/Method	Accracy	Sensitivity	Specificity
SVM	0.65	0.68	0.62
BrainNetCNN	0.67	0.68	0.67
3D-ResNet	0.56	0.58	0.62
3D-AlexNet	0.66	0.64	0.73
Ours	0.71	0.66	0.69

4 Conclusion

In this paper, an efficient fused attention subnet model is proposed to classify ASD and neurotypical subjects. As the crucial component of the model, the residual attention module can effectively mask the redundant regions of the original feature map to achieve higher performance. Multiple sets of controlled experiments are used to prove that the method is superior to machine learning methods and a variety of deep learning classification models. Future directions include modifying the architecture to incorporate multimodal brain MRI. Also, incorporating phenotypic data, such as behavioral characteristics, to further improve model classification accuracy is an interesting future research direction.

References

1. Lanillos, P., Oliva, D., Philippsen, A.: A review on neural network models of schizophrenia and autism spectrum disorder. Neural Netw. **122**, 338–363 (2020)

2. Zwaigenbaum, L., Bauman, M.L., Stone, W.L., et al.: Early identification of autism spectrum disorder: recommendations for practice and research. Pediatrics **136**(Suppl 1), S10-40 (2015)
3. Landa, R.J., Gross, A.L., Stuart, E.A., et al.: Developmental trajectories in children with and without autism spectrum disorders: the first 3 years. Child Dev **84**(2), 429–442 (2013)
4. Rudie, J.D., Hernandez, L.M., Brown, J.A., et al.: Autism -associated promoter variant in MET impacts functional and structural brain networks. Neuron **75**(5), 904–915 (2012)
5. Tyszka, J.M., Kennedy, D.P., Paul, L.K., et al.: Largely typical patterns of resting-state functional connectivity in high-functioning adults with autism. Cereb Cortex **24**(7), 1894–1905 (2014)
6. Lambinp, ., et al.: Radiomics: extracting more information from medical images using advanced feature analysis. Eur. J. Cancer **48**(4), 441–446 (2012)
7. Cortes, C., Vapnik, V.: Support-vector networks. Mach. Learn. **20**, 273–297 (1995)
8. Wang, C., Xiao, Z., Wang, B., Wu, J.: Identifification of autism based on svm-rfe and stacked sparse auto-encoder. IEEE Access **7**, 118 030–118 036 (2019)
9. Yao, Z., et al.: Resting-state time-varying analysis reveals aberrant variations of functional connectivity in autism. Front. Hum. Neurosci. **10**, 463 (2016)
10. Cao, B., Kong, X., Yu, P.S.: A review of heterogeneous data mining for brain disorder identifification. Brain Inf. **2**(4), 253–264 (2015)
11. Volden, J.: Autism spectrum disorder. In: Cummings, L. (ed.) Research in Clinical Pragmatics. PPPP, vol. 11, pp. 59–83. Springer, Cham (2017). https://doi.org/10.1007/978-3-319-474 89-2_3
12. Ohno, Y., et al.: Machine learning for lung ct texture analysis: improvement of inter-observer agreement for radiological finding classification in patients with pulmonary diseases. Eur. J. Radiol. (2020). https://doi.org/10.1016/j.ejrad.2020.109410
13. Al-Masni, M.A., Al-Antari, M.A., Park, J.M., et al.: Simultaneous detection and classification of breast masses in digital mammograms via a deep learning YOLO-based CAD system. Comput. Methods Programs Biomed. **157**, 85–94 (2018)
14. Jain, S.M.: Detection of autism using magnetic resonance imaging data and graph convolutional neural networks detection of autism using magnetic resonance imaging data and graph convolutional neural networks. Mater Dissertation, Rochester Institute of Technology 2018)
15. Brown, C.J., Kawahara, J., Hamarneh, G.: Connectome priors in deep neural networks to predict autism. In: 2018 IEEE 15th International Symposium on Biomedical Imaging (ISBI 2018), pp. 110–113, Washington, DC, USA, April 2018
16. Ahmed, M.R., Zhang, Y., Liu, Y., Liao, H.: Single volume image generator and deep learning-based ASD classification. IEEE J. Biomed. Health Inf. **24**(11), 3044–3054 (2020). https://doi.org/10.1109/JBHI.2020.2998603
17. Lingyu, X., Liu, Y., Jie, Y., Li, X., Xuan, Y., Cheng, H., Li, J.: Characterizing autism spectrum disorder by deep learning spontaneous brain activity from functional near-infrared spectroscopy. J. Neurosci. Meth. **331**, 108538 (2020). https://doi.org/10.1016/j.jneumeth.2019.108538
18. Jinlong, H., Cao, L., Li, T., Liao, B., Dong, S., Li, P.: Interpretable learning approaches in resting-state functional connectivity analysis: the case of autism spectrum disorder. Comput. Math. Meth. Med. **2020**, 1–12 (2020). https://doi.org/10.1155/2020/1394830
19. Reem, H., Ahmed, S., Ali, M.: A Robust DWT-CNN Based CAD System for Early Diagnosis of Autism Using Task-based fMRI. Med. Phys. **30**, 2315–2326 (2020)
20. Li, L., Xu, M., Wang, X.: Attention Based Glaucoma Detection: A Large-scale Database and CNN. arXiv:1903.10831v3 [cs.CV] 21 Apr 2019
21. Ypsilantis, P.-P., Montana, G.: Learning what to look in chest x-rays with a recurrent visual attention model. arXiv:1701.06452 (2017)

22. Kensho, H., Hirokatsu, K.: Yutaka Satoh. Can Spatiotemporal 3D CNNs Retrace the History of 2D CNNs and ImageNet. National Institute of Advanced Industrial Science and Technology (AIST). arXiv:1711.09577v2 [cs.CV] 2 Apr 2018

23. Kensho, H., Hirokatsu, K., Yutaka, S.: Towards good practice for action recognition with spatiotemporal 3D convolutions. 2018 24th International Conference on Pattern Recognition (ICPR), 20–24(August 2018), 2516–2522

24. Wang, F., Jiang, M., Qian, C., et al.: Residual Attention Network for Image Classification. arXiv:1704.06904v1 [cs.CV] 23 Apr 2017

25. He, K., Zhang, X., Ren, S., Sun, J.: Deep residual learning for image recognition. Proceedings of the IEEE Conference on Computer Vision and Pattern Recognition, pp. 770–778 (2016)

26. Di Martino, A., et al.: The autism brain imaging data exchange: towards large-scale evaluation of the intrinsic brain architecture in autism. Molecul. Psychiatry 19(6), 659–667 (2014)

CEID: Benchmark Dataset for Designing Segmentation Algorithms of Instruments Used in Colorectal Endoscopy

Wanwan Han[1], Guanghui Yue[1(✉)], Lvyin Duan[1], Xue Bai[2], Jingfeng Du[2(✉)], Tianwei Zhou[3], and Tianfu Wang[1]

[1] School of Biomedical Engineering, Health Science Centre,
Shenzhen University, Shenzhen, China
yueguanghui@szu.edu.cn
[2] Department of Gastroenterology and Hepatology,
Shenzhen University General Hospital, Shenzhen, China
[3] College of Management, Shenzhen University, Shenzhen, China

Abstract. Recently, a large number of computer-assisted methods have been reported for colorectal lesions (e.g., polyp, inflammation, perforation, etc.) detection, segmentation, and classification in endoscopy to improve the operating efficiency of clinicians and surgical robots. However, few works specially involve endoscopic instruments which play a great role in lesion screening, tracking, and diagnosis. To promote the development of this field, we create a colorectal endoscopic instrument dataset (CEID) in this paper, which consists of 1032 images containing colorectal procedure instruments, such as snares, titanium clips, entry needles, high frequency electrotomes and biopsy forceps. The segmentation mask of each image was labeled and verified by two experienced gastroenterologists. Furthermore, we selected 5 classic general-purpose segmentation algorithms built for the medical image segmentation task and 2 specific-purpose segmentation algorithms built for the digestive lesion segmentation task, and tested their performance on the collected dataset. Experimental results demonstrate that, our dataset is capable of verifying different segmentation networks, and both kinds of methods cannot fully meet the clinical needs, leaving a large potential for further improvements. Benchmarking using the dataset provides an opportunity for researchers to contribute to the field of automatic instrument segmentation in colorectal endoscopy.

Keywords: Colorectal endoscopic instruments · Image segmentation · Deep learning

1 Introduction

A survey by the American Cancer Society shows that colorectal cancer has become one of the main killers threatening human life, with the third highest incidence rate and the second highest mortality rate in the world [1]. Currently, early screening and treatment of colorectal diseases (e.g., inflammation, vascular disease, and polyps) are clinically

© Springer Nature Switzerland AG 2021
Y. Peng et al. (Eds.): ICIG 2021, LNCS 12889, pp. 618–629, 2021.
https://doi.org/10.1007/978-3-030-87358-5_50

considered as an effective way to prevent colorectal cancer. In disease screening and treatment, endoscopy plays a vital role as it facilitates gastroenterologist to observe the morphological characteristics of lesions [2]. During colorectal endoscopy, a variety of instruments are used in lesion screening, detection, and surgery. For example, the charged thermal biopsy forceps and snare are used to scald and cut the polyp in colorectal polypectomy, respectively.

Further, with the rapid development of computer technology, the surgical robots have gradually entered clinical. For example, Da Vinci Surgical Robot is used for laparoscopic surgery [3]. Specially, instruments segmentation and tracking can effectively improve the intelligent operation system of robotic. In view of these, automatically segmenting the instrument area has important significance for colorectal disease diagnosis since it can either provide a prior knowledge for the follow-up task, e.g., assist surgical robot implement instrument or lesion tracking. Unfortunately, researchers paid little attention on designing instrument segmentation algorithms in endoscopic images, while mainly focused on proposing new lesion segmentation algorithms in recent years. For example, considering that polyps are varied in shapes, sizes, colors and textures, Nguyen et al. [4] proposed a multi-model deep segmentation network named MED-Net by combining a multi-scale encoder and a multi-scale decoder. The network obtains multi-level contextual information to improve the prediction accuracy by extracting discriminative features at different receptive fields and multi-scales. Similarity, Sun et al. [5] introduced the dilated convolution into UNet [6] to extract features at multi scales for fully obtaining the morphological characteristics of polyps. To further improve the segmentation accuracy, Jha et al. [7] introduced the residual module into UNet++ [8], and obtained richer semantic features by increasing the network depth.

Although many segmentation algorithms have been proposed, they do not tackle the instrument segmentation challenge well. There are two possible reasons. On the one hand, the collected endoscopic images are usually with bleeding, blurring, weak contours, feces, specular reflections and ambiguous areas between instruments and human tissues, affected by multiple factors, e.g., preoperative preparations, physiological activities of patients, and operation habits of endoscopists. On the other hand, there are different types of diseases in clinic, the instruments used for different diagnosis and treatment tasks are quite diverse in sizes, types, surfaces. These make the segmentation tasks more challenging. Therefore, it is urgent and important to design specific segmentation algorithms for colorectal endoscopic instruments. Much to our regret, this task does not receive sufficient attention, and even its prior work, i.e., constructing segmentation dataset, are extremely scarce in the literature.

To further promote the development of this field, we provide a comprehensive colorectal endoscopic instrument dataset (CEID) and give some discussion and analysis regarding this dataset by testing several recently reported segmentation algorithms in this paper. Specifically, we first carefully investigated the clinical endoscopic procedure and selected 1032 images with various instruments. Then, each image was labeled and verified by two experimental gastroenterologists. Finally, we conducted extensive experiments to discuss the necessity of designing specific segmentation algorithm for colorectal endoscopic instruments. The main contributions of this paper are three-folds:

- With the motivation mentioned above, this paper creates a colorectal endoscopic instrument dataset (with 1032 images and their segmentation masks), including varieties of instruments, such as endoscope transparent caps, titanium clips, biopsy forceps, entry needles, high-frequency electrotomes, etc.
- This paper rigorously selected five classic general-purpose and two specific-purpose segmentation algorithms, and carried out segmentation experiments on the created dataset. It presents the qualitative and quantitative experimental results, and gives detailed analysis and discussion, correspondingly.
- This paper concludes that, existing segmentation methods are still much space for improvement and have more prediction errors especially when the image covers bleeding, mirror reflections, instrument blurs, air bubbles, and color distortions. Future work needs to develop specific segmentation algorithms for endoscopic instruments.

The reminder of this paper is organized as follows. Section 2 introduces the related work. Section 3 details the construction procedure of the proposed dataset. Section 4 gives the experiment settings, experimental results and discussion. Section 5 concludes this paper.

2   Related Work

Recently, the endoscopic vision has received increasing attention of researchers in computer and medical fields. Since 2015, MICCAI (Medical Image Computing and Computer Assisted Intervention) Society has organized a series of challenges in endoscopic instrument segmentation. In 2015, MICCAI set up the "Endoscopic Vision Instrument Sub-challenge", including instrument segmentation and tracking tasks in robotic laparoscopic surgery systems. The goal of this challenge is to improve the operation accuracy of robotic surgery through instrument segmentation and tracking technology [3]. For this purpose, the challenge organizer released laparoscopy dataset for verifying and comparing different segmentation algorithms. By further considering the clinical environment, MICCAI launched the "Robot Instrument Segmentation Sub-Challenge" in 2017, where more video sequences with instrument motion and complex background recorded by Da Vinci Xi systems were added [9]. This sub-challenge consists of binary segmentation, multi-label segmentation and instrument recognition. Similarly, MICCAI organized the "Robotic Scene Segmentation challenge" in 2018, in which the dataset was expanded to 19 video sequences (recorded by Da Vinci X or Xi system) by adding a set of anatomical objects as compared to the dataset used in the challenge 2017 [10]. In 2019, MICCAI further enriched the competition contents according to the clinical needs and launched the "Robust Medical Instrument Segmentation (ROBUST-MIS) challenge" [11]. Specifically, this challenge consists of three tasks, i.e., binary segmentation, multiple instance detection and multiple instance segmentation. The dataset included 10040 images, which acquired from 10 rectal resection procedures, 10 proctocolectomy procedures, and 10 procedures of sigmoid resection procedures.

Table 1 briefly summarizes the recently reported datasets in the instrument segmentation task, the partial content of the table refer to this paper [12]. From the table, we have the following observations. First, some datasets are specifically targeted at robotic surgery system, where partial images are generated by computer rendering. It should be noted that, the segmentation algorithms trained on the rendering dataset cannot be always effective on the real-word dataset due to the intrinsic difference between two kinds of datasets. Second, almost all datasets are concurrently built for segmenting instruments used for disease diagnosis and surgery on multiple abdominal organs, such as stomach, heart, colorectum, liver, etc. No dataset is specifically proposed for colorectal endoscopic instrument segmentation. Until recently, Jha et al. [12] released a slightly relevant dataset. However, the dataset contains 590 images captured from the whole digestive tract, and only very few of them are colorectal endoscopy images. Given that both the instruments (i.e., the foreground) and organs surface (i.e., background) are quite different, the dataset collected from different abdominal organs seems unsuitable for designing an instrument

Table 1. Datasets of Endoscopic Instrument Segmentation.

Dataset	Instrument	Task	Surgery Scene	Type
Instrument segmentation and tracking (2015) [3]	Rigid and robotic instruments	Segmentation and tracking	Laparoscopy	220 images 27 video sequences
Robotic Instrument Segmentation (2017) [9]	Robotic surgical instruments	Binary segmentation, multi-label segmentation and instrument recognition	Abdominal porcine	10 video sequences
Robotic Scene Segmentation (2018) [10]	Robotic surgical instruments	Multi-instance segmentation	Robotic nephrectomy	19 video sequences
Robust Medical instrument segmentation (2019) [11]	Laparoscopic instrument	Binary segmentation, multiple instance detection and multiple instance segmentation	Laparoscopy	10040 images
Kvasir-Instrument (2020) [12]	Diagnostic and therapeutic tools in endoscopic images	Binary segmentation, detection and localization	Gastroscopy and colonoscopy	590 images
Colorectal Endoscopic Instrument Dataset (**Ours**)	Diagnostic and therapeutic tools in endoscopic images	Binary segmentation, detection and localization	colonoscopy	1032 images

segmentation method in colorectal endoscopy. Therefore, it is of significance to create colorectal endoscopic instrument segmentation datasets specifically. Such a dataset will provide a good experimental benchmark for future research.

3   Colorectal Endoscopic Instrument Dataset

3.1   Dataset Details

Our dataset consists of 1032 colorectal endoscopic images recorded by electronic gastroenteroscopy Olympus290. All images were collected in the General Hospital of Shenzhen University from 2018 to 2020. In order to meet clinical practice, the endoscopic dataset contains various image contents, e.g., bleeding, mirror reflections, faeces, and various distortions, e.g., motion blur, color change. Meanwhile, it covers majority of the screening and surgical tools used in the surgery process, including endoscopic transparent caps, titanium clips, biopsy forceps, entry needles, high frequency electrotome, etc. For each image, two experienced gastroenterologists carefully label and verify its segmentation mask. Detailed information about labelling procedure can be found in Sect. 3.2. To protect privacy, we removed all patient information and cropped the image uniformly to a size of 900×900 pixels. Figure 1 shows some samples of the created dataset. As can be seen, the selected images are with diverse instruments, which are different in color, size, location, shape, etc.

3.2   Labelling Procedure

In this paper, we selected one widely used annotation software, i.e., labelme [13], to generate the binary mask of each endoscopic image. The instrument region was manually labeled and saved into JSON files, which were further converted into the corresponding binary segmentation mask through the built-in code of labelme software. To be specific, the labeling procedure of each image was conducted by two professional gastroenterologists and could be systematically divided into three stages:

- First, one gastroenterologist rigorously selects the image with clinical significance, and coarsely points out the location of instruments.
- Then, the same gastroenterologist finely marks the instrument position in the pixel level by the labelme software.
- Finally, another gastroenterologist validates and modifies (if needed) the binary mask to determine the final segmentation ground truth.

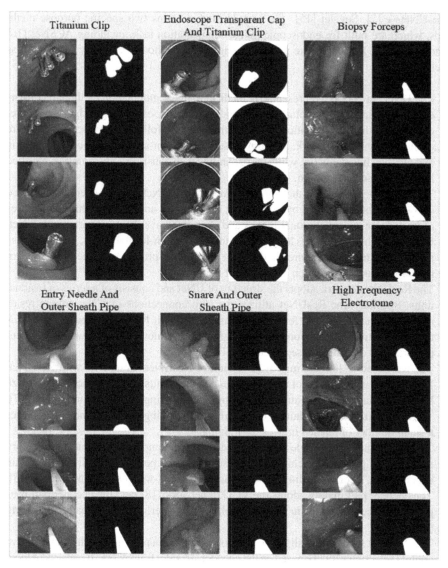

Fig. 1. Typical samples of the collected dataset: we list the color image and its binary mask for each type of instruments here (please zoom in for the better view)(Color figure online)

4   Experiments

To investigate the necessity of designing specific segmentation algorithms for instruments, we select two kinds of segmentation algorithms and test them on the collected dataset. The first kind contains five general-purpose methods, which are built for the medical image segmentation task, including UNet [6], UNet++ [8], ResUNet [14],

ResUNet++ [7], SegNet [15]. The second kind contains two specific-purpose methods, which are built for endoscopic image segmentation task, including ACSNet [16] and PraNet [17]. To facilitate understanding, these methods are briefly introduced as below.

- The UNet network is a representative medical image segmentation method. It consists of a contracting path to capture context and a symmetric expanding path to enable precise localization [6]. Specifically, the contracting path follows the typical architecture of a convolutional network, including a series of down-sampling, pooling operation and rectified linear unit [6], while the expanding path consists of up-sampling, rectified linear unit and convolution.
- The UNet++ network is the improved version of UNet. It is a deeply-supervised encoder-decoder network by connecting the encoder and decoder through a series of nested dense convolutional blocks and skip pathways [8]. Compared with UNet, UNet++ not only integrates low-level features with high-level features, but also incorporates the structural features in different depth. This promotes the network to learn more important information at each layer features.
- The ResUNet network adopts the structure of UNet and consists of a series of residual units. Specially, the ResUNet utilizes the skip connections of UNet among residual units to combine low levels information and high levels information. It facilitate information propagation without degradation, achieving comparable ever better performance on semantic segmentation [14].
- The ResUNet + + is the improved version of ResUNet. Compared with ResUNet, ResUNet + + network not only includes residual units, but also includes squeeze blocks, excitation blocks, atrous spatial pyramid pooling and attention modules [7]. The network takes full advantage of deep residual learning and UNet and only requires a small number of labeled images for training.
- The SegNet network was designed for reducing the computational time and memory usage on the premise of achieving good segmentation performance. It consists of an encoder part, a corresponding decoder part and a pixel-wise classification layer [15]. The encoder part mainly adopts the VGG16 network [18], and the decoder part uses pooling indices computed in the max-pooling step to perform non-linear up-sampling [15].
- The ACSNet was specifically proposed for polyp segmentation, which is an adaptive context selection network based on the encoder-decoder framework. It consists of local context attention module, global context module and adaptive selection module. The local context attention module delivers local context information from encoder layers to decoder layers, and the global context module obtains global context information. The adaptive selection module adaptively selects context information and aggregates these information [16].
- The PraNet utilizes parallel partial decoder and reverse attention for polyp segmentation. Specially, the parallel partial decoder is used to generate the high-level global map, which delivers semantic information through cascading multi-level features forward for enhances the performance of segmentation. The reverse attention module facilitates learning boundary information.

4.1 Experimental Settings

To ensure the comparison fairness, the source codes of all selected competing methods here are either provided by the associated authors or downloaded from the GitHub website marked with high usage rate. All methods are retrained on the collected dataset using a graphic station with NVIDIA TU102 GPU and Intel(R) Xeon(R) Silver 4210R CPU @ 2.40GHz.

All experiments is implemented in Pytorch and trained with the Adam optimizer. During the training stage of all experiment, we consistently use data processing and training methods used in PraNet network. The batch size is set to 16, each image is resized to 352×352 and then fed into selected competing models to train. We divide the dataset into training set and testing set for UNet network[1], UNet++ network[2], ResUNet network[3], ResUNet++ network[3], SegNet network[4], ACSNet network[5] and PraNet network[6]. The training set and testing set are approximately with the ratio of 8:2, i.e., 825 images in training set and 207 images in testing set.

Four evaluation criteria, i.e., Dice similarity coefficient (Dice), Intersection over Union (IoU), Sensitivity and Precision, are selected for comparing the performance among competing methods in this paper. For all criteria, higher evaluation values indicate better segmentation accuracy. Their mathematical expressions are sequentially expressed from Eq. (1) to Eq. (4):

$$Dice = \frac{2TP}{FP + 2TP + FN} \tag{1}$$

$$IoU = \frac{TP}{FP + TP + FN} \tag{2}$$

$$Sensitivity = \frac{TP}{TP + FN} \tag{3}$$

$$Precision = \frac{TP}{TP + FP} \tag{4}$$

TP (or FP) indicates the number of positive samples that are correctly classified (or misclassified), as well as TN (or FN) for negative samples.

---

[1] https://github.com/milesial/Pytorch-UNet.

[2] https://github.com/4uiiurz1/pytorch-nested-UNet.

[3] https://github.com/rishikksh20/ResUNet.

[4] https://github.com/say4n/pytorch-segnet.

[5] https://github.com/ReaFly/ACSNet.

[6] https://github.com/DengPingFan/PraNet.

4.2 Experimental Results and Analysis

The qualitative and quantitative results are shown in Fig. 2 and Table 2, respectively. Due to the limited space, we only present partial segmentation results here. In spite of this, the results, to the great extent, involve all instrument types in our dataset, including snares, titanium clips, entry needles, high frequency electrotomes, and biopsy forceps. From Fig. 2, we have the following observations. First, the general-purpose segmentation methods are usually inferior to the specific-purpose segmentation methods (see the intuitive comparison among the first five columns and the last two columns). Second, both kinds of methods perform weakly in blurred images (see the first row), and perform effectively in clear and simple images (see the eighth, ninth and eleventh rows). Third, most of the methods cannot accurately segment instrument boundary when the scenes are with multiple instruments or ambiguous areas between instruments and human tissues (see the second, third, fourth, fifth and seventh rows).

To give more insightful analysis, we further list the quantitative results in Table 2. For convenient expression, we only compare the Dice value for conclusion here. Comparison results on other evaluation criteria can also come to a similar conclusion. As can be seen, the general-purposed methods, i.e., ResUNet, UNet, ResUNet++, UNet++ and SegNet (with the Dice values of 0.748, 0.831, 0.844, 0.869 and 0.896, respectively), perform lower than the specific-purpose methods, i.e., ACSNet and PraNet (with the Dice values of 0.908 and 0.913, respectively). One possible reason is that UNet and UNet++ have the dense and complicated concatenations, which make network redundant and hard to train. Similarity, ResUNet, ResUNet++ and SegNet cannot simultaneously deal with local and global features, thereby missing partial task-related information, causing poor segmentation performance (especially on the instrument boundary). In contrast, ACSNet and PraNet respectively attempt to extract more context information and utilize reverse attention for obtaining better results. Nevertheless, almost all these methods produce prediction errors in cases of bleeding, mirror reflections, instrument blurs, air bubbles, and color distortions. There are two possible reasons:

- The appearance of different instruments (e.g., snares, titanium clips, entry needles, high frequency electrotomes, and biopsy forceps) are quite different, and the instrument number, color, size and type are uncertain in the endoscopic image. This requires the segmentation algorithm to adaptively learn multi-scale and multi-level information by fully considering color, shape features as well as semantic features. Much to our regret, the selected methods are either fail to obtain multi-scale features or insufficient to extract all task-related features simultaneously.
- The image usually has complex contents and multiple distortions during endoscopy and surgery, such as bleeding, reflections, faeces, bubbles, color bias, blurs, contrast change etc. These make the segmentation task more challenging. How to effectively deal with these challenges remains an open question currently.

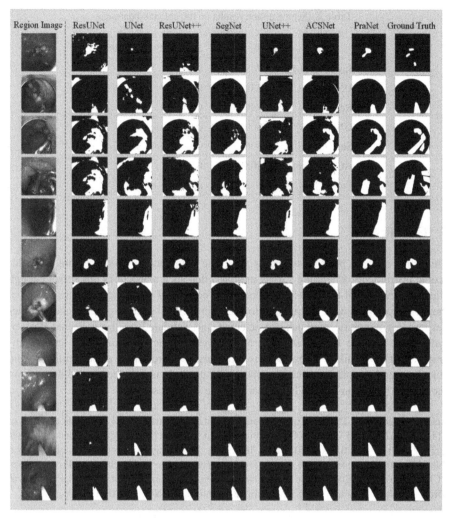

Fig. 2. Segmentation results of some typical samples in the dataset (please zoom in for the better view)

Through the analysis of experimental results, it is clear that there is still a large space for research on the colorectal endoscopy instrument segmentation. In the further research, we will extend this work and propose a specific and effective segmentation network via analysis of the characteristics of colorectal endoscopic instruments as well as the endoscopic scene information. Such a work will help to improve the operation efficiency of clinicians and surgical robots, and promote the development of intelligent medicine.

Table 2. Segmentation results on the collected dataset

	Dice	IoU	Sensitivity	Precision
ResUNet [14]	0.748	0.636	0.901	0.663
UNet [6]	0.831	0.762	0.825	0.684
ResUNet++ [7]	0.844	0.762	0.840	0.851
UNet++ [8]	0.869	0.802	0.868	0.713
SegNet [15]	0.896	0.835	0.879	0.920
ACSNet [16]	0.908	0.861	0.907	0.935
PraNet [17]	0.913	0.859	0.911	0.925

5 Conclusion

This paper makes a prior investigation about the segmentation task of colorectal endo-scopic instruments. Literature survey indicates that such a task does not attract enough attention. In view of this, we first collect 1032 colorectal endoscopic images and label them by two experienced gastroenterologist. Then, several general-purpose and specific-purpose segmentation methods are selected and validated on the collected dataset. Finally, we provide some discussion and analysis in view of qualitative and quanti-tative results. Overall speaking, there is still a large research space of designing specific colorectal endoscopic instrument segmentation algorithms, and the created dataset can served as a basic comparison benchmark for the future research.

Acknowledgement. This work was supported in part by National Natural Science Foundation of China (No. 62001302), in part by Guangdong Basic and Applied Basic Research Foundation (Nos. 2021A1515011348, 2019A1515111205), in part by Natural Science Foundation of Shenzhen (No. JCYJ20190808145011259), in part by Shenzhen Science and Technology Program (No. RCBS20200714114920379), and in part by Open Project Program of State Key Laboratory of Virtual Reality Technology and Systems, Beihang University (No. VRLAB2021C05).

References

1. Siegel, R.L., Miller, K.D., Goding Sauer, A., et al.: Colorectal cancer statistics. CA: A Cancer J. Clin. **70**(1),145–164 (2020)
2. Iddan, G., Meron, G., Glukhovsky, A., et al.: Wireless capsule endoscopy. Nature **405**(6785), 417 (2000)
3. Bodenstedt, S., Allan, M., Agustinos, A., et al.: Comparative evaluation of instrument segmentation and tracking methods in minimally invasive surgery. arXiv:1805.02475 (2018)
4. Nguyen, N.Q., Vo, D.M., Lee, S.W.: Contour-aware polyp segmentation in colonoscopy images using detailed upsamling encoder-decoder networks. IEEE Access **8**, 99495–99508 (2020)
5. Sun, X., Zhang, P., Wang, D., et al.: Colorectal polyp segmentation by U-Net with dila-tion convolution. In: 2019 18th IEEE International Conference On Machine Learning And Applications (ICMLA), pp. 851–858. IEEE (2019)

6. Ronneberger, O., Fischer, P., Brox, T.: U-net: Convolutional networks for biomedical image segmentation. In: International Conference on Medical Image Computing and Computer-Assisted Intervention. Springer, Cham (2015). https://doi.org/10.1007/978-3-319-24574-4_28

7. Jha, D., Smedsrud, P.H., Riegler, M.A., et al.: ResUNet++: an advanced architecture for medical image segmentation. In: 2019 IEEE International Symposium on Multimedia (ISM), pp. 225–2255. IEEE (2019)

8. Zhou, Z., Rahman Siddiquee, M.M., Tajbakhsh, N., Liang, J.: UNet++: A nested u-net architecture for medical image segmentation. In: Stoyanov, D., Taylor, Z., Carneiro, G., Syeda-Mahmood, T., Martel, A., Maier-Hein, L., Tavares, J.M.R.S., Bradley, A., Papa, J.P., Belagiannis, V., Nascimento, J.C., Lu, Z., Conjeti, S., Moradi, M., Greenspan, H., Madabhushi, A. (eds.) DLMIA/ML-CDS -2018. LNCS, vol. 11045, pp. 3–11. Springer, Cham (2018). https://doi.org/10.1007/978-3-030-00889-5_1

9. Allan, M., Shvets, A., Kurmann, T., et al.: robotic instrument segmentation challenge. arXiv: 1902.06426 (2019)

10. Allan, M., Kondo, S., Bodenstedt, S., et al.: 2018 robotic scene segmentation challenge. arXiv: 2001.11190 (2020)

11. Ross, T., Reinke, A., Full, P.M., et al.: Robust medical instrument segmentation challenge 2019. arXiv:2003.10299 (2020)

12. Jha, D., Ali, S., Emanuelsen, K., et al.: Kvasir-Instrument: diagnostic and therapeutic tool segmentation dataset in gastrointestinal endoscopy. In: International Conference on Multimedia Modeling, pp. 218–229. Springer, Cham (2021). https://doi.org/10.1007/978-3-030-67835-7_19

13. Russell, B.C., Torralba, A., Murphy, K.P., et al.: LabelMe: a database and web-based tool for image annotation. Int. J. Comput. Vision **77**(1–3), 157–173 (2008)

14. Zhang, Z., Liu, Q., Wang, Y.: Road extraction by deep residual u-net. IEEE Geosci. Remote Sens. Lett. **15**(5), 749–753 (2018)

15. Badrinarayanan, V., Kendall, A., Cipolla, R.: Segnet: A deep convolutional encoder-decoder architecture for image segmentation. IEEE Trans. Pattern Anal. Mach. Intell. **39**(12), 2481–2495 (2017)

16. Zhang, R., Li, G., Li, Z., et al.: Adaptive context selection for polyp segmentation. In: International Conference on Medical Image Computing and Computer-Assisted Intervention, pp. 253–262. Springer, Cham (2020). https://doi.org/10.1007/978-3-030-59725-2_25

17. Fan, D.P., Ji, G.P., Zhou, T., et al.: Pranet: Parallel reverse attention network for polyp segmentation. In: International Conference on Medical Image Computing and Computer-Assisted Intervention, pp. 263–273. Springer, Cham (2020). https://doi.org/10.1007/978-3-030-59725-2_26

18. Simonyan, K., Zisserman, A.: Very deep convolutional networks for large-scale image recognition. arXiv:1409.1556 (2014)

CD Loss: A Class-Center Based Distribution Loss for Discriminative Feature Learning in Medical Image Classification

Yanhong Zhou[1,2,3], Jie Du[1,2,3]($\boxtimes$), Yujian Liu[1,2,3], Yali Qiu[1,2,3], and Tianfu Wang[1,2,3]

[1] Health Science Center, School of Biomedical Engineering,
Shenzhen University, Shenzhen 518060, China
[2] National-Regional Key Technology Engineering Laboratory for Medical Ultrasound,
Shenzhen University, Shenzhen 518060, China
[3] Marshall Laboratory of Biomedical Engineering, Shenzhen University,
Shenzhen 518060, China

Abstract. Accurate classification of medical images plays an essential role in the early diagnosis of disease. Although deep learning has achieved great success in medical images, it remains challenging due to the critical issue of significant intra-class variation and inter-class similarity caused by the diversity of imaging modalities and clinical pathologies. For this purpose, we propose a Class-center based Distribution loss (CD-loss) to guide the deep convolution neural networks (DCNNs) to extract more discriminative features for better classification accuracy. In detail, our CD-loss aims to force the extracted features from medical image data follow the distribution of that extracted from natural image data. That is because in general, there is less significant intra-class variation and inter-class similarity in natural images as that in medical images due to their different imaging mechanisms. In addition, the available medical images are usually very limited, and state-of-the-art (SOTA) metric learning loss functions easily suffer from over-fitting on such small data. On the contrary, our CD-loss extracts discriminative features not only based on the small medical image data but also the large natural image data to reduce over-fitting. To appreciate the performance of the proposed loss, in this experiment, several SOTA metric learning loss functions are used for comparison. The results demonstrate the effectiveness of our method in terms of classification accuracy and F1-scores.

Keywords: Medical image classification · Metric learning · Loss function · Discriminative feature learning

---

Supported by National Natural Science Foundation of China No. 62006160, Educational Commission of Guangdong Province 2020KQNCX062, Shenzhen Fundamental Research Program 20200813102946001.

Y. Peng et al. (Eds.): ICIG 2021, LNCS 12889, pp. 630–640, 2021.
https://doi.org/10.1007/978-3-030-87358-5_51

1   Introduction

The classification of medical images using computer-aided diagnosis (CAD) system is useful in reducing mortality rates of disease [2,23]. Deep learning technology has developed rapidly, especially deep convolutional neural networks (DCNNs, e.g., GoogleNet [19], ResNet [7], DenseNet [8], Inception v3 [20]) that have made great progress in image classification. Although compared to traditional handcrafted features, these methods get much higher accuracy, they have not achieved the same success in medical image classification as they have done in the ImageNet Challenge [14]. That is because there is a critical issue in medial images: significant intra-class variation and inter-class similarity caused by the diversity of imaging modalities and clinical pathologies [5]. For instance, as shown in Fig. 1, there is a big visual difference between two COVID CT images (i.e., Fig. 1(a) and (b)). Similar results are also observed on two NON-COVID CT images (e.g., Fig. 1(c) and Fig. 1(d)). But images with different labels (e.g., Fig. 1(a) and Fig. 1(c), or Fig. 1(b) and Fig. 1(d)) share many visual similarities.

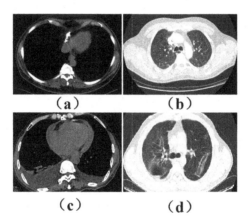

(a)   (b)

(c)   (d)

Fig. 1. Examples show the intra-class variation and inter-class similarity in medical images.

To resolve the intra-class variation and inter-class similarity issue, metric learning has attracted lots of attentions. Metric learning aims at extracting discriminative feature representations that clusters similar samples while separating dissimilar samples in the feature space. In literatures [6,16,22], metric learning loss functions are designed for feature learning. Different from the traditional Cross Entropy loss (CE-loss), metric learning losses show their superiorities in feature extraction. In detail, the CE-loss cannot analyze the distribution in samples and classes, which only measures the difference between the predicted probability distribution and the target distribution [9]. On the contrary, metric learning losses concentrate on data distribution to discover the differences between classes and find the main common patterns within classes. Consequently, incorporating metric learning losses with CE-loss can guide the DCNN models to extract more discriminative features for better classification performance.

For instance, in literature [6,16,22], CE+Contrastive loss, CE+Triplet loss and CE+Center loss are proposed. However, to minimize the distance between samples within classes and maximize the distances between classes, CE+Contrastive loss and CE+Triplet loss only concentrate on the pair of samples, which easily causes an unstable training process and sub-optimal solution [22]. Through minimizing the distances between samples and the class center, CE+Center loss is more stable than CE+Contrastive and CE+Triplet losses, because the class center moves slightly in every iterations during training. However, different from natural images, medical images usually have very limited samples and CE+Center loss may easily suffers from over-fitting.

In this paper, a Class-center based Distribution loss (CD-loss) is proposed in the embedding layer of DCNNs for better feature learning in medical image classification. Due to the different imaging mechanisms, there is no significant intra-class variation and inter-class similarity in natural images as that in medical images [15]. Moreover, it is easy to collect a large amount of natural images for classification. Hence, in this work, CD-loss is proposed to force the features extracted from medical images follow the distribution of that learned from natural images through minimizing the distances between samples in medical images and class center in natural images. Under this way, our CD-loss is more stable than the pair-based losses (e.g., CE+Contrastive loss and CE+Triplet loss) and reduces over-fitting compared to CE+Center loss. The experiments have been conducted to compare our CD-loss with several SOTA losses under some popular DCNN models. The main contributions of this work are summarized as follows:

i) The proposed CD-loss can be involved into any DCNNs models for better feature learning;

ii) In order to improve the performance of DCNNs on medical image classification, our CD-loss is proposed for extracting discriminative features of medical images by learning the data distribution of natural images.

iii) Different from existing metric learning loss functions, our CD-loss reduces the intra-class distance and increases the inter-class distance based on both medical and natural images to reduce over-fitting.

2   Related Work

DCNN models use various strategies to increase the performance of medical image classification, when the training data is limited. One method is called transfer learning [21], which transfers knowledge learned in a certain domain to a different but related domain. In medical image classification, in order to reduce over-fitting on small data, the model can be firstly trained on a large natural image dataset (e.g., ImageNet) and then fine-tuned on the small medical image data. For instance, in literature [12], 92% of accuracy is achieved on a small pneumonia X-rays image dataset through transfer learning. However, if there are differences between natural images and medical images, only sharing model parameters may have a little boost on model performance [1,11]. Another method is called data augmentation [4,24], such as rotations, flips, translations or using generative adversarial network (GAN) to generate synthetic images. However, these synthetic images may be similar to the primal ones and the improvements by using these enhancement methods may be limited [10]. Moreover, existing DCNN models usually take the traditional CE-loss in the training process, considering the difference between the predicted and target labels rather than analyzing the distribution of samples [9].

In the past decades, metric learning has been applied on face recognition tasks [3], in which loss functions that enlarge the distances of different faces and narrow the distances of same faces in the feature space are designed. Recently, metric learning loss functions are also designed for discriminative feature learning in natural image classification, including Contrastive loss [6], Triplet loss [16], Center loss [22]. Contrastive loss encourages similar pairs to be close and dissimilar pairs to have distance of at least margin m from each other. Triplet loss makes the distance between an anchor and a positive sample greater than the distance between an anchor and a negative sample. Center loss maintains a class center for each class and then makes all samples to be close to their center. Very recently, these losses are also involved in medical image classification to resolve the issue of significant intra-class variation and inter-class similarity. For instance, a Siamese neural network with Contrastive loss is proposed for COVID-19 diagnosis [17]. This structure is also used in heart disease classification [13]. However, Contrastive loss and Triplet loss are both pair-based losses which are unstable during training [22]. For Center loss that uses class center only, the model is stable for training. However, all these methods do not consider the issue of small data in medical images, and hence they easily suffer from over-fitting.

3 Proposed Method

3.1 Overview of the Proposed Method

Figure 2 presents a brief flowchart for the classification of medical images by using our CD-loss. Our method consists of two parts: DCNNs layers and metric learning layers. Our CD-loss is involved in the metric learning layer for discriminative feature learning. In the first step, DCNN models are trained on a natural image dataset to learn one discriminative data distribution, i.e., under this data distribution, a higher classification accuracy can be easily obtained. Then the target medical image data are forced to follow the discriminative feature distribution by closing the medical samples to the class center in natural images. Specifically, one natural image dataset (noted by A) is selected since it is easy to get a good classification performance. The DCNN model trained on A is then fine-tuned based on our CD-loss for the target medical image dataset (noted by B). For a new medical image dataset (e.g., C or D), the DCNN model can be further fine-tuned based on our CD-loss rather than retraining the DCNN model to improve the classification accuracy of the model. It is worth noting that different from traditional transfer learning, in this work, not only model parameters but also data distribution are shared between natural and medical images.

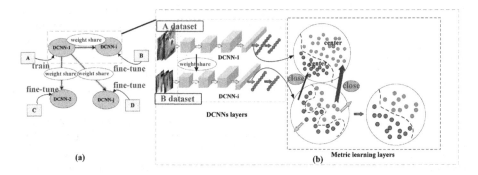

Fig. 2. (a): Architecture of the model which has n DCNN components. DCNN-i, (i = 1, ..., n), represents i-th DCNN convolution. The parameters between them and DCNN-1 are shared. (b): Architecture of the proposed loss in the DCNN.

3.2   CD-Loss for Intra-class Variation

In order to achieve high classification accuracy on medical image datasets, an effective model that is insensitive to small data needs to be designed. Due to the large amount of data in natural images, the distribution in the feature space is more conducive to DCNNs for classification. Our goal is to make the small medical image data have discriminative features as that in natural image data. In this work, CD-loss for intra-class variation is proposed to extract discriminative feature representation. It is hoped that the sum of the distance between the medical samples and the class center in natural images should to be as small as possible, that is, minimizing the intra-class distance.

Let $X = \{x_i | i = 1, 2, ..., N\}$ to be the set of training samples and $Y = \{y_i | i = 1, 2, ..., N\}$ to be the set of labels of X, where N is the total number of training samples. For a sample x_i in medical images, the associated labels of x_i , c_{y+}, c_{y-} are y_i, y_+ and y_- respectively. The intra-class distance is defined by,

$$D_+ = ||f(x_i) - c_{y+}||_2, if\ y_i = y_+ \tag{1}$$

$$D_- = ||f(x_i) - c_{y-}||_2, if\ y_i = y_- \tag{2}$$

where $f(x_i)$ represents the output of the fully connected layer of DCNN model for the target B dataset, c_{y+} represents the center of the positive samples in the A dataset, while c_{y-} represents the center of the negative samples in A.

Consequently, the CD-loss for intra-class variation is defined by,

$$L_{intra} = \frac{1}{2} \sum_{n=1}^{N} (D_+^2 + D_-^2) \tag{3}$$

Through minimizing the L_{intra} loss (i.e., Eq. (3)), the samples in medical image data (B) are all close to the class center with the same label in natural image data (A).

3.3 CD-Loss for Inter-class Similarity

In Sect. 3.2, L_{intra} loss is designed for reducing the intra-class variation. In this subsection, the CD-loss for inter-class similarity is proposed for maximizing the distances between classes. For binary classification, x_i is one training sample in the target B dataset, and c_y is one class center in A dataset. The associated labels of x_i and c_y are y_i and y_c respectively, where $y_i \neq y_c$. The CD-loss for inter-class similarity is defined by,

$$L_{inter} = \max(m - ||f(x_i) - c_y||_2^2, 0), if\ y_i \neq y_c \qquad (4)$$

where $f(x_i)$ represents the output of the fully connected layer of this network. m is a hyper-parameter, which indicates the degree of dissimilarity. Minimizing L_{inter} is equivalent to forcing the distances between samples and the class centers with different labels to m, as shown in Fig. 3.

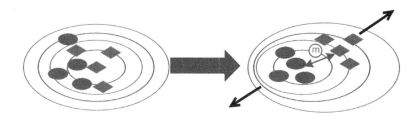

Fig. 3. An example on feature space, in which similar images get closer and dissimilar images are far away from each other.

3.4 CD-Loss for both Intra-class Variation and Inter-class Similarity

In order to simultaneously resolve the issue of significant intra-class variation and inter-class similarity in medical image classification, Class-Center based Distribution loss (CD-loss) is proposed, which incorporates Eq. (3) and (4). The CD-loss is formulated by,

$$L_{CD} = \frac{1}{2N}((\sum_{n=1}^{N_+} (yD_+^2 + (1-y)\max{(m - D_+^2, 0)}^2) \qquad (5)$$

$$+ \sum_{n=1}^{N_-} ((1-y)D_-^2 + y\max{(m - D_-^2, 0)}^2))$$

where N_+ and N_- represent the number of positive samples and negative samples, respectively. Obviously, minimizing Eq. (5) makes the samples with the same label into a cluster (following the distribution in natural images) and the samples with different labels are far away from each other.

For better classification, the following loss function is adopted,

$$L_{final} = \lambda_1 L_{CD} + \lambda_2 L_{CE} \tag{6}$$

where λ_1 and λ_2 are hyper-parameters, and L_{CE} represents the Cross Entropy loss.

4 Experiments and Results

4.1 Experimental Settings

Four datasets are used in our experiments, including one natural image dataset and three medical image datasets. The natural image dataset is the Cats vs. Dogs, and three medical image datasets are the COVID19-CT [25], ChestXRay2017 [12] and BreakHis datasets [18], respectively. The Cats vs. Dogs dataset contains 25,000 images, including 12500 images of cat and 12500 images of dog. The ratio of splitting training and testing sets of this dataset is 7:3. This dataset is used as the A dataset in our proposed method since all comparison models can obtain more than 99% in this dataset. The splitting ratio of training and testing sets of BreakHis 40X is 8:2 (see Table 1 for details). Four popular loss functions are chosen for comparison, including CE-loss, CE+Contrastive loss, CE+Triplet loss and CE+Center loss. Each loss is evaluated with Accuracy and F1-scores as the measurement. All comparison models are trained for 100 epochs until convergence and the max scores are recorded. In addition, the hyperparameters λ_1 and λ_2 associated with CE-loss and metric learning losses are tuned in the range of [0.0001, 0.1] with step of 0.0001 and [0.1, 1] with step of 0.1 for all compared metric learning models, respectively.

Table 1. The data properties of the one natural image dataset and three medical image datasets.

Dataset type	Dasetset	Training instances	Test instances	total
Natural image dataset	Cats vs. Dogs[a]	17500	7500	25000
Medical image datasets	COVID19-CT[b]	425	203	628
	ChestXray2017[c]	8232	624	8656
	BreakHis 40X[d]	1596	399	1995

[a]https://www.kaggle.com/c/dogs-vs-cats/data
[b]https://github.com/UCSD-AI4H/COVID-CT
[c]https://data.mendeley.com/datasets/rscbjbr9sj/2
[d]https://web.inf.ufpr.br/vri/databases/breast-cancer-histopathological-database-breakhis/

Table 2. Comparisons between the proposed loss and SOTA losses on medical images datasets

COVID19-CT					
Method	CE	CE+Contrastive	CE+Triplet	CE+Center	CE+CD(our)
Accuracy	82.75%	85.22 %	83.47%	84.73%	**86.20%**
F1 scores	81.86%	84.53%	83.82%	83.82%	**85.10%**
ChestXray2017					
Method	CE	CE+Contrastive	CE+Triplet	CE+Center	CE+CD(our)
Accuracy	86.05%	87.17%	86.37%	88.30%	**90.22%**
F1 scores	89.94%	90.63%	88.21%	91.38%	**92.36%**
BreakHis 40X					
Method	CE	CE+Contrastive	CE+Triplet	CE+Center	CE+CD(our)
Accuracy	74.43%	79.94%	80.94%	80.95%	**81.70%**
F1 scores	80.23%	84.17%	86.02%	**87.29%**	85.77 %

Table 3. Ablation experiments of our CD-loss on COVID19-CT

DenseNet	CD-intra[a]	CD-inter[b]	Accuracy	F1 scores
√	√		83.74%	82.53%
√		√	82.75%	81.28%
√	√	√	**86.20%**	**85.10%**

[a]CD-loss for intra-class variation;
[b]CD-loss for inter-class similarity.

4.2 Effectiveness of the CD-Loss Approach

This section evaluates the effectiveness of the proposed CD-loss. Table 2 shows that our CD-loss achieves the best performance in most of experiments, compared to other four SOTA losses in terms of overall accuracy and F1-scores.

In detail, compared to the traditional CE-loss, our CD-loss (as well as other metric learning losses) improves the overall classification accuracy up to 7.27% (BreakHis 40X). This verifies the effectiveness of metric learning. Compared to the SOTA metric learning losses, our CD-loss also gets the highest classification accuracy and the improvement is up to 3.85% (ChestXray2017). That is mainly because our CD-loss extracts discriminative features not only based on the small medical image data but also the large natural image data.

The ablation experiment of our CD-loss in Table 3 shows that in medical image classification, both intra-class variation and inter-class similarity issues negatively influence the classification performance. Our CD-loss simultaneously resolves these two significant issues through incorporating CD-intra and CD-inter.

4.3   Generalizability of the CD-Loss Approach

In order to evaluate the generalization of our CD-loss, four DCNN models are used as backbone networks with different losses on dataset COVID19-CT, as shown in Table 4. Table 4 shows that on four different DCNN models (including GoogleNet, ResNet, DenseNet and Inception v3), our CD-loss consistently out-performs all other compared losses in most experiments. Hence, our CD-loss can effectively improve the feature learning capability of DCNN models with high generalizability.

Table 4. Classification performance of various model architectures on COVID19-CT.

Model	Loss	Accuracy	F1 Scores
GoogleNet	CE	80.78%	79.14%
	CE+Contrastive	82.75%	82.41%
	CE+Triplet	83.25%	81.31%
	CE+Center	81.28%	80.40%
	CE+CD(our)	**83.74%**	**82.53%**
ResNet	CE	78.32%	77.08%
	CE+Contrastive	79.80%	77.59%
	CE+Triplet	80.78%	77.45%
	CE+Center	80.29%	79.38%
	CE+CD(our)	**81.77%**	**79.77%**
DenseNet	CE	82.75%	81.86%
	CE+Contrastive	85.22%	84.53%
	CE+Triplet	83.74%	82.54%
	CE+Center	84.73%	83.28%
	CE+CD(our)	**86.20%**	**85.10%**
Inception v3	CE	79.80%	78.97%
	CE+Contrastive	82.75%	81.86%
	CE+Triplet	**84.72%**	82.68%
	CE+Center	81.77%	82.12%
	CE+CD(our)	83.74%	**83.52%**

5   Conclusion

In this paper, a Class-center based Distribution loss (CD-loss) is proposed for resolving the issue of significant intra-class variation and inter-class similarity in medical image classification. Although existing metric learning losses can resolve this significant issue, their performances are easily influenced by the fact that medical images usually have very limited training samples. Hence in this work, our CD-loss is proposed to extract discriminative features based on both small medical image data and large natural image data to reduce over-fitting. The experimental results show that our CD-loss outperforms both traditional CE-loss and metric learning losses (including Contrastive, Triplet and Center losses) in terms of overall accuracy and F1-scores. Moreover, our CD-loss can be involved in any DCNN models to improve the feature learning capability with high generalizability. In the future, we would like to improve our CD-loss to be fit for segmentation or object detection tasks.

References

1. Altae-Tran, H., Ramsundar, B., Pappu, A.S., Pande, V.: Low data drug discovery with one-shot learning. ACS Cent. Sci. **3**(4), 283–293 (2017)
2. Anand, V., Koundal, D.: Computer-assisted diagnosis of thyroid cancer using medical images: a survey. In: Singh, P.K., Kar, A.K., Singh, Y., Kolekar, M.H., Tanwar, S. (eds.) Proceedings of ICRIC 2019. LNEE, vol. 597, pp. 543–559. Springer, Cham (2020). https://doi.org/10.1007/978-3-030-29407-6_39
3. Chopra, S., Hadsell, R., LeCun, Y.: Learning a similarity metric discriminatively, with application to face verification. In: 2005 IEEE Computer Society Conference on Computer Vision and Pattern Recognition, vol. 1, pp. 539–546. IEEE (2005)
4. Ding, J., Chen, B., Liu, H., Huang, M.: Convolutional neural network with data augmentation for SAR target recognition. IEEE Geosci. Remote Sens. Lett. **13**(3), 364–368 (2016)
5. Ghasemi, M., Kelarestaghi, M., Eshghi, F., Sharifi, A.: FDSR: a new fuzzy discriminative sparse representation method for medical image classification. Artif. Intell. Med. **106**, 101876 (2020)
6. Hadsell, R., Chopra, S., LeCun, Y.: Dimensionality reduction by learning an invariant mapping. In: 2006 IEEE Computer Society Conference on Computer Vision and Pattern Recognition, vol. 2, pp. 1735–1742. IEEE (2006)
7. He, K., Zhang, X., Ren, S., Sun, J.: Deep residual learning for image recognition. In: Proceedings of the IEEE Conference on Computer Vision and Pattern Recognition, pp. 770–778 (2016)
8. Huang, G., Liu, Z., Van Der Maaten, L., Weinberger, K.Q.: Densely connected convolutional networks. In: Proceedings of the IEEE Conference on Computer Vision and Pattern Recognition, pp. 4700–4708 (2017)
9. Huang, Z., Zhou, Q., Zhu, X., Zhang, X.: Batch similarity based triplet loss assembled into light-weighted convolutional neural networks for medical image classification. Sensors **21**(3), 764 (2021)
10. Huang, Z., Zhu, X., Ding, M., Zhang, X.: Medical image classification using a light-weighted hybrid neural network based on PCANet and DenseNet. IEEE Access **8**, 24697–24712 (2020)
11. Kearnes, S., Goldman, B., Pande, V.: Modeling industrial ADMET data with multitask networks. arXiv preprint arXiv:1606.08793 (2016)
12. Kermany, D.S., et al.: Identifying medical diagnoses and treatable diseases by image-based deep learning. Cell **172**(5), 1122–1131 (2018)
13. Khaneja, A., Srivastava, S., Rai, A., Cheema, A., Srivastava, P.K.: Analysing risk of coronary heart disease through discriminative neural networks. arXiv preprint arXiv:2008.02731 (2020)

14. Ma, X., et al.: Understanding adversarial attacks on deep learning based medical image analysis systems. Pattern Recogn. **110**, 107332 (2021)
15. Meng, Z., Zhao, Z., Su, F.: Multi-classification of breast cancer histology images by using gravitation loss. In: ICASSP 2019–2019 IEEE International Conference on Acoustics, Speech and Signal Processing, pp. 1030–1034. IEEE (2019)
16. Schroff, F., Kalenichenko, D., Philbin, J.: FaceNet: a unified embedding for face recognition and clustering. In: Proceedings of the IEEE Conference on Computer Vision and Pattern Recognition, pp. 815–823 (2015)
17. Shorfuzzaman, M., Hossain, M.S.: MetaCOVID: a Siamese neural network framework with contrastive loss for n-shot diagnosis of COVID-19 patients. Pattern Recogn. **113**, 107700 (2021)
18. Spanhol, F.A., Oliveira, L.S., Petitjean, C., Heutte, L.: A dataset for breast cancer histopathological image classification. IEEE Trans. Biomed. Eng. **63**(7), 1455–1462 (2015)
19. Szegedy, C., et al.: Going deeper with convolutions. In: Proceedings of the IEEE Conference on Computer Vision and Pattern Recognition, pp. 1–9 (2015)
20. Szegedy, C., Vanhoucke, V., Ioffe, S., Shlens, J., Wojna, Z.: Rethinking the inception architecture for computer vision. In: Proceedings of the IEEE Conference on Computer Vision and Pattern Recognition, pp. 2818–2826 (2016)
21. Torrey, L., Shavlik, J.: Transfer learning. In: Handbook of Research on Machine Learning Applications and Trends: Algorithms, Methods, and Techniques, pp. 242–264. IGI global (2010)
22. Wen, Y., Zhang, K., Li, Z., Qiao, Yu.: A discriminative feature learning approach for deep face recognition. In: Leibe, B., Matas, J., Sebe, N., Welling, M. (eds.) ECCV 2016. LNCS, vol. 9911, pp. 499–515. Springer, Cham (2016). https://doi.org/10.1007/978-3-319-46478-7_31
23. Yang, S., Liu, X., Zheng, Z., Wang, W., Ma, X.: Fusing medical image features and clinical features with deep learning for computer-aided diagnosis. arXiv preprint arXiv:2103.05855 (2021)
24. Zhang, H.P., et al.: Value of contrast-enhanced ultrasound in the differential diagnosis of gallbladder lesion. World J. Gastroenterol. **24**(6), 744 (2018)
25. Zhao, J., Zhang, Y., He, X., Xie, P.: COVID-CT-dataset: a CT scan dataset about COVID-19. arXiv preprint arXiv:2003.13865 (2020)

Pruning the Seg-Edge Bilateral Constraint Fully Convolutional Network for Iris Segmentation

Hui Zhang[1], Junxing Hu[2], Jing Liu[1], Zhaofeng He[3(✉)], Xingguang Li[1], and Lihu Xiao[1]

[1] Beijing IrisKing Co., Ltd., Beijing, China
[2] Institute of Automation Chinese Academy of Sciences, Beijing, China
[3] Beijing University of Posts and Telecommunications, Beijing, China
zhaofenghe@bupt.edu.cn

Abstract. Iris semantic segmentation in less-constrained scenarios is the basis of new generation of iris recognition technology. In this paper, we reexamined our approach iris segmentation framework, named Seg-Edge bilateral constraint network (SEN), which contains an edge map generating network which passes detailed edge information from low level convolutional layers to iris semantic segmentation analysis layers and segmentation-edge bilateral constraint structure for focusing on interesting objects. To reduce the number of network parameters, we propose pruning filters and corresponding feature maps that are identified as useless by l_1-norm and l_2-norm, which results in a lightweight iris segmentation network while keeping the performance almost intact or even better. A novel l_1-norm or [l_1-norm, l_2-norm] clustering based pruning method is proposed to improve pruning effect and avoid the time consuming manual design. Experimental results suggest that the proposed SEN structure outperforms the state-of-the-art iris segmentation methods, and the clustering based pruning methods outperform manual design in both compression ratio and accuracy.

Keywords: Iris segmentation · Bilateral constraint domain transform · Model pruning

1 Introduction

Iris recognition is a reliable identification technique due to the stability and uniqueness of the iris in biometrics. In the last decades, iris recognition has been widely used in mines, prison, banks, police and entry and exit control. However, the traditional iris recognition only can be used under strictly limited conditions and asks for highly cooperated users. The user friendliness iris recognition system inevitably leads to a decline in iris image quality, which seriously affects the difficulty of iris image preprocessing. For example, it is more difficult to locate iris parts in defocus blur, motion blur, occlusion, or reflection iris images than

---

H. Zhang and J. Hu—These authors contribute equally to this article.

Y. Peng et al. (Eds.): ICIG 2021, LNCS 12889, pp. 641–653, 2021.
https://doi.org/10.1007/978-3-030-87358-5_52

in high quality iris images. In fact, the performance of iris segmentation [1–3] directly affects the performance of iris recognition. The higher the segmentation accuracy, the more precise the retained iris information.

Traditional iris segmentation methods usually includes preprocessing, denoising, boundary detection, and post-processing. There are several typical methods for iris segmentation. Daugman [1] proposes using an integro-differential operator to detect eyelids and locate iris boundaries. Wildes [2] presents exploiting a circular Hough transform to localize iris boundaries in iris images. He et al. [4] propose the method which is inspired by Hooke's law.

In the past few years, some algorithms based on neural network are proposed for the pixel level iris segmentation. Proença [5] exploits the neural network with one hidden layer. Tan et al. [6] use a typical 3-layer feed-forward neural network. Liu et al. [7] propose a multi-scale fully convolutional network. We proposed the Seg-Edge bilateral constraint network (SEN) for iris segmentation in [8], which improves the average segmentation errors over the state-of-the-arts by 2.22% and 22.03% on UBIRIS.v2 [9] and CASIA.v4-distance [10] dataset respectively.

To reduce the computational complexity and model size, we study the network pruning base on the l_1-norm and l_2-norm of feature maps. The pruning foundation includes: filters corresponding to feature maps with small l_1-norm or l_2-norm values extract little information and contribute little to the segmentation task; filters corresponding to feature maps with large different l_1-norm and l_2-norm values may contain valid information for segmentation. We prose a novel l_1-norm and l_2-norm clustering based pruning strategy, which not only save thousands of hours for manual design, but also achieve better accuracy with larger compression ratio.

2   Related Work

2.1   Semantic Segmentation

With the development of deep learning methods, the semantic segmentation has attracted more and more attention. The appearance of Fully Convolutional Networks (FCN) [11] leads to a rapid increase in the number of end-to-end semantic segmentation networks. The FCN model transforms all of the fully connected layers to convolutional layers which allows the input image of any size. SegNet [12] is an encoder-decoder structure, but it uses max-pooling indices to enhance location information. The DeepLab model proposed in [13] uses atrous convolution and fully connected Conditional Random Field to avoid the reduction of the spatial resolution of feature maps. The atrous convolution effectively enlarges the field-of-view of filters to incorporate a larger context without increasing the number of parameters and the amount of computation. DeepLab v2 [14] uses Atrous Spatial Pyramid Pooling (ASPP) with multiple sampling rates to robustly segment objects.

2.2   Model Pruning

For network model compression, a lot of methods have been proposed. LeCun et al. [15] propose Optimal Brain Damage to remove unimportant weights from a network. They use second-derivative information to make a tradeoff between network complexity and training set error. Han et al. [16] remove the connection whose weight is lower than a threshold after an initial training phase and converts a dense, fully-connected layer to a sparse layer. Li et al. [17] present removing filters together with their connecting feature maps to reduce the computation cost. Under the guidance of l_1-norm, this approach does not produce sparse connectivity patterns and not need the additional regularization.

3   Proposed Methods

3.1   Seg-Edge Bilateral Constraint Network

The structure of Seg-Edge bilateral constraint network (SEN) is shown in Fig. 1. It is composed of three components: backbone; iris edge map using rich convolutional features (RCF); bilateral constraint domain transform (BCT).

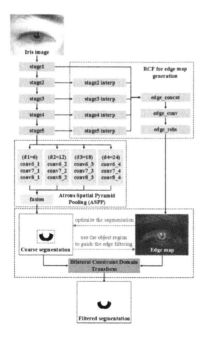

Fig. 1. The architecture of the proposed Seg-Edge bilateral constraint network (SEN).

Backbone Structure. We exploit the FCN model DeepLab v2 [14] as the backbone structure. The 'stage1' to 'stage5' in Fig. 1 stands for a bunch of convolutional layers of VGG-16. See [8] for more details.

Rich Convolutional Features for Edge Map Generation. Low-level convolutional layers contains richer edge features at different scales and sharpness degrees. We exploit all of them to predict the edge map following [18]. For medial convolutional layers, the method rescales their outputs to the original size, denoted as 'stage2 interp' to 'stage5 interp' in Fig. 1. A concat layer concatenates them in the channel dimension to one output. A convolutional layer with 1×1 kernel is used to produce the iris edge prediction.

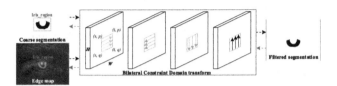

Fig. 2. Illustration of the bilateral constraint domain transform. The black dashed arrow indicates the forward propagation. The red dashed arrow indicates the back propagation. The red dashed box indicates the iris region, in which the edge map and the coarse segmentation are recursively filtered across rows and columns. (Color figure online)

Bilateral Constraint Domain Transform. We propose a novel bilateral constraint domain transform (BDT) structure in [8]. The iris edge map generated from intermediate convolutional layers can pass more detailed edge information to segmentation results. We use the iris region produced by coarse segmentation to constrain the edge filtering scope, which allows the edge filtering to focus on the interesting object parts. As illustrated in Fig. 2, the BDT recursively filters inputs across rows and columns through K iterations.

During the forward propagation, the filtering is performed along with four directions (left to right, right to left, top to bottom, and bottom to top) in sequence. For 2-D inputs of height, H and width W, the output $y_{i,j}$ is computed as: $y_{i,j} = (1-w_{i,j})x_{i,j}+w_{i,j}y_{i,j-1} i = p, ..., q \quad (1 \leq p \leq q \leq H), j = s, ..., t \quad (2 \leq s \leq t \leq W)$, where $x_{i,j}$ is the pixel value at (i,j) of the coarse iris segmentation, p and q are the lower and upper bound of the iris region in the vertical direction, s and t are the bound in the horizontal direction. The weight $w_{i,j} \in [0,1]$ is a feedback coefficient which is related to the iris edge map.

During the backward propagation, the segmentation errors at the output $y_{i,j}$ are back propagated through the BDT onto its inputs. To avoid the interference from the non-iris area and constrain the edge filtering inside the object region, we add the same limitation to both the coarse segmentation and the edge map. The derivative is calculated as:

$$\frac{\partial L}{\partial x_{i,j}} \leftarrow (1 - w_{i,j})\frac{\partial L}{\partial y_{i,j}}; \qquad \frac{\partial L}{\partial y_{i,j-1}} \leftarrow \frac{\partial L}{\partial y_{i,j-1}} + w_{i,j}\frac{\partial L}{\partial y_{i,j}}$$

$$\frac{\partial L}{\partial w_{i,j}} \leftarrow \frac{\partial L}{\partial w_{i,j}} + (y_{i,j-1} - x_{i,j})\frac{\partial L}{\partial y_{i,j}}; \qquad \frac{\partial L}{\partial g_{i,j}} \leftarrow -\frac{\sqrt{2}\,\sigma_s}{\sigma_k\,\sigma_r}w_{i,j}\frac{\partial L}{\partial w_{i,j}}$$

$$\sigma_k = \sqrt{3}\sigma_s \frac{2^{K-k}}{\sqrt{4^K - 1}}; i = q, ..., p(1 \leq p \leq q \leq H), j = t, ..., s(2 \leq s \leq t \leq W)$$

3.2 Iris Segmentation Model Pruning

To reduce the parameters and floating point operations (FLOP) of model, the model pruning is an intuitive and efficient way. We adopt the l_1-norm based pruning strategy in [17] as the basic pruning method. The original pruning method needs one layer by one layer experiments and manual design, which is time consuming and difficult to operate. To overcome the drawback of manual design and improve pruning effectiveness, we propose clustering based methods to determine the pruning ratio with less human intervention.

Pruning Filters in a Single Layer. It is crucial to determine the pruning object and the corresponding importance measure. We first prune the single layer to observe its sensitivity to pruning. To avoid producing sparse connectivity patterns and the additional regularization, we use the filter of the convolutional layer as the pruning object following [17]. The procedure of pruning is as follow: Step 1: For the ith convolutional layer, let $f_{i,j}$ denotes jth filter, calculate its l_1-norm $l_{ij} = \sum |f_{i,j}|$; Step 2: Sort filters by l_{ij}; Step 3: Prune m filters with the smallest l_{ij} and connecting feature maps; Step 4: Create a new model with the remaining filter weights and retrain it. We compare the pruned models and retrained pruned models with the original model. Some layers are sensitive to pruning as we can not recover the accuracy after pruning them.

Pruning Filters Across Multiple Layers by Manual Setting. For layers which are sensitive to pruning, we prune fewer or no filters of them. We adopt the *one-shot* pruning method which prunes filters across multiple layers at once and retrains the model [17]. We decide which filters can be pruned based on the single layer pruning experimental results.

Pruning Filters Across Multiple Layers by l_1-norm Clustering. We propose directly calculating the pruning ratio of each layer in the original model by using the clustering method. The k-means clustering is adopted. The clustering based pruning avoids manually setting thresholds which brings a lot of conveniences for practical usage. The pruning ratio (p_i) for the i-th layer is calculated as:

- Step 1: Calculate the l_1-norm l_{ij} of the j-th filter.
- Step 2: Sort all filters of the layer by the l_1-norm.
- Step 3: Prune 50% filters with the smallest l_1-norm and test the pruned model without retraining. The layer whose pruned model has small accuracy loss will be pruned more, otherwise less pruning.
- Step 4: Cluster the filters into C_i categories by l_{ij}, and a_c is the c-th category. The $(C_i + 1)$-quantiles are used as initial centers for the repeatability.
- Step 5: Sort clusters by l_{ij}, and a_1 has the smallest value.

– Step 6: If the layer is compressed less, $p_i = num\,(a_1)/o_i$. If the layer is compressed more, $p_i = \sum_{c=1}^{C_i-1} num\,(a_c)/o_i, C_i \geq 3$. where o_i is the number of output channels for the i-th layer, $num(\cdot)$ is used to count filter numbers.

Pruning Filters Across Multiple Layers by l_1-norm and l_2-norm Clustering. As demonstrated in paper [17] and our previous experiments, it may have little effect on segmentation results to prune the filters whose outputs are relatively small l_1-norm or l_2-norm values. The l_1-norm and the l_2-norm of one feature map usually show similar distribution. However, there are still some feature maps have different l_1-norm and l_2-norm value distribution, as shown in Fig. 3. If l_1-norm ($/l_2$-norm) is large while l_2-norm ($/l_1$-norm) is small, corresponding filters of this map may include important information for segmentation. Pruning filters just based on l_1-norm may possibly delete these important filters. So, we consider both l_1-norm and l_2-norm for clustering. The l_1-norm and l_2-norm are contacted to form a vector $[l_1$-norm, l_2-norm$]$. Figure 4 shows some examples of clustering result.

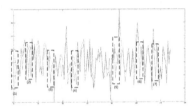

Fig. 3. An example l_1-norm and l_2-norm value distribution (conv2-2). Seven black dashed boxes illustrate some obviously inconsistent distributed of l_1-norm and l_2-norm.

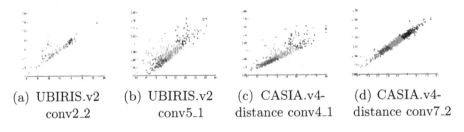

(a) UBIRIS.v2 conv2_2   (b) UBIRIS.v2 conv5_1   (c) CASIA.v4-distance conv4_1   (d) CASIA.v4-distance conv7_2

Fig. 4. Examples of $[l_1$-norm, l_2-norm$]$ clustering results.

The pruning ratio for the i-th convolutional layer is calculated as follows:

– Step 1: Calculate the l_1-norm l_{ij}^1 and l_2-norm l_{ij}^2 of the j-th filter respectively.
– Step 2: Sort all filters of the layer by the l_1-norm.
– Step 3: Same as step 3) in Sect. 3.2.

- Step 4: Calculate the mean of l_i^1 and l_i^2 for each layer respectively. α is a hyper-parameter and $\alpha = 4$ in our experiments, l_{ij}^1 and l_{ij}^2 are computed as:
  - if $l_{ij}^1 - mean(l_i^1) > \alpha * mean(l_i^1)$, $l_{ij}^1 = mean(l_i^1) + \alpha * mean(l_i^1)$;
  - if $mean(l_i^1) - l_{ij}^1 > \alpha * mean(l_i^1)$, $l_{ij}^1 = mean(l_i^1) - \alpha * mean(l_i^1)$;
  - if $l_{ij}^2 - mean(l_i^2) > \alpha * mean(l_i^2)$, $l_{ij}^2 = mean(l_i^2) + \alpha * mean(l_i^2)$;
  - if $mean(l_i^2) - l_{ij}^2 > \alpha * mean(l_i^2)$, $l_{ij}^2 = mean(l_i^2) - \alpha * mean(l_i^2)$.
- Step 5: Normalize l_{ij}^1 and l_{ij}^2 respectively by minimax normalization.
- Step 6: Cluster into C_i categories by $[l_{ij}^1, l_{ij}^2]$, and a_c is the c-th category.
- Step 7: Sort all clusters by l_{ij}^1 or $l_{ij}^1 + l_{ij}^2$, and a_1 has the smallest value.
- Step 8: Same as Step 6 in Sect. 3.2.

4   Experiments and Results

4.1   Datasets

We evaluate algorithms on two datasets: One is a subset of UBIRIS.v2 [9], which contains 500 images for training and 445 images for testing, short as UBIRIS; One is a subset of CASIA.v4-distance [10], which contains 300 images for training and 100 images for testing, short as CASIA.

4.2   Experimental Results

The accuracies of models are measured by the average segmentation error $ASE = (\sum_{i,j \in (H,W)} G(i,j) \oplus M(i,j))/(N \times H \times W)$, where N is the total number of the test images, H and W are height and width, G and M are the ground truth mask and the generated iris mask respectively. $\oplus$ represents an exclusive OR operation to compute the segmentation error. The comparational results of proposed SEN with other methods are listed in Table 1.

Table 1. Comparisons of the ASE with other methods.

Method	UBIRIS (%)	CASIA (%)
Proposed SEN	**0.88**	**0.46**
MFCNs [7]	0.90	0.59
RTV-L^1 [19]	1.21	0.68
Tan et al. [20]	1.31	–
Tan and Kumar [21]	1.72	0.81
Proença [5]	1.87	–
Tan and Kumar [6]	1.90	1.13

Table 2. Pruning ratios (%) of manual setting strategies. 'LY' indicates layer number. 1–21 indicate 21 layers from conv1_1 to conv7_4. 'PR' indicates pruning ratio.

Prune_1	LY	1	2	3	4	5	6	7	8	9	10	11	12	13	14	15	16	17	18	19	20	21
UBIRIS	PR	10	0	0	0	0	0	0	0	0	0	0	0	0	0	0	30	0	70	0	0	0	0
Prune_1	LY	1	2	3	4	5	6	7	8	9	10	11	12	13	14	15	16	17	18	19	20	21
CASIA	PR	0	0	30	0	10	0	0	0	0	0	0	0	0	0	0	0	0	40	0	0	60
Prune_2	LY	1	2	3	4	5	6	7	8	9	10	11	12	13	14	15	16	17	18	19	20	21
UBIRIS	PR	0	0	0	0	0	0	0	0	0	0	50	50	50	50	50	50	50	50	50	50	50
Prune_2	LY	1	2	3	4	5	6	7	8	9	10	11	12	13	14	15	16	17	18	19	20	21
CASIA	PR	0	0	0	0	0	0	0	0	0	0	50	50	50	50	50	50	50	50	50	50	50
Prune_3	LY	1	2	3	4	5	6	7	8	9	10	11	12	13	14	15	16	17	18	19	20	21
UBIRIS	PR	0	0	0	0	0	0	0	0	0	0	0	0	0	0	50	50	50	50	50	50	50
Prune_3	LY	1	2	3	4	5	6	7	8	9	10	11	12	13	14	15	16	17	18	19	20	21
CASIA	PR	0	0	0	0	0	0	0	0	0	0	0	0	0	0	50	50	50	50	50	50	50

Table 3. The best ASE of retraining process are reported. 'Params' and 'FLOP' indicate the reduced percentage of parameters and FLOP for each pruning strategies.

Strategy	UBIRIS (%)			CASIA (%)		
	ASE	Params	FLOP	ASE	Params	FLOP
Prune_1	**0.926**	2.79	2.75	**0.489**	8.19	9.11
Prune_2	0.979	58.28	46.15	0.494	58.28	46.15
Prune_3	0.928	33.31	26.38	0.494	33.31	26.38

Pruning Results Based on Manual Setting. We design three different pruning strategies in total, and the design procedure is as follow:

a) After sorting filters by l_1-norm, we prune the smallest filters of each convolutional layer independently with different pruning ratios in the range of 10% to 90%, and evaluate the ASE of pruned model, seeing Fig. 5. Pruning some single layers may even improve the performance. We first prune these filters and retrain. The pruned layers and corresponding pruning ratios of models are denoted as Prune_1 as follows: (i) For UBIRIS, we prune 10%, 30%, 70% of conv1_1, conv7_1, conv7_2, respectively.

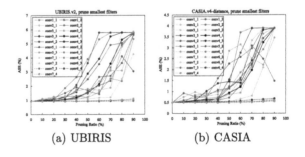

(a) UBIRIS   (b) CASIA

Fig. 5. The ASE after pruning filters with the smallest weights sum for each layer.

(ii) For CASIA, we prune 30%, 10%, 40%, 60% of conv2_1, conv3_1, conv6_3, conv7_4, respectively.

b) We retrain all pruned models and results are listed in Fig. 6. Some layers are sensitive to pruning, as we can not recover their accuracies even using small pruning ratios, such as conv2_2 layer. We empirically prune 50% filters of each layer from conv5_1 to the end of the model, denoted as Prune_2. Table 3 demonstrates that the ASE of the pruned model for the CASIA can be restored. But we can not restore the ASE for the UBIRIS.v2 because the layers of the fifth stage are sensitive to pruning for this dataset (seeing Fig. 6).

c) Based on the result of (2), we prune 50% filters of each layer from conv6_1 to conv7_4, denoted as Prune_3.

In conclusion, details of these three pruning strategy Prune_1, Prune_2, and Prune_3 are listed in Table 2, and results are shown in the Table 3. As a trade-off between the accuracy and the number of parameters, the proper pruning strategy for UBIRIS and CASIA is Prune_1 and Prune_2 respectively.

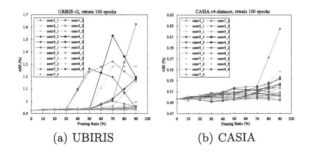

(a) UBIRIS   (b) CASIA

Fig. 6. The ASE after retraining the pruned models.

Pruning Results Based on l_1-norm Clustering. As a trade-off between the accuracy and the number of parameters, we regard the pruning 50% filters as an appropriate pruning ratio. For results at 50% pruning ratio, we set the upper limit 10% for $loss_{ASE}$ (the loss of ASE). For the pruning method only using l_1-norm, the k-means is used to cluster sorted filters in each layer of the original models. Experimental results indicate 3 clusters is the best choice. Clustering results for models are shown in Table 4.

Following the clustering results, the pruning strategy PruneCl_1 ($loss_{ASE} \geq$ 10%: pruning less) is designed. We also find that some layers have large $loss_{ASE}$ so that not pruning them may lead to better results. Therefore, we add three strategies as PruneCl_2 ($loss_{ASE} \geq$ 10%: not pruning), PruneCl_3 ($10\% \leq loss_{ASE} < 50\%$: pruning less, $loss_{ASE} \geq 50\%$: not pruning), PruneCl_4 ($10\% \leq loss_{ASE} < 100\%$: pruning less, $loss_{ASE} \geq 100\%$: not pruning). Table 5 lists the detailed pruning ratios. We prune these filters and retrain, results are in Table 6.

Table 4. Clustering results of l_1-norm: the number of samples in each category

Layer	UBIRIS			CASIA			Layer	UBIRIS			CASIA		
	Cat 1	Cat 2	Cat 3	Cat 1	Cat 2	Cat 3		Cat 1	Cat 2	Cat 3	Cat 1	Cat 2	Cat 3
conv1_1	32	19	13	31	20	13	conv5_2	152	259	101	182	261	69
conv1_2	15	18	31	16	17	31	conv5_3	131	253	128	138	250	124
conv2_1	49	41	38	46	37	45	conv6_1	436	433	155	209	510	305
conv2_2	41	44	43	41	44	43	conv7_1	388	455	181	2	519	503
conv3_1	77	135	44	79	137	40	conv6_2	257	516	251	254	500	270
conv3_2	86	113	57	84	110	62	conv7_2	2	574	448	137	537	350
conv3_3	80	120	56	86	117	53	conv6_3	241	516	267	234	512	278
conv4_1	211	229	72	219	217	76	conv7_3	2	511	511	2	523	499
conv4_2	193	236	83	213	218	81	conv6_4	209	489	326	200	494	330
conv4_3	194	256	62	213	248	51	conv7_4	2	502	520	2	513	509
conv5_1	195	245	72	201	245	66							

Table 5. Pruning ratios (%) obtained by l_1-norm clustering. 'LY' indicates layer No.

PruneCl_1	LY	1	2	3	4	5	6	7	8	9	10	11	12	13	14	15	16	17	18	19	20	21
UBIRIS	PR	50	20	40	30	30	30	30	40	40	40	40	30	30	80	80	80	60	70	50	70	50
PruneCl_2	LY	1	2	3	4	5	6	7	8	9	10	11	12	13	14	15	16	17	18	19	20	21
UBIRIS	PR	0	0	0	0	0	0	0	0	0	0	0	0	0	80	80	80	60	70	50	70	50
PruneCl_3	LY	1	2	3	4	5	6	7	8	9	10	11	12	13	14	15	16	17	18	19	20	21
UBIRIS	PR	50	0	40	0	0	30	0	0	0	0	0	0	0	80	80	80	60	70	50	70	50
PruneCl_4	LY	1	2	3	4	5	6	7	8	9	10	11	12	13	14	15	16	17	18	19	20	21
UBIRIS	PR	50	20	40	0	30	30	0	40	40	0	0	30	30	80	80	80	60	70	50	70	50
PruneCl_1	LY	1	2	3	4	5	6	7	8	9	10	11	12	13	14	15	16	17	18	19	20	21
CASIA	PR	50	30	40	30	30	30	30	40	40	40	40	40	30	70	50	70	70	70	50	70	50
PruneCl_2	LY	1	2	3	4	5	6	7	8	9	10	11	12	13	14	15	16	17	18	19	20	21
CASIA	PR	0	0	0	0	0	0	0	0	0	0	0	0	0	70	50	70	70	70	50	70	50
PruneCl_3	LY	1	2	3	4	5	6	7	8	9	10	11	12	13	14	15	16	17	18	19	20	21
CASIA	PR	0	30	40	0	0	0	0	0	0	0	0	0	0	70	50	70	70	70	50	70	50
PruneCl_4	LY	1	2	3	4	5	6	7	8	9	10	11	12	13	14	15	16	17	18	19	20	21
CASIA	PR	0	30	40	0	30	30	0	40	0	0	0	0	0	70	50	70	70	70	50	70	50

Table 6. Accuracy result of pruning by l_1-norm clustering.

Strategy	UBIRIS (%)			CASIA (%)		
	ASE	Params	FLOP	ASE	Params	FLOP
PruneCl_1	0.961	74.18	70.15	0.520	72.91	69.51
PruneCl_2	0.930	47.41	37.54	0.500	44.58	35.31
PruneCl_3	0.939	48.62	45.88	0.512	44.89	40.05
PruneCl_4	0.959	65.79	61.54	0.512	50.13	47.71

Table 7. Clustering results of [l_1-norm, l_2-norm]: the number of samples in each category for all layers of UBIRIS and CASIA model respectively

Layer	UBIRIS			CASIA			Layer	UBIRIS			CASIA		
	Cat 1	Cat 2	Cat 3	Cat 1	Cat 2	Cat 3		Cat 1	Cat 2	Cat 3	Cat 1	Cat 2	Cat 3
conv1_1	32	20	12	33	19	12	conv5_2	204	245	63	205	242	65
conv1_2	15	18	31	15	18	31	conv5_3	141	250	121	143	251	118
conv2_1	56	60	12	27	41	60	conv6_1	487	393	144	227	507	290
conv2_2	36	51	41	26	59	43	conv7_1	443	419	162	208	499	317
conv3_1	91	114	51	89	117	50	conv6_2	270	502	252	264	491	269
conv3_2	101	97	58	94	101	61	conv7_2	292	500	232	255	473	296
conv3_3	90	115	51	81	111	64	conv6_3	265	519	240	258	509	257
conv4_1	201	224	87	211	211	90	conv7_3	227	483	314	196	446	382
conv4_2	208	239	65	206	234	72	conv6_4	230	494	300	250	498	276
conv4_3	192	245	75	201	248	63	conv7_4	242	505	277	227	500	297
conv5_1	206	219	87	214	219	79							

Table 8. Pruning ratios (%) obtained by [l_1-norm, l_2-norm] clustering.

UBIRIS	LY	1	2	3	4	5	6	7	8	9	10	11
	PR	50.00	23.44	40.63	28.13	35.55	41.02	31.64	39.26	38.48	37.50	40.23
	LY	12	13	14	15	16	17	18	19	20	21	
	PR	39.84	27.54	85.94	84.18	75.39	77.44	76.56	69.34	70.70	72.95	
CASIA	LY	1	2	3	4	5	6	7	8	9	10	11
	PR	46.88	23.44	42.19	23.44	31.64	34.38	31.64	43.36	40.23	39.26	41.80
	LY	12	13	14	15	16	17	18	19	20	21	
	PR	40.04	27.93	71.68	69.04	73.73	71.09	73.93	62.70	73.05	71.00	
CASIA without conv1_1 pruning	LY	1	2	3	4	5	6	7	8	9	10	11
	PR	0	23.44	42.19	23.44	31.64	34.38	31.64	43.36	40.23	39.26	41.80
	LY	12	13	14	15	16	17	18	19	20	21	
	PR	40.04	27.93	71.68	69.04	73.73	71.09	73.93	62.70	73.05	71.00	

Pruning Results Based on l_1-norm and l_2-norm Clustering. For the pruning method using l_1-norm and l_2-norm, we also use k-means to cluster $[l_{ij}^1, l_{ij}^2]$ of filters into $K = 3$ clusters each layer. Clustering results for models are shown in Table 7. Following the clustering results, prune strategies for UBIRIS and CASIA are designed are illustrate in Table 8. We prune these filters and retrain, results are listed in Table 9. The pruning ratio of Params and FLOP of this strategy is the largest. But the *ASE* for UBIRIS.v2 are better than the manual designed strategies Prune_2 which have much smaller pruning ratios (see Table 3) and l_1-norm clustering based strategies PruneCl_1, PruneCl_4 which have smaller pruning ratios (see Table 6).

Results of two datasets show different changing situations with strategy changes. We infer that the different is due to the different of the visible and the near infrared images. The near infrared images include more detailed texture. So the conv1_1 layer may contain more detailed or finer low-level perceptual information that cannot be pruned. To verify the conjecture, we conduct an experiment without pruning the conv1_1, as the 3rd row of Table 8. The result is listed in Table 9. It is a little better than using the PruneCl12 pruning strategy.

Table 9. Result of pruning by [l_1-norm, l_2-norm] clustering.

Strategy	ASE(%)	Params (%)	FLOP (%)
UBIRIS	0.947	75.87	72.34
CASIA	0.530	74.58	70.62
CASIA without pruning conv1_1	0.520	74.55	68.79

5   Conclusions

In this paper, we reviewed our proposed Seg-Edge bilateral constraint network for iris segmentation. The iris edge map generated from convolutional layers optimizes the iris segmentation by aligning it with the iris boundary. The iris region produced by the segmentation limits the scope which makes the edge filtering pay more attention to the interesting target. The proposed clustering based pruning method is not only a substitute for time and computing resources consuming manual design, but also a better pruning method achieving much better segmentation accuracy and larger pruning ratio.

Acknowledgement. This work was supported by National Key Research and Development Program of China No. 2020AAA0140002.

References

1. Daugman, J.: High confidence visual recognition of persons by a test of statistical independence. TPAMI **15**(11), 1148–1161 (1993)
2. Wildes, R.: Iris recognition: an emerging biometric technology. Proc. IEEE **85**(9), 1348–1363 (1997)
3. Ma, L., Tan, T., Wang, Y., Zhang, D.: Personal identification based on iris texture analysis. TPAMI **25**(12), 1519–1533 (2003)
4. He, Z., Tan, T., Sun, Z., Qiu, X.: Toward accurate and fast iris segmentation for iris biometrics. TPAMI **31**(9), 1670–1684 (2009)
5. Proenca, H.: Iris recognition: on the segmentation of degraded images acquired in the visible wavelength. TPAMI **32**(8), 1502–1516 (2010)
6. Tan, C., Kumar, A.: Unified framework for automated iris segmentation using distantly acquired face images. TIP **21**(9), 4068–4079 (2012)
7. Liu, N., Li, H., Zhang, M., Liu, J., Sun, Z., Tan, T.: Accurate iris segmentation in non-cooperative environments using fully convolutional networks. In: ICB (2016)
8. Hu, J., Zhang, H., Xiao, L., Liu, J., Li, X., Li, L.: Seg-edge bilateral constraint network for iris segmentation. In: CVPR, pp. 5872–5881 (2017)
9. Proenca, H., Filipe, S., Santos, R., Oliveira, J., Alexandre, L.A.: The ubiris. v2: a database of visible wavelength iris images captured on-the-move and at-a-distance. TPAMI **32**(8), 1529–1535 (2010)
10. Casia.v4 database. http://www.cbsr.ia.ac.cn/china/Iris%20Databases%20CH.asp
11. Long, J., Shelhamer, E., Darrell, T.: Fully convolutional networks for semantic segmentation. In: CVPR, pp. 3431–3440 (2015)

12. Badrinarayanan, V., Handa, A., Cipolla, R.: Segnet: a deep convolutional encoder-decoder architecture for robust semantic pixel-wise labelling, arXiv preprint arXiv:1505.07293 (2015)
13. Chen, L.C., Papandreou, G., Kokkinos, I., Murphy, K., Yuille, A.L.: Semantic image segmentation with deep convolutional nets and fully connected CRFs, arXiv preprint arXiv:1412.7062 (2014)
14. Chen, L.C., Papandreou, G., Kokkinos, I., Murphy, K., Yuille, A.L.: Deeplab: semantic image segmentation with deep convolutional nets, atrous convolution, and fully connected CRFs. TPAMI **40**(4), 834–848 (2018)
15. LeCun, Y., Denker, J.S., Solla, S.A.: Optimal brain damage. In: Advances in Neural Information Processing Systems, pp. 598–605 (1990)
16. Han, S., Pool, J., Tran, J., Dally, W.J.: Learning both weights and connections for efficient neural network. In: Advances in Neural Information Processing Systems, pp. 1135–1143 (2015)
17. Li, H., Kadav, A., Durdanovic, I., Samet, H., Graf, H.P.: Pruning filters for efficient convnets, arXiv preprint arXiv:1608.08710 (2016)
18. Chen, L.C., Barron, J.T., Papandreou, G., Murphy, K., Yuille, A.L.: Semantic image segmentation with task-specific edge detection using CNNs and a discriminatively trained domain transform. In: CVPR, pp. 4545–4554 (2016)
19. Zhao, Z., Ajay, K.: An accurate iris segmentation framework under relaxed imaging constraints using total variation model. In: ICCV, pp. 3828–3836 (2015)
20. Tan, T., He, Z., Sun, Z.: Efficient and robust segmentation of noisy iris images for non-cooperative iris recognition. Image Vis. Comput. **28**(2), 223–230 (2010)
21. Tan, C., Kumar, A.: Towards online iris and periocular recognition under relaxed imaging constraints. TIP **22**(10), 3751–3765 (2013)

CAB-Net: Channel Attention Block Network for Pathological Image Cell Nucleus Segmentation

Meixuan Li[1], Huijie Fan[2,3(⊠)], and Dawei Yang[1]

[1] School of Information Technology and Engineering, Shenyang Ligong University, Shenyang 110159, Liaoning, China
[2] State Key Laboratory of Robotics, Shenyang Institute of Automation, Chinese Academy of Sciences, Shenyang 110016, China
fanhuijie@sia.cn
[3] Institutes for Robotics and Intelligent Manufacturing, Chinese Academy of Sciences, Shenyang 110016, China

Abstract. In histopathological image analysis, cell nucleus segmentation plays an important role in the clinical analysis and diagnosis of cancer. However, due to the different morphology of cells, uneven staining and the existence of a large number of dense nuclei, it is still challenging to accurately segment the nucleus. In order to learn more specific key feature information during the training process, this paper proposed a network model called the CAB-Net that uses channel attention to enhance the learning of feature information on each channel. The network uses the channel attention mechanism to extract the key features in each channel, generates weights to judge the importance of the features, and then weights them into the original image. This aims to strengthen the extraction of key information, thereby generating a more characteristic feature map, and enabling the model to make more accurate judgments. We added a boundary smoothness constraint, in order to better identify cell nuclei with unclear boundaries and achieve more accurate cell nucleus segmentation. The experimental results show that the method in this paper achieves good performance on the cell segmentation data set.

Keywords: Nucleus segmentation · Attention models · Deep learning

1 Introduction

After effective processing, pathological images play an important role in the diagnosis and prevention of cancer. The segmentation of cell nucleus can extract morphological features such as the shape, characteristics, cell position and density information of the cell nucleus. The precise segmentation of cell nuclei is also the basis for cell detection, classification and tumor grading, which is of great significance to the pathological diagnosis of many diseases, and is the key basis for judging the occurrence of lesions. However, due to the huge differences between different pathological images [14], cells also have different states, uneven cell staining and huge differences between different nuclear scanning devices, there

© Springer Nature Switzerland AG 2021
Y. Peng et al. (Eds.): ICIG 2021, LNCS 12889, pp. 654–663, 2021.
https://doi.org/10.1007/978-3-030-87358-5_53

are still many challenges to the precise segmentation of cell nuclei. Traditional medical image segmentation methods have big defects, such as not considering spatial features and being too sensitive to noise, not being able to balance the contradiction between detection accuracy and noise resistance, and oversegmentation, which cannot achieve accurate segmentation. Compared with traditional segmentation [11], the deep learning methods [3] show better performance in the process of medical image segmentation and diagnosis.

In most cases, traditional convolutional neural network segmentation methods use image blocks around pixels as input to classify pixels. This method has low computational efficiency, high storage consumption and too small receptive field. In recent years, some effective solutions have been proposed for the above problems. For example, Long et al. [5] proposed the Fully Convolutional Networks (FCN) structure for pixel-level classification and prediction of images. The network structure uses ResNet [9] as the backbone encoder. Its two branches are used for cell nucleus segmentation and cell nucleus contour segmentation. This method can realize the pixellevel classification of images and shows good performance. Ronneberger et al. [6] proposed a U-net network structure that is very suitable for medical image segmentation, the U-net network structure not only has a compressed path to capture contextual information, but also a symmetrical extended path that provides precise positioning, these allow the network to obtain contextual information at a higher resolution. But the results obtained by the above methods are still not satisfactory. This is because pooling is used in FCN to reduce the image size to increase the receiving field, and then upsampling is used to enlarge the image size, in this process of first reducing and then increasing, some information will be lost. However, in real training, u-net often reduces network performance due to different types of cells and different shades of staining results, resulting in insufficient feature extraction and the segmentation result is not fine enough.

In order to extract better features, we proposed a full-resolution Channel Attention [8] Block Network (CAB-Net) for pathological image segmentation, as shown in Fig. 1. The proposed model has three advantages:

- We have designed a channel attention block which use the attention mechanism to enhance the features on each channel, useful information from a large amount of characteristic information.
- In order to make the cell contour segmentation smoother, we added boundary smoothing loss [2] to enhance boundary recognition. It makes the features belonging to contour pixels more similar to enhance the difference between contour pixels and background pixels, and enhances the segmentation of cell nucleus boundaries.
- We use a dilated convolution [10] in the convolutional layer to increase the receiving field. So that, each convolution can output a larger range of information.

In addition, because there is no upsample layer in our network, we make the input and output feature maps of the entire network have the same resolution to better preserve edge and other information to improve the performance of the network.

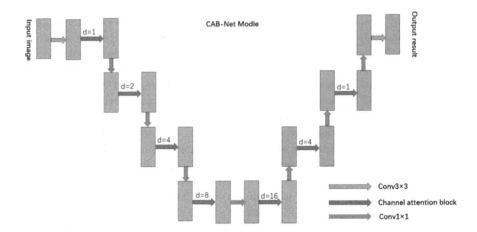

Fig. 1. Diagram of our method network model. The d in each channel attention block stands for dilation factors.

2 Method

The structure diagram of the network model proposed in this paper is shown in Fig. 1. The network is composed of 3×3 convolutional layers at the beginning and end, and 7 channel attention block layers in the middle. There is a 1×1 convolutional layer behind each block layer, which is used to compress the number of features. In order not to lose the resolution and increase the receiving field, the dilated convolution is used in each block layer of the network. But the same dilatation rate will cause a lot of information in adjacent pixels to be ignored, so we use a different dilatation ratefor each block layer. As shown in Fig. 1, the dilated rate of each block layer from front to back is set to 1, 2, 4, 8, 16, 4, and 1, respectively. The last two layers set the dilated rate to 4 and 1 in order to solve the problem of gridding artifacts caused by the dilated rate of the same multiple.

2.1 Channel Attention Block

In order to extract better features, we designed a channel attention block to the network, which is a channel-based attention mechanism. Generally speaking, the essence of attention is to imitate human visual attention. It applies the learned image feature weights to the original features to extract important information while ignoring other unimportant information. Channel attention is to pay attention to the weight of different channels. It is the attention that acts on the channel scale. In the $C \times H \times W$ feature map, the weight of the plane $H \times W$ is the same, but the weight of C in the channel attention is different. Therefore, the attention of the channel is to let each C learn different weights in the dimension of the channel, so as to judge the importance of each feature, obtain the required features, and improve the efficiency of the task.

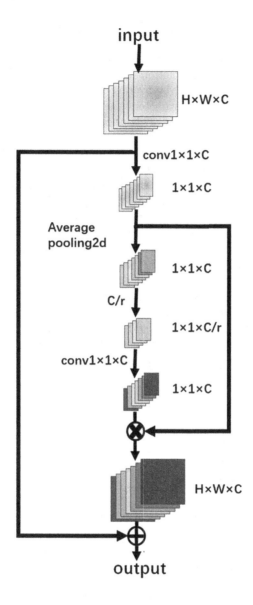

Fig. 2. The specific implementation framework of channel attention block in our method.

The specific structure of the channel attention block layer is shown in Fig. 2. First, perform 1×1 convolution operation on the feature map, the purpose is to realize the information interaction between channels, so that the number of channels becomes C, and the input is converted to $1 \times 1 \times C$ output. The function of this step is equivalent to obtaining global information, that is, the result of this layer shows the numerical distribution of the C feature maps of this layer.

We use this output result to construct a smooth average of all pixels through averagepooling2d, integrate the feature information into the channel, further enhance the feature information, and pass the information more completely to the next module for feature extraction. After that, perform C/r conversion on the feature information obtained by averagepooling2d, r represents the scaling parameter, which is a variable parameter (the value of r in this article is 16), and its purpose is to reduce the number of channels and reduce the amount of calculation, followed by the feature more compact and more convenient extraction of useful features. Then use convolution transformation to change its output to the same $1 \times 1 \times C$ output as the original output for subsequent calculations. The last is a reweight operation. We treat the weight of the calculated output as the importance of each channel, and then multiply them channel by channel to the previous feature, which is the $1 \times 1 \times C$ feature output after the conv1 $\times$ 1 operation, get new features on the channel. However, the resulting feature information is too single to be convincing, so it needs to be added to the original feature map to enhance the features and obtain the final output for feature extraction.

To sum up, it is the implementation process of the entire channel attention block. Since different channels have different importance in the feature map, each channel should have a weight value. We judge its importance by learning the weights of different channels, and add the weights to the original features as judgments to filter and extract useful features and suppress features that have little effect, so as to achieve enhanced feature processing.

2.2   Loss Function

The most commonly used loss function in image segmentation is the cross-entropy loss function. The loss function checks and predicts each pixel separately and is defined as:

$$\mathcal{L}_{CE} = -\frac{1}{N} \sum_{i=1}^{N} \sum_{m=1}^{M} \omega_i h_i^{(m)} \log p_i^{(m)} \tag{1}$$

Where M is the number of categories, N is the number of all pixels, $p_i^{(m)}$ is the probability that pixel i belongs to category m, and $h_i^{(m)}$ (0 or 1) is the category label of m. However, the cross-entropy loss function usually does not consider the spatial relationship between pixels, and cannot distinguish the feature difference between background pixels and boundary pixels well. Literature [4] adds the variance term to the original cross-entropy loss function, which solves the problem that the cross-entropy loss function does not consider the spatial relationship between pixels. The formula is as follows:

$$\mathcal{L}_{var} = \frac{1}{C} \sum_{c=1}^{C} \frac{1}{|S_c|} \sum_{i=1}^{|S_c|} (\mu_c - t_i)^2 \tag{2}$$

Where C represents the instance number, $|S_c|$ is the number of pixels belonging to C, t_i is the probability that pixel i belongs to the correct category, and μ_i is the average of the probability of S_c pixels.

However, the above-mentioned cross-entropy function cannot distinguish the background and the boundary well. So we added a boundary smoothing constraint to increase the difference between background pixels and boundary pixels. Boundary smoothing constraint is to strengthen the intra-class consistency and inter-class difference of background and boundary through regularization of do-main-invariant, contour-relevant, and background-relevan embedding. First, we get the results of contour and background embedding by performing weighted average pooling on the binary contour mask and the binary background mask. It is worth noting that since we only want to enhance the discrimination of pixels around the border, the background pixel sampling range of the binary background mask is only around the border. Because it is considered that if the above embedding is directly constraint, it may be too strict, so the embedding network is used to transfer the feature E to the low-dimensional space to calculate the distance of d (E_x, E_y), where (x, y) is randomly obtained in the all domain, he resulting loss is defined as follows:

$$\ell_{ED}(x,y) = \begin{cases} d(E_x, E_y), & if \gamma(E_x) = \gamma(E_y) \\ (\max(0, \zeta - d(E_x, E_y)))^2, & if \gamma(E_x) \neq \gamma(E_y) \end{cases} \tag{3}$$

Among them, $\gamma(E)$ represents the category of E, 0 represents contour features, 1 represents background features, and ζ is a pre-defined distance margin we set to 10 in this article. The final $\mathcal{L}_{smooth}$ is the he average of $\ell_{ED}(x,y)$ and C represents the number of combinations. The formula is as follows:

$$\mathcal{L}_{smooth} = \sum_{x=1}^{q} \sum_{y=x+1}^{q} \ell_{ED}(x,y)/C \tag{4}$$

Our overall loss function expression is as follows:

$$\mathcal{L}_{cab} = \mathcal{L}_{CE} + a\mathcal{L}_{var} + b\mathcal{L}_{smooth} \tag{5}$$

3 Experiments

3.1 Dataset

We use the public data set Multi-Organ [13] to evaluate our proposed model and compare it with the most popular methods. This data set contains 30 histopathological images stained with hematoxylin-eosin (H&E) at a resolution of 1000 × 1000. They come from multiple hospitals and are composed of different types of cancer from different organs, and each type of cell nucleus has a different appearance. According to previous work methods, the four organs in the data set are used as the training set and the training set of the same organ respectively, and the remaining three organs are used as the training set of different organs.

3.2   Evaluation Metrics

For the evaluation, we use the same metric as the reference [4], including four different metrics for evaluation, which are the set similarity metric Dice coefficient, the harmonic mean F1-Score of precision and recall, and the aggregate Jaccard index AJI. And the average Hausdorff distance. For detailed definitions of these indicators, see [1, 7, 15].

3.3   Implementation Details

First, we normalize [12] the dyeing of the image to reduce the chromatic aberration of the dyed image. Due to the insufficient number of data sets, we expanded the data through methods such as flipping, mirroring, and scaling. In the training process, set the output number of each layer of feature maps to 24, randomly crop an image of 208×208 pixels, and use a batch size of 4 as the input. The weights in the loss function are set to 1 and 0.005 respectively ($a = 1$, $b = 0.005$). The set training period is 300 epoch, and the learning rate is 0.001.

3.4   Results and Comparison

In order to prove the effectiveness of the proposed model, we compare with the CNN3 model [7], the u-net model [6] and the FullNet&varCE model on the Multi-Organ dataset. We divide the test set into two test data same organ test and different organ test, to verify the generalization ability of the model.

As shown in Table 1 and Table 2, $M_{\mathcal{L}_{smooth}}$ represents the model without $\mathcal{L}_{smooth}$. We observed that the model without $\mathcal{L}_{smooth}$ also got better results,

Table 1. Same organ test set

Method	F1	Dice	H	AJI
CNN3 [7]	0.8222	0.7031	7.93	0.5154
U-net [6]	0.8510	0.7962	6.89	0.5815
FullNet varCE [4]	0.8552	0.8007	6.54	0.5964
CAB-Net ($M_{\mathcal{L}_{smooth}}$)	0.8596	0.8057	**6.34**	0.6052
CAB-Net	**0.8602**	**0.8061**	6.35	**0.6133**

Table 2. Different organ test set

Method	F1	Dice	H	AJI
CNN3 [7]	0.8327	0.8051	**8.03**	0.4989
U-net [6]	0.8401	0.7732	10.57	0.5481
FullNet varCE [4]	0.8639	0.8054	8.16	0.6164
CAB-Net ($M_{\mathcal{L}_{smooth}}$)	0.8650	0.8069	8.05	0.6184
CAB-Net	**0.8659**	**0.8074**	8.07	**0.6220**

proving the effectiveness of the channel attention block model. And because $\mathcal{L}_{smooth}$ enhances the categorical features of border and background pixels, which makes the difference between border pixels and background pixels more obvious, so the model after adding lsmooth has a higher AJI value, which proves that our model has good effects in over-segmentation and under-segmentation. And the indicators in Table 1 and Table 2 also have good results, and show better generalization performance in Table 2.

Finally, we compared the results with the paper [4], as shown in Fig. 3. We observed that we can better predict clustered nuclei and accurately separate them (as shown in the first two rows of Fig. 3), and can better locate the nuclei and determine whether there are nuclei (as shown in the last two rows of Fig. 3). In short, it can be proved that our method can better identify cell nuclei, segment partially adhered cell nuclei, and has better segmentation performance on the da-taset Multi-Organ, which proves the effectiveness of our method.

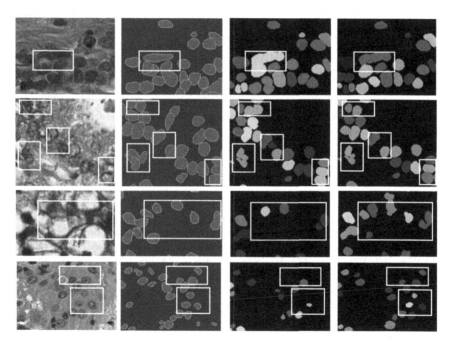

Fig. 3. From left to right are input images, the ground truth, Fullnet-var results [4] and our results.

4   Conclusion

This paper proposed a method of cell nucleus segmentation based on the network structure of channel attention block (CAB-Net). This method mainly uses the attention mechanism to extract feature information into each channel, and then uses methods such as average pooling to enhance the features. The purpose is to make effective features have a larger weight in the feature map, and invalid features have a smaller weight in the feature map, so as to obtain a more characteristic feature map to train the model to obtain better results. The boundary smoothness constraint is applied in the model to enhance the characteristics of the boundary by increasing the difference between the boundary and the background pixels, and separate the smooth boundary. Dilated convolution is also added to the network to increase the receptive field of the model. The method proposed in this paper strengthens the transfer of features, makes more effective use of features, and reduces the number of parameters to a certain extent. Finally, this method can achieve better performance on the Multi-Organ nuclei segmentation dataset.

Acknowledgments. This work is supported by the National Natural Science Foundation of China (61873259,61821005), and the Youth Innovation Promotion Association of Chinese Academy of Sciences(2019203), and the Education Department of Liaoning PResearch on Target Tracking Algorithm Based on Siamese Network (No.: LG201915); Shenyang Ligong University: Design and implementation of multi-target tracking algorithm based on deep learning.

References

1. Huang, G., Liu, Z., Van Der Maaten, L., Weinberger, K.Q.: Densely connected convolutional networks. In: Proceedings of CVPR, pp. 2261–2269. CVPR (2017)
2. Liu, Q., Dou, Q., Heng, P.-A.: Shape-aware meta-learning for generalizing prostate MRI segmentation to unseen domains. In: Martel, A.L., et al. (eds.) MICCAI 2020. LNCS, vol. 12262, pp. 475–485. Springer, Cham (2020). https://doi.org/10.1007/978-3-030-59713-9_46
3. Garcia-Garcia, A., Orts, S., Oprea, S., Villena Martinez, V., Rodríguez, J.: A Review on Deep Learning Techniques Applied to Semantic Segmentation (2017)
4. Qu, H., Yan, Z., Riedlinger, G.M., De, S., Metaxas, D.N.: Improving nuclei/gland instance segmentation in histopathology images by full resolution neural network and spatial constrained loss. In: Shen, D., et al. (eds.) MICCAI 2019. LNCS, vol. 11764, pp. 378–386. Springer, Cham (2019). https://doi.org/10.1007/978-3-030-32239-7_42
5. Long, J., Shelhamer, E., Darrell, T.: Fully convolutional networks for semantic segmentation. In: Proceedings of CVPR, pp. 3431–3440 (2015)
6. Ronneberger, O., Fischer, P., Brox, T.: U-Net: convolutional networks for biomedical image segmentation. In: Navab, N., Hornegger, J., Wells, W.M., Frangi, A.F. (eds.) MICCAI 2015. LNCS, vol. 9351, pp. 234–241. Springer, Cham (2015). https://doi.org/10.1007/978-3-319-24574-4_28

7. Kumar, N., Verma, R., Sharma, S., Bhargava, S., Vahadane, A., Sethi, A.: A dataset and a technique for generalized nuclear segmentation for computational pathology. IEEE Trans. Med. Imaging **36**(7), 1550–1560 (2017)
8. Hu, J., Shen, L., Albanie, S., Sun, G., Wu, E.: Squeeze-and-excitation networks. IEEE Trans. Pattern Anal. Mach. Intell. **42**, 2011–2023 (2020). https://doi.org/10.1109/TPAMI.2019.2913372
9. He, K., Zhang, X., Ren, S., Sun, J.: Deep residual learning for image recognition. In: Proceedings of CVPR, pp. 770–778 (2016) https://doi.org/10.1109/CVPR.2016.90
10. Yu, F., Koltun, V., Funkhouser, T.A.: Dilated residual networks. In: Proceedings of CVPR, vol. 2, p. 3 (2017)
11. Jiang, F., Gu, Q., Hao, H.Z., Li, N., Guo, Y.W., Chen, D.X.: Survey on content-based image segmentation methods. Ruan Jian Xue Bao/J. Softw. **28**(1), 160–183 (2017). https://doi.org/10.13328/j.cnki.jos.005136. (in Chinese)
12. Macenko, M., Niethammer, M., Marron, J.S., et al.: A method for normalizing histology slides for quantitative analysis. In: Proceedings of IEEE International Symposium on Biomedical Imaging, pp. 1107–1110 (2009)
13. Kumar, N., et al.: A multi-organ nucleus segmentation challenge. IEEE Trans. Med. Imaging (2019). https://doi.org/10.1109/TMI.2019.2947628
14. Zhang, X., Xing, F., Su, H., Yang, L., Zhang, S.: High-throughput histopathological image analysis via robust cell segmentation and hashing. Med. Image Anal. **26**(1), 306–315 (2015)
15. Qu, H., Wu, P., Huang, Q., et al.: Weakly supervised deep nuclei segmentation using points annotation in histopathology images. In: International Conference on Medical Imaging with Deep Learning, pp. 390–400 (2019)

Region Context Aggregation Network for Multi-organ Segmentation on Abdominal CT

Yinuo Wang[1], Bo Liu[1,2]([✉]), Fugen Zhou[1,2], and Xiangzhi Bai[1,2]

[1] Beihang University, Beijing, People's Republic of China
bo.liu@buaa.edu.cn
[2] Beijing Advanced Innovation Center for Biomedical Engineering, Beihang University, Beijing 100083, People's Republic of China

Abstract. Pointing at the problem of the automatic segmentation of multiple abdominal organs on CT, we propose a coarse-to-fine based 3D network, named as RCANet, which could effectively refine the coarse segmentation by an end-to-end learning strategy through exploring more contextual information. Our network consists of several simple but useful modules which are helpful to represent the relation between voxels and object regions more effectively. First, we learn a 3D coarse segmentation map through a classical 3D UNet. Second, we use a region concentration block (RCB) to extract the global context information of each object region. Last, we augment the combination of each voxels and its affiliated region by utilizing a region aggregation module (RAM) and obtain the final segmentation result. In our paper, we demonstrate the advantages of RCANet on TCIA public dataset with the improvement on some small organs and on average compared with some advanced methods.

Keywords: Multi-organ segmentation · Coarse-to-fine network · CT segmentation

1 Introduction

CT-based segmentation of abdominal multi-organs plays a significant role in visual enhancement, disease diagnosis, operation planning and postoperative evaluation [16] More specifically, the patient-specific anatomical segmentation map is required for the planning of the radiotherapy and serves as an auxiliary visual reference during an image-guided surgery [9], thereby avoiding extra damage to organs at risk. For patients who suffer from esophagorespiratory fistula (ERF), expandable metallic stents placement is a safe and effective palliative treatment. Before the placement, it is necessary to assess the airway stricture and the relationship between the fistula and the surrounding tissue by CT segmentation, so as to prevent the compression of surrounding organs caused by the expansion of expandable metallic stents [13]. Besides, in the interventional treatment of abdominal cancer, segmentation of organs is needed to navigate puncture needles and catheters through human vessels and organs [24].

© Springer Nature Switzerland AG 2021
Y. Peng et al. (Eds.): ICIG 2021, LNCS 12889, pp. 664–674, 2021.
https://doi.org/10.1007/978-3-030-87358-5_54

In recent years, lots of deep learning-based organ and lesion segmentation methods have emerged thick and fast, being used to replace traditional tiring and time-consuming manual delineation. UNet, a single path network structure, defines the network structure paradigm of most medical image segmentation and performs well in many different tasks [11]. UNet++ extends the network topology, so that the network can integrate the information of different scale features and learn the importance of various scales [25]. Also based on UNet, some previous works introduce dense connection block, which establishes the information flow between non-adjacent layers through more skip connections [2,8,22]. This kind of module is more conducive to the transmission and learning of features. Some other works adopt the inception-like block [5] or ASPP block to replace the original convolution kernel, so as to reconcile features and capture context information of different scales. In addition, coarse-to-fine strategies [12,17,18,26] are brought to handle the GPU memory limitation by roughly locating the organs of interest in the first stage and further refining the segmentation masks in the second stage. These usually improve the segmentation accuracy but need to train multiple network. Recently advanced attention mechanisms are proved to be capable of capturing the most discriminant part of the features in the network [7,9,10,15,18,23]. Embedded as gates in the path of skip connections, common attention modules can generate attentive features at multiple scales, assisting the network in focusing the regions which are more relevant to the target classes.

When UNet and its derivative structure are applied to different tasks, it is doubted that a single model can excellently handle various task. Isensee et al. propose nnU-Net [6], which is almostly based on the pure structure of 2d or 3d UNet. According to the author's experience, a set of criteria is designed, which can automatically select the appropriate preprocessing scheme, the network hyper parameters, the inference strategy and the post-processing method for various inputs. Using this framework, the author win the highest average dice score in ten organ segmentation competitions of the decathlon medical segmentation challenge [14]. Pointing at similar problems, some researches on neural architecture search (NAS) have been applied on medical image segmentation [3,19], but they are limited by the complicated setting of search space, as well as the slightly worse accuracy.

Influenced by some works which use coarse-to-fine strategies [12,17,18,20,26] and some other works which focus on promoting the representation by aggregating the contextual pixels [1,21], we propose a coarse-to-fine and attention mechanism based 3D network, named as RCANet. It extracts the coarse segmentation map by a generic 3d UNet and then renovates the representation between voxels and regions using the proposed region context aggregation(RCA) module. Different from the coarse-to-fine principle mentioned above, our approach needs no extra network and makes refinement on the whole prediction map, which can downsize the whole network stream and be easily used on any 3d backbone. The RCA module could generates region contextual representation from the coarse features and then enhance the voxel-region relation through combining the region contextual representation. As shown schematically in Fig. 1, the

RCA module can be divided into the region concentration block (RCB) and the region aggregation module(RAM), which correspond to the two functions above. We perform a complete set of experiment and evaluation on a public dataset. From the result analysis, we find that the RCA module can promisingly improve the overall segmentation performance of multiple organs. Besides, it can especially improve the segmentation performance of some organs with complex shape (duodenum) or small size (gallbladder, esophagus).

2   Method

2.1   Base Network

We use a generic 3d UNet as a base network that generates a coarse segmentation and two kinds of representation. As shown in Fig. 1, given an input image I, the base network first use the network parameters Θ to output a coarse segmentation map $M_{coarse} = f(I, \Theta)$ that we use to compute an auxiliary loss. Second, the base network generates what we call transit features which contain sufficient high-level and low-level features of the input volume. Third, a set of auxiliary features are produced by the base network, dividing into K feature maps. Each of the feature map indicates the subordinating degree of voxels to the class k.

2.2   Region Context Aggregation Module

To effectively improve the coarse segmentation map, we propose a post-processing module connected to the base network. The whole network integrates the coarse segmentation information extracted by 3d UNet, and then merge the contextual voxels into a region contextual representation, which is utilized to better describe the relation of voxels and target regions, and finally refine the coarse segmentation map.

First, we exploit the RCB shown in Fig. 2 to structure region Contextual Representation. Specifically, given the transit features $T \in \mathbb{R}^{C \times D \times H \times W}$ and the auxiliary features $A \in \mathbb{R}^{K \times D \times H \times W}$, the RCB reshapes and normalizes the A with the softmax function, and then multiplies it by reshaped T to obtain the region Contextual Representation $R \in \mathbb{R}^{C \times K}$. Here, C, K, D, H, W denote the number of channels, the number of classes, depth, height and width of feature map respectively. The process can be formulated as follows:

$$R_k = \sum_{i=1}^{DHW} \frac{exp(A_{ki}/t)}{\sum_{j=1}^{DHW} exp(A_{kj}/t)} T_i \tag{1}$$

where A_{ki} indicates the subordinating degree of a voxel i to a region object k. The temperature factor t is generally set to 1. This representation not only enables voxels to concentrate on each object region from a global aspect, but also enables the object regions' distribution to be more comprehensively and correctly consistent with the contextual voxels, resulting in mutual promotion.

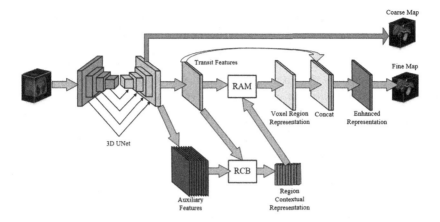

Fig. 1. An Overview of the region context aggregation Network. Given an input CT patch, we first use a 3d UNet to get the coarse segmentation map and coarse features. Then the RCA module consisting of RCB and RAM is applied to construct the region contextual representation and adjust the relation between voxels and object regions. Then the enhanced relation representation is concatenated with coarse features to generate a refined segmentation map.

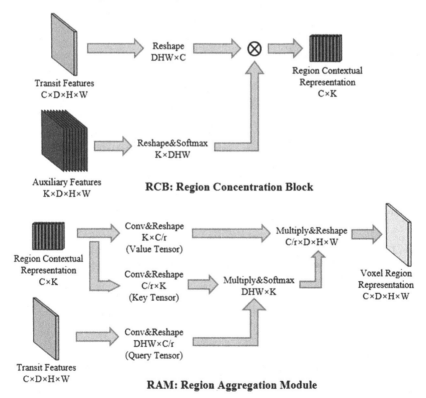

Fig. 2. The details of the region concentration block and the region aggregation module.

Second, in RAM, a query tensor is converted from transit features with a 1×1 Conv-Instance Normalization-ReLU operation. Meanwhile, a value tensor and a key tensor is separately converted from R with two 1×1 Conv-IN-ReLU operations. The channel C is shrunk to C/r due to the need of reducing the 3d network's parameters. And a matrix multiplication and normalization is applied to the reshaped query tensor and key tensor to calculate a refined relation, which is then multiplied by the value tensor to generate the voxel region representation:

$$V_{ci} = \rho \left(\sum_{k=0}^{K} (\frac{exp(\beta\,(R_{kc})\,\gamma\,(T_i))}{\sum_{j=0}^{K}(exp(\beta\,(R_{kc})\,\gamma\,(T_i)))}\alpha\,(R_{kc})') \right) \tag{2}$$

where $\alpha\,(\cdot),\beta\,(\cdot),\gamma\,(\cdot),\rho\,(\cdot)$ indicate transformation functions of 1×1 Conv-IN-ReLU operation. The voxel region representation takes advantages of regional contextual information and reconstructs voxel-level features. It is finally concatenated with transit features to generate an enhanced representation, after which the final refinement is achieved. In this way, the approach can fully mine the relevant contextual information on the basis of coarse segmentation, in order to correct some wrong classified voxels.

3   Experiments and Results

3.1   Dataset and Preprocessing

Our experiment was performed on the abdominal multi-organ segmentation dataset of TCIA, which contains 43 cases of abdominal CT. The size of original transverse section is 512×512, the spacing of transverse section is in the range of 0.66×0.66 mm to 0.98×0.98 mm, and the thickness of transverse section is in the range of 0.5 to 1.0 mm. Each case contains $K = 9$ labels consisting of the manual annotations of eight anatomical structures extended by [2] (spleen, left kidney, gallbladder, esophagus, liver, stomach, pancreas, duodenum), plus background.

In order to remove the redundant padding and improve the network computing efficiency, we refer to Gibson's method [2] to crop the region of interest in CT scans, and then resample each scan to size of $144 \times 144 \times 144$.

Table 1. Dice scores of previous methods, baseline 3d Unet, 3d Unet with ASPP module and our approach on TCIA validation set. Various datasets and cross-validation setting preclude direct comparisons.

Average Dice Score (%)	Spleen	Left Kidney	Gallbladder	Esophagus	Liver	Stomach	Pancreas	duodenum	Avg.
DenseVNet [2]	95	93	73	71	95	87	75	63	81.5
Global FCN U-Net [4]	94.5	94.3	73.5	59.9	95.6	87	68.8	54.3	78.48
Hybrid-OBELISK+CNN [4]	94.4	94.2	75.3	63.3	95.4	86.8	70.2	53.8	79.17
3d Unet	96.38	96.08	84.20	74.16	96.50	91.22	**82.20**	71.88	86.57
3d Unet + ASPP	96.06	95.88	82.60	73.88	96.44	92.06	81.96	71.50	86.29
Our method	**96.54**	**96.16**	**85.26**	**75.42**	**96.60**	**92.14**	82.16	**73.32**	**87.20**

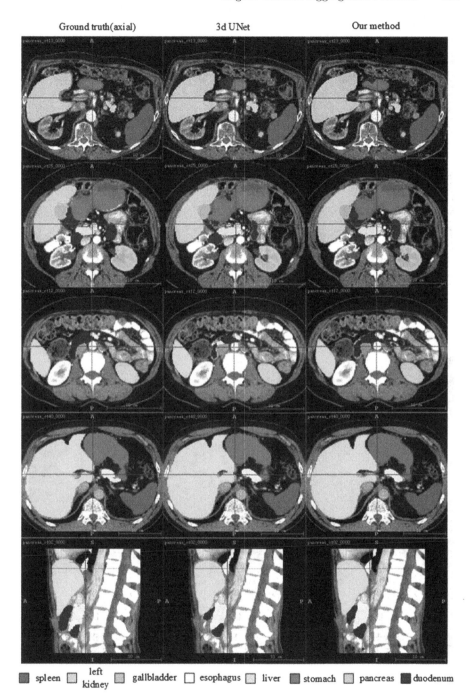

Fig. 3. Visualization of axial and sagittal planes of several prediction maps. Ground truth annotations, the results from 3d UNet and our approach are displayed from left to right.

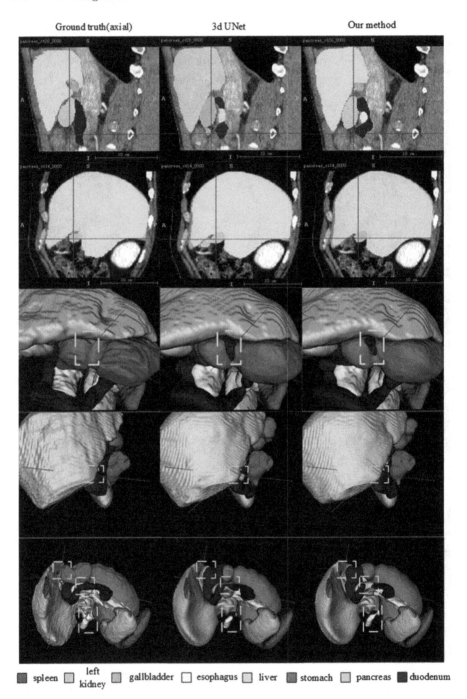

Fig. 4. Visualization of sagittal planes and 3d surface rendering of several prediction maps. Ground truth annotations, the results from 3d UNet and our approach are displayed from left to right.

Table 2. Comparison of 95% Hausdorff Distance of 3d UNet and our approach on TCIA validation set.

Average 95% Hausdorff Distance (mm)	Spleen	Left Kidney	Gallbladder	Esophagus	Liver	Stomach	Pancreas	Duodenum	Avg.
3d Unet	**2.620**	2.114	**5.676**	5.636	5.226	9.436	5.164	17.866	6.717
3d Unet + ASPP	2.826	2.228	6.834	5.954	3.988	**8.670**	5.132	17.884	6.689
Our method	2.712	**2.106**	5.726	**5.418**	**3.594**	9.196	**4.954**	**15.396**	**6.137**

3.2 Implementation

All experiments were performed using Pytorch 1.8 with a NVIDIA GeForce RTX 3090 with 24 GB memory. According to [6], for each scan, we first truncated the intensity values at the 99.5 and 0.05 percentile to filter unnecessary regions, and then normalized the intensity values by subtracting their mean and dividing by their standard deviation.

In the training stage, we randomly cropped 3d sub-volumes of size $128 \times 128 \times 128$ from CT scans as the input of the network. To avoid the over-fitting of limited training data, we adopted some data augmentation techniques, including random rotation, scaling, gamma augmentation, flipping, adding white Gaussian noise and Gaussian blurring. Since 3d network produces large memory consumption, we chose a small batch size of 2 and replaced batch normalization with instance normalization. We trained our network for 250 epochs. Each epoch contained 250 iterations. We chose the stochastic gradient descent algorithm as the optimizer with an initial learning rate of 0.01 and a momentum of 0.99. Besides, downsampling is performed with strided convolutions and upsampling is performed with transposed convolutions. The width of the transit features is set to 32, same as the width of the second last features in the base network. The loss function in our approach is the sum of dice loss and cross entropy loss, which can be formulated as:

$$L = \lambda_1 L_1 + \lambda_2 L_2 \tag{3}$$

where L_1 and L_2 represent the loss of coarse segmentation and fine segmentation respectively. Both λ_1 and λ_2 are set to 0.5 in our experiment.

In the test stage, we analyzed the accuracy of our method using a 5-fold cross-validation over 43 subjects. For each test image in each fold, we analyzed the performance of each organ segmentation using Dice coefficient and 95% Hausdorff distance.

3.3 Result Analysis

We display axial plane, sagittal plane and 3d surface rendering of several prediction maps in validation set by ITK-SNAP software, and carefully compare the results of 3d UNet and our approach with the ground truth labels. In Fig. 3, the first and second row show partial segmentation results of stomach and duodenum, exhibiting that our approach can represent the relationship between the two adjacent organs more accurately compared with baseline 3d UNet. In the third and fourth row of Fig. 3, we observe that our approach can better describe the shape of duodenum, and can also segment some details of the liver more correctly. In the fifth row, it is clear that our approach's segmentation of esophagus has a more comparable shape to the corresponding part of ground truth. Similarly, We can see in the 3d surface rendering of Fig. 4 that, there are some mistakenly classified voxels on the side of stomach, and our approach can effectively reduce the volume of mistaken area and push voxels to the correct class. As shown in Table 1, though the difference of dataset and cross-validation setting precludes direct comparison, our method outperforms many other advanced methods such as DenseVnet [2] and OBELISK [4] on the whole. As listed in Table.1, compared with the base 3d UNet and the 3d Unet with an ASPP head, our method obtains improvement in seven of the eight organs in total on dice scores. Among them, the dice scores of gallbladder, esophagus and duodenum are improved more than 1%, which shows that our method optimizes the segmentation of organs with complex shapes or small size. The data in Table 2 shows that our method reduces 95% Hausdorff distance on most organs, which means that the segmentation results produced by our method have fine robustness on the edge of most organs. However, our approach is mainly based on the coarse features produced by the base network, so it may still be restricted by the performance of base network prediction to some extent, which we will take into consideration in our next work. From the analysis above and experimental quantitative results, we can find that our approach significantly improves the segmentation performance of some important tubular organs(such as esophagus and duodenum) and some small organs (such as gallbladder).

4   Discussion and Conclusion

The RCANet presented in this paper provides a simple yet effective coarse-to-fine method on an important medical image segmentation task. It improves the performance of the algorithm based on the most advanced baseline framework while it takes less than twenty seconds to make a segmentation prediction for a test CT volume. As shown in the quantitative results, our approach is effective for most organs tested.

In conclusion, we propose a region context aggregation module connected to the 3d UNet for multi-organ segmentation's improvement on abdominal CT scans. Our experiments and results show that our approach can grab ample contextual information from coarse features through structuring and enhancing the affinity between CT voxels and object regions, resulting in better performance on predicting the segmentation map.

Acknowledgement. This work was supported by the National Key R&D Program of China under Grant No. 2018YFA0704100 and 2018YFA0704101, the National Natural Science Foundation of China under Grant No. 61601012.

References

1. Fu, J., et al.: Dual attention network for scene segmentation. In: Proceedings of the IEEE/CVF Conference on Computer Vision and Pattern Recognition, pp. 3146–3154 (2019)
2. Gibson, E., et al.: Automatic multi-organ segmentation on abdominal CT with dense V-networks. IEEE Trans. Med. Imaging **37**(8), 1822–1834 (2018)
3. Guo, D., et al.: Organ at risk segmentation for head and neck cancer using stratified learning and neural architecture search. In: Proceedings of the IEEE/CVF Conference on Computer Vision and Pattern Recognition, pp. 4223–4232 (2020)
4. Heinrich, M.P., Oktay, O., Bouteldja, N.: Obelisk-Net: fewer layers to solve 3D multi-organ segmentation with sparse deformable convolutions. Med. Image Anal. **54**, 1–9 (2019)
5. Ibtehaz, N., Rahman, M.S.: MultiresuNet: rethinking the U-net architecture for multimodal biomedical image segmentation. Neural Netw. **121**, 74–87 (2020)
6. Isensee, F., Jaeger, P.F., Kohl, S.A., Petersen, J., Maier-Hein, K.H.: nnU-Net: a self-configuring method for deep learning-based biomedical image segmentation. Nat. Methods **18**(2), 203–211 (2021)
7. Li, C., et al.: ANU-Net: attention-based nested u-net to exploit full resolution features for medical image segmentation. Comput. Graph. **90**, 11–20 (2020)
8. Li, X., Chen, H., Qi, X., Dou, Q., Fu, C.W., Heng, P.A.: H-DenseUnet: hybrid densely connected UNet for liver and tumor segmentation from CT volumes. IEEE Trans. Med. Imaging **37**(12), 2663–2674 (2018)
9. Liu, Y., et al.: CT-based multi-organ segmentation using a 3D self-attention u-net network for pancreatic radiotherapy. Med. Phys. **47**(9), 4316–4324 (2020)
10. Oktay, O., et al.: Attention U-Net: learning where to look for the pancreas. arXiv preprint arXiv:1804.03999 (2018)
11. Ronneberger, O., Fischer, P., Brox, T.: U-Net: convolutional networks for biomedical image segmentation. In: Navab, N., Hornegger, J., Wells, W.M., Frangi, A.F. (eds.) MICCAI 2015. LNCS, vol. 9351, pp. 234–241. Springer, Cham (2015). https://doi.org/10.1007/978-3-319-24574-4_28
12. Roth, H.R., et al.: A multi-scale pyramid of 3D fully convolutional networks for abdominal multi-organ segmentation. In: Frangi, A.F., Schnabel, J.A., Davatzikos, C., Alberola-López, C., Fichtinger, G. (eds.) MICCAI 2018. LNCS, vol. 11073, pp. 417–425. Springer, Cham (2018). https://doi.org/10.1007/978-3-030-00937-3_48
13. Shin, J.H., Kim, J.H., Song, H.Y.: Interventional management of esophago respiratory fistula. Korean J. Radiol. **11**(2), 133 (2010)
14. Simpson, A.L., et al.: A large annotated medical image dataset for the development and evaluation of segmentation algorithms. arXiv preprint arXiv:1902.09063 (2019)
15. Sinha, A., Dolz, J.: Multi-scale self-guided attention for medical image segmentation. IEEE J. Biomed. Health Inform. **25**(1), 121–130 (2020)
16. Sykes, J.: Reflections on the current status of commercial automated segmentation systems in clinical practice (2014)
17. Wang, W., et al.: A fully 3D cascaded framework for pancreas segmentation. In: 2020 IEEE 17th International Symposium on Biomedical Imaging (ISBI), pp. 207–211. IEEE (2020)
18. Wang, Y., Zhou, Y., Shen, W., Park, S., Fishman, E.K., Yuille, A.L.: Abdominal multi-organ segmentation with organ-attention networks and statistical fusion. Med. Image Anal. **55**, 88–102 (2019)

19. Yan, X., Jiang, W., Shi, Y., Zhuo, C.: MS-NAS: multi-scale neural architecture search for medical image segmentation. In: Martel, A.L., et al. (eds.) MICCAI 2020. LNCS, vol. 12261, pp. 388–397. Springer, Cham (2020). https://doi.org/10.1007/978-3-030-59710-8_38

20. Zhang, F., et al.: ACFNet: attentional class feature network for semantic segmentation. In: Proceedings of the IEEE/CVF International Conference on Computer Vision, pp. 6798–6807 (2019)

21. Zhang, H., Zhang, H., Wang, C., Xie, J.: Co-occurrent features in semantic segmentation. In: Proceedings of the IEEE/CVF Conference on Computer Vision and Pattern Recognition, pp. 548–557 (2019)

22. Zhang, J., Jin, Y., Xu, J., Xu, X., Zhang, Y.: MDU-Net: multi-scale densely connected U-Net for biomedical image segmentation. arXiv preprint arXiv:1812.00352 (2018)

23. Zhang, Z., Fu, H., Dai, H., Shen, J., Pang, Y., Shao, L.: ET-Net: a generic edge-attention guidance network for medical image segmentation. In: Shen, D., et al. (eds.) MICCAI 2019. LNCS, vol. 11764, pp. 442–450. Springer, Cham (2019). https://doi.org/10.1007/978-3-030-32239-7_49

24. Zhong, W., et al.: Celiac plexus block for treatment of pain associated with pancreatic cancer: a meta-analysis. Pain Pract. **14**(1), 43–51 (2014)

25. Zhou, Z., Rahman Siddiquee, M.M., Tajbakhsh, N., Liang, J.: UNet++: a nested U-Net architecture for medical image segmentation. In: Stoyanov, D., et al. (eds.) DLMIA/ML-CDS -2018. LNCS, vol. 11045, pp. 3–11. Springer, Cham (2018). https://doi.org/10.1007/978-3-030-00889-5_1

26. Zhu, Z., Xia, Y., Shen, W., Fishman, E., Yuille, A.: A 3D coarse-to-fine framework for volumetric medical image segmentation. In: 2018 International Conference on 3D Vision (3DV), pp. 682–690. IEEE (2018)

A Reversible Digital Watermarking Algorithm Based on Medical Images via Threshold Segmentation and Contrast Enhancement

Jin Pang[1], Xingjie Huang[1], Ru Zhang[2], Jianyi Liu[2(✉)], Yue Wang[2], and Youqiang Sun[2]

[1] State Grid Information and Telecommunication Branch, Beijing, China
[2] Beijing University of Posts and Telecommunications, Beijing, China
{Zhangru,liujy,youqiang_sun}@bupt.edu.cn

Abstract. With the popularization of the Internet, the information is more convenient to acquire and transmit via network. But the privacy protection under the digital environment should be paid more and more attention. Now, in the paperless hospital, the reversible digital watermarking technology is adopted to embed the electronic cases into medical images of patients as watermark form, which can ensure the privacy protection. However, the existing reversible digital watermarking algorithm usually pursues the peak signal-to-noise ratio, which makes it difficult to consider the embedding capacity and image quality. To solve these problems, a reversible digital watermarking algorithm based on threshold segmentation for image contrast enhancement is proposed. In the proposed model, the Ostu threshold segmentation is applied to the gradient amplitude of the image to obtain the pixel threshold, and the bidirectional scanning is used to determine the foreground area. Meanwhile, the square column displacement between peak-pixel and zero-pixel value is used to avoid pixel overflow. The redundant information is added in the process of embedding to ensure the accuracy of information extraction. The experimental results show that the algorithm can keep a higher embedding capacity and make the embedded image with a higher visual quality.

Keywords: Reversible digital watermarking · Threshold segmentation · Contrast enhancement · Medical images

1 Introduction

With the arrival of the era of big data, information communication and sharing are becoming more and more convenient. Online healthcare systems and telemedicine are rapidly evolving, and digital medical images are playing an increasingly important role in medical clinical diagnosis. Through the Internet, digital medical images can be used for remote medical diagnosis between hospitals and healthcare entities, as well as allow patients to have access to their own medical files [1]. At the same time, people pay more attention to privacy and the need for privacy protection are increasing. Some scholars have suggested that patients' privacy information and diagnostic information,

© Springer Nature Switzerland AG 2021
Y. Peng et al. (Eds.): ICIG 2021, LNCS 12889, pp. 675–690, 2021.
https://doi.org/10.1007/978-3-030-87358-5_55

such as Electronic Patient Records, can be embedded in medical images in the form of watermarks to ensure that the privacy information is invisible to third parties. To achieve this process, how to ensure that the medical image can be restored without distortion at the receiving end is a key problem, which can be solved by reversible digital watermarking algorithm (RDWA) [2]. The embedding process does not affect the visual quality of medical images, especially the region of interest, and original medical images can be restored accurately when extracting information. How to improve the embedding capacity while ensuring the invisibility of reversible watermarking becomes the next research hotspot [3].

Digital watermarking technology has also made great progress in theoretical research. The earliest digital watermarking scheme used the Least Significant Bit (LSB) [4] of gray pixel value to embed the watermarking information. The encrypted image obtained by this embedding method cannot be recovered accurately at the receiving end. In military, medical and other fields, image content is extremely sensitive, and minor changes may affect people's judgment, then bringing serious consequences. People are eager to recover the original carrier image without damage after information extraction, so reversible digital watermarking technology is produced. Reversible digital watermarking technology can be also called as Reversible Data Hiding (RDH). The earliest reversible digital watermarking algorithm was proposed by American scholar Barton in a patent during 1997 [5]. Since then, scholars have carried out many researches on reversible digital watermarking technology, and its application fields are increasingly extensive, such as image authentication [5], stereo image coding [6, 7], error concealment in video frames [8], vector image restoration in computer-aided design (CAD) engineering graphics [9] and other scenarios.

Based on in-depth study and research on the current reversible image watermarking technology, this paper focuses on how to propose a reversible digital watermarking algorithm with larger embedding capacity and higher visual quality for medical images.

The rest of this paper is organized as follows: Sect. 2 analyzes the related work on reversible watermarking; the proposed model and background are given in detail; Sect. 4 gives the experiments of the comparison of the proposed model and existing method; the conclusion and feature work of this paper are given in Sect. 5.

2 Related Work

Reversible Digital Watermarking Algorithm based on Histogram Shift: Reversible digital watermarking based on HS technology was first proposed by Ni et al. [10]. The basic idea of the HS based reversible watermarking is that the peak point and zero point are first located in the constructed gray histogram, then the information is embedded by moving the square column between the peak-point and zero-point. Many scholars have researched reversible digital watermarking algorithms based on spatial histogram shift. Lin et al. [11] proposed a multi-layer reversible digital water marking algorithm based on histogram shift of difference images. The multi-layer embedding strategy can improve the embedding capacity and keep the distortion small. Kim et al. [12] divided the original image into N equal-sized sub-images, the strongest spatial correlation sub-image is selected as the reference image, and used the histogram shift of

$N-1$ difference images to achieve reversible digital watermarking. Alavianmehr et al. [13] proposed an algorithm based on histogram shift in integer wavelet domain. After the low-frequency subband coefficient matrix is partitioned, the inverse s-scan is used to obtain the adjacent coefficient difference, and the embedding capacity of the algorithm is controlled by adjusting the embedding level (EL). Without attack, the original image can be recovered without damage. Huang et al. [14] used the quadtree decomposition method to divide each area of the original image into blocks of different sizes according to the smoothness degree, and embedded bit information in each block using histogram shifting technology. When maintaining the same peak signal to noise ratio (PSNR), the embedding capacity of the algorithm is significantly higher than that of the algorithm with fixed block size. Tai et al. [15] adopted a binary tree structure to determine the peak point for embedding information. The information that the sender and receiver need to share is only the level number of the binary tree. To some extent, the algorithm solves the common shortcoming of HS, that is, it must provide the peak point and zero point in the form of additional information. Qin et al. [16] designed a high image quality reversible digital watermarking algorithm by combining adaptive pixel selection, image inpainting based on partial differential equation and histogram shift technology. Wang et al. [17] transformed the HS-based multiple embedding problem into a problem of balancing embedding rate and distortion, and used GA algorithm to search for the optimal peak-point and zero-point of multiple embedding. Compared with the algorithm in reference [18], the quality of the encrypted image obtained by this algorithm is higher. Li et al. [19] proposed a general framework for constructing reversible digital water-marking algorithm based on HS. A reversible digital watermarking algorithm can be obtained by modifying the shifting function and embedding function. The framework has the potential to provide reversible digital watermarking algorithm, but it also has its limitations. For example, it cannot produce adaptive embedding and location map free algorithm.

Reversible Digital Watermarking Algorithm for Contrast Enhancement: PSNR has been used to evaluate the invisibility of digital watermarking algorithms for a long time. However, the evaluation of image quality by PSNR is different from subjective perception, because PSNR calculates the pixel difference between two images, and fails to consider the structural information of the image itself and visual features of human eyes [20]. Taking advantage of this, Wu et al. [21] firstly proposed a reversible digital watermarking algorithm to enhance image contrast. By constantly shifting and embedding the two highest bins in the histogram and their outside columns, the height of the two highest columns in each cycle was reduced to achieve histogram equalization. Wu et al. [22] also applied the idea in the literature [21] threshold was regarded as the background area. The part greater than or equal to the threshold value is regarded as the foreground area (usually the area of interest), and the contrast of the foreground area image is enhanced. Because there are some points or regions with small pixel value in the foreground area of medical image, the fore-ground area obtained by this method is smaller than the actual foreground area, which limits the amount of information embedded in the image to a certain extent. Gao et al. [23] proposed a reversible digital watermarking algorithm based on con-trolled contrast enhancement and integer wavelet domain coefficient extension. By limiting the size of Relative Contrast Error (RCE) to control the embedding process, the visual distortion caused by excessive Contrast enhancement can be avoided to a certain ex-tent. Kim et al. [24] achieved information embedding and histogram equalization by moving bins between the peak point and zero-point in each round of embedding. In addition, the location map is used to record whether the pixel value corresponds to the original zero point or the zero-point generated by the shift, and the location map is generated in each round of the loop. Compared with the previous algorithm, this algo-rithm can not only avoid the overflow of pixel value, but also cleverly realizes the automatic closure of the loop process by taking advantage of the gradually increasing feature of the location map. For natural images, the algorithm achieves good results in enhancing image contrast and avoids excessive enhancement.

The main work and research results are as follows: a reversible digital watermarking algorithm based on threshold segmentation and histogram equalization is proposed. Considering that the foreground region is spatially continuous in the medical image, which contains both substantial and non-substantial regions. So, the OSTU threshold segmentation algorithm is applied to obtain the contour of the foreground region on the gradient amplitude, and the whole foreground region is determined by two-way scanning. And the histogram equalization is achieved by moving the columns between the highest and lowest columns. To reduce the size of the location map, the lowest adjacent column on the side near the highest column is selected as the lowest column of the current round when there are multiple lowest columns at the same time. Simulation results show that this algorithm can achieve adaptive cyclic embedding, which can not only obtain a large embedding capacity, but also make the embedded image have a high visual quality.

3   The Proposed Method

For the lacking visual quality of the original image, if keep the original image quality, that cannot get a good visual experience. Different from the existing reversible digital watermarking techniques, the contrast-enhanced reversible digital watermarking technique can improve the image quality to some extent. The method's essence is histogram shift. By embedding bit information m at the peak point, $m \in \{0, 1\}$ and the number of 0 and 1 is roughly equal, the height of peak bins is repeatedly reduced, and histogram equalization is finally achieved.

3.1   The Threshold Segmentation of Ostu

Ostu segmentation algorithm [25], also called the maximum inter-class variance method or Ozu method. This method uses the idea of clustering to divide images into two categories according to pixel gray value, and maximize the variance between the two categories while keeping the minimum internal variance of each category. And the appropriate gray value can be calculated by calculating the variance.

If the image size is $M \times N$, and the n_j represented the number of pixels with the value of j, then:

$$M \times N = n_0 + n_1 + \ldots + n_{l-1} \tag{1}$$

While set the segmentation threshold as T, then the pixels are divided into two categories: background pixel p_1 and foreground pixel p_2, $p_1 \in [0, T]$, $p_2 \in [T + 1, l - 1]$. The proportion of the background pixels in the whole image is θ_1, the average gray value is μ_1, and the proportion of the foreground pixels in the whole image is θ_2, the average gray value is μ_2. The average gray level of the whole image is μ, the variance between classes is recorded as τ.

$$\theta_1 + \theta_2 = 1 \tag{2}$$

$$\mu_1 = \sum_{j=0}^{T} j * \Pr(j|C_0) = \sum_{j=0}^{T} j * \frac{P_j}{\sum_{j=0}^{T} P_j} \tag{3}$$

$$\mu_2 = \sum_{j=T+1}^{l-1} j * \Pr(j|C_1) = \sum_{j=T+1}^{l-1} j * \frac{P_j}{\sum_{j=T+1}^{l-1} P_j} \tag{4}$$

$$\mu = \mu_1 * \theta_1 + \mu_2 * \theta_2 \tag{5}$$

$$\tau = \theta_1 * (\mu - \mu_1)^2 + \theta_2 * (\mu - \mu_2)^2 \tag{6}$$

Substitute the Eq. (5) into Eq. (6) to obtain a simplified formula for inter-class variance:

$$\tau = \theta_1 * \theta_2 * (\mu_1 - \mu_2)^2 \tag{7}$$

Substitute $T \in [0, l - 1]$ into Eq. (7) successively, the foreground area and background area are segmented by the T, which make the makes the maximum value of τ. Then the T is called the best threshold.

The gray difference between the two parts after threshold segmentation are influenced by the inter-class variance, the variance is higher and the difference greater. If some pixels in the foreground area are divided into the background area, or the pixels that should be classified into the background area are classified into the foreground area, the inter-class variance will decrease. Therefore, OSTU algorithm can play the role of automatic threshold segmentation.

3.2 Gradient Amplitude

The image edge refers to the part where the brightness changes significantly in the local of an image. The edge has two attributes: amplitude and direction: the amplitude reflects the intensity of the edge of an image; the pixel changes slowly along the edge direction, while the pixel changes drastic along the vertical edge direction. These changes can be detected by differential operator, the detection process also relies on the calculation of the first derivative, and the finite difference value of the first partial derivative in the 2×2 neighborhood can be regarded as the approximate calculation result of the first derivative. The calculations are shown below:

$$f'_m(m, n) \approx G_m = \frac{f(m + 1, n) - f(m, n) + f(m + 1, n + 1) - f(m, n + 1)}{2} \tag{8}$$

$$f'_n(m, n) \approx G_n = \frac{f(m, n+1) - f(m, n) + f(m+1, n+1) - f(m+1, n)}{2} \qquad (9)$$

The gradient amplitude can be calculated from the first partial derivative:

$$D(m, n) = \sqrt{G_m(m, n)^2 + G_n(m, n)^2} \qquad (10)$$

Image noise is sensitive to the calculation of derivative. The derivative calculation will amplify image noise and increase the number of false edges in detection results when the noise is not controlled. Therefore, before using the finite difference method to calculate the gradient amplitude, noise reduction is needed. In this section, Gaussian Filter is used for image smoothing to suppress image noise.

3.3   Histogram Equalization

The essence of histogram equalization is histogram shift technique [26]. To achieve the quantitative equilibrium effect, the height of the peak column is continuously reduced by moving the column during each embedding stage. For the peak square column, there are two cases of moving to the left or right. When the peak-point is less than the zero-point, the square column moves to the right, and the change of pixel value during embedding is shown in Eq. (11). When the peak-point is more than the zero-point, the square column between the peak-point and the zero-point in the embedding process moves to the left, and the pixel is modified according to the Eq. (12).

$$p' = \begin{cases} p + m, & p = Mx \\ p + 1, & Mx < p < Mn \\ p, & p < Mx \ or \ p \geq Mn \end{cases} \qquad (11)$$

$$p' = \begin{cases} p - m, & p = Mx \\ p - 1, & Mn < p < Mx \\ p, & p \leq Mn \ or \ p > Mx \end{cases} \qquad (12)$$

In the equations, $m \in \{0, 1\}$ is the bit which need embedded, the Mx means the peak-point, the Mn is the zero-point. When there is more than one peak-point in an embedding stage, the one with the smallest pixel is selected as the peak-point during the current round of embedding. When there are multiple zero-points, the height of adjacent column on the side of each zero-point in the histogram close to the peak-point is obtained, and the one with the smallest height of adjacent column is selected as the zero-point embedded in this round.

In the process of histogram shift, to ensure that the cover image in the extraction stage can be recovered without damage. So, it is necessary to use the tag sequence S to record the pixels whose pixel value p is equal to zero-point Mn and its adjacent pixel value Mn + 1 or Mn − 1. When the peak-point is less than the zero-point, the marking rules are shown in Eq. (13). When the peak-point is greater than the zero-point, the marking rules are shown in Eq. (14).

$$S_i = \begin{cases} 0, & p = Mn \\ 1, & p = Mn - 1 \ and \ Mx < Mn \end{cases} \qquad (13)$$

$$S_i = \begin{cases} 0, & p = Mn \\ 1, & p = Mn + 1 \ and \ Mx > Mn \end{cases} \tag{14}$$

Among the Equations, the S_i is the value of the i th in S.

In the process of extraction and recovery, the pixels which between the zero-point and the peak-point are processed, when the peak point is less than the zero-point, the watermark bits are extracted from the peak-point and its adjacent pixels, as shown in Eq. (15).

$$m = \begin{cases} 0, & p = Mx \\ 1, & p = Mx + 1 \ and \ Mx < Mn \end{cases} \tag{15}$$

The cover pixels are recovered in a opposite direction to the histogram shift of the embedding process. When the pixel value p' is Mn, it's needs to recover the pixel according to the tag sequence S, as shown in Eq. (16).

$$p_0 = \begin{cases} p' - 1, & Mx < p' < Mn \\ p' - 1, & p' = Mn \ and \ S_i = 1 \\ p', & p' = Mn \ and \ S_i = 0 \\ p', & p' \le Mx \ or \ p' > Mn \end{cases} \tag{16}$$

When the peak-point is larger than the zero-point, the watermark extraction is shown in Eq. (17), and the recovery of cover pixels are shown in Eq. (18).

$$m = \begin{cases} 0, & p = Mx \\ 1, & p = Mx - 1 \ and \ Mx > Mn \end{cases} \tag{17}$$

$$p_0 = \begin{cases} p' + 1, & Mx < p' < Mn \\ p' + 1, & p' = Mn \ and \ S_i = 1 \\ p', & p' = Mn \ and \ S_i = 0 \\ p', & p' < Mx \ or \ p' \ge Mn \end{cases} \tag{18}$$

3.4 The Termination Condition of Round

When the loop of embedding ends, the modified pixel value p' is taken as the initial pixel value p of the new loop embedding process. To ensure the reversibility of the model, the peak-point Mx and zero-point Mn used in the last round of embedding process are respectively converted into 8-bit binary representation Mn. And the Mn is connected as the first part of additional information before the watermark bits to be embedded in the round.

For the peak-point and zero-point used in the last embedding process, after converting them into binary representation, then the first 16 pixels of the cover image are embedded by LSB method. And the 16 pixels are connected to the x_n of the additional information in this round, then the watermark bit is embedded before embedding. Since the peak-point and the zero-point cannot be equal, to identify the first round, set the x_n to sixteen '0' in the first round. In the extraction and recovery stage, when the first 16 bits extracted in a certain extraction round are all '0', it means that the round is the last one.

The tag sequence S is used to record pixels whose pixel value is equal to zero-point M_n and its adjacent pixel $M_n + 1$ or $M_n - 1$. To ensure the lossless recovery of the carrier image, it is necessary to embed the marker sequence into the carrier image. Here, we connect S as part of the additional information before the watermark bit to be embedded. The content of additional information is shown in Fig. 1.

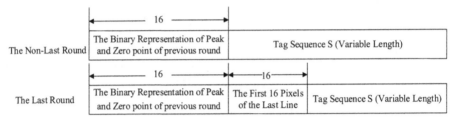

Fig. 1. Additional Information Composition.

As the loop of the embedding increases, the number of pixels at the point where the pixel is equal to zero gradually increases, so the length of the tag sequence S becomes larger and larger. When the number of peak-points is less than the length of the additional information, the embedding ends and the previous round is the last round.

3.5 The Embedding Stage

The watermark embedding stage includes the following steps:

Step 1. A Gaussian filter with 3×3 template size is constructed to smooth the image and calculate the gradient amplitude of the image;

Step 2. The Ostu threshold segmentation algorithm is used to process the gradient amplitude matrix, and a binary matrix BW with the same size as the original image is obtained;

Step3. The binary matrices $BW1$ and $BW2$ are constructed. Search each row of BW, obtain the leftmost coordinate *left* and rightmost coordinate *right*. Then set the value as 1 from *left* to *right*, and set the values on both sides to 0. Each column of BW is scanned to obtain the top and bottom coordinates with the value of 1 in each column. Set the value of $BW2$ corresponding column between top and bottom to 1, and the value on both sides is 0;

Step 4. The binary matrix BW is constructed. Search the $BW1$ and $BW2$ synchronously. If the values at the same position in the two matrices are all 1, then the value under the corresponding coordinate in BW is set to 1 (foreground), otherwise it is set to 0 (background);

Step 5. The histogram is constructed from the pixels of the foreground, and the peak-points and zero-points in the histogram are obtained. According to the selected peak-point and zero-point, the moving direction of the straight square column is determined;

Step 6. Get the tag sequence S. If the square column is moved to the right, add a tag to S according to Eq. (13); on the contrary, when the square column moves to the left, add tag according to Eq. (14);

Step 7. The peak-point Mx and zero-point Mn used in the last round of embedding process are respectively converted into 8-bit binary representation x_n. The x_n in the first round is filled with sixteen '0'. The peak-point and zero-point of the last round are converted into binary sequence, then use the LSB method to hide the sequence in the first pixels of the cover image. And connect the LSB of the original pixel after the x_n of the additional information;

Step 8. Before each loop, the additional information is embedded. Each line of cover image I and binary matrix BW is scanned synchronously. For pixels in the foreground area, when the square column moves to the right, the pixel is modified and information bits are embedded according to Eq. (11). If the square column is moved to the left, move the square column to embed the information bit according to Eq. (12);

Step 9. Repeat Step5 to Step8 until the embedding bits in a loop is less than the number of additional information bits, and the last round of the loop is the last round of embedding.

3.6 The Extraction and Recovery Stage

The steps of watermark extraction and cover recovery are as follows:

Step 1. In the first loop of extraction, the first 16 pixels of the last line of the embedded image is obtained to constitute the peak-point and zero-point of this loop;

Step 2. Each line of embedded image I and binary matrix BW is scanned synchronously. When the peak-points are less than the zero-points, information is extracted from the pixels of the foreground area according to Eq. (15). When the peak-points are more than the zero-points, the information is extracted from the pixels of the foreground area according to Eq. (17);

Step 3. The first 16 bits of each loop of information extraction constituted the peak-points and zero-points of the next round of extraction. If the first round is extracted, the first 16 pixels of the last line of the embedded image is recovered by LSB method with the extracted bits from the 17th to the 32th;

Step 4. The remaining information bit R is composed of the tag sequence S and the watermark bit, that is, the first round of extraction S starts from the 33 th bit of extraction, and the remaining rounds of S start from the 17 th bit;

Step 5. Scan each line of embedded image I and binary matrix BW synchronously. If the peak-points are less than the zero-points, recover the pixels in the foreground area according to Eq. (16). If the peak-points are more than the zero-points, the pixels in the foreground area are recovered according to Eq. (18);

Step 6. The bits of the tag sequence S used for pixel restoration are removed, and the remaining bits in R are the watermark bits extracted by the round;

Step 7. Step 2 to Step 6 are repeated until all the first 16bits of an extraction are 0, that means this round is the last round of extraction and the extraction is terminated.

4   The Results and Analysis of Experiments

4.1   Experiment Dataset and Environment

In this section, we used the MRI, CT and X-Ray Images of the Partners Infectious Disesase Images and Emicrobes Digital Library as the cover images. The images are shown in Fig. 2. All experiments were performed on a personal desktop computer with a 3GHz i5 processor and 8GB of RAM. The software used in the experiment is MATLAB R2016A under Windows 10 OS.

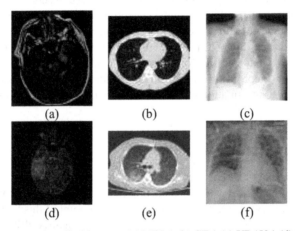

Fig. 2. Different types of medical images. (a) MRI-1 (b) CT-1 (c) XRAY-1 (d) MRI -2 (e) CT-2 (f) XRAY-2

4.2   Control Experiment and Analysis

Visual Effects and Load

Compared with the general reversible watermarking, the reversible watermarking with the enhanced contrast cannot only ensure the similarity between the embedded image and the original image, but also obtain a better visual effect on the recovery image and has a higher embedding capacity. To verify the effectiveness of the proposed model, we compared with the algorithms in literature [22, 24] and [27]. In the experiment, parameters are set according to the reference [27]. L_T sets 32, and the number of rounds L is 60. The parameters used in all experiments were the same. Embedded images are obtained after embedding by different watermark algorithms, the images shown in Fig. 3. The embedded bits and SSIM of different embedded images by difference models are shown in Table 1.

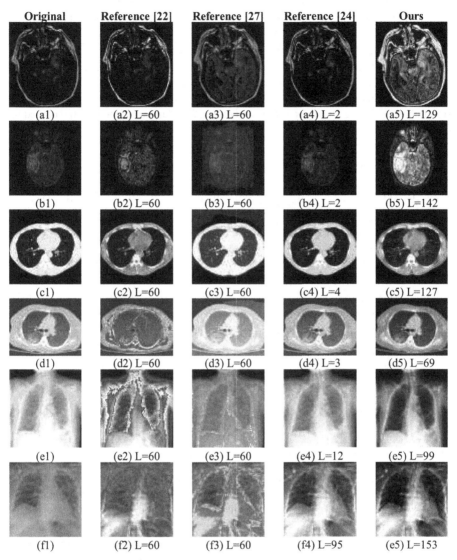

Original	Reference [22]	Reference [27]	Reference [24]	Ours
(a1)	(a2) L=60	(a3) L=60	(a4) L=2	(a5) L=129
(b1)	(b2) L=60	(b3) L=60	(b4) L=2	(b5) L=142
(c1)	(c2) L=60	(c3) L=60	(c4) L=4	(c5) L=127
(d1)	(d2) L=60	(d3) L=60	(d4) L=3	(d5) L=69
(e1)	(e2) L=60	(e3) L=60	(e4) L=12	(e5) L=99
(f1)	(f2) L=60	(f3) L=60	(f4) L=95	(e5) L=153

Fig. 3. The original cover images and the embedded images by different models. (a ~ f1) the original cover images (a ~ f2) the embedded images by reference [22] (a ~ f3) the embedded images by reference [27] (a ~ f4) the embedded images by reference [24] (a ~ f5) the embedded images by Ours.

The enhancement effect of the method in reference [22] for some images is not obvious, as shown in Fig. 3 (a2). However, for most cover images, as shown in Fig. 3 (b2), (d2) and (e2), excessive enhancement occurs when this method is used. As the method in reference [27] does not segment the image, the distortion is spread over the whole pixel range, resulting in a noise like fuzzy area in the background area of the image, as shown in Fig. 3 (b3), (c3) and (d3). This method does not enhance the contrast of X-Ray images, but also causes excessive sharpening of the substantial areas of the images. Literature [24] takes brightness maintenance as the basic point. Therefore, for most images, the algorithm has fewer rounds of embedding, and the image contrast is not significantly enhanced. However, for Fig. 3 (f4), the enhancement effect of the algorithm is relatively ideal. Compared with the above three models, the proposed model in this paper has a larger number of rounds embedding times, and the contrast of the image is significantly enhanced, so the better visual effect [28] can be obtained for the embedded images.

Table 1. The SSIM and embedding bits of different methods.

Methods	Metric	Reference [22]	Reference [27]	Reference [24]	Ours
MRI-1	Embedding bits	22212	150568	102812	407283
	SSIM	0.974	0.742	1.000	0.386
MRI-2	Embedding bits	101361	82448	88004	144326
	SSIM	0.666	0.516	1.000	0.352
CT-1	Embedding bits	141675	104163	102292	196163
	SSIM	0.931	0.920	1.000	0.956
CT-2	Embedding bits	186913	76169	76774	231061
	SSIM	0.724	0.916	1.000	0.938
XRAY-1	Embedding bits	195361	86249	25799	141398
	SSIM	0.799	0.908	0.999	0.860
XRAY-2	Embedding bits	245887	152349	275174	380995
	SSIM	0.670	0.655	0.758	0.593

As can be seen from Table 1, for the same cover image, the proposed model has the highest embedding bits than others, which can satisfy the embedding requirements. The method in reference [24] can achieve a high SSIM [29] value, the embedded image has the similar structure with cover image. However, for the image with low brightness in the substantive area of the image, as shown in Fig. 3 (a4), maintaining a high structure similarity with the original image cannot achieve the effect of contrast enhancement. The algorithm in reference [27] was applied to MRI-2 images, and the SSIM value obtained was relatively low. As can be seen from Fig. 3 (b3), the structural characteristics of the substantial area of the image were significantly changed, and the visual quality of the packed image was low. Although the SSIM value obtained by the method in reference [22] in MRI-1 dataset is higher than the reference [27], but it can be seen from Fig. 3 (a2) that the image contrast is not significantly enhanced. The SSIM value obtained by this method on CT-2 and XRAY-1 datasets are low, and the image structure is obvious changed, and the experience threshold does not make a good effect here. The proposed model in this paper is applied to CT-1 and CT-2 datasets, and obtain a higher SSIM value. However, the SSIM value of MRI-1 and MRI-2 datasets are low, because the brightness of the original images are low. The brightness of the image is significantly improved after embedding the watermark by using the proposed model, so that the content of the substantial area can be more clearly.

Quantitative Evaluation Comparison

The quantization evaluation REE, RCE, RMBE and RSS [30] are used to evaluate the performance of the different models. The parameters of reference [27] L_T set 32, set the rounds L to 60. The L of the reference [22] is also 60. The termination conditions of the proposed model and reference [24] are determined by the number of peak-points and the amount of additional information. The quantitative comparison results of the four models are shown in Fig. 4, where the abscissa of the figures represent CT-1, CT-2, MRA-1, MRA-2, XRAT-1, and XRAT-2 datasets.

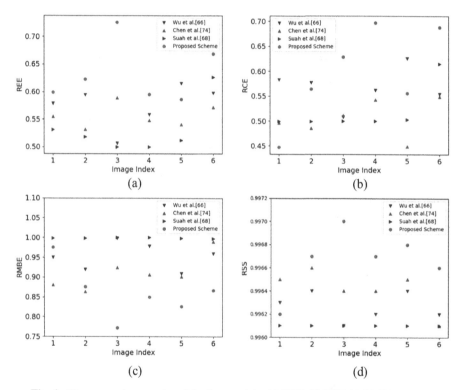

Fig. 4. The comparison results of the four models. (a) REE (b) RCE (c) RMBE (d) RSS

The REE value of the proposed model in this paper are all larger than 0.5 on the six images, except for image XRAY-1, the REE value of the proposed model is the largest for the same image. Which indicating that pixel of the cover image has been enhanced. As for the second metric, the proposed model also has the larger values of REC than other models expect CT-1 and the contrast of these images has been enhanced obviously. Although part of the models is higher than the proposed model, the over-enhancement is presented. Reference [24] is a reversible digital watermarking algorithm based on brightness preservation, and its RMBE is close to 1 in all images. In the process of image contrast enhancement, the proposed model sacrifices the maintenance of the average brightness of the image, so RMBE fluctuates between different images, but all of them are above 0.75. The proposed model sacrifices the maintenance of the average brightness of the image to some extent in the process of enhancing the image contrast, so RMBE fluctuates between different images, but all of them are above 0.75. In addition, for the six images, the RSS of the proposed model are all close to 1, which can ensure the structural similarity between the embedded image and the original cover image.

5 Conclusion

In this paper, a reversible digital watermarking algorithm based on threshold segmentation and histogram equalization. Considering that the foreground area is spatially continuous in the medical image, which contains both substantial and non-substantial regions, we apply the maximum inter-class variance algorithm to the gradient amplitude matrix of the image to obtain the image threshold. In addition, the horizontal and vertical scanning mode enables the model to obtain a relatively continuous embedded region. The termination of the embedding round is controlled by embedding additional information with increasing length. Simulation results show that the proposed model can achieve adaptive cyclic embedding, which can not only obtain a large embedding capacity, but also the embedded image with a high visual quality.

In the proposed model, histogram shift is used to control the watermark embedding, although the image contrast is enhanced, the local brightness of some images is uneven. In the future work, we need to control the brightness of the local area, and enhance the visual quality of the image.

Acknowledgements. The authors would like to thank the anonymous referees for their valuable comments and helpful suggestions. The work is supported by Science and Technology Project of the Headquarters of State Grid Corporation of China, and "The research and technology for collaborative defense and linkage disposal in network security devices" (5700-202152186A-0-0-00).

References

1. Aparna, P., Kishore, P.V.V.: Biometric-based efficient medical image watermarking in E-healthcare application. IET Image Proc. **13**(3), 421–428 (2019)
2. Ghafoor, R., Saleem, D., Jamal, S.S., et al.: Survey on reversible watermarking techniques of echocardiography. Secur. Commun. Netw. **2021** (2021). https://doi.org/10.1145/2743065.2743102
3. Chen, Y., Li, Z., Wang, L., et al.: High-capacity reversible watermarking algorithm based on the region of interest of medical images. In: IEEE International Conference on Signal Processing (ICSP), pp. 1158–1162. Beijing, China (2018)
4. Rachael, O., Misra, S., Ahuja, R., et al.: Image steganography and steganalysis based on least significant bit (LSB). In: 1st International Conference on Emerging Trends in Information Technology, pp. 1100–1111. Delhi, India (2020)

5. Barton, J.M.: Method and apparatus for embedding authentication information within digital data, Patent: 6523114 (US) (2003)
6. Coltuc, D., Caciula, I.: Stereo embedding by reversible watermarking: further results. In: 2009 International Symposium on Signals, Circuits and Systems (ISSCS), Iasi, Romania (2009)
7. Tong, X., Shen, G., Xuan, G., et al.: Stereo image coding with histogram-pair based reversible data hiding. In: 13th International Workshop on Digital-Forensics and Watermarking, pp. 201–214. Taipei, Taiwan (2015)
8. Chung, K.-L., Huang, Y.-H., Chang, P.-C., et al.: Reversible data hiding-based approach for intra-frame error concealment in H.264/AVC. IEEE Trans. Circuits Syst. Video Technol. **20**(11), 1643–1647 (2010)
9. Peng, F., Lei, Y.-Z., Long, M., et al.: A reversible watermarking scheme for two-dimensional CAD engineering graphics based on improved difference expansion. CAD Comput. Aided Des. **43**(8), 1018–1024 (2011)
10. Ni, Z., Shi, Y.-Q., Ansari, N., et al.: Reversible data hiding. IEEE Trans. Circuits Syst. Video Technol. **16**(3), 354–361 (2006)
11. Lin, C.-C., Tai, W.-L., Chang, C.-C.: Multilevel reversible data hiding based on histogram modification of difference images. Pattern Recogn. **41**(12), 3582–3591 (2008)
12. Kim, K.-S., Lee, M.-J., Lee, H.-Y., et al.: Reversible data hiding exploiting spatial correlation between sub-sampled images. Pattern Recogn. **42**(11), 3083–3096 (2009)
13. Alavianmehr, M.A., Rezaei, M., Helfroush, M.S, et al.: A semi-fragile lossless data hiding scheme based on multi-level histogram shift in image integer wavelet transform domain. In: International Symposium on Telecommunications, pp. 976–981. Tehran, Iran (2012)
14. Huang, H.-C., Fang, W.-C.: Integrity preservation and privacy protection for medical images with histogram-based reversible data hiding. In: Proceedings of the 2011 IEEE/NIH Life Science Systems and Applications Workshop, pp. 108–111 (2011)
15. Tai, W.-L., Yeh, C.-M., Chang, C.-C.: Reversible data hiding based on histogram modification of pixel differences. IEEE Trans. Circuits Syst. Video Technol. **19**(6), 906–910 (2009)
16. Qin, C., Chang, C.-C., Huang, Y.-H., et al.: An inpainting-assisted reversible steganographic scheme using a histogram shifting mechanism. IEEE Trans. Circuits Syst. Video Technol. **23**(7), 1109–1118 (2013)
17. Wang, J., Ni, J., Zhang, X., et al.: Rate and distortion optimization for reversible data hiding using multiple histogram shifting. IEEE Trans. Cybern. **47**(2), 315–326 (2017)
18. Wu, H.-T., Huang, J.: Reversible image watermarking on prediction errors by efficient histogram modification. Signal Process **92**(12), 3000–3009 (2012)
19. Li, X., Li, B., Yang, B., et al.: General framework to histogram-shifting-based reversible data hiding. IEEE Trans. Image Process **22**(6), 2181–2191 (2013)
20. Yang, Y., Zhang, W.M., Hou, D.D., et al.: Research and prospect of reversible data hiding method with contrast enhancement. Chin. J. Netw. Inf. Secur. **2**(4), 12–20 (2016)
21. Wu, H.-T., Dugelay, J.-L., Shi, Y.-Q.: Reversible image data hiding with contrast enhancement. IEEE Signal Process Lett. **22**(1), 81–85 (2015)
22. Wu, H.-T., Huang, J., Shi, Y.-Q.: A reversible data hiding method with contrast enhancement for medical images. J. Vis. Commun. Image Represent **31**, 146–153 (2015)
23. Gao, G., Shi, Y.-Q.: Reversible data hiding using controlled contrast enhancement and integer wavelet transform. IEEE Signal Process Lett. **22**(11), 2078–2082 (2015)
24. Kim, S., Lussi, R., Qu, X., et al.: Reversible data hiding with automatic brightness preserving contrast enhancement. IEEE Trans. Circuits Syst .Video Technol. **29**(8), 2271–2284 (2018)
25. Han, C.: OSTU image segmentation algorithm of Fruit Fly Optimization Algorithm. Comput. Model. New Technol. **18**(11), 358–363 (2014)
26. Kalyani, J., Chakraborty, M.: Contrast enhancement of MRI images using histogram equalization techniques. In: 2020 International Conference on Computer, Electrical and Communication Engineering, Kolkata, India (2020)

27. Chen, H., Ni, J., Hong, W., et al.: Reversible data hiding with contrast enhancement using adaptive histogram shifting and pixel value ordering. Signal Process Image Commun. **46**, 1–16 (2016)
28. Wang, Z., Bovik, A.C., Sheikh, H.R., et al.: Image quality assessment: from error visibility to structural similarity. IEEE Trans. Image Process **13**(4), 600–612 (2004)
29. Hore, A., Ziou, D.: Image quality metrics: PSNR vs. SSIM. In: International Conference on Pattern Recognition (ICPR), pp. 2366–2369 (2010)
30. Gao, M.-Z., Wu, Z.-G., Wang, L.: Comprehensive evaluation for HE based contrast enhancement techniques. Smart Innov. Syst. Technol. **21**, 331–338 (2013)

EMISTA-Based Quantitative PET Reconstruction

Linlin Zhao and Huafeng Liu[✉]

State Key Laboratory of Modern Optical Instrumentation, College of Optical Science
and Engineering, Zhejiang University, Hangzhou 310027, China
liuhf@zju.edu.cn

Abstract. As an important tool for cancer diagnosis and brain function imaging, PET is widely used in clinical fields where quantitative accuracy takes an important role. Several methods have been suggested to improve the quantification performance of PET by introducing quantitative coefficients, taking advantages of the time-of-flight (TOF) information, or modeling the point spread function (PSF). However, some physical effects such as photon attenuation limit the quantification potential, which should be focused on. In this paper, we proposed a novel method based on the combination of the expectation maximization (EM) and the learning ability of neural networks, achieving the quantification of PET reconstruction from raw sinogram data without attenuation correction (AC). The EM module was utilized to recover less-accurate PET images without the consideration of attenuation. And these rough images were finely adjusted by the network module which has strong nonlinearity to improve the quantitative performance. The proposed method was evaluated on simulated phantom data and compared to several existing reconstruction methods. It turns out that our method has great potential of high-quality PET image reconstruction.

Keywords: Quantitative PET reconstruction · Non-attenuation correction · Neural network

1 Introduction

As a medical imaging method for disease diagnosis and therapy tracking, positron emission tomography (PET) achieves non-invasive molecular-level information presentation of specific targets [1]. The spatial distribution of the radiotracer can be reconstructed via reconstruction algorithms such as expectation maximization (EM) [2], total variation (TV) [3] and neural networks [4–6], of which the quantification of the radioactivity is a very important goal, especially for the tumors detection and brain functions imaging [7].

Supported in part by the National Key Technology Research and Development Program of China (No: 2016YFC1300302, 2017YFE0104000), the National Natural Science Foundation of China (No: U1809204, 61701436), and by the Key Research and Development Program of Zhejiang Province (No: 2021C03029).

Y. Peng et al. (Eds.): ICIG 2021, LNCS 12889, pp. 691–703, 2021.
https://doi.org/10.1007/978-3-030-87358-5_56

The rapid development of quantitative PET technology in recent years has made it widely used in tissue and organ diagnosis [8], quantitative analysis of biomolecules of protein [9], and drug development [10] which promotes the quantitative accuracy of PET in return. A previous research achieved the quantitative results by introducing and estimating a quantitative coefficient in the forward modeling process of PET [11]. Some studies attempted to use the time-of-flight (TOF) information to increase the signal-to-noise ratio, thus enhancing the quantification ability [12]. And there were also researches focusing on introducing the point spread function (PSF) into the reconstruction model of the PET imaging [13,14]. However, the quantification potential of PET is still limited by many factors such as the physical effects of imaging, tracer dynamics and motion, among which the photon attenuation seriously affects the accuracy of PET. Several methods have been proposed to obtain an attenuation map from transmission sources, computed tomography (CT) or magnetic resonance (MR) images used for attenuation correction (AC). The AC was conducted using transmission PET scans in the early years [15], while currently achieved by hybrid imaging systems such as PET/CT [16] and PET/MRI [17], and neural networks in the image domain [18].

In this paper, we proposed a novel method, dubbed EMISTA, which contained an EM reconstruction module and an ISTA quantification module, to directly reconstruct the PET images from the sinograms with non-attenuation correction (sinograms$_{NAC}$). We also evaluated the reconstruction quality, quantification performance and generalization ability of EMISTA. The sinograms$_{NAC}$ was served as the input of EMISTA. PET images were first reconstructed by the EM module, and then quantified by the ISTA module to be more similar to the ground truth. Considering the sparsity of images as prior knowledge, the rough quantitative PET images were finely adjusted by using the strong nonlinearity of EMISTA. As expected, the quantitative PET images recovered from sinograms$_{NAC}$ using EMISTA can accurately reflect the real activity distribution.

2   Materials and Methods

2.1   Methods

The measured sinograms y can be modeled as a collection of independent Poisson random variables and its mean $\bar{y}$ has an affine transform related to the unknown PET activity images:

$$\bar{y} = Gx + s + r, \tag{1}$$

where $\bar{y} \in \mathbb{R}^{M \times 1}$ denotes the mean of the measurements, $G \in \mathbb{R}^{M \times N}$ is the system matrix of projection, the element g_{ij} in the ith row and the jth column of G denotes the probability that the annihilation photons of the voxel j will be detected by the detector i, $x \in \mathbb{R}^{N \times 1}$ denotes the unknown PET activity distribution images, $s \in \mathbb{R}^{M \times 1}$ and $r \in \mathbb{R}^{M \times 1}$ are the photons of the scatter

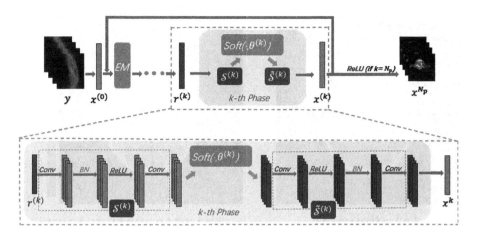

Fig. 1. The structure schematic diagram of EMISTA. There are N_p phases in a epoch with an EM module and an ISTA module.

events and random events, respectively, and the photons of the scatter events are ignored in this paper.

Given the measurements $\bar{y}$, to acquire the unknown images x is a common inverse problem. In the process of accurate reconstruction of PET images, however, ill-posed problems are inevitably encountered. The expectation maximization-driven iteration shrinkage-thresholding algorithm (EMISTA) net we proposed is used to accurately reconstruct images. EMISTA consists of a data fidelity term $\mathcal{F}(x)$ and a regularization term $\mathcal{R}(x)$ which results in the minimization problem by

$$\hat{x} = \arg\min_x \mathcal{F}(x) + \mathcal{R}(x). \tag{2}$$

The optimization problem of Eq. 2 can be solved iteratively in two steps, $\mathcal{F}(x)$ reconstruction and $\mathcal{R}(x)$ quantification. The data fidelity term $\mathcal{F}(x)$ used for estimating the activity distribution of PET (r^k) can be solved by the standard EM-surrogate of Poisson log-likelihood function [19]:

$$\begin{aligned} r^k &= \arg\min_x \mathcal{F}(x) \\ &= \arg\min_x f(x) + \frac{\beta}{2}\|x - x^{(k-1)}\|_2^2. \end{aligned} \tag{3}$$

To solve the optimization equation above, some transformation has been taken for $\mathcal{F}(x)$:

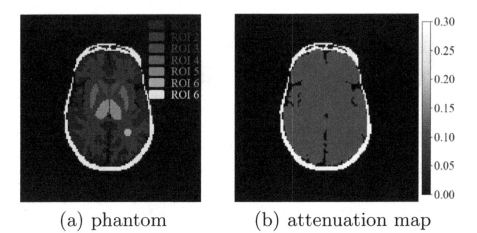

(a) phantom   (b) attenuation map

Fig. 2. The brain phantom with seven ROIs and attenuation map.

$$\mathcal{F}(x) = f(x) + \frac{\beta}{2}\|x - x^{k-1}\|_2^2$$

$$= \sum_{i=1}^{n_d}[Gx]_i + r_i - y_i \log([Gx]_i + r_i) + \frac{\beta}{2}\sum_{j=1}^{n_d}(x_j - x_j^{(k-1)})^2$$

$$\leq \sum_{j=1}^{n_d}\{-e_j(x^{(k')}) \log(x_j^{(k')}) + g_j x_j + \frac{\beta}{2}(x_j - x_j^{(k-1)})^2\} \qquad (4)$$

$$= \sum_{j=1}^{n_d} Q_j(x_j),$$

where k' denotes the k'th iteration, $e_j(x^{(k')}) = \sum_{i=1}^{n_d} g_{ij}\frac{y_i}{\bar{y}_i(x^{(k')})}$, g_{ij} is the element in the ith row and the jth column of G, and the n_d is the number of layers. To obtain the optimum solution of $\mathcal{F}(x)$, the differential of $Q_j(x_j)$, $\frac{\partial Q_j(x_j)}{\partial x_j}$, should be zero, which is equivalent to solving the following quadratic formula:

$$\beta x_j^2 + (g_j - \beta x_j^{(k-1)})x_j - e_j(x^{(k')})x_j^{(k')} = 0, \qquad (5)$$

and the solution of optimization problem Eq. 3 is equivalent to the root of Eq. 5 whose form is as the following equation according to [19]:

$$r_j^{(k)} = \begin{cases} \dfrac{\sqrt{\lambda^2 + \beta\nu} - \lambda}{\beta}, & \lambda < 0 \\[2ex] \dfrac{\nu}{\sqrt{\lambda^2 + \beta\nu} + \lambda}, & \lambda \geq 0, \end{cases} \qquad (6)$$

where $\lambda = \frac{1}{2}(g_j - \beta x_j^{(k-1)})$, $\nu = e_j(x^{(k')})x_j^{(k')}$, $g_j = \sum_{i=1}^{n_d} g_{ij}$. The initialization images x_0 and the output images of the network iteration $x^{(k-1)}$ are updated by Eq. 6.

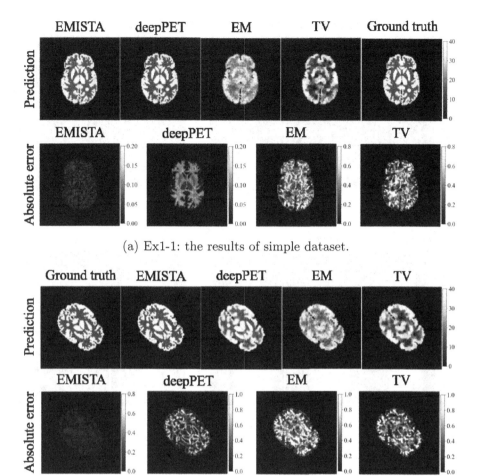

(a) Ex1-1: the results of simple dataset.

(b) Ex1-2:the results of complicated dataset.

Fig. 3. The reconstructed images and corresponding Abs% images of four methods for two datasets.

The regularization $\mathcal{R}(x)$ can be model by the following formula [20]:

$$x^{(k)} = \arg\min_{x} \frac{1}{2}\|x - r^{(k)}\|_2^2 + \gamma\|\psi x\|_1, \tag{7}$$

where γ denotes the regularization parameter, ψ is a sparse transform, and ψx is a sparse vector. In order to improve the quantitative accuracy of reconstructed images and take full advantages of the learning ability of the network, the sparse transform ψ is replaced by the general nonlinear transform, denoted by $\mathcal{S}(\cdot)$ whose parameters are learnable. $\mathcal{S}(\cdot)$ is designed as a combination of two convolutional layers separated by a batch normalization later and an activation layer. Therefore, the Eq. 7 becomes:

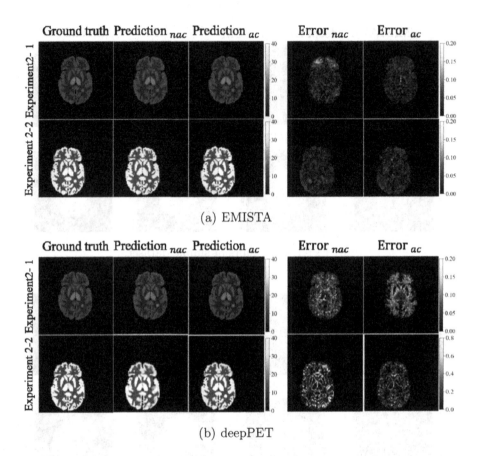

(a) EMISTA

(b) deepPET

Fig. 4. Reconstructed results of EMISTA and deepPET in the condition with or without AC

$$x^{(k)} = \arg\min_{x} \frac{1}{2}\|x - r^{(k)}\|_2^2 + \gamma\|\mathcal{S}(x)\|_1. \tag{8}$$

According to Theorom 1 in [20], the following approximation can be taken:

$$\|\mathcal{S}(x) - \mathcal{S}(r^{(k)})\|_2^2 \approx \alpha\|x - r^k\|_2^2, \tag{9}$$

where α is a factor that is only related to $\mathcal{S}(\cdot)$. Substituting $\|x - r^k\|_2^2$ in Eq. 8 by this approximation, we can obtain the following equation:

$$x^{(k)} = \arg\min_{x} \frac{1}{2}\|\mathcal{S}(x) - \mathcal{S}(r^{(k)})\|_2^2 + \theta\|\mathcal{S}(x)\|_1, \tag{10}$$

where $\theta = \alpha\gamma$. It is obvious that the optimization problem of Eq. 10 can be reshaped to the soft threshold version:

$$\mathcal{S}(x^{(k)}) = soft(\mathcal{S}(r^{(k)}), \theta). \tag{11}$$

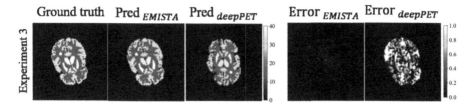

Fig. 5. The reconstructed results of the complicated dataset by the model trained for the simple dataset.

To restore the image $x^{(k)}$ from $\mathcal{S}(x^{(k)})$, the inverse operator of $\mathcal{S}$ is introduced here, which is denoted as $\widetilde{\mathcal{S}}$, such that $\widetilde{\mathcal{S}} \circ \mathcal{S} = I$, where I is an identity operator. Therefore, the optimization problem of Eq. 10 can be efficiently solved by the following form:

$$x^{(k)} = \widetilde{\mathcal{S}}(soft(\mathcal{S}(r^{(k)}), \theta)). \tag{12}$$

It is noted that there is an initialization operation before the first iteration, which is realized by computing an initial matrix Q_{init} as:

$$Q_{init} = \arg\min_{Q} \|Qy - x\|_F^2 + \lambda\|Q\|_F^2 = xy^\top(yy^\top + \lambda I)^{-1}, \tag{13}$$

where Q_{init} denotes the initial matrix to be computed, x and y are the PET images and sinograms of training data, I is the identity matrix.

The whole structure of our network is shown in Fig. 1. There are N_p phases; each contains two modules: the EM reconstruction and the ISTA quantification. EM algorithm generates reconstructed images from the initial images x_0 or the output of last phase $x^{(k-1)}$, which are served as the input of the ISTA module. The image r^k reconstructed by the EM module is less-accurate, since the measurements $\bar{y}$ contains attenuation information while the system matrix G only represents the probability. Therefore, the ISTA learns the attenuation mechanism between the low-accuracy quantitative images and the ground truth, subsequently, and provides a high-accuracy one as the input of the EM module of the next iteration.

2.2 Data Acquisition

Two simulated datasets were used in the current study, which were the simple dataset and the complicated dataset. The simple dataset included two types of image-sinogram pairs, and was based on a two-dimension brain phantom slice from Zubal [21]. The phantom was divided into seven regions of interest (ROI) as shown in Fig. 2(a), which were gray matter (ROI1), white mat5er (ROI2), caudate nucleus (ROI3), putamen (ROI4), thalamus (ROI5), artificially added tumors (ROI6) and skull (ROI7). The ^{18}F-labeled fluorodeoxyglucose ([^{18}F]-FDG) was served as the radioactive tracer. And the activity distribution of different ROIs was simulated by COMKAT toolbox [22] according to the activity

Table 1. The mean and standard deviation of PSNR and SSIM of reconstructed images in all experiments.

	Approach	PSNR	SSIM	Approach	PSNR	SSIM
Ex1-1	EMISTA	39.78 ± 3.16	0.9983 ± 0.0016	EM	18.05 ± 0.64	0.8506 ± 0.0189
	deepPET	35.91 ± 2.06	0.9973 ± 0.0016	TV	16.84 ± 1.04	0.7548 ± 0.0729
Ex1-2	EMISTA	35.18 ± 4.01	0.9942 ± 0.0099	EM	17.98 ± 1.87	0.8375 ± 0.0405
	deepPET	23.01 ± 1.52	0.9443 ± 0.0173	TV	16.80 ± 2.30	0.7509 ± 0.1056
Ex2-1	EMISTA_{nac}	39.78 ± 3.16	0.9983 ± 0.0016	deepPET_{nac}	35.91 ± 2.06	0.9973 ± 0.0016
	EMISTA_{ac}	39.80 ± 3.06	0.9983 ± 0.0017	deepPET_{ac}	37.78 ± 2.82	0.9981 ± 0.0011
Ex2-2	EMISTA_{nac}	35.18 ± 4.01	0.9942 ± 0.0099	deepPET_{nac}	23.01 ± 1.52	0.9443 ± 0.0173
	EMISTA_{ac}	35.01 ± 3.96	0.9941 ± 0.0105	deepPET_{ac}	23.26 ± 1.62	0.9464 ± 0.0189
Ex3	EMISTA	32.61 ± 9.66	0.9178 ± 0.1545	deepPET	13.19 ± 1.73	0.4601 ± 0.2028

curves. Then, the CT values of different ROIs were converted into attenuation coefficients through the following equation, and the attenuation map is shown in Fig. 2(b).

$$
\mu^{PET} = \begin{cases}
\mu_{H_2O}^{PET} \dfrac{CT + 1000}{1000} & , CT \leq 0HU \\
\mu_{H_2O}^{PET} + CT \dfrac{\mu_{H_2O}^{CT}(\mu_{Bone}^{PET} - \mu_{H_2O}^{PET})}{1000(\mu_{Bone}^{CT} - \mu_{H_2O}^{CT})} & , CT > 0HU,
\end{cases}
\tag{14}
$$

where $\mu_{H_2O}^{PET} = 0.096\,\text{cm}^{-1}$, $\mu_{Bone}^{PET} = 0.172\,\text{cm}^{-1}$, $\mu_{H_2O}^{CT} = 0.184\,\text{cm}^{-1}$ and $\mu_{Bone}^{CT} = 0.428\,\text{cm}^{-1}$. It is worth noting that we ignored the distribution of the skull when simulating the activity distribution, but took it into account when generating the attenuation map. Subsequently, the sinograms were projected from the activity distribution images by the Michigan Image Reconstruction Toolbox with a simple strip-integral system model [23]. The Toolbox generated a system matrix firstly, and then projected the activity images obtained above, containing 160 angles and 128 detector bins, as well as considering the attenuation and 10% Poisson noise. In this way, the first set of image-sinograms$_{NAC}$ pairs was generated. In addition, the other set of data, namely image-sinograms$_{AC}$ pairs, were simulated with the same conditions except without the attenuation information. The mean photon number of both sinograms$_{NAC}$ and sinograms$_{AC}$ in one sinogram image was about 4.00×10^5. Although the number of the photons was almost the same, the relative distribution of the photons was completely different between the sinograms$_{NAC}$ and the sinograms$_{AC}$.

The complicated dataset was based on 60 new phantoms derived from the Zubal phantom by random manipulations including rotation, translation and scaling. The PET activity images, sinogramss$_{NAC}$ and sinogramss$_{AC}$ were produced in the same way as aforementioned. And the mean photon number in one sinogram image of simulated sinograms was about 4.00×10^5.

Table 2. The mean and standard deviation of Abs% of different ROIs between the ground truth and the predicted images in the Ex1 and Ex2.

		EMISTA		deepPET		EM	TV
		NAC	AC	NAC	AC	NAC	NAC
Dataset1	ROI1	3.41 ± 1.80	3.52 ± 1.98	3.90 ± 2.03	3.41 ± 2.19	29.14 ± 5.75	37.74 ± 7.50
	ROI2	4.06 ± 1.50	4.05 ± 1.72	6.65 ± 2.89	5.11 ± 3.19	46.97 ± 17.04	50.03 ± 6.00
	ROI3	3.49 ± 1.03	3.47 ± 2.16	5.22 ± 3.58	4.57 ± 3.74	37.65 ± 5.64	53.30 ± 6.33
	ROI4	3.44 ± 2.11	3.23 ± 1.94	5.71 ± 4.17	5.04 ± 4.18	38.31 ± 5.21	48.09 ± 7.20
	ROI5	3.66 ± 2.07	3.37 ± 2.04	5.15 ± 3.27	4.39 ± 3.46	33.56 ± 6.04	41.68 ± 7.95
	ROI6	3.85 ± 2.47	3.35 ± 2.18	4.50 ± 3.10	4.08 ± 3.13	44.67 ± 5.61	48.85 ± 10.41
	Total	3.75 ± 1.59	3.76 ± 1.54	5.42 ± 1.64	4.38 ± 1.82	38.80 ± 6.90	44.76 ± 5.20
Dataset2	ROI1	6.11 ± 4.66	5.73 ± 3.70	16.12 ± 2.37	13.51 ± 2.11	31.20 ± 5.11	36.14 ± 9.86
	ROI2	7.29 ± 5.54	8.97 ± 7.66	31.08 ± 8.65	19.28 ± 5.72	38.15 ± 13.84	52.68 ± 10.05
	ROI3	5.11 ± 4.17	4.88 ± 4.34	16.58 ± 3.99	14.49 ± 2.74	41.88 ± 6.73	51.12 ± 9.55
	ROI4	6.45 ± 4.62	5.69 ± 4.81	14.46 ± 5.19	11.20 ± 2.97	42.45 ± 6.48	47.90 ± 8.12
	ROI5	5.16 ± 4.49	5.02 ± 4.23	11.36 ± 2.47	10.12 ± 2.46	38.27 ± 6.99	40.18 ± 11.41
	ROI6	6.65 ± 6.80	6.26 ± 6.27	16.91 ± 5.39	11.97 ± 3.28	48.61 ± 5.51	48.16 ± 8.59
	Total	6.65 ± 4.84	7.30 ± 5.40	23.30 ± 5.26	16.15 ± 3.65	35.67 ± 5.78	45.31 ± 7.61

3   Experiments and Results

3.1   Experiment and Training Procedure

In this paper, we studied the potential of EMISTA to reconstruct quantitative PET images, and compared it with deepPET [24] and two conventional iteration methods, EM and TV. All the methods carried out on two datasets to 1) evaluate the quality and quantitative accuracy of the reconstructed images from sinograms$_{NAC}$ 2) analysis the impact of attenuation. In order to further verify the learning ability of our method for the attenuation mechanism, we compared the reconstructed results from sinograms$_{NAC}$ and sinograms$_{AC}$. Peak signal to noise ratio (PSNR) and structural similarity (SSIM) [25] were implemented to evaluate the reconstruction performance. And the voxel-wise percent difference defined as the following formulation was applied to evaluate the quantification performance.

$$Abs_\% = \frac{|x - x_{rec}|}{x} \times 100, \tag{15}$$

where x and x_{rec} are the labels and reconstruction images.

In Experiment 1 (Ex1), 1800 pairs of activity images and sinograms$_{NAC}$ of each dataset were used for training, and 200 pairs of each dataset (Ex1-1 and Ex1-2) for validation and test which were equally divided into two non-overlapping parts. The neural networks were trained with the Adam optimizer and the learning rate dropped to half every 20 epochs in all experiments. The initial learning rate was set to 10^{-3} in EMISTA and deepPET. In addition more hyper-parameters in EMISTA needed fine tuning, such as the soft threshold θ, the layer n_d in one epoch and the number of the iterations N_p. The λ in Eq. 13 also needed to be well-designed, which was set to 1 to make the training, the

Table 3. The mean and standard deviation of Abs% of different ROIs between the ground truth and the prediction of EMISTA and deepPET in the Ex3.

	ROI1	ROI2	ROI3	ROI4	ROI5	ROI6	TOTAL
EMISTA	17.44 ± 24.93	18.36 ± 24.99	17.82 ± 25.63	17.71 ± 25.75	18.48 ± 26.01	17.83 ± 25.41	17.96 ± 25.14
deepPET	60.82 ± 15.73	64.57 ± 20.64	52.47 ± 20.22	54.88 ± 19.11	42.77 ± 21.01	60.13 ± 23.73	61.48 ± 17.24

validation and the test datasets having almost the same initialization results. To enhance the learning ability, the initialization matrix was computed only using a half of the training data. Furthermore, 1800 image-sinograms$_{NAC}$ pairs or image-sinograms$_{AC}$ pairs of each dataset (Ex2-1 and Ex2-2) were used for training and 200 pairs for validation and test in Ex2.

3.2   Results

The Ex1 was carried out on both datasets to recover quantitative PET images from sinograms$_{NAC}$ using EMISTA and three compared methods. The representative reconstructed images and Abs% images are shown in Fig. 3. The reconstruction performance described by the PSNR and SSIM is displayed in Table 1, and the quantitative results of different ROIs described by Abs% are shown in Table 2. As can be seen in Ex1-1 of Fig. 3 and Table 1, EMISTA is able to clearly reconstruct the activity distribution and capture the details, and the Abs% images (Fig. 3(a)) and the mean values of Abs% (Table 2) prove excellent quantitative accuracy of our approach. However, the two conventional methods, EM and TV, show poor reconstruction and quantification ability. It is noted that although deepPET can reconstruct PET images clearly, the reconstruction quality and quantification performance of PET images are still worse than EMISTA's. Next, we researched on the complicated dataset with the same experimental settings in Ex1-2. When the dataset becomes complicated, the reconstructed images of EMISTA are still clear, containing tiny details, while the images of deepPET get blurry at the outline and the boundary of each ROI (Fig. 3(b)). And the mean Abs% of deepPET becomes so large that it could not be accepted in clinical, while the quantification performance of EMISTA is only slightly worse than tested on the simple dataset (Table 1 and Table 2). It is noted that the results of quantitative reconstruction deteriorate mostly due to the less-accurate assessments of the activity distribution in ROI2 in all methods.

In order to further verify the quantification potential of our method without the step of AC on both datasets, we analyzed the quantitative metrics of the reconstructed images from sinograms$_{NAC}$ and sinograms$_{AC}$. The representative reconstructed images and Abs% images of EMISTA and deepPET are shown in Fig. 4. Regardless of whether the sinograms are clean or not, the reconstructed results of EMISTA are almost indistinguishable (Fig. 3(a)). And the quantitative results in Table 2 also show that the total Abs% of reconstructed images from sinograms$_{NAC}$ and sinograms$_{AC}$ are comparable. The mean Abs% of NAC and AC of two datasets are 3.75%, 3.76%, 6.65% and 7.30%. Therefore, EMISTA can not only reconstruct the PET images from the sinogram domain, but also learn the implicit attenuation information during the reconstruction process. However, the reconstruction results of deepPET from the sinogram$_{NAC}$ are much worse than those from the sinograms$_{AC}$ (Fig. 4(b), Table 1 and Table 2). Not only the boundary of the reconstructed image becomes blurred, but also the quantitative accuracy is greatly decreased.

Finally in Ex3, the model trained with the simple dataset of Ex1-1 was used to recover the images of the complicated dataset of Ex1-2. The reconstructed results shown in Fig. 5 indicates that EMISTA has stronger generalization ability to reconstruct the quantitative PET images clearly while deepPET hardly recovers the outline of images. The quantitative results are shown in Table 3 and demonstrate the robustness of proposed method. Even though the PSNR and SSIM of images decrease compared to Ex1-2 (Table 1) and Abs$_\%$ of images increase slightly using EMISTA, EMISTA still guarantees the accuracy of quantitative PET images, which is promising for clinical practice.

4   Conclusion

In this paper, we proposed a novel method, dubbed EMISTA, to directly obtain quantitative PET images recovered from sinograms$_{NAC}$, which contains an EM reconstruction module and an ISTA quantification module. EMISTA utilizes the EM module to recover less-accurate images with the restriction of system matrix, and rough images are finely adjusted by the ISTA module which has strong learning ability to improve the quantification performance. We evaluated the reconstruction quality, quantification performance and generalization of EMISTA. And it is proved that EMISTA has the advantages of direct reconstruction from sinograms$_{NAC}$ even if the images are complicated. Furthermore, our method has excellent generalization ability. In conclusion, the study shows promising results that might make it possible to obtain PET images recovered from sinograms$_{NAC}$.

References

1. Zaidi, H., Karakatsanis, N.: Towards enhanced PET quantification in clinical oncology. Br. J. Radiol. **91**, 20170508 (2017)
2. De Pierro, A.R.: A modified expectation maximization algorithm for penalized likelihood estimation in emission tomography. IEEE Trans. Med. Imaging **14**(1), 132–137 (1995)
3. Zhang, Z., Liu, H.: Nonlocal total variation based dynamic PET image reconstruction with low-rank constraints. Phys. Scr. **94**(6), 065202 (2019)
4. Xie, N., et al.: Penalized-likelihood PET image reconstruction using 3D structural convolutional sparse coding. IEEE Trans. Biomed. Eng. (2020). https://doi.org/10.1109/TBME.2020.3042907

5. Cui, J., Yu, H., Chen, S., Chen, Y., Liu, H.: Simultaneous estimation and segmentation from projection data in dynamic PET. Med. Phys. **46**, 1245–1259 (2019)
6. Cui, J., Qin, Z., Chen, S., Chen, Y., Liu, H.: Structure and tracer kinetics-driven dynamic PET reconstruction. IEEE Trans. Radiat. Plasma Med. Sci. **4**, 400–409 (2020)
7. Tozaki, T., Senda, M., Sakamoto, S., Matsumoto, K.: Computer assisted diagnosis method of whole body cancer using FDG-PET images. In: Proceedings 2003 International Conference on Image Processing (Cat. No. 03CH37429), vol. 2, pp. II–1085 (2003). https://doi.org/10.1109/ICIP.2003.1246874
8. Emond, E.C., Groves, A.M., Hutton, B.F., Thielemans, K.: Effect of positron range on PET quantification in diseased and normal lungs. Phys. Med. Biol. **64**(20), 205010 (2019)
9. Miederer, M., Pektor, S., Miederer, I., Bausbacher, N., Diken, M.: Iodine-124 PET quantification of organ-specific delivery and expression of NIS-encoding RNA. EJNMMI Res. **11**(1), 1–8 (2021)
10. Seo, Y.: Quantification of SPECT and PET for drug development. Curr. Radiopharm. **1**(1), 17–21 (2008)
11. Madsen, M.T.: Emission tomography: the fundamentals of PET and SPECT. Shock **23**(11), 5341–9 (2005)
12. Karp, J.S., Surti, S., Daube-Witherspoon, M.E., Muehllehner, G.: Benefit of time-of-flight in PET: experimental and clinical results. J. Nucl. Med. **49**(3), 462 (2008)
13. Alessio, A.M., Kinahan, P.E., Lewellen, T.K.: Modeling and incorporation of system response functions in 3-D whole body PET. IEEE Trans. Med. Imaging **25**(7), 828–837 (2006)
14. Panin, V.Y., Kehren, F., Michel, C., Casey, M.: Fully 3-D PET reconstruction with system matrix derived from point source measurements. IEEE Trans. Med. Imaging **25**(7), 907–921 (2006)
15. García-Pérez, P., Espaa, S.: Simultaneous emission and attenuation reconstruction in time-of-flight PET using a reference object. EJNMMI Phys. **7**(1), 3 (2020)
16. Alessio, A.M., Kohlmyer, S., Branch, K., Chen, G., Kinahan, P.: Cine CT for attenuation correction in cardiac PET/CT. J. Nucl. Med. **48**(5), 794–801 (2007)
17. Fei, B., et al.: MR/PET quantification tools: registration, segmentation, classification, and MR-based attenuation correction. Med. Phys. **39**(10), 6443–6454 (2012)
18. Bortolin, K., Arabi, H., Zaidi, H.: Deep learning-guided attenuation and scatter correction without using anatomical images in brain PET/MRI. In: 2019 IEEE Nuclear Science Symposium and Medical Imaging Conference (NSS/MIC), pp. 1–3. IEEE (2019)
19. Lim, H., Chun, I.Y., Dewaraja, Y.K., Fessler, J.A.: Improved low-count quantitative PET reconstruction with an iterative neural network. IEEE Trans. Med. Imaging **39**(11), 3512–3522 (2020)
20. Zhang, J., Ghanem, B.: ISTA-Net: interpretable optimization-inspired deep network for image compressive sensing. In: 2018 IEEE/CVF Conference on Computer Vision and Pattern Recognition, pp. 1828–1837. IEEE (2018)
21. Zubal, I.G.: Computerized three-dimensional segmented human anatomy. Med. Phys. **21**(2), 299 (1999)
22. Muzic, R.F., Cornelius, S.: Comkat: compartment model kinetic analysis tool. J. Nucl. Med. **42**(4), 636–645 (2001)
23. Fessler, J.A.: Penalized weighted least-squares image reconstruction for positron emission tomography. IEEE Trans. Med. Imaging **13**(2), 290–300 (1994)

24. Häggström, I., Schmidtlein, C.R., Campanella, G., Fuchs, T.J.: Deeppet: a deep encoder-decoder network for directly solving the PET image reconstruction inverse problem. Med. Image Anal. **54**, 253–262 (2019)
25. Horé, A., Ziou, D.: Image quality metrics: PSNR vs. SSIM. In: 2010 20th International Conference on Pattern Recognition, pp. 2366–2369 (2010). https://doi.org/10.1109/ICPR.2010.579

Bootstrap Knowledge Distillation for Chest X-ray Image Classification with Noisy Labelling

Minli Li[1] and Jian Xu[1,2,3]([✉])

[1] South China University of Technology, Guangzhou, China
{seminli_li,jianxu}@scut.edu.cn
[2] Guangdong Tourism Strategy and Policy Research Center South China University of Technology, Guangzhou, China
[3] State Key Laboratory of Subtropical Building Science, Guangzhou, China

Abstract. Chest X-ray images classification provides an essential way for lung disease diagnosis. However, this task is challenging due to the lack of professional knowledge and high annotation cost on Chest X-ray images. A common solution for medical data annotation is to use Natural Language Processing (NLP) techniques to extract labels from radiology reports. However, due to the complex structure of radiology reports, NLP based annotation will inevitably bring noisy labels into data, making analysis very difficult. Most existing methods seek to train a classification model (such as convolutional neural network) directly on the original data and ignore the noisy labels, which, however, may lead to very limited diagnosis performance. In this work, we propose a novel Bootstrap Knowledge Distillation (BKD) method, which seeks to improve the label qualities gradually, thereby degrade the noise level of the whole dataset. We theoretically analyze that the distribution of distilled labels will gradually approach to the unseen real labels distribution. Extensive experimental results on real-world Chest X-ray datasets demonstrate the effectiveness of the proposed method.

Keywords: Chest X-ray image classification · Bootstrap knowledge distillation · Noisy labels · Deep learning · Multi-label learning

1 Introduction

Chest X-ray (CXR) images are the most common medical images and are often used for diagnosing multiple chests related diseases [1–3], as shown in Fig. 1. Due to the complex and indistinguishable textures and structures in CXR images, identifying and distinguishing the various chest diseases in CXR images are very difficult tasks even to professional radiologists [5,6]. Recently, some methods have been proposed to address these tasks, which, however, have two main challenges.

First, existing expert-diagnosis methods and computer-aided diagnosis methods are hard to guarantee to achieve good performance on CXR , because of lacking exact professional knowledge and large clean datasets. For expert-diagnosis

© Springer Nature Switzerland AG 2021
Y. Peng et al. (Eds.): ICIG 2021, LNCS 12889, pp. 704–715, 2021.
https://doi.org/10.1007/978-3-030-87358-5_57

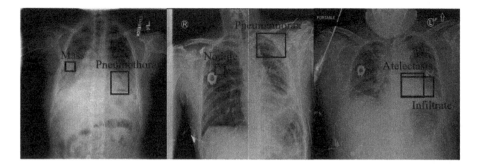

Fig. 1. Chest X-ray images indicate multiple diseases.

methods, radiologists may make mistakes or biased decisions even with long-term clinical training and professional guidance. To address this, deep convolutional neural networks (CNNs) have been used for computer-aided diagnosis [4,6–8,10–12]. Wang et al. [6] proposes a weakly-supervised multi-label image classification method to detect thoracic diseases. Wong et al. [17] uses the concatenation of segmentation network outputs and original images to detect disease, which only needs very few positive samples, thus is suitable for the class imbalance issues. However, these methods often require a large clean dataset to obtain satisfactory performance, since they can fully memorize all the noisy label [14].

Second, collecting a high quality dataset is time consuming and expensive, especially in medical field. Existing datasets, such as CheXpert [5] and Chest X-ray14 [6], are both extracted from radiology reports by NLP technology. Due to the capacity limitation of the current NLP technique, it is difficult to guarantee to obtain clean labels, especially for a large-scale dataset. Recent approaches dealing with noisy labels can be divided into the following three directions. 1) Several methods (e.g. [20]) estimate some noise transition matrix to characterize the noise in the training data. 2) The methods training on selected samples, such as Co-teaching [21] strategy and MentorNet [22], try to select clean instances out of the noise. 3) Veit et al. [23] and Raykar et al. [9] conduct labels cleaning which require a well-designed network architecture. However, these methods directly trained on Chest X-ray images would lead to poor performance.

In this paper, we propose a novel algorithm called Bootstrap Knowledge Distillation (BKD) for Chest X-ray image classification. Our idea is to transform the distribution of noisy labels to be close to the real distribution and avoid learning the noise transition matrix. Specifically, we continuously clean the noisy labels with the guidance of a constantly improving teacher model. Then, we distill knowledge from a single teacher model to a single student model, which is different from transitional distilling methods [16] using an ensemble model to guide training a light model.

In summary, we make the following contributions:

– We propose a bootstrap algorithm based on knowledge distillation to constantly guide a student model learning from noisy labels by a teacher model.

– We theoretically analyze the proposed method and prove that it can continuously transform the distribution of noisy labels to be closer to the distribution of real labels.
– Experimental results on both CheXpert and ChestX-ray14 datasets show the effectiveness of our proposed method.

2   Methods

2.1   Problem Definition

In this paper, we consider lung disease classification on CXR images as a multi-label learning problem. Throughout the paper, we use the following notations. Let $\mathcal{X}$ be the input space and $\mathcal{Y} \in [0,1]^L$ be the label space, where L is the number of labels. Let $\mathcal{D} = \{(x_i, y_i)\}_{i=1}^N$ be the training samples, where $y_i = (y_i^1, \ldots, y_i^L)$, N is the number of data samples, and $y_i^l \in [0,1]$ is the probability of lth label for the ith data samples. For convenience, we denote $[0,1]$ by Δ. We assume that dataset $\mathcal{D}$ contains a portion of noisy data $\mathcal{D}_n$ and a portion of clean data $\mathcal{D}_c$, i.e., $\mathcal{D} = \mathcal{D}_n \cup \mathcal{D}_c$.

We denote a classifier by $f = \sigma(g) : \mathcal{X} \mapsto \mathcal{Y}$, where g is often a deep neural network, and $\sigma : \mathbb{R}^L \mapsto \Delta^L$ is the sigmoid operation and denote the output of model for label l by f^l, then $f(x) = (f^1, f^2, \ldots, f^L)$. For the multi-label learning setting, we aim to train a classifier for predicting multi labels. To this end, we simply perform a weighted linear sum of the cross entropy losses for each individual label,

$$\mathcal{L}_{\mathcal{D}}(f(x), y) = \frac{1}{NL} \sum_{i=1}^N \sum_{l=1}^L y_i^l \log f^l(x_i). \tag{1}$$

Due to the high collecting and annotating costs, CXR datasets often contain noises and missing labels, hence challenging for the multi-label learning. Most existing methods choose to ignore noisy labels which inevitably limit its performance. In contrast, we propose a bootstrap knowledge distillation method to iteratively reduce label noises in Sect. 2.2.

2.2   Bootstrap Knowledge Distillation

In this section, we develop a bootstrap knowledge distillation algorithm to continuously transform the distribution of noisy labels to be closer to the distribution of real labels without estimating a noise transition matrix. Bootstrapping means improving by one's own guidance and knowledge distillation is to transform knowledge from one to the other.

Our algorithm requires training an initial teacher model on a clean dataset. On the process of learning, we use the combination of original noisy labels and the output predictions of current teacher model as pseudo labels to guide training a student model at each time step. Intuitively, as the training process progresses,

Algorithm 1. Bootstrap Knowledge Distillation

Require: Dataset $\mathcal{D}_0 = \mathcal{D}_c \cup \mathcal{D}_n$, model f_0 trained on $\mathcal{D}_c$, maximum step $T_{\max}$, maximum epoch $E_{\max}$, initialize $\lambda = \lambda_0$, λ update step size $\lambda_s \in [0, \lambda_0]$.
   for $t = 1, 2, \ldots, T_{\max}$ **do**
      use model f_{t-1} to predict s_{t-1}
      if the AUC score on validation set of model f_{t-1} is better than f_{t-2} **then**
         $y_t^\lambda = \lambda y + (1 - \lambda)s_{t-1}(x)$
         create dataset $\mathcal{D}_t = \{(x, y_t^\lambda)|x \in \mathcal{D}\}$
      else
         $\mathcal{D}_t = \mathcal{D}_{t-1}$
      end if
      train a model f_t on dataset $\mathcal{D}_t$ with maximum epoch $E_{\max}$
      update λ: $\lambda = \max(\lambda - \lambda_s, 0)$
   end for

---

the prediction of our teacher model becomes more reliable, thus provides better guidance to the student model.

Concretely, at each time step t, we transfer the knowledge of teacher model f_{t-1} to a student model f_t which trained on the entire noisy dataset $\mathcal{D}$ using the following loss [18],

$$\mathcal{L}_{\mathrm{KD}}^t(f_t(x), y) = \lambda \mathcal{L}_{\mathcal{D}}(f_t(x), y) + (1 - \lambda)\mathcal{L}_{\mathcal{D}}(f_t(x), s_{t-1}(x))$$
$$= \mathcal{L}_{\mathcal{D}}(f_t(x), \lambda y + (1 - \lambda)s_{t-1}(x)), \qquad (2)$$

where $s_{t-1}(x) = \sigma(g_{t-1}(x)/T')$, T' is the temperature [16] and we simply set it to 1 in this work; $\lambda \in [0, 1]$ is a weight to balance the primary label y and teacher model output $f_{t-1}(x)$; $\mathcal{L}_{\mathcal{D}}$ is the cross entropy loss in Eq. (1).

In Eq. (2), the target label is composed by the original noisy labels y and model f_{t-1} trained at last time step, we denote a surrogate dataset by $\mathcal{D}_t = \{(x, y_t^\lambda)|x \in \mathcal{D}\}$, where $y_t^\lambda = \lambda y + (1 - \lambda)s_{t-1}(x)$. Then the student model f_t is trained on surrogate dataset $\mathcal{D}_t$ using the following loss,

$$\mathcal{L}_{\mathrm{KD}}^t(f_t(x), y) = \mathcal{L}_{\mathcal{D}_t}(f_t(x), y_t^\lambda). \qquad (3)$$

Note that our method initialized from a model trained on a clean dataset, ensuring that the student network can perform better than the teacher model with a suitable λ, theoretical analysis is provided in Sect. 2.3. It is difficult to compute the optimal value of λ in practice. Intuitively, the prediction of teacher model becomes more and more reliable, the value of weight λ becomes smaller. We decrease λ with step size λ_s.

The process of bootstrap knowledge distillation is shown in Algorithm 1. Next, we provide the theoretical analysis to further demonstrate the effectiveness of the proposed method in Sect. 2.3.

2.3   Theoretical Analysis

We analyze bootstrap knowledge distillation in this section. We use ℓ_2-norm to measure the distance between two label sets:

$$D(Y, Y^*) = \mathbb{E}_i[\|y_i - y_i^*\|^2], \ y_i \in Y \text{ and } y_i^* \in Y^*. \tag{4}$$

Let Y denotes the arbitrary predicted labels on the unseen test dataset $\mathcal{D}_{test}$, and Y^* denotes the corresponding unknown true labels. Then $D(Y, Y^*)$, denoted by D_y, represents the prediction performance of the corresponding arbitrary model.

Definition 1. *[27] The square loss of the learner f on an example x can be composited into a bias term $\ell_2(y^*, y_m)$ and a variance term $\mathbb{E}_{\mathcal{D}}[\ell_2(y_m, f(x))]$, where $y_m = \mathbb{E}_{\mathcal{D}}[f(x)]$, y^* is the unseen true label, $\mathcal{D}$ is the entire training dataset.*

Proposition 1. *At each time step t, we assume the variance term of D_y and $D_{s_{t-1}}$ are independent, leading to the distance $D_{y_t^\lambda}$ is smaller than both the distance D_y and $D_{s_{t-1}}$,*

$$\min_\lambda D_{y_t^\lambda} < \min\{D_y, D_{s_{t-1}}\} \tag{5}$$

where s_{t-1} and y are the labels output from model f_{t-1} and true labels, respectively. $D_{y_t^\lambda}$ can reach its optimal $D_{y_t^{\lambda^*}}$, if and only if $\lambda^* = \frac{D_{s_{t-1}}}{D_{s_{t-1}} + D_y}$.

The proof of Proposition 1 is supplied in appendix.

From Proposition 1, the distance between pseudo labels and true labels becomes smaller if we use a suitable λ when performing knowledge distillation. By bootstrap knowledge distilling, we transform the distribution of original labels to the distribution of real labels without learning a noise transition matrix. Intuitively, we continuously perturb the original labels to be closer to unknown real labels with the guidance of a teacher model.

3   Experiment

3.1   Datasets

CheXpert. Irvin et al. [5] released a dataset which contains 224,316 chest radiographs of 65,240 patients. The CheXpert dataset consists of 14 labeled observations. In this work, we focus on the evaluation of 5 observations including Atelectasis, Consolidation, Cardiomegaly, Edema, and Effusion for better comparing with baselines. The training set is annotated by NLP technology, which leads to noisy labels in the resulting dataset. The validation set contains 200 studies from 200 patients. Three board-certified radiologists vote for the labels of data in the validation set, providing strong ground truth. The test set of CheXpert is not published.

ChestX-Ray14. Wang et al. [6] released a dataset which contains 112,120 frontal-view X-ray images of 30,805 unique patients with the text-mined fourteen disease image labels, where each image can have multi-labels, mined from the associated radiological reports using NLP. Fourteen common thoracic pathologies include Atelectasis, Consolidation, Infiltration, Pneumothorax, Edema, Emphysema, Fibrosis, Effusion, Pneumonia, Pleural thickening, Cardiomegaly, Nodule, Mass and Hernia. Both validation set and test set are extracted by NLP technology, hence noisy labels exist in the entire dataset.

3.2 Implement Details

We follow the architecture in baselines [5,13] and use DenseNet-121 in our network. All experiments are implemented with PyTorch [28].

For CheXpert dataset, we use the certain part of data as the clean dataset to train the initial teacher model. At the next steps, the model should be trained using the entire dataset. Therefore, we carry out three kinds of approaches to generate the entire dataset, mapping all of the uncertain labels to 0 (U-Zeros), or all to 1 (U-Ones), or all to the output probability of auxiliary model (Self-Train), thinking of them as the noisy data of the dataset. Using these three datasets respectively, we train the network for 5 epochs at each time step, and images are fed into the network with 320×320 pixels.

For Chest X-ray14 dataset, there is no clean sub-dataset for training the initial teacher model. Thus, we use a pre-trained model with the same architecture as our network to choose a clean sub-dataset. According to the predictions of the pre-trained model on the entire dataset, we regard those whose output probability is larger than 0.55 and ground truth is 1 as certain positive, and those whose output probability is smaller than 0.45 and ground truth label is 0 as certain negative and the rest as uncertain labels. Next, we train the first teacher model using the certain dataset. At each time step, we train the network for 15 epochs, and images are fed into the network with 224×224 pixels.

We use Adam optimizer with default β-parameter of β_1=0.9, β_2=0.999, and learning rate is initialized to 1e-4. We save checkpoint for every 4800 iterations. We choose the output of the top 1 model or the ensemble of top 5 models as our final prediction results. We empirically initialize λ=0.6 and decrease continuously with λ_s=0.1. The sensitivity of λ_s will be analyzed in supplementary material.

3.3 Results

We evaluate all approaches using the area under the receiver operating characteristic curve (AUC) metric.

Results on CheXpert. The validation AUC scores achieved by approaches which use uncertain labels in different manners (U-Ones, U-Zeros, U-SelfTrained) are shown in Table 1. We compare our method with the baseline [5] which shares the same network architecture with ours. The baseline method trains a CNN and takes the ensemble of 30 checkpoints by computing the mean of the output probabilities over the 30 models as the final prediction result.

The results in Table 1 show both our ensemble model using 5 checkpoints and model without ensemble can outperform the baseline on mean AUC scores. In "U-Ones" and "U-Zeros" cases: (1) Our method greatly improves the performance in the detection of "Cardiomegaly" and "Consolidation", hinting that "U-Ones" and "U-Zeros" which cause noisy labels in training data will limit the capacity of the classifier; (2) In the detection of "Atelectasis", the performance of our method is worse than "U-Ones" but better than "U-Zeros", indicating that most of the uncertain labels are likely to be positive.

While continuously using the prediction of teacher model as pseudo labels, our method can be regarded as a self-trained approach. Compared with baselines, our approach can better assign labels for those whose labels are uncertain.

Table 1. AUC scores on the validation set of CheXpert dataset.

Methods		Ate-	Card-	Conso-	Edema	Effusion	Mean
U-Ones	30× ensemble [5]	0.858	0.832	0.899	**0.941**	0.934	0.893
	Ours w/o ensemble	**0.863**	0.856	0.920	0.931	0.937	0.901
	Ours 5× ensemble	0.846	0.858	0.926	0.939	**0.944**	**0.903**
U-Zeros	30× ensemble [5]	0.811	0.840	0.932	0.929	0.931	0.889
	Ours w/o ensemble	0.822	0.860	0.922	0.920	0.938	0.892
	Ours 5× ensemble	0.825	0.860	0.936	0.921	0.935	**0.895**
U-SelfTrained	Self-trained [5]	0.833	0.831	0.939	0.935	0.932	0.894
	Ours w/o ensemble	0.851	**0.884**	0.926	0.935	0.941	**0.907**
	ours 5× ensemble	0.836	0.881	**0.948**	0.930	0.934	0.906

"Ate-":"Atelectasis", "Card-":"Cardiomegaly", "Conso":"Consolidation".

Results on ChestX-ray14. The performance of our method on ChestX-ray14 dataset is shown in Table 2. We compare the results of our method with three best published results. Wang et al. [6] proposed a weakly-supervised based multi-label classification. Yao et al. [10] exploited the dependencies between labels to improve the performance of classifier. Rajpurkar et al. [13] used the same CNN architecture as ours to perform multi-label classification. The results show that our method focusing on noisy labels outperforms baseline methods on most Pathologies.

4   Sensitivity Study of λ_s

To evaluate the sensitivity of growth step size λ_s, we set different $\lambda_s \in \{0.01, 0.05, 0.10\}$ of λ and show mean AUC scores on the CheXpert Dataset in Table 3. In order to limit the cost of time, we perform the distillation process 5 times (i.e., $T_{max} = 5$) for each λ_s. As shown in Table 3, the AUC score is slightly higher than the other two when $\lambda_s = 0.10$. At the early stage, the performance of the student model improves greatly, hence the change of optimal λ is large, leading to better performance with the large step size λ_s.

Table 2. AUC scores on all 14 pathologies in the ChestX-ray14 dataset.

Pathology	Wang et al. [6]	Yao et al. [10]	CheXNet [13]	Ours
Atelectasis	0.716	0.772	0.8094	**0.835**
Cardiomegaly	0.807	0.904	**0.925**	0.918
Effusion	0.784	0.859	0.864	**0.886**
Infiltration	0.609	0.695	**0.735**	0.715
Mass	0.706	0.792	0.868	**0.868**
Nodule	0.671	0.717	0.780	**0.801**
Pneumonia	0.633	0.713	0.768	**0.780**
Pneumothorax	0.806	0.841	0.889	**0.891**
Consolidation	0.708	0.788	0.790	**0.819**
Edema	0.835	0.882	0.888	**0.899**
Emphysema	0.815	0.829	**0.937**	0.933
Fibrosis	0.769	0.767	0.805	**0.851**
Pleural Thickening	0.708	0.765	**0.806**	0.791
Hernia	0.767	0.914	0.917	**0.972**
Mean	0.738	0.803	0.841	**0.854**

Table 3. Mean AUC score for different λ_s

λ_s	0.01	0.05	0.10
Mean AUC	0.900	0.905	0.906

5   More Discussions

We show AUC scores of different disease of U-Ones and U-Zeros approaches during the training process in Fig. 2 and Fig. 3, respectively. From the results, mean AUC grows gradually while AUC for each disease is fluctuating. The possible reason is that, according to Sect. 1, the optimal λ may be different for different diseases, while the proposed method uses the same λ for every label. Furthermore, in the future, we will perform a greedy strategy such as line search to find the optimal λ with low cost of time for different labels.

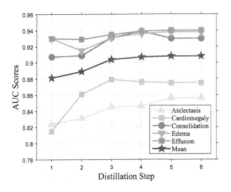

Fig. 2. AUC for approach "U-Ones".   **Fig. 3.** AUC for approach "U-Zeros".

6   Conclusion

In this paper, we have proposed a bootstrap knowledge distillation algorithm to deal with noisy labels in CXR images classification. Our key idea is to continuously use a teacher model to correct the noisy labels to be close to the real labels. We theoretically analyze that with bootstrap knowledge distillation, the distribution of noisy labels are guided towards the unknown real labels distribution. Experimental results demonstrate the effectiveness of considering the noisy labels in CXR images classification.

Acknowledgements. This work was partially supported by Guangdong University Characteristic Innovation Project (2017WTSCX002), Guangdong Natural Science Foundation Doctoral Research Project (2018A030310365), International Cooperation open Project of State Key Laboratory of Subtropical Building Science, South China University of Technology (2019ZA02), Science and Technology Program of Guangzhou, China under Grants 202007030007.

A   Theoretical Analysis

Proposition 1. *At each time step t, we assume the variance term of D_y and $D_{s_{t-1}}$ are independent, leading to the distance $D_{y_t^\lambda}$ is smaller than both the distance D_y and $D_{s_{t-1}}$,*

$$\min_\lambda D_{y_t^\lambda} < \min\{D_y, D_{s_{t-1}}\} \tag{6}$$

where s_{t-1} and y are the labels output from model f_{t-1} and true labels respectively. $D_{y_t^\lambda}$ can reach its optimal

$$D_{y_t^{\lambda^*}} = \min_\lambda D_{y_t^\lambda} = \frac{D_y \cdot D_{s_{t-1}}}{D_y + D_{s_{t-1}}}, \tag{7}$$

if and only if $\lambda^* = \frac{D_{s_{t-1}}}{D_{s_{t-1}} + D_y}$.

Proof. At time step $t = 0$, we train a model f_0 from a clean dataset $\mathcal{D}_c$, the expected prediction error can be composed into the bias term and variance term.

$$\mathbb{E}_{\mathcal{D}_{\text{test}}}[\ell(s_0, y^*)] = \ell(\bar{s}_0, y^*) + \mathbb{E}_{\mathcal{D}_{\text{test}}}[\ell(\bar{s}_0, s_0)] \tag{8}$$

where $\ell(\cdot, \cdot)$ is ℓ_2 distance, $\bar{s}_0 = \mathbb{E}_{\mathcal{D}_{\text{test}}}[s_0]$. Since the high capacity of CNN model, we make a reasonable assumption that the bias term $\ell(s_0, y^*)$ is close to zero . Also, the variance term of D_y and D_{s_0} is independent. This leads to

$$\ell(\bar{s}_0, y^*) = 0 \Rightarrow \bar{s}_0 \approx y^* \tag{9}$$

$$\mathbb{E}_{\mathcal{D}_{\text{test}}}[\ell(s_0, y^*)] \approx \mathbb{E}_{\mathcal{D}_{\text{test}}}[\ell(s_0, \bar{s}_0)] \triangleq D_{s_0} \tag{10}$$

$$\begin{aligned}
\mathbb{E}_{\mathcal{D}_{\text{test}}}[(y - y^*)^T(s_0 - y^*)] &= \mathbb{E}_{\mathcal{D}_{\text{test}}}[y - y^*]^T \mathbb{E}_{\mathcal{D}_{\text{test}}}[s_0 - y^*] \\
&= \mathbb{E}_{\mathcal{D}_{\text{test}}}[y - y^*]^T \mathbb{E}_{\mathcal{D}_{\text{test}}}[s_0 - \bar{s}_0] \\
&= \mathbb{E}_{\mathcal{D}_{\text{test}}}[y - y^*]^T \mathbf{0} = 0
\end{aligned} \tag{11}$$

Due to Eqs. (9)–(11), we have

$$\begin{aligned}
D_{y_1^\lambda} &= \mathbb{E}_{\mathcal{D}_{\text{test}}}[\|y_1^\lambda - y^*\|^2] \\
&= \mathbb{E}_{\mathcal{D}_{\text{test}}}[\|\lambda y + (1-\lambda)s_0 - y^*\|^2] \\
&= \mathbb{E}_{\mathcal{D}_{\text{test}}}[\|\lambda(y - y^*) + (1-\lambda)(s_0 - y^*)\|^2] \\
&= \lambda^2 D_y + (1-\lambda)^2 D_{s_0}
\end{aligned} \tag{12}$$

Since to Eq. (12), when $\lambda = \dfrac{D_{t-1}}{D_{s_{t-1}} + D_y}$, $D_{y_1^\lambda}$ reach its minimum,

$$D_{y_1^{\lambda *}} = \min_\lambda D_{y_1^\lambda} = \frac{D_y \cdot D_{s_0}}{D_y + D_{s_0}} \tag{13}$$

At each time step t, we train model f_t from a dataset $\mathcal{D}_t = \{(x, y_t^\lambda)\}$. We assume $\ell(\bar{s}_t, y_t^\lambda)$ is close to zero, where $s_t = f_t(x)$, $\bar{s}_t = \mathbb{E}_{\mathcal{D}_{\text{test}}}[s_t]$, this leads to $\mathbb{E}_{\mathcal{D}_{\text{test}}}[s_t] \approx y_t^\lambda$, so that the distance between s_t and y is approximate to $D_{y_t^\lambda}$.

$$\begin{aligned}
D_{s_t} &= \mathbb{E}_{\mathcal{D}_{\text{test}}}[\ell(s_t, y^*)] \\
&= \ell(\bar{s}_t, y_t^\lambda) + \mathbb{E}_{\mathcal{D}_{\text{test}}}[\ell(s_t, y^*)] \\
&\approx \mathbb{E}_{\mathcal{D}_{\text{test}}}[\ell(y_t^\lambda, y^*)] \\
&= D_{y_t^\lambda}
\end{aligned} \tag{14}$$

As Eqs. (9)–(12), we have

$$\min_\lambda D_{y_t^\lambda} < \min\{D_y, D_{s_{t-1}}\} \tag{15}$$

and

$$D_{y_t^{\lambda *}} = \min_\lambda D_{y_t^\lambda} = \frac{D_y \cdot D_{s_{t-1}}}{D_y + D_{s_{t-1}}} \tag{16}$$

if and only if $\lambda^* = \dfrac{D_{s_{t-1}}}{D_{s_{t-1}} + D_y}$. $\qquad\qquad\square$

References

1. Cai, J., Lu, L., et al.: Iterative attention mining for weakly supervised thoracic disease pattern localization in chest X-rays. In: MICCAI (2018)
2. Wang, X., Peng, Y., Lu, L., et al.: TieNet: text-image embedding network for common thorax disease classification and reporting in chest X-rays. In: CVPR (2018)
3. Tang, Y., Wang, X., et al.: Attention-guided curriculum learning for weakly supervised classification and localization of thoracic diseases on chest radiographs. In: MICCAI (2018)
4. Chartrand, G., Cheng, P.M., Vorontsov, E., et al.: Deep learning: a primer for radiologists. Radiographics 37(7), 2113–2131 (2017)
5. Irvin, J., Rajpurkar, P., Ko, M., et al.: CheXpert: A Large Chest Radiograph Dataset with Uncertainty Labels and Expert Comparison. arXiv: 1901.07031 (2019)
6. Wang, X., Peng, Y., Lu, L., et al.: ChestX-ray8: hospital-scale chest x-ray database and benchmarks on weakly-supervised classification and localization of common thorax diseases. In: CVPR 2097–2106 (2017)
7. Milletari, F., et al.: CFCM: segmentation via coarse to fine context memory. In: MICCAI (2018)
8. Xie, Y., et al.: Transferable multi-model ensemble for benign-malignant lung nodule classification on chest CT. In: MICCAI (2017)
9. Raykar, V.C., et al.: Learning from crowds. JMLR 11(4), 1297–1322 (2010)
10. Yao, L., et al.: Learning to diagnose from scratch by exploiting dependencies among labels. arXiv preprint arXiv:1710.10501 (2017)
11. Kumar, P., Monika, G., Muktabh, M.S.: Boosted cascaded convnets for multilabel classification of thoracic diseases in chest radiographs. In: ICIAR (2018)
12. Han, Z., et al.: Towards automatic report generation in spine radiology using weakly supervised framework. In: MICCAI (2018)
13. Rajpurkar, P., et al.: Chexnet: Radiologist-level pneumonia detection on chest x-rays with deep learning. arXiv preprint arXiv:1711.05225 (2017)
14. Zhang, C., et al.: Understanding deep learning requires rethinking generalization. arXiv preprint arXiv:1611.03530 (2016)
15. Vapnik, V., Rauf, I.: Learning using privileged information: similarity control and knowledge transfer. JMLR 16, 2023–2049 (2015)
16. Hinton, G., Vinyals, O., Dean, J.: Distilling the knowledge in a neural network. arXiv preprint arXiv:1503.02531 (2015)
17. Wong, K.C.L., et al.: Building disease detection algorithms with very small numbers of positive samples. In: MICCAI (2017)
18. Li, Y., Yang, J., Song, Y., et al.: Learning from noisy labels with distillation. In: CVPR, pp. 1910–1918 (2017)
19. Lopez-Paz, D., Bottou, L., Schölkopf, B., et al.: Unifying distillation and privileged information. arXiv preprint arXiv:1511.03643 (2015)
20. Goldberger, J., Ehud, B.-R.: Training deep neural-networks using a noise adaptation layer. In: ICLR (2017)
21. Han, B., et al.: Co-teaching: Robust training of deep neural networks with extremely noisy labels. In: NeurIPS (2018)
22. Jiang, L., et al.: Mentornet: Learning data-driven curriculum for very deep neural networks on corrupted labels. arXiv preprint arXiv:1712.05055 (2017)

23. Veit, A., et al.: Learning from noisy large-scale datasets with minimal supervision. In: CVPR (2017)
24. Natarajan, N., et al.: Learning with noisy labels. In: NeurIPS (2013)
25. Reed, S., et al.: Training deep neural networks on noisy labels with bootstrapping. arXiv preprint arXiv:1412.6596 (2014)
26. Arpit, D., et al.: A closer look at memorization in deep networks. In: ICML (2017)
27. Pedro, D.: A unified bias-variance decomposition and its applications. In: ICML (2000)
28. Paszke, A., et al.: Pytorch: Tensors and dynamic neural networks in python with strong gpu acceleration (2017)

Multi-modal Fusion with Dense Connection for Acute Bilirubin Encephalopathy Classification

Xiangjun Chen[1(✉)], Zhaohui Wang[1], Yuefu Zhan[2], and Peizhong Wang[1]

[1] School of Computer Science and Cyberspace Security, Hainan University, Haikou, China
[2] Hainan Women and Children's Medical Center, Haikou, China

Abstract. Bilirubin is a metabolite of red blood cells. When the bilirubin content exceeds the normal value, it will cause acute bilirubin encephalopathy (ABE), and rapidly deteriorate to kernicterus if without intervene, which has a case fatality rate as high as 10%. Recently, deep learning approaches have been widely applied in structural magnetic resonance image analysis. This study aims to develop a method based on deep learning to effectively classify ABE. Since most current medical image research only relies on single modal, which leads to the model unable to learn complementary features from multi-modality MRIs. Motivated by this issue, a convolutional neural network incorporating multi-modal fusion with dense connection is designed to learn the multi-level features of MRI for ABE classification. Moreover, the attention module was introduced into the dense connection to address the issue of class imbalance in the medical image. By exploring several dense connection strategies and designing ablation experiments, the rationality of the proposed method was demonstrated.

Keywords: Acute bilirubin encephalopathy (ABE) · Multi-modal fusion · Dense connection · Convolutional neural network (CNN).

1 Introduction

Neonatal jaundice is one of the most clinically concerning issues. It is mainly caused by the accumulation of neurotoxic unconjugated bilirubin in newborns that cannot be effectively controlled, due to premature birth and other factors [1]. Neonatal jaundice can predispose a newborn to develop hyperbilirubinemia if not appropriately treated, though mostly benign, they may progress to acute bilirubin encephalopathy (ABE). ABE is extremely easy to deteriorate to kernicterus with a high mortality rate. Even if fortunately cured, survivors usually develop lifelong neurologic sequelae [2]. Based on years of surveys, up to 8–9% of newborns have severe ABE, of which 0.9% developed kernicterus due to lack of appropriate diagnosis [3]. Early diagnosis and rapid intervention can reverse ABE. Thus efficient diagnosis is the key to minimize the incidence of bilirubin-induced neurologic dysfunction.

The evaluation of neonatal jaundice is typically achieved by measuring the total serum bilirubin concentration. Nevertheless, since it is difficult to directly measure the

© Springer Nature Switzerland AG 2021
Y. Peng et al. (Eds.): ICIG 2021, LNCS 12889, pp. 716–728, 2021.
https://doi.org/10.1007/978-3-030-87358-5_58

bilirubin level in the brain, it will cause a fairly high false-positive rate [4]. Therefore, there is an urgent need to directly detect subtle changes in the patient's brain through non-invasive methods to assess the level of brain damage caused by ABE. Magnetic resonance imaging (MRI) provides a lot of information about the structure of soft tissue due to the high resolution of the images [5]. T2-weighted, T1-weighted, and fluid attenuation inversion recovery images are common modalities of MRI. Since these modalities can provide complementary information, it is becoming the common modality used to evaluate the neonatal brain affected by bilirubin toxicity. Whereas assessing the level of brain damage caused by ABE based on MRI is an intractable task. Recently, researchers have realized that newborns with normal myelination also have high signal intensity similar to those of newborns with ABE [6], as shown in Fig. 1. Besides, some lesion regions, e.g. brainstem auditory and vestibular are too small to be seen on MRI [7]. Consequently, it is difficult to yield accurate diagnosis only through the naked eye assessment strategy of radiologists.

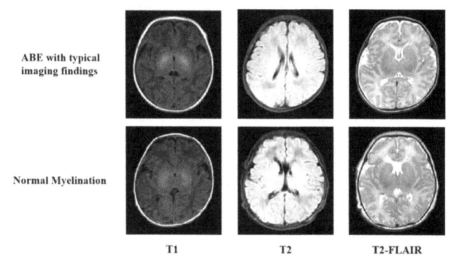

Fig. 1. The ABE with typical imaging findings are shown in the upper row, the normal myelination is shown in the lower row. The normal myelination has a similar signal intensity in the globus pallidus, subthalamic nuclei, hippocampus, and cerebellum to newborns with ABE.

With the advent of radiomics, various image features which are difficult to be recognized by radiologists can be identified. The introduction of radiomics enables medical images to be transformed into extractable features, with the purpose of improving the capability of characterizing disease-induced pathology in detail with high-throughput quantitative measurements [8]. Some disease researches have similar imaging features with ABE for reference despite the current ABE level assessment based on radiomics is rare, such as brain tumors. Specifically, an abnormal MRI in newborns with ABE is characterized by bilateral hyperintensity in the globus pallidus region [9], which is similar to the hyperintensity in the tumor region of brain tumor patients. Several years ago, some radiomics models based on machine learning have been proposed to classify brain tumors, e.g. a multi-step scheme consists of ROIs definition, feature extraction, and classification was proposed by zacharaki et al. [10] for brain tumor detection. Note-worthy, ROIs must be manually selected in a machine learning-based method, which cannot avoid subjective intervention. Moreover, due to the radiographic data character-istics as structural complexity and high dimensionality, machine learning-based brain tumor analysis is challenging.

As a subset of machine learning, deep learning which deals with learning complex features automatically and representations of the data with deep levels of abstraction can achieve a higher performance than machine learning methods. Given the excel-lent performance in processing images, deep learning-based approaches, particularly Convolutional neural networks (CNNs), have become more prominent for brain tumor classification. To name a few, Pan et al. [11] proposed a brain tumor detection method that uses a CNNs structure. The performance is compared with a SVM and the results show an enormous improvement with the use of the CNNs. Additionally, a method based on CNNs and a genetic algorithm is proposed by Anaraki et al. [12] to noninvasively classify different grades of Glioma. In particular, the structure of the CNNs is evolved using GA. In general, CNNs-based tumor classification dispense with manual selection ROIs. Hence, applying the CNNs to the newborns with ABE which have abnormal sig-nals in the lesion regions can also improve the diagnostic performance. Currently, the deep learning model enables to achieve outperforms radiologists in the field of medical image analyses. Nevertheless, most current medical image classification task incorpo-rates the above methods, single modality are adopted as the input to train individual model, which leads to the model unable to learn cross-modal interdependencies from multi-modality MRIs.

Compared to single modality, multi-modality can extract features from different modalities and bring complementary information, which can contribute to better data representation [13]. Thus, multi-modality fusion is extensively applied in medical image classification. In general, fusion strategies based on deep learning are generally divided into input-level [14], decision-level [15], and layer-level [16]. In the input-level fusion strategy, multi-modal images are fused channel by channel as the multi-channel inputs before fed into the model. Since the input-level fusion just directly concatenates the modalities, the relationship among the different modalities cannot be exploited. In a decision-level fusion strategy, each modality is applied as the single input of the model. The outputs of each path will be integrated to get the result. Although compared to input-level fusion, decision-level fusion can capture complementary information from each modality, but the strategy only learns the independent feature representation [17], and still cannot learn complex relationships among modalities. The layer-level fusion strategy allows several modalities to be adopted as a single input to train the individual model, and then these extracted individual features will be fused before the decision layer, and the fused feature map will be fed into the decision layer to acquire the result. Despite compared to the decision-level fusion, the layer-level fusion has a slightly smaller memory overhead but is still fails to demonstrate an overwhelming superiority. Motivated by the recent success of densenet [18] in the medical image domain [19, 20], the proposed method introduces dense connections among the different layers in the layer-level fusion strategy to learn intricate relationships among modalities, which can help the model capture more valuable features than simply integrating each modality.

Whereas due to the lesions occupy a few pixels of the MRI, there is a significant imbalance between lesion and background class [21], the pure dense connection is not suitable for medical image data with extremely class imbalance. The features extracted by the model have equal contributions to each node of the network layer, so training with the class imbalanced data will bias the results towards classes with a large region [22]. To solve this problem, partitioning the regions of the lesion is a preliminary task in medical image classification by non-deep learning methods. Nevertheless, the end-to-end training strategy of deep learning cannot achieve manual segmentation of lesions. Motivated by this issue, the proposed method introduces an attention mechanism in dense connection as a tool to capture the most informative feature representation. The attention mechanism will allow the model to learn more effective information in the data through training. The principle is to form attention by masking the key information by attaching a weight matrix to the image.

In this paper, the multi-modal fusion strategy is applied to ABE classification to learn the multi-modal features of MRI, which aims to replace the method of assessing ABE based on manual screening with a deep learning model. The layer-level fusion strategy was adopted to learn complementary information from different modalities, and dense connections are introduced among each modality to fully exploit the feature representation. It is worth mentioning that the attention mechanism is integrated into the dense connection to refine the feature map through dense connection, which can greatly solve the issue of image class imbalance by highlighting the characteristics of pivotal regions. The results of several ablation experiments demonstrate that the proposed method achieved excellent classification performance.

The leftover of the paper is organized as follows: Section 2 discusses the proposed method in detail; In Sect. 3, the experiment and discussion including the dataset are presented. Finally, the conclusion of this work is described in Sect. 4.

2 Proposal Network

In this section, the overall structure of the proposed method is first introduced, and then the components of the fusion strategy, including the fusion with dense connection and the attention module are presented in detail. Finally, the dense connection with attention is described in detail.

2.1 Overview of the Framework

The framework of the proposed method is shown in Fig. 2. The three modalities (T1, T2, and T2 flair) of neonatal brain MRI as input, and feeds them into three independent paths respectively. while the output is two predicted labels (1) newborn with ABE and (2) normal myelination group. These three paths are updated during the training phase together, and the training process of the model is a supervised end-to-end format.

Specifically, these modalities will be fed to individual paths to extract features. The dense connections between the different paths is to capture complex relationships among

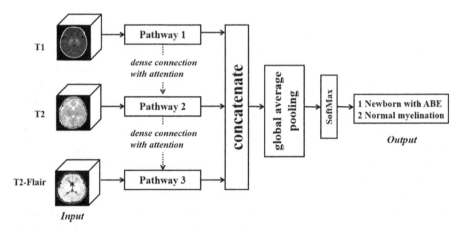

Fig. 2. The framework of the proposed method

modalities, which is to be discussed in Sect. 2.2. Moreover, to redistribute the weights of the features extracted from the upper path before they are concatenated into the lower path through the dense connection, the attention module was introduced into the dense connection, which is to be discussed in Sects. 2.3 and 2.4. After the feature extraction phase, the feature maps of each path will be fused. Worth noting, to reduce the number of parameters while regularizing the entire network to alleviate over-fitting, after feature fusion, the fully connected layer is replaced by global average pooling and fed to the SoftMax classifier for classification.

2.2 Multi-modal Fusion with Dense Connection

Given the layer-level fusion strategy cannot capture complex relationships between modalities, the proposed method extends the concept of dense connectivity in DenseNet [19] to the network constructed by multi-paths. Each modality has a single path, and dense connections occur among layers across different paths. The selection of dense connection strategy will be discussed in detail in Sect. 3.2. Instead of construct extremely deep or wide architectures, this strategy can exploit the potential of the model by feature reuse, yielding condensed models with performance equivalent to the deep models. It can also alleviate the issue of vanishing gradient by improving the flow of information and gradients throughout the model. Thus DenseNet allows for improved effectiveness in the layer-level fusion network.

For simplicity, only the scheme of two modalities is considered, despite an extension to N modalities is straightforward. Denote the output of the i th layer in paths A and B as X_i^A and X_i^B, respectively. Denote the combined operation including the BN layer, the ReLU layer and the convolutional layer as H. As shown in Fig. 3, each layer in path B accepts the feature maps of all the previous layers of the corresponding layer in path A, and concatenate them in the channel dimension, where [...] denotes a concatenation operation. In general, the output of the i th layer in a path B can be defined as follows:

$$X_i^B = H([X_{i-1}^B, X_{i-2}^A ... X_0^A]) \tag{1}$$

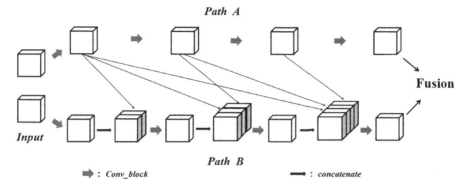

Fig. 3. The dense connection strategy in dual path

The dense connections are intractable for images with extremely class imbalances, despite it can capture complex relationships between modalities. Since the extracted features have equal contributions to each node of the network layer, the conventional dense connection strategy will result in the feature maps without prominent lesion regions being concatenated into the lower path. To allow the features extracted by the upper path to be refined before being concatenated into the lower path through the dense connection, the proposed method introduces the attention module among the dense connection to highlight the informative features and mask redundant regions.

2.3 Attention Module

The principle of attention mechanism is to form attention through a mask with a weight parameter, i.e. applied the feature map to autonomously learn the weight distribution, and then adopt the learned weights to element-wise add to the original features to highlight the regions related to the classification task.

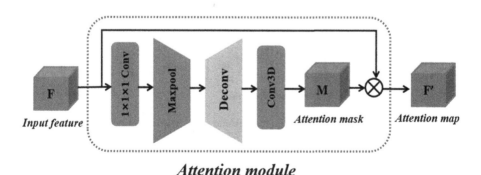

Attention module

Fig. 4. The structure of the attention module

The proposed method incorporates the attention module into dense connection to adjust feature maps, the structure of the attention module is shown in Fig. 4. Given an intermediate feature map F as input, the attention module sequentially infers an attention map M. The attention process can be summarized as:

$$F` = M \otimes F \tag{2}$$

where $\otimes$ denotes element-wise multiplication, F` denotes the features after being adjusted. Specifically, the input of the attention module is the original feature F before dense connection, which is represented by the tensor (size: $680 \times 600 \times 24$). As shown in Fig. 4, to compress the original feature channel, the input tensor is first fed to one convolutional layer with a kernel size of $1 \times 1 \times 1$, then a max-pooling operation is applied to compress the features. The same depth of deconvolution operation is adopted to upsample the features. Afterward, the convolution operation is adopted to further extract the features to obtain attention mask M. Finally, a $680 \times 600 \times 24$ attention map F` can be yielded by element-wise multiplication of the original feature F and the attention mask M, the values of which range from 0 to 1. The yielded attention maps are used to weight the original feature maps before dense connection. This is to be discussed in the next section.

2.4   Dense Connection with Attention

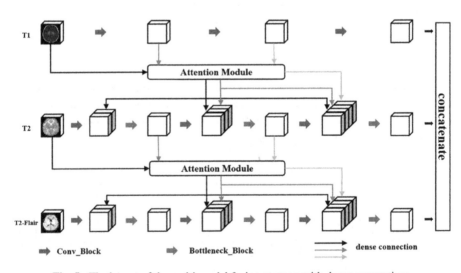

Fig. 5. The layout of the multi-modal fusion strategy with dense connections.

As shown in Fig. 5, instead of directly concatenating the feature maps, the proposed method introduced the attention module to refine all of the feature maps before dense connections. By focusing on the most contributory information and mask redundant regions to optimize network performance and save computing resources.

Specifically, the three modalities of neonatal brain MRI are fed as independent inputs to the three paths respectively, each modal is represented by the tensor (size: $680 \times$

600×24). The input of the top path is T1 modal MRI, three convolutional blocks are constructed to extract features and produced feature maps, the architecture of the convolution block is shown in Fig. 6A. Since the high-dimensional characteristics of MRI, the 3D convolution kernels can fully extract the spatial features of the image while retaining the original network structure. Consequently, the convolution kernel with a size of $3 \times 3 \times 3$ is selected in the convolution block. Note that all convolutional layers in the model are followed by batch normalization and ReLU function for increasing the nonlinearity of the model, such that the convergence rate can be sped up.

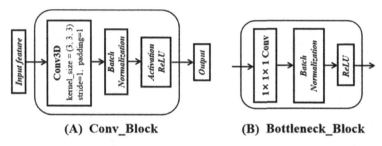

(A) Conv_Block   **(B) Bottleneck_Block**

Fig. 6. The structure of the convolution block and the bottleneck block

On the other hand, as the input of the middle path, T2 modal also extracts features by three convolutional blocks. Unlike the top path, each layer in the middle path accepts densely connected features from the top path containing attention modules and concatenates them in the channel dimension. As shown in Eq. (3), assuming that each layer of the top path produces K feature maps, the number of input channels in the i th layer in the middle path can be denoted by:

$$K0 + (i-1) * K \tag{3}$$

From Eq. (3), with the layers go deeper, the number of channels of the concatenated feature maps will gradually increase. To compress the number of channels to the same as before concatenating, a bottleneck block is introduced after each concatenating. As shown in Fig. 6B, the bottleneck block consists of $1 \times 1 \times 1$ convolution, BN, and ReLU functions.

Since the fusion strategy based on the dense connection between the bottom path and the middle path is the same as above, the specific details will not be repeated. After the feature extraction phase, the individual feature representations learned from these three independent paths will be fused. Finally, the result of the fusion will be fed to the decision layer to obtain the predicted label.

3   Experiments and Discussion

3.1   Datasets

In this work, a large-scale acute bilirubin encephalopathy (ABE) database contains 650 MRIs of the newborn brain (1–12 months) with 300 positive and 350 negative samples was introduced to evaluate the proposed method. The protocol included the T1-weighted, T2-weighted, and T2-weighted fluid-attenuated inversion recovery (FLAIR) imaging in the axial direction. Each confirmed sample is diagnosed by qualified radiologists, taking the consideration of both morphologic and functional analysis. Besides, the blood indicators of each subject are collected, including significant clinical indicators related to ABE level such as total serum bilirubin concentration, mean red blood cell hemoglobin, etc. to eliminate false-positive samples. The proposed method merges the 24 slices images with the.dicom format of each sample into a complete brain image with the.nii format (size: 680 × 600 × 24) as the input of the model. Figure 7 shows imaging in the axial direction of the three sequences in the database.

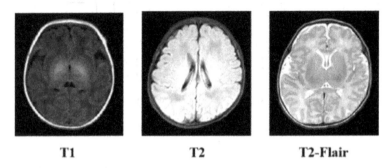

T1   **T2**   **T2-Flair**

Fig. 7. Sample of the database. Each sample incorporates three sequences: T1-weighted, T2-weighted, T2-weighted fluid-attenuated inversion recovery.

3.2   Classification Results and Discusion

In this section, two experiments are implemented to demonstrate the performance of the proposed method and the rationality of the design. Firstly, to adopt the optimal dense connection strategy, several connection strategies based on the layer-level fusion strategy were considered. In another experiment, the rationality of the structure was demonstrated through three sets of ablation experiments.

This experiment applies end-to-end supervised learning where the parameters were randomly initialized at the beginning and optimized by the cross-entropy loss and Adam optimizer with a learning rate of 0.001, and momentum of 0.9. The confusion matrix is obtained by comparing the classified labels and gold-standard labels, from which true negative (TN), false negative (FN), true positive (TP), and false positive (FP) are calculated to quantify the performance of the proposed method. Then, the accuracy, sensitivity, and specificity of the model are calculated as follows:

$$
\begin{aligned}
\text{accracy} &= \frac{TP + TN}{TP + TN + FP + FN} \\
\text{sensitivity} &= \frac{TP}{TP + FN} \\
\text{specificity} &= \frac{TN}{TN + FP}
\end{aligned}
\tag{4}
$$

Exploration of Dense Connection Strategy: Three dense connection strategies were considered to evaluate the impact of different strategies on performance. As shown in Tabel 1, the accuracy of the model, the number of parameters, and training time (single epoch) is introduced as metrics to evaluate the model. For simplicity, only the scenario of two modalities is considered.

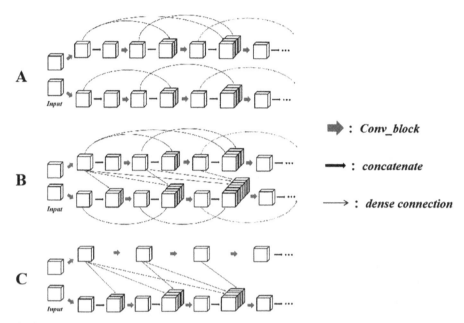

Fig. 8. Different dense connection strategies: (A) Dense connections in a single path (B) Hyper dense connection (C) Our dense connection strategy.

First, the dense connection in Densenet [18] is extended to the dual path. As shown in Fig. 8A, the output of each layer incorporates feature maps from all previous layers. In this scenario, the concatenate of the feature maps only occurs inside the path, which leads to the information unable to be reused between different modalities. Thus the superiority of multi-modal fusion has not been fully demonstrated.

Second, to address the shortcoming of the first strategy that the relationship between the modalities cannot be captured, the concept of dense connectivity is extended to multi-modal settings that dense connection is introduced among different paths. As shown in Fig. 8B, dense connection concatenates feature maps between different layers and different paths. Since under this hyperdense connection strategy, the bottom path must concatenate features from different paths on the premise of concatenating features from all previous layers. Thus the experimental results demonstrate that the hyperdense connection strategy has geometric multiple increases in memory overhead and training time compared to the first connection strategy, despite it can achieve a certain improvement in accuracy. In this case, as the number of fused modalities increases, the issue of vanishing/exploding gradients will occur with a high probability.

Combining the shortcomings of the above strategies, the proposed method is put forward. The study found that dense connection inside the path can strengthen feature propagation within the path [18], but it has no effect on capturing the complex relationship between modalities. Thus, simply abandon the dense connection inside the path, and choose a strategy with less memory consumption on the premise of making full use of complementary information between multi-modal as much as possible. As shown in Fig. 8C, the dense connections only occur between layers across different paths. Compared to the hyperdense strategy, this scheme obtains much less memory overhead and training time, despite its accuracy is lower. Under comprehensive trade-offs, this proposal is selected as the dense connection scheme in the fusion strategy.

Table 1. Performance of different dense connection strategies.

Metrics/Strategy	DenseNet	Hyper dense	Ours
Accuracy	54.19%	78.48%	75.26%
Params	7,538,560	10,349,450	5,230,700
Training time (sec)	24.57 (± 9.45)	38.27 (± 4.32)	19.62 (± 5.64)

Ablation Experiment: In this experiment, the rationality of the model structure was validated by three sets of ablation experiments. First, to demonstrate the superiority of multi-modal fusion, single modal (T1-weighted) MRI as input to train the network. Experimentally, compared with multi-modal fusion, single-modal cannot capture the complex features of the newborn's brain from different views. Therefore, the performance of the model is inferior to the classification based on multi-modal fusion. Second, to demonstrate the necessity of introducing dense connections into multi-modal fusion, a structure containing three modalities without dense connections is used for feature extraction. Since the model cannot reuse features from different modalities through dense connections between paths, it cannot learn more valuable information between modalities. In this case, the performance of the model is slightly inferior to that of multi-modal fusion with dense connections. Finally, a dense connection-based multi-modal fusion strategy without attention module is designed to verify the ability of the attention module to highlight key features. Table 2 compares the model metrics of the proposed method with different scheme.

Table 2. Performance of different structures.

Metrics/Method	Accracy	Sensitivity	Specificity
Single modal	59.16%	56.71%	62.26%
Multi-modal	60.83%	60.00%	61.81%
Multi-modal & dense connection	65.83%	63.76%	68.62%
Ours	75.26%	81.25%	70.00%

4 Conclusion

In this paper, a multi-modal fusion strategy is proposed for acute bilirubin encephalopathy (ABE) classification. To capture complex relationships between modalities, the dense connection is introduced among different paths, and several connection strategies are designed to select the optimal scheme. Moreover, to address the issue of class imbalance in the medical image, the feature maps are adjusted by the attention module. Three groups of ablation experiments were designed to demonstrate the rationality of the model structure. There were still has limitations of the proposed method. Although abandon the dense connection inside the path, it was still computational expensive to train parameters. Consequently, the future work incorporates trade-off network parameters and settings to achieve the best classification effect, and design multimodal networks to effectively combine different modalities to exploit the latent relationship between different modalities.

References

1. Iskander, I., Gamaleldin, R.: Acute bilirubin encephalopathy: some lessons learned. Semin. Perinatol. **45**, 151353-1–151353-6 (2021)
2. Shapiro, S.M.: Chronic bilirubin encephalopathy: diagnosis and outcome. Semin. Fetal Neonatal. Med. **15**, 157–163 (2010)
3. Wei, K.L., Yang, Y.J., Yao, Y.J., Du, L.Z., Wang, Q.H., Wang, R.H., et al.: Epidemiologic survey on hospitalized neonates in China. Transl. Pediatr. **1**, 15–22 (2012)
4. Maisels, M.J.: Managing the jaundiced newborn: a persistent challenge. CMAJ **187**, 335–343 (2015)
5. Vijayalaxmi, M., Fatahi, O.: Speck, Magnetic resonance imaging (MRI): A review of genetic damage investigations. Mutation Res.- Rev. Mutation Res. **764**, 51–63 (2015) (Elsevier)
6. Barkovich, A.J.: MR of the normal neonatal brain: assessment of deep structures. AJNR Am. J. Neuroradiol. **19**, 1397–1403 (1998)
7. Ahdab-Barmada, M., Moossy, J.: Kernicterus reexamined. Pediatrics **71**, 463–464 (1983)
8. Lambin, P., Rios-Velazquez, E., Leijenaar, R., Carvalho, S., van Stiphout, R.G., Granton, P., et al.: Radiomics: extracting more information from medical images using advanced feature analysis. Eur. J. Cancer. **48**, 441–446 (2012)
9. Wisnowski, J.L., Panigrahy, A.: Magnetic resonance imaging abnormalities in advanced acute bilirubin encephalopathy highlight dentato-thalamo-cortical pathways. J. Pediatr. **174**, 260–263 (2016)
10. Zacharaki, E.I., Wang, S., Chawla, S., Yoo, D.S., Wolf, R., Melhem, E.R.: MRI-based classification of brain tumor type and grade using SVM-RFE. 2009 IEEE International Symposium on Biomedical Imaging: From Nano to Macro June 2009, pp. 1035–1038
11. Pan, Y., Huang, W., Lin, Z., Zhu, W., Zhou, J., Wong, J.: Brain tumor grading based on neural networks and convolutional neural networks. In: 2015 37th Annual International Conference of the IEEE Engineering in Medicine and Biology Society (EMBC), pp. 699–702 (2015)
12. Amin, K.A., Moosa, A., Foad, K.: Magnetic resonance imaging-based brain tumor grades classification and grading via convolutional neural networks and genetic algorithms. Biocybern. Biomed. Eng. **39**, 63–74 (2019)
13. Tongxue, Z., Su, R., Stephane, C.: A review: deep learning for medical image segmentation using multi-modality fusion. Array **3–4**, 100004 (2019)

14. Wang, G., Li, W., Ourselin, S., Vercauteren, T.: Automatic brain tumor segmentation using cascaded anisotropic convolutional neural networks. In: International MICCAI Brainlesion Workshop, pp. 178–190. Springer (2017). https://doi.org/10.1007/978-3-319-75238-9_16

15. Nie, D., Wang, L., Gao, Y., Sken, D.: Fully convolutional networks for multimodality isointense infant brain image segmentation. In: 2016 IEEE 13th International Symposium on Biomedical Imaging (ISBI), pp. 1342–1345. IEEE (2016)

16. Chen, L., Wu, Y., Dsouza, A.M., Abidin, A.Z., Wismüller, A., Xu, C.: Mri tumor segmentation with densely connected 3d cnn. In: Medical Imaging 2018: Image Processing, vol. 10574, pp. 105741F. International Society for Optics and Photonics (2018)

17. Rokach, L.: Ensemble-based classifiers. Artif. Intell. Rev. **33**(1–2), 1–39 (2010)

18. Huang, G., Liu, Z.: Laurens van der Maaten. Densely Connected Convolutional Networks. arXiv:1608.06993v5 [cs.CV] 28 Jan 2018

19. Li, X., Chen, H., Qi, X., Dou, Q., Fu, C.-W., Heng, P.A.: HDenseUNet: Hybrid densely connected UNet for liver and liver tumor segmentation from CT volumes. arXiv:1709.07330 (2017)

20. Yu, L., et al.: Automatic 3D cardiovascular MR segmentation with densely-connected volumetric convnets. In: Descoteaux, M., Maier-Hein, L., Franz, A., Jannin, P., Collins, D.L., Duchesne, S. (eds.) MICCAI 2017. LNCS, vol. 10434, pp. 287–295. Springer, Cham (2017). https://doi.org/10.1007/978-3-319-66185-8_33

21. Alessandro, B., Claudio, M., Francesco, T.: Addressing class imbalance in deep learning for small lesion detection on medical images. Comput. Biol. Med. **120**, 103735 (2020)

22. Li, S., Song, W., Qin, H., Hao, A.: Deep variance network: an iterative, improved CNN framework for unbalanced training datasets. Pattern Recognit. **81**, 294–308 (2018)

3-D Convolutional Neural Network Driven by Dimensionality Reduction for Hyperspectral Blood Cells Classification

Yuan Li[1], Hong Huang[1(✉)], Jian Wu[2], and Yiming Tang[1]

[1] Key Laboratory of Optoelectronic Technology and Systems of the Education Ministry of China, Chongqing University, Chongqing 400044, China
hhuang@cqu.edu.cn

[2] Chongqing University Cancer Hospital, 181 Hanyu Road, Shapingba District, Chongqing 4000030, China

Abstract. Recent developments in convolutional neural network (CNN) led to an interest in the classification of blood cells hyperspectral images (HSI). However, traditional CNN algorithms cannot explore the intrinsic geometric structures of blood cells HSI, which may cause a limit in classification accuracy. To address this issue, this paper proposed a three-dimensional (3-D) convolutional neural network driven by dimensionality reduction termed 3DDRNet. 3DDRNet first designs a optimization criteria to compact intraclass neighbors and separate interclass samples in low-dimensional embedding space. Then, a 3-D convolutional neural network is used to extract spatial-spectral features for classification. Experimental results on the Bloodcell1-3 and Bloodcell2-2 datasets demonstrate that the proposed 3DDRNet can achieve better classification results than many state-of-the-art methods.

The GitHub Respository: https://github.com/jmjkx/MyConference.

Keywords: Blood cells · Hyperspectral image · Deep learning · Convolutional neural network · Dimensionality reduction

1 Introduction

Red and white blood cells are essential components of human blood [1,2]. Their amount in the blood is closely related to the physiological state of the human body, and too little or too much number of white blood cells has deleterious effects on immune system. In clinical diagnosis, how to count red and white blood cells in blood smear has immense value [3]. In the early stage, scientists tried to count blood cells by microscope and the resistivity of blood cells, but its accuracy and efficiency were limited. With the rapid development of information technology, computer-assisted counting is widely used in blood cells classification, which is contributed to its high efficiency and speed.

The computer-assisted counting methods include geometric counting methods and statistical counting methods [4]. Typical geometric methods include

© Springer Nature Switzerland AG 2021
Y. Peng et al. (Eds.): ICIG 2021, LNCS 12889, pp. 729–741, 2021.
https://doi.org/10.1007/978-3-030-87358-5_59

distance classifiers and linear classifiers, but these methods are not effective for microscopic images with nonlinear distribution. Statistical analysis methods include parameter estimation method, gradient method, bayesian criterion method, maximum likelihood method, and support vector machine (SVM) [5–7]. These methods have better classification ability in the case of a larger number of samples. However, when encountering data with complex structures, they need the statistical distribution of samples to obtain the prior probability and class distribution probability density function [8].

Recently, convolutional neural network (CNN) models have achieved great success for medical application [9–11]. Kermany et al. [12] utilized transfer convolutional neural network to demonstrate performance comparable to that of human experts in classifying age-related macular degeneration and diabetic macular edema. Liskowski et al. [13] proposed a supervised segmentation technique that uses a deep neural network pretrained to segment retinal blood vessels. Khashman et al. [14] compared three different neural network methods to classify subtypes of blood cells with RGB images. However, these CNN methods are based on traditional optical imaging [15,16], which cannot reflect the complex biological structures of blood cells.

As an emerging imaging modality [17–19], hyperspectral imagery (HSI) offers great potential for contactless blood cells counts [20,21]. It simultaneously contains spatial structures and spectral information [22,23], which can acquire various and massive information from blood cells samples. Thus, the combination of CNN and HSI has become a new trend [24]. Huang et al. [25] proposed a modulated Gabor filter convolutional neural network (MGCNN) model combining modulated Gabor filter with convolutional neural network, which achieved better blood cells classification results than traditional neural network. Wei et al. [26] developed a dual channel CNN combining typical CNN features with end-to-end net features, which achieved better classification performance of blood cells. However, hyperspectral images have high spectral resolution and hundreds of bands, which contain complex geometric structures. They are easy to cause Hughes phenomena [27,28], especially in cases where there is limited availability of labeled training samples. Traditional CNN cannot explore the intrinsic geometric structures of HSI, and their classification performances are restricted [29,30].

To overcome the above drawbacks, we proposed a 3-D convolutional neural network driven by dimensionality reduction (3DDRNet) for classification of blood cells HSI. 3DDRNet first constructs two graphs to represent the intraclass and interclass similarities of blood cells. Then, an objective optimization function is designed to reveal the intrinsic geometric structures of hyperspectral data. By compacting the intraclass samples and separating the interclass samples, 3DDRNet obtains a projection matrix to map the blood cells feature into low-dimensional space. At last, these embedding features are sent to a subsequent 3-D convolutional neural network (3DCNN) to extract spatial-spectral features for classification.

This paper is organized as follows. Section 2 details our proposed method. In Sect. 3, the experimental results on the Bloodcell1-3 and Bloodcell2-2 datasets are presented to indicate the capability of the 3DDRNet method. Section 4 provides some concluding remarks and suggestions for future work.

2   Proposed Method

Traditional 3DCNN methods use original HSI data, and they cannot reveal the intrinsic geometric structures. To overcome this drawback, a 3DDRNet model is proposed. As shown in Fig. 1, an optimization criteria is designed to build a projection matrix for dimensionality reduction. Then, all the high-dimensional blood cells data will be sent into the projection matrix, and embedding features in low-dimensional space are obtained. At last, a 3DCNN model is constructed for these embedding features to classify the samples.

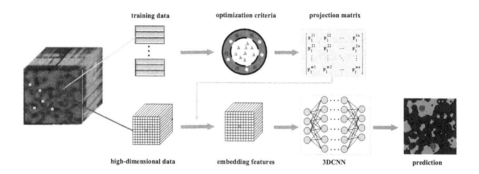

Fig. 1. The architecture of the proposed 3DDRNet.

For convenience, let us suppose a dataset $\mathbf{X} = [\mathbf{x}_1, \mathbf{x}_2, \cdots, \mathbf{x}_n] \in \Re^{D \times n}$, where D and n are the number of bands and samples in HSI, respectively. The corresponding class label of $\mathbf{x}_i$ is denoted as $l_i \in \{1, 2, \cdots, q\}, i \in \{1, 2, \ldots, n\}$, where q is the number of class.

The optimization criteria first constructs an intrinsic graph $\mathbf{G}$ and a penalty graph $\mathbf{G}^P$ to effectively represent the interclass and intraclass structures of data. Under graph $\mathbf{G}$, each sample $\mathbf{x}_i$ is connected with the intraclass neighbors from the same class. The similarity weight w_{ij} between $\mathbf{x}_i$ and $\mathbf{x}_j$ is formulated as

$$w_{i,j} = \begin{cases} 1, \mathbf{x}_i \in N_1(\mathbf{x}_j) \text{ or } \mathbf{x}_j \in N_1(\mathbf{x}_i) \quad \text{and} \quad l_i = l_j \\ 0, \quad otherwise \end{cases} \tag{1}$$

where $N_1(\mathbf{x}_i)$ denotes the k_w intraclass neighbor points of $\mathbf{x}_i$, and k_w is the intraclass similarity of data.

For penalty graph $\mathbf{G}^P$, it connects the marginal points from different classes. The penalty weight $w_{i,j}^P$ between $\mathbf{x}_i$ and $\mathbf{x}_j$ is set as

$$w_{ij}^P = \begin{cases} 1, \mathbf{x}_i \in N_2(\mathbf{x}_j) \text{ or } \mathbf{x}_j \in N_2(\mathbf{x}_i) \quad \text{and} \quad l_i \neq l_j \\ 0, \quad otherwise \end{cases} \tag{2}$$

where $N_2(\mathbf{x}_i)$ represents the k_b interclass neighbor points of $\mathbf{x}_i$, and k_b interclass neighbor points mean the interclass similarity of data that need to be avoided in low-dimensional embedding space.

Suppose $\mathbf{V}$ represents a projection matrix. To enhance intraclass compactness and interclass separability, the objective function can be calculated as

$$\min_{\mathbf{V}} J(\mathbf{V}) = \min_{\mathbf{V}} \frac{\sum_{i=1}^{n}\sum_{j=1}^{n}\left\|\mathbf{V}^T\mathbf{x}_i - \mathbf{V}^T\mathbf{x}_j\right\|_2^2 w_{ij}}{\sum_{i=1}^{n}\sum_{j=1}^{n}\left\|\mathbf{V}^T\mathbf{x}_i - \mathbf{V}^T\mathbf{x}_j\right\|_2^2 w_{ij}^P} \qquad (3)$$

$$= \min_{\mathbf{V}} \frac{tr[\mathbf{V}^T\mathbf{S}_w\mathbf{V}]}{tr[\mathbf{V}^T\mathbf{S}_b\mathbf{V}]}$$

where $\mathbf{S}_w = \mathbf{X}\mathbf{L}_w\mathbf{X}^T$, $\mathbf{S}_b = \mathbf{X}\mathbf{L}_b\mathbf{X}^T$, $\mathbf{L}_w = \mathbf{D}_w - \mathbf{W}$, $\mathbf{L}_b = \mathbf{D}_b - \mathbf{W}^P$, $\mathbf{D}_w = diag([\sum_{j=1}^{N} w_{ij}]_{i=1}^{N})$, $\mathbf{D}_b = diag([\sum_{j=1}^{N} w_{ij}^P]_{i=1}^{N})$. The optimization problem in Eq. 3 can be solved by using Lagrange multiplier method. Then, the optimization projection matrix $\mathbf{V} = [\mathbf{v}_1, \mathbf{v}_2, \dots, \mathbf{v}_m]$ is able to be obtained, where m is the m largest eigenvalues of $\mathbf{S}_w^{-1}\mathbf{S}_b$. Through the proposed optimization criteria, the embedding features can be expressed as $\mathbf{Y} = \mathbf{V}^T\mathbf{X} \in \Re^{m \times n}$.

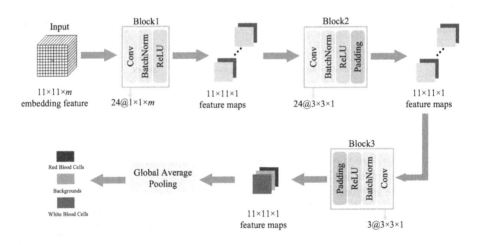

Fig. 2. The detailed architecture of the proposed 3DCNN model

After the embedding features are obtained, a 3DCNN is performed for further feature extraction and classification. Figure 2 shows the detailed architecture of the network. To take full advantage of spatial-spectral information provided by the embedding features, the proposed 3DCNN takes 3-D cubes of size $11 \times 11 \times m$ as input, and m is the dimension of the embedding features. Subsequently, three blocks are designed. In Block1, a 3-D convolutional layer with size $1 \times 1 \times m$ is designed to extract spatial-spectral features. A batch normalization layer is performed to standardize the output of the convolutional layer. Then, the feature maps with size $11 \times 11 \times 1$ are obtained by rectified linear unit (ReLU) action function. In Block2, the feature maps from Block1 are sent to a 3-D convolutional layer with size $3 \times 3 \times 1$. Similar to Block1, a batch normalization layer and a ReLU action function are performed to obtain deep spatial-spectral features. At the end of this block, a padding layer is performed to make the feature maps have same length as the inputs of Block2. The structures of Block3 is the same as Block2, and it further extracts the instrinsic spatial-spectral features. Through processing with the three blocks, the instrinsic spatial-spectral features with size $11 \times 11 \times 1$ were acquired. At last, a global average pooling layer is developed to classify these instrinsic features.

3 Experiment

3.1 Data Description

1) Bloodcell1-3 Data: The dataset is a hyperspectral image collected by composing the VariSpec Liquid Crystal Tunable Filters (LCTFS) with the microscope and silicon charge-coupled equipment. The size of Bloodcell1-3 is 973×799, including 33 bands. There are three classes in this dataset, which cover red blood cells, white blood cells, and backgrounds. The HSI in false color and its corresponding ground truth are shown in Fig. 3.

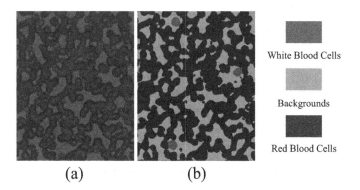

Fig. 3. Bloodcell1-3 image. (a) HSI in false color. (b) Corresponding labels.

2) Bloodcell2-2 Data: This dataset is collected by composing VariSpec LCTFS with a microscope and silicon charge-coupled devices. It contains 33 bands and 3 classes in total, and the image size is 462×451 pixels. The HSI in false color and its corresponding ground truth are shown in Fig. 4.

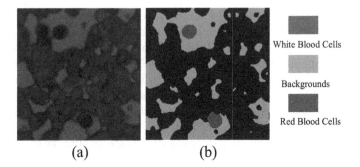

White Blood Cells

Backgrounds

Red Blood Cells

(a)   (b)

Fig. 4. Bloodcell2-2 image. (a) HSI in false color. (b) Corresponding labels.

3.2   Experimental Setup

In the experiments, the values of k_b and k_w were obtained by conducting a grid search. For Bloodcell1-3 dataset, k_b and k_w were set to 8 and 9. For Bloodcell2-2 dataset, k_b and k_w were set to 26 and 4, respectively. HSI datasets were randomly divided into training set, valid set, and test set. To obtain embedding features, we combined training set and valid set to learn the projection matrix. Then, all samples were projected to obtain the embedding features. After that, the proposed 3DCNN was employed for classification in all experiments. When the training process was finished, we chose the model with the best performance on the validation set for prediction.

The proposed 3DDRNet was compared with several algorithms, such as nearest neighborhood (NN), support vector machine (SVM), one-dimensional convolutional neural network (1DCNN), two-dimensional convolutional neural network (2DCNN) and 3DCNN. The former two methods are conventional methods, while the latter three algorithms are deep learning (DL) algorithms. For SVM, we selected a radial basis function (RBF) kernel, and obtained the parameters by a grid search. In each experiment, the overall classification accuracies (OAs) were used to evaluate classification performance. The epoch and batch sizes were set as 1000 and 256, respectively. The standard stochastic gradient descent (SGD) was adopted for optimization, and the learning rate was set as 5×10^{-3}. To robustly evaluate the results in different training conditions, the experiments were randomly repeated ten times.

The proposed optimization criteria algorithm was implemented in Matlab2019b. The traditional methods were implemented with scikit-learn package 0.21.4 in Python 3.6. The deep learning methods were employed using PyTorch 1.6 on a desktop workstation server with two Intel Xeon 3.6 GHz CPU processors, 256 GB memory, and 6 NVIDIA RTX TITAN GPU cards.

3.3   Analysis of Embedding Dimension

To explore the influence of embedding dimension m on the classification performance of 3DDRNet, experiments were performed with different embedding dimensions. In each class, 160 samples (80 training samples and 80 valid samples) were randomly selected for training, and 2000 samples were employed for classification. The embedding dimension was selected at a range of $\{1, 2, 3..., 31, 32\}$. Figure 5 compares the OAs of 3DDRNet with different dimensions on the Bloodcell1-3 and Bloodcell2-2 datasets.

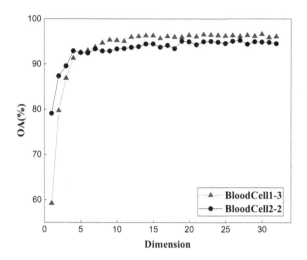

Fig. 5. OAs of 3DDRNet with different embedding dimensions on the Bloodcell1-3 and Bloodcell2-2 datasets.

As can be seen from Fig. 5, some conclusions can be obtained. As the embedding dimension increases, the OAs on the two datasets both increases gradually. This is because when the dimension of embedding features increases, the feature information will be excessive. However, when the embedding dimension increases to a certain extent, the OAs of most algorithms tend to be stable. This is for the reason that the information of features in the embedding space is near saturation. To achieve better classification results, the embedding dimension was set to 30 and 27 corresponding to Bloodcell1-3 and Bloodcell2-2, respectively.

3.4 Convergence Experiment

In this subsection, the convergence of 3DDRNet was analyzed under different numbers of iterations on Bloodcell1-3 dataset. In each class, 80 training samples were selected randomly. The remaining samples were exploited to build test set. As can be seen in Fig. 6, in the first 100 iterations, when the value of loss function decreases, the number of iterations rises. After 100 iterations, the rate of loss value decline decreased. Moreover, the OAs have a rapid improvement in the first 100 iterations, and then reach a relatively stable state after 800 iterations. Therefore, 3DDRNet converges within 800 iterations.

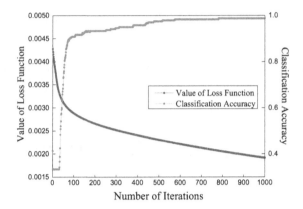

Fig. 6. Classification accuracy and convergence curve versus a different number of iterations for 3DDRNet on Bloodcell1-3 dataset.

3.5   Classification Results

Table 1. Classification result of different methods for the Bloodcell1-3 dataset[OA ± STD(%)].

NTr	NVa	NTe	NN	SVM	1DCNN	2DCNN	3DCNN	3DDRNet
10	10	2000	62.11 ± 1.70	68.46 ± 2.65	65.07 ± 5.89	66.77 ± 13.74	91.42 ± 2.09	**92.80 ± 1.99**
20	20	2000	62.63 ± 1.72	72.45 ± 1.09	75.06 ± 4.80	79.63 ± 6.44	93.31 ± 1.58	**93.72 ± 1.34**
30	30	2000	65.22 ± 1.38	74.65 ± 1.34	76.84 ± 6.36	82.92 ± 7.90	94.27 ± 0.53	**94.49 ± 0.75**
40	40	2000	65.31 ± 1.44	75.23 ± 1.51	82.40 ± 1.55	83.18 ± 8.05	95.15 ±0.70	**95.40 ± 0.67**
50	50	2000	66.66 ± 1.45	76.16 ± 0.95	79.67 ± 2.89	87.41 ± 5.26	95.18 ± 0.48	**95.28 ± 0.49**
60	60	2000	67.06 ± 1.21	76.39 ± 0.98	82.14 ± 1.44	90.51 ± 2.98	95.93 ± 0.73	**96.04 ± 0.61**
70	70	2000	67.01 ± 0.67	77.93 ± 0.83	81.56 ± 1.13	90.21 ± 1.45	95.92 ± 0.93	**95.97 ± 0.58**
80	80	2000	67.63 ± 0.93	77.68 ± 0.93	82.86 ± 1.52	91.82 ± 1.84	96.17 ± 0.39	**96.24 ± 0.58**

In this section, the experiments were conducted on Bloodcell1-3 and Bloodcell2-2 datasets to evaluate the classification performance of different classification methods. In order to demonstrate the classification performance under different training conditions, we randomly selected NTr (NTr = 10, 20, 30, 40, 50, 60, 70, and 80) training samples, NVa (NVa = 10, 20, 30, 40, 50, 60, 70, and 80) valid samples, and NTe (NTe = 2000) test samples from each class. The classification results on the Bloodcell1-3 dataset under different training conditions are shown as Table 1.

As revealed in Table 1, most OAs for every algorithm are improved as the number of training samples increases. It indicates that a larger number of training set contains more effective information for classification. In most cases, DL algorithms achieve better OAs than traditional methods. Because DL algorithms

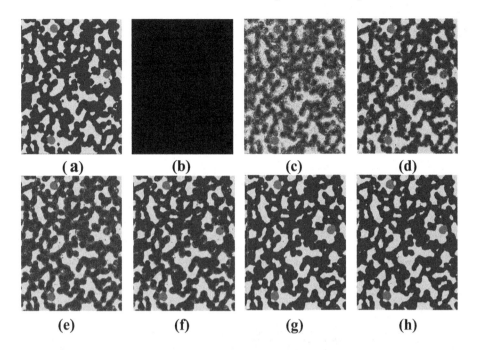

Fig. 7. Classification maps for different methods for the Bloodcell1-3 dataset. (a) ground truth, (b) training samples, (c) NN, (d) SVM, (e) 1DCNN, (f) 2DCNN, (g) 3DCNN, (h) 3DDRNet.

have better capabilities of feature extraction, which is beneficial for classification. In DL methods, the classification performances of 1DCNN, 2DCNN, and 3DCNN increase in turn. It is for reason that 1DCNN can only extract spectral information for prediction and 3DCNN has a better ability of spatial-spectral feature extraction. The 3DDRNet algorithm achieved better classification results than other methods, because it compacts the intraclass data and separates the interclass data to optimize the high-dimensional data from HSI.

In order to analyze the classification performances of different methods on each class, 160 samples per class were randomly selected for training and the rest were for testing. Figure 7 shows the corresponding classification maps of different methods for the Bloodcell1-3 HSI. The 3DDRNet produces more homogenous areas and smoother classification maps than other methods. The possible reason for this is 3DDRNet explores the intrinsic geometric structures of the high-dimensional data and enhances the ability of classification.

From the classification result of Bloodcell2-2 dataset in Table 2, it is apparent that the 3DDRNet model achieves better classification performance. It is because 3DDRNet compacts the intraclass data and separates the interclass data by designing a projection matrix, which is more beneficial to classification.

Figure 8 shows the corresponding classification maps of different methods for the Bloodcell2-2 hyperspectral image. The experiment setup is the same as Fig. 7. Compared with other methods, the classificationmap of the 3DDRNet was smoother and had more homogenous than those of other methods. It demonstrates that the proposed 3DDRNet explores the intrinsic geometric structures of the high-dimensional data from HSI by compacting the intraclass data and separating the interclass data.

Table 2. Classification result of different methods for the Bloodcell2-2 dataset[OA ± STD(%)].

NTr	NVa	NTe	NN	SVM	1DCNN	2DCNN	3DCNN	3DDRNet
10	10	2000	76.60 ± 2.21	81.72 ± 1.26	73.48 ± 5.79	77.53 ± 4.36	89.25 ± 2.33	**90.01 ± 2.03**
20	20	2000	79.41 ± 2.55	83.46 ± 1.37	81.95 ± 1.36	81.58 ± 2.61	92.19 ± 1.57	**92.24 ± 1.30**
30	30	2000	79.92 ± 1.01	83.62 ± 1.06	83.52 ± 2.22	85.47 ± 1.81	92.82 ± 1.21	**93.04 ± 1.01**
40	40	2000	80.34 ± 1.48	84.83 ± 0.98	84.74 ± 2.19	83.18 ± 8.05	94.34 ± 0.66	**94.41 ± 0.74**
50	50	2000	80.62 ± 1.70	84.13 ± 2.02	84.46 ± 1.15	88.23 ± 1.55	95.01 ± 0.86	**95.03 ± 0.81**
60	60	2000	81.84 ± 1.07	85.64 ± 1.31	85.23 ± 1.19	87.90 ± 1.67	95.45 ± 0.54	**95.63 ± 0.48**
70	70	2000	81.87 ± 1.64	86.78 ± 1.84	85.11 ± 1.69	89.26 ± 1.74	95.44 ± 0.76	**95.49 ± 1.30**
80	80	2000	81.28 ± 0.94	77.96 ± 0.58	86.22 ± 1.02	91.07 ± 1.24	**96.06 ± 0.60**	95.85 ± 0.63

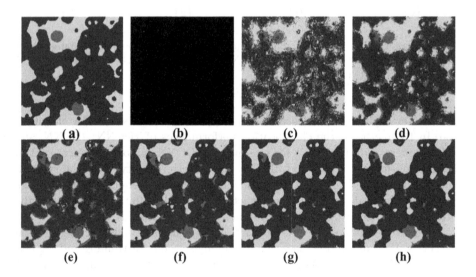

Fig. 8. Classification maps for different methods for the Bloodcell2-2 dataset. (a) ground truth, (b) training samples, (c) NN, (d) SVM, (e) 1DCNN, (f) 2DCNN, (g) 3DCNN, (h) 3DDRNet.

4   Conclusion

In this paper, we proposed a deep learning method called 3DDRNet to learn the low-dimensional embedding features for blood cells HSI classification. 3DDR-Net designs a optimization criteria to compact the intraclass data and separate the interclass data, which explores the intrinsic geometric structures of high-dimensional data from blood cells HSI. Then, a 3DCNN is proposed to extract spatial-spectral features for classification. As a result, the proposed method can effectively extract the discriminant features, which is able to improve classification performance. The experimental results on the Bloodcell1-3 and Bloodcell2-2 datasets show that the proposed algorithm performs better than many state-of-the-art methods in the term of OAs. Our future work will focus on exploring graph structures of blood cells HSI by graph convolutional neural network.

Acknowledgments. The authors would like to thank Professors Li Wei of Beijing Institute of Technology for providing us with the blood cells hyperspectral image. Thanks to the anonymous reviewers and the associate editor for their insightful comments and suggestions. This work was supported in part by the National Science Foundation of China under Grant 42071302, the Innovation Program for Chongqing Overseas Returnees under Grant cx2019144, and the Higher Education and Research Grants of NVIDIA.

Author contributions. Yuan Li: Methodology, Validation, Data curation, Writing-review, Writing-original draft. **Hong Huang:** Supervision, Investigation, Methodology, Validation, Formal analysis, Writing-review & editing. **Jian Wu:** Methodology, Formal analysis, Validation, Writing-review. **Yiming Tang:** Formal analysis, Validation, Writing-review

Conflict of Interest. The authors declare that they have no known competing financial interests or personal relationships that could have appeared to influence the work reported in this paper.

References

1. Zhang, Q.M., et al.: Landscape and dynamics of single immune cells in hepatocellular carcinoma. Cell **179**(4), 829–845 (2019)
2. Sabatino, J.J., Probstel, A.K., Zamvil, S.S.: B cells in autoimmune and neurodegenerative central nervous system diseases. Nat. Rev. Neurosci. **20**(12), 728–745 (2019)
3. Henry, B.M., et al.: Red blood cell distribution width (RDW) predicts COVID-19 severity: a prospective, observational study from the cincinnati SARS-CoV-2 emergency department cohort. Diagnostics **10**(9), 168 (2020)
4. Nazlibilek, S., Karacor, D., Ercan, T., Sazli, M.H., Kalender, O., Ege, Y.: Automatic segmentation, counting, size determination and classification of white blood cells. Measurement **55**, 58–65 (2014)
5. Sato, T., Suzuki, R., Sunaga, R.: Maximum likelihood estimation of red blood cell aggregation degree based on calculation of local flow vector in blood circuit. Electr. Commun. Jpn. **101**(12), 13–20 (2018)
6. Mansourian, M., Kazemi, I., Kelishadi, R.: Pediatric metabolic syndrome and cell blood counts: bivariate bayesian modeling. J. Trop. Pediatr. **60**(1), 61–67 (2014)
7. Tai, W.L., Hu, R.M., Han, C.W.H., Chen, R.M., Tsai, J.J.P: Blood cell image classification based on hierarchical SVM. In: 2011 IEEE International Symposium on Multimedia, pp. 129–136. IEEE, Dana Point (2011)

8. Liang, G.B., Hong, H.C., Xie, W.F., Zheng, L.X.: Combining convolutional neural network with recursive neural network for blood cell image classification. IEEE Access **6**, 36188–36197 (2018)
9. Topol, E.J.: High-performance medicine: the convergence of human and artificial intelligence. Nat. Med. **25**(1), 44–56 (2019)
10. Apostolopoulos, I.D., Mpesiana, T.A.: Covid-19: automatic detection from X-ray images utilizing transfer learning with convolutional neural networks. Phys. Eng. Sci. Med. **43**(2), 635–640 (2020). https://doi.org/10.1007/s13246-020-00865-4
11. Dey, R., Lu, Z.J., Hong, Y.: Diagnostic classification of lung nodules using 3D neural networks. In: IEEE 15th International Symposium on Biomedical Imaging, pp. 774–778. IEEE, Washington DC (2018)
12. Kermany, D.S., et al.: Identifying medical diagnoses and treatable diseases by image-based deep learning. Cell **172**(5), 1122–1131 (2018)
13. Liskowski, P., Krawiec, K.: Segmenting retinal blood vessels with deep neural networks. IEEE Trans. Med. Imaging **35**(11), 2369–2380 (2016)
14. Khashman, A.: Investigation of different neural models for blood cell type identification. Neural Comput. Appl. **21**(6), 1177–1183 (2012)
15. Xu, K.J., Huang, H., Deng, P.F., Li, Y.: Deep feature aggregation framework driven by graph convolutional network for scene classification in remote sensing. IEEE Transactions on Neural Networks and Learning Systems (2021). https://doi.org/10.1109/TNNLS.2021.3071369
16. Xu, K.J., Huang, H., Deng, P.F.: Remote sensing image scene classification based on global-local dual-branch structure model. IEEE Geoscience and Remote Sensing Letters (2021). https://doi.org/10.1109/LGRS.2021.3075712
17. Khan, M.J., Khan, H.S., Yousaf, A., Khurshid, K., Abbas, A.: Modern trends in hyperspectral image analysis: a review. IEEE Access **6**, 14118–14129 (2018)
18. Lu, G.L., Fei, B.W.: Medical hyperspectral imaging: a review. J. Biomed. Opt. **19**(1), 010901 (2014)
19. Jansen-Winkeln, B., et al.: Feedforward artificial neural network-based colorectal cancer detection using hyperspectral imaging: a step towards automatic optical biopsy. Cancers **13**(5), 967 (2021)
20. Li, X., Li, W., Xu, X.D., Hu, W.: Cell classification using convolutional neural networks in medical hyperspectral imagery. In: 2nd International Conference on Image. Vision and Computing, pp. 501–504. IEEE, Chengdu (2017)
21. Chang, L., Li, W., Li, Q.L.: Guided filter-based medical hyperspectral image restoration and cell classification. J. Med. Imaging Health Inform. **8**(4), 826–835 (2018)
22. Ran, Q., Chang, L., Li, W., Xu, X.F.: Spatial-spectral blood cell classification with microscopic hyperspectral imagery. In: Yu, J., Wang, Z., Hang, W., Zhao, B., Hou, X., Xie, M., Shimura, T. (eds.) AOPC 2017: Optical Spectroscopy and Imaging, LNCS, vol. 10461, UNSP 1046102. SPIE, Beijing (2017). https://doi.org/10.1117/12.2281268
23. Pu, C.Y., Huang, H., Luo, L.Y.: Classification of hyperspectral image with attention mechanism-based dual-path convolutional network. IEEE Geosci. Remote Sens. Lett. **9**, 1–5 (2021)
24. Li, Z.Y., Huang, H., Duan, Y.L., Shi, G.Y.: DLPNet: a deep manifold network for feature extraction of hyperspectral imagery. Neural Netw. **129**, 7–18 (2020)
25. Huang, Q., Li, W., Zhang, B.C., Li, Q.L., Tao, R., Lovell, N.H.: Blood cell classification based on hyperspectral imaging with modulated gabor and CNN. IEEE J. Biomed. Health Inform. **24**(1), 160–170 (2020)

26. Wei, X.L., Li, W., Zhang, M.M., Li, Q.L.: Medical hyperspectral image classification based on end-to-end fusion deep neural network. IEEE Trans. Instrum. Meas. **68**(11), 4481–4492 (2019)
27. Shi, G.Y., Huang, H., Wang, L.H.: Unsupervised dimensionality reduction for hyperspectral imagery via local geometric structures feature learning. IEEE Geosci. Remote Sens. Lett. **17**(8), 1425–1429 (2020)
28. Duan, Y.L., Huang, H., Tang, Y.X.: Local constraint-based sparse manifold hypergraph learning for dimensionality reduction of hyperspectral image. IEEE Trans. Geosci. Remote Sens. **59**(1), 613–628 (2021)
29. Shi, G.Y., Luo, F.L., Tang, Y.M., Li, Y.: Dimensionality reduction of hyperspectral image based on local constrained manifold structure collaborative preserving embedding. Remote Sens. **13**(7), 1363 (2021)
30. Ravi, D., Fabelo, H., Callico, G.M., Yang, G.Z.: Manifold embedding and semantic segmentation for intraoperative guidance with hyperspectral brain imaging. IEEE Trans. Med. Imaging **19**(1), 010901 (2014)

Deep Learning-Based Regional Sub-models Integration for Parkinson's Disease Diagnosis Using Diffusion Tensor Imaging

Hengling Zhao[1], Chih-Chien Tsai[2,3], Ce Zhu[1], Mingyi Zhou[1], Jiun-Jie Wang[2,3], and Yipeng Liu[1(✉)]

[1] School of Information and Communication Engineering, University of Electronic Science and Technology of China, Chengdu, China
yipengliu@uestc.edu.cn
[2] Department of Medical Imaging and Radiological Science, Chang Gung University, Taoyuan City, Taiwan
[3] Healthy Aging Research Center, Chang Gung University, Taoyuan City, Taiwan

Abstract. Parkinson's disease (PD) is a neurodegenerative disease. PD patients may have serious movement disorders and mental problems. The current diagnosis requires a professionally trained medical doctor to take a long period for it. Different doctors may even have different accuracies. Recently advances in deep learning-based medical image classification make it is possible to diagnose PD automatically. Different from most of the existing works on magnetic resonance images, we use diffusion tensor imaging (DTI) in that it can reflect functional data of the brain. We propose a sub-models integration framework based on convolutional neural networks (CNNs) for Parkinson's disease. Each sub-region of the brain is used to train a unique CNN model, named sub-model, and the selective stacking algorithm is used to screen these sub-models. It obtains the classification accuracy of 92.4% on the cross-validation dataset. In addition, it can provide that which sub-regions play a role in the judgment of the final result so that this framework has stronger practical application than an end-to-end model.

Keywords: Parkinson's disease · Diffusion tensor imaging · Deep learning · Regional · Sub-models · Integration

1 Introduction

Parkinson's disease (PD) is one of the most common neurodegenerative diseases in clinical. However, there is no efficient diagnostic tool for it. PD patients not only have a movement disorder but may also have a mental problem such as sleep problem, depression, memory impairment, and fatigue. It can be worse as time goes on, and brings great pain to the patients and their families.

This work was supported in part by the National Natural Science Foundation of China (NSFC) under Grant 62020106011 and Grant U19A2052 and in part by the Sichuan Science and Technology Program under Grant 2019YFH008.

Y. Peng et al. (Eds.): ICIG 2021, LNCS 12889, pp. 742–753, 2021.
https://doi.org/10.1007/978-3-030-87358-5_60

Doctors usually make diagnosis of the disease based on the patient's clinical performance. Studies [2] show that early (within five years) PD was diagnosed with no more than 26% accuracy in patients who had not been treated or who did not respond well to drugs. Even when PD patients responded well to drugs, the accuracy was the only 53%. Because of the irreversibility of early neurodegenerative diseases, it is of great clinical significance to find a biomarker for early diagnosis of neurodegenerative diseases.

Hirschauer et al. [10] used Parkinson's Progression Markers Initiative (PPMI) subject data (consists of six clinical examinations and neuroimaging measurements of two regions of interest) to diagnose PD patients and the prediction accuracy is high through the probabilistic neural network, support vector machine (SVM), k-nearest neighbors algorithm, and classification tree. Frid et al. [7,18] used speech data and SVM technique to detect PD patients, obtaining good prediction results. Such methods reduce the reliance on medical experts compared to previous methods of manually tagging features. Gallicchio et al. [8] adopted deep echo state networks to analyze the whole time-series collected from a tablet device during the sketching of spiral tests, which is a convenient diagnosis method. Pereira et al. [16] used a pen equipped with a special sensor to perform handwriting tests on patients to obtain biological characteristics, and then used convolutional neural networks to diagnose these characteristic data [17]. The above works used the biological and behavioral characteristics of Parkinson's disease to diagnose patients, and the accuracy of diagnosis of Parkinson's disease in the early clinical stage is not high.

In the diagnostic work using traditional magnetic resonance imaging (MRI), many image-based volume measurement methods are used to detect relevant brain tissues [3,5,21]. But the loss of volume is not unique to Parkinson's disease and appears only in its advanced stages. As a new technique of MRI, diffusion tensor image (DTI) can well reflect the functional characteristics in space, which is widely used in the study of neurodegenerative diseases [1,4,11,15,23,24]. Therefore, we utilize DTI for PD diagnosis. A major limitation of the use of diffusion tensor magnetic resonance imaging in the clinical diagnosis of Parkinson's disease is that the selection of a specific region of interest (ROI) in the basal ganglia region focuses on white matter lesions [9]. Vaillancourt et al. found a reduction of fractional anisotropy (FA) scores in the substantia nigra tail of PD patients [22], although there were still many of the same values as those observed in healthy subjects [6,12]. Lu et al. found that PD patients showed increased diffusion in multiple cortical areas extending beyond the basal ganglia, which also proved that the measurement of water diffusion in the brain could be used in the clinical evaluation of Parkinson's disease [13]. Thus finding the brain regions with the best diagnostic performance is a major focus of research in the Parkinson's field. In this paper, we cut the brain DTI data into 116 brain regions, to find the areas which are more responsive to Parkinson's disease.

This framework firstly split the brain DTI data into 116 brain regions, and then use deep convolutional networks to supervise and train 90 brain regions except the cerebellum to obtain 90 deep learning models. The next step is using the greedy algorithm to screen these sub-regional models, and finally, the weighted average of the results of the selected region combination is the final result. Our contributions are as follows:

- Used diffusion tensor images to reflect brain functional activity data for diagnosis.
- The framework can provide more intermediate information than the previous end-to-end method, that is, which sub-regions display the patients are at risk of illness.
- The single sub-regional model with low accuracy is robust, and then they are integrated to have better classification effect and stronger practical application value.

2   Dataset

2.1   Description of Data

DTI data used in this study come from the PPMI database[1]. The PPMI [14] is an observational clinical study designed to identify PD biomarkers for diagnosis and comprehensive evaluating. Data type includes clinical markers, advanced imaging, and biological samples. DTI is a new technique of MRI, whose measure indices including fractional anisotropy (FA), mean diffusivity (MD), axial diffusivity (AD) and radial diffusivity (RD), and FA is used in this study. FA provides an anisotropy measure of water diffusion presumably reflecting preferential directions of fiber orientation. There are 282 samples including 206 PD patients and 76 healthy control (HC) and the FA data have been processed as shown in Sect. 2.2.

2.2   Data Processing

Because the scanned brain coordinates of each patient are different, each DTI sample needs to be corrected to the same standard coordinates. Utilizing Statistical Parametric Mapping (SPM8) software in MATLAB get an averaged group template from all patients' high-resolution T1 images, and this process will produce a transformation matrix for each patient. There is Montreal Neurological Institute (MNI) template in this software that can split the brain into 116 standard brain network map areas, so we can split each patient brain into 116 regions just apply each inversed transformation matrix in the standard brain network coordinates. The data in 116 brain areas are inputs for our proposed diagnostic frame. However, since the cerebellar regions of brain images are too small to be extracted by convolutional neural networks (CNNs) for information features, and the cerebellum is generally considered to have a relatively small correlation with the diagnosis of PD, we only select images from other regions of the brain (regions other than the cerebellum) as the input, and the number of input regions is 90.

---

[1] https://www.ppmi-info.org/access-data-specimens/download-data/.

3   Model

Our model mainly consists of two modules: 1) sub-region diagnosis using CNNs, 2) finding the best combination of sub-regions. An overview is shown in Fig. 1, where the AUC_n is the area under the ROC curve of the n-th sub-region. The whole algorithm flow is summarized as follows:

1. Utilize CNNs to diagnose 90 brain regions respectively in the cross-validation dataset.
2. Get 90 optimal sub-regional combinations with different numbers from 1 to 90 using selective stacking algorithm in Sect. 3.2.
3. Choose the combination having best result as the finally optimal combination, and apply it to the test dataset.

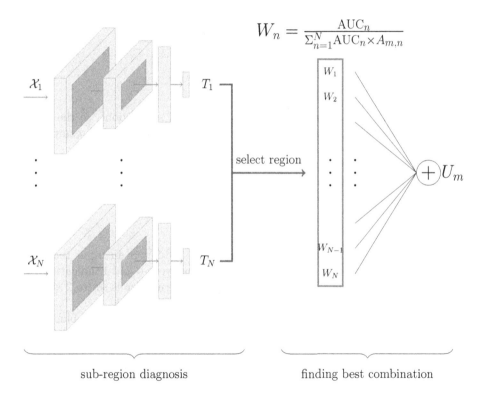

$$W_n = \frac{AUC_n}{\Sigma_{n=1}^{N} AUC_n \times A_{m,n}}$$

sub-region diagnosis   finding best combination

Fig. 1. The whole algorithm operation diagram

3.1   Sub-regional Diagnosis

CNNs have been used for medical image processing, and some studies [19,20] have obtained good results by using the ROI to reduce overfitting. In this module,

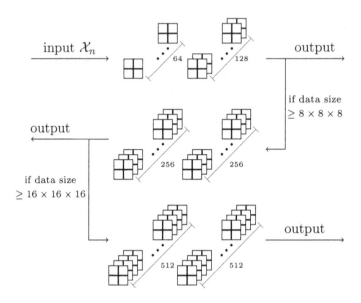

Fig. 2. Adaptive CNN model

we apply CNNs with different structures to different sub-regions, so the architecture of the whole network is adaptive. As shown in Fig. 2, as the complexity of the input data increases, the corresponding network will be deeper.

A CNN model including convolutional blocks, fully-connected layers and a softmax layer, the latter two are used for classification. The forward propagation process of a CNN model is expressed as:

$$y_n = h_\theta(\mathcal{X}_n) \tag{1}$$

where θ represents parameter in CNN, $\mathcal{X}_n \in \mathbb{R}^{R_1 \times R_2 \times R_3}$ is an input tensor of the n-th ROI and y_n is the corresponding output between 0 and 1 indicating PD probability. As shown in Fig. 2, each convolutional kernel size is set to $2 \times 2 \times 2$, and each convolutional layer owns 64–512 convolutional kernels.

At last, we adopt the weighted score combination method to combine these sub-regional models (called sub-models). We weighted the results of each sub-model according to the AUC value of each sub-region.

Firstly, the probability results of every sub-models are binarized as

$$T_n = \begin{cases} 0 & \text{if } Y_n < \alpha, \\ 1 & \text{otherwise,} \end{cases} \tag{2}$$

where α is segmentation threshold generally 0.5. Then the binary result T_n in a combination with m sub-regions is weighted by the AUC_n as

$$S_n = T_n \times \frac{\text{AUC}_n}{\sum_{n=1}^{N} \text{AUC}_n \times A_{m,n}}, \tag{3}$$

where Am, n represents whether the n-th sub-region is selected by the sub-regional combination and is formulated as

$$A_{m,n} = \begin{cases} 1 & \text{if } h_\theta^n \in \mathbb{H}_m, \\ 0 & \text{otherwise,} \end{cases} \tag{4}$$

where $\mathbb{H}_m$ represents the set of m sub-models. Finally, each sub-regional combination can obtain a score U_m which is formulated as

$$U_m = \Sigma_{n=1}^N S_n \times A_{m,n}. \tag{5}$$

U_m is used to calculate the combination AUC of this combination, which is the evaluation index in selective stacking algorithm.

Input:
$\mathbb{H}_N = \{h_\theta^1, ..., h_\theta^N\}$: A arrangement of N sub-models from large to small according AUC.
$\mathbb{H}_m$: Combination of selected sub-models, where m is the number of models in it.
$\bar{\mathbb{H}}_m$: Combination of unselected sub-models.
N: The number of all sub-regions, here is 90 in this study
Output: $\mathbb{H}_m$
1 **for** $m \leftarrow 1$ **to** N **do**
2       $\mathbb{H}_m \leftarrow \{h_\theta^1, ..., h_\theta^m\}$;
3   **repeat**
4           $\mathbb{H}_{m-1} \leftarrow \mathbb{H}_m - h_\theta^j$, where h_θ^j is the sub-model whose contribution is the least in $\mathbb{H}_m$;
5           $\mathbb{H}_m \leftarrow \mathbb{H}_{m-1} + h_\theta^k$, where h_θ^k is the sub-model whose contribution is the most in $\bar{\mathbb{H}}_m$;
6   **until** $j{=}k$;
7 **end**

Algorithm 1: Selective Stacking

3.2 Sub-regional Model Screening

Some studies show that just a part of regions in the brain is connected to PD and because adding too many irrelevant features may lead to overfitting of models, we screen sub-regional models to reduce redundant data and alleviate overfitting. We determined the diagnostic contribution of each sub-region according to the value of AUC and the combination whose AUC is the highest is the optimal combination.

It's an NP-hard problem for finding the globally optimal combination of all sub-models, so we designed a selective stacking method to screen the combination and the algorithm is shown in Algorithm 1. After discarding a sub-model h_θ^j, the selected sub-regional combination having the highest combination AUC means the contribution of sub-model h_θ^j is the least. After adding-in a sub-model h_θ^k, the selected sub-regional combination having the highest combination AUC means the contribution of sub-model h_θ^k is the most.

Generally speaking, the weights of individual sub-regions differ greatly, and the contribution of some sub-regions is significantly greater than that of other sub-regions. The convergence speed of the algorithm is very fast, and the running time of the whole selective stacking algorithm does not need a long time. We can get a model combination with 90 sub-regions through Algorithm 1, and choose one combination with the best performance (highest value of AUC) as the finally optimal combination.

4   Experiment

We randomly select 232 samples for 10-fold cross-validation and 50 samples as the blind test dataset. The process of the sub-regional diagnosis and finding the best combination are just related to the cross-validation dataset. Thus the results of the test dataset are reliable. The split of the dataset is proportional and the number of samples in PD and HC is shown in Table 1. Because the DTI dataset is unbalanced and not very large, we adopt some operations to avoid over-fitting, and the details are in Sect. 4.1. The experiment results of the cross-validation and the blind test dataset are in Sect. 4.2.

Table 1. The detailed numbers of samples in the cross-validation dataset and the blind test dataset.

	Cross-validation	Blind test
PD	170	36
HC	62	14

4.1   Data Augmentation

The HC samples are far less than PD samples, thus when training the model, we randomly select a part of HC samples, which are added noise, to join the training. This operation avoids the model bias towards PD patients. Besides, all samples are added random noise in the training process to avoid over-fitting, because there are only about 200 samples in training.

4.2   Results

The cross-validation accuracy of all 90 sub-models on FA data is shown in Table 2. The sub-region with the best model performance is Lingual_R (81.56%), that with the worst model performance is Pallidum_L (55.43%). On the whole,

Table 2. The accuracy of each sub-regional model in the cross-validation dataset.

Regions	Accuracy	Regions	Accuracy
Lingual_R	81.52%	Frontal_Inf_Oper_L	70.65%
Angular_L	80.43%	Temporal_Pole_Mid_L	70.65%
Frontal_Sup_Orb_R	80.43%	Occipital_Mid_L	70.65%
SupraMarginal_L	80.43%	Occipital_Mid_R	70.65%
Cingulum_Mid_R	79.35%	Precuneus_L	70.65%
Precuneus_R	79.35%	Frontal_Mid_L	70.65%
Cingulum_Ant_L	78.26%	Frontal_Inf_Orb_L	70.65%
Postcentral_R	78.26%	Parietal_Sup_R	69.57%
Insula_R	78.26%	Temporal_Sup_R	69.57%
Lingual_L	78.26%	Cuneus_R	69.57%
Frontal_Sup_Medial_L	78.26%	Frontal_Inf_Tri_L	69.57%
Temporal_Mid_L	77.17%	Thalamus_L	69.57%
Frontal_Inf_Oper_R	76.09%	Precentral_R	69.57%
Cingulum_Ant_R	76.09%	Olfactory_R	68.48%
Cingulum_Post_R	76.09%	Frontal_Sup_L	68.48%
Occipital_Sup_R	76.09%	Parietal_Inf_R	68.48%
SupraMarginal_R	76.09%	Hippocampus_R	68.48%
Frontal_Inf_Tri_R	76.09%	Frontal_Mid_Orb_R	68.48%
Heschl_L	75%	Caudate_R	68.48%
Temporal_Sup_L	75%	Temporal_Inf_R	68.48%
Paracentral_Lobule_L	75%	Temporal_Pole_Mid_R	68.48%
Frontal_Mid_Orb_L	75%	Temporal_Pole_Sup_L	68.48%
Putamen_R	75%	Olfactory_L	68.48%
Cingulum_Mid_L	73.91%	Fusiform_L	67.39%
Occipital_Inf_L	73.91%	Postcentral_L	66.3%
Rolandic_Oper_R	73.91%	Frontal_Sup_R	66.3%
Insula_L	73.91%	Cingulum_Post_L	65.22%
Caudate_L	72.83%	Precentral_L	65.22%
Frontal_Mid_R	72.83%	Thalamus_R	65.22%
Temporal_Inf_L	72.83%	Parietal_Inf_L	65.22%
Calcarine_L	72.83%	Pallidum_R	63.04%
Amygdala_R	72.83%	Temporal_Pole_Sup_R	63.04%
Frontal_Sup_Medial_R	72.83%	ParaHippocampal_R	63.04%
Cuneus_L	72.83%	Calcarine_R	63.04%
Fusiform_R	71.74%	Angular_R	63.04%
Rolandic_Oper_L	71.74%	Frontal_Mid_Orb_R	61.96%
Paracentral_Lobule_R	71.74%	Frontal_Sup_Orb_L	61.96%
ParaHippocampal_L	71.74%	Supp_Motor_Area_L	61.96%
Occipital_Sup_L	71.74%	Parietal_Sup_L	60.87%
Heschl_R	71.74%	Rectus_L	60.87%
Frontal_Mid_Orb_L	71.74%	Supp_Motor_Area_R	60.87%
Frontal_Inf_Orb_R	71.74%	Temporal_Mid_R	59.78%
Hippocampus_L	71.74%	Amygdala_L	56.52%
Putamen_L	71.74%	Rectus_R	56.52%
Occipital_Inf_R	70.65%	Pallidum_L	55.43%

most of the deep learning models of sub-regions have achieved certain results in the prediction of PD.

After getting models of every sub-regions, we use the Algorithm 1 to screen the sub-models and obtain the best combination (the final model in this study). The best combination includes 8 sub-regions: Precuneus_R ,Insula_R, Frontal_Sup_Orb_R, Lingual_R, Frontal_Inf_Oper_R, Occipital_Inf_L, Precentral_L, Temporal_Pole_Mid_R. As shown in Fig. 3, the locations of the selected sub-regions and their corresponding weights were shown in the real brain, with darker colors representing higher AUC. The ROC curve and AUC of the final model in the cross-validation dataset are shown in Fig. 4. The predicted accuracy, sensitivity, specificity are shown in Table 3, which indicates that our proposed deep learning-based sub-models integration framework has a great performance in the cross-validation dataset.

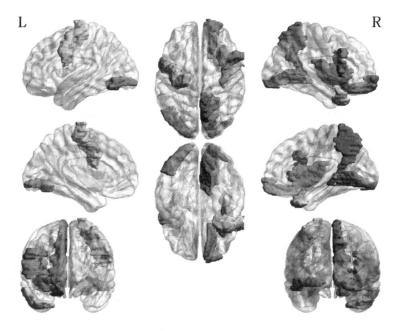

Fig. 3. Visualization of the best combination. 'L' is the left side of the brain, 'R' is the right of that.

Table 3. Three performance indicators for the cross-validation dataset. Sensitivity is the true positive sample percentage of the total positive sample, specificity is the true negative sample percentage of the total negative sample, and higher both of above values are better.

Accuracy (%)	Sensitivity (%)	Specificity (%)
92.4	92.6	91.7

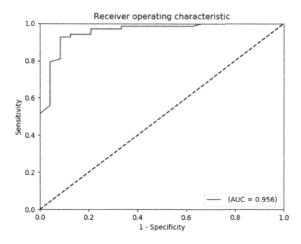

Fig. 4. The ROC curve of the best combination with 8 sub-regions in the cross-validation dataset.

Then, we apply the final model on the blind test dataset and use the confusion matrix and some classification indicators (given in Table 4) to evaluate it. Positive predictive value (PPV) is called precision, which is the true positive sample percentage of the predicted positive sample. True positive rate (TPR) is called recall (equal to sensitivity in Table 3), which is the true positive sample percentage of the total positive sample. F1 score is calculated by precision and recall, which is formulated as

$$F1 = \frac{2 \times precision \times recall}{precision + recall}.$$

Table 4. Confusion matrix and classification indicators of the blind test dataset. The values in blue are the higher the better.

		Actual class			
	Total	PD	HC	Prevalence $= 72\%$	**ACC $=$ 80.0%**
Predicted class	PD	35	9	**PPV $=$ 79.5%**	FDR $= 20.5\%$
	HC	1	5	FOR $= 16.7\%$	**NPV $=$ 83.3%**
		TPR $=$ 97.2%	FPR $= 64.3\%$	LR+ $= \frac{TPR}{FPR}$	**F1 $=$ 87.45%**
		FNR $= 2.8\%$	**TNR $=$ 35.7%**	LR$- = \frac{FNR}{TNR}$	

5   Conclusion

In this study, we propose a deep learning-based sub-models integration framework using DTI to detect PD patients and assist doctors to diagnose. This model attained 92.4% accuracy in the cross-validation dataset, and give the visualization of the chosen sub-regions and their corresponding degree of importance. In the blind test dataset, this model obtained 80% accuracy, where the sensitivity (TPR, recall) is up to 97.2%. Because the PPMI dataset is not large enough and unbalanced, the specificity (TNR) on the blind test dataset is only 35.7%. We have achieved higher accuracy and specificity in a better quality (larger and more balanced) dataset. The above results are in preparation and will be written in a journal edition.

References

1. Acosta-Cabronero, J., Alley, S., Williams, G.B., Pengas, G., Nestor, P.J.: Diffusion tensor metrics as biomarkers in Alzheimer's disease. PLoS ONE **7**(11), e49072 (2012)
2. Adler, C.H., et al.: Low clinical diagnostic accuracy of early vs advanced Parkinson disease: clinicopathologic study. Neurology **83**(5), 406–412 (2014)
3. Carlesimo, G., Piras, F., Assogna, F., Pontieri, F., Caltagirone, C., Spalletta, G.: Hippocampal abnormalities and memory deficits in Parkinson disease: a multimodal imaging study. Neurology **78**(24), 1939–1945 (2012)
4. Chang, C.C., et al.: Clinical significance of the pallidoreticular pathway in patients with carbon monoxide intoxication. Brain **134**(12), 3632–3646 (2011)
5. Choi, S.H., Jung, T.M., Lee, J.E., Lee, S.K., Sohn, Y.H., Lee, P.H.: Volumetric analysis of the substantia innominata in patients with Parkinson's disease according to cognitive status. Neurobiol. Aging **33**(7), 1265–1272 (2012)
6. Cochrane, C.J., Ebmeier, K.P.: Diffusion tensor imaging in parkinsonian syndromes: a systematic review and meta-analysis. Neurology **80**(9), 857–864 (2013)
7. Frid, A., et al.: Computational diagnosis of Parkinson's disease directly from natural speech using machine learning techniques. In: 2014 IEEE International Conference on Software Science, Technology and Engineering, pp. 50–53. IEEE (2014)
8. Gallicchio, C., Micheli, A., Pedrelli, L.: Deep echo state networks for diagnosis of Parkinson's disease. arXiv preprint arXiv:1802.06708 (2018)
9. Gattellaro, G., et al.: White matter involvement in idiopathic Parkinson disease: a diffusion tensor imaging study. Am. J. Neuroradiol. **30**(6), 1222–1226 (2009)
10. Hirschauer, T.J., Adeli, H., Buford, J.A.: Computer-aided diagnosis of Parkinson's disease using enhanced probabilistic neural network. J. Med. Syst. **39**(11), 1–12 (2015)
11. Kendi, A.K., Lehericy, S., Luciana, M., Ugurbil, K., Tuite, P.: Altered diffusion in the frontal lobe in Parkinson disease. Am. J. Neuroradiol. **29**(3), 501–505 (2008)
12. Kikuchi, A., et al.: Hypometabolism in the supplementary and anterior cingulate cortices is related to dysphagia in Parkinson's disease: a cross-sectional and 3-year longitudinal cohort study. BMJ Open **3**(3), e002249 (2013)
13. Lu, C.S., et al.: Alterations of diffusion tensor MRI parameters in the brains of patients with Parkinson's disease compared with normal brains: possible diagnostic use. Eur. Radiol. **26**(11), 3978–3988 (2016)
14. Marek, K., et al.: The Parkinson progression marker initiative (PPMI). Prog. Neurobiol. **95**(4), 629–635 (2011)
15. Menke, R.A., et al.: MRI characteristics of the substantia nigra in Parkinson's disease: a combined quantitative T1 and DTI study. Neuroimage **47**(2), 435–441 (2009)

16. Pereira, C.R., et al.: A step towards the automated diagnosis of Parkinson's disease: analyzing handwriting movements. In: 2015 IEEE 28th International Symposium on Computer-Based Medical Systems, pp. 171–176. IEEE (2015)
17. Pereira, C.R., Weber, S.A., Hook, C., Rosa, G.H., Papa, J.P.: Deep learning-aided Parkinson's disease diagnosis from handwritten dynamics. In: 2016 29th SIBGRAPI Conference on Graphics, Patterns and Images (SIBGRAPI), pp. 340–346. IEEE (2016)
18. Sakar, B.E., et al.: Collection and analysis of a Parkinson speech dataset with multiple types of sound recordings. IEEE J. Biomed. Health Inform. **17**(4), 828–834 (2013)
19. Sun, W., Zheng, B., Qian, W.: Automatic feature learning using multichannel ROI based on deep structured algorithms for computerized lung cancer diagnosis. Comput. Biol. Med. **89**, 530–539 (2017)
20. Tajbakhsh, N., et al.: Convolutional neural networks for medical image analysis: full training or fine tuning? IEEE Trans. Med. Imaging **35**(5), 1299–1312 (2016)
21. Tessitore, A., et al.: Regional gray matter atrophy in patients with Parkinson disease and freezing of gait. Am. J. Neuroradiol. **33**(9), 1804–1809 (2012)
22. Vaillancourt, D., et al.: High-resolution diffusion tensor imaging in the substantia nigra of de novo Parkinson disease. Neurology **72**(16), 1378–1384 (2009)
23. Wang, J., et al.: Microstructural changes in patients with progressive supranuclear palsy: a diffusion tensor imaging study. J. Magn. Reson. Imaging **32**(1), 69–75 (2010)
24. Zhang, Y., et al.: Diffusion tensor imaging of cingulum fibers in mild cognitive impairment and Alzheimer disease. Neurology **68**(1), 13–19 (2007)

Individual-Specific Connectome Fingerprint Based Classification of Temporal Lobe Epilepsy

Yao Meng[1,2], Jinming Xiao[1,2], Siqi Yang[1,2], Qiang Xu[3], Zhiqiang Zhang[3], and Wei Liao[1,2(✉)]

[1] The Clinical Hospital of Chengdu Brain Science Institute, School of Life Science and Technology, University of Electronic Science and Technology of China, Chengdu 611731, People's Republic of China
weiliao@uestc.edu.cn

[2] MOE Key Lab for Neuroinformation, High-Field Magnetic Resonance Brain Imaging Key Laboratory of Sichuan Province, University of Electronic Science and Technology of China, Chengdu 611731, People's Republic of China

[3] Department of Medical Imaging, Jinling Hospital, Nanjing University School of Medicine, Nanjing, China

Abstract. Non-lesional temporal lobe epilepsy (TLE) is a syndrome of epilepsies that have no clear morphological change and cannot be diagnosed by structural imaging. TLE has been found extensive disruption in cortical functional connectome based on inaccurate traditional group-level atlas. In the present study, we utilized a well-recognized individualized functional parcellation method which achieve more accurate definition of functional areas compare to traditional group-level atlas to identify functional regions of interest (ROIs). Based on the individualized ROIs, we constructed individual-specific connectome fingerprint. By the aid of machine learning algorithm, we extract core features of individualized functional connectome and fed it into support vector machine to classify TLE patients. We parcellated the cerebral cortex to individual-specific functional networks and further identified 73 homologous functional ROIs utilized in the subsequent group-level analysis. The individualized connectome achieved better performance in the classification model in terms of multiple evaluating metrics compare to connectome fingerprint based on group-level atlas. This study verified the feasibility of individual-level parcellation method in the application of TLE classification and may provide potential imaging biomarkers for TLE.

Keywords: Individual-specific · Functional connectome · Temporal lobe epilepsy

1 Introduction

Temporal lobe epilepsy (TLE) is a major type in epilepsy syndromes with majority patients found with hippocampal sclerosis [1]. But about 30% cases cannot be diagnosed with normal structural magnetic resonance imaging (MRI), that is, non-lesional TLE [2]. Without clearly visible cortical morphology change the functional activity could be the key aspect to study the pathology of non-lesional TLE.

© Springer Nature Switzerland AG 2021
Y. Peng et al. (Eds.): ICIG 2021, LNCS 12889, pp. 754–761, 2021.
https://doi.org/10.1007/978-3-030-87358-5_61

Functional magnetic resonance imaging (fMRI) is a technique to detect the neurovascular coupling signal which reflect brain functional activity. This technique has been extensively used in the study of cortical dysfunction and pathological process in lots of neurological and psychiatric diseases considering the excellent spatial and reasonable time resolution. TLE exhibited significant dysfunctional connectivity between brain regions which measured by resting-state fMRI (rs-fMRI) [3].

Traditional connectome analyses usually based on group-level atlas to parcellate the brain to areas to define the node [4]. This practice ignored the inter-subject variability in terms of functional topography which bring inaccurate definition of network nodes and may yield problematic representations of the connectome. Several studies have explored the method to define individual-specific function ROIs [4, 5, 7, 8], and some studies also shown the benefit in relating cognitive characteristics with brain circuitry and finding potential disease biomarkers [9, 10].

In the present study, we utilized a well-established individual-level functional parcellation algorithm to construct individualized connectome fingerprint. Based on the connectome, we introduced machine learning model to classify TLE patients. We also evaluated the model performance of individualized ROIs compared to traditional group-level based atlas.

2 Materials and Methods

2.1 Participants

This retrospective study was approved by the local medical ethics committee at Jinling Hospital, Nanjing University School of Medicine, China. Written informed consent was obtained from all participants. The patients were diagnosed with non-lesional temporal lobe epilepsy (TLE, n = 47, 27 males, age = 26.5 ± 8.38 years) and 78 age- and sex-matched healthy controls (HC) (39 males, age = 25.5 ± 6.27 years) were recruited through Jinling Hospital, Nanjing University School of Medicine, Nanjing, China. All included patients had negative presentation on diagnostic magnetic resonance imaging (MRI), and following criteria: (a) typical symptoms of TLE, such as automatism (hand, oral), autonomic symptoms, olfactory hallucination, déjà vu, and complex partial seizures with aura; (b) specific patterns of electrophysiological activity recorded by scalp electroencephalogram (EEG); (c) no abnormalities on diagnostic MRI; (d) no progressive diseases, tumors, or previous neurosurgery. All patients were diagnosed as TLE according to the International League Against Epilepsy (ILAE) classification [11].

2.2 Data Acquisition

All participants underwent structural and functional MRI scans with a Siemens Trio 3T scanner (Siemens, Munich, Germany) at Jinling Hospital, Nanjing, China. Foam padding was used to minimize head motion. All participants were required to keep their eyes closed, and to keep their head still. Functional images were acquired using an echo-planar imaging sequence aligned along the anterior commissure-posterior commissure line. High resolution T1-weighted (T1w) image was acquired in the sagittal orientation using a magnetization-prepared rapid gradient-echo sequence. The detailed scan parameter described in previous studies [12]. All TLE patients were in an interictal state during the entire scan process.

2.3 Data Processing

Structural data were used FreeSurfer (version 6.0.1, https://surfer.nmr.mgh.harvard.edu) to perform skull stripping, volumetric labeling, intensity normalization, white matter segmentation, surface atlas registration, and surface extraction and reconstruction. Functional data were preprocessed using the Computational Brain Imaging Group (CBIG) pipeline (https://github.com/ThomasYeoLab/CBIG) [13, 14] that combined the FMRIB Software Library (FSL) (version 5.0.9), FreeSurfer, and additional censoring steps [15, 16]. The first four frames were excluded to ensure steady-state longitudinal magnetization, and then slice-timing and motion correction were performed. Boundary-based registration was utilized to register fMRI volumes to T1w images. Nuisance signals including six head motion parameters, averaged signals from cerebrospinal fluid, white matter, and global brain signal, as well as their temporal derivatives (18 regressors in total) were regressed out. Participants with a mean frame-wise displacement (FD) [17] larger than 0.5 mm were excluded from all further analyses, and motion contaminated time frames (FD > 0.5 mm) and neighboring time frames were substituted by the least square interpolation of neighboring clean frames. Functional image data were then bandpass filtered (band width 0.01–0.08 Hz) [13]. Functional data were projected to a standard surface-based space ("fsaverage6" space) and then smoothed along the cortical surface with a Gaussian kernel (full width at half maximum, FWHM = 6 mm). In consideration of computational loading, the functional data downsampled to relative low-resolution standard space ("fsaverage4" space).

2.4 Individual-Level Functional ROIs Identification

Individual-level Networks Identification. Briefly, based on a group-level functional atlas [18] with 18 networks, the parcellation algorithm [4] that guided by group-level atlas and take consideration of the influence of the spatial distribution of inter-individual variability and signal-to-noise ratio (SNR) parcellated the cortical surface into 18 networks on individual level. As iterations proceed, the final parcellation scheme completely driven by the individual's functional data.

Individual-Level ROIs Identification. The identification process of individualized functional ROIs was described in [19]. The individualized networks derived from previous step were segmented further to small patches using a clustering algorithm. These patches were matched to 116 cortical ROIs derived from the group-level atlas. According to specific rules of matching, ROIs will be classified in individual-level.

2.5 Functional Connectome Calculation and Feature Selection

For group-level analysis, ROIs consistently identified in all participants were enrolled to perform subsequent analysis. The ROI's signal was defined by the mean time series of all vertices located in the specific ROI. Functional connectivity between two ROIs was defined by computing the Pearson correlation of corresponding ROI signals then Fisher-Z transformed to Z values.

The features used in subsequent classification was extracted by least absolute shrinkage and select operator (LASSO).

2.6 Classification Model

Support vector machine was utilized to classify the TLE patients and HC based on the functional connectome features. Leave-one-out-alone strategy was deployed to achieve cross validation. To determine the statistical power and significant level of classification model, permutation testing was deployed.

3 Results

3.1 Demographics

Two groups have matched age, sex, mean FD. All participants were right-handed. The detailed demographic information was list in Table 1.

Table 1. Demographic and clinical characteristics of participants

Demographics	TLE (n = 47)	HC (n = 78)	Statistics
Age	26.5 ± 8.38	25.5 ± 6.27	–
Sex (male/female)	27/20	39/39	$\chi^2 = 0.65$ ($p = 0.42$)
Mean FD (mm)	0.13	0.14	$t_{123} = 0.79$ ($p = 0.43$)
Duration of epilepsy (months)	95.9 ± 80.71	–	–
Age at seizure onset (years)	8.8 ± 6.52	–	–

3.2 Individualized Functional ROIs

All participants went through 10 iterations to yield the individual-level networks parcellation. In the process, networks gradually differ from group-level atlas and converge to final individual-specific map (Fig. 1).

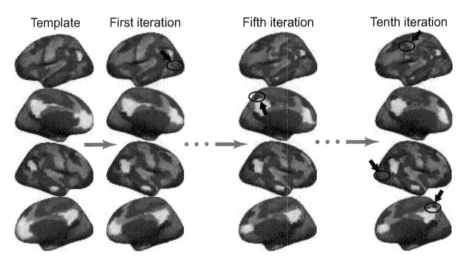

Fig. 1. The individual-level network identification iteration process from an example participant. The black circle and arrow highlight some example area that have significant difference between group atlas and individualized network parcellation.

After the identification process of individual-level functional ROIs, 73 ROIs was enrolled in the subsequent analysis (Fig. 2B). Most ROIs were retained with some areas stay unrecognized which mainly distributed in association cortex such as insula, lateral frontal cortex, lateral temporal lobe and temporal-parietal conjunction area (Fig. 2B). The average FC matrix shown that individualized ROIs yield stronger within network

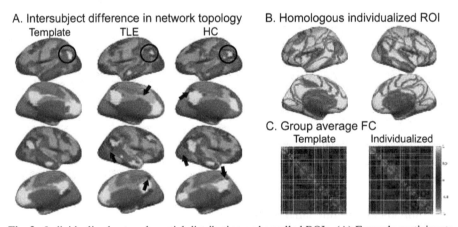

Fig. 2. Individualized network spatial distribution and enrolled ROIs. (A) Example participants from both groups show distinct network distribution. The black circle and arrow highlight some example area that have significant difference between group atlas and individualized network parcellation in both TLE and HC groups. (B) The consensus ROIs (n = 73) enrolled on group level from identified individual-level ROIs. (C) The average functional connectivity matrices across participants based on group atlas (template) and individualized ROIs (individualized).

connectivity which catering to the fundamental hypothesis of functional connectome (Fig. 2C).

3.3 Classification Performance

Features fed into the classification model extract from functional connectome using LASSO algorithm. The detailed metrics for evaluating classification model performance listed in Table 2. Briefly, in contrast to connectome constructed by traditional group atlas, individual-level ROIs improved the model extensively. The classification model utilizing individualized ROIs yield greater area under the receive operator curve (AUC of ROC, Table 2 and Fig. 3).

Table 2. Metrics of classification model performance

	Accuracy	Precision	Recall	F1-score	AUC of ROC	Statistical Significance (p value)
Individualized	0.83	0.83	0.70	0.76	0.89	<0.001
Template	0.74	0.69	0.57	0.62	0.78	0.004

4   Discussions

In the light of individualized functional parcellation technique, we parcellated the cerebral cortex to macroscale networks and further into areas on individual-level. Based on the more accurate functional area definition, we constructed connectome fingerprint and by the aid of machine learning classified TLE patients. The individualized ROIs improved the classification accuracy and other performance metrics. This may inform that the better representation of brain connectivity affords more precise pathological biomarkers.

The group-level functional atlas is the fundamental tool for the community to study the connectome topology and probe potential connectivity biomarkers. But the functional areas definition has great variability in terms of location and size [6]. The variability has inhomogeneous spatial distribution that association cortex shows greater inter-subject variation and primary cortex more uniform across cohorts [6]. In the present study we utilized a well-recognized individual-level parcellation method [4] that yield more accurate area definition. This practice improved the performance of the model in contrast to group-level atlas in the classification of TLE. This may help us better understand the key connection to diagnose and probe the pathological circuity of non-lesional TLE.

The individualized technique deployed in this study also have limitations. Because of the inter-subject variability, some areas in association cortex not included in the connectome construction and classification analysis. And by the consideration of the situation of patients, the acquisition volume of function data stays relatively low and may affect the stability of individual functional ROIs identification.

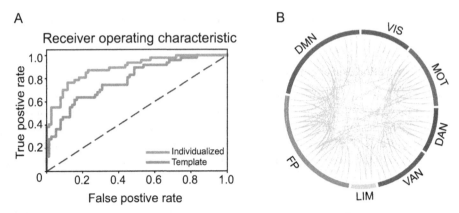

Fig. 3. Receive operator characteristic and the edges contribute to classification. (A) The receive operator characteristic of both individualized and group-level atlas connectome-based models. (B) The edges contributed to classification process in the individualized connectome model.

5   Conclusions

Individualized functional ROIs has been identified for TLE patients and HC. Based on the more accurate ROIs definition, individualized functional connectome outperformed traditional group-level atlas in terms of TLE classification in present study. The individualized ROIs may help us to find more precise connectivity biomarkers in non-lesional TLE and other neurological diseases.

Acknowledgments. We are grateful to all the participants in this study. This study was funded by the National Natural Science Foundation of China (61871077, 62036003, and U1808204), and the Excellent Youth Foundation of Sichuan Scientific Committee (2020JDJQ0016).

References

1. Engel, J.: Introduction to temporal lobe epilepsy. Epilepsy Res. **26**, 141–150 (1996). https://doi.org/10.1016/S0920-1211(96)00043-5
2. Fan, Z., et al.: Diagnosis and surgical treatment of non-lesional temporal lobe epilepsy with unilateral amygdala enlargement. Neurol. Sci. **42**(6), 2353–2361 (2020). https://doi.org/10.1007/s10072-020-04794-8
3. Haneef, Z., Lenartowicz, A., Yeh, H.J., et al.: Effect of lateralized temporal lobe epilepsy on the default mode network. Epilepsy Behav. **25**, 350–357 (2012). https://doi.org/10.1016/j.yebeh.2012.07.019
4. Wang, D., Buckner, R.L., Fox, M.D., et al.: Parcellating cortical functional networks in individuals. Nat Neurosci **18**, 1853–1860 (2015). https://doi.org/10.1038/nn.4164
5. Cui, Z., Li, H., Xia, C.H., et al.: Individual variation in functional topography of association networks in youth. Neuron **106**, 340-353.e8 (2020). https://doi.org/10.1016/j.neuron.2020.01.029
6. Mueller, S., Wang, D., Fox, M.D., et al.: Individual variability in functional connectivity architecture of the human brain. Neuron **77**, 586–595 (2013). https://doi.org/10.1016/j.neuron.2012.12.028

7. Dickie, E.W., Ameis, S.H., Shahab, S., et al.: Personalized intrinsic network topography mapping and functional connectivity deficits in autism spectrum disorder. Biol. Psychiat. **84**, 278–286 (2018). https://doi.org/10.1016/j.biopsych.2018.02.1174

8. Schaefer, A., Kong, R., Gordon, E.M., et al.: Local-global parcellation of the human cerebral cortex from intrinsic functional connectivity MRI. Cereb. Cortex **28**, 3095–3114 (2018). https://doi.org/10.1093/cercor/bhx179

9. Wang, D., Li, M., Wang, M., et al.: Individual-specific functional connectivity markers track dimensional and categorical features of psychotic illness. Mol. Psychiatry **25**, 2119–2129 (2020). https://doi.org/10.1038/s41380-018-0276-1

10. Fan, Y., Li, L., Peng, Y., et al.: Individual-specific functional connectome biomarkers predict schizophrenia positive symptoms during adolescent brain maturation. Hum. Brain Mapp. **42**, 1475–1484 (2021). https://doi.org/10.1002/hbm.25307

11. Scheffer, I.E., Berkovic, S., Capovilla, G., et al.: ILAE classification of the epilepsies: position paper of the ILAE commission for classification and terminology. Epilepsia **58**, 512–521 (2017). https://doi.org/10.1111/epi.13709

12. Meng, Y., Yang, S., Chen, H., et al.: Systematically disrupted functional gradient of the cortical connectome in generalized epilepsy: initial discovery and independent sample replication. Neuroimage **230**, 117831 (2021). https://doi.org/10.1016/j.neuroimage.2021.117831

13. Kong, R., Li, J., Orban, C., et al.: Spatial Topography of individual-specific cortical networks predicts human cognition, personality, and emotion. Cereb. Cortex **29**, 2533–2551 (2019). https://doi.org/10.1093/cercor/bhy123

14. Li, J., Kong, R., Liégeois, R., et al.: Global signal regression strengthens association between resting-state functional connectivity and behavior. Neuroimage **196**, 126–141 (2019). https://doi.org/10.1016/j.neuroimage.2019.04.016

15. Power, J.D., Mitra, A., Laumann, T.O., et al.: Methods to detect, characterize, and remove motion artifact in resting state fMRI. Neuroimage **84**, 320–341 (2014). https://doi.org/10.1016/j.neuroimage.2013.08.048

16. Gordon, E.M., Laumann, T.O., Adeyemo, B., et al.: Generation and evaluation of a cortical area parcellation from resting-state correlations. Cereb Cortex **26**, 288–303 (2016). https://doi.org/10.1093/cercor/bhu239

17. Power, J.D., Barnes, K.A., Snyder, A.Z., et al.: Spurious but systematic correlations in functional connectivity MRI networks arise from subject motion. Neuroimage **59**, 2142–2154 (2012). https://doi.org/10.1016/j.neuroimage.2011.10.018

18. Thomas Yeo, B.T., Krienen, F.M., Sepulcre, J., et al.: The organization of the human cerebral cortex estimated by intrinsic functional connectivity. J. Neurophysiol. **106**, 1125–1165 (2011). https://doi.org/10.1152/jn.00338.2011

19. Li, M., Wang, D., Ren, J., et al.: Performing group-level functional image analyses based on homologous functional regions mapped in individuals. PLoS Biol. **17**, e2007032 (2019). https://doi.org/10.1371/journal.pbio.2007032

Multi-atlas Segmentation Combining Multi-task Local Label Learning and Semi-supervised Label Propagation

Bo Li[1], Qiang Zheng[1(✉)], Kun Zhao[2], Honglun Li[3], Chaoqing Ma[1], Shuanhu Wu[1], and Xiangrong Tong[1]

[1] School of Computer and Control Engineering, Yantai University, Yantai 264205, China
zhengqiang@ytu.edu.cn
[2] Beijing Advanced Innovation Centre for Biomedical Engineering, School of Biological Science and Medical Engineering, Beihang University, Beijing, China
[3] Departments of Medical Oncology and Radiology, Affiliated Yantai Yuhuangding Hospital of Qingdao University Medical College, Yantai 264000, China

Abstract. Multi-atlas based segmentation methods have achieved great success in hippocampal segmentation due to their promising performance. However, the correlation between voxels in the target image is often ignored. In this study, an image segmentation method based on multi-atlas is proposed by combining the multi-task learning method with the semi-supervised label propagation algorithm. Both multi-task learning and semi-supervised label propagation can take advantage of the correlation between voxels in the target image. Specifically, instead of training an independent model for each voxel to be segmented in the target images, the multi-task learning method trains a joint classification model for a multi-task-voxel cluster in a target image patch, followed by majority voting to obtain a probabilistic segmentation for the central voxel. The probabilistic map is then used to guide a semi-supervised label propagation algorithm to get the final segmentation results. The proposed method was applied to hippocampus segmentation in MR images and compared with state-of-the-art multi-atlas segmentation methods. Experimental results demonstrated that our method had better segmentation performance for the hippocampal segmentation.

Keywords: Multi-atlas · Hippocampus segmentation · Multi-task learning · Label propagation

1 Introduction

The hippocampal segmentation from magnetic resonance (MR) brain images is of great importance in a variety of neurodegenerative diseases studies [1, 2]. There are a series of methods approved for hippocampal segmentation in recent years. Especially, the Multi-atlas based image segmentation (MAIS) is an automatic medical image segmentation technique, which has been successfully adopted in hippocampus segmentation studies with competitive segmentation performance [3–10], and frequently used to reveal

© Springer Nature Switzerland AG 2021
Y. Peng et al. (Eds.): ICIG 2021, LNCS 12889, pp. 762–772, 2021.
https://doi.org/10.1007/978-3-030-87358-5_62

the complex anatomical structures, morphological changes, pathological regions, and image-based interventions [11, 12]. Briefly, the MAIS method aligns the multi-atlas images and its labels with the target image, and then performs label fusion to obtain the segmentation result of the target image.

In the last few decades, the topic of great interest based on MAIS methods was label fusion strategies [12–16] rather than image registration [17–19]. Specifically, majority voting (MV) is the most primitive label fusion strategy [20], while more complicated label fusion strategy, such as metric learning, joint label fusion [21] and dictionary learning [22]. Besides, the label fusion can also be implemented in the pattern recognition framework, in which the multi-atlas images and their labels are taken as training data, and a classification model is established by support vector machines (SVM) [6], linear regression models [8], and artificial neural networks (ANNs) [23] etc. However, the existing MAIS methods implement the label fusion independently for each individual voxel in the target image without considering correlations between them. Besides, the relationship between voxels is of great concern for label fusion [10]. Therefore, we assume that the segmentation accuracy of the MAIS would improve significantly if the correlations between voxels were considered sufficiently.

However, the existing MAIS methods implement the label fusion independently for each individual voxel in the target image without considering correlations between them. On one hand, the training of the pattern recognition model is implemented voxel by voxel in the target image, lacking joint training of neighbour voxels. On the other hand, the spatial consistency between the voxels in the target image is not taken into consideration. Therefore, the multi-atlas image segmentation framework needs a better solution to improve the segmentation accuracy.

In this paper, a novel label fusion strategy was proposed by combining a multi-task local label learning method and a label propagation method. We validated our approach using 35 imaging data and labels downloaded from the Alzheimer's disease Neuroimaging Initiative (ADNI) database (adni.loni.usc.edu) [24]. Specifically, multi-task learning is to leverage useful information contained in the multiple related tasks and jointly train the pattern recognition model for the neighbour voxels in a patch in the target image, followed by majority voting to obtain a probabilistic segmentation for the central voxel in the target image patch. Then, the semi-supervised label propagation algorithm propagates the reliable segmentation information on the probabilistic map under the constraint of consistent regularization in local and global space.

2   Method

The proposed MAIS method consists of a multi-task local label learning method for probabilistic map computation and a semi-supervised label propagation method for hippocampal segmentation. The method is abbreviated as MTL-SSLP.

2.1   MAIS Based on Multi-task Learning

Given an image T to be segmented and M aligned atlas images and their labels $L_i = (I_i, E_i)$, $i = 1,...,M$ with I_i and E_i being the ith atlas image and label respectively, under the framework of pattern recognition, a multi-task classification model is established to obtain the probabilistic segmentation results of the image to be segmented. Instead of training a single-task pattern recognition model independently upon each voxel x in the target image, we constructed a 7-task learning model upon its 6-connected neighborhoods $N_6(x)$ (named multi-task-voxel cluster, Fig. 1 (a)), followed by majority voting of the predicted labels in the multi-task-voxel cluster to calculate the final probabilistic value of the central voxel x.

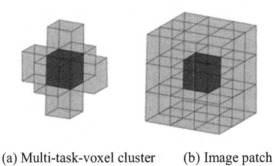

(a) Multi-task-voxel cluster   (b) Image patch

Fig. 1. Multi-task-voxel cluster $N_6(x)$ in (a) and image patch $N_{26}(x)$ in (b). The red boxes represent the central voxels.

Specifically, we constructed a shared feature space for training each multi-task learning model by extracting 26-connected neighborhoods $N_{26}(x)$ (named image patch, Fig. 1 (b)) from each atlas image. The texture image features calculation for each image patch is same as the method described in [5]. The training data for each task were determined from the shared feature space by a k-NN (k nearest neighbor classification) strategy, which chose the same K nearest positive and negative training samples for each task from the shared feature space. Figure 2 shows the multi-task learning framework for probabilistic segmentation.

Regarding the multi-task learning model, multi-task lasso model with logistic loss function was adopted in our study [25] as follows:

$$\min_{W,C} \sum_{i=1}^{t} \sum_{j=1}^{n_i} \log\left(1 + \exp\left(-Y_{i,j}\left(W_i^T X_{i,j} + C_i\right)\right)\right) + \rho_1 \|W\|_1 + \rho_{L2} \|W\|_F^2 \quad (1)$$

where $X_{i,j}$ represents the sample j of the i-th task, $Y_{i,j}$ represents its corresponding label, W_i and C_i are the model for task i, the regularization parameter ρ_1 controls sparsity, and the optional ρ_{L2} regularization parameter controls the $\ell 2$-norm penalty. Figure 3 shows the relationships among X, Y, W, and C, where W is the parameter matrix sized $d * t$, and C is the t-dimension vector. For a testing sample X corresponding to task i, the predicted label y can be computed as follows:

$$Y = X^T \cdot W_i + C_i \quad (2)$$

After the calculation of the multi-task learning model, a probabilistic segmentation map is obtained by majority voting of the predicted labels in the multi-task-voxel cluster.

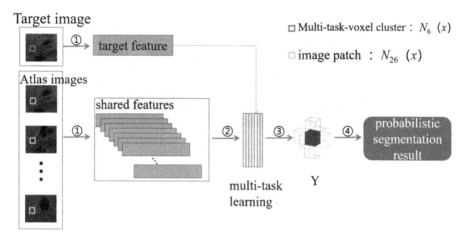

Fig. 2. Multi-task learning framework for probabilistic segmentation. ① Target image and atlas image features extraction. ② Joint training of the multi-task learning model based on the shared feature space. ③ The probabilistic value of the central voxel was calculated by majority voting of the predicted labels in the multi-task-voxel cluster. ④ The probabilistic map calculation.

$$Y = X^T \cdot W_i + C_i$$

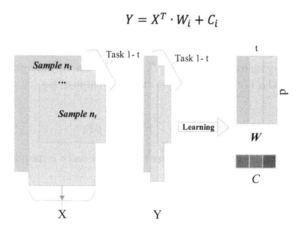

Fig. 3. The framework of multi-task learning model. X represents the training samples; Y represents the corresponding labels. W and C are the model for each task.

In the next section, the semi-supervised label propagation algorithm is adopted to optimize the probabilistic segmentation results by updating the voxels without 100% votes in the hippocampus or background defined inside the narrowband (red area in Fig. 4). Figure 4 compares narrowband obtained by MV and MTL classification model. The narrowband (red area in Fig. 4) obtained by MTL are obviously more precise than MV.

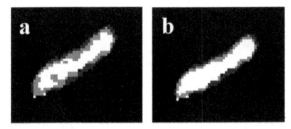

Fig. 4. The probability segmentation maps by MV in (a) and multi-task learning in (b). The subsequent semi-supervised label propagation was implemented in the red region (narrow band). (Color figure online)

2.2 Semi-supervised Label Propagation

To further improve segmentation accuracy, under the constraint of local and global consistency of the image, a semi-supervised label propagation algorithm based on the graph is used to refine the above probabilistic segmentation results [26].

Given the probabilistic segmentation map Y_0, the semi-supervised label propagation was implemented by optimizing the following function:

$$E(Y) = Y^T(L - S)Y + \alpha(Y - Y_0)^T(Y - Y_0) \tag{3}$$

where Y is matrix of the final segmentation result maps, L is an identity matrix, S is a normalized similarity matrix to characterizes similarity among different voxels, L-S is a Laplacian matrix and α is a parameter. The implementation of Eq. (3) can be performed as follows:

$$Y^{n+1} = (1 - \beta)SY^n + \beta Y_0 \tag{4}$$

where β ($0 < \beta < 1$) is a trade-off parameter related to α *and n* is the number of iteration steps.

2.3 Improving Computational Efficiency

A bounding box generation and atlas selection was performed before multi-atlas based label fusion to reduce the computation cost. First, all images were linearly registered into the standard space of MINI152 (1 mm * 1 mm * 1 mm), a box large enough to cover the hippocampus in the space was determined following the procedure described in [6]. Then, by calculating the normalized mutual information between the target image and each atlas set image, 20 most similar atlas sets were selected for each target image after nonlinear registration [10]. The initial segmentation result of the image to be segmentation is obtained by MV based on the selected atlas images. Finally, MTL_SSLP was used to segment the voxels whose foreground or background were not 100% votes in majority voting [8].

3 The Experimental Results

3.1 Image Data

In this study, 35 MRI images were used, which were downloaded from ADNI database. The ADNI MRI scans were acquired using a sagittal 3D MP-RAGE T1-w sequence (TR = 2,400 ms, minimum full TE, TI = 1,000 ms, FOV = 240 mm, voxel size of 1.25 × 1.25 × 1.2 mm^3) [11].

3.2 Evaluation of Segmentation Accuracy

In our study, nine indicators (Dice, precision, recall, Jaccard, Harsdorff distance (HD), average distance (MD), and average symmetric surface distance (ASSD)) were calculated to measure the difference between label A obtained by manual segmentation by experts and label B obtained by the proposed segmentation method. The calculation formula is as follows:

$$\text{Dice} = 2\frac{V(A\cap B)}{V(A)+V(B)}, \text{Jaccard} = \frac{V(A\cap B)}{V(A\cup B)}, \text{Precision} = \frac{V(A\cap B)}{V(B)}, \text{Recall} = \frac{V(A\cap B)}{V(A)},$$

$$\text{MD} = mean_{e\in\partial A}(min_{f\in\partial B}d(e,f)),$$

$$\text{ASSD} = \left(mean_{e\in\partial A}\left(\min_{f\in\partial B}d(e,f)\right)+mean_{e\in\partial B}(\min_{f\in\partial A}d(e,f))\right)/2,$$

(5)

$$\text{HD} = max(H(A,B),H(B,A)), where\ H(A,B) = max_{e\in\partial A}min_{f\in\partial B}d(e,f)),$$

$$\text{RMSD} = \frac{\sqrt{D_A^2 + D_B^2}}{card\{\partial A\}+card\{\partial B\}}, where\ D_A^2 = \sum_{e\in\partial A}(\min_{f\in\partial B}min\ d(e,f)),$$

HD95: It's the same formula as HD, but delete 5% of the points that are largest distance in the data.

3.3 Parameter Tuning

The parameters of multi-task learning model were determined by an internal parametric setting of 5-fold cross-validation. We compared different values of training sample K in Table 1 (the number of positive and negative samples in the training), obtaining that the optimal $K = 140$ with Dice = 0.882 and 0.884 for left and right hippocampus segmentation.

Table 1. Experimental results under different K values. The bold values represent the best results.

K	Dice	
	Left	Right
100	0.880	0.883
200	0.880	0.882
140	**0.882**	**0.884**

3.4 Experimental Results

We set up five groups of contrast experiments, including Nonlocal patch (NLP) [27], Majority Voting (MV) [20], Metric learning (ML) [9], Local Label Learning (LLL) [6] and Random Local Binary Pattern (RLBP) [8]. Set the optimal parameters they recommend for each study. The leave-one-out cross-validation was adopted for the 35 data. Table 2 shows the comparison of results.

Table 2. Nine indices for experimental comparison in hippocampus segmentation. The bold values represent the best results. The segmentation methods are respectively: Majority Voting (MV), Nonlocal patch (NLP), Metric learning (ML), Local Label Learning (LLL), Random Local Binary Pattern (RLBP), and our method (MTL-SSLP).

		MV	NLP	RLBP	ML	LLL	MTL-SSLP
Dice	Left	0.8591	0.8777	0.8836	0.8837	0.8819	**0.8839**
	Right	0.8633	0.8801	0.8856	0.8857	0.8837	**0.8860**
Jaccard	Left	0.7546	0.7829	0.7922	0.7924	0.7896	**0.7926**
	Right	0.7602	0.7865	0.7952	0.7954	0.7921	**0.7957**
Precision	Left	0.8445	0.8667	0.8731	**0.8762**	0.8703	0.8681
	Right	0.8493	0.8701	0.8776	**0.8795**	0.8749	0.8749
Recall	Left	0.8790	0.8922	0.8962	0.8931	0.8959	**0.9020**
	Right	0.8821	0.8928	0.8964	0.8945	0.8954	**0.8998**
MD	Left	0.3004	0.2550	0.2670	0.2668	0.2529	**0.2357**
	Right	0.3033	0.2652	0.2752	0.2707	0.2686	**0.2491**
HD	Left	3.5851	3.4328	3.4799	**3.4241**	3.4321	3.4590
	Right	3.7225	3.4827	3.3152	3.2950	**3.2906**	3.4169
HD95	Left	1.4351	1.3328	1.2173	1.2496	1.2100	**1.138**
	Right	1.4639	1.2954	1.1365	1.1352	1.1984	**1.0821**
ASSD	Left	0.3596	0.3155	0.2888	0.2924	0.2959	**0.2877**
	Right	0.3648	0.3209	0.2938	0.2965	0.3064	**0.2887**
RMSD	Left	0.6690	0.6200	0.5889	0.5950	0.5925	**0.5862**
	Right	0.6740	0.6196	0.5835	0.5858	0.5981	**0.5678**

The mean value of 9 indicators for hippocampus segmentation assessment using different label fusion methods showed that our method achieved better segmentation. The voxel correlation information in the target image can be used to improve the performance of label fusion. A randomly selected subject and its with 3D segmentation of the left hippocampus by different segmentation methods were shown in Fig. 5, which demonstrated the best segmentation by the proposed MTL-SSLP method. The overall trend of all subjects regarding Dice index is shown in Fig. 6, and the proposed MTL-SSLP method obtains the best performance in hippocampus segmentation.

Besides, we compared the computational cost of different methods under comparison. The average time of label fusion when segmenting a subject was MV (0.03 min), NLP (3.73 min), RLBP (10.95 min), ML (46.18 min), LLL (4.8 min), MTL-SSLP (14.43 min). Compared with the single-task learning method, this study's multi-task learning method needs more computation, but faster than ML method.

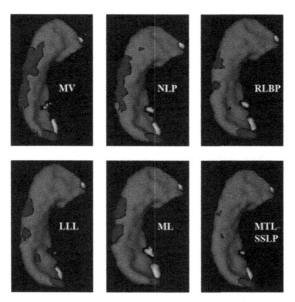

Fig. 5. The 3D segmentation results of hippocampus by different methods (Red indicates manual and segmentation results are overlap. Blue is the result of the manual. Green is the result of the segmentation.). The segmentation methods are respectively: Majority Voting (MV), Nonlocal patch (NLP), Metric learning (ML), Local Label Learning (LLL), Random Local Binary Pattern (RLBP), and our method (MTL-SSLP). (Color figure online)

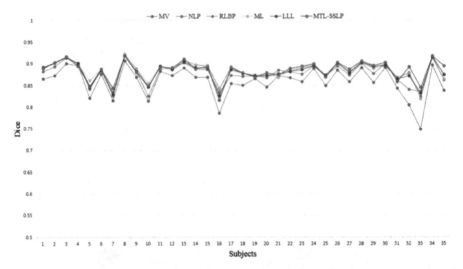

Fig. 6. Dice Comparison under different methods on all data. X-coordinate represents number of subjects, and y-coordinate represents the value of Dice. Majority Voting (MV), Nonlocal patch (NLP), Random Local Binary Pattern (RLBP), Metric learning (ML), Local Label Learning (LLL) and our method (MTL-SSLP).

4   Conclusion and Discussion

MAIS method has achieved good performance in most image segmentation studies, but most existing MAIS methods usually ignore the potential correlation between voxels in the target image. In this study, an image segmentation method based on multi-atlas is proposed by combining the multi-task learning method with the semi-supervised label propagation algorithm, aiming to integrate correlation between voxels in the image to be segmentation and improve image segmentation accuracy. Multi-task learning is to leverage useful information contained in the multiple related tasks and jointly train the pattern recognition model for the neighbor voxels in a patch in the target image. Semi-supervised label propagation method is to propagate the reliable segmentation information on the probabilistic map regularized by local and global spatial consistency. Both of them can effectively use the correlation between image voxels and provide more effective prediction in image segmentation.

The experimental results on EADC-ADNI dataset demonstrated that our method could obtain better performance in segmenting hippocampus. The segmentation performance of the MAIS method can be further improved by improving image registration and more effective atlas selection methods.

Acknowledgments. This work was supported by National Natural Science Foundation of China (61802330, 61802331, 61801415), Natural Science Foundation of Shandong Province (ZR2018BF008).

References

1. Zhao, K., et al.: Independent and reproducible hippocampal radiomic biomarkers for multisite Alzheimer's disease: diagnosis, longitudinal progress and biological basis. Sci. Bull. **65**(13) (2020)
2. Li, H., Habes, M., Wolk, D.A., Fan, Y.: A deep learning model for early prediction of Alzheimer's disease dementia based on hippocampal magnetic resonance imaging data. Alzheimer's Dementia J. Alzheimer's Assoc. **15**(8) (2019)
3. Hao, Y., Jiang, T., Yong, F.: Iterative multi-atlas based segmentation with multi-channel image registration and Jackknife context model. In: Proceedings/IEEE International Symposium on Biomedical Imaging: from Nano to Macro. IEEE International Symposium on Biomedical Imaging, pp. 900–903 (2012)
4. Hao, Y., Jiang, T. and Fan, Y.: Shape-constrained multi-atlas based segmentation with multi-channel registration. In: Proceedings of SPIE - The International Society for Optical Engineering, vol. 8314, no. 3, p. 124 (2012)
5. Hao, Y., et al.: Local label learning (L3) for multi-atlas based segmentation. Brainnetome Center 831481 (2012)
6. Hao, Y., et al.: Local label learning (LLL) for subcortical structure segmentation: application to hippocampus segmentation. Hum. Brain Mapp. **35**(6) (2014)
7. Eugenio, I.J., Sabuncu, M.R.: Multi-atlas segmentation of biomedical images: a survey. Med. Image Anal. **24**(1) (2015)
8. Zhu, H., Cheng, H., Fan, Y.: Random local binary pattern based label learning for multi-atlas segmentation. Med. Imaging (2015)
9. Zhu, H., Cheng, H., Yang, X., Fan, Y.: Metric learning for multi-atlas based segmentation of hippocampus. Neuroinformatics **15**(1), 41–50 (2016). https://doi.org/10.1007/s12021-016-9312-y
10. Zheng, Q., Wu, Y., Fan, Y.: Integrating semi-supervised and supervised learning methods for label fusion in multi-atlas based image segmentation. Front. Neuroinform. (2018)
11. Tiwari, A., Srivastava, S., Pant, M.: Brain tumor segmentation and classification from magnetic resonance images: review of selected methods from 2014 to 2019. Pattern Recogn. Lett. **131** (2020)
12. Avendi, M.R., Kheradvar, A., Jafarkhani, H.: A combined deep-learning and deformable-model approach to fully automatic segmentation of the left ventricle in cardiac MRI. Med. Image Anal. **30** (2016)
13. Zhang, L., Wang, Q., Gao, Y., Li, H., Wu, G., Shen, D.: Concatenated spatially-localized random forests for hippocampus labeling in adult and infant MR brain images. Neurocomputing **229** (2017)
14. Zu, C., et al.: Robust multi-atlas label propagation by deep sparse representation. Pattern Recogn. **63** (2017)
15. Yang, X., Fan, Y.: Coupled dictionary learning for joint MR image restoration and segmentation. Med. Imaging (2018)
16. Yang, X., Fan, Y.: Feature extraction using convolutional neural networks for multi-atlas based image segmentation. Med. Imaging (2018)
17. Alvén, J., Norlén, A., Enqvist, O., Kahl, F.: Überatlas: fast and robust registration for multi-atlas segmentation. Pattern Recogn. Lett. **80** (2016)
18. Doshi, J., et al.: MUSE: MUlti-atlas region segmentation utilizing ensembles of registration algorithms and parameters, and locally optimal atlas selection. NeuroImage **127** (2016)
19. Alchatzidis, S., Sotiras, A., Zacharaki, E.I., Paragios, N.: A discrete MRF framework for integrated multi-atlas registration and segmentation. Int. J. Comput. Vis. **121**(1), 169–181 (2016). https://doi.org/10.1007/s11263-016-0925-2

20. Rohlfing, T., Brandt, R., Menzel, R., Maurer Jr, C.R.: Evaluation of atlas selection strategies for atlas-based image segmentation with application to confocal microscopy images of bee brains. NeuroImage **21**(4) (2004)

21. Wang, H., Suh, J.W., Das, S.R., Pluta, J.B., Craige, C., Yushkevich, P.A: Multi-atlas segmentation with joint label fusion. IEEE Trans. Pattern Anal. Mach. Intell. **35**(3) (2013)

22. Roy, S., et al.: Subject-specific sparse dictionary learning for atlas-based brain MRI segmentation. IEEE J. Biomed. Health Inform. **19**(5) (2015)

23. Amoroso, N., et al.: Hippocampal unified multi-atlas network (HUMAN): protocol and scale validation of a novel segmentation tool. Phys. Med. Biol. **60**(22) (2015)

24. Khan, A.R., Cherbuin, N., Wen, W., Anstey, K.J., Sachdev, P., Beg, M.F.: Optimal weights for local multi-atlas fusion using supervised learning and dynamic information (SuperDyn): Valid. Hippocampus Segment. NeuroImage **56**(1) (2011)

25. Zhou, J., Chen, J. and Ye, J.: MALSAR: multi-task learning via structural regularization. Arizona State University (2011).http://www.MALSAR.org

26. Zhou, D., Bousquet, O., Lal, T.N., Weston, J., Olkopf, B.S.: Learning with local and global consistency. Adv. Neural Inf. Process. Syst. **16**(3) (2004)

27. Coupé, P., Manjón, J.V., Fonov, V., Pruessner, J., Robles, M., Collins, D.L.: Patch-based segmentation using expert priors: application to hippocampus and ventricle segmentation. NeuroImage **54**(2) (2011)

HPCSeg-Net: Hippocampus Segmentation Network Integrating Autofocus Attention Mechanism and Feature Recombination and Recalibration Module

Bin Liu[1], Qiang Zheng[1(✉)], Kun Zhao[2], Honglun Li[3], Chaoqing Ma[1], Shuanhu Wu[1], and Xiangrong Tong[1]

[1] School of Computer and Control Engineering, Yantai University, Yantai 264205, China
zhengqiang@ytu.edu.cn
[2] Beijing Advanced Innovation Centre for Biomedical Engineering, School of Biological Science and Medical Engineering, Beihang University, Beijing, China
[3] Departments of Medical Oncology and Radiology, Affiliated Yantai Yuhuangding Hospital of Qingdao University Medical College, Yantai 264000, China

Abstract. The analysis of hippocampus morphology based on magnetic resonance images is of great significance in the diagnosis of Alzheimer's disease and other neurological diseases, where accurate segmentation of the hippocampus is the premise. In this paper, a novel HPCSeg-Net was proposed for hippocampus segmentation based on the U-Net framework, which adopted a cascaded autofocus attention mechanism and adaptive feature recombination and recalibration module. The cascaded autofocus attention mechanism, which includes autofocus block and attention block, was devised for skip connection and semantic gap reduction between contracting and expansive pathways. The autofocus block was to generate powerful features by parallelizing multiple convolutional layers with different dilation rates, while the followed attention block was to suppress irrelevant areas around the hippocampus and highlighting the salient features. Moreover, feature recombination employed linear expansion and compression to generate complex semantic segmentation features, while the feature recalibration module was to collect context information and preserve spatial information. The experiments implemented on 133 studies from the ADNI dataset demonstrated that the proposed HPCSeg-Net could achieve competitive segmentation performance (average Dice index > 0.89) compared to multi-atlas segmentation methods.

Keywords: Hippocampal segmentation · U-Net · Autofocus · Attention · Feature recombination and recalibration

© Springer Nature Switzerland AG 2021
Y. Peng et al. (Eds.): ICIG 2021, LNCS 12889, pp. 773–782, 2021.
https://doi.org/10.1007/978-3-030-87358-5_63

1 Introduction

Hippocampal morphological change is one of the typical hallmarks of Alzheimer's disease (AD) [1, 2], where the volume or shape features have been widely applied in classifying AD and normal controls (NCs) [3, 4]. In hippocampus morphology-related analysis, hippocampus segmentation from magnetic resonance images (MRI) is an important premise. However, it is still challenging to accurately and rapidly segment the hippocampus due to its irregular shape and blurred boundary in MRI scans.

Among hippocampus segmentation methods, multi-atlas based image segmentation (MAIS), including majority voting (MV) [5], non-local patch (NLP) [6], local label learning (LLL) [7], random local binary pattern (RLBP) [8] and metric learning (ML) [9], random forests (RF) [10], integrated semi-supervised label propagation and random forests (RF-SSLP) [11] etc., are representative methods with high accuracy, which has been widely applied in a variety of brain MRI analysis. The MAIS workflow typically consists of image registration and label fusion, but both components suffer from high computation costs despite its considerable segmentation accuracy.

In recent years, deep learning has been solidly established as a robust technique, particularly in medical image segmentation. Pereira et al. [12] proposed feature recombination and recalibration block to generate more complex features, preserve spatial meaning, and achieve good brain tumor segmentation results. Zeng et al. [13] used 3D dense full convolution neural network to segment the hippocampus of premature infants and aged groups. Cao et al. [14] proposed a multi-task deep learning (MDL) method for joint hippocampus segmentation and clinical score regression using MRI. Liu et al. [4] proposed a multi-model deep learning framework based on convolutional neural network, which simultaneously completed the two tasks of Alzheimer's disease classification and hippocampus segmentation. The U-Net model caused the semantic gap problem [15] and the class imbalance in hippocampal segmentation makes the network unable to extract enough fine-grained information.

In our study, a novel HPCSeg-Net was proposed for hippocampus segmentation based on the U-Net framework, which adopted a cascaded autofocus attention mechanism and adaptive feature recombination and recalibration module. The cascaded autofocus attention mechanism, which includes autofocus block and attention block, was devised for skip connection and semantic gap reduction between contracting and expansive pathways. The autofocus block was to generate powerful features by parallelizing multiple convolutional layers with different dilation rates, while the followed attention block was to suppress irrelevant areas around the hippocampus and highlighting the salient features. Moreover, feature recombination employed linear expansion and compression to generate complex semantic segmentation features, while the feature recalibration module was to collect context information and preserve spatial information. Based on the data provided by the EADC–ADNI (European Alzheimer's Disease Consortium and Alzheimer's Disease Neuroimaging Initiative) harmonized segmentation protocol (www.hippocampal-protocol.net), we validated the proposed HPCSeg-Net in segmenting the hippocampal in MRI scans. Experimental results demonstrate that HPCSeg-Net could achieve competitive segmentation performance when comparing to multi-atlas segmentation methods.

2   Methods

2.1   The Proposed HPCSeg-Net for Hippocampus Segmentation

In our study, the HPCSeg-Net is established based on U-Net [16] framework, As shown in Fig. 1, other than the U-Net framework, there are three submodules: 1) AF Block (Autofocus Block); 2) Atte Block (Attention Block); 3) RR Block (Recombination and Recalibration Block). Specifically, the cascaded AF block and Atte block were employed for skip connection and semantic gap reduction between contracting and expansive pathways, while the RR block was devised to replace the standard convolutions in both contracting and expansive pathways.

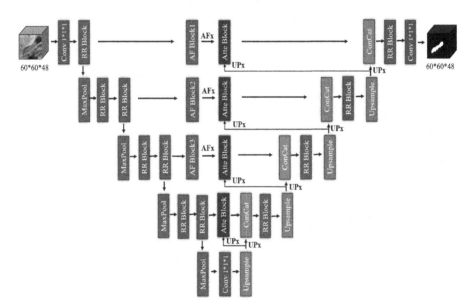

Fig. 1. The framework of HPCSeg-Net. Atte Block = Attention Block; RR Block = Recombination and Recalibration Block; AF Block = Autofocus Block. AF Block 1, AF Block 2 and AF Block 3 represent the autofocus Block with the number of parallels dilated convolution. UPx represents the feature map after Upsample, AFx represents the feature map after the AF block. Encoder: the down-sampling by Maxpool is performed with the kernels of $2 \times 2 \times 2$ and stride 2; Decoder: the up-sampling by Upsample is performed with the scale-factor of 2; Finally, outputs are converted to probabilistic segmentation of the hippocampal regions by applying softmax, and the probability output is converted to a binary mask.

Autofocus (AF) Block. The AF block [17] adopted in the proposed HPCSeg-Net was shown in Fig. 2(a). In our study, the AF block was added to the first three skip connections, in which, the attention mechanism can capture the importance of each scale when dealing with different positions of the image. In each AF block, multiple convolution layers with different dilation rates were used parallelly to obtain multi-scale information, generating multiple tensors with the same number of channels (F_k). The feature map is generated by

Softmax with a tensor with K channels, one for each scale (λ_k). The tensor F_k of different scales is multiplied by the corresponding attention map λ_k voxel. (the attention weights λ_k are shared across all channels of tensor for different dilated convolution). The multiple tensors were then merged through an attention mechanism. Given the fact that the feature map becomes smaller in the down-sampling pathway, we adopt a decreased number of parallel dilated convolution strategies (from top to bottom is 3, 2 and 1 respectively). The AF block was not added in the deep layer of skip connection due to a small-sized feature map ($8 \times 8 \times 6$ in our study), otherwise the parallel convolutions with different dilation rates will cause a decreased accuracy.

Attention (Atte) Block. Followed by the AF block and inspired by the attention gate model [18], an Atte block was added to the skip connection, consisting of convolutional layers, batch normalized (BN), and ReLU activation and sigmoid. As shown in Fig. 2(b), UPx represents the feature map after Upsample, and AFx represents the feature map after the autofocus layer. After fusing the features UPX and AFx, the weight matrix Λ was obtained by sigmoid operation. Finally, features from irrelevant regions were suppressed by multiplying weight matrix Λ to AFx through the attention mechanism.

Recombination and Recalibration (RR) Block. The RR block [12] was also adopted in our study. The architecture of RR Block is shown in Fig. 2(c). Additionally, considering

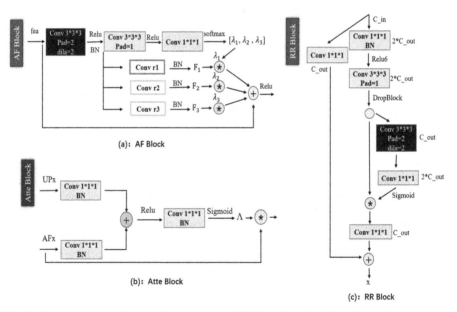

Fig. 2. The three submodules used in the proposed HPCSeg-Net. (a) AF Block: r1, r2, r3 represent different dilation rates (2, 4, 6 respectively), $\lambda_1, \lambda_2, \lambda_3$ represent an attention map that corresponds to the k-th scale, F_1, F_2, F_3 represent the output tensor of the different scale. (b) Atte Block: UPx represents the feature map after Upsample, AFx represents the feature map after the autofocus block, and Λ represents the weight matrix (c) RR Block: C_in represents the input channel and C_out represents the output channel.

the over-parameterization, the RR block was revised by adding a DropBlock [19] to the 3 × 3 × 3 convolution in the trunk branch. The DropBlock is a structured form of dropout mechanism that is particularly useful for the regularization of convolutional networks. In the down-sampling and up-sampling stages of the hippocampus segmentation model, the RR block was used to replace the standard convolutions to generate fine-grained information and collect contextual information while preserving spatial information.

2.2 Loss Function

In this study, the Dice loss function in (1) was used in the HPCSeg-Net model with values ranging from 0 to 1.

$$DiceLoss = 1 - \frac{2|A \cap B|}{|A| + |B|} \tag{1}$$

where A represents manual segmentation and B represents automatic segmentation using the deep learning model.

2.3 Data Preprocessing

All images were affinely registered to the MNI152 template ($1 \times 1 \times 1$ mm^3). Considering the small volume of the hippocampus relative to the human brain, the number of voxels is much smaller than that of background voxels, leading to serious class-imbalance problems. In order to reduce the background voxels, a box big sufficient to cover the hippocampus is determined in this space [7], and crop each MR image into an image patch with a size of 60 × 60 × 48 (Fig. 3). Additionally, the right hippocampus was flipped to the left side in the training process (Fig. 4) for data augmentation.

The input of the HPCSeg-Net is an image patch with the size of 60 × 60 × 48. In order to learn deeper features through multiple down-sampling, the image patch was changed to 64 × 64 × 48 by a zero-padding.

Fig. 3. Hippocampal patch generation in MRI (Sagittal) (60 × 60 × 48).

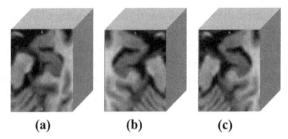

Fig. 4. Hippocampus flip. (a) Left hippocampus; (b) Right hippocampus; (c) Right hippocampus after flipping.

2.4 Evaluation

In order to evaluate the segmentation performance of the HPCSeg-Net proposed in this study, Dice similarity coefficient in (2) was calculated as follows

$$Dice(A, B) = \frac{2|A \cap B|}{|A| + |B|} \tag{2}$$

where A was hippocampus segmentation by deep learning model, B was the manual segmentation. In our study, Dice (A, B) represents the overlap between manual segmentation and automated segmentaton by HPCSeg-Net.

3 Experiments and Result

3.1 Dataset

In order to test the performance of the HPCSeg-Net, the brain MR images and hippocampal segmentation labels of 133 subjects obtained from EADC-ADNI were used in this paper, consisting of 98 subjects from a preliminary release and 35 subjects from a final release. The ADNI MRI scans were acquired using a sagittal 3D MP-RAGE T1-w sequence (TR = 2,400 ms, minimum full TE, TI = 1,000 ms, FOV = 240 mm, voxel size of $1.25 \times 1.25 \times 1.2$ mm^3) [20]. More details about the image capture program can be found on the ADNI website (www.adni-info.org). In this study, the preliminary release of the 133 subjects was divided into the training set (80 subjects) and validation set (18 subjects), the final release of the 35 subjects was used as the test set.

3.2 Implementation

Pytorch deployed on NVIDIA Geforce RTX 2080 GPU was used to implement HPCSeg-Net. The learning rate was set to 1×10^{-4}, and decayed by 10% every 30 epochs. In DropBlock, the block-size = 4, drop-prob = 0.1, the batch size was set to 2, and the training time was set to 70 epochs.

3.3 Result

On the test set, the hippocampus segmentation accuracy of the HPCSeg-Net was summarized in Table 1, with an average segmentation accuracy of 0.8908. Moreover, the proposed HPCSeg-Net was also compared with MAIS methods, including MV, LLL, NLP, RLBP, ML, RF and RF-SSLP. The experimental results in Table 2 demonstrated that the proposed HPCSeg-Net could achieve the best performance in hippocampus segmentation.

Table 1. Hippocampus segmentation accuracy of the HPCSeg-Net

	Left	Right	Average
Dice	0.892	0.8896	0.8908

Table 2. The Dice index of different hippocampal segmentation methods, including majority voting (MV), non-local patch (NLP), local label learning (LLL), random local binary pattern (RLBP), metric learning (ML), random forests (RF), integrated semi-supervised label propagation and random forests (RF-SSLP) and HPCSeg-Net. Best results in bold.

	Left hippocampus	Right hippocampus	Average
MV	0.8602	0.8633	0.8618
NLP	0.8777	0.8802	0.8790
LLL	0.8820	0.8838	0.8829
RLBP	0.8836	0.8857	0.8846
ML	0.8838	0.8858	0.8848
RF	0.8850	0.8857	0.8853
RF-SSLP	0.8898	**0.8908**	0.8903
HPCSeg-Net	**0.8920**	0.8896	**0.8908**

Moreover, a subject was randomly selected from the test set, and its 2D and 3D segmentation comparison under different methods was presented in Figs. 5 and 6, respectively. A higher consistency between manual segmentation and automated segmentation by HPCSeg-Net was observed.

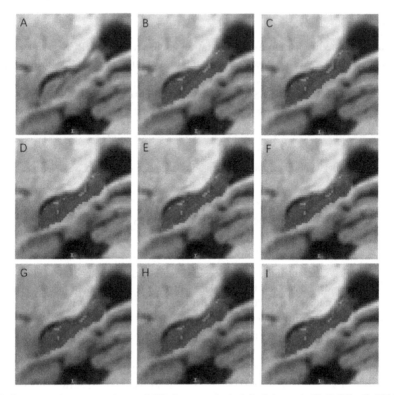

Fig. 5. Segmentation comparison of 2D images. A (original image), B (MV), C (NLP), D (LLL), E (RLBP), F (ML), G (RF), H (RF-SSLP), I (HPCSeg-Net). Red: manual segmentation, Green: algorithm segmentation results, Blue: overlap between manual segmentation and algorithm segmentation results. (Color figure online)

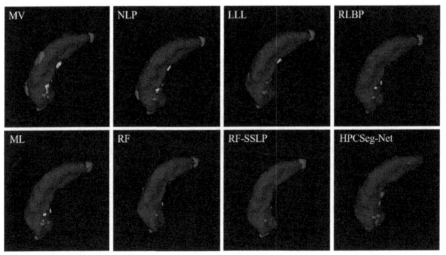

Fig. 6. Segmentation comparison of 3D images. Red: manual segmentation results, Green: algorithm segmentation results, Blue: overlap between manual segmentation and algorithm segmentation results. (Color figure online)

4 Discussion and Conclusion

In order to segment the hippocampus accurately and efficiently, we proposed a novel hippocampal segmentation method HPCSeg-Net integrating a cascaded autofocus attention mechanism and adaptive feature recombination and recalibration module. Specifically, the feature recombination and recalibration module were used to replace the standard convolutions to obtain informative fine-grained semantic information. Additionally, an autofocus module with different dilated convolution was added to the skip connection to obtain multi-scale information and reduce the semantic gap. The experimental results demonstrated a better performance when comparing with the MAIS methods. The proposed HPCSeg-Net can achieve an average Dice index of 89.08%.

The segmentation efficiency of the proposed method was also compared in our study. We counted the average running time of 70 MR images segmented by the MAIS methods in 35 subjects, including MV (0.03 min), NLP (3.73 min), RLBP (10.95 min), ML (46.18 min), LLL (4.8 min), RF (46.7 min) and RF-SSLP (48 min). Comparing with the MAIS methods, the proposed HPCSeg-Net in this study takes only 0.35 min to segment the 70 MR images in test set, and the average segmentation time is less than 1 s. Meanwhile, the segmentation can achieve the best performance comparing with MAIS methods. The results demonstrated that the proposed HPCSeg-Net is better than the MAIS methods in segmentation performance and computational cost.

From Figs. 5 and 6, some boundary voxels of the hippocampus were not perfectly segmented for both multi-atlas segmentation and the HPCSeg-Net. A suggestion to further improve the accuracy is adding a loss function focusing on boundary learning. In addition, the accuracy of hippocampal segmentation could be further improved by adding more training data.

In conclusion, the HPCSeg-Net proposed in this paper improves hippocampal segmentation in MR images in both segmentation accuracy and computational efficiency, which could help calculate its volume and measure its shape accurately and rapidly in medical image analysis.

Acknowledgments. This work was supported by National Natural Science Foundation of China (61802330, 61802331, 61801415), Natural Science Foundation of Shandong Province (ZR2018BF008).

References

1. Shi, F., et al.: Hippocampal volume and asymmetry in mild cognitive impairment and Alzheimer's disease: meta-analyses of MRI studies. Hippocampus **19**, 1055–1064 (2009)
2. Zhao, K., et al.: Independent and reproducible hippocampal radiomic biomarkers for multisite Alzheimer's disease: diagnosis, longitudinal progress and biological basis. Sci. Bull. **65**, 1103–1113 (2020)
3. Lin, W., et al.: Convolutional neural networks-based MRI image analysis for the Alzheimer's disease prediction from mild cognitive impairment. Front. Neurosci. **12**, 777 (2018)
4. Liu, M., et al.: A multi-model deep convolutional neural network for automatic hippocampus segmentation and classification in Alzheimer's disease. NeuroImage **208**, 116459 (2020)

5. Rohlfing, T., et al.: Evaluation of atlas selection strategies for atlas-based image segmentation with application to confocal microscopy images of bee brains. Neuroimage **21**, 1428–1442 (2004)

6. Coupé, P., et al.: Patch-based segmentation using expert priors: application to hippocampus and ventricle segmentation. Neuroimage **54**, 940–954 (2011)

7. Hao, Y., et al.: Local label learning (LLL) for subcortical structure segmentation: application to hippocampus segmentation. Hum. Brain Mapp. **35**, 2674–2697 (2014)

8. Zhu, H., et al.: Random local binary pattern based label learning for multi-atlas segmentation. In: Medical Imaging 2015: Image Processing, p. 94131B. International Society for Optics and Photonics (2015)

9. Zhu, H., et al.: Metric learning for multi-atlas based segmentation of hippocampus. Neuroinformatics **15**, 41–50 (2017)

10. Han, X.: Learning-boosted label fusion for multi-atlas auto-segmentation. In: Wu, G., Zhang, D., Shen, D., Yan, P., Suzuki, K., Wang, F. (eds.) MLMI 2013. LNCS, vol. 8184, pp. 17–24. Springer, Cham (2013). https://doi.org/10.1007/978-3-319-02267-3_3

11. Zheng, Q., et al.: Integrating semi-supervised and supervised learning methods for label fusion in multi-atlas based image segmentation. Front. Neuroinform. **12**, 69 (2018)

12. Pereira, S., Alves, V., Silva, C.A.: Adaptive feature recombination and recalibration for semantic segmentation: application to brain tumor segmentation in MRI. In: Frangi, A.F., Schnabel, J.A., Davatzikos, C., Alberola-López, C., Fichtinger, G. (eds.) MICCAI 2018. LNCS, vol. 11072, pp. 706–714. Springer, Cham (2018). https://doi.org/10.1007/978-3-030-00931-1_81

13. Zeng, D., et al.: Hippocampus segmentation for preterm and aging brains using 3D densely connected fully convolutional networks. IEEE Access **8**, 97032–97044 (2020)

14. Cao, L., et al.: Multi-task neural networks for joint hippocampus segmentation and clinical score regression. Multimedia Tools Appl. **77**(22), 29669–29686 (2018). https://doi.org/10.1007/s11042-017-5581-1

15. Ibtehaz, N., Rahman, M.S.: MultiResUNet: rethinking the U-Net architecture for multimodal biomedical image segmentation. Neural Netw. **121**, 74–87 (2020)

16. Ronneberger, O., Fischer, P., Brox, T.: U-net: convolutional networks for biomedical image segmentation. In: Navab, N., Hornegger, J., Wells, W.M., Frangi, A.F. (eds.) MICCAI 2015. LNCS, vol. 9351, pp. 234–241. Springer, Cham (2015). https://doi.org/10.1007/978-3-319-24574-4_28

17. Qin, Y., et al.: Autofocus layer for semantic segmentation. In: Frangi, A.F., Schnabel, J.A., Davatzikos, C., Alberola-López, C., Fichtinger, G. (eds.) MICCAI 2018. LNCS, vol. 11072, pp. 603–611. Springer, Cham (2018). https://doi.org/10.1007/978-3-030-00931-1_69

18. Oktay, O., et al.: Attention U-Net: learning where to look for the pancreas. arXiv preprint arXiv:1804.03999 (2018)

19. Ghiasi, G., et al.: Dropblock: a regularization method for convolutional networks. arXiv preprint arXiv:1810.12890 (2018)

20. Jack Jr., C.R., et al.: The Alzheimer's disease neuroimaging initiative (ADNI): MRI methods. J. Magn. Resonan. Imaging Off. J. Int. Soc. Magn. Resonan. Med. **27**, 685–691 (2008)

Uncertainty-Based Visual Guidance for Interactive Medical Volume Segmentation Editing

Sheng Shi, Bowei Zhou, Yibo Song, and Li Chen[(✉)]

School of Software, Tsinghua University, Beijing 100084, China
chenlee@tsinghua.edu.cn

Abstract. The existing automatic medical volume segmentation methods are usually not accurate enough, and manually editing the segmentation result is still very tedious. The paper proposes a novel editing framework for medical volume data segmentation by providing users simple and convenient 3D interactions under the visual guidance of segmentation uncertainty measurements. In the system, the volume data will be visualized in a combination of volume rendering and surface rendering. Since it is hard for users to obtain volume data information as context from surface rendering, we have designed uncertainty metrics based on mesh shape descriptors and volume image structure descriptors. The measures are mapped and rendered on the segmentation boundary mesh to indicate the uncertainty of the current segmentation boundary, which can guide users in finding a optimal editing region to start editing. Existing interactive volume segmentation editing methods usually have a demand of per-slice 2D interactions which are inconvenient and time-consuming. Compared to these methods, our system allows users to use sketch-based interactions to generate editing slices of custom shapes, and refine the contours on 2D slices to edit the current medical segmentation result. The edit results will be propagated to the 3D volume using Laplacian mesh editing techniques, which makes only a few slice interactions required. The experiments have shown that our method can effectively improve the accuracy of segmentation results. Compared with the similar methods, the number of interactions is also effectively reduced.

Keywords: Volume segmentation · Interactive segmentation · Visualization · Uncertainty measure

1 Introduction

Volume data segmentation is a typical problem in the field of image segmentation. It has a wide range of applications, especially in digital medical field. However, medical volume data are complex and the boundaries of segmentation targets such as tumors are often unclear. As a result, the existing automatic segmentation methods are usually not accurate enough, and manually editing the segmentation result is still necessary.

Volume data segmentation editing methods can be classified into two types: 2D and 3D editing. Compared to 3D volume rendering and surface rendering, the original

© Springer Nature Switzerland AG 2021
Y. Peng et al. (Eds.): ICIG 2021, LNCS 12889, pp. 783–796, 2021.
https://doi.org/10.1007/978-3-030-87358-5_64

volume data can be displayed more accurately on 2D slices. However, it needs the user to have a good understanding of the 3D structure of the volume data, and can identify the foreground objects that need to be segmented. In addition, it is difficult to propagate the results of 2D slice segmentation to the 3D volume. For more complex data, users often need to label a large number of slices, which is very time-consuming. The operations in 3D view are very intuitive, for the user can directly see the shape of the reconstructed volume. However, it is difficult to display the context information of the original volume data in the 3D view, which makes it difficult for the user to determine where to start editing and in which direction to edit.

The interactive segmentation editing method proposed in this paper allows users to interactively generate curved editing surfaces by cutting on the segmentation target. Compared to traditional methods of operating on a plane, the generated curved editing surface can be adapted to different shapes of segmentation targets, which can reduce the number of interactions required. By finding the intersection of the surface and the segmentation, we can get a contour line. Users can easily adjust the segmentation by adjusting this contour. We apply Laplacian mesh editing techniques to propagate this edition to the 3D volume. At the same time, a mesh optimization method is applied to make the segmentation result closer to the boundary of the target in the volume data.

In addition, in the process of interactive editing, it is often difficult for a user to determine where to edit by observing the mesh of 3D segmentation. Existing works have taken the idea of propagating edits on a few 2D slices to 3D, such as the work of Heckel et al. [1]. But there is less work to give users visual segmentation guidance, which can be very helpful in the segmentation editing process. In this paper, based on the user guidance, we have designed a segmentation uncertainty measure based on mesh shape descriptors and volume image structure descriptors. And users are prompted by the mesh-based visualization technology to further improve the segmentation interactive editing process and reduce the number of user interactions.

The main contributions of this paper are:

- A novel editing framework for 3D medical data segmentation by the visual guidance of segmentation uncertainty measurements;
- A measurement method for the 3D segmentation uncertainty and visual hints for generating editing surfaces by volume-surface fused rendering;
- A propagation mechanism from 2D slice contour edits to 3D segmentation boundary based on volume data feature constrains.

Segmentation editing experiments on volume medical data show that the framework proposed in this paper can provide users with useful visual guidance. Users can edit the segmentation easily and efficiently, and the segmentation accuracy after editing is improved. Compared with similar software, it can also reduce editing time and interaction times.

2 Overview of the Method

The pipeline of the interaction framework proposed in this paper is as follows:

Step 1: Generating segmentation results using automatic methods. As the proposed method is a method for editing the segmentation, it can be combined with any volume segmentation algorithm, such as U-net [2].

Step 2: Visualizing the segmentation results with the principle of Focus + Context using volume-surface fused rendering. Volume rendering provides an overview of the raw data, and the mesh provides detailed features of the segmentation results.

Step 3: Computing and visualizing the uncertainty measure of the segmentation. The measure is mapped on the mesh, which can assist users in finding areas of interest.

Step 4: Generating editing slice by drawing a stroke on the mesh and adjusting segmentation results on the slice.

Step 5: Propagating edits of 2D slices to the 3D segmentation boundary through an optimization algorithm. This step uses Laplacian mesh optimization as the basic framework while incorporating the volume data information into the optimization method.

Repeat Step 2 to Step 5 until the segmentation accuracy is high enough.

Three key techniques are used in the above pipeline. We are going to introduce them in the next three sections.

3   Uncertainty-Based Visual Guidance

This paper attempts to calculate the mesh shape descriptors and volume image structure descriptors. By designing a variety of visualization methods, users would be guided in finding the region of interest that may have problems during the editing stage (Figs. 1 and 2).

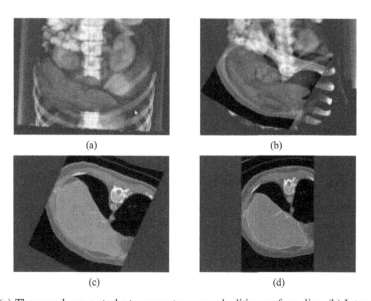

(a)   (b)

(c)   (d)

Fig. 1. (a) The user draws a stroke to generate a curved editing surface slice. (b) Intersect with the segmentation mesh. (c) Generate a segmentation contour. (d) Contour editing mode on a 2D slice.

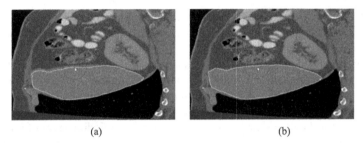

(a)   (b)

Fig. 2. Edit the contour on a 2D slice. (a) Use the brush tool to drag and modify the contour. (b) Editing results.

3.1 Preprocessing

This paper uses the method of Lempitsky et al. [3] to smooth the mesh generated by the marching cubes algorithm. The method mainly uses the second-order gradient constraint to optimize and reconstruct the original data field, so that the optimized volume data field F satisfies:

$$\int \left(\frac{\partial^2 F}{\partial x^2}\right)^2 + \left(\frac{\partial^2 F}{\partial y^2}\right)^2 + \left(\frac{\partial^2 F}{\partial z^2}\right)^2 dV \rightarrow min \tag{1}$$

This optimization problem is a quadratic programming problem, which can be solved using a linear least squares method.

3.2 Local Shape Feature of the Segmentation Boundary

In this paper, the mesh vertex normal vector is selected as the shape descriptor to describe the local shape in the neighborhood near each vertex. We apply the method of Panozzo et al. [4] to calculate the segmentation boundary normal. This method supports calculating shape features at the vertices of the mesh on multiple scales, and the noise can be effectively reduced by controlling the scale. The main idea is to use the quadratic polynomial to fit at the vertices, to obtain the parametric surface in the local coordinate system. The first-order partial derivative is used to calculate the tangent vector, as well as the normal vector.

3.3 Structural Feature of the Volume

The volume data is essentially the sampling result of the spatial scalar field, and the shape features are contained in the volume image information. It is possible to use image processing algorithms to extract the normal vector features. The relationship between the normal vector and the gradient in the volume data $I(x, y, z)$ is as follows:

$$g = \left(g_x, g_y, g_z\right)^T = \left(\frac{\partial I}{\partial x}, \frac{\partial I}{\partial y}, \frac{\partial I}{\partial z}\right)^T \tag{2}$$

$$n = \frac{g}{|g|} \tag{3}$$

This method needs to calculate the first-order gradient g of the volume data. Since the volume gradient uses differential for numerical approximation, the gradient calculation is highly sensitive to noise, and the noise influence needs to be considered, to improve the accuracy of the gradient.

In order to reduce the influence of noise on the gradient calculation, a common method is to smooth the volume firstly. To improve the efficiency and reduce the memory consumption, referring to the work of Rieger et al. [5], we use the Gaussian derivatives-based filtering method to calculate the gradient.

The gradient is calculated using convolution as follows:

$$g_x = I(x, y, x) \cdot G_x(\sigma_D) \tag{4}$$

where g_x is a first-order Gaussian differential kernel, as well as g_y and g_z. σ_D is the standard deviation of the Gaussian kernel, and also determines the size of the convolution kernel as the scale parameter of the algorithm. After these calculations, we get the normal features of the volume.

3.4 Segmentation Uncertainty Measure

By comparing the mesh shape feature and volume structure feature, we can measure the accuracy of the current segmentation. Cosine similarity is defined by the comparison of the segmentation boundary normal $n_M(V)$, and the volume gradient $g_I(V)$:

$$\text{Sim}(V) = \frac{n_M(V) \cdot g_I(V)}{|n_M(V)||g_I(V)|} \tag{5}$$

Due to the uncertainty of the positive/negative of the volume gradient, the length of the above cosine distance is taken, and the segmentation uncertainty on the vertex V is defined as follows:

$$\alpha(V) = 1 - |\text{Sim}(V)| \tag{6}$$

For the segmentation uncertainty metric proposed in this subsection, its value and its spatial distribution can be used as a measure of the current segmentation, participating in the segmentation editing guidance process.

3.5 Visualization

In this paper, the mesh-based visualization is used to visualize the volume data information and the segmentation uncertainty measure on the surface of the mesh to provide editing guidance for the user. Using the mesh as the target of editing visualization is more intuitive than the volume data.

Volume Intensity Visualization. Volume intensity gives users the most impression. Referring to the work of Ijiri et al. [6], plotting the intensity of the volume data on the mesh can guide users to find out the segmentation errors. When viewing the segmentation result in this mode, users need to pay attention to the region where the intensity of the mesh surface changes abruptly. These mutations often indicate that the segmentation boundary spans different volume data regions and needs further editing so that the boundary roughly coincides with the edge in the volume data. Through the method of slice interaction, users can further confirm whether there is an error.

Volume Gradient Visualization. In order to calculate the normal information of the volume data, the volume gradient is calculated as above using a Gaussian differential kernel-based convolution method. The color coding is performed according to the gradient length, and the gradient information is visualized on the surface of the mesh for the user to check the current segmentation, as shown in Fig. 3. By observing this visualization, the user can get the gradient information corresponding to each region in the segmentation mesh. If there is a region that is obviously discontinuous on the volume, it indicates that there is a gradient mutation.

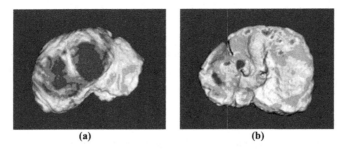

(a)   (b)

Fig. 3. Volume gradient visualization.

Uncertainty Visualization. The segmentation uncertainty metric is defined by the cosine distance of the normal vectors in Eq. (6). The visualization is shown in Fig. 4. The uncertainty may present some patterns, which is more visually obvious than the gradient and other metrics. Here are some examples of these patterns.

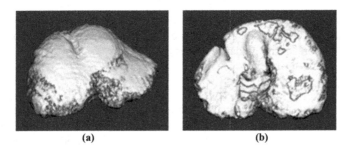

(a)   (b)

Fig. 4. Uncertainty visualization

4   Editing Slice Generation

Classical triaxial slicing method has limitations for specific volume data structures, typically tubular structures such as bones and blood vessels. Referring to the mesh editing framework proposed by Ijiri et al. [6], the framework in this paper implements a generation method of slices by drawing strokes with user interaction, extending along the line of sight and intersecting the volume data. In this way, the user can have better control over the position and shape of the slices.

The line drawn by the user on the screen can be regarded as a polyline consisting of a number of points. The polyline is extended along the line of sight and intersects with the volume rendering texture to construct a curved editing surface slice in the volume rendering space, as shown in Fig. 5. The intensity data of the original volume is displayed on the slice for the user to check.

At the same time, the cutting surface also intersects the segmentation mesh to get a contour curve that can be drawn on the slice generated in the previous step. The isosurface mesh is usually large in data size. In order to improve the algorithm efficiency, this step uses the GPU parallelizing mesh intersection method to find the intersection contour. These steps generate a curved editing surface which is difficult for the user to edit directly, so consider expanding it into a plane. The final result is shown in Fig. 1. The editing framework of this paper implements a brush tool for the user to edit the segmentation contour on the slice. The modified contour vertices will participate in the mesh optimization stage, which will be propagated to the 3D segmentation mesh.

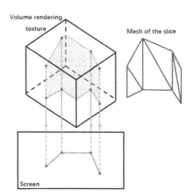

Fig. 5. Curved surface slice generated by user's stroke.

5   Edit Propagation Algorithm

The process of propagating the user's edits on the 2D slice to the 3D segmentation boundary needs to preserve the local shape of the mesh. It is implemented using mesh optimization method. The Laplacian mesh deformation method proposed by Sorkine et al. [7] meets the requirements of edit propagation, for its goal is to minimize the local shape changes of the mesh during the mesh deformation process. We choose it as the basic optimization framework and combine the volume data information into the optimization method.

The energy function designed in this paper is as follows:

$$E(V') = \|L(V') - T(V')\delta_0\|^2 + \omega\|MV' - C\|^2 - \kappa G(V') \tag{7}$$

where V' is the optimized vertex coordinate. $L(V')$, $T(V')$ and $G(V')$ represent the Laplacian coordinate, the local verterx transformation, and the volume gradient of V', respectively. δ_0 is the initial Laplacian coordinate. M is the vertex linear combination parameter, and C is the control point obtained by user interaction. ω and κ are weighting parameters.

The method deforms the mesh by minimizing the change in Laplacian coordinates of the mesh vertices and constraining the position of the control points. In order to make the deformed vertices closer to the volume data edges, a volume gradient constraint is added to the optimization function. The advantage is that the Laplacian operator of the mesh can maintain the local shape feature of the mesh, so that the deformation result is more natural. And the volume gradient constraint is introduced, to improve the segmentation precision.

The problem with this approach is that the existence of volume gradient constraints breaks the linearity of the Laplacian framework. Volume gradient functions are usually non-convex and non-smooth, which cannot be optimized by the classical gradient descent methods. Therefore, the semi-quadratic decomposition algorithm is introduced in this paper, to decompose the problem. Auxiliary variable and slack variable are introduced to replace the non-convex terms in the original function, and the two sub-problems are optimized separately. After the replacement, the energy function becomes Eq. (8), since $G(V')$ is non-convex, the auxiliary variable P and the slack variable are introduced. The auxiliary variable P is used to replace the V' in the non-convex function $G(V')$, and the $\|V' - P\|^2$ term is added so that P is as close as possible to the replaced V'. As approaches infinity, there is E' approaches E.

$$E'(V') = \|L(V') - T(V')\delta_0\|^2 + \omega\|MV' - C\|^2 - \kappa G(P) + \theta\|V' - P\|^2 \tag{8}$$

The optimization problem can be split into two sub-problems. Sub-problem 1 takes the vertex coordinates V' as an unknown variable and P as a known auxiliary variable. At this point the equation is a linear equation that can be solved using a least squares framework. Sub-problem 2 takes the auxiliary variable P as an unknown variable and V' as a known variable. This problem is independent of each vertex. Here, the neighborhood search method is used to search along the normal direction within a certain range near the vertex, and try to search for a position with a higher gradient to minimize the energy function. Through this decomposition, we decompose the non-convex optimization problem into a linear optimization problem and a neighborhood search problem. By iterative optimization, these two processes can approximate the solution of the original problem.

6 Experiment

6.1 Interactive Editing Example

This section demonstrates the segmentation editing process and mesh optimization effects of the framework proposed by this paper through a case study of kidney segmentation editing. First, the user loads the CT data and the segmentation data, and determines the position and shape of the target kidney by observing the volume rendering and the segmentation mesh. The region of interest is found by drawing and generating slices. An under-segmented region is shown in Fig. 6a. Through 3D observation, it is obvious that the contour generated according to the current segmentation is inconsistent with the edge structure in the volume data.

The user enters the contour editing mode on the 2D slice, and the contour is adjusted by using the brush tool, to match the boundary in the slice image, as shown by the green and yellow contours in Fig. 6c. Before starting the mesh optimization, the user adjusts the radius of the editing area, and the system displays the current editing area size in real time, as shown in Fig. 6d. Adjusting the editing area will change the number of vertices participating in the optimization, which will affect the time consumption the optimization algorithm.

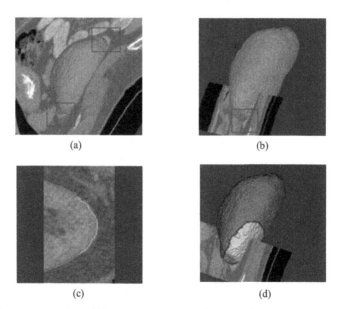

(a)

(b)

(c)

(d)

Fig. 6. Kidney segmentation editing process. (a) Look for the region of interest. (b) Draw a slice for the area. (c) Edit the contour in the 2D contour editing mode, green is the initial contour, and yellow is the edited contour. (d) Adjust the size of the propagation area, the blue boundary is a fixed contour, and the yellow is the area to be optimized. (Color figure online)

In the experiment, the role of the Laplacian framework is that the mesh deforms to the boundary according to the contour constraint, and meanwhile drives other vertices in the editing area (yellow) on both sides of the slices to move in a why that maintains the original shape of the mesh. The effect of the volume gradient is that, with the progress of iteration, the mesh locally produces a slight deformation, changing the local shape of the original mesh, so that some of the vertices are closer to the boundary. The algorithm tends to converge at the end of the optimization process. The results are shown in Fig. 7.

(a)   (b)

Fig. 7. The result of editing propagation optimization. (a) Before. (b) After.

6.2 Uncertainty Measure Guidance Example

The data used in this experiment was obtained from the LiTS CT dataset [8]. The system reads the CT data and the segmentation result, and performs the smoothing algorithm to the segmentation mesh. It is not easy for the user to decide where to start the segmentation editing when viewing the mesh shown in Fig. 8a. Through the intensity visualization as shown in Fig. 8b, the user finds that the intensity of volume on the mesh surface is unevenly distributed, which may be because the corresponding region crosses the boundary structure in the volume data. Select the area in Fig. 8c and use the interactive

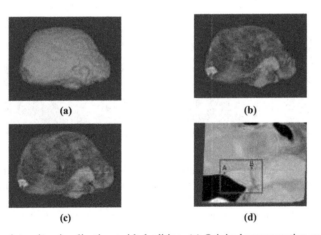

(a)   (b)

(c)   (d)

Fig. 8. Volume intensity visualization guided editing. (a) Original segmentation results. (b) The intensity visualization. (c) Find a region of interest and generate a slice by stroke. (d) The under-segmented area.

method to generate the slice. In Fig. 8d, the slice shows that there is an error with the AB segment of the current segmentation boundary. The boundary at point A fails to extend along the obvious black boundary, but enters the interior of the segmentation target, resulting in an abrupt change of the intensity of the mesh surface. It can be further edited using the 2D slice editing method.

In addition, the user can switch to the uncertainty visualization mode. The user can easily distinguish the areas that need attention from the uncertainty visualization view in Fig. 9a. The two segmentation uncertainty patterns described above are shown in Fig. 9b to f. The "contour" patterns in (b) and (c) show the rib structure near the liver, providing the user with a volume data context. The user can determine whether the region near the rib matches the segmentation boundary based on a priori knowledge of the medical data. The "noise" pattern in (d), (e), and (f) shows that there may be errors. In this region, the volume structure is relatively uniform, which makes the volume gradient fail to show an obvious distribution trend. Then the user should observe the 2D contour by

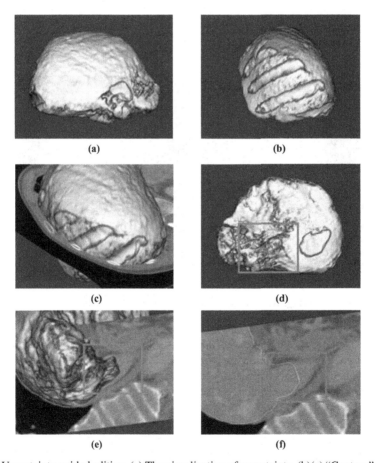

Fig. 9. Uncertainty guided editing. (a) The visualization of uncertainty. (b)(c) "Contour" pattern. (d)(e)(f) "Noise" pattern.

further slicing the similar region, and uses the previous method to edit and correct the segmentation error region.

6.3 Comparisons

For comparison, the commercial software TurtleSeg [9] was used to segment the same liver data. TurtleSeg also performs interactive editing based on contours.

The software's segmentation process is:

Step 1: Observe the target through volume rendering and triaxial view.
Step 2: Select a slice to mark the initial contour.
Step 3: The system gives the recommended slices according to the user's marks.
Step 4: The user repeatedly marks the contour of the slices recommended by the system.
Step 5: The algorithm reconstructs the surface based on all the contours to generate the segmentation result.

The contour interaction is based on the 3D live wire algorithm [10], which can automatically fit the boundary in the 2D slice for extension, as shown in Fig. 10.

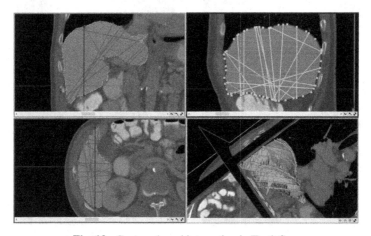

Fig. 10. Contour-based interaction in TurtleSeg.

For the same liver data, TurtleSeg and our method were used for segmentation, 10 contour interactions were used respectively. The experimental results show that using the editing method of this paper can achieve better editing results. Since the method supports the user to generate slices by brush strokes freely, the user can select the most suitable view to edit the target. While TurtleSeg cannot choose the shape of the slice arbitrarily. Some structures cannot provide a priori information through user interaction, resulting in poor editing results. For interaction efficiency, TurtleSeg needs to mark or adjust each contour, so the interaction time for the contour is longer, and the user needs more interactions to mark the contour on the 2D slice. Since the system provides a slice recommendation function to guide the user to select an interaction location, this part is less time consuming. Due to the adjustment based on the existing segmentation results, the method in this paper takes less time on a single contour. But compared with TurtleSeg, the time of finding the region of interest is longer, and users have to determine the location of the error by repeatedly generating the contour. In general, the proposed method can reduce the interaction time compared to the commercial software TurtleSeg, and also has advantages in segmentation editing (Fig. 11 and Table 1).

Table 1. Comparison with TurtleSeg

	Ours	TurtleSeg
Single contour editing time	2–3 min	5–6 min
Searching the editing area	Manual	Automatic or manual
Editing times	The segmentation times decrease with the improvement of pre-segmentation quality	With the increase of segmentation times, it becomes more difficult to improve the segmentation quality
Segmentation accuracy	The accuracy of editing area is improved obviously, which is affected by the initial segmentation	The precision of fine structure is not enough, and the contour is difficult to cover all

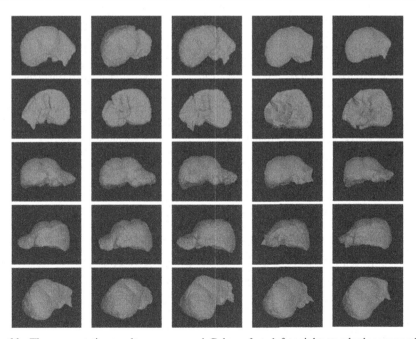

Fig. 11. The segmentation results are compared. Column from left to right: standard segmentation result (manual annotation), pre-segmentation result (level set) used in this method, editing result (10 interactions), TurtleSeg segmentation result (10 interactions), TurtleSeg segmentation result (20 interactions).

7 Conclusions

The paper proposes a volume data segmentation editing method based on uncertainty guidance. In order to assist users to edit the segmentation, this paper designed a series of uncertainty measures and mapped them on the surface of the segmentation mesh. With the assistance of the uncertainty measure guidance, users can easily find out proper regions to start editing. The system allows users to draw and generate a curved editing surface slice in the 3D view. Then, users can edit the segmentation on the slice and propagate the edits to the 3D mesh. Users repeat editing as above several times to complete the segmentation.

Through experiments, we verified the effectiveness of slice editing and uncertainty guidance. Compared to similar commercial softwares, the method we proposed also takes less interaction time on editing.

Acknowledgements. This research is partially supported by the National Key R&D Program of China (Grant No. 2017YFB1304301) and National Natural Science Foundation of China (Grant Nos. 61972221, 61572274).

References

1. Heckel, F., Moltz, J.H., Tietjen, C., Hahn, H.K.: Sketch-based editing tools for tumour segmentation in 3D medical images. In: Computer Graphics Forum, vol. 32, pp. 144–157. Wiley Online Library (2013)
2. Ronneberger, O., Fischer, P., Brox, T.: U-Net: convolutional networks for biomedical image segmentation. In: Navab, N., Hornegger, J., Wells, W.M., Frangi, A.F. (eds.) MICCAI 2015. LNCS, vol. 9351, pp. 234–241. Springer, Cham (2015). https://doi.org/10.1007/978-3-319-24574-4_28
3. Lempitsky, V.: Surface extraction from binary volumes with higher-order smoothness (2010)
4. Kronenberger, M., Wirjadi, O., Hagen, H.: Empirical comparison of curvature estimators on volume images and triangle meshes. IEEE Trans. Visual. Comput. Graph. (2018)
5. Rieger, B., Timmermans, F.J., Van Vliet, L.J., Verbeek, P.W.: On curvature estimation of ISO surfaces in 3D gray-value images and the computation of shape descriptors. IEEE Trans. Pattern Anal. Mach. Intell. **26**(8), 1088–1094 (2004)
6. Ijiri, T., Yokota, H.: Contour-based interface for refining volume segmentation. In: Computer Graphics Forum, vol. 29, pp. 2153–2160. Wiley Online Library (2010)
7. Sorkine, O., Cohen-Or, D., Lipman, Y., Alexa, M., Rössl, C., Seidel, H.-P.: Laplacian surface editing. In: Proceedings of the 2004 Eurographics/ACM SIGGRAPH Symposium on Geometry Processing, pp. 175–184. ACM (2004)
8. Christ, P., Ettlinger, F., Grün, F., Lipkova, J., Kaissis, G.: LiTS-liver tumor segmentation challenge. In: ISBI and MICCAI (2017)
9. Turtleseg Homepage. http://www.turtleseg.org/. Accessed 15 May 2021
10. Poon, M., Hamarneh, G., Abugharbieh, R.: Efficient interactive 3D livewire segmentation of complex objects with arbitrary topology. Comput. Med. Imaging Graph. **32**(8), 639–650 (2008)

Semi-supervised Yolo Network for Induced Pluripotent Stem Cells Detection

Xinglie Wang[1], Jinqi Liao[2], Guanghui Yue[1], Liangge He[1], Mingzhu Li[1],
Enmin Liang[1], Tianfu Wang[1], Guangqian Zhou[2(✉)], and Baiying Lei[1(✉)]

[1] National-Regional Key Technology Engineering Laboratory for Medical Ultrasound,
Guangdong Key Laboratory for Biomedical Measurements and Ultrasound Imaging, School of
Biomedical Engineering, Health Science Center, Shenzhen University, Shenzhen, China
leiby@szu.edu.cn

[2] Department of Medical Cell Biology and Genetics, Guangdong Key Laboratory of Genomic
Stability and Disease Prevention, Shenzhen Key Laboratory of Anti-Aging and Regenerative
Medicine, and Shenzhen Engineering Laboratory of Regenerative Technologies for Orthopaedic
Diseases, Health Science Center, Shenzhen University, Shenzhen 518060, China
gqzhou@szu.edu.cn

Abstract. Induced pluripotent stem cells (iPSCs) have broad prospects in clinical
and industrial applications, and the automatic identification of iPSCs is essential
to optimize the iPSCs manufacturing. However, the challenge of obtaining large
amounts of labeled images has limited the use of image analysis in the field of
iPSCs. In this paper, we propose Semi-Yolo, a simple yet effective semi-supervised
learning (SSL) network that combines mean-teacher SSL paradigm and the Yolo
object detection network for the iPSCs identification. The designed burn-in stage
in Semi-Yolo makes full use of available labeled images, providing good initialization for both student and teacher model. Then in the teacher-student mutual
learning stage, the gradually progressing teacher model of Semi-Yolo generates
highly confident pseudo labels for unlabeled images, which provides extra training
data to update the student model in a mutually-beneficial manner. Together with
a Mosaic data augmentation technique to increase the diversity of our data, Semi-
Yolo achieves favorable detection performance on the collected iPSCs detection
dataset. Extensive experimental results on our dataset demonstrates the effectiveness of Semi-Yolo with great improvement compared to supervised baseline, which shows better detection precision and faster detection speed than the
state-of-the-art SSL object detection algorithm.

Keywords: Induced pluripotent stem cells · Object detection · Semi-supervised
learning · Mosaic data augmentation

1 Introduction

Induced pluripotent stem cells (iPSCs), as a type of pluripotent stem cells derived from
adult somatic cells, have great potential in disease modelling, regenerative medicine such
as organ synthesis and tissue repairing [1, 2]. However, iPSCs derivation and culturing

© Springer Nature Switzerland AG 2021
Y. Peng et al. (Eds.): ICIG 2021, LNCS 12889, pp. 797–808, 2021.
https://doi.org/10.1007/978-3-030-87358-5_65

are typically a time-consuming and inefficient process, taking about 4 weeks for human cells, with efficiencies around 0.01–0.1% [3]. Early identification of iPSCs in microscopy view helps optimize the reprogramming process of iPSCs, which indicates the urgent need to develop an automatic and efficient method to detect iPSCs in microscopy images for further researches.

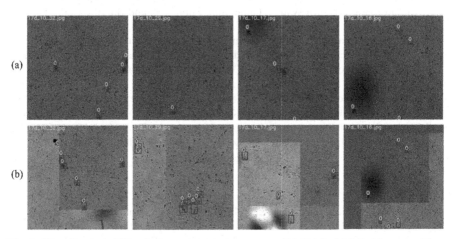

Fig. 1. Visualization of Mosaic data augmentation strategy. (a) Original labeled images without Mosaic augmentation. (b) Training images with Mosaic augmentation.

With the recent tremendous progress, object detection algorithm has been widely used in the field of medical image analysis such as the mitosis detection in breast cancer histology images [4, 5], which is able to detect the mitosis cells in a fast and accurate way. However, the identification of iPSCs is a much more challenging task compared to the aforementioned researches. Firstly, cell staining technique will lead to massive death of iPSCs, which is not supposed to happen during the iPSCs production. Secondly, the inefficient process of iPSC derivation indicates that it is expensive and time-consuming to obtain large amount of labeled data.

Semi-supervised learning (SSL) method has received growing attention as it provides an effective way for using unlabeled data to improve model performance [6–10]. Yet, these advances have primarily applied in the field of image classification, rather than object detection where labeling cost is relatively more expensive. When it comes to medical image labeling, the cost will rise further as labels need more rigorous verification from experienced experts or researchers. On the other hand, the majority of recent researches on object detection focus on building a stronger and more efficient model for natural images datasets [11–16], only a few related works of SSL object detection [17–20]. As for the identification of iPSCs, most previous works concentrate on building classification algorithms to classify the quality of iPSCs colonies based on manually cropped and fully annotated images [21–25]. Object detection methods and SSL technique haven't been applied on the iPSCs related researches.

In this work, we leverage knowledge learned from existing SSL methods on natural images analysis for iPSCs identification under microscopic bright-field images. We propose a SSL method named Semi-Yolo for iPSCs detection that combines mutual beneficial teacher-student learning manner, self-training strategy (via pseudo label) and high efficient Yolo v5 network [10, 16]. In our method, (i) we adopt a burn-in stage to train student network for better initialize the teacher and student model. (ii) We use the exponential moving average (EMA) to update teacher model in teacher-student mutual learning stage, thus a more stable teacher network can be obtained to generate pseudo labels. (iii) We apply a simple data augmentation for both images with ground-truth label and the corresponding images of pseudo labels generated by teacher model, which extends the distribution of our data to alleviate the problem of insufficient labeled data.

To the best of our knowledge, this is the first semi-supervised object detection algorithm proposed in the field of iPSCs identification since SSL has great potential for solving the problem of insufficient labeled images. We highlight the contributions of this paper as follows:

- We build a SSL detection method for non-invasive iPSC identification to alleviate the data labeling burden without bringing damage to iPSCs colonies.
- We adopt a two-stage training procedure, including a burn-in stage and a teacher-student mutual learning stage to accelerate the training process and make full use of the unlabeled data for improving detection result.
- We employ a simple and effective Mosaic data augmentation method to extend the data distribution for further improving the performance of our method.

2 Related Work

2.1 iPSCs Identification

Tokunaga *et al.* [21] firstly introduced supervised machine learning into the identification of iPSCs, which indicates that morphologies play a key role in distinguishing iPSCs from differentiated cells. Henry Joutsijoki *et al.* [22] utilized k-nearest neighbors algorithm together with scaled invariant feature transformation based features in iPSCs colonies images classification, which obtained the best accuracy of 62.4%. Then with the boosting of deep-learning methods, Kimmel *et al.* [23] developed a fully supervised vector-based convolutional neural networks (CNNs) for distinguishing characteristics of iPSC colonies. Ariel Waiseman *et al.* [24] used CNNs on accurate classification of iPSCs differentiation along with cell staining technique. These works mostly focused on the supervised classification task of manually cropped iPSCs colony images, some of them even used cell staining technique to improve the performance.

2.2 Object Detection

Object detection deals with detecting instances of semantic objects of a certain class in digital images or videos. Mainstream object detection frameworks include Region-based object detector [11–13], Yolo [14–16], etc. These popular object detectors have achieved tremendous performance improvements over the last few years based on large amounts of fully labeled datasets. Apart from the application in natural scene, some previous works have adopted object detection algorithm on medical objects detection in a supervised manner [4, 5].

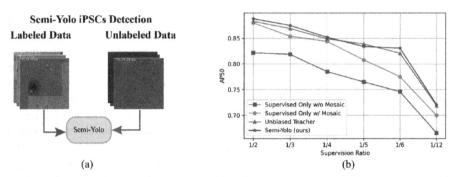

Fig. 2. (a) Illustration of the proposed Semi-Yolo for iPSCs detection, where both labeled and unlabeled data are used to train the SSL iPSCs detector. (b) Our proposed Semi-Yolo method (red curve) has significant improvement compared to the supervised method (blue and orange curve) and better comprehensive performance than Unbiased Teacher [20]. (Color figure online)

2.3 Semi-supervised Learning for Object Detection

Most of the previous works of semi-supervised learning are focused on classification [6–9]. Only a few researches utilized SSL technique on object detection task with the great complexity in architecture design of object detectors [17–20]. Jeong *et al.* [18] designed a consistency-based SSL method for object detection, which used a consistency constraint as a tool to make full use of unlabeled data. Sohn *et al.* [19] proposed a simple SSL teacher-student framework to generate highly confident pseudo labels for unlabeled images, which updates the model by enforcing consistency via strong augmentation. Liu *et al.* [20] transferred the teacher-student architecture on object detection to build a better semi-supervised object detector named Unbiased Teacher, in which they replaced the standard cross-entropy loss with multi-class Focal loss [26] to address the pseudo-labeling bias issue.

3   Method

Figure 3 illustrates the proposed SSL detection network Semi-Yolo for iPSCs detection, based on mutual beneficial teacher-student learning manner and self-training strategy (via pseudo label). We adopt Yolo v5 as the basic model of teacher and student network. In the burn-in stage, we train the student network with available labeled data augmented by the Mosaic data augmentation strategy for specific epochs. When entering the teacher-student mutual learning stage, we duplicate the best weights of student model in the previous stage to initialize the teacher model. In this stage, teacher model is used to generate high confident pseudo labels to train student model, and the student model is updated with the learned knowledge in student model. As a result, the student model and teacher model are evolved successively with the gradually improved pseudo labels and knowledge from student model, respectively.

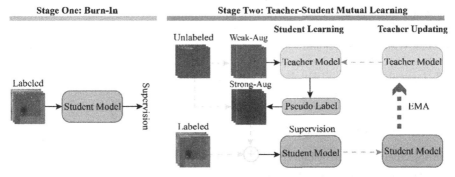

Fig. 3. Overview of the proposed Semi-Yolo framework for iPSCs detection. The Semi-Yolo contains two stage of training. In the burn-in stage, we train the student Yolo network with Mosaic augmented labeled data for proper epochs. In the teacher-student mutual learning stage, the fixed teacher model is used to generate highly confident pseudo labels, which will be fused with labeled data to train the student model. After weights of the student model have been updated with gradient descent, the teacher model is refined as an EMA of its previous weights and the updated student's weight.

3.1 Mosaic Data Augmentation

Mosaic data augmentation was firstly proposed by the Yolo v5 network, which attracts broad attention as its magic power demonstrated in [15]. As shown in Fig. 1, Mosaic represents a powerful data augmentation method that randomly mixes 4 training images with random affine transformation such as image rotation, image scaling and image translation. Thus, objects with different contexts, various scales, and multiple perspectives are mixed in single images. This enhances the ability of object detector of recognizing the target objects in complex scenes, especially for the bright-field microscopy images of iPSCs colonies as showed in Fig. 1. The background of these microscopy images are full of dead cells and miscellaneous cells, while the illumination is also uneven, resulting in shadow blocks.

3.2 Burn-In Stage

Unlike the common classification and segmentation tasks, SSL object detection algorithm in pseudo label manner requires highly confident pseudo labels from unlabeled images, which indicates the significance of a good initialization of teacher network.

In this paper, we adopt a burn-in stage to train the student network with available labeled images $I_s = \left\{ x_i^s, y_i^s \right\}_{i=1}^{N_s}$ for pre-set epochs. s denotes the supervised information, N_s is the number of supervised data, i is an index of the labeled images. Given a labeled image x^s, a set of object coordinates and corresponding category information are stored in the annotation y^s. Since we use the Yolo algorithm as the basic network of student model, the supervision loss contains three terms: the bounding box loss $\mathcal{L}^{box}$, the object loss $\mathcal{L}^{obj}$ and the category classification loss $\mathcal{L}^{cls}$. The supervised loss of burn-in stage is written as follows:

$$\mathcal{L}_{sup} = \sum_i \left(\mathcal{L}^{box}\left(x_i^s, y_i^s\right) + \mathcal{L}^{obj}\left(x_i^s, y_i^s\right) + \mathcal{L}^{cls}\left(x_i^s, y_i^s\right) \right). \tag{1}$$

When transferring to the teacher-student learning stage, we firstly duplicate the weights θ of student model to initialize the teacher model for the following training process. With the using of burn-in stage, we can cut down the time of generating pseudo labels and update the student model with pseudo labels compared to the teacher-student SSL methods applied in the classification task, which generates pseudo labels from scratch.

3.3   Teacher-Student Mutual Learning

The objective of SSL algorithm contains an auxiliary task, which explores the unlabeled data to improve the performance of main task with well-learned knowledge. To leverage the unsupervised data as in Unbiased Teacher, where the student model is optimized by using the pseudo labels generated by the teacher model as well as the true labels, and the teacher model is gradually updated by transferring the weights of learned student model with EMA manner. With the continuously knowledge exchanging between the student model and the teacher model, the performance of both models getting is improved in the teacher-student mutual learning stage. As presented in [10], injecting noise in the student model for forcing it to learn harder from the pseudo labels leads to better generalization of student model. Thus, we perform weak augmentation on the unlabeled data as the input of teacher model for generating more precise pseudo labels, and the data trained in student model is augmented strongly for improving the robustness of the student model.

Student Model Training in Mutual Learning Stage. To leverage the unsupervised data $I_u = \left\{ x_j^u \right\}_{j=1}^{N_u}$, we follow the self-training paradigm for generating pseudo labels $\hat{y}^u$ of the given unlabeled images x^u to train the student, where j is the index of unlabeled images, N_u is the total number of unlabeled images. To prevent the student model from consecutively degenerating with overwhelming low-confident pseudo labels, we introduce a confidence threshold ξ of the bounding boxes predicted by teacher model to discard the noisy pseudo labels. If there are no predicted bounding boxes with confidence scores above the threshold ξ in an unlabeled image, we will skip the image for student model training and keep it for the next round of pseudo labels generation. Except the data of pseudo labels, we mix the supervised data and the unsupervised data together for training the student by following the setting in Mean Teacher [9]. Both supervised data and unsupervised data are used for training the student model. Also, the loss of student training process consists of supervised learning loss and unsupervised loss, which can be written as follows:

$$\mathcal{L}_m = \mathcal{L}_{sup} + \lambda_u \sum_j \left(\mathcal{L}^{box}\left(x_j^u, \hat{y}_j^u\right) + \mathcal{L}^{obj}\left(x_j^u, \hat{y}_j^u\right) + \mathcal{L}^{cls}\left(x_j^u, \hat{y}_j^u\right) \right) \qquad (2)$$

where subscript m in loss $\mathcal{L}_m$ means teacher-student mutual learning stage, $\mathcal{L}_{sup}$ is defined in Eq. (1). λ_u is the weight of the unsupervised loss, we use λ_u to optimize the gradient information learned from unsupervised data.

Teacher Model Updating via Exponential Moving Average. EMA has demonstrated its effectiveness of obtaining more stable weights of model in previous works [10, 20]. For the sake of generating more precise pseudo labels of iPSCs colonies, we utilize EMA to update the weights of teacher model. Thus, our gradually updating teacher model can be considered as the temporal ensemble of the student model in different training epochs. The weights of teacher model update process can be written as follows:

$$\theta_t = \alpha\theta_{t-1} + (1 - \alpha)\theta_s \tag{3}$$

where α is the smoothing coefficient hyperparameter, θ_{t-1} and θ_t are the weights of teacher model before and after EMA updating, respectively, while θ_s is the weights of current student model.

4 Experiments

4.1 Experimental Setting-Up

As there is no available open dataset of iPSCs detection, we culture iPSCs and collect bright-field microscopy images from 17th to 18th day since we perform the reprogrammed procedure on foreskin tissue of boys. All the cells are cultured in six-well plates incubated with LN521 (Biolamina, LN321-03) at 37 °C. During the image acquisition process, the microscope magnification is set to 4 times, and the imaging mode is set as bright-field. We collect total number of 813 images at the same resolution 2048 × 2048 in the 17th and 18th day after cell reprogramming procedure started. We divide the data into training, validation and testing set as shown in Table 1.

Table 1. Summary of self-collected iPSCs detection dataset.

Data	Day	Image	Object
Training set	17th–8th	602	1763
Validation set	18th	106	322
Testing set	18th	105	350

To evaluate the performance of all deep learning detection algorithm in a fair way, we choose the "Adam" optimizer with the same learning rate 10^{-4}. The total number of epoch for training is set to 200, while the batch-size is 8. All models in this study are trained on single NVIDIA GeForce GTX 1080 Ti graphics card. We use AP50 (the area under precision-recall curve as the threshold of Intersection Over Union (IOU) set as 0.5) as evaluation metric, and the performance is evaluated on the teacher model. Note that we scale the resolution of all the images to 640 × 640 for better calculating efficiency in all experiments.

4.2 Comparison with Different Methods

We evaluate the efficacy of our proposed Semi-Yolo network on our self-collected iPSCs detection dataset. We carry out our experiments by randomly sampling $1/n$ images

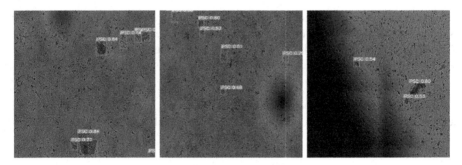

Fig. 4. Detection examples of our self-collected iPSCs identification dataset.

in training set as supervised data, while the rest of $(1 - 1/n)$ images are regarded as unsupervised data, $n \in \{2, 3, 4, 5, 6, 12\}$ by dropping their labels. We adopt the smallest version of Yolo v5 with total 283 layers as the basic detector of supervised learning as well as the basic model of the teacher and student models of Semi-Yolo. For both Unbiased Teacher and Semi-Yolo, the smooth coefficient α, confidence threshold ξ, unsupervised loss weight λ_u are set to the same 0.9996, 0.85 and 0.5, respectively. The number of burn-in epoch is set as 80. The experimental results of AP50 are presented in Fig. 2 (b) and Table 2.

As illustrated in Table 2, Mosaic data augmentation improves the performance of supervised method with a large margin. Semi-Yolo improves the detection results of iPSCs colonies significantly compared to the supervised settings. In addition, Semi-Yolo has better comprehensive performance compared to the state-of-the-art SSL object detection method Unbiased Teacher in terms of AP50, while the inference speed is about 9 times faster than Unbiased Teacher.

Table 2. Comparison in AP50 for different methods on iPSCs detection. We report the result with different proportions of images server as supervised set. "Supervised" refers to results trained with available labeled images, Mosaic Supervised means the implementation of Mosaic augmentation. We also perform data augmentation on Unbiased Teacher and Semi-Yolo network. The last column is the average inference speeds of each method for millisecond per image (ms/img).

	1/12	1/6	1/5	1/4	1/3	1/2	ms/img
Supervised	0.666	0.746	0.766	0.785	0.819	0.822	6.2
Mosaic supervised	0.700	0.775	0.808	0.844	0.854	0.880	7.2
Unbiased teacher	0.719	0.821	**0.839**	0.849	0.869	0.883	61
Semi-Yolo (ours)	**0.721**	**0.831**	0.834	**0.852**	**0.875**	**0.888**	**6.6**

4.3 Ablation Study

We carry out ablation study on the key components of our proposed Semi-Yolo network. The study analyzes the Semi-Yolo performance of 1) training with or without burn-in stage; 2) training with or without Mosaic data augmentation; 3) different ratios of labeled images; 4) the hyperparameters α, smoothing coefficient of EMA, and ξ, the confidence threshold of pseudo label, and λ_u, the weight of unsupervised loss.

Impact of Burn-in Stage. As shown in Fig. 3, we only train the student network with available supervised data in burn-in stage. While in teacher-student mutual learning stage, additional task including generating pseudo labels and optimize student model with pseudo labels and true labels. Thus, using burn-in stage to train the student model will accelerate the network training significantly. Experimental results in Table 3 indicates that using burn-in strategy improves most results except for the one using 1/5 images as supervised data.

Impact of Mosaic Data Augmentation. The power of Mosaic augmentation has been illustrated in the supervised results in Fig. 2 (a). By using Mosaic, the detection results of the supervised learning models improve remarkably. To further explore the impact of Mosaic data augmentation on Semi-Yolo, we train Semi-Yolo without Mosaic, while other settings stay unchanged as shown in Table 2. The results are presented in the second row of Table 3. Obviously, Mosaic boosts the detection performance as illustrated in the second row and the fourth row of Table 3.

Table 3. Ablation Study of burn-in stage and Mosaic augmentation. Except for burn-in stage and Mosaic augmentation, other hyperparameters are set to the same values in our experiments.

Burn-in	Mosaic	1/12	1/6	1/5	1/4	1/3	1/2
✓		0.643	0.670	0.735	0.788	0.774	0.857
	✓	0.715	0.827	0.839	0.847	0.862	0.884
✓	✓	0.721	0.831	0.834	0.852	0.875	0.888

Hyperparameter α. We study the impact of EMA smoothing coefficient α of different values using 1/3 images as unlabeled data. The results are summarized in Fig. 4. $\alpha = 0$ means EMA is not implemented according to Eq. (3). We observe that with the using of EMA, all the results are improved compared to $\alpha = 0$, and the best performance of Semi-Yolo is obtained when $\alpha = 0.99$. Figure 5 (a) indicates that the model will degenerate without using EMA (Blue curve), while α is larger than 0.9, the model will keep improving steadily until the end of training.

Hyperparameter ξ and λ_u. We further test the impact of confidence threshold of pseudo label ξ and the weight of unsupervised loss λ_u with 1/3 images as unlabeled data, the other settings are kept unchanged as the experiments in Table 2.

As presented in Fig. 5, the model performs best with confidence threshold $\xi = 0.85$ in Fig. 6 (a). The proper confidence threshold leads to better performance by learning knowledge from the true iPSCs colonies while neglect objects of false positive. The comparison results of different unsupervised loss weights are presented in Fig. 6 (b), which shows that model achieves highest AP50 value with $\lambda_u = 0.5$.

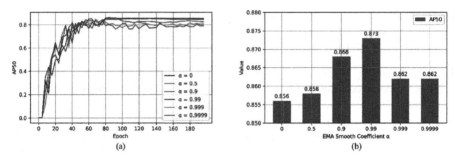

Fig. 5. AP50 of Semi-Yolo with different values of EMA smoothing coefficient $\alpha \in$ {0, 0.5, 0.9, 0.99, 0.999, 0.9999}.

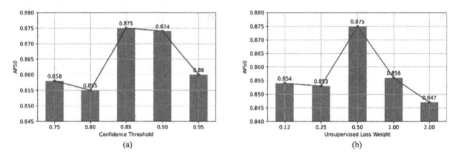

Fig. 6. AP50 of Semi-Yolo with different values of confidence threshold of pseudo label $\xi \in$ {0.75, 0.80, 0.85, 0.90, 0.95} and the weight of unsupervised loss $\lambda_u \in$ {0.12, 0.25, 0.5, 1.0, 2.0}.

5 Conclusion

In this paper, we propose an effective semi-supervised object detection method named Semi-Yolo for iPSCs identification. The Mosaic data augmentation extends the data distribution by randomly mixing 4 images in a single image, which alleviates the insufficient labeled data in the medical image analysis field. The two training procedures include the burn-in stage and teacher-student mutual learning stage makes full use of the unsupervised data via a pseudo label self-training manner, which obtains promising detection performance improvement for iPSCs identification compared to the supervised method. By exploiting high-speed Yolo network, our proposed Semi-Yolo can identify the iPSCs colonies in bright-field microscopy images at a remarkable speed of about 6.6 ms per image.

Acknowledgment. This work was supported partly by National Natural Science Foundation of China (Nos. 61871274, U1909209, and No. 62001302), Key Laboratory of Medical Image Processing of Guangdong Province (No. K217300003), Guangdong Pearl River Talents Plan (2016ZT06S220), Guangdong Basic and Applied Basic Research Foundation (Nos. 2021A1515011348, 2019A1515111205), Shenzhen Peacock Plan (Nos. KQTD2016 053112051497 and KQTD2015033016104926), and Shenzhen Key Basic

Research Project (JCYJ20170818094109846), Natural Science Foundation of Shenzhen (Nos. JCYJ20190808145011259, RCBS20200714114920379).

References

1. Takahashi, K., Yamanaka, S.: Induction of pluripotent stem cells from mouse embryonic and adult fibroblast cultures by defined factors. Cell **126**(4), 663–676 (2006)
2. Mahla, R.S.: Stem cells applications in regenerative medicine and disease therapeutics. Int. J. Cell Biol. **2016** (2016)
3. Zhou, T., Benda, C., Dunzinger, S., et al.: Generation of human induced pluripotent stem cells from urine samples. Nat. Protoc. **7**(12), 2080 (2012)
4. Albarqouni, S., Baur, C., Achilles, F., et al.: AggNet: deep learning from crowds for mitosis detection in breast cancer histology images. IEEE Trans. Med. Imaging **35**(5), 1313–1321 (2016)
5. Li, Z., Dong, M., Wen, S., et al.: CLU-CNNs: object detection for medical images. Neurocomputing **350**, 53–59 (2019)
6. Lee, D.-H.: Pseudo-label: the simple and efficient semi-supervised learning method for deep neural networks. In: Workshop on Challenges in Representation Learning, ICML 2013, vol. 3, no. 2 (2013)
7. Rasmus, A., Valpola, H., Honkala, M., et al.: Semi-supervised learning with ladder networks. arXiv preprint arXiv:1507.02672 (2015)
8. Laine, S., Aila, T.: Temporal ensembling for semi-supervised learning. arXiv preprint arXiv:1610.02242 (2016)
9. Tarvainen, A., Valpola, H.: Mean teachers are better role models: weight-averaged consistency targets improve semi-supervised deep learning results. arXiv preprint arXiv:1703.01780 (2017)
10. Xie, Q., Luong, M.-T., Hovy, E., et al.: Self-training with noisy student improves imagenet classification. In: Proceedings of the IEEE/CVF Conference on Computer Vision and Pattern Recognition, 2020, pp. 10687–10698 (2020)
11. Girshick, R., Donahue, J., Darrell, T., et al.: Rich feature hierarchies for accurate object detection and semantic segmentation. In: Proceedings of the IEEE Conference on Computer Vision and Pattern Recognition, 2014, pp. 580–587 (2014)
12. Girshick, R.: Fast R-CNN. In: Proceedings of the IEEE International Conference on Computer Vision, 2015, pp. 1440–1448 (2015)
13. Ren, S., He, K., Girshick, R., et al.: Faster R-CNN: towards real-time object detection with region proposal networks. Adv. Neural. Inf. Process. Syst. **2015**, 91–99 (2015)
14. Redmon, J., Farhadi, A.: Yolov3: an incremental improvement. arXiv preprint arXiv:1804.02767 (2018)
15. Bochkovskiy, A., Wang, C.-Y., Liao, H.-Y.M.: YOLOv4: optimal speed and accuracy of object detection. arXiv preprint arXiv:2004.10934 (2020)
16. Jocher, G.: Yolo network from ultralytics LLC. https://github.com/ultralytics/yolov5. Accessed 29 Apr 2020
17. RoyChowdhury, A., Chakrabarty, P., Singh, A., et al.: Automatic adaptation of object detectors to new domains using self-training. In: Proceedings of the IEEE/CVF Conference on Computer Vision and Pattern Recognition, 2019, pp. 780–790 (2019)
18. Jeong, J., Lee, S., Kim, J., et al.: Consistency-based semi-supervised learning for object detection (2019)
19. Sohn, K., Zhang, Z., Li, C.-L., et al.: A simple semi-supervised learning framework for object detection. arXiv preprint arXiv:2005.04757 (2020)

20. Liu, Y.-C., Ma, C.-Y., He, Z., et al.: Unbiased teacher for semi-supervised object detection. arXiv preprint arXiv:2102.09480 (2021)
21. Tokunaga, K., Saitoh, N., Goldberg, I.G., et al.: Computational image analysis of colony and nuclear morphology to evaluate human induced pluripotent stem cells. Sci. Rep. **4**, 6996 (2014)
22. Joutsijoki, H., Haponen, M., Rasku, J., et al.: Machine learning approach to automated quality identification of human induced pluripotent stem cell colony images. In: Computational and mathematical methods in medicine, 2016 (2016)
23. Kavitha, M.S., Kurita, T., Park, S.-Y., et al.: Deep vector-based convolutional neural network approach for automatic recognition of colonies of induced pluripotent stem cells. PloS ONE **12**(12) (2017)
24. Waisman, A., La Greca, A., Möbbs, A.M., et al.: Deep learning neural networks highly predict very early onset of pluripotent stem cell differentiation. Stem Cell Reports **12**(4), 845–859 (2019)
25. Liu, G., David, B.T., Trawczynski, M., et al.: Advances in pluripotent stem cells: history, mechanisms, technologies, and applications. Stem Cell Rev. Rep. **16**(1), 3–32 (2020)
26. Lin, T.-Y., Goyal, P., Girshick, R., et al.: Focal loss for dense object detection. In: Proceedings of the IEEE Conference on Computer Vision and Pattern Recognition 2017, pp. 2980–2988 (2017)

Corona Virus Disease (COVID-19) Detection in CT Images Using Synergic Deep Learning

Yiwei Gao[1], Hongjie Hu[2($\boxtimes$)], and Huafeng Liu[1($\boxtimes$)]

[1] State Key Lab of Modern Optical Instrumentation, Zhejiang University,
Hangzhou 310027, China
liuhf@zju.edu.cn
[2] Department of Radiology, Sir Run Run Shaw Hospital, Zhejiang University,
Hangzhou 310016, China
hongjiehu@zju.edu.cn

Abstract. During the global COVID-19 outbreak, it is very important to automatically screen for COVID-19 from chest computed tomography (CT). However, due to slight differences between COVID-19 and other viral pneumonia in chest CT, accurate screening checking COVID-19 remains a huge challenge. We present a deep learning scheme to automatically diagnose COVID-19 from chest CT. In this effort, a Synergic Deep Learning (SDL) model is proposed, which has two main modules. One is a module with 2 Resnet-50, which is used to learn and extract features from the image; the other is a synergic network, which is used to judge whether the input of the two networks mentioned above are of the same type and perform modulation. The proposed method achieves an accuracy of 95.11% in distinguishing COVID-19 from Non-COVID-19 with AUC = 0.9919, which is better than using a single Resnet-50. In addition, when it works in the multi-classification problem of the community acquired pneumonia (CAP), pneumonia, lung infection and COVID-19, it also has outstanding performance with accuracy of 88.56%, AUC = 0.9128.

Keywords: COVID-19 · Deep learning · Synergic deep learning ·
Classification · Chest CT

1 Introduction

In the process of the spread of COVID-19 around the world, in order to quickly complete its diagnosis and reduce the damage of COVID-19 to global economic life as much as possible, many researchers have focused on the use of deep learning methods for detection [1]. Most of them propose methods for the analysis of chest CT scans, with particular reference to the problem of distinguishing between COVID-19 and other pneumonia, i.e. pneumonia (CAP) and interstitial lung disease (IDL) [2]. Wang et al. [3]. propose a framework for fast COVID-19 screening in 3D chest CT images, which allows to reveal the presence of pneumonia and, in case, to determine whether it is caused by COVID-19 or by other viruses. Han et al. [4]. propose a novel attention

© Springer Nature Switzerland AG 2021
Y. Peng et al. (Eds.): ICIG 2021, LNCS 12889, pp. 809–819, 2021.
https://doi.org/10.1007/978-3-030-87358-5_66

based deep 3D multiple instance learning (AD3D-MIL) to classify CT scans into three classes. Some efforts focus on the COVID-19 lesion segmentation or accurate lung lobe segmentation. Zhou et al. [5] present a method that can segment and quantify the regions of infection due to COVID-19 on CT scans. In addition, there are some efforts devote to the development of various methodologies to analyze lung ultrasonography (LUS) sequences or CXR images. Roy et al. [6]. propose a study regarding the application of the deep learning methodologies for the analysis of LUS images. Oh et al. [7]. find that the globally distributed localized intensity variation can be a discriminatory feature for the detection of COVID-19 signs in chest X-rays. Consequently, they propose and train a patch-based deep neural network architecture. Although several methods mentioned above have their merits, there are still some problems that cannot be ignored. Insufficient datasets may result in poor accuracy and insufficient generalization ability, therefore it will lead to low sensitivity to COVID-19 prediction.

In this paper, a Synergic Deep Learning (SDL) [8–10] scheme is proposed to recognize COVID-19 from CT images. Our proposed model consists of 2 pre-trained residual neural networks (ResNet-50) and 1 synergic network. Each ResNet-50 learns image representation and classification, and connects the learned image representation as the input of the synergic network, which has a fully connected structure to predict whether the pair of input images belong to the same class or not. Therefore, under the supervision of the classification error of each ResNet-50 and the cooperative error of two ResNet-50, the SDL model can be trained in an end-to-end manner. Our results show that the SDL model has achieved good performance on the CT images diagnosis task of COVID-19.

2   Materials and Methods

2.1   Dataset

The CT images used in the experiment were from patients with confirmed COVID-19 and patients without COVID-19, among which patients with non-COVID-19 included other patients with pneumonia and normal people. Specifically, our data included 213 cases with COVID-19 and 335 cases with non-COVID-19.

Finally, 548 patients (mean age, 42.5 ± 16.1 years; range, 3–81 years, male 278, female 270) were enrolled into this study, including 213 patients (mean age, 50.7 ± 14.7 years; range, 8–81 years; male 115, female 98) with clinical diagnosed COVID-19 (COVID-positive group) and 335 patients (mean age, 31.2 ± 10.0 years; range, 3–69 years; male 163, female 172) without COVID-19 (COVID-negative group) [11, 12]. The main clinical symptoms for these patients were fever, cough, fatigue, and diarrhea. The all CT images are divided into training set, cross-validation set and test set according to the ratio of 6:2:2. The specific number is shown in Table 1.

Table 1. The specific number of CT data

Image data collection				
Hospitals	COVID-19		Non-COVID-19	
	Cases	Images	Cases	Number of CT sets
I	8	10	202	236
II	6	6	73	100
III	184	700		
IV	12	16	60	132
V	3	3		
Total	213	735	335	486

2.2 Method

The proposed synergic deep learning model is represented by SDL, which consists of three main modules: image pair input layer, 2 ResNet-50 components (the reason why we called it SDL^2) and 1 synergic network. Figure 1 [9, 10] shows the architecture of SDL^2. The input to the SDL^2 model is a set of randomly selected images, not a single image. Each ResNet-50 component of any network structure can independently learn the representation from the image under the supervision of the true label of the input images. A synergic network with a fully connected structure is used to verify whether the input pairs belong to the same category, and if there is a synergic error, the corrective feedback is given. Then, we delve into the three modules of the SDL^2 model.

Unlike traditional Deep Convolutional Neural Networks (DCNN), the proposed synergic model simultaneously accepts n input images randomly selected from the training set. Each image and its class label are input into the ResNet-50 component together, and each pair of images has a corresponding synergic label, which the synergic network will use. In order to unify the image size, we use bicubic interpolation to adjust the size of each image to $224 \times 224 \times 3$.

Due to the powerful representation ability of the residual network, we adopted a pre-trained 50-layer residual neural network (ResNet-50) as the initialization of each DCNN component, denoted as ResNet50-A and ResNet50-B.

We use the image sequence $X = \{x^{(1)}, x^{(2)}, \ldots, x^{(N)}\}$ and the corresponding category label sequence $Y = \{y^{(1)}, y^{(2)}, \ldots, y^{(N)}\}$ to train each ResNet-50 component, thus finding a set of parameters θ via minimizing the subsequent cross entropy loss

$$l(\theta) = -\frac{1}{N}\left[\sum_{i=0}^{N}\sum_{j=1}^{k} l\{y(i) = j\} \log \frac{e^{z_j^{(i)}}}{\Sigma_{l=1}^{k} e^{z_i^{(i)}}}\right] \tag{1}$$

where k is the number of categories, and $Z^{(i)} = F(x^{(i)}, \theta)$ represents the forward calculation. This optimization problem can be solved by using the mini-batch stochastic gradient descent (mini-batch SGD) algorithm. The obtained parameter set for ResNet-50 is represented by $\theta^{(A)}$ and $\theta^{(B)}$. These parameters are not shared between different ResNet-50 components.

In order to further supervise the training of each ResNet-50 component by the synergic label of each pair of images, we designed a synergic network consisting of an embedding layer, a fully connected learning layer and an output layer. Let a pair of images (x_A, x_B) be input into two ResNet-50 components (ResNet50-A, ResNet50-B). The output of the second penultimate fully connected layer in the ResNet-50 is defined as the deep image features learned by the ResNet-50, which can be obtained through forward calculation, and the form is as follows:

$$f_A = F\left(x_A, \theta^{(i)}\right) \tag{2}$$

$$f_B = F\left(x_B, \theta^{(j)}\right) \tag{3}$$

Then, the deep features of the two images are connected as $f_{A \cdot B}$ and input into the synergic network. The corresponding expected output is the synergic label of the image pair, which is defined as follows:

$$y_s(x_A, x_B) = \begin{cases} 1 \text{ if } y_A = y_B \\ 0 \text{ if } y_A \neq y_B \end{cases} \tag{4}$$

It is convenient to monitor the cooperative signal by adding another sigmoid layer and using the following binary cross entropy loss:

$$l_s\left(\theta^s\right) = y_s \log \hat{y}_s + (1 - y_s) \log (1 - \hat{y}_s) \tag{5}$$

Among them, θ^S is the parameter of the synergic network, $\hat{y} = F\left(f_{A \circ B}, \theta^S\right)$ is the forward calculation of the synergic network. The synergic network verifies whether the input image pairs belong to the same category, and if there is a synergic error, it provides correction feedback.

The proposed SDL^2 model consists of 2 ResNet-50 components and a synergic network. During end-to-end training, the parameters of each DCNN component and each synergic network can be updated to

$$\theta^{(A)}(t + 1) = \theta^{(A)} \cdot (t) - \eta(t) \cdot \Delta^{(A)} \tag{6}$$

$$\theta^{(B)}(t + 1) = \theta^{(B)} \cdot (t) - \eta(t) \cdot \Delta^{(B)} \tag{7}$$

$$\theta^{S(A,B)}(t + 1) = \theta^{S(A,B)} \cdot (t) - \eta(t) \tag{8}$$

where $\eta(t)$ is the variable learning rate, S(A, B) represents the synergic network between ResNet50-A and ResNet50-B.

$$\Delta^{(A)} = \frac{\partial l^{(A)}\left(\theta^{(A)}\right)}{\partial \theta^{(A)}} + \lambda \frac{\partial l^{S(A,B)}\left(\theta^{S(A,B)}\right)}{\partial \theta^{S(A,B)}} \tag{9}$$

$$\Delta^{(B)} = \frac{\partial l^{(B)}\left(\theta^{(B)}\right)}{\partial \theta^{(B)}} + \lambda \frac{\partial l^{S(A,B)}\left(\theta^{S(A,B)}\right)}{\partial \theta^{S(A,B)}} \tag{10}$$

$$\Delta^{S(A,B)} = \frac{\partial l^{S(A,B)}\left(\theta^{S(A,B)}\right)}{\partial \theta^{S(A,B)}} \tag{11}$$

λ represents the trade-off between the subversion of the classification error and the coordination error. Algorithm 1 summarizes the training process of the SDL^2 model. When the trained SDL^2 model is applied to the classification of the test image x, Each ResNet-50 component gives a prediction vector $P(A) = (P(A)_1, P(A)_2 \ldots \ldots P(A)_M)$, $P(B) = (P(B)_1, P(B)_2 \ldots \ldots P(B)_M)$ which is the activations in its last fully connected layer. The class label of the test image can be predicted as results.

$$y = \arg\max\left(\sum_{i=1}^{M} P(A)_i + P(B)_i\right) \tag{12}$$

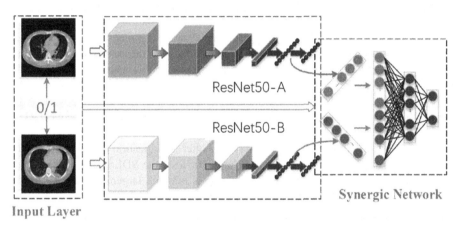

Fig. 1. Architecture of the SDL^2 model of dual DCNNs and a synergic network

3 Results

3.1 Preprocessing

Data are pre-processed in the following steps before feeding them into the network. First, we reshape all CT images to the same size of $224 \times 224 \times 3$. Then, we conduct "width/center" (width: 1600, center: -500) scaling in CT images for contrast enhancement. After comprehensive consideration, we truncate the CT image into the window $[-1300, 300]$, which sets the intensity value above 300 to 300, and below -1300 to -1300. Under the choice of this width/center, the lesion area of the lungs is most prominent in the CT image, which can minimize the influence of other combinations and blood vessels.

In order to remove the influence of the bed board area, it is necessary to segment the lungs on the CT image. First, the pre-processed CT image was segmented by the fill water method, and then the corrosion and opening and closing operations were performed successively to remove the area of the bed with large differences, and only extract the complete lung area. And choose an image with complete lung space as input.

The image is binarized first, and the pixel values below 100 are set to 0. Next, the corrosion algorithm is used to remove the noise, the closed operation is used to remove the hole at the edge, and the open operation is used to remove the area of the bed board below. Finally, the effective area is extracted by the fill water method, and a CT image of only the lung area is obtained.

We have used this method for segmentation on data sets from different sources and found that although the original CT images have large differences in the table, they can be effectively segmented through this method to extract effective parts.

3.2 Comparison with Resnet-50

In order to better evaluate the advantages of the SDL^2 network, we compared it with the train results of a single Resnet-50 network on the cross-validation set, and the results are shown in Fig. 2. In order to better show the changes in the training process, we selected the results of each iteration to show the difference between the convergence speed and accuracy of the SDL^2 network during the training process compared to the Resnet-50 network. In the figure, we can clearly see that the accuracy of the SDL^2 network on the cross-validation set is significantly higher than that of the Resnet-50 network. After the last iteration, its accuracy on the cross-validation set reached 0.9494 and 0.9474, respectively.

It is obvious that the SDL^2 network has a better optimization effect in improving the accuracy of the network. As for the change of loss, the SDL^2 network can reach a fast convergence rate even when the initial loss is much larger than the Resnet-50

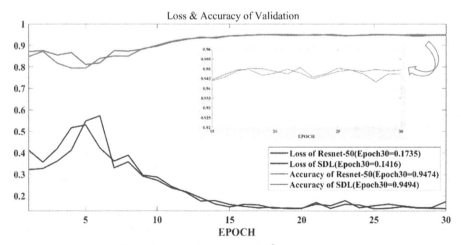

Fig. 2. Loss & accuracy of SDL^2 and Resnet-50

network. After the 16th iteration, the loss of the SDL^2 network is less than the loss of the Resnet-50 network. The results have also been kept lower. After the last iteration, its losses on the cross-validation set are 0.1416 and 0.1735, respectively.

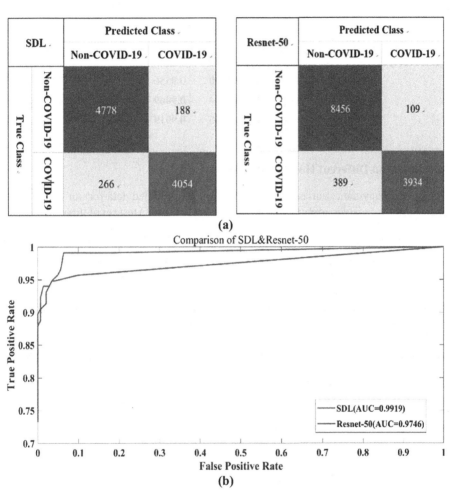

(a)

(b)

Fig. 3. Confusion matrix (a) and ROC curve (b) of SDL^2 and Resnet-50

We also drew the confusion matrix and ROC curve of the two models on the test set (Fig. 3) to analyze their specific performance, and calculated multiple comparison indicators based on the confusion matrix, which are listed in Table 2. From the above analysis, it can be seen that compared with Resnet-50, SDL^2 has higher accuracy and higher sensitivity and AUC value. Those results show that SDL^2 is indeed far better than Resnet-50 in classification performance.

Table 2. Metric of SDL^2 and Resnet-50

Metric	Method	
	Resnet-50	SDL^2
Accuracy	0.9463	**0.9511**
Sensitive	0.9100	**0.9384**
Specificity	**0.9780**	0.9621
Precision	**0.9730**	0.9556
F1	0.9404	**0.9469**
AUC	0.9746	**0.9919**

3.3   Result on Different Hospitals of SDL^2

Due to our many data sources, a total of 5 hospitals provided data for our experiment. Therefore, we consider applying the trained model to the data test set of these 5 hospitals to determine the performance of the model on the data of different hospitals and analyze the possible causes of classification errors. The results are shown in Table 3. The data of the latter two hospitals only contain CT images of COVID-19 patients, and the ROC curve of the model in the data of the first three hospitals is also drawn (Fig. 4).

The analysis shows that, except for Hospital V, the SDL^2 model has a relatively excellent performance on the data of the other 4 hospitals, reaching a higher accuracy rate (I: 0.9947, II: 0.942, III: 0.9849, IV: 0.8931) and AUC value (II: 0.9256, IV: 0.8918). However, the model performed poorly in the data from Hospital V. We guess that this may be related to the lack of COVID-19 data, and the only three COVID-19 data are mostly from patients with mild illness. In mild patients, the lesion area of lung CT is not obvious, so they are more likely to be misclassified.

Table 3. Metric of data from different hospitals

Metric	Hospital				
	I	II	III	IV	V
Accuracy	0.9447	0.9420	0.9849	0.8931	0.7741
Sensitive	0.2736	0.5774	/	0.9329	/
Specificity	0.9702	0.9684	/	0.6228	/
Precision	0.26	0.5694	/	0.9439	/
F1	0.2667	0.5734	/	0.9383	/
AUC	0.7416	0.9256	/	0.8918	/

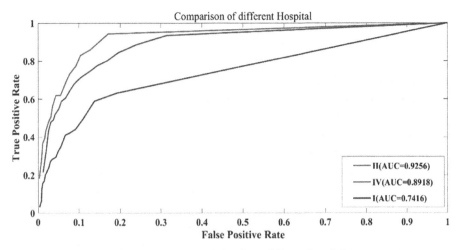

Fig. 4. ROC curve of data from different hospitals

3.4 Result on Different Lung Diseases and COVID-19 of SDL^2

In the data of the two hospitals of I and II, the specific prevalence of Non-COVID-19 patients was marked, and we screened out 3 types of lung diseases: community-acquired pneumonia (CAP), pneumonia, and Pulmonary infection. Since the labeling does not cover every case, it is impossible to determine whether the unlabeled patient is a healthy person with the disease, so normal conditions cannot be added to the multi-classification task.

Table 4. Metric of different lung disease and COVID-19

Metric	Classes			
	CAP	Pneumonia	Pulmonary infections	COVID-19
Accuracy	**0.88554**			
Sensitive	0.9460	0.6958	0.8359	**0.7349**
Specificity	0.7497	0.9562	0.9932	**0.9962**
Precision	0.9094	0.7748	0.8425	**0.9172**
F1	0.9273	0.7332	0.8392	**0.8160**
AUC	0.9164	0.8133	0.8999	**0.9128**

Therefore, our labels are divided into 4 categories: CAP, pneumonia, Pulmonary infection and COVID-19. And adopt the same data division method and parameter values, train it on the SDL^2 network, the accuracy on the training set can reach 0.9028; and test the trained model on the test set, and get 4 kinds of confusion matrix (Fig. 5.), and calculated different indicators in Table 4 based on this. At the same time, their corresponding ROC curves are drawn, as shown in Fig. 6.

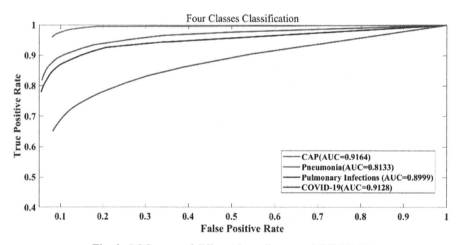

		Predicted Class			
		CAP	Pneumonia	Pulmonary Infections	COVID-19
True Class	CAP	2120	98	17	6
	Pneumonia	161	382	1	5
	Pulmonary Infections	18	3	107	0
	COVID-19	32	10	2	122

Fig. 5. Confusion matrix of different lung disease and COVID-19

Four Classes Classification

CAP(AUC=0.9164)
Pneumonia(AUC=0.8133)
Pulmonary Infections (AUC=0.8999)
COVID-19(AUC=0.9128)

True Positive Rate

False Positive Rate

Fig. 6. ROC curve of different lung disease and COVID-19

Analyzing the data shows that the SDL^2 model we proposed also has a relatively excellent performance on multi-classification problems. Its overall classification accuracy reaches 0.8855, and it has a good AUC value in the identification and diagnosis of

4 diseases, and it exceeds 0.9 in CAP and COVID-19, and in the diagnosis of the other two lung diseases inferior to them, but also got a value of more than 0.8. The reason may be that the data volume of CAP and COVID-19 is much larger than the other two lung diseases, and the model will also tend to the group with large data volume when classifying.

Acknowledgements. This work is supported in part by the National Key Technology Research and Development Program of China (No: 2016YFC1300302, 2017YFE0104000), the National Natural Science Foundation of China (No: U1809204, 61701436), and by the Key Research and Development Program of Zhejiang Province (No: 2021C03029).

References

1. Apostolopoulos, I.D., Mpesiana, T.A.: COVID-19: automatic detection from X-ray images utilizing transfer learning with convolutional neural networks. Phys. Eng. Sci. Med. **43**(2), 635–640 (2020)
2. Özkaya, U. Barstugan, M., Ozturk, S.: Coronavirus (COVID-19) classification using CT images by machine learning methods. arXiv (2020)
3. Wang, X., et al.: A weakly-supervised framework for COVID-19 classification and Lesion localization from chest CT. IEEE Trans. Med. Imaging **39**(8), 2615–2625 (2020)
4. Han, Z., et al.: Accurate screening of COVID-19 using attention-based deep 3D multiple instance learning. IEEE Trans. Med. Imaging **39**(8), 2584–2594 (2020)
5. Zhou, L., Li, Z., Zhou, J., Li, H., Gao, X.: A rapid, accurate and machine-agnostic segmentation and quantification method for CT-based COVID-19 diagnosis. IEEE Trans. Med. Imaging **39**(8), 2638–2652 (2020)
6. Roy, S., Menapace, W., Oei, S., Luijten, B., Demi, L.: Deep learning for classification and localization of COVID-19 markers in point-of-care lung ultrasound. IEEE Trans. Med. Imaging **39**(8), 2676–2687 (2020)
7. Oh, Y., Park, S., Ye, J.C.: Deep learning COVID-19 features on CXR using limited training data sets. IEEE Trans. Med. Imaging **39**(8), 2688–2700 (2020)
8. Schelb, P., et al.: Classification of cancer at prostate MRI: deep learning versus clinical PI-RADS assessment. Radiology **293**(3), 607–617 (2019)
9. Zhang, J., Xie, Y., Wu, Q., Xia, Y.: Skin Lesion classification in dermoscopy images using synergic deep learning. In: Frangi, A.F., Schnabel, J.A., Davatzikos, C., Alberola-López, C., Fichtinger, G. (eds.) MICCAI 2018. LNCS, vol. 11071, pp. 12–20. Springer, Cham (2018). https://doi.org/10.1007/978-3-030-00934-2_2
10. Zhang, J., Xie, Y., Wu, Q., Xia, Y.: Medical image classification using synergic deep learning. Med. Image Anal. **54**, 10–19 (2019)
11. Butt, C., Gill, J., Chun, D., Babu, B.A.: Deep learning system to screen coronavirus disease 2019 pneumonia. Appl. Intell. **5** (2020)
12. Wang, S., et al.: A deep learning algorithm using CT images to screen for Corona virus disease (COVID-19). medRxiv, p. 2020.02.14.20023028 (2020)

Eye Movement Event Detection Based on Path Signature

Haidong Gao, Yinwei Zhan$^{(\boxtimes)}$, Fuyu Ma, and Zilin Chen

School of Computer Science and Technology, Guangdong University of Technology,
100 Waihuanxi Road, Higher Education Megacenter, Guangzhou 510006, China
ywzhan@gdut.edu.cn

Abstract. Eye movement event detection is a demanding technique in cognitive behavior analysis and HCI. Since an eye movement trajectory is a natural path, we try to introduce path signature (PS) to better explore eye movement events; PS is a feature that can highly summarize path information. For this, a multi-input network (MINN) combining 1D-CNN and bidirectional long short-term memory (BiLSTM) is constructed to classify gaze samples as fixation, saccade, smooth pursuit or noise. MINN requires two inputs of local features and global features respectively. The local features include the speed and direction of the gaze trajectory and the global features are the PS's of the gaze trajectory. Experiments on GazeCom, the biggest eye movement event detection dataset, show that our approach with PS outperforms the state-of-the-art methods that do not use PS.

Keywords: Eye movement event detection · Path signature · Deep learning

1 Introduction

Eye movement event detection is important for many eye tracking applications when understanding of perceptual processes is required. In eye movement research, the goal of event detection is to robustly extract event including fixation, saccade and smooth pursuit from the stream of raw data samples via an eye tracker [27]. Most methods to date are based on hand tuned thresholds and criteria. However, it is difficult to extract universal features and design appropriate classifiers because of the diversity of eye movement data. There have been some works that try to use deep learning to automatically detect eye movement events. Hoppe and Bulling [6] introduces convolutional neural networks (CNN) to learn features directly from Fourier transformed eye movement data, which achieves the average F1 score 0.55 for eye movement event recognition. Startsev et al. [18] extract the speed and direction of each gaze point at different temporal

Supported by Science and Technology Planning Projects of Guangdong Province, China, with grant numbers 2019B010150002 and 2020B0101130019.

Y. Peng et al. (Eds.): ICIG 2021, LNCS 12889, pp. 820–830, 2021.
https://doi.org/10.1007/978-3-030-87358-5_67

scales as features, and construct a neural network combining CNN and BiLSTM as the classifier. Their result is much better than Hoppe's. However, using the speed and direction of gaze as features only represents the local information of the eye movement trajectory, while ignoring the global information of the eye movement trajectory.

PS is a feature that uses a set of numbers to express path information, which is simple and effective. PS was proposed in [2] in the form of noncommutative formal power series and then used to solve differential equations driven by rough paths [14,15]. Since 2005, PS has been used in voice compression [16], handwritten character recognition [8,21–25], human motion recognition [10,26] and quantitative finance [5,11–13].

In this paper, we introduce PS into eye movement event detection. For this, we present a multi-input neural network (MINN) based on CNN and BiLSTM to detect the three major eye movement event classes, fixation, saccade and smooth pursuit, as well as potential noise. Differing from the work in[18], we not only use the speed and direction of the gaze to describe the local information of the eye trajectory, but also use PS as a feature to describe the global information of the eye trajectory. In addition, each feature sequence has its own input channel instead of being integrated together into the neural network. We measure the performance of each feature combination on a public dataset named Gaze-Com [4]. The result shows that the combination of feature sequences including PS performs much better than the combination without PS. Our method achieves average F1 score as 0.846, which is the best result compared with state-of-the-art methods.

2   Related Works

Eye movement event detection methods are mainly divided into three categories: threshold methods, machine learning methods and deep learning methods. Speed and dispersion are the two most commonly used features in the threshold methods. A typical method based on speed threshold is Velocity-Threshold Identification (I-VT) [17]. When the speed of a gaze point is greater than the threshold, I-VT judges it as a saccade point, and the remaining points are labeled as fixation points. A method named Velocity and Velocity Threshold Identification (I-VVT) introduces a second lower thresholds on the basis of I-VT to detect smooth pursuit event [7]. If the speed of the gaze point is bigger than the high threshold, it is considered a saccade point. If it is bigger than the lower threshold and smaller than the higher threshold, it is regarded as smooth pursuit point. The rest points are labeled as fixation points. Dispersion-Threshold Identification (I-DT) is a typical dispersion threshold based method [17]. The fixation points are detected by setting thresholds on the horizontal and vertical coordinates. If the horizontal and vertical coordinates do not exceed the threshold within a fixed time, it is considered to be a fixation point, and the remaining points are considered to be saccade points. Velocity and Dispersion-Threshold Identification (I-VDT) combines I-VT and I-DT, using speed threshold to detect saccade and use dispersion threshold to detect fixation [7].

However, all the threshold methods have the disadvantage that requires the user to manually set the threshold. In recent years, the trend of using machine learning and deep learning to handle classification tasks is increasing. The work [19] uses Bayesian classifier to automatically classify viewpoints with the distance between viewpoints as features. The work in [20] uses sliding window to extract the shape feature of smooth pursuit and input the features into a KNN classifier to get the classification results. A method proposed in [1] uses CNN to extract temporal characteristics of the eye positions and local visual features, and then classifies the eye movement event via a support vector machine.

Another work in [9] proposed smooth pursuit detection algorithm based on sliding windows, each window being classified based on four criteria. If all the criteria are satisfied, gaze points in the window is labeled as smooth pursuit. But this method requires a set of already detected saccades. Later, Zemblys, et al. [27] summarized 14 common features related to eye movement event detection and compared the importance of these features under random forest classifier.

There are a few methods to detect eye movement event by using deep learning. The work in [6] uses the sliding window to carry out fast Fourier transform on eye movement data, and decomposes the signal into components of different frequencies, which are fed into convolutional neural network for training and testing. Their network architecture is simple, including only a convolutional layer, a max pooling layer and a fully connected layer. The average of F1 score for fixation, saccade and smooth pursuit are 0.63, 0.53 and 0.55 respectively. Another deep learning method is proposed in [18], in which the network consists of three one-dimensional convolution layers, one BiLSTM layer and three completely connected layers. As for the input of this network, velocity and direction at 5 different scales are extracted from the eye movement data. The result of training and testing on GazeCome is much better than [6], according to their report.

3 Path Signature

In this section, we will give a briefly introduction to the mathematical definition of path signature. For the detail refer to [3]. For a d dimensional path $X :$ $[a, b] \rightarrow \mathbb{R}^d$, where $[a, b]$ is a time interval, denote the coordinate paths by $X = (X^1, \cdots, X^d)$, each $X^i \rightarrow \mathbb{R}$ being a real-valued path. For any single index $i \in \{1, \cdots, d\}$, the *one-fold iterative integral* is defined as

$$S(X)^i_{a,t} = \int_{a<s<t} dX^i_s = X^i_t - X^i_a. \tag{1}$$

Now for any $i, j \in \{1, \cdots, d\}$, the *double iterated integral* is defined as

$$S(X)^{i,j}_{a,t} = \int_{a<s<t} S(X)^i_{a,s} dX^j_s = \int_{a<r<s<t} dX^i_r dX^j_s. \tag{2}$$

Further, for any integer $k \geq 1$, the *k-fold iterated integral* of X with indexes $i_1, \cdots, i_k \in \{1, \cdots, d\}$ is defined as

$$
\begin{aligned}
S(X)_{a,t}^{i_1,\cdots,i_k} &= \int_{a<s<t} S(X)_{a,s}^{i_1,\cdots,i_{k-1}} dX_s^{i_k} \\
&= \int_{a<t_k<t} \cdots \int_{a<t_1<t_2} dX_{t_1}^{i_1} \cdots dX_{t_k}^{i_k}.
\end{aligned}
\tag{3}
$$

The Definition of PS. The signature of a path $X : [a,b] \to \mathbb{R}^d$, denoted by $S(X)_{a,b}$, is the collection (infinite series) of all the iterated integrals of X:

$$
S(X)_{a,b} = (1, S(X)_{a,b}^1, \cdots, S(X)_{a,b}^d, S(X)_{a,b}^{1,1}, S(X)_{a,b}^{1,2}, \cdots).
\tag{4}
$$

The k-th level PS is the collection of all the *k-fold iterated integral* of path X. For example, the first level PS of X is $S(X)_{a,b}^1, \cdots, S(X)_{a,b}^d$, and the second level PS of X is $S(X)_{a,b}^{1,1}, S(X)_{a,b}^{1,2}, \cdots, S(X)_{a,b}^{d,d}$.

Since the signature of a path is a infinite series, we often truncate $S(X)$ at level m to make sure the dimension of path signature in a reasonable range. Empirically, the value range of m is $[2,5]$, because high-level PS characterizes more detailed information in the path, which leads to an increase in computational cost. The dimension of $S(X)_{t_1,t_2}$ truncated at level m is calculated through

$$
M(m) = 1 + d + \cdots + d^m = \frac{1 - d^{m+1}}{1 - d}.
\tag{5}
$$

4   MINN: A Multi-input Network

4.1   Feature Representation for Gaze Trajectory

In eye movement event, each gaze position is expressed as three-dimensional coordinate (t, x, y), where t is timestamp, x and y are the horizontal and vertical coordinates respectively. Then the eye movement trajectory E of N gaze points can be expressed as

$$
E = \begin{bmatrix} t_1 & t_2 & t_3 & \cdots & t_N \\ x_1 & x_2 & x_3 & \cdots & x_N \\ y_1 & y_2 & y_3 & \cdots & y_N \end{bmatrix}
\tag{6}
$$

We first extract the speed and direction features of E. The speed of gaze point at time t is calculated via

$$
v_{t;\Delta t} = \frac{\sqrt{(x_{t+\Delta t} - x_t)^2 + (y_{t+\Delta t} - y_t)^2}}{\Delta t},
\tag{7}
$$

and its direction is

$$
d_{t;\Delta t} = \arctan \frac{y_{t+\Delta t} - y_t}{x_{t+\Delta t} - x_t}.
\tag{8}
$$

where $\Delta t > 0$ is the span of time.

We use the mirror padding to pad Δt gaze samples on the end of the eye movement trajectory to handle the case of $t + \Delta t > N$. By calculating the speed and direction of each gaze point in the eye movement trajectory, we can get the speed sequence

$$V_{\Delta t} = (v_{1;\Delta t}, v_{2;\Delta t}, \cdots, v_{N;\Delta t})^{T}, \tag{9}$$

and the direction sequence

$$D_{\Delta t} = (d_{1;\Delta t}, d_{2;\Delta t}, \cdots, d_{N;\Delta t})^{T}. \tag{10}$$

Inspired by [18], we extract the speed and the direction of the gaze at 5 different time spans $\Delta t = 4, 8, 16, 32$ and 64, and get correspondingly the speed sequences

$$V = (V_4, V_8, V_{16}, V_{32}, V_{64}) \tag{11}$$

and the direction sequences

$$D = (D_4, D_8, D_{16}, D_{32}, D_{64}), \tag{12}$$

which are used as the speed feature and direction feature of the eye movement trajectory, respectively.

However, the speed and the direction of gaze can only characterize the local features of the eye movement trajectory, but not the global information of the eye movement trajectory, especially the shape of eye movement trajectory. Thus, we connect every gaze position to obtain the eye movement trajectory and then extract PS of the trajectory as the third eye movement feature descriptor.

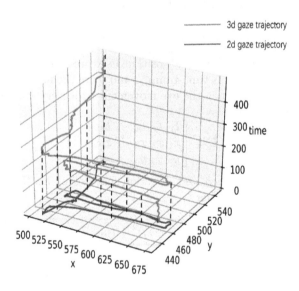

Fig. 1. 2D and 3D representation for gaze trajectory.

The PS of 2D eye movement trajectory can be uniquely represented if the path contains no part that exactly retraces itself. However, it is inevitable that some parts of eye movement trajectory retrace themselves due to the repeated observation of the region of interest (as shown in Fig. 1). This leads to long-term back and forth saccade that may be recognized as short-term smooth pursuit. Thus, we add the time dimension to the gaze point coordinates, and then extract the features of the three dimensional eye movement trajectory. By sliding over an eye movement trajectory E, we can extract path signature within the sliding window at every position. Assume the window size is $w = 2\Delta t + 1$. The eye movement data sequence within the window at position n is

$$e_n = \begin{bmatrix} t_{n-\Delta t} \cdots t_n \cdots t_{n+\Delta t} \\ x_{n-\Delta t} \cdots x_n \cdots x_{n+\Delta t} \\ y_{n-\Delta t} \cdots y_n \cdots y_{n+\Delta t} \end{bmatrix} \tag{13}$$

The path signature is calculated from e_n, resulting in a feature vector $S(e_n)|m$. Thus, the eye movement trajectory can be represented as a PS sequence

$$P_m = (S(e_1)|m, S(e_2)|m, \cdots, S(e_N)|m). \tag{14}$$

We use the mirror padding to pad Δt gaze samples on each side of the eye movement trajectory to handle the cases of $n - \Delta t < 0$ and the case of $n + \Delta t > N$.

4.2   MINN Network Architecture

In this work, we implement a composite structure network that consists of two input layers, six one-dimension convolutional layers, two time-distributed dense (FC) layers and two BiLSTM layer; see Fig. 2. The data received by each input layer is a sequence of features or a combination of several feature sequences, and the output is a sequence of labels. The convolutional part behind the first input layer contains three one-dimensional convolutional (conv1D) layers with the kernel size of 3 and a batch normalization operation before activation. There are 64, 32 and 16 filters in the three conv1D layers respectively. Higher level features are extracted by the following time-distributed dense layers and then fed into the BiLSTM layer of 32 units. All the layers between the second input layer and the concatenate layer are exactly the same as the layers between the first input layer and the concatenate layer. The outputs of the two BiLSTM layer are connected together by the concatenate layer and fed into the following time-distributed dense layer which contains 5 units. All the conv1D layers and time-distributed dense layers before BiLSTM, except for the first convolutional layer of each convolutional layer, are preceded by dropout to prevent overfitting, and use rectified linear units (ReLUs) as activation function. The two BiLSTM layer has 32 units and uses tanh as activation function. According to the number of classes, the last time-distributed dense layer has five units and uses softmax as activation function, and the output of this layer is a sequence of labels.

We use a sliding window to input each feature sequence into MINN. In order to minimize the border effects, the whole data sequence is mirror-padded by

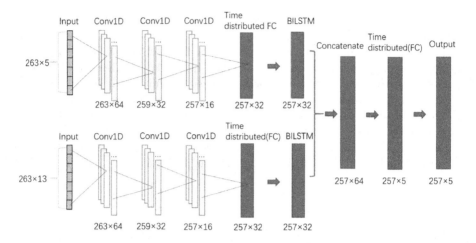

Fig. 2. The MINN network architecture. The first input is V as in (11) and the second input is P_2 as in (14).

three samples on each side and each convolutional layers in MINN uses valid padding. So when we generate the labels for the input data, the neighboring input sequences overlap by six samples, but the output sequences do not.

5   Experiment and Analysis

5.1   Dataset

Our experiments are conducted on GazeCom which was recorded with an SR Research EyeLink II. It consists of 18 videos, around 20 s each. The total number of individual labels is about 4.3 million. Event-wise, the dataset contains 38629 fixations, 39217 saccades and 4631 smooth pursuits, a few noise and unknown points totally. Most of the data are recorded 250 Hz and a few data are recorded 500 Hz. For the convenience of training and testing MINN, we resample all the data recorded 500 Hz 250 Hz by down 2 sampling.

5.2   Implementation Details

The truncate number m is set to 2 when extracting PS and the size of sliding window w is set to 31. The size of the sliding window used to segment the feature sequence is set to 257. In order to test the performance of each kind of features, we input each feature sequence and their different combinations into MINN. When only one feature is used to detect eye movement event, we close one of the input channels of MINN to make it a single input structure. When two kinds of features are used as inputs, these two types of features are respectively input into MINN from the two input layers. When using all the three features, we input speed and direction to one of the input layers, and PS into the other input layer.

When training MINN, the training batch size is set to 1000. All the convolutional and fully connected layers of MINN are initialized with random weights from a normal distribution, and the training epochs is set to 200. RMSprop optimizer with default parameters from the Keras framework is used as optimizer, and categorical cross-entropy is used as the loss function.

5.3 Evaluation

We use "leave-one-out" cross-validation strategy to identify the performance of classifier. The experiment is run 18 times, each time training on all the data for 17 videos and testing on all the eye movement data collected for the remaining video clip. The criteria we used for evaluating the quality of the classifier are accuracy and F1 score. The F1 score is a number that belongs to $[0, 1]$ which can be regarded as a harmonic average of model precision p and recall r, i.e.

$$F1 = \frac{2pr}{p + r}. \tag{15}$$

5.4 Comparison of Feature Combinations

As discussed above, the main ingredients of the features in our work are PS, speed and direction. To make their performances comparative, we conduct a series of experiments on these features individually and respectively their combinations. Seven cases are processed: PS, speed, direction, speed with direction, PS with speed, PS with direction, and PS with speed and direction. See Fig. 3 for the accuracies and Fig. 4 for the losses. Note that the combination of speed and direction was discussed in [18], the latest work on deep learning based eye movement events detection.

From Fig. 3 and Fig. 4 we can see that the individual PS feature is much better than the individual direction feature, but slightly worse than the individual speed feature, while any combination with PS feature is much better than that without PS feature. Therefore, the PS feature is competitive in identifying eye movement events.

5.5 Comparison with State-of-the-Art Methods

The comparison results of our method with the state-of-art methods are listed in Table 1, which show that MINN has the best recognition effect for each eye movement event, and only the recognition effect of fixation is slightly lower than 1DCNN-BiLSTM. But the batch size and training epochs of MINN are much smaller than 1DCNN-BiLSTM. This means that MINN can achieve very good results in a very small amount of time.

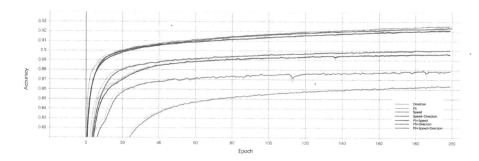

Fig. 3. Accuracy curve of each feature combinations

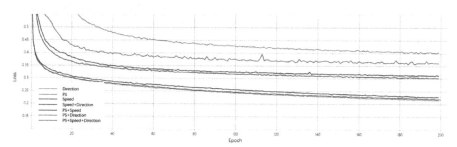

Fig. 4. Loss curve of each feature combinations

Table 1. Comparison of our method with the state-of-art methods

	Accuracy	Average F1 Score	Fixation	Saccade	Smooth Pursuit
MINN	0.9255	0.846	0.928	0.896	0.716
1DCNN-BiLSTM [18]	0.9002	0.830	0.939	0.893	0.703
Larsson [9]	0.8541	0.730	0.912	0.861	0.459
I-VDT [7]	0.7384	0.606	0.882	0.676	0.321

6   Conclusion

In this paper, we introduce PS into eye movement event detection, and construct a multi-input neural network based on CNN and BiLSTM. By adding PS to characterize the global information of the eye movement trajectory, our method significantly improves the recognition rate of eye movement events. The average F1 score reaches 0.846, which outperforms the existing methods.

References

1. Anantrasirichai, N., Gilchrist, I.D., Bull, D.R.: Fixation identification for low-sample-rate mobile eye trackers. In: 2016 IEEE International Conference on Image Processing (ICIP), pp. 3126–3130. IEEE (2016)

2. Chen, K.T.: Integration of paths-a faithful representation of paths by noncommutative formal power series. Trans. Am. Math. Soc. **89**(2), 395–407 (1958)
3. Chevyrev, I., Kormilitzin, A.: A primer on the signature method in machine learning. arXiv preprint arXiv:1603.03788 (2016)
4. Dorr, M., Martinetz, T., Gegenfurtner, K.R., Barth, E.: Variability of eye movements when viewing dynamic natural scenes. J. Vis. **10**(10), 28 (2010)
5. Gyurkó, L.G., Lyons, T., Kontkowski, M., Field, J.: Extracting information from the signature of a financial data stream. arXiv preprint arXiv:1307.7244 (2013)
6. Hoppe, S., Bulling, A.: End-to-end eye movement detection using convolutional neural networks. arXiv preprint arXiv:1609.02452 (2016)
7. Komogortsev, O.V., Karpov, A.: Automated classification and scoring of smooth pursuit eye movements in the presence of fixations and saccades. Behav. Res. Methods **45**(1), 203–215 (2012). https://doi.org/10.3758/s13428-012-0234-9
8. Lai, S., Jin, L.: Offline writer identification based on the path signature feature. In: 2019 International Conference on Document Analysis and Recognition (ICDAR), pp. 1137–1142. IEEE (2019)
9. Larsson, L., Nyström, M., Andersson, R., Stridh, M.: Detection of fixations and smooth pursuit movements in high-speed eye-tracking data. Biomed. Signal Process. Control **18**, 145–152 (2015)
10. Li, C., Zhang, X., Liao, L., Jin, L., Yang, W.: Skeleton-based gesture recognition using several fully connected layers with path signature features and temporal transformer module. In: Proceedings of the AAAI Conference on Artificial Intelligence, vol. 33, pp. 8585–8593 (2019)
11. Lyons, T., Nejad, S., Arribas, I.P.: Nonparametric pricing and hedging of exotic derivatives. arXiv preprint arXiv:1905.00711 (2019)
12. Lyons, T., Nejad, S., Arribas, I.P.: Numerical method for model-free pricing of exotic derivatives using rough path signatures. arXiv preprint arXiv:1905.01720 (2019)
13. Lyons, T., Ni, H., Oberhauser, H.: A feature set for streams and an application to high-frequency financial tick data. In: Proceedings of the 2014 International Conference on Big Data Science and Computing, pp. 1–8 (2014)
14. Lyons, T., Qian, Z., Qian, Z., et al.: System Control and Rough Paths. Oxford University Press, Oxford (2002)
15. Lyons, T.J., Caruana, M., Lévy, T.: Differential Equations Driven by Rough Paths. Springer, Heidelberg (2007). https://doi.org/10.1007/978-3-540-71285-5
16. Lyons, T.J., Sidorova, N.: Sound compression-a rough path approach. Signs **10**(1), X1 (2005)
17. Salvucci, D.D., Goldberg, J.H.: Identifying fixations and saccades in eye-tracking protocols. In: Proceedings of the 2000 Symposium on Eye Tracking Research & Applications, pp. 71–78 (2000)
18. Startsev, M., Agtzidis, I., Dorr, M.: 1D CNN with BLSTM for automated classification of fixations, saccades, and smooth pursuits. Behav. Res. Methods **51**(2), 556–572 (2019)
19. Tafaj, E., Kasneci, G., Rosenstiel, W., Bogdan, M.: Bayesian online clustering of eye movement data. In: Proceedings of the Symposium on Eye Tracking Research and Applications, pp. 285–288 (2012)
20. Vidal, M., Bulling, A., Gellersen, H.: Detection of smooth pursuits using eye movement shape features. In: Proceedings of the Symposium on Eye Tracking Research and Applications, pp. 177–180 (2012)

21. Xie, Z., Sun, Z., Jin, L., Feng, Z., Zhang, S.: Fully convolutional recurrent network for handwritten Chinese text recognition. In: 2016 23rd International Conference on Pattern Recognition (ICPR), pp. 4011–4016. IEEE (2016)
22. Yang, W., Jin, L., Liu, M.: Character-level Chinese writer identification using path signature feature, dropstroke and deep CNN. arXiv preprint arXiv:1505.04922 (2015)
23. Yang, W., Jin, L., Liu, M.: Deepwriterid: an end-to-end online text-independent writer identification system. IEEE Intell. Syst. **31**(2), 45–53 (2016)
24. Yang, W., Jin, L., Tao, D., Xie, Z., Feng, Z.: Dropsample: a new training method to enhance deep convolutional neural networks for large-scale unconstrained handwritten Chinese character recognition. Pattern Recogn. **58**, 190–203 (2016)
25. Yang, W., Jin, L., Xie, Z., Feng, Z.: Improved deep convolutional neural network for online handwritten Chinese character recognition using domain-specific knowledge. In: 2015 13th International Conference on Document Analysis and Recognition (ICDAR), pp. 551–555. IEEE (2015)
26. Yang, W., Lyons, T., Ni, H., Schmid, C., Jin, L.: Developing the path signature methodology and its application to landmark-based human action recognition. arXiv preprint arXiv:1707.03993 (2017)
27. Zemblys, R., Niehorster, D.C., Komogortsev, O., Holmqvist, K.: Using machine learning to detect events in eye-tracking data. Behav. Res. Methods **50**(1), 160–181 (2017). https://doi.org/10.3758/s13428-017-0860-3

Author Index

\

Printed in the United States
by Baker & Taylor Publisher Services